The Founders' Constitution

The Founders' Constitution

Edited by
Philip B. Kurland
and
Ralph Lerner

VOLUME THREE

Article 1, Section 8, Clause 5,
through Article 2, Section 1

Liberty Fund
Indianapolis

This book is published by Liberty Fund, Inc., a foundation established to encourage study of the ideal of a society of free and responsible individuals.

The cuneiform inscription that serves as our logo and as the design motif for our endpapers is the earliest-known written appearance of the word "freedom" (*amagi*), or "liberty." It is taken from a clay document written about 2300 B.C. in the Sumerian city-state of Lagash.

Philip B. Kurland was the William R. Kenan, Jr., Distinguished Service Professor in the College and professor in the Law School, University of Chicago.

Ralph Lerner is the Benjamin Franklin Professor in the College and professor in the Committee on Social Thought, University of Chicago.

Printed in the United States of America

04 03 02 01 P 5 4 3 2

Library of Congress Cataloging-in-Publication Data

The Founders' Constitution / edited by Philip B. Kurland and Ralph Lerner.
p. cm.
Originally published: Chicago: University of Chicago Press, 1987.
Includes bibliographical references and index.
Contents: v. 1. Major themes—v. 2. Preamble through Article 1, Section 8, Clause 4—v. 3. Article 1, Section 8, Clause 5, through Article 2, Section 1—v. 4. Article 2, Section 2, through Article 7—v. 5. Amendments I–XII.
ISBN 0-86597-279-6 (set: pbk.: alk. paper)—ISBN 0-86597-302-4 (v. 1: pbk.: alk. paper)—ISBN 0-86597-303-2 (v. 2: pbk.: alk. paper)
1. Constitutional history—United States—Sources. I. Kurland, Philip B. II. Lerner, Ralph.

KF4502 .F68 2000
342.73′029—dc21 99-052811

ISBN 0-86597-304-0 (v. 3 pbk.: alk. paper)
ISBN 0-86597-305-9 (v. 4 pbk.: alk. paper)
ISBN 0-86597-306-7 (v. 5 pbk.: alk. paper)

Liberty Fund, Inc.
8335 Allison Pointe Trail, Suite 300
Indianapolis, Indiana 46250-1684

Cover design by Erin Kirk New, Watkinsville, Georgia

Printed and bound by Edwards Brothers, Inc., Ann Arbor, Michigan

To Julie, Martha, and Ellen

Contents

VOLUME THREE: ARTICLE 1, SECTION 8, CLAUSE 5, THROUGH ARTICLE 2, SECTION 1
(For detailed contents, see box at opening of each item or group of items listed below)

Note on References

References to documents follow a consistent pattern both in the cross-references (in the detailed tables of contents) and in the indexes. Where a document in volume 1 is being cited, reference is to chapter and document number: thus, for example, ch. 15, no. 23. Where the document is to be found in one of the subsequent volumes, which are organized by Constitutional article, section, and clause, or by amendment, reference is in this mode: 1.8.8, no. 12; or, Amend. I (religion), no. 66. Each document heading consists of its serial number in that particular chapter; an author and title (or letter writer and addressee, or speaker and forum); date of publication, writing, or speaking; and, where not given in the first part of the heading, an identification of the source of the text being reprinted. These sources are presented in short-title form, the author of the source volume being presumed (unless otherwise noted) to be the first proper name mentioned in the document heading. Thus, for example, in the case of a letter from Alexander Hamilton to Governor George Clinton, "Papers 1:425–28" would be understood to refer to the edition fully described under "Hamilton, Papers" in the list of short titles found at the back of each volume.

A somewhat different form has been followed in the case of the proceedings of the Constitutional Convention that met in Philadelphia from late May to mid-September of 1787. As might be expected, we have included many extracts from the various records kept by the participants while they were deliberating over the shape and character of a new charter of government. For any particular chapter or unit, those extracts have been grouped as a single document, titled "Records of the Federal Convention," and placed undated in that chapter's proper time slot. The bracketed note that precedes each segment within that selection of the "Records" lists the volume and opening page numbers in the printed source (Max Farrand's edition), the name of the participant whose notes are here being reproduced (overwhelmingly Madison, but also Mason, Yates, others, and the Convention's official Journal), and the month and day of 1787 when the reported transaction took place.

Article 1, Section 8, Clause 5

To coin Money, regulate the Value thereof, and of foreign Coin, and fix the Standard of Weights and Measures;

1

William Blackstone, Commentaries 1:264–68
1765

Secondly, the regulation of weights and measures. These, for the advantage of the public, ought to be universally the same throughout the kingdom; being the general criterions which reduce all things to the same or an equivalent value. But, as weight and measure are things in their nature arbitrary and uncertain, it is therefore expedient that they be reduced to some fixed rule or standard: which standard it is impossible to fix by any written law or oral proclamation; for no man can, by words only, give another an adequate idea of a foot-rule, or a pound-weight. It is therefore necessary to have recourse to some visible, palpable, material standard; by forming a comparison with which, all weights and measures may be reduced to one uniform size: and the prerogative of fixing this standard, our antient law vested in the crown; as in Normandy it belonged to the duke. This standard was originally kept at Winchester: and we find in the laws of king Edgar, near a century before the conquest, an injunction that the one measure, which was kept at Winchester, should be observed throughout the realm. Most nations have regulated the standard of measures of length by comparison with the parts of the human body; as the palm, the hand, the span, the foot, the cubit, the ell, (*ulna,* or arm) the pace, and the fathom. But, as these are of different dimensions in men of different proportions, our antient historians inform us, that a new standard of longitudinal measure was ascertained by king Henry the first; who commanded that the *ulna* or antient ell, which answers to the modern yard, should be made of the exact length of his own arm. And, one standard of measures of length being gained, all others are easily derived from thence; those of greater length by multiplying, those of less by subdividing, that original standard. Thus, by the statute called *compositio ulnarum et perticarum,* five yards and an half make a perch; and the yard is subdivided into three feet, and each foot into twelve inches; which inches will be each of the length of three grains of barley. Superficial measures are derived by squaring those of length; and measures of capacity by cubing them. The standard of weights was originally taken from corns of wheat, whence the lowest denomination of weights we have is still called a grain; thirty two of which are directed, by the statute called *compositio mensurarum,* to compose a penny weight, whereof twenty make an ounce, twelve ounces a pound, and so upwards. And upon these principles the first standards were made; which, being originally so fixed by the crown, their subsequent regulations have been generally made by the king in parliament. Thus, under king Richard I, in his parliament holden at Westminster, *A.D.* 1197, it was ordained that there shall be only one weight and one measure throughout the kingdom, and that the custody of the assise or standard of weights and measures shall be committed to certain persons in every city and borough; from whence the antient office of the king's aulnager seems to have been derived, whose duty it was, for a certain fee, to measure all cloths made for sale, till the office was abolished by the statute 11 & 12 W. III. c. 20. In king John's time this ordinance of king Richard was frequently dispensed with for money; which occasioned a provision to be made for inforcing it, in the great charters of king John and his son. These original standards were called *pondus regis,* and *mensura domini regis;* and are directed by a variety of subsequent statutes to be kept in the exchequer, and all weights and measures to be made conformable thereto. But, as sir Edward Coke observes, though this hath so often by authority of parliament been enacted, yet it could never be effected; so forcible is custom with the multitude, when it hath gotten an head.

Thirdly, as money is the medium of commerce, it is the king's prerogative, as the arbiter of domestic commerce, to give it authority or make it current. Money is an universal medium, or common standard, by comparison with which the value of all merchandize may be ascertained: or it is a sign, which represents the respective values of all commodities. Metals are well calculated for this sign, because they are durable and are capable of many subdivisions: and a precious metal is still better calculated for this purpose, because it is the most portable. A metal is also the most proper for a common measure, because it can easily be reduced to the same standard in all nations: and every particular nation fixes on it it's own impression, that the weight and standard (wherein consists the intrinsic value) may both be known by inspection only.

As the quantity of precious metals increases, that is, the more of them there is extracted from the mine, this universal medium or common sign will sink in value, and grow less precious. Above a thousand millions of bullion are calculated to have been imported into Europe from America within less than three centuries; and the quantity is daily increasing. The consequence is, that more money must be given now for the same commodity than was given an hundred years ago. And, if any accident was to diminish the quantity of gold and silver, their value would proportionably rise. A horse, that was formerly worth ten pounds, is now perhaps worth twenty; and, by any failure of current specie, the price may be reduced to what it was. Yet is the horse in reality neither dearer nor cheaper at one time than another: for, if the metal which constitutes the coin was formerly twice as scarce as at present, the commodity was then as dear at half the price, as now it is at the whole.

The coining of money is in all states the act of the sovereign power; for the reason just mentioned, that it's value may be known on inspection. And with respect to coinage in general, there are three things to be considered therein; the materials, the impression, and the denomination.

With regard to the materials, sir Edward Coke lays it down, that the money of England must either be of gold or silver; and none other was ever issued by the royal authority till 1672, when copper farthings and half-pence were coined by king Charles the second, and ordered by proclamation to be current in all payments, under the value of six-pence, and not otherwise. But this copper coin is not upon the same footing with the other in many respects, particularly with regard to the offence of counterfeiting it.

As to the impression, the stamping thereof is the unquestionable prerogative of the crown: for, though divers bishops and monasteries had formerly the privilege of coining money, yet, as sir Matthew Hale observes, this was usually done by special grant from the king, or by prescription which supposes one; and therefore was derived from, and not in derogation of, the royal prerogative. Besides that they had only the profit of the coinage, and not the power of instituting either the impression or denomination; but had usually the stamp sent them from the exchequer.

The denomination, or the value for which the coin is to pass current, is likewise in the breast of the king; and, if any unusual pieces are coined, that value must be ascertained by proclamation. In order to fix the value, the weight, and the fineness of the metal are to be taken into consideration together. When a given weight of gold or silver is of a given fineness, it is then of the true standard, and called sterling metal; a name for which there are various reasons given, but none of them entirely satisfactory. And of this sterling metal all the coin of the kingdom must be made by the statute 25 Edw. III. c. 13. So that the king's prerogative seemeth not to extend to the debasing or inhancing the value of the coin, below or above the sterling value: though sir Matthew Hale appears to be of another opinion. The king may also, by his proclamation, legitimate foreign coin, and make it current here; declaring at what value it shall be taken in payments. But this, I apprehend, ought to be by comparison with the standard of our own coin; otherwise the consent of parliament will be necessary. There is at present no such legitimated money; Portugal coin being only current by private consent, so that any one who pleases may refuse to take it in payment. The king may also at any time decry, or cry down, any coin of the kingdom, and make it no longer current.

2

Robert Morris to President of Congress
15 Jan. 1782
Jefferson Papers 7:160–68

Finding by the Act of the United States in Congress of the seventh Instant that I am Instructed to prepare and report a Table of Rates at which the different Species of foreign Coins most likely to circulate within the United States shall be received at the Treasury I have been induced again to turn my Attention to an Object which has employed my Thoughts very frequently and which would have been long since submitted to Congress had I not been prevented by other Business and much delayed by those Things relating to this Business which depended upon others. I shall now pray Leave to deliver my Sentiments somewhat at large on this Subject.

The United States labor under many Inconveniences and even Disadvantages which may at present be remedied but which if suffered to continue would become incurable and lead to pernicious Consequences. It is very fortunate for us that the Weights and Measures used throughout America are the same. Experience has shewn in other Countries that the Efforts of the Legislator to Change Weights and Measures altho fully seconded by the more enlightened Part of the Community have been so strongly opposed by the popular Habits and Prejudices that Ages have elapsed without producing the desired Effect. I repeat therefore that it is happy for us to have throughout the Union the same Ideas of a Mile and an Inch a Hogshead and a Quart, a Pound an Ounce. So far our commercial Dealings are simplified and brought down to the level of every Capacity. With respect to our Money the Case is very widely different. The Ideas annexed to a Pound a Shilling and a Penny are almost as various as the States themselves. Calculations are therefore as necessary for our inland Commerce as upon foreign Exchanges and the commonest Things become intricate where Money has any thing to do with them. A Farmer in New hampshire for Instance can readily form an Idea of a Bushell of Wheat in South Carolina weighing sixty Pounds and placed at one hundred Miles from Charlestown but if he were told that in such Situation it is worth twenty one Shillings and eight Pence, he would be obliged to make many Enquiries and form some Calculations before he could know that this Sum meant in general what he would call four Shillings. And even then he would have to enquire what Kind of Coin that four Shillings was paid in before he could estimate it in his own Mind according to the Ideas of Money which he had imbibed. Difficulties of this Sort do not occur to Farmers alone, they are perplexing to most Men and troublesome to all. It is however a fortunate Circumstance that Money is so much in the Power of the Sovereign as that he can easily lead the People into new Ideas of it and even if that were not the Case yet the loose State in which our Currency has been for some Years past has opened the Way for receiving any Impressions on that Subject. As we are now shaking off the Inconveniencies of a depreciating Medium the present Moment seems to be that in which a general Currency can best be established so as that in a few Months the same Names of Money will mean the same Things in the several Parts of the United States.

Another Inconvenience which admits of the same easy Remedy and which would indeed be cured by the very same Act is the Want of a legal Tender. This is as necessary for the Purposes of Jurisprudence as a general Currency is for those of Commerce. For altho there is great Impropriety not to say Injustice in compelling a Man to receive a Part of his Debt in discharge of the whole yet it is both Just and proper that the Law should protect the honest Debtor who is willing to pay against the vexatious Suits of an Oppressive Creditor who refuses to receive the full Value.

The Nature Value and Use of Money have always occasioned strong Temptations to the Commission of Fraud and of Consequence the Practice of counterfeiting is coeval with that of Coining. No Government can Guard its Subjects entirely against the wicked Ingenuity which has been exercised in this respect. But it has always been the Object of every wise Government to take all the Precautions against it which are within the Compass of human Ability. These Precautions will be most effectual where the Coins are few and simple because they by that Means become familiar to all Ranks and Degrees of Men but where the Coins are so numerous that the Knowledge of them is a kind of Science the lower Order of Citizens are constantly injured by those who carry on the Business of debasing sweating clipping counterfeiting and the like. It is therefore to be lamented that we have so many different Coins in the United States.

It is not necessary to mention what is in every Body's Mouth that the precious Metals were first used as Bullion and that the Inconvenience of weighing and the Difficulty of Assaying introduced the Practice of Coining in Order that the weight and fineness might be known at the first View and of Consequence the Value be instantly ascertained. It is equally unnecessary to observe that the great Privilege of declaring this Value by particular Marks has among all Nations been vested exclusively in the Sovereign. A Trust so important could not indeed be vested any where else because the Danger of abusing it was too great. And History informs us that Sovereigns themselves have not on this Occasion behaved with that Integrity which was alike due to their Subjects and to themselves to the Interests of their People and to their own personal Glory. Experience has already told us that the advantage of Gold as a Coin is in this Country very considerably diminished for every distinct Piece must be weighed before it can be safely received. Both Gold and Silver Coins are indeed preferable, in one respect to common Bullion that the Standard is presumed to be just and consequently they are received without the Delays and Expences of assaying. It must however be remembered that they are all foreign Coins and of Course we are not only exposed to the Tricks of Individuals but should it suit the Interest or Convenience of any Sovereign to make base Money for us there is Nothing to prevent it. If for Instance the King of England or any of his Birmingham Artists should coin Guineas worth but sixteen shillings Sterling our Citizens would readily and freely receive them at twenty one Shillings Sterling. It is my Duty to mention to Congress Information I have received that Guineas of base Metal are coined at Birmingham so well as to escape any common Attention. Now there can be no Doubt but that every such Guinea received here would be a national Loss to us of an English Crown. How much we suffer in this Way at present it is impossible to estimate.

What I have already had the Honor to observe contains some of the reasons why it appears to me highly necessary that an American Coin should be adopted without Delay and to these Reasons it may be added that there is a want of small Money for the common Occasions of Trade and that it is more felt by our Soldiery than any other Persons. For the little Pay which they do receive being either in Gold or at best in Dollars the Sutlers and others with whom they have Dealings continually take the Advantage of their want of Change and rate the Prices of their Goods accordingly.

Shortly after my Appointment finding that there was a considerable Quantity of public Copper at Boston I ordered it round to this Place. It has safely arrived and will when coined amount to a considerable Sum. The necessary Machinery of a Mint can be easily made and there are Persons who can perform the whole Business. I must pray leave therefore to submit to Congress some few more particular remarks on this Subject as introductory to a Plan for an American Coin.

Altho most Nations have coined Copper yet that Metal is so impure that it has never been considered as constituting the Money Standard. This is affixed to the two precious Metals because they alone will admit of having their intrinsic Value precisely ascertained. But Nations differ very much in the relation they have established between Gold and Silver. In some European Countries an Ounce of pure Gold passes for fifteen Ounces of pure Silver. In others for fourteen. In China it passes for much less. The Standard therefore which is affixed to both Metals is in Reality affixed to neither. In England Gold is to Silver nearly in the Proportion of one to fifteen and in France nearly of one to fourteen. If a Man carries fourteen ounces of Gold from France to England he receives two hundred and ten Ounces of Silver which in France purchase fifteen ounces of Gold so that he gains on that Exchange one ounce of Gold. In like Manner he who carries from England fourteen Ounces of Silver to France receives one Ounce of Gold which in England purchases fifteen Ounces of Silver wherefore he gains on that Exchange one Ounce of Silver. If it be then supposed that the Coins of these two Countries were alike pure it must follow that in a short Time all the gold Coin of full Weight would be in England and all the silver Coin of full weight in France. But the light Silver circulating in England and the light Gold in France the real Standard of Coin in each would be different from the legal and seek a Medium of fourteen and an half of Silver for one of Gold altho the legal Standard might still be in the one Place fifteen and in the other fourteen.

The Demand which Commerce might make for any one of the precious Metals in Preference of the other would vary this real Standard from Time to Time and in every Payment a Man would get more or less of real Value for his Debt according as he were paid in the Coin of greater or lesser Value in relation to the real Standard. If for Instance the Debt were contracted when the Silver was to Gold as one to fifteen and paid when as one to fourteen; if the Debt were paid in Silver he would gain one thirtieth and if in Gold he would loose one thirtieth. In England the Money Standard is rather affixed to Gold than to Silver because all Payments are made in the former and in France it is rather affixed to Silver than to Gold.

Arguments are unnecessary to shew that the Scale by which every thing is to be measured ought to be as fixed as the Nature of Things will permit of. Since therefore a Money Standard affixed to both the precious Metals will not give this certain Scale it is better to make use of one only. Gold is more valuable than Silver and so far must have the Preference but it is from that very Circumstance the more exposed to fraudulent Practices. Its Value rendering it more portable is an Advantage. But it is an Advantage which Paper possesses in a much greater Degree and of Consequence the commercial Nation of England has had recourse to Paper for the Purposes of it's Trade altho the Mass of circulating Coin is Gold. It will always be in our Power to carry a Paper Circulation to every proper Extent. There can be no doubt therefore that our Money Standard ought to be affixed to Silver.

But Silver is liable like every Thing else to a Change of Value, if there is a Demand for it, to export, the Value will rise, if the Contrary it will fall, and so far it cannot be considered as a fixed Measure of Value. Before this Objection be considered it will be proper to make a few reflexions on another Part of the present Subject but in this Place I remark that if the Objection cannot be removed we must not suffer it to preponderate because it weighs alike against every other Metal.

To Coin Money is a certain Expence and of Course it is an Expence which must be borne by the People. In England the Coin when melted will sell as Bullion for just as much as its Weight in other Coin. The Expence of Coinage is paid by the Crown and of Course it is raised by Taxes from the People. In France the Coinage instead of being expensive yields a Profit. The Price given for Metal at the Mint is about eight Pr. Cent less than the same Quantity will yield when coined at the french Standard. Both of these Methods are liable to Objections. When Commerce demands an Exportation of Bullion from England the Coin of the Kingdom goes out in common with others; this increases of Course the National Expence of Coinage. Laws to prevent the Exportation or Importation of any Thing so valuable as Money are always Nugatory because they always *can* be eluded and therefore when private Interest requires they always *will* be eluded. That the Guineas of England therefore are not continually going away is to be attributed to the extraordinary Value affixed to Gold which has been just mentioned and which banishes silver continually. In France the People are not liable to this Inconvenience because their Money passing for more than its Value in Bullion, Bullion will always be exported in Preference of Coin. But for the same Reason there is always a strong Temptation to imitate their Coin and send it for the Purchase of their Commodities. It would be both impossible and unnecessary to distinguish the True from the false because both would be of equal intrinsic Value. The Place at which they were struck would be indifferent to the Receiver, of Consequence the foreigner who made french Coin would gain by his Trade and the french Nation would loose proportionately.

The Money paid for Coining or the Coinage of France has however this Advantage that the Money is a Standard which does not fluctuate with the Price of Bullion. This Coinage is as has been said about eight Pr. Cent. When Bullion is below ninety two it is carried to the Mint when above ninety two to the Broker or Silver Smith. The Coin still continues fixed nor will it bear Exportation until Bullion rises to an hundred when the french Coin would be as liable to Exportation as the English. In that Case it would be exported on one Hand, while on the other no more would have been coined for a considerable Period because to make the eight Pr. Cent Coinage it is necessary that the Mint Price should be ninety two. The Coin therefore could not long be exported if at all but would soon resume it's Value. The Price of Bullion must float between ninety two and an hundred while the Coin would preserve its fixed Quality as Money.

Hence then it appears proper that the Price of Coining should be defrayed by the Coinage because first it is natural and proper that the Price should be paid when the Benefit is received and that the Citizen in Return for the Advantage of being ascertained in the Value of the Medium of Commerce by the Sovereign should pay for ascertaining it just as that he should pay for the fashion of the Plate he uses or the Construction of the Cart he employs. Secondly it is right that Money should acquire a Value, as Money distinct from that which it Possesses as a Commodity in Order that it should be a fixed Rule whereby to Measure the Value of all other Things and thirdly it is wise to prevent the Exportation of the Coin which would involve an unnecessary national Expence and also to prevent the Imitation of it abroad so as to create a national Loss: For both which Purposes it is proper that the Coinage should only defray the Expence without making any considerable Profit. The Laws usual in all Countries with respect to the Money will then fully operate the Effect intended.

In Order that a Coin may be perfectly intelligible to the whole People it must have some Affinity to the former Currency. This therefore will be requisite in the present Case. The Purposes of Commerce require that the lowest divisible Point of Money or what is more properly called the Money Unit should be very small because by that Means Price can be brought in the smallest Things to bear a Proportion to the Value. And altho it is not absolutely necessary yet it is very desirable that Money should be increased in a decimal Ratio because by that Means all Calculations of Interest Exchange Insurance and the like are rendered much more simple and accurate and of Course more within the Power of the great Mass of People. Wherever such Things require much Labor Time and Reflection the greater Number who do not know are made the Dupes of the lesser Number who do.

The various Coins which have circulated in America have undergone different Changes in their Value so that there is hardly any which can be considered as a general Standard unless it be spanish Dollars. These pass in Georgia at five Shillings in North Carolina and New York at eight Shillings in Virginia and the four Eastern states at six Shillings in all the other States except South Carolina at seven Shillings and six Pence and in South Carolina at thirty two Shillings and six Pence: The Money Unit of a new Coin to agree without a Fraction with all these different Values of a Dollar except the last will be the fourteen hundred and fortieth Part of a Dollar equal to the sixteen hundreth Part of a Crown. Of these Units twenty four will be a Penny of Georgia, fifteen will be a Penny of North Carolina, or New York, twenty will be a Penny of Virginia and the four Eastern States sixteen will be a Penny of all the other States except South Carolina and forty eight will be thirteen Pence of South Carolina.

It has been already observed that to have the Money Unit very small is advantageous to Commerce but there is no Necessity that this Money Unit be exactly represented in Coin it is sufficient that its Value be precisely known. On the present Occasion two Copper Coins will be proper the one of eight Units and the other of five. These may be called an eight and a five two of the former will make a Penny Proclamation or Pennsylvania Money and three a Penny Georgia Money, of the latter three will make a Penny York Money and four a Penny lawful or Virginia Money. The Money Unit will be equal to a quarter of a Grain of fine Silver in coined Money. Proceeding thence in a decimal Ratio one hundred would be the lowest Silver Coin and might be called a Cent. It would contain twenty five Grains of fine Silver to which may be added two Grains of Copper and the whole would weigh one Penny Weight three Grains. Five of these would make a Quint or five hundred Units weighing five Penny Weight fifteen Grains and ten would make a Mark or one thousand Units weighing Seven Penny weight six Grains.

If the Mint Price of fine Silver be established at 22,237. Units per Pound. This being coined would be four Times 5,760 Grains or 23,040 Units. The difference is 803. Units and therefore the Coinage is 803 on 23,040 or somewhat more than 3⁴⁸⁄₁₀₀ P. Cent, which would be about the Expence attending it. A Dollar contains by the best Assays which I have been able to get about 373 Grains of fine Silver and that at the Mint Price would be 1,440 Units. In like Manner if Crowns contain from 414. to 415 Grains of fine Silver they would at the Mint Price be worth 1600 Units.

When such a Coin shall have been established the Value of all others would be easily ascertained because Nothing more would be necessary than to have them assayed at the Mint. The Advantage of Possessing legal Money in Preference of any other would induce People to carry foreign Coin to the Mint until a sufficiency were struck for the circulating Medium. The remainder of the foreign Silver together with the Gold should be left entirely to the Operations of Commerce as Bullion.

In the present Moment it is by no Means of such Consequence to establish the relative Value of different Coins as to provide a Standard of our own by which in future to estimate them. If the Value were now sought they must all be estimated in Dollars because Dollars are called for in the several requisitions of Congress. Without noticing the Preference thus given to one foreign Coin over another it is sufficient to observe that if a greater Alloy should be introduced by the Spanish Government into their Dollars our interior regulations as to Money would be overturned and certainly we have no Security that this will not happen. There is not any great Inconvenience from leaving Matters on their present footing until they can be remedied by the Operations of a Mint for it is not to be supposed that all the Money raised by Taxes in a State is to be brought out of it. I expect that there will be very little Occasion to transport money from Place to Place. It is much easier to negotiate than to carry it and if any Species of Money is generally received within a State at the same Rate in which it is paid in Taxes there will be no Difficulty in expending it at its Value. Whenever Money shall be struck by Authority of the United States then indeed it will be proper to receive in Taxes no other Coin.

If Congress are of Opinion with me that it will be proper to Coin Money I will immediately obey their Orders and establish a Mint. And I think I can say with Safety that no better Moment could be chosen for the Purpose than the present. Neither will any thing have a greater tendency to restore public Credit for altho it is possible that the new Money will at first be received with Diffidence by some Yet when it has been fairly assayed it will gain full Confidence from all; and the Advantage of holding the only Money which can Pay Debts or Discharge

Taxes will soon give it the Preference over all and indeed banish all other from Circulation. Whereas fixing a Relation of Value now on whatever Principles attempted might give Offence to the Power whose Coin should in any Instance be reduced from its present numerary Value among us.

3

ROBERT MORRIS TO THOMAS JEFFERSON
1 May 1784

Jefferson Papers 7:189–92

I have received your favor of the twenty sixth Instant for which I pray you to accept my Thanks. Enclosed you have the Copy of my Letter of the fifteenth of January 1782. to Congress and also Mr. Governeur Morris's Letter to Mr. Helmly of the thirtieth of April 1783. I will add to these such Observations as have occurred on your Notes which agreably to your Desire are herewith returned.

I agree with you as to your Idea of a Money Unit in the first and second Points but to the third must submit an Alteration. Premising however that in this Letter I shall adopt the Term *Unit* in the Sense in which you have used it viz: as the largest Silver Coin instead of that Sense in which it is applied in my Letter viz. as the lowest fractional Money of Account not represented precisely by any Coin, similar in this Respect to the Portugueze Rea. I think then the third Proposition would stand best in this Way *That its Parts be so correspondent to the present Money of Account as to be of easy Adoption to the People.*

I take it to be a self Evident Proposition that any Coin may be Circulated at a Rate nearly proportioned to it's intrinsic Worth and in that Point of View it is unimportant what the Size or Standard shall be. But the present Object is to go farther and adopt such a Coin as shall become exclusively the circulating Medium and a new Money of Account. It is true that Dollars form our general Circulation but they are not any where the Money of Account. No Merchants Books are kept in Dollars few if any Purchases are made at a Rate specified in Dollars and Parts of Dollars. Let it be supposed then that a Dollar be taken as the *Unit* and divided into an hundred Parts and that a Merchant desirous of adopting the New Coin should balance his Books to open them in it. Let it be a Merchant of Boston and let the first Sum he wants to reduce be £365. this would be expressed thus in the new Coin 1216.66⅔. His first Essay therefore would oblige him to combine both Vulgar and decimal fractions. If the same Essay be made on the Books of any other Merchant it would be attended with the same Effect. It is therefore of little Avail that the unit be nearly or even exactly of the Value of known Coins unless it's Parts correspond with the present Money of Account.

In this Letter you will find enclosed my original Letter to Congress of the twenty third of April 1783. together with the Specimens of a Coin there mentioned. These you will be so kind as to deliver to the Secretary of Congress after you have done with them and as the Reasoning on such Subjects is facilitated by a Reference to visible Objects let us take the largest of those Silver Coins as the Money *Unit* divisible into a thousand Parts each containing ¼ of a Grain of pure Silver. Here then we have a Piece of Money of convenient Size containing 250 grains of pure Silver, and worth about two thirds of a Dollar viz: 4/2 Virginia Money. The smallest Copper Piece is worth one Farthing Virginia Money and £365. is expressed thus 1752. Suppose we add 6.d.¼ it will then stand 1752.125. Trials upon other Currencies will shew that all Sums can be brought to agree not only *nearly* but *exactly* to this unless in a very few Cases indeed where 1/15 of the small Copper Piece must be rejected. The Objection you State against this Coin is that the Unit is divided into 1000 Parts whereas you would divide a Unit one third larger into no more than 100 Parts but we must consider that the 1/100 of a Dollar is not sufficiently small to be rejected in any Matter of Accot. and then when the Poor are Purchasers or Venders it does not admit of the Divisibility necessary for their Affairs. The Rea of Portugal is 1/800 of a Dollar and is not found to make any Difficulty in Calculations or Entries but on the contrary to occasion much Convenience. Names are of little Consequence but they are not quite indifferent. Suppose that we call the largest Piece a Dollar the smallest a Shilling and that the Shilling be divisible into an hundred Pence. If a Gold Coin be struck it may be made equal to five Dollars and it's value about that of a Pistole. This might be called a Pound and would be exactly 20/10 of the Currency of New Hampshire Massachusetts Rhodes Island Connecticut and Virginia. In point of Size I believe that these Pieces of Money would be convenient and I do not think it of small Consequence that the lowest fractional Part be a Quantity of pure Silver equal to an established Weight because in considering foreign Exchanges we can by that Means always bring the Money of Account of foreign Nations to an exact analogy with our own.

On the whole there are but two Points in which we differ the first is as to the Value of the lowest fractional Part of the Money Unit for we agree that it should proceed from thence upwards in a decimal Ratio. The second is as to the Proportion which Gold should bear to Silver. I wish this to be rather too small than too large because I think the Bank Paper may supply the Place of Gold and not of Silver. If therefore we give more for Silver and less for Gold the Gold will be exported and the Silver will stay. To this I add that our direct Means of importing Bullion is Gold from Lisbon and not Silver from the Spanish Territories because the latter will probably continue to be shut against us and we know by Experience that Silver was exported to England in Preference to Gold while our legal Proportion was the same as theirs because theirs being too high Silver always was worth more at Market than the Mint Price. To shew that this continues to be the Case I will observe that the lowest Price Current of Dollars yet received from England is for old Dollars 63/9 and for new Dollars 62/6. per Pound, altho neither of them are so fine as the Sterling Standard which according to Law is worth but 62/. Hence you will see that the *actual* is below the *legal* Proportion and the fixing of the legal Proportion so high is the Cause why all but light Silver is banished from Circulation. If the Piece of five Dollars were made to contain 84 Grains of pure Gold and seven of Alloy this would establish a Proportion of 1. to 14. $^{37}/_{42}$ and would be attended with this Advantage that the Piece would weigh exactly three Pennyweight nineteen Grains, without any fractions of a Grain either in the pure [gold or in the] Alloy. The Quantity of Alloy in the Silver is not material to the Value but if it be sufficiently hard all Alloy beyond that Point renders it more liable to Imitation by a baser Composition. Let the Plan be what it may I think it would be advantageous to make the different Pieces of Money consist of Weights represented by a Number of Pennyweights or Grains without Fractions and also to have in each Piece an integral Number of Grains of pure Metal.

I do not think it will be necessary to cause Assays of the different Coins to be made because I have already a Work more perfect in its Kind than any Assays we can have made. It is the Production of a Person employed by the french Court for the Purpose and the only Difficulty in the Application of it consists in the Difference between their Weights and ours. This however is easily surmounted by Approximation. I should suppose that Congress might adopt (before their Adjournment) a Plan for the Coinage and certainly it is an Object which merits immediate Attention. So far from being attached to the Plan which I have held out I am ready to confess that the Subject is not so familiar as I could wish and that I am not for that Reason competent to a decisive Judgment. All which I can pretend to is a general Sketch to be matured by the Wisdom of Congress but I wish that it may meet their speedy Determination.

There is one Point on which you have not said any Thing but which appears to be of Importance viz: how the Expence is to be defrayed. Supposing you to be with me in Opinion that it ought to be by what is called *Coinage* I would hint that the Price to be given for fine Silver or *Mint Price* should be established and if you make a Golden Coin that of Gold also. If the Mint Price of an Ounce of fine Gold be fixed at 28. Dollars this at the Rate of 84. Grains for 5 Dollars would when coined amount to 28.571. being a little more than two per Cent Difference.

I must intreat your Excuse for the Crudeness of this hasty Production which is not so attentively digested as it might have been because I am unwilling to delay it.

4

WHARTON v. MORRIS
1 Dall. 125 (Pa. 1785)

The bond is made payable in current money of Pennsylvania; but, I would ask, what is the *current money of Pennsylvania?* For my part, I know of none, that can properly be so called, for current and lawful are synonymous. In Great Britain, the king, by his proclamation, may render any species of coin a lawful currency. But here, it can only be done by an act of assembly; and except in the temporary laws for supporting the former emissions of paper-money, there is no pretence that the legislature has ever interfered upon this subject. The expressions in the 2d section of the act of the 27th January 1777 (P.L. p. 6), cannot be construed to make the Spanish milled dollars a legal tender, as they are only mentioned by words of reference; but that which was declared to be a lawful tender, and consequently became the legal currency of the land, was the money emitted under the authority of congress.

To that species of money, therefore, the bond must be taken to relate; and the jury will either reduce the penalty to gold or silver, according to the scale of depreciation; or, if they think it more equitable, they will find a verdict for the value of the tobacco, and give the plaintiffs legal interest from the day of the sale.

5

THOMAS JEFFERSON, PROPOSITIONS RESPECTING COINAGE
13 May 1785

Papers 7:194–98, 202

First. The value of silver compared with gold. Second. The weight or size of the several pieces of money that are to be made. Third. The money arithmetic, or the mode in which it is to be counted; and fourth, The charges of coinage are to be considered.

1. In France, 1 grain of pure gold is counted worth 15 grains of silver. In Spain, 16 grains of silver are exchanged for 1 of gold, and in England 15⅕. In both of the kingdoms last mentioned, gold is the prevailing money; because silver is undervalued. In France silver prevails. Sundry advantages would arise to us from a system by which silver might become the prevailing money. This would operate as a bounty to draw it from our neighbours, by whom it is not sufficiently esteemed. Silver is not exported so easily as gold, and it is a more useful metal.

Certainly our exchange should not be more than 15 grains of silver for one of gold. It has been alledged by the late financier, that we should not give more than 14½; perhaps 14¾ would be a better medium, considering the quantity of gold that may be expected from Portugal.

2. The weight, size or value of the several pieces of money that shall be made, or rather the most convenient value of the money unit, is a question not easily determined, considering that most of the citizens of the United States, are accustomed to count in pounds, shillings and pence; and that those sums are of different values in the different states: hence they convey no distinct ideas. The money of the United States should be equally fitted to all. The late financier has proposed to make gold and silver

pieces of particular weight; and there is a very simple process, by which the imaginary money of the several states may be translated into such pieces, or vice versa. He proposes that the money unit be one quarter of a grain of pure silver. That the smallest coin be of copper, which shall be worth 5 of those units. The smallest silver coin to be worth 100 units; another to be worth 500; another of 1000; and thus increasing decimally.

The objections to this plan are, that it introduces a coin unlike in value to any thing now in use. It departs from the national mode of keeping accounts, and tends to preserve inconvenient prejudices. Whence it must prevent national uniformity in accounts; a thing greatly to be desired.

Another plan has been offered, which proposes, that the money unit be one dollar; and the smallest coin is to be of copper, of which 200 shall pass for one dollar. This plan also proposes, that the several pieces shall increase in a decimal ratio; and that all accounts be kept in decimals, which is certainly by much the most short and simple mode.

In favour of this plan it is urged, that a dollar, the proposed unit, has long been in general use. Its value is familiar. This accords with the national mode of keeping accounts, and may in time produce the happy effect of uniformity in counting money throughout the union.

3. The money arithmetic, though an important question, is one that can admit of little dispute. All accomptants must prefer decimals.

4. What is the best mode of defraying the expence of coinage? Different nations have adopted different systems. The British value their silver when coined, no higher than bullion. Hence it follows, that the expence of the mint, increasing the civil list, must be paid by a general tax; and tradesmen are disposed to work up the current coin, by which the tax is increased and continued. In some other countries silver or gold when coined, are valued above the price of bullion; whence tradesmen are discouraged from melting or working up the current coin, and the mint is rather profitable than burdensome. Certainly there are good and conclusive reasons, why we should value the national coin above the price of bullion; but there is a certain point beyond which we may not proceed, lest we encourage counterfeits, or private imitations of our coin. It has been proposed to make a difference of $2\frac{1}{2}$ per cent. nearly, as an allowance for the coinage of gold, and of 3.013 per cent. for the coinage of silver. It is probable that 3 per cent. would more than defray the expence of coining silver, in which case it would be a temptation to private imitation, and would operate against the free circulation of the money, as being valued too high. It is to be remembered that silver coin ought to be encouraged, and probably 2 per cent. or $2\frac{1}{4}$ per cent. would be a proper difference between silver coined and bullion. The same difference to be made in the price of gold. If this does not fully pay the expences of the mint, there will be a much larger gain on the coinage of copper; and if there should remain a small balance against the mint, its operation will not be unfavourable.

The coinage of copper is a subject that claims our immediate attention. From the small value of the several pieces of copper coin, this medium of exchange has been too much neglected. The more valuable metals are daily giving place to base British halfpence, and no means are used to prevent the fraud. This disease, which is neglected in the beginning, because it appears trifling, may finally prove very destructive to commerce. It is admitted that copper may at this instant be purchased in America at $\frac{1}{8}$ of a dollar the pound. British halfpence made at the tower are 48 to the pound. Those manufactured at Birmingham, and shipped in thousands for our use, are much lighter, and they are of base metal. It can hardly be said that 72 of them are worth a pound of copper. Hence it will follow, that we give for British halfpence, about six times their value. There are no materials from which we can estimate the weight of halfpence that have been imported from Britain since the late war. But we have heard of sundry shipments being ordered, to the nominal amount of 1000 guineas; and we are told, that no packet arrives from England, without some hundred weight of base halfpence. It is a very moderate computation which states our loss on the last twelve months, at 30,000 dollars, by the commerce of vile coin. The whole expence of a mint would not have amounted to half of that sum, and the whole expence of domestic coinage would remain in the country.

The following forms of money are submitted.

	Dollars.	
1 piece of gold of	5	
1 piece of silver of	1	containing 362 grains pure silver. This is the unit or money of account.
	dol.	
1 ditto,	$\frac{1}{2}$ or .5	
1 ditto,	$\frac{1}{4}$ or .25	
1 ditto,	$\frac{1}{10}$ or .1	
1 ditto,	$\frac{1}{20}$ or .05	
1 piece of copper of	$\frac{1}{100}$ or .01	
1 ditto,	$\frac{1}{200}$ or .005	

The quantity of pure silver being fixed that is to be in the unit or dollar, and the relation between silver and gold being fixed, all the other weights must follow.

When it is considered, that the Spaniards have been reducing the weight of their dollars, and that instead of 385.5 the grains of pure silver in the old Mexican dollar, the new dollars have not more than 365 grains, it will hardly be thought that 362 grains of pure silver is too little for the federal coin, which is to be current in all payments for one dollar. Some of the old dollars will admit of a second coinage; but the new ones will not. If the value of gold compared to that of silver, be fixed at 15 to one, and the alloy in each be $\frac{1}{12}$, the weight of the several denominations will be readily determined.

The price of bullion is immediately determined by the per centage that is charged towards the expences of the mint.

If the United States determine to adhere to the dollar as their money of account, and to simplify accounts by the use of decimals, there is nothing to prevent the immediate commencement of a coinage of copper.

Let the copper pieces, of which 100 are to pass for a dollar, contain each 131 grains of pure copper, or 44 of them weigh one pound. In this case our copper coin, when compared with the money of account, will be 6 per cent. better than that of Great-Britain. There will remain a sufficient profit on the coinage.

Copper at the best quality in plates, may be purchased in Europe at 10d. ½ sterling. In cutting blanks there will be a waste of 22 per cent. Those clippings are worth 7d. ½ per pound. Thence the blanks will cost 11d. ½ nearly; it may be stated at 1s.9d. New-York money per pound, exclusive of the expence of cutting them, which is not great, as one man can readily cut 100 weight in a day.

The operation, improperly called milling, by which the sharp edges are worn off from the coppers, is not more expensive than cutting the blanks.

In the process of coining copper, eight artists or labourers may be required.

One engraver, 1 labourer for the blank press.

One smith, 5 labourers for the coining press.

By those people 100 weight of copper may readily be coined every day, or the value of 44 dollars. Deducting the necessary expences, there may be saved 30 per cent.

. . . . .

The advantages of coining money in this country are, first, those which arise from the same operation in all other countries; and secondly, that of reducing all our currencies to one. The advantages from the coin here proposed are, first, that none other will effect the object already mentioned of banishing other currencies, because that alone applies without fractions to them all. Secondly, that the minuteness of its lowest denomination would render it an accurate measure of the smallest variations of quantity or quality in any commodity. Thirdly, that the decimal proportion of its parts would render all calculations in it easy, as appears in the calculations and consequent rates of exchange above mentioned: And lastly, that few figures would be used for the largest sum, while at the same time the smallest sums would be comprehended. For if the lowest denomination be of considerable value, recourse must be had to fractions, as in England, where the penny is divided into fourths, eights, and sometimes sixteenths, and even then without sufficient accuracy; whereas the lowest denomination of the coin here proposed will be about 1/27 of a penny sterling.

Lastly, as to the names above chosen, they, like all other names, are arbitrary, and better may perhaps be substituted. The word crown occurred from the following idea of an impression for the gold coin—An Indian, his right foot on a crown, a bow in his left-hand, in his right-hand thirteen arrows; and the inscription Manus inimica Tyrannis.

6

RECORDS OF THE FEDERAL CONVENTION

[*2:136, 144, 159, 167; Committee of Detail*]

16. S & H.D. in C. ass. shall have the exclusive Right of coining Money—regulating its Alloy & Value—fixing the Standard of Weights and Measures throughout U.S.

. . . . .

10. To (regulate)* The exclusive right of coining money (Paper prohibit) no State to be perd. in future to emit Paper Bills of Credit witht. the App: of the Natl. Legisle nor to make any (Article) Thing but Specie a Tender in paymt of debts

. . . . .

. . . of coining Money—fixing the Standard of Weights and Measures—of determining in what Species of Money the public Treasury shall be supplied.

. . . . .

The Legislature of the United States shall have the (Right and) Power . . . to coin Money, to regulate the (Alloy and) Value of foreign Coin; to fix the Standard of Weights and Measures; . . .

[*2:308; Madison, 16 Aug.*]

for coining money. agd. to nem. con.

for regulating foreign coin. d. do.

for fixing the standard of weights & measures. do. do.

[*2:569, 595; Committee of Style*]

Sect. I. The Legislature shall have power . . .

To coin money;

To regulate the value of foreign coin;

To fix the standard of weights and measures; . . .

. . . . .

[e] To coin money, regulate the value thereof, and of foreign coin, and fix the standard of weights and measures.

*[EDITORS' NOTE.— Words in parentheses were crossed out in the original.]

7

JAMES MADISON, FEDERALIST, NO. 42, 285
22 Jan. 1788

All that need be remarked on the power to coin money, regulate the value thereof, and of foreign coin, is that by providing for this last case, the Constitution has supplied a material omission in the articles of confederation. The authority of the existing Congress is restrained to the regulation of coin *struck* by their own authority, or that of the respective States. It must be seen at once, that the proposed uniformity in the *value* of the current coin might be destroyed by subjecting that of foreign coin to the different regulations of the different States.

The punishment of counterfeiting the public securities as well as of the current coin, is submitted of course to that authority, which is to secure the value of both.

The regulation of weights and measures is transferred from the articles of confederation, and is founded on like considerations with the preceding power of regulating coin.

8

JOHN JAY TO GEORGE WASHINGTON
13 Nov. 1790

Correspondence 3:406–7

The Constitution gives power to the Congress "to coin money, regulate the value thereof, and of foreign coin; to provide for the punishment of counterfeiting the securities and current coin of the United States." If the word *current* had been omitted, it might have been doubted whether the Congress could have punished the counterfeiting of foreign coin. Mexican dollars have long been known in our public acts as *current* coin. The 55th section of the act "to provide more effectually for the collection of the duties," etc., enumerates a variety of foreign coins which shall be received for the duties and fees mentioned in it.

The late penal act (as it is generally called) provides punishment for counterfeiting paper, but not coin, foreign or domestic. Whether this omission was accidental or designed, I am uninformed. It appears to me more expedient that this offence, as it respects current coin, should be punished in a uniform manner throughout the nation, rather than be left to State laws and State courts.

The Constitution provides, that "no State shall coin money, nor make any thing but gold or silver coin a *tender* in payment of debts." Must not this gold and silver coin be such only as shall be either struck or made current by the Congress? At present, I do not recollect any act which designates, unless perhaps by implication, what coins shall be a *legal* tender between citizen and citizen.

9

ST. GEORGE TUCKER, BLACKSTONE'S COMMENTARIES
1:APP. 261–62
1803

By the former articles of confederation it was agreed that the United States in congress assembled, should have the sole and exclusive right and power of regulating the alloy and value of coin struck by their own authority, or by that of the respective states; and fixing the standard of weights and measures throughout the United States. By the present constitution the respective states are interdicted from coining money. All the powers mentioned in this clause are branches of the royal prerogative in England, but are with much greater propriety vested in the legislative department by the federal constitution. The history of England affords numberless instances, where this prerogative has been exercised to the great oppression of the subject. The power of debasing the value of the coin, at pleasure, has in fact been frequently used as an expedient for raising a revenue, and is accordingly reckoned as one of the indirect modes of taxation, by the author of the treatise on political economy: for if the government gives coin of an inferior standard, for purer coin of the same weight, as is generally done in these cases; or if it receives more for the coin, than the value of the bullion, and the expence of the coinage, as is likewise frequently practised, the difference is an acquisition of revenue, paid by him who brings his bullion to the mint. According to the principles of our constitution, therefore, such a tax can not be imposed but by the representatives of the people.

Mr. Barrington, in his readings upon the English statutes, doubts whether the regulation of weights and measures be practicable, by law. He remarks, that in England it has been attempted by at least six different statutes, all of which have been ineffectual. He quotes an observation of Montesquieu's that it is the mark of a little mind in a legislature to attempt regulations of this kind. In England, perhaps, the attempt has not succeeded from some defect in the system. That proposed by Mr. Jefferson, when secretary of state, appears to be perfectly simple, and, I should apprehend, easily practicable: and the standard of measure, especially, may be obtained with a mathematical exactness sufficient for all the purposes of commerce, and even of arts and sciences.

It appears by the journals of the senate of the United States, March the 1st, 1791. "That a proposition had been made to the national assembly of France for obtaining a standard of measure, which shall at all times be invariable, and communicable to all nations, and at all times. That a similar proposition had been submitted to the British parliament: as the avowed object of these is to introduce an uniformity in the weights and measures of commercial nations; and as a coincidence of regulation by the government of the United States on so interesting a subject would be desirable, the senate resolved, that it would not be eligible at that time to introduce any alterations in the weights and measures of the United States."

10

Joseph Story, Commentaries on the Constitution 3:§§ 1112–17
1833

§ 1112. Under the confederation, the continental congress had delegated to them, "the sole and exclusive right and power of regulating the alloy and value of coin struck by their own authority, or by that of the states," and "fixing the standard of weights and measures throughout the United States." It is observable, that, under the confederation, there was no power given to regulate the value of foreign coin, an omission, which in a great measure would destroy any uniformity in the value of the current coin, since the respective states might, by different regulations, create a different value in each. The constitution has, with great propriety, cured this defect; and, indeed, the whole clause, as it now stands, does not seem to have attracted any discussion in the convention. It has been justly remarked, that the power "to coin money" would, doubtless, include that of regulating its value, had the latter power not been expressly inserted. But the constitution abounds with pleonasms and repetitions of this nature.

§ 1113. The grounds, upon which the general power to coin money, and regulate the value of foreign and domestic coin, is granted to the national government, cannot require much illustration in order to vindicate it. The object of the power is to produce uniformity of value throughout the Union, and thus to preclude us from the embarrassments of a perpetually fluctuating and variable currency. Money is the universal medium or common standard, by a comparison with which the value of all merchandise may be ascertained, or, it is a sign, which represents the respective values of all commodities. It is, therefore, indispensable for the wants and conveniencies of commerce, domestic as well as foreign. The power to coin money is one of the ordinary prerogatives of sovereignty, and is almost universally exercised in order to preserve a proper circulation of good coin of a known value in the home market. In order to secure it from debasement it is necessary, that it should be exclusively under the control and regulation of the government; for if every individual were permitted to make and circulate, what coin he should please, there would be an opening to the grossest frauds and impositions upon the public, by the use of base and false coin. And the same remark applies with equal force to foreign coin, if allowed to circulate freely in a country without any control by the government. Every civilized government, therefore, with a view to prevent such abuses, to facilitate exchanges, and thereby to encourage all sorts of industry and commerce, as well as to guard itself against the embarrassments of an undue scarcity of currency, injurious to its own interests and credits, has found it necessary to coin money, and affix to it a public stamp and value, and to regulate the introduction and use of foreign coins. In England, this prerogative belongs to the crown; and, in former ages, it was greatly abused; for base coin was often coined and circulated by its authority, at a value far above its intrinsic worth; and thus taxes of a burthensome nature were laid indirectly upon the people. There is great propriety, therefore, in confiding it to the legislature, not only as the more immediate representatives of the public interests, but as the more safe depositaries of the power.

§ 1114. The only question, which could properly arise under our political institutions, is, whether it should be confided to the national, or to the state government. It is manifest, that the former could alone give it complete effect, and secure a wholesome and uniform currency throughout the Union. The varying standards and regulations of the different states would introduce infinite embarrassments and vexations in the course of trade; and often subject the innocent to the grossest frauds. The evils of this nature were so extensively felt, that the power was unhesitatingly confided by the articles of confederation exclusively to the general government, notwithstanding the extraordinary jealousy, which pervades every clause of that instrument. But the concurrent power thereby reserved to the states, (as well as the want of a power to regulate the value of foreign coin,) was, under that feeble pageant of sovereignty, soon found to destroy the whole importance of the grant. The floods of depreciated paper money, with which most of the states of the Union, during the last war, as well as the revolutionary war with England, were inundated, to the dismay of the traveller and the ruin of commerce, afford a lively proof of the mischiefs of a currency exclusively under the control of the states.

§ 1115. It will be hereafter seen, that this is an exclusive power in congress, the states being expressly prohibited from coining money. And it has been said by an eminent statesman, that it is difficult to maintain, on the face of the constitution itself and independent of long continued practice, the doctrine, that the states, not being at liberty to coin money, can authorize the circulation of bank paper, as currency, at all. His reasoning deserves grave consideration, and is to the following effect. The states cannot coin money. Can they, then, coin that, which becomes the actual and almost universal substitute for money? Is not the right of issuing paper, intended for circulation in the place, and as the representative of metallic currency, derived merely from the power of coining and regulating the metallic currency? Could congress, if it did not possess the power of coining money and regulating the value of foreign coins, create a bank with the power to circulate bills? It would be difficult to make it out. Where, then, do the states, to whom all control over the metallic currency is altogether prohibited, obtain this power? It is true, that in other countries, private bankers, having no legal authority over the coin, issue notes for circulation. But this they do always with the consent of government, express or implied; and government restrains and regulates all their operations at its pleasure. It would be a startling proposition in any other part of the world, that the prerogative of coining money, held by government, was liable to be defeated, counteracted, or impeded by another prerogative, held in other hands, of authorizing a paper circulation. It is further to be observed, that the states cannot issue bills of credit; not that they cannot make them a legal tender; but that they cannot issue them at all. This is a clear indication of the intent of the constitution to restrain the states, as well from establishing a paper circulation, as from interfering with the metallic circulation. Banks have been created by states with no capital whatever, their notes being put in circulation simply on the credit of the state. What are the issues of such banks, but bills of credit issued by the state?

§ 1116. Whatever may be the force of this reasoning, it is probably too late to correct the error, if error there be, in the assumption of this power by the states, since it has an inveterate practice in its favour through a very long period, and indeed ever since the adoption of the constitution.

§ 1117. The other power, "to fix the standard of weights and measures," was, doubtless, given from like motives of public policy, for the sake of uniformity, and the convenience of commerce. Hitherto, however, it has remained a dormant power, from the many difficulties attendant upon the subject, although it has been repeatedly brought to the attention of congress in most elaborate reports. Until congress shall fix a standard, the understanding seems to be, that the states possess the power to fix their own weights and measures; or, at least, the existing standards at the adoption of the constitution remain in full force. Under the confederation, congress possessed the like exclusive power. In England, the power to regulate weights and measures is said by Mr. Justice Blackstone to belong to the royal prerogative. But it has been remarked by a learned commentator on his work, that the power cannot, with propriety, be referred to the king's prerogative; for, from Magna Charta to the present time, there are above twenty acts of parliament to fix and establish the standard and uniformity of weights and measures.

SEE ALSO:

Articles of Confederation, art. 9, 1 Mar. 1781
Gouverneur Morris to William Hemsley, 30 Apr. 1783, Jefferson Papers 7:169–72
Thomas Jefferson, Some Thoughts on Coinage, Mar. 1784, Papers 7:173–75
Thomas Jefferson, Notes on Coinage, Mar.–May 1784, Papers 7:175–85
Thomas Jefferson, Notes for Reply to Robert Morris, 7–9 May 1784, Papers 7:193–94
An Act Establishing a Mint, and Regulating the Coins of the United States, 1 Stat. 246 (1792)
An Act to Authorize the Issuing of Treasury Notes, 2 Stat. 766 (1812)

Article 1, Section 8, Clause 6

To provide for the Punishment of counterfeiting the Securities and current Coin of the United States:

1

RECORDS OF THE FEDERAL CONVENTION

[*2:315; Madison, 17 Aug.*]

Mr. Governr Morris thought it would be necessary to extend the authority farther, so as to provide for the punishment of counterfeiting in general. Bills of exchange for example might be forged in one State and carried into another:

It was suggested by some other member that *foreign* paper might be counterfeited by Citizens; and that it might be politic to provide national authority for the punishment of it. . . .

Mr. Elseworth enlarged the motion so as to read "to define and punish piracies and felonies committed on the high seas, counterfeiting the securities and current coin of the U. States, and offences agst. the law of Nations" which was agreed to, nem. con.

2

St. George Tucker, Blackstone's Commentaries 1:App. 262–64 1803

This power seems to be a natural incident to two others, of which we have before taken notice: the power of borrowing money on the credit of the United States, and that of coining money, and regulating the value thereof.

But congress appear to have extended the interpretation of this article much further than it might have been supposed it would bear: and possibly much further than the framers of the constitution intended. I allude to the act of 5 cong. c. 78, to punish frauds committed on the bank of the United States, which inflicts the penalty of fine and imprisonment, for forging or counterfeiting any bill or note, issued by order of the president, directors and company of the bank of the United States.

The right of congress to establish this company or corporation, with exclusive privileges, was warmly contested when the bill for establishing the bank was introduced into congress. 1 cong. 3 sess. c. 10. The same congress had at their first session agreed to an amendment of the constitution, declaring, that the powers not delegated to the United States, by the constitution, nor prohibited by it to the states, are reserved to the states respectively, or to the people. The advocates for the bill were challenged to produce the clause in the constitution which gave congress power to erect a bank. It nevertheless passed both houses. The president of the United States hesitated; it is said that he consulted his constitutional advisers upon the subject. That two of them were of opinion the bill was unconstitutional. It nevertheless, received his assent on the last day, that the constitution allowed him to deliberate upon it. Had he turned to the journals of the convention (as on another occasion,) it has been confidently said, he would there have seen, that the proposition to authorise congress to establish a bank, had been made in convention and rejected: of this, he can not be supposed to have been ignorant, as he presided in the convention, when it happened; the journals of that body were then a secret, and in his keeping. If it was proper to resort to those journals to give a proper interpretation to the constitution in one instance, it surely was equally proper in the other; and if the rejection of one proposition in that body, was a sufficient reason for rejecting the same, when made by either house of congress, it seems difficult to assign a reason why the other should not have been treated in the same manner.

If it were, in fact, an unconstitutional exercise of power in congress to pass a law establishing the bank, nothing can manifest the impropriety of over-stepping the limits of the constitution, more than the act which we have just noticed. It shows that the most unauthorised acts of government may be drawn into precedents to justify other unwarrantable usurpations.

3

State v. Randall *2 Aiken 89 (Vt. 1827)*

Hutchinson, J.: . . . The motion in arrest is now to be considered; and the first and second points urged will be disposed of together. The first point is, that the courts of the United States have jurisdiction of the offence charged. The second is, that the State Court has no such jurisdiction; and the reason assigned in argument is, that the courts of the United States have a paramount jurisdiction.

That the courts of the United States have this paramount jurisdiction, is inferred from the constitutional power of congress to legislate upon this subject, and from their having in fact so legislated. The power of congress upon this subject is comprised in the 8th section, article 1st, of the constitution, on the 27th page of our Statute Book, and is in these words;—"The congress shall have power to provide for the punishment of counterfeiting the securities and current coin of the United States." Whatever power upon this subject is not given to congress, by the above section, yet remains in the several states: for this is all that gives any such power, and the 12th article of the amendments, is as follows: "The powers not delegated to the United States by the constitution, not prohibited by it to the states, are reserved to the states respectively, or to the people."

Now, it is not, nor can it be, pretended, that bank notes are a current coin, and within that expression of the constitution. Nor is it easy to conceive how they can be termed the securities of the United States. The United States have not issued them, nor are they holden to pay them. The United States own some shares in the bank stock, and in this they are like other stock-holders, but not the individual stockholders, but the bank, or whole body of stockholders, who act by their agents, the President and Directors, issue the bills, and must pay them when returned for payment. Those are the securities of the United States, which are issued by their direction, and for which they receive a consideration, and which they must pay and redeem. Such are various certificates, indents and notes issued by the officers of the United States, under some law of congress, showing a debt due from the United States; such were the treasury notes issued in the time of the late war.

If congress have any right to legislate upon that subject, they derive it by implication merely. It is inferred from their right to establish a bank; but it has been a subject of great doubt whether they have that right. And, if that right be doubtful, their right to give jurisdiction to the United States' courts of the offence of counterfeiting the bank bills, must be no less doubtful.

But, if it were a conceded point, that congress have such a right to legislate upon this subject, we cannot admit, that by that merely, the state Legislatures are deprived of such right. The congress of the United States have never so understood the constitution, and great practical difficulty would result from such a construction.

The constitution, article 3d, section 2d, defines to what the judicial power of the United States shall extend; and among other things, says, it shall extend to controversies between a state and citizens of another state, between citizens of different states, between citizens of the same state, claiming lands under grants of different states, &c. Suppose congress had never passed any law giving the jurisdiction of these subjects to any particular court of the United States, or had never established any courts to whom such jurisdiction could be given, can it be pretended that these cases would be out of the pale of the law? That no action could be maintained in the courts of this state in favour of a citizen of Massachusetts, against a citizen of this state? No actions between our own citizens claiming lands under grants from different states? It is impossible that a court should so decide. In the provisions made by congress, adapted to these cases, they consider that the state courts hold jurisdiction, till some law of congress transfers the exclusive jurisdiction to the courts of the United States. Their provisions are contained in the 11th section of the judiciary act. That gives no jurisdiction whatever to the courts of the United States, in cases of common law and equity, unless the sum or value in controversy exceeds five hundred dollars, exclusive of costs: and the original jurisdiction is given in those cases only *in concurrence with the courts of the several states.* And a part of the same section gives to the circuit courts exclusive cognizance of all crimes and offences cognizable under the authority of the United States, except where said act otherwise provides, or the laws of the United States should otherwise direct, and concurrent jurisdiction with the district courts, of the crimes and offences cognizable therein. The expression, *offences cognizable under the authority of the United States,* implies, that congress must have power from the constitution to make, and in fact make, laws for the punishment of crimes, before the circuit courts can take cognizance of the same; and the exception which follows, takes out of this jurisdiction every case taken out and placed elsewhere by the same, or any other act of congress.

The foregoing views have been fully sanctioned by the supreme court of the United States, in the case of *Houston* vs. *Moore, 5 Wheaton,* page 1. A statute of Pennsylvania, of March 1814, enacted, among other things, "that every non-commissioned officer and private of the militia, who shall have neglected or refused to serve when called into actual service, in pursuance of any order or requisition of the President of the United States, shall be liable to the penalties defined in the act of the congress of the United States, passed on the 28th of February, 1795." *Houston* was called to go into actual service and refused, and was fined by a court martial, ordered under the state authority, and the fine was levied of his property; and he brought his action of trespass for taking his property, which was decided against him in the highest court of the state; and the decisions comprised in a bill of exceptions were revised upon a writ of error, brought to the supreme court of the United States, and the question to be decided was, whether the state statute was constitutional? It was decided so to be, and the judgment was affirmed. This is a long report, and the question of concurrent jurisdiction of the United States' courts and state courts fully examined; and the result drawn, is, that where congress may give jurisdiction to the courts of the United States, yet have not done it, the state courts retain jurisdiction; or, if exclusive jurisdiction is not given to the United States' courts, the state courts retain concurrent jurisdiction.

The cases alluded to, of state bankrupt laws and steam boat grants, rest upon other parts of the constitution, and have little or no analogy to the present question. The state bankrupt laws fall within a section of the constitution which negatives the power of a state to pass laws of the nature therein named; one of which is a law impairing the obligation of contracts. And the steam boat grants import an exclusive privilege, which interferes with the powers of congress to regulate commerce with foreign nations, and among the several states, and with the powers actually exercised by congress in regulating the coasting trade.

Hence we have arrived at the conclusion, that even if congress have the power and right to give exclusive jurisdiction over this offence to the courts of the United States, until they shall have done so, the jurisdiction remains in the state courts, by force of the laws of the several states, as fully as if congress had no power to legislate upon the subject.

But it is said, that congress have legislated upon the subject, and made provision for the punishment of the same offence; and the act of congress is produced. See the statute of 1816, *Ingersol's Digest,* page 93. The terms of the body of this statute are sufficiently extensive to confer entire jurisdiction over this offence to the courts of the United States; but the whole statute must be construed together, or the correct inference will not be drawn. And the statute contains the following proviso: "Provided that nothing herein contained, shall be construed to deprive the courts of the individual states of a jurisdiction, under the laws of the individual states, over any offence declared punishable by this act." The necessary construction of this statute is, that congress admit, or concede the previous power of the states to enact laws, and their courts to execute them, over this offence, and give jurisdiction to the courts of the United States, *sub modo,* and so as not to interfere with that previous jurisdiction of the state courts. The 17th of *John. Rep.* pages 4th and 261st, is cited to show, that congress cannot give jurisdiction to the state courts. Probably they cannot give such jurisdiction, but it is unnecessary now to decide that question. It is sufficient for the present case, if the courts of this state would have had jurisdiction, had not congress interfered at all, and that the interference of congress expressly leaves the state courts enjoying all the rights of jurisdiction they had before the act of congress passed. The distinction between the conferring a jurisdiction by congress, and the refusal to take away a jurisdiction already enjoyed, is too obvious to require elucidation.

Other acts of congress, of an earlier date, punishing the counterfeiting of United States' bank bills contain each the same proviso. In fact, that subject has never by congress been taken from the jurisdiction of the state courts, where they held the same by their own laws.

Furthermore, congress have the most conclusive right to legislate upon the subject of counterfeiting the coins, and may give exclusive jurisdiction for the punishment thereof to the courts of the United States. Upon this they have legislated, and have given jurisdiction to the courts of the United States, but not exclusive; for they have added a proviso similar to the other, expressly leaving a concurrent jurisdiction in the state courts, under the state laws. See said *Ingersol's Digest,* page 163.

This concurrent jurisdiction has always been exercised by the state courts ever since the organization of the federal government, both over the subject of counterfeiting the coins and the bills of the United States' Bank. Many convictions have been had, and prisoners punished corporeally, and by confinement to hard labour, and otherwise, according to the laws of the several states. We should be afraid, at this late period, to decide that all these convictions have been *coram non judice,* and prepare the way for all the prisoners to bring their actions of trespass against those who inflicted the punishments, and even against the judges themselves.

Besides, during all this time, no person has ever appealed to the paramount jurisdiction of the United States' courts for redress, nor has any branch of the United States' government furnished an intimation, that these proceedings were wrong. The practice, therefore, universal in itself, is supported by general approbation; and a contrary practice would be attended with such incalculable inconvenience, that no state tribunal ought ever to take the lead in attempting a change. What could be done in case of a change? Congress have made no provision for such an event. Their laws punish by confinement to hard labour; but they have made no provision for any place for such confinement. The marshal may hire, if he can; otherwise there is no place within his control. It would require an entirely new regulation of United States' prisons, if the jurisdiction of the courts of the United States were to become and be considered as exclusive over all the crimes of which they may take jurisdiction.

The object of the Federal Compact does not require such a course. That object is to unite the strength of all the states for the common support and defence of their national rights. To effect this, the judicial power of the courts of the United States should extend to all those matters that may affect the general union, and tend to support its integrity and harmony. Their jurisdiction should extend over such crimes as necessarily affect the Union, or the Federal Government as such. Hence their criminal code is almost exclusively of this description. The statutes of the United States provide for the punishment of treason against the United States; piracy, murder or robbery upon the high seas, or a territory under the sole jurisdiction of the United States, forgery of the publick securities of the United States, stealing, altering, &c. the records of the United States' courts, perjury committed in the courts of the United States; resisting the officers of the United States in their official duties; the counterfeiting the coins of the United States, &c. &c. So far as this last offence is an attack upon the Mint of the United States, or upon the Treasury, by creating a liability that counterfeit coins make a part of the national funds, it is not only proper, but necessary that there should be a tribunal for their punishment, without depending upon the state courts. But, so far as the crime bears principally upon the rights of the citizens of the individual states, it is at least, safe and proper to permit the state courts, under the state laws, to punish such offence. The cases might be too numerous to receive a proper attention from the high tribunals of the United States, so few in number as are provided, and so remote may be the officers whose duty it might be to prosecute. But, be this as it may, congress, while they give a jurisdiction to the courts of the United States over the counterfeiting the coins and the bills of the United States' bank, say expressly, that they will not take from the state courts any jurisdiction they may have, by the laws of the individual states, over the same offences.

But there is urged upon the Court the hardship, and even absurdity, that a man should be liable to be arraigned before two distinct tribunals, for the same offence. The difficulty in this, like other concurrent jurisdictions, is rather imaginary than real. The court that first has jurisdiction, by commencement of the prosecution, will retain the same till a decision is made; and a decision in one court will bar any farther prosecution for the same offence, in that or any other court. It is like the case of civil suits for matters over five hundred dollars, between citizens of different states. The creditor may sue, at his election, either before the court of the state, or of the United States; but, when he has made such election, the debtor is safe from any liability to be called before the other court. So, if goods are stolen in one county, and carried by the thief through several counties, he is liable to be prosecuted in either of those counties; but, when prosecuted in one, that puts an end to his liability for that offence.

Sufficient, perhaps, is said, even if the crime charged were clearly comprised in the United States' statute, for then the jurisdictions would be concurrent; but the crime of which the respondent stands convicted by the jury is clearly not contained in said statute. It is contended, however, that, although the same act is not punished by the United States' law, yet congress having legislated upon the subject, all is to be considered as included; what is not expressed is to be considered as merged in what is expressed: or, in other words, congress having affixed a punishment to the forging and passing these counterfeit bills, it is a virtual enactment, that no other transaction concerning them shall be made penal. This argument is plausible, and may be applied with correctness and force to certain cases where the very enactment implies a negative of all other provisions. For instance, the laws of congress, regulating the coasting trade and prescribing requisites that must be complied with by all who embark in that trade, necessarily imply that the trade may be pursued with no other restraints from government than those prescribed. So of the laws regulating foreign commerce, so far as relates to the requisitions of our own government. But those who sail within the jurisdiction of any foreign government, must not consider our government as warranting that there shall be no new requisitions there. The same may be said of statutes in general, that confer rights unconditionally. No condition can be lawfully added afterwards. But, should courts decide that a statute of the United States' congress, providing for the punishment merely of the original counterfeiting of coins or bank bills, divests each state of the power to pass a law, to punish the passing, to her own citizens, such counterfeit coins or bills, this would be narrowing down the sovereignty of the individual states to a small compass. Just so, should congress, as in the present case, provide a punishment for making and passing, but none for the having in possession, with intent to pass. The powers of a state, necessary to prevent a continual depredation upon her citizens, by fraud and deception, should never be thus narrowed down by implication merely. It is soon enough for the state courts to relinquish their jurisdiction over such offences, where it is expressly conferred by the statute of the state, when some act of congress transfers the exclusive jurisdiction to the courts of the United States.

The decision of the Court is, that the state court has jurisdiction of the offence charged, and of which the respondent has been found guilty.

Another objection urged in arrest, is, that the statute, upon which the indictment is founded, is so repugnant to itself as to be wholly void. (*See the statute, p.* 261.) So far as need be recited, it is as follows: "That if any person shall counterfeit, or cause or procure to be counterfeited, or aid or assist in counterfeiting, any bill or note issued, or to be issued, by the president, directors and company of the bank of the United States, or shall alter any such bill or note, issued or to be issued, as aforesaid, or shall utter, pass, or give in payment, or offer to pass or give in payment, or procure to be offered, passed, or given in payment, or have in his possession, with an intention to utter, pass or give in payment, any such *counterfeited,* or altered bill or note, knowing the same to be *counterfeited* or altered, every person so offending, on conviction, shall be punished," &c. The repugnancy objected to, is created by the use of the word *counterfeited.* It is said, that the expression, a counterfeited bill, imports the true bill, in imitation of which some spurious bill is made; and that the expression in the indictment, "had in his possession a certain false, forged and *counterfeited* bank note, with an intention to utter, pass and give in payment the same, which was made in imitation of, and did purport to be a bank note, issued, &c." imports the charge of having in his possession the true bill, not the spurious one; and that the alleging it to be false and forged, (words not in the statute) does not help the case, but adds to the repugnancy. The respondent's counsel, in support of this objection, have cited the *4th of Cranch R.* 167, *United States* vs. *Cantrill.* That was a motion in arrest, for two reasons assigned, one to the indictment itself, and one to the statute on which it was predicated. It was submitted without argument, and the court decided, that the judgment ought to be arrested for reasons assigned in the record. In adverting to the reasons, the statute is recited as follows. "If any person shall utter or publish, as true, any false, forged or counterfeited bill or note, issued by order of the president, directors and company of the bank of the United States, and signed by the president, and counter-signed by the cashier," &c. This recital furnishes reason enough for the arrest, for such a statute punishes the publishing as true, bills actually issued by order of the president, &c. and actually signed by the President, &c. Such bills may be said to be counterfeited, according to the strict interpretation of that word, but they cannot be called false and forged; nor ought people to be punished for passing them. It is not so easy to see the force of the other objection, nor is it certain that the court intended to sanction it. The charge is, that the defendant [had] "a certain false, forged and counterfeit paper, purporting to be a bank bill of the United States, for ten dollars, signed by *Thomas Willing,* president, and *G. Simpson,* cashier, &c." It is said, that this means and imports, that the false and counterfeit bill was in fact signed by *Thomas Willing,* and so of the cashier. This is not the necessary construction, and it is obvious the person who drafted the indictment, intended the word *signed* should refer to the true bill, which the counterfeit purported to be. Remove the comma that precedes the word *signed,* and such would be the necessary construction, and the objection would vanish. And it would seem hardly proper to quash an indictment upon so nice a point as would depend upon the punctuation, which is always in some degree arbitrary.

Possibly another objection might have had weight, though it does not appear to be noticed. The expression is, a bill of the United States, not of the bank of the United States. This was a failure to declare within the statute. At any rate, the United States' statute was considered to be a nullity, and congress passed another upon the same subject.

It is suggested, that the same repugnancy exists in the statute of this state, above recited, as in that of the United States. If the word *counterfeit* had been used instead of the word *counterfeited,* in the two last places where it occurs, in what is herein before recited, the difficulty would all be removed, with regard to that part of the statute. The word is used in its proper sense where it first occurs in the section. The expressions, "shall counterfeit, or procure to be counterfeited, or assist in counterfeiting," mean the making or procuring to be made, or assisting to make a false and counterfeit bill, in imitation of a true bill, issued, &c. and the expression, "had in his possession a counterfeit bill, knowing the same to be counterfeit, and with intention of uttering, &c." would be a consistent and proper description of the crime intended to be punished. And wherever the word *altered* is used in the section, it is used in a consistent and proper sense. It is obvious, that the legislature, in this statute, used the word *counterfeited* in the sense of *counterfeit,* in the part applicable to this indictment. Now the question is, shall the Court sanction this use of the word, or decide the statute void, for its repugnant use of the word? In *Swift's Dig. 1st vol. p.* 12, several rules of construing statutes are collected, which may be of use upon this question.

1st. We must consider the subject matter, and affix to the words used, a meaning correspondent to the subject to which they are applied. In applying this rule, it is plain the object of the legislature was, to provide for the punishment of every kind of traffick in spurious bank bills. They begin by describing, in proper language, the making of them, and then proceed, in as proper language, to describe the passing them and having them in possession with intent to pass, till they come to the word which should characterize the spurious bill, and there use the word *counterfeited.* To construe this as meaning a true bill, or the one of which a counterfeit was passed, or intended to be passed, would be changing the subject matter entirely. If there can be no mistake, either by the Court, or those who read the statute to learn what conduct is prohibited, as to what the legislature intended by the word *counterfeited,* we ought to construe it as they intended it. Words are but signs of ideas, and the same words are frequently used, in some degree, in different senses. The ancient forms of declarations for assault and battery, show that the word *entreat* was then used in the same sense as we now use the word *treat.*

A second rule from the same author is, "The cotemporaneous exposition of a statute is to be regarded; such as the opinion of the sages of the law who lived at the time it was made." In applying this rule, we observe, that the statute of 1797, made upon this subject, and which was in operation twenty years, used the word *counterfeited* in the same place and sense as this statute. Very many indictments were framed, and convictions had upon that statute. Some were met with demurrers, others with motions in arrest. The ablest counsel in the several counties were employed to defend, and it is not known that any indictment failed, through the insufficiency of that statute. Either the counsel thought it no objection, and did not move it, or it was overruled. Every State's Attorney found difficulty upon the subject. But the indictments were drawn much upon the plan of these 2d and 4th counts, describing the spurious bill, and then saying, that it was made in imitation of, and did then and there purport to be, a bank note of, &c. issued, &c. describing the true bill, imitated by the spurious one. But in a count for uttering, &c. the expression, *knowing the same to be counterfeited,* was necessarily used, for such was the statute.

A third rule from the same author is, that "Words and phrases, the meaning of which has been ascertained in a statute, are, when used in a subsequent statute, to be understood in the same sense."

After the statute of 1797 had been in operation twenty years, and the word *counterfeited* had been considered as meaning the same as the word *counterfeit,* not only in the statute, but in indictments founded upon it, in all, or nearly all the counties of the state, the revision of the criminal code was submitted to a respectable judiciary committee, who reported, and the legislature enacted, the law now in question, placing the word *counterfeited* where it must be understood in the same sense as in said former statute, from which this was nearly copied. Here then, is virtually an enactment of the legislature, that the word *counterfeited* in that statute shall mean the same as *counterfeit.*

It is worthy of observation, that though congress passed a new law to remedy the evils in the old one, as before mentioned, yet the word *counterfeited* is used in the same sense as in our statute, three times in the statute of the United States, now in force, to punish the counterfeiting the publick securities; and once in the act to punish the *counterfeiting* of bank bills.

4

STATE v. TUTT

2 Bailey 44 (S.C. 1830)

HARPER, J. delivered the opinion of the Court.

In support of the first ground in arrest of judgment, the reasoning of the prisoner's counsel has been to this effect. That the act of Congress establishing the Bank of the United States, provides for punishing the counterfeiting, or the uttering and publishing as true, of any counterfeit note, bill, order or check of that institution, by fine and imprisonment. That it has been decided that the general Government had constitutional power to establish the bank, and it was necessarily incident to that power, that it should be able to protect its paper from forgery. That, at least the Court will be unwilling to question the power of the government in a case like the present; and having legislated on the subject, its legislation must be exclusive. That the Federal Government possesses exclusive power in three instances. 1st. Where the power is granted exclusively in terms; 2d. Where it is granted to the Government, and prohibited to the States; and 3d. Where the power is granted, and having been exercised by legislation on the subject, the exercise of similar power by the States would be repugnant and incompatible. That to the last class belongs the power in question: And the act of Congress having fixed the punishment of counterfeiting bank notes, or uttering them as true, it is repugnant and incompatible that a different punishment should be prescribed by the act of the State. Will you say that the punishment shall be accumulative, and that the party may be tried first in one Court, and then in the other, in violation of the privilege of a citizen not to be twice put in jeopardy for the same offence, or shall a conviction under one jurisdiction be a bar to trial in the other? Many absurd and inconvenient consequences would follow this view of the subject. Then a pardon by the Governor before trial, must be a bar to a prosecution in the Federal Court, or a pardon of the President in the State Court. That it is true, the act saves the jurisdiction of the State Courts over such offences; but if the legislation of Congress has covered the whole ground, and thus become exclusive, it had no right to delegate such jurisdiction. The case of Houston *v.* Moore, 5 Wheat. 1. was principally relied on in support of these views.

The constitution expressly grants to Congress the power to punish the offence of *counterfeiting* the securities and current coin of the United States. Yet, in the case of the State *v.* Antonio, 2 Treadw. 776, which was a prosecution for *uttering and publishing* forged coin, the Constitutional Court held that its jurisdiction was not ousted. The Court intimates its impression, (the grant to Congress being of the power to punish *counterfeiting*) that if the jurisdiction to punish the *uttering and publishing*, were exclusive in either the Federal or State tribunals, it appertained rather to the latter. This seems not to be without reason. The offence against the Government of the United States consists in discrediting its currency. That against the State in defrauding its citizens. The offence against the State is certainly of the more palpable and dangerous character. The framers of the Constitution may have supposed that the power of punishing the actual forgery, was a sufficient security to the general Government, while to the States, it belonged to protect their citizens from the consequences of passing and circulating spurious coin. If this reasoning has any weight with respect to the uttering of forged coin, it would seem intitled to still more with respect to forged bank notes. The power to establish a bank, is an implied one, as being necessary and proper to carry the granted powers into effect, and from this implied power is implied the further power to protect the paper of the bank by punishing the circulating of spurious paper. The necessity of this implication may perhaps be doubted. The injury to the bank, of circulating forged paper is, that its genuine paper may be discredited, and its circulation impeded. But this cannot take place to a great extent, and is trifling, compared with the injury a State may sustain, if it be deprived of the power of protecting its citizens from being inundated by a spurious currency; injuring their property, depraving their morals and embarrassing their intercourse.

Suppose, that instead of the fine and imprisonment imposed by the act, Congress had thought a trifling fine of a few dollars sufficient for the protection of the bank, must the State abandon all power of protecting its citizens? The argument, from necessity, seems much stronger in favor of the power of the States. On this question, however, I do not think it necessary to give a definitive opinion.

The grant of a power to Congress which is not prohibited to the States, is likely to be the source of many difficult questions in our jurisprudence. Among these will probably be, whether the same act of an individual may not constitute a distinct and separate offence against each Government, and be punishable by each. We have held in some instances, that the same act may constitute two distinct offences against our own Government. The question whether, if both Governments provided for the punishment of the same offence, the law of the State shall be null, and superseded by the law of the general Government, seems to be decided by the case of Houston *v.* Moore. But there is this distinction between that case and the present. In that, the act punished by the law of the State, was certainly and exclusively an offence against the general Government; a refusal by a militiaman to obey the orders of the president, which the State undertook to punish. Here, certainly there is an offence against the State, and a very different one from that committed against the United States. These difficulties, however, do not arise in the case before us, as the jurisdiction of the States is expressly saved by the act of Congress in question. The law of Congress for punishing the counterfeiting of coin, enacts that it shall not be construed to deprive the Courts of the individual States, of jurisdiction under the laws of the State, over offences made punishable by the act. Justice Story in the case of Houston *v.* Moore, recognizes the jurisdiction of the States under this saving. He refers to the practice of the several States, particularly of Pennsylvania. The cases of White *v.* Commonwealth, 4 Binn. 408, and Livingston *v.* Van Ingen, 9 Johns. 507, are referred to in a note. I believe that most of the States have similar cases, and in none of them has their authority been called in question. The saving under the law establishing the bank, is in a different form, and renders the question less disputable. It is in the form of a proviso: "provided that nothing herein contained shall be construed to deprive the Courts of the individual States of a jurisdiction under the laws of the several States, over any offence declared punishable by this act." Congress makes it a condition of its legislation, that it shall not interfere with the jurisdiction of the States. It is certainly true, that the general Government cannot confer a jurisdiction on the States where it was not possessed before. But in the case we are considering, there was unquestionably a jurisdiction in the first instance. The State is supposed to have lost it, because Congress having a concurrent jurisdiction, and having exercised it, its laws being supreme, have come in collision with the law of the State. But Congress itself has declared that its laws shall not come into collision with the law of the State; but if there be any repugnancy or incompatibility, the law of the State shall have effect. It seems to me, therefore, that if either law be inoperative within this State, it is clearly the law of Congress; and that by virtue of its own provisions.

SEE ALSO:

Records of the Federal Convention, Farrand 2:168, 182, 312, 570, 595; 4:52

State v. *Antonio*, 2 Treadway 776 (S.C. 1816)

Joseph Story, Commentaries on the Constitution 3:§ 1118 (1833)

Article 1, Section 8, Clause 7

To establish Post Offices and post Roads;

1

Records of the Federal Convention

[*2:615; Madison, 14 Sept.*]

Docr. Franklin moved to add after the words "post roads" Art I Sect. 8. "a power to provide for cutting canals where deemed necessary"

Mr Wilson 2ded. the motion

Mr Sherman objected. The expense in such cases will fall on the U— States, and the benefit accrue to the places where the canals may be cut.

Mr Wilson. Instead of being an expence to the U. S. they may be made a source of revenue.

Mr. Madison suggested an enlargement of the motion into a power "to grant charters of incorporation where the interest of the U.S. might require & the legislative provisions of individual States may be incompetent". His primary object was however to secure an easy communication between the States which the free intercourse now to be opened, seemed to call for—The political obstacles being removed, a removal of the natural ones as far as possible ought to follow. Mr. Randolph 2ded. the proposition.

Mr King thought the power unneccessary.

Mr Wilson. It is necessary to prevent *a State* from obstructing the *general* welfare.

Mr King—The States will be prejudiced and divided into parties by it—In Philada. & New York, It will be referred to the establishment of a Bank, which has been a subject of contention in those Cities. In other places it will be referred to mercantile monopolies.

Mr. Wilson mentioned the importance of facilitating by canals, the communication with the Western Settlements—As to Banks he did not think with Mr. King that the power in that point of view would excite the prejudices & parties apprehended. As to mercantile monopolies they are already included in the power to regulate trade.

Col: Mason was for limiting the power to the single case of Canals. He was afraid of monopolies of every sort, which he did not think were by any means already implied by the Constitution as supposed by Mr. Wilson.

The motion being so modified as to admit a distinct question specifying & limited to the case of canals.

N— H— no— Mas. no. Ct. no— N— J— no— Pa ay. Del. no— Md. no. Va. ay. N— C— no— S— C. no— Geo. ay. [Ayes—3; noes—8.]

2

John Jay to George Washington
21 Sept. 1788

John Jay Papers, Columbia University

Your Ideas relative to the Diffusion of Intelligence and useful Information by means of news Papers and the Press, appear to me exceedingly just; nor do I percieve any good Objection to preferring the Stages to Post Riders for the Transportation of the mail, on the contrary I think the Ballance of advantages is clearly in favor of the former.

How far it was the Duty of the Post office to recieve and forward news papers is a Question respecting which I confess I have Doubts. If I am rightly informed the Post Riders were formerly *permitted* to carry news Papers on such Terms as might be settled between them and the Printers. The Number of Printers and of news Papers are now so great, that if the latter were admitted into the Mail the Expense to the public would be considerably enhanced; and it seems but reasonable that as the Printers (as well as the public) would derive much advantage from such a Regulation, they should contribute somewhat to it.

The Direction of the Post Office, instead of being as hitherto, consigned chiefly to a committee, and managed without much System, should I think be regulated by Law, and put under the Superintendence, and in some Degree under the controul of the Executive. The Public are not well satisfied on this Head, as Matters now stand, and there is but little Reason to expect any important change during the Existence of the present Government. The succeeding one will have an opportunity of doing a very *acceptable* Service to their Constituents by regulating the Post office in a proper Manner; and the more of *such* things they may have to do, the better.

3

HOUSE OF REPRESENTATIVES, POST OFFICE BILL
6–7 Dec. 1791, 3, 5 Jan. 1792
Annals 3:229–41, 303–10

[*6 Dec. 1791*]

Mr. LIVERMORE observed that the Legislative body being empowered by the Constitution "to establish post offices and post roads," it is as clearly their duty to designate the roads as to establish the offices; and he did not think they could with propriety delegate that power, which they were themselves appointed to exercise. Some gentlemen, he knew, were of opinion that the business of the United States could be better transacted by a single person than by many; but this was not the intention of the Constitution. It was provided that the Government should be administered by Representatives, of the people's choice; so that every man, who has the right of voting, shall be in some measure concerned in making every law for the United States. The establishment of post roads he considered as a very important object; but he did not wish to see them so diffused as to become a heavy charge where the advantage resulting from them would be but small; nor, on the other hand, for the sake of bringing a revenue into the Treasury, consent to straiten them so as to check the progress of information. If the post office were to be regulated by the will of a single person, the dissemination of intelligence might be impeded, and the people kept entirely in the dark with respect to the transactions of Government; or the Postmaster, if vested with the whole power, might branch out the offices to such a degree as to make them prove a heavy burden to the United States. In many instances the expense is productive of a benefit sufficient to counterbalance it; in others, no public benefit arises, but some individuals reap a private advantage from the institution, whilst it is injurious to others. The most material point, in his opinion, was to determine the road itself; if the House gave up that, they might as well leave all the rest of the business to the discretion of the Postmaster, and permit him to settle the rates of postage, and every other particular relative to the post office, by saying, at once, "there shall be a Postmaster General, who shall have the whole government of the post office, under such regulations as he from time to time shall be pleased to enact."

Mr. SEDGWICK felt himself by no means disposed to resign all the business of the House to the President, or to any one else; but he thought that the Executive part of the business ought to be left to Executive officers. He did not, for his part, know the particular circumstances of population, geography, &c., which had been taken into the calculation by the select committee, when they pointed out the roads delineated in the bill; but he would ask, whether they understood the subject so thoroughly as the Executive officer would, who being responsible to the people for the proper discharge of the trust reposed in him, must use his utmost diligence in order to a satisfactory execution of the delegated power? As to the constitutionality of this delegation, it was admitted by the committee themselves who brought in the bill; for if the power was altogether indelegable, no part of it could be delegated; and if a part of it could, he saw no reason why the whole could not. The second section was as unconstitutional as the first, for it is there said, that "it shall be lawful for the Postmaster General to establish such other roads as post roads, as to him may seem necessary."

Congress, he observed, are authorized not only to establish post offices and post roads, but also to borrow money; but is it understood that Congress are to go in a body to borrow every sum that may be requisite? Is it not rather their office to determine the principle on which the business is to be conducted, and then delegate the power of carrying their resolves into execution? They are also empowered to coin money, and if no part of their power be delegable, he did not know but they might be obliged to turn coiners, and work in the Mint themselves. Nay, they must even act the part of executioners, in punishing piracies committed on the high seas. In the delegation of power, the whole purpose, in his opinion, is answered, when the rules by which the business is to be conducted are pointed out by law; nor could he discover anything in the Constitution to restrict the House from adopting this mode of conducting business.

Mr. HARTLEY.—I cannot agree with the gentleman from Massachusetts, that as often as this business had been agitated, there had been a majority in the House in favor of leaving it to the Executive to designate the post roads. Nay, so far as my recollection (which is perhaps not so good as that gentleman's) serves me, we uniformly have had a majority for Congress to point out the post roads.

The Constitution seems to have intended that we should exercise all the powers respecting the establishing post roads we are capable of; but the gentleman says we are not competent to this duty, that it must be intrusted to the Executive.

Sir, in many questions concerning the property or geography of the United States, we had full information on this floor from every quarter. The people's interests and circumstances have been known, however distinctly or differently situated.

On the subject of the post office there has been much discussion. Almost the whole of the roads here stated have appeared in bills before, and though the gentleman (who made the motion for striking out) may not perfectly understand all the roads, yet if he will be so good as to attend to the gentlemen who represent the different parts of the Union, he ought to be satisfied. Unless they are prejudiced, they can certainly give the best information. If it were left to the President or Postmaster General, neither is acquainted with all the roads contemplated; they must depend in a great measure on the information of others.

We represent the people, we are constitutionally vested with the power of determining upon the establishment of post roads; and, as I understand at present, ought not to delegate the power to any other person.

A General Post Office is intended to be established by the bill, and the collection of the revenue is put under the superintendence of a Postmaster General; the minutiae is submitted to him. I should imagine there ought to be a limitation of the law in point of time, say three, four, or five years; when we come to the proper place, a motion to that purpose may be made. No one in the United States has a greater respect for the President than myself, and I hold that the several Departments are filled with gentlemen of the first abilities and fitness, but we are not to confine ourselves to a view of the moment. This bill has the complexion of a perpetual law; we must have some regard to consequences. If the amendment takes place, the office as well as revenue will be thrown into the power of the Executive, who may increase the roads and offices as far as the revenues go. The revenue of the post office is at present not great, but if proper seeds are now sown, it may hereafter be productive. In Great Britain, much has been obtained from the post office, and most of the European nations count upon it as a considerable branch of revenue. Will it be prudent for us to grant this power to the Executive, in the latitude contended for? We must not suppose that this country will always remain incorrupt; we shall share the fate of other nations. Through the medium of the post office a weighty influence may be obtained by the Executive; this is guarded against in England by prohibiting officers in the Post Office Department from interfering at elections. There is no such guard or caution in the present bill. By the amendment, we are unnecessarily parting with our revenues, and throwing an improper balance into the Executive scale, and which our constituents do not expect from us. The Senate heretofore have disagreed with us, but if they will take the same pains we have, the means of information is within their reach; upon a review, they may probably change their sentiments. This is a law of experiment, let us try it a few years. If, upon experience, we find ourselves incompetent to the duty, we must (if the Constitution will admit) grant the power to the Executive; or, if the Constitution will not allow such a delegation, submit the article for amendment in a constitutional way. I am against the amendment.

Mr. B. BOURNE was in favor of the amendment, which he thought both expedient and constitutional. In speaking of *post offices and post roads,* the Constitution, he observed, speaks in general terms, as it does of *a mint, excises, &c.* In passing the excise law, the House, not thinking themselves possessed of sufficient information, empowered the President to mark out the districts and surveys; and if they had a right to delegate such power to the Executive, the further delegation of the power of marking out the roads for the conveyance of the mail, could hardly be thought dangerous. The Constitution meant no more than that Congress should possess the exclusive right of doing that, by themselves or by any other person, which amounts to the same thing. The business he thought much more likely to be well executed by the President, or the Postmaster General, than by Congress. He had himself been of the committee who framed the bill, but could not tell whether the roads marked out in it were better than any other, except so far as relates to the State which he represents; and he imagined the other members of the committee were in a similar predicament. The President having opportunities of obtaining information from the different members of the House, from the Postmaster General, and from others, will be more competent to determine the proper road. It will be occasionally necessary to change the route, and lay out new roads, and he could see no inconvenience from intrusting either the President or the Postmaster General with the necessary powers for these purposes. At all events, the House could guard against any apprehended danger, by the insertion of such a clause as had been proposed, [by Mr. HARTLEY,] limiting the operation of the bill to three, four, or five years. At the expiration of that term, the power would revert to Congress, and they might then retain the exercise of it in their own hands, if they found that any improper use had been made of it.

Mr. WHITE made several observations on the expediency and constitutionality of the measure. No individual could possess an equal share of information with that House on the subject of the geography of the United States. He disapproved of the amendment for many other reasons, and particularly its approximation to the custom of England. Such advances towards Monarchy, if not checked in season, he was apprehensive would tend to unhinge the present Government. If this Government retains its present Republican form, it will be owing to the members of this House. It is easy to see what hand could be made of the post offices, if ever they are under the direction of an improper person. At the time of a general election, for instance, how easy would it be for this man to dictate to particular towns and villages, "If you do not send such a man to Congress, you shall have no post office; but if you elect my friend, you shall have a post office, and the roads shall be run agreeably to your wishes." Another improper use may be made of this power by the interception of letters, and checking the regular channel of information throughout the country. Upon the whole, he was clearly for rejecting the motion for striking out the words in the bill.

Mr. LAURANCE observed, that the revenues arising from the post office would not, perhaps, produce a sufficient sum to defray the expenses of the establishment. If this should be the fact, he would prefer the amendment, but if the revenue should increase from time to time, he should have no objection to the addition of posts and roads in proportion to such increase. The consequence of establishing so extensive a system all at once, as was contemplated in the bill, might be, that the revenue would fall short, and then additional taxes must be laid to pay off the deficiency; however, upon the whole, if he could be satisfied that the revenues of the Department would be sufficient to defray the expenses of it, he would be against striking out the clause in the bill.

Mr. PAGE.—If the motion before the committee succeeds, I shall make one which will save a deal of time and money, by making a short session of it; for if this House can, with propriety, leave the business of the post office to the President, it may leave to him any other business of legislation; and I may move to adjourn and leave all the objects of legislation to his sole consideration and direction. But how the President should be better acquainted with the proper places for post offices and post roads than the Representatives of the people, I cannot conceive. In Virginia, for instance, cannot the ten Representatives say, with more certainty, what post roads would be proper in that State than any one man? I look upon the motion as unconstitutional, and if it were not so, as having a mischievous tendency, which I am willing to believe the member who made it is not aware of.

In reply to Mr. SEDGWICK, he said, he heard but two arguments on which any stress was laid, viz: that the President's greater responsibility pointed him out as the proper person to be intrusted with the important business of establishing post offices and post roads, and that his superior knowledge of this subject ought to induce the committee to leave it to him alone; but as to the responsibility, how that can be greater than the responsibility of the members of this House, when he is appointed by Electors for a longer term than they are; and they elected by the people themselves, and accountable to them every two years, is to me inconceivable; and as to his superior knowledge, granting that he possessed it, which I cannot grant, can there be a greater paradox than the assertion that the President's knowledge alone is greater than that very knowledge, aided by the united information of both Houses of Congress, collected and presented to him in the bill? Sir, if the clause which it is said we should strike out, instead of communicating the sense of this House to the President, took away his right of approving or rejecting it, there might be some weight in the argument drawn from the supposition of his superior knowledge; but as this is not, and cannot be the case, and so far from it, that the clause submits the matter to the most mature deliberation of the President and Senate, it must be paradoxical to say that we lose the advantage of superior wisdom and knowledge of the subject, if we do not leave it to the President alone. But we are told that the motion is not unconstitutional. I think it is; but who is there that denies it is contrary to the interest and spirit of a free Government? The people, however, may think with the member who made the motion, that the President (that is, the man who is now their President) understands this matter, and can do it better than their Representatives; and they may think the whole business of Government might be safely intrusted to him; but they are too wise to make the experiment, and understand the nature of their Government so well as to complain that Congress too often commits to Heads of Departments what the Constitution requires at their hands. The President himself, if I mistake not, views the subject before us in the light I do, or he would not so repeatedly have called on us to make it a peculiar object of our deliberation.

Mr. STEELE would not take up the time of the House in considering whether the motion was constitutional or not; but he was apprehensive it would be burdensome to impose the duty on the President, who must feel very disagreeable to hear that after he had exerted his utmost abilities to give satisfaction, discontents had taken place. He hoped the gentleman from New York, who had hitherto shown himself so staunch a friend to the present Constitution, would not oppose the diffusion of knowledge and information amongst the people, upon an idea of a supposed deficiency in the revenue of the Post Office, for it might very soon increase to a sum more than sufficient for the expenses of the establishment.

Mr. VINING said, that since this subject had been before the last House, during the recess, he had seen many lights thrown on it, and he was convinced that the members were as fully competent to judge of the matter as any one man could be; this, he thought a fact not now to be disputed, as well as that more satisfaction would be given to the country in general. There is no analogy between the United States and Great Britain, when the subject of the post roads and post offices are to be considered. This country, from its great extent and uncultivated state, as well as from a thousand other causes, is not at all similar to the situation of Great Britain; therefore, any attempt to imitate their regulations would be improper. With regard to the regulation being given to the President, two things should be considered; to a good President it would be a burden; to a bad President, a dangerous power of establishing offices and roads in those places only where his interest would be promoted, and removing others of long standing, in order to harrass those he might suppose inimical to his ambitious views. The Constitution has certainly given us the power of establishing posts and roads, and it is not even implied that it should be transferred to the President; his powers are well defined; we create offices, and he fills them with such persons as he approves of, with the advice of the Senate. Having thus far stated his opinion, he would vote against the amendment to the bill; and when the first section was got over, he would propose a clause to be inserted in the second section, which he hoped would meet the ideas of the gentleman from New York, viz: that the cross-roads and offices should be so regulated as not to exceed the surplusage of the revenue of the general establishment. The doubt of the bill's not passing the Senate, should have no weight in his mind; he would rather fifty bills should be lost than shrink from his trust; and he hoped the House of Representatives would show their firmness in the present instance; and if the Senate should afterwards reject the bill, as they had done before, let them be answerable for their own conduct: they can do these things more gracefully than this House, as they are not seen in the act. Mr. V. concluded, by drawing another argument from that part of the Speech of the President, at the opening of the present session, which respects the post office and post roads, wherein he so warmly recommends it to the Legislature to take up the subject. This expression is as strong an argument as can possibly be adduced, to show that he had no other conception of the matter than that it was the peculiar privilege of the Legislature.

Mr. BARNWELL was not surprised that a diversity of opinions should prevail on such a subject; but that there should be any question respecting the constitutionality of the amendment astonished him. It was very natural to suppose members from the same State would differ in opinion, and this showed the greater degree of necessity there was to vest the power in the hands of a high responsible officer to determine upon it; for, by doing so, there would be less partiality exhibited in the delineation of the roads, &c. But, if left to the House, it would be almost impossible to reconcile any line to all parties; for the members from each State would probably be guided more by the principle of domestic convenience than by a sense of general good. In reply to Mr. V.'s argument, that it would be a burden to a good President, he thought it would be a pleasure to him to render service to his country. Upon the whole, he was in favor of Mr. SEDGWICK's motion.

Mr. GERRY took a general view of most of the arguments in favor of the motion; replied to each; and concluded, by asking why the commercial interest only should be accommodated, and the inland inhabitants excluded from the advantages of post roads? Why one class of citizens should be preferred to another? The diffusion of knowledge and information is as necessary to one as to the other; and the revenue from the post office would increase from year to year, to defray the expense of the additional post roads which are proposed in the bill.

Mr. STEELE defended the committee who had reported the bill, and explained the grounds on which they had proceeded in laying out the roads for the general advantage of the United States, rather than to accommodate a few trading places only on the sea coast; and with regard to the route to Charleston, to which Mr. BARNWELL had objected, he said it would cause letters to arrive there four or five days sooner than by the old route.

Mr. BENSON observed, that the constitutionality of the amendment is denied, and it is said that the Legislature alone is competent to establish post offices and post roads; notwithstanding this, there is not a single post office designated by the bill. Much has been observed respecting the Legislative and Executive powers, and the committee are cautioned against delegating the powers of the Legislature to the Supreme Executive. Without attempting a definition of their powers, or determining their respective limits, which he conceived it was extremely difficult to do, he would only observe that much must necessarily be left to the discretion of the Legislature. He was very doubtful whether it would ever be in the power of the House to form any bill that would give satisfaction. This he spoke from experience; for it had been often tried in the old Congress, and was as often defeated by the partial and local clauses proposed by the different members. For these reasons, he believed it would be better to delegate the power, and let the regulations be made by the President, than to be enacting supplementary laws year after year, at the instance of individual members.

[*7 Dec.*]

Mr. WHITE observed, that there was a necessity for changing many of the present routes of the post, and although gentlemen have said that information on the subject cannot be so well obtained from this House as from the Executive, because no one member knows all the roads, yet it must be allowed that every road is known to some of the members. The people of the United States have suffered too long under the present establishment; four hundred and eighty-six thousand inhabitants, on the western side of the river Potomac, in the State of Virginia, are deprived of the benefit of a post road: will any gentleman say that nearly half a million of persons shall not have the privilege of a post office, or the means of information? He would not go into any lengthy observations, as the subject had been so fully discussed yesterday. He declared his opinion that the House had a right to send a person to lay out the post roads, agreeably to their directions, and therefore hoped the amendment would be negatived, and that the bill would be gone through with, with such reasonable amendments as might be suggested.

Mr. LIVERMORE said, that gentlemen had drawn arguments from the second clause of the bill before it was yet under consideration, from which they endeavored to prove an absurdity in the first clause, and thus take an uncandid advantage of the liberality of the committee in leaving the appointment of the deputy postmasters and branching offices to the Postmaster General. If, however, there be any defect in the second clause, it can be amended when we come to it; but to attempt to bring forward this section as a bar to the adoption of the first, is an unfair mode of proceeding, and seems as if intended to throw the bill out at any rate. With regard to what has been said of the responsibility of a high Executive officer, he did not deny the wisdom and integrity of the President, who would, no doubt, conduct this as well as he had always done any subject committed to his care; but this would be a very troublesome business to impose upon him, and those who are desirous of doing it, are not acting a friendly part. The Constitution has pointed out one certain mode for the Legislature to proceed in, and it is more proper for the House to determine on the subject than any one man; let the experiment be made for three years, or for ten years, and it will always be found in our power to amend the defects in the system as they arise to our view.

Mr. MADISON said, that the arguments which are offered by the gentlemen who are in favor of the amendment, appear to be drawn rather from theory than any line of practice which had hitherto governed the House. However difficult it may be to determine with precision the exact boundaries of the Legislative and Executive powers, he was of opinion that those arguments were not well founded, for they admit of such construction as will lead to blending those powers so as to leave no line of separation whatever. The greatest obstacle to the due exercise of the powers vested in the Legislature by the bill, which has been mentioned, is the difficulty of accommodating the regulations to the various interests of the different parts of the Union; and this is said to be almost impracticable. But it may be remembered, that similar embarrassments appeared when the impost and tonnage bills were under consideration; on those subjects, the members were obliged to be governed, in a great degree, by mutual information and reciprocal confidence. In respect to the establishment and arrangements of the different ports of entry and clearance, and other objects, that was a business of much greater importance and difficulty than this; but it was accomplished. The Constitution has not only given the Legislature the power of creating offices, but it expressly restrains the Executive from appointing officers, except such as are provided for by law. As has been well observed by the gentleman from Delaware, the President is invested with the power of filling those offices; but does it follow that we are to delegate to him the power to create them? The reference to the appointments and arrangements made by the Executive, pursuant to the powers delegated to the Executive by the excise law, cannot be considered as a parallel case; no similar exigency exists to justify a similar delegation. The danger of infringing on the powers of the Executive, which has been suggested, and the caution to the House against touching on the appointment of officers, is a species of reasoning on the subject, which may be carried so far as to say that we ought not to make any appointments by law; and yet this has been done as in the instance of the appointment of the Commissioners for purchasing in the public debt, all of whom were appointed by the act making provision for the reduction of the public debt. Where is the necessity of departing from the principles of the Constitution in respect to the post office and post roads, more than in all other cases? The subject is expressly committed to Legislative determination by the Constitution. If the second section of the bill requires amendment, it can be rectified when it comes before us; and with respect to future cases, should there be a necessity for additional post roads, they can be provided for by supplementary laws; and therefore no reason on that account can be urged for delaying the provision proposed by the bill. He concluded by saying, that there did not appear to be any necessity for alienating the powers of the House; and that if this should take place, it would be a violation of the Constitution.

Mr. SEDGWICK would make a few observations, which he felt himself obliged to submit to the consideration of the Committee, as well to defend himself as his motion, from the unwarrantable attacks which gentlemen had made on both.

The powers of the Constitution, he was sorry to say, were made in debate to extend or contract, as seemed, for the time being, to suit the convenience of the arguments of gentlemen. The member from Virginia, [Mr. MADISON] had discovered an additional quality of unconstitutionality involved in the motion under consideration. It was *that the creation of offices was by the Constitution confined solely to the Legislature*. This position was undoubtedly just, if by it was meant *that the powers and duties of offices must be defined by law*. But he understood the gentleman to extend his meaning much further, and to have declared, in substance, *that all offices, however subordinate and dependent, must be numerically provided for by law*. The gentleman had, with his usual accuracy and precision, foreseen the application of his principle to the power which, on the same subject, had been delegated by the excise law, by which the Executive was authorized to parcel the whole country into districts, and to appoint the various officers necessary to execute the law. Nothing more was in that instance done, than to define the powers and duties annexed to the offices, but the limits to which their authority was to extend, and their number, was very properly left with the Executive. In that instance, such a delegation was indispensably necessary; nor was it, in his opinion, less necessary in the multifarious arrangements of post offices. That gentleman had supposed this necessity had in that instance justified the expedients; if so, the same conclusion might be drawn on the present occasion. But, for his part, if he should assume that member's opinions, he should be incapable of deriving consolation from the same source; for that there never has as yet been, and probably never would exist in the administration of this Government, a necessity so urgent as to authorize an usurpation of power. The motion before the committee was constitutional, or the reverse; if the latter, the same was true of the existing act in the instance alluded to. That in either instance, a supposed necessity could not justify the infraction of a Constitution which the members were under every obligation of duty, and their oaths, solemnly pledged, to support. Gentlemen should be very cautious how, on slight grounds, they assent to principles, which, if they were true, would evince that the Government had scattered through the whole country, officers who are daily seizing on the property of the citizens, by the assumption of unconstitutional powers. It was true, as had been observed by his friend from New York, [Mr. BENSON] that it was impossible precisely to define a boundary line between the business of Legislative and Executive; but from his own experience, as a public man, and from reflection, he was induced to believe, that as a general rule, the establishment of principles was the peculiar province of the former, and the execution of them, that of the latter. He would, therefore, at least, generally, as much as possible, avoid going into detail. In adopting this as a general rule of conduct, he was not influenced by considerations which gentlemen in opposition to his motion had suggested—the preeminently great and good character of the MAN who was now called by unanimous suffrage to administer the Executive—for he had always considered that, with sagacious minds, that should be the season of political caution, when the Executive was in the hands of one to whom all hearts justly bowed. From the nature of the business to be transacted, he had drawn his conclusion; he thought an Executive officer, responsible to the public for the performance of an important and interesting trust, would inquire with more scrupulous caution, and decide with more justice, than could be expected from a popular assembly, who, from the nature of things, would be more remiss than consisted with a just determination; and he appealed to those gentlemen who were members of the last House, for a recollection of that apathy and torpor which prevailed on a former attempt to demark the post roads. He observed that the opposition to his motion on the ground of unconstitutionality, came with an ill grace from the gentleman who had reported the bill; for, by one section, the Postmaster General was expressly authorized to establish post roads not provided for by the bill, upon a condition that does not at all affect the present question; and by another section, the same officer was authorized to appoint, unrestrained, all his deputies, each of whom is to establish and keep an office. This, in his opinion, was not only expedient but indispensably necessary. It was, however, a delegation of power, attended by all those circumstances which rendered, in the opinion of that gentleman, the present motion unconstitutional. He said, no gentleman had contended for carrying into execution the principles they attempted to establish, to an extent to which they would go. *That no road can be a post road but such as shall be established by law.* The bill establishes the road from place to place, leaving the intermediate distance untouched; as for instance, from Boston to Worcester. Between those two points is, or is not, a post road, if the bill should become a law, established? If the former part of the dilemma is embraced, then also by the motion, if adopted, will a post road be established from Maine to Georgia. For he supposed it impossible to make any well-founded distinction between the one case and the other. His motion then would as effectually establish a post road in the intermediate space as the bill in its present form; and all the objections which had been made to the former, would apply with equal force to the latter. Gentlemen had spoken in strong terms of the disinterestedness, information, and respectability of the members of the House, and of the popular confidence which resulted therefrom. No man had a more respectable opinion of the Representatives of the people than himself; he need not, however, observe to them, that they were men, subject to like passions and imperfections with their fellow-citizens. It could not have escaped the reflection of the committee, that the gentlemen who composed it, had a very important interest in establishing the directions of the post; that on the declarations of men thus interested, we must rely for the justness of our ultimate conclusions; on evidence of interested individuals, individuals who are, by their relation to the subject of inquiry, excluded, on principles of law, from all credit, must we rely for a knowledge of those facts which are to direct our judgment.

Mr. Boudinot and Mr. Gerry made some remarks, and then the question being taken, Mr. Sedgwick's motion was negatived.

[*3 Jan. 1792*]

A motion was made by Mr. Fitzsimons to allow the proprietors of stages employed in conveying the mail, to carry passengers also, without being liable to molestation or impediment, on any of the post roads.

Against this motion it was urged, that the General Government has no right to make any such provision; and that even if it possessed the power, such an exertion of it would be unjust, as it would interfere with the private rights of individuals, who, under the laws of some States, (Maryland and Virginia, for instance) enjoy the exclusive privilege of driving stages for the conveyance of travelers. Under the faith of the State laws, which were in existence before the establishment of the present Government, and have not yet been abrogated, these citizens vested a considerable property in this business, in hopes of reaping an adequate advantage from their undertaking. In many instances, it was made a condition in the contract, that they should make and repair the roads at their own private expense: the terms they complied with; but they would not have thus expended their money, or established the stages at all, if they had not obtained a monopoly to secure them in the exclusive enjoyment of the benefits; and to this monopoly the public are indebted for the cheap and easy conveyance which those stages at present afford for private passengers and the mail of the United States. Many of the original proprietors have made transfers of their right, for considerable sums of money; nor can the right, thus acquired by the present proprietors, be impaired, without an open violation of private contracts, and the invasion of a property lawfully purchased, and guaranteed by the State Legislatures,—a property, which Congress have no right to take for the public use, without making an adequate compensation.

That clause of the Constitution which empowers the Federal Government to establish post offices and post roads, cannot, it was said, be understood to extend farther than the conveyance of intelligence, which is the proper object of the Post Office establishment. It gives no power to send men and baggage by post. The State Governments have always possessed the power of stopping or taxing passengers; that power they have never given up; and the proposition now made to wrest it from them, might be viewed as an attempt to lay the State Legislatures prostrate at the feet of the General Government, and will give a shock to every State in the Union.

If, by the construction of that clause of the Constitution, which authorizes Congress to make all laws necessary for carrying into execution the several powers vested in them, they should establish the proposed regulations for the conveyance of the mail, they may proceed farther, and so regulate the post roads, as to prevent passengers from traveling on them; they may say what weights shall be carried on those roads, and at what seasons of the year; they may remove every thing that stands in their way—they may level buildings to the ground, under pretence of making more convenient roads; they may abolish tolls and turnpikes; they may, where an established ferry has been kept for a hundred years past in the most convenient place for crossing a river, give the post-rider authority to set up a new one beside it, and ruin the old establishment; they may say, that the person who carries the mail shall participate in every privilege that is now exclusively enjoyed by any man or body of men, and allege, as a reason for these encroachments, that they are only necessary encouragements to carry the mail of the United States. In short, the ingenuity of man can not devise any new proposition so strange and inconsistent, as not to be reducible within the pale of the Constitution, by such a mode of construction. If this were once admitted, the Constitution would be an useless and dead letter; and it would be to no purpose, that the States, in Convention assembled, had framed that instrument to guide the steps of Congress: as well might they at once have said, "There shall be a Congress, who shall have full power and authority to make all laws, which to their wisdom shall seem meet and proper."

But the States will never submit to this new regulation; nor will the individuals concerned tamely suffer an invasion of those rights, which they enjoy under the State laws. A contest will undoubtedly ensue; and the present proprietors of the stages will not fail to stop any new stage-wagons that carry passengers along their roads, whether they carry the mail or not. It would be unwise in Congress to enter into a contest where the advantage is but trifling, and the risk much greater perhaps than they are aware of. It is easy to blow a small spark into an extensive flame; and prudence ought to caution them against raising a ferment, which may be productive of the most serious consequences.

In favor of the motion it was urged that the Constitution, in authorizing Congress to establish post offices and post roads, and to make all laws necessary for carrying into execution the several powers intrusted to them, has conferred on them ample powers respecting the point in question. If the post roads belong to the United States, then every citizen of the United States has as good a right to use them, under the regulations of Congress, as the citizens of any particular State, through which they happen to run. If they belong to the individual States, and are subject to their regulation, the same authority that limits the use of them to particular wagons, may also say that those wagons shall carry nothing else but passengers, and thus even the mail itself may be prevented from passing.

It was thought hard that a citizen of the United States should be prevented from traveling through an individual State in a stage-wagon, unless the wagon belonged to that State. If a right exists in the State Legislature to impose a tax in this instance, they may farm it out at a high rate, and make it amount to what they please: they may proceed further, and oblige every citizen of the United States who travels within their boundaries, to purchase a certificate to entitle him to pass.

If the House meant to establish the post office at all, and to have the roads free, it was thought necessary to make such a provision as the one under consideration. If not, the Postmaster General may be obliged to adopt the less convenient mode of having the mail carried every where on horseback; even in this case, the State Legislatures may subject the post-horses to a tax, upon the same principle as the post-carriages.

The question, it was said, could not involve any controversy between the United States and the individual States. It was merely a judicial question, and determinable in a Court of Law, whether a State has a right to grant and support such a monopoly. Other monopolies had existed before the establishment of the General Government, but had been since done away; the duty of tonnage, for instance, which had been granted in some States for the improvement of navigation.

As to the infringement of contracts made before the adoption of the Constitution, if the different Conventions had agreed upon that ground, the Constitution itself would never have been adopted, as it abrogated not only several private contracts, but even certain parts of the State Constitutions themselves. But the evil, in the present case, would be great indeed, if the States were allowed a power of repealing or annulling the principles of the Constitution, under cover of acts that existed previous to its formation.

The laws of the United States must be general: they must operate equally throughout the Union, nor be clogged with any incumbrances or restrictions in any one State more than another. The power of barely establishing post roads would prove a mere nullity, unless accompanied with a power of making them useful. The stages are a public convenience to the citizens of the United States traveling along those roads; and if the State Legislatures exercise the power of stopping and taxing those carriages at their pleasure, the utility of this mode of conveyance, together with that of the roads themselves, will be in a great measure destroyed. If, to prevent this evil, and the better to accommodate the citizens of the United States, and to facilitate the conveyance of the public mail, Congress found it necessary to establish turnpike-roads from one end of the Continent to the other, the Constitution gave them full power to make such regulations and it hoped they would soon adopt the measure.

[5 *Jan.*]

A motion was made and seconded further to amend the said bill, by inserting, after the ——— section, the following clause:

> "*And be it further enacted,* That it shall be lawful for the carriages, by which the mail shall be conveyed, to receive passengers to or from any place or places, and through any State or States, upon all roads declared to be post roads, by the laws of the United States."

Mr. Clark objected to the proposition. He thought it would give rise to a contest between the State and General Governments, which he conceived was unnecessary, and had better be avoided.

Mr. Seney also objected to it. Before such a clause was agreed to, it certainly was incumbent on the gentlemen in favor of it to show that the regulations in the several States which would be affected by it, had or would obstruct the transportation of the mail. Except this was made to appear, it ought to be well considered how far the interference with those privileges would tend to disturb the tranquility of the Government.

Mr. Livermore said he had no doubts on this subject. The right of Congress to send the mail in that way which will be most for the public advantage, cannot be controverted. Let gentlemen consider what would be the consequence, if similar monopolies existed in all the other States; it would entirely render nugatory the power of Congress to establish post offices and post roads. The consequences of this are easily to be conceived. It is said, that the persons vested with these exclusive privileges have contracted on as easy terms as the Postmaster General could have contracted with any other persons; but it does not follow that they will not extort in future—it certainly destroys all competition, and leaves the United States entirely in the power of these persons. He hoped that the House would not hesitate to adopt the proposition.

Mr. SENEY replied to Mr. LIVERMORE, in a few remarks, in which he justified the States of Maryland and Virginia for granting the monopolies in question.

Mr. GERRY said he was in favor of the proposition. He asserted that the power to establish post roads was coeval with that of establishing post offices; if the former power is not in Congress, they have already proceeded too far in exercising the latter power. It has been said, that the States had a right to grant these monopolies—to this he conceded that they had, previous to the adoption of the Constitution; but, in consequence of that event, all such laws are null and void of course. It is become necessary for Congress to carry their power in this respect into execution; for he had been informed, from good authority, that the Postmaster General could not contract with these persons upon the same terms that he could with others. He instanced other inconveniences and disadvantages resulting from this situation of things, especially by an unnecessary detention of the mail for two days every week. Congress ought to define and declare their powers, that those States which have passed laws incompatible therewith may repeal them. With respect to the power of establishing post offices, none of the States claim a participation of that power; and as to the establishing post roads, if the States possess any power in that case, Congress certainly possesses concurrent power; and therefore this Government may certainly make the necessary regulations, where the States have either made improper regulations, or no regulations at all. He conceived that justice to individuals, and to the United States, rendered it absolutely necessary for Congress to exercise the power.

Mr. NILES inquired, what is the import of the present question? Is it not, sir, whether you may carry your mail through any of the States, on foot, on horseback, or in a stage coach? It is not contended that any law of any State can, constitutionally, prevent this. The States, by adopting the Constitution, have ceded their right to you, and of course divested themselves of all right to prevent you from exercising it. But, sir, the question is simply, whether Congress have a right to authorize the carrier of the mail to carry passengers, on hire, through those States where an exclusive right of carrying passengers for hire has been granted by the State Government, and still exists. You are empowered by the Constitution to establish post offices and post roads, and to do whatever may be *necessary* and *proper* to carry that power into effect. Now, sir, is it necessary, in order to the transportation of your mail, that you should erect stage-coaches for the purpose of transporting passengers? What has your mail to do with passengers transported for hire? Why, sir, nothing more than this—by granting to the carrier of your mail a right to carry passengers for hire, the carriage of the mail may be a little less expensive. Does this consideration render it *necessary* and *proper* for you to violate the laws of the States? If not, you will, by so doing, violate their rights, and overleap the bounds of your own. This matter *may* occasion a legal adjudication, in order to which the Judiciary must determine, whether you have a *constitutional right* to establish this regulation, and this will depend on the question whether it be *necessary* and *proper*. A curious *discretionary law* question! Such a one as I presume never entered the thought of the States when they adopted the Constitution. But, sir, if the trifling pecuniary saving proposed by this regulation, entitles it to the character of a *necessary* one, or, in the sense of the Constitution, a *proper* one, and so a constitutional one, what may not Congress do under the idea of *propriety?* It may be *proper,* for the sake of a more advantageous contract for carrying the mail, to authorize the carrier to erect ferry-boats, for the transportation both of the mail and of passengers—or to grant the right of driving herds of cattle over toll bridges and turnpike roads, toll free, in violation both of legal and prescriptive rights—to erect posthouses under peculiar regulations, and with exclusive right. What, sir, may not be construed as *proper* to be done by Congress? Under this idea, the whole powers vested in Congress by the Constitution will be found in the magic word *proper;* and the States might have spared, as nugatory, all their deliberations on the Constitution, and have constituted a Congress, with general authority to legislate on every subject, and in any manner it might think *proper.* What rights, then, remain to the States? None, sir, but the *empty* denomination of Republican Governments. I consider the proposition as an attack upon the rights of the States, and shall therefore give my vote against it.

Mr. BARNWELL said he had no doubt of the constitutionality of the proposition; but he was of opinion that the present was not the most eligible time to exercise the power. Still he was of opinion that Congress ought now to declare that it would exercise it at the expiration of the contracts which at present exist between particular States and individuals, and he moved a proviso to that effect, as follows:

> "*Provided,* That whenever any exclusive privilege of conveying passengers for hire in stage carriages, on any of the roads established by this law, hath been heretofore granted by any of the States for a term of years, such exclusive privilege shall continue and be of full force and effect, agreeable to the conditions thereof, until such term shall expire."

Mr. LAURANCE was in sentiment with Mr. BARNWELL, and seconded his motion for adding a proviso, as above.

Mr. CLARK objected to the proviso; it was legislating on a subject of which the House was entirely ignorant. We do not know how long those contracts are to exist; why should we, then, interfere in a business which we ought not to do any thing about. We may set aside the law, or the State may abrogate it, but in either case the proprietors would be entitled to a full indemnification. For his part, he thought the House was getting into a maze—the bill has long been under consideration, and we seem to make no progress. I could wish that the whole bill was buried, and that we might hear no more of post offices and post roads.

Mr. VENABLE controverted the constitutionality of an interference on the part of Congress in respect to these monopolies. He observed, that the Constitution was totally silent on the subject of passengers; it simply relates to the transportation of letters. And he conceived that the operation of the proposition would be to create monopolies on the part of the United States.

[It was here contended that the proviso was not in order. The Speaker said it was not in order. An appeal was then made to the House, which voted that the proviso was in order, and it was then discussed.]

Mr. Wadsworth said he was opposed to both the clause and the proviso; he conceived there was no occasion for either. The State of Connecticut has granted exclusive privileges to run stages in that State, but has reserved to itself the power to annihilate those contracts at pleasure; and, whenever the General Government shall make provision for transporting the mail on those roads, those exclusive privileges will cease; and he did not know but that this was the case in other States.

Mr. Livermore said the proviso was the most extraordinary one he had ever heard in his life—we in the first place, in effect, abrogate certain laws of particular States, and then by a proviso confirm those very laws.

Mr. Laurance contended that, however extraordinary the proviso may appear, it was strictly proper. Contracts are not to be violated—once formed, they are sacred. The States had a right to form those contracts, and to grant those privileges, and therefore the persons enjoying them cannot be deprived of them; and though the General Government has undoubtedly a right to take the most eligible methods for the transportation of the mail, yet the rights of these people ought not to be violated.

Mr. Gerry opposed the proviso. It recognised the right of the respective States to pass such laws as the first part of the clause intends to abrogate, not only before, but subsequent to the adoption of the Constitution, which he conceived involved an absurdity. On the general subject, he said, that these monopolies were a tax, not only on the citizens of other States, but of every State in the Union. He conceived that no State possesses the power of taxing the people of the United States.

Mr. Benson remarked, that the proviso was improper and unnecessary. Should any consequences result from agreeing to the first part of the clause, they will arise between the individual claiming the privileges and the State which granted them, and must be settled by a judicial decision.

Mr. Sturges said he should vote in favor of the proviso, though he conceived that Congress had a right to make such a law as would, in its operation, entirely supercede these contracts.

4

Thomas Jefferson to James Madison
6 Mar. 1796
Works 8:226–27

P.S. Have you considered all the consequences of your proposition respecting post roads? I view it as a source of boundless patronage to the executive, jobbing to members of Congress & their friends, and a bottomless abyss of public money. You will begin by only appropriating the surplus of the post office revenues; but the other revenues will soon be called into their aid, and it will be a scene of eternal scramble among the members, who can get the most money wasted in their State; and they will always get most who are meanest. We have thought, hitherto, that the roads of a State could not be so well administered even by the State legislature as by the magistracy of the county, on the spot. What will it be when a member of N H is to mark out a road for Georgia? Does the power to *establish* post roads, given you by Congress, mean that you shall *make* the roads, or only *select* from those already made, those on which there shall be a post? If the term be equivocal, (& I really do not think it so,) which is the safest construction? That which permits a majority of Congress to go to cutting down mountains & bridging of rivers, or the other, which if too restricted may refer it to the states for amendment, securing still due measure & proportion among us, and providing some means of information to the members of Congress tantamount to that ocular inspection, which, even in our county determinations, the magistrate finds cannot be supplied by any other evidence? The fortification of harbors were liable to great objection. But national circumstances furnished some color. In this case there is none. The roads of America are the best in the world except those of France & England. But does the state of our population, the extent of our internal commerce, the want of sea & river navigation, call for such expense on roads here, or are our means adequate to it? Think of all this, and a great deal more which your good judgment will suggest, and pardon my freedom.

5

St. George Tucker, Blackstone's Commentaries
1:App. 264–65
1803

7. Congress have power to establish post-offices, and post-roads. And this is one of those cases, in which I have supposed that the states may possess a concurrent, but subordinate authority, to that of the federal government.

Concurrent, inasmuch, as there seems to be nothing in the constitution, nor in the nature of the thing itself, which may not be exercised by both, at the same time, without prejudice, or interference; subordinate, because wherever any power is expressly granted to congress, it is to be taken, for granted, that it shall not be contravened by the authority of any particular state. If, therefore, any state should find it necessary to establish post-offices on any road, which is not an established post-road, under the laws of the United States, there seems to be no constitutional objection to its doing so, until congress should think proper to exert its constitutional right to establish a communication by post, between the same places. . . . I put this case merely to shew how far the exercise of these concurrent powers may be reconciled: it is much to be desired that a question of such delicacy may never occur between any state, and the federal government.

The post-office, under proper regulations, is one of the most beneficial establishments which can be introduced by any government; by providing the means of intercourse between the citizens of remote parts of the confederation, on such a regular footing, as must contribute greatly to the convenience of commerce, and to the free, and frequent communication of facts, and sentiments between individuals. Hence the revenue arising from this source will always be more easily collected, and more cheerfully paid, than any other whatever. It appears, that notwithstanding the many unprofitable branches, into which the post-roads have been divided for the convenience of the people of the United States, there still remains a considerable sum that is annually brought into the federal treasury.

It seems reasonable that the product of this branch of the revenue should be, exclusively, applied to the extention of its benefits, until they shall completely pervade every part of the union.

6

William Rawle, A View of the Constitution of the United States 103–4 1829 (2d ed.)

The power to establish *post offices and post roads,* has a necessary connexion with the promotion of commerce and the general welfare of the Union.

A regular system of free and speedy communication, is of vital importance to the mercantile interest, but on a wider scale we must also admit it to be of the first consequence to the general benefit. In time of peace, it tends to keep the people duly informed of their political interests; it assists the measures of government, and the private intercourse of individuals. During a war, the rapid communication of intelligence, by means of the post, and the greater facility of transferring bodies of men or munitions of war, to different places, by the aid of good roads, are evident advantages. If these establishments should in practice produce no revenue, the expense would be properly chargeable to the Union, and the proceeds of taxation in the common forms be justly applied to defray it. If, however, as has proved to be the case, the post office yields a revenue, which is with the other revenues of the United States applicable only to the general service, it is obvious, that no state ought to interfere by establishing a post office of its own. This is therefore an exclusive power so far as relates to the conveyance of letters, &c. In regard to post roads, it is unnecessary, and therefore would be unwarrantable in congress where a sufficient road already exists, to make another; and on the other hand, no state has a power to deny or obstruct the passage of the mail, or the passage of troops, or the property of the United States over its public roads.

The power given to congress, in respect to this subject, was brought into operation soon after the Constitution was adopted, and various provisions have at different times been enacted, founded on the principle of its being an exclusive power.

It has been made a constitutional question, whether congress has a right to open a new mail road through a state or states for general purposes, involving the public benefit, and the same doubt has been extended to the right of appropriating money in aid of canals through states. If we adhere to the words of the text, we are confined to post roads; but it appears to the author to be one of those implied powers which may fairly be considered as within the principles of the Constitution, and which there is no danger in allowing. The general welfare may imperiously require communications of either of these descriptions. A state is bound to consult only its own immediate interests, and not to incur expense for the benefit of other states. The United States are bound to uphold the general interest at the general expense. To restrain them to pointing out the utility of the measure, and calling on particular states to execute it, would be partially to recall the inefficiency of the old government and to violate the main principle of the present one. If any political evil could result from the procedure, it would present a strong argument against the allowance of the power; but good roads, and facile, aquatic communications, while they promote the prosperity of the country, cannot be seriously alleged to affect the sovereignty of the states, or the liberties of the people. It is doubtful whether tolls for passage on it, can be constitutionally exacted.

7

Joseph Story, Commentaries on the Constitution 3:§§ 1119–42, 1144–45 1833

§ 1119. The next power of congress is, "to establish post-offices and post-roads." The nature and extent of this power, both theoretically and practically, are of great importance, and have given rise to much ardent controversy. It deserves, therefore, a deliberate examination. It was passed over by the Federalist with a single remark, as a power not likely to be disputed in its exercise, or to be deemed dangerous by its scope. The "power," says the Federalist, "of establishing post-roads must, in every view, be a harmless power; and may, perhaps, by judicious management, become productive of great public conveniency. Nothing, which tends to facilitate the intercourse between the states, can be deemed unworthy of the public care." One cannot but feel, at the present time, an inclination to smile at the guarded caution of these expressions, and the hesitating avowal of the importance of the power. It affords, perhaps, one of the most striking proofs, how much the growth and prosperity of the country have outstripped the most sanguine anticipations of our most enlightened patriots.

§ 1120. The post-office establishment has already become one of the most beneficent, and useful establishments under the national government. It circulates intelligence of a commercial, political, intellectual, and private nature, with incredible speed and regularity. It thus administers, in a very high degree, to the comfort, the interests, and the necessities of persons, in every rank and station of life. It brings the most distant places and persons, as it were, in contact with each other; and thus softens the anxieties, increases the enjoyments, and cheers the solitude of millions of hearts. It imparts a new influence and impulse to private intercourse; and, by a wider diffusion of knowledge, enables political rights and duties to be performed with more uniformity and sound judgment. It is not less effective, as an instrument of the government in its own operations. In peace, it enables it without ostentation or expense to send its orders, and direct its measures for the public good, and transfer its funds, and apply its powers, with a facility and promptitude, which, compared with the tardy operations, and imbecile expedients of former times, seem like the wonders of magic. In war it is, if possible, still more important and useful, communicating intelligence vital to the movements of armies and navies, and the operations and duties of warfare, with a rapidity, which, if it does not always ensure victory, at least, in many instances, guards against defeat and ruin. Thus, its influences have become, in a public, as well as private view, of incalculable value to the permanent interests of the Union. It is obvious at a moment's glance at the subject, that the establishment in the hands of the states would have been wholly inadequate to these objects; and the impracticability of a uniformity of system would have introduced infinite delays and inconveniences; and burthened the mails with an endless variety of vexatious taxations, and regulations. No one, accustomed to the retardations of the post in passing through independent states on the continent of Europe, can fail to appreciate the benefits of a power, which pervades the Union. The national government is that alone, which can safely or effectually execute it, with equal promptitude and cheapness, certainty and uniformity. Already the post-office establishment realizes a revenue exceeding two millions of dollars, from which it defrays all its own expenses, and transmits mails in various directions over more than one hundred and twenty thousand miles. It transmits intelligence in one day to distant places, which, when the constitution was first put into operation, was scarcely transmitted through the same distance in the course of a week. The rapidity of its movements has been in a general view doubled within the last twenty years. There are now more than eight thousand five hundred post-offices in the United States; and at every session of the legislature new routes are constantly provided for, and new post-offices established. It may, therefore, well be deemed a most beneficent power, whose operations can scarcely be applied, except for good, and accomplish in an eminent degree some of the high purposes set forth in the preamble of the constitution, forming a more perfect union, providing for the common defence, and promoting the general welfare.

§ 1121. Under the confederation, (art. 9,) congress was invested with the sole and exclusive power of "establishing and regulating post-offices *from one state to another* throughout the United States, and exacting such postage on the papers passing through the same, as may be requisite to defray the expenses of the said office." How little was accomplished under it will be at once apparent from the fact, that there were but seventy-five post-offices established in all the United States in the year 1789; that the whole amount of postage in 1790 was only $37,935; and the number of miles travelled by the mails only 1875. This may be in part attributable to the state of the country, and the depression of all the commercial and other interests of the country. But the power itself was so crippled by the confederation, that it could accomplish little. The national government did not possess any power, except to establish post-offices from state to state, (leaving perhaps, though not intended, the whole interior post-offices in every state to its own regulation,) and the postage, that could be taken, was not allowed to be beyond the actual expenses; thus shutting up the avenue to all improvements. In short, like every other power under the confederation, it perished from a jealousy, which required it to live, and yet refused it appropriate nourishment and sustenance.

§ 1122. In the first draft of the constitution, the clause stood thus, "Congress shall have power to establish post-offices." It was subsequently amended by adding the words "and post-roads," by the vote of six states against five; and then, as amended, it passed without opposition. It is observable, that the confederation gave only the power to establish and regulate *post-offices;* and therefore the amendment introduced a new and substantive power, unknown before in the national government.

§ 1123. Upon the construction of this clause of the constitution, two opposite opinions have been expressed. One maintains, that the power to establish post-offices and post-roads can intend no more, than the power to direct, where post-offices shall be kept, and on what roads the mails shall be carried. Or, as it has been on other occasions expressed, the power to establish post-roads is a power to designate, or point out, what roads shall be mail-roads, and the right of passage or way along them, when so designated. The other maintains, that although these modes of exercising the power are perfectly constitutional; yet they are not the whole of the power, and do not exhaust it. On the contrary, the power comprehends the right to make, or construct any roads, which congress may deem proper for the conveyance of the mail, and to keep them in due repair for such purpose.

§ 1124. The grounds of the former opinion seem to be as follows. The power given under the confederation never practically received any other construction. Congress never undertook to make any roads, but merely designated those existing roads, on which the mail should pass. At the adoption of the constitution there is not the slightest evidence, that a different arrangement, as to the limits of the power, was contemplated. On the contrary, it was treated by the Federalist, as a harmless power, and not requiring any comment. The practice of the government, since the adoption of the constitution, has conformed to this view. The first act passed by congress, in 1792, is entitled "an act to establish post-offices and post-roads." The first section of this act established many post-offices as well as post-roads. It was continued, amended, and finally repealed, by a series of acts from 1792 to 1810; all of which acts have the same title, and the same provisions declaring certain roads to be post-roads. From all of which it is manifest, that the legislature supposed, that they had established post-roads in the sense of the constitution, when they declared certain roads, then in existence, to be post-roads, and designated the routes, along which the mails were to pass. As a farther proof upon this subject, the statute book contains many acts passed at various times, during a period of more than twenty years, discontinuing certain post-roads. A strong argument is also derivable from the practice of continental Europe, which must be presumed to have been known to the framers of the constitution. Different nations in Europe have established posts, and for mutual convenience have stipulated a free passage for the posts arriving on their frontiers through their territories. It is probable, that the constitution intended nothing more by this provision, than to enable congress to do by law, without consulting the states, what in Europe can be done only by treaty or compact. It was thought necessary to insert an express provision in the constitution, enabling the government to exercise jurisdiction over ten miles square for a seat of government, and of such places, as should be ceded by the states for forts, arsenals, and other similar purposes. It is incredible, that such solicitude should have been expressed for such inconsiderable spots, and yet, that at the same time, the constitution intended to convey by implication the power to construct roads throughout the whole country, with the consequent right to use the timber and soil, and to exercise jurisdiction over them. It may be said, that, unless congress have the power, the mail-roads might be obstructed, or discontinued at the will of the state authorities. But that consequence does not follow; for when a road is declared by law to be a mail-road, the United States have a right of way over it; and, until the law is repealed, such an interest in the use of it, as that the state authorities could not obstruct it. The terms of the constitution are perfectly satisfied by this limited construction, and the power of congress to make whatever roads they may please, in any state, would be a most serious inroad upon the rights and jurisdiction of the states. It never could have been contemplated.

§ 1125. The grounds, upon which the other opinion is maintained, are as follows: This is not a question of implied power; but of express power. We are not now looking to what are properly incidents, or means to carry into effect given powers; but are to construe the terms of an express power. The words of the constitution are, "Congress shall have power to establish post-offices and post-roads." What is the true meaning of these words? There is no such known sense of the word "establish," as to "direct," "designate," or "point out." And if there were, it does not follow, that a special or peculiar sense is to be given to the words, not conformable to their general meaning, unless that sense be required by the context, or, at least, better harmonizes with the subject matter, and objects of the power, than any other sense. That cannot be pretended in the present case. The received general meanings, if not the only meanings of the word "establish," are, to settle firmly, to confirm, to fix, to form or modify, to found, to build firmly, to erect permanently. And it is no small objection to any construction, that it requires the word to be deflected from its received and usual meaning; and gives it a meaning unknown to, and unacknowledged by lexicographers. Especially is it objectionable and inadmissible, where the received and common meaning harmonizes with the subject matter; and if the very end were required, no more exact expression could ordinarily be used. In legislative acts, in state papers, and in the constitution itself, the word is found with the same general sense now insisted on; that is, in the sense of, to create, to form, to make, to construct, to settle, to build up with a view to permanence. Thus, our treaties speak of establishing regulations of trade. Our laws speak of *establishing* navy-hospitals, where land is to be purchased, work done, and buildings erected; of *establishing* trading-houses with the Indians, where houses are to be erected and other things done. The word is constantly used in a like sense in the articles of confederation. The authority is therein given to congress of *establishing* rules in cases of captures; of *establishing* courts of appeal in cases of capture; and, what is directly in point, of *establishing* and *regulating post-offices*. Now, if the meaning of the word here was simply to point out, or designate post-offices, there would have been an end of all further authority, except of regulating the post-offices, so designated and pointed out. Under such circumstances, how could it have been possible under that instrument (which declares, that every power not *expressly* delegated shall be retained by the states) to find any authority to carry the mail, or to make contracts for this purpose? much more to prohibit any other persons under penalties from conveying letters, despatches, or other packets from one place to another of the United States? The very first act of the continental congress on this subject was, "for *establishing* a post," (not a post office;) and it directed, "that a line of posts be appointed under the direction of the post-master general, from Falmouth, in New-England, to Savannah, in Georgia, with as many cross-posts, as he shall think fit;" and it directs the necessary expenses of the *"establishment"* beyond the revenue to be paid out by the United Colonies. Under this, and other supplementary acts, the establishment continued until October, 1782, when, under the articles of confederation, the establishment was re-organized, and, instead of a mere appointment and designation of post-offices, provision was made, "that a continued communication of posts throughout the United States shall be *established* and maintained," &c.; and many other regulations were made wholly incompatible with the narrow construction of the words now contended for.

§ 1126. The constitution itself also uniformly uses the word "establish" in the general sense, and never in this peculiar and narrow sense. It speaks in the preamble of one motive being, "to *establish* justice," and that the people do *ordain* and *establish* this constitution. It gives power to *establish* an uniform rule of naturalization and uniform laws on the subject of bankruptcies. Does not this authorize congress to make, create, form, and construct laws on these subjects? It declares, that the judicial power shall be vested in one supreme court and in such inferior courts, as congress may, from time to time, *ordain* and *establish.* Is not a power to *establish* courts a power to create, and make, and regulate them? It declares, that the ratification of nine states shall be sufficient for the *establishment* of this constitution between the states so ratifying the same. And in one of the amendments, it provides, that congress shall make no law respecting an *establishment* of religion. It is plain, that to construe the word in any of these cases, as equivalent to *designate,* or *point out,* would be absolutely absurd. The clear import of the word is, to create, and form, and fix in a settled manner. Referring it to the subject matter, the sense, in no instance, can be mistaken. To establish courts is to create, and form, and regulate them. To establish rules of naturalization is to frame and confirm such rules. To establish laws on the subject of bankruptcies is to frame, fix, and pass them. To establish the constitution is to make, and fix, and erect it, as a permanent form of government. In the same manner, to establish post-offices and post-roads is to frame and pass laws, to erect, make, form, regulate, and preserve them. Whatever is necessary, whatever is appropriate to this purpose, is within the power.

§ 1127. Besides; upon this narrow construction, what becomes of the power itself? If the power be to *point out,* or *designate post-offices,* then it supposes, that there already exist some offices, out of which a designation can be made. It supposes a power to select among things of the same nature. Now, if an office does not already exist at the place, how can it be designated, as a post-office? If you cannot create a post-office you can do no more, than mark out one already existing. In short, these rules of strict construction might be pressed still farther; and, as the power is only given to designate, not offices, but post-offices, the latter must be already in existence; for otherwise the power must be read, to designate what offices shall be used, as post-offices, or at what places post-offices shall be recognised; either of which is a departure from the supposed literal interpretation.

§ 1128. In the next place, let us see, what upon this narrow interpretation becomes of the power in another aspect. It is to establish post-offices. Now, the argument supposes, that this does not authorize the purchase or erection of a building for an office; but it does necessarily suppose the authority to erect or create an office; to regulate the duties of the officer; and to fix a place, (*officina*) where his business is to be performed. It then unavoidably includes, not merely a power to designate, but a power to create the thing intended, and to do all other acts to make the thing effectual; that is, to create the whole system appropriate to a post-office establishment. Now, this involves a plain departure from the very ground of the argument. It is no longer a power to designate a thing, or mark out a route; but it is a power to create, and fix every other thing necessary and appropriate to post-offices. The argument, therefore, resorts to implications in order to escape from its own narrow interpretation; and the very power to designate becomes a power to create offices and frame sys-tems, and institute penalties, and raise revenue, and make contracts. It becomes, in fact, the very thing, which the other argument supposes to be the natural sense, viz. the power to erect, and maintain a post-office establishment.

§ 1129. Under any other interpretation, the power itself would become a mere nullity. If resort be had to a very strict and critical examination of the words, the power "to establish post-offices" imports no more, than the power to create the offices intended; that done, the power is exhausted; and the words are satisfied. The power to create the office does not necessarily include the power to carry the mail, or regulate the conveyance of letters, or employ carriers. The one may exist independently of the other. A state might without absurdity possess the right to carry the mail, while the United States might possess the right to designate the post-offices, at which it should be opened, and provide the proper officers; or the converse powers might belong to each. It would not be impracticable, though it would be extremely inconvenient and embarrassing. Yet, no man ever imagined such a construction to be justifiable. And why not? Plainly, because constitutions of government are not instruments to be scrutinized, and weighed, upon metaphysical or grammatical niceties. They do not turn upon ingenious subtleties; but are adapted to the business and exigencies of human society; and the powers given are understood in a large sense, in order to secure the public interests. Common sense becomes the guide, and prevents men from dealing with mere logical abstractions. Under the confederation, this very power to establish post-offices was construed to include the other powers already named, and others far more remote. It never entered into the heads of the wise men of those days, that they possessed a power to create post-offices, without the power to create all the other things necessary to make post-offices of some human use. They did not dream of post-offices without posts, or mails, or routes, or carriers. It would have been worse than a mockery. Under the confederation, with the strict limitation of powers, which that instrument conferred, they put into operation a large system for the appropriate purposes of a post-office establishment. No man ever doubted, or denied the constitutionality of this exercise of the power. It was largely construed to meet the obvious intent, for which it was delegated. The words of the constitution are more extensive, than those of the confederation. In the latter, the words to establish *"post-roads"* are not to be found. These words were certainly added for some purpose. And if any, for what other purpose, than to enable congress to lay out and make roads?

§ 1130. Under the constitution congress has, without any questioning, given a liberal construction to the power to establish post-offices and post-roads. It has been truly said, that in a strict sense, "this power is executed by the single act of making the establishment. But from this has been inferred the power and duty of carrying the mail along the post-road from one post-office to another. And from this implied power has been again inferred the right to punish those, who steal letters from the post-office, or rob the mail. It may be said with some plausibility, that the right to carry the mail, and to punish those, who rob it, is not indispensably necessary to the establishment of a post-office and a post-road. This right is indeed essential to the beneficial exercise of the power; but not indispensably necessary to its existence."

§ 1131. The whole practical course of the government upon this subject, from its first organization down to the present time, under every administration, has repudiated the strict and narrow construction of the words above mentioned. The power to establish post-offices and post-roads has never been understood to include no more, than the power to point out and designate post-offices and post-roads. Resort has been constantly had to the more expanded sense of the word "establish;" and no other sense can include the objects, which the post-office laws have constantly included. Nay, it is not only not true, that these laws have stopped short of an exposition of the words sufficiently broad to justify the making of roads; but they have included exercises of power far more remote from the immediate objects. If the practice of the government is, therefore, of any weight in giving a constitutional interpretation, it is in favour of the liberal interpretation of the clause.

§ 1132. The fact, if true, that congress have not hitherto made any roads for the carrying of the mail, would not affect the right, or touch the question. It is not doubted, that the power has been properly carried into effect, by making certain state roads post-roads. When congress found those roads suited to the purpose, there could be no constitutional reason for refusing to establish them, as mail-routes. The exercise of authority was clearly within the scope of the power. But the argument would have it, that, because this exercise of the power, clearly within its scope, has been hitherto restrained to making existing roads post-roads, therefore congress cannot proceed constitutionally to make a post-road, where no road now exists. This is clearly what lawyers call a *non sequitur.* It might with just as much propriety be urged, that, because congress had not hitherto used a particular means to execute any other given power, therefore it could not now do it. If, for instance, congress had never provided a ship for the navy, except by purchase, they could not now authorize ships to be built for a navy, or *à converso.* If they had not laid a tax on certain goods, it could not now be done. If they had never erected a custom-house, or court-house, they could not now do it. Such a mode of reasoning would be deemed by all persons wholly indefensible.

§ 1133. But it is not admitted, that congress have not exercised this very power with reference to this very object. By the act of 21st of April, 1806, (ch. 41,) the president was authorized to cause to be opened a road from the frontier of Georgia, on the route from Athens to New-Orleans; and to cause to be opened a road or roads through the territory, then lately ceded by the Indians to the United States, from the river Mississippi to the Ohio, and to the former Indian boundary line, which was established by the treaty of Greenville; and to cause to be opened a road from Nashville, in the state of Tennessee, to Natchez, in the Mississippi territory. The same remark applies to the act of 29th of March, 1806, (ch. 19,) "to regulate the laying out and making a road from Cumberland, in the state of Maryland, to the state of Ohio." Both of these acts were passed in the administration of President Jefferson, who, it is well known, on other occasions maintained a strict construction of the constitution.

§ 1134. But passing by considerations of this nature, why does not the power to establish post-offices and post-roads include the power to make and construct them, when wanted, as well as the power to establish a navy-hospital, or a custom-house, a power to make and construct them? The latter is not doubted by any persons; why then is the former? In each case, the sense of the ruling term "establish" would seem to be the same; in each, the power may be carried into effect by means short of constructing, or purchasing the things authorized. A temporary use of a suitable site or buildings may possibly be obtained with, or without hire. Besides; why may not congress purchase, or erect a post-office building, and buy the necessary land, if it be in their judgment advisable? Can there be a just doubt, that a power to establish post-offices includes this power, just as much, as a power to establish custom-houses would to build the latter? Would it not be a strange construction to say, that the abstract office might be created, but not the officina, or place, where it could be exercised? There are many places peculiarly fit for local post-offices, where no suitable building might be found. And, if a power to construct post-office buildings exists, where is the restraint upon constructing roads?

§ 1135. It is said, that there is no reason, why congress should be invested with such a power, seeing that the state roads may, and will furnish convenient routes for the mail. When the state-roads do furnish such routes, there can certainly be no sound policy in congress making other routes. But there is a great difference between the policy of exercising a power, and the right of exercising it. But, suppose the state-roads do not furnish (as in point of fact they did not at the time of the adoption of the constitution, and as hereafter, for many exigencies of the government in times of war and otherwise, they may not) suitable routes for the mails, what is then to be done? Is the power of the general government to be paralyzed? Suppose a mail-road is out of repair and founderous, cannot congress authorize the repair of it? If they can, why then not make it originally? Is the one more a means to an end, than the other? If not, then the power to carry the mails may be obstructed; nay, may be annihilated by the neglect of a state. Could it have been the intention of the constitution, in the exercise of this most vital power, to make it dependent upon the will, or the pleasure of the states?

§ 1136. It has been said, that when once a state-road is made a post-road by an act of congress, the national government have acquired such an interest in the use of it, that it is not competent for the state authorities to obstruct it. But how can this be made out? If the power of congress is merely to select or designate the mail-roads, what interest in the use is acquired by the national government any more, than by any travellers upon the road? Where is the power given to acquire it? Can it be pretended, that a state may not discontinue a road, after it has been once established, as a mail-road? The power has been constantly exercised by the states ever since the adoption of the constitution. The states have altered, and discontinued, and changed such roads at their pleasure. It would be a most truly alarming inroad upon state sovereignty to declare, that a state-road could never be altered or discontinued after it had once become a mail-road. That would be to supersede all state authority over their own roads. If the states can discontinue their roads, why not obstruct them? Who shall compel them to repair them, when discontinued, or to keep them at any time in good repair? No one ever yet contended, that the national government possessed any such compulsive authority. If, then, the states may alter or discontinue their roads, or suffer them to go out of repair, is it not obvious, that the power to carry the mails may be retarded or defeated in a great measure by this constitutional exercise of state power? And, if it be the right and duty of congress to provide adequate means for the transportation of the mails, wherever the public good requires it, what limit is there to these means, other than that they are appropriate to the end?

§ 1137. In point of fact, congress cannot be said, in any exact sense, to have yet executed the power to establish post-roads, if by that power we are to understand the designation of particular state-roads, on which the mails shall be carried. The general course has been to designate merely the towns, between which the mails shall be carried, without ascertaining the particular roads at all. Thus, the Act of 20th of February, 1792, ch. 7, (which is but a sample of the other acts,) declares, that "the following roads be established, as post-roads, namely, from Wiscasset in the District of Maine to Savannah in Georgia, by the following route, to wit: Portland, Portsmouth, Newburyport, Ipswich, Salem, Boston, Worcester," &c. &c.; without pointing out any road between those places, on which it should be carried. There are different roads from several of these places to the others. Suppose one of these roads should be discontinued, could the mail-carriers insist upon travelling it?

§ 1138. The truth is, that congress have hitherto acted under the power to a very limited extent only; and will forever continue to do so from principles of public policy and economy, except in cases of an extraordinary nature. There can be no motive to use the power, except for the public good; and circumstances may render it indispensable to carry it out in particular cases to its full limits. It has already occurred, and may hereafter occur, that post-roads may be important and necessary for the purpose of the Union, in peace as well as in war, between places, where there is not any good state-road, and where the amount of travel would not justify any state in an expenditure equal to the construction of such a state-road. In such cases, as the benefit is for the Union, the burthen ought to be borne by the Union. Without any invidious distinction, it may be stated, that the winter mail-route between Philadelphia, and Baltimore, and Washington, by the way of the Susquehannah and Havre de Grace, has been before congress under this very aspect. There is no one, who will doubt the importance of the best post-road in that direction; (the nearest between the two cities;) and yet it is obvious, that the nation alone can be justly called upon to provide the road.

§ 1139. Let a case be taken, when state policy or state hostility shall lead the legislature to close up, or discontinue a road, the nearest and the best between two great states, rivals perhaps for the trade and intercourse of a third state, shall it be said, that congress has no right to make, or repair a road for keeping open for the mail the best means of communication between those states? May the national government be compelled to take the most inconvenient and indirect routes for the mail? In other words, have the states a power to say, how, and upon what roads the mails shall, and shall not travel? If so, then in relation to post-roads, the states, and not the Union, are supreme.

§ 1140. But it is said, that it would be dangerous to allow any power in the Union to lay out and construct post-roads; for then the exercise of the power would supersede the state jurisdiction. This is an utter mistake. If congress should lay out and construct a post-road in a state, it would still be a road within the ordinary territorial jurisdiction of the state. The state could not, indeed, supercede, or obstruct, or discontinue it, or prevent the Union from repairing it, or the mails from travelling on it. But subject to these incidental rights, the right of territory and jurisdiction, civilly and criminally, would be complete and perfect in the state. The power of congress over the road would be limited to the mere right of passage and preservation. That of the state would be general, and embrace all other objects. Congress undoubtedly has power to purchase lands in a state for any public purposes, such as forts, arsenals, and dock-yards. So, they have a right to erect hospitals, custom-houses, and court-houses in a state. But no person ever imagined, that these places were thereby removed from the general jurisdiction of the state. On the contrary, they are universally understood for all other purposes, not inconsistent with the constitutional rights and uses of the Union, to be subject to state authority and rights.

§ 1141. The clause respecting cessions of territory for the seat of government, and for forts, arsenals, dock-yards, &c. has nothing to do with the point. But if it had, it is favourable to the power. That clause was necessary for the purpose of ousting the state jurisdiction in the specified cases, and for vesting an *exclusive* jurisdiction in the general government. No general or *exclusive* jurisdiction is either required, or would be useful in regard to post-roads. It would be inconvenient for congress to assemble in a place, where it had not exclusive jurisdiction. And an exclusive jurisdiction would seem indispensable over forts, arsenals, dock-yards, and other places of a like nature. But surely it will not be pretended, that congress could not erect a fort, or magazine, in a place within a state, unless the state should cede the territory. The only effect would be, that the jurisdiction in such a case would not be exclusive. Suppose a state should prohibit a sale of any of the lands within its boundaries by its own citizens, for any public purposes indispensable for the Union, either military or civil, would not congress possess a constitutional right to demand, and appropriate land within the state for such purposes, making a just compensation? Exclusive jurisdiction over a road is one thing; the right to make it is quite another. A turnpike company may be authorized to make a road; and yet may have no jurisdiction, or at least no exclusive jurisdiction over it.

§ 1142. The supposed silence of the Federalist proves nothing. That work was principally designed to meet objections, and remove prejudices. The post-office establishment in its nature, and character, and purposes, was so generally deemed useful and convenient, and unexceptionable, that it was wholly unnecessary to expound its value, or enlarge upon its benefits.

. . . . .

§ 1144. This question, as to the right to lay out and construct post-roads, is wholly distinct from that of the more general power to lay out and make canals, and military and other roads. The latter power may not exist at all; even if the former should be unquestionable. The latter turns upon a question of implied power, as incident to given powers. The former turns upon the true interpretation of words of express grant. Nobody doubts, that the words "establish post-roads," may, without violating their received meaning in other cases, be construed so, as to include the power to lay out and construct roads. The question is, whether that is the true sense of the words, as used in the constitution. And here, if ever, the rule of interpretation, which requires us to look at the nature of the instrument, and the objects of the power, as a national power, in order to expound its meaning, must come into operation.

§ 1145. But whatever be the extent of the power, narrow or large, there will still remain another inquiry, whether it is an exclusive power, or concurrent in the states. This is not, perhaps, a very important inquiry, because it is admitted on all sides, that it can be exercised only in subordination to the power of congress, if it be concurrent in the states. A learned commentator deems it concurrent, inasmuch as there seems nothing in the constitution, or in the nature of the thing itself, which may not be exercised by both governments at the same time, without prejudice or interference; but subordinate, because, whenever any power is expressly granted to congress, it is to be taken for granted, that it is not to be contravened by the authority of any particular state. A state might, therefore, establish a post-road, or postoffice, on any route, where congress had not established any. On the other hand, another learned commentator is of opinion, that the power is exclusive in congress, so far as relates to the conveyance of letters, &c. It is highly improbable, that any state will attempt any exercise of the power, considering the difficulty of carrying it into effect, without the co-operation of congress.

SEE ALSO:

William Blackstone, Commentaries 1:311 (1765)

Records of the Federal Convention, Farrand 1:243; 2:135, 144, 159, 167–68, 303, 322, 328, 569, 595

An Act to Establish the Post-Office of the United States, 1 Stat. 733 (1799)

Article 1, Section 8, Clause 8

To promote the Progress of Science and useful Arts, by securing for limited Times to Authors and Inventors the exclusive Right to their respective Writings and Discoveries;

1

An Act for Preventing the Frequent Abuses in Printing Seditious Treasonable and Unlicensed Books and Pamphlets and for Regulating Printing and Printing Presses
14 Chas. 2, c. 33 (1662)

(See Amend. I [speech and press], no. 1)

2

An Act for the Encouragement of Learning, by Vesting the Copies of Printed Books in the Author's or Purchasers of Such Copies
8 Anne, c. 19 (1709)

Whereas *printers, booksellers, and other persons have of late frequently taken the liberty of printing, reprinting, and publishing, or causing to be printed, reprinted, and published, books and other writings, without the consent of the authors or proprietors of such books and writings, to their very great detriment, and too often to the ruin of them and their families:* for preventing therefore such practices for the future, and for the encouragement of learned men to compose and write useful books; may it please your Majesty, that it may be enacted, and be it enacted by the Queen's most excellent majesty, by and with the advice and consent of the lords spiritual and temporal, and commons, in this present parliament assembled, and by the authority of the same, That from and after the tenth day of *April,* one thousand seven hundred and ten, the author of any book or books already printed, who hath not transferred to any other the copy or copies of such book or books, share or shares thereof, or the bookseller or booksellers, printer or printers, or other person or persons, who hath or have purchased or acquired the copy or copies of any book or books, in order to print or reprint the same, shall have the sole right and liberty of printing such book and books for the term of one and twenty years, to commence from the said tenth day of *April,* and no longer; and that the author of any book or books already composed, and not printed and published, or that shall hereafter be composed, and his assignee or assigns, shall have the sole liberty of printing and reprinting such book and books for the term of fourteen years, to commence from the day of the first publishing the same, and no longer; and that if any other bookseller, printer, or other person whatsoever, from and after the tenth day of *April,* one thousand seven hundred and ten, within the times granted and limited by this act, as aforesaid, shall print, reprint, or import, or cause to be printed, reprinted, or imported, any such book or books, without the consent of the proprietor or proprietors thereof first had and obtained in writing, signed in the presence of two or more credible witnesses; or knowing the same to be so printed or reprinted, without the consent of the proprietors, shall sell, publish, or expose to sale, or cause to be sold, published, or exposed to sale, any such book or books, without such consent first had and obtained, as aforesaid: then such offender or offenders shall forfeit such book or books, and all and every sheet or sheets, being part of such book or books, to the proprietor or proprietors of the copy thereof, who shall forthwith damask, and make waste paper of them; and further, That every such offender or offenders shall forfeit one penny for every sheet which shall be found in his, her, or their custody, either printed or printing, published, or exposed to sale, contrary to the true intent and meaning of this act; the one moiety thereof to the Queen's most excellent majesty, her heirs and successors, and the other moiety thereof to any person or persons that shall sue for the same, to be recovered in any of her Majesty's courts of record at *Westminster,* by action of debt, bill, plaint, or information, in which no wager of law, essoin, privilege, or protection, or more than one imparlance shall be allowed.

II. *And whereas many persons may through ignorance offend against this act, unless some provision be made, whereby the property in every such book, as is intended by this act to be secured to the proprietor or proprietors thereof, may be ascertained, as likewise the consent of such proprietor or proprietors for the printing or reprinting of such book or books may from time to time be known;* be it therefore further enacted by the authority aforesaid, That nothing in this act contained shall be construed to extend to subject any bookseller, printer, or other person whatsoever, to the forfeitures or penalties therein mentioned, for or by reason of the printing or reprinting of any book or books without such consent, as aforesaid, unless the title to the copy of such book or books hereafter published shall, before such publication, be entred in the register book of the company of stationers, in such manner as hath been usual, which register book shall at all times be kept at the hall of the said company, and unless such consent of the proprietor or proprietors be in like manner entred as aforesaid, for every of which several entries, six pence shall be paid, and no more; which said register book may, at all seasonable and convenient time, be resorted to, and inspected by any bookseller, printer, or other person, for the purposes before-mentioned, without any fee or reward; and the clerk of the said company of stationers shall, when and as often as thereunto required, give a certificate under his hand of such entry or entries, and for every such certificate may take a fee not exceeding six pence.

III. Provided nevertheless, That if the clerk of the said company of stationers for the time being, shall refuse or neglect to register, or make such entry or entries, or to give such certificate, being thereunto required by the author or proprietor of such copy or copies, in the presence of two or more credible witnesses, That then such person and persons so refusing, notice being first duly given of such refusal, by an advertisement in the *Gazette,* shall have the like benefit, as if such entry or entries, certificate or certificates had been duly made and given; and that the clerks so refusing, shall, for any such offence, forfeit to the proprietor of such copy or copies the sum of twenty pounds, to be recovered in any of her Majesty's courts of record at *Westminster,* by action of debt, bill, plaint, or information, in which no wager of law, essoin, privilege or protection, or more than one imparlance shall be allowed.

IV. Provided nevertheless, and it is hereby further enacted by the authority aforesaid, That if any bookseller or booksellers, printer or printers, shall, after the said five and twentieth day of *March,* one thousand seven hundred and ten, set a price upon, or sell, or expose to sale, any book or books at such a price or rate as shall be conceived by any person or persons to be too high and unreasonable; it shall and may be lawful for any person or persons, to make complaint thereof to the lord archbishop of *Canterbury* for the time being, the lord chancellor, or lord keeper of the great seal of *Great Britain* for the time being, the lord bishop of *London* for the time being, the lord chief justice of the court of *Queen's Bench,* the lord chief justice of the court of *Common Pleas,* the lord chief baron of the court of *Exchequer* for the time being, the vice chancellors of the two universities for the time being, in that part of *Great Britain* called *England;* the lord president of the sessions for the time being, the lord chief justice general for the time being, the lord chief baron of the *Exchequer* for the time being, the rector of the college of *Edinburgh* for the time being, in that part of *Great Britain* called *Scotland;* who, or any one of them, shall and have hereby full power and authority, from time to time, to send for, summon, or call before him or them such bookseller or booksellers, printer or printers, and to examine and enquire of the reason of the dearness and inhauncement of the price or value of such book or books by him or them so sold or exposed to sale; and if upon such enquiry and examination it shall be found, that the price of such book or books is inhaunced, or any wise too high or unreasonable, then and in such case the said archbishop of *Canterbury,* lord chancellor or lord keeper, bishop of *London,* two chief justices, chief baron, vice chancellors of the universities, in that part of *Great Britain* called *England,* and the said lord president of the sessions, lord justice general, lord chief baron, and the rector of the college of *Edinburgh,* in that part of *Great Britain* called *Scotland,* or any one or more of them, so enquiring and examining, have hereby full power and authority to reform and redress the same, and to limit and settle the price of every such printed book and books, from time to time, according to the best of their judgments, and as to them shall seem just and reasonable; and in case of alteration of the rate or price from what was set or demanded by such bookseller or booksellers, printer or printers, to award and order such bookseller and booksellers, printer and printers, to pay all the costs and charges that the person or persons so complaining shall be put unto, by reason of such complaint, and of the causing such rate or price to be so limited and settled; all which shall be done by the said archbishop of *Canterbury,* lord chancellor or lord keeper, bishop of *London,* two chief justices, chief baron, vice chancellors of the two universities, in that part of *Great Britain* called *England,* and the said lord president of the sessions, lord justice general, lord chief baron, and rector of the college of *Edinburgh,* in that part of *Great Britain* called *Scotland,* or any one of them, by writing under their hands and seals, and thereof publick notice shall be forthwith given by the said bookseller or booksellers, printer or printers, by an advertisement in the *Gazette;* and if any bookseller or booksellers, printer or printers, shall, after such settlement made of the said rate and price, sell, or expose to sale, any book or books, at a higher or greater price, than what shall have been so limited and settled, as aforesaid, then, and in every such case such bookseller and booksellers, printer and printers, shall forfeit the sum of five pounds for every such book so by him, her, or them sold or exposed to sale; one moiety thereof to the Queen's most excellent majesty, her heirs and successors, and the other moiety to any person or persons that shall sue for the same, to be recovered, with costs of suit, in any of her Majesty's courts of record at *Westminster,* by action of debt, bill, plaint or information, in which no wager of law, essoin, privilege, or protection, or more than one imparlance shall be allowed.

V. Provided always, and it is hereby enacted, That nine copies of each book or books, upon the best paper, that from and after the said tenth day of *April,* one thousand seven hundred and ten, shall be printed and published, as aforesaid, or reprinted and published with additions, shall, by the printer and printers thereof, be delivered to the warehouse keeper of the said company of stationers for the time being, at the hall of the said company, before such publication made, for the use of the royal library, the libraries of the universities of *Oxford* and *Cambridge,* the libraries of the four universities in *Scotland,* the library of *Sion College* in *London,* and the library commonly called the library belonging to the faculty of advocates at *Edinburgh* respectively; which said warehouse keeper is hereby required within ten days after demand by the keepers of the respective libraries, or any person or persons by them or any of them authorized to demand the said copy, to deliver the same, for the use of the aforesaid libraries; and if any proprietor, bookseller, or printer, or the said warehouse keeper of the said company of stationers, shall not observe the direction of this act therein, that then he and they so making default in not delivering the said printed copies, as aforesaid, shall forfeit, besides the value of the said printed copies, the sum of five pounds for every copy not so delivered, as also the value of the said printed copy not so delivered, the same to be recovered by the Queen's majesty, her heirs and successors, and by the chancellor, masters, and scholars of any of the said universities, and by the president and fellows of *Sion College,* and the said faculty of advocates at *Edinburgh,* with their full costs respectively.

VI. Provided always, and be it further enacted, That if any person or persons incur the penalties contained in this act, in that part of *Great Britain* called *Scotland,* they shall be recoverable by any action before the court of session there.

VII. Provided, That nothing in this act contained, do extend, or shall be construed to extend to prohibit the importation, vending, or selling of any books in *Greek, Latin,* or any other foreign language printed beyond the seas; any thing in this act contained to the contrary notwithstanding.

VIII. And be it further enacted by the authority aforesaid, That if any action or suit shall be commenced or brought against any person or persons whatsoever, for doing or causing to be done any thing in pursuance of this act, the defendants in such action may plead the general issue, and give the special matter in evidence; and if upon such action a verdict be given for the defendant, or the plaintiff become nonsuited, or discontinue his action, then the defendant shall have and recover his full costs, for which he shall have the same remedy as a defendant in any case by law hath.

IX. Provided, That nothing in this act contained shall extend, or be construed to extend, either to prejudice or confirm any right that the said universities, or any of them, or any person or persons have, or claim to have, to the printing or reprinting any book or copy already printed, or hereafter to be printed.

X. Provided nevertheless, That all actions, suits, bills, indictments, or informations for any offence that shall be committed against this act, shall be brought, sued, and commenced within three months next after such offence committed, or else the same shall be void and of none effect.

XI. Provided always, That after the expiration of the said term of fourteen years, the sole right of printing or disposing of copies shall return to the authors thereof, if they are then living, for another term of fourteen years.

3

William Blackstone, Commentaries 2:406
1766

Now the identity of a literary composition consists intirely in the *sentiment* and the *language;* the same conceptions, cloathed in the same words, must necessarily be the same composition: and whatever method be taken of conveying that composition to the ear or the eye of another, by recital, by writing, or by printing, in any number of copies or at any period of time, it is always the identical work of the author which is so conveyed; and no other man can have a right to convey or transfer it without his consent, either tacitly or expressly given. This consent may perhaps be tacitly given, when an author permits his work to be published, without any reserve of right, and without stamping on it any marks of ownership: it is then a present to the public, like the building of a church, or the laying out a new highway: but, in case of a bargain for a single impression, or a sale or gift of the copyright, the reversion is plainly continued in the original proprietor, or the whole property transferred to another.

The Roman law adjudged, that if one man wrote any thing, though never so elegantly, on the paper or parchment of another, the writing should belong to the original owner of the materials on which it was written: meaning certainly nothing more thereby, than the mere mechanical operation of writing, for which it directed the scribe to receive a satisfaction; especially as, in works of genius and invention, such as a picture painted on another man's canvas, the same law gave the canvas to the painter. We find no other mention in the civil law of any property in the works of the understanding, though the sale of literary copies, for the purposes of recital or multiplication, is certainly as antient as the times of Terence, Martial, and Statius. Neither with us in England hath there been any direct determination upon the right of authors at the common law. But much may be gathered from the frequent injunctions of the court of chancery, prohibiting the invasion of this property: especially where either the injunctions have been *perpetual,* or have related to unpublished manuscripts, or to such antient books, as were not within the provisions of the statute of queen Anne. Much may also be collected from the several legislative recognitions of copyrights; and from those adjudged cases at common law, wherein the crown hath been considered as invested with certain prerogative copyrights; for, if the crown is capable of an exclusive right in any one book, the subject seems also capable of having the same right in another.

But, exclusive of such copyright as may subsist by the rules of the common law, the statutes 8 Ann. c. 19. hath protected by additional penalties the property of authors and their assigns for the term of fourteen years; and hath directed that if, at the end of that term, the author himself be living, the right shall then return to him for another term of the same duration: and a similar privilege is extended to the inventors of prints and engravings, for the term of fourteen years, by the statute 8 Geo. II. c. 13. Both which appear to have been copied from the exception in the statute of monopolies, 21 Jac. I. c. 3. which allows a royal patent of privilege to be granted for fourteen years to any inventor of a new manufacture, for the sole working or making of the same; by virtue whereof a temporary property becomes vested in the patentee.

4

MASSACHUSETTS CONSTITUTION OF 1780, CH. 5, SEC. 2

Wisdom and knowledge, as well as virtue, diffused generally among the body of the people, being necessary for the preservation of their rights and liberties; and as these depend on spreading the opportunities and advantages of education in the various parts of the country, and among the different orders of the people, it shall be the duty of legislatures and magistrates, in all future periods of this commonwealth, to cherish the interests of literature and the sciences, and all seminaries of them; especially the university at Cambridge, public schools and grammar schools in the towns; to encourage private societies and public institutions, rewards and immunities, for the promotion of agriculture, arts, sciences, commerce, trades, manufactures, and a natural history of the country; to countenance and inculcate the principles of humanity and general benevolence, public and private charity, industry and frugality, honesty and punctuality in their dealings; sincerity, good humor, and all social affections, and generous sentiments, among the people.

5

JAMES MADISON, ACT SECURING COPYRIGHT FOR AUTHORS, VIRGINIA HOUSE OF DELEGATES
16 Nov. 1785

Papers 8:418–19

I. *BE it enacted by the General Assembly,* That the author of any book or pamphlet already printed, being a citizen of any one of the United States, who has not transferred to any other person or persons the copy or copies of such book, or pamphlet, share, or shares thereof, his heirs and assigns, or the person or persons who have purchased or acquired such copy or copies, share or shares, in order to print or reprint the same, his heirs and assigns shall have the exclusive right of printing and re-printing such book or pamphlet, within this commonwealth, for the term of twenty-one years, to be computed from the first publication thereof; and that the author of any book or pamphlet already composed and not printed or published, or that shall hereafter be composed, being a citizen, as aforesaid, his heirs and assigns shall have the exclusive right of printing and re-printing such book or pamphlet, within this commonwealth, for the like term of twenty-one years, to be computed from the first publication thereof. And if any person or persons whatsoever, shall print, re-print, or cause to be printed or re-printed, within this commonwealth, any such book or pamphlet; or shall import into this commonwealth, from any foreign kingdom or state, any printed or re-printed copies of such book or pamphlet, without the consent of the author or proprietor thereof first obtained in writing, signed in presence of two credible witnesses at least; or who, knowing the same to be so printed, re-printed, or imported, without such consent first had and obtained, shall publish, sell, or expose to sale, or cause to be published, sold, or exposed to sale, any copy or copies of any such book or pamphlet; the person or persons offending herein, shall forfeit to the party injured, double the value of all the copies so printed, re-printed, or imported; or so published, sold, or exposed to sale; to be recovered at the suit of such party, in any court of record within this commonwealth.

II. *Provided nevertheless,* That no person shall be entitled to the benefit of this act, until he shall have registered the title of such book or pamphlet with the clerk of the council, and procured a certificate of such registry from the said clerk; which certificate the clerk is hereby required to give, taking only three shillings for his trouble.

6

RECORDS OF THE FEDERAL CONVENTION

[*2:321; Journal, 18 Aug.*]
To secure to literary authors their copy rights for a limited time
To establish an University
To encourage, by proper premiums and provisions, the advancement of useful knowledge and discoveries
To establish seminaries for the promotion of literature and the arts and sciences
To grant charters of incorporation
To grant patents for useful inventions
To secure to authors exclusive rights for a certain time
To establish public institutions, rewards and immunities for the promotion of agriculture, commerce, trades, and manufactures.

[*2:505; Journal, 5 Sept.*]
"To promote the progress of science and useful arts by securing for limited times to Authors and Inventors the exclusive right to their respective writings and discoveries.
agreed

[*2:595; Committee of Style*]
To promote the progress of science and useful arts, by securing for limited times to authors and inventors the exclusive right to their respective writings and discoveries.

7

JAMES MADISON, FEDERALIST, NO. 43, 288
23 Jan. 1788

The utility of this power will scarcely be questioned. The copy right of authors has been solemnly adjudged in Great Britain to be a right at common law. The right to useful inventions, seems with equal reason to belong to the inventors. The public good fully coincides in both cases, with the claims of individuals. The States cannot separately make effectual provision for either of the cases, and most of them have anticipated the decision of this point, by laws passed at the instance of Congress.

8

JAMES RUMSEY TO THOMAS JEFFERSON
6 June 1789
Jefferson Papers 15:171–72

My letters mention that their was a Committee of Congress appointed to bring in a bill for Establishing an office for granting Exclusive Wrights to inventors &c. This is a business that is at present upon, but a bad footing, in any part of the world; England I believe has fixed it on the best Establishment, yet it is far short of being Equitable, or Encorgeing to ingenious men, which I suppose was the object such laws was intended to imbrace. The dispute between Mr. Fitch and myself has Caused many of the gentlemen of our Country to be very tenacious about giveing grants, so much so that the assembly of New York, and Some others, would not give me a grant for the principle of my boiler, but only for one formed like the drawing laid before them (which was intended only to Explain its principle more Clearly than Expressions Could,) alledgeing that any other kind of grant, would Cut of others from improveing on it, and so I think it ought for a limmited time, or what will a grant be worth, if Every form that a machine Can be put into should intitle a different person to use the same principle; there is no machine Extent but what might be Varied as often as their is days in a year, and still answer nearly the same purpose. Such machines as are already in use (and their principles not under any restrictions by patents,) then Every person Improveing on such machines ought to have a grant for such improvement and no more, but where the principle itself is new I humbly Conceive that it ought to be secured to the inventor for a Limmited time. otherwise but few persons will spend their money and time in makeing new discoveries, knowing that the first person that Varies the form of his invention, will be intitled to receive Eaqueal advantages from it with himself. The french method of haveing new inventions Exammined by a Committee of philosophical Charactors, before grants Can be obtained, is certainly a good one, as it has a tendency to prevent many simple projectors from ruining themselves by the too Long persuit of projects that they know but little about.

I have troubled you Sir with these remarks, not only because I am deeply interested myself in haveing a just and permanent Establishment of this business made, but because I wish my Countrymen to have such Encouragement given to them, as to Cause them to out Strip the world in arts and Sciences. And knowing you Could throw great light upon the Subject on your return to america was still a greater inducement for me to wish to draw your attention towards that object.—I meet with many delays in geting forward my Experiment. It will be ten days yet before I can have the Vessel Launched, by the time She gets to London I Expect to have the machinery ready to put into her. What time it may take to fix it is uncertain, but hope not long; I have a dread Comes on me as the day approaches on which I have so much at Stake, yet Every reveiw I take of my plan Confirms me more and more in its Success.

9

Alexander Hamilton, Report on Manufactures
5 Dec. 1791

Papers 10:338–40

First. To constitute a fund for paying the bounties which shall have been decreed.

Secondly. To constitute a fund for the operations of a Board, to be established, for promoting Arts, Agriculture, Manufactures and Commerce. Of this institution, different intimations have been given, in the course of this report. An outline of a plan for it shall now be submitted.

Let a certain annual sum, be set apart, and placed under the management of Commissioners, not less than three, to consist of certain Officers of the Government and their Successors in Office.

Let these Commissioners be empowered to apply the fund confided to them—to defray the expences of the emigration of Artists, and Manufacturers in particular branches of extraordinary importance—to induce the prosecution and introduction of useful discoveries, inventions and improvements, by proportionate rewards, judiciously held out and applied—to encourage by premiums both honorable and lucrative the exertions of individuals, And of classes, in relation to the several objects, they are charged with promoting—and to afford such other aids to those objects, as may be generally designated by law.

The Commissioners to render [to the Legislature] an annual account of their transactions and disbursments; and all such sums as shall not have been applied to the purposes of their trust, at the end of every three years, to revert to the Treasury. It may also be enjoined upon them, not to draw out the money, but for the purpose of some specific disbursment.

It may moreover be of use, to authorize them to receive voluntary contributions; making it their duty to apply them to the particular objects for which they may have been made, if any shall have been designated by the donors.

There is reason to believe, that the progress of particular manufactures has been much retarded by the want of skilful workmen. And it often happens that the capitals employed are not equal to the purposes of bringing from abroad workmen of a superior kind. Here, in cases worthy of it, the auxiliary agency of Government would in all probability be useful. There are also valuable workmen, in every branch, who are prevented from emigrating solely by the want of means. Occasional aids to such persons properly administered might be a source of valuable acquisitions to the country.

The propriety of stimulating by rewards, the invention and introduction of useful improvements, is admitted without difficulty. But the success of attempts in this way must evidently depend much on the manner of conducting them. It is probable, that the placing of the dispensation of those rewards under some proper discretionary direction, where they may be accompanied by *collateral expedients,* will serve to give them the surest efficacy. It seems impracticable to apportion, by general rules, specific compensations for discoveries of unknown and disproportionate utility.

The great use which may be made of a fund of this nature to procure and import foreign improvements is particularly obvious. Among these, the article of machines would form a most important item.

The operation and utility of premiums have been adverted to; together with the advantages which have resulted from their dispensation, under the direction of certain public and private societies. Of this some experience has been had in the instance of the Pennsylvania society, [for the Promotion of Manufactures and useful Arts;] but the funds of that association have been too contracted to produce more than a very small portion of the good to which the principles of it would have led. It may confidently be affirmed that there is scarcely any thing, which has been devised, better calculated to excite a general spirit of improvement than the institutions of this nature. They are truly invaluable.

In countries where there is great private wealth much may be effected by the voluntary contributions of patriotic individuals, but in a community situated like that of the United States, the public purse must supply the deficiency of private resource. In what can it be so useful as in prompting and improving the efforts of industry?

10

Levi Lincoln, Patents for Inventions
26 May 1802

1 Ops. Atty. Gen. 110

The authority given by law to grant patents is unquestionably confined to the citizens of the United States. The privilege is a monopoly in derogation of common right, and, as it is not, ought not to be extended to foreigners. Were it to be, it would be subject to endless abuses, privations, and embarrassments to our citizens. I have no doubt on the question.

11

St. George Tucker, Blackstone's Commentaries 1:App. 265–67 1803

8. Congress have power to promote the progress of science and useful arts, by securing for limited times to authors and inventors the exclusive right to their respective writings and discoveries. C. U. S. Art. 1, Sect. 8.

This is another branch of federal authority, in which I presume the states may possess some degree of concurrent right within their respective territories; but as the security which the state could afford, would necessarily fall short of that which an authority co-extensive with the union may give, it is scarcely probable that the protection of the laws of any particular state will hereafter be resorted to; more especially, as the act of 2 Cong. c. *55,* declares, that "where any state before it's adoption of the present form of government shall have granted an exclusive right to any invention, the party claiming that right, shall not be capable of obtaining an exclusive right under that act, but on relinquishing his right under such particular state, and of such relinquishment his obtaining an exclusive right under that act, shall be sufficient evidence." But this act does not appear to extend to copy-rights: the exclusive right to which is secured by an act passed, 1 Cong. 2 Sess. c. 15, amended by the act of 7 Cong. c. 36, for fourteen years; and if at the expiration of that term, the author being living, the same exclusive right shall be continued to him and his heirs, for other fourteen years. But the exclusive rights of other persons to their inventions, is limited to fourteen years, only, by the act first mentioned. Aliens, who have resided two years in the United States, are moreover entitled to the benefit of a patent for any new invention, by virtue of the act of 6 Cong. c. 25.

Whether it was under this clause of the constitution, or not, that the first secretary of the treasury grounded his opinion of the right of congress to establish trading companies, for the purpose of encouraging arts and manufactures; or whether it was under this clause, that the establishment of a company for the discovery of mines, minerals, and metals, was contemplated by the authors of that scheme; or whether it was from a conviction of the unconstitutionality of the proposition, in both cases, that neither of them took effect, I cannot presume to determine: but, certainly, if this clause of the constitution was relied upon, as giving congress a power to establish such monopolies, nothing could be more fallacious than such a conclusion. For the constitution not only declares the object, but points out the express *mode* of giving the encouragement; viz. "by securing for a limited time to authors and inventors, the exclusive right to their respective writings, and discoveries." Nothing could be more superfluous, or incompatible, with the object contended for, than these words, if it was, indeed, the intention of the constitution to authorise congress, to adopt any other mode which they might think proper.

12

Thomas Jefferson to Isaac McPherson 13 Aug. 1813 *Writings 13:333–35*

It has been pretended by some, (and in England especially,) that inventors have a natural and exclusive right to their inventions, and not merely for their own lives, but inheritable to their heirs. But while it is a moot question whether the origin of any kind of property is derived from nature at all, it would be singular to admit a natural and even an hereditary right to inventors. It is agreed by those who have seriously considered the subject, that no individual has, of natural right, a separate property in an acre of land, for instance. By an universal law, indeed, whatever, whether fixed or movable, belongs to all men equally and in common, is the property for the moment of him who occupies it, but when he relinquishes the occupation, the property goes with it. Stable ownership is the gift of social law, and is given late in the progress of society. It would be curious then, if an idea, the fugitive fermentation of an individual brain, could, of natural right, be claimed in exclusive and stable property. If nature has made any one thing less susceptible than all others of exclusive property, it is the action of the thinking power called an idea, which an individual may exclusively possess as long as he keeps it to himself; but the moment it is divulged, it forces itself into the possession of every one, and the receiver cannot dispossess himself of it. Its peculiar character, too, is that no one possesses the less, because every other possesses the whole of it. He who receives an idea from me, receives instruction himself without lessening mine; as he who lights his taper at mine, receives light without darkening me. That ideas should freely spread from one to another over the globe, for the moral and mutual instruction of man, and improvement of his condition, seems to have been peculiarly and benevolently designed by nature, when she made them, like fire, expansible over all space, without lessening their density in any point, and like the air in which we breathe, move, and have our physical being, incapable of confinement or exclusive appropriation. Inventions then cannot, in nature, be a subject of property. Society may give an exclusive right to the profits arising from them, as an encouragement to men to pursue ideas which may produce utility, but this may or may not be done, according to the will and convenience of the society, without claim or complaint from anybody. Accordingly, it is a fact, as far as I am informed, that England was, until we copied her, the only country on earth which ever, by a general law, gave a legal right to the exclusive use of an idea. In some other countries it is sometimes done, in a great case, and by a special and personal act, but, generally speaking, other nations have thought that these monopolies produce more embarrassment than advantage to society; and it may be observed that the nations which refuse monopolies of invention, are as fruitful as England in new and useful devices.

Considering the exclusive right to invention as given not of natural right, but for the benefit of society, I know well the difficulty of drawing a line between the things which are worth to the public the embarrassment of an exclusive patent, and those which are not. As a member of the patent board for several years, while the law authorized a board to grant or refuse patents, I saw with what slow progress a system of general rules could be matured.

13

William Rawle, A View of the Constitution of the United States 104–6
1829 (2d ed.)

At common law, it seems to have been a question whether the inventor of any new art or improvement had such a special property in it, as to entitle him to pursue another who made use of it after the inventor had made it public. But there was no doubt that if another person had fallen on the same invention, without a knowledge of the first, he would be entitled to the benefit of his own talents. It has however been deemed in many countries politic and wise, to secure to the first inventor a reward for the time and study employed in such pursuits. In England, the king undertook, on the score of royal prerogative, to grant exclusive privileges of making and selling articles of domestic manufacture, and of importing foreign articles, by which protection to such inventors was occasionally obtained. But this practice began to be abused, and such licenses or monopolies, often conferred as rewards on particular favourites, or used merely to promote the interest of the crown, had increased in the reign of Elizabeth and James I. to an alarming degree, and therefore, by an act passed in the twenty-first year of the reign of the latter, all such grants are declared to be void; in the fifth section, however, a proviso is introduced, which is the foundation of the present system in that country relative to patents, by allowing them to be granted to the authors of any new inventions for a term not exceeding fourteen years.

In respect to what is termed literary property; the right which a person may be supposed to have in his own original compositions,—the same doubts as to the common law are entertained, and the protection of a statute has been likewise extended, which at the same time disposed of the common law question, as to those who complied with its forms, by declaring that the author should have the benefit of it for fourteen years, and no longer, unless he was still living at the expiration of the first term, when it might be renewed for fourteen years more. But as the author might not avail himself of the benefit of the statute, the question remained unsettled till the year 1774, when a small majority of the twelve Judges decided against it. This interesting question merits much consideration. At present it is sufficient to say, that as from the nature of our Constitution, no new rights can be considered as created by it, but its operation more properly is the organization and distribution of a conceded power in relation to rights already existing, we must regard these provisions as at least the evidence of opinion, that such a species of property, both in the works of authors and in the inventions of artists, had a legal existence.

In some of the states, prior to the adoption of the general Constitution, acts of the legislature in favour of meritorious discoveries and improvements, had been passed; but their efficacy being confined to the boundaries of the states, was of little value, and there can be no doubt that, as soon as congress legislated on the subject, (which was as early as the second session, 1790,) all the state provisions ceased; although in the act of 21 Feb. 1793, it is cautiously provided that the applicant for the benefit of the protection of the United States, shall surrender his right under any state law; of which his obtaining a patent shall be sufficient evidence.

14

Joseph Story, Commentaries on the Constitution 3:§§ 1147–50
1833

§ 1147. This power did not exist under the confederation; and its utility does not seem to have been questioned. The copyright of authors in their works had, before the revolution, been decided in Great Britain to be a common law right; and it was regulated and limited under statutes passed by parliament upon that subject. The right to useful inventions seems, with equal reason, to belong to the inventors; and, accordingly, it was saved out of the statute of monopolies in the reign of King James the First, and has ever since been allowed for a limited period, not exceeding fourteen years. It was doubtless to this knowledge of the common law and statuteable rights of authors and inventors, that we are to attribute this constitutional provision. It was beneficial to all parties, that the national government should possess this power; to authors and inventors, because, otherwise, they would have been subjected to the varying laws and systems of the different states on this subject, which would impair, and might even destroy the value of their rights; to the public, as it would promote the progress of science and the useful arts, and admit the people at large, after a short interval, to the full possession and enjoyment of all writings and inventions without restraint. In short, the only boon, which could be offered to inventors to disclose the secrets of their discoveries, would be the exclusive right and profit of them, as a monopoly for a limited period. And authors would have little inducement to prepare elaborate works for the public, if their publication was to be at a large expense, and, as soon as they were published, there would be an unlimited right of depredation and piracy of their copyright. The states could not separately make effectual provision for either of the cases; and most of them, at the time of the adoption of the constitution, had anticipated the propriety of such a grant of power, by passing laws on the subject at the instance of the continental congress.

§ 1148. The power, in its terms, is confined to authors and inventors; and cannot be extended to the introducers of any new works or inventions. This has been thought by some persons of high distinction to be a defect in the constitution. But perhaps the policy of further extending the right is questionable; and, at all events, the restriction has not hitherto operated as any discouragement of science or the arts. It has been doubted, whether congress has authority to decide the fact, that a person is an author or inventor in the sense of the constitution, so as to preclude that question from judicial inquiry. But, at all events, such a construction ought never to be put upon the terms of any general act in favour of a particular inventor, unless it be inevitable.

§ 1149. It has been suggested, that this power is not exclusive, but concurrent with that of the states, so always, that the acts of the latter do not contravene the acts of congress. It has, therefore, been asserted, that where congress go no farther than to secure the right to an author or inventor, the state may regulate the use of such right, or restrain it, so far as it may deem it injurious to the public. Whether this be so or not may be matter for grave inquiry, whenever the question shall arise directly in judgment. At present, it seems wholly unnecessary to discuss it theoretically. But, at any rate, there does not seem to be the same difficulty in affirming, that, as the power of congress extends only to authors and inventors, a state may grant an exclusive right to the possessor or introducer of an art or invention, who does not claim to be an inventor, but has merely introduced it from abroad.

§ 1150. In the first draft of the constitution the clause is not to be found; but the subject was referred to a committee, (among other propositions,) whose report was accepted, and gave the clause in the very form, in which it now stands in the constitution. A more extensive proposition, "to establish public institutions, rewards, and immunities for the promotion of agriculture, commerce, and manufactures" was (as has been before stated) made, and silently abandoned. Congress have already, by a series of laws on this subject, provided for the rights of authors and inventors; and, without question, the exercise of the power has operated as an encouragement to native genius, and to the solid advancement of literature and the arts.

15

WHEATON v. PETERS
8 Pet. 591 (1834)

Mr Justice M'LEAN delivered the opinion of the court.

After stating the case, he proceeded:

Some of the questions which arise in this case are as novel, in this country, as they are interesting. But one case involving similar principles, except a decision by a state court, has occurred; and that was decided by the circuit court of the United States for the district of Pennsylvania, from whose decree no appeal was taken.

The right of the complainants must be first examined. If this right shall be sustained as set forth in the bill, and the defendants shall be proved to have violated it, the court will be bound to give the appropriate redress.

The complainants assert their right on two grounds.

First, under the common law.

Secondly, under the acts of congress.

And they insist, in the first place, that an author was entitled, at common law, to a perpetual property in the copy of his works, and in the profits of their publication; and to recover damages for its injury, by an action on the case, and to the protection of a court of equity.

In support of this proposition, the counsel for the complainants have indulged in a wide range of argument, and have shown great industry and ability. The limited time allowed for the preparation of this opinion, will not admit of an equally extended consideration of the subject by the court.

Perhaps no topic in England has excited more discussion, among literary and talented men, than that of the literary property of authors. So engrossing was the subject, for a long time, as to leave few neutrals, among those who were distinguished for their learning and ability. At length the question, whether the copy of a book or literary composition belongs to the author at common law, was brought before the court of king's bench, in the great case of Miller v. Taylor, reported in 4 Burr. 2303. This was a case of great expectation; and the four judges, in giving their opinions, seriatim, exhausted the argument on both sides. Two of the judges, and lord Mansfield, held, that, by the common law, an author had a literary property in his works; and they sustained their opinion with very great ability. Mr. Justice Yeates, in an opinion of great length, and with an ability, if equalled, certainly not surpassed, maintained the opposite ground.

Previous to this case, injunctions had issued out of chancery to prevent the publication of certain works, at the instance of those who claimed a property in the copyright, but no decision had been given. And a case had been commenced, at law, between Tonson and Collins, on the same ground, and was argued with great ability, more than once, and the court of king's bench were about to take the opinion of all the judges, when they discovered that the suit had been brought by collusion, to try the question, and it was dismissed.

This question was brought before the house of lords, in the case of Donaldson v. Beckett and others, reported in 4 Burr. 2408.

Lord Mansfield, being a peer, through feelings of delicacy, declined giving any opinion. The eleven judges gave their opinions on the following points. 1st. Whether at common law an author of any book or literary composition, had the sole right of first printing, and publishing the same for sale; and might bring an action against any person who printed, published and sold the same, without his consent? On this question there were eight judges in the affirmative, and three in the negative.

2d. If the author had such right originally, did the law take it away, upon his printing and publishing such book or literary composition; and might any person, afterward, reprint and sell, for his own benefit, such book or literary composition, against the will of the author? This question was answered in the affirmative, by four judges, and in the negative by seven.

3d. If such action would have lain, at common law, is it taken away by the statute of 8 Anne; and is an author, by the said statute, precluded from every remedy, except on the foundation of the said statute, and on the terms of the conditions prescribed thereby? Six of the judges, to five, decided that the remedy must be under the statute.

4th. Whether the author of any literary composition, and his assigns, had the sole right of printing and publishing the same in perpetuity, by the common law? Which question was decided in favour of the author, by seven judges to four.

5th. Whether this right is any way impeached, restrained or taken away, by the statute 8 Anne? Six to five judges, decided that the right is taken away by the statute. And the lord chancellor, seconding lord Camden's motion to reverse, the decree was reversed.

It would appear from the points decided, that a majority of the judges were in favour of the common law right of authors, but that the same had been taken away by the statute.

The title and preamble of the statute, 8 Anne, ch. 19, is as follows: "An act for the encouragement of learning, by vesting the copies of printed books in the authors or purchasers of such copies, during the times therein mentioned.

"Whereas printers, booksellers and other persons, have of late frequently taken the liberty of printing, reprinting, and publishing, or causing to be printed, reprinted and published, books and other writings without the consent of the authors or proprietors of such books and writings, to their very great detriment, and too often to the ruin of them and their families," &c.

In 7 Term Rep. 627, lord Kenyon says, "all arguments in the support of the rights of learned men in their works, must ever be heard with great favour by men of liberal minds to whom they are addressed. It was probably on that account, that when the great question of literary property was discussed, some judges of enlightened understanding went the length of maintaining, that the right of publication rested exclusively in the authors and those who claimed under them for all time; but the other opinion finally prevailed, which established that the right was confined to the times limited by the act of parliament. And, that, I have no doubt, was the right decision."

And in the case of the University of Cambridge v. Pryer, 16 East, 319, lord Ellenborough remarked, "it has been said that the statute of 8 Anne has three objects: but I cannot subdivide the two first; I think it has only two. The counsel for the plaintiffs contended that there was no right at common law; and perhaps there might not be; but of that we have not particularly any thing to do."

From the above authorities, and others which might be referred to if time permitted, the law appears to be well settled in England, that, since the statute of 8 Anne, the literary property of an author in his works can only be asserted under the statute. And that, notwithstanding the opinion of a majority of the judges in the great case of Miller v. Taylor was in favour of the common law right before the statute, it is still considered, in England, as a question by no means free from doubt.

That an author, at common law, has a property in his manuscript, and may obtain redress against any one who deprives him of it, or by improperly obtaining a copy endeavours to realize a profit by its publication, cannot be doubted; but this is a very different right from that which asserts a perpetual and exclusive property in the future publication of the work, after the author shall have published it to the world.

The argument that a literary man is as much entitled to the product of his labour as any other member of society, cannot be controverted. And the answer is, that he realizes this product by the transfer of his manuscripts, or in the sale of his works, when first published.

A book is valuable on account of the matter it contains, the ideas it communicates, the instruction or entertainment it affords. Does the author hold a perpetual property in these? Is there an implied contract by every purchaser of his book, that he may realize whatever instruction or entertainment which the reading of it shall give, but shall not write out or print its contents.

In what respect does the right of an author differ from that of an individual who has invented a most useful and valuable machine? In the production of this, his mind has been as intensely engaged, as long, and, perhaps, as usefully to the public, as any distinguished author in the composition of his book.

The result of their labours may be equally beneficial to society, and in their respective spheres they may be alike distinguished for mental vigour. Does the common law give a perpetual right to the author, and withhold it from the inventor? And yet it has never been pretended that the latter could hold, by the common law, any property in his invention, after he shall have sold it publicly.

It would seem, therefore, that the existence of a principle may well be doubted, which operates so unequally. This is not a characteristic of the common law. It is said to be founded on principles of justice, and that all its rules must conform to sound reason.

Does not the man who imitates the machine profit as much by the labour of another, as he who imitates or republishes a book? Can there be a difference between the types and press with which one is formed, and the instruments used in the construction of the others?

That every man is entitled to the fruits of his own labour must be admitted; but he can enjoy them only, except by statutory provision, under the rules of property, which regulate society, and which define the rights of things in general.

But, if the common law right of authors were shown to

exist in England, does the same right exist, and to the same extent, in this country?

It is clear, there can be no common law of the United States. The federal government is composed of twenty-four sovereign and independent states; each of which may have its local usages, customs and common law. There is no principle which pervades the union and has the authority of law, that is not embodied in the constitution or laws of the union. The common law could be made a part of our federal system, only by legislative adoption.

When, therefore, a common law right is asserted, we must look to the state in which the controversy originated. And in the case under consideration, as the copyright was entered in the clerk's office of the district court of Pennsylvania, for the first volume of the book in controversy, and it was published in that state; we may inquire, whether the common law, as to copyrights, if any existed, was adopted in Pennsylvania.

It is insisted, that our ancestors, when they migrated to this country, brought with them the English common law, as a part of their heritage.

That this was the case, to a limited extent, is admitted. No one will contend, that the common law, as it existed in England, has ever been in force in all its provisions, in any state in this Union. It was adopted, so far only as its principles were suited to the condition of the colonies: and from this circumstance we see, what is common law in one state, is not so considered in another. The judicial decisions, the usages and customs of the respective states, must determine, how far the common law has been introduced and sanctioned in each.

In the argument, it was insisted, that no presumption could be drawn against the existence of the common law, as to copyrights, in Pennsylvania, from the fact of its never having been asserted, until the commencement of this suit.

It may be true, in general, that the failure to assert any particular right, may afford no evidence of the non existence of such right. But the present case may well form an exception to this rule.

If the common law, in all its provisions, has not been introduced into Pennsylvania, to what extent has it been adopted? Must not this court have some evidence on this subject. If no right, such as is set up by the complainants, has heretofore been asserted, no custom or usage established, no judicial decision been given, can the conclusion be justified, that, by the common law of Pennsylvania, an author has a perpetual property in the copyright of his works.

These considerations might well lead the court to doubt the existence of this law in Pennsylvania; but there are others of a more conclusive character.

The question respecting the literary property of authors, was not made a subject of judicial investigation in England until 1760; and no decision was given until the case of Miller v. Taylor was decided in 1769. Long before this time, the colony of Pennsylvania was settled. What part of the common law did Penn and his associates bring with them from England?

The literary property of authors, as now asserted, was then unknown in that country. Laws had been passed, regulating the publication of new works under license. And the king, as the head of the church and the state, claimed the exclusive right of publishing the acts of parliament, the book of common prayer, and a few other books.

No such right at the common law had been recognized in England, when the colony of Penn was organized. Long afterwards, literary property became a subject of controversy, but the question was involved in great doubt and perplexity; and a little more than a century ago, it was decided by the highest judicial court in England, that the right of authors could not be asserted at common law, but under the statute. The statute of 8 Anne was passed in 1710.

Can it be contended, that this common law right, so involved in doubt as to divide the most learned jurists of England, at a period in her history, as much distinguished by learning and talents as any other; was brought into the wilds of Pennsylvania by its first adventurers. Was it suited to their condition?

But there is another view still more conclusive.

In the eighth section of the first article of the constitution of the United States it is declared, that congress shall have power "to promote the progress of science and useful arts, by securing for limited times, to authors and inventors, the exclusive right to their respective writings and discoveries." And in pursuance of the power thus delegated, congress passed the act of the 30th of May, 1790.

This is entitled "an act for the encouragement of learning, by securing the copies of maps, charts and books, to the authors and proprietors of such copies, during the times therein mentioned."

In the first section of this act, it is provided, "that from and after its passage, the author and authors of any map, chart, book or books, already printed within these United States, being a citizen, &c. who hath or have not transferred to any other person the copyright of such map, chart, book or books, &c. shall have the sole right and liberty of printing, reprinting, publishing and vending such map, book or books, for fourteen years."

In behalf of the common law right, an argument has been drawn from the word *secure,* which is used in relation to this right, both in the constitution and in the acts of congress. This word, when used as a verb active, signifies to protect, insure, save, ascertain, &c.

The counsel for the complainants insist that the term, as used, clearly indicates an intention, not to originate a right, but to protect one already in existence.

There is no mode by which the meaning affixed to any word or sentence, by a deliberative body, can be so well ascertained, as by comparing it with the words and sentences with which it stands connected. By this rule the word *secure,* as used in the constitution, could not mean the protection of an acknowledged legal right. It refers to inventors, as well as authors, and it has never been pretended by any one, either in this country or in England, that an inventor has a perpetual right, at common law, to sell the thing invented.

And if the word *secure* is used in the constitution, in reference to a future right, was it not so used in the act of congress?

But, it is said, that part of the first section of the act of congress, which has been quoted, a copyright is not only recognized as existing, but that it may be assigned, as the rights of the assignee are protected, the same as those of the author.

As before stated, an author has, by the common law a property in his manuscript; and there can be no doubt that the rights of an assignee of such manuscript, would be protected by a court of chancery. This is presumed to be the copyright recognized in the act, and which was intended to be protected by its provisions. And this protection was given as well to books published under such circumstances, as to manuscript copies.

That congress, in passing the act of 1790, did not legislate in reference to existing rights, appears clear, from the provision that the author, &c. "shall have the sole right and liberty of printing," &c. Now if this exclusive right existed at common law, and congress were about to adopt legislative provisions for its protection, would they have used this language? Could they have deemed it necessary to vest a right already vested. Such a presumption is refuted by the words above quoted, and their force is not lessened by any other part of the act.

Congress, then, by this act, instead of sanctioning an existing right, as contended for, created it. This seems to be the clear import of the law, connected with the circumstances under which it was enacted.

From these considerations it would seem, that if the right of the complainants can be sustained, it must be sustained under the acts of congress. Such was, probably, the opinion of the counsel who framed the bill, as the right is asserted under the statues, and no particular reference is made to it as existing at common law. The claim, then, of the complainants, must be examined in reference to the statues under which it is asserted.

There are but two statutes which have a bearing on this subject; one of them has already been named, and the other was passed the 29th of April, 1802.

The first section of the act of 1790, provides, that an author, or his assignee, "shall have the sole right and liberty of printing, reprinting, publishing and vending such map, chart, book or books, for the term of fourteen years, from the recording of the title thereof in the clerk's office, as hereinafter directed: and that the author, &c. in books not published, &c. shall have the sole right and liberty of printing, reprinting, publishing, and vending such map, chart, book or books, for the like term of fourteen years, from the time of recording the title thereof in the clerk's office, as aforesaid. And at the expiration of the said term, the author, &c. shall have the same exclusive right continued to him, &c. for the further term of fourteen years: provided he or they shall cause the title thereof to be a second time recorded, and published in the same manner as is hereinafter directed, and that within six months before the expiration of the first term of fourteen years."

The third section provides, that "no person shall be entitled to the benefit of this act, &c. unless he shall first deposit, &c., a printed copy of the title in the clerk's office, &c." "And such author or proprietor shall within two months from the date thereof, cause a copy of said record to be published in one or more of the newspapers printed in the United States, for the space of four weeks."

And the fourth section enacts that "the author, &c. shall, within six months after the publishing thereof, deliver or cause to be delivered to the secretary of state, a copy of the same to be preserved in his office."

The first section of the act of 1802 provides, that "every person who shall claim to be the author, &c., before he shall be entitled to the benefit of the act entitled an act for the encouragement of learning, by securing the copies of maps, charts and books, to the authors and proprietors of such copies, during the time therein mentioned, he shall, in addition to the requisites enjoined in the third and fourth sections of said act, if a book or books, give information by causing the copy of the record which by said act he is required to publish, to be inserted in the page of the book next to the title."

These are substantially the provisions by which the complainants' right must be tested. They claim under a renewal of the term, but this necessarily involves the validity of the right under the first as well as the second term. In the language of the statute, the "same exclusive right" is continued the second term that existed the first.

It will be observed, that a right accrues under the act of 1790, from the time a copy of the title of the book is deposited in the clerk's office. But the act of 1802 adds another requisite to the accruing of the right, and that is, that the record made by the clerk, shall be published in the page next to the title page of the book.

And it is argued with great earnestness and ability, that these are the only requisites to the perfection of the complainants' title. That the requisition of the third section to give public notice in the newspapers, and that contained in the fourth to deposit a copy in the department of state; are acts subsequent to the accruing of the right, and whether they are performed or not, cannot materially affect the title.

The case is compared to a grant with conditions subsequent, which can never operate as a forfeiture of the title. It is said also, that the object of the publication in the newspapers, and the deposit of the copy in the department of state was merely to give notice to the public; and that such acts, not being essential to the title, after so great a lapse of time, may well be presumed. That if neither act had been done, the right of the party having accrued, before either was required to be done, it must remain unshaken.

This right, as has been shown, does not exist at common law—it originated, if at all, under the acts of congress. No one can deny that when the legislature are about to vest an exclusive right in an author or an inventor, they have the power to prescribe the conditions on which such right shall be enjoyed; and that no one can avail himself of such right who does not substantially comply with the requisitions of the law.

This principle is familiar, as it regards patent rights; and it is the same in relation to the copyright of a book. If any difference shall be made, as it respects a strict conformity to the law, it would seem to be more reasonable to make the requirement of the author, rather than the inventor.

The papers of the latter are examined in the department of state, and require the sanction of the attorney-general; but the author takes every step on his own responsibility, unchecked by the scrutiny or sanction of any public functionary.

The acts required to be done by an author, to secure his right, are in the order in which they must naturally transpire. First, the title of the book is to be deposited with the clerk, and the record he makes must be inserted in the first or second page; then the public notice in the newspapers is to be given; and within six months after the publication of the book, a copy must be deposited in the department of state.

A right undoubtedly accrues on the record being made with the clerk, and the printing of it as required; but what is the nature of that right. Is it perfect? If so, the other two requisites are wholly useless.

How can the author be compelled either to give notice in the newspaper, or deposit a copy in the state department. The statute affixes no penalty for a failure to perform either of these acts; and it provides no means, by which it may be enforced.

But we are told they are unimportant acts. If they are indeed wholly unimportant, congress acted unwisely in requiring them to be done. But whether they are important or not, is not for the court to determine, but the legislature; and in what light they were considered by the legislature, we can learn only by their official acts.

Judging then of these acts by this rule, we are not at liberty to say they are unimportant, and may be dispensed with. They are acts which the law requires to be done, and may this court dispense with their performance?

But the inquiry is made, shall the non performance of these subsequent conditions operate as a forfeiture of the right?

The answer is, that this is not a technical grant of precedent and subsequent conditions. All the conditions are important; the law requires them to be performed; and, consequently, their performance is essential to a perfect title. On the performance of a part of them, the right vests; and this was essential to its protection under the statute: but other acts are to be done, unless congress have legislated in vain, to render the right perfect.

The notice could not be published until after the entry with the clerk, nor could the book be deposited with the secretary of state until it was published. But these are acts not less important than those which are required to be done previously. They form a part of the title, and until they are performed, the title is not perfect.

The deposit of the book in the department of state, may be important to identify it at any future period, should the copyright be contested, or an unfounded claim of authorship asserted.

But, if doubts could be entertained whether the notice and deposit of the book in the state department, were essential to the title, under the act of 1790; on which act my opinion is principally founded; though I consider it in connexion with the other act; there is, in the opinion of three of the judges, no ground for doubt under the act of 1802. The latter act declares that every author, &c., before he shall be entitled to the benefit of the former act, shall, "in addition to the requisitions enjoined in the third and fourth sections of said act, if a book, publish," &c.

Is not this a clear exposition of the first act? Can an author claim the benefit of the act of 1790, without performing "the requisites enjoined in the third and fourth sections of it." If there be any meaning in language, the act of 1802, the three judges think, requires these requisites to be performed "in addition" to the one required by that act, before an author, &c. "shall be entitled to the benefit of the first act."

The rule by which conditions precedent and subsequent are construed, in a grant, can have no application to the case under consideration; as every requisite, in both acts, is essential to the title.

A renewal of the term of fourteen years can only be obtained by having the title page recorded with the clerk, and the record published on the page next to that of the title, and public notice given within six months before the expiration of the first term.

In opposition to the construction of the above statutes, as now given, the counsel for the complainants refered to several decisions in England, on the construction of the statute of 8 Anne, and other statutes.

In the case of Beckford v. Hood, 7 Term Rep. 620, the court of king's bench decided, "that an author, whose work is pirated before the expiration of twenty-eight years from the first publication of it, may maintain an action on the case for damages, against the offending party, although the work was not entered at Stationers' Hall." But this entry was necessary only to subject the offender to certain penalties, provided in the statute of 8 Anne. The suit brought was not for the penalties, and consequently, the entry of the work at Stationers' Hall, was not made a question in the case. In the case of Blackwell v. Harper, 2 Atk. 95, lord Hardwicke is reported to have said, upon the act of 8 Anne, c. 19, "the clause of registering with the Stationers' Company, is relative to the penalty, and the property cannot vest without such entry;" for the words are, "that nothing in this act shall be construed to subject any bookseller, &c. to the forfeitures, &c. by reason of printing any book, &c. unless the title to the copy of such book, hereafter published, shall, before such publication, be entered in the register book of the Company of Stationers."

The very language quoted by his lordship shows, that the entry was not necessary to an investiture of the title, but to the recovery of the penalties provided in the act against those who pirated the work.

His lordship decided in the same case, that "under an act of parliament, providing that a certain inventor shall have the sole right and liberty of printing and reprinting certain prints for the term of fourteen years, and to commence from the day of first publishing thereof, which shall be truly engraved with the name of the proprietor on each plate, and printed on every such print or prints," the property in the prints vests absolutely in the engraver, though the day of publication is not mentioned."

The authority of this case is seriously questioned in the case of Newton v. Cowie, 4 Bingham, 241. And it would seem, from the decision of lord Hardwicke, that he had doubts of the correctness of the decision, as he decreed an injunction, without by-gone profits. And lord Alvany, in the case of Harrison v. Hogg, cited in 4 Bing. 242, said "that he was glad he was relieved from deciding on the same act, as he was inclined to differ from lord Hardwicke."

By a reference to the English authorities in the construction of statutes, somewhat analogous to those under which the complainants set up their right, it will be found that the decisions often conflict with each other; but it is believed that no settled construction has been given to any British statute, in all respects similar to those under consideration, which is at variance with the one now given. If, however, such an instance could be found, it would not lessen the confidence we feel in the correctness of the view which we have taken.

The act of congress under which Mr. Wheaton, one of the complainants, in his capacity of reporter, was required to deliver eighty copies of each volume of his reports to the department of state, and which were, probably, faithfully delivered, does not exonerate him from the deposit of a copy under the act of 1790. The eighty volumes were delivered for a different purpose; and cannot excuse the deposit of the one volume as specially required.

The construction of the acts of congress being settled, in the further investigation of the case it would become necessary to look into the evidence and ascertain whether the complainants have not shown a substantial compliance with every legal requisite. But on reading the evidence we entertain doubts, which induce us to remand the cause to the circuit court, where the facts can be ascertained by a jury.

And the case is accordingly remanded to the circuit court, with directions to that court to order an issue of facts to be examined and tried by a jury, at the bar of said court, upon this point, viz. whether the said Wheaton as author, or any other person as proprietor, had complied with the requisites prescribed by the third and fourth sections of the said act of congress, passed the 31st day of May, 1790, in regard to the volumes of Wheaton's Reports in the said bill mentioned, or in regard to one or more of them in the following particulars, viz, whether the said Wheaton or proprietor did, within two months from the date of the recording thereof in the clerk's office of the district court, cause a copy of the said record to be published in one or more of the newspapers printed in the resident states, for the space of four weeks; and whether the said Wheaton or proprietor after the publishing thereof, did deliver or cause to be delivered to the secretary of state of the United States, a copy of the same to be preserved in his office, according to the provisions of the said third and fourth sections of the said act.

And if the said requisites have not been complied with in regard to all the said volumes, then the jury to find in particular in regard to what volumes they or either of them have been so complied with.

It may be proper to remark that the court are unanimously of opinion, that no reporter has or can have any copyright in the written opinions delivered by this court; and that the judges thereof cannot confer on any reporter any such right.

Mr. Justice THOMPSON, dissenting.

It is matter of regret with me, at any time to dissent from an opinion pronounced by a majority of this court, and where my mind is left balancing, after a full examination of the case, my habitual respect for the opinion of my brethren may justify a surrender of my own. But where no such apology is left to me to rest upon, it becomes a duty to adhere to my own opinion; and I shall proceed to assign the reasons which have led me to a conclusion different from that at which a majority of the court has arrived.

It is unnecessary for me to state any thing more with respect to the bill and answer, than barely to observe that the complainants in the court below rest their claim, both upon the statutory and the common law right. The bill charges, that all the provisions of the acts of congress have been complied with; that every thing has been done which was required by those acts in order to entitle them to the benefit thereof; and that if it were otherwise, the orator, Henry Wheaton, has, as the author of said reports, the property in the copy of the same, and the sole right to enjoy and dispose of the same.

It would be improper in the present stage of this cause to examine the evidence which was before the court below, touching certain questions of fact which it is alleged are required by the acts of congress in order to entitle the complainants to the benefit of those acts, have been complied with. An issue has been directed to inquire into those matters. Nor is it deemed necessary to examine whether the publication of the Condensed Reports by the defendants, is a violation of the complainants' copyright, if they have complied with all the requisites of the acts of congress. This would seem necessarily implied, by the ordering of the issue; for such inquiries would be useless, if the right secured under those acts has not been violated.

I shall therefore confine myself to an examination of the common law right, and the effect and operation of the acts of congress upon such right.

I think I may assume as a proposition not to be questioned, that in England, prior to the statute of Anne, the right of an author to the benefit and profit of his work, is recognized by the common law. No case has been cited on the argument, and none has fallen under my observation, at all throwing in doubt this general proposition. Whenever the question has been there agitated, it has been in connection with the operation of the statute upon this right. The case of Miller v. Taylor, 4 Burr. 2303, decided in the year 1769, was the first determination in the court of king's bench upon the common law right of literary property. In that case the broad question is stated and examined, whether the copy of a book or literary composition belongs to the author by the common law; and three of the judges, including lord Mansfield, decided in the affirmative. Mr. Justice Yeates dissented. But I am not aware that upon this abstract question a contrary decision has ever been made in England. This would seem to be sufficient to put at rest that general question, and render it unnecessary to go into a very particular examination of the reasons and grounds upon which the decision was founded. The elaborate examination bestowed upon the question by the judges in that case, has brought into view, on both sides of the question, the main arguments of which the point is susceptible. The great principle on which the author's right rests, is, that it is the fruit of production of his own labour, and which may, by the labour of the faculties of the mind, establish a right of property, as well as by the faculties of the body; and it is difficult to perceive any well founded objection to such a claim of right. It is founded upon the soundest principles of justice, equity and public policy. Blackstone, in his Commentaries, 2d vol. 405, has succinctly stated the principle, that when a man, by the exertion of his rational powers, has produced an original work, he seems to have clearly a right to dispose of that identical work as he pleases; and any attempt to vary the disposition he has made of it, appears to be an invasion of that right. That the identity of a literary composition consists entirely in the sentiment and the language. The same conception, clothed in the same words, must necessarily be the same composition; and whatever method be taken to exhibit that composition to the ear or to the eye of another, by recital, by writing, or by printing, in any number of copies, or at any period of time, it is always the identical work of the author which is so exhibited; and no other man, it has been thought, can have a right to exhibit it, especially for profit, without the author's consent. The origin of this right is not probably to be satisfactorily ascertained, and indeed if it could, it might be considered an objection to its existence as a common law right; but from the time of the invention of printing, in the early part of the fifteenth century, such a right seems to have been recognized. The historical account of the recognition of the right, is to be collected from the discussions in Miller v. Taylor. The Stationers' Company was incorporated in the year 1556, and from that time to the year 1640, the crown exercised an unlimited authority over the press, which was enforced by the summary process of search, confiscation and imprisonment, given to the Stationers' Company, and executed by the then supreme jurisdiction of the star chamber. In the year 1640 the star chamber was abolished; and the existence of copyrights before that period, upon principles of usage, can only be looked for in the Stationers' Company, or the star chamber or acts of state; and the evidence on this point says Mr. Justice Wills, is liable to little suspicion. It was indifferent to the views of government whether the property of an innocent book licensed, was open or private property.

It was certainly against the power of the crown to allow it as private property, without being protected by any royal privilege. It could be done only on principles of private justice, moral fitness and public convenience, which, when applied to a new subject, make common law, without a precedent; much more when received and approved by usage. And in this case of Miller v. Taylor, it was found by the special verdict, "that before the reign of her late majesty, queen Anne, it was usual to purchase from authors the *perpetual copyright* of their books, and to assign the same from hand to hand for valuable consideration, and to make the same the subject of family settlements, for the provision of wives and children." This usage is evidence of the common law, and shows that the copyright was considered and treated as property, transferable from party to party; and property, too, of a permanent nature, suitable for family settlement and provisions.

Common law, says lord Coke, 1 Inst. 1, 2, is sometimes called right, common right, common justice. And lord Mansfield says, the common law is drawn from the principles of right and wrong, the fitness of things, convenience and policy. And it is upon these principles that the copyright of authors is protected. After the year 1640, when the press became subject to license, the various ordinances and acts of parliament referred to in Miller v. Taylor, and collected in Maugham's treatise on the Law of Literary Property, p. 13—16, necessarily imply, and presuppose, the existence of a common law right in the author.

The common law, says an eminent jurist, 2 Kent's Comm. 471, includes those principles, usages and rules of action, applicable to the government and security of person and property which do not rest for their authority upon any express and positive declaration of the will of the legislature. A great proportion of the rules and maxims which constitute the immense code of the common law, grew into use by gradual adoption, and received, from time to time, the sanction of the courts of justice, without any legislative act or interference. It was the application of the dictates of natural justice, and of cultivated reason, to particular cases. In the just language of Sir Matthew Hale, the common law of England is not the product of the wisdom of some one man, or society of men, in any one age, but of the wisdom, counsel, experience and observation of many ages of wise and observing men. And, in accordance with these sound principles, and as applicable to the subject of copyright, are the remarks of Mr. Christian, in his notes to Blackstone's Commentaries, 2 Bl. Comm. 406, and note. Nothing, says he, is more erroneous, than the practice of referring the origin of moral rights, and the system of natural equity, to the savage state, which is supposed to have preceded civilized establishments, in which literary composition, and, of consequence, the right to it, could have no existence. But the true mode of ascertaining a moral right, is to inquire whether it is such as the reason, the cultivated reason of mankind must necessarily assent to. No proposition seems more conformable to that criterion, than that every one should enjoy the reward of his labour, the harvest where he has sown, or the fruit of the tree which he has planted. Whether literary property is sui generis, or under whatever denomination of rights it may be classed, it seems founded upon the same principle of general utility to society, which is the basis of all other moral rights and obligations. Thus considered, an author's copyright ought to be esteemed an invaluable right, established in sound reason and abstract morality.

It is unnecessary, for the purpose of showing my views upon this branch of the case, to add any thing more. In my judgment, every principle of justice, equity, morality, fitness and sound policy concurs, in protecting the literary labours of men, to the same extent that property acquired by manual labour is protected. The objections to the admission of the common law right of authors, are generally admitted to be summed up, in all their force and strength, by Mr. Justice Yeates, in the case of Miller v. Taylor. These objections may be classed under two heads: the one founded upon the nature of the property or subject matter of the right claimed; and the other on the presumed abandonment of the right by the author's publication.

The first appears to me to be too subtle and metaphysical to command the assent of any one, or to be adopted as the ground of deciding the question. It seems to be supposed, that the right claimed is to the ideas contained in the book. The claim, says Mr. Justice Yeates, is to the style and ideas of the author's composition; and it is a well established maxim, that nothing can be an object of property which has not a corporal substance. The property claimed is all ideal; a set of ideas which have no bounds or marks whatever—nothing that is capable of a visible possession—nothing that can sustain any one of the qualities or incidents of property. Their whole existence is in the mind alone. Incapable of any other modes of acquisition or enjoyment than by mental possession or apprehension; safe and invulnerable from their own immateriality, no trespass can reach them, no tort affect them; no fraud or violence diminish or damage them. Yet these are the phantoms which the author would grasp and confine to himself; and these are what the defendant is charged with having robbed the plaintiff of.

He asks, can sentiments themselves (apart from the paper on which they are contained) be taken in execution for a debt; or if the author commits treason or felony, or is outlawed, can the ideas be forfeited? Can sentiments be seized; or, by any act whatever be vested in the crown? If they cannot be seized, the sole right of publishing them cannot be confined to the author. How strange and singular, says he, must this extraordinary kind of property be, which cannot be visibly possessed, forfeited or seized, nor is susceptible of any external injury, nor, consequently, of any specific or possible remedy.

These, and many other similar declarations are made by Mr. Justice Yeates, to illustrate his view of the nature of a copyright. And he seems to treat the question, as if the claim was to a mere idea, not embodied or exhibited in any tangible form or shape. No such pretension has ever been set up, that I am aware of, by any advocate of the right to literary property. And this view of it would hardly deserve a serious notice, had it not been taken by a distinguished judge. Lord Mansfield, in the case of Miller v. Taylor, in defining the nature of the right or copyright says, "I use the word copy in the technical sense in which that name or term has been used for ages, to signify an incorporeal right to the sole printing and publishing of something intellectual, communicated by letters;" and this is the sense in which I understand the term copyright always to be used, when spoken of as property.

The other objection urged by Mr. Justice Yeates, that the publication by the author is an abandonment of the exclusive right, rests upon more plausible grounds, but is equally destitute of solidity.

This would seem, according to his view of the case, the main point in the cause. The general question, he says, is, whether, after a voluntary and *general publication* of an author's work by himself, or by his authority, the author has a sole and perpetual property in that work, so as to give him a right to confine every subsequent publication to himself, or his assigns, for ever.

And he lays down this general proposition. That the right of publication must for ever depend on the claimant's property in the thing to be published. Whilst the subject of publication continues his own exclusive property, he will so long have the sole and perpetual right to publish it. But whenever that property ceases, or by any act or event becomes common, the right of publication will be equally common. The particular terms in which Mr. Justice Yeates states his proposition, are worthy of notice. He puts the case upon its being a *general publication,* the meaning of which undoubtedly is, that the publication is without any restriction expressed or implied, as to the use to be made of it by the party into whose hands it might come, by purchase or otherwise. Unless such was his meaning, the proposition, I presume, no one will contend, can be maintained. Suppose an express contract made with a party who shall purchase a book, that he shall not republish it; this surely would be binding upon him.

So, if the bookseller should give a like notice of the author's claim, and a purchase of a book made without any express stipulation not to republish, the law would imply an assent to the condition. And any circumstances from which such an undertaking could be reasonably inferred, would lead to the same legal consequences. The nature of the property, and the general purposes for which it is published and sold, show the use which is to be made of it. The usual and common object which a person has in view in the purchase of a book is for the instruction, information or entertainment to be derived from it, and not for republication of the work. It is the use of it for these purposes which is implied in the sale and purchase. And this use is in subordination to the antecedent and higher right of the author; and comes strictly within the maxim, sic utere tuo ut alienam non laedas. But the case is not left to rest on any implied notice of the author's claim, and the conditions on which he makes it public. This is contained on the title page of the very book purchased, and cannot be presumed to escape the notice of the purchaser. It is there, in terms, announced, that the author claims the right of publication; and whoever purchases, therefore, does it with notice of such claim, and is bound to use it in subordination thereto. Mr. Justice Yeates admits, that every man is entitled to the fruits of his own labour; but that he can be entitled to it only, subject to the general rights of mankind, and the general rules of property; and that there must be a limitation to such right, otherwise the rights of others are infringed. The force of such limitation upon the right, is now readily perceived. If the right exists, it is a common law right, growing out of the natural justice of the case; being the result of a man's own labour. He thinks the statute of Anne fixes a just limitation. But suppose no statute had been passed on the subject; where would have been the limitation? The right existing, who would have authority to say where it should end? It must necessarily be without limitation, and it is no infringement of the rights of others. They enjoy it for the purpose intended, and according to the nature of the property. The purchaser of the book has a right to all the benefit resulting from the information or amusement he can derive from it. And if, in consequence thereof, he can write a book on the same subject, he has a right so to do. But this is a very different use of the property from the taking and publishing of the very language and sentiment of the author; which constitute the identity of his work.

Mr. Justice Yeates puts the effect of a publication upon the ground of intent in the author. The act of publication, says he, when voluntarily done by the author, is virtually and necessarily a gift to the public. And he must be deemed to have so intended it. But no such intention can surely be inferred, when the contrary intention is inscribed upon the first page of the book, which cannot escape notice.

The case of Percival v. Phipps, 2 Ves. and Beam. 19, recognizes the implied prohibition against publishing the work of another, arising from the very nature of the property. It was held in that case, that private letters, having the character of literary composition, were within the spirit of the act protecting literary property, and that by sending a letter, the writer did not give the receiver authority to publish it; and this is the doctrine of Lord Hardwicke in Pope v. Carl, 2 Atk. 342, where it is said that familiar letters may form a literary composition, in which the author retains his copyright, and does not, by sending them to the person to whom they are addressed, authorize him, or a third person, to use them for the purpose of profit, by publishing them against the interest and intention of the author. That by sending the letter, though he parts with the property of the paper, he does not part with the property of copyright in the composition.

But how stands the case, with respect to the effect of publication by the author, according to Mr. Justice Yeates' own rule. He says, "in all abandonments of such kind of property, two circumstances are necessary," an actual relinquishing of the possession, and an *intention* to relinquish it. That the author's name being inserted in the title page is no reason against the abandonment; for many of our best and noblest authors have published their works from more generous views than pecuniary profit. Some have written for fame, and the benefit of mankind. That the omission of the author's name can make no difference; for, if the property be absolutely his, he has no occasion to add his name to the title page. He cannot escape, it seems, from calling the copyright *property,* although a mere *idea;* and resorts again to his favourite theory, that it has no indicia, no distinguishing marks to denote his proprietary interest therein; and hard, says he, would be the law, that should adjudge a man guilty of a crime, when he had no possibility of knowing that he was doing the least wrong to any individual. That he could not know who was the proprietor of these intellectual ideas, they not having any earmarks upon them, or tokens of a particular proprietor.

If, as Mr. Justice Yeates admits, it is a question of *intention* whether the author meant to abandon his work to the public, and relinquish all private or individual claims to it, no possible doubt can exist as to the conclusion in the present case. Would a jury hesitate a moment upon the question under the evidence before the court? The right set up and stamped upon the title *page* of the book, shuts the door against any inference, that the publication was intended to be a gift to the public.

Mr. Justice Yeates admits, that so long as a literary composition is in manuscript, and remains under the sole dominion of the author, it is his exclusive property. It would seem, therefore, that the *idea* when once reduced to writing, is susceptible of identity, and becomes the subject of property. But property, without the right to use it, is empty sound, says Mr. Justice Aston in Miller v. Taylor. And, indeed, it would seem a mere mockery for the law to recognize any thing as property, which the owner could not use safely and securely for the purposes for which it was intended, unless interdicted, by the principles of morality or public policy.

It is not necessary that I should go into any particular examination of the construction of the statute of Anne, or to what extent it may affect the common law right of authors in England; because, as I shall hereafter show, that statute was never considered in force in Pennsylvania. The mere common law right, uninfluenced by that statute, is alone drawn in question under this branch of the case. And the decision in the case of Miller v. Taylor, would seem to put that question at rest in England, at that day. Mr. Justice Yeates, in aid of his opinion, relied much upon that statute: arguing that from the title, which is an "act for the encouragement of learning, by *vesting* the copies of printed books in the authors or purchasers of such copies, during the times therein mentioned;" and from the provision in the act, that the *sole right* should be vested, &c. for twenty-one years, and *no longer;* the right was *created,* and limited by the act, and did not rest upon the common law. The other three judges, however, maintained, that an author's right was not derived from the statute, but, that he had an original perpetual common law right and property in his work, and that the statute was only cumulative, and giving additional remedies for a violation of the right. That the preamble in the act proceeds upon the ground of a right of property in the author having been violated; and that the act was intended as a confirmation of such right. And that from the remedy enacted against the violation of the right being only temporary, it might be argued, that it afforded an implication, that there existed no right but what was secured by the act. To guard against which, there is an express saving in the ninth section of the act. "Provided that nothing in this act contained, shall extend or be construed to extend either to prejudice or confirm *any right,* that the said universities or any of them, *or any person or persons,* have or claim to have to the printing or reprinting, any book or copy already printed, or hereafter to be printed." That the words *any right,* manifestly meant any *other* right, than the term secured by the act. It may be observed here, that whatever may be the just weight to be given to the term *"vested"* and the words *"no longer,*" as used in the statute of Anne, and so much relied on by Mr. Justice Yeates, have no application to our acts of congress; no such term or provision being used. A writ of error was brought in this case of Miller v. Taylor, but afterwards abandoned, and the law was considered settled, until called in question in Donaldson v. Beckett, 4 Burr. 2408, which came before the house of lords in the year 1774, upon an appeal from a decree of the court of chancery, founded upon the judgment in Miller v. Taylor.

Upon this appeal certain questions were propounded to the twelve judges. Lord Mansfield, however gave no opinion, it being very unusual, as the reporter states, from reasons of delicacy, for a peer to support his own judgment upon appeal to the house of lords. This statement necessarily implies, however, that he had not changed his opinion. There were, therefore, eleven judges who voted upon the questions.

One of the questions propounded was: whether, at common law, an author of any book or literary composition, had the sole right of *first printing* and publishing the same for sale, and might bring an action against any person who printed, published and sold the same without his consent.

Upon this question ten voted in the affirmative, and one in the negative.

Another question was: if the author had such right originally, *did the law take it away upon his printing and publishing* such book or literary composition, and might any person, afterwards, reprint and sell, for his own benefit, such book or literary composition, against the will of the author.

Upon this question seven were in the negative, and four in the affirmative.

The vote upon these two questions settled the point, that, by the common law, the author of any literary composition, and his assigns, had the sole right of printing and publishing the same in perpetuity.

Another question propounded was: if an action would have lain, at common law, is it taken away by the statute of Anne? and is an author, by the said statute, precluded from every remedy, except on the foundation of the statute, and on the terms and conditions prescribed thereby?

Upon this question, six voted in the affirmative, and five in the negative; and it will be perceived, that if lord Mansfield had voted on this question, and in conformity with his opinion in Miller v. Taylor, the judges would have been equally divided.

That the law in England has not been considered as settled, in conformity with the vote on this last question, is very certain. For it is the constant practice, in chancery, to grant injunctions to restrain printers from publishing the works of others, which practice can only be sustained on the ground that the penalties given by the statute, are not the only remedy that can be resorted to. In Miller v. Taylor, lord Mansfield says, the whole jurisdiction exercised by the court of chancery, since 1710, the date of the statute of Anne, against pirates of copies, is an authority that authors had a property antecedent, to which the act gives a temporary additional *security.* It can stand upon no other foundation. And in the case of Beckford v. Hood, 7 Term Rep. 616, it was decided, that an author whose work is pirated before the expiration of the time limited in the statute, may maintain an action on the case for damages, against the offending party. Lord Kenyon says, the question is, whether the right of property being vested in authors for certain periods, the common law remedy for a violation of it, does not attach within the time limited by the act of parliament. Within those periods, the act says, that the author shall have the sole right and liberty of printing, &c. Thus the statute having vested that right in the author, the common law gives the remedy by action in the case for violation of it; and that the meaning of the act in creating the penalties, was to give an accumulative remedy. And in this all the judges concurred. And Mr. Justice Grose observes, that in the great case of Miller v. Taylor, Mr. Justice Yeates gave his opinion against the common law right of authors; but he was decidedly of opinion, that an exclusive right of property was vested by the statute for the time limited; and he says, that by the decision in the house of lords of Donaldson v. Beckett, the common law right of action is not considered as taken away by the statute of Anne, but that it could not be exercised beyond the time limited by that statute: and it is worthy of notice that this action on the case, for damages, was sustained, although the work was not entered at Stationers' Hall, nor the author's name affixed to the first publication. This, lord Kenyon observes, was to serve as a notice and warning to the public, that none might ignorantly incur the penalties and forfeitures given against such as pirate the works of others. But calling on a party who has injured the civil property of another, for a remedy in damages, cannot properly fall under the description for a forfeiture or penalty.

From this view of the law, as it stands in England, it is very clear that, previous to the statute of Anne, the perpetual common law right of authors, was undisputed. That after that statute, in the case of Miller v. Taylor, it was held, that this common law right remained unaffected by the statute, which only gave a cumulative remedy. That the subsequent case of Donaldson v. Beckett, limited the right to the times mentioned in the statute. But that for all violations of the right during that time, all the common law remedies continued, although no entry of the work at Stationers' Hall had been made, according to the provisions of the statute. Such entry being necessary, only for the purpose of subjecting the party violating the right, to the penalties given by the act.

I do not deem it necessary particularly to inquire, whether, as an abstract question, the same reasons do not exist for the protection of mechanical inventions, as the production of mental labour. The inquiry is not, whether it would have been wise to have recognized an exclusive right to mechanical inventions. It is enough, when we are inquiring what the law is, and not what it ought to have been, to find that no such principle ever has been recognized by any judicial decision. The argument was urged with great earnestness by Mr. Justice Yeates in Miller v. Taylor, but repudiated by lord Mansfield and the other judges. With respect to copyrights, however, the law has been considered otherwise; and the original common law right fully established, though modified in some respects by the statute of Anne.

I shall proceed, now, to some notice of the light in which copyrights have been viewed in this country.

It appears from the journals of the old congress (8 Journals 257), that this question was brought before that body by sundry papers and memorials on the subject of literary *property;* and which were referred to a committee, of which Mr. Madison was one; and on the 27th of May, 1783, the following resolution was reported and adopted.

"Resolved, that it be recommended to the several states, to *secure* to the authors or publishers of any new books not hitherto printed, being citizens of the United States, and to their executors, administrators and assigns, the copyright of such books for a certain time, not less than fourteen years from the first publication; and to *secure* to the said authors, if they shall survive the term first mentioned, and to their executors, administrators and assigns, the copyright of such books for another term or time, not less than fourteen years; such copy or exclusive right of printing, publishing and vending the same, to be *secured* to the original authors or publishers, their executors, administrators and assigns, by such laws and such restrictions, as to the several states may seem proper."

This right is here treated and dealt with as property already existing; and not as creating any thing which had previously no being. It is spoken of as something tangible, that might pass to executors and administrators, and transferable by assignment. And the recommendation to the state was, to pass laws to *secure* such a right.

It must be presumed, that congress understood the light in which this subject was viewed in the mother country. And it is deserving of notice, that Mr. Madison, one of the committee, afterwards wrote the number in the Federalist, where this subject is discussed; and where it is expressly asserted, that this has been adjudged in England to be a right at common law.

And it is worthy of remark also, that no mention is here made of any right in mechanical inventions: and although the arts and sciences are connected in the same clause in the constitution, and placed under the legislative power of congress, it does not, by any means follow, that they were considered as standing on the same footing.

Several of the states had already passed laws on this subject; and many others, in compliance with the recommendation of congress, did the same.

The state of Massachusetts, as early as March, 1783, passed a law, entitled, "an act for the purpose of *securing* to authors, the exclusive right and benefit of publishing their literary productions for twenty-one years." The preamble to this act shows, in a strong and striking manner, the views entertained at that day in this enlightened state, of the value of this right. "Whereas, the improvement of knowledge, the progress of civilization, the public weal of the community, and the advancement of human happiness greatly depend on the efforts of learned and ingenious persons, in the various arts and sciences; as the principal encouragement such persons can have, to make great and beneficial exertions of this nature, must exist in the legal security of the fruits of their study and industry, to themselves; and as such security is one of the natural rights of all men, there being no *property* more peculiarly a man's own, than that which is produced by the labour of his mind: therefore, to encourage learned and ingenious persons to write useful books, for the benefit of mankind, be it enacted," &c. The act then proceeds to declare, that all books, treatises, and other literary works, &c., shall be the sole property of the author or authors, being subjects of the United States of America, their heirs and assigns, for the full and complete term of twenty-one years from the date of their first publication. And certain penalties are affixed to a violation of the right, with a proviso, that the act shall not be construed to extend in favour, or for the benefit of any author, or subject of any other of the United States, until the state of which such author is a subject, shall have passed similar laws for securing to authors the exclusive right and benefit of publishing their literary productions. 1 Laws Mass. 94.

This act recognizes in the fullest and most unqualified manner, the natural right which an author has to the productions and labour of his own mind. And it is worthy of notice, that the act does not recognize as a natural right, or in any manner provide for the protection of mechanical inventions; thereby showing the distinction between mental and manual labour in the view of that legislature, although it is now attempted to put them on the same footing.

The state of Connecticut had, previously, in the same year (January, 1783), passed an act for the encouragement of literature and genius, containing the following preamble: "whereas it is perfectly agreeable to the principles of natural justice and equity, that every author should be *secured* in receiving the profits that may arise from the sale of his works; and such security may encourage men of learning and genius to publish their writings, which may do honour to their country, and service to mankind." Certain provisions are then made for the security of such right, which it is unnecessary here to be particularly noticed.

There is a like proviso as in the Massachusetts act; that the benefit of the law is not to extend to authors, inhabitants of, or residing in other states, until such states have passed similar laws. Statutes of Conn. 474. This law is also confined to literary productions, and in no manner extending to mechanical labours.

In the colony of New York, in the year 1786, a law "to promote literature" was passed, reciting, "whereas, it is agreeable to the principles of natural equity and justice, that every author should be *secured* in receiving the profits that may arise from the sale of his works; and such security may encourage persons of learning and genius to publish their writings, which may do honour to their country, and service to mankind;" and then making provision, for securing to authors the sole right of printing, publishing and selling their works for fourteen years. With a proviso to the fourth section of the act, recognizing a common law right; but leaving it open and unaffected in cases not coming within the act: viz., "provided, that nothing in this act shall extend to, affect, prejudice or confirm the rights which any person may have to the printing or publishing of any books or pamphlets at *common law,* in cases not mentioned in this act."

The state of Virginia also, in the year 1785, passed a similar law, for *securing* to authors of literary works, an exclusive property therein, for a limited time. 1 Rev. Code, 534. Like laws for the same purpose were passed by other states, which are not necessary here to be noticed; enough having been referred to, to show the light in which literary property was viewed in this country; and that such laws were passed, with a view to protect and secure a pre-existing right, founded on the eternal rules and principles of natural right and justice, and recognized by the common law.

But under the existing governments of the United States, before the adoption of the present constitution, adequate protection could not be given to authors throughout the United States, by any general law. It depended on the legislatures of the several states; and this led to the provisions in the present constitution, giving to congress power "to promote the progress of science and the useful arts, by *securing,* for limited times, to authors and inventors, the exclusive right to their respective writings and discoveries." Constit. art 1, sect. 8.

It has been argued at the bar, that, as the promotion of the progress of science and the useful arts, is here united in the same clause in the constitution, the rights of authors and inventors were considered as standing on the same footing; but this, I think, is a non sequitur. This article is to be construed distributively, and must have been so understood; for when congress came to execute this power by legislation, the subjects are kept distinct, and very different provisions are made respecting them. All the laws relative to inventions, purport to be acts to promote the progress of the useful arts. They do not use any language which implies or presupposes any existing prior right *to be secured;* but clearly imply that the whole exclusive right is created by the law, and ends with the expiration of the patent. The first law, passed in the year 1790, 1 Story's Ed. 80, requires that the specification shall be so particular, as not only to distinguish the invention or discovery from other things before known and used, but also to enable a workman, or other person, skilled in the art or manufacture, to make, construct, or use the same, *to the end that the public may have the full benefit thereof, after the expiration of the patent term.* This is the consideration demanded by the public, for the protection during the time mentioned in the patent; and the books furnish no case, that I am aware of, where an action has been attempted to be sustained upon any supposed common law right of the inventor.

But the case is quite different with respect to copyrights. All the laws on this subject purport to be made for *securing* to authors and proprietors such copyright. They presuppose the existence of a right, which is to be secured, and not a right originally created by the act. The security provided by the act is for a limited time. But there is no intimation that at the expiration of that time the copy becomes common, as in the case of an invention. The right, at the expiration of the time limited in the acts of congress, is left to the common law protection, without the additional security thrown around it by the statutes; and stands upon the same footing as it did before the statutes were passed. The protection for a limited time by the aid of penalties, against the violators of the right, proceeds upon the ground that the author, within that time, can so multiply his work, and reap such profits therefrom, as to enable him to rest upon his common law right, without the extraordinary aid of penal laws.

In the Federalist, No. 43, written by Mr. Madison, who reported the resolution referred to, in the old congress, this clause in the constitution is under consideration, and the writer observes: that the utility of this power will scarcely be questioned. *The copyright of authors has been solemnly adjudged in Great Britain, to be a right at common law.* The right to useful inventions seems, with equal reason, to belong to the inventors. The public good fully coincides, in both cases, with the claims of individuals. The states cannot separately make effectual provision for either of the cases; and most of them have anticipated the decision of this point, by laws passed at the instance of congress.

Although it is here said, that the right to useful inventions seems with equal reason to belong to the inventors, as the copyright to authors: yet it is not pretended that the common law equally recognizes them. But the contrary is necessarily implied, when it is expressly said that the copyright, has been adjudged to be a common law right, but is silent as to inventors' rights.

The common law right of authors is expressly recognized by Mr. Justice Story in his Commentaries. In noticing this article in the constitution, he says, "this power did not exist under the confederation, and its utility does not seem to have been questioned. The copyright of authors in their works had, before the revolution, been decided in Great Britain to be a common law right, and it was regulated and limited under statutes passed by parliament upon that subject." 3 Story's Com. 48. If these statutes do not affect the right in the case now before the court, it remains and is to be viewed as a common law right.

The judge in the court below, who decided this case, seems to place much reliance on what he considers a doubt, suggested by chancellor Kent, as to the existence of the common law right. Let us see what he does say. "It was," says he, "for some time the prevailing and better opinion in England, that authors had an exclusive copyright at common law, as permanent as the property of an estate; and that the statute of Anne, protecting by penalties that right for fourteen years, was only an additional sanction, and made in affirmance of the common law. This point came at last to be questioned, and it became the subject of a very serious litigation in the court of king's bench. It was decided in Miller v. Taylor, 1769, that every author had a common law right in perpetuity, independent of statute, to the exclusive printing and publishing his original compositions. The court was not unanimous, and the subsequent decision of the house of lords, in Donaldson v. Beckett, in February 1774, settled this very litigated question against the opinion of the king's bench, by establishing, that the common law right of action, *if any existed,* could not be exercised beyond the time limited by the statute of Anne," 2 Com. 375, second ed. It is here fully admitted, that by the decision in Miller v. Taylor, every author had a common law right in perpetuity, to the publishing of his original composition. And, if it was intended to intimate, that the subsequent decision, in Donaldson v. Beckett, overruled this decision, as to the common law right; I apprehend, this must be a mistake, according to the report of the case in 4 Burr. I understand the decision then was, by ten of the judges, that at common law an author had the sole right of *first printing* and publishing his work, and by seven judges to four, that such right continued after his *first publication.* It is true, it was decided by six to five of the judges, that the common law right of action could not be exercised beyond the time limited by the statute of Anne. But with the construction of this statute, we have no concern, if it was not in force in Pennsylvania. The settlement of the common law right is the material point, and that is admitted, by chancellor Kent, to have been decided in favour of the author. There is certainly considerable obscurity in the report of this case, as to how far it has modified the common law remedy: this arises probably from the manner in which the questions were propounded by the house of lords to the judges.

I do not perceive how it becomes necessary in this case to decide the question, whether we have here any code of laws, known and regarded as the common law of the United States. This case presents a question respecting the right of property, and in such cases the state laws form the rules of decision in the courts of the United States; and the case now before the court must be governed by the law of copyright in the state of Pennsylvania. The complainants, though citizens of New York, are entitled to the benefit of those laws for the protection of their property; and have a right to prosecute their suit in the courts of the United States.

If, by the common law of England, an author has the copyright in his literary compositions, it becomes necessary to inquire whether that law is in force in the state of Pennsylvania.

It was very properly admitted by the court below, on the trial of this cause, that when the American colonies were first settled by our ancestors, it was held as well by the settlers, as by the judges and lawyers of England, that they brought with them, as a birthright and inheritance, so much of the common law as was applicable to their local situation and change of circumstances; and that each colony judged for itself, what parts of the common law were applicable to its new condition. Mr. Justice Story recognizes the same principle in his Commentaries, vol. 1, 137 to 140. Englishmen, says he, removing to another country, must be deemed to carry with them those rights and privileges which belong to them in their native country; and that the plantations formed in this country were to be deemed a part of the ancient dominions, and the subjects inhabiting them to belong to a common country, and to retain their former rights and privileges. That the universal principle has been (and the practice has conformed to it), that the common law is our birthright and inheritance, and that our ancestors brought hither with them, upon their immigration, all of it which was applicable to their situation. The whole structure of our present jurisprudence stands upon the original foundation of the common law. The old congress, in the year 1774, unanimously resolved, that the respective colonies are entitled to the common law of England. 1 Story's Com. 140, and note.

The colony of Pennsylvania was settled about the year 1682; at which period, and down to the time of the case of Miller v. Taylor, 1769, the whole course of the British government, as well in parliament, as in the star chamber, and court of chancery, proceeded, in relation to the regulation of copyrights, upon the ground of an existing common law right in authors: and which was so universally acknowledged, that it was not contested in a court of justice until that case; and then solemnly, and upon the most mature deliberation, decided to be a common law right, notwithstanding the statute of Anne passed in the year 1710. And the subsequent decision of Donaldson v. Beckett, turned entirely upon the construction of that act, which it was supposed limited the remedy to the time prescribed in the act for the protection of the copyright. So that at the time of the settlement of Pennsylvania, and for nearly a century thereafter, the common law right with all the common law remedies attached to it, was the received and acknowledged doctrine in England. And if the common law was brought into Pennsylvania, by the first settlers, the law of copyright formed a part of it, and was in force there, and has so continued ever since, not having been abolished or modified by any legislature in that state. But the existence of the common law in Pennsylvania, is not left to inference upon the general principles applicable to emigrants, before alluded to; there is positive legislation on the subject.

We find, as early as the year 1718, a law in that colony with a recital, "whereas king Charles II., by his royal charter to William Penn, for erecting this country into a province, did declare it to be his will and pleasure, that the laws for regulating and governing of property, within the said province, as well for the descent and enjoyment of lands, as for the enjoyment and succession of goods and chattels, and likewise as to felonies, should be and continue the same as they should be, for the time being, by the general course of the law in the kingdom of England, until the said laws shall be altered by the said William Penn, his heirs and assigns, and by the free men of the said province, their delegates or deputies, or the greater part of them: and whereas it is a settled point, that as the common law is the birthright of all English subjects, so it ought to be their rule in the British dominions. But acts of parliament have been adjudged not to extend to these plantations, unless they are particularly named as such: now, therefore," &c.: and certain statutes relating to crimes are adopted; and this question came under the consideration of the supreme court of that state, in the case of Morris's Lessee v. Van Dorin, 1 Dall. 64, in the year 1782, and chief justice M'Kean, in pronouncing the judgment of the court, says: this state has had her government for above a hundred years, and it is the opinion of the court, that the common law of England has always been in force in Pennsylvania. That all statutes made in Great Britain before the settlement of Pennsylvania, have no force here, unless they are convenient, and adapted to the circumstances of the country; and that all statutes made *since the settlement of Pennsylvania,* have no force here, unless the colonies are particularly named; and he adds, that the spirit of the act of 1718 supports this opinion.

With respect to English statutes which have been considered in force in Pennsylvania, we have the most satisfactory evidence in the report of the judges of the supreme court of that state, made under an act of the legislature passed April 7th, 1807, 3 Binn. 395, by which the judges were required to examine, and report, which of the English statutes are in force in that commonwealth; and upon this subject the report states: "with respect to English statutes, enacted since the settlement of Pennsylvania, it has been assumed, as a principle, that they do not extend here, unless they have been recognized by our acts of assembly, or adopted by long continued practice in courts of justice. Of the latter description there are very few; and those, it is supposed, were introduced from a sense of their evident utility. As English statutes, they had no obligatory force; but, from long practice, they may be considered as incorporated with the law of our country."

From this review of the law, I think I have shown, that, by the common law of England, down, at least, to the decision in the case of Donaldson v. Beckett, an author was considered as having an exclusive right, in perpetuity, to his literary compositions. That this right, as a branch of the common law, was brought into Pennsylvania with the first settlers, as early as the year 1682. That whatever effect and operation the statute of Anne may have been deemed to have had upon the common law in England, that statute never having been in force in Pennsylvania, the common law right remains unaffected by it. And with this view of the law, and the rights of an author, I proceed to consider the acts of congress which have been passed on this subject.

Observing, in the first place, that we are bound to presume that congress understood the nature and character of this claim of authors to the enjoyment of the fruits of their literary labours, and the ground upon which it rested. This is useful and necessary, to conduct us to a right understanding of their legislation. A knowledge of the mischief is necessary, to a just and correct view of the remedy intended to be applied.

But the knowledge of congress on this subject is not left open to presumption. The question, as to its being an exclusive and perpetual right, was brought directly to the view of congress.

Three acts have been passed on this subject; and being not only in pari materia, but connected with each other by their very titles and objects, are to be construed together, and explained by each other.

The last act on the subject was passed in the year 1831, and is entitled "an act to amend the several acts respecting copyrights, approved February 3d, 1831." And the report of the judiciary committee, to whom the subject was referred, shows in what point of light the subject was presented to congress.

Your committee, says the report, believe that the just claims of authors, require from our legislation a *protection,* not less than what is proposed in the bill reported. From the first principles of proprietorship *in property, an author has an exclusive and perpetual right,* in preference to any other, to the fruits of his labour. Though the nature of literary property is peculiar, it is not the less real and valuable. If labour and effort in producing what before was not possessed or known will give title, then the literary man has title, perfect and absolute, and should have his reward.

The object of the law, and to which the attention of congress was specially drawn, was the *protection* of property; claimed and admitted to be exclusive and perpetual in the author.

It may be useful, preliminarily, to notice a few of the settled rules by which statutes are to be construed.

In construing statutes, three points are to be regarded; the old law, the mischief, and the remedy; and the construction should be such, if possible, to suppress the mischief, and advance the remedy. 1 Bl. Com. 87; Bac. Ab. Stat. 1, pl. 31, 32.

An affirmative statute does not abrogate the common law.

If a thing is at common law, a statute cannot restrain it, unless it be in negative words. Plowd. 113; 2 Kent's Com. 462; 2 Mason 451; 1 Inst. 111, 115; 10 Mod. 118. Bac. Abr. Stat. 9.

Where a statute gives a remedy, where there was one by the common law, and does not imply a negative of the common law remedy, there will be two concurrent remedies. In such case, the statute remedy is accumulative. 2 Bac. 803, 805; 2 Inst. 200; Com. Dig. Action upon Statute, 6.

Considering the common law right of the author established, and with these rules of construing statutes kept in view, I proceed to the consideration of the acts of congress.

The first law was passed in the year 1790 (1 vol. Story's ed. of Laws of United States, 94), and is entitled, "an act for the encouragement of learning, by *securing* the copies of maps, charts and books, to the authors and proprietors of such copies, during the times therein mentioned."

The first section declares, that the author of any book or books already printed, being a citizen of the United States, and who hath not transferred the copyright to any other person, and any other person, being a citizen of the United States, &c. who hath purchased, or legally acquired the copyright of such book, in order to print, reprint, publish or vend the same, shall have the *sole right* and liberty of printing, reprinting publishing and vending the same, for fourteen years *from the recording of the title thereof* in the clerk's office, as hereinafter directed. The like provision is made, with respect to books or manuscripts not printed, or thereafter composed. The title, and this section of the act, obviously consider and treat this copyright as property; something that is capable of being transferred; and the right of the assignee is protected equally with that of the author; and the object of the act, and all its provisions purport to be for *securing* the right. Protection is the avowed and real purpose for which it is passed. There is nothing here admitting the construction, that a new right is created. The provision in no way or manner deals with it as such. It in no manner limits or withdraws from the right, any protection it before had. It is a forced and unreasonable interpretation, and in violation of all the well settled rules of construction, to consider it as restricting, limiting or abolishing any pre-existing right. Statutes are not presumed to make any alteration in the common law, further or otherwise, than the act expressly declares. And, therefore, when the act is general, the law presumes it did not intend to make any alteration; for if such was the intention, the legislature would have so expressed it. 11 Mod. 148; 19 Vin. 512, Stat. E. 6, pl. 12. And hence the rule is laid down in Plowden, if a thing is at common law, a statute cannot restrain it, unless it be in negative words. It is in every sense an affirmative statute, and does not abrogate the common law.

The cumulative security or protection given by the statute, attaches *from the recording of the title of the book in the clerk's office of the district court where the author or proprietor shall reside.* If the statute should be considered as creating a new right, that right vests upon recording the title. This is the only prerequisite, or condition precedent, to the vesting the right. Whatever it is that is given by the statute, and the other requirements in the third and fourth sections, of publishing in the newspaper within two months from the date of the record, and delivering a copy of the book to the secretary of state within six months from the publication; cannot be construed as prerequisites or conditions precedent to the vesting. These provisions cannot be considered in any other light than as directory. In no other view can these sections of the law be made consistent with the provisions of the first section. The benefit of the act, so far as respects the exclusive right, takes effect from the time of recording the title in the clerk's office: but the publication in the newspaper may be made at any time within two months, and the copy delivered to the secretary of state within six months. What would be the situation of the author if his copyright should be violated before the expiration of the time allowed him for these purposes? Would he have no remedy? The second section declares in terms, that if any person, from and after the *recording the title,* shall, without the consent of the author or proprietor, print or reprint, &c., he thereby incurs the penalties given by the act. Both the right and the remedy therefore given by the act, attach on the recording of the title. And this construction is not at all affected by any thing contained in the third section of the act; which declares, that no person shall be entitled to the benefit of this act, unless he shall have deposited a printed copy of the title in the clerk's office. This is in perfect harmony with the first and second sections; and, although the requirement to publish a copy of the record in the newspaper is in the same section, it is in a separate and distinct clause, and no more required to be considered a prerequisite, than if it was in a distinct section: and so it was considered by Mr. Justice Washington in Ewer v. Coxe, 4 Wash. C. C. Rep. 490; and he also in that case considered the requirement in the fourth section to deliver a copy to the secretary of state as directory, and not as a condition: and indeed the result of his opinion was, that if the author's copyright depended upon the act of 1790, it would be complete by a deposite of a copy of the title in the clerk's office. But that the act of 1802 not only added another requisite, viz. causing a copy of the record to be inserted at full length in the title page, but made the publication in the newspaper, and the delivery of a copy of the book to the secretary of state, prerequisites, although not made so by the act of 1790. Mr. Justice Washington is fully supported in his construction of the act of 1790 by the case of Nichols v. Ruggles, 3 Day, 145, decided in the supreme court of errors of the state of Connecticut, where it is held, that the provisions of the statute, which require the author to publish the title of his book in a newspaper, and to deliver a copy of the work to the secretary of state, are merely directory, and constitute no part of the essential requisites for securing the copyright. This case was decided in the year 1808, and I do not find any reference to the act of 1802. This can only be accounted for upon the supposition, that, in the opinion of the counsel and court, this act did not at all affect the construction of the act of 1790; for had it been supposed that the act of 1802 made the publication in a newspaper, and a delivery of a copy of the work to the secretary of state, prerequisites to the vesting of the copyright, it would necessarily have led to a different result on the motion for a new trial. Judge Hopkinson, who tried the cause now before the court, thinks the act of 1790 will not admit of the construction given to it by judge Washington; but that under that act the publication in a newspaper and delivery of a copy of the work to the secretary of state, are prerequisites to the establishment of the right; and such I understand to be the opinion of a majority of this court, by which the construction of the act of 1790 by judge Washington is overruled. I have already attempted to show that this construction of the act of 1790 cannot be sustained; nor do I think that the act of 1802 will aid that construction of the act of 1790, and in this I understand my brother M'Lean concurs: so that upon this question, as to the effect of the act of 1802 upon the act of 1790, the court is equally divided, and the decision of the cause rests upon the act of 1790. A brief notice, however, of the act of 1802, 2 Story's Ed. Laws U.S. 866, may not be amiss.

It purports so far as it relates to the present question, to be a supplement to the act of 1790, and declares that the author or proprietor of a book, before he shall be entitled to the benefit of that act, shall, in addition to the requisites enjoined in the third and fourth section of said act, give information, by causing a copy of the record, required to be published in a newspaper, to be inserted at full length in the title page or in the page immediately following the title page of the book. It is to be observed, that this purports to be a supplementary act, the office of which is only to add something to the original act, but not to alter or change the provisions which it already contains. It leaves the original act precisely as it was, and only superadds to its provisions the matter of the supplement; and both, when taken together, will receive the same construction as if originally incorporated in the same act. This is the natural and rational view of the matter. Suppose this new requisite had been in the original act, how would it stand? If it was in a separate and distinct section, it would run thus: that the author, before he shall be entitled to the benefit of this act, shall insert at full length, in the title page of the book, a copy of the record of the title. This could not change the construction of the act as to the publication in the newspaper, or delivery of a copy of the book to the secretary of state. Nor could it have any such effect, if it followed immediately after the prerequisite of depositing a printed copy of the title of the book in the clerk's office; and this would have been the natural place for the provision, if it had been inserted in the original act.

Judge Washington, in Ewer v. Coxe, says that the supplemental act declares that the person seeking to obtain this right shall perform this new requisition, in addition to those prescribed in the third and fourth sections of the act of 1790, *and that he must perform the whole before he shall be entitled to the benefit of the act.* I find no such declaration in the act. The second section, which relates to prints, does contain this declaration, but it has no application to books.

If the act of 1802 is intended as a legislative construction of the act of 1790, and is clearly erroneous, it cannot be binding upon the court.

The act of 1831, being in pari materia, may be taken into consideration in construing the previous acts which it purports to amend; and we find in this act only two prerequisites imposed upon an author, to entitle him to the benefit of the act, viz. to deposit a printed copy of the title of the book in the clerk's office of the district court of the district wherein the author or proprietor shall reside, and to give information of the copyright being secured, by inserting on the title page, or the page immediately following, the entry therein directed, viz. "entered according to the act of congress," &c. And these being prerequisites under the former laws, it is fairly to be concluded that they were the only prerequisites, and that the other requirements are merely directory; and if so, the complainants in the court below, have shown all that the acts of congress require to vest the copyright. The title has been recorded in the clerk's office, and a copy of the record inserted in the title page of the book.

But if the complainants in the court below have not made out a complete right under the acts of congress, there is no ground upon which the common law remedy can be taken from them. If there be a common law right, there certainly must be a common law remedy. The statute contains nothing in terms, having any reference to the common law right; and if such right is considered abrogated, limited or modified by the acts of congress, it must be by implication; and to so construe these acts, is in violation of the established rules of construction, that where a statute gives a remedy in the affirmative without a negative expressed or implied, for a matter which was actionable at common law, the party may sue at common law, as well as upon the statute. 1 Chitty's Pl. 144. This is a well settled principle, and fully recognized and adopted in the case of Almy v. Harris, 5 Johns. Rep. 175.

Whatever effect the statute of Anne may have had in England, as to limiting or abridging the common law right there; no such effect, upon any sound rules of interpretation, can grow out of our acts of congress. There is a wide difference in the phraseology of the laws. The statute of Anne contains negative words. It declares that the author shall have the sole right and liberty of printing, &c. for the time contained in the statute, and *no longer;* and these are the words upon which the advocates for the limitation of the common law right mainly rest: and it was, for a long time, considered by the ablest judges in England, that even these strong words did not limit or abridge the common law right; and the question, at this day, is not considered free from doubt.

This act, and the construction which it had received in England, were well known and understood when the act of congress was passed, and no such limitation is inserted or intended, or any matter at all repugnant to the continuance of the common law right, in its full extent. These laws proceed on the ground that the common law remedy was insufficient to protect the right, and provide additional security, by means of penalties, for the violation of it. Congress having before them the statute of Anne, and apprized of the doubt entertained in England as to its effect upon the common law right, if it had been intended to limit or abridge that right, some plain and explicit provision to that effect would doubtless have been made; and not having been made, is, to my mind, satisfactory evidence that no such effect was intended.

If the present action was to recover the penalties given by the statute, it might be incumbent on the appellants to show that all the requirements in the acts of congress had been complied with. This would be resorting to the new statutory remedy, and the party must bring himself within the statute, in order to entitle him to that remedy. But admitting that the right depends upon the statute, and is limited to the time therein prescribed, the remedy by injunction continues during that time. This is admitted by Mr. Justice Yeates, in Miller v. Taylor. The author, says he, has certainly a property in the copy of his book, during the term the statute has allowed; and whilst that term exists, it is like a lease, a grant, or any other common law right; and will equally entitle him to all common law remedies for the enjoyment of that right. He may, I should think, file an injunction bill to stop the printing. But I may say with more positiveness, he might bring an action to recover satisfaction for the injury done, contrary to law, under the statute. And the same doctrine is laid down by the whole court, in Beckford v. Wood, 7 Term Rep. 616. Lord Kenyon says: the statute vests the right in authors for certain periods; and within those periods, the act says, the author shall have the sole right and liberty of printing, &c.; and the statute having vested the right in the author, the common law gives the remedy by action on the case for a violation of it; and that the act, by creating the penalties, meant to give an accumulative remedy.

The language in the statute of Anne, which is considered as vesting the right, is the same as in the act of congress. In the former, it is considered as necessarily implied in the declaration that the author shall have the *sole right* during such time, &c. And in the act of congress, there is the same declaration, that the author shall have the *sole right* of printing, &c. from the time of recording the title in the clerk's office. The right being thus vested at the time, draws after it the common law remedy. And there is no more reason for contending, that the remedy given by the statute, supersedes the common law remedy under the act of congress, than under the statute of Anne. The statute remedy is through the means of penalties in both cases.

The term for which the copyright is secured in the case now before the court has not expired; and according to the admitted and settled doctrine in England, under the statute of Anne, the common law remedy exists during that period.

Upon the whole, in whatever light this case is viewed, whether as a common law right, or depending on the act of congress, I think the appellants are entitled to the remedy sought by the bill; and that the decree of the court below ought to be reversed, the injunction made perpetual, and an account taken according to the prayer in the bill, without directing an issue to try any matter of fact, touching the right.

Mr. Justice Baldwin also dissented from the opinion of the court.

SEE ALSO:

Pope v. *Curl,* 26 Eng. Rep. 608 (Ch. 1741)
Miller v. *Taylor,* 4 Burr. 2303, 2310–2407 (K.B. 1769)
Donaldsons v. *Becket,* 4 Burr. 2408–17 (H.L. 1774)
Universities Copyright Act, 15 Geo. 3, c. 53 (1775)
Thomas Paine, An Act for Incorporating the American Philosophical Society, 1780, Life 4:43–46
Noah Webster to James Madison, 5 July 1784, Madison Papers 8:96
George Washington, First Annual Address, 8 Jan. 1790, Richardson 1:66
An Act to Promote the Progress of the Useful Arts, 10 Apr. 1790, 1 Stat. 109
An Act for the Encouragement of Learning, by Securing the Copies of Maps, Charts, and Books, to the Authors and Proprietors of Such Copies, 31 May 1790, 1 Stat. 124
Nichols v. *Ruggles,* 3 Day 145 (Conn. 1808)
Livingston v. *Van Ingen,* 9 Johns. R. 507 (N.Y. 1812)
Evans v. *Robinson,* 8 Fed. Cas. 886, no. 4,571 (C.C.D.Md. 1813)
Evans v. *Jordan,* 9 Cranch 199 (1815)
Evans v. *Eaton,* 3 Wheat. 454 (1818)
Evans v. *Eaton,* 7 Wheat. 356 (1822)
Ewer v. *Coxe,* 8 Fed. Cas. 917, no. 4,584 (C.C.E.D.Pa. 1824)
Thomas Jackson Oakley, Thomas Addis Emmet, & William Wirt, Arguments before the Supreme Court in *Gibbons* v. *Ogden,* 9 Wheat. 1 (1824)
Pennock v. *Dialogue,* 2 Pet. 1 (1829)
Noah Webster, Origins of the Copy-Right Laws in the United States, 1831, Political Papers 173–77
Grant v. *Raymond,* 6 Pet. 218 (1832)

Article 1, Section 8, Clause 9

To constitute Tribunals inferior to the supreme Court;

1

William Blackstone, Commentaries 1:257
1765

III. Another capacity, in which the king is considered in domestic affairs, is as the fountain of justice and general conservator of the peace of the kingdom. By the fountain of justice the law does not mean the *author* or *original,* but only the *distributor.* Justice is not derived from the king, as from his *free gift;* but he is the steward of the public, to dispense it to whom it is *due.* He is not the spring, but the reservoir; from whence right and equity are conducted, by a thousand chanels, to every individual. The original power of judicature, by the fundamental principles of society, is lodged in the society at large: but as it would be impracticable to render complete justice to every individual, by the people in their collective capacity, therefore every nation has committed that power to certain select magistrates, who with more ease and expedition can hear and determine complaints; and in England this authority has immemorially been exercised by the king or his substitutes. He therefore has alone the right of erecting courts of judicature: for, though the constitution of the kingdom hath entrusted him with the whole executive power of the laws, it is impossible, as well as improper, that he should personally carry into execution this great and extensive trust: it is consequently necessary, that courts should be erected, to assist him in executing this power; and equally necessary, that, if erected, they should be erected by his authority. And hence it is, that all jurisdictions of courts are either mediately or immediately derived from the crown, their proceedings run generally in the king's name, they pass under his seal, and are executed by his officers.

2

RECORDS OF THE FEDERAL CONVENTION

[*1:124; Madison, 5 June*]

Mr. Rutlidge havg. obtained a rule for reconsideration of the clause for establishing *inferior* tribunals under the national authority, now moved that that part of the clause in propos. 9. should be expunged: arguing that the State Tribunals might and ought to be left in all cases to decide in the first instance the right of appeal to the supreme national tribunal being sufficient to secure the national rights & uniformity of Judgmts: that it was making an unnecessary encroachment on the jurisdiction of the States, and creating unnecessary obstacles to their adoption of the new system.—Mr. Sherman 2ded. the motion.

Mr. Madison observed that unless inferior tribunals were dispersed throughout the Republic with *final* jurisdiction in *many* cases, appeals would be multiplied to a most oppressive degree; that besides, an appeal would not in many cases be a remedy. What was to be done after improper Verdicts in State tribunals obtained under the biassed directions of a dependent Judge, or the local prejudices of an undirected jury? To remand the cause for a new trial would answer no purpose. To order a new trial at the supreme bar would oblige the parties to bring up their witnesses, tho' ever so distant from the seat of the Court. An effective Judiciary establishment commensurate to the legislative authority, was essential. A Government without a proper Executive & Judiciary would be the mere trunk of a body without arms or legs to act or move.

Mr. Wilson opposed the motion on like grounds. he said the admiralty jurisdiction ought to be given wholly to the national Government, as it related to cases not within the jurisdiction of particular states, & to a scene in which controversies with foreigners would be most likely to happen.

Mr. Sherman was in favor of the motion. He dwelt chiefly on the supposed expensiveness of having a new set of Courts, when the existing State Courts would answer the same purpose.

Mr. Dickinson contended strongly that if there was to be a National Legislature, there ought to be a national Judiciary, and that the former ought to have authority to institute the latter.

On the question for Mr. Rutlidge's motion to strike out "inferior tribunals"

Massts. divided, Cont. ay. N. Y. divd. N. J. ay. Pa. no. Del. no. Md. no. Va. no. N. C. ay. S. C. ay. Geo ay [Ayes—5; noes—4; divided—2.]

Mr. Wilson & Mr. Madison then moved, in pursuance of the idea expressed above by Mr. Dickinson, to add to Resol: 9. the words following "that the National Legislature be empowered to institute inferior tribunals". They observed that there was a distinction between establishing such tribunals absolutely, and giving a discretion to the Legislature to establish or not establish them. They repeated the necessity of some such provision.

Mr. Butler. The people will not bear such innovations. The States will revolt at such encroachments. Supposing such an establishment to be useful, we must not venture on it. We must follow the example of Solon who gave the Athenians not the best Govt. he could devise; but the best they wd. receive.

Mr. King remarked as to the comparative expence that the establishment of inferior tribunals wd. cost infinitely less than the appeals that would be prevented by them.

On this question as moved by Mr. W. and Mr. M.

Mass. Ay. Ct. no. N. Y. divid. N. J. ay. Pa. ay. Del. ay. Md. ay. Va. ay. N. C. ay. S. C. no. Geo. ay. [Ayes—8; noes—2; divided—1.]

[*1:128; Pierce, 5 June*]

Mr. Rutledge was of opinion that it would be right to make the adjudications of the State Judges, appealable to the national Judicial.

Mr. Madison was for appointing the Judges by the Senate.

Mr. Hamilton suggested the idea of the Executive's appointing or nominating the Judges to the Senate which should have the right of rejecting or approving.

[*2:45; Madison, 18 July*]

12. Resol: "that Natl. Legislature be empowered to appoint inferior tribunals"

Mr. Butler could see no necessity for such tribunals. The State Tribunals might do the business.

Mr. L. Martin concurred. They will create jealousies & oppositions in the State tribunals, with the jurisdiction of which they will interfere.

Mr. Ghorum. There are in the States already federal Courts with jurisdiction for trial of piracies &c. committed on the Seas. no complaints have been made by the States or the Courts of the States. Inferior tribunals are essential to render the authority of the Natl. Legislature effectual

Mr. Randolph observed that the Courts of the States can not be trusted with the administration of the National laws. The objects of jurisdiction are such as will often place the General & local policy at variance.

Mr. Govr. Morris urged also the necessity of such a provision

Mr. Sherman was willing to give the power to the Legislature but wished them to make use of the State Tribunals whenever it could be done. with safety to the general interest.

Col. Mason thought many circumstances might arise not now to be foreseen, which might render such a power absolutely necessary.

On question for agreeing to 12. Resol: empowering the National Legislature to appoint "inferior tribunals". Agd. to nem. con.

3

LUTHER MARTIN, GENUINE INFORMATION
1788
Storing 2.4.58

Among other powers given to this government in the eighth section, it has that of appointing tribunals *inferior* to the *supreme court;* to this power there was an opposition. It was urged, that there, was no occasion for *inferior* courts of the *general government* to be appointed in the different States, and that such ought not to be admitted—That the different *State judiciaries* in the respective States would be *competent to,* and *sufficient for,* the cognizance in the *first instance* of all cases that should arise under the laws of the general government, which being by this system made the supreme law of the States, would be binding on the different State judiciaries—That by giving an *appeal* to the *supreme court* of the United States, the *general government* would have a *sufficient* check over their decisions, and security for the enforcing of their laws—That to have *inferior* courts appointed under the authority of Congress in the different States, would eventually *absorb* and *swallow up* the *State judiciaries,* by drawing all business from them to the courts of the general government, which the *extensive* and *undefined* powers, legislative and judicial, of which it is possessed, would *easily enable* it to do—That it would *unduly* and *dangerously* increase the *weight* and *influence* of Congress in the *several States,* be productive of a *prodigious number of officers,* and be attended with an *enormous* additional and unnecessary *expence*—That the judiciaries of the respective States not having power to decide upon the laws of the general government, but the determination on those laws being *confined* to the judiciaries appointed under the authority of Congress in the *first instance,* as well as on *appeal,* there would be a necessity for *judges* or magistrates of the general government, and those to a considerable number, in *each county* of *every State*—That there would be a necessity for courts to be holden by them in each county, and that these courts would stand in need of all the proper officers, such as *sheriffs, clerks* and others commissioned, under the authority of the general government: in fine, that the administration of justice, as it will relate to the laws of the general government would require in each State all the magistrates, courts, officers and expence, which is now found necessary in the respective States for the administration of justice as it relates to the laws of the State governments. But here again we were overruled by a majority, who *assuming* it as a *principle* that the general government and the State governments (as long as they should exist) would be at *perpetual variance* and enmity, and that their *interests* would constantly be *opposed* to each other, insisted for that reason that the *State judges* being citizens of their respective States, and holding their commissions under them, ought not, though *acting on oath,* to be *entrusted* in the administration of the laws of the general government.

4

ST. GEORGE TUCKER, BLACKSTONE'S COMMENTARIES
1:APP. 267–68
1803

9. Congress is moreover authorised to constitute tribunals inferior to the supreme court. [C.U.S. Art. 1. § 8.] The third article of the constitution further declares, that the judicial power of the United States shall be vested in one supreme court, and in such inferior courts, as congress may from time to time, ordain, and establish. . . .The establishment of courts, is in England, a branch of the royal prerogative, which has in that country been, from time to time, very much abused; as in the establishment of the famous courts of high-commission, and of the star-chamber; two of the most infamous engines of oppression and tyranny, that ever were erected in any country. "The judges of which (as the statute for suppressing the former declares) undertook to punish, where no law did warrant, and the proceedings, and censures of which were an intollerable burthen upon the subject, and the means to introduce an arbitrary power and government." In England there are also courts of special-commission of *oyer and terminer,* (I do not here speak of the ordinary commissions of *oyer and terminer* and general gaol delivery, under which, courts are held by the judges of the courts of Westminster-hall, at the assizes, in every county,) occasionally constituted for the special purpose of trying persons accused of treason, or rebellion, the judges of which, are frequently some of the great officers of state, associated with some of the judges of Westminster-hall, and others, whose commission determines as soon as the trial is over. Most of the state trials, have been had before courts thus constituted: and the number of convictions and condemnations in those courts is a sufficient proof how very exceptionable such tribunals are: or rather how dangerous to the lives and liberties of the people, a power to select particular persons, as judges for the trial of state offences, must be, in any country, and under any possible form of government. In these cases, the offence is not only in theory, against the crown and government, but often, in fact, against the person, authority, and life of the ruling monarch. His great officers of state share with him in danger, and too probably in apprehension, and resentment. These are the judges, he selects, and from their hands expects security for himself and them. Whilst the frailties of human nature remain, can such a tribunal be deemed impartial? Wisely, then, did the constitution of the United States deny to the executive magistrate a power so truly formidable: wisely was the supreme federal legislature made the depositary of the power of establishing courts, inferior to the supreme court; and most wisely was it provided, that the judges of those courts, when once appointed by the president with the advice of the senate, should depend only on their good behaviour for their continuance in of-

fice, and be placed at once beyond the reach of hope or fear, where they might hold the balance of justice steadily in their hands.

These considerations induce a conviction in my mind, that this clause of the constitution does not authorise the establishment of occasional, or temporary courts, but courts of a permanent constitution and duration. Courts that could neither be affected in their conduct nor in their existence by the ferments or changes, or parties; and which might remain a monument to all posterity of the wisdom of that policy, which separates the judiciary from the executive and legislative departments, and places it beyond the influence or control of either.

5

AMERICAN INSURANCE CO. v. CANTER
1 Pet. 511 (1828)

[MARSHALL, C.J.] The plaintiffs filed their libel in this cause in the District Court of South Carolina, to obtain restitution of 356 bales of cotton, part of the cargo of the ship Point a Petre; which had been insured by them on a voyage from New-Orleans to Havre de Grace, in France. The Point a Petre was wrecked on the coast of Florida, the cargo saved by the inhabitants, and carried into Key West, where it was sold for the purpose of satisfying the salvors; by virtue of a decree of a Court, consisting of a notary and five jurors, which was erected by an Act of the territorial legislature of Florida. The owners abandoned to the underwriters, who having accepted the same, proceeded against the property; alleging that the sale was not made by order of a Court competent to change the property.

David Canter claimed the cotton as a *bona fide* purchaser, under the decree of a competent Court, which awarded seventy-six per cent. to the salvors, on the value of the property saved.

The District Judge pronounced the decree of the territorial Court a nullity, and awarded restitution to the libellants of such part of the cargo as he supposed to be identified by the evidence; deducting therefrom a salvage of fifty per cent.

The libellants and claimant both appealed. The Circuit Court reversed the decree of the District Court, and decreed the whole cotton to the claimant, with costs; on the ground that the proceedings of the Court at Key West were legal and transferred the property to the purchaser.

From this decree the libellants have appealed to this Court.

The cause depends, mainly, on the question whether the property in the cargo saved, was changed by the sale at Key West. The conformity of that sale to the order under which it was made, has not been controverted. Its validity has been denied, on the ground that it was ordered by an incompetent tribunal.

The tribunal constituted by an Act of the territorial legislature of Florida, passed on the 4th July 1823, which is inserted in the record. That Act purports to give the power which has been exercised; consequently the sale is valid, if the territorial legislature was competent to enact the law.

The course which the argument has taken, will require, that, in deciding this question, the Court should take into view the relation in which Florida stands to the United States.

The Constitution confers absolutely on the government of the Union, the powers of making war, and of making treaties; consequently, that government possesses the power of acquiring territory, either by conquest or by treaty.

The usage of the world is, if a nation be not entirely subdued, to consider the holding of conquered territory as a mere military occupation, until its fate shall be determined at the treaty of peace. If it be ceded by the treaty, the acquisition is confirmed, and the ceded territory becomes a part of the nation to which it is annexed; either on the terms stipulated in the treaty of cession, or on such as its new master shall impose. On such transfer of territory, it has never been held, that the relations of the inhabitants with each other undergo any change. Their relations with their former sovereign are dissolved, and new relations are created between them and the government which has acquired their territory. The same Act which transfers their country, transfers the allegiance of those who remain in it; and the law, which may be denominated political, is necessarily changed, although that which regulates the intercourse, and general conduct of individuals, remains in force, until altered by the newly created power of the state.

On the 2d of February 1819, Spain ceded Florida to the United States. The 6th article of the treaty of cession, contains the following provision—"The inhabitants of the territories, which his Catholic majesty cedes to the United States by this treaty, shall be incorporated in the Union of the United States, as soon as may be consistent with the principles of the federal Constitution; and admitted to the enjoyment of the privileges, rights, and immunities of the citizens of the United States."

This treaty is the law of the land, and admits the inhabitants of Florida to the enjoyment of the privileges, rights, and immunities, of the citizens of the United States. It is unnecessary to inquire, whether this is not their condition, independent of stipulation. They do not, however, participate in political power; they do not share in the government, till Florida shall become a state. In the mean time, Florida continues to be a territory of the United States; governed by virtue of that clause in the Constitution, which empowers Congress "to make all needful rules and regulations, respecting the territory, or other property belonging to the United States."

Perhaps the power of governing a territory belonging to the United States, which has not, by becoming a state acquired the means of self-government, may result necessarily from the facts, that it is not within the jurisdiction of any particular state, and is within the power and jurisdiction of the United States. The right to govern, may be the inevitable consequence of the right to acquire territory. Whichever may be the source whence the power is derived, the possession of it is unquestioned. In execution of it, Congress, in 1822, passed "an Act for the establishment of a territorial government in Florida;" and, on the 3d of March 1823, passed another Act to amend the Act of 1822. Under this Act, the territorial legislature enacted the law now under consideration.

The 5th section of the Act of 1823, creates a territorial legislature, which shall have legislative powers over all rightful objects of legislation; but no law shall be valid, which is inconsistent with the laws and Constitution of the United States.

The 7th section enacts "That the judicial power shall be vested in two Superior Courts, and in such inferior Courts, and justices of the peace, as the legislative council of the territory may from time to time establish." After prescribing the place of cession, and the jurisdictional limits of each Court, the Act proceeds to say; "within its limits herein described, each Court shall have jurisdiction in all criminal cases, and exclusive jurisdiction in all capital offences; and original jurisdiction in all civil cases of the value of one hundred dollars, arising under and cognizable by the laws of the territory, now in force therein, or which may, at any time, be enacted by the legislative council thereof."

The 8th section enacts "That each of the said Superior Courts shall moreover have and exercise the same jurisdiction within its limits, in all cases arising under the laws and Constitution of the United States, which, by an Act to establish the judicial Courts of the United States, approved the 24th of September 1789, and an Act in addition to the Act, entitled an Act to establish the judicial Courts of the United States, approved the 2d of March 1793, was vested in the Court of Kentucky district."

The powers of the territorial legislature extend to all rightful objects of legislation, subject to the restriction, that their laws shall not be "inconsistent with the laws and Constitution of the United States." As salvage is admitted to come within this description, the Act is valid, unless it can be brought within the restriction.

The counsel for the libellants contend, that it is inconsistent with both the law and the Constitution; that it is inconsistent with the provisions of the law, by which the territorial government was created, and with the amendatory Act of March 1823. It vests, they say, in an inferior tribunal, a jurisdiction, which is, by those Acts, vested exclusively in the Superior Courts of the territory.

This argument requires an attentive consideration of the sections which define the jurisdiction of the Superior Courts. The 7th section of the Act of 1823, vests the whole judicial power of the territory "in two Superior Courts, and in such inferior Courts, and justices of the peace, as the legislative council of the territory may from time to time establish." This general grant is common to the superior and inferior Courts, and their jurisdiction is concurrent, except so far as it may be made exclusive in either, by other provisions of the statute. The jurisdiction of the Superior Courts, is declared to be exclusive over capital offences; on every other question over which those Courts may take cognizance by virtue of this section, concurrent jurisdiction may be given to the inferior Courts. Among these subjects, are "all civil cases arising under and cognizable by the laws of the territory, now in force therein, or which may at any time be enacted by the legislative council thereof."

It has been already stated, that all the laws which were in force in Florida while a province of Spain, those excepted which were political in their character, which concerned the relations between the people and their sovereign, remained in force, until altered by the government of the United States. Congress recognises this principle, by using the words "laws of the territory now in force therein." No laws could then have been in force, but those enacted by the Spanish government. If among these, a law existed on the subject of salvage, and it is scarcely possible there should not have been such a law, jurisdiction over cases arising under it, was conferred on the Superior Courts, but that jurisdiction was not exclusive. A territorial Act, conferring jurisdiction over the same cases on an inferior Court, would not have been inconsistent with this section.

The 8th section extends the jurisdiction of the Superior Courts, in terms which admit of more doubt. The words are "That each of the said Superior Courts, shall moreover have and exercise the same jurisdiction, within its limits, in all cases arising under the laws and Constitution of the United States, which, by an Act to establish the judicial Courts of the United States, was vested in the Court of the Kentucky district."

The 11th section of the Act declares "That the laws of the United States, relating to the revenue and its collection, and all other public Acts of the United States, not inconsistent or repugnant to this Act, shall extend to, and have full force and effect, in the territory aforesaid."

The laws which are extended to the territory by this section, were either for the punishment of crime, or for civil purposes. Jurisdiction is given in all criminal cases, by the 7th section, but in civil cases, that section gives jurisdiction only in those which arise under and are cognizable by the laws of the territory: consequently all civil cases arising under the laws which are extended to the territory by the 11th section, are cognizable in the territorial Courts, by virtue of the 8th section; and, in those cases, the Superior Courts may exercise the same jurisdiction as is exercised by the Court for the Kentucky district.

The question suggested by this view of the subject, on which the case under consideration must depend, is this:—

Is the admiralty jurisdiction of the District Courts of the United States vested in the Superior Courts of Florida under the words of the 8th section, declaring that each of the said Courts "shall moreover have and exercise the same jurisdiction within its limits, in all cases arising under the laws and Constitution of the United States," which was vested in the Courts of the Kentucky district?

It is observable, that this clause does not confer on the territorial Courts all the jurisdiction which is vested in the Court of the Kentucky district, but that part of it only which applies to "cases arising under the laws and Constitution of the United States." Is a case of admiralty of this description?

The Constitution and laws of the United States, give jurisdiction to the District Courts over all cases in admiralty; but jurisdiction over the case, does not constitute the case itself. We are therefore to inquire, whether cases in admiralty, and cases arising under the laws and Constitution of the United States, are identical.

If we have recourse to that pure fountain from which all the jurisdiction of the Federal Courts is derived, we find language employed which cannot well be misunderstood. The Constitution declares, that "the judicial power shall extend to all cases in law and equity, arising under this Constitution, the laws of the United States, and treaties made, or which shall be made, under their authority; to all cases affecting ambassadors, or other public ministers, and consuls; to all cases of admiralty and maritime jurisdiction."

The Constitution certainly contemplates these as three distinct classes of cases; and if they are distinct, the grant of jurisdiction over one of them does not confer jurisdiction over either of the other two. The discrimination made between them, in the Constitution, is, we think, conclusive against their identity. If it were not so, if this were a point open to inquiry, it would be difficult to maintain the proposition that they are the same. A case in admiralty does not, in fact, arise under the Constitution or laws of the United States. These cases are as old as navigation itself; and the law, admiralty and maritime as it has existed for ages, is applied by our Courts to the cases as they arise. It is not then to the 8th section of the territorial law that we are to look for the grant of admiralty and maritime jurisdiction, to the territorial Courts. Consequently, if that jurisdiction is exclusive, it is not made so by the reference to the District Court of Kentucky.

It has been contended, that by the Constitution the judicial power of the United States extends to all cases of admiralty and maritime jurisdiction; and that the whole of this judicial power must be vested "in one Supreme Court, and in such inferior Courts as Congress shall from time to time ordain and establish." Hence it has been argued, that Congress cannot vest admiralty jurisdiction in Courts created by the territorial legislature.

We have only to pursue this subject one step further, to perceive that this provision of the Constitution does not apply to it. The next sentence declares, that "the Judges both of the Supreme and inferior Courts, shall hold their offices during good behaviour." The Judges of the Superior Courts of Florida hold their offices for four years. These Courts, then, are not constitutional Courts, in which the judicial power conferred by the Constitution on the general government, can be deposited. They are incapable of receiving it. They are legislative Courts, created in virtue of the general right of sovereignty which exists in the government, or in virtue of that clause which enables Congress to make all needful rules and regulations, respecting the territory belonging to the United States. The jurisdiction with which they are invested, is not a part of that judicial power which is defined in the 3d article of the Constitution, but is conferred by Congress, in the execution of those general powers which that body possesses over the territories of the United States. Although admiralty jurisdiction can be exercised in the states in those Courts, only, which are established in pursuance of the third article of the Constitution; the same limitation does not extend to the territories. In legislating for them, Congress exercises the combined powers of the general, and of a state government.

We think, then, that the Act of the territorial legislature, erecting the Court by whose decree the cargo of the Point a Petre was sold, is not "inconsistent with the laws and Constitution of the United States," and is valid. Consequently, the sale made in pursuance of it changed the property, and the decree of the Circuit Court, awarding restitution of the property to the claimant, ought to be affirmed with costs.

SEE ALSO:

Records of the Federal Convention, Farrand 1:95, 118, 231, 292; 2:38–39, 133, 144, 168, 313, 570, 595

Archibald Maclaine, North Carolina Ratifying Convention, 26 July 1788, Elliot 4:94

William Wirt, Tenure of Office of a Judge in Michigan, 21 Sept. 1824, 1 Ops. Atty. Gen. 696

Article 1, Section 8, Clause 10

To define and punish Piracies and Felonies committed on the high Seas, and Offences against the Law of Nations;

1

Edmund Randolph, James Duane, John Witherspoon, Report to Congress Nov. 1781

Journals 21:1136–37

On a report of a committee, consisting of Mr. [Edmund] Randolph, Mr. [James] Duane, Mr. [John] Witherspoon, appointed to prepare a recommendation to the states to enact laws for punishing infractions of the laws of nations:

> The committee, to whom was referred the motion for a recommendation to the several legislatures to enact punishments against violators of the law of nations, report:
>
> That the scheme of criminal justice in the several states does not sufficiently comprehend offenses against the law of nations:
>
> That a prince, to whom it may be hereafter necessary to disavow any transgression of that law by a citizen of the United States, will receive such disavowal with reluctance and suspicion, if regular and adequate punishment shall not have been provided against the transgressor:
>
> That as instances may occur, in which, for the avoidance of war, it may be expedient to repair out of the public treasury injuries committed by individuals, and the property of the innocent be exposed to reprisal, the author of those injuries should compensate the damage out of his private fortune.

Resolved, That it be recommended to the legislatures of the several states to provide expeditious, exemplary and adequate punishment:

First. For the violation of safe conducts or passports, expressly granted under the authority of Congress to the subjects of a foreign power in time of war:

Secondly. For the commission of acts of hostility against such as are in amity, league or truce with the United States, or who are within the same, under a general implied safe conduct:

Thirdly. For the infractions of the immunities of ambassadors and other public ministers, authorised and received as such by the United States in Congress assembled, by animadverting on violence offered to their persons, houses, carriages and property, under the limitations allowed by the usages of nations; and on disturbance given to the free exercise of their religion: by annulling all writs and processes, at any time sued forth against an ambassador, or other public minister, or against their goods and chattels, or against their domestic servants, whereby his person may be arrested: and,

Fourthly. For infractions of treaties and conventions to which the United States are a party.

The preceding being only those offences against the law of nations which are most obvious, and public faith and safety requiring that punishment should be co-extensive with such crimes:

Resolved, That it be farther recommended to the several states to erect a tribunal in each State, or to vest one already existing with power to decide on offences against the law of nations, not contained in the foregoing enumeration, under convenient restrictions.

Resolved, That it be farther recommended to authorise

suits to be instituted for damages by the party injured, and for compensation to the United States for damage sustained by them from an injury done to a foreign power by a citizen.

2

RESPUBLICA v. DE LONGCHAMPS

1 Dall. 111 (Pa. 1784)

MCKEAN, Chief Justice.—This is a case of the first impression in the United States. It must be determined on the principles of the laws of nations, which form a part of the municipal law of Pennsylvania; and, if the offences charged in the indictment have been committed, there can be no doubt, that those laws have been violated. The words used in the minister's house (which is to be considered as a foreign domicil, where the minister resides in full representation of his sovereign, and where the laws of the state do not extend), may be compared to the same words applied to the judges, in a court of justice, where they sit in representation of the majesty of the people of Pennsylvania. In that case, the offender would be immediately committed to jail, without the preliminary process of an indictment by a grand jury; and, in the case before us, if the offender is convicted, he may certainly be punished by fine and imprisonment.

In actions of slander, words were formerly construed in the mildest sense they would admit; but reason has superseded such forced interpretations, and words are now to be taken according to their ordinary import and meaning. Those expressed by the defendant, are evidently of a tendency so opprobrious and violent, that they cannot fail to aggravate the outrage which has been committed.

As to the assault, this is, perhaps, one of that kind, in which the insult is more to be considered, than the actual damage; for, though no great bodily pain is suffered by a blow on the palm of the hand, or the skirt of the coat, yet these are clearly within the legal definition of assault and battery, and among gentlemen, too often, induce duelling, and terminate in murder. As, therefore, anything attached to the person, partakes of its inviolability, de Longchamps' striking Monsieur Marbois' cane, is a sufficient justification of that gentleman's subsequent conduct.

BRYAN, Justice.—The distinction between a consul and a member of the legation, is not warranted in this case; for Monsieur Marbois never ceased to be the latter. As secretary to the legation, his authority descends from a high source, his commission being made out in the same form as the minister's, and signed in the same manner, by the king his master.

The jury, at first, found the defendant guilty of the assault only; but, the court desiring them to reconsider the matter, they returned with a verdict against him on both counts.

The sentence of the court was suspended, in consequence of a case stated by his Excellency the President, and the Honorable Supreme Executive Council, for the opinion of the judges. It was argued in open court, on the 10th and 12th of July, by five counsel, two for the affirmative, and three for the negative; and on the 7th of October, the prisoner being brought before the court, the Chief Justice stated the case, repeated the answers of the judges, and finally, pronounced the judgment of the court, in the following manner.

MCKEAN, Chief Justice.—Charles Julian de Longchamps: You have been indicted for unlawfully and violently threatening and menacing bodily harm and violence to the person of the Honorable Francis Barbe de Marbois, secretary to the legation from France, and counsul-general of France to the United States of America, in the mansion-house of the minister plenipotentiary of France; and for an assault and battery committed upon the said secretary and consul, in a public street in the city of Philadelphia. To this indictment, you have pleaded, that you were not guilty, and for a trial put yourself upon the country; an unbiassed jury, upon a fair trial, and clear evidence, have found you guilty.

These offences having been thus legally ascertained and fixed upon you, his Excellency the President, and the Honorable the Supreme Executive Council, attentive to the honor and interest of this state, were pleased to inform the judges of this court, as they had frequently done before, that the minister of France had earnestly repeated a demand, that you, having appeared in his house in the uniform of a French regiment, and having called yourself an officer in the troops of his Majesty, should be delivered up to him for these outrages, as a Frenchman, to be sent to France; and wished us in this stage of your prosecution, to take into mature consideration, and in the most solemn manner to determine:—

1. Whether you could be legally delivered up by council, according to the claim made by the late minister of France?

2. If you could not be thus legally delivered up, whether your offences in violation of the law of nations, being now ascertained and verified according to the laws of this commonwealth, you ought not to be imprisoned, until his most Christian Majesty shall declare, that the reparation is satisfactory?

3. If you can be imprisoned, whether any legal act can be done by council, for causing you to be so imprisoned?

To these questions we have given the following answers in writing:—

"In compliance with the request of his Excellency the President, and the Honorable the Supreme Executive Council, we postponed passing sentence upon Charles Julian de Longchamps, until we had maturely considered the three questions above proposed for our determination. On the 10th and 12th days of July, the several questions were argued before the court by five counsel, two on the affirmative and three on the negative side. We have kept the matter under advisement until this day, and now deliver our opinion thereupon.

"1. And as to the first question, we answer, that it is our opinion, that, in this case, Charles Julian de Longchamps cannot be legally delivered up by council, according to the claim made by the minister of France. Though, we think, cases may occur, where council could, *pro bono publico,* and to prevent atrocious offenders evading punishment, deliver them up to the justice of the country to which they belong, or where the offences were committed.

"2. Punishments must be inflicted in the same county where the criminals were tried and convicted, unless the record of the attainder be removed into the supreme court, which may award execution in the county where it sits; they must be such as the laws expressly prescribe; or where no stated or fixed judgment is directed, according to the legal direction of the court; but judgments must be certain and definite in all respects. Therefore, we conclude, that the defendant cannot be imprisoned, until his most Christian Majesty shall declare that the reparation is satisfactory.

"3. The answer to the last question is rendered unnecessary, by the above answer to the second question."

The foregoing answers having been given, it only remains for the court to pronounce sentence upon you. This sentence must be governed by a due consideration of the enormity and dangerous tendency of the offences you have committed, of the wilfulness, deliberation and malice wherewith they were done, of the quality and degree of the offended and offender, the provocation given, and all other circumstances which may any way aggravate or extenuate the guilt.

The first crime in the indictment is an infraction of the law of nations. This law, in its full extent, is a part of the law of this state, and is to be collected from the practice of different nations, and the authority of writers. The person of a public minister is sacred and inviolable. Whoever offers any violence to him, not only affronts the sovereign he represents, but also hurts the common safety and well-being of nations—he is guilty of a crime against the whole world.

All the reasons, which establish the independency and inviolability of the person of a minister, apply likewise to secure the immunities of his house. It is to be defended from all outrage; it is under a peculiar protection of the laws; to invade its freedom, is a crime against the state and all other nations.

The *comites* of a minister, or those of his train, partake also of his inviolability. The independence of a minister extends to all his household; these are so connected with him, that they enjoy his privileges and follow his fate. The secretary to the embassy has his commission from the sovereign himself; he is the most distinguished character in the suit of a public minister, and is, in some instances, considered as a kind of public minister himself. Is it not, then, an extraordinary insult, to use threats of bodily harm to his person, in the domicil of the minister plenipotentiary? If this is tolerated, his freedom of conduct is taken away, the business of his sovereign cannot be transacted, and his dignity and grandeur will be tarnished.

You then have been guilty of an atrocious violation of the law of nations; you have grossly insulted gentlemen, the peculiar objects of this law (gentlemen of amiable characters, and highly esteemed by the government of this state), in a most wanton and unprovoked manner: and it is now the interest as well as duty of the government, to animadvert upon your conduct with a becoming severity—such a severity as may tend to reform yourself, to deter others from the commission of the like crime, preserve the honor of the state, and maintain peace with our great and good ally, and the whole world.

A wrong opinion has been entertained concerning the conduct of Lord Chief Justice Holt and the court of king's bench, in England, in the noted case of the Russian ambassador. They detained the offenders, after conviction, in prison, from term to term, until the Czar Peter was satisfied, without ever proceeding to judgment; and from this, it has been inferred, that the court doubted, whether they could inflict any punishment for an infraction of the law of nations. But this was not the reason. The court never doubted, that the law of nations formed a part of the law of England, and that a violation of this general law could be punished by them; but no punishment less than death would have been thought by the Czar an adequate reparation for the arrest of his ambassador. This punishment they could not inflict, and such a sentence as they could have given, he might have thought a fresh insult. Another expedient was, therefore, fallen upon. However, the princes of the world, at this day, are more enlightened, and do not require impracticable nor unreasonable reparations for injuries of this kind.

The second offense charged in the indictment, namely, the assault and battery, need no observations.

Upon the whole, THE COURT, after a most attentive consideration of every circumstance in this case, do award, and direct me to pronounce the following sentence:—

That you pay a fine of one hundred French crowns to the commonwealth; that you be imprisoned until the 4th day of July 1786, which will make a little more than two years' imprisonment in the whole; that you then give good security to keep the peace, and be of good behavior to all public ministers, secretaries to embassies and consuls, as well as to all the liege people of Pennsylvania, for the space of seven years, by entering into a recognisance, yourself in a thousand pounds, and two securities in five hundred pounds each: that you pay the costs of this prosecution, and remain committed until this sentence be complied with.

3

RECORDS OF THE FEDERAL CONVENTION

[*2:315, Madison, 17 Aug.*]

"To declare the law and punishment of piracies and felonies &c" &c considered.

Mr. Madison moved to strike out "and punishment" &c-

Mr. Mason doubts the safety of it, considering the strict rule of construction in criminal cases. He doubted also the propriety of taking the power in all these cases wholly from the States.

Mr Governr Morris thought it would be necessary to extend the authority farther, so as to provide for the punishment of counterfeiting in general. Bills of exchange for example might be forged in one State and carried into another:

It was suggested by some other member that *foreign* paper might be counterfeited by Citizens; and that it might be politic to provide by national authority for the punishment of it.

Mr Randolph did not conceive the expunging "the punishment" would be a constructive exclusion of the power. He doubted only the efficacy of the word "declare".

Mr Wilson was in favor of the motion– Strictness was not necessary in giving authority to enact penal laws; though necessary in enacting & expounding them.

On motion for striking out "and punishment" as moved by Mr Madison

N. H. no. Mas. ay. Ct no. Pa ay. Del. ay– Md no. Va. ay. N– C– ay. S– C. ay– Geo. ay. [Ayes—7; noes—3.]

Mr Govr Morris moved to strike out "declare the law" and insert "punish" before "piracies". and on the question

N– H– ay. Mas– ay. Ct. no. Pa. ay. Del. ay. Md ay. Va. no. N. C– no. S. C– ay. Geo– ay. [Ayes—7; noes—3.]

Mr. Madison, and Mr. Randolph moved to insert, "define &." before "punish".

Mr. Wilson thought "felonies" sufficiently defined by Common law.

Mr. Dickenson concurred with Mr Wilson

Mr Mercer was in favor of the amendment.

Mr Madison. felony at common law is vague. It is also defective. One defect is supplied by Stat: of Anne as to running away with vessels which at common law was a breach of trust only. Besides no foreign law should be a standard farther than is expressly adopted—If the laws of the States were to prevail on this subject, the citizens of different States would be subject to different punishments for the same offence at sea—There would be neither uniformity nor stability in the law—The proper remedy for all these difficulties was to vest the power proposed by the term "define" in the Natl. legislature.

Mr Govr. Morris would prefer *designate* to *define,* the latter being as he conceived, limited to the preexisting meaning. ——— It was said by others to be applicable to the creating of offences also, and therefore suited the case both of felonies & of piracies. The motion of Mr. M. & Mr. R was agreed to.

Mr. Elseworth enlarged the motion so as to read "to define and punish piracies and felonies committed on the high seas, counterfeiting the securities and current coin of the U. States, and offences agst. the law of Nations" which was agreed to, nem con.

[*2:614; Madison, 14 Sept.*]

To define & punish piracies and felonies on the high seas, and "punish" offences against the law of nations.

Mr. Govr. Morris moved to strike out "punish" before the words "offences agst. the law of nations." so as to let these be *definable* as well as punishable, by virtue of the preceding member of the sentence.

Mr. Wilson hoped the alteration would by no means be made. To pretend to *define* the law of nations which depended on the authority of all the Civilized Nations of the World, would have a look of arrogance. that would make us ridiculous.

Mr. Govr The word *define* is proper when applied to *offences* in this case; the law of nations being often too vague and deficient to be a rule.

On the question to strike out the word "punish" it passed in the affirmative

N— H. ay. Mas— no. Ct. ay. N— J. ay. Pa. no. Del. ay Md. no. Va. no. N. C— ay—S— C— ay. Geo— no. [Ayes—6; noes—5.]

4

JAMES MADISON, FEDERALIST, NO. 42, 280–81 22 Jan. 1788

The power to define and punish piracies and felonies committed on the high seas, and offences against the law of nations, belongs with equal propriety to the general government; and is a still greater improvement on the articles of confederation. These articles contain no provision for the case of offences against the law of nations; and consequently leave it in the power of any indiscreet member to embroil the confederacy with foreign nations. The provision of the foederal articles on the subject of piracies and felonies, extends no farther than to the establishment of courts for the trial of these offences. The definition of piracies might perhaps without inconveniency, be left to the law of nations; though a legislative definition of them, is found in most municipal codes. A definition of felonies on the high seas is evidently requisite. Felony is a term of loose signification even in the common law of England; and of various import in the statute law of that kingdom. But neither the common, nor the statute law of that or of any other nation ought to be a standard for the proceedings of this, unless previously made its own by legislative adoption. The meaning of the term as defined in the codes of the several States, would be as impracticable as the former would be a dishonorable and illegitimate guide. It is not precisely the same in any two of the States; and varies in each with every revision of its criminal laws. For the sake of certainty and uniformity therefore, the power of defining felonies in this case, was in every respect necessary and proper.

5

James Wilson, Of the Law of Nations, Lectures on Law
1791
Works 1:148–67

The law of nature, when applied to states or political societies, receives a new name, that of the law of nations. This law, important in all states, is of peculiar importance in free ones. The States of America are certainly entitled to this dignified appellation. A weighty part of the publick business is transacted by the citizens at large. They appoint the legislature, and, either mediately or immediately, the executive servants of the publick. As the conduct of a state, both with regard to itself and others, must greatly depend upon the character, the talents, and the principles of those, to whom the direction of that conduct is intrusted; it is highly necessary that those who are to protect the rights, and to perform the duties of the commonwealth, should be men of proper principles, talents, and characters: if so, it is highly necessary that those who appoint them should be able, in some degree at least, to distinguish and select those men, whose principles, talents, and characters are proper. In order to do this, it is greatly useful that they have, at least, some just and general knowledge of those rights that are to be protected, and of those duties that are to be performed. Without this, they will be unable to form a rational conjecture, concerning the future conduct of those whom they are to elect. Nay, what is more; without some such general and just knowledge, they will be unable to form a rational judgment, concerning the past and present conduct of those whom they have already elected; and, consequently, will be unable to form a rational determination whether, at the next election, they should reappoint them, or substitute others in their place. As the practice of the law of nations, therefore, must, in a free government, depend very considerably on the acts of the citizens, it is of high import that, among those citizens, its knowledge be generally diffused.

But, if the knowledge of the law of nations is greatly useful to those who appoint, it must surely be highly necessary to those who are appointed, the publick servants and stewards of the commonwealth. Can its interests be properly managed, can its character be properly supported, can its happiness be properly consulted, by those who know not what it owes to others, what it owes to itself, what it has a right to claim from others, and what it has a right to provide for itself? In a free commonwealth, the path to publick service and to publick honour is open to all. Should not all, therefore, sedulously endeavour to become masters of such qualifications, as will enable them to tread this path with credit to themselves, and with advantage to their country?

In the United States, a system of republicks, the law of nations acquires an importance still more peculiar and distinguished. In the United States, the law of nations operates upon peculiar relations, and upon those relations with peculiar energy. Well am I justified, on every account, in announcing the dignity and greatness of the subject, upon which I am now to enter.

On all occasions, let us beware of being misled by names. Though the law, which I am now to consider, receives a new appellation; it retains, unimpaired, its qualities and its power. The law of nations, as well as the law of nature, is of obligation indispensable: the law of nations, as well as the law of nature, is of origin divine.

The opinions of many concerning the law of nations have been very vague and unsatisfactory; and if such have been the opinions, we have little reason to be surprised, that the conduct of nations has too often been diametrically opposite to the law, by which it ought to have been regulated. In the judgment of some writers, it would seem, for instance, that neither the state which commences an unjust war, nor the chief who conducts it, derogates from the general sanctity of their respective characters. An ardent love of their country they seem to have thought a passion too heroick, to be restrained within the narrow limits of systematick morality; and those have been too often considered as the greatest patriots, who have contributed most to gratify the publick passion for conquest and power. States, as well as monarchs, have too frequently been blinded by ambition. Of this there is scarcely a page in ancient or in modern history, relating to national contentions, but will furnish the most glaring proofs. The melancholy truth is, that the law of nations, though founded on the most solid principles of natural obligation, has been but imperfectly viewed in theory, and has been too much disregarded in practice.

The profound and penetrating Bacon was not inattentive to the imperfect state, in which he found the science of the law of nations. As, in another science, that enlightened philosophical guide pointed to the discoveries of a Newton; so in this, in all probability, he laid a foundation for the researches of a Grotius. For we have reason to believe, as we are told by Barbeyrac, that it was the study of the works of Lord Bacon, that first inspired Grotius with the design of writing a system concerning the law of nations. In this science Grotius did much; for he was well qualified to do much. Extensive knowledge, prodigious reading, indefatigable application to study, all these were certainly his. Yet with all these, he was far from being as successful in law, as Sir Isaac Newton was in philosophy. He was unfortunate in not setting out on right and solid principles. His celebrated book of the Rights of War and Peace is indeed useful; but it ought not to be read without a due degree of caution: nor ought all his doctrines to be received, without the necessary grains of allowance. At this we ought not to wonder, when we consider the extent, the variety, and the importance of his subject, and that, before his time, it was little known, and much neglected. His opinion concerning the source and the obligation of the law of nations is very defective. He separates that law from the law of nature, and assigns to it a different origin. "When many men," says he, "at different times and places, unanimously affirm the same thing for truth; this should be ascribed to a general cause. In the subjects treated of by us, this cause can be no other than either a just inference drawn from the principles of nature, or a universal consent. The first discovers to us the law of nature, the second the law of nations." The law of nations, we see, he traces from the principle of universal consent. The consequence of this is, that the law of nations would be obligatory only upon those by whom the consent was given, and only by reason of that consent. The farther consequence would be, that the law of nations would lose a part, and the greatest part, of its obligatory force, and would also be restrained as to the sphere of its operations. That it would lose the greatest part of its obligatory force, sufficiently appears from what we have said at large concerning the origin and obligation of natural law, evincing it to be the will of God. That it would be restrained as to the sphere of its operations, appears from what Grotius himself says, when he explains his meaning in another place. He qualifies the universality of his expression by adding these words, "at least the most civilized nations;" and he afterwards says that this addition is made "with reason." On the *least* civilized nations, therefore, the law of nations would not, according to his account of it, be obligatory.

I admit that there are laws of nations—perhaps it is to be wished that they were designated by an appropriate name; for names, after all, will have their influence on operations—I freely admit that there are laws of nations, which are founded altogether upon consent. National treaties are laws of nations, obligatory solely by consent. The customs of nations become laws solely by consent. Both kinds are certainly voluntary. But the municipal laws of a state are not more different from the law of nature, than those voluntary laws of nations are, in their source and power, different from the law of nations, properly so called. Indeed, those voluntary laws of nations are as much under the control of the law of nations, properly so called, as municipal laws are under the control of the law of nature. The law of nations, properly so called, is the law of nature applied to states and sovereigns. The law of nations, properly so called, is the law of states and sovereigns, obligatory upon them in the same manner, and for the same reasons, as the law of nature is obligatory upon individuals. Universal, indispensable, and unchangeable is the obligation of both.

But it will naturally be asked, if the law of nations bears, as from this account it bears, the same relation to states, which the law of nature bears to individuals, if the law of nature and the law of nations are accompanied with the same obligatory power, and are derived from the same common source; why should the law of nations have a distinct name? Why should it be considered as a separate science? Some have thought that the difference was only in name; and if only in name, there could surely be no solid reason for establishing even that difference. Of those, who thought so, Puffendorff was one. "Many," says he, "assert the law of nature and of nations to be the very same thing, differing no otherwise than in external denomination. Thus Mr. Hobbes divides natural law, into the natural law of men, and the natural law of states, commonly called the law of nations. He observes, that the precepts of both are the same; but that as states, when once instituted, assume the personal properties of men, what we call the law of nature, when we speak of particular men, we denominate the law of nations, when we apply it to whole states, nations, or people. This opinion," continues Puffendorff, "we, for our part, readily subscribe to; nor do we conceive, that there is any other voluntary or positive law of nations, properly vested with a true and legal force, and obliging as the ordinance of a superiour power." By the way, we may here observe, that, with regard to the law of nations, Grotius and Puffendorff seem to have run into contrary extremes. The former was of opinion, that the whole law of nations took its origin and authority from consent. The latter was of opinion, that every part of the law of nations was the same with the law of nature, that no part of it could receive its obligatory force from consent; because, according to his favourite notion of law, no such thing could exist without the intervention of a superior power. The truth seems to lie between the two great philosophers. The law of nations, properly so called, or, as it may be termed, the natural law of nations, is a part, and an important part, of the law of nature. The voluntary law of nations falls under the class of laws that are positive. If a particular name had been appropriated to this last species of law, it is probable that much confusion and ambiguity, on this subject, would have been avoided; and the distinction between the different parts of that law, comprehended, at present, under the name of the law of nations, would have been as clearly marked, as uniformly preserved, and as familiarly taken, as the well known and well founded distinction between natural and municipal law. But to return.

As Puffendorff thought that the law of nature and the law of nations were precisely the same, he has not, in his book on these subjects, treated of the law of nations separately; but has every where joined it with the law of nature, properly so called. His example has been followed by the greatest part of succeeding writers. But the imitation of it has produced a confusion of two objects, which ought to have been viewed and studied distinctly and apart. Though the law of nations, properly so called, be a part of the law of nature; though it spring from the same source, and though it is attended with the same obligatory power; yet it must be remembered that its application is made to very different objects. The law of nature is applied to individuals: the law of nations is applied to states. The important difference between the objects, will occasion a proportioned difference in the application of the law. This difference in the application renders it fit that the law of nature, when applied to states, should receive an appropriate name, and should be taught and studied as a separate science.

Though states or nations are considered as moral persons; yet the nature and essence of these moral persons differ necessarily, in many respects, from the nature and essence of the individuals, of whom they are composed. The application of a law must be made in a manner suitable to its object. The application, therefore, of the law of nature to nations must be made in a manner suitable to nations: its application to individuals must be made in a manner suitable to individuals. But as nations differ from individuals; the application of the law suitable to the former, must be different from its application suitable to the latter. To nations this different application cannot be made with accuracy, with justness, and with perspicuity, without the aid of new and discriminating rules. These rules will evince, that, on the principles themselves of the law of nature, that law, when applied to nations, will prescribe decisions different from those which it would prescribe, when applied to individuals. To investigate those rules; to deduce, from the same great and leading principles, applications differing in proportion to the difference of the persons to which they are applied, is the object of the law of nations, considered as a science distinct and separate from that of the law of nature.

Having given you this general idea and description of the law of nations; need I expatiate on its dignity and importance? The law of nations is the law of sovereigns. In free states, such as ours, the sovereign or supreme power resides in the people. In free states, therefore, such as ours, the law of nations is the law of the people. Let us again beware of being misled by an ambiguity, sometimes, such is the structure of language, unavoidable. When I say that, in free states, the law of nations is the law of the people; I mean not that it is a law made by the people, or by virtue of their delegated authority; as, in free states, all municipal laws are. But when I say that, in free states, the law of nations is the law of the people; I mean that, as the law of nature, in other words, as the will of nature's God, it is indispensably binding upon the people, in whom the sovereign power resides; and who are, consequently, under the most sacred obligations to exercise that power, or to delegate it to such as will exercise it, in a manner agreeable to those rules and maxims, which the law of nature prescribes to every state, for the happiness of each, and for the happiness of all. How vast—how important—how interesting are these truths! They announce to a free people how exalted their rights; but, at the same time, they announce to a free people how solemn their duties are. If a practical knowledge and a just sense of these rights and these duties were diffused among the citizens, and properly impressed upon their hearts and minds; how great, how beneficial, how lasting would be their fruits! But, unfortunately, as there have been and there are, in arbitrary governments, flatterers of princes; so there have been and there are, in free governments, flatterers of the people. One distinction, indeed, is to be taken between them. The latter herd of flatterers persuade the people to make an improper use of the power, which of right they have: the former herd persuade princes to make an improper use of power, which of right they have not. In other respects, both herds are equally pernicious. Both flatter to promote their private interests: both betray the interests of those whom they flatter.

It is of the highest, and, in free states, it is of the most general importance, that the sacred obligation of the law of nations should be accurately known and deeply felt. Of all subjects, it is agreeable and useful to form just and adequate conceptions; but of those especially, which have an influence on the practice and morality of states. For it is a serious truth, however much it has been unattended to in practice, that the laws of morality are equally strict with regard to societies, as to the individuals of whom the societies are composed. It must be owing either to ignorance, or to a very unjustifiable disregard to this great truth, that some transactions of publick bodies have often escaped censure, nay, sometimes have received applause, though these transactions have been such, as none of the individuals composing those bodies would have dared to introduce into the management of his private affairs; because the person introducing them would have been branded with the most reproachful of names and characters. It has been long admitted, by those who have been the best judges of private life and manners, that integrity and sound policy go hand in hand. It is high time that this maxim should find an establishment in the councils of states, and in the cabinets of princes. Its establishment there would diffuse far and wide the most salutary and benign effects.

Opinions concerning the extent of the law of nations have not been less defective and inadequate, than those concerning its origin and obligatory force. Some seem to have thought, that this law respects and regulates the conduct of nations only in their intercourse with each other. A very important branch of this law—that containing the duties which a nation owes itself—seems to have escaped their attention. "The general principle," says Burlamaqui, "of the law of nations, is nothing more than the general law of sociability, which obliges nations to the same duties as are prescribed to individuals. Thus the law of natural equality, which prohibits injury and commands the reparation of damage done; the law of beneficence, and of fidelity to our engagements, are laws respecting nations, and imposing, both on the people and on their respective sovereigns, the same duties as are prescribed to individuals." Several other writers concerning the law of nations appear to have formed the same imperfect conceptions with regard to its extent. Let us recur to what the law of nature dictates to an individual. Are there not duties which he owes to himself? Is he not obliged to consult and promote his preservation, his freedom, his reputation, his improvement, his perfection, his happiness? Now that we have seen the law of nature as it respects the duties of individuals, let us see the law of nations as it respects the duties of states, to themselves: for we must recollect that the law of nations is only the law of nature judiciously applied to the conduct of states. From the duties of states, as well as of individuals, to themselves, a number of corresponding rights will be found to arise.

A state ought to attend to the preservation of its own

existence. In what does the existence of a state consist? It consists in the association of the individuals, of which it is composed. In what consists the preservation of this existence? It consists in the duration of that association. When this association is dissolved, the state ceases to exist; though all the members, of whom it was composed, may still remain. It is the duty of a state, therefore, to preserve this association undissolved and unimpaired. But in this, as in many other instances, a difference between the nature of states and the nature of individuals will occasion, for the reasons already mentioned, a proportioned difference in the application of the law of nature. Nations, as well as men, are taught by the law of nature, gracious in its precepts, to consider their happiness as the great end of their existence. But without existence there can be no happiness: the means, therefore, must be secured, in order to secure the end. But yet, between the duty of self-preservation required from a state, and the duty of self-preservation required from a man, there is a most material difference; and this difference is founded on the law of nature itself. A nation has a right to assign to its existence a voluntary termination: a man has not. What can be the reasons of this difference? Several may be given. By the voluntary act of the individuals forming the nation, the nation was called into existence: they who bind, can also untie: by the voluntary act, therefore, of the individuals forming the nation, the nation may be reduced to its original nothing. But it was not by his own voluntary act that the man made his appearance upon the theatre of life; he cannot, therefore, plead the right of the nation, by his own voluntary act to make his exit. He did not make; therefore, he has no right to destroy himself. He alone, whose gift this state of existence is, has the right to say when and how it shall receive its termination.

Again; though nations are considered as moral persons, and, in that character, as entitled, in many respects, to claim the rights, and as obliged, in many respects, to perform the duties of natural persons; yet we must always remember that of natural persons those moral persons are composed; that for the sake of natural persons those moral persons were formed; and that while we suppose those moral persons to live, and think, and act, we know that they are natural persons alone, who really exist or feel, who really deliberate, resolve, and execute. Now none of these observations resulting from the nature and essence of the nation, can be applied, with any degree of propriety, to the nature and essence of the man: and, therefore, the inferences drawn from these observations, with regard to the case of the nation, are wholly inapplicable to the case of the man.

One of these inferences is, that as it was for the happiness of the members that the moral existence of the nation was produced; so the happiness of the members may require this moral existence to be annihilated. Can this inference be applied to the man?

Further; there may be a moral certainty, that, of the voluntary dissolution of the nation, the necessary consequence will be an increase of happiness. Can such a consequence be predicted, with moral certainty, concerning the voluntary death of the man?

This instance shows, in a striking manner, how, on some occasions, the law of nature, when applied to a nation, may dictate or authorize a measure of conduct very different from that, which it would authorize and dictate with regard to a man.

As it is, in general, the duty of a state to preserve itself; so it is, in general, its duty to preserve its members. This is a duty which it owes to them, and to itself. It owes it to them, because their advantage was the final cause of their joining in the association, and engaging to support it; and they ought not to be deprived of this advantage, while they fulfil the conditions, on which it was stipulated. This duty the nation owes to itself, because the loss of its members is a proportionable loss of its strength; and the loss of its strength is proportionably injurious both to its security, and to its preservation. The result of these principles is, that the body of a nation should not abandon a country, a city, or even an individual, who has not forfeited his rights in the society.

The right and duty of a state to preserve its members are subject to the same limitations and conditions, as its right and duty to preserve itself. As, for some reasons, the society may be dissolved; so, for others, it may be dismembered. A part may be separated from the other parts; and that part may either become a new state, or may associate with another state already formed. An illustration of this doctrine may be drawn from a recent instance, which has happened in the commonwealth of Virginia. The district of Kentucky has, by an amiable agreement, been disjoined from the rest of the commonwealth, and has been formed into a separate state. It is a pleasure, perhaps I may add it is a laudable pride, to be able to furnish, to the world, the first examples of carrying into practice the most sublime parts of the most sublime theories of government and law.

When a nation has a right, and is under an obligation to preserve itself and its members; it has, by a necessary consequence, a right to do everything, which, without injuring others, it can do, in order to accomplish and secure those objects. The law of nature prescribes not impossibilities: it imposes not an obligation, without giving a right to the necessary means of fulfilling it. The same principles, which evince the right of a nation to do every thing, which it lawfully may, for the preservation of itself and of its members, evince its right, also, to avoid and prevent, as much as it lawfully may, every thing which would load it with injuries, or threaten it with danger.

It is the right, and generally it is the duty, of a state, to form a constitution, to institute civil government, and to establish laws. If the constitution formed, or the government instituted, or the laws established shall, on experience, be found weak, or inconvenient, or pernicious; it is the right, and it is the duty of the state to strengthen, or alter, or abolish them. These subjects will be fully treated in another place.

A nation ought to know itself. It ought to form a just estimate of its own situation, both with regard to itself and to its neighbours. It ought to learn the excellencies, and the blemishes likewise of its own constitution. It ought to review the instances in which it has already attained, and it ought to ascertain those in which it falls short of, a practicable degree of perfection. It ought to find out what improvements are peculiarly necessary to be promoted, and what faults it is peculiarly necessary to avoid. Without a discriminating sagacity of this kind, the principle of imitation, intended for the wisest purposes in states as well as in individuals, would be always an uncertain, sometimes a dangerous guide. A measure extremely salutary to one state, might be extremely injurious to another. What, in one situation, would be productive of peace and happiness, might, in another, be the unfortunate cause of infelicity and war. Above all things, the genius and manners of the people ought to be carefully consulted. The government ought to be administered agreeably to this genius and these manners; but how can this be done, if this genius and these manners are unknown? This duty of self-knowledge is of vast extent and of vast importance, in nations as well as in men.

To love and to deserve honest fame, is another duty of a people, as well as of an individual. The reputation of a state is not only a pleasant, it is also a valuable possession. It attracts the esteem, it represses the unfriendly inclinations of its neighbours. This reputation is acquired by virtue, and by the conduct which virtue inspires. It is founded on the publick transactions of the state, and on the private behaviour of its members.

A state should avoid ostentation, but it should support its dignity. This should never be suffered to be degraded among other nations. In transactions between states, an attention to this object is of much greater importance than is generally imagined. Even the marks and titles of respect, to which a nation, and those who represent a nation, are entitled, ought not to be considered as trivial: they should be claimed with firmness: they should be given with alacrity. The dignity, the equality, the mutual independence, and the frequent intercourse of nations render such a tenour of conduct altogether indispensable.

It is the duty of a nation to intrust the management of its affairs only to its wisest and best citizens. The immense importance of this duty is easily seen; but it is not sufficiently regarded. The meanest menial of a family will not be received without examination and cautious inquiry. The most important servants of the publick will be voted in without consideration and without care. In electioneering, as it is called, we frequently find warm recommendations and active intrigues in favour of candidates for the highest offices, to whom the recommenders and intriguers would not, if put to the test, intrust the management of the smallest part of their own private interest. An election ground, the great theatre of original sovereignty, on which nothing but inviolable integrity and independent virtue should be exhibited, is often and lamentably transformed into a scene of the vilest and lowest debauchery and deception. An election maneuvre, an election story, are names appropriated to a conduct, which, in other and inferiour transactions, would be branded, and justly branded, with the most opprobrious appellations. Even those, who may be safely trusted every where else, will play false at elections. The remarks, which I have made concerning general elections, may be too often made, with equal truth, concerning other appointments to offices. But these things ought not to be. When the obligation and the importance of the great national duty required at elections—a duty prescribed by him who made us free—a duty prescribed that we may continue free—when all this shall be sufficiently diffused, and known, and felt; these things will not be. The people will then elect conscientiously; and will require conscientious conduct from those whom they elect.

A nation ought to encourage true patriotism in its members. The first step towards this encouragement is to distinguish between its real and its pretended friends. The discrimination, it is true, is often difficult, sometimes impracticable: but it is equally true, that it may frequently be made. Let the same care be employed, let the same pains be taken, to ascertain the marks of deceit and the marks of sincerity in publick life, and in intriguing for publick office, which are usually taken and employed in private life, and in solicitations for acts of private friendship. The care and pains will sometimes, indeed, be fruitless; but they will sometimes, too, be successful; at all times, they will be faithful witnesses, that those, who have employed them, have discharged their duty.

If a nation establish itself, or extend its establishment in a country already inhabited by others; it ought to observe strict justice, in both instances, with the former inhabitants. This is a part of the law of nations, that very nearly concerns the United States. It ought, therefore, to be well understood. The whole earth is allotted for the nourishment of its inhabitants, but it is not sufficient for this purpose, unless they aid it by labour and culture. The cultivation of the earth, therefore, is a duty incumbent on man by the order of nature. Those nations that live by hunting, and have more land than is necessary even for the purposes of hunting, should transfer it to those who will make a more advantageous use of it: those who will make this use of it ought to pay, for they can afford to pay, a reasonable equivalent. Even when the lands are no more than sufficient for the purposes of hunting, it is the duty of the new inhabitants, if advanced in society, to teach, and it is the duty of the original inhabitants, if less advanced in society, to learn, the arts and uses of agriculture. This will enable the latter gradually to contract, and the former gradually to extend their settlements, till the science of agriculture is equally improved in both. By these means, the intentions of nature will be fulfilled; the old and the new inhabitants will be reciprocally useful; peace will be preserved, and justice will be done.

It is the duty of a nation to augment its numbers. The performance of this duty will naturally result from the discharge of its other duties: by discharging them, the number of persons born in the society will be increased; and strangers will be incited to wish a participation in its blessings. Among other means of increasing the number of citizens, there are three of peculiar efficacy. The first is, easily to receive all strangers of good character, and to communicate to them the advantages of liberty. The state will be thus filled with citizens, who will bring with them commerce and the arts, and a rich variety of manners and characters. Another means conducive to the same end is, to encourage marriages. These are the pledges of the state. A third means for augmenting the number of inhabitants is, to preserve the rights of conscience inviolate. The right of private judgment is one of the greatest advantages of mankind; and is always considered as such. To be deprived of it is insufferable. To enjoy it lays a foundation for that peace of mind, which the laws cannot give, and for the loss of which the laws can offer no compensation.

A nation should aim at its perfection. The advantage and improvement of the citizens are the ends proposed by the social union. Whatever will render that union more perfect will promote these ends. The same principles, therefore, which show that a man ought to pursue the perfection of his nature, will show, likewise, that the citizens ought to contribute every thing in their power towards the perfection of the state. This right involves the right of preventing and avoiding every thing, which would interrupt or retard the progress of the state towards its perfection. It also involves the right of acquiring every thing, without which its perfection cannot be promoted or obtained.

Happiness is the centre, to which men and nations are attracted: it is, therefore, the duty of a nation to consult its happiness. In order to do this, it is necessary that the nation be instructed to search for happiness where happiness is to be found. The impressions that are made first, sink deepest; they frequently continue through life. That seed, which is sown in the tender minds of youth, will produce abundance of good, or abundance of evil. The education of youth, therefore, is of prime importance to the happiness of the state. The arts, the sciences, philosophy, virtue, and religion, all contribute to the happiness, all, therefore, ought to receive the encouragement, of the nation. In this manner, publick and private felicity will go hand in hand, and mutually assist each other in their progress.

When men have formed themselves into a state or nation, they may reciprocally enter into particular engagements, and, in this manner, contract new obligations in favour of the members of the community; but they cannot, by this union, discharge themselves from any duties which they previously owed to those, who form no part of the union. They continue under all the obligations required by the universal society of the human race—the great society of nations. The law of that great and universal society requires, that each nation should contribute to the perfection and happiness of the others. It is, therefore, a duty which every nation owes to itself, to acquire those qualifications, which will fit and enable it to discharge those duties which it owes to others. What those duties are, we shall now very concisely and summarily inquire.

The first and most necessary duty of nations, as well as of men, is to do no wrong or injury. Justice is a sacred law of nations. If the law of the great society of nations requires, as we have seen it to require, that each should contribute to the perfection and happiness of others; the first degree of this duty surely is, that each should abstain from every thing, which would positively impair that perfection and happiness. This great principle prohibits one nation from exciting disturbances in another, from seducing its citizens, from depriving it of its natural advantages, from calumniating its reputation, from debauching the attachment of its allies, from fomenting or encouraging the hatred of its enemies. If, however, a nation, in the necessary prosecution of its own duties and rights, does what is disagreeable or even inconvenient to another, this is not to be considered as an injury; it ought to be viewed as the unavoidable result, and not as the governing principle of its conduct. If, at such conduct, offence is taken, it is the fault of that nation, which takes, not of that nation, which occasions it.

But nations are not only forbidden to do evil; they are also commanded to do good to one another. The duties of humanity are incumbent upon nations as well as upon individuals. An individual cannot subsist, at least he cannot subsist comfortably, by himself. What is true concerning one, is true concerning all. Without mutual good offices and assistance, therefore, happiness could not be procured, perhaps existence could not be preserved. Hence the necessity of the duties of humanity among individuals. Every one is obliged, in the first place, to do what he can for himself; in the next, to do what he can for others; beginning with those with whom he is most intimately connected. The consequence is, that each man is obliged to give to others every assistance, for which they have a real occasion, and which he can give without being wanting to himself. What each is obliged to perform for others, from others he is entitled to receive. Hence the advantage as well as the duty of humanity. These principles receive an application to states as well as to men. Each nation owes to every other the duties of humanity. It is true, there may be some difference in the application, in this as well as in other instances: but the principles of the application are the same. A nation can subsist by itself more securely and more comfortably than an individual can; therefore the duty of mutual assistance will not, at all periods, be equally indispensable, or return with equal frequency. But when it becomes, as it may become, equally indispensable; and when it returns, as it may return, with equal frequency; it ought, in either case, to be equally performed. One individual may attack another daily: a longer time is necessary for the aggression of one nation upon another. The assistance, therefore, which ought to be given to the individual daily, will be necessary for the nation only at more distant intervals of time. But between nations, what the duties of humanity lose in point of frequency, they gain in point of importance, in proportion, perhaps, to the difference between a single individual, and all those individuals of whom the nation is composed.

One nation ought to give to another, not only the assistance necessary to its preservation, but that also which is necessary to its perfection, whenever it is wanted, and whenever, consistently with other superiour duties, it can be given. The case in which assistance ought to be demanded, and those in which it ought to be given, must be decided respectively by that nation which demands, and by that of which the demand is made. It is incumbent on each to decide properly; not to demand, and not to refuse, without strong and reasonable cause.

It may, perhaps, be uncommon, but it is certainly just, to say that nations ought to love one another. The offices of humanity ought to flow from this pure source. When this happily is the case, then the principles of affection and of friendship prevail among states as among individuals: then nations will mutually support and assist each other with zeal and ardour; lasting peace will be the result of unshaken confidence; and kind and generous principles, of a nature far opposite to mean jealousy, crooked policy, or cold prudence, will govern and prosper the affairs of men. And why should not this be the case? When a number of individuals, by the social union, become fellow citizens, can they, by that union, devest themselves of that relation, which subsists between them and the other—the far greater—part of the human species? With regard to those, can they cease to be men?

The love of mankind is an important duty and an exalted virtue. Much has been written, much has been said concerning the power of *intellectual* abstraction, which man possesses, and which distinguishes him so eminently from the inferiour orders of animals. But little has been said, and little has been written, concerning another power of the human mind, still more dignified, and, beyond all comparison, more amiable—I may call it the power of *moral* abstraction.

All things in nature are individuals. But when a number of individuals have a near and striking resemblance, we, in our minds, class them together, and refer them to a species, to which we assign a name. Again; when a number of species have a resemblance, though not so near and striking, we, in the same manner, class them also together, and refer them to a genus, to which we likewise assign a name. Different genera may have a resemblance, though still less close and striking; we refer them to a higher genus, till we arrive at *being*, the highest genus of all. This is the progress of intellectual abstraction.

We are possessed of a moral power, similar in its nature and in its progress—a principle of good will as well as of knowledge. This principle of benevolence is indeed primarily and chiefly directed towards individuals, those especially, with whom we are or wish to be most intimately connected. But this principle, as well as the other, is capable of abstraction, and of embracing general objects. The culture, the improvement, and the extension of this principle ought to have made, in the estimation of philosophers, as important a figure among the moral, as the other has made among the intellectual powers and operations of the mind; for it is susceptible of equal culture, of equal improvement, and of equal extension.

"After having," says the illustrious Neckar, in his book concerning the importance of religious opinions, "proved myself a citizen of France, by my administration, as well as my writings, I wish to unite myself to a fraternity still more extended, that of the whole human race. Thus, without dispersing our sentiments, we may be able to communicate ourselves a great way off, and enlarge, in some measure, the limits of our circle. Glory be to our thinking faculties for it! to that spiritual portion of ourselves, which can take in the past, dart into futurity, and intimately associate itself with the destiny of men of all countries and of all ages!"

To the same purpose is the sentiment of Cicero, in his beautiful treatise on the nature and offices of friendship. "In tracing the social laws of nature," says he, "it seems evident, that man, by the frame of his moral constitution, is supposed to consider himself as standing in some degree of social relation to the whole species in general; and that this principle acts with more or less vigour, according to the distance at which he is placed with respect to any particular community or individual of his kind."

This principle of benevolence and sociability, which is not confined to one sect or to one state, but ranges excursive through the whole expanded theatre of men and nations, instead of being always acknowledged and always recommended, as it ought to have been, has been altogether omitted by some philosophers: by some, its existence seems to have been doubted or denied.

"Some sort of union," says Rutherforth, in his institutes of natural law, "there is between all nations: they are all included in the collective idea of mankind, and are frequently spoken of under this general name. But this is not a social union: the several parts of the collective idea, whether we consider the great body of mankind as made up of individuals or of nations, are not connected, as the several parts of a civil society are, by compact among themselves: the connexion is merely notional, and is only made by the mind, for its own convenience."

The very enlarged active power, concerning which I speak, is, to this day, so far as I know, without an appropriated name. The term *philanthropy* approaches near, but does not reach it. We sometimes call it *patriotism,* by a figurative extension of that term, which, in its proper meaning, denotes a circle of benevolence limited by the state, of which one is a member. When we speak of the most exalted of all characters, of the man who possesses this virtue, we generally describe him, by a metaphor, a "citizen of the world." A "man of the world," which would be the more natural expression, though it is in common use, is used to convey a very different idea.

If the general observations, which I have before made concerning the nature, the structure, and the evidence of language, be well founded, the particular remarks I have now made will appear to be striking and just.

This power of moral abstraction should be exercised and cultivated with the highest degree of attention and zeal. It is as necessary to the progress of exalted virtue, as the power of intellectual abstraction is to the progress of extensive knowledge. The progress of the former will be accompanied with a degree of pleasure, of utility, and of excellence, far superiour to any degree of those qualities, which can accompany the latter. The purest pleasures of mathematical learning spring from the source of accurate and extended intellectual abstraction. But those pleasures, pure as they are, must yield the palm to those, which arise from abstraction of the moral kind.

By this power, exerted in different proportions, the commonwealth of Pennsylvania, the empire of the United States, the civilized and commercial part of the world, the inhabitants of the whole earth, become objects of a benevolence the warmest, and of a spirit the most patriotick; for custom, the arbitress of language, has not yet authorized a more appropriate epithet. By this power, a number of individuals, who, considered separately, may be so minute, so unknown, or so distant, as to elude the operations of our benevolence, yet, comprehended under one important and distinguished aspect, may become a general and complex object, which will warm and dilate the soul. By this power the capacity of our nature is enlarged; men, otherwise invisible, are rendered conspicuous; and become known to the heart as well as to the understanding.

This enlarged and elevated virtue ought to be cultivated by nations with peculiar assiduity and ardour. The sphere of exertion, to which an individual is confined, is frequently narrow, however enlarged his disposition may be. But the sphere, to the extent of which a state may exert herself, is often comparatively boundless. By exhibiting a glorious example in her constitution, in her laws, in the administration of her constitution and laws, she may diffuse reformation, she may diffuse instruction, she may diffuse happiness over this whole terrestrial globe.

How often and how fatally are expressions and sentiments perverted! How often and how fatally is perverted conduct the unavoidable and inveterate effect of perverted sentiment and expression! What immense treasures have been exhausted, what oceans of human blood have been shed, in France and England, by force of the expression "natural enemy!" 'Tis an unnatural expression. The antithesis is truly in the thought: for natural enmity forms no title in the genuine law of nations, part of the law of nature. It is adopted from a spurious code.

The foregoing rules and maxims of national law, though they are the sacred, the inviolable, and the exalted precepts of nature, and of nature's Author, have been long unknown and unacknowledged among nations. Even where they have been known and acknowledged, their calm still voice has been drowned by the solicitations of interest, the clamours of ambition, and the thunder of war. Many of the ancient nations conceived themselves to be under no obligations whatever to other states or the citizens of other states, unless they could produce in their favour a connexion formed and cemented by a treaty of amity.

At last, however, the voice of nature, intelligible and persuasive, has been heard by nations that are civilized: at last it is acknowledged that mankind are all brothers: the happy time is, we hope, approaching, when the acknowledgment will be substantiated by a uniform corresponding conduct.

How beautiful and energetick are the sentiments of Cicero on this subject. "It is more consonant to nature," that is, as he said a little before, to the law of nations, "to undertake the greatest labours, and to undergo the severest trouble, for the preservation and advantage of all nations, if such a thing could be accomplished, than to live in solitary repose, not only without pain, but surrounded with all the allurements of pleasure and wealth. Every one of a good and great mind, would prefer the first greatly before the second situation in life." "It is highly absurd to say, as some have said, that no one ought to injure a parent or a brother, for the sake of his own advantage; but that another rule may be observed concerning the rest of the citizens: such persons determine that there is no law, no bonds of society among the citizens, for the common benefit of the commonwealth. This sentiment tends to dissolve the union of the state. Others, again, admit that a social regard is to be paid to the citizens, but deny that this regard ought to be extended in favour of foreigners: such persons would destroy the common society of the human race; and if this common society were destroyed, the destruction would involve, in it, the fate also of beneficence, liberality, goodness, justice. Which last virtue is the mistress and the queen of all the other virtues." By justice here, Cicero clearly means that universal justice, which is the complete accomplishment of the law of nature.

It has been already observed, that there is one part of the law of nations, called their voluntary law, which is founded on the principle of consent: of this part, publick compacts and customs received and observed by civilized states form the most considerable articles.

Publick compacts are divided into two kinds—treaties and sponsions. Treaties are made by those who are empowered, by the constitution of a state, to represent it in its transactions with other nations. Sponsions are made by an inferiour magistrate or officer, on behalf of the state, but without authority from it. Such compacts, therefore, do not bind the state, unless it confirms them after they are made. These take place chiefly in negotiations and transactions between commanding officers, during a war.

Though the power of making treaties is usually, it is not necessarily annexed to sovereign power. Some of the princes and free cities of Germany, though they hold of the emperour and the empire, have nevertheless the right of making treaties with foreign nations: this right, as well as several other rights of sovereignty, the constitution of the empire has secured to them.

With a policy, wiser and more profound, because it shuts the door against foreign intrigues with the members of the union, no state comprehended within our national government, can enter into any treaty, alliance, or confederation.

It is in the constitution or fundamental laws of every nation, that we must search, in order to discover what power it is, which has sufficient authority to contract, with validity, in the name of the state.

A treaty is valid, if there has been no essential defect in the manner, in which it has been made; and, in order to guard against essential defects, it is only necessary that there be sufficient power in the contracting parties, that their mutual consent be given, and that that consent be properly declared.

It is a truth certain in the law of nature, that he who has made a promise to another, has given to that other a perfect right to demand the performance of the promise. Nations and the representatives of nations, therefore, ought to preserve inviolably their treaties and engagements: by not preserving them, they subject themselves to all the consequences of violating the perfect right of those, to whom they were made. This great truth is generally acknowledged; but too frequently an irreligious disregard is shown to it in the conduct of princes and states. But such a disregard is weak as well as wicked. In publick as in private life, among sovereigns as among individuals, honesty is the best policy, as well as the soundest morality. Among merchants, credit is wealth; among states and princes, good faith is both respectability and power.

A state, which violates the sacred faith of treaties, violates not only the voluntary, but also the natural and necessary law of nations; for we have seen that, by the law of nature, the fulfilment of promises is a duty as much incumbent upon states as upon men. Indeed it is more incumbent on the former than on the latter; for the consequences both of performing and of violating the engagements of the former, are generally more important and more lasting, than any which can flow from engagements performed or violated by individuals. Hence the strict propriety, as well as the uncommon beauty of the sentiment—that if good faith were banished from every other place, she should find an inviolable sanctuary at least in the bosoms of princes.

Every treaty should be illuminated by perspicuity and candour. A tricking minister is, in real infamy, degraded as much below a vulgar cheat, as the dignity of states is raised above that of private persons. Ability and address in negotiation may be used to avoid, never to accomplish a surprise.

Fraud in the subsequent interpretation, is equally base and dishonourable as fraud in the original structure of treaties. In the scale of turpitude, it weighs equally with the most flagrant and notorious perfidy.

Treaties and alliances are either personal or real. The first relate only to the contracting parties, and expire with those who contract. The second relate to the state, in whose name and by whose authority the contract was made, and are permanent as the state itself, unless they determine, at another period, by their own limitation.

Every treaty or alliance made with a commonwealth is, in its own nature, real; for it has reference solely to the body of the state. When a free people make an engagement, it is the nation which contracts. Its stipulations depend not on the lives of those, who have been the instruments in forming the treaty: nor even on the lives of those citizens, who were alive when the treaty was formed. They change; but the commonwealth continues the same.

Hence the stability and the security of treaties made with commonwealths. By the faithful observance of their treaties, the Cantons of Switzerland have rendered themselves respectable and respected over all Europe. Let it be mentioned to the honour of the parliament of Great Britain, that it has frequently thanked its king for his zeal and attachment to the treaties, in which he has engaged the nation.

The corruption of the best things and institutions, however, always degenerates into the worst. The citizens of Carthage prostituted the character of their republick to such a degree, that, if we may believe the testimony of an enemy, *Punica fides* became proverbial, over the ancient world, to denote the extreme of perfidy.

As the United States have surpassed others, even other commonwealths, in the excellence of their constitution and government; it is reasonably to be hoped, that they will surpass them, likewise, in the stability of their laws, and in their fidelity to their governments.

In the great chart of the globe of credit, we hope to see American placed as the very antipode of Carthaginian faith.

6

ST. GEORGE TUCKER, BLACKSTONE'S COMMENTARIES 1:APP. 268–69 1803

The definition of piracies, says the author of the Federalist, might perhaps, without inconvenience, be left to the law of nations: though a legislative definition of them is found in most municipal codes. A definition of felonies on the high seas is evidently requisite, being a term of loose signification, even in the common law of England. The true ground of granting these powers to congress seems to be, the immediate and near connection and relation which they have to the regulation of commerce with foreign nations, which must necessarily be transacted by the communication on the high seas; and the right of deciding upon questions of war and peace, where the law of nations, is the only guide. Under this head, of offences against the law of nations, the violation of the rights of ambassadors, as also of passports, and safe conducts is included. The act of 1 cong. 2 sess. c. 9, embraces the whole.

And here we may remark by the way, the very guarded manner in which congress are vested with authority to legislate upon the subject of crimes, and misdemeanors. They are not entrusted with a general power over these subjects, but a few offences are selected from the great mass of crimes with which society may be infested, upon which, only, congress are authorised to prescribe the punishment, or define the offence. All felonies and offences committed upon land, in all cases not expressly enumerated, being reserved to the states respectively. From whence this corollary seems to follow. That all crimes cognizable by the federal courts (except such as are committed in places, the exclusive jurisdiction of which has been ceded to the federal government) must be previously defined, (except treason,) and the punishment thereof previously declared, by the federal legislature.

7

THE SCHOONER EXCHANGE v. MCFADDON *7 Cranch 116 (1812)*

MARSHALL Ch. J. Delivered the opinion of the Court as follows:

This case involves the very delicate and important inquiry, whether an American citizen can assert, in an

American court, a title to an armed national vessel, found within the waters of the United States.

The question has been considered with an earnest solicitude, that the decision may conform to those principles of national and municipal law by which it ought to be regulated.

In exploring an unbeaten path, with few, if any, aids from precedents or written law, the court has found it necessary to rely much on general principles, and on a train of reasoning, founded on cases in some degree analogous to this.

The jurisdiction of *courts* is a branch of that which is possessed by the nation as an independent sovereign power.

The jurisdiction of the nation within its own territory is necessarily exclusive and absolute. It is susceptible of no limitation not imposed by itself. Any restriction upon it, deriving validity from an external source, would imply a diminution of its sovereignty to the extent of the restriction, and an investment of that sovereignty to the same extent in that power which could impose such restriction.

All exceptions, therefore, to the full and complete power of a nation within its own territories, must be traced up to the consent of the nation itself. They can flow from no other legitimate source.

This consent may be either express or implied. In the latter case, it is less determinate, exposed more to the uncertainties of construction; but, if understood, not less obligatory.

The world being composed of distinct sovereignties, possessing equal rights and equal independence, whose mutual benefit is promoted by intercourse with each other, and by an interchange of those good offices which humanity dictates and its wants require, all sovereigns have consented to a relaxation in practice, in cases under certain peculiar circumstances, of that absolute and complete jurisdiction within their respective territories which sovereignty confers.

This consent may, in some instances be tested by common usage, and by common opinion, growing out of that usage.

A nation would justly be considered as violating its faith, although that faith might not be expressly plighted, which should suddenly and without previous notice, exercise its territorial powers in a manner not consonant to the usages and received obligations of the civilized world.

This full and absolute territorial jurisdiction being alike the attribute of every sovereign, and being incapable of conferring extra-territorial power, would not seem to contemplate foreign sovereigns nor their sovereign rights as its objects. One sovereign being in no respect amenable to another; and being bound by obligations of the highest character not to degrade the dignity of his nation, by placing himself or its sovereign rights within the jurisdiction of another, can be supposed to enter a foreign territory only under an express license, or in the confidence that the immunities belonging to his independent sovereign station, though not expressly stipulated, are reserved by implication, and will be extended to him.

This perfect equality and absolute independence of sovereigns, and this common interest impelling them to mutual intercourse, and an interchange of good offices with each other, has given rise to a class of cases in which every sovereign is understood to wa[i]ve the exercise of a part of that complete exclusive territorial jurisdiction, which has been stated to be the attribute of every nation.

1st. One of these is admitted to be the exemption of the person of the sovereign from arrest or detention within a foreign territory.

If he enters that territory with the knowledge and license of its sovereign, that license, although containing no stipulation exempting his person from arrest, is universally understood to imply such stipulation.

Why has the whole civilized world concurred in this construction? The answer cannot be mistaken. A foreign sovereign is not understood as intending to subject himself to a jurisdiction incompatible with his dignity, and the dignity of his nation, and it is to avoid this subjection that the license has been obtained. The character to whom it is given, and the object for which it is granted, equally require that it should be construed to impart full security to the person who has obtained it. This security, however, need not be expressed; it is implied from the circumstances of the case.

Should one sovereign enter the territory of another, without the consent of that other, expressed or implied, it would present a question which does not appear to be perfectly settled, a decision of which is not necessary to any conclusion to which the Court may come in the cause under consideration. If he did not thereby expose himself to the territorial jurisdiction of the sovereign, whose dominions he had entered, it would seem to be because all sovereigns impliedly engage not to avail themselves of a power over their equal, which a romantic confidence in their magnanimity has placed in their hands.

2d. A second case, standing on the same principles with the first, is the immunity which all civilized nations allow to foreign ministers.

Whatever may be the principle on which this immunity is established, whether we consider him as in the place of the sovereign he represents, or by a political fiction suppose him to be extra-territorial, and, therefore, in point of law, not within the jurisdiction of the sovereign at whose Court he resides; still the immunity itself is granted by the governing power of the nation to which the minister is deputed. This fiction of exterritoriality could not be erected and supported against the will of the sovereign of the territory. He is supposed to assent to it.

This consent is not expressed. It is true that in some countries, and in this among others, a special law is enacted for the case. But the law obviously proceeds on the idea of prescribing the punishment of an act previously unlawful, not of granting to a foreign minister a privilege which he would not otherwise possess.

The assent of the sovereign to the very important and extensive exemptions from territorial jurisdiction which are admitted to attach to foreign ministers, is implied from the considerations that, without such exemption, every sovereign would hazard his own dignity by employing a public minister abroad. His minister would owe temporary and local allegiance to a foreign prince, and would be less competent to the objects of his mission. A sovereign committing the interests of his nation with a foreign power, to the care of a person whom he has selected for that purpose, cannot intend to subject his minister in any degree to that power; and therefore, a consent to receive him, implies a consent that he shall possess those privileges which his principal intended he should retain—privileges which are essential to the dignity of his sovereign, and to the duties he is bound to perform.

In what cases a minister, by infracting the laws of the country in which he resides, may subject himself to other punishment than will be inflicted by his own sovereign, is an enquiry foreign to the present purpose. If his crimes be such as to render him amenable to the local jurisdiction, it must be because they forfeit the privileges annexed to his character; and the minister, by violating the conditions under which he was received as the representative of a foreign sovereign, has surrendered the immunities granted on those conditions; or, according to the true meaning of the original assent, has ceased to be entitled to them.

3d. A third case in which a sovereign is understood to cede a portion of his territorial jurisdiction is, where he allows the troops of a foreign prince to pass through his dominions.

In such case, without any express declaration waiving jurisdiction over the army to which this right of passage has been granted, the sovereign who should attempt to exercise if would certainly be considered as violating his faith. By exercising it, the purpose for which the free passage was granted would be defeated, and a portion of the military force of a foreign independent nation would be diverted from those national objects and duties to which it was applicable, and would be withdrawn from the control of the sovereign whose power and whose safety might greatly depend on retaining the exclusive command and disposition of this force. The grant of a free passage therefore implies a waiver of all jurisdiction over the troops during their passage, and permits the foreign general to use that discipline, and to inflict those punishments which the Government of his army may require.

But if, without such express permit, an army should be led through the territories of a foreign prince, might the jurisdiction of the territory be rightfully exercised over the individuals composing this army?

Without doubt, a military force can never gain immunities of any other description than those which war gives, by entering a foreign territory against the will of its sovereign. But if his consent, instead of being expressed by a particular license, be expressed by a general declaration that foreign troops may pass through a specified tract of country, a distinction between such general permit and a particular license is not perceived. It would seem reasonable that every immunity which would be conferred by a special license, would be in like manner conferred by such general permit.

We have seen that a license to pass through a territory implies immunities not expressed, and it is material to enquire why the license itself may not be presumed?

It is obvious that the passage of an army through a foreign territory will probably be at all times inconvenient and injurious, and often would be eminently dangerous to the sovereign through whose dominion it passed. Such a practice would break down some of the most decisive distinctions between peace and war, and would reduce a nation to the necessity of resisting by war, an act not absolutely hostile in its character, or of exposing itself to the stratagems and frauds of a power whose integrity might be doubted, and who might enter the country under deceitful pretexts. It is for reasons like these that the general license to foreigners to enter the dominions of a friendly power, is never understood to extend to a military force; and an army marching into the dominions of another sovereign, may justly be considered as committing an act of hostility; and if not opposed by force, acquires no privilege by its irregular and improper conduct. It may however well be questioned whether any other than the sovereign power of the state be capable of deciding that such military commander is without a license.

But the rule which is applicable to armies, does not appear to be equally applicable to ships of war entering the ports of a friendly power. The injury inseparable from the march of an army through an inhabited country, and the dangers often, indeed generally, attending it, do not ensue from admitting a ship of war, without special license, into a friendly port. A different rule therefore with respect to this species of military force has been generally adopted. If, for reasons of state, the ports of a nation generally, or any particular ports be closed against vessels of war generally, or the vessels of any particular nation, notice is usually given of such determination. If there be no prohibition, the ports of a friendly nation are considered as open to the public ships of all powers with whom it is at peace, and they are supposed to enter such ports and to remain in them while allowed to remain, under the protection of the government of the place.

In almost every instance, the treaties between civilized nations contain a stipulation to this effect in favor of vessels driven in by stress of weather or other urgent necessity. In such cases the sovereign is bound by compact to authorize foreign vessels to enter his ports. The treaty binds him to allow vessels in distress to find refuge and asylum in his ports, and this is a license which he is not at liberty to retract. It would be difficult to assign a reason for withholding from a license thus granted, any immunity from local jurisdiction which would be implied in a special license.

If there be no treaty applicable to the case, and the sovereign, from motives deemed adequate by himself, permits his ports to remain open to the public ships of foreign friendly powers, the conclusion seems irresistable, that they enter by his assent. And if they enter by his assent necessarily implied, no just reason is perceived by the Court for distinguishing their case from that of vessels which enter by express assent.

In all cases of exemption which have been reviewed, much has been implied, but the obligation of what was implied has been found equal to the obligation of that which was expressed. Are there reasons for denying the application of this principle to ships of war?

In this part of the subject a difficulty is to be encountered, the seriousness of which is acknowledged, but which the Court will not attempt to evade.

Those treaties which provide for the admission and safe departure of public vessels entering a port from stress of weather or other urgent cause, provide in like manner for the private vessels of the nation; and where public vessels enter a port under the general license which is implied merely from the absence of a prohibition, they are, it may be urged, in the same condition with merchant vessels entering the same port for the purposes of trade who cannot thereby claim any exemption from the jurisdiction of the country. It may be contended, certainly with much plausibility if not correctness, that the same rule, and same principle are applicable to public and private ships; and since it is admitted that private ships entering without special license become subject to the local jurisdiction, it is demanded on what authority an exception is made in favor of ships of war.

It is by no means conceded, that a private vessel really availing herself of an asylum provided by treaty, and not attempting to trade, would become amenable to the local jurisdiction, unless she committed some act forfeiting the protection she claims under compact. On the contrary, motives may be assigned for stipulating, and according immunities to vessels in cases of distress, which would not be demanded for, or allowed to those which enter voluntarily and for ordinary purposes. On this part of the subject, however, the Court does not mean to indicate any opinion. The case itself may possibly occur, and ought not to be prejudged.

Without deciding how far such stipulations in favor of distressed vessels, as are usual in treaties, may exempt private ships from the jurisdiction of the place, it may safely be asserted, that the whole reasoning upon which such exemption has been implied in other cases, applies with full force to the exemption of ships of war in this.

"It is impossible to conceive," says Vattel, "that a Prince who sends an ambassador or any other minister can have any intention of subjecting him to the authority of a foreign power; and this consideration furnishes an additional argument, which completely establishes the independency of a public minister. If it cannot be reasonably presumed that his sovereign means to subject him to the authority of the prince to whom he is sent, the latter, in receiving the minister, consents to admit him on the footing of independency; and thus there exists between the two princes a tacit convention, which gives a new force to the natural obligation."

Equally impossible is it to conceive, whatever may be the construction as to private ships, that a prince who stipulates a passage for his troops, or an asylum for his ships of war in distress, should mean to subject his army or his navy to the jurisdiction of a foreign sovereign. And if this cannot be presumed, the sovereign of the port must be considered as having conceded the privilege to the extent in which it must have been understood to be asked.

To the Court, it appears, that where, without treaty, the ports of a nation are open to the private and public ships of a friendly power, whose subjects have also liberty without special license, to enter the country for business or amusement, a clear distinction is to be drawn between the rights accorded to private individuals or private trading vessels, and those accorded to public armed ships which constitute a part of the military force of the nation.

The preceding reasoning, has maintained the propositions that all exemptions from territorial jurisdiction, must be derived from the consent of the sovereign of the territory; that this consent may be implied or expressed; and that when implied, its extent must be regulated by the nature of the case, and the views under which the parties requiring and conceding it must be supposed to act.

When private individuals of one nation spread themselves through another, as business or caprice may direct, mingling indiscriminately with the inhabitants of that other, or when merchant vessels enter for the purpose of trade, it would be obviously inconvenient and dangerous to society, and would subject the laws to continual infraction, and the government to degradation, if such individuals or merchants did not owe temporary and local allegiance, and were not amenable to the jurisdiction of the country. Nor can the foreign sovereign have any motive for wishing such exemption. His subjects thus passing into foreign countries, are not employed by him, nor are they engaged in national pursuits. Consequently there are powerful motives for not exempting persons of this description from the jurisdiction of the country in which they are found, and no one motive for requiring it. The implied license, therefore, under which they enter can never be construed to grant such exemption.

But in all respects different is the situation of a public armed ship. She constitutes a part of the military force of her nation; acts under the immediate and direct command of the sovereign; is employed by him in national objects. He has many and powerful motives for preventing those objects from being defeated by the interference of a foreign state. Such interference cannot take place without affecting his power and his dignity. The implied license therefore under which such vessel enters a friendly port, may reasonably be construed, and it seems to the Court, ought to be construed, as containing an exemption from the jurisdiction of the sovereign, within whose territory she claims the rights of hospitality.

Upon these principles, by the unanimous consent of nations, a foreigner is amenable to the laws of the place; but certainly in practice, nations have not yet asserted their jurisdiction over the public armed ships of a foreign sovereign entering a port open for their reception.

Bynkershoek, a jurist of great reputation, has indeed maintained that the property of a foreign sovereign is not distinguishable by any legal exemption from the property of an ordinary individual, and has quoted several cases in which courts have exercised jurisdiction over causes in which a foreign sovereign was made a party defendant.

Without indicating any opinion on this question, it may safely be affirmed, that there is a manifest distinction between the private property of the person who happens to be a prince, and that military force which supports the sovereign power, and maintains the dignity and the independence of a nation. A prince, by acquiring private property in a foreign country, may possibly be considered as subjecting that property to the territorial jurisdiction; he may be considered as so far laying down the prince, and assuming the character of a private individual; but this he cannot be presumed to do with respect to any portion of that armed force, which upholds his crown, and the nation he is entrusted to govern.

The only applicable case cited by Bynkershoek, is that of the Spanish ships of war seized in Flushing for a debt due from the king of Spain. In that case, the states general interposed; and there is reason to believe, from the manner in which the transaction is stated, that, either by the interference of government, or the decision of the court, the vessels were released.

This case of the Spanish vessel is, it is believed, the only case furnished by the history of the world, of an attempt made by an individual to assert a claim against a foreign prince, by seizing the armed vessels of the nation. That this proceeding was at once arrested by the government, in a nation which appears to have asserted the power of proceeding in the same manner against the private property of the prince, would seem to furnish no feeble argument in support of the universality of the opinion in favor of the exemption claimed for ships of war. The distinction made in our own laws between public and private ships would appear to proceed from the same opinion.

It seems then to the Court, to be a principle of public law, that national ships of war, entering the port of a friendly power open for their reception, are to be considered as exempted by the consent of that power from its jurisdiction.

Without doubt, the sovereign of the place is capable of destroying this implication. He may claim and exercise jurisdiction either by employing force, or by subjecting such vessels to the ordinary tribunals. But until such power be exerted in a manner not to be misunderstood, the sovereign cannot be considered as having imparted to the ordinary tribunals a jurisdiction, which it would be a breach of faith to exercise. Those general statutory provisions therefore which are descriptive of the ordinary jurisdiction of the judicial tribunals, which give an individual whose property has been wrested from him, a right to claim that property in the courts of the country, in which it is found, ought not, in the opinion of this Court, to be so construed as to give them jurisdiction in a case, in which the sovereign power has impliedly consented to wa[i]ve its jurisdiction.

The arguments in favor of this opinion which have been drawn from the general inability of the judicial power to enforce its decisions in cases of this description, from the consideration, that the sovereign power of the nation is alone competent to avenge wrongs committed by a sovereign, that the questions to which such wrongs give birth are rather questions of policy than of law, that they are for diplomatic, rather than legal discussion, are of great weight, and merit serious attention. But the argument has already been drawn to a length, which forbids a particular examination of these points.

The principles which have been stated, will now be applied to the case at bar.

In the present state of the evidence and proceedings, the Exchange must be considered as a vessel which was the property of the Libellants, whose claim is repelled by the fact, that she is now a national armed vessel, commissioned by, and in the service of the emperor of France. The evidence of this fact is not controverted. But it is contended, that it constitutes no bar to an enquiry into the validity of the title, by which the emperor holds this vessel. Every person, it is alleged, who is entitled to property brought within the jurisdiction of our Courts, has a right to assert his title in those Courts, unless there be some law taking his case out of the general rule. It is therefore said to be the right, and if it be the right, it is the duty of the Court, to enquire whether this title has been extinguished by an act, the validity of which is recognized by national or municipal law.

If the preceding reasoning be correct, the Exchange, being a public armed ship, in the service of a foreign sovereign, with whom the government of the United States is at peace, and having entered an American port open for her reception, on the terms on which ships of war are generally permitted to enter the ports of a friendly power, must be considered as having come into the American territory, under an implied promise, that while necessarily within it, and demeaning herself in a friendly manner, she should be exempt from the jurisdiction of the country.

If this opinion be correct, there seems to be a necessity for admitting that the fact might be disclosed to the Court by the suggestion of the Attorney for the United States.

I am directed to deliver it, as the opinion of the Court, that the sentence of the Circuit Court, reversing the sentence of the District Court, in the case of the Exchange be reversed, and that of the District Court, dismissing the libel be affirmed.

8

Brown v. United States

8 Cranch 110 (1814)

(See 1.8.11, no. 15)

9

United States v. Smith

5 Wheat. 153 (1820)

Story, J., delivered the opinion of the court.

The act of congress upon which this indictment is founded provides, "that if any person or persons whatsoever, shall, upon the high seas, commit the crime of piracy, as defined by the law of nations, and such offender or offenders shall be brought into, or found in the United States, every such offender or offenders shall, upon conviction thereof, &c., be punished with death."

The first point made at the bar is, whether this enactment be a constitutional exercise of the authority delegated to congress upon the subject of piracies. The constitution declares, that congress shall have power "to define and punish piracies and felonies committed on the high seas, and offences against the law of nations." The argument which has been urged in behalf of the prisoner is, that congress is bound to define, in terms, the offence of piracy, and is not at liberty to leave it to be ascertained by judicial interpretation. If the argument be well founded, it seems admitted by the counsel that it equally applies to the 8th section of the act of congress of 1790, c. 9, which declares, that robbery and murder committed on the high seas shall be deemed piracy; and yet, notwithstanding a series of contested adjudications on this section, no doubt has hitherto been breathed of its conformity to the constitution.

In our judgment, the construction contended for proceeds upon too narrow a view of the language of the constitution. The power given to congress is not merely "to define and punish piracies;" if it were, the words "to define," would seem almost superfluous, since the power to punish piracies would be held to include the power of ascertaining and fixing the definition of the crime. And it has been very justly observed, in a celebrated commentary, that the definition of piracies might have been left, without inconvenience, to the law of nations, though a legislative definition of them is to be found in most municipal codes. The Federalist, No. 42, p. 276. But the power is also given "to define and punish felonies on the high seas, and offences against the law of nations." The term "felonies" has been supposed, in the same work, not to have a very exact and determinate meaning in relation to offences at the common law committed within the body of a county. However this may be, in relation to offences on the high seas, it is necessarily somewhat indeterminate, since the term is not used in the criminal jurisprudence of the admiralty in the technical sense of the common law. See 3 Inst. 112; Hawk. P. C. c. 37; Moore, 576. Offences, too, against the law of nations, cannot, with any accuracy, be said to be completely ascertained and defined in any public code recognized by the common consent of nations. In respect, therefore, as well to felonies on the high seas as to offences against the law of nations, there is a peculiar fitness in giving the power to define as well as to punish; and there is not the slightest reason to doubt that this consideration had very great weight in producing the phraseology in question.

But supposing congress were bound, in all the cases included in the clause under consideration, to define the offence, still, there is nothing which restricts it to a mere logical enumeration, in detail, of all the facts constituting the offence. Congress may as well define by using a term of a known and determinate meaning, as by an express enumeration of all the particulars included in that term. That is certain which is by necessary reference made certain. When the act of 1790 declares that any person who shall commit the crime of robbery, or murder, on the high seas shall be deemed a pirate, the crime is not less clearly ascertained than it would be by using the definitions of these terms as they are found in our treatises of the common law. In fact, by such a reference, the definitions are necessarily included, as much as if they stood in the text of the act. In respect to murder, where "malice aforethought" is of the essence of the offence, even if the common-law definition were quoted in express terms, we should still be driven to deny that the definition was perfect, since the meaning of "malice aforethought" would remain to be gathered from the common law. There would then be no end to our difficulties, or our definitions, for each would involve some terms which might still require some new explanation. Such a construction of the constitution is, therefore, wholly inadmissible. To define piracies, in the sense of the constitution, is merely to enumerate the crimes which shall constitute piracy; and this may be done either by a reference to crimes having a technical name, and determinate extent, or by enumerating the acts in detail, upon which the punishment is inflicted.

It is next to be considered, whether the crime of piracy is defined by the law of nations with reasonable certainty. What the law of nations on this subject is, may be ascertained by consulting the works of jurists, writing professedly on public law; or by the general usage and practice of nations; or by judicial decisions recognizing and enforcing that law. There is scarcely a writer on the law of nations, who does not allude to piracy as a crime of a settled and determinate nature; and whatever may be the diversity of definitions, in other respects, all writers concur in holding that robbery, or forcible depredations upon the sea, *animo furandi*, is piracy. The same doctrine is held by all the great writers on maritime law, in terms that admit of no reasonable doubt. The common law, too, recognizes and punishes piracy as an offence, not against its own municipal code, but as an offence against the law of nations, (which is part of the common law,) as an offence against the universal law of society, a pirate being deemed an enemy of the human race. Indeed, until the statute of 28th of Henry VIII., c. 15, piracy was punishable in England only in the admiralty, as a civil law offence; and that statute, in changing the jurisdiction, has been universally admitted not to have changed the nature of the offence. Hawk. P. C. c. 37, s. 2; 3 Inst. 112. Sir Charles Hedges, in his charge at the admiralty sessions, in the case of Rex *v.* Dawson, 5 State Trials, declared, in emphatic terms, that "piracy is only a sea term for robbery, piracy being a robbery committed within the jurisdiction of the admiralty." Sir Leoline Jenkins, too, on a like occasion, declared that "a robbery, when committed upon the sea, is what we call piracy;" and he cited the civil law writers, in proof. And it is manifest, from the language of Sir William Blackstone, 4 Bl. Comm. 73, in his comments on piracy, that he considered the common-law definition as distinguishable in no essential respect from that of the law of nations. So that, whether we advert to writers on the common law, or the maritime law, or the law of nations, we shall find that they universally treat of piracy as an offence against the law of nations, and that its true definition, by that law, is robbery upon the sea. And the general practice of all nations in punishing all persons, whether natives or foreigners, who have committed this offence against any persons whatsoever, with whom they are in amity, is a conclusive proof that the offence is supposed to depend, not upon the particular provisions of any municipal code, but upon the law of nations, both for its definition and punishment. We have, therefore, no hesitation in declaring that piracy, by the law of nations, is robbery upon the sea, and that it is sufficiently and constitutionally defined by the 5th section of the act of 1819.

Another point has been made in this case, which is, that the special verdict does not contain sufficient facts upon which the court can pronounce that the prisoner is guilty of piracy. We are of a different opinion. The special verdict finds that the prisoner is guilty of the plunder and robbery charged in the indictment; and finds certain additional facts from which it is most manifest that he and his associates were, at the time of committing the offence, freebooters upon the sea, not under the acknowledged authority, or deriving protection from the flag or commission of any government. If, under such circumstances, the offence be not piracy, it is difficult to conceive any which would more completely fit the definition.

It is to be certified to the circuit court, that upon the facts stated, the case is piracy, as defined by the law of nations, so as to be punishable under the act of congress of the 3d of March, 1819.

LIVINGSTON, J., dissented. In a case affecting life, no apology can be necessary for expressing my dissent from the opinion which has just been delivered.

The only question of any importance in this case is whether the act of the 3d of March, 1819, be a constitutional exercise of the power delegated to congress of "defining and punishing piracies?" The act declares, that any person who shall commit on the high seas the crime of piracy, as defined by the law of nations, shall be punished with death. The special power here given to define piracy, can be attributed to no other cause, than to the uncertainty which it was known existed on this subject in the laws of nations, and which it must have been the intention of the framers of the constitution to remove, by conferring on the national legislature the power which has been mentioned. It was well known to the members of the federal convention, that in treatises on the law of nations, or in some of them, at least, definitions of piracy might be found; but it must have been as well known to them that there was not such a coincidence on this subject, as to render a reference to that code a desirable or safe mode of proceeding, in a criminal and especially in a capital case. If it had been intended to adopt the definition or definitions of this crime, so far as they were to be collected from the different commentators on this code, with all the uncertainty and difficulty attending a research for that purpose, it might as well at once have been adopted as a standard, by the constitution itself. The object, therefore, of referring its definition to congress was, and could have been no other than, to enable that body to select from sources it might think proper, and then to declare, and with reasonable precision to define, what act or acts should constitute this crime; and having done so, to annex to it such punishment as might be thought proper. Such a mode of proceeding would be consonant with the universal practice in this country, and with those feelings of humanity which are ever opposed to the putting in jeopardy the life of a fellow-being, unless for the contravention of a rule which has been previously prescribed, and in language so plain and explicit as not to be misunderstood by any one. Can this be the case, or can a crime be said to be defined, even to a common intent, when those who are desirous of information on the subject are referred to a code, without knowing with any certainty where it is to be found, and from which even those to whom it may be accessible, can with difficulty decide, in many cases, whether a particular act be piracy or not? Although it cannot be denied that some writers on the law of nations do declare what acts are deemed piratical, yet it is certain that they do not all agree; and if they did, it would seem unreasonable to impose upon that class of men, who are the most liable to commit offences of this description, the task of looking beyond the written law of their own country for a definition of them. If in criminal cases every thing is sufficiently certain, which by reference may be rendered so, which was an argument used at bar, it is not perceived why a reference to the laws of China, or to any other foreign code, would not have answered the purpose quite as well as the one which has been resorted to. It is not certain, that, on examination, the crime would not be found to be more accurately defined in the code thus referred to, than in any writer on the law of nations; but the objection to the references in both cases is the same: that it is the duty of congress to incorporate into their own statutes a definition in terms, and not to refer the citizens of the United States for rules of conduct to the statutes or laws of any foreign country, with which it is not to be presumed that they are acquainted. Nor does it make any difference in this case, that the law of nations forms part of the law of every civilized country. This may be the case to a certain extent; but as to criminal cases, and as to the offence of piracy in particular, the law of nations could not be supposed of itself to form a rule of action, and therefore, a reference to it, in this instance, must be regarded in the same light, as a reference to any other foreign code. But it is said, that murder and robbery have been declared to be punishable by the laws of the United States, without any definition of what act or acts shall constitute either of these offences. This may be; but both murder and robbery, with arson, burglary, and some other crimes, are defined by writers on the common law, which is part of the law of every State in the Union, of which, for the most obvious reasons, no one is allowed to allege his ignorance in excuse for any crime he may commit. Nor is there any hardship in this, for the great body of the community have it in their power to become acquainted with the criminal code under which they live; not so when acts which constitute a crime are to be collected from a variety of writers, either in different languages, or under the disadvantage of translations, and from a code with whose provisions even professional men are not always acquainted. By the same clause of the constitution, congress have power to punish offences against the law of nations, and yet it would hardly be deemed a fair and legitimate execution of this authority, to declare that all offences against the law of nations, without defining any one of them, should be punished with death. Such mode of legislation is but badly calculated to furnish that precise and accurate information, in criminal cases, which it is the duty and ought to be the object of every legislature to impart.

Upon the whole, my opinion is, that there is not to be found in the act that definition of piracy which the constitution requires, and that, therefore, judgment on the special verdict ought to be rendered for the prisoner.

10

The Antelope
10 Wheat. 66 (1825)

(See 1.9.1, no. 25)

11

James Kent, Commentaries
1:1–4, 15–19, 171–76
1826

When the United States ceased to be a part of the British empire, and assumed the character of an independent nation, they became subject to that system of rules which reason, morality, and custom had established among the civilized nations of Europe, as their public law. During the war of the American revolution, Congress claimed cognizance of all matters arising upon the law of nations, and they professed obedience to that law, "according to the general usages of Europe." By this law we are to understand that code of public instruction, which defines the rights and prescribes the duties of nations, in their intercourse with each other. The faithful observance of this law is essential to national character, and to the happiness of mankind. According to the observation of the President de Montesquieu, it is founded on the principle, that different nations ought to do each other as much good in peace, and as little harm in war, as possible, without injury to their true interests. But, as the precepts of this code are not defined in every case with perfect precision, and as nations have no common civil tribunal to resort to for the interpretation and execution of this law, it is often very difficult to ascertain, to the satisfaction of the parties concerned, its precise injunctions and extent; and a still greater difficulty is the want of adequate pacific means to secure obedience to its dictates.

There has been a difference of opinion among writers, concerning the foundations of this law. It has been considered by some as a mere system of positive institutions, founded upon consent and usage; while others have insisted that the law of nations was essentially the same as the law of nature, applied to the conduct of nations, in the character of moral persons, susceptible of obligation and laws. We are not to adopt either of these theories as exclusively true. The most useful and practical part of the law of nations is, no doubt, instituted or positive law, founded on usage, consent, and agreement. But it would be improper to separate this law entirely from natural jurisprudence, and not to consider it as deriving much of its force, and dignity, and sanction, from the same principles of right reason, and the same view of the nature and constitution of man, from which the science of morality is deduced. There is a natural and a positive law of nations. By the former, every state, in its relations with other states, is bound to conduct itself with justice, good faith, and benevolence; and this application of the law of nature has been called by Vattel, the necessary law of nations, because nations are bound by the law of nature to observe it; and it is termed by others, the internal law of nations, because it is obligatory upon them in point of conscience.

We ought not, therefore, to separate the science of public law from that of ethics, nor to encourage the dangerous suggestion, that governments are not as strictly bound by the obligations of truth, justice, and humanity, in relation to other powers, as they are in the management of their own local concerns. States, or bodies politic, are to be considered as moral persons, having a public will, capable and free to do right and wrong, inasmuch as they are collections of individuals, each of whom carries with him into the service of the community, the same binding law of morality and religion which ought to control his conduct in private life. The law of nations is a complex system, composed of various ingredients. It consists of general principles of right and justice, equally suitable to the government of individuals in a state of natural equality, and to the relation and conduct of nations; of a collection of usages and customs, the growth of civilization and commerce; and of a code of conventional or positive law. In the absence of these latter regulations, the intercourse and conduct of nations are to be governed by principles fairly to be deduced from the rights and duties of nations, and the nature of moral obligation; and we have the authority of the lawyers of antiquity, and of some of the first masters in the modern school of public law, for placing the moral obligation of nations and of individuals on similar grounds, and for considering individual and national morality as parts of one and the same science.

The law of nations, so far as it is founded on the principles of natural law, is equally binding in every age, and upon all mankind. But the Christian nations of Europe, and their descendants on this side of the Atlantic, by the vast superiority of their attainments in arts, and science, and commerce, as well as in policy and government; and, above all, by the brighter light, the more certain truths, and the more definite sanction, which Christianity has communicated to the ethical jurisprudence of the ancients, have established a law of nations peculiar to themselves. They form together a community of nations, united by religion, manners, morals, humanity, and science, and united also by the mutual advantages of commercial intercourse, by the habit of forming alliances and treaties with each other, of interchanging ambassadors, and of studying and recognising the same writers and systems of public law.

. . . . .

Thus stood the law of nations at the age of Grotius. It had been rescued, to a very considerable extent, from the cruel usages and practices of the northern barbarians. It had been restored to some degree of science and civility by the influence of Christianity, the study of the Roman law, and the spirit of commerce. It had grown greatly in value and efficacy, from the intimate connexion and constant intercourse of the modern nations of Europe, who were derived from a common origin, and were governed by similar institutions, manners, laws, and religion. But it was still in a state of extreme disorder, and its principles were but little known, and less observed. It consisted of a series of undigested precedents, without order or authority. Grotius has, therefore, been justly considered as the father of the law of nations; and he arose like a splendid luminary, dispelling darkness and confusion, and imparting light, and guides, and security, to the intercourse of nations. It is said that Lord Bacon first suggested the necessity of such a work as that of Grotius, reducing the law of nations to the certainty and precision of a regular science. Grotius has himself fully explained the reasons which led him to undertake his necessary, and most useful, and immortal work. He found the sentiment universally prevalent, not only among the vulgar, but among men of reputed widsom and learning, that war was a stranger to all justice, and that no commonwealth could be governed without injustice. The saying of Euphemus in Thucydides, he perceived to be in almost every one's mouth, that nothing which was useful was unjust. Many persons, who were friends to justice in private life, made no account of it in a whole nation, and did not consider it as applicable to rulers. He perceived a horrible licentiousness and cruelty in war, throughout the Christian world, of which barbarians might be ashamed. When men took up arms, there was no longer any reverence for law either human or divine, and it seemed as if some malignant fury was sent forth into the world, with a general license for the commission of all manner of wickedness and crime.

The object of Grotius was to correct these false theories and pernicious maxims, by showing a community of sentiment among the wise and learned of all nations and ages, in favour of the natural law of morality. He likewise undertook to show that justice was of perpetual obligation, and essential to the well being of every society, and that the great commonwealth of nations stood in need of law, and the observance of faith, and the practice of justice. His object was to digest in one systematic code, the principles of public right, and to supply authorities for almost every case in the conduct of nations; and he had the honour of reducing the law of nations to a system, and of producing a work which has been resorted to as the standard of authority in every succeeding age. The more it is studied, the more will our admiration be excited at the consummate execution of the plan, and the genius and erudition of the author. There was no system of the kind extant, that had been produced by the ancient philosophers of Greece, or by the primitive Christians. The work of Aristotle on the rights of war, and the writings of the Romans on their fecial law, had not survived the wreck of ancient literature; and the treatises of some learned moderns on public law, were most imperfect, and exceedingly defective in illustrations from history, and in omitting to place their decisions upon the true foundations of equity and justice. Grotius, therefore, went purposely into the details of history and the usages of nations, and he resorted to the testimony of philosophers, historians, orators, poets, civilians, and divines, because they were the materials out of which the science of morality was formed; and when many men, at different times and places, unanimously affirmed the same thing for truth, it ought to be ascribed to some universal cause. His unsparing citation of authorities, in support of what the present age may consider very plain and undisputed truths, has been censured by many persons as detracting from the value of the work. On the other hand, the support that he gave to those truths, by the concurrent testimony of all nations and ages, has been justly supposed to contribute to the reverence for the principles of international justice, which has since distinguished the European nations.

Among the disciples of Grotius, Puffendorf has always held the first rank. His work went more at large into the principles of natural law, and combined the science of ethics with what may be more strictly called the law of nations. It is copious in detail, but of very little practical value in teaching us what the law of nations is at this day. It is rather a treatise on moral philosophy than on international law; and the same thing may be said of the works of Wolfius, Burlamaqui, and Rutherforth. The Summary of the Law of Nations, by Professor Martens, is a treatise of greater practical utility, but it is only a very partial view of the system, being confined to the customary and conventional law of the modern nations of Europe. Bynkershoeck's treatise on the law of war, has always been received as of great authority, on that particular branch of the science of the law of nations, and the subject is ably and copiously discussed. The work is replete with practical illustration, though too exclusive in its references to the ordinances of his own country, to render his authority very unquestionable. The most popular, and the most elegant writer on the law of nations, is Vattel, whose method has been greatly admired. He has been cited, for the last half century, more freely than any one of the public jurists; but he is very deficient in philosophical precision. His topics are loosely, and often tediously and diffusively discussed, and he is not sufficiently supported by the authority of precedents, which constitute the foundation of the positive law of nations. There is no one work which combines, in just proportions, and with entire satisfaction, an accurate and comprehensive view of the necessary and of the instituted law of nations, and in which principles are sufficiently supported by argument, authority, and examples. Since the age of Grotius, the code of war has been vastly enlarged and improved, and its rights better defined, and its severities greatly mitigated. The rights of maritime capture, the principles of the law of prize, and the duties and privileges of neutrals, have grown into very important titles in the system of national law. We now appeal to more accurate, more authentic, more precise, and more commanding evidence of the rules of public law, by a reference to the decisions of those tribunals, to whom, in every country, the administration of that branch of jurisprudence is specially intrusted. We likewise appeal to the official documents and ordinances of particular states, which have professed to reduce into a systematic code, for the direction of their own tribunals, and for the information of foreign powers, the law of nations, on those points which relate particularly to the rights of commerce, and the duties of neutrality. But in the absence of higher and more authoritative sanctions, the ordinances of foreign states, the opinions of eminent statesmen, and the writings of distinguished jurists, are regarded as of great consideration on questions not settled by conventional law. In cases where the principal jurists agree, the presumption will be very great in favour of the solidity of their maxims; and no civilized nation, that does not arrogantly set all ordinary law and justice at defiance, will venture to disregard the uniform sense of the established writers on international law. England and the United States have been equally disposed to acknowledge the authority of the works of jurists, writing professedly on public law, and the binding force of the general usage and practice of nations, and the still greater respect due to judicial decisions recognising and enforcing the law of nations. In all our foreign negotiations, and domestic discussions of questions of national law, we have paid the most implicit respect to the practice of Europe, and the opinions of her most distinguished civilians. In England, the report, made in 1753, to the king, in answer to the Prussian memorial, is very satisfactory evidence of the obedience shown to the great standing authorities on the law of nations, to which I have alluded. And in a case which came before Lord Mansfield, in 1764, in the K. B. he referred to a decision of Lord Talbot, who had declared that the law of nations was to be collected from the practice of different nations, and the authority of writers; and who had argued from such authorities as Grotius, Barbeyrac, Bynkershoeck, Wiquefort, &c. in a case where British authority was silent. The most celebrated collections and codes of maritime law, such as the *Consolato del Mare,* the laws of Oleron, the laws of the Hanseatic league, and, above all, the marine ordinances of Lewis XIV., are also referred to, as containing the most authentic evidence of the immemorial and customary law of Europe.

. . . . .

The Congress of the United States, during the time of the American war, discovered great solicitude to maintain inviolate the obligations of the law of nations, and to have infractions of it punished in the only way that was then lawful, by the exercise of the authority of the legislatures of the several states. They recommended to the states to provide expeditious, exemplary, and adequate punishment, for the violation of safe conducts or passports, granted under the authority of Congress, to the subjects of a foreign power in time of war; and for the commission of acts of hostility against persons in amity or league with the United States; and for the infractions of treaties and conventions to which the United States were a party; and for infractions of the immunities of ambassadors, and other public ministers.

Piracy is robbery, or a forcible depredation on the high seas, without lawful authority, and done *animo furandi.* It is the same offence at sea with robbery on land; and all the writers on the law of nations, and on the maritime law of Europe, agree in this definition of piracy. Pirates have been regarded by all civilized nations as the enemies of the human race, and the most atrocious violators of the universal law of society. They are every where pursued and punished with death; and the severity with which the law has animadverted upon this crime, arises from its enormity and danger, the cruelty that accompanies it, the necessity of checking it, the difficulty of detection, and the facility with which robberies may be committed upon pacific traders, in the solitude of the ocean. Every nation has a right to attack and exterminate them without any declaration of war; for though pirates may form a loose and temporary association among themselves, and re-establish in some degree those laws of justice which they have violated with the rest of the world, yet they are not considered as a national body, or entitled to the laws of war as one of the community of nations. They acquire no rights by conquest; and the law of nations, and the municipal law of every country, authorize the true owner to reclaim his property taken by pirates, wherever it can be found; and they do not recognise any title to be derived from an act of piracy. The principle, that *a piratis et latronibus capta dominium non mutant,* is the received opinion of ancient civilians, and modern writers on general jurisprudence; and the same doctrine was maintained in the English courts of common law prior to the great modern improvements made in the science of the law of nations.

By the constitution of the United States, Congress were authorized to define and punish piracies and felonies committed on the high seas, and offences against the law of nations. In pursuance of this authority, it was declared by the act of Congress of April 30th, 1790, sec. 8. that murder or robbery committed on the high seas, or in any river, haven, or bay, out of the jurisdiction of any particular state, or any other offence, which, if committed within the body of a county, would, by the laws of the United States, be punishable with death, should be adjudged to be piracy and felony, and punishable with death. It was further declared, that if any captain or mariner should piratically and feloniously run away with any vessel, or any goods or merchandise to the value of fifty dollars; or should yield up any such vessel voluntarily to pirates; or if any seaman should forcibly endeavour to hinder his commander from defending the ship or goods committed to his trust, or should make a revolt in the ship; every such offender should be adjudged a pirate and felon, and be punishable with death. Accessaries to such piracies before the fact, are punishable in like manner; but accessaries after the fact are only punishable with fine and imprisonment. And, by the act of March 3d, 1819, sec. 5. (and which act was made perpetual by the act of 15th of May, 1820, sec. 2.) Congress declared, that if any person on the high seas should commit the crime of *piracy, as defined by the law of nations,* he should, on conviction, suffer death. It was again declared, by the act of Congress of 15th of May, 1820, sec. 3. that if any person upon the high seas, or in any open roadstead, or bay, or river, where the sea ebbs and flows, commits the crime of robbery in and upon any vessel, or the lading thereof, or the crew, he should be adjudged a pirate. So, if any person concerned in any particular enterprise, or belonging to any particular crew, should land, and commit robbery on shore, such an offender should also be adjudged a pirate. The statute, in this respect, seems to be only declaratory of the law of nations; for, upon the doctrine of the case of *Lindo* v. *Rodney,* such plunder and robbery ashore, by the crew, and with the aid of vessels, is a marine case, and of admiralty jurisdiction.

Under these legislative provisions, it has been made a question, whether it was sufficient to refer to the law of nations for a definition of piracy, without giving the crime a precise definition in terms. The point was settled in the case of the *United States* v. *Smith;* and it was there held not to be necessary to give by statute a more logical enumeration in detail of all the facts constituting the offence, and that Congress might as well define it by using a term of a known and determinate meaning, as by expressly mentioning all the particulars included in that term. The crime of piracy was defined by the law of nations with reasonable certainty, and it does not depend upon the particular provisions of any municipal code for its definition and punishment. Robbery on the high seas is, therefore, piracy by the act of Congress, as well as by the law of nations.

There can be no doubt of the right of Congress to pass laws punishing pirates, though they may be foreigners, and may have committed no particular offence against the United States. It is of no importance for the purpose of giving jurisdiction on *whom* or *where* a piratical offence has been committed. A pirate, who is one by the law of nations, may be tried and punished in any country where he may be found, for he is reputed to be out of the protection of all laws and privileges. The statute of any government may declare an offence committed on board its own vessels to be piracy, and such an offence will be punishable exclusively by the nation which passes the statute. But piracy, under the law of nations, is an offence against all nations, and punishable by all. In the case of the *United States* v. *Palmer,* it was held, that the act of Congress of 1790 was intended to punish offences against the United States, and not offences against the human race; and that the crime of robbery, committed by a person who was not a citizen of the United States, on the high seas, on board of a ship belonging exclusively to subjects of a foreign state, was not piracy under the act, and was not punishable in the courts of the United States. The offence, in such a case, must, therefore, be left to be punished by the nation under whose flag the vessel sailed, and within whose particular jurisdiction all on board the vessel were. This decision was according to the law and practice of nations, for it is a clear and settled principle, that the jurisdiction of every nation extends to its own citizens, on board of its own public and private vessels at sea. The case applied only to the fact of robbery committed at sea, on board of a foreign vessel, at the time belonging exclusively to subjects of a foreign state; and it was not intended to decide, that the same offence, committed on board of a vessel not belonging to the subjects of any foreign power, was not piracy. The same court, afterwards, in the case of the *United States* v. *Klintock,* admitted, that murder or robbery, committed on the high seas, by persons on board of a vessel not at the time belonging to the subjects of any foreign power, but in possession of a crew acting in defiance of all law, and acknowledging obedience to no government or flag whatsoever, fell within the purview of the act of Congress, and was punishable in the courts of the United States. Persons of that description were pirates, and proper objects for the penal code of all nations. The act of Congress did not apply to offences committed against the particular sovereignty of a foreign power; or to murder or robbery committed in a vessel belonging at the time, in fact as well as in right, to the subject of a foreign state, and, in virtue of such property, subject at the time to his control. But it applied to offences committed against all nations, by persons who, by common consent, were equally amenable to the laws of all nations.

It was further held, in the case of the *United States* v. *Pirates,* and in the case of the *United States* v. *Holmes,* in pursuance of the same principle, that the moment a vessel assumed a piratical character, and was taken from her officers, and proceeded on a piratical cruise, she lost all claim to national character, and the crew, whether citizens or foreigners, were equally punishable, under the act of Congress, for acts of piracy; and it would be immaterial what was the national character of the vessel before she assumed a piratical character. Piracy is an offence within the criminal jurisdiction of all nations. It is against all, and punished by all; and the plea of *autrefois acquit,* resting on a prosecution instituted in the courts of any civilized state, would be a good plea in any other civilized state. As the act of Congress of 1790, declares every offence committed at sea to be piracy, which would be punishable with death if committed on land, it may be considered as enlarging the definition of piracy, so as not only to include every offence which is piracy by the law of nations, and the act of Congress of 1819, but other offences which were not piracy until made so by statute.

12

William Rawle, A View of the Constitution of the United States 106–9
1829 (2d ed.)

The regulation of foreign commerce appertains to congress alone, and the punishment of offences committed on the high seas is an unavoidable incident to this power: as soon as the Constitution was adopted, the power of the states in this respect was at an end. But the principle of this exclusive jurisdiction might perhaps be further extended. After the territorial boundaries of a nation are left, the sea becomes the common property of all nations, and the rights and privileges relative thereto being regulated by the law of nations and treaties, properly belong to the national jurisdiction, and would be inconveniently retained by the states which, in this respect, form only parts of the nation.

It does not seem to have been necessary to define the crime of piracy. There is no act on which the universal sense of nations has been so fully and distinctly expressed, as there is no act which is so universally punished. The pirate is the enemy of all nations, and all nations are the enemy of the pirate.

Felony is a term derived from the common law of England, and when committed on the high seas, amounts to piracy. The power to define either may have been introduced to authorize congress to qualify and reduce the acts which should amount to either. It is coupled with the power to punish, and this power extends not merely to citizens of the United States, but to all others except the citizens or subjects of a foreign state sailing under its flag and committing acts which amount to piracy; but general piracy committed by persons on board of a vessel, acting in defiance of all law, and acknowledging obedience to no government, are punishable in our courts, and in the courts of all nations.

By the high seas we are to understand not only the ocean out of sight of land, but waters on the sea coast beyond the boundaries of low water mark, although in a roadstead or bay, within the jurisdiction or limits of one of the states or of a foreign government.

A power to *define and to punish offences against the law of nations* is contained in the same paragraph, but it is doubtful whether the power to punish ought to be considered as an exclusive one. The law of nations forms a part of the common law of every civilized country; violations of it may be committed as well on land as at sea, and while the jurisdiction of the separate states is admitted to be withdrawn from them in regard to acts committed on the sea, it does not seem to follow that it is superseded as to those on shore.

Such acts may be of various kinds, and although the most prominent subjects under this head are those which relate to the persons and privileges of ambassadors, yet in many other particulars, infringements of the law of nations may be proper subjects of state jurisdiction. But even if an outrage were committed on a diplomatic character, and he preferred the redress to be obtained from a state court to that afforded by the courts of the United States, it is not perceived that this clause would prohibit him from so doing; yet whether the power is exclusive or not, on which some further remarks will be made, the power to define and to punish this class of offences is with great propriety given to congress. The United States being alone responsible to foreign nations for all that affects their mutual intercourse, and tends to promote the general relations of good order and just demeanour, it rests with them alone to declare what shall constitute such crimes, and to prescribe suitable punishments.

When such laws are made, they become binding rules of decision as well on the state courts as on the courts of the United States; but if cases arise for which no such statutory provision has been made, both these descriptions of courts are thrown upon those general principles, which being enforced by other nations, those nations have a right to require us to apply and enforce in their favour, or for the benefit of their citizens and subjects.

13

UNITED STATES v. BENNER

24 Fed. Cas. 1084, no. 14,568 (C.C.E.D.Pa. 1830)

(See 2.2.2–3, no. 33)

14

JOSEPH STORY, COMMENTARIES ON THE CONSTITUTION 3:§§ 1153–62 1833

---

§ 1153. By the confederation the sole and exclusive power was given to congress "of appointing courts for the trial of piracies and felonies committed on the high seas." But there was no power expressly given to define and punish piracies and felonies. Congress, however, proceeded to pass an ordinance for the erection of a court for such trials, and prescribed the punishment of death upon conviction of the offence. But they never undertook to define, what piracies or felonies were. It was taken for granted, that these were sufficiently known and understood at the common law; and that resort might, in all such cases, be had to that law, as the recognised jurisprudence of the Union.

§ 1154. If the clause of the constitution had been confined to piracies, there would not have been any necessity of conferring the power to define the crime, since the power to punish would necessarily be held to include the power of ascertaining and fixing the definition of the crime. Indeed, there would not seem to be the slightest reason to define the crime at all; for piracy is perfectly well known and understood in the law of nations, though it is often found defined in mere municipal codes. By the law of nations, robbery or forcible depredation upon the sea, *animo furandi*, is piracy. The common law, too, recognises, and punishes piracy as an offence, not against its own municipal code, but as an offence against the universal law of nations; a pirate being deemed an enemy of the human race. The common law, therefore, deems piracy to be robbery on the sea; that is, the same crime, which it denominates robbery, when committed on land. And if congress had simply declared, that piracy should be punished with death, the crime would have been sufficiently defined. Congress may as well define by using a term of a known and determinate meaning, as by an express enumeration of all the particulars included in that term; for that is certain, which, by reference, is made certain. If congress should declare murder a felony, no body would doubt, what was intended by murder. And, indeed, if congress should proceed to declare, that homicide, "with malice aforethought," should be deemed murder, and a felony; there would still be the same necessity of ascertaining, from the common law, what constituted malice aforethought. So, that there would be no end to difficulties or definitions; for each successive definition might involve some terms, which would still require some new explanation. But the true intent of the constitution in this part, was, not merely to define piracy, as known to the law of nations, but to enumerate what crimes in the national code should be deemed piracies. And so the power has been practically expounded by congress.

§ 1155. But the power is not merely to define and punish piracies, but *felonies,* and *offences* against *the law of nations;* and on this account, the power to define, as well as to punish, is peculiarly appropriate. It has been remarked, that felony is a term of loose signification, even in the common law; and of various import in the statute law of England. Mr. Justice Blackstone says, that felony, in the general acceptation of the English law, comprises every species of crime, which occasioned at common law the forfeiture of lands and goods. This most frequently happens in those crimes, for which a capital punishment either is, or was liable to be inflicted. All offences now capital by the English law are felonies; but there are still some offences, not capital, which are yet felonies, (such as suicide, petty larceny, and homicide by chance medley;) that is, they subject the committers of them to some forfeiture, either of lands or goods. But the idea of capital punishment has now become so associated, in the English law, with the idea of felony, that if an act of parliament makes a new offence felony, the law implies, that it shall be punished with death, as well as with forfeiture.

§ 1156. Lord Coke has given a somewhat different account of the meaning of felony; for he says *"ex vi termini significat quodlibet capitale crimen felleo animo perpetratum;"* (that is, it signifies every capital offence committed with a felonious intent;) "in which sense murder is said to be done *per feloniam,* and is so appropriated by law, as that *felonice* cannot be expressed by any other word. This has been treated as a fanciful derivation, and not as correct, as that of Mr. J. Blackstone, who has followed out that of Spelman.

§ 1157. But whatever may be the true import of the word felony at the common law, with reference to municipal offences, in relation to offences on the high seas, its meaning is necessarily somewhat indeterminate; since the term is not used in the criminal jurisprudence of the Admiralty in the technical sense of the common law. Lord Coke long ago stated, that a pardon of felonies would not pardon piracy, for "piracy or robbery on the high seas was no felony, whereof the common law took any knowledge, &c.; but was only punishable by the civil law, &c.; the attainder by which law wrought no forfeiture of lands or corruption of blood." And he added, that the statute of 28 Henry 8, ch. 15, which created the High Commission Court for the trial of "all treasons, felonies, robberies, murders, and confederacies, committed in or upon the high sea, &c.," did not alter the offence, or make the offence felony, but left the offence as it was before the act, viz. felony only by the civil law.

§ 1158. Offences against the law of nations are quite as important, and cannot with any accuracy be said to be completely ascertained, and defined in any public code, recognized by the common consent of nations. In respect, therefore, as well to felonies on the high seas, as to offences against the law of nations, there is a peculiar fitness in giving to congress the power to define, as well as to punish. And there is not the slightest reason to doubt, that this consideration had very great weight with the convention, in producing the phraseology of the clause. On either subject it would have been inconvenient, if not impracticable, to have referred to the codes of the states, as well from their imperfection, as their different enumeration of the offences. Certainty, as well as uniformity, required, that the power to define and punish should reach over the whole of these classes of offences.

§ 1159. What is the meaning of "high seas" within the intent of this clause does not seem to admit of any serious doubt. The phrase embraces not only the waters of the ocean, which are out of sight of land, but the waters on the sea coast below low water mark, whether within the territorial boundaries of a foreign nation, or of a domestic state. Mr. Justice Blackstone has remarked, that the *main sea* or high sea begins at the low water mark. But between the high water mark and the low water mark, where the tide ebbs and flows, the common law and the admiralty have *divisum imperium,* an alternate jurisdiction, one upon the water, when it is full sea; the other upon the land, when it is an ebb. He doubtless here refers to the waters of the ocean on the sea-coast, and not in creeks and inlets. Lord Hale says, that the sea is either that, which lies within the body of the county or without. That, which lies without the body of a county, is called the main sea, or ocean. So far, then, as regards the states of the Union, "high seas" may be taken to mean that part of the ocean, which washes the sea-coast, and is without the body of any county, according to the common law; and, so far as regards foreign nations, any waters on their sea-coast, below low-water mark.

§ 1160. Upon the propriety of granting this power to the national government, there does not seem to have been any controversy; or if any, none of a serious nature. It is obvious, that this power has an intimate connexion and relation with the power to regulate commerce and intercourse with foreign nations, and the rights and duties of the national government in peace and war, arising out of the law of nations. As the United States are responsible to foreign governments for all violations of the law of nations, and as the welfare of the Union is essentially connected with the conduct of our citizens in regard to foreign nations, congress ought to possess the power to define and punish all such offences, which may interrupt our intercourse and harmony with, and our duties to them.

§ 1161. Whether this power, so far as it concerns the law of nations, is an exclusive one, has been doubted by a learned commentator. As, up to the present time, that question may be deemed for most purposes to be a mere speculative question, it is not proposed to discuss it, since it may be better reasoned out, when it shall require judicial decision.

§ 1162. The clause, as it was originally reported in the first draft of the constitution, was in substance, though not in language, as it now stands. It was subsequently amended; and in the second draft stood in its present terms. There is, however, in the Supplement to the Journal, an obscure statement of a question put, to strike out the word "punish," seeming to refer to this clause, which was carried in the affirmative by the vote of six states against five. Yet the constitution itself bears testimony, that it did not prevail.

15

Case of Jose Ferreira dos Santos

2 Marshall's C.C. 493 (C.C.D.Va. 1835)

(See 4.2.2, no. 9)

SEE ALSO:

Records of the Federal Convention, Farrand 2:143, 168, 312, 570, 595

Edmund Randolph, Who Privileged from Arrest, 26 June 1792, 1 Ops. Atty. Gen. 26

James Iredell, Charge to Grand Jury, (C.C.D.Md., 1793) Life 2:392

Henfield's Case, 11 Fed. Cas. 1099, no. 6,360 (C.C.D.Pa. 1793)

William Bradford, Respect Due to Consuls, 20 Feb. 1794, 1 Ops. Atty. Gen. 41

House of Representatives, Sequestration of British Debts, 27–28 Mar., 10–11 Apr. 1794, Annals 4:537–41, 543–49, 553–54, 569–70, 589–90

James Iredell, Charge to Grand Jury (C.C.D.Pa., 12 Apr. 1796), Life 2:467–74

Charles Lee, Consular Privileges, 21 Nov. 1797, 1 Ops. Atty. Gen. 77

Charles Lee, Actions against Foreigner, 29 Dec. 1797, 1 Ops. Atty. Gen. 81

Charles Lee, Service of Process aboard a British Ship-of-War, 11 Mar. 1799, 1 Ops. Atty. Gen. 87

United States v. *McGill,* 4 Dall. 426 (C.C.D.Pa. 1806)

United States v. *Hand,* 26 Fed. Cas. 103, no. 15,297 (C.C.D.Pa. 1810)

Richard Rush, Prosecutions for Piracy, 29 Aug. 1815, 1 Ops. Atty. Gen. 185

The Nereide, 9 Cranch 388 (1815)

L'Invincible, 1 Wheat. 238 (1816)

United States v. *Palmer,* 3 Wheat. 610 (1818)

The Estrella, 4 Wheat. 298 (1819)

United States v. *Wiltberger,* 5 Wheat. 76 (1820)

United States v. *Klintock,* 5 Wheat. 144 (1820)

United States v. *The Pirates,* 5 Wheat. 184 (1820)

United States v. *Holmes,* 5 Wheat. 412 (1820)

William Wirt, Foreign Requisitions—Law of Nations, 20 Nov. 1821, 1 Ops. Atty. Gen. 510

The Bello Corunes, 6 Wheat. 151 (1821)

William Wirt, Statutory Piracy, 28 Nov. 1825, 2 Ops. Atty. Gen. 19

The Marianna Flora, 11 Wheat. 1 (1826)

James Kent, Commentaries 1:21, 23–44 (1826)

United States v. *Grush,* 26 Fed. Cas. 48, no. 15,268 (C.C.D.Mass. 1829)

Article 1, Section 8, Clause 11

To declare War, grant Letters of Marque and Reprisal, and make Rules concerning Captures on Land and Water;

1

William Blackstone, Commentaries 1:249–51 1765

III. Upon the same principle the king has also the sole prerogative of making war and peace. For it is held by all the writers on the law of nature and nations, that the right of making war, which by nature subsisted in every individual, is given up by all private persons that enter into society, and is vested in the sovereign power: and this right is given up not only by individuals, but even by the intire body of people, that are under the dominion of a sovereign. It would indeed be extremely improper, that any number of subjects should have the power of binding the supreme magistrate, and putting him against his will in a state of war. Whatever hostilities therefore may be committed by private citizens, the state ought not to be affected thereby; unless that should justify their proceedings, and thereby become partner in the guilt. Such unauthorized voluntiers in violence are not ranked among open enemies, but are treated like pirates and robbers: according to that rule of the civil law; *hostes hi sunt qui nobis, aut quibus nos, publice bellum decrevimus: caeteri latrones aut praedones sunt.* And the reason which is given by Grotius, why according to the law of nations a denunciation of war ought always to precede the actual commencement of hostilities, is not so much that the enemy may be put upon his guard, (which is matter rather of magnanimity than right) but that it may be certainly clear that the war is not undertaken by private persons, but by the will of the whole community; whose right of willing is in this case transferrèd to the supreme magistrate by the fundamental laws of society. So that, in order to make war completely effectual, it is necessary with us in England that it be publicly declared and duly proclaimed by the king's authority; and, then, all parts of both the contending nations, from the highest to the lowest, are bound by it. And, wherever the right resides of beginning a national war, there also must reside the right of ending it, or the power of making peace. And the same check of parliamentary impeachment, for improper or inglorious conduct, in beginning, conducting, or concluding a national war, is in general sufficient to restrain the ministers of the crown from a wanton or injurious exertion of this great prerogative.

IV. But, as the delay of making war may sometimes be detrimental to individuals who have suffered by depredations from foreign potentates, our laws have in some respect armed the subject with powers to impel the prerogative; by directing the ministers of the crown to issue letters of marque and reprisal upon due demand: the prerogative of granting which is nearly related to, and plainly derived from, that other of making war; this being indeed only an incomplete state of hostilities, and generally ending in a formal denunciation of war. These letters are grantable by the law of nations, whenever the subjects of one state are oppressed and injured by those of another; and justice is denied by that state to which the oppressor belongs. In this case letters of marque and reprisal (words in themselves synonimous and signifying a taking in return) may be obtained, in order to seise the bodies or goods of the subjects of the offending state, until satisfaction be made, wherever they happen to be found. Indeed this custom of reprisals seems dictated by nature herself; and accordingly we find in the most antient times very notable instances of it. But here the necessity is obvious of calling in the sovereign power, to determine when reprisals may be made; else every private sufferer would be a judge in his own cause. And, in pursuance of this principle, it is with us declared by the statute 4 Hen.V. c. 7. that, if any subjects of the realm are oppressed in time of truce by any foreigners, the king will grant marque in due form, to all that feel themselves grieved. Which form is thus directed to be observed: the sufferer must first apply to the lord privy-seal, and he shall make out letters of request under the privy seal; and, if, after such request of satisfaction made, the party required do not within convenient time make due satisfaction or restitution to the party grieved, the lord chancellor shall make him out letters of marque under the great seal; and by virtue of these he may attack and seise the property of the aggressor nation, without hazard of being condemned as a robber or pirate.

2

ARTICLES OF CONFEDERATION, ART. 9
1 Mar. 1781

ARTICLE IX. The united states in congress assembled, shall have the sole and exclusive right and power of determining on peace and war, except in the cases mentioned in the sixth article—of sending and receiving ambassadors—entering into treaties and alliances, provided that no treaty of commerce shall be made whereby the legislative power of the respective states shall be restrained from imposing such imposts and duties on foreigners as their own people are subjected to, or from prohibiting the exportation or importation of any species of goods or commodities, whatsoever—of establishing rules for deciding in all cases, what captures on land or water shall be legal, and in what manner prizes taken by land or naval forces in the service of the united states shall be divided or appropriated—of granting letters of marque and reprisal in times of peace—appointing courts for the trial of piracies and felonies committed on the high seas and establishing courts for receiving and determining finally appeals in all cases of captures, provided that no member of congress shall be appointed a judge of any of the said courts.

3

CONTINENTAL CONGRESS
Apr. 1781
Journals 19:361

Be it ordained, and it is hereby ordained, by the United States in Congress assembled, that the following instructions be observed by the captains or commanders of private armed vessels commissioned by letters of marque or general reprisals, or otherwise, by the authority of the United States in Congress assembled:

I. You may by force of arms attack, subdue, and seize all ships, vessels and goods, belonging to the King or Crown of Great Britain, or to his subjects, or others inhabiting within any of the territories or possessions of the aforesaid King of Great Britain, on the high seas, or between high-water and low-water marks. And you may also annoy the enemy by all means in your power, by land as well as by water, taking care not to infringe or violate the laws of nations, or laws of neutrality.

II. You are to pay a sacred regard to the rights of neutral powers, and the usage and customs of civilized nations; and on no pretence whatever, presume to take or seize any ships or vessels belonging to the subjects of princes or powers in alliance with these United States; except they are employed in carrying contraband goods or soldiers to our enemies; and in such case you are to conform to the stipulations contained in the treaties subsisting between such princes or powers and these states: and you are not to capture, seize or plunder any ships or vessels of our enemies, being under the protection of neutral coasts, nations, or princes, under the pains and penalties expressed in a proclamation issued by the Congress of the United States, the 9th day of May, in the year of our Lord one thousand seven hundred and seventy-eight.

III. You shall permit all neutral vessels freely to navigate on the high seas, or coasts of America, except such as are employed in carrying contraband goods or soldiers to the enemies of these United States.

4

RECORDS OF THE FEDERAL CONVENTION

[*1:19; Madison, 29 May*]

[Mr. Randolph] then proceeded to enumerate the defects: 1. that the confederation produced no security agai[nst] foreign invasion; congress not being permitted to prevent a war nor to support it by th[eir] own authority—Of this he cited many examples; most of whi[ch] tended to shew, that they could not cause infractions of treaties or of the law of nations, to be punished: that particular states might by their conduct provoke war without controul; and that neither militia nor draughts being fit for defence on such occasions, enlistments only could be successful, and these could not be executed without money.

[*2:318; Madison, 17 Aug.*]

"To make war"

Mr Pinkney opposed the vesting this power in the Legislature. Its proceedings were too slow. It wd. meet but once a year. The Hs. of Reps. would be too numerous for such deliberations. The Senate would be the best depositary, being more acquainted with foreign affairs, and most capable of proper resolutions. If the States are equally represented in Senate, so as to give no advantage to large States, the power will notwithstanding be safe, as the small have their all at stake in such cases as well as the large States. It would be singular for one authority to make war, and another peace.

Mr Butler. The Objections agst the Legislature lie in a great degree agst the Senate. He was for vesting the power in the President, who will have all the requisite qualities, and will not make war but when the Nation will support it.

Mr. Madison and Mr Gerry moved to insert *"declare,"* striking out *"make"* war; leaving to the Executive the power to repel sudden attacks.

Mr Sharman thought it stood very well. The Executive shd. be able to repel and not to commence war. "Make" better than "declare" the latter narrowing the power too much.

Mr Gerry never expected to hear in a republic a motion to empower the Executive alone to declare war.

Mr. Elseworth. there is a material difference between the cases of making *war,* and making *peace.* It shd. be more easy to get out of war, than into it. War also is a simple and overt declaration. peace attended with intricate & secret negociations.

Mr. Mason was agst giving the power of war to the Executive, because not safely to be trusted with it; or to the Senate, because not so constructed as to be entitled to it. He was for clogging rather than facilitating war; but for facilitating peace. He preferred *"declare"* to *"make"*.

On the Motion to insert *declare*—in place of *Make,* it was agreed to.

N. H. no. Mas. abst. Cont. no.* Pa ay. Del. ay. Md. ay. Va. ay. N. C. ay. S. C. ay. Geo- ay. [Ayes—7; noes—2; absent—1.]

Mr. Pinkney's motion to strike out whole clause, disagd. to without call of States.

Mr Butler moved to give the Legislature power of peace, as they were to have that of war.

Mr Gerry 2ds. him. 8 Senators may possibly exercise the power if vested in that body, and 14 if all should be present; and may consequently give up part of the U. States. The Senate are more liable to be corrupted by an Enemy than the whole Legislature.

*On the remark by Mr. King that *"make"* war might be understood to "conduct" it which was an Executive function, Mr. Elseworth gave up his objection and the vote of Cont was changed to—ay.

On the motion for adding "and peace" after "war"

N. H. no. Mas. no. Ct. no. Pa. no. Del. no. Md. no. Va. no. N. C. no S. C. no. Geo. no. [Ayes—0; noes—10.]

5

PIERCE BUTLER, SOUTH CAROLINA LEGISLATURE
16 Jan. 1788

Elliot: 4:263

Maj. Pierce Butler (one of the delegates of the Federal Convention) was one of a committee that drew up this clause, and would endeavor to recollect those reasons by which they were guided. It was at first proposed to vest the sole power of making peace or war in the Senate; but this was objected to as inimical to the genius of a republic, by destroying the necessary balance they were anxious to preserve. Some gentlemen were inclined to give this power to the President; but it was objected to, as throwing into his hands the influence of a monarch, having an opportunity of involving his country in a war whenever he wished to promote her destruction. The House of Representatives was then named; but an insurmountable objection was made to this proposition—which was, that negotiations always required the greatest secrecy, which could not be expected in a large body. The honorable gentleman then gave a clear, concise opinion on the propriety of the proposed Constitution.

6

JAMES WILSON, LEGISLATIVE DEPARTMENT, LECTURES ON LAW
1791

Works 1:433–34

One great end of the national government is to "provide for the common defence." Defence presupposes an attack. We all know the instruments by which an attack is made by one nation upon another. We all, likewise, know the instruments necessary for defence when such an attack is made. That nation, which would protect herself from hostilities, or maintain peace, must have it in her power—such is the present situation of things—to declare war. The power of declaring war, and the other powers naturally connected with it, are vested in congress. To provide and maintain a navy—to make rules for its government—to grant letters of marque and reprisal—to make rules concerning captures—to raise and support armies—to establish rules for their regulation—to provide for organizing, arming, and disciplining the militia, and for calling them forth in the service of the Union—all these are powers naturally connected with the power of declaring war. All these powers, therefore, are vested in congress.

As the law is now received in England, the king has the sole prerogative of making war. On this very interesting power, the constitution of the United States renews the principles of government, known in England before the conquest. This indeed, as we are told by a well informed writer, may be accounted the chief difference between the Anglo-Saxon and the Anglo-Norman government. In the former, the power of making peace and war was invariably possessed by the wittenagemote; and was regarded as inseparable from the allodial condition of its members. In the latter, it was transferred to the sovereign: and this branch of the feudal system, which was accommodated, perhaps, to the depredations and internal commotions prevalent in that rude period, has remained in subsequent ages, when, from a total change of manners, the circumstances, by which it was recommended, have no longer any existence.

7

Thomas Jefferson, The Anas
Nov. 1793
Works 1:325–30

Nov. 8. 93. . . . R. [Attorney-General Edmund Randolph] & myself opposed the right of the Presidt. to declare anything future on the qu. shall there or shall there not be war? & that no such thing was intended; that H.'s constrn [Hamilton's construction] of the effect of the proclmn would have been a determn of the question of the *guarantee* which we both denied to have intended, & I had at the time declared the Executive incompetent to. R. said he meant that forn natns. should understand it as an intimation of the Pr.'s opn that neutrality would be our interest. I declared my meaning to have been that forn nations should understand no such thing, that on the contrary I would have chosen them to be doubtful & to come & bid for our neutrality. I admitted the Presidt. havg. recd. the natn. at the close of Congr. in a state of peace, was bound to preserve them in that state till Congr. shd. meet again, & might proclaim anything which went no farther. The Pres. decld. he nevr. had an idea that he could bind Congress agt. declaring war, or that anything containd. in his proclmn could look beyd. the first day of their meeting. His main view was to keep our people in peace, he apologized for the use of the term neutrality in his answers, & justifd. it by having submitted the first of them (that to the merchts wherein it was used) to our considn, & we had not objected to the term. He concluded in the end that Colo. H. should prepare a paragraph on this subject for the speech, & it should then be considered. We were here called to dinner.

After dinner the *renvoi* of Genet was proposed by himself. I opposed it on these topics. France the only nation on earth sincerely our friend.—The measure so harsh a one that no precedt. is producd. where it has not been followed by war. Our messenger has now been gone 84. days, conseqly. we may hourly expect the return & to be relieved by their revocation of him. Were it now resolved on, it would be 8. or 10. days before the matter on which the order shd. be founded could be selected, arranged, discussed, & forwarded. This wd. bring us within 4 or 5. days of the meeting of Congress. Wd. it not be better to wait & see how the pulse of that body, new as it is, would beat. They are with us now, probably but such a step as this may carry many over to Genet's side. Genet will not obey the order, &c., &c. The Presidt. asked me what I would do if Genet sent the accusn to us to be communicd. to Congr. as he threatd. in the lre to Moultrie? I sd. I wd. not send it to Congr., but either. put it in the newsp. or send it back to him to be publd. if he pleased. Other questions & answers were put & returned in a quicker altercation than I ever before saw the President use. Hamilton was for the *renvoi.* Spoke much of the dignity of the nation, that they were now to form their character, that our conduct now would tempt or deter other forn. min. from treatg us in the same manner, touched on the Pr's personal feelings—did not believe Fr. wd. make it a cause of war, if she did we ought to do what was right & meet the consequences &c. Knox on the same side, & said he thot it very possible Mr. Genet would either declare us a departmt. of France, or levy troops here & endeavor to reduce us to obedce. R. of my opn, & argued chiefly on the resurrection of popularity to Genet which might be prodd. by this measure. That at present he was dead in the public opn if we would but leave him so. The Presidt. lamented there was not unanimity among us; that as it was we had left him exactly where we found him. & so it ended.

Nov. 15. 1793. E. R. tells me, that Ham. in conversn with him yesterday said "Sir, if all the people in America were now assembled, & to call on me to say whether I am a friend to the French revolution, I would declare that *I have it in abhorrence.*"

Nov. 21. We met at the President's. The manner of explaining to Congress the intentions of the Proclmn was the matter of debate. E. R. produced his way of stating it. This expressed it's views to have been 1. to keep our citizens quiet. 2. to intimate to foreign nations that it was the Pr's opn that the interests & disposns of this country were for peace. Hamilton produced his statement in which he declared his intention to be to say nothing which could be laid hold of for any purpose, to leave the proclamation to explain itself. He entered pretty fully into all the argumentation of Pacificus, he justified the right of the Presidt to declare his opinion for a *future neutrality,* & that there existed no circumstances to oblige the U. S. to enter into the war on account of the guarantee, and that in agreeing to the proclmn he meant it to be understood as conveying both declarations, viz, neutrality, & that the *casus foederis* on the guarantee did not exist. Notwithstanding these declns of the Presidt. he admitted the Congress might declare war. In like manner they might declare war in the face of a treaty, & in direct infraction of it. Among other positions laid down by him, this was with great positiveness, that the constn having given power to the Presidt. & Senate to make treaties, they might make a treaty of neutrality which should take from Congress the right to declare war in that particular case, and that under the form of a treaty they might exercise any powers whatever, even those exclusively given by the constn to the H. of representatives. R. opposed this position, & seemed to think that where they undertook to do acts by treaty (as to settle a tariff of duties) which were exclusively given to the legislature, that an act of the legislature would be necessary to confirm them, as happens in England when a treaty interferes with duties establd by law.—I insisted that in givg to the Prest. & Senate a power to make treaties, the constn meant only to authorize them to carry into effect by way of treaty any powers they might constitutionally exercise. I was sensible of the weak points in this position, but there were still weaker in the other hypotheses, and if it be impossible to discover a rational measure of authority to have been given by this clause, I would rather suppose that the cases which my hypothesis would leave unprovided, were not thought of by the Convention, or if thought of, could not be agreed on, or were thought on and deemed unnecessary to be invested in the government. Of this last description were treaties of neutrality, treaties of offensive & defensive &c. In every event I would rather construe so narrowly as to oblige the nation to amend and thus declare what powers they would agree to yield, than too broadly & indeed so broadly as to enable the Executive and Senate to do things which the constn forbids. On the question Which form of explaining the principles of the proclmn should be adopted? I declared for R.'s, tho' it gave to that instrumt. more objects than I had contemplated. K declared for H's. The Presidt. said he had had but one object, the keeping our people quiet till Congress should meet, that nevertheless to declare he did not mean a decln of neutrality in the technical sense of the phrase might perhaps be crying *peccavi* before he was charged. However he did not decide between the two draughts.

8

JAMES MADISON TO THOMAS JEFFERSON
2 Apr. 1798
Writings 6:312–14

The President's message is only a further development to the public, of the violent passions, & heretical politics, which have been long privately known to govern him. It is to be hoped however that the H. of Rep will not hastily eccho them. At least it may be expected that before war measures are instituted, they will recollect the principle asserted by 62 vs. 37, in the case of the Treaty, and insist on a full communication of the intelligence on which such measures are recommended. The present is a plainer, if it be not a stronger case, and if there has been sufficient defection to destroy the majority which was then so great & so decided, it is the worst symptom that has yet appeared in our Councils. The constitution supposes, what the History of all Govts demonstrates, that the Ex. is the branch of power most interested in war, & most prone to it. It has accordingly with studied care, vested the question of war in the Legisl. But the Doctrines lately advanced strike at the root of all these provisions, and will deposit the peace of the Country in that Department which the Constitution distrusts as most ready without cause to renounce it. For if the opinion of the P. not the facts & proofs themselves are to sway the judgment of Congress, in declaring war, and if the President in the recess of Congrs. create a foreign mission, appt. the minister, & negociate a War Treaty, without the possibility of a check even from the Senate, untill the measures present alternatives overruling the freedom of its judgment; if again a Treaty when made obliges the Legis. to declare war contrary to its judgment, and in pursuance of the same doctrine, a law declaring war, imposes a like moral obligation, to grant the requisite supplies until it be formally repealed with the consent of the P. & Senate, it is evident that the people are cheated out of the best ingredients in their Govt., the safeguards of peace which is the greatest of their blessings. I like both your suggestions in the present crisis. Congress ought clearly to prohibit arming, & the P. ought to be brought to declare on what ground he undertook to grant an indirect licence to arm. The first instructions were no otherwise legal than as they were in pursuance of the law of Nations, & consequently in execution of the law of the land. The revocation of the instructions is a virtual change of the law, & consequently a usurpation by the Ex. of a legislative power. It will not avail to say that the law of Nations leaves this point undecided, & that every nation is free to decide it for itself. If this be the case, the regulation being a Legislative not an Executive one, belongs to the former, not the latter Authority; and comes expressly within the power, "to define the law of Nations," given to Congress by the Constitution. I do not expect however that the Constitutional party in the H. of R. is strong eno- to do what ought to be done in the present instance. Your 2d idea that an adjournment for the purpose of consulting the constituents on the subject of war, is more practicable because it can be effected by that branch alone if it pleases, & because an opposition to such a measure will be more striking to the public eye. The expedient is the more desirable as it will be utterly impossible to call forth the sense of the people generally before the season will be over, especially as the Towns, &c., where there can be most despatch in such an operation are on the wrong side, and it is to be feared that a partial expression of the public voice, may be misconstrued or miscalled, an evidence in favor of the war party. On what do you ground the idea that a decln of war requires ⅔ of the Legislature? The force of your remark however is not diminished by this mistake, for it remains true, that measures are taking or may be taken by the Ex. that will end in war, contrary to the wish of the Body which alone can declare it.

9

Charles Lee, Treason
21 Aug. 1798
1 Ops. Atty. Gen. 84

Having taken into consideration the acts of the French republic relative to the United States, and the laws of Congress passed at the last session, it is my opinion that there exists not only an *actual* maritime war between France and the United States, but a maritime war *authorized* by both nations. Consequently, France is our enemy; and to aid, assist, and abet that nation in her maritime warfare, will be treason in a citizen or any other person within the United States not commissioned under France. But in a French subject, commissioned by France, acting openly according to this commission, such assistance will be hostility. The former may be tried and punished according to our laws; the latter must be treated according to the laws of war.

I have thought it my duty to make this communication in consequence of the information you received from Rhode Island, of the intentions of a Frenchman, whose name I do not now call to mind, who is said to be somewhere in this country, on the business of buying ships and supplies of a military kind, for the West Indies. He should be apprehended and tried as a traitor, unless he has a commission, and acts according to it; in which case he should be treated as an enemy, and confined as a prisoner of war.

10

Bas v. Tingy
4 Dall. 37 (1800)

The Judges delivered their opinions *seriatim* in the following manner.

Moore, Justice. This case depends on the construction of the act, for the regulation of the navy. It is objected, indeed, that the act applies only to future wars; but its provisions are obviously applicable to the present situation of things, and there is nothing to prevent an immediate commencement of its operation.

It is, however, more particularly urged, that the word "enemy" cannot be applied to the French; because the section in which it is used, is confined to such a state of war, as would authorize a re-capture of property belonging to a nation in amity with the United States, and such a state of war, it is said, does not exist between America and France. A number of books have been cited to furnish a glossary on the word enemy; yet, our situation is so extraordinary, that I doubt whether a parallel case can be traced in the history of nations. But, if words are the representatives of ideas, let me ask, by what other word the idea of the relative situation of America and France could be communicated, than by that of hostility, or war? And how can the characters of the parties engaged in hostility or war, be otherwise described than by the denomination of enemies? It is for the honor and dignity of both nations, therefore, that they should be called enemies; for, it is by that description alone, that either could justify or excuse, the scene of bloodshed, depredation and confiscation, which has unhappily occurred; and, surely, congress could only employ the language of the act of June 13, 1798, towards a nation whom she considered as an enemy.

Nor does it follow, that the act of March 1799, is to have no operation, because all the cases in which it might operate, are not in existence at the time of passing it. During the present hostilities, it affects the case of recaptured property belonging to our own citizens, and in the event of a future war it might also be applied to the case of recaptured property belonging to a nation in amity with the United States. But it is further to be remarked, that all the expressions of the act may be satisfied, even at this very time: for by former laws the re-capture of property, belonging to persons resident within the United States is authorized; those residents may be aliens; and, if they are subjects of a nation in amity with the United States, they answer completely the description of the law.

The only remaining objection, offered on behalf of the plaintiff in error, supposes, that, because there are no repealing or negative words, the last law must be confined to future cases, in order to have a subject for the first law to regulate. But if two laws are inconsistent, (as, in my judgment, the laws in question are) the latter is a virtual repeal of the former, without any express declaration on the subject.

On these grounds, I am clearly of opinion, that the decree of the circuit court ought to be affirmed.

Washington, Justice. It is admitted, on all hands, that the defendant in error is entitled to some compensation: but the plaintiff in error contends, that the compensation should be regulated by the act of the 28th June 1798, (4 vol. p. 154. s. 2.) which allows only one-eight for salvage; while the defendant in error refers his claim to the act of the 2d March, (ibid. 456. s. 7.) which makes an allowance of one half, upon a re-capture from the enemy, after an adverse possession of ninety-six hours.

If the defendant's claim is well founded, it follows, that the latter law must virtually have worked a repeal of the former; but this has been denied for a variety of reasons:

1st. Because the former law relates to re-captures from the French, and the latter law relates to re-captures from the enemy; and it is said that "the enemy" is not descriptive of France or of her armed vessels, according to the correct and technical understanding of the word.

The decision of this question must depend upon another; which is, whether, at the time of passing the act of congress of the 2d of March 1799, there subsisted a state of war between the two nations? It may, I believe, be safely laid down, that every contention by force between two nations, in external matters, under the authority of their respective governments, is not only war, but public war. If it be declared in form, it is called solemn, and is of the perfect kind; because one whole nation is at war with another whole nation; and all the members of the nation declaring war, are authorized to commit hostilities against all the members of the other, in every place, and under every circumstance. In such a war all the members act under a general authority, and all the rights and consequences of war attach to their condition.

But hostilities may subsist between two nations, more confined in its nature and extent; being limited as to places, persons, and things; and this is more properly termed imperfect war; because not solemn, and because those who are authorized to commit hostilities, act under special authority, and can go no farther than to the extent of their commission. Still, however, it is public war, because it is an external contention by force between some of the members of the two nations, authorized by the legitimate powers. It is a war between the two nations, though all the members are not authorized to commit hostilities such as in a solemn war, where the government restrain the general power.

Now, if this be the true definition of war, let us see what was the situation of the United States in relation to France. In March 1799, congress had raised an army; stopped all intercourse with France; dissolved our treaty; built and equipt ships of war; and commissioned private armed ships; enjoining the former, and authorizing the latter, to defend themselves against the armed ships of France, to attack them on the high seas, to subdue and take them as prize, and to re-capture armed vessels found in their possession. Here, then, let me ask, what were the technical characters of an American and French armed vessel, combating on the high seas, with a view the one to subdue the other, and to make prize of his property? They certainly were not friends, because there was a contention by force; nor were they private enemies, because the contention was external, and authorized by the legitimate authority of the two governments. If they were not our enemies, I know not what constitutes an enemy.

2d. But, secondly, it is said, that a war of the imperfect kind, is more properly called acts of hostility, or repriszal, and that congress did not mean to consider the hostility subsisting between France and the United States, as constituting a state of war.

In support of this position, it has been observed, that in no law prior to March 1799, is France styled our enemy, nor are we said to be at war. This is true; but neither of these things were necessary to be done: because as to France, she was sufficiently described by the title of the French republic; and as to America, the degree of hostility meant to be carried on, was sufficiently described without declaring war, or declaring that we were at war. Such a declaration by congress, might have constituted a perfect state of war, which was not intended by the government.

3d. It has, likewise, been said, that the 7th section of the act of March 1799, embraces cases which, according to pre-existing laws, could not then take place, because no authority had been given to re-capture friendly vessels from the French; and this argument was strongly and forcibly pressed.

But, because every case provided for by this law was not then existing, it does not follow, that the law should not operate upon such as did exist, and upon the rest whenever they should arise. It is a permanent law, embracing a variety of subjects, not made in relation to the present war with France only, but in relation to any future war with her, or with any other nation. It might then very properly allow salvage for re-capturing of American vessels from France, which had previously been authorized by law, though it could not immediately apply to the vessels of friends: and whenever such a war should exist between the United States and France, or any other nation, as according to the law of nations, or special authority, would justify the re-capture of friendly vessels, it might on that event, with similar propriety, apply to them, which furnishes, I think, the true construction of the act.

The opinion which I delivered at New York, in *Talbot* v. *Seeman,* was, that although an *American* vessel could not justify the re-taking of a neutral vessel from the *French,* because neither the sort of war that subsisted, nor the special commission under which the American acted, authorized the proceeding; yet, that the 7th section of the act of 1799, applied to recaptures from *France as an enemy,* in all cases authorized by congress. And on both points, my opinion remains unshaken; or rather has been confirmed by the very able discussion which the subject has lately undergone in this court, on the appeal from my decree. Another reason has been assigned by the defendant's counsel, why the former law is not to be regarded as repealed by the latter, to wit: that a subsequent affirmative general law cannot repeal a former affirmative special law, if both may stand together. This ground is not taken, because such an effect involves an indecent censure upon the legislature for passing contradictory laws, since the censure only applies where the contradiction appears in the same law; and it does not follow, that a provision which is proper at one time may not be improper at another, when circumstances are changed: but the ground of argument is, that a change ought not to be presumed. Yet, if there is sufficient evidence of such a change in the legislative will, and the two laws are in collision, we are forced to presume it.

What then is the evidence of legislative will? In fact and in law we are at war: an *American* vessel fighting with a *French* vessel, to subdue and make her prize, is fighting with an enemy accurately and technically speaking: and if this be not sufficient evidence of the legislative mind, it is explained in the same law. The sixth and the ninth sections of the act speak of *prizes,* which can only be of property taken at sea from *an enemy, jure belli;* and the 9th section speaks of prizes as taken from *an enemy,* in so many words, alluding to prizes which had been previously taken: but no prize could have been then taken except *from France:* prizes taken from France were, therefore, taken from *the enemy.* This then is a legislative interpretation of the word enemy; and if the enemy as to prizes, surely they preserve the same character as to re-captures. Besides, it may be fairly asked, why should the rate of salvage be different in such a war as the present, from the salvage in a war more solemn or general? And it must be recollected, that the occasion of making the law of March 1799, was not only to raise the salvage, but to apportion it to the hazard in which the property re-taken was placed; a circumstance for which the former salvage law had not provided.

The two laws, upon the whole, cannot be rendered consistent, unless the court could wink so hard as not to see and know, that in fact, in the view of congress, and to every intent and purpose, the possession by a French armed vessel of an American vessel, was the possession of an *enemy:* and, therefore, in my opinion, the decree of the circuit court ought to be affirmed.

Chase, Justice. The Judges agreeing unanimously in their opinion, I presumed that the sense of the court would have been delivered by the president; and therefore, I have not prepared a formal argument on the occasion. I find no difficulty, however, in assigning the general reasons, which induce me to concur in affirming the decree of the circuit court.

An American public vessel of war re-captures an American merchant vessel from a French privateer, after 96 hours possession, and the question is stated, what salvage ought to be allowed? There are two laws on the subject: by the first of which, only one-eight of the value of the re-captured property is allowed; but by the second, the re-captor is entitled to a moiety. The re-capture happened after the passing of the latter law; and the whole controversy turns on the single question, whether France was at that time an enemy? If France was an enemy, then the law obliges us to decree one half of the value of ship and cargo for salvage: but if France was not an enemy, then no more than one-eighth can be allowed.

The decree of the Circuit Court (in which I presided) passed by consent; but although I never gave an opinion, I have never entertained a doubt on the subject. Congress is empowered to declare a general war, or congress may wage a limited war; limited in place, in objects, and in time. If a general war is declared, its extent and operations are only restricted and regulated by the *jus belli,* forming a part of the law of nations; but if a partial law is waged, its extent and operation depend on our municipal laws.

What then is the nature of the contest subsisting between America and France? In my judgment, it is a limited, partial, war. Congress has not declared war in general terms; but congress has authorized hostilities on the high seas by certain persons in certain cases. There is no authority given to commit hostilities on land; to capture unarmed French vessels, nor even to capture French armed vessels lying in a French port; and the authority is not given indiscriminately, to every citizen of America, against every citizen of France, but only to citizens appointed by commissions, or exposed to immediate outrage and violence. So far it is, unquestionably, a partial war; but, nevertheless, it is a public war, on account of the public authority from which it emanates.

There are four acts, authorized by our government, that are demonstrative of a state of war. A belligerent power has a right, by the law of nations, to search a neutral vessel; and, upon suspicion of a violation of her neutral obligations, to seize and carry her into port for further examination. But by the acts of congress, an American vessel is authorized: 1st. To resist the search of a French public vessel: 2d. To capture any vessel that should attempt by force, to compel submission to a search: 3d. To re-capture any American vessel seized by a French vessel: and 4th, To capture any French armed vessel wherever found on the high seas. This suspension of the law of nations, this right of capture and re-capture, can only be authorized by an act of the government, which is, in itself, an act of hostility. But still it is a restrained, or limited hostility; and there are, undoubtedly, many rights attached to a general war, which do not attach to this modification of the powers of defence and aggression. Hence, whether such shall be the denomination of the relative situation of America and France, has occasioned great controversy at the bar; and, it appears, that Sir William Scott, also, was embarrassed in describing it, when he observed, "that in the present state of hostility (if so it may be called) between America and France," it is the practice of the English court of Admiralty, to restore re-captured American property, on payment of a salvage. *Rob. Rep.* 54. *The Santa Cruz.* But, for my part, I cannot perceive the difficulty of the case. As there may be a public general war, and a public qualified war; so there may, upon correspondent principles, be a general enemy, and a partial enemy. The designation of "enemy" extends to a case of perfect war; but as a general designation, it surely includes the less, as well as the greater, species of warfare. If congress had chosen to declare a general war, France would have been a general enemy; having chosen to wage a partial war, France was, at the time of the capture, only a partial enemy; but still she was an enemy.

It has been urged, however, that congress did not intend the provisions of the act of March 1799, for the case of our subsisting qualified hostility with France, but for the case of a future state of a general war with any nation: I think, however, that the contrary appears from the terms of the law itself, and from the subsequent repeal. In the 9th section it is said, that all the money accruing, "or which has already accrued from the sale of prizes," shall constitute a fund for the half-pay of officers and seamen. Now, at the time of making this appropriation, no prizes, (which *ex vi termini* implies a capture in a state of war) had been taken from any nation but France, those which had been taken, were not taken from France as a friend; they must consequently have been taken from her as an enemy; and the restrospective provision of the law can only operate on such prizes. Besides, when the 13th section regulates "the bounty given by the United States on any national ship of war, taken from the enemy, and brought into port," it is obvious, that even if the bounty has no relation to previous captures, it must operate from the moment of passing the act, and embraces the case of a national ship of war, taken from France as an enemy, according to the existing qualified state of hostilities. But the repealing act, passed on the 3d of March 1800, (subsequent to the re-capture in the present case) ought to silence all doubt, as to the intention of the legislature; for, if the act of March 1799, did not apply to the French republic as an enemy, there could be no reason for altering, or repealing, that part of it, which regulates the rate of salvage on re-captures.

The acts of congress have been analysed to show, that a war is not openly denounced against France, and that France is no where expressly called the enemy of America: but this only proves the circumspection and prudence of the legislature. Considering our national prepossessions in favour of the French republic, congress had an arduous task to perform, even in preparing for necessary defence, and just retaliation. As the temper of the people rose, however, in resentment of accumulated wrongs, the language and the measures of the government became more and more energetic and indignant; though hitherto the popular feeling may not have been ripe for a solemn declaration of war; and an active and powerful opposition in our public councils, has postponed, if not prevented that decisive event, which many thought would have best suited the interest, as well as the honour of the United States. The progress of our contest with France, indeed, resembles much the progress of our revolutionary contest; in which, watching the current of public sentiment, the patriots of that day proceeded, step by step, from the supplicatory language of petitions for a redress of grievances, to the bold and noble declaration of national independence.

Having, then, no hesitation in pronouncing, that a partial war exists between America and France, and that France was an enemy, within the meaning of the act of March 1799, my voice must be given for affirming the decree of the circuit court.

Paterson, Justice. As the case appears on the record, and has been accurately stated by the counsel and by the judges, who have delivered their opinions, it is not necessary to recapitulate the facts. My opinion shall be expressed in a few words. The United States and the French republic are in a qualified state of hostility. An imperfect war, or a war, as to certain objects, and to a certain extent, exists between the two nations; and this modified warfare is authorised by the constitutional authority of our country. It is war *quoad hoc.* As far as congress tolerated and authorised the war on our part, so far may we proceed in hostile operations. It is a maritime war, a war at sea as to certain purposes, The national armed vessels of France attack and capture the national armed vessels of the United States; and the national armed vessels of the United States are expressly authorised and directed to attack, subdue, and take, the national armed vessels of France, and also to recapture American vessels. It is therefore a public war between the two nations qualified, on our part, in the manner prescribed by the constitutional organ of our country. In such a state of things it is scarcely necessary to add, that the term *"enemy,"* applies; it is the appropriate expression, to be limited in its signification, import, and use, by the qualified nature and operation of the war on our part. The word enemy proceeds the full length of the war, and no farther. Besides, the intention of the legislature as to the meaning of this word, enemy, is clearly deducible from the act for the government of the navy, passed the 2d of March 1799. This act embraces the past, present, and future, and contains passages, which point the character of enemy at the *French,* in the most clear and irresistible manner. I shall select one paragraph, namely, that which refers to prizes taken by our public vessels, anterior to the passing of the latter act. The word prizes in this section can apply to the *French,* and the *French* only. This is decisive on the subject of legislative intention.

11

ALEXANDER HAMILTON, THE EXAMINATION, NO. 1
17 Dec. 1801
Papers 25:454–57

The Message of the President, by whatever motives it may have been dictated, is a performance which ought to alarm all who are anxious for the safety of our Government, for the respectability and welfare of our nation. It makes, or aims at making, a most prodigal sacrifice of constitutional energy, of sound principle, and of public interest, to the popularity of one man.

The first thing in it which excites our surprise, is the very extraordinary position, that though *Tripoli had declared war in form* against the United States, and had enforced it by actual hostility, yet that there was not power, for want of *the sanction of Congress,* to capture and detain her cruisers with their crews.

When the newspapers informed us, that one of these cruisers, after being subdued in a bloody conflict, had been liberated and permitted quietly to return home, the imagination was perplexed to divine the reason. The conjecture naturally was, that pursuing a policy, too refined perhaps for barbarians, it was intended by that measure to give the enemy a strong impression of our magnanimity and humanity. No one dreampt of a scruple as to the *right* to seize and detain the armed vessel of an open and avowed foe, vanquished in battle. The enigma is now solved, and we are presented with one of the most singular paradoxes, ever advanced by a man claiming the character of a statesman. When analyzed, it amounts to nothing less than this, that *between* two nations there may exist a state of complete war on the one side—of peace on the other.

War, of itself, gives to the parties a mutual right to kill in battle, and to capture the persons and property of each other. This is a rule of natural law; a necessary and inevitable consequence of the state of war. This state between two nations is completely produced by the act of one—it requires no concurrent act of the other. It is impossible to conceive the idea, that one nation can be in full war with another, and this other not in the same state with respect to its adversary. The moment therefore that two nations are, in an absolute sense, at war, the public force of each may exercise every act of hostility, which the general laws of war authorise, against the persons and property of the other. As it respects this conclusion, the distinction between offensive and defensive war, makes no difference. That distinction is only material to discriminate the agressing nation from that which defends itself against attack. The war is offensive on the part of the state which makes it; on the opposite side it is defensive: but the rights of both, as to the measure of hostility, are equal.

It will be readily allowed that the Constitution of a particular country may limit the Organ charged with the direction of the public force, in the use or application of that force, even in time of actual war: but nothing short of the strongest negative words, of the most express prohibitions, can be admitted to restrain that Organ from so employing it, as to derive the fruits of actual victory, by making prisoners of the persons and detaining the property of a vanquished enemy. Our Constitution happily is not chargeable with so great an absurdity. The framers of it would have blushed at a provision, so repugnant to good sense, so inconsistent with national safety and inconvenience. That instrument has only provided affirmatively, that, "The Congress shall have power to declare War;" the plain meaning of which is that, it is the peculiar and exclusive province of Congress, *when the nation is at peace,* to change that state into a state of war; whether from calculations of policy or from provocations or injuries received: in other words, it belongs to Congress only, *to go to War.* But when a foreign nation declares, or openly and avowedly makes war upon the United States, they are then by the very fact, already *at war,* and any declaration on the part of Congress is nugatory: it is at least unnecessary. This inference is clear in principle, and has the sanction of established practice. It is clear in principle, because it is self-evident, that a declaration by one nation against another, produce[s] at once a complete state of war between both; and that no declaration on the other side can at all vary their relative situation: and in practice it is well known, that nothing is more common, than when war is declared by one party, to prosecute mutual hostilities, without a declaration by the other.

The doctrine of the Message includes the strange absurdity, that, without a declaration of war by Congress, our public force may destroy the life, but may not restrain the liberty, or seize the property of an enemy. This was exemplified in the very instance of the Tripolitan corsair. A number of her crew were slaughtered in the combat, and after she was subdued she was set free with the remainder. But it may perhaps be said, that she was the assailant, and that resistance was an act of mere defence, and self-preservation. Let us then pursue the matter a step further. Our ships had blockaded the Tripolitan Admiral in the bay of Gibraltar; suppose, he had attempted to make his way out, without first firing upon them: if permitted to do it, the blockade was a farce; if hindered by force, this would have amounted to more than a mere act of defence; and if a combat had ensued, we should then have seen an unequivocal illustration of the unintelligible right, to take the life but not to abridge the liberty, or capture the property of an enemy.

Let us suppose an invasion of our territory, previous to a declaration of war by Congress. The principle avowed in the Message would authorize our troops to kill those of the invader, if they should come within the reach of their bayonets, perhaps to drive them into the sea, and drown them; but not to disable them from doing harm, by the milder process of making them prisoners, and sending them into confinement. Perhaps it may be replied, that the same end would be answered by disarming and leaving them to starve. The merit of such an argument would be complete by adding, that should they not be famished, before the arrival of their ships, with a fresh supply of arms, we might then, if able, disarm them a second time, and send them on board their fleet, to return safely home.

The inconvenience of the doctrine in practice, is not less palpable than its folly in theory. In every case it presents a most unequal warfare. In the instance which has occurred, the vanquished Barbarian got off with the loss of his guns. Had he been victorious, the Americans, whose lives might have been spared, would have been doomed to wear out a miserable existence in slavery and chains. Substantial benefits would have rewarded his success; while on our side, life, liberty and property, were put in jeopardy, for an empty triumph. This, however, was a partial inconvenience—cases may arise in which evils of a more serious and comprehensive nature wou'd be the fruits of this visionary and fantastical principle. Suppose that, in the recess of Congress, a foreign maritime power should unexpectedly declare war against the United States, and send a fleet and army to seize Rhode-Island, in order from thence to annoy our trade and our seaport towns. Till the Congress should assemble and declare war, which would require time, our ships might, according to the hypothesis of the Message, be sent by the President to fight those of the enemy as often as they should be attacked, but not to capture and detain them: If beaten, both vessels and crews whould be lost to the United States: if successful, they could only disarm those they had overcome, and must suffer them to return to the place of common rendezvous, there to equip anew, for the purpose of resuming their depredations on our towns and our trade.

Who could restrain the laugh of derision at positions so preposterous, were it not for the reflection that in the first magistrate of our country, they cast a blemish on our national character? What will the world think of the fold when such is the shepherd?

12

St. George Tucker, Blackstone's Commentaries 1:App. 269–72 1803

11. The power of declaring war, with all its train of consequences, direct and indirect, forms the next branch of the powers confided to congress; and happy it is for the people of America that it is so vested. The term war, embraces the extremes of human misery and iniquity, and is alike the offspring of the one and the parent of the other.

What else is the history of war from the earliest ages to the present moment but an afflicting detail of the sufferings and calamities of mankind, resulting from the ambition, usurpation, animosities, resentments, piques, intrigues, avarice, rapacity, oppressions, murders, assassinations, and other crimes, of the few possessing power! How rare are the instances of a just war! How few of those which are thus denominated have had their existence in a national injury! The personal claims of the sovereign are confounded with the interests of the nation over which he presides, and his private grievances or complaints are transferred to the people; who are thus made the victims of a quarrel in which they have no part, until they become principals in it, by their sufferings. War would be banished from the face of the earth, were nations instead of princes to decide upon their necessity. Injustice can never be the collective sentiment of a people emerged from barbarism. Happy the nation where the people are the arbiters of their own interest and their own conduct! Happy were it for the world, did the people of all nations possess this power.

In England the right of making war is in the king. In Sweden it was otherwise after the death of Charles XII. until the revolution in 1772, when from a limited monarchy, Sweden became subject to a despot. With us the representatives of the people have the right to decide this important question, conjunctively with the supreme executive who may, on this occasion as on every other, (except a proposal to amend the constitution,) exercise a qualified negative on the joint resolutions of congress; but this negative is unavailing if two thirds of the congress should persist in an opposite determination; so that it may be in the power of the executive to prevent, but not to make, a declaration of war.

The several states are not only prohibited from declaring war, but even from engaging in it, without consent of congress, unless actually invaded, or in such imminent danger as will not admit of delay. This is certainly a very wise prohibition. . . . in fact, every barrier which can be opposed to the hasty engaging in war, is so much gained in favour of the interests of humanity. Upon the same principle it seems to be, that the states are likewise prohibited from granting letters of marque and reprisal: a measure which not unfrequently precedes a declaration of war where individuals of one nation are oppressed or injured by those of another, and justice is denied by the state to which the author of such oppression or injury belongs. Did the several states possess the power of declaring war, or of commencing hostility without the consent of the whole, the union could never be secure of peace, and since the whole confederacy is responsible for any such act, it is strictly consonant with justice and sound policy, that the whole should determine on the occasion which may justify involving the nation in a war. The keeping up troops or ships of war in time of peace, is also prohibited to the several states upon the same principle. For these kinds of preparations for hostility are such as frequently may provoke, and even justify hostility on the part of other nations. But whenever war is actually declared, this prohibition ceases, and any state may adopt such additional measures for it's own peculiar defence as it's resources will enable it to do. The prohibition to emit bills of credit, must, however, infallibly narrow the means of recurring to these resources; a consequence which probably was not adverted to by the state conventions, as I do not recollect any amendments proposed on that subject.

The power of declaring war, with all it's immediate consequences, was granted to congress under the former confederation, and nearly the same restrictions against engaging in war, keeping up troops and vessels of war in time of peace, were laid upon the individual states by the same instrument.

Among the amendments proposed by the convention of this state, and some others, to the constitution, there was one, "that no declaration of war should be made, nor any standing army or regular troops be raised or kept up, in time of peace, without the consent of two-thirds of the members present in both houses. And that no soldier should be enlisted for a longer term than four years, except in time of war, and then for no longer term than the continuance of the war." North-Carolina, as well as some other of the states, concurred in proposing similar amendments, but none has yet been made in this respect.

One of the most salutary provisions of the constitution, under this head, appears to be, that no appropriation of money to the use of an army, shall be for a longer term than two years. Perhaps it would have been better to have limited such an appropriation to a single year. But inasmuch as no appropriation can be made for a longer time than the period affixed for the duration of congress, it will be in the power of the people, should the reasons of such an appropriation be disapproved by them, to remove their representatives, on a new election, from a trust which they may appear willing to betray. It is, therefore, to be hoped, that such a consideration will afford a sufficient check to the proceedings of congress, in regard to the raising and supporting armies. With regard to a navy, the nature of such an establishment, to have any good effect, must be permanent. It would, therefore, have been extremely unwise to impose any prohibitions on that subject.

13

LITTLE v. BAREME

2 Cranch 170 (1804)

MARSHALL, C. J., delivered the opinion of the court.

The Flying Fish, a Danish vessel, having on board Danish and neutral property, was captured on the 2d of December, 1799, on a voyage from Jeremie to St. Thomas's, by the United States frigate Boston, commanded by Captain Little, and brought into the port of Boston, where she was libelled as an American vessel that had violated the non-intercourse law.

The judge, before whom the cause was tried, directed a restoration of the vessel and cargo as neutral property, but refused to award damages for the capture and detention, because, in his opinion, there was probable cause to suspect the vessel to be American.

On an appeal to the circuit court this sentence was reversed, because The Flying Fish was on a voyage from, not to, a French port and was therefore, had she even been an American vessel, not liable to capture on the high seas.

During the hostilities between the United States and France, an act for the suspension of all intercourse between the two nations was annually passed. That under which The Flying Fish was condemned, declared every vessel owned, hired or employed, wholly or in part, by an American, which should be employed in any traffic or commerce with or for any person resident within the jurisdiction, or under the authority, of the French republic, to be forfeited, together with her cargo; the one half to accrue to the United States, and the other to any person or persons, citizens of the United States, who will inform and prosecute for the same.

The 5th section of this act authorizes the President of the United States to instruct the commanders of armed vessels "to stop and examine any ship or vessel of the United States on the high seas, which there may be reason to suspect to be engaged in any traffic or commerce contrary to the true tenor of the act, and if upon examination it should appear that such ship or vessel is bound, or sailing to, any port or place within the territory of the French republic or her dependencies, it is rendered lawful to seize such vessel, and send her into the United States for adjudication."

It is by no means clear that the President of the United States, whose high duty it is to "take care that the laws be faithfully executed," and who is commander-in-chief of the armies and navies of the United States, might not, without any special authority for that purpose, in the then existing state of things, have empowered the officers commanding the armed vessels of the United States, to seize and send into port for adjudication, American vessels which were forfeited by being engaged in this illicit commerce. But when it is observed that the general clause of the 1st section of the "act, which declares that such vessels may be seized, and may be prosecuted in any district or circuit court, which shall be holden within or for the district where the seizure shall be made," obviously contemplates a seizure within the United States; and that the 5th section gives a special authority to seize on the high seas, and limits that authority to the seizure of vessels bound, or sailing to, a French port, the legislature seem to have prescribed that the manner in which this law shall be carried into execution, was to exclude a seizure of any vessel not bound to a French port. Of consequence, however strong the circumstances might be, which induced Captain Little to suspect The Flying Fish to be an American vessel, they could not excuse the detention of her, since he would not have been authorized to detain her had she been really American.

It was so obvious, that if only vessels sailing to a French port could be seized on the high seas, that the law would be very often evaded, that this act of congress appears to have received a different construction from the executive of the United States; a construction much better calculated to give it effect.

A copy of this act was transmitted by the secretary of the navy to the captains of the armed vessels, who were ordered to consider the 5th section as a part of their instructions. The same letter contained the following clause: "A proper discharge of the important duties enjoined on you, arising out of this act, will require the exercise of a sound and an impartial judgment. You are not only to do all that in you lies to prevent all intercourse, whether direct or circuitous, between the ports of the United States and those of France or her dependencies, where the vessels are apparently as well as really American, and protected by American papers only, but you are to be vigilant that vessels or cargoes really American, but covered by Danish or other foreign papers, and bound to or from French ports, do not escape you."

These orders, given by the executive under the construction of the act of congress made by the department to which its execution was assigned, enjoin the seizure of American vessels sailing from a French port. Is the officer who obeys them liable for damages sustained by this misconstruction of the act, or will his orders excuse him? If his instructions afford him no protection, then the law must take its course, and he must pay such damages as are legally awarded against him; if they excuse an act not otherwise excusable, it would then be necessary to inquire whether this is a case in which the probable cause which existed to induce a suspicion that the vessel was American, would excuse the captor from damages when the vessel appeared in fact to be neutral.

I confess the first bias of my mind was very strong in favor of the opinion that though the instructions of the executive could not give a right, they might yet excuse from damages. I was much inclined to think that a distinction ought to be taken between acts of civil and those of military officers; and between proceedings within the body of the country and those on the high seas. That implicit obedience which military men usually pay to the orders of their superiors, which indeed is indispensably necessary to every military system, appeared to me strongly to imply the principle that those orders, if not to perform a prohibited act, ought to justify the person whose general duty it is to obey them, and who is placed by the laws of his country in a situation which in general requires that he should obey them. I was strongly inclined to think that where, in consequence of orders from the legitimate authority, a vessel is seized with pure intention, the claim of the injured party for damages would be against that government from which the orders proceeded, and would be a proper subject for negotiation. But I have been convinced that I was mistaken, and I have receded from this first opinion. I acquiesce in that of my brethren, which is, that the instructions cannot change the nature of the transaction, or legalize an act which, without those instructions, would have been a plain trespass.

It becomes, therefore, unnecessary to inquire whether the probable cause afforded by the conduct of The Flying Fish to suspect her of being an American would excuse Captain Little from damages for having seized and sent her into port, since, had she been an American, the seizure would have been unlawful.

Captain Little, then, must be answerable in damages to the owner of this neutral vessel, and as the account taken by order of the circuit court is not objectionable on its face, and has not been excepted to by counsel before the proper tribunal, this court can receive no objection to it.

14

The Schooner Exchange v. McFaddon

7 Cranch 116 (1812)

(See 1.8.10, no. 7)

15

Brown v. United States

8 Cranch 110 (1814)

Marshall, *Ch. J.* delivered the opinion of the Court, as follows:

The material facts in this case are these:

The *Emulous* owned by John Delano and others, citizens of the United States, was chartered to a company carrying on trade in Great Britain, one of whom was an American citizen, for the purpose of carrying a cargo from Savannah to Plymouth. After the cargo was put on board, the vessel was stopped in port by the embargo of the 4th of April, 1812. On the 25th of the same month, it was agreed between the master of the ship and the agent of the shippers, that she should proceed with her cargo to New Bedford, where her owners resided, and remain there without prejudice to the charter party. In pursuance of this agreement, the Emulous proceeded to New Bedford, where she continued until after the declaration of war. In October or November, the ship was unloaded and the cargo, except the pine timber, was landed. The pine timber was floated up a salt water creek, where, at low tide, the ends of the timber rested on the mud, where it was secured from floating out with the tide, by impediments fastened in the entrance of the creek. On the 7th of November, 1812, the cargo was sold by the agent of the owners, who is an American citizen, to the Claimant, who is also an American citizen. On the 19th of April, a libel was filed by the attorney for the United States, in the district Court of Massachusetts, against the said cargo, as well on behalf of the United States of America as for and in behalf of John Delano and of all other persons concerned. It does not appear that this seizure was made under any instructions from the president of the United States; nor is there any evidence of its having his sanction, unless the libels being filed and prosecuted by the law officer who represents the government, must imply that sanction.

On the contrary, it is admitted that the seizure was made by an individual, and the libel filed at his instance, by the district attorney who acted from his own impressions of what appertained to his duty. The property was claimed by Armitz Brown under the purchase made in the preceding November.

The district Court dismissed the libel. The Circuit Court reversed this sentence, and condemned the pine timber as enemy property forfeited to the United States. From the sentence of the Circuit Court, the Claimant appealed to this Court.

The material question made at bar is this. Can the pine timber, even admitting the property not to be changed by the sale in November, be condemned as prize of war?

The cargo of the Emulous having been legally acquired and put on board the vessel, having been detained by an embargo not intended to act on foreign property, the vessel having sailed before the war, from Savannah, under a stipulation to re-land the cargo in some port of the United States, the re-landing having been made with respect to the residue of the cargo, and the pine timber having been floated into shallow water, where it was secured and in the custody of the owner of the ship, an American citizen, the Court cannot perceive any solid distinction, so far as respects confiscation, between this property and other British property found on land at the commencement of hostilities. It will therefore be considered as a question relating to such property generally, and to be governed by the same rule.

Respecting the power of government no doubt is entertained. That war gives to the sovereign full right to take the persons and confiscate the property of the enemy wherever found, is conceded. The mitigations of this rigid rule, which the humane and wise policy of modern times has introduced into practice, will more or less affect the exercise of this right, but cannot impair the right itself. That remains undiminished, and when the sovereign authority shall chuse to bring it into operation, the judicial department must give effect to its will. But until that will shall be expressed, no power of condemnation can exist in the Court.

The questions to be decided by the Court are:

1st. May enemy's property, found on land at the commencement of hostilities, be seized and condemned as a necessary consequence of the declaration of war?

2d. Is there any legislative act which authorizes such seizure and condemnation?

Since, in this country, from the structure of our government, proceedings to condemn the property of an enemy found within our territory at the declaration of war, can be sustained only upon the principle that they are instituted in execution of some existing law, we are led to ask,

Is the declaration of war such a law? Does that declaration, by its own operation, so vest the property of the enemy in the government, as to support proceedings for its seizure and confiscation, or does it vest only a right, the assertion of which depends on the will of the sovereign power?

The universal practice of forbearing to seize and confiscate debts and credits, the principle universally received, that the right to them revives on the restoration of peace, would seem to prove that war is not an absolute confiscation of this property, but simply confers the right of confiscation.

Between debts contracted under the faith of laws, and property acquired in the course of trade, on the faith of the same laws, reason draws no distinction; and, although, in practice, vessels with their cargoes, found in port at the declaration of war, may have been seized, it is not believed that modern usage would sanction the seizure of the goods of an enemy on land, which were acquired in peace in the course of trade. Such a proceeding is rare, and would be deemed a harsh exercise of the rights of war. But although the practice in this respect may not be uniform, that circumstance does not essentially affect the question. The enquiry is, whether such property vests in the sovereign by the mere declaration of war, or remains subject to a right of confiscation, the exercise of which depends on the national will: and the rule which applies to one case, so far as respects the operation of a declaration of war on the thing itself, must apply to all others over which war gives an equal right. The right of the sovereign to confiscate debts being precisely the same with the right to confiscate other property found in the country, the operation of a declaration of war on debts and on other property found within the country must be the same. What then is this operation?

Even *Bynkershoek,* who maintains the broad principle, that in war every thing done against an enemy is lawful; that he may be destroyed, though unarmed and defenceless; that fraud, or even poison, may be employed against him; that a most unlimited right is acquired to his person and property; admits that war does not transfer to the sovereign a debt due to his enemy; and, therefore, if payment of such debt be not exacted, peace revives the former right of the creditor; "because," he says, "the occupation which is had by war consists more in fact than in law." He adds to his observations on this subject, "let it not, however, be supposed that it is only true of actions, that they are not condemned *ipso jure,* for other things also belonging to the enemy may be concealed and escape condemnation."

Vattel says, that "the sovereign can neither detain the persons nor the property of those subjects of the enemy who are within his dominions at the time of the declaration."

It is true that this rule is, in terms, applied by *Vattel* to the property of those only who are personally within the territory at the commencement of hostilities; but it applies equally to things in action and to things in possession; and if war did, of itself, without any further exercise of the sovereign will, vest the property of the enemy in the sovereign, his presence could not exempt it from this operation of war. Nor can a reason be perceived for maintaining that the public faith is more entirely pledged for the security of property trusted in the territory of the nation in time of peace, if it be accompanied by its owner, than if it be confided to the care of others.

Chitty, after stating the general right of seizure, says, "But, in strict justice, that right can take effect only on those possessions of a belligerent which have come to the hands of his adversary after the declaration of hostilities."

The modern rule then would seem to be, that tangible property belonging to an enemy and found in the country at the commencement of war, ought not to be immediately confiscated; and in almost every commercial treaty an article is inserted stipulating for the right to withdraw such property.

This rule appears to be totally incompatible with the idea, that war does of itself vest the property in the belligerent government. It may be considered as the opinion of all who have written on the *jus belli,* that war gives the right to confiscate, but does not itself confiscate the property of the enemy; and their rules go to the exercise of this right.

The constitution of the United States was framed at a time when this rule, introduced by commerce in favor of moderation and humanity, was received throughout the civilized world. In expounding that constitution, a construction ought not lightly to be admitted which would give to a declaration of war an effect in this country it does not possess elsewhere, and which would fetter that exercise of entire discretion respecting enemy property, which may enable the government to apply to the enemy the rule that he applies to us.

If we look to the constitution itself, we find this general reasoning much strengthened by the words of that instrument.

That the declaration of war has only the effect of placing the two nations in a state of hostility, of producing a state of war, of giving those rights which war confers; but not of operating, by its own force, any of those results, such as a transfer of property, which are usually produced by ulterior measures of government, is fairly deducible from the enumeration of powers which accompanies that of declaring war. "Congress shall have power"—"to declare war, grant letters of marque and reprisal, and make rules concerning captures on land and water."

It would be restraining this clause within narrower limits than the words themselves import, to say that the power to make rules concerning captures on land and water, is to be confined to captures which are exterritorial. If it extends to rules respecting enemy property found within the territory, then we perceive an express grant to congress of the power in question as an independent substantive power, not included in that of declaring war.

The acts of congress furnish many instances of an opinion that the declaration of war does not, of itself, authorize proceedings against the persons or property of the enemy found, at the time, within the territory.

War gives an equal right over persons and property: and if its declaration is not considered as prescribing a law respecting the person of an enemy found in our country, neither does it prescribe a law for his property. The act concerning alien enemies, which confers on the president very great discretionary powers respecting their persons, affords a strong implication that he did not possess those powers by virtue of the declaration of war.

The "act for the safe keeping and accommodation of prisoners of war," is of the same character.

The act prohibiting trade with the enemy, contains this clause:

"And be it further enacted, That the president of the United States be, and he is hereby authorized to give, at any time within six months after the passage of this act, passports for the safe transportation of any ship or other property belonging to British subjects, and which is now within the limits of the United States."

The phraseology of this law shows that the property of a British subject was not considered by the legislature as being vested in the United States by the declaration of war; and the authority which the act confers on the president, is manifestly considered as one which he did not previously possess.

The proposition that a declaration of war does not, in itself, enact a confiscation of the property of the enemy within the territory of the belligerent, is believed to be entirely free from doubt. Is there in the act of congress, by which war is declared against Great Britain, any expression which would indicate such an intention?

That act, after placing the two nations in a state of war, authorizes the president of the United States to use the whole land and naval force of the United States to carry the war into effect, and "to issue to private armed vessels of the United States, commissions or letters of marque and general reprisal against the vessels, goods and effects of the government of the united kingdom of Great Britain and Ireland, and the subjects thereof."

That reprisals may be made on enemy property found within the United States at the declaration of war, if such be the will of the nation, has been admitted; but it is not admitted that, in the declaration of war, the nation has expressed its will to that effect.

It cannot be necessary to employ argument in showing that when the attorney for the United States institutes proceedings at law for the confiscation of enemy property found on land, or floating in one of our creeks, in the care and custody of one of our citizens, he is not acting under the authority of letters of marque and reprisal, still less under the authority of such letters issued to a private armed vessel.

The "act concerning letters of marque, prizes and prize goods," certainly contains nothing to authorize this seizure.

There being no other act of congress which bears upon the subject, it is considered as proved that the legislature has not confiscated enemy property which was within the United States at the declaration of war, and that this sentence of condemnation cannot be sustained.

One view, however, has been taken of this subject which deserves to be further considered.

It is urged that, in executing the laws of war, the executive may seize and the Courts condemn all property which, according to the modern law of nations, is subject to confiscation, although it might require an act of the legislature to justify the condemnation of that property which, according to modern usage, ought not to be confiscated.

This argument must assume for its basis the position that modern usage constitutes a rule which acts directly upon the thing itself by its own force, and not through the sovereign power. This position is not allowed. This usage is a guide which the sovereign follows or abandons at his will. The rule, like other precepts of morality, of humanity, and even of wisdom, is addressed to the judgment of the sovereign; and although it cannot be disregarded by him without obloquy, yet it may be disregarded.

The rule is, in its nature, flexible. It is subject to infinite modification. It is not an immutable rule of law, but depends on political considerations which may continually vary.

Commercial nations, in the situation of the United States, have always a considerable quantity of property in the possession of their neighbors. When war breaks out, the question, what shall be done with enemy property in our country, is a question rather of policy than of law. The rule which we apply to the property of our enemy, will be applied by him to the property of our citizens. Like all other questions of policy, it is proper for the consideration of a department which can modify it at will; not for the consideration of a department which can pursue only the law as it is written. It is proper for the consideration of the legislature, not of the executive or judiciary.

It appears to the Court, that the power of confiscating enemy property is in the legislature, and that the legislature has not yet declared its will to confiscate property which was within our territory at the declaration of war. The Court is therefore of opinion that there is error in the sentence of condemnation pronounced in the Circuit Court in this case, and doth direct that the same be reversed and annulled, and that the sentence of the District Court be affirmed.

STORY, *J.*

In this case, I have the misfortune to differ in opinion from my brethren; and as the grounds of the decree were fully stated in an opinion delivered in the Court below, I shall make no apology for reading it in this place.

"This is a prize allegation filed by the district attorney, in behalf of the United States, and of John Delano, against 550 tons of pine timber, part of the cargo of the American ship Emulous, which was seized as enemies' property, about the 5th day of April, 1813, after the same had been discharged from said ship, and while afloat in a creek or dock at New Bedford, where the tide ebbs and flows.

From the evidence in this case, it appears that the ship Emulous is owned by the said John Delano, John Johnson, Levi Jenny, and Joshua Delano of New Bedford, and citizens of the United States. On the 3d day of February 1812, the owners, by their agents, entered into a charter-party with Elijah Brown as agent of Messrs. Christopher Idle, Brother and Co. and James Brown, of London, merchants, for said ship, to proceed from the port of Charleston, South Carolina, (where the ship then lay,) to Savannah, in Georgia, and there take on board a cargo of timber and staves, at a certain freight stipulated in the charter-party, and proceed with the same to Plymouth, in England, 'for orders to unload there or at any other of his majesty's dock-yards in England.' The ship accordingly proceeded to Savannah, took on board the agreed cargo, and was there stopped by the embargo laid by Congress on the 4th of April 1812. On the 25th of the same April, it was agreed between Mr. E. Brown and the master of the ship, that she should proceed with the cargo to, and lay at New Bedford, without prejudice to the charter-party. The ship accordingly proceeded for New Bedford, and arrived there in the latter part of May 1812, where, it seems, the cargo was finally, but the particular time is not stated, unloaded by the owners of the ship, the staves put into a warehouse, and the timber into a salt water creek or dock, where it has ever since remained, waterborne, under the custody of said John Delano, by whom the subsequent seizure was made, for his own benefit and the benefit of the United States. On the 7th November, 1812, Mr. Elijah Brown, as agent for the British owners, (one of whom, James Brown, is his brother,) sold the whole cargo to the present claimant, Mr. Armitz Brown (who it should seem is also his brother) for 2433 dollars and 67 cents, payable in nine months, for which the claimant gave his note accordingly. The master of the ship, Capt. Allen, swears that, at the time of entering into the charter-party, Mr. Elijah Brown stated to him that the British owners had contracted with the British government to furnish a large quantity of timber to be delivered in some of his majesty's dock-yards.

Besides the claim of Mr. Brown, there is a claim interposed by the owners of the ship Emulous, praying for an allowance to them of their expenses and charges in the premises.

A preliminary exception has been taken to the libel for a supposed incongruity in blending the rights of the United States and of the informer in the manner of a *qui tam* action at the common law.

I do not think this exception is entitled to much consideration. It is, at most, but an irregularity which cannot affect the nature of the proceedings, or oust the jurisdiction of this Court. If the informer cannot legally take any interest, the United States have still a right, if their title is otherwise well founded, to claim a condemnation: Nor would a proceeding of this nature be deemed a fatal irregularity in Courts having jurisdiction of seizures, whose proceedings are governed by much more rigid rules than those of the admiralty. It is a principle clearly settled at the common law, that any person might seize uncustomed goods to the use of himself and the king, and thereupon inform of the seizure; and if, in the exchequer, the informer be not entitled to any part, the whole shall, on such information, be adjudged to the king. For this doctrine we have the authority of lord Hale. *Harg. law tracts,* 227. And the solemn judgment of the Court, in *Roe v. Roe, Hardr.* 185.—and *Malden v. Bartlett, Parker,* 105. The same rule most undoubtedly exists in the prize Court, and, as I apprehend, applies with greater latitude. All property captured belongs originally to the crown; and individuals can acquire a title thereto in no other manner than by grant from the crown. *The Elsebe,* 5. *Rob.* 173.—11. *East,* 619.—*The Maria Francoise.* 6. *Rob.* 282. This, however, does not preclude the right to seize; on the contrary, it is an indisputable principle in the English prize Courts, that a subject may seize hostile property for the use of the crown, wherever it is found; and it rests in the discretion of the crown whether it will or will not ratify and consummate the seizure by proceeding to condemnation. But to the prize Court it is a matter of pure indifference whether the seizure proceeded originally from the crown, or has been adopted by it; and whether the crown would take *jure coronae,* by its transcendant prerogative, or *jure admiralitatis,* as a power annexed by its grant to the office of lord high admiral. The cases of captures by noncommissioned vessels, by commanders on foreign stations, anterior to war, by private individuals in port or on the coasts, and by naval commanders on shore on unauthorised expeditions, are all very strong illustrations of the principle. *The Aquila,* 1. *Rob.* 37.—*The Twee Gesuster,* 2. *Rob.* 284, *note.*—*The Rebeckah,* 1. *Rob.* 227.—*The Gertruyda,* 2. *Rob.* 211.—*The Melomane,* 5. *Rob.* 41.—*The Charlotte,* 4. *Rob.* 282.—*The Richmond,* 5. *Rob.* 325.—*Thorshaven,* 1. *Edw.* 102.—*Hale in Harg. law tracts, ch.* 28. *p.* 245. And in cases where private captors seek condemnation to themselves, it is the settled course of the Court, on failure of their title, to decree condemnation to the crown or the admiralty, as the circumstances require. *The Walsingham Packet,* 2. *Rob.* 77.—*The Etrusco,* 4. *Rob.* 262. *note.—and the cases cited supra.* Nor can I consider these principles of the British Courts a departure from the law of nations. The authority of *Puffendorf* and *Vattel* are introduced to shew that private subjects are not at liberty to seize the property of enemies without the commission of the sovereign, and if they do they are considered as pirates. But when attentively considered, it strikes me that, taking the full scope of these authors, they will not be found to support so broad a position. *Puff. B.* 8. *ch.* 6. § 21.—*Vattel, B.* 3. *ch.* 15. § 223, 224, 225, 226, 227. *Vattel* himself admits (§ 234.) that the declaration of war, which enjoins the subjects at large to attack the enemy's subjects, implies a general order; and that to commit hostilities on our enemy without an order from our sovereign after the war, is not a violation so much of the law of nations as of the public law applicable to the sovereignty of our own nation, (§ 225.) And he explicitly states, (§ 226.) that, by the law of nations, when once two nations are engaged in war, all the subjects of the one may commit hostilities against those of the other, and do them all the mischief authorized by the state of war. All that he contends for is, that though, by the declaration, all the subjects in general are ordered to attack the enemy, yet that by custom this is usually restrained to persons acting under commission; and that the general order does not invite the subjects to undertake any offensive expedition without a commission or particular order; (§ 227.) and that if they do, they are not usually treated by the enemy in a manner as favorable as other prisoners of war, (§ 226.) And *Vattel* (§ 227.) explicitly declares, that the declaration of war "authorizes, indeed, and even obliges every subject, of whatever rank, to secure the persons and *things* belonging to the enemy, when they fall into his hands. And he then goes on to state cases in which the authority of the sovereign may be presumed, (§ 228.) The whole doctrine of Vattel, fairly considered, amounts to no more than this, that the subject is not required, by the mere declaration of war, to originate predatory expeditions against the enemy;

that he is not authorized to wage war contrary to the will of his own sovereign; and that, though the ordinary declaration of war imports a general authority to attack the enemy and his property, yet custom has so far restrained its meaning, that it is in general confined to persons acting under the particular or constructive commission of the sovereign. If, therefore, the subject do undertake a predatory expedition, it is an infringement of the public law of his own country, whose sovereignty he thus invades, but it is not a violation of the law of nations of which the enemy has a right to complain. But if the property of the enemy *fall* into the hands of a subject, he is bound to secure it.

For every purpose applicable to the present case, it does not seem necessary to controvert these positions; and, whatever may be the correctness of the others, I am perfectly satisfied that the position is well founded, that no subject can legally commit hostilities, or capture property of an enemy, when, either expressly or constructively, the sovereign has prohibited it. But suppose he does, I would ask if the sovereign may not ratify his proceedings; and thus, by a retroactive operation, give validity to them? Of this there seems to me no legal doubt. The subject seizes at his peril, and the sovereign decides, in the last resort, whether he will approve or disapprove of the act. *Thorshaven,* 1, *Edw.* 102. The authority of *Puffendorf* is still less in favor of the position of the Claimant's counsel. In the section cited (*book* 8, *ch.* 6, *sec.* 21.) Puffendorf considers the question to whom property captured in war belongs; a question also examined by *Vattel* in the 229th section of the book and chapter above referred to. In the course of that discussion, Puffendorf observes, 'that it may be very justly questioned, whether every thing taken in war, by *private hostilities,* and by the bravery of private subjects that have no commission to warrant them, belongeth to them that take it. For this is also a part of the war, to appoint what persons are to act in a hostile manner against the enemy, and how far: and, in consequence, no private person hath power to make devastations in an enemy's country or to carry off spoil or plunder without permission from his sovereign: and the sovereign is to decide how far private men, when they are permitted, are to use that liberty of plunder; and whether they are to be the sole proprietors in the booty or only to share a part of it: so that all a private adventurer in war can pretend to, is no more than what his sovereign will please to allow him; for to be a soldier and to act offensively, a man must be commissioned by public authority.'

As to the point upon which Puffendorf here expresses his doubts, I suppose that no person, at this day, entertains any doubts. It is now clear, as I have already stated, that all captures in war enure to the sovereign, and can become private property only by his grant. But is there any thing in Puffendorf to authorize the doctrine, that the subject so seizing property of the enemy, is guilty of a very enormous crime—of the odious crime of piracy? And is there, in this language, any thing to show that the sovereign may not adopt the acts of his subjects, in such a case, and give them the effect of full and perfect ratification? It has not been pretended, that I recollect, that Grotius supports the position contended for. To me it seems pretty clear that his opinions lean rather the other way; viz: to support the indiscriminate right of captors to all property captured by them. *Grotius, lib.* 3, *ch.* 6, *sec.* 2, *sec.* 10, *sec.* 12. *Bynkershoek* has not discussed the question in direct terms. In one place (*Bynk. Pub. Juris, ch.* 3,) he says, that he is not guilty of any crime, by the laws of war, who invades a hostile shore in hopes of getting booty. It is true that, in another place (*id. ch.* 20,) he admits, in conformity to his doctrine elsewhere, (*id. ch.* 17,) that if an uncommissioned cruizer should sail for the purpose of making hostile captures, she might be dealt with as a pirate, if she made any captures except in self-defence. But this he expressly grounds upon the municipal edicts of his own country in relation to captures made by its own subjects. And he says, every declaration of war not only permits but expressly orders all subjects to injure the enemy by every possible means; not only to avert the danger of capture, but to capture and strip the enemy of all his property. And, looking to the general scope of his observations, (*id. ch.* 3, 4, *&* *ch.* 16 *&* 17.) I think it may, not unfairly, be argued that, independent of particular edicts, the subjects of hostile nations might lawfully seize each other's property wherever found: at least, he states nothing from which it can be inferred that the sovereign might not avail himself of property captured from the enemy by uncommissioned subjects. On the whole, I hold that the true doctrine of the law of nations, found in foreign jurists, is, that private citizens cannot acquire to themselves a title to hostile property, unless it is seized under the commission of their sovereign; and that, if they depredate upon the enemy, they act upon their peril, and may be liable to punishment, unless their acts are adopted by their sovereign. That, in modern times, the mere declaration of war is not supposed to clothe the citizens with authority to capture hostile property, but that they may lawfully seize hostile property in their own defence, and are bound to secure, for the use of the sovereign, all hostile property which falls into their hands. If the principles of British prize law go further, I am free to say that I consider them as the law of this country.

I have been led into this discussion of the doctrine of foreign jurists, farther than I originally intended; because the practice of this Court in prize proceedings must, as I have already intimated, be governed by the rules of admiralty law disclosed in English reports, in preference to the mere *dicta* of elementary writers. I thought it my duty, however, to notice these authorities, because they seem generally relied on by the Claimant's counsel. In my judgment, the libel is well and properly brought; at least for all the purposes of justice between the parties before the Court; and I overrule the exception taken to its sufficiency.

Having disposed of this objection, I come now to consider the objection made by the United States against the sufficiency of the claim of Mr. Brown; and I am entirely satisfied that his claim must be rejected. It is a well known rule of the prize Court, that the *onus probandi* lies on the Claimant; he must make out a good and sufficient title before he can call upon the captors to shew any ground for the capture. *The Walsingham packet,* 2, *Rob.* 77. If, therefore, the Claimant make no title, or trace it only by illegal transactions, his claim must be rejected, and the Court left to dispose of the cause, as the other parties may establish their rights. In the present case, Mr. Brown claims a title by virtue of a contract and sale made by alien enemies since the war: I say by alien enemies; for it is of no importance what the character of the agent is: the transaction must have the same legal construction as though made by the aliens themselvs. Now admitting that this sale was not colorable, but *bona fide,* which, however, I am not, at present, disposed to believe, still it was a contract made with enemies, pending a known war; and therefore invalid. No principle of national or municipal law is better settled, than that all contracts with an enemy, made during war, are utterly void. This principle has grown hoary under the reverend respect of centuries; (19, *Edw.* 4, 6, *cited Theol. Dig. lib.* 1, *ch.* 6, *sec.* 21. *Ex parte Bonsmaker,* 13, *Ves. jun.* 71—*Briston v. Towers,* 6, *T. R.* 45,) and cannot now be shaken without uprooting the very foundations of national law. *Bynk. Quaest. Pub. Juris, ch.* 3.

I, therefore, altogether reject the claim interposed by Mr. Brown. What, then, is to be done with the property? It is contended, on the part of the United States, that it ought to be condemned to the United States, with a recompense, in the nature of salvage, to be awarded to Mr. Delano. On the part of the Claimant's counsel (who, under the circumstances, must be considered as arguing as *amicus curiae* to inform the conscience of the Court) it is contended, 1st. That this Court, as a Court of prize, has no proper jurisdiction over the cause. 2d. That if it have jurisdiction, it cannot award condemnation to the United States, for several reasons. 1st. Because, by the law of nations, as now understood, no government can lawfully confiscate the debts, credits, or visible property of alien enemies, which have been contracted or come into the country during peace. 2d. Because, if the law of nations does not, the common law does afford such immunity from confiscation to property situated like the present. 3d. Because, if the right to confiscate exist, it can be exercised only by a positive act of congress, who have not yet legislated to this extent. 4th. Because, if the last position be not fully accurate, yet, at all events, this process, being a high prerogative power, ought not to be exercised, except by express instructions from the president, which are not shown in this case.

Some of these questions are of vast importance and most extensive operation; and I am exceedingly obliged to the gentlemen who have argued them with so much ability and learning, for the light which they have thrown upon a path so intricate and obscure. I have given these questions as much consideration as the state of my health and the brevity of time would allow; and I shall now give them a distinct and separate discussion, that I may at least disclose the sources of my errors, if any, and enable those who unite higher powers of discernment with more extensive knowledge, to give a more exact and just opinion.

And first . . . As to the jurisdiction of this Court in matters of prize.

This depends partly on the prize act of 26th June, 1812, ch. 107, § 6, and partly on the true extent and meaning of the admiralty and maritime jurisdiction conferred on the Courts of the United States. The act of 26th June, 1812, ch. 107, provides that in all cases of captured vessels, goods and effects which shall be brought within the jurisdiction of the United States, the district Court shall have exclusive original cognizance thereof, as in civil causes of admiralty and maritime jurisdiction. The act of 18th June, 1812, ch. 102, declaring war, authorizes the president to issue letters of marque and reprisal to private armed ships against the vessels, goods and effects of the British government and its subjects; and to use the whole land and naval force of the United States to carry the war into effect. In neither of these acts is there any limitation as to the places where captures may be made on the land or on the seas; and, of course, it would seem that the right of the Courts to adjudicate respecting captures would be co-extensive with such captures, wherever made, unless the jurisdiction conferred is manifestly confined by the former act to captures made by private armed vessels. It is not, however, necessary closely to sift this point, as it may now be considered as settled law, that the Courts of the United States, under the judicial act of 30th September, 1789, ch. 20, have, by the delegation of all civil causes of admiralty and maritime jurisdiction, at least as full jurisdiction of all causes of prize as the admiralty in England. *Glass and al. v. the sloop Betsey and al.* 3 *Dall.* 6. *Talbot v. Janson.* 3 *Dall.* 133. *Penhallow and al. v. Doane's administrators.* 3 *Dall.* 54. *Jennings v. Carson,* 4 *Cranch,* 2. Over what captures, then, has the admiralty jurisdiction as a prize Court? This is a question of considerable intricacy, and has not as yet, to my knowledge, been fully settled. It has been doubted whether the admiralty has an inherent jurisdiction of prize, or obtains it by virtue of the commission usually issued on the breaking out of war. That the exercise of the jurisdiction is of very high antiquity and beyond the time of memory, seems to be incontestible. It is found recognized in various articles of the black book of the admiralty, in public treaties and proclamations of a very early date, and in the most venerable relics of ancient jurisprudence. See *Robb. Coll. Marit. Intro. p.* 6, 7. *Id. Instructions,* 3 *H.* 8, *p.* 10, *art.* 18, *&c. Id. p.* 12, *note letter. Edw.* 3, *A. D.* 1343. *Treaty Henry* 7 *and Charles* 8, *A. D.* 1497. *Rob. Coll. Marit. p.* 83 *and p.* 98, *art.* 8. *Rob. Coll. Mar. p.* 189, *note. Roughton, art.* 19, 20, *&c. &c. passim.* In *Lindo v. Rodney, Doug.* 613, *note,* Lord *Mansfield,* in discussing the subject, admits the immemorial antiquity of the prize jurisdiction of the admiralty; but leaves it uncertain whether it was coeval with the instance jurisdiction, and whether it is constituted by special commission, or only called into exercise thereby. After the doubts of so eminent a judge, it would not become me to express a decided opinion. But taking the fact that, in the earliest times, the jurisdiction is found in the possession of the admiralty, independent of any known special commission; that, in other countries, and especially in France, upon whose ancient prize ordinances the administration of prize law seems, in a great measure, to have been modelled, *(Vide Ordin. of France, A. D.* 1400, *Rob. Coll. Marit. p.* 75. *Ordin. of France, A. D.* 1584. *Id. p.* 105. *Treaty Henry* 7 *and Charles* 8. *Id. p.* 83, and *Rob. note, Id.* 105*)* the jurisdiction has uniformly belonged to the admiralty; there seems very strong reason to presume that it always constituted an ordinary and not an extraordinary branch of the admiralty powers: and so I apprehend it was considered by the Supreme Court of the United States, in *Glass and al. v. the Betsey,* 3 *Dall.* 6.

However this question may be, as to the right of the admiralty to take cognizance of mere captures made on the land, exclusively by land forces, as to which I give no opinion, it is very clear that its jurisdiction is not confined to mere captures at sea. The prize jurisdiction does not depend upon locality, but upon the subject matter. The words of the prize commission contain authority to proceed upon all and all manner of captures, seizures, prizes and reprisals of all ships and goods that are and shall be taken. The admiralty, therefore, not only takes cognizance of all captures made at sea, in creeks, havens and rivers, but also of all captures made on land, where the same have been made by a naval force, or by co-operation with a naval force. This exercise of jurisdiction is settled by the most solemn adjudications. *Key and Hubbard v. Pearse,* cited in *Le Caux v. Eden, Doug.* 606. *Lindo v. Rodney, Doug.* 613, *note. The capture of the Cape of Good Hope,* 2 *Rob.* 274. *The Stella del Norte,* 5 *Rob.* 349. *The island of Trinidad,* 5 *Rob.* 92. *Thorshaven,* 1 *Edw.* 102. *The capture of Chrinsurah,* 1 *Deten.* 179. *The Rebeckah,* 1 *Rob.* 227. *The Gertruyda,* 2 *Rob.* 211. *The Maria Francoise,* 6 *Rob.* 282.

Such, then, being the acknowledged extent of the prize jurisdiction of the admiralty, it is, at least in as ample an extent, conferred on the Courts of the United States. For the determination, therefore, of the case before the Court, it is not necessary to claim a more ample jurisdiction; for the capture or seizure, though made in port, was made while the property was waterborne. Had it been landed and remained on land, it would have deserved consideration whether it could have been proceeded against as prize, under the admiralty jurisdiction, or whether, if liable to seizure and condemnation in our Courts, the remedy ought not to have been pursued by a process applicable to municipal confiscations. On these points I give no opinion. See the case of the *Oester Eems* cited in the *Two Friends,* 1 *Rob.* 284, *note. Hale de Portubus Maris, &c. in Harg. Law tracts, ch.* 28, *p.* 245, *&c. Parker Rep.* 267.

Having disposed of the question as to the jurisdiction of this Court, I come to one of a more general nature; viz. Whether, by the modern law of nations, the sovereign has a right to confiscate the debts due to his enemy, or the goods of his enemy found within his territory at the commencement of the war. I might spare myself the consideration of the question as to *debts;* but, as it has been ably argued, I will submit some views respecting it, because they will illustrate and confirm the doctrine applicable to goods. It seems conceded, and indeed is quite too clear for argument, that, in former times, the right to confiscate *debts* was admitted as a doctrine of national law. It had the countenance of the civil law. (*Dig. lib.* 44. *tit.* 4.—*id. lib.* 49, *tit.* 15,)—of *Grotius,* (*De jure belli et pacis, lib.* 3, *ch.* 2, *§* 2, *ch.* 6. *§* 2 *ch.* 7, *§* 3 *and* 4, *ch.* 13, *§* 1, 2.)—of *Puffendorf,* (*De jure Nat. et Nat. lib.* 8, *ch.* 6, *§* 23,)—and lastly of *Bynkershoek;* (*Quaest. Pub. Juris, lib.* 1, *ch.* 7.) who is himself of the highest authority, and pronounces his opinion in the most explicit manner. Down to the year 1737, it may be considered as the opinion of jurists that the right was unquestionable. It is, then, incumbent on those who assume a different doctrine, to prove that, since that period, it has by the general consent of nations, become incorporated into the code of public law. I take upon me to say that no jurist of reputation can be found who has denied the right of confiscation of enemies debts. *Vattel* has been supposed to be the most favorable to the new doctrine. He certainly does not deny the right to confiscate; and if he may be thought to hesitate in admitting it, nothing more can be gathered from it than that he considers that, in the present times, a relaxation of the rigor of the law has been in practice among the sovereigns of Europe. *Vattel, lib.* 3, *ch.* 5, *§* 77. Surely a relaxation of the law in practice cannot be admitted to constitute an abolition in principle, when the principle is asserted, as late as 1737, by Bynkershoek, and the relaxation shewn by Vattel in 1775. In another place, however, Vattel, speaking on the subject of reprisals, admits the right to seize the property of the nation or its subjects by way of reprisal, and, if war ensues, to confiscate the property so seized. The only exception he makes, is of property which has been deposited in the hands of the nation, and intrusted to the public faith; as is the case of property in the public funds. *Vattel, lib.* 2, *ch.* 18, *§* 342, 343, 344. The very exception evinces pretty strongly the opinion of Vattel as to the general rule. Of the character of Vattel as a jurist, I shall not undertake to express an opinion. That he has great merit is conceded; though a learned civilian, sir James MacIntosh, informs us that he has fallen into great mistakes in important 'practical discussion of public law.' *Discourse on the law of nations, p.* 32, *note.* But if he is singly to be opposed to the weight of Grotius and Puffendorf, and, above all, Bynkershoek, it will be difficult for him to sustain so unequal a contest. I have been pressed with the opinion of a very distinguished writer of our own country on this subject.—*Camillus, No.* 18 *to* 23, *on the British treaty of* 1794. I admit, in the fullest manner, the great merit of the argument which he has adduced against the confiscation of private debts due to enemy subjects. Looking to the measure not as of strict right, but as of sound policy and national honor, I have no hesitation to say that the argument is unanswerable. He proves incontrovertibly what the highest interest of nations dictates with a view to permanent policy: but I have not been able to perceive the proofs by which he overthrows the ancient principle. In respect to the opinion of Grotius, quoted by him in No. 20, as indicating a doubt by Grotius of his own principles, I cannot help thinking that the learned writer has himself fallen into a mistake. Grotius, in the place referred to, lib. 3, ch. 20, § 16. is not adverting to the right of confiscation, but merely to the general results of a treaty of peace. He says (§ 15.) that, after a peace, no action lies for damages done in the war; but (§ 16,) that debts due before the war are not, by the mere operations of the war, *released,* but remain suspended during the war, and the right to recover them revives at the peace. It is impossible to doubt the meaning of Grotius, when the preceding and succeeding sections are taken in connexion. Grotius, therefore, is not inconsistent with himself, nor is 'Bynkershoek more inconsistent;' for the latter explicitly avows the same doctrine, but considers it inapplicable to debts confiscated during the war; for these are completely extinguished. *Bynk. Quaest. Pub. Juris, ch.* 7.

It is supposed by the same learned writer, that the principle of confiscating debts had been abandoned for more than a century. That the practice was intermitted, is certainly no very clear proof of an abandonment of the principle. Motives of policy and the general interests of commerce may combine to induce a nation not to inforce its strict rights, but it ought not therefore to be construed to release them. It may, however, be well doubted if the practice is quite so uniform as it is supposed. The case of the Silesia loan, which exercised the highest talents of the English nation, is an instance to the contrary, almost within half a century, (in 1752,) In the very elaborate discussions of national law to which that case gave birth, there is not the slightest intimation that the law of nations prohibited a sovereign from confiscating debts due to his enemies, even where the debts were due from the nation; though there is a very able statement of its injustice in that particular case: and the English memorial admits that when sovereigns or states borrow money from foreigners, it is very commonly expressed in the contract, that it should not be seized as reprisals, or in case of war. Now it strikes me that this very circumstance shews in a strong light the general opinion as to the ordinary right of confiscation. The stipulations of particular treaties of the United States have been cited, in corroboration of their general doctrine, by the claimant's counsel. These treaties certainly shew the opinion of the government as to the impolicy of enforcing the right of confiscation against debts and actions. See *treaty with Great Britain,* 1794, *art.* 10—*with France* 1778, *art.* 20—*with Holland, 8th October* 1782, *art.* 18—*with Prussia,* 11*th July* 1799, *art.* 23—*with Morocco,* 1787, *art.* 24— But I cannot admit them to be evidence for the purpose for which they have been introduced. It may be argued with quite as much if not greater force, that these stipulations imply an acknowledgement of the general right of confiscation, and provide for a liberal relaxation between the parties. I hold, with Bynkershoek, (*Quaest. Pub. Jur. ch.* 7.) that where such treaties exist, they must be observed; where there are none, the general right prevails. It has been further supposed, that the common law of England is against the right of confiscating debts; and the declaration of *Magna Charta,* ch. 30, has been cited to shew the liberal views of the British constitution. This declaration, so far as is necessary to the present purpose, is as follows: 'If they' (i. e. foreign merchants,) 'be of a land making war against us, and be found in our realm at the beginning of the war, they shall be attached without harm of body or goods (*rerum*) until it be known unto us, or our chief justice, how our merchants be entreated, then in the land making war against us, and if our merchants be well entreated there, theirs shall be likewise with us.' I quote the translation of *lord Coke,* (2, *Just.* 27.)—This would certainly seem to be a very liberal provision; and if its true construction applied to all property and persons, as well transiently in the country as domiciled and fixed there, it would certainly be entitled to all the encomiums which it has received. *Montesq. Spirit of Laws, lib.* 20, *ch.* 14. How far it is now considered as binding, in relation to vessels and goods found within the realm at the commencement of the war, I shall hereafter consider. It will be observed, however, that this article of *Magna Charta,* does not protect the debts or property of foreigners who are *without the realm:* it is confined to foreigners *within* the realm upon the public faith on the breaking out of the war. Now it seems to be the established rule of the common law, that all *choses in action,* belonging to an enemy, are forfeitable to the crown; and that the crown is at liberty, at any time during the war, to institute a process, and thereby appropriate them to itself. This was the doctrine of the year books, and stands confirmed by the solemn decision of the exchequer, in *the Attorney General v. Weeden, Parker Rep.* 267.—*Maynard's Edw.* 2, *cited ibid.*—It is a prerogative of the crown which, I admit, has been very rarely enforced; (See *lord Alvanley's* observations in *Furtado v. Rodgers,* 3, *Bos. and Pub.* 191,) but its existence cannot admit of a legal doubt. On a review of authorities, I am entirely satisfied that, by the rigor of the law of nations and of the common law, the sovereign of a nation may lawfully confiscate the debts of his enemy, during war, or by way of reprisal: and I will add, that I think this opinion fully confirmed by the judgement of the Supreme Court in *Ware v. Hylton,* 3, *Dall.* 199, where the doctrine was explicitly asserted by some of the judges, reluctantly admitted by others, and denied by none.

In respect to the *goods* of an enemy found within the dominions of a belligerent power, the right of confiscation is most amply admitted by Grotius, and Puffendorf, and Bynkershoek, and Burlamaqui, and Rutherforth and Vattel. *See Grotius,* and *Puffendorf,* and *Bynkershoek ubi supra;* and *Bynk. Qu. Pub. Jur. c.* 4, and 6. 2, *Burlam. p.* 209, *sec.* 12, *p.* 219, *sec.* 2, *p.* 221, *sec.* 11. *Ruth. lib.* 2, *c.* 9, *p.* 558 *to* 573. Such, also, is the rule of the common law. *Hale* in *Harg. law tracts, p.* 245, *c.* 18. *Vattel* has indeed contended (and in this he is followed by *Azuni, Part.* 2, *ch.* 4, *art.* 2, *sec.* 7,) that the sovereign declaring war, can neither detain the persons nor the property of those subjects of the enemy who are within his dominions at the time of the declaration, because they came into the country upon the public faith. This exception (which, in terms, is confined to the property of persons who are within the country,) seems highly reasonable in itself, and is an extension of the rule in *Magna Charta.* But, even limited as it is, it does not seem followed in practice; and Bynkershoek is an authority the other way. *Bynk. Quaest. Pub. Jur. c.* 2, 3, 7. In England, the provision in *Magna Charta* seems, in practice, to have been confined to foreign merchants domiciled there; and not extended to others who came to ports of the realm for occasional trade. Indeed, from the language of some authorities, it would seem that the clause was inserted, not so much to benefit foreign merchants, as to provide a remedy for their own subjects, in cases of hostile injuries of foreign countries. (See the opinion of Ch. J. *Lee* in *Key v. Pearse,* cited *Doug.* 606, 607.) However this may be, it is very certain that Great Britain has uniformly seized, as prize, all vessels and cargoes of her enemies found afloat in her ports at the commencement of war. Nay, she has proceeded yet farther, and, in contemplation of hostilities, laid embargoes on foreign vessels and cargoes, that she might, at all events, secure the prey. It cannot be necessary for me to quote authorities on this point. In the articles respecting the *droits of admiralty* in 1665, there is a very formal recognition of the rights of the crown to all vessels and cargoes seized before hostilities. *The Rebeckah*, 1, *Rob.* 227, and *id.* 230, *note* (*a.*) This exercise of hostile right—of the *summum jus*, is so far, indeed, from being obsolete, that it is in constant operation, and, in the present hostilities, has been applied to the property of the citizens of the United States. Of a similar character, is the detention of American seamen found in her service at the commencement of the war, as prisoners of war; a practice which violates the spirit, though not the letter, of *Magna Charta;* and, certainly, can, in equity and good faith, find few advocates. Of the right of Great Britain thus to seize vessels and cargoes found in her ports on the breaking out of war, I do not find any denial in authorities which are entitled to much weight; and I, therefore, consider the rule of the law of nations to be, that every such exercise of authority is lawful, and rests in the sound discretion of the sovereign of the nation.

The next question is, whether congress (for with them rests the sovereignty of the nation as to the right of making war, and declaring its limits and effects) have authorized the seizure of enemies' property afloat in our ports. The act of 18th June, 1812, ch. 102, is in very general terms, declaring war against Great Britain, and authorizing the president to employ the public forces to carry it into effect. Independent of such express authority, I think that, as the executive of the nation, he must, as an incident of the office, have a right to employ all the usual and customary means acknowledged in war, to carry it into effect. And there being no limitation in the act, it seems to follow that the executive may authorize the capture of all enemies' property, wherever, by the law of nations, it may be lawfully seized. In cases where no grant is made by congress, all such captures, made under the authority of the executive, must enure to the use of the government. That the executive is not restrained from authorizing captures on land, is clear from the provisions of the act. He may employ and actually has employed the land forces for that purpose; and no one has doubted the legality of the conduct. That captures may be made, within our own ports, by commissioned ships, seems a natural result of the language—of the generality of expression in relation to the authority to grant letters of marque and reprisal to private armed vessels, which the act does not confine to captures on the high seas, and is supported by the known usage of Great Britain in similar cases. It would be strange indeed, if the executive could not authorize or ratify a capture in our own ports, unless by granting a commission to a public or private ship. I am not bold enough to interpose a limitation where congress have not chosen to make one; and I hold, that, by the act declaring war, the executive may authorize all captures which, by the modern law of nations, are permitted and approved. It will be at once perceived, that in this doctrine I do not mean to include the right to confiscate debts due to enemy subjects. This, though a strictly national right, is so justly deemed odious in modern times, and is so generally discountenanced, that nothing but an express act of congress would satisfy my mind that it ought to be included among the fair objects of warfare; more especially as our own government have declared it unjust and impolitic. But if congress should enact such a law, however much I might regret it, I am not aware that foreign nations, with whom we have no treaty to the contrary, could, on the footing of the rigid law of nations, complain, though they might deem it a violation of the modern policy.

On the whole, I am satisfied that congress have authorized a seizure and condemnation of enemy property found in our ports under the circumstances of the present case. And the executive may lawfully authorize proceedings to enforce the confiscation of the same property before the proper tribunals of the United States. The district attorney is, for this purpose, the proper agent of the executive and of the United States. From the character and duties of his station, he is bound to guard the rights of the United States, and to secure their interests. Whenever he choses to institute proceedings on behalf of the United States, it is presumed by Courts of law that he has the sanction of the proper authorities; and that presumption will avail, until the executive or the legislature disavow the proceedings, and sanction a restoration of the property.

I have taken up more time than I originally intended, in discussing the various subjects submitted in the argument. An apology will be found in their extraordinary importance. If I shall have successfully shewn that the principles of prize law, as admitted in England and in the United States, have the sanction of the principles of public law and public jurists, I shall not regret the labor that has been employed, although, in this particular case, I may pronounce an erroneous sentence.

I reverse the decree of the district Court, and condemn the 550 tons of timber to the United States; subject, however, to the right of the owners of the *Emulous* to a reimbursement of their actual charges and expenses for the custody of the property, which I shall reserve for further consideration; and I shall order the said property to be sold, and the proceeds brought into Court to abide the further order of the Court."

Such is the opinion which I had the honor to pronounce in the Circuit Court; and upon the most mature reflection, I adhere to it. The argument in this Court, urged on behalf of the Claimant, has put in controversy the same points which were urged before me. But as the opinion of this Court admits many of the principles for which I contended, I shall confine my additional remarks to such as have been overruled by my brethren.

It seems to have been taken for granted in the argument of counsel that the opinion held in the Circuit Court proceeded, in some degree, upon a supposition that a declaration of war operates *per se* an *actual confiscation* of enemy's property found within our territory. To me this is a perfectly novel doctrine. It was not argued, on either side, in the Circuit Court, and certainly never received the slightest countenance from the Court. I disclaim, therefore, any intention to support a doctrine which I always supposed to be wholly untenable. I go yet further, and admit that a declaration of war does not, of itself, import a confiscation of enemies' property within or without the country, on the land or on the high seas. The title of the enemy is not by war divested, but remains *in proprio vigore,* until a hostile seizure and possession has impaired his title. All that I contend for is, that a declaration of war gives a right to confiscate enemies' property, and enables the power to whom the execution of the laws and the prosecution of the war are confided, to enforce that right. If, indeed, there be a limit imposed as to the extent to which hostilities may be carried by the executive, I admit that the executive cannot lawfully transcend that limit; but if no such limit exist, the war may be carried on according to the principles of the modern law of nations, and enforced when, and where, and on what property the executive chooses.

In no act whatsoever, that I recollect, have congress declared the confiscation of enemies' property. They have authorized the president to grant letters of marque and general reprisal, which he may revoke and annul at his pleasure: and even as to captures actually made under such commissions, no absolute title by confiscation vests in the captors, until a sentence of condemnation. If, therefore, British property had come into our ports since the war, and the president had declined to issue letters of marque and reprisal, there is no act of congress which, in terms, declares it confiscated and subjects it to condemnation. If, nevertheless, it be confiscable, the right of confiscation results not from the express provisions of any statute, but from the very state of war, which subjects the hostile property to the disposal of the government. But until the title should be divested by some overt act of the government and some judicial sentence, the property would unquestionably remain in the British owners, and if a peace should intervene, it would be completely beyond the reach of subsequent condemnation.

There is, then, no distinction recognized by any act of congress, between enemies' property which was within our ports at the commencement of war, and enemies' property found elsewhere. Neither are declared *ipso facto* confiscated; and each, as I contend, are merely confiscable.

I will now consider what, in point of law, is the operation of the acts of Congress made in relation to the present war.

The act of 18th June, 1812, ch. 102, declares war to exist between Great Britain and the United States, and authorizes the president of the United States to use the land and naval force of the United States to carry the same into effect; and further authorizes him to issue letters of marque, &c. to private armed vessels, against the vessels, goods and effects of the government of Great Britain and the subjects thereof.

The prize act of 26th June, 1812, ch. 107, confers the power on the president to issue instructions to private armed vessels, for the regulation of their conduct. The act of 6th July, 1812, ch. 128, authorizes the president to make regulations, &c. for the support and exchange of prisoners of war. The act of 6th July, 1812, ch. 129, respecting trade with the enemy, authorizes the president to grant passports for the property of British subjects within the limits of the United States during the space of six months, and protects certain British packets, &c. with despatches, from capture. The act of 3d March, 1813, ch. 203, vests in the president the power of retaliation for any violation of the rules and usages of civilized warfare by Great Britain.

These are all the acts which confer powers, or make provisions touching the management of the war. In no one of them is there the slightest limitation upon the executive powers growing out of a state of war; and they exist, therefore, in their full and perfect vigour. By the constitution, the executive is charged with the faithful execution of the laws; and the language of the act declaring war authorizes him to carry it into effect. In what manner, and to what extent, shall he carry it into effect? What are the legitimate objects of the warfare which he is to wage? There is no act of the legislature defining the powers, objects or mode of warfare: by what rule, then, must he be governed? I think the only rational answer is by the law of nations as applied to a state of war. Whatever act is legitimate, whatever act is approved by the law, or hostilities among civilized nations, such he may, in his discretion, adopt and exercise; for with him the sovereignty of the nation rests as to the execution of the laws. If any of such acts are disapproved by the legislature, it is in their power to narrow and limit the extent to which the rights of war shall be exercised; but until such limit is assigned, the executive must have all the right of modern warfare vested in him, to be exercised in his sound discretion, or he can have none. Upon what principle, I would ask, can he have an implied authority to adopt one and not another? The best manner of annoying, injuring and pressing the enemy, must, from the nature of things, vary under different circumstances; and the executive is responsible to the nation for the faithful discharge of his duty, under all the changes of hostilities.

But it is said that a declaration of war does not, of itself, import a right to confiscate enemies' property found within the country at the commencement of war. I cannot admit this position in the extent in which it is laid down. Nothing, in my judgment, is more clear from authority, than the right to seize hostile property afloat in our ports at the commencement of war. It is the settled practice of nations, and the modern rule of Great Britain herself, applied (as appears from the affidavits in this very cause) to American property in the present war; applied, also, to property not merely on board of ships, but to spars floating alongside of them—I forbear, however, to press this point, because my opinion in the Court below contains a full discussion of it.

It is also said that a declaration of war does not carry with it the right to confiscate property found in our country at the commencement of war, because the constitution itself, in giving congress the power "to declare war, grant letters of marque and reprisal, and make rules concerning captures on land and water," has clearly evinced that the power to declare war did not, *ex vi terminorum,* include a right to capture property every where, and that the power to make rules concerning captures on land and water, may well be considered as a substantive power as to captures of property *within our own territory.* In my judgment, if this argument prove any thing, it proves too much. If the power to make rules respecting captures, &c. be a substantive power, it is equally applicable to all captures, wherever made, on land or on water. The terms of the grant import no limitation as to place; and I am not aware how we can place around them a narrower limit than the terms import. Upon the same construction, the power to grant letters of marque and reprisal is a substantive power; and a declaration of war could not, of itself, authorize any seizure whatsoever of hostile property, unless this power was called into exercise. I cannot, therefore, yield assent to this argument. The power to declare war, in my opinion, includes all the powers incident to war, and necessary to carry it into effect. If the constitution had been silent as to letters of marque and captures, it would not have narrowed the authority of congress. The authority to grant letters of marque and reprisal, and to regulate captures, are ordinary and necessary incidents to the power of declaring war. It would be utterly ineffectual without them. The expression, therefore, of that which is implied in the very nature of the grant, cannot weaken the force of the grant itself. The words are merely explanatory, and introduced *ex abundanti cautela.* It might be as well contended; that the power "to provide and maintain a navy," did not include the power to regulate and govern it, because there is in the constitution an express provision to this effect. And yet I suppose that no person would doubt that congress, independent of such express provision, would have the power to regulate and govern the navy; and if they should authorize the executive "to provide and maintain a navy," it seems to me as clear that he must have the incidental power to make rules for its government. In truth, it is by no means unfrequent in the constitution to add clauses of a special nature to general powers which embrace them, and to provide affirmatively for certain powers, without meaning thereby to negative the existence of powers of a more general nature. The power to provide "for the common defence and general welfare," could hardly be doubted to include the power "to borrow money;" the power "to coin money," to include the power "to regulate the value therof;" and the power "to raise and support armies," to include the power "to make rules for the government and regulation" thereof. On the other hand, the affirmative power "to define and punish piracies and felonies committed on the high seas," has never been supposed to negative the right to punish other offences on the high seas; and congress have actually legislated to a more enlarged extent. I cannot therefore persuade myself that the argument against the doctrine for which I contend, is at all affected by any provision in the constitution.

The opinion of my brethren seems to admit that the effect of hostilities is to confer all the rights which war confers; and it seems tacitly to concede, that, by virtue of the declaration of war, the executive would have a right to seize enemies' property which should actually come within our territory during the war. Certainly no such power is given directly by any statute. And if the argument be correct, that the power to make captures on land or water must be expressly called into exercise by congress, before the executive can, even after war, enforce a capture and condemnation, it will be very difficult to support the concession. Suppose a British ship of war or merchant ship should now come within our ports, there is no statute declaring such ship actually confiscated. There is no express authority either for the navy or army to make a capture of her; and although the executive might authorize a private armed ship so to do, yet it would depend altogether on the will of the owners of the ship, whether they would so do or not. Can it be possible that the executive has not the power to authorize such seizure? And if he may authorize a seizure by the army or navy, why not by private individuals if they will volunteer for the purpose?

The act declaring war has authorized the executive to employ the land and naval force of the United States, to carry it into effect. When and where shall he carry it into effect? Congress have not declared that any captures shall be made on land; and if this be a substantive power, not included in a declaration of war, how can the executive make captures on land, when congress have not expressed their will to this effect? The power to employ the army and navy might well be exercised in preventing invasion, and in the common defence, without unnecessarily including a right to capture, if the right to capture be not an incident of war: and upon what ground, then, can the executive plan and execute foreign expeditions or foreign captures? Upon what ground can he authorize a Canadian campaign, or seize a British fort or territory, and occupy it by right of capture and conquest I am utterly at a loss to perceive, unless it be that the power to carry the war into effect, gives every incidental power which the law of nations authorizes and approves in a state of war. I am at a loss to perceive how the power exists, to seize and capture enemy's property which was without our territory at the commencement of the war, and not the power to seize that which was within our territory at the same period. Neither are expressly given nor denied (except as to private armed ships,) and how can either be assumed except as an incident of war, acknowledged upon national and public principles? It may be suggested that the executive, "as commander in chief of the army and navy," has the power to make foreign conquests. But this is utterly inadmissible, if the right to authorize captures resides as a substantive power in congress, and does not follow as an incident of a declaration of war: and certainly the rights of the "commander in chief" must be restrained to such acts as are allowed by the laws. Besides, the same difficulty meets us here as in the former case; if his powers, as commander in chief, authorize him to make captures without the territory, why not within the territory?

The acts respecting alien enemies and prisoners of war, have been supposed, even in a state of *actual* war, to confer new powers on the executive. I cannot accede to the inference in the extent to which it is claimed. In general, these acts may be deemed mere regulations of war, limiting and directing the discretion of the executive; and it cannot be doubted that Congress had a perfect right to prescribe such regulations. To regulate the exercise of the rights of war as to enemies, does not, however, imply that such rights have not an independent existence. Besides, it is clear that the act respecting alien enemies applies only to aliens resident within the country; and not to the property of aliens, who are not so resident. I might answer, in the same manner, the argument drawn from the act of 6th July 1812, ch. 129, § 4, and the act of 3d of March 1813, ch. 203.—But even admitting that these acts did confer some new powers, still, as these powers do not respect the present case, I cannot consider them as affording even a legislative implication against the existence of the powers for which I contend.

It has been supposed that my opinion assumes for its basis the position, that modern usage constitutes a rule which acts directly on the thing itself by its own force, and not through the sovereign power. Certainly I do not admit this supposition to be correct. My argument proceeds upon the ground, that when the legislative authority, to whom the right to declare war is confided, has declared war in its most unlimited manner, the executive authority, to whom the execution of the war is confided, is bound to carry it into effect. He has a discretion vested in him, as to the manner and extent; but he cannot lawfully transcend the rules of warfare established among civilized nations. He cannot lawfully exercise powers or authorize proceedings which the civilized world repudiates and disclaims. The sovereignty, as to declaring war and limiting its effects, rests with the legislature. The sovereignty, as to its execution, rests with the president. If the legislature do not limit the nature of the war, all the regulations and rights of general war attach upon it. I do not, therefore, contend that modern usage of nations constitutes a rule acting on enemies' property, so as to produce confiscation of itself, and not through the sovereign power: on the contrary, I consider enemies' property in no case whatsoever confiscated by the mere declaration of war; it is only liable to be confiscated at the discretion of the sovereign power having the conduct and execution of the war. The modern usage of nations is resorted to merely as a limitation of this discretion, not as conferring the authority to exercise it. The sovereignty to execute it is supposed already to exist in the president, by the very terms of the constitution: and I would again ask, if this general power to confiscate enemies' property does not exist in the executive, to be exercised in his discretion, how is it possible that he can have authority to seize and confiscate any enemies' property coming into the country since the war, or found in the enemies' territory?—Yet I understood the opinion of my brethren to proceed upon the tacit acknowledgement that the executive may seize and confiscate such property, under the circumstances which I have stated.

16

JAMES KENT, COMMENTARIES 53–67
1826

As war cannot lawfully be commenced on the part of the United States, without an act of Congress, such an act is, of course, a formal official notice to all the world, and equivalent to the most solemn declaration.

When war is duly declared, it is not merely a war between this and the adverse government in their political characters. Every man is, in judgment of law, a party to the acts of his own government, and a war between the governments of two nations, is a war between all the individuals of the one, and all the individuals of which the other nation is composed. Government is the representative of the will of all the people, and acts for the whole society. This is the theory in all governments, and the best writers on the law of nations concur in the doctrine, that when the sovereign of a state declares war against another sovereign, it implies that the whole nation declares war, and that all the subjects of the one, are enemies to all the subjects of the other. Very important consequences concerning the obligations of subjects, are deducible from this principle.

When hostilities have commenced, the first objects that naturally present themselves for detention and capture, are the persons and property of the enemy, found within the territory at the breaking out of the war. According to strict authority, a state has a right to deal as an enemy with persons and property so found within its power, and to confiscate the property, and detain the persons as prisoners of war. No one, says Bynkershoeck, ever required that notice should be given to the subjects of the enemy, to withdraw their property, or it would be forfeited. The practice of nations is to appropriate it at once, without notice, if there be no special convention to the contrary. But, though Bynkershoeck lays down this, as well as other rules of war, with great harshness and severity, he mentions several instances arising in the 17th, and one as early as the 15th century, of stipulations in treaties, allowing foreign subjects a reasonable time after the war breaks out, to recover and dispose of their effects, or to withdraw them. Such stipulations have now become an established *formula* in commercial treaties. Emerigon considers such treaties as an affirmance of common right, or the public law of Europe, and the general rule laid down by some of the later publicists, is in conformity with that provision. The sovereign who declares war, says Vattel, can neither detain those subjects of the enemy who are within his dominions at the time of the declaration of war, nor their effects. They came into the country under the sanction of public faith. By permitting them to enter his territories, and continue there, the sovereign tacitly promised them protection and security for their return. He is, therefore, to allow them a reasonable time to retire with their effects, and if they stay beyond the time, he has a right to treat them as disarmed enemies, unless detained by sickness, or other insurmountable necessity, and then they are to be allowed a further time. It has been frequently provided by treaty, that foreign subjects should be permitted to remain, and continue their business, notwithstanding a rupture between the governments, so long as they conducted innocently; and when there was no such treaty, such a liberal permission has been often announced in the very declaration of war. Sir Michael Foster mentions several instances of such declarations by the King of Great Britain, and he says that aliens were thereby enabled to acquire personal chattels, and to maintain actions for the recovery of their personal rights, in as full a manner as alien friends.

Besides those stipulations in treaties, which have softened the rigours of war by the civilizing spirit of commerce, many governments have made special provision, in their own laws and ordinances, for the security of the persons and property of enemy's subjects, found in the country at the commencement of war.

It was provided by *magna charta,* that, upon the breaking out of war, foreign merchants found in England, and belonging to the country of the enemy, should be attached, "without harm of body or goods," until it be known how English merchants were treated by the enemy; and "if our merchants," said the charter, "be safe and well treated there, theirs shall be likewise with us." It has been deemed extraordinary, that such a liberal provision should have found a place in a treaty between a feudal king and his barons; and Montesquieu, was struck with admiration at the fact, that a protection of that kind should have been made one of the articles of English liberty. But this provision was confined to the effects of alien merchants, who were within the realm at the commencement of the war, and it was understood to be confined to the case of merchants domiciled there. It was accompanied also with one very ominous qualification, and it was at least equalled, if not greatly excelled, by an ordinance of Charles V. of France, a century afterwards, which declared that foreign merchants, who should be in France at the time of the declaration of war, should have nothing to fear, for they should have liberty to depart freely, with their effects. The spirit of the provision in magna charta, was sustained by a resolution of the judges, in the time of Henry VIII., when they resolved, that if a Frenchman came to England before the war, neither his person nor goods should be seized. The statute of staples, of 27 Edw. III. c. 17. made a still more liberal and precise enactment in favour of foreign merchants, residing in England when war commenced between their prince and the king of England. They were to have convenient warning of forty days, by proclamation, to depart the realm, with their goods, and if they could not do it within that time, by reason of accident, they were to have forty days more to pass with their merchandise, and with liberty, in the mean time, to sell the same. The act of Congress of the 6th of July, 1798, c. 73. was dictated by the same humane and enlightened policy. It authorized the President, in case of war, to direct the conduct to be observed towards subjects of the hostile nation, and being aliens, and within the United States, and in what cases, and upon what security, their residence should be permitted; and it declared, in reference to those who were to depart, that they should be allowed such reasonable time as might be consistent with the public safety, and according to the dictates of humanity and national hospitality, "for the recovery, disposal and removal of their goods and effects, and for their departure."

But however strong the current of authority in favour of the modern and milder construction of the rule of national law on this subject, the point seems to be no longer open for discussion in this country; and it has been definitively settled, in favour of the ancient and sterner rule, by the Supreme Court of the United States. The effect of war upon British property, found in the United States, on land, at the commencement of the war, was learnedly discussed, and thoroughly considered, in the case of *Brown;* and the Circuit Court of the United States, at Boston, decided, as upon a settled rule of the law of nations, that the goods of the enemy found in the country, and all the vessels and cargoes found afloat in our ports, at the commencement of hostilities, were liable to seizure and confiscation; and the exercise of the right rested in the discretion of the sovereign of the nation. When the case was brought up, on appeal, before the Supreme Court of the United States, the broad principle was assumed, that war gave to the sovereign full right to take the persons, and confiscate the property of the enemy, wherever found; and that the mitigations of this rigid rule, which the wise and humane policy of modern times had introduced into practice, might, more or less, affect the exercise of the right, but could not impair the right itself. Commercial nations have always considerable property in the possession of their neighbours; and, when war breaks out, the question what shall be done with enemy's property found in the country, is one rather of policy than of law, and is one properly addressed to the consideration of the legislature, and not to the courts of law. The strict right of confiscation of that species of property existed in Congress, and without a legislative act authorizing its confiscation, it could not be judicially condemned; and the act of Congress of 1812, declaring war against Great Britain, was not such an act. Until some statute directly applying to the subject, be passed, the property would continue under the protection of the law, and might be claimed by the British owner, at the restoration of peace.

Though this decision established the right, contrary to much of modern authority and practice, yet a great point was gained over the rigour and violence of the ancient doctrine, by making the exercise of the right to depend upon a special act of Congress.

The practice, so common in modern Europe, of imposing embargoes at the breaking out of hostility, has, apparently, the effect of destroying that protection to property, which the rule of faith and justice gives to it, when brought into the country in the course of trade, and in the confidence of peace. Sir William Scott, in the case of the *Boedes Lust,* explains this species of embargo to be an act of a hostile nature, and amounting to an implied declaration of war, though liable to be explained away and annulled, by a subsequent accommodation between the nations. The seizure is at first equivocal, and if the matter in dispute terminates in reconciliation, the seizure becomes a mere civil embargo, but if it terminates otherwise, the subsequent hostilities have a retroactive effect, and render the embargo a hostile measure, *ab initio.* The property detained is deemed enemy's property, and liable to condemnation. This species of reprisal for some previous injury, is laid down in the books as a lawful measure, according to the usage of nations; but it is often reprobated, and it cannot well be distinguished from the practice of seizing property found within the territory upon the declaration of war. It does not differ in substance from the conduct of the Syracusans, in the time of Dionysius the Elder, (and which Mitford considered to be a gross violation of the law of nations,) for they voted a declaration of war against Carthage, and immediately seized the effects of Carthaginian traders in their warehouses, and Carthaginian richly laden vessels in their harbour, and then sent a herald to Carthage to negotiate. But this act of the Syracusans, near four hundred years before the Christian aera, was no more than what is the ordinary practice in England, according to the observation of Lord Mansfield, in *Lindo* v. *Rodney.* "Upon the declaration of war or hostilities, all the ships of the enemy," he says, "are detained in our ports, to be confiscated, as the property of the enemy, if no reciprocal agreement is made."

Another question respecting the effect of a declaration of war upon property, arose in the case of the *Rapid.* It was held, that, after the commencement of war, an American citizen could not lawfully send a vessel to the enemy's country, to bring home his own property, without rendering it liable to seizure *in transitu,* as enemy's property. Every thing that issues from a hostile country, is, *prima facie,* the property of the enemy, and a citizen cannot lawfully be concerned in any commercial intercourse with the enemy. The English courts were formerly inclined to allow goods, in the enemy's country at the beginning of the war, to be brought home; but it is now the settled law, that it cannot be done safely, without a license from the government.

The claim of a right to confiscate debts, contracted by individuals in time of peace, and which remain due to subjects of the enemy at the declaration of war, rests very much upon the same principle as that concerning enemy's tangible property, found in the country at the opening of the war; though I think the objection to the right of confiscation, in this latter case, is much stronger. In former times, the right to confiscate debts was admitted as a doctrine of national law, and Grotius, Puffendorf and Bynkershoeck pronounce in favour of it. It had the countenance of the civil law, and even Cicero, in his *Offices,* when stating the cases in which promises are not to be kept, mentions that of the creditor becoming the enemy of the country of the debtor. Down to the year 1737, the general opinion of jurists was in favour of the right; but Vattel says, that a relaxation of the rigour of the rule has since taken place among the sovereigns of Europe, and that, as the custom has been generally received, he who should act contrary to it, would injure the public faith, for strangers trusted his subjects only from a firm persuasion that the general custom would be observed. There has frequently been a stipulation in modern treaties, that debts should not be confiscated in the event of war; and these conventional provisions are evidence of the sense of the governments which are parties to them, and that the right of confiscation of debts and things in action, is against good policy, and ought to be discontinued. The recent treaty between the United States and Colombia contains such a provision; but the treaty between the United States and Great Britain in 1795, went further, and contained the explicit declaration, that it was "unjust and impolitic" that the debts of individuals should be impaired by national differences. A very able discussion of this assumed right to confiscate debts, was made by General Hamilton, in the numbers of *Camillus,* published in 1795. He examined the claim to confiscate private debts, or private property in banks, or in the public funds, on the grounds of reason and principle, on those of policy and expediency, on the opinion of jurists, on usage, and on conventional law; and his argument against the justice and policy of the claim was exceedingly powerful. He contended it to be against good faith for a government to lay its hands on private property, acquired by the permission, or upon the invitation of the government, and under a necessarily implied promise of protection and security. Vattel says, that every where, in case of a war, funds credited to the public are exempt from confiscation and seizure. Emerigon and Martens make the same declaration. The practice would have a very injurious influence upon the general sense of the inviolability and sanctity of private contracts; and with debtors who had a nice and accurate sense of justice and honour, the requisition of government would not be cheerfully or readily obeyed. Voltaire has given a striking instance of the impracticability of confiscating property deposited in trust with a debtor, and of the firmness of Spanish faith. When war was declared between France and Spain, in 1684, the king of Spain endeavoured to seize the property of the French in Spain, but not a single Spanish factor would betray his French correspondent.

Notwithstanding the weight of modern authority, and of argument, against this claim of right on the part of the sovereign, to confiscate the debts and funds of the subjects of his enemy during war, the judicial language in this country is decidedly in support of the right. In the case of *Brown* v. *The United States,* already mentioned, Judge Story, in the Circuit Court in Massachusetts, laid down the right to confiscate debts, and enemy's property found in the country, according to the rigorous doctrine of the elder jurists; and he said the opinion was fully confirmed by the judgment of the Supreme Court in *Ware* v. *Hylton,* where the doctrine was explicitly asserted by some of the judges, reluctantly admitted by others, and denied by none. Chief Justice Marshall, in delivering the opinion of the Supreme Court, in the case of *Brown,* observed, that between debts contracted under the faith of laws, and property acquired in the course of trade on the faith of the same laws, reason drew no distinction, and the right of the sovereign to confiscate debts, was precisely the same with the right to confiscate other property found in the country. This right, therefore, was admitted to exist as a settled and decided right, *stricto jure,* though, at the same time, it was conceded to be the universal practice, to forbear to seize and confiscate debts and credits. We may, therefore, lay it down as a principle of public law, so far as the same is understood and declared by the highest judicial authorities in this country, that it rests in the discretion of the legislature of the Union, by a special law for that purpose, to confiscate debts contracted by our citizens, and due to the enemy; but as it is asserted by the same authority, this right is contrary to universal practice, and it may, therefore, well be considered as a naked and impolitic right, condemned by the enlightened conscience and judgment of modern time.

If property should have been wrongfully taken by the state before the war, and be in the country at the opening of the war, such property cannot be seized, but must be restored; because, to confiscate that species of enemy's property, would be for the government to take advantage of its own wrong. The celebrated *Report* of the English law officers of the crown in 1753, *in Answer to the Prussian Memorial,* stated, that French ships, taken before the war of 1741, were, during the heat of the war with France, as well as afterwards, restored by sentences of the admiralty courts, to the French owners. No such property was ever attempted to be confiscated, for had it not been for the wrong done, the property would not have been within the king's dominions. And yet even such property is considered to be subject to the rule of vindictive retaliation; and Sir Wm. Scott observed, in the case of the *Santa Cruz,* that it was the constant practice of England, to condemn property seized before the war, if the enemy condemns—and to restore, if the enemy restores.

One of the immediate and important consequences of the declaration of war, is the absolute interruption and interdiction of all commercial correspondence, intercourse, and dealing, between the subjects of the two countries. The idea that any commercial intercourse, or pacific dealing, can lawfully subsist between the people of the powers at war, except under the clear and express sanction of the government, and without a special license, is utterly inconsistent with the new class of duties growing out of a state of war. The interdiction flows, necessarily, from the principle already stated, that a state of war puts all the members of the two nations respectively in hostility to each other; and to suffer individuals to carry on a friendly or commercial intercourse, while the two governments were at war, would be placing the act of government, and the acts of individuals, in contradiction to each other. It would counteract the operations of war, and throw obstacles in the way of public efforts, and lead to disorder, imbecility, and treason. Trading supposes the existence of civil contracts and relations, and a reference to courts of justice; and it is, therefore, necessarily, contradictory to a state of war. It affords aid to the enemy in an effectual manner, by enabling the merchants of the enemy's country to support their government, and it facilitates the means of conveying intelligence, and carrying on a traitorous correspondence with the enemy. These considerations apply with peculiar force to maritime states, where the principal object is to destroy the marine and commerce of the enemy, in order to force them to peace. It is a well settled doctrine in the English courts, and with the English jurists, that there cannot exist, at the same time, a war for arms, and a peace for commerce. The war puts an end at once to all dealing, and all communication, with each other, and places every individual of the respective governments, as well as the governments themselves, in a state of hostility. This is equally the doctrine of all the authoritative writers on the law of nations, and of the maritime ordinances of all the great powers of Europe. It is equally the received law of this country, and was so decided frequently by the Congress of the United States during the revolutionary war, and again by the Supreme Court of the United States during the course of the last war; and it is difficult to conceive of a point of doctrine more deeply or extensively rooted in the general maritime law of Europe, and in the universal and immemorial usage of the whole community of the civilized world.

It follows, as a necessary consequence of the doctrine of the illegality of all intercourse or traffic, without express permission, that all contracts with the enemy, made during war, are utterly void. The insurance of enemy's property is an illegal contract, because it is a species of trade and intercourse with the enemy. The drawing of a bill of exchange, by an alien enemy, on a subject of the adverse country, is an illegal and void contract, because it is a communication and contract. The purchase of bills on the enemy's country, or the remission and deposit of funds there, is a dangerous and illegal act, because it may be cherishing the resources and relieving the wants of the enemy. The remission of funds, in money or bills, to subjects of the enemy, is unlawful. The inhibition reaches to every communication, direct or circuitous. All endeavours at trade with the enemy, by the intervention of third persons, or by partnerships, have equally failed, and no artifice has succeeded to legalize the trade, without the express permission of the government. Every relaxation of the rule tends to corrupt the allegiance of the subject, and prevents the war from fulfilling its end. The only exception to this strict and rigorous rule of international jurisprudence, is the case of ransom bills, and they are contracts of necessity, founded on a state of war, and engendered by its violence. It is also a further consequence of the inability of the subjects of the two states, to commune or carry on any correspondence or business together, that all commercial partnerships existing between the subjects of the two parties, prior to the war, are dissolved by the mere force and act of the war itself; though other contracts existing prior to the war, are not extinguished, but the remedy is only suspended, and this from the inability of an alien enemy to sue, or to sustain, in the language of the civilians, a *persona standi in judicio.* The whole of this doctrine respecting the illegality of any commercial intercourse between the inhabitants of two nations at war, was extensively reviewed, and the principal authorities, ancient and modern, foreign and domestic, were accurately examined, and the positions which have been laid down established, in the case of *Griswold* v. *Waddington,* decided in the Supreme Court of this state, and afterwards affirmed on error.

This strict rule has been carried so far in the British

admiralty, as to prohibit a remittance of supplies even to a British colony, during its temporary subjection to the enemy, and when the colony was under the necessity of supplies, and was only very partially and imperfectly supplied by the enemy. The same interdiction of trade applies to ships of truce, or cartel ships, which are a species of navigation intended for the recovery of the liberty of prisoners of war. Such a special and limited intercourse is dictated by policy and humanity, and it is indispensable that it be conducted with the most exact and exclusive attention to the original purpose, as being the only condition upon which the intercourse can be tolerated. All trade, therefore, by means of such vessels, is unlawful, without the express consent of both the governments concerned. It is equally illegal for an ally of one of the belligerents, and who carries on the war conjointly, to have any commerce with the enemy. A single belligerent may grant licenses to trade with the enemy, and dilute and weaken his own rights at pleasure, but it is otherwise when allied nations are pursuing a common cause. The community of interest, and object, and action, creates a mutual duty not to prejudice that joint interest; and it is a declared principle of the law of nations, founded on very clear and just grounds, that one of the belligerents may seize, and inflict the penalty of forfeiture, on the property of a subject of a co-ally, engaged in a trade with the common enemy, and thereby affording him aid and comfort, whilst the other ally was carrying on a severe and vigorous warfare. It would be contrary to the implied contract in every such warlike confederacy, that neither of the belligerents, without the other's consent, should do any thing to defeat the common object.

In the investigation of the rules of the modern law of nations, particulary with regard to the extensive field of maritime capture, reference is generally and freely made to the decisions of the English courts. They are in the habit of taking accurate and comprehensive views of general jurisprudence, and they have been deservedly followed by the courts of the United States, on all the leading points of national law. We have a series of judicial decisions in England, and in this country, in which the usages and the duties of nations are explained and declared with that depth of research, and that liberal and enlarged inquiry, which strengthens and embellishes the conclusions of reason. They contain more intrinsic argument, more full and precise details, more accurate illustrations, and are of more authority, than the more loose *dicta* of elementary writers. When those courts in this country, which are charged with the administration of international law, have differed from the English adjudications, we must take the law from domestic sources; but such an alternative is rarely to be met with, and there is scarcely a decision in the English prize courts at Westminster, on any general question of public right, that has not received the express approbation and sanction of our national courts. We have attained the rank of a great commercial nation, and war, on our part, is carried on upon the same principles of maritime policy, which have directed the forces and animated the councils of the naval powers of Europe. When the United States formed a component part of the British empire, our prize law and theirs was the same, and after the revolution it continued to be the same, as far as it was adapted to our circumstances, and was not varied by the power which was capable of changing it. The great value of a series of judicial decisions, in prize cases, and on other questions depending on the law of nations, is that they liquidate, and render certain and stable, the loose general principles of that law, and show their application, and how they are understood in the country where the tribunals are sitting. They are, therefore, deservedly received with very great respect, and as presumptive, though not conclusive evidence of the law in the given case. This was the language of the Supreme Court of the United States, so late as 1815, and the decisions of the English High Court of Admiralty, especially since the year 1789, have been consulted and uniformly respected by that court, as enlightened commentaries on the law of nations, and affording a vast variety of instructive precedents for the application of the principles of that law.

17

WILLIAM RAWLE, A VIEW OF THE CONSTITUTION OF THE UNITED STATES 109–11
1829 (2d ed.)

The power of *declaring war,* with all its train of consequences, direct and indirect, forms the next branch of powers exclusively confided to congress.

The right of using force, or of making war, belongs to nations, so far as it is necessary for their defence and the support of their rights. But the evils of war are certain, and the event doubtful, and therefore both wisdom and humanity require, that every possible precaution should be used before a nation is plunged into it. In monarchies, the king generally possesses this power, and it is as often exercised for his own aggrandizement as for the good of the nation. Republics, though they cannot be wholly exonerated from the imputation of ambition, jealousies, causeless irritations, and other personal passions, enter into war more deliberately and reluctantly.

It is not easy to perceive where this power could, with us, be more prudently placed. But it must be remembered, that we may be involved in a war without a formal declaration of it. In the year 1800, we were engaged in a qualified, but public, war with France; qualified, because it was only waged on the high seas—public, because the whole nation was involved in it. It was founded on the hostile measures authorized by congress against France, by reason of her unjust aggressions on our commerce—yet there was no declaration of war. In such a war we may also be involved by the conduct of the executive, without the participation of the legislature. The intercourse with foreign nations, the direction of the military and naval power, being confided to the president, his errors or misconduct may draw hostilities upon us. No other restraint appears to exist, than that of withholding the supplies to carry it on, which indeed congress can in no case grant beyond the term of two years. But in England, the king is, in this respect, equally dependent on the parliament, and its history shows that this dependence is not always adequate to prevent unpopular wars.

The several states are, by another clause, prohibited from engaging in war, unless actually invaded, or in such imminent danger as will not admit of delay.

But although congress alone can subject us to the dubious results of formal war, a smaller portion of the government can restore us to peace. Hostilities may be terminated by a truce, which the president alone (it is conceived) may make. The duration of a truce is indefinite. It suspends all hostilities while it continues in force; but it does not revive treaties which were broken by the commencement of the war, or restore rights of any sort, which were suspended by it. It may be general or partial—it may extend to all places and to all the mutual forces of the belligerents, or it may be confined to particular places or particular armaments. When it ceases, it is unnecessary to repeat the declaration of war. But before its conventual termination, unless some fresh cause of complaint should have arisen, it would be inconsistent with good faith to renew hostilities.

Treaties, by which peace is completely restored, may, as already shown, be made by the president and senate alone, without the concurrence, and against the will of the house of representatives.

It has been made a subject of doubt, whether the power to make war and peace, should not be the same, and why a smaller part of the government should be entrusted with the latter, than the former. Sufficient reasons may certainly be assigned for the distinction. Peace is seldom effected without preparatory discussions, often of length and difficulty, the conduct of which, of course, belongs only to the president and senate. War is always an evil; peace is the cure of that evil. War should always be avoided as long as possible, and although it may happen to be brought on us as before observed, without the previous assent of congress, yet a regular and formal war should never be entered into, without the united approbation of the whole legislature. But although a peace is seldom obnoxious and unacceptable to the public, yet its necessity or propriety may not always be apparent, and a public disclosure of the urgent motives that really exist in favour of it, may be prejudicial. The people have, in such case, a stronger motive for relying on the wisdom and justice of the president and senate, than in the case of ordinary treaties. They are less likely than a larger body to be influenced by partial views or occasional inflammation, and the very circumstance of the smallness of their numbers increase their responsibility to public opinion.

18

Joseph Story, Commentaries on the Constitution 3:§§ 1164–72
1833

§ 1164. A similar exclusive power was given to congress by the confederation. That such a power ought to exist in the national government, no one will deny, who believes, that it ought to have any powers whatsoever, either for offence or defence, for the common good, or for the common protection. It is, therefore, wholly superfluous to reason out the propriety of granting the power. It is self-evident, unless the national government is to be a mere mockery and shadow. The power could not be left without extreme mischief, if not absolute ruin, to the separate authority of the several states; for then it would be at the option of any one to involve the whole in the calamities and burthens of warfare. In the general government it is safe, because there it can be declared only by the majority of the states.

§ 1165. The only practical question upon this subject would seem to be, to what department of the national government it would be most wise and safe to confide this high prerogative, emphatically called the last resort of sovereigns, *ultima ratio regum.* In Great Britain it is the exclusive prerogative of the crown; and in other countries, it is usually, if not universally, confided to the executive department. It might by the constitution have been confided to the executive, or to the senate, or to both conjointly.

§ 1166. In the plan offered by an eminent statesman in the convention, it was proposed, that the senate should have the sole power of declaring war. The reasons, which may be urged in favour of such an arrangement, are, that the senate would be composed of representatives of the states, of great weight, sagacity, and experience, and that being a small and select body, promptitude of action, as well as wisdom, and firmness, would, as they ought, accompany the possession of the power. Large bodies necessarily move slowly; and where the co-operation of different bodies is required, the retardation of any measure must be proportionally increased. In the ordinary course of legislation this may be no inconvenience. But in the exercise of such a prerogative, as declaring war, despatch, secresy, and vigour are often indispensable, and always useful towards success. On the other hand it may be urged in reply, that the power of declaring war is not only the highest sovereign prerogative; but that it is in its own nature and effects so critical and calamitous, that it requires the utmost deliberation, and the successive review of all the councils of the nation. War, in its best estate, never fails to impose upon the people the most burthensome taxes, and personal sufferings. It is always injurious, and sometimes subversive of the great commercial, manufacturing, and agricultural interests. Nay, it always involves the prosperity, and not unfrequently the existence, of a nation. It is sometimes fatal to public liberty itself, by introducing a spirit of military glory, which is ready to follow, wherever a successful commander will lead; and in a republic, whose institutions are essentially founded on the basis of peace, there is infinite danger, that war will find it both imbecile in defence, and eager for contest. Indeed, the history of republics has but too fatally proved, that they are too ambitious of military fame and conquest, and too easily devoted to the views of demagogues, who flatter their pride, and betray their interests. It should therefore be difficult in a republic to declare war; but not to make peace. The representatives of the people are to lay the taxes to support a war, and therefore have a right to be consulted, as to its propriety and necessity. The executive is to carry it on, and therefore should be consulted, as to its time, and the ways and means of making it effective. The co-operation of all the branches of the legislative power ought, upon principle, to be required in this the highest act of legislation, as it is in all others. Indeed, there might be a propriety even in enforcing still greater restrictions, as by requiring a concurrence of two thirds of both houses.

§ 1167. This reasoning appears to have had great weight with the convention, and to have decided its choice. Its judgment has hitherto obtained the unqualified approbation of the country.

§ 1168. In the convention, in the first draft of the constitution, the power was given merely "to make war." It was subsequently, and not without some struggle, altered to its present form. It was proposed to add the power "to make peace;" but this was unanimously rejected; upon the plain ground, that it more properly belonged to the treaty-making power. The experience of congress, under the confederation, of the difficulties, attendant upon vesting the treaty-making power in a large legislative body, was too deeply felt to justify the hazard of another experiment.

§ 1169. The power to declare war may be exercised by congress, not only by authorizing general hostilities, in which case the general laws of war apply to our situation; or by partial hostilities, in which case the laws of war, so far as they actually apply to our situation, are to be observed. The former course was resorted to in our war with Great Britain in 1812, in which congress enacted, "that war be, and hereby is declared to exist, between the United Kingdom of Great Britain and Ireland and the dependencies thereof, and the United States of America and their territories." The latter course was pursued in the qualified war of 1798 with France, which was regulated by divers acts of congress, and of course was confined to the limits prescribed by those acts.

§ 1170. The power to declare war would of itself carry the incidental power to grant letters of marque and reprisal, and make rules concerning captures. It is most probable, that an extreme solicitude to follow out the powers enumerated in the confederation occasioned the introduction of these clauses into the constitution. In the former instrument, where all powers, not *expressly* delegated, were prohibited, this enumeration was peculiarly appropriate. But in the latter, where incidental powers were expressly contemplated, and provided for, the same necessity did not exist. As has been already remarked in another place, and will abundantly appear from the remaining auxiliary clauses to the power to declare war, the constitution abounds with pleonasms and repetitions, sometimes introduced from caution, sometimes from inattention, and sometimes from the imperfections of language.

§ 1171. But the express power "to grant letters of marque and reprisal" may not have been thought wholly unnecessary, because it is often a measure of peace, to prevent the necessity of a resort to war. Thus, individuals of a nation sometimes suffer from the depredations of foreign potentates; and yet it may not be deemed either expedient or necessary to redress such grievances by a general declaration of war. Under such circumstances the law of nations authorizes the sovereign of the injured individual to grant him this mode of redress, whenever justice is denied to him by the state, to which the party, who has done the injury, belongs. In this case the letters of marque and reprisal (words used as synonymous, the latter (reprisal) signifying, a taking in return, the former (letters of marque) the passing the frontiers in order to such taking,) contain an authority to seize the bodies or goods of the subjects of the offending state, wherever they may be found, until satisfaction is made for the injury. This power of reprisal seems indeed to be a dictate almost of nature itself, and is nearly related to, and plainly derived from that of making war. It is only an incomplete state of hostilities, and often ultimately leads to a formal denunciation of war, if the injury is unredressed, or extensive in its operations.

§ 1172. The power to declare war is exclusive in congress; and (as will be hereafter seen,) the states are prohibited from engaging in it, unless in cases of actual invasion or imminent danger thereof. It includes the exercise of all the ordinary rights of belligerents; and congress may therefore pass suitable laws to enforce them. They may authorize the seizure and condemnation of the property of the enemy within, or without the territory of the United States; and the confiscation of debts due to the enemy. But, until laws have been passed upon these subjects, no private citizens can enforce any such rights; and the judiciary is incapable of giving them any legitimate operation.

SEE ALSO:

Records of the Federal Convention, Farrand 1:292; 2:143, 144, 168, 313, 322, 326, 328, 505, 570, 595
Respublica v. *Sparhawk,* 1 Dall. 357 (Pa. 1788)
Penhallow v. *Doane,* 3 Dall. 54 (1795)
Talbot v. *Jansen,* 3 Dall. 133 (1795)
An Act respecting Enemy Aliens, 1 Stat. 577 (1798)
Charles Lee, Prize Ship and Crew, 20 Sept. 1798, 1 Ops. Atty. Gen. 85
Talbot v. *Seeman,* 1 Cranch 1 (1801)
John Stanley, 1 May 1802, Cunningham 1:287–88
The Emulous, 8 Fed. Cas. 697, no. 4,479 (C.C.D.Mass. 1813), rev'd *Brown* v. *United States,* 8 Cranch 110 (1814)
Russel v. *Skipworth,* 6 Binney 241 (Pa. 1814)
The Venus, 8 Cranch 253 (1814)
Almeida v. *Certain Slaves,* 1 Fed. Cas. 538, no. 255 (D.S.C. 1814)
Thirty Hogsheads of Sugar v. *Boyle,* 9 Cranch 191 (1815)
The Eleanor, 2 Wheat. 345 (1817)
The Estrella, 4 Wheat. 298 (1819)
Griswold v. *Waddington,* 16 Johns. R. 438 (N.Y. 1819)

Article 1, Section 8, Clause 12

To raise and support Armies, but no Appropriation of Money to that Use shall be for a longer Term than two Years;

1

Bill of Rights, sec. 6
1 W. & M., 2d sess., c. 2, 16 Dec. 1689

That the raising or keeping a standing army within the kingdom in time of peace, unless it be with consent of parliament, is against law.

2

Montesquieu, Spirit of Laws, bk. 5, ch. 19
1748

Thirdly, it may be inquired, whether civil and military employments should be conferred on the same person. In republics I think they should be joined, but in monarchies separated. In the former it would be extremely dangerous to make the profession of arms a particular state, distinct from that of civil functions; and in the latter, no less dangerous would it be to confer these two employments on the same person.

In republics a person takes up arms only with a view to defend his country and its laws; it is because he is a citizen he makes himself for a while a soldier. Were these two distinct states, the person who under arms thinks himself a citizen would soon be made sensible he is only a soldier.

In monarchies, they whose condition engages them in the profession of arms have nothing but glory, or at least honor or fortune, in view. To men, therefore, like these, the prince should never give any civil employments; on the contrary, they ought to be checked by the civil magistrate, that the same persons may not have at the same time the confidence of the people and the power to abuse it.

We have only to cast an eye on a nation that may be justly called a republic, disguised under the form of monarchy, and we shall see how jealous they are of making a separate order of the profession of arms, and how the military state is constantly allied with that of the citizen, and even sometimes of the magistrate, to the end that these qualities may be a pledge for their country, which should never be forgotten.

The division of civil and military employments, made by the Romans after the extinction of the republic, was not an arbitrary thing. It was a consequence of the change which happened in the constitution of Rome; it was natural to a monarchical government; and what was only commenced under Augustus, succeeding emperors were obliged to finish, in order to temper the military government.

Procopius, therefore, the competitor of Valens the emperor, was very much to blame when, conferring the proconsular dignity upon Hormisdas, a prince of the blood royal of Persia, he restored to this magistracy the military command of which it had been formerly possessed; unless, indeed, he had very particular reasons for so doing. A person that aspires to the sovereignty concerns himself less about what is serviceable to the state than what is likely to promote his own interest.

3

William Blackstone, Commentaries 1:254
1765

In this capacity therefore, of general of the kingdom, the king has the sole power of raising and regulating fleets and armies. Of the manner in which they are raised and regulated I shall speak more, when I come to consider the military state. We are now only to consider the prerogative of enlisting and of governing them: which indeed was disputed and claimed, contrary to all reason and precedent, by the long parliament of king Charles I; but, upon the restoration of his son, was solemnly declared by the statute 13 Car. II. c. 6. to be in the king alone: for that the sole supreme government and command of the militia within all his majesty's realms and dominions, and of all forces by sea and land, and of all forts and places of strength, ever was and is the undoubted right of his majesty, and his royal predecessors, kings and queens of England; and that both or either house of parliament cannot, nor ought to, pretend to the same.

4

James Burgh, Political Disquisitions
2:341–49, 389–91, 399–407
1774

General Reflections on Standing Armies in free Countries in Times of Peace.

In a survey of public abuses, it would be unpardonable to overlook that of a standing army in times of peace, one of the most hurtful, and most dangerous of abuses.

The very words, Army, War, Soldier, &c. entering into a humane and christian ear, carry with them ideas of hatred, enmity, fighting, bloodshed, mangling, butchering, destroying, unpeopling, and whatever else is horrible, cruel, hellish. My inestimable friend, the late great and good Dr. *Hales,* was used to say, that if any thing might be called the peculiar disgrace of human nature, and of our world, it is war; that a set of wretched worms, whose whole life, when it holds out the best, is but a moment, a dream, a vision of the night, should shorten this their short span, should assemble by thousands and myriads, travel over vast countries, or cross unmeasurable oceans, armed with swords and spears and infernal fire, and when they meet immediately fall to butchering one another, only because a couple of frantic and mischievous fiends in human shape, commonly called kings, have fallen out they know not about what, and have ordered them to go and make havock of one another.

Yet such is the turn of mind of those who are at the head of the world, that they bestow more attention upon the art of war, that is, the art of destroying their fellow-creatures, than upon the improvement of all the liberal arts and sciences, and outvie one another in keeping up bands of those butchers of mankind commonly called standing armies, to the number of many thousands; and so prevalent is this infatuation, that even we, though surrounded by the ocean, must mimick the kingdoms on the continent, and beggar ourselves by keeping up an army of near 50,000 in times of profound peace.

The whole art of war from beginning to end is, at best, but a scene of folly and absurdity. Two kings, already possessed of more territory than they know how to govern, fall out about a province. They immediately take up arms. Immediately half a continent is deluged in blood. They carry on their infernal hatred, while either of them can find in the purses of their beggared subjects any money to squander, or while they can find any more of their miserable people, who, being by the fell ravage of war stripped of all, are glad to throw themselves into the army, to get a morsel of bread. And when the two mighty belligerant powers, the two venomous worms, have carried on the contest almost to the destruction of both, the point in dispute remains undecided as before, or they see, that it might have been infinitely better decided by arbitration of indifferent states, without the spilling of one drop of christian blood.

War is not a more proper method of deciding controversies between kings, than single combat between individuals. All that can be determined by fighting is, that the conqueror is the best fighter of the two; not that he has justice on his side. As I should conclude that private person, who chose rather to decide a quarrel by a duel, than to appeal to the laws of his country, or stand to arbitration of a few friends, a ruffian and a murderer; so I do not hesitate to pronounce every king a butcher of mankind who chooses rather to appeal to the *ratio ultima regum,* than to arbitration of neutral princes.

Standing armies first become necessary, or the pretence of their necessity plausible, when the disbanded troops, called *tard-venus,* in *France,* took to plundering and mischief in times of peace. Then the neighbouring princes pretended they must be upon an equal foot with *France.* But what is that to *England,* surrounded by the sea, and guarded by a fleet equal to all the maritime force of *Europe?*

In former times we had no mercenary army. It was the militia that went to the holy war, that conquered *France,* &c. So at *Rome* there was no mercenary army in the best times of the republic. Our *Hen.* VII. raised no small jealousy by his 100 yeomen of the guards, augmented by him from 50, the whole standing army of his times. In the days of *Ch.* II. the army was got to 5,000; in our times to near 50,000. There can no account be given of this alarming increase, but the increase of corruption, and decrease of attention to liberty. And now, our patriotic parliaments have made the army a sacred establishment, and the sinking fund a temporary expedient.

An army, in a free country, says judge *Blackstone,* "ought only to be enlisted for a short and limited time. The soldiers should live intermixed with the people. No separate camp, no barracks, no inland fortresses should be allowed." Yet it is notorious, that our soldiers are enlisted for life, on pain of death, if they desert; and that camps, barracks, and inland forts, are very common in our pretended free country. The mere slavery of a soldier's life, and the rigorous discipline, and *Turkish* severities, so great a number of brave, and freeborn *English* subjects are exposed to in the army, are sufficient to render it the abhorrence of every true *English* spirit, and the peculiar disgrace of our country, and our times. See *Blackstone's* COMMENTARIES, 1. 415, where the learned author (no malecontent) shews the peculiar danger to liberty from enslaving so many subjects, (and thereby exciting their envy against their countrymen, who enjoy what they are for ever deprived of) and then arming those slaves, to enable them to reduce the rest to their condition, of which ill policy history furnishes many terrible examples.

"In a land of liberty it is extremely *dangerous* to make a distinct order of the profession of arms. In absolute monarchies, this is necessary for the safety of the prince, and arises from the main principle of their constitution, which is, that of governing by fear: but in free states, the profession of a soldier, taken singly and merely as a profession, is justly an object of jealousy.—The laws, therefore, and constitution of these kingdoms know no such state as that of a perpetual standing soldier, bred up to no other profession, than that of war." Yet we see gentlemen breed up their sons for the army as regularly as for law, physic, or divinity; and, while in *France,* the land of slaves, the soldiery are engaged only for a certain time, ours are for life; that they may be effectually separated from the people, and attached to another interest.

The judge goes on to shew, that in the *Saxon* times, the military force was under the absolute command of the dukes, or heretochs, who were elected by the people. This the judge, as if he were fascinated in favour of prerogative, sees in a dangerous light. "This large share of power, says he, thus conferred by the people, though intended to preserve the liberty of the subject, was perhaps unreasonably detrimental to the prerogative of the crown." And then he mentions one instance of its being abused. But will any *Englishman,* understanding what he says, gravely declare, that he thinks an armed force safer, in respect of liberty, in the hands of a *king,* than of a number of subjects elected by the *people?* Yet this very author prefers a militia to an army. If all this be either consistent with the fundamental principles of liberty, or with itself, it is to be understood in some manner, which I own to be out of my reach.

"Those, who have the command of the arms in a country, says *Aristotle,* are masters of the state, and have it in their power to make what revolutions they please." Οἱ τῶν ὅπλων κυρίοι, κ. τ. λ.

The soldiery are themselves bound for life, under the most abject slavery. For what is more perfect slavery, than for a man to be, without relief, obliged to obey the command of another, at the hazard of his life, if he obeys, and under the penalty of certain death if he disobeys, while the smallest misbehaviour may bring upon him the most painful and disgraceful punishment? The sense of their own remediless condition may naturally be expected to excite in them the same disposition, which shews itself in the negroes in *Jamaica,* and the eunuchs in the eastern seraglios.

In the mutiny-act, it is always mentioned, that keeping up an army in time of peace, without consent of parliament, is unlawful. But there is no such clause for keeping up *marines.* Yet marines are as much an army as any other men; are mostly at land; and may, at any time, be applied to the enslaving of the people, as readily as the soldiery. 'Tis true, their number is at present inconsiderable; but that is entirely at the disposal of government.

Lord *Hinton's* arguments against a reduction of the army, *A. D.* 1738.

1. The army is only a change made in the management of the armed force of the nation, which was formerly kept up in the guise of a militia.

Ans. The army is the very creature of the court; and therefore likely to execute every order of the court. The army is detached from the people for life, and enslaved for life. A militia continues still a part of the people, and is to return and mix with the people again, which must keep up in their minds both an awe and an affection for the people.

2. Now all the countries about have regular disciplined armies.

Ans. This is no reason for our keeping up an army, who are separated from all our neighbors. It is a reason for our keeping up a fleet, and a militia.

3. Our militia cannot be trusted. Our people are otherwise employed, than in learning military discipline.

Ans. The army are, on no account, preferable to a militia, but their being more thoroughly trained. Let the militia then be thoroughly disciplined. Fifty days exercise at different times in the year, will train them thoroughly. Let them have pay for those days, and carry on their business the rest of the year as at present. And let every male be trained; and then see, whether enemies will invade, or tumults disturb.

4. The army has not yet enslaved us. Experience shows us, that a standing army is not unfriendly to liberty.

Ans. We ought to depend on the *constitution* for the safety of our liberties; not on the moderation of the individuals, who command our army. If our army has not yet enslaved us; we know, that the far greatest part of the world has been enslaved by armies. But it is much to be questioned, whether we are not already so far enslaved, that the people could not now obtain of government what they requested, though the undoubted sense of the people was known to government.

5. An annual army is different from a standing army. The former may be dissolved, whenever it pleases parliament to give over providing for it.

Ans. There is no difference, as to the liberty of the subject, whether the army be on one foot, or the other; whether it be established by law, or whether it be constantly kept, and certainly never to be reduced.

6. An army is necessary to keep the peace. Turbulent people raise tumults about matters, which have had even the sanction of parliament, as excises, turnpikes, suppression of gin, &c.

Ans. Good government is a surer way to keep the peace, than keeping up a formidable and expensive army. The people may judge wrong, or be misled occasionally. But it is mal-administration that sets up popular demagogues, who could not excite the people to tumults, if government did not afford some cause for discontent. The sanction of parliament neither will nor ought to satisfy the people, unless the people be satisfied of the independency of the members, who compose it. So much for lord *Hinton's* arguments.

"Whatever it may be called, that government is certainly, and necessarily, a military government where the army is the strongest power in the country. And it is eternally true, that a free parliament and a standing army are absolutely incompatible."

"It is the interest of favourites to advise the king to govern by an *army:* for if he prevails (over his subjects) then they are sure to have what heart can wish; and if he fail, yet they are but where they were; they had nothing, and they can lose nothing."

Every officer in the army, almost, is an addition to the power and influence of the ministry. And every addition to their power and influence is a step toward aristocracy or absolute monarchy.

"All armies whatsoever, says *Davenant,* if they are over large, tend to the dispeopling of a country, of which our neighbour nation is a sufficient proof; where in one of the best climates in *Europe* men are wanting to till the ground. For children do not proceed from intemperate pleasures taken loosely and at random, but from a regular way of living, where the father of the family desires to rear up, and provide for the offspring he shall beget."

When a country is to be enslaved, the army is the instrument to be used. No nation ever was enslaved but by an army. No nation ever kept up an army in times of peace, which did not lose its liberties.

"An army is so forcible, and, at the same time, so coarse an instrument, that any hand, that wields it, may, without much dexterity, perform any operation, and gain any ascendancy in human society."

Mr. *Hume* calls the army a mortal distemper in the *British* government, of which it must at last inevitable perish.

It was *Walpole's* custom, if a borough did not elect his man for their member, to send them a messenger of *Satan* to buffet them, a company of soldiers to live upon them.

In this way a standing army may be used as an instrument in the hand of a wicked minister for crushing liberty.

. . . . .

A Militia, with the Navy, the only proper Security of a free People in an insular Situation, both against foreign Invasion and domestic Tyranny.

A standing army, as those on the continent, continues, of course, from year to year, without any new appointment, and is a part of the constitution. Our courtiers affect to call the *British* land-establishment a parliamentary army, and would deceive us into the notion of a difference between a standing army and a parliamentary. The *British* land-forces, say they, are appointed from year to year, not only as to their number, but their subsistence; so that the parliament's neglecting to provide for their subsistence would be annihilating the army at once. But is the army the less a grievance for its being on this foot, than if it were on the same with those of *France* or *Spain?* Suppose that for twenty years together, we should have no parliament called. At the end of that period, could the grievance and loss to the nation be estimated as at all less upon the whole, than it would have been, if the king had at the beginning of the twenty years, declared by edict, that there should be no parliament during that period? This would be a bolder stroke of tyranny, than merely neglecting, from year to year, or refusing, to let the writs be issued; but the people would be as really deprived of the advantages of parliaments by one proceeding, as by the other.

"No kingdom can be secured otherwise than by arming the people. The possession of arms is the distinction between a freeman and a slave. He, who has nothing, and who himself belongs to another, must be defended by him, whose property he is, and needs no arms. But he, who thinks he is his own master, and has what he can call his own, ought to have arms to defend himself, and what he possesses; else he lives precariously, and at discretion. And though for a while, those, who have the sword in their power, abstain from doing him injury, yet by degrees he will be awed into submission to every arbitrary command. Our ancestors" [the *Caledonii, see Tacit. &c.*] "by being always armed, and frequently in action, defended themselves against the *Romans, Danes* and *English,* and maintained their liberty against the incroachments of their own princes."

"We all know, that the only way of enslaving a people, is by keeping up a standing army; that by standing forces all limited monarchies have been destroyed; without them none; that so long as any standing forces are allowed in a nation, pretences will never be wanting to increase them; that princes have never suffered a militia to be put upon any good foot, lest standing armies should appear unnecessary."

. . . . .

Nothing will make a nation so unconquerable as a militia, or every man's being trained to arms. For every *Briton* having in him by birth the principal part of a soldier, I mean the heart; will want but little training beyond what he will have as a militia-man, to make him a complete soldier. A standing army, though numerous, might be routed in one engagement, if an engagement should happen in consequence of a *French* invasion. Whereas the militia of *Britain* would be a million of men; which would render a descent from *France* an operation of war not to be thought of.

"All the force, which the *French* can throw over to this country, before our fleet can come to our assistance, must be so inconsiderable, that their landing would deserve the name of a surprize, rather than of an invasion;" says one, who will hardly be suspected of intending to derogate from the importance of the army; I mean, *John,* duke of *Argyle.*

De Wit proposed to the *French* king, during the first *Dutch* war, an invasion of *England.* The king replied, that such an attempt would be fruitless, and would unite all the jarring parties in *England* against the enemy. "We shall have," says he, "in a few days after our landing, 50,000 men (meaning the militia) upon us."

Mr. *Fletcher* adds afterwards what follows.

"The essential quality of a militia consistent with freedom, is, that the officers be named, and preferred, and they, and the soldiers maintained, not by the prince but the people, who send them out. Ambitious princes [and he would have added, if he had fore-known the late duke of *Newcastle*'s opposition to the establishment of the militia, *corrupt ministers*] have always endeavoured to discredit the militia, and render it burdensome to the people, by never suffering it to be upon any right, or even tolerable footing; all to persuade the necessity of standing forces. In the battle of *Naseby,* the number of forces was equal on both sides; and all circumstances equal. In the parliament's army only nine officers had ever seen actual service, and most of the soldiers were *London* prentices, drawn out of the city two months before. In the king's army there were above 1000 officers, who had served abroad; yet the regulars were routed by the prentices. A good militia is of such importance to a nation, that it is the chief part of the constitution of every free government. For, though, as to other things, the constitution be ever so slight, a good militia will always preserve the public liberty; and in the best constitution ever known, as to all other parts of government, if the militia be not upon a right foot, the liberty of the people must perish. The militia of antient *Rome* made her mistress of the world. Standing armies enslaved her. The *Lacedaemonians* continued 800 years free, because they had a good militia. The *Swiss* are the freest people in our times, and like to continue such the longest, because they have the best militia."

However a corrupt government may intend to defeat the design of a militia by totally perverting it from its original intention and use, this ought not to hinder all men of property from learning the use of arms. There is no law against a free subject's acquiring any laudable accomplishment. And if the generality of housekeepers were only half-disciplined, a designing prince, or ministry, would hardly dare to provoke the people by an open attack on their liberties, lest they should find means to be completely instructed in the exercise of arms before the chain could be rivetted. But without the people's having some knowledge of arms, I see not what is to secure them against slavery, whenever it shall please a daring prince, or minister, to resolve on making the experiment. See the histories of all the nations of the world.

The militia-act is long and intricate; whereas there was nothing necessary, but to direct, that every third man in every parish in *England,* whose house had 10 or more windows, should be exercised in his own parish, by an experienced serjeant,   times every year, the days to be appointed; and every third part of every parish to be upon the list for three years, and free six years, so that in nine years every such housekeeper in *England* might have had all the knowledge he could acquire by   field-days. The men never to be drawn out of their respective parishes, but to resist an invasion, quell an insurrection, or for some necessary purpose. Every healthy housekeeper of 10 windows and above, under 50, who refused to enlist and attend the exercising days, to be fined. No hirelings to be accepted. The commanders to be the men of largest property in each county.

A country, in which every man of property could defend his property, could have no occasion for a dangerous standing army, and would be incomparably more secure against invasion, than it could be with a standing army of 50,000 men scattered over a whole empire.

Lord *Lyttelton* thinks the militia (the only permanent military force, our ancestors knew) was commanded by the heretoch of every county, who was annually chosen into his office by the freeholders in the folkmote, or county-court; and that after the *Norman* times, this command devolved upon the earl of each county.

A militia consisting of any others than the men of *property* in a country, is no militia; but a mungrel army.

Men of business and property will never choose to enter into the militia, if they may be called from their homes, and their business, for three years together, subject to martial law all the while.

Brigadier general *Townshend,* in his Dedication of the "*Plan of Discipline composed for the Militia of the county of Norfolk,*" affirms, that he has made some persons masters of that exercise "in two or three mornings, so as to perform it with grace and spirit;" and that the common men learned it in "seven or eight days time, some in less."

The same gentleman complains heavily of the "discouragements, slights, delays, evasions, and unnatural treatment" of the militia-act from those, whose duty it was to see it executed according to its intention. One would think the old militia law might have directed our government to avoid sending the militia out of their respective counties. This was always expressly guarded against, and was never to be done, but in the case of foreign invasion.

The single circumstance of the national militia's being first settled by the great and good *Alfred,* ought to prejudice all friends to liberty in its favour. That able politician lord *Molesworth* thinks a militia infinitely preferable to an army, both on the score of safety from tyranny at home, and of invasion from abroad. Judge *Blackstone* gives the preference to a militia. The *Polish* militia serve but 40 days in the year.

Queen *Elizabeth's* whole reign may be almost called a state of defensive and offensive war; in *England* as well as in *Ireland;* in the *Indies* as well as in *Europe;* she ventured to go through this state, if it was a venture, without the help of a standing army. The people of *England* had seen none from the days of *Richard* II. and this cautious queen might perhaps imagine that the example of his reign and those of other countries where standing armies were established, would beget jealousies in the minds of her people, and diminish that affection, which she esteemed and found to be the greatest security of her person, and the greatest strength of her government. Whenever she wanted troops, her subjects flocked to her standard; and her reign affords most illustrious proofs, that all the ends of security and of glory too may be answered in this island without the charge and danger of the expedient just mentioned. This assertion will not be contradicted by those who recollect in how many places and on how many occasions her forces fought and conquered the best disciplined veteran troops in *Europe.*

The militia was established by *Alfred,* and fell into decay under the *Stuarts.* A proof, that a militia is good, and ought to be kept up. The *Stuarts* were friends to standing armies. A demonstration, that standing armies are dangerous. *James* II. at his accession declared the militia useless; and demanded supplies for keeping an army, he was to raise. It is well known what armies *Charles* I. raised, and in what bloody business he employed them. *Charles* II. had, at the beginning of his reign, about 5,000 men. Toward the end of his reign, the army was increased to near 8,000. *James* II. at the time of *Monmouth*'s rebellion, had on foot 15,000 men. At the prince of *Orange*'s arrival, 30,000 regular troops.

The command of the militia was only put in the hands of the crown, when the nation was in a state of insanity, and every man ready to lay down his head on a block, for the king [*Ch.* II.]' to chop it off, if he pleased. As it is regulated by 30 *Geo.* II. c. 25, it remains too much on the same foot. For it is officered by the lord lieutenant, the deputy-lieutenants and other principal land-holders, under a commission from the crown, which places it, as every thing else is, too much under the power of the court.

The first commission of array is thought to have been in the times of *Hen.* V. When he went to *France, A. D.* 1415, he impowered commissioners to take an account of all the freemen in each county, who were able to bear arms, to divide them into companies, and to have them in readiness for resisting the enemy.

"The citizens, and country gentlemen soon became excellent officers;" says Mr. *Hume.* This shews what a militia may in a short time be brought to. For what is a militia-man, but a soldier, engaged for a limited time, and less completely trained? And what is a soldier, but a militia-man completely disciplined, and enslaved for life? The principal part of a soldier is the heart; and that almost every *Briton* has by birth without training. A militia-man is a free citizen; a soldier, a slave for life. Which is most likely to shew the most courage and the greatest attachment to his country?

"The militia—if it could not preserve liberty to the people, preserved at least the power, if ever the inclination should arise, of recovering it."

"Against insurrections at home, the sheriff of every county has the power of the militia in him, and if he be negligent to suppress them with the *posse comitatus,* he is fineable. Against invasions from abroad, every man would be ready to give his assistance. There would be little need to raise forces, when every man would be ready to defend himself, and to fight *pro aris et focis.*" What would this honest man have said if he had been told, that the time would come, when it would be called necessary to keep up a standing army in this free country, surrounded with the ocean, in peace as well as war, to the formidable number of above 40,000, a number superior to that with which *Alexander* conquered the world?

Why must the *British* soldiery be enslaved for life, any more, than the sailors on board the navy? Were the militia put upon a right foot, the same individuals might serve either by sea or land, during a certain short period, and then return to their respective station. I know the court-sycophants will object to this, That a soldier requires a great deal of training and reviewing, before he comes to have the cool courage necessary in action, &c. But this is all pretence. We hardly ever have had, or can have occasion for any soldiery. Our wars with *France* in old times are now by all parties confessed to have been merely the loss of so much blood and treasure without possibility of advantage to this island. And our continental wars since the Revolution we have been drawn into chiefly by the unfortunate circumstance of our having on our throne a set of princes connected with the continent. There is no advantage we have ever gained by war, which would not have been greater, and cost us incomparably less, if we had kept to the sea. For we never can have a nation for our enemy that is not commercial, and we can certainly at any time force a commercial nation to yield to reasonable terms by attacking their commerce, their foreign settlements, their coast-towns, their fisheries, &c. And by sea we may always command the superiority. For every *Briton* is born with the heart of a soldier and a sailor in him; and wants but little training to be equal on either element, to any veteran of any country. Accordingly we never hear of the common men, in either service, shewing any appearance of cowardice.

"Immediately after the mutiny bill had passed the lower house, Mr. *Thomas Pitt,* elder brother of Mr. *William Pitt,* then paymaster general, moved, on the 9th of *March,* 1749, for leave to bring in a bill to limit respective times, beyond which no noncommissioned officer or soldier, now, or who hereafter may be such in his majesty's land-service, shall be compelled to continue in the said service. The motion was seconded by Sir *Francis Dashwood;* but very poorly supported in numbers. And at last, on the 19th of *April,* it was, upon a division of 139 against 82, put off for two months, so that it was no more heard of. Had this limitation taken place, such a rotation of soldiers would have ensued among the common people, that in a few years every peasant, labourer, and inferior tradesman in the kingdom would have understood the exercise of arms; and perhaps the people in general would have concluded, that a standing army, on whose virtue the constitution of *Great Britain* seems to depend, was altogether unnecessary."

Those incendiaries who go about to destroy our constitution, have not blushed in the same breath to admit, that standing armies have been generally the instruments of overturning free governments, and to affirm that a standing army is necessary to be kept in ours; if you ask them against whom, they answer you very frankly, against the people; if you ask them why, they answer you with the same frankness, because of the levity and inconstancy of the people. This is the evil; an army is the remedy. Our army is not designed, according to these doctors of slavery, against the enemies of the nation. We are confident that the present army is incapable of being employed to such purposes, and abhors an imputation which might have been justly cast on *Cromwell's* army, but is very unjustly insinuated against the present.

5

Adam Smith, Wealth of Nations, bk. 5, ch. 1, pt. 1
1776

Men of republican principles have been jealous of a standing army as dangerous to liberty. It certainly is so, wherever the interest of the general and that of the principal officers are not necessarily connected with the support of the constitution of the state. The standing army of Caesar destroyed the Roman republic. The standing army of Cromwel turned the long parliament out of doors. But where the sovereign is himself the general, and the principal nobility and gentry of the country the chief officers of the army; where the military force is placed under the command of those who have the greatest interest in the support of the civil authority, because they have themselves the greatest share of that authority, a standing army can never be dangerous to liberty. On the contrary, it may in some cases be favourable to liberty. The security which it gives to the sovereign renders unnecessary that troublesome jealousy, which, in some modern republics, seems to watch over the minutest actions, and to be at all times ready to disturb the peace of every citizen. Where the security of the magistrate, though supported by the principal people of the country, is endangered by every popular discontent; where a small tumult is capable of bringing about in a few hours a great revolution, the whole authority of government must be employed to suppress and punish every murmur and complaint against it. To a sovereign, on the contrary, who feels himself supported, not only by the natural aristocracy of the country, but by a well-regulated standing army, the rudest, the most groundless, and the most licentious remonstrances can give little disturbance. He can safely pardon or neglect them, and his consciousness of his own superiority naturally disposes him to do so. That degree of liberty which approaches to licentiousness can be tolerated only in countries where the sovereign is secured by a well-regulated standing army. It is in such countries only, that the public safety does not require, that the sovereign should be trusted with any discretionary power, for suppressing even the impertinent wantonness of this licentious liberty.

6

George Washington, Sentiments on a Peace Establishment
2 May 1783
Writings 26:374–76, 388–91

A Peace Establishment for the United States of America may in my opinion be classed under four different heads Vizt:

First. A regular and standing force, for Garrisoning West Point and such other Posts upon our Northern, Western, and Southern Frontiers, as shall be deemed necessary to awe the Indians, protect our Trade, prevent the encroachment of our Neighbours of Canada and the Florida's, and guard us at least from surprizes; Also for security of our Magazines.

Secondly. A well organized Militia; upon a Plan that will pervade all the States, and introduce similarity in their Establishment Manoeuvres, Exercise and Arms.

Thirdly. Establishing Arsenals of all kinds of Military Stores.

Fourthly. Accademies, one or more for the Instruction of the Art Military; particularly those Branches of it which respect Engineering and Artillery, which are highly essential, and the knowledge of which, is most difficult to obtain. Also Manufactories of some kinds of Military Stores.

Upon each of these, and in the order in which they stand, I shall give my sentiments as concisely as I can, and with that freedom which the Committee have authorized.

Altho' a *large* standing Army in time of Peace hath ever been considered dangerous to the liberties of a Country, yet a few Troops, under certain circumstances, are not only safe, but indispensably necessary. Fortunately for us our relative situation requires but few. The same circumstances which so effectually retarded, and in the end conspired to defeat the attempts of Britain to subdue us, will now powerfully tend to render us secure. Our *distance* from the European States in a great degree frees us of apprehension, from their numerous regular forces and the Insults and dangers which are to be dreaded from their Ambition.

But, if our danger from those powers was more imminent, yet we are too poor to maintain a standing Army adequate to our defence, and was our Country more populous and rich, still it could not be done without great oppression of the people. Besides, as soon as we are able to raise funds more than adequate to the discharge of the Debts incurred by the Revolution, it may become a Question worthy of consideration, whether the surplus should not be applied in preparations for building and equipping a Navy, without which, in case of War we could neither protect our Commerce, nor yield that Assistance to each other, which, on such an extent of Sea-Coast, our mutual Safety would require.

. . . . .

Were it not totally unnecessary and superfluous to adduce arguments to prove what is conceded on all hands the Policy and expediency of resting the protection of the Country on a respectable and well established Militia, we might not only shew the propriety of the measure from our peculiar local situation, but we might have recourse to the Histories of Greece and Rome in their most virtuous and Patriotic ages to demonstrate the Utility of such Establishments. Then passing by the Mercinary Armies, which have at one time or another subverted the liberties of allmost all the Countries they have been raised to defend, we might see, with admiration, the Freedom and Independence of Switzerland supported for Centuries, in the midst of powerful and jealous neighbours, by means of a hardy and well organized Militia. We might also derive useful lessons of a similar kind from other Nations of Europe, but I believe it will be found, the *People of this Continent* are too well acquainted with the Merits of the subject to require information or example. I shall therefore proceed to point out some general outlines of their duty, and conclude this head with a few particular observations on the regulations which I conceive ought to be immediately adopted by the States at the instance and recommendation of Congress.

It may be laid down as a primary position, and the basis of our system, that every Citizen who enjoys the protection of a free Government, owes not only a proportion of his property, but even of his personal services to the defence of it, and consequently that the Citizens of America (with a few legal and official exceptions) from 18 to 50 Years of Age should be borne on the Militia Rolls, provided with uniform Arms, and so far accustomed to the use of them, that the Total strength of the Country might be called forth at a Short Notice on any very interesting Emergency, for these purposes they ought to be duly organized into Commands of the same formation; (it is not of *very* great importance, whether the Regiments are large or small, provided a sameness prevails in the strength and composition of them and I do not know that a better establishment, than that under which the Continental Troops now are, can be adopted. They ought to be regularly Mustered and trained, and to have their Arms and Accoutrements inspected at certain appointed times, not less than once or twice in the course of every [year] but as it is obvious, amongst such a Multitude of People (who may indeed be useful for temporary service) there must be a great number, who from domestic Circumstances, bodily defects, natural awkwardness or disinclination, can never acquire the habits of Soldiers; but on the contrary will injure the appearance of any body of Troops to which they are attached, and as there are a sufficient proportion of able bodied young Men, between the Age of 18 and 25, who, from a natural fondness for Military parade (which passion is almost ever prevalent at that period of life) might easily be enlisted or drafted to form a Corps in every State, capable of resisting any sudden impression which might be attempted by a foreign Enemy, while the remainder of the National forces would have time to Assemble and make preparations for the Field. I would wish therefore, that the former, being considered as a *denier resort,* reserved for some great occasion, a judicious system might be adopted for forming and placing the latter on the best possible Establishment. And that while the Men of this description shall be viewed as the Van and flower of the American Forces, ever ready for Action and zealous to be employed whenever it may become necessary in the service of their Country; they should meet with such exemptions, privileges or distinctions, as might tend to keep alive a true Military pride, a nice sense of honour, and a patriotic regard for the public. Such sentiments, indeed, ought to be instilled into our Youth, with their earliest years, to be cherished and inculcated as frequently and forcibly as possible.

It is not for me to decide positively, whether it will be ultimately most interesting to the happiness and safety of the United States, to form this Class of Soldiers into a kind of Continental Militia, selecting every 10th 15th or 20th. Man from the Rolls of each State for the purpose; Organizing, Officering and Commissioning those Corps upon the same principle as is now practiced in the Continental Army. Whether it will be best to comprehend in this body, all the Men fit for service between some given Age and no others, for example between 18 and 25 or some similar description, or whether it will be preferable in every Regiment of the proposed Establishment to have one additional Company inlisted or drafted from the best Men for 3, 5, or 7 years and distinguished by the name of the additional or light Infantry Company, always to be kept complete. The Companies might then be drawn together occasionally and formed into particular Battalions or Regiments under Field Officers appointed for that Service. One or other of these plans I think will be found indispensably necessary, if we are in earnest to have an efficient force ready for Action at a moments Warning. And I cannot conceal my private sentiment, that the formation of additional, or light Companies will be most consistent with the genius of our Countrymen and perhaps in their opinion most consonant to the spirit of our Constitution.

I shall not contend for names or forms, it will be altogether essential, and it will be sufficient that perfect Uniformity should be established throughout the Continent, and pervade, as far as possible, every Corps, whether of standing Troops or Militia, and of whatever denomination they may be. To avoid the confusion of a contrary practice, and to produce the happy consequences which will attend a uniform system of Service, in case Troops from the different parts of the Continent shall ever be brought to Act together again, I would beg leave to propose, that Congress should employ some able hand, to digest a Code of Military Rules and regulations, calculated immediately for the Militia and other Troops of the United States; And as it should seem the present system, by being a little simplified, altered, and improved, might be very well adopted to the purpose; I would take the liberty of recommending, that measures should be immediately taken for the accomplishment of this interesting business, and that an Inspector General should be appointed to superintend the execution of the proposed regulations in the several States.

7

ALEXANDER HAMILTON, CONTINENTAL CONGRESS REPORT ON A MILITARY PEACE ESTABLISHMENT
18 June 1783
Papers 3:378–83

The Committee observe with respect to a military peace establishment, that before any plan can with propriety be adopted, it is necessary to inquire what powers exist for that purpose in the confederation.

By the 4th. clause of the 6th article it is declared that "no vessels of war shall be kept up by any state in time of peace, except such number only as shall be deemed necessary by the United States in Congress assembled, for the defence of such state or its trade; nor shall any body of forces be kept up by any state in time of peace, except such number only, as in the judgment of the United States in Congress assembled shall be deemed requisite to garrison the forts necessary for the defence of such state."

By the 5th. clause of the 9th article, The United States in Congress assembled are empowered generally (and without mention of peace or war) "to build and equip a navy, to agree upon the number of land forces, and to make requisitions from each state for its quota, in proportion to the number of white inhabitants in each state, which requisition shall be binding, and thereupon the legislature of each state, shall appoint the Regimental officers, raise the men and clothe arm and equip them in a soldierlike manner at the expence of the United States and the officers and men so cloathed armed and equipped shall march to the place appointed and within the time agreed on by the United States in Congress assembled."

By the 4th. clause of the same article the United States are empowered "to appoint all officers of the land forces except regimental officers, to appoint all officers of the naval forces, and to commission all officers whatever in the service of the United States, making rules for the government and regulation of the said land and naval forces and directing their operations."

It appears to the Committee that the terms of the first clause are rather restrictive on the particular states than directory to the United States, intended to prevent any state from keeping up forces land or naval without the approbation and sanction of the Union, which might endanger its tranquillity and harmony, and not to contravene the positive power vested in the United States by the subsequent clauses, or to deprive them of the right of taking such precautions as should appear to them essential to the general security. A distinction that this is to be provided for in time of war, by the forces of the Union, in time of peace, by those of each state would involve, besides other inconveniences, this capital one, that when the forces of the Union should become necessary to defend its rights and repel any attacks upon them, the United States would be obliged to *begin to create* at the very moment they would have occasion *to employ* a fleet and army. They must wait for an actual commencement of hostilities before they would be authorised to prepare for defence, to raise a single regiment or to build a single ship. When it is considered what a length of time is requisite to levy and form an army and still more to build and equip a navy, which is evidently a work of leisure and of peace requiring a gradual preparation of the means—there cannot be presumed so improvident an intention in the Confederation as that of obliging the United States to suspend all provision for the common defence 'till a declaration of war or an invasion. If this is admitted it will follow that they are at liberty to make such establishments in time of peace as they shall judge requisite to the common safety. This is a principle of so much importance in the apprehension of the Committee to the welfare of the union, that if any doubt should exist as to the true meaning of the first-mentioned clause, it will in their opinion be proper to admit such a construction as will leave the general power, vested in the United States by the other clauses, in full force; unless the states respectively or a Majority of them shall declare a different interpretation. The Committee however submit to Congress, (in conformity to that spirit of Candour and to that respect for the sense of their constituents, which ought ever to characterize their proceedings) the propriety of transmitting the plan which they may adopt to the several states to afford an opportunity of signifying their sentiments previous to its final execution.

The Committee, are of opinion, if there is a con[s]titutional power in the United States for that purpose, that there are conclusive reasons in favour of foederal in preference to state establishments.

First there are objects for which separate provision cannot conveniently be made; posts within certain districts, the ju[r]isdiction and property of which are not yet constitutionally ascertained—territory appertaining to the United States not within the original claim of any of the states—the navigation of the Missippi and of the lakes—the rights of the fisheries and of foreign commerce; all which belonging to the United States depending on the laws of nations and on treaty, demand the joint protection of the Union, and cannot with propriety be trusted to separate establishments.

Secondly, the fortifications proper to be established ought to be constructed with relation to each other on a general and well-digested system and their defence should be calculated on the same principles. This is equally important in the double view of safety and oeconomy. If this is not done under the direction of the United States, each state following a partial and disjointed plan, it will be found that the posts will have no mutual dependence or support—that they will be improperly distributed, and more numerous than is necessary as well as less efficacious—of course more easily reduced and more expensive both in the construction and defence.

3dly. It happens, that from local circumstances particular states, if left to take care of themselves, would be in possession of the chief part of the standing forces and of the principal fortified places of the union; a circumstance inconvenient to them and to the United States—to them, because it would impose a heavy exclusive burthen in a matter the benefit of which will be immediately shared by their neighbours and ultimately by the states at large—to the United States, because it confides the care of the safety of the *whole* to a *part,* which will naturally be unwilling as well as unable to make such effectual provision at its particular expence, as the common welfare requires—because a single state from the peculiarity of its situation, will in a manner keep the keys of the United States—because in fine a considerable force in the hands of a few states may have an unfriendly aspect on the confidence and harmony which ought carefully to be maintained between the whole.

4thly. It is probable that a provision by the Congress of the forces necessary to be kept up will be based upon a more systematic and oeconomical plan than a provision by the states separately; especially as it will be of importance as soon as the situation of affairs will permit, to establish founderies, manufactaries of arms, powder &c; by means of which the labour of a part of the troops applied to this purpose will furnish the United States with those essential articles on easy terms, and contribute to their own support.

5thly. There must be a corps of Artillery and Engineers kept on foot in time of peace, as the officers of this corps require science and long preliminary study, and cannot be formed on an emergency; and as the neglect of this institution would always oblige the United States to have recourse to foreigners in time of war for a supply of officers in this essential branch—an inconvenience which it ought to be the object of every nation to avoid. Nor indeed is it possible to dispense with the service of such a corps in time of peace, as it will be indispensable not only to have posts on the frontier; but to have fortified harbours for the reception and protection of the fleet of the United States. This corps requiring particular institutions for the instruction and formation of the officers cannot exist upon separate establishments without a great increase of expence.

6thly. It appears from the annexed papers No. 1 to 4, to be the concurrent opinion of the Commander in Chief, the Secretary at War, the Inspector General and the Chief Engineer, not only that some militia establishment is indispensable but that it ought in all respects to be under the authority of the United States as well for military as political reasons. The plan hereafter submitted on considerations of oeconomy is less extensive than proposed by either of them.

The Committee upon these principles submit the following plan.

The Military peace establishment of the United States to consist of four regiments of infantry, and, one of Artillery incorporated in a corps of Engineers, with the denomination of the corps of Engineers.

Each Regiment of infantry to consist of two batalions, each batalion of four companies, each company of 64 rank and file, with the following, commissioned and Non commissioned officers, pay, rations and cloathing; to be however recruited to one hundred & twenty eight rank & file in time of war, preserving the proportion of corporals to privates.

8

RICHARD HENRY LEE TO JAMES MONROE
5 Jan. 1784
Letters 2:287–88

You are perfectly right Sir in your observation concerning the consequence of a standing army—that it has constantly terminated in the destruction of liberty—It has not only *been* constantly so, but I think it clear from the construction of human nature, that it will always *be* so—And it is realy unfortunate for human freedom, safety, and happiness, that so many plausible arguments are ever at hand to support a system which both reason & experience prove to be productive of the greatest human evils, Slavery—But it may well be questioned, why, to avoid possible ills, should we adopt measures which in their nature produce the highest evil? The spirit of the 4th section of the 6th article of the Confederation plainly discourages the idea of standing army, by the special injunctions concerning a well regulated militia, which is indeed the best defence, and only proper security for a free people to venture upon. To guard our frontiers from Indian invasion, to prevent irregular settlements, and to secure the possessions of foreign powers from the encroachments of our people which may provoke foreign or indian wars; seem to be the reasons assigned for the adoption of this mischief working system, a standing military force. But surely it is the business of other powers to secure their own possessions and punish the violators of them—And it would be as new as it would be improper to keep a standing army to prevent the encroachments of our own citizens upon foreign states—it will ever be sufficient to disavow such proceedings and to give the Culprits up to justice, or punish them ourselves. As to the protection of our own frontiers, it would seem best to leave it to the people themselves, as hath ever been the case, and if at any time the frontier men should be too hard pressed, they may be assisted by the midland militia. This will always secure to us a hardy set of men on the frontiers, used to arms, and ready to assist against invasions on other parts. Whereas, if they are protected by regulars, security will necessarily produce inattention to arms, and the whole of our people becoming disused to War, render the Curse of a standing army Necessary. In this light the Indians may be considered as a useful people, as it is surely fortunate for a free community to be under some necessity of keeping the whole body acquainted with the use of Arms.

9

RECORDS OF THE FEDERAL CONVENTION

[*2:329; Madison, 18 Aug.*]

Mr. Ghorum moved to add "and support" after "raise". Agreed to nem. con. and then the clause agreed to nem. con- as amended.

Mr Gerry took notice that there was no check here agst. standing armies in time of peace. The existing Congs. is so constructed that it cannot of itself maintain an army. This wd. not be the case under the new system. The people were jealous on this head, and great opposition to the plan would spring from such an omission. He suspected that preparations of force were now making agst. it. (he seemed to allude to the activity of the Govr. of N. York at this crisis in disciplining the militia of that State.) He thought an army dangerous in time of peace & could never consent to a power to keep up an indefinite number. He proposed that there shall not be kept up in time of peace more than thousand troops. His idea was that the blank should be filled with two or three thousand.

[*2:509; Madison, 5 Sept.*]

To the (2) clause Mr. Gerry objected that it admitted of appropriations to an army. for two years instead of one, for which he could not conceive a reason—that it implied there was to be a standing army which he inveighed against as dangerous to liberty, as unnecessary even for so great an extent of Country as this. and if necessary, some restriction of the number & duration ought to be provided: Nor was this a proper time for such an innovation. The people would not bear it.

Mr Sherman remarked that the appropriations were permitted only, not required to be for two years. As the Legislature is to be biennally elected, it would be inconvenient to require appropriations to be for one year, as there might be no Session within the time necessary to renew them. He should himself he said like a reasonable restriction on the number and continuance of an army in time of peace.

The clause (2). was agreed to nem: con:

[*2:616; Madison, 14 Sept.*]

Col: Mason, being sensible that an absolute prohibition of standing armies in time of peace might be unsafe, and wishing at the same time to insert something pointing out and, guarding against the danger of them, moved to preface the clause (Art I sect. 8) "To provide for organizing, arming and disciplining the Militia &c" with the words "And that the liberties of the people may be better secured against the danger of standing armies in time of peace" Mr. Randolph 2ded. the motion

Mr Madison was in favor of it. It did not restrain Congress from establishing a military force in time of peace if found necessary; and as armies in time of peace are allowed on all hands to be an evil, it is well to discountenance them by the Constitution, as far as will consist with the essential power of the Govt. on that head.

Mr Govr. Morris opposed the motion as setting a dishonorable mark of distinction on the military class of Citizens

Mr Pinkney & Mr. Bedford concurred in the opposition.

On the question

N. H—no—Mas—no—Ct no. N—J—no. Pa. no. Del. no. Maryd no Va ay— N. C. no. S. C. no. Geo. ay.

[Ayes—2; noes—9.]

10

FEDERAL FARMER, NO. 3
10 Oct. 1787
Storing 2.8.39

The power in the general government to lay and collect internal taxes, will render its powers respecting armies, navies and the militia, the more exceptionable. By the constitution it is proposed that congress shall have power "to raise and support armies, but no appropriation of money to that use shall be for a longer term than two years; to provide and maintain a navy; to provide for calling forth the militia to execute the laws of the union, suppress insurrections, and repel invasions: to provide for organizing, arming, and disciplining the militia: reserving to the states the right to appoint the officers, and to train the militia according to the discipline prescribed by congress;" congress will have unlimited power to raise armies, and to engage officers and men for any number of years; but a legislative act applying money for their support can have operation for no longer term than two years, and if a subsequent congress do not within the two years renew the appropriation, or further appropriate monies for the use of the army, the army will be left to take care of itself. When an army shall once be raised for a number of years, it is not probable that it will find much difficulty in getting congress to pass laws for applying monies to its support. I see so many men in America fond of a standing army, and especially among those who probably will have a large share in administering the federal system; it is very evident to me, that we shall have a large standing army as soon as the monies to support them can be possibly found. An army is a very agreeable place of employment for the young gentlemen of many families. A power to raise armies must be lodged some where; still this will not justify the lodging this power in a bare majority of so few men without any checks; or in the government in which the great body of the people, in the nature of things, will be only nominally represented. In the state governments the great body of the people, the yeomanry, etc. of the country, are represented: It is true they will chuse the members of congress, and may now and then chuse a man of their own way of thinking; but it is impossible for forty, or thirty thousand people in this country, one time in ten to find a man who can possess similar feelings, views, and interests with themselves: Powers to lay and collect taxes and to raise armies are of the greatest moment; for carrying them into effect, laws need not be frequently made, and the yeomanry, etc of the country ought substantially to have a check upon the passing of these laws; this check ought to be placed in the legislatures, or at least, in the few men the common people of the country, will, probably, have in congress, in the true sense of the word, "from among themselves." It is true, the yeomanry of the country possess the lands, the weight of property, possess arms, and are too strong a body of men to be openly offended—and, therefore, it is urged, they will take care of themselves, that men who shall govern will not dare pay any disrespect to their opinions. It is easily perceived, that if they have not their proper negative upon passing laws in congress, or on the passage of laws relative to taxes and armies, they may in twenty or thirty years be by means imperceptible to them, totally deprived of that boasted weight and strength: This may be done in a great measure by congress, if disposed to do it, by modelling the militia. Should one fifth, or one eighth part of the men capable of bearing arms, be made a select militia, as has been proposed, and those the young and ardent part of the community, possessed of but little or no property, and all the others put upon a plan that will render them of no importance, the former will answer all the purposes of an army, while the latter will be defenceless. The state must train the militia in such form and according to such systems and rules as congress shall prescribe: and the only actual influence the respective states will have respecting the militia will be in appointing the officers. I see no provision made for calling out the *posse commitatus* for executing the laws of the union, but provision is made for congress to call forth the militia for the execution of them—and the militia in general, or any select part of it, may be called out under military officers, instead of the sheriff to enforce an execution of federal laws, in the first instance and thereby introduce an entire military execution of the laws. I know that powers to raise taxes, to regulate the military strength of the community on some uniform plan, to provide for its defence and internal order, and for duly executing the laws, must be lodged somewhere; but still we ought not so to lodge them, as evidently to give one order of men in the community, undue advantages over others; or commit the many to the mercy, prudence, and moderation of the few. And so far as it may be necessary to lodge any of the peculiar powers in the general government, a more safe exercise of them ought to be secured, by requiring the consent of two-thirds or three-fourths of congress thereto—until the federal representation can be increased, so that the democratic members in congress may stand some tolerable chance of a reasonable negative, in behalf of the numerous, important, and democratic part of the community.

11

A DEMOCRATIC FEDERALIST
17 Oct. 1787

Storing 3.5.10–12

But Mr. Wilson has not stopped here—he has told us that a STANDING ARMY, that *great support of tyrants,* not only was not dangerous, but that it was *absolutely necessary.*—O! my much respected fellow citizens! and are you then reduced to such a degree of insensibility, that assertions like these will not rouse your warmest resentment and indignation? Are we then, after the experience of past ages, and the result of the enquiries of the best and most celebrated patriots have taught us to dread a standing army above all earthly evils, are we then to go over all the thread-bare common place arguments that have been used without success by the advocates of tyranny, and which have been for a long time past so gloriously refuted! Read the excellent *Burgh* in his political disquisitions, on this hackneyed subject, and then say, whether you think that a standing army is necessary in a free country? Even Mr. Hume, an *aristocratical* writer, has candidly confessed, that *an army is a mortal distemper in a government, of which it must at last inevitably perish* (2d Burgh 349) and the Earl of Oxford (*Oxford* the friend of France, and the *pretender,* the attainted *Oxford*) said in the British parliament, in a speech on the mutiny bill; that "while he had breath, he would speak for the liberties of his country, and against courts martial and a standing army in peace as dangerous to the constitution," (*Ibid* page 455 [356]). Such were the speeches even of the enemies to liberty, when Britain had yet a right to be called free. But, says Mr. Wilson, "It is necessary to maintain the appearance of strength even in times of the most profound tranquillity." And what is this more than a thread-bare hackneyed argument, which has been answered over and over in different ages, and does not deserve even the smallest consideration?—Had we a standing army, when the British invaded our peaceful shores? Was it a standing army that gained the battles of Lexington, and Bunker's Hill, and took the ill fated Burgoyne? Is not a well regulated *militia* sufficient for every purpose of internal defence? And which of you, my fellow citizens, is afraid of any invasion from foreign powers, that our brave militia would not be able immediately to repel?

Mr. Wilson says that *he does not know of any nation in the world which has not found it necessary to maintain the appearance of strength in a season of the most profound tranquility:* if by this *equivocal* assertion, he has meant to say that there is no nation in the world without a *standing army in time of peace,* he has been mistaken. I need only adduce the example of Switzerland, which, like us, is a *republic,* whose *thirteen* cantons, like our thirteen States, are under a *federal government,* and which besides is surrounded by the most powerful nations in Europe, all jealous of its liberty and prosperity: And yet that nation has preserved its freedom for many ages, with the sole help of a militia, and has never been known to have a standing army, except when in actual war.—Why should we not follow so glorious an example, and are we less able to defend our liberty without an army, than that brave but small nation, which with its militia alone has hitherto defied all Europe?

It is said likewise, that *a standing army is not a new thing in America—Congress even at this moment have a standing army on foot.*—I answer, that *precedent* is not *principle*—Congress have no right to keep up a standing army in time of peace:—If they do, it is an infringement of the liberties of the people—*wrong* can never be justified by *wrong*—but it is well known that the assertion is groundless, the few troops that are on the banks of the Ohio, were sent for the express purpose of repelling the invasion of the savages, and protecting the inhabitants of the frontiers.—It is our misfortune that we are never at peace with those inhuman butchers of their species, and while they remain in our neighbourhood, we are always, with respect to them, in a state of war—as soon as the danger is over, there is no doubt but Congress will disband their handful of soldiers:—it is therefore not true, that Congress keep up a standing army in a time of peace and profound security.

12

ALEXANDER HAMILTON, FEDERALIST, NO. 8, 44–50
20 Nov. 1787

Assuming it therefore as an established truth that the several States, in case of disunion, or such combinations of them as might happen to be formed out of the wreck of the general confederacy, would be subject to those vicissitudes of peace and war, of friendship and enmity with each other, which have fallen to the lot of all neighbouring nations not united under one government, let us enter into a concise detail of some of the consequences, that would attend such a situation.

War between the States, in the first periods of their separate existence, would be accompanied with much greater distresses than it commonly is in those countries, where regular military establishments have long obtained. The disciplined armies always kept on foot on the continent of Europe, though they bear a malignant aspect to liberty and oeconomy, have notwithstanding been productive of the signal advantage, of rendering sudden conquests impracticable, and of preventing that rapid desolation, which used to mark the progress of war, prior to their introduction. The art of fortification has contributed to the same ends. The nations of Europe are incircled with chains of fortified places, which mutually obstruct invasion. Campaigns are wasted in reducing two or three frontier garrisons, to gain admittance into an enemy's country. Similar impediments occur at every step, to exhaust the strength and delay the progress of an invader. Formerly an invading army would penetrate into the heart of a neighbouring country, almost as soon as intelligence of its approach could be received; but now a comparatively small force of disciplined troops, acting on the defensive with the aid of posts, is able to impede and finally to frustrate the enterprises of one much more considerable. The history of war, in that quarter of the globe, is no longer a history of nations subdued and empires overturned, but of towns taken and retaken, of battles that decide nothing, of retreats more beneficial than victories, of much effort and little acquisition.

In this country the scene would be altogether reversed. The jealousy of military establishments, would postpone them as long as possible. The want of fortifications leaving the frontiers of one State open to another, would facilitate inroads. The populous States would with little difficulty overrun their less populous neighbours. Conquests would be as easy to be made, as difficult to be retained. War therefore would be desultory and predatory. PLUNDER and devastation ever march in the train of irregulars. The calamities of individuals would make the principal figure in the events, which would characterise our military exploits.

This picture is not too highly wrought, though I confess, it would not long remain a just one. Safety from external danger is the most powerful director of national conduct. Even the ardent love of liberty will, after a time, give way to its dictates. The violent destruction of life and property incident to war—the continual effort and alarm attendant on a state of continual danger, will compel nations the most attached to liberty, to resort for repose and security, to institutions, which have a tendency to destroy their civil and political rights. To be more safe they, at length, become willing to run the risk of being less free.

The institutions alluded to are STANDING ARMIES, and the correspondent appendages of military establishments. Standing armies it is said are not provided against in the new constitution; and it is therefore inferred, that they may exist under it.* Their existence however from the very terms of the proposition, is, at most, problematical & uncertain. But standing armies, it may be replied, must inevitably result from a dissolution of the confederacy. Frequent war and constant apprehension, which requires a state of as constant preparation, will infallibly produce them. The weaker States or confederacies, would first have recourse to them, to put themselves upon an equality with their more potent neighbours. They would endeavour to supply the inferiority of population and resources, by a more regular and effective system of defence, by disciplined troops and by fortifications. They would, at the same time, be necessitated to strengthen the executive arm of government; in doing which, their constitutions would acquire a progressive direction towards monarchy. It is of the nature of war to increase the executive at the expence of the legislative authority.

The expedients which have been mentioned, would soon give the States or confederacies that made use of

*This objection will be fully examined in its proper place, and it will be shown that the only rational precaution which could have been taken on this subject has been taken; and a much better one than is to be found in any constitution that has been heretofore framed in America, most of which contain no guard at all on this subject.

them, a superiority over their neighbours. Small States, or States of less natural strength, under vigorous governments, and with the assistance of disciplined armies, have often triumphed over larger States, or States of greater natural strength, which have been destitute of these advantages. Neither the pride, nor the safety of the more important States, or confederacies, would permit them long to submit to this mortifying and adventitious inferiority. They would quickly resort to means similar to those by which it had been effected, to reinstate themselves in their lost pre-eminence. Thus we should in a little time see established in every part of this country, the same engines of despotism, which have been the scourge of the old world. This at least would be the natural course of things, and our reasonings will be the more likely to be just, in proportion as they are accommodated to this standard.

These are not vague inferrences drawn from supposed or speculative defects in a constitution, the whole power of which is lodged in the hands of the people, or their representatives and delegates, but they are solid conclusions drawn from the natural and necessary progress of human affairs.

It may perhaps be asked, by way of objection to this, why did not standing armies spring up out of the contentions which so often distracted the ancient republics of Greece? Different answers equally satisfactory may be given to this question. The industrious habits of the people of the present day, absorbed in the pursuits of gain, and devoted to the improvements of agriculture and commerce are incompatible with the condition of a nation of soldiers, which was the true condition of the people of those republics. The means of revenue, which have been so greatly multiplied by the encrease of gold and silver, and of the arts of industry, and the science of finance, which is the offspring of modern times, concurring with the habits of nations, have produced an intire revolution in the system of war, and have rendered disciplined armies, distinct from the body of the citizens, the inseparable companion of frequent hostility.

There is a wide difference also, between military establishments in a country, seldom exposed by its situation to internal invasions, and in one which is often subject to them, and always apprehensive of them. The rulers of the former can have no good pretext, if they are even so inclined, to keep on foot armies so numerous as must of necessity be maintained in the latter. These armies being, in the first case, rarely, if at all, called into activity for interior defence, the people are in no danger of being broken to military subordination. The laws are not accustomed to relaxations, in favor of military exigencies—the civil state remains in full vigor, neither corrupted nor confounded with the principles or propensities of the other state. The smallness of the army renders the natural strength of the community an overmatch for it; and the citizens, not habituated to look up to the military power for protection, or to submit to its oppressions, neither love nor fear the soldiery: They view them with a spirit of jealous acquiescence in a necessary evil, and stand ready to resist a power which they suppose may be exerted to the prejudice of their rights. The army under such circumstances, may usefully aid the magistrate to suppress a small faction, or an occasional mob, or insurrection; but it will be unable to enforce encroachments against the united efforts of the great body of the people.

In a country, in the predicament last described, the contrary of all this happens. The perpetual menacings of danger oblige the government to be always prepared to repel it—its armies must be numerous enough for instant defence. The continual necessity for their services enhance the importance of the soldier, and proportionably degrades the condition of the citizen. The military state becomes elevated above the civil. The inhabitants of territories, often the theatre of war, are unavoidably subjected to frequent infringements on their rights, which serve to weaken their sense of those rights; and by degrees, the people are brought to consider the soldiery not only as their protectors, but as their superiors. The transition from this disposition to that of considering them as masters, is neither remote, nor difficult: But it is very difficult to prevail upon a people under such impressions, to make a bold, or effectual resistance, to usurpations, supported by the military power.

The kingdom of Great Britain falls within the first description. An insular situation, and a powerful marine, guarding it in a great measure against the possibility of foreign invasion, supercede the necessity of a numerous army within the kingdom. A sufficient force to make head against a sudden descent, till the militia could have time to rally and embody, is all that has been deemed requisite. No motive of national policy has demanded, nor would public opinion have tolerated a large number of troops upon its domestic establishment. There has been, for a long time past, little room for the operation of the other causes, which have been enumerated as the consequences of internal war. This peculiar felicity of situation has, in a great degree, contributed to preserve the liberty, which that country to this day enjoys, in spite of the prevalent venality and corruption. If, on the contrary, Britain had been situated on the continent, and had been compelled, as she would have been, by the situation, to make her military establishments at home co-extensive with those of the other great powers of Europe, she, like them, would in all probability, be at this day a victim to the absolute power of a single man. 'Tis possible, though not easy, that the people of that island may be enslaved fom other causes, but it cannot be by the powers of an army so inconsiderable as that which has been usually kept up in that kingdom.

If we are wise enough to preserve the Union, we may for ages enjoy an advantage similar to that of an insulated situation. Europe is at a great distance from us. Her colonies in our vicinity, will be likely to continue too much disproportioned in strength, to be able to give us any dangerous annoyance. Extensive military establishments cannot, in this position, be necessary to our security. But if we should be disunited, and the integral parts should either remain separated, or which is most probable, should be thrown together into two or three confederacies, we should be in a short course of time, in the predicament of the continental powers of Europe—our liberties would be a prey to the means of defending ourselves against the ambition and jealousy of each other.

This is an idea not superficial or futile, but solid and weighty. It deserves the most serious and mature consideration of every prudent and honest man of whatever party. If such men will make a firm and solemn pause, and mediate dispassionately on the importance of this interesting idea, if they will contemplate it, in all its attitudes, and trace it to all its consequences, they will not hesitate to part with trivial objections to a constitution, the rejection of which would in all probability put a final period to the Union. The airy phantoms that flit before the distempered imaginations of some of its adversaries, would quickly give place to the more substantial forms of dangers real, certain, and formidable.

13

JAMES WILSON, PENNSYLVANIA RATIFYING CONVENTION
11 Dec. 1787
Elliot 2:520–21

I proceed to another objection that is taken against the power, given to Congress, of raising and keeping up standing armies. I confess I have been surprised that this objection was ever made; but I am more so that it is still repeated and insisted upon. I have taken some pains to inform myself how the other governments of the world stand with regard to this power, and the result of my inquiry is, that there is not one which has not the power of raising and keeping up standing armies. A government without the power of defence! it is a solecism.

I well recollect the principle insisted upon by the patriotic body in Great Britain; it is, that, in time of peace, a standing army ought not to be kept up without the consent of Parliament. Their only apprehension appears to be, that it might be dangerous, were the army kept up without the concurrence of the representatives of the people. Sir, we are not in the millennium. Wars may happen; and when they do happen, who is to have the power of collecting and appointing the force, then become immediately and indispensably necessary?

It is not declared, in this Constitution, that the Congress shall raise and support armies. No, sir: if they are not driven to it by necessity, why should we suppose they would do it by choice, any more than the representatives of the same citizens in the state legislatures? For we must not lose sight of the great principle upon which this work is founded. The authority here given to the general government flows from the same source as that placed in the legislatures of the several states.

It may be frequently necessary to keep up standing armies in time of peace. The present Congress have experienced the necessity, and seven hundred troops are just as much a standing army as seventy thousand. The principle which sustains them is precisely the same. They may go further, and raise an army, without communicating to the public the purpose for which it is raised. On a particular occasion they did this. When the commotions existed in Massachusetts, they gave orders for enlisting an additional body of two thousand men. I believe it is not generally known on what perilous tenure we held our freedom and independence at that period. The flames of internal insurrection were ready to burst out in every quarter; they were formed by the correspondents of state officers, (to whom an allusion was made on a former day,) and from one end to the other of the continent, we walked on ashes, concealing fire beneath our feet; and ought Congress to be deprived of power to prepare for the defence and safety of our country? Ought they to be restricted from arming, until they divulge the motive which induced them to arm? I believe the *power* of raising and keeping up an army, in time of peace, is essential to every government. No government can secure its citizens against dangers, internal and external, without possessing it, and sometimes carrying it into execution. I confess it is a power in the exercise of which all wise and moderate governments will be as prudent and forbearing as possible. When we consider the situation of the United States, we must be satisfied that it will be necessary to keep up some troops for the protection of the western frontiers, and to secure our interest in the internal navigation of that country. It will be not only necessary, but it will be economical on the great scale. Our enemies, finding us invulnerable, will not attack us; and we shall thus prevent the occasion for larger standing armies.

14

ALEXANDER HAMILTON, FEDERALIST, NO. 23, 146–51
18 Dec. 1787

The necessity of a Constitution, at least equally energetic with the one proposed, to the preservation of the Union, is the point, at the examination of which we are now arrived.

This enquiry will naturally divide itself into three branches—the objects to be provided for by a Foederal Government—the quantity of power necessary to the accomplishment of those objects—the persons upon whom that power ought to operate. Its distribution and organization will more properly claim our attention under the succeeding head.

The principal purposes to be answered by Union are these—The common defence of the members—the preservation of the public peace as well against internal convulsions as external attacks—the regulation of commerce with other nations and between the States—the superintendence of our intercourse, political and commercial, with foreign countries.

The authorities essential to the care of the common defence are these—to raise armies—to build and equip fleets—to prescribe rules for the government of both—to direct their operations—to provide for their support. These powers ought to exist without limitation: *Because it is impossible to foresee or define the extent and variety of national exigencies, or the correspondent extent & variety of the means which may be necessary to satisfy them.* The circumstances that endanger the safety of nations are infinite; and for this reason no constitutional shackles can wisely be imposed on the power to which the care of it is committed. This power ought to be co-extensive with all the possible combinations of such circumstances; and ought to be under the direction of the same councils, which are appointed to preside over the common defence.

This is one of those truths, which to a correct and unprejudiced mind, carries its own evidence along with it; and may be obscured, but cannot be made plainer by argument or reasoning. It rests upon axioms as simple as they are universal. The *means* ought to be proportioned to the *end;* the persons, from whose agency the attainment of any *end* is expected, ought to possess the *means* by which it is to be attained.

Whether there ought to be a Foederal Government intrusted with the care of the common defence, is a question in the first instance open to discussion; but the moment it is decided in the affirmative, it will follow, that that government ought to be cloathed with all the powers requisite to the complete execution of its trust. And unless it can be shewn, that the circumstances which may affect the public safety are reducible within certain determinate limits; unless the contrary of this position can be fairly and rationally disputed, it must be admitted, as a necessary consequence, that there can be no limitation of that authority, which is to provide for the defence and protection of the community, in any matter essential to its efficacy; that is, in any matter essential to the *formation, direction* or *support* of the NATIONAL FORCES.

Defective as the present Confederation has been proved to be, this principle appears to have been fully recognized by the framers of it; though they have not made proper or adequate provision for its exercise. Congress have an unlimited discretion to make requisitions of men and money—to govern the army and navy—to direct their operations. As their requisitions were made constitutionally binding upon the States, who are in fact under the most solemn obligations to furnish the supplies required of them, the intention evidently was, that the United States should command whatever resources were by them judged requisite to "the common defence and general welfare." It was presumed that a sense of their true interests, and a regard to the dictates of good faith, would be found sufficient pledges for the punctual performance of the duty of the members to the Foederal Head.

The experiment has, however demonstrated, that this expectation was ill founded and illusory; and the observations made under the last head, will, I imagine, have sufficed to convince the impartial and discerning, that there is an absolute necessity for an entire change in the first principles of the system: That if we are in earnest about giving the Union energy and duration, we must abandon the vain project of legislating upon the States in their collective capacities: We must extend the laws of the Foederal Government to the individual citizens of America: We must discard the fallacious scheme of quotas and requisitions, as equally impracticable and unjust. The result from all this is, that the Union ought to be invested with full power to levy troops; to build and equip fleets, and to raise the revenues, which will be required for the formation and support of an army and navy, in the customary and ordinary modes practiced in other governments.

If the circumstances of our country are such, as to demand a compound instead of a simple, a confederate instead of a sole government, the essential point which will remain to be adjusted, will be to discriminate the OBJECTS, as far as it can be done, which shall appertain to the different provinces or departments of power; allowing to each the most ample authority for fulfilling the objects committed to its charge. Shall the Union be constituted the guardian of the common safety? Are fleets and armies and revenues necessary to this purpose? The government of the Union must be empowered to pass all laws, and to make all regulations which have relation to them. The same must be the case, in respect to commerce, and to every other matter to which its jurisdiction is permitted to extend. Is the administration of justice between the citizens of the same State, the proper department of the local governments? These must possess all the authorities which are connected with this object, and with every other that may be allotted to their particular cognizance and direction. Not to confer in each case a degree of power, commensurate to the end, would be to violate the most obvious rules of prudence and propriety, and improvidently to trust the great interests of the nation to hands, which are disabled from managing them with vigour and success.

Who so likely to make suitable provisions for the public defence, as that body to which the guardianship of the public safety is confided—which, as the center of information, will best understand the extent and urgency of the dangers that threaten—as the representative of the WHOLE will feel itself most deeply interested in the preservation of every part—which, from the responsibility implied in the duty assigned to it, will be most sensibly impressed with the necessity of proper exertions—and which, by the extension of its authority throughout the States, can alone establish uniformity and concert in the plans and measures, by which the common safety is to be secured? Is there not a manifest inconsistency in devolving upon the Foederal Government the care of the general defence, and leaving in the State governments the *effective* powers, by which it is to be provided for? Is not a want of co-operation the infallible consequence of such a system? And will not weakness, disorder, an undue distribution of the burthens and calamities of war, an unnecessary and intolerable increase of expence, be its natural and inevitable concomitants? Have we not had unequivocal experience of its effects in the course of the revolution, which we have just accomplished?

Every view we may take of the subject, as candid enquirers after truth, will serve to convince us, that it is both unwise and dangerous to deny the Foederal Government an unconfined authority, as to all those objects which are intrusted to its management. It will indeed deserve the most vigilant and careful attention of the people, to see that it be modelled in such a manner, as to admit of its being safely vested with the requisite powers. If any plan which has been, or may be offered to our consideration, should not, upon a dispassionate inspection, be found to answer this description, it ought to be rejected. A government, the Constitution of which renders it unfit to be trusted with all the powers, which a free people *ought to delegate to any government,* would be an unsafe and improper depository of the NATIONAL INTERESTS, wherever THESE can with propriety be confided, the co-incident powers may safely accompany them. This is the true result of all just reasoning upon the subject. And the adversaries of the plan, promulgated by the Convention, ought to have confined themselves to showing that the internal structure of the proposed government, was such as to render it unworthy of the confidence of the people. They ought not to have wandered into inflammatory declamations, and unmeaning cavils about the extent of the powers. The POWERS are not too extensive for the OBJECTS of Foederal administration, or in other words, for the management of our NATIONAL INTERESTS; nor can any satisfactory argument be framed to shew that they are chargeable with such an excess. If it be true, as has been insinuated by some of the writers on the other side, that the difficulty arises from the nature of the thing, and that the extent of the country will not permit us to form a government, in which such ample powers can safely be reposed, it would prove that we ought to contract our views, and resort to the expedient of separate Confederacies, which will move within more practicable spheres. For the absurdity must continually stare us in the face of confiding to a government, the direction of the most essential national interests, without daring to trust it with the authorities which are indispensable to their proper and efficient management. Let us not attempt to reconcile contradictions, but firmly embrace a rational alternative.

I trust, however, that the impracticability of one general system cannot be shewn. I am greatly mistaken, if any thing of weight, has yet been advanced of this tendency; and I flatter myself, that the observations which have been made in the course of these papers, have sufficed to place the reverse of that position in as clear a light as any matter still in the womb of time and experience can be susceptible of. This at all events must be evident, that the very difficulty itself drawn from the extent of the country, is the strongest argument in favor of an energetic government; for any other can certainly never preserve the Union of so large an empire. If we embrace the tenets of those, who oppose the adoption of the proposed Constitution, as the standard of our political creed, we cannot fail to verify the gloomy doctrines, which predict the impracticability of a national system, pervading the entire limits of the present Confederacy.

15

ALEXANDER HAMILTON, FEDERALIST, NO. 24, 152–57
19 Dec. 1787

To the powers proposed to be conferred upon the Foederal Government in respect to the creation and direction of the national forces, I have met with but one specific objection; which if I understand it rightly is this—that proper provision has not been made against the existence of standing armies in time of peace; an objection which I shall now endeavour to shew rests on weak and unsubstantial foundations.

It has indeed been brought forward in the most vague and general form, supported only by bold assertions—without the appearance of argument—without even the sanction of theoretical opinions, in contradiction to the practice of other free nations, and to the general sense of America, as expressed in most of the existing constitutions. The propriety of this remark will appear the moment it is recollected that the objection under consideration turns upon a supposed necessity of restraining the LEGISLATIVE authority of the nation, in the article of military establishments; a principle unheard of except in one or two of our state constitutions, and rejected in all the rest.

A stranger to our politics, who was to read our newspapers, at the present juncture, without having previously inspected the plan reported by the Convention, would be naturally led to one of two conclusions: either that it contained a positive injunction that standing armies should be kept up in time of peace, or that it vested in the EXECUTIVE the whole power of levying troops, without subjecting his discretion in any shape to the controul of the legislature.

If he came afterwards to peruse the plan itself, he would be surprised to discover that neither the one nor the other was the case—that the whole power of raising armies was lodged in the *legislature,* not in the *executive;* that this legislature was to be a popular body, consisting of the representatives of the people, periodically elected; and that, instead of the provision he had supposed in favour of standing armies, there was to be found, in respect to this object, an important qualification even of the legislative discretion, in that clause which forbids the appropriation of money for the support of an army for any longer period than two years: a precaution, which, upon a nearer view of it, will appear to be a great and real security against the keeping up of troops without evident necessity.

Disappointed in his first surmise, the person I have supposed would be apt to pursue his conjectures a little further. He would naturally say to himself, it is impossible that all this vehement and pathetic declamation can be without some colorable pretext. It must needs be, that this people so jealous of their liberties, have in all the preceding models of the constitutions, which they have established, inserted the most precise and rigid precautions on this point, the omission of which in the new plan has given birth to all this apprehension and clamour.

If under this impression he proceeded to pass in review the several State Constitutions, how great would be his disappointment to find that *two* only of them* contained an interdiction of standing armies in time of peace; that the other eleven had either observed a profound silence on the subject, or had in express terms admitted the right of the legislature to authorise their existence.

Still however he would be persuaded that there must be some plausible foundation for the cry raised on this head. He would never be able to imagine, while any source of information remained unexplored, that it was nothing more than an experiment upon the public credulity, dictated either by a deliberate intention to deceive or by the overflowings of a zeal too intemperate to be ingenuous. It would probably occur to him that he would be likely to find the precautions he was in search of in the primitive compact between the States. Here, at length, he would expect to meet with a solution of the enigma. No doubt he would observe to himself the existing confederation must contain the most explicit provisions against military establishments in time of peace; and a departure from this model in a favourite point has occasioned the discontent which appears to influence these political champions.

If he should now apply himself to a careful and critical survey of the articles of confederation, his astonishment would not only be increased but would acquire a mixture of indignation at the unexpected discovery that these articles instead of containing the prohibition he looked for, and tho' they had with a jealous circumspection restricted the authority of the State Legislatures in this particular, had not imposed a single restraint on that of the United States. If he happened to be a man of quick sensibility or ardent temper, he could now no longer refrain from regarding these clamours as the dishonest artifices of a sinister and unprincipled opposition to a plan which ought at least to receive a fair and candid examination from all sincere lovers of their country! How else, he would say, could the authors of them have been tempted to vent such loud censures upon that plan, about a point, in which it seems to have conformed itself to the general sense of America as declared in its different forms of government, and in which it has even superadded a new and powerful guard unknown to any of them? If on the contrary he happened to be a man of calm and dispassionate feelings—he would indulge a sigh for the frailty of human nature; and would lament that in a matter so interesting to the happiness of millions the true merits of the question should be perplexed and entangled by expedients so unfriendly to an impartial and right determination. Even such a man could hardly forbear remarking that a conduct of this kind has too much the appearance of an intention to mislead the people by alarming their passions rather than to convince them by arguments addressed to their understandings.

But however little this objection may be countenanced even by precedents among ourselves, it may be satisfactory to take a nearer view of its intrinsic merits. From a close examination it will appear that restraints upon the discretion of the Legislature in respect to military establishments in time of peace would be improper to be imposed, and if imposed, from the necessities of society would be unlikely to be observed.

Though a wide ocean separates the United States from Europe; yet there are various considerations that warn us against an excess of confidence or security. On one side of us and stretching far into our rear are growing settlements subject to the dominion of Britain. On the other side and extending to meet the British settlements are colonies and establishments subject to the dominion of Spain. This situation and the vicinity of the West-India islands belonging to these two powers create between them, in respect to their American possessions, and in relation to us, a common interest. The savage tribes on our western frontier ought to be regarded as our natural enemies their natural allies; because they have most to fear from us and most to hope from them. The improvements in the art of navigation have, as to the facility of communication, rendered distant nations in a great measure neighbours. Britain and Spain are among the principal maritime powers of Europe. A future concert of views between these nations ought not to be regarded as improbable. The increasing remoteness of consanguinity is every day diminishing the force of the family compact between France and Spain. And politicians have ever with great reason considered the ties of blood as feeble and precarious links of political connection. These circumstances combined admonish us not to be too sanguine in considering ourselves as intirely out of the reach of danger.

Previous to the revolution, and even since the peace, there has been a constant necessity for keeping small garrisons on our western frontier. No person can doubt that these will continue to be indispensible, if it should only be against the ravages and depredations of the Indians. These garrisons must either be furnished by occasional detachments from the militia, or by permanent corps in the pay of the government. The first is impracticable; and if practicable, would be pernicious. The militia would not long, if at all, submit to be dragged from their occupations and families to perform that most disagreeable duty in times of profound peace. And if they could be prevailed upon, or compelled to do it, the increased expence of a frequent rotation of service and the loss of labor, and dis-

*This statement of the matter is taken from the printed collections of state constitutions—Pennsylvania and North-Carolina are the two which contain the interdiction in these words—"as standing armies in time of peace are dangerous to liberty, *they ought not* to be kept up." This is in truth rather a *caution* than a *prohibition*. New-Hampshire, Massachusetts, Delaware, and Maryland, have in each of their bills of rights a clause to this effect—"standing armies are dangerous to liberty, and ought not to be raised or kept up *without the consent of the legislature*"; which is a formal admission of the authority of the legislature. NEW YORK has no bill of her rights and her Constitution says not a word about the matter. No bills of rights appear annexed to the constitutions of the other States, except the foregoing, and their constitutions are equally silent. I am told, however, that one or two states have bills of right which do not appear in this collection, but that those also recognize the right of the legislative authority in this respect.

concertion of the industrious pursuits of individuals, would form conclusive objections to the scheme. It would be as burthensome and injurious to the public, as ruinous to private citizens. The latter resource of permanent corps in the pay of government amounts to a standing army in time of peace; a small one indeed, but not the less real for being small. Here is a simple view of the subject that shows us at once the impropriety of a constitutional interdiction of such establishments, and the necessity of leaving the matter to the discretion and prudence of the legislature.

In proportion to our increase in strength, it is probable, nay it may be said certain, that Britain and Spain would augment their military establishments in our neighbourhood. If we should not but be willing to be exposed in a naked and defenceless condition to their insults or encroachments, we should find it expedient to increase our frontier garrisons in some ratio to the force by which our western settlements might be annoyed. There are and will be particular posts the possession of which will include the command of large districts of territory and facilitate future invasions of the remainder. It may be added that some of those posts will be keys to the trade with the Indian nations. Can any man think it would be wise to leave such posts in a situation to be at any instant seized by one or the other of two neighbouring and formidable powers? To act this part would be to desert all the usual maxims of prudence and policy.

If we mean to be a commercial people or even to be secure on our Atlantic side, we must endeavour as soon as possible to have a navy. To this purpose these must be dock-yards and arsenals, and, for the defence of these, fortifications and probably garrisons. When a nation has become so powerful by sea, that it can protect its dock-yards by its fleets, this supersedes the necessity of garrisons for that purpose; but where naval establishments are in their infancy, moderate garrisons will in all likelihood be found an indispensible security against descents for the destruction of the arsenals and dock-yards, and sometimes of the fleet itself.

16

ALEXANDER HAMILTON, FEDERALIST, NO. 25, 158–63
21 Dec. 1787

It may perhaps be urged, that the objects enumerated in the preceding number ought to be provided for by the State Governments, under the direction of the Union. But this would be in reality an inversion of the primary principle of our political association; as it would in practice transfer the care of the common defence from the foederal head to the individual members: A project oppressive to some States, dangerous to all, and baneful to the confederacy.

The territories of Britain, Spain and of the Indian nations in our neighbourhood, do not border on particular States; but incircle the Union from MAINE to GEORGIA. The danger, though in different degrees, is therefore common. And the means of guarding against it ought in like manner to be the objects of common councils and of a common treasury. It happens that some States, from local situation, are more directly exposed. NEW-YORK is of this class. Upon the plan of separate provisions, New-York would have to sustain the whole weight of the establishments requisite to her immediate safety, and to the mediate or ultimate protection of her neighbours. This would neither be equitable as it respected New-York, nor safe as it respected the other States. Various inconveniences would attend such a system. The States, to whose lot it might fall to support the necessary establishments, would be as little able as willing, for a considerable time to come, to bear the burthen of competent provisions. The security of all would thus be subjected to the parsimony, improvidence or inability of a part. If the resources of such part becoming more abundant and extensive, its provisions should be proportionably enlarged, the other States would quickly take the alarm at seeing the whole military force of the Union in the hands of two or three of its members; and those probably amongst the most powerful. They would each choose to have some counterpoise; and pretences could easily be contrived. In this situation, military establishments, nourished by mutual jealousy, would be apt to swell beyond their natural or proper size; and being at the separate disposal of the members, they would be engines for the abridgment, or demolition of the national authority.

Reasons have been already given to induce a supposition, that the State Governments will too naturally be prone to a rivalship with that of the Union, the foundation of which will be the love of power; and that in any contest between the foederal head and one of its members, the people will be most apt to unite with their local government: If in addition to this immense advantage, the ambition of the members should be stimulated by the separate and independent possession of military forces, it would afford too strong a temptation, and too great facility to them to make enterprises upon, and finally to subvert the constitutional authority of the Union. On the other hand, the liberty of the people would be less safe in this state of things, than in that which left the national forces in the hands of the national government. As far as an army may be considered as a dangerous weapon of power, it had better be in those hands, of which the people are most likely to be jealous, than in those of which they are least likely to be jealous. For it is a truth which the experience of all ages has attested, that the people are always most in danger, when the means of injuring their rights are in the possession of those of whom they entertain the least suspicion.

The framers of the existing confederation, fully aware of the danger to the Union from the separate possession of military forces by the States, have in express terms, prohibited them from having either ships or troops, unless with the consent of Congress. The truth is, that the existence of a Foederal Government and military establishments, under State authority, are not less at variance with each other, than a due supply of the foederal treasury and the system of quotas and requisitions.

There are other lights besides those already taken notice of, in which the impropriety of restraints on the discretion of the national Legislature will be equally manifest. The design of the objection, which has been mentioned, is to preclude standing armies in time of peace; though we have never been informed how far it is desired the prohibition should extend; whether to raising armies as well as to *keeping them up* in a season of tranquility or not. If it be confined to the latter, it will have no precise signification, and it will be ineffectual for the purpose intended. When armies are once raised, what shall be denominated "keeping them up," contrary to the sense of the constitution? What time shall be requisite to ascertain the violation? Shall it be a week, a month, or a year? Or shall we say, they may be continued as long as the danger which occasioned their being raised continues? This would be to admit that they might be kept up *in time of peace* against threatening, or impending danger; which would be at once to deviate from the literal meaning of the prohibition, and to introduce an extensive latitude of construction. Who shall judge of the continuance of the danger? This must undoubtedly be submitted to the national government—and the matter would then be brought to this issue, that the national government, to provide against apprehended danger, might, in the first instance, raise troops, and might afterwards keep them on foot, as long as they supposed the peace or safety of the community was in any degree of jeopardy. It is easy to perceive, that a discretion so latitudinary as this, would afford ample room for eluding the force of the provision.

The supposed utility of a provision of this kind, must be founded upon a supposed probability, or at least possibility, of a combination between the executive and the legislative in some scheme of usurpation. Should this at any time happen, how easy would it be to fabricate pretences of approaching danger? Indian hostilities instigated by Spain or Britain, would always be at hand. Provocations to produce the desired appearances, might even be given to some foreign power, and appeased again by timely concessions. If we can reasonably presume such a combination to have been formed, and that the enterprize is warranted by a sufficient prospect of success; the army when once raised, from whatever cause, or on whatever pretext, may be applied to the execution of the project.

If to obviate this consequence, it should be resolved to extend the prohibition to the *raising* of armies in time of peace, the United States would then exhibit the most extraordinary spectacle, which the world has yet seen—that of a nation incapacitated by its constitution to prepare for defence, before it was actually invaded. As the ceremony of a formal denunciation of war has of late fallen into disuse, the presence of an enemy within our territories must be waited for as the legal warrant to the government to begin its levies of men for the protection of the State. We must receive the blow before we could even prepare to return it. All that kind of policy by which nations anticipate distant danger, and meet the gathering storm, must be abstained from, as contrary to the genuine maxims of a free government. We must expose our property and liberty to the mercy of foreign invaders, and invite them, by our weakness, to seize the naked and defenceless prey, because we are afraid that rulers, created by our choice—dependent on our will—might endanger that liberty, by an abuse of the means necessary to its preservation.

Here I expect we shall be told, that the Militia of the country is its natural bulwark, and would be at all times equal to the national defence. This doctrine in substance had like to have lost us our independence. It cost millions to the United States, that might have been saved. The facts, which from our own experience forbid a reliance of this kind, are too recent to permit us to be the dupes of such a suggestion. The steady operations of war against a regular and disciplined army, can only be successfully conducted by a force of the same kind. Considerations of oeconomy, not less than of stability and vigor, confirm this position. The American Militia, in the course of the late war, have by their valour on numerous occasions, erected eternal monuments to their fame; but the bravest of them feel and know, that the liberty of their country could not have been established by their efforts alone, however great and valuable they were. War, like most other things, is a science to be acquired and perfected by diligence, by perseverance, by time, and by practice.

All violent policy, contrary to the natural and experienced course of human affairs, defeats itself. Pennsylvania at this instant affords an example of the truth of this remark. The bill of rights of that State declares, that standing armies are dangerous to liberty, and ought not to be kept up in time of peace. Pennsylvania, nevertheless, in a time of profound peace, from the existence of partial disorders in one or two of her counties, has resolved to raise a body of troops; and in all probability, will keep them up as long as there is an appearance of danger to the public peace. The conduct of Massachusetts affords a lesson on the same subject, though on different ground. That State (without waiting for the sanction of Congress as the articles of the confederation require) was compelled to raise troops to quell a domestic insurrection, and still keeps a corps in pay to prevent a revival of the spirit of revolt. The particular constitution of Massachusetts opposed no obstacle to the measure; but the instance is still of use to instruct us, that cases are likely to occur under our governments, as well as under those of other nations, which will sometimes render a military force in time of peace essential to the security of the society; and that it is therefore improper, in this respect, to controul the legislative discretion. It also teaches us, in its application to the United States, how little the rights of a feeble government are likely to be respected, even by its own constituents. And it teaches us, in addition to the rest, how unequal parchment provisions are to a struggle with public necessity.

It was a fundamental maxim of the Lacedemonian commonwealth, that the post of Admiral should not be conferred twice on the same person. The Pelopponesian confederates, having suffered a severe defeat at sea from the Athenians, demanded Lysander, who had before served with success in that capacity, to command the combined fleets. The Lacedemonians, to gratify their allies, and yet preserve the semblance of an adherence to their ancient institutions, had recourse to the flimsy subterfuge of investing LYSANDER with the real power of Admiral, under the nominal title of Vice-Admiral. This instance is selected from among a multitude that might be cited to confirm the truth already advanced and illustrated by domestic examples; which is, that nations pay little regard to rules and maxims calculated in their very nature to run counter to the necessities of society. Wise politicians will be cautious about fettering the government with restrictions, that cannot be observed; because they know that every breach of the fundamental laws, though dictated by necessity, impairs that sacred reverence, which ought to be maintained in the breasts of rulers towards the constitution of a country, and forms a precedent for other breaches, where the same plea of necessity does not exist at all, or is less urgent and palpable.

17

ALEXANDER HAMILTON, FEDERALIST, NO. 26, 164–71
22 Dec. 1787

It was a thing hardly to be expected, that in a popular revolution the minds of men should stop at that happy mean, which marks the salutary boundary between POWER and PRIVILEGE, and combines the energy of government with the security of private rights. A failure in this delicate and important point is the great source of the inconveniences we experience; and if we are not cautious to avoid a repetition of the error, in our future attempts to rectify and ameliorate our system, we may travel from one chimerical project to another; we may try change after change; but we shall never be likely to make any material change for the better.

The idea of restraining the Legislative authority, in the means of providing for the national defence, is one of those refinements, which owe their origin to a zeal for liberty more ardent than enlightened. We have seen however that it has not had thus far an extensive prevalency: That even in this country, where it has made its first appearance, Pennsylvania and North-Carolina are the only two States by which it has been in any degree patronised: And that all the others have refused to give it the least countenance; wisely judging that confidence must be placed some where; that the necessity of doing it is implied in the very act of delegating power; and that it is better to hazard the abuse of that confidence, than to embarrass the government and endanger the public safety, by impolitic restrictions on the Legislative authority. The opponents of the proposed Constitution combat in this respect the general decision of America; and instead of being taught by experience the propriety of correcting any extremes, into which we may have heretofore run, they appear disposed to conduct us into others still more dangerous and more extravagant. As if the tone of government had been found too high, or too rigid, the doctrines they teach are calculated to induce us to depress, or to relax it, by expedients which upon other occasions have been condemned or forborn. It may be affirmed without the imputation of invective, that if the principles they inculcate on various points could so far obtain as to become the popular creed, they would utterly unfit the people of this country for any species of government whatever. But a danger of this kind is not to be apprehended. The citizens of America have too much discernment to be argued into anarchy. And I am much mistaken if experience has not wrought a deep and solemn conviction in the public mind, that greater energy of government is essential to the welfare and prosperity of the community.

It may not be amiss in this place concisely to remark the origin and progress of the idea which aims at the exclusion of military establishments in time of peace. Though in speculative minds it may arise from a contemplation of the nature and tendency of such institutions fortified by the events that have happened in other ages and countries; yet as a national sentiment it must be traced to those habits of thinking, which we derive from the nation from whom the inhabitants of these States have in general sprung.

In England for a long time after the Norman conquest the authority of the monarch was almost unlimited. Inroads were gradually made upon the prerogative, in favour of liberty, first by the Barons and afterwards by the people, 'till the greatest part of its most formidable pretensions became extinct. But it was not 'till the revolution in 1688, which elevated the Prince of Orange to the throne of Great Britain, that English liberty was completely triumphant. As incident to the undefined power of making war, an acknowledged prerogative of the crown, Charles IId. had by his own authority kept on foot in time of peace a body of 5,000 regular troops. And this number James IId. increased to 30,000; which were paid out of his civil list. At the revolution, to abolish the exercise of so dangerous an authority, it became an article of the bill of rights then framed, that "the raising or keeping a standing army within the kingdom in time of peace, *unless with the consent of Parliament,* was against law."

In that kingdom, when the pulse of liberty was at its highest pitch, no security against the danger of standing armies was thought requisite, beyond a prohibition of their being raised or kept up by the mere authority of the executive magistrate. The patriots, who effected that memorable revolution, were too temperate and too well informed, to think of any restraint in the legislative discretion. They were aware that a certain number of troops for guards and garrisons were indispensable, that no precise bounds could be set to the national exigencies; that a power equal to every possible contingency must exist somewhere in the government; and that when they referred the exercise of that power to the judgement of the legislature, they had arrived at the ultimate point of precaution, which was reconciliable with the safety of the community.

From the same source, the people of America may be said to have derived a hereditary impression of danger to liberty from standing armies in time of peace. The circumstances of a revolution quickened the public sensibility on every point connected with the security of popular rights; and in some instances raised the warmth of our zeal beyond the degree which consisted with the due temperature of the body politic. The attempts of two of the states to restrict the authority of the legislature in the article of military establishments are of the number of these instances. The principles, which had taught us to be jealous of the power of an hereditary monarch, were by an injudicious excess extended to the representatives of the people in their popular assemblies. Even in some of the States, where this error was not adopted, we find unnecessary declarations, that standing armies ought not to be kept up, in time of peace WITHOUT THE CONSENT OF THE LEGISLATURE—I call them unnecessary, because the reason, which had introduced a similar provision into the English bill of rights, is not applicable to any of the state constitutions. The power of raising armies at all, under those constitutions, can by no construction be deemed to reside any where else, than in the legislatures themselves; and it was superfluous, if not absurd, to declare that a matter should not be done without the consent of a body, which alone had the power of doing it. Accordingly in some of those constitutions, and among others in that of this State of New-York; which has been justly celebrated both in Europe and in America as one of the best of the forms of government established in this country, there is a total silence upon the subject.

It is remarkable, that even in the two States, which seem to have mediated an interdiction of military establishments in time of peace, the mode of expression made use of is rather cautionary than prohibitory. It is not said, that standing armies *shall not be* kept up, but that they *ought not* to be kept up in time of peace. This ambiguity of terms appears to have been the result of a conflict between jealousy and conviction, between the desire of excluding such establishments at all events, and the persuasion that an absolute exclusion would be unwise and unsafe.

Can it be doubted that such a provision, whenever the situation of public affairs was understood to require a departure from it, would be interpreted by the Legislature into a mere admonition and would be made to yield to the necessities or supposed necessities of the State? Let the fact already mentioned with respect to Pennsylvania decide. What then (it may be asked) is the use of such a provision, if it cease to operate, the moment there is an inclination to disregard it?

Let us examine whether there be any comparison, in point of efficacy, between the provision alluded to and that which is contained in the New Constitution, for restraining the appropriations of money for military purposes to the period of two years. The former by aiming at too much is calculated to effect nothing; the latter, by steering clear of an imprudent extreme, and by being perfectly compatible with a proper provision for the exigencies of the nation, will have a salutary and powerful operation.

The Legislature of the United States will be *obliged* by this provision, once at least in every two years, to deliberate upon the propriety of keeping a military force on foot; to come to a new resolution on the point; and to declare their sense of the matter, by a formal vote in the face of their constituents. They are not *at liberty* to vest in the executive department permanent funds for the support of an army; if they were even incautious enough to be willing to repose in it so improper a confidence. As the spirit of party, in different degrees, must be expected to infect all political bodies, there will be no doubt persons in the national Legislature willing enough to arraign the measures and criminate the views of the majority. The provision for the support of a military force will always be a favourable topic for declamation. As often as the question comes forward, the public attention will be roused and attracted to the subject, by the party in opposition: And if the majority should be really disposed to exceed the proper limits the community will be warned of the danger and will have an opportunity of taking measures to guard against it. Independent of parties in the national Legislature itself, as often as the period of discussion arrived, the state Legislature, who will always be not only vigilant but suspicious and jealous guardians of the rights of the citizens, against incroachments from the Foederal government, will constantly have their attention awake to the conduct of the national rulers and will be ready enough, if any thing improper appears, to sound the alarm to the people and not only to be the VOICE but if necessary the ARM of their discontent.

Schemes to subvert the liberties of a great community *require time to* mature them for execution. An army so large as seriously to menace those liberties could only be formed by progressive augmentations; which would suppose, not merely a temporary combination between the legislature and executive, but a continued conspiracy for a series of time. Is it probable that such a combination would exist at all? Is it probable that it would be persevered in and transmitted along, through all the successive variations in the representative body, which biennial elections would naturally produce in both houses? Is it presumable, that every man, the instant he took his seat in the national senate, or house of representatives, would commence a traitor to his constituents and to his country? Can it be supposed, that there would not be found one man, discerning enough to detect so atrocious a conspiracy, or bold or honest enough to apprise his constituents of their danger? If such presumptions can fairly be made, there ought to be at once an end of all delegated authority. The people should resolve to recall all the powers they have heretofore parted with out of their own hands; and to divide themselves into as many states as there are counties, in order that they may be able to manage their own concerns in person.

If such suppositions could even be reasonably made, still the concealment of the design, for any duration, would be impracticable. It would be announced by the very circumstance of augmenting the army to so great an extent in time of profound peace. What colorable reason could be assigned in a country so situated, for such vast augmentations of the military force? It is impossible that the people could be long deceived; and the destruction of the project and of the projectors would quickly follow the discovery.

It has been said that the provision, which limits the appropriation of money for the support of an army to the period of two years would be unavailing; because the executive, when once possessed of a force large enough to awe the people into submission, would find resources in that very force sufficient to enable him to dispense with supplies from the acts of the legislature. But the question again recurs: Upon what pretence could he be put into possession of a force of that magnitude in time of peace? If we suppose it to have been erected, in consequence of some domestic insurrection, or foreign war, then it becomes a case not within the principle of the objection; for this is levelled against the power of keeping up troops in time of peace. Few persons will be so visionary, as seriously to contend, that military forces ought not to be raised to quell a rebellion, or resist an invasion; and if the defence of the community, under such circumstances, should make it necessary to have an army, so numerous as to hazard its liberty, this is one of those calamities for which there is neither preventative nor cure. It cannot be provided against by any possible form of government: It might even result from a simple league offensive and defensive; if it should ever be necessary for the confederates or allies to form an army for common defence.

But it is an evil infinitely less likely to attend us in an united than in a disunited state; nay it may be safely asserted that it is an evil altogether unlikely to attend us in the better situation. It is not easy to conceive a possibility, that dangers so formidable can assail the whole Union, as to demand a force considerable enough to place our liberties in the least jeopardy; especially if we take into our view the aid to be derived from the militia, which ought always to be counted upon, as a valuable and powerful auxiliary. But in a state of disunion (as has been fully shewn in another place) the contrary of this supposition would become not only probable but almost unavoidable.

18

ALEXANDER HAMILTON, FEDERALIST, NO. 28, 176–80
26 Dec. 1787

That there may happen cases, in which the national government may be necessitated to resort to force, cannot be denied. Our own experience has corroborated the lessons taught by the examples of other nations; that emergencies of this sort will sometimes arise in all societies, however constituted; that seditions and insurrections are unhappily maladies as inseparable from the body politic, as tumours and eruptions from the natural body; that the idea of governing at all times by the simple force of law (which we have been told is the only admissible principle of republican government) has no place but in the reveries of those political doctors, whose sagacity disdains the admonitions of experimental instruction.

Should such emergencies at any time happen under the national government, there could be no remedy but force. The means to be employed must be proportioned to the extent of the mischief. If it should be a slight commotion in a small part of a State, the militia of the residue would be adequate to its suppression: and the natural presumption is, that they would be ready to do their duty. An insurrection, whatever may be its immediate cause, eventually endangers all government: Regard to the public peace, if not to the rights of the Union, would engage the citizens, to whom the contagion had not communicated itself, to oppose the insurgents: And if the general government should be found in practice conducive to the prosperity and felicity of the people, it were irrational to believe that they would be disinclined to its support.

If on the contrary the insurrection should pervade a whole State, or a principal part of it, the employment of a different kind of force might become unavoidable. It appears that Massachusetts found it necessary to raise troops for repressing the disorders within that State; that Pennsylvania, from the mere apprehension of commotions among a part of her citizens, has thought proper to have recourse to the same measure. Suppose the State of New-York had been inclined to re-establish her lost jurisdiction over the inhabitants of Vermont; could she have hoped for success in such an enterprise from the efforts of the militia alone? Would she not have been compelled to raise and to maintain a more regular force for the execution of her design? If it must then be admitted that the necessity of recurring to a force different from the militia in cases of this extraordinary nature, is applicable to the State governments themselves, why should the possibility that the national government might be under a like necessity in similar extremities, be made an objection to its existence? Is it not surprising that men, who declare an attachment to the union in the abstract, should urge, as an objection to the proposed constitution, what applies with tenfold weight to the plan for which they contend; and what as far as it has any foundation in truth is an inevitable consequence of civil society upon an enlarged scale? Who would not prefer that possibility to the unceasing agitations and frequent revolutions which are the continual scourges of petty republics?

Let us pursue this examination in another light. Suppose, in lieu of one general system, two or three or even four confederacies were to be formed, would not the same difficulty oppose itself to the operations of either of these confederacies? Would not each of them be exposed to the same casualties; and, when these happened, be obliged to have recourse to the same expedients for upholding its authority, which are objected to a government for all the States? Would the militia in this supposition be more ready or more able to support the federal authority than in the case of a general union? All candid and intelligent men must upon due consideration acknowledge that the principle of the objection is equally applicable to either of the two cases; and that whether we have one government for all the States, or different governments for different parcels of them, or even if there should be an intire separation of the States, there might sometimes be a necessity to make use of a force constituted differently from the militia to preserve the peace of the community, and to maintain the just authority of the laws against those violent invasions of them which amount to insurrections and rebellions.

Independent of all other reasonings upon the subject, it is a full answer to those who require a more peremptory provision against military establishments in time of peace, that the whole power of the proposed government is to be in the hands of the representatives of the people. This is the essential, and after all the only efficacious security for the rights and privileges of the people which is attainable in civil society.

If the representatives of the people betray their constituents, there is then no resource left but in the exertion of that original right of self-defence, which is paramount to all positive forms of government; and which, against the usurpations of the national rulers, may be exerted with infinitely better prospect of success, than against those of the rulers of an individual State. In a single State, if the persons entrusted with supreme power became usurpers, the different parcels, subdivisions or districts, of which it consists, having no distinct government in each, can take no regular measures for defence. The citizens must rush tumultuously to arms, without concert, without system, without resource; except in their courage and despair. The usurpers, cloathed with the forms of legal authority, can too often crush the opposition in embryo. The smaller the extent of territory, the more difficult will it be for the people to form a regular or systematic plan of opposition; and the more easy will it be to defeat their early efforts. Intelligence can be more speedily obtained of their preparations and movements; and the military force in the possession of the usurpers, can be more rapidly directed against the part where the opposition has begun. In this situation, there must be a peculiar coincidence of circumstances to ensure success to the popular resistance.

The obstacles to usurpation and the facilities of resistance increase with the increased extent of the state; provided the citizens understand their rights and are disposed to defend them. The natural strength of the people in a large community, in proportion to the artificial strength of the government, is greater than in a small; and of course more competent to a struggle with the attempts of the government to establish a tyranny. But in a confederacy the people, without exaggeration, may be said to be entirely the masters of their own fate. Power being almost always the rival of power; the General Government will at all times stand ready to check the usurpations of the state governments; and these will have the same disposition towards the General Government. The people, by throwing themselves into either scale, will infallibly make it preponderate. If their rights are invaded by either, they can make use of the other, as the instrument of redress. How wise will it be in them by cherishing the Union to preserve to themselves an advantage which can never be too highly prised!

It may safely be received as an axiom in our political system, that the state governments will in all possible contingencies afford complete security against invasions of the public liberty by the national authority. Projects of usurpation cannot be masked under pretences so likely to escape the penetration of select bodies of men as of the people at large. The Legislatures will have better means of information. They can discover the danger at a distance; and possessing all the organs of civil power and the confidence of the people, they can at once adopt a regular plan of opposition, in which they can combine all the resources of the community. They can readily communicate with each other in the different states; and unite their common forces for the protection of their common liberty.

The great extent of the country is a further security. We have already experienced its utility against the attacks of a foreign power. And it would have precisely the same effect against the enterprises of ambitious rulers in the national councils. If the foederal army should be able to quell the resistance of one state, the distant states would be able to make head with fresh forces. The advantages obtained in one place must be abandoned to subdue the opposition in others; and the moment the part which had been reduced to submission was left to itself its efforts would be renewed and its resistance revive.

We should recollect that the extent of the military force must at all events be regulated by the resources of the country. For a long time to come, it will not be possible to maintain a large army: and as the means of doing this increase, the population and natural strength of the community will proportionably increase. When will the time arrive, that the foederal Government can raise and maintain an army capable of erecting a despotism over the great body of the people of an immense empire; who are in a situation, through the medium of their state governments, to take measures for their own defence with all the celerity, regularity and system of independent nations? The apprehension may be considered as a disease, for which there can be found no cure in the resources of argument and reasoning.

19

James Iredell, Marcus, Answers to Mr. Mason's Objections to the New Constitution
1788

Pamphlets 363–66

The subject of a standing army has been exhausted in so masterly a manner in two or three numbers of the Federalist (a work which I hope will soon be in every body's hands) that but for the sake of regularity in answering Mr. Mason's objections, I should not venture upon the same topic, and shall only presume to do so, with a reference for fuller satisfaction to that able performance. It is certainly one of the most delicate and proper cases for the consideration of a free people, and so far as a jealousy of this kind leads to any degree of caution not incompatible with the public safety, it is undoubtedly to be commended. Our jealousy of this danger has descended to us from our British ancestors; in that country they have a Monarch, whose power being limited, and at the same time his prerogatives very considerable, a constant jealousy of him is both natural and proper. The two last of the Stuarts having kept up a considerable body of standing forces in time of peace for the clear and almost avowed purpose of subduing the liberties of the people, it was made an article of the bill of rights at the revolution, "That the raising or keeping a standing army within the kingdom in time of peace, unless it be with the consent of Parliament, is against law;" but no attempt was made, or I dare say even thought of, to restrain the Parliament from exercise of that right. An army has been kept on foot annually by authority of Parliament, and I believe ever since the revolution they have had some standing troops; disputes have frequently happened about the number, but I don't recollect any objection by the most zealous patriot, to the keeping up of any at all. At the same time, notwithstanding the above practice of an annual vote (arising from a very judicious caution), it is still in the power of Parliament to authorize the keeping up of any number of troops for an indefinite time, and to provide for their subsistence for any number of years. Considerations of prudence, not constitutional limits to their authority, alone restrain such an exercise of it—our Legislature however will be strongly guarded, though that of Great Britain is without any check at all. No appropriations of money for military services can continue longer than two years. Considering the extensive services the general government may have to provide for upon this vast continent, no forces with any serious prospect of success could be attempted to be raised for a shorter time. Its being done for so short a period, if there were any appearance of ill designs in the government, would afford time enough for the real friends of their country to sound an alarm, and when we know how easy it is to excite jealousy of any government, how difficult for the people to distinguish from their real friends, those factious men who in every country are ready to disturb its peace for personal gratifications of their own, and those desperate ones to whom every change is welcome, we shall have much more reason to fear that the government may be overawed by groundless discontents, than that it should be able, if contrary to every probability such a government could be supposed willing, to effect any designs for the destruction of their own liberties as well as those of their constituents; for surely we ought ever to remember, that there will not be a man in the government but who has been either mediately or immediately recently chosen by the people, and that for too limited a time to make any arbitrary designs consistent with common sense, when every two years a new body of representatives with all the energy of popular feelings will come, to carry the strong force of a severe national control into every department of government. To say nothing of the one-third to compose the Senate coming at the same time, warm with popular sentiments, from their respective assemblies. Men may be sure to suggest dangers from any thing, but it may truly be said that those who can seriously suggest the danger of a premeditated attack on the liberties of the people from such a government as this, could with ease assign reasons equally plausible for mistrusting the integrity of any government formed in any manner whatever; and really it does seem to me, that all their reasons may be fairly carried to this position, that inasmuch as any confidence in any men would be unwise, as we can give no power but what may be grossly abused, we had better give none at all, but continue as we are, or resolve into total anarchy at once, of which indeed our present condition falls very little short. What sort of a government would that be which, upon the most certain intelligence that hostilities were meditated against it, could take no method for its defence till after a formal declaration of war, or the enemy's standard was actually fixed upon the shore? The first has for some time been out of fashion, but if it had not, the restraint these gentlemen recommend, would certainly have brought it into disuse with every power who meant to make war upon America. They would be such fools as to give us the only warning we had informed them we would accept of, before we would take any steps to counteract their designs. The absurdity of our being prohibited from preparing to resist an invasion till after it had actually taken place* is so glaring, that no man can consider it for a moment without being struck with astonishment to see how rashly, and with how little consideration gentlemen, whose characters are certainly respectable, have suffered themselves to be led away by so delusive an idea. The example of other countries, so far from warranting any such limitation of power, is directly against it. That of England has already been particularly noticed. In our present articles of confederation there is no such restriction. It has been observed by the Federalist, that Pennsylvania and North Carolina appear to be the only States in the Union which have attempted any restraint of the Legislative authority in this particular, and that their restraint appears rather in the light of a caution than a prohibition; but notwithstanding that, Pennsylvania had been obliged to raise forces in the very face of that article of her bill of rights. That great writer from the remoteness of his situation, did not know that North Carolina had equally violated her bill of rights in a similar manner. The Legislature of that State in November, 1785, passed an act for raising 200 men for the protection of a county called Davidson county against hostilities from the Indians; they were to continue for *two years* from the time of their first rendezvous, unless sooner disbanded by the Assembly, and were to be subject to the same "rules with respect to their government as were established in the time of the late war by the Congress of the United States for the government of the Continental army." These are the very words of the act. Thus, from the examples of the only two countries in

*Those gentlemen who gravely tell us that the militia will be sufficient for this purpose, do not recollect that they themselves do not desire we shall rely solely on a militia in case of actual war, and therefore in the case I have supposed they cannot be deemed sufficient even by themselves, for when the enemy landed it would undoubtedly be a time of war, but the misfortune would be, that they would be prepared; we not. Certainly all possible encouragement should be given to the training of our militia, but no man can really believe that they will be sufficient, without the aid of any regular troops, in time of foreign hostility. A powerful militia may make fewer regulars necessary, but will not make it safe to dispense with them altogether.

the world that I believe ever attempted such a restriction, it appears to be a thing incompatible with the safety of government. Whether their restriction is to be considered as a caution or a prohibition, in less than five years after peace the caution has been disregarded, or the prohibition disobeyed. Can the most credulous or suspicious men require stronger proof of the weakness and impolicy of such restraints?

20

BRUTUS, NO. 8
10 Jan. 1788
Storing 2.9.96–101

The power to raise armies, is indefinite and unlimited, and authorises the raising forces, as well in peace as in war. Whether the clause which impowers the Congress to pass all laws which are proper and necessary, to carry this into execution, will not authorise them to impress men for the army, is a question well worthy consideration? If the general legislature deem it for the general welfare to raise a body of troops, and they cannot be procured by voluntary enlistments, it seems evident, that it will be proper and necessary to effect it, that men be impressed from the militia to make up the deficiency.

These powers taken in connection, amount to this: that the general government have unlimitted authority and controul over all the wealth and all the force of the union. The advocates for this scheme, would favor the world with a new discovery, if they would shew, what kind of freedom or independency is left to the state governments, when they cannot command any part of the property or of the force of the country, but at the will of the Congress. It seems to me as absurd, as it would be to say, that I was free and independent, when I had conveyed all my property to another, and was tenant to will to him, and had beside, given an indenture of myself to serve him during life.—The power to keep up standing armies in time of peace, has been justly objected, to this system, as dangerous and improvident. The advocates who have wrote in its favor, have some of them ridiculed the objection, as though it originated in the distempered brain of its opponents, and others have taken pains to shew, that it is a power that was proper to be granted to the rulers in this constitution. That you may be enabled to form a just opinion on this subject. I shall first make some remarks, tending to prove, that this power ought to be restricted, and then animadvert on the arguments which have been adduced to justify it.

I take it for granted, as an axiom in politic, that the people should never authorise their rulers to do any thing, which if done, would operate to their injury.

It seems equally clear, that in a case where a power, if given and exercised, will generally produce evil to the community, and seldom good—and which, experience has proved, has most frequently been exercised to the great injury, and very often to the total destruction of the government; in such a case, I say, this power, if given at all, should if possible be so restricted, as to prevent the ill effect of its operation.

Let us then enquire, whether standing armies in time of peace, would be ever beneficial to our country—or if in some extraordinary cases, they might be necessary; whether it is not true, that they have generally proved a scourge to a country, and destructive of their liberty.

I shall not take up much of your time in proving a point, in which the friends of liberty, in all countries, have so universally agreed. The following extract from Mr. Pultney's speech, delivered in the house of commons of Great-Britain, on a motion for reducing the army, is so full to the point, and so much better than any thing I can say, that I shall be excused for inserting it. He says, "I have always been, and always shall be against a standing army of any kind; to me it is a terrible thing, whether under that of a parliamentary, or any other designation; a standing army is still a standing army by whatever name it is called; they are a body of men distinct from the body of the people; they are governed by different laws, and blind obedience, and an entire submission to the orders of their commanding officer, is their only principle; the nations around us, sir, are already enslaved, and have been enslaved by those very means; by means of their standing armies they have every one lost their liberties; it is indeed impossible that the liberties of the people in any country can be preserved where a numerous standing army is kept up. Shall we then take our measures from the example of our neighbours? No, sir, on the contrary, from their misfortunes we ought to learn to avoid those rocks upon which they have split.

"It signifies nothing to tell me that our army is commanded by such gentlemen as cannot be supposed to join in any measures for enslaving their country; it may be so; I have a very good opinion of many gentlemen now in the army; I believe they would not join in any such measures; but their lives are uncertain, nor can we be sure how long they will be kept in command, they may all be dismissed in a moment, and proper tools of power put in their room. Besides, sir, we know the passions of men, we know how dangerous it is to trust the best of men with too much power. Where was a braver army than that under Jul. Caesar? Where was there ever an army that had served their country more faithfully? That army was commanded generally by the best citizens of Rome, by men of great fortune and figure in their country, yet that army enslaved their country. The affections of the soldiers towards their country, the honor and integrity of the under officers, are not to be depended on. By the military law the administration of justice is so quick, and the punishment so severe, that neither the officer nor soldier dare dispute the orders of his supreme commander; he must not consult his own inclination. If an officer were commanded to pull his own father out of this house, he must do it; he dares not disobey; immediate death would be the sure consequence of the least grumbling: and if an officer were sent into the court of request, accompanied by a body of musketeers with screwed bayonets, and with orders to tell us what we ought to do, and how we were to vote: I know what would be the duty of this house; I know it would be our duty to order the officer to be hanged at the door of the lobby; but I doubt, sir, I doubt much, if such a spirit could be found in the house, or in any house of commons that will ever be in England.

"Sir, I talk not of imaginary things? I talk of what has happened to an English house of commons, from an English army; not only from an English army, but an army that was raised by that very house of commons, an army that was paid by them, and an army that was commanded by generals appointed by them; therefore do not let us vainly imagine, that an army, raised and maintained by authority of parliament, will always be so submissive to them. If an army be so numerous as to have it in their power to overawe the parliament, they will be submissive as long as the parliament does nothing to disoblige their favourite general; but when that case happens, I am afraid, that in place of the parliament's dismissing the army, the army will dismiss the parliament."—If this great man's reasoning be just, it follows, that keeping up a standing army, would be in the highest degree dangerous to the liberty and happiness of the community—and if so, the general government ought not to have authority to do it; for no government should be empowered to do that which if done, would tend to destroy public liberty.

21

Brutus, no. 9
17 Jan. 1788
Storing 2.9.105–14

That standing armies are dangerous to the liberties of a people was proved in my last number—If it was necessary, the truth of the position might be confirmed by the history of almost every nation in the world. A cloud of the most illustrious patriots of every age and country, where freedom has been enjoyed, might be adduced as witnesses in support of the sentiment. But I presume it would be useless, to enter into a laboured argument, to prove to the people of America, a position, which has so long and so generally been received by them as a kind of axiom.

Some of the advocates for this new system controvert this sentiment, as they do almost every other that has been maintained by the best writers on free government.—Others, though they will not expressly deny, that standing armies in times of peace are dangerous, yet join with these in maintaining, that it is proper the general government should be vested with the power to do it. I shall now proceed to examine the arguments they adduce in support of their opinons.

A writer, in favor of this system, treats this objection as a ridiculous one. He supposes it would be as proper to provide against the introduction of Turkish janizaries, or against making the Alcoran a rule of faith.

From the positive, and dogmatic manner, in which this author delivers his opinions, and answers objections made to his sentiments—one would conclude, that he was some pedantic pedagogue who had been accustomed to deliver his dogmas to pupils, who always placed implicit faith in what he delivered.

But, why is this provision so ridiculous? because, says this author, it is unnecessary. But, why is it unnecessary? "because, the principles and habits, as well as the power of the Americans are directly opposed to standing armies; and there is as little necessity to guard against them by positive constitutions, as to prohibit the establishment of the Mahometan religion." It is admitted then, that a standing army in time of peace, is an evil. I ask then, why should this government be authorised to do evil? If the principles and habits of the people of this country are opposed to standing armies in time of peace, if they do not contribute to the public good, but would endanger the public liberty and happiness, why should the government be vested with the power? No reason can be given, why rulers should be authorised to do, what, if done, would oppose the principles and habits of the people, and endanger the public safety, but there is every reason in the world, that they should be prohibited from the exercise of such a power. But this author supposes, that no danger is to be apprehended from the exercise of this power, because, if armies are kept up, it will be by the people themselves, and therefore, to provide against it, would be as absurd as for a man to "pass a law in his family, that no troops should be quartered in his family by his consent." This reasoning supposes, that the general government is to be exercised by the people of America themselves—But such an idea is groundless and absurd. There is surely a distinction between the people and their rulers, even when the latter are representatives of the former.—They certainly are not identically the same, and it cannot be disputed, but it may and often does happen, that they do not possess the same sentiments or pursue the same interests. I think I have shewn, that as this government is constituted, there is little reason to expect, that the interest of the people and their rulers will be the same.

Besides, if the habits and sentiments of the people of America are to be relied upon, as the sole security against the encroachment of their rulers, all restrictions in constitutions are unnecessary; nothing more is requisite, than to declare who shall be authorized to exercise the powers of government, and about this we need not be very careful—for the habits and principles of the people will oppose every abuse of power. This I suppose to be the sentiments of this author, as it seems to be of many of the advocates of this new system. An opinion like this, is as directly opposed to the principles and habits of the people of America, as it is to the sentiments of every writer of reputation on the science of government, and repugnant to the principles of reason and common sense.

The idea that there is no danger of the establishment of a standing army, under the new constitution, is without foundation.

It is a well known fact, that a number of those who had an agency in producing this system, and many of those who it is probable will have a principal share in the administration of the government under it, if it is adopted, are avowedly in favour of standing armies. It is a language common among them, "That no people can be kept in order, unless the government have an army to awe them into obedience; it is necessary to support the dignity of government, to have a military establishment." And there will not be wanting a variety of plausible reason[s] to justify the raising one, drawn from the danger we are in from the Indians on our frontiers, or from the European provinces in our neighbourhood. If to this we add, that an army will afford a decent support, and agreeable employment to the young men of many families, who are too indolent to follow occupations that will require care and industry, and too poor to live without doing any business[:] we can have little reason to doubt, but that we shall have a large standing army, as soon as this government can find money to pay them, and perhaps sooner.

A writer, who is the boast of the advocates of this new constitution, has taken great pains to shew, that this power was proper and necessary to be vested in the general government.

He sets out with calling in question the candour and integrity of those who advance the objection, and with insinuating, that it is their intention to mislead the people, by alarming their passions, rather than to convince them by arguments addressed to their understandings.

The man who reproves another for a fault, should be careful that he himself be not guilty of it. How far this writer has manifested a spirit of candour, and has pursued fair reasoning on this subject, the impartial public will judge, when his arguments pass before them in review.

He first attempts to shew, that this objection is futile and disingenuous, because the power to keep up standing armies, in time of peace, is vested, under the present government, in the legislature of every state in the union, except two. Now this is so far from being true, that it is expressly declared, by the present articles of confederation, that no body of forces "shall be kept up by any state, in time of peace, except such number only, as in the judgment of the United States in Congress assembled, shall be deemed requisite to garrison the forts necessary for the defence of such state." Now, was it candid and ingenuous to endeavour to persuade the public, that the general government had no other power than your own legislature have on this head; when the truth is, your legislature have no authority to raise and keep up any forces?

He next tells us, that the power given by this constitution, on this head, is similar to that which Congress possess under the present confederation. As little ingenuity is manifested in this representation as in that of the former.

I shall not undertake to enquire whether or not Congress are vested with a power to keep up a standing army in time of peace; it has been a subject warmly debated in Congress, more than once, since the peace; and one of the most respectable states in the union, were so fully convinced that they had no such power, that they expressly instructed their delegates to enter a solemn protest against it on the journals of Congress, should they attempt to exercise it.

But should it be admitted that they have the power, there is such a striking dissimilarity between the restrictions under which the present Congress can exercise it, and that of the proposed government, that the comparison will serve rather to shew the impropriety of vesting the proposed government with the power, than of justifying it.

It is acknowledged by this writer, that the powers of Congress, under the present confederation, amount to little more than that of recommending. If they determine to raise troops, they are obliged to effect it through the authority of the state legislatures. This will, in the first instance, be a most powerful restraint upon them, against ordering troops to be raised. But if they should vote an army, contrary to the opinion and wishes of the people, the legislatures of the respective states would not raise them. Besides, the present Congress hold their places at the will and pleasure of the legislatures of the states who send them, and no troops can be raised, but by the assent of nine states out of the thirteen. Compare the power proposed to be lodged in the legislature on this head, under this constitution, with that vested in the present Congress, and every person of the least discernment, whose understanding is not totally blinded by prejudice, will perceive, that they bear no analogy to each other. Under the present confederation, the representatives of nine states, out of thirteen, must assent to the raising of troops, or they cannot be levied: under the proposed constitution, a less number than the representatives of two states, in the house of representatives, and the representatives of three states and an half in the senate, with the assent of the president, may raise any number of troops they please. The present Congress are restrained from an undue exercise of this power, from this consideration, they know [that] the state legislatures, through whose authority it must be carried into effect, would not comply with the requisition for the purpose, if it was evidently opposed to the public good: the proposed constitution authorizes the legislature to carry their determinations into execution, without the intervention of any other body between them and the people. The Congress under the present form are amenable to, and removable by, the legislatures of the respective states, and are chosen for one year only: the proposed constitution does not make the members of the legislature accountable to, or removeable by the state legislatures at all; and they are chosen, the one house for six, and the other for two years; and cannot be removed until their time of service is expired, let them conduct [themselves] ever so badly.—The public will judge, from the above comparison, how just a claim this writer has to that candour he affects to possess. In the mean time, to convince him, and the advocates for this system, that I possess some share of candor, I pledge myself to give up all opposition to it, on the head of standing armies, if the power to raise them be restricted as it is in the present confederation; and I believe I may safely answer, not only for myself, but for all who make the objection, that they will be satisfied with less.

22

JAMES MADISON, FEDERALIST, NO. 41, 269–76
19 Jan. 1788

Security against foreign danger is one of the primitive objects of civil society. It is an avowed and essential object of the American Union. The powers requisite for attaining it, must be effectually confided to the foederal councils.

Is the power of declaring war necessary? No man will answer this question in the negative. It would be superfluous therefore to enter into a proof of the affirmative. The existing confederation establishes this power in the most ample form.

Is the power of raising armies, and equipping fleets necessary? This is involved in the foregoing power. It is involved in the power of self-defence.

But was it necessary to give an INDEFINITE POWER of raising TROOPS, as well as providing fleets; and of maintaining both in PEACE, as well as in WAR?

The answer to these questions has been too far anticipated, in another place, to admit an extensive discussion of them in this place. The answer indeed seems to be so obvious and conclusive as scarcely to justify such a discussion in any place. With what colour of propriety could the force necessary for defence, be limited by those who cannot limit the force of offence? If a Federal Constitution could chain the ambition, or set bounds to the exertions of all other nations: then indeed might it prudently chain the discretion of its own Government, and set bounds to the exertions for its own safety.

How could a readiness for war in time of peace be safely prohibited, unless we could prohibit in like manner the preparations and establishments of every hostile nation? The means of security can only be regulated by the means and the danger of attack. They will in fact be ever determined by these rules, and by no others. It is in vain to oppose constitutional barriers to the impulse of self-preservation. It is worse than in vain; because it plants in the Constitution itself necessary usurpations of power, every precedent of which is a germ of unnecessary and multiplied repetitions. If one nation maintains constantly a disciplined army ready for the service of ambition or revenge, it obliges the most pacific nations, who may be within the reach of its enterprizes, to take corresponding precautions. The fifteenth century was the unhappy epoch of military establishments in time of peace. They were introduced by Charles VII. of France. All Europe has followed, or been forced into the example. Had the example not been followed by other nations, all Europe must long ago have worne the chains of a universal monarch. Were every nation except France now to disband its peace establishment, the same event might follow. The veteran legions of Rome were an overmatch for the undisciplined valour of all other nations, and rendered her mistress of the world.

Not less true is it, that the liberties of Rome proved the final victim to her military triumphs, and that the liberties of Europe, as far as they ever existed, have with few exceptions been the price of her military establishments. A standing force therefore is a dangerous, at the same time that it may be a necessary provision. On the smallest scale it has its inconveniences. On an extensive scale, its consequences may be fatal. On any scale, it is an object of laudable circumspection and precaution. A wise nation will combine all these considerations; and whilst it does not rashly preclude itself from any resource which may become essential to its safety, will exert all its prudence in diminishing both the necessity and the danger of resorting to one which may be inauspicious to its liberties.

The clearest marks of this prudence are stamped on the proposed Constitution. The Union itself which it cements and secures, destroys every pretext for a military establishment which could be dangerous. America, united with a handful of troops, or without a single soldier, exhibits a more forbidding posture to foreign ambition, than America disunited, with an hundred thousand veterans ready for combat. It was remarked on a former occasion, that the want of this pretext had saved the liberties of one nation in Europe. Being rendered by her insular situation and her maritime resources, impregnable to the armies of her neighbours, the rulers of Great-Britain have never been able, by real or artificial dangers, to cheat the public into an extensive peace establishment. The distance of the United States from the powerful nations of the world, gives them the same happy security. A dangerous establishment can never be necessary or plausible, so long as they continue a united people. But let it never for a moment be forgotten, that they are indebted for this advantage to their Union alone. The moment of its dissolution will be the date of a new order of things. The fears of the weaker or the ambition of the stronger States or Confederacies, will set the same example in the new, as Charles VII. did in the old world. The example will be followed here from the same motives which produced universal imitation there. Instead of deriving from our situation the precious advantage which Great-Britain has derived from hers, the face of America will be but a copy of that of the Continent of Europe. It will present liberty every where crushed between standing armies and perpetual taxes. The fortunes of disunited America will be even more disastrous than those of Europe. The sources of evil in the latter are confined to her own limits. No superior powers of another quarter of the globe intrigue among her rival nations, inflame their mutual animosities, and render them the instruments of foreign ambition, jealousy and revenge. In America, the miseries springing from her internal jealousies, contentions and wars, would form a part only of her lot. A plentiful addition of evils would have their source in that relation in which Europe stands to this quarter of the earth, and which no other quarter of the earth bears to Europe. This picture of the consequences of disunion cannot be too highly coloured, or too often exhibited. Every man who loves peace, every man who loves his country, every man who loves liberty, ought to have it ever before his eyes, that he may cherish in his heart a due attachment to the Union of America, and be able to set a due value on the means of preserving it.

Next to the effectual establishment of the Union, the best possible precaution against danger from standing armies, is a limitation of the term for which revenue may be appropriated to their support. This precaution the Constitution has prudently added. I will not repeat here the observations, which I flatter myself have placed this subject in a just and satisfactory light. But it may not be improper to take notice of an argument against this part of the Constitution, which has been drawn from the policy and practice of Great-Britain. It is said that the continuance of an army in that kingdom, requires an annual vote of the Legislature; whereas the American Constitution has lengthened this critical period to two years. This is the form in which the comparison is usually stated to the public: But is it a just form? Is it a fair comparison? Does the British Constitution restrain the Parliamentary discretion to one year? Does the American impose on the Congress appropriations for two years? On the contrary, it cannot be unknown to the authors of the fallacy themselves, that the British Constitution fixes no limit whatever to the discretion of the Legislature, and that the American ties down the Legislature to two years, as the longest admissible term.

Had the argument from the British example been truly stated, it would have stood thus: The term for which supplies may be appropriated to the army-establishment, though unlimited by the British Constitution, has nevertheless in practice been limited by parliamentary discretion, to a single year. Now if in Great-Britain, where the House of Commons is elected for seven years; where so great a proportion of the members are elected by so small a proportion of the people; where the electors are so corrupted by the Representatives, and the Representatives so corrupted by the Crown, the Representative body can possess a power to make appropriations to the army for an indefinite term, without desiring, or without daring, to extend the term beyond a single year; ought not suspicion herself to blush in pretending that the Representatives of the United States, elected FREELY, by the WHOLE BODY of the people, every SECOND YEAR, cannot be safely entrusted with a discretion over such appropriations, expressly limited to the short period of TWO YEARS?

A bad cause seldom fails to betray itself. Of this truth, the management of the opposition to the Federal Government is an unvaried exemplification. But among all the blunders which have been committed, none is more striking than the attempt to enlist on that side, the prudent jealousy entertained by the people, of standing armies. The attempt has awakened fully the public attention to that important subject; and has led to investigations which must terminate in a thorough and universal conviction, not only that the Constitution has provided the most effectual guards against danger from that quarter, but that nothing short of a Constitution fully adequate to the national defence, and the preservation of the Union, can save America from as many standing armies as it may be split into States or Confederacies; and from such a progressive augmentation of these establishments in each, as will render them as burdensome to the properties and ominous to the liberties of the people; as any establishment that can become necessary, under a united and efficient Government, must be tolerable to the former, and safe to the latter.

The palpable necessity of the power to provide and maintain a navy has protected that part of the Constitution against a spirit of censure, which has spared few other parts. It must indeed be numbered among the greatest blessings of America, that as her Union will be the only source of her maritime strength, so this will be a principal source of her security against danger from abroad. In this respect our situation bears another likeness to the insular advantage of Great-Britain. The batteries most capable of repelling foreign enterprizes on our safety, are happily such as can never be turned by a perfidious government against our liberties.

The inhabitants of the Atlantic frontier are all of them deeply interested in this provision for naval protection, and if they have hitherto been suffered to sleep quietly in their beds; if their property has remained safe against the predatory spirit of licencious adventurers; if their maritime towns have not yet been compelled to ransome themselves from the terrors of a conflagration, by yielding to the exactions of daring and sudden invaders, these instances of good fortune are not to be ascribed to the capacity of the existing government for the protection of those from whom it claims allegiance, but to causes that are fugitive and fallacious. If we except perhaps Virginia and Maryland, which are peculiarly vulnerable on their Eastern frontiers, no part of the Union ought to feel more anxiety on this subject than New-York. Her sea coast is extensive. The very important district of the state is an island. The state itself is penetrated by a large navigable river for more than fifty leagues. The great emporium of its commerce, the great reservoir of its wealth, lies every moment at the mercy of events, and may almost be regarded as a hostage, for ignominious compliances with the dictates of a foreign enemy, or even with the rapacious demands of pirates and barbarians. Should a war be the result of the precarious situation of European affairs, and all the unruly passions attending it, be let loose on the ocean, our escape from insults and depredations, not only on that element but every part of the other bordering on it, will be truly miraculous. In the present condition of America, the states more immediately exposed to these calamities, have nothing to hope from the phantom of a general government which now exists; and if their single resources were equal to the task of fortifying themselves against the danger, the object to be protected would be almost consumed by the means of protecting them.

23

BRUTUS, NO. 10
24 Jan. 1788
Storing 2.9.115–27

The liberties of a people are in danger from a large standing army, not only because the rulers may employ them for the purposes of supporting themselves in any usurpations of power, which they may see proper to exercise, but there is great hazard, that any army will subvert the forms of the government, under whose authority, they are raised, and establish one, according to the pleasure of their leader.

We are informed, in the faithful pages of history, of such events frequently happening.—Two instances have been mentioned in a former paper. They are so remarkable, that they are worthy of the most careful attention of every lover of freedom.—They are taken from the history of the two most powerful nations that have ever existed in the world; and who are the most renowned, for the freedom they enjoyed, and the excellency of their constitutions:—I mean Rome and Britain.

In the first, the liberties of the commonwealth was destroyed, and the constitution overturned, by an army, lead by Julius Cesar, who was appointed to the command, by the constitutional authority of that commonwealth. He changed it from a free republic, whose fame had sounded, and is still celebrated by all the world, into that of the most absolute despotism. A standing army effected this change, and a standing army supported it through a succession of ages, which are marked in the annals of history, with the most horrid cruelties, bloodshed, and carnage;—The most devilish, beastly, and unnatural vices, that ever punished or disgraced human nature.

The same army, that in Britain, vindicated the liberties of that people from the encroachments and despotism of a tyrant king, assisted Cromwell, their General, in wresting from the people, that liberty they had so dearly earned.

You may be told, these instances will not apply to our case:—But those who would persuade you to believe this, either mean to deceive you, or have not themselves considered the subject.

I firmly believe, no country in the world had ever a more patriotic army, than the one which so ably served this country, in the late war.

But had the general who commanded them, been possessed of the spirit of a Julius Cesar or a Cromwell, the liberties of this country, had in all probability, terminated with the war; or had they been maintained, might have cost more blood and treasure, than was expended in the conflict with Great-Britain. When an anonimous writer addressed the officers of the army at the close of the war, advising them not to part with their arms, until justice was done them—the effect it had is well known. It affected them like an electric shock. He wrote like Cesar; and had the commander in chief, and a few more officers of rank, countenanced the measure, the desperate resolution had been taken, to refuse to disband. What the consequences of such a determination would have been, heaven only knows.—The army were in the full vigor of health and spirits, in the habit of discipline, and possessed of all our military stores and apparatus. They would have acquired great accessions of strength from the country.—Those who were disgusted at our republican forms of government (for such there then were, of high rank among us) would have lent them all their aid.—We should in all probability have seen a constitution and laws, dictated to us, at the head of an army, and at the point of a bayonet, and the liberties for which we had so severely struggled, snatched from us in a moment. It remains a secret, yet to be revealed, whether this measure was not suggested, or at least countenanced, by some, who have had great influence in producing the present system.—Fortunately indeed for this country, it had at the head of the army, a patriot as well as a general; and many of our principal officers, had not abandoned the characters of citizens, by assuming that of soldiers, and therefore, the scheme proved abortive. But are we to expect, that this will always be the case? Are we so much better than the people of other ages and of other countries, that the same allurements of power and greatness, which led them aside from their duty, will have no influence upon men in our country? Such an idea, is wild and extravagant.—Had we indulged such a delusion, enough has appeared in a little time past, to convince the most credulous, that the passion for pomp, power and greatness, works as powerfully in the hearts of many of our better sort, as it ever did in any country under heaven.—Were the same opportunity again to offer, we should very probably be grossly disappointed, if we made dependence, that all who then rejected the overture, would do it again.

From these remarks, it appears, that the evil to be feared from a large standing army in time of peace, does not arise solely from the apprehension, that the rulers may employ them for the purpose of promoting their own ambitious views, but that equal, and perhaps greater danger, is to be apprehended from their overturning the constitutional powers of the government, and assuming the power to dictate any form they please.

The advocates for power, in support of this right in the proposed government, urge that a restraint upon the discretion of the legislatures, in respect to military establishments in time of peace, would be improper to be imposed, because they say, it will be necessary to maintain small garrisons on the frontiers, to guard against the depredations of the Indians, and to be prepared to repel any encroachments or invasions that may be made by Spain or Britain.

The amount of this argument striped of the abundant verbages with which the author has dressed it, is this:

It will probably be necessary to keep up a small body of troops to garrison a few posts, which it will be necessary to maintain, in order to guard against the sudden encroachments of the Indians, or of the Spaniards and British; and therefore, the general government ought to be invested with power to raise and keep up a standing army in time of peace, without restraint; at their discretion.

I confess, I cannot perceive that the conclusion follows from the premises. Logicians say, it is not good reasoning to infer a general conclusion from particular premises: though I am not much of a Logician, it seems to me, this argument is very like that species of reasoning.

When the patriots in the parliament in Great-Britain, contended with such force of argument, and all the powers of eloquence, against keeping up standing armies in time of peace, it is obvious, they never entertained an idea, that small garrisons on their frontiers, or in the neighbourhood of powers, from whom they were in danger of encroachments, or guards, to take care of public arsenals would thereby be prohibited.

The advocates for this power farther urge that it is necessary, because it may, and probably will happen, that circumstances will render it requisite to raise an army to be prepared to repel attacks of an enemy, before a formal declaration of war, which in modern times has fallen into disuse. If the constitution prohibited the raising an army, until a war actually commenced, it would deprive the government of the power of providing for the defence of the country, until the enemy were within our territory. If the restriction is not to extend to the raising armies in cases of emergency, but only to the keeping them up, this would leave the matter to the discretion of the legislature; and they might, under the pretence that there was danger of an invasion, keep up the army as long as they judged proper—and hence it is inferred, that the legislature should have authority to raise and keep up an army without any restriction. But from these premises nothing more will follow than this, that the legislature should not be so restrained, as to put it out of their power to raise an army, when such exigencies as are instanced shall arise. But it does not thence follow, that the government should be empowered to raise and maintain standing armies at their discretion as well in peace as in war. If indeed, it is impossible to vest the general government with the power of raising troops to garrison the frontier posts, to guard arsenals, or to be prepared to repel an attack, when we saw a power preparing to make one, without giving them a general and indefinite authority, to raise and keep up armies, without any restriction or qualification, then this reasoning might have weight; but this has not been proved nor can it be.

It is admitted that to prohibit the general government, from keeping up standing armies, while yet they were authorised to raise them in case of exigency, would be an insufficient guard against the danger. A discretion of such latitude would give room to elude the force of the provision.

It is also admitted that an absolute prohibition against raising troops, except in cases of actual war, would be improper; because it will be requisite to raise and support a small number of troops to garrison the important frontier posts, and to guard arsenals; and it may happen, that the danger of an attack from a foreign power may be so imminent, as to render it highly proper we should raise an army, in order to be prepared to resist them. But to raise and keep up forces for such purposes and on such occasions, is not included in the idea, of keeping up standing armies in times of peace.

It is a thing very practicable to give the government sufficient authority to provide for these cases, and at the same time to provide a reasonable and competent security against the evil of a standing army—a clause to the following purpose would answer the end:

As standing armies in time of peace are dangerous to liberty, and have often been the means of overturning the best constitutions of government, no standing army, or troops of any description whatsoever, shall be raised or kept up by the legislature, except so many as shall be necessary for guards to the arsenals of the United States, or for garrisons to such posts on the frontiers, as it shall be deemed absolutely necessary to hold, to secure the inhabitants, and facilitate the trade with the Indians: unless when the United States are threatened with an attack or invasion from some foreign power, in which case the legislature shall be authorised to raise an army to be prepared to repel the attack; provided that no troops whatsoever shall be raised in time of peace, without the assent of two thirds of the members, composing both houses of the legislature.

A clause similar to this would afford sufficient latitude to the legislature to raise troops in all cases that were really necessary, and at the same time competent security against the establishment of that dangerous engine of despotism a standing army.

The same writer who advances the arguments I have noticed, makes a number of other observations with a view to prove that the power to raise and keep up armies, ought to be discretionary in the general legislature; some of them are curious; he instances the raising of troops in Massachusetts and Pennsylvania, to shew the necessity of keeping a standing army in time of peace; the least reflection must convince every candid mind that both these cases are totally foreign to his purpose—Massachusetts raised a body of troops for six months, at the expiration of which they were to disband of course; this looks very little like a standing army. But beside, was that commonwealth in a state of peace at that time? So far from it that they were in the most violent commotions and contents, and their legislature had formally declared that an unnatural rebellion existed within the state. The situation of Pennsylvania was similar; a number of armed men had levied war against the authority of the state, and openly avowed their intention of withdrawing their allegiance from it. To what purpose examples are brought, of states raising troops for short periods in times of war or insurrections, on a question concerning the propriety of keeping up standing armies in times of peace, the public must judge.

24

FEDERAL FARMER, NO. 18
25 Jan. 1788
Storing 2.8.220

In the present state of mankind, and of conducting war, the government of every nation must have power to raise and keep up regular troops: the question is, how shall this power be lodged? In an entire government, as in Great-Britain, where the people assemble by their representatives in one legislature, there is no difficulty, it is of course properly lodged in that legislature: But in a confederated republic, where the organization consists of a federal head, and local governments, there is no one part in which it can be solely, and safely lodged. By art. 1. sect. 8. "congress shall have power to raise and support armies." &c. By art. 1 sect. 10. "no state, without the consent of congress, shall keep troops, or ships of war, in time of peace." It seems fit the union should direct the raising of troops, and the union may do it in two ways; by requisitions on the states, or by direct taxes—the first is most conformable to the federal plan, and safest; and it may be improved, by giving the union power, by its own laws and officers, to raise the states quota that may neglect, and to charge it with the expence; and by giving a fixed quorum of the state legislatures power to disapprove the requisition. There would be less danger in this power to raise troops, could the state governments keep a proper controul over the purse and over the militia; but after all the precautions we can take, without evidently fettering the union too much, we must give a large accumulation of powers to it, in these and other respects. There is one check, which, I think, may be added with great propriety—that is, no land forces shall be kept up, but by legislative acts annually passed by congress, and no appropriation of monies for their support shall be for a longer term than one year. This is the constitutional practice in Great-Britain, and the reasons for such checks in the United States appear to be much stronger. We may also require that these acts be passed by a special majority, as before mentioned. There is another mode still more guarded, and which seems to be founded in the true spirit of a federal system: it seems proper to divide those powers we can with safety, lodge them in no one member of the government alone; yet substantially to preserve their use, and to ensure duration to the government, by modifying the exercise of them—it is to empower congress to raise troops by direct levies, not exceeding a given number, say 2000 in time of peace, and 12,000 in a time of war, and for such further troops as may be wanted, to raise them by requisitions qualified as before mentioned. By the above recited clause no state shall keep troops, &c. in time of peace—this clearly implies, it may do it in time of war: this must be on the principle, that the union cannot defend all parts of the republic, and suggests an idea very repugnant to the general tendency of the system proposed, which is to disarm the state governments: a state in a long war may collect forces sufficient to take the field against the neighbouring states. This clause was copied from the confederation, in which it was of more importance than in the plan proposed, because under this the separate states, probably, will have but small revenues.

25

JAMES MADISON, FEDERALIST, NO. 46, 320–22
29 Jan. 1788

The only refuge left for those who prophecy the downfall of the State Governments, is the visionary supposition that the Foederal Government may previously accumulate a military force for the projects of ambition. The reasonings contained in these papers must have been employed to little purpose indeed, if it could be necessary now to disprove the reality of this danger. That the people and the States should for a sufficient period of time elect an uninterrupted succession of men ready to betray both; that the traitors should throughout this period, uniformly and systematically pursue some fixed plan for the extension of the military establishment; that the governments and the people of the States should silently and patiently behold the gathering storm, and continue to supply the materials, until it should be prepared to burst on their own heads, must appear to every one more like the incoherent dreams of a delirious jealousy, or the misjudged exaggerations of a counterfeit zeal, than like the sober apprehensions of genuine patriotism. Extravagant as the supposition is, let it however be made. Let a regular army, fully equal to the resources of the country be formed; and let it be entirely at the devotion of the Foederal Government; still it would not be going too far to say, that the State Governments with the people on their side would be able to repel the danger. The highest number to which, according to the best computation, a standing army can be carried in any country, does not exceed one hundredth part of the whole number of souls; or one twenty-fifth part of the number able to bear arms. This proportion would not yield in the United States an army of more than twenty-five or thirty thousand men. To these would be opposed a militia amounting to near half a million of citizens with arms in their hands, officered by men chosen from among themselves, fighting for their common liberties, and united and conducted by governments possessing their affections and confidence. It may well be doubted whether a militia thus circumstanced could ever be conquered by such a proportion of regular troops. Those who are best acquainted with the late successful resistance of this country against the British arms will be most inclined to deny the possibility of it. Besides the advantage of being armed, which the Americans possess over the people of almost every other nation, the existence of subordinate governments to which the people are attached, and by which the militia officers are appointed, forms a barrier against the enterprizes of ambition, more insurmountable than any which a simple government of any form can admit of. Notwithstanding the military establishments in the several kingdoms of Europe, which are carried as far as the public resources will bear, the governments are afraid to trust the people with arms. And it is not certain that with this aid alone, they would not be able to shake off their yokes. But were the people to possess the additional advantages of local governments chosen by themselves, who could collect the national will, and direct the national force; and of officers appointed out of the militia, by these governments and attached both to them and to the militia, it may be affirmed with the greatest assurance, that the throne of every tyranny in Europe would be speedily overturned, in spite of the legions which surround it. Let us not insult the free and gallant citizens of America with the suspicion that they would be less able to defend the rights of which they would be in actual possession, than the debased subjects of arbitrary power would be to rescue theirs from the hands of their oppressers. Let us rather no longer insult them with the supposition, that they can ever reduce themselves to the necessity of making the experiment, by a blind and tame submission to the long train of insidious measures, which must precede and produce it.

The argument under the present head may be put into a very concise form, which appears altogether conclusive. Either the mode in which the Foederal Government is to be constructed will render it sufficiently dependant on the people, or it will not. On the first supposition, it will be restrained by that dependence from forming schemes obnoxious to their constituents. On the other supposition it will not possess the confidence of the people, and its schemes of usurpation will be easily defeated by the State Governments; who will be supported by the people.

26

A [MARYLAND] FARMER, NO. 2
29 Feb. 1788
Storing 5.1.41–45

It will be asked how has *England* preserved her liberties, with at least an apparent standing army?—I answer, she did loose them; but as there was no standing army until lately, she regained them again:—She lost them under the Tudors, who broke the then oppressive power of the aristocracy, but the unparalleled avarice of Henry VIIth, the boundless extravagance of Henry VIIIth, the short reign of Edward VIth, (which was but the sickly blaze of a dying candle) the bigotry of that weak woman Mary, who had no other object than religious persecution, and lastly the parsimony of Elizabeth, who had no children of her own to provide for, and who hated her legal successor and his family—all conspired to prevent their establishing a military standing force, sufficient to secure their usurpations; and the nation recovered from their paroxism under the Stuarts, who were too weak and too wicked to command even respect, nothwithstanding their dignity.—On the revolution in 1688, the patriots of that day formed some glorious bulwarks, which seem as yet to have secured them from the evils and danger of their present standing army, though still in my opinion, they hold their remaining liberties by a very precarious tenure indeed, as the first enterprizing and popular Prince will most probably convince them.

Let us now examine these defences and compare them with those of the proposed constitution.

In *England,* by their bill of rights, a standing army is declared to be contrary to their constitution, and a militia the only natural and safe defence of a free people—This keeps the jealousy of the nation constantly awake, and has proved the foundation of all the other checks.

In the American constitution, there is no such declaration, or check at all.

In *England,* the military are declared by their constitution to be in *all* cases subordinate to the civil power; and consequently the civil officers have always been active in supporting this pre-eminence.

In the American constitution, there is no such declaration.

In *England,* the mutiny bill can only be passed from year to year, or on its expiration every soldier is as free, and the equal by law of the first general officer of the land.

In *America,* the articles of war (which is the same thing) has been already considered as *perpetual* (as I am well informed) under even the present Congress, although the constitutions of all the States positively forbid any standing troops at all, much less laws for them.

In *England,* the appropriation of money for the support of their army must be from year to year; in America it may be for double the period.

How favorable is this contrast to Britain—that Britain which we lavished our blood and treasure to separate ourselves from, as a country of slavery—But we then held different sentiments from those now become so fashionable; for this I appeal to the constitutions of the several States.

In the declaration of rights of *Massachusetts,* sect. 17.—The people have a right to keep and to bear arms for the common defence. And as in time of peace, armies are dangerous to liberty, they ought not to be maintained without the consent of the legislature, and the military power shall always be held in exact subordination to the civil authority, and be governed by it.

Sect. 27. In time of peace, no soldier ought to be quartered in any house without the consent of the owner; and in time of war, such quarters ought not to be made but by the civil magistrate, in a manner ordained by the legislature.

Declaration of rights of *Pennsylvania,* sect. 13.—That the people have a right to bear arms for the defence of themselves and the State; and as standing armies in the time of peace, are dangerous to liberty, they ought not to be kept up: And that the military should be kept under strict subordination to, and governed by civil power.

Declaration of rights of *Maryland,* sect. 25.—That a well regulated militia is the proper and natural defence of a free government.

Sect. 26. That standing armies are dangerous to liberty, and ought not to be raised or kept without consent of the legislature.

Sect. 27. That in all cases and at all times the military ought to be under strict subordination to, and controul of the civil power.

Sect. 28. That no soldier ought to be quartered in any house in time of peace, without the consent of the owner; and in time of war, in such manner only as the legislature shall direct.

Declaration of rights of *Delaware,* in the same words as *Maryland.*

Declaration of rights of *North-Carolina,* sect. 17.—That the people have a right to bear arms for the defence of the State; and as standing armies in time of peace are dangerous to liberty, they ought not to be kept up; and that the military should be kept under strict subordination to, and governed by the civil power.

Constitution of *South-Carolina,* sect. 42.—That the military be subordinate to the civil power of the State.

But we are told by *Aristides,* that our poverty is our best security against many standing troops.—Are *we then, and our posterity,* always to be poor? This security would certainly cease with our poverty; but the truth is, our poverty instead of preventing will be the first cause of the increase of a standing army.—Our poverty will render the people less able to pay the few troops it is admitted we must keep.—This expence added to the immense public and private debts, which an efficient government seems to be requisite to enforce payment of, together with the onerous and complicated civil governments, both Continental and State, will be productive of future uneasiness and discontent.—The most sanguine among us must expect some turbulence and commotion; let the smallest appearance of commotion peep out again in any part of the Continent, and there is not a rich man in the United States, who will think himself or his property safe, until *both* are surrounded with standing troops. This is the only public purpose for which *these* men ever did, or ever will willingly contribute their money. But then, according to their laudable custom, they must have interest for their advances;—this increases the public burthens—Commotion is followed by commotion, until the spirit of the people is broken and sunk by the halter, the scaffold, and a regular standing army.—

27

Debate in Virginia Ratifying Convention
14 June 1788
Elliot 3:380–95, 400–402

[Mr. Mason.] No man has a greater regard for the military gentlemen than I have. I admire their intrepidity, perseverance, and valor. But when once a standing army is established in any country, the people lose their liberty. When, against a regular and disciplined army, yeomanry are the only defence,—yeomanry, unskilful and unarmed,—what chance is there for preserving freedom? Give me leave to recur to the page of history, to warn you of your present danger. Recollect the history of most nations of the world. What havoc, desolation, and destruction, have been perpetrated by standing armies! An instance within the memory of some of this house will show us how our militia may be destroyed. Forty years ago, when the resolution of enslaving America was formed in Great Britain, the British Parliament was advised by an artful man, who was governor of Pennsylvania, to disarm the people; that it was the best and most effectual way to enslave them; but that they should not do it openly, but weaken them, and let them sink gradually, by totally disusing and neglecting the militia. [Here Mr. Mason quoted sundry passages to this effect.] This was a most iniquitous project. Why should we not provide against the danger of having our militia, our real and natural strength, destroyed? The general government ought, at the same time, to have some such power. But we need not give them power to abolish our militia. If they neglect to arm them, and prescribe proper discipline, they will be of no use. I am not acquainted with the military profession. I beg to be excused for any errors I may commit with respect to it. But I stand on the general principles of freedom, whereon I dare to meet any one. I wish that, in case the general government should neglect to arm and discipline the militia, there should be an express declaration that the state governments might arm and discipline them. With this single exception, I would agree to this part, as I am conscious the government ought to have the power.

They may effect the destruction of the militia, by rendering the service odious to the people themselves, by harassing them from one end of the continent to the other, and by keeping them under martial law.

The English Parliament never pass a mutiny bill but for one year. This is necessary; for otherwise the soldiers would be on the same footing with the officers, and the army would be dissolved. One mutiny bill has been here in force since the revolution. I humbly conceive there is extreme danger of establishing cruel martial regulations. If, at any time, our rulers should have unjust and iniquitous designs against our liberties, and should wish to establish a standing army, the first attempt would be to render the service and use of militia odious to the people themselves—subjecting them to unnecessary severity of discipline in time of peace, confining them under martial law, and disgusting them so much as to make them cry out, "Give us a standing army!" I would wish to have some check to exclude this danger; as, that the militia should never be subject to martial law but in time of war. I consider and fear the natural propensity of rulers to oppress the people. I wish only to prevent them from doing evil. By these amendments I would give necessary powers, but no unnecessary power. If the clause stands as it is now, it will take from the state legislatures what divine Providence has given to every individual—the means of self-defence. Unless it be moderated in some degree, it will ruin us, and introduce a standing army.

Mr. Madison. Mr. Chairman, I most cordially agree, with the honorable member last up, that a standing army is one of the greatest mischiefs that can possibly happen. It is a great recommendation for this system, that it provides against this evil more than any other system known to us, and, particularly, more than the old system of confederation. The most effectual way to guard against a standing army, is to render it unnecessary. The most effectual way to render it unnecessary, is to give the general government full power to call forth the militia, and exert the whole natural strength of the Union, when necessary. Thus you will furnish the people with sure and certain protection, without recurring to this evil; and the certainty of this protection from the whole will be a strong inducement to individual exertion. Does the organization of the government warrant a belief that this power will be abused? Can we believe that a government of a federal nature, consisting of many coëqual sovereignties, and particularly having one branch chosen from the people, would drag the militia unnecessarily to an immense distance? This, sir, would be unworthy the most arbitrary despot. They have no temptation whatever to abuse this power; such abuse could only answer the purpose of exciting the universal indignation of the people, and drawing on themselves the general hatred and detestation of their country.

I cannot help thinking that the honorable gentleman has not considered, in all its consequences, the amendment he has proposed. Would this be an equal protection, sir, or would it not be a most partial provision? Some states have three or four states in contact. Were this state invaded, as it is bounded by several states, the militia of three or four states would, by this proposition, be obliged to come to our aid; and those from some of the states would come a far greater distance than those of others. There are other states, which, if invaded, could be assisted by the militia of one state only, there being several states which border but on one state. Georgia and New Hampshire would be infinitely less safe than the other states. Were we to adopt this amendment, we should set up those states as butts for invasions, invite foreign enemies to attack them, and expose them to peculiar hardships and dangers. Were the militia confined to any limited distance from their respective places of abode, it would produce equal, nay, more inconveniences. The principles of equality and reciprocal aid would be destroyed in either case.

I cannot conceive that this Constitution, by giving the general government the power of arming the militia, takes it away from the state governments. The power is concurrent, and not exclusive. Have we not found, from experience, that, while the power of arming and governing the militia has been solely vested in the state legislatures, they were neglected and rendered unfit for immediate service? Every state neglected too much this most essential object. But the general government can do it more effectually. Have we not also found that the militia of one state were almost always insufficient to succor its harassed neighbor? Did all the states furnish their quotas of militia with sufficient promptitude? The assistance of one state will be of little avail to repel invasion. But the general head of the whole Union can do it with effect, if it be vested with power to use the aggregate strength of the Union. If the regulation of the militia were to be committed to the executive authority alone, there might be reason for providing restrictions. But, sir, it is the legislative authority that has this power. They must make a law for the purpose.

The honorable member is under another mistake. He wishes martial law to be exercised only in time of war, under an idea that Congress can establish it in time of peace. The states are to have the authority of training the militia according to the congressional discipline; and of governing them at all times when not in the service of the Union. Congress is to govern such part of them as may be employed in the actual service of the United States; and such part only can be subject to martial law. The gentlemen in opposition have drawn a most tremendous picture of the Constitution in this respect. Without considering that the power was absolutely indispensable, they have alarmed us with the possible abuse of it, but have shown no inducement or motive to tempt them to such abuse. Would the legislature of the state drag the militia of the eastern shore to the western frontiers, or those of the western frontiers to the eastern shore, if the local militia were sufficient to effect the intended purpose? There is something so preposterous, and so full of mischief, in the idea of dragging the militia unnecessarily from one end of the continent to the other, that I think there can be no ground of apprehension. If you limit their power over the militia, you give them a pretext for substituting a standing army. If you put it in the power of the state governments to refuse the militia, by requiring their consent, you destroy the general government, and sacrifice particular states. The same principles and motives which produce disobedience to requisitions, will produce refusal in this case.

The restrictions which the honorable gentlemen mentioned to be in the British constitution are all provisions against the power of the executive magistrate; but the House of Commons may, if they be so disposed, sacrifice the interest of their constituents in all those cases. They may prolong the duration of mutiny bills, and grant supplies to the king to carry on an impolitic war. But they have no motives to do so; for they have strong motives to do their duty. We have more ample security than the people of Great Britain. The powers of the government are more limited and guarded, and our representatives are more responsible than the members of the British House of Commons.

Mr. Clay apprehended that, by this power, our militia might be sent to the Mississippi. He observed that the sheriff might raise the *posse comitatus* to execute the laws. He feared it would lead to the establishment of a military government, as the militia were to be called forth to put the laws into execution. He asked why this mode was preferred to the old, established custom of executing the laws.

Mr. Madison answered, that the power existed in all countries; that the militia might be called forth, for that purpose, under the laws of this state and every other state in the Union; that public force must be used when resistance to the laws required it, otherwise society itself must be destroyed; that the mode referred to by the gentleman might not be sufficient on every occasion, as the sheriff must be necessarily restricted to the *posse* of his own county. If the *posse* of one county were insufficient to overcome the resistance to the execution of the laws, this power must be resorted to. He did not, by any means, admit that the old mode was superseded by the introduction of the new one. And it was obvious to him, that, when the civil power was sufficient, this mode would never be put in practice.

Mr. HENRY. Mr. Chairman, in my judgment the friends of the opposition have to act cautiously. We must make a firm stand before we decide. I was heard to say, a few days ago, that the sword and purse were the two great instruments of government; and I professed great repugnance at parting with the purse, without any control, to the proposed system of government. And now, when we proceed in this formidable compact, and come to the national defence, the sword, I am persuaded we ought to be still more cautious and circumspect; for I feel still more reluctance to surrender this most valuable of rights.

The honorable member who has risen to explain several parts of the system was pleased to say, that the best way of avoiding the danger of a standing army, was, to have the militia in such a way as to render it unnecessary; and that, as the new government would have power over the militia, we should have no standing army—it being unnecessary. This argument destroys itself. It demands a power, and denies the probability of its exercise. There are suspicions of power on one hand, and absolute and unlimited confidence on the other. I hope to be one of those who have a large share of suspicion. I leave it to this house, if there be not too small a portion on the other side, by giving up too much to that government. You can easily see which is the worst of two extremes. Too much suspicion may be corrected. If you give too little power to-day, you may give more to-morrow. But the reverse of the proposition will not hold. If you give too much power to-day, you cannot retake it to-morrow: for to-morrow will never come for that purpose. If you have the fate of other nations, you will never see it. It is easier to supply deficiencies of power than to take back excess of power. This no man can deny.

But, says the honorable member, Congress will keep the militia armed; or, in other words, they will do their duty. Pardon me if I am too jealous and suspicious to confide in this remote possibility. My honorable friend went on a supposition that the American rulers, like all others, will depart from their duty without bars and checks. No government can be safe without checks. Then he told us they had no temptation to violate their duty, and that it would be their interest to perform it. Does he think you are to trust men who cannot have separate interests from the people? It is a novelty in the political world (as great a novelty as the system itself) to find rulers without private interests, and views of personal emoluments, and ambition. His supposition, that they will not depart from their duty, as having no interest to do so, is no satisfactory answer to my mind. This is no check. The government may be most intolerable and destructive, if this be our only security.

My honorable friend attacked the honorable gentleman with universal principles—that, in all nations and ages, rulers have been actuated by motives of individual interest and private emoluments, and that in America it would be so also. I hope, before we part with this great bulwark, this noble palladium of safety, we shall have such checks interposed as will render us secure. The militia, sir, is our ultimate safety. We can have no security without it. But then, he says that the power of arming and organizing the militia is concurrent, and to be equally exercised by the general and state governments. I am sure, and I trust in the candor of that gentleman, that he will recede from that opinion, when his recollection will be called to the particular clause which relates to it.

As my worthy friend said, there is a positive partition of power between the two governments. To Congress is given the power of "arming, organizing, and disciplining the militia, and governing such part of them as may be employed in the service of the United States." To the state legislatures is given the power of "appointing the officers, and training the militia according to the discipline prescribed by Congress." I observed before, that, if the power be concurrent as to arming them, it is concurrent in other respects. If the states have the right of arming them, &c., concurrently, Congress has a concurrent power of appointing the officers, and training the militia. If Congress have that power, it is absurd. To admit this mutual concurrence of powers will carry you into endless absurdity—that Congress has nothing exclusive on the one hand, nor the states on the other. The rational explanation is, that Congress shall have exclusive power of arming them, &c., and that the state governments shall have exclusive power of appointing the officers, &c. Let me put it in another light.

May we not discipline and arm them, as well as Congress, if the power be concurrent? so that our militia shall have two sets of arms, double sets of regimentals, &c.; and thus, at a very great cost, we shall be doubly armed. The great object is, that every man be armed. But can the people afford to pay for double sets of arms, &c.? Every one who is able may have a gun. But we have learned, by experience, that, necessary as it is to have arms, and though our Assembly has, by a succession of laws for many years, endeavored to have the militia completely armed, it is still far from being the case. When this power is given up to Congress without limitation or bounds, how will your militia be armed? You trust to chance; for sure I am that that nation which shall trust its liberties in other hands cannot long exist. If gentlemen are serious when they suppose a concurrent power, where can be the impolicy to amend it? Or, in other words, to say that Congress shall not arm or discipline them, till the states shall have refused or neglected to do it? This is my object. I only wish to bring it to what they themselves say is implied. Implication is to be the foundation of our civil liberties; and when you speak of arming the militia by a concurrence of power, you use implication. But implication will not save you, when a strong army of veterans comes upon you. You would be laughed at by the whole world, for trusting your safety implicitly to implication.

The argument of my honorable friend was, that rulers might tyrannize. The answer he received was, that they will not. In saying that they would not, he admitted they might. In this great, this essential part of the Constitution, if you are safe, it is not from the Constitution, but from the virtues of the men in government. If gentlemen are willing to trust themselves and posterity to so slender and improbable a chance, they have greater strength of nerves than I have.

The honorable gentleman, in endeavoring to answer the question why the militia were to be called forth to execute the laws, said that the civil power would probably do it. He is driven to say, that the civil power may do it instead of the militia. Sir, the military power ought not to interpose till the civil power refuse. If this be the spirit of your new Constitution, that the laws are to be enforced by military coercion, we may easily divine the happy consequences which will result from it. The civil power is not to be employed at all. If it be, show me it. I read it attentively, and could see nothing to warrant a belief that the civil power can be called for. I should be glad to see the power that authorizes Congress to do so. The sheriff will be aided by military force. The most wanton excesses may be committed under color of this; for every man in office, in the states, is to take an oath to support it in all its operations. The honorable gentleman said, in answer to the objection that the militia might be marched from New Hampshire to Georgia, that the members of the government would not attempt to excite the indignation of the people. Here, again, we have the general unsatisfactory answer, that they will be virtuous, and that there is no danger.

Will gentlemen be satisfied with an answer which admits of dangers and abuses if they be wicked? Let us put it out of their power to do mischief. I am convinced there is no safety in the paper on the table as it stands now. I am sorry to have an occasion to pass a eulogium on the British government, as gentlemen may object to it. But how natural it is, when comparing deformities to beauty, to be struck with the superiority of the British government to that system! In England, self-love—self-interest—powerfully stimulates the executive magistrate to advance the prosperity of the nation. In the most distant part, he feels the loss of his subjects. He will see the great advantage of his posterity inseparable from the felicity of his people. Man is a fallen creature, a fallible being, and cannot be depended on without self-love. Your President will not have the same motives of self-love to impel him to favor your interests. His political character is but transient, and he will promote, as much as possible, his own private interests. He will conclude, the constant observation has been that he will abuse his power, and that it is expected. The king of England has a more permanent interest. His stock, his family, is to continue in possession of the same emolument. The more flourishing his nation, the more formidable and powerful is he. The sword and purse are not united, in that government, in the same hands, as in this system. Does not infinite security result from a separation?

But it is said that our Congress are more responsible than the British Parliament. It appears to me that there is no real, but there may be some specious responsibility. If Congress, in the execution of their unbounded powers, shall have done wrong, how will you come at them to punish them, if they are at the distance of five hundred miles? At such a great distance, they will evade responsibility altogether. If you have given up your militia, and Congress shall refuse to arm them, you have lost every thing. Your existence will be precarious, because you depend on others, whose interests are not affected by your infelicity. If Congress are to arm us exclusively, the man of New Hampshire may vote for or against it, as well as the Virginian. The great distance and difference between the two places render it impossible that the people of that country can know or pursue what will promote our convenience. I therefore contend that, if Congress do not arm the militia, we ought to provide for it ourselves.

Mr. NICHOLAS. Mr. Chairman, the great object of government, in every country, is security and public defence. I suppose, therefore, that what we ought to attend to here, is, what is the best mode of enabling the general government to protect us. One of three ways must be pursued for this purpose. We must either empower them to employ, and rely altogether on, a standing army; or depend altogether on militia; or else we must enable them to use the one or the other of these two ways, as may be found most expedient. The least reflection will satisfy us that the Convention has adopted the only proper method. If a standing army were alone to be employed, such an army must be kept up in time of peace as would be sufficient in war. The dangers of such an army are so striking that every man would oppose the adoption of this government, had it been proposed by it as the only mode of defence. Would it be safe to depend on militia alone, without the agency of regular forces, even in time of war? Were we to be invaded by a powerful, disciplined army, should we be safe with militia? Could men unacquainted with the hardships, and unskilled in the discipline of war,—men only inured to the peaceable occupations of domestic life,—encounter with success the most skilful veterans, inured to the fatigues and toils of campaigns? Although some people are pleased with the theory of reliance on militia, as the sole defence of a nation, yet I think it will be found, in practice, to be by no means adequate. Its inadequacy is proved by the experience of other nations. But were it fully adequate, it would be unequal. If war be supported by militia, it is by personal service. The poor man does as much as the rich. Is this just? What is the consequence when war is carried on by regular troops? They are paid by taxes raised from the people, according to their property; and then the rich man pays an adequate share.

But, if you confine yourselves to militia alone, the poor man is oppressed. The rich man exempts himself by furnishing a substitute. And, although it be oppressive to the poor, it is not advantageous to the rich? For what he gives would pay regular troops. It is therefore neither safe nor just to depend entirely on militia. As these two ways are ineligible, let us consider the third method. Does this Constitution put this on a proper footing? It enables Congress to raise an army when necessary, or to call forth the militia when necessary. What will be the consequence of their having these two powers? Till there be a necessity for an army to be raised, militia will do. And when an army will be raised, the militia will still be employed, which will render a less numerous army sufficient. By these means, there will be a sufficient defence for the country, without having a standing army altogether, or oppressing the people. The worthy member has said, that it ought to be a part of the Constitution that the militia ought not to go out of the state without the consent of the state legislature. What would be the consequence of this? The general defence is trusted to the general government. How is it to protect the Union? It must apply to the state governments before it can do it. Is this right? Is it not subjecting the general will to the particular will, and exposing the general defence to the particular caprice of the members of the state governments? This would entirely defeat the power given to Congress to provide for the general defence; and unless the militia were to aid in the execution of the laws when resisted, the other powers of Congress would be nugatory. But he has said that this idea is justified by the English history; for that the king has the power of the sword, but must apply to the commons for the means of using it—for the purse. This is not a similar case. The king and commons are parts of the same government. But the general government is separate and perfectly distinct from the individual governments of the states. Should Congress be obliged to apply to the particular states for the militia, they may be refused, and the government overturned. To make the case similar, he ought to show us that the king and Parliament were obliged to call on some other power to raise forces, and provide for the means of carrying on war; for, otherwise, there is no similitude.

If the general government be obliged to apply to the states, a part will be thereby rendered superior to the whole. What are to be the effects of the amendments proposed? To destroy one of the most beneficial parts of the Constitution, put an obstacle in the way of the general government, and put it in the power of the state governments to take away the aid of the militia. Who will be most likely to want the aid of the militia? The Southern States, from their situation. Who are the most likely to be called for? The Eastern States, from their strength, &c. Should we put it in the power of particular states to refuse the militia, it ought to operate against ourselves. It is the height of bad policy to alter this part of the system. But it is said, the militia are to be disarmed. Will they be worse armed than they are now? Still, as my honorable friend said, the states would have power to arm them. The power of arming them is concurrent between the general and state governments; for the power of arming them rested in the state governments before: and although the power be given to the general government, yet it is not given exclusively; for, in every instance where the Constitution intends that the general government shall exercise any power exclusively of the state governments, words of exclusion are particularly inserted. Consequently, in every case where such words of exclusion are not inserted, the power is concurrent to the state governments and Congress, unless where it is impossible that the power should be exercised by both. It is, therefore, not an absurdity to say, that Virginia may arm the militia, should Congress neglect to arm them. But it would be absurd to say that we should arm them after Congress had armed them, when it would be unnecessary; or that Congress should appoint the officers, and train the militia, when it is expressly excepted from their powers.

But his great uneasiness is, that the militia may be under martial law when not on duty. A little attention will be sufficient to remove this apprehension. The Congress is to have power "to provide for the arming, organizing, and disciplining the militia, and for governing such part of them as may be employed in the service of the United States." Another part tells you that they are to provide for calling them forth, to execute the laws of the Union, suppress insurrections, and repel invasions. These powers only amount to this—that they can only call them forth in these three cases, and that they can only govern such part of them as may be in the actual service of the United States. This causes a sufficient security that they will not be under martial law but when in actual service. If, sir, a mutiny bill has continued since the revolution, recollect that this is done under the present happy government. Under the new government, no appropriation of money, to the use of raising or supporting an army, shall be for a longer term than two years. The President is to command. But the regulation of the army and navy is given to Congress. Our representatives will be a powerful check here. The influence of the commons, in England, in this case, is very predominant. But the worthy member on the other side of the house has said that the militia are the great bulwark of the nation, and wishes to take no step to bring them into disuse. What is the inference? He wishes to see the militia employed. The Constitution provides what he wants. This is, to bring them frequently into use. If he expects that, by depriving the general government of the power of calling them into more frequent use, they will be rendered more useful and expert, he is greatly deceived. We ought to part with the power to use the militia to somebody. To whom? Ought we not to part with it for the general defence? If you give it not to Congress, it may be denied by the states. If you withhold it, you render a standing army absolutely necessary; for if they have not the militia, they must have such a body of troops as will be necessary for the general defence of the Union.

It was said, by the gentleman, that there was something singular in this government, in saying that the militia shall be called forth to execute the laws of the Union. There is a great difference between having the power in three cases, and in all cases. They cannot call them forth for any other purpose than to execute the laws, suppress insurrections, and repel invasions. And can any thing be more demonstrably obvious, than that the laws ought to be enforced if resisted, and insurrections quelled, and foreign invasions repelled? But it is asked, Why has not the Constitution declared that the civil power shall be employed to execute the laws? Has it said that the civil power shall not be employed? The civil officer is to execute the laws on all occasions; and, if he be resisted, this auxiliary power is given to Congress of calling forth the militia to execute them, when it shall be found absolutely necessary.

From his argument on this occasion, and his eulogium

on the executive magistrate of Britain, it might be inferred that the executive magistrate here was to have the power of calling forth the militia. What is the idea of those gentlemen who heard his argument on this occasion? Is it not that the President is to have this power—that President, who, he tells us, is not to have those high feelings, and that fine sensibility, which the British monarch possesses? No, sir, the President is not to have this power. God forbid we should ever see a public man in this country who should have this power. Congress only are to have the power of calling forth the militia. And will the worthy member say that he would trust this power to a prince, governed by the dictates of ambition, or mere motives of personal interest, sooner than he would trust it in the hands of Congress? I will trust Congress, because they will be actuated by motives of fellow-feeling. They can make no regulations but what will affect themselves, their friends, and relations. But I would not trust a prince, whose ambition and private views would be the guide of his actions. When the government is carried on by representatives, and persons of my own choice, whom I can follow when far removed, who can be displaced at stated and short periods,—I can safely confide the power to them. It appears to me that this power is essentially necessary; for, as the general defence is trusted to Congress, we ought to intrust fully the means. This cannot be fully done without giving the power of calling forth the militia; and this power is sufficiently guarded.

Mr. MADISON. Mr. Chairman, the honorable gentleman has laid much stress on the maxim, that the purse and sword ought not to be put in the same hands, with a view of pointing out the impropriety of vesting this power in the general government. But it is totally inapplicable to this question. What is the meaning of this maxim? Does it mean that the sword and purse ought not to be trusted in the hands of the same government? This cannot be the meaning; for there never was, and I can say there never will be, an efficient government, in which both are not vested. The only rational meaning is, that the sword and purse are not to be given to the same member. Apply it to the British government, which has been mentioned. The sword is in the hands of the British king; the purse in the hands of the Parliament. It is so in America, as far as any analogy can exist. Would the honorable member say that the sword ought to be put in the hands of the representatives of the people, or in other hands independent of the government altogether? If he says so, it will violate the meaning of that maxim. This would be a novelty hitherto unprecedented. The purse is in the hands of the representatives of the people. They have the appropriation of all moneys. They have the direction and regulation of land and naval forces. They are to provide for calling forth the militia; and the President is to have the command, and, in conjunction with the Senate, to appoint the officers. The means ought to be commensurate to the end. The end is general protection. This cannot be effected without a general power to use the strength of the Union.

We are told that both sides are distinguished by these great traits, confidence and distrust. Perhaps there may be a less or greater tincture of suspicion on one side than the other. But give me leave to say that, where power can be safely lodged, if it be necessary, reason commands its cession. In such case, it is imprudent and unsafe to withhold it. It is universally admitted that it must be lodged in some hands or other. The question, then, is, in what part of the government it ought to be placed; and not whether any other political body, independent of the government, should have it or not. I profess myself to have had a uniform zeal for a republican government. If the honorable member, or any other person, conceives that my attachment to this system arises from a different source, he is greatly mistaken. From the first moment that my mind was capable of contemplating political subjects, I never, till this moment, ceased wishing success to a well-regulated republican government. The establishment of such in America was my most ardent desire. I have considered attentively (and my consideration has been aided by experience) the tendency of a relaxation of laws and a licentiousness of manners.

If we review the history of all republics, we are justified in the supposition that, if the bands of the government be relaxed, confusion will ensue. Anarchy ever has produced, and I fear ever will produce, despotism. What was the state of things that preceded the wars and revolutions in Germany? Faction and confusion. What produced the disorders and commotions of Holland? The like causes. In this commonwealth, and every state in the Union, the relaxed operation of the government has been sufficient to alarm the friends of their country. The rapid increase of population in every state is an additional reason to check dissipation and licentiousness. Does it not strongly call for the friends of republican government to endeavor to establish a republican organization? A change is absolutely necessary. I can see no danger in submitting to practice an experiment which seems to be founded on the best theoretic principles.

But the honorable member tells us there is not an equal responsibility delineated, on that paper, to that which is in the English government. Calculations have been made here, that, when you strike off those entirely elected by the influence of the crown, the other part does not bear a greater proportion to the number of their people, than the number fixed in that paper bears to the number of inhabitants in the United States. If it were otherwise, there is still more responsibility in this government. Our representatives are chosen for two years. In Great Britain, they are chosen for seven years. Any citizen may be elected here. In Great Britain, no one can be elected, to represent a county, without having an estate of the value of six hundred pounds sterling a year; nor to represent a corporation, without an annual estate of three hundred pounds. Yet we are told, there is no sympathy or fellow-feeling between the people here and their representatives; but that in England they have both. A just comparison will show that, if confidence be due to the government there, it is due tenfold here.

. . . . .

GOV. RANDOLPH. Mr. Chairman, our attention is summoned to this clause respecting the militia, and alarms are thrown out to persuade us that it involves a multiplicity of danger. It is supposed by the honorable gentleman lately up, and another gentleman, that the clause for calling forth the militia to suppress insurrections, repel invasions, and execute the laws of the Union, implies that, instead of using civil force in the first instance, the militia are to be called forth to arrest petty offenders against the laws. Ought not common sense to be the rule of interpreting this Constitution? Is there an exclusion of the civil power? Does it provide that the laws are to be enforced by military coercion in all cases? No, sir. All that we are to infer is, that when the civil power is not sufficient, the militia must be drawn out. Who are they? He says (and I cheerfully acquiesce in the rectitude of the assertion) that they are the bulwarks of our liberties. Shall we be afraid that the people, this bulwark of freedom, will turn instruments of slavery? The officers are to be appointed by the states. Will you admit that they will act so criminally as to turn against their country? The officers of the general government are attached to it, because they derive their appointment from it. Admitting the militia officers to be corrupt, what is to make them be in favor of the general government? Will not the same reason attach them to the state governments? But it is feared that the militia are to be subjected to martial law when not in service. They are only to be called out in three cases, and only to be governed by the authority of Congress when in the actual service of the United States; so that their articles of war can no longer operate upon them than when in the actual service of the Union.

Can it be presumed that you can vest the supreme power of the United States with the power of defence, and yet take away this natural defence from them? You risk the general defence by withholding this power.

The honorable gentleman, speaking of responsibility, has mistaken facts. He says the king cannot pardon offenders found guilty on impeachment. The king can pardon after impeachment, though not before. He says, further, that in America every thing is concealed, whereas in England the operations of the government are openly transacted. In England, those subjects which produce impeachments are not opinions. No man ever thought of impeaching a man for an opinion. It would be impossible to discover whether the error in opinion resulted from a wilful mistake of the heart, or an involuntary fault of the head. What are the occasions of impeachments most commonly? Treaties. Are these previously known? No. Till after they are presented to the public eye, they are not known. Those who advised a treaty are not known till then. There ought not to be a publication on the subject of negotiations till they are concluded. So that, when he thinks there is a greater notoriety in this case in England than here, I say he is mistaken. There will be as much notoriety in America as in England. The spirit of the nation occasions the notoriety of their political operations, and not any constitutional requisition. The spirit of liberty will not be less predominant in America, I hope, than there. With respect to a standing army, I believe there was not a member in the federal Convention, who did not feel indignation at such an institution. What remedy, then, could be provided? Leave the country defenceless? In order to provide for our defence, and exclude the dangers of a standing army, the general defence is left to those who are the objects of defence. It is left to the militia, who will suffer if they become the instruments of tyranny. The general government must have power to call them forth when the general defence requires it. In order to produce greater security, the state governments are to appoint the officers. The President, who commands them when in actual service of the Union, is appointed secondarily by the people. This is a further security. Is it not incredible that men who are interested in the happiness of their country—whose friends, relations, and connections, must be involved in the fate of their country—should turn against their country? I appeal to every man whether, if any of our own officers were called upon to destroy the liberty of their country, he believes they would assent to such an act of suicide. The state governments, having the power of appointing them, may elect men who are the most remarkable for their virtue of attachment to their country.

Mr. GEORGE MASON, after having read the clause which gives Congress power to provide for arming, organizing, and disciplining the militia, and governing those in actual service of the Union, declared it as his firm belief, that it included the power of annexing punishments, and establishing necessary discipline, more especially as the construction of this, and every other part of the Constitution, was left to those who were to govern. If so, he asked if Congress could not inflict the most ignominious punishments on the most worthy citizens of the community. Would freemen submit to such indignant treatment? It might be thought a strained construction, but it was no more than Congress might put upon it. He thought such severities might be exercised on the militia as would make them wish the use of the militia to be utterly abolished, and assent to the establishment of a standing army. He then adverted to the representation, and said it was not sufficiently full to take into consideration the feelings and sentiments of all the citizens. He admitted that the nature of the country rendered a full representation impracticable. But he strongly urged that impracticability as a conclusive reason for granting no powers to the government but such as were absolutely indispensable, and these to be most cautiously guarded.

28

ST. GEORGE TUCKER, BLACKSTONE'S COMMENTARIES 1:APP. 272–75 1803

The objects of this clause of the constitution, although founded upon the principle of our state bill of rights, Art. 8, declaring, "that a well regulated militia, composed of the body of the people trained to arms, is the proper, natural, and safe defence of a free state," were thought to be dangerous to the state governments. The convention of Virginia, therefore, proposed the following amendment to the constitution; "that each state respectively should have the power to provide for organizing, arming, and disciplining it's own militia, whenever congress should neglect to provide for the same." . . . A further amendment proposed, was, "that the militia should not be subject to martial law, except when in actual service, in time of war, rebellion, or invasion." . . . A provision manifestly implied in the words of the constitution. As to the former of these amendments, all room for doubt, or uneasiness upon the subject, seems to be completely removed, by the fourth article of amendments to the constitution, since ratified, viz. "That a militia being necessary to the security of a free state, the right of the people to keep, and bear arms, shall not be infringed." . . . To which we may add, that the power of arming the militia, not being prohibited to the states, respectively, by the constitution, is, consequently, reserved to them, concurrently with the federal government. In pursuance of these powers, an act passed, 2 Cong. 1 Sess. c. 33, to provide for the national defence, by establishing an uniform militia throughout the United States; and the system of organization thereby established, has been carried into effect in Virginia, and probably in all the other states of the union.

Uniformity in the system of organization, and discipline of the militia, the constitutional defence of a free government is certainly desirable, and must be attended with beneficial effects, whenever the occasion may again require the co-operation of the militia of the states respectively. The want of power over these subjects, was one of the defects of the former system of government under the confederation; and the consequent want of uniformity of organization, and of discipline, among the several corps of militia drawn together from the several states, together with the uncertainty and variety of the periods of service, for which those corps were severally embodied, produced a very large portion of those disgraces, which attended the militia of almost every state, during the revolutionary war; and, thus contributed to swell the national debt, to an enormous size, by a fruitless expence. By authorising the federal government to provide for all these cases, we may reasonably hope, that the future operations of the militia of the confederated states, will justify the opinion, that they are the most safe, as well as most natural defence of a free state. An opinion, however, which will never be justified, if the duty of arming, organizing, training, and disciplining them, be neglected: a neglect the more unpardonable, as it will pave the way for standing armies; the most formidable of all enemies to genuine liberty in a state.

We have seen that the appointment of the officers of the militia, and the authority of training them, are expressly reserved to the states, by this article: this was considered as a most important check to any possible abuse of power in the federal government, whenever the aid of the militia should be required by it.

Notwithstanding this wise precaution in the constitution, the fifth congress appear to have disregarded it, by authorising the president of the United States, to enlist and organize volunteers, or special corps of militia, whose officers HE was authorised to appoint, either by *his own authority,* or with the concurrence of the senate; they were likewise to be trained and disciplined in the manner which he should direct, and be liable to be called upon to do duty, at any time that he should judge proper, within two years after their acceptance, and be exempted, during the time of their engagement, from all militia duty, which might be required of them by the laws of the United States, or of any state, and from every fine, penalty, or disability, provided to enforce the performance of any duty or service in the militia. . . . The number of these corps was at first unlimited, and the president was authorised to sell or lend them artillery, small-arms, accoutrements, from the public arsenals. L. U. S. 5 Cong. c. 64. Sec. 3, and c. 74. . . . As these select corps were not called into actual service by those acts, but were only liable to be called upon at the pleasure of the president, it seems impossible to view them in any other light, than as a part of the militia of the states, separated by an unconstitutional act of congress, from the rest, for the purpose of giving to the president powers, which the constitution expressly denied him, and an influence the most dangerous that can be conceived, to the peace, liberty, and happiness of the United States.

29

JOSEPH STORY, COMMENTARIES ON THE CONSTITUTION 3:§§ 1174–87
1833

§ 1174. The power to raise armies is an indispensable incident to the power to declare war; and the latter—would be literally *brutum fulmen* without the former, a means of mischief without a power of defence. Under the confederation congress possessed no power whatsoever to raise armies; but only "to agree upon the number of land forces, and to make requisitions from each state for its quota, in proportion to the number of white inhabitants in such state;" which requisitions were to be binding; and thereupon the legislature of each state were to appoint the regimental officers, raise the men, and clothe, arm, and equip them in a soldier-like manner, at the expense of the United States. The experience of the whole country, during the revolutionary war, established, to the satisfaction of every statesman, the utter inadequacy and impropriety of this system of requisition. It was equally at war with economy, efficiency, and safety. It gave birth to a competition between the states, which created a kind of auction of men. In order to furnish the quotas required of them, they outbid each other, till bounties grew to an enormous and insupportable size. On this account many persons procrastinated their enlistment, or enlisted only for short periods. Hence, there were but slow and scanty levies of men in the most critical emergencies of our affairs; short enlistments at an unparalleled expense; and continual fluctuations in the troops, ruinous to their discipline, and subjecting the public safety frequently to the perilous crisis of a disbanded army. Hence also arose those oppressive expedients for raising men, which were occasionally practised, and which nothing, but the enthusiasm of liberty, could have induced the people to endure. The burthen was also very unequally distributed. The states near the seat of war, influenced by motives of self-preservation, made efforts to furnish their quotas, which even exceeded their abilities; while those at a distance were exceedingly remiss in their exertions. In short, the army was frequently composed of three bodies of men; first, raw recruits; secondly, persons, who were just about completing their term of service; and thirdly, of persons, who had served out half their term, and were quietly waiting for its determination. Under such circumstances, the wonder is not, that its military operations were tardy, irregular, and often unsuccessful; but, that it was ever able to make head-way at all against an enemy, possessing a fine establishment, well appointed, well armed, well clothed, and well paid. The appointment, too, by the states, of all regimental officers, had a tendency to destroy all harmony and subordination, so necessary to the success of military life.

§ 1175. There is great wisdom and propriety in relieving the government from the ponderous and unwieldy machinery of the requisitions and appointments under the confederation. The present system of the Union is *general* and direct, and capable of a uniform organization and action. It is essential to the common defence, that the national government should possess the power to raise armies; build and equip fleets; prescribe rules for the government of both; direct their operations; and provide for their support.

§ 1176. The clause, as originally reported, was "to raise armies;" and subsequently it was, upon the report of a committee, amended, so as to stand in its present form; and as amended it seems to have encountered no opposition in the convention. It was, however, afterwards assailed in the state conventions, and before the people, with incredible zeal and pertinacity, as dangerous to liberty, and subversive of the state governments. Objections were made against the general and indefinite power to raise armies, not limiting the number of troops; and to the maintenance of them in peace, as well as in war.

§ 1177. It was said, that congress, having an unlimited power to raise and support armies, might, if in their opinion the general welfare required it, keep large armies constantly on foot, and thus exhaust the resources of the United States. There is no control on congress, as to numbers, stations, or government of them. They may billet them on the people at pleasure. Such an unlimited authority is most dangerous, and in its principles despotic; for being unbounded, it must lead to despotism. We shall, therefore, live under a government of military force. In respect to times of peace, it was suggested, that there is no necessity for having a standing army, which had always been held, under such circumstances, to be fatal to the public rights and political freedom.

§ 1178. To these suggestions it was replied with equal force and truth, that to be of any value, the power must be unlimited. It is impossible to foresee, or define the extent and variety of national exigencies, and the correspondent extent and variety of the national means necessary to satisfy them. The power must be co-extensive with all possible combinations of circumstances, and under the direction of the councils entrusted with the common defence. To deny this would be to deny the means, and yet require the end. These must, therefore, be unlimited in every matter essential to its efficacy, that is, in the formation, direction, and support of the national forces. This was not doubted under the confederation; though the mode adopted to carry it into effect was utterly inadequate and illusory. There could be no real danger from the exercise of the power. It was not here, as in England, where the executive possessed the power to raise armies at pleasure; which power, so far as respected standing armies in time of peace, it became necessary to provide by the bill of rights, in 1688, should not be exercised without the consent of parliament. Here the power is exclusively confined to the legislative body, to the representatives of the states, and of the people of the states. And to suppose it will not be safe in their hands, is to suppose, that no powers of government, adapted to national exigencies, can ever be safe in any political body. Besides, the power is limited by the necessity (as will be seen) of biennial appropriations. The objection, too, is the more strange, because there are but two constitutions of the thirteen states, which attempt in any manner to limit the power; and these are rather cautions for times of peace, than prohibitions. The confederation itself contains no prohibition or limitation of the power. Indeed, in regard to times of war, it seems utterly preposterous to impose any limitations upon the power; since it is obvious, that emergencies may arise, which would require the most various, and independent exercises of it. The country would otherwise be in danger of losing both its liberty and its sovereignty, from its dread of investing the public councils with the power of defending it. It would be more willing to submit to foreign conquest, than to domestic rule.

§ 1179. But in times of peace the power may be at least equally important, though not so often required to be put in full exercise. The United States are surrounded by the colonies and dependencies of potent foreign governments, whose maritime power may furnish them with the means of annoyance, and mischief, and invasion. To guard ourselves against evils of this sort, it is indispensable for us to have proper forts and garrisons, stationed at the weak points, to overawe or check incursions. Besides; it will be equally important to protect our frontiers against the Indians, and keep them in a state of due submission and control. The garrisons can be furnished only by occasional detachments of militia, or by regular troops in the pay of the government. The first would be impracticable, or extremely inconvenient, if not positively pernicious. The militia would not, in times of profound peace, submit to be dragged from their occupations and families to perform such a disagreeable duty. And if they would, the increased expenses of a frequent rotation in the service; the loss of time and labour; and the breaking up of the ordinary employments of life; would make it an extremely ineligible scheme of military power. The true and proper recourse should, therefore, be to a permanent, but small standing army for such purposes. And it would only be, when our neighbours should greatly increase their military force, that prudence and a due regard to our own safety would require any augmentation of our own. It would be wholly unjustifiable to throw upon the states the defence of their own frontiers, either against the Indians, or against foreign foes. The burthen would often be disproportionate to their means, and the benefit would often be largely shared by the neighbouring states. The common defence should be provided for out of the common treasury. The existence of a federal government, and at the same time of military establishments under state authority, are not less at variance with each other, than a due supply of the federal treasury, and the system of quotas and requisitions.

§ 1180. It is important also to consider, that the surest means of avoiding war is to be prepared for it in peace. If a prohibition should be imposed upon the United States against raising armies in time of peace, it would present the extraordinary spectacle to the world of a nation incapacitated by a constitution of its own choice from preparing for defence before an actual invasion. As formal denunciations of war are in modern times often neglected, and are never necessary, the presence of an enemy within our territories would be required, before the government would be warranted to begin levies of men for the protection of the state. The blow must be received, before any attempts could be made to ward it off, or to return it. Such a course of conduct would at all times invite aggression and insult; and enable a formidable rival or secret enemy to seize upon the country, as a defenceless prey; or to drain its resources by a levy of contributions, at once irresistible and ruinous. It would be in vain to look to the militia for an adequate defence under such circumstances. This reliance came very near losing us our independence, and was the occasion of the useless expenditure of many millions. The history of other countries, and our past experience, admonish us, that a regular force, well disciplined and well supplied, is the cheapest, and the only effectual means of resisting the inroads of a well disciplined foreign army. In short, under such circumstances the constitution must be either violated, (as it in fact was by the states under the confederation,) or our liberties must be placed in extreme jeopardy. Too much precaution often leads to as many difficulties, as too much confidence. How could a readiness for war in time of peace be safely prohibited, unless we could in like manner prohibit the preparations and establishments of every hostile nation? The means of security can be only regulated by the means and the danger of attack. They will, in fact, ever be determined by these rules, and no other. It will be in vain to oppose constitutional barriers to the impulse of self-preservation.

§ 1181. But the dangers from abroad are not alone those, which are to be guarded against in the structure of the national government. Cases may occur, and indeed are contemplated by the constitution itself to occur, in which military force may be indispensable to enforce the laws, or to suppress domestic insurrections. Where the resistance is confined to a few insurgents, the suppression may be ordinarily, and safely confided to the militia. But where it is extensive, and especially if it should pervade one, or more states, it may become important and even necessary to employ regular troops, as at once the most effective, and the most economical force. Without the power to employ such a force in time of peace for domestic purposes, it is plain, that the government might be in danger of being overthrown by the combinations of a single faction.

§ 1182. The danger of an undue exercise of the power is purely imaginary. It can never be exerted, but by the representatives of the people of the states; and it must be safe there, or there can be no safety at all in any republican form of government. Our notions, indeed, of the dangers of standing armies in time of peace, are derived in a great measure from the principles and examples of our English ancestors. In England, the king possessed the power of raising armies in the time of peace according to his own good pleasure. And this prerogative was justly esteemed dangerous to the public liberties. Upon the revolution of 1688, parliament wisely insisted upon a bill of rights, which should furnish an adequate security for the future. But how was this done? Not by prohibiting standing armies altogether in time of peace; but (as has been already seen) by prohibiting them *without the consent of parliament.* This is the very proposition contained in the constitution; for congress can alone raise armies; and may put them down, whenever they choose.

§ 1183. It may be admitted, that standing armies may prove dangerous to the state. But it is equally true, that the want of them may also prove dangerous to the state. What then is to be done? The true course is to check the undue exercise of the power, not to withhold it. This the constitution has attempted to do by providing, that "no appropriation of money to that use shall be for a longer term than two years." Thus, unless the necessary supplies are voted by the representatives of the people every two years, the whole establishment must fall. Congress may indeed, by an act for this purpose, disband a standing army at any time; or vote the supplies only for one year, or for a shorter period. But the constitution is imperative, that no appropriation shall prospectively reach beyond the biennial period. So that there would seem to be every human security against the possible abuse of the power.

§ 1184. But, here again it was objected, that the executive might keep up a standing army in time of peace, notwithstanding no supplies should be voted. But how can this possibly be done? The army cannot go without supplies; it may be disbanded at the pleasure of the legislature; and it would be absolutely impossible for any president, against the will of the nation, to keep up a standing army in *terrorem populi.*

§ 1185. It was also asked, why an appropriation should not be annually made, instead of biennially, as is the case in the British parliament. The answer is, that congress may in their pleasure limit the appropriation to a single year; but exigencies may arise, in which, with a view to the advantages of the public service and the pressure of war, a biennial appropriation might be far more expedient, if not absolutely indispensable. Cases may be supposed, in which it might be impracticable for congress, in consequence of public calamities, to meet annually for the despatch of business. But the supposed example of the British parliament proves nothing. That body is not restrained by any constitutional provision from voting supplies for a standing army for an unlimited period. It is the mere practice of parliament, in the exercise of its own discretion, to make an annual vote of supplies. Surely, if there is no danger in confiding an unlimited power of this nature to a body chosen for seven years, there can be none in confiding a limited power to an American congress, chosen for two years.

§ 1186. In some of the state conventions an amendment was proposed, requiring, that no standing army, or regular forces be kept up in time of peace, except for the necessary protection and defence of forts, arsenals, and dockyards, without the consent of two thirds of both houses of congress. But it was silently suffered to die away with the jealousies of the day. The practical course of the government on this head has allayed all fears of the people, and fully justified the opinions of the friends of the constitution. It is remarkable, that scarcely any power of the national government was at the time more strongly assailed by appeals to popular prejudices, or vindicated with more full and masculine discussion. The Federalist gave it a most elaborate discussion, as one of the critical points of the constitution. In the present times the subject attracts no notice, and would scarcely furnish a topic, even for popular declamation. Ever since the constitution was put into operation, congress have restrained their appropriations to the current year; and thus practically shown the visionary nature of these objections.

§ 1187. Congress in 1798, in expectation of a war with France, authorized the president to accept the services of any companies of volunteers, who should associate themselves for the service, and should be armed, clothed, and equipped at their own expense, and to commission their officers. This exercise of power was complained of at the time, as a virtual infringement of the constitutional authority of the states in regard to the militia; and, as such, it met with the disapprobation of a learned commentator. His opinion does not, however, seem since to have received the deliberate assent of the nation. During the late war with Great Britain, laws were repeatedly passed, authorizing the acceptance of volunteer corps of the militia under their own officers; and eventually, the president was authorized, with the consent of the senate, to commission officers for such volunteer corps. These laws exhibit the decided change of the public opinion on this subject; and they deserve more attention, since the measures were promoted and approved under the auspices of the very party, which had inculcated an opposite opinion. It is proper to remark, that the Federalist maintained, that the disciplining and effective organization of the whole militia would be impracticable; that the attention of the government ought particularly to be directed to the formation of a select corps of moderate size, upon such principles, as would really fit them for service in case of need; and that such select corps would constitute the best substitute for a large standing army, and the most formidable check upon any undue military powers; since it would be composed of citizens well disciplined, and well instructed in their rights and duties.

SEE ALSO:

Generally 1.8.13–16; Amends. II, III
Samuel Adams, Boston Gazette, 5 Dec. 1768, Writings 1:257–59
Samuel Adams, Boston Gazette, 12 Dec. 1768, Writings 1:264–68
Joseph Warren to Samuel Adams, 26 May 1775, Life 495–96
Samuel Adams to James Warren, 7 Jan. 1776, Writings 3:250–51
Records of the Federal Convention, Farrand 2:143, 158, 167, 168, 323, 334, 505, 570, 595, 640
Tench Coxe, An Examination of the Constitution, Fall, 1787, Pamphlets 150–51
A Federal Republican, 28 Oct. 1787, Storing 3.6.20–21
Thomas McKean, Pennsylvania Ratifying Convention, 11 Dec. 1787, Elliot 2:536–37
Debate in Massachusetts Ratifying Convention, 24 Jan. 1788, Elliot 2.97
Impartial Examiner, no. 1, 27 Feb. 1788, Storing, 5.14.8
Debate in Virginia Ratifying Convention, 6, 9 June 1788, Elliot 3:77, 78–79, 178–79
Debate in North Carolina Ratifying Convention, 26 July 1788, Elliot 4:95–100
George Washington, First Annual Address, 8 Jan. 1790, Richardson 1:65
Kentucky Constitution of 1792, art. 12, c. 24, Thorpe 3:1275
George Washington, Seventh Annual Address, 8 Dec. 1795, Richardson 1:184
House of Representatives, Provisional Army, 8 May 1798, Annals 8:1631–42
House of Representatives, Volunteer Corps, 10–11, 13 Jan. 1812, Annals 23:728–49, 750–54

Article 1, Section 8, Clause 13

To provide and maintain a Navy;

1

Records of the Federal Convention

[*2:143, 158, 168; Committee of Detail*]

5. To make war . . . & equip Fleets.

. . . . .

The Legislature of U.S. shall have the exclusive Power— . . . of equiping a Navy—

. . . . .

. . . to build and equip Fleets . . .

[*2:330; Madison, 18 Aug.*]

Instead of "to build and equip fleets"—"to provide & maintain a navy" agreed to nem. con as a more convenient definition of the power.

[*2:570, 595; Committee of Style*]

To provide & maintain a navy;

2

John Jay, Federalist, no. 4, 19–23 7 Nov. 1787

The extension of our own commerce in our own vessels, cannot give pleasure to any nations who possess territories on or near this Continent, because the cheapness and excellence of our productions, added to the circumstance of vicinity, and the enterprize and address of our merchants and navigators, will give us a greater share in the advantages which those territories afford, than consists with the wishes or policy of their respective Sovereigns.

Spain thinks it convenient to shut the Mississippi against us on the one side, and Britain excludes us from the St. Laurence on the other; nor will either of them permit the other waters, which are between them and us, to become the means of mutual intercourse and traffic.

From these and such like considerations, which might if consistent with prudence, be more amplified and detailed, it is easy to see that jealousies and uneasinesses may gradually slide into the minds and cabinets of other nations; and that we are not to expect they should regard our advancement in union, in power and consequence by land and by sea, with an eye of indifference and composure.

The People of America are aware that inducements to war, may arise out of these circumstances, as well as from others not so obvious at present; and that whenever such inducements may find fit time and opportunity for operation, pretences to colour and justify them will not be wanting. Wisely therefore do they consider Union and a good national Government as necessary to put and keep them in *such a situation* as instead of *inviting* war, will tend to repress and discourage it. That situation consists in the best possible state of defence, and necessarily depends on the Government, the arms and the resources of the country.

As the safety of the whole is the interest of the whole, and cannot be provided for without Government, either one or more or many, let us inquire whether one good Government is not, relative to the object in question, more competent than any other given number whatever.

One Government can collect and avail itself of the talents and experience of the ablest men, in whatever part of the Union they may be found. It can move on uniform principles of policy—It can harmonize, assimilate, and protect the several parts and members, and extend the benefit of its foresight and precautions to each. In the formation of treaties it will regard the interest of the whole, and the particular interests of the parts as connected with that of the whole. It can apply the resources and power of the whole to the defence of any particular part, and that more easily and expeditiously than State Governments, or separate confederacies can possibly do, for want of concert and unity of system. It can place the militia under one plan of discipline, and by putting their officers in a proper line of subordination to the Chief Magistrate, will as it were consolidate them into one corps, and thereby render them more efficient than if divided into thirteen or into three or four distinct independent bodies.

What would the militia of Britain be, if the English militia obeyed the Government of England, if the Scotch militia obeyed the Government of Scotland, and if the Welch militia obeyed the Government of Wales! Suppose an invasion—would those three Governments (if they agreed at all) be able with all their respective forces, to operate against the enemy so effectually as the single Government of Great Britain would?

We have heard much of the fleets of Britain, and the time may come, if we are wise, when the fleets of America may engage attention. But if one national Government had not so regulated the navigation of Britain as to make it a nursery for seamen—if one national Government had not called forth all the national means and materials for forming fleets, their prowess and their thunder would never have been celebrated. Let England have its navigation and fleet—Let Scotland have its navigation and fleet—Let Wales have its navigation and fleet—Let Ireland have its navigation and fleet—Let those four of the constituent parts of the British empire be under four independent Governments, and it is easy to perceive how soon they would each dwindle into comparative insignificance.

Apply these facts to our own case—Leave America divided into thirteen, or if you please into three or four independent Governments, what armies could they raise and pay, what fleets could they ever hope to have? If one was attacked would the other[s] fly to its succour, and spend their blood and money in its defence? Would there be no danger of their being flattered into neutrality by specious promises, or seduced by a too great fondness for peace to decline hazarding their tranquillity and present safety for the sake of neighbours, of whom perhaps they have been jealous, and whose importance they are content to see diminished? Altho' such conduct would not be wise it would nevertheless be natural. The history of the States of Greece, and of other Countries abound with such instances, and it is not improbable that what has so often happened, would under similar circumstances happen again.

But admit that they might be willing to help the invaded State or Confederacy. How and when, and in what proportion shall aids of men and money be afforded? Who shall command the allied armies, and from which of them shall he receive his orders? Who shall settle the terms of peace, and in case of disputes what umpire shall decide between them, and compel acquiescence? Various difficulties and inconveniences would be inseparable from such a situation; whereas one Government watching over the general and common interests, and combining and directing the powers and resources of the whole, would be free from all these embarrasments, and conduce far more to the safety of the people.

But whatever may be our situation, whether firmly united under one national Government, or split into a number of confederacies, certain it is, that foreign nations will know and view it exactly as it is; and they will act towards us accordingly. If they see that our national Government is efficient and well administered—our trade prudently regulated—our militia properly organized and disciplined—our resources and finances discreetly managed—our credit re-established—our people free, contented, and united, they will be much more disposed to cultivate our friendship, than provoke our resentment. If on the other hand they find us either destitute of an effectual Government, (each State doing right or wrong as to its rulers may seem convenient), or split into three or four independent and probably discordant republics or confederacies, one inclining to Britain, another to France, and a third to Spain, and perhaps played off against each other by the three, what a poor pitiful figure will America make in their eyes! How liable would she become not only to their contempt, but to their outrage; and how soon would dear bought experience proclaim, that when a people or family so divide, it never fails to be against themselves.

3

ALEXANDER HAMILTON, FEDERALIST, NO. 11, 65–73
24 Nov. 1787

(See vol. 1, ch. 7, no. 13)

4

DEBATE IN VIRGINIA RATIFYING CONVENTION
14 June 1788
Elliot 3:428–30

MR. GRAYSON. Mr. Chairman, I conceive that the power of providing and maintaining a navy is at present dangerous, however warmly it may be urged by gentlemen that America ought to become a maritime power. If we once give such power, we put it in the hands of men whose interest it will be to oppress us. It will also irritate the nations of Europe against us. Let us consider the situation of the maritime powers of Europe: they are separated from us by the Atlantic Ocean. The riches of all those countries come by sea. Commerce and navigation are the principal sources of their wealth. If we become a maritime power, we shall be able to participate in their most beneficial business. Will they suffer us to put ourselves in a condition to rival them? I believe the first step of any consequence, which will be made towards it, will bring war upon us. Their ambition and avarice most powerfully impel them to prevent our becoming a naval nation. We should, on this occasion, consult our ability. Is there any gentleman here who can say that America can support a navy? The riches of America are not sufficient to bear the enormous expense it must certainly occasion. I may be supposed to exaggerate, but I leave it to the committee to judge whether my information be right or not.

It is said that shipwrights can be had on better terms in America than in Europe; but necessary materials are so much dearer in America than in Europe, that the aggregate sum would be greater. A seventy-four gun ship will cost you ninety-eight thousand pounds, including guns, tackle, &c. According to the usual calculation in England, it will cost you the further sum of forty-eight thousand pounds to man it, furnish provisions, and pay officers and men. You must pay men more here than in Europe, because, their governments being arbitrary, they can command the services of their subjects without an adequate compensation; so that, in all, the expenses of such a vessel would be one hundred and forty thousand pounds in one year. Let gentlemen consider, then, the extreme difficulty of supporting a navy, and they will concur with me, that America cannot do it. I have no objection to such a navy as will not excite the jealousy of the European countries. But I would have the Constitution to say, that no greater number of ships should be had than would be sufficient to protect our trade. Such a fleet would not, probably, offend the Europeans. I am not of a jealous disposition; but when I consider that the welfare and happiness of my country are in danger, I beg to be excused for expressing my apprehensions. Let us consider how this navy shall be raised. What would be the consequence under those general words, "to provide and maintain a navy"? All the vessels of the intended fleet would be built and equipped in the Northern States, where they have every necessary material and convenience for the purpose. Will any gentleman say that any ship of war can be raised to the south of Cape Charles? The consequence will be that the Southern States will be in the power of the Northern States.

We should be called upon for our share of the expenses, without having equal emoluments. Can it be supposed, when this question comes to be agitated in Congress, that the Northern States will not take such measures as will throw as much circulating money among them as possible, without any consideration as to the other states? If I know the nature of man, (and I believe I do,) they will have no consideration for us. But, supposing it were not so, America has nothing at all to do with a fleet. Let us remain for some time in obscurity, and rise by degrees. Let us not precipitately provoke the resentment of the maritime powers of Europe. A well-regulated militia ought to be the defence of this country. In some of our constitutions it is said so. This Constitution should have inculcated the principle. Congress ought to be under some restraint in this respect. Mr. Grayson then added, that the Northern States would be principally benefited by having a fleet; that a majority of the states could vote the raising a great navy, or enter into any commercial regulation very detrimental to the other states. In the United Netherlands there was much greater security, as the commercial interest of no state could be sacrificed without its own consent. The raising a fleet was the daily and favorite subject of conversation in the Northern States. He apprehended that, if attempted, it would draw us into a war with Great Britain or France. As the American fleet would not be competent to the defence of all the states, the Southern States would be most exposed. He referred to the experience of the late war, as a proof of what he said. At the period the Southern States were most distressed, the Northern States, he said, were most happy. They had privateers in abundance, whereas we had but few. Upon the whole, he thought we should depend on our troops on shore, and that it was very impolitic to give this power to Congress without any limitation.

Mr. Nicholas remarked that the gentleman last up had made two observations—the one, that we ought not to give Congress power to raise a navy; and the other, that we had not the means of supporting it. Mr. Nicholas thought it a false doctrine. Congress, says he, has a discretionary power to do it when necessary. They are not bound to do it in five or ten years, or at any particular time. It is presumable, therefore, that they will postpone it until it be proper.

Mr. Grayson had no objection to giving Congress the power of raising such a fleet as suited the circumstances of the country. But he could not agree to give that unlimited power which was delineated in that paper.

5

George Washington, Eighth Annual Address
7 Dec. 1796
Richardson 1:201

To an active external commerce the protection of a naval force is indispensable. This is manifest with regard to wars in which a State is itself a party. But besides this, it is in our own experience that the most sincere neutrality is not a sufficient guard against the depredations of nations at war. To secure respect to a neutral flag requires a naval force organized and ready to vindicate it from insult or aggression. This may even prevent the necessity of going to war by discouraging belligerent powers from committing such violations of the rights of the neutral party as may, first or last, leave no other option. From the best information I have been able to obtain it would seem as if our trade to the Mediterranean without a protecting force will always be insecure and our citizens exposed to the calamities from which numbers of them have but just been relieved.

These consideratious invite the United States to look to the means, and to set about the gradual creation of a navy. The increasing progress of their navigation promises them at no distant period the requisite supply of seamen, and their means in other respects favor the undertaking. It is an encouragement, likewise, that their particular situation will give weight and influence to a moderate naval force in their hands. Will it not, then, be advisable to begin without delay to provide and lay up the materials for the building and equipping of ships of war, and to proceed in the work by degrees, in proportion as our resources shall render it practicable without inconvenience, so that a future war of Europe may not find our commerce in the same unprotected state in which it was found by the present?

6

House of Representatives, Protection of Trade
22 June 1797
Annals 7:363–66.

(See 2.2.1, no. 8)

7

Bas v. Tingy
4 Dall. 37 (1800)

(See 1.8.11, no. 10)

8

Joseph Story, Commentaries on the Constitution 3:§§ 1189–91
1833

§ 1189. Under the confederation congress possessed the power "to build and equip a navy." The same language was adopted in the original draft of the constitution; and it was amended by substituting the present words, apparently without objection, as more broad and appropriate. In the convention, the propriety of granting the power seems not to have been questioned. But it was assailed in the state conventions as dangerous. It was said, that commerce and navigation are the principal sources of the wealth of the maritime powers of Europe; and if we engaged in commerce, we should soon become their rivals. A navy would soon be thought indispensable to protect it. But the attempt on our part to provide a navy would provoke these powers, who would not suffer us to become a naval power. Thus, we should be immediately involved in wars with them. The expenses, too, of maintaining a suitable navy would be enormous; and wholly disproportionate to our resources. If a navy should be provided at all, it ought to be limited to the mere protection of our trade. It was further urged, that the Southern states would share a large portion of the burthens of maintaining a navy, without any corresponding advantages.

§ 1190. With the nation at large these objections were not deemed of any validity. The necessity of a navy for the protection of commerce and navigation was not only admitted, but made a strong ground for the grant of the power. One of the great objects of the constitution was the encouragement and protection of navigation and trade. Without a navy, it would be utterly impossible to maintain our right to the fisheries, and our trade and navigation on the lakes, and the Mississippi, as well as our foreign commerce. It was one of the blessings of the Union, that it would be able to provide an adequate support and protection for all these important objects. Besides; a navy would be absolutely indispensable to protect our whole Atlantic frontier, in case of a war with a foreign maritime power. We should otherwise be liable, not only to the invasion of strong regular forces of the enemy; but to the attacks and incursions of every predatory adventurer. Our maritime towns might all be put under contribution; and even the entrance and departure from our own ports be interdicted at the caprice, or the hostility of a foreign power. It would also be our cheapest, as well as our best defence; as it would save us the expense of numerous forts and garrisons upon the sea-coast, which, though not effectual for all, would still be required for some purposes. In short, in a maritime warfare without this means of defence, our commerce would be driven from the ocean, our ports would be blockaded, our sea-coast infested with plunderers, and our vital interests put at hazard.

§ 1191. Although these considerations were decisive with the people at large in favour of the power, from its palpable necessity and importance to all the great interests of the country, it is within the memory of all of us, that the same objections for a long time prevailed with a leading party in the country, and nurtured a policy, which was utterly at variance with our duties, as well as our honour. It was not until during the late war with Great Britain, when our little navy, by a gallantry and brilliancy of achievement almost without parallel, had literally fought itself into favour, that the nation at large began to awake from its lethargy on this subject, and to insist upon a policy, which should at once make us respected and formidable abroad, and secure protection and honour at home. It has been proudly said by a learned commentator on the laws of England, that the royal navy of England hath ever been its greatest defence and ornament. It is its ancient and natural strength; the floating bulwark of the island; an army, from which, however strong and powerful, no danger can be apprehended to liberty. Every American citizen ought to cherish the same sentiment, as applicable to the navy of his own country.

Article 1, Section 8, Clause 14

To make Rules for the Government and Regulation of the land and naval Forces;

1

Records of the Federal Convention

[*2:330; Madison, 18 Aug.*]

"To make rules for the Government and regulation of the land & naval forces,"—added from the existing Articles of Confederation.

Mr. L. Martin and Mr. Gerry now regularly moved "provided that in time of peace the army shall not consist of more than   thousand men."

Genl. Pinkney asked whether no troops were ever to be raised untill an attack should be made on us?

Mr. Gerry. if there be no restriction, a few States may establish a military Govt.

Mr. Williamson, reminded him of Mr. Mason's motion for limiting the appropriation of revenue as the best guard in this case.

Mr. Langdon saw no room for Mr. Gerry's distrust of the Representatives of the people.

Mr. Dayton. preparations for war are generally made in peace; and a standing force of some sort may, for ought we know, become unavoidable. He should object to no restrictions consistent with these ideas.

The motion of Mr. Martin & Mr. Gerry was disagreed to nem. con.

[*2:570, 595; Committee of Style*]

To make rules for the government and regulation of the land and naval forces.

2

House of Representatives, Army Regulations Jan. 1806

Annals 15:326–27

The House went into a Committee of the Whole on the bill for establishing rules and articles for the government of the Armies of the United States.

The bill was taken up by sections.

On reaching the eighth article, which authorizes a court martial to punish with death or otherwise any one "who, being present at any mutiny or sedition, does not use his utmost endeavor to suppress the same, or coming to the knowledge of any intended mutiny, does not, without delay, give information thereof to his commanding officer," Mr. G. W. Campbell moved to strike out the words "death or otherwise."

Messrs. Varnum and Nelson opposed the motion, which was disagreed to without a division.

In a subsequent article, Mr. G. W. Campbell moved to strike out that part, which authorizes a court martial to punish with death any one who offers violence to his officer.

In support of this amendment, Mr. Campbell reprobated the idea of the lives of citizens being in the power of a court martial. He compared soldiers to mere machines, from the severity of the military law; he said almost every article in the bill was stained with blood; he drew a parallel between them and the civil penal laws; and that when men know how small offences subjected them to death, they would be deterred from or disgusted in serving their country.

Mr. SOUTHARD and Mr. COOK followed with similar observations and arguments, in favor of the amendment.

This was strenuously opposed by Mr. R. NELSON, Mr. SMILIE, Mr. MACON, and Mr. TALLMADGE.

These gentlemen represented the necessity of the bill standing as it had hitherto done in this respect. They drew a picture of the Army without discipline, where every soldier might think himself at his own disposal—of an army being ordered to attack the enemy, and an officer refusing, and drawing his sword on his commanding officer. The necessity of a code of laws for the military differing from the civil law was demonstrated; and having, by the law as it stands, gone through the Revolutionary war with success, and in peace found no ill consequence arising therefrom, they thought it neither prudent nor safe to adopt the amendment.

Mr. TALLMADGE said, that in the Revolutionary war, the disobedience of soldiers to their officers' commands, had, at one time gone to such a length as threatened a mutiny. The Adjutant General, Lee, was struck by a soldier on being ordered to do his duty. The commander ordered him to be tried by a general court martial. He was found guilty and sentenced to be shot. The army was drawn up, to attend the execution; upon the spot appointed for that purpose General Lee interceded in behalf of the soldier, who was, in consequence pardoned. This, however, produced a good effect in the army. Mr. TALLMADGE, brought forward other instances of danger, when soldiers were not subject to severe laws. Soldiers, he observed, were a description of men that must be ruled with severity—and though officers were invested with this authority, they were ever careful in exerting it. So far from it, that an officer had an esteem for the soldiers he commands—while the soldier himself, acting up to the tenor of his duty, respected his officer.

The question being now called for on Mr. CAMPBELL'S amendment, was lost. The affirmative only 20.

3

JOSEPH STORY, COMMENTARIES ON THE CONSTITUTION 3:§§ 1192–93
1833

§ 1192. The next power of congress is "to make rules for the government and regulation of the land and naval forces." This is a natural incident to the preceding powers to make war, to raise armies, and to provide and maintain a navy. Its propriety, therefore, scarcely could be, and never has been denied, and need not now be insisted on. The clause was not in the original draft of the constitution; but was added without objection by way of amendment. It was without question borrowed from a corresponding clause in the articles of confederation, where it was with more propriety given, because there was a prohibition of all implied powers. In Great Britain, the king, in his capacity of generalissimo of the whole kingdom, has the sole power of regulating fleets and armies. But parliament has repeatedly interposed; and the regulation of both is now in a considerable measure provided for by acts of parliament. The whole power is far more safe in the hands of congress, than of the executive; since otherwise the most summary and severe punishments might be inflicted at the mere will of the executive.

§ 1193. It is a natural result of the sovereignty over the navy of the United States, that it should be exclusive. Whatever crimes, therefore, are committed on board of public ships of war of the United States, whether they are in port or at sea, they are exclusively cognizable and punishable by the government of the United States. The public ships of sovereigns, wherever they may be, are deemed to be extraterritorial, and enjoy the immunities from the local jurisdiction belonging to their sovereign.

SEE ALSO:

Generally 1.8.12; 1.8.13; 1.8.15; Amend. V

Article 1, Section 8, Clause 15

To provide for calling forth the Militia to execute the Laws of the Union, suppress Insurrections and repel Invasions;

1

William Blackstone, Commentaries 1:395
1765

In a land of liberty it is extremely dangerous to make a distinct order of the profession of arms. In absolute monarchies this is necessary for the safety of the prince, and arises from the main principle of their constitution, which is that of governing by fear: but in free states the profession of a soldier, taken singly and merely as a profession, is justly an object of jealousy. In these no man should take up arms, but with a view to defend his country and it's laws: he puts not off the citizen when he enters the camp; but it is because he is a citizen, and would wish to continue so, that he makes himself for a while a soldier. The laws therefore and constitution of these kingdoms know no such state as that of a perpetual standing soldier, bred up to no other profession than that of war: and it was not till the reign of Henry VII, that the kings of England had so much as a guard about their persons.

2

Virginia Declaration of Rights, sec. 13
12 June 1776

13. That a well regulated militia, composed of the body of the people, trained to arms, is the proper, natural, and safe defence of a free state; that standing armies, in time of peace, should be avoided, as dangerous to liberty; and that, in all cases, the military should be under strict subordination to, and governed by, the civil power.

3

Delaware Declaration of Rights and Fundamental Rules, secs. 18–20
11 Sept. 1776

18. That a well regulated Militia is the proper, natural and safe Defense of a free Government.

19. That standing Armies are dangerous to Liberty, and ought not to be raised or kept up without the Consent of the Legislature.

20. That in all Cases and at all Times the Military ought to be under strict Subordination to and governed by the Civil Power.

4

JOHN ADAMS TO THOMAS JEFFERSON
26 May 1777
Cappon 1:5

I had this Morning, the Pleasure of your Favour of the Sixteenth inst, by the Post; and rejoice to learn that your Battallions, were so far fill'd, as to render a Draught from the Militia, unnecessary. It is a dangerous Measure, and only to be adopted in great Extremities, even by popular Governments. Perhaps, in Such Governments Draughts will never be made, but in Cases, when the People themselves see the Necessity of them. Such Draughts are widely different from those made by Monarchs, to carry on Wars, in which the People can see, no Interest of their own nor any other object in View, than the Gratification of the Avarice, Ambition, Caprice, Envy, Revenge, or Vanity of a Single Tyrant. Draughts in the Massachusetts, as they have been there managed, have not been very unpopular, for the Persons draughted are commonly the wealthiest, who become obliged to give large Premiums, to their poorer Neighbours, to take their Places.

5

RECORDS OF THE FEDERAL CONVENTION

[*1:54; Madison, 31 May*]

The last clause of Resolution 6. authorizing an exertion of the force of the whole agst. a delinquent State came next into consideration.

Mr. Madison, observed that the more he reflected on the use of force, the more he doubted the practicability, the justice and the efficacy of it when applied to people collectively and not individually.—, A Union of the States containing such an ingredient seemed to provide for its own destruction. The use of force agst. a State, would look more like a declaration of war, than an infliction of punishment, and would probably be considered by the party attacked as a dissolution of all previous compacts by which it might be bound. He hoped that such a system would be framed as might render this recourse unnecessary, and moved that the clause be postponed. This motion was agreed to nem. con.

[*1:61; McHenry, 31 May*]

And to call forth the force of the union against any member of the union failing to fulfil its duty under the articles thereof.

postponed.

Mr. E. Gery thought this clause "ought to be expressed so as the people might not understand it to prevent their being alarmed".

This idea rejected on account of its *artifice*, and because the system without such a declaration gave the government the means to secure itself.

[*1:245; Madison, 15 June*]

6. . . . that if any State, or any body of men in any State shall oppose or prevent ye. carrying into execution such acts or treaties, the federal Executive shall be authorized to call forth ye power of the Confederated States, or so much thereof as may be necessary to enforce and compel an obedience to such Acts, or an Observance of such Treaties.

[*2:382; Journal, 23 Aug.*]

It was moved and seconded to strike the following words out of the 18 clause of the 1st section 7 article

"enforce treaties"

which passed in the affirmative

It was moved and seconded to alter the first part of the 18 clause of the 1st section, 7 article to read

"To provide for calling forth the militia to execute the laws "of the Union, suppress insurrections, and repel invasions"

which passed in the affirmative

On the question to agree to the 18th clause of the 1st section, 7 article, as amended

it passed in the affirmative.

6

BRUTUS, NO. 4
29 Nov. 1787
Storing 2.9.50

If then this government should not derive support from the good will of the people, it must be executed by force, or not executed at all; either case would lead to the total destruction of liberty.—The convention seemed aware of this, and have therefore provided for calling out the militia to execute the laws of the union. If this system was so framed as to command that respect from the people, which every good free government will obtain, this provision was unnecessary—the people would support the civil magistrate. This power is a novel one, in free governments—these have depended for the execution of the laws on the Posse Comitatus, and never raised an idea, that the people would refuse to aid the civil magistrate in executing those laws they themselves had made.

7

JAMES WILSON, PENNSYLVANIA RATIFYING CONVENTION
11 Dec. 1787
Elliot 2:521–22

It is said that Congress should not possess the power of calling out the militia, to execute the laws of the Union, suppress insurrections, and repel invasions; nor the President have the command of them when called out for such purposes.

I believe any gentleman, who possesses military experience, will inform you that men without a uniformity of arms, accoutrements, and discipline, are no more than a mob in a camp; that, in the field, instead of assisting, they interfere with one another. If a soldier drops his musket, and his companion, unfurnished with one, takes it up, it is of no service, because his cartridges do not fit it. By means of this system, a uniformity of arms and discipline will prevail throughout the United States.

I really expected that, for this part of the system at least, the framers of it would have received plaudits instead of censures, as they here discover a strong anxiety to have this body put upon an effective footing, and thereby, in a great measure, to supersede the necessity of raising or keeping up standing armies.

The militia formed under this system, and trained by the several states, will be such a bulwark of internal strength, as to prevent the attacks of foreign enemies. I have been told that, about the year 1744, an attack was intended by France upon Massachusetts Bay, but was given up on reading the militia law of the province.

If a single state could deter an enemy from such attempts, what influence will the proposed arrangement have upon the different powers of Europe?

In every point of view, this regulation is calculated to produce good effects. How powerful and respectable must the body of militia appear under general and uniform regulations! How disjointed, weak, and inefficient are they at present! I appeal to military experience for the truth of my observations.

8

LUTHER MARTIN, GENUINE INFORMATION
1788
Storing 2.4.60

This section proceeds further to give a power to the Congress to provide for the calling forth the militia, to execute the laws of the union, suppress insurrections and repel invasions. As to *giving such a power* there was no objection; but it was thought by some, that this power *ought* to be given with certain *restrictions.* It was thought that not more than a certain *part* of the militia of any one State, ought to be obliged to *march out* of the same, or be *employed out* of the same, at any *one time,* without the consent of the legislature of such State. This *amendment* I endeavored to obtain; but it met with the same fate, which attended almost every attempt to *limit* the powers given to the general government, and *constitutionally* to guard against *their abuse,* it was not adopted. As it now stands, the Congress will have the power, if they please, to march the *whole* militia of Maryland to the *remotest* part of the union, and keep them in service as long as they think proper, without being in any respect *dependent* upon the *government of Maryland* for this *unlimitêd exercise of power over its citizens. All of whom,* from the *lowest* to the *greatest,* may, during such service, be *subjected* to *military* law, and *tied up* and *whipped* at the *halbert* like the *meanest* of *slaves.*

9

ALEXANDER HAMILTON, FEDERALIST, NO. 29, 181–87
9 Jan. 1788

The power of regulating the militia and of commanding its services in times of insurrection and invasion are natural incidents to the duties of superintending the common defence, and of watching over the internal peace of the confederacy.

It requires no skill in the science of war to discern that uniformity in the organization and discipline of the militia would be attended with the most beneficial effects, whenever they were called into service for the public defence. It would enable them to discharge the duties of the camp and of the field with mutual intelligence and concert; an advantage of peculiar moment in the operations of an army: And it would fit them much sooner to acquire the degree of proficiency in military functions, which would be essential to their usefulness. This desirable uniformity can only be accomplished by confiding the regulation of the militia to the direction of the national authority. It is therefore with the most evident propriety that the plan of the Convention proposes to empower the union "to provide for organizing, arming and disciplining the militia, and for governing such part of them as may be employed in the service of the United States, *reserving to the states respectively the appointment of the officers and the authority of training the militia according to the discipline prescribed by Congress.*"

Of the different grounds which have been taken in opposition to the plan of the Convention, there is none that was so little to have been expected, or is so untenable in itself, as the one from which this particular provision has been attacked. If a well regulated militia be the most natural defence of a free country, it ought certainly to be under the regulation and at the disposal of that body which is constituted the guardian of the national security. If standing armies are dangerous to liberty, an efficacious power over the militia, in the body to whose care the protection of the State is committed, ought as far as possible to take away the inducement and the pretext to such unfriendly institutions. If the foederal government can command the aid of the militia in those emergencies which call for the military arm in support of the civil magistrate, it can the better dispense with the employment of a different kind of force. If it cannot avail itself of the former, it will be obliged to recur to the latter. To render an army unnecessary will be a more certain method of preventing its existence than a thousand prohibitions upon paper.

In order to cast an odium upon the power of calling forth the militia to execute the Laws of the Union, it has been remarked that there is no where any provision in the proposed Constitution for calling out the POSSE COMITATUS to assist the magistrate in the execution of his duty; whence it has been inferred that military force was intended to be his only auxiliary. There is a striking incoherence in the objections which have appeared, and sometimes even from the same quarter, not much calculated to inspire a very favourable opinion of the sincerity or fair dealing of their authors. The same persons who tell us in one breath that the powers of the federal government will be despotic and unlimited, inform us in the next that it has not authority sufficient even to call out the POSSE COMITATUS. The latter fortunately is as much short of the truth as the former exceeds it. It would be as absurd to doubt that a right to pass all laws *necessary* and *proper* to execute its declared powers would include that of requiring the assistance of the citizens to the officers who may be entrusted with the execution of those laws; as it would be to believe that a right to enact laws necessary and proper for the imposition and collection of taxes would involve that of varying the rules of descent and alienation of landed property or of abolishing the trial by jury in cases relating to it. It being therefore evident that the supposition of a want of power to require the aid of the POSSE COMITATUS is entirely destitute of colour, it will follow that the conclusion which has been drawn from it, in its application to the authority of the federal government over the militia is as uncandid as it is illogical. What reason could there be to infer that force was intended to be the sole instrument of authority merely because there is a power to make use of it when necessary? What shall we think of the motives which could induce men of sense to reason in this manner? How shall we prevent a conflict between charity and judgment?

By a curious refinement upon the spirit of republican jealousy, we are even taught to apprehend danger from the militia itself in the hands of the federal government. It is observed that select corps may be formed, composed of the young and ardent, who may be rendered subservient to the views of arbitrary power. What plan for the regulation of the militia may be pursued by the national government is impossible to be foreseen. But so far from viewing the matter in the same light with those who object to select corps as dangerous, were the Constitution ratified, and were I to deliver my sentiments to a member of the federal legislature from this State on the subject of a militia establishment, I should hold to him in substance the following discourse:

"The project of disciplining all the militia of the United States is as futile as it would be injurious, if it were capable of being carried into execution. A tolerable expertness in military movements is a business that requires time and practice. It is not a day or even a week that will suffice for the attainment of it. To oblige the great body of the yeomanry and of the other classes of the citizens to be under arms for the purpose of going through military exercises and evolutions as often as might be necessary, to acquire the degree of perfection which would intitle them to the character of a well regulated militia, would be a real grievance to the people, and a serious public inconvenience and loss. It would form an annual deduction from the productive labour of the country to an amount which, calculating upon the present numbers of the people, would not fall far short of the whole expence of the civil establishments of all the States. To attempt a thing which would abridge the mass of labour and industry to so considerable an extent would be unwise; and the experiment, if made, could not succeed, because it would not long be endured. Little more can reasonably be aimed at with respect to the people at large than to have them properly armed and equipped; and in order to see that this be not neglected, it will be necessary to assemble them once or twice in the course of a year.

"But though the scheme of disciplining the whole nation must be abandoned as mischievous or impracticable; yet it is a matter of the utmost importance that a well digested plan should as soon as possible be adopted for the proper establishment of the militia. The attention of the government ought particularly to be directed to the formation of a select corps of moderate size upon such principles as will really fit it for service in case of need. By thus circumscribing the plan it will be possible to have an excellent body of well trained militia ready to take the field whenever the defence of the State shall require it. This will not only lessen the call for military establishments; but if circumstances should at any time oblige the government to form an army of any magnitude, that army can never be formidable to the liberties of the people, while there is a large body of citizens little if at all inferior to them in discipline and the use of arms, who stand ready to defend their own rights and those of their fellow citizens. This appears to me the only substitute that can be devised for a standing army; the best possible security against it, if it should exist."

Thus differently from the adversaries of the proposed constitution should I reason on the same subject; deducing arguments of safety from the very sources which they represent as fraught with danger and perdition. But how the national Legislature may reason on the point is a thing which neither they nor I can foresee.

There is something so far fetched and so extravagant in the idea of danger to liberty from the militia, that one is at a loss whether to treat it with gravity or with raillery; whether to consider it as a mere trial of skill, like the paradoxes of rhetoricians, as a disingenuous artifice to instill prejudices at any price or as the serious offspring of political fanaticism. Where in the name of common sense are our fears to end if we may not trust our sons, our brothers, our neighbours, our fellow-citizens? What shadow of danger can there be from men who are daily mingling with the rest of their countrymen; and who participate with them in the same feelings, sentiments, habits and interests? What reasonable cause of apprehension can be inferred from a power in the Union to prescribe regulations for the militia and to command its services when necessary; while the particular States are to have the *sole and exclusive appointment of the officers*? If it were possible seriously to indulge a jealousy of the militia upon any conceivable establishment under the Foederal Government, the circumstance of the officers being in the appointment of the States ought at once to extinguish it. There can be no doubt that this circumstance will always secure to them a preponderating influence over the militia.

In reading many of the publications against the Constitution, a man is apt to imagine that he is perusing some ill written tale or romance; which instead of natural and agreeable images exhibits to the mind nothing but frightful and distorted shapes—Gorgons Hydras and Chimeras dire—discoloring and disfiguring whatever it represents and transforming every thing it touches into a monster.

A sample of this is to be observed in the exaggerated and improbable suggestions which have taken place respecting the power of calling for the services of the militia. That of New-Hampshire is to be marched to Georgia, of Georgia to New Hampshire, of New-York to Kentuke and of Kentuke to Lake Champlain. Nay the debts due to the French and Dutch are to be paid in Militia-men instead of Louis d'ors and ducats. At one moment there is to be a large army to lay prostrate the liberties of the people; at another moment the militia of Virginia are to be dragged from their homes five or six hundred miles to tame the republican contumacy of Massachusetts; and that of Massachusetts is to be transported an equal distance to subdue the refractory haughtiness of the aristocratic Virginians. Do the persons, who rave at this rate, imagine, that their art or their eloquence can impose any conceits or absurdities upon the people of America for infallible truths?

If there should be an army to be made use of as the engine of despotism what need of the militia? If there should be no army, whither would the militia, irritated by being called upon to undertake a distant and hopeless expedition for the purpose of rivetting the chains of slavery upon a part of their countrymen direct their course, but to the seat of the tyrants, who had meditated so foolish as well as so wicked a project; to crush them in their imagined intrenchments of power and to make them an example of the just vengeance of an abused and incensed people? Is this the way in which usurpers stride to dominion over a numerous and enlightened nation? Do they begin by exciting the detestation of the very instruments of their intended usurpations? Do they usually commence their career by wanton and disgustful acts of power calculated to answer no end, but to draw upon themselves universal hatred and execration? Are suppositions of this sort the sober admonitions of discerning patriots to a discerning people? Or are they the inflammatory ravings of chagrined incendiaries or distempered enthusiasts? If we were even to suppose the national rulers actuated by the most ungovernable ambition, it is impossible to believe that they would employ such preposterous means to accomplish their designs.

In times of insurrection or invasion it would be natural and proper that the militia of a neighbouring state should be marched into another to resist a common enemy or to guard the republic against the violences of faction or sedition. This was frequently the case in respect to the first object in the course of the late war; and this mutual succour is indeed a principal end of our political association. If the power of affording it be placed under the direction of the union, there will be no danger of a supine and listless inattention to the dangers of a neighbour, till its near approach had superadded the incitements of self preservation to the too feeble impulses of duty and sympathy.

10

A [NEW HAMPSHIRE] FARMER, NO. 1
11 Jan. 1788
Storing 4.17.4

Standing armies are dangerous *in time of peace to the liberties of a free people*, provided they are kept and voted their continuance yearly, they soon get ingrafted into and become a part of the Constitution, therefore they ought not to be kept up, on any pretext whatsoever, any longer than till the enemy are driven from our doors. War is justifiable on no other principle than self-defence, it is at best a curse to any people; it is comprehensive of most, if not all the mischiefs that do or can afflict mankind; it depopulates nations; lays waste the finest countries; destroys arts and sciences, it many times ruins the best men, and advances the worst, it effaces every trace of virtue, piety and compassion, and introduces all kind of corruption in public affairs; and in short, is pregnant with so many evils, that it ought ever to be avoided if possible; nothing but self-defence can justify it. An army, either in peace or war, is like the locust and caterpillers of Egypt; they bear down all before them—and many times, by designing men, have been used as an engine to destroy the liberties of a people, and reduce them to the most abject slavery. I have both summered and wintered with an army: You, my friends, in general, know nothing of the evils that attend it; guard and secure it well in your Bill of Rights, that it may not be in the power of any set of men to trample your liberties under their feet with it. Organize your militia, arm them well, and under Providence they will be a sufficient security. I have once born arms in defence of my country;—I am now willing to risque myself and property, together with my liberties and privileges, (with a well regulated militia) and when they are invaded, I will gird on my sword and appear in their defence. And, if my children after me will not do it, let them loose theirs with their heads into the bargain.

11

Federal Farmer, no. 18
25 Jan. 1788
Storing 2.8.217

These corps, not much unlike regular troops, will ever produce an inattention to the general militia; and the consequence has ever been, and always must be, that the substantial men, having families and property, will generally be without arms, without knowing the use of them, and defenceless; whereas, to preserve liberty, it is essential that the whole body of the people always possess arms, and be taught alike, especially when young, how to use them; nor does it follow from this, that all promiscuously must go into actual service on every occasion. The mind that aims at a select militia, must be influenced by a truly anti-republican principle; and when we see many men disposed to practice upon it, whenever they can prevail, no wonder true republicans are for carefully guarding against it. As a farther check, it may be proper to add, that the militia of any state shall not remain in the service of the union, beyond a given period, without the express consent of the state legislature.

12

Luther Martin, Letters, no. 3
14 Mar. 1788
Essays 358–59

That a system may enable government wantonly to exercise power over the militia, to call out an unreasonable number from any particular state without its permission, and to march them upon, and continue them in, remote and improper services; that the same system should enable the government totally to discard, render useless, and even disarm, the militia, when it would remove them out of the way of opposing its ambitious views, is by no means inconsistent, and is really the case in the proposed constitution. In both these respects it is, in my opinion, highly faulty, and ought to be amended. In the proposed system the general government has a power not only without the consent, but contrary to the will of the state government, to call out the whole of its militia, without regard to religious scruples, or any other consideration, and to continue them in service as long as it pleases, thereby subjecting the freemen of a whole state to martial law and reducing them to the situation of slaves. It has also, by another clause, the powers by which only the militia can be organized and armed, and by the neglect of which they may be rendered utterly useless and insignificant, when it suits the ambitious purposes of government. Nor is the suggestion unreasonable, even if it had been made, that the government might improperly oppress and harass the militia, the better to reconcile them to the idea of regular troops, who might relieve them from the burthen, and to render them less opposed to the measures it might be disposed to adopt for the purpose of reducing them to that state of insignificancy and uselessness. When the Landholder declared that "I contended the powers and authorities of the new constitution must destroy the liberties of the people," he for once stumbled on the truth, but even this he could not avoid coupling with an assertion utterly false. I never suggested that "the same powers could be safely entrusted to the old Congress;" on the contrary, I opposed many of the powers as being of that nature that, in my opinion, they could not be entrusted to any government whatever consistent with the freedom of the states and their citizens, and I earnestly recommended, what I wish my fellow citizens deeply to impress on your minds, that in altering or amending our federal government no greater powers ought to be given than experience has shown to be necessary, since it will be easy to delegate further power when time shall dictate the expediency or necessity, but powers once bestowed upon a government, should they be found ever so dangerous or destructive to freedom, cannot be resumed or wrested from government but by another revolution.

13

Debate in Virginia Ratifying Convention
14 June 1788
Elliot 3:378–79

Mr. Clay wished to be informed why the Congress were to have power to provide for calling forth the militia, to put the laws of the Union into execution.

Mr. Madison supposed the reasons of this power to be so obvious that they would occur to most gentlemen. If resistance should be made to the execution of the laws, he said, it ought to be overcome. This could be done only in two ways—either by regular forces or by the people. By one or the other it must unquestionably be done. If insurrections should arise, or invasions should take place, the people ought unquestionably to be employed, to suppress and repel them, rather than a standing army. The best way to do these things was to put the militia on a good and sure footing, and enable the government to make use of their services when necessary.

Mr. George Mason. Mr. Chairman, unless there be some restrictions on the power of calling forth the militia, to execute the laws of the Union, suppress insurrections, and repel invasions, we may very easily see that it will produce dreadful oppressions. It is extremely unsafe, without some alterations. It would be to use the militia to a very bad purpose, if any disturbance happened in New Hampshire, to call them from Georgia. This would harass the people so much that they would agree to abolish the use of the militia, and establish a standing army. I conceive the general government ought to have power over the militia, but it ought to have some bounds. If gentlemen say that the militia of a neighboring state is not sufficient, the government ought to have power to call forth those of other states, the most convenient and contiguous. But in this case, the consent of the state legislatures ought to be had. On *real* emergencies, this consent will never be denied, each state being concerned in the safety of the rest. This power may be restricted without any danger. I wish such an amendment as this—that the militia of any state should not be marched beyond the limits of the adjoining state; and if it be necessary to draw them from one end of the continent to the other, I wish such a check, as the consent of the state legislature, to be provided. Gentlemen may say that this would impede the government, and that the state legislatures would counteract it by refusing their consent. This argument may be applied to all objections whatsoever. How is this compared to the British constitution? Though the king may declare war, the Parliament has the means of carrying it on. It is not so here. Congress can do both. Were it not for that check in the British government, the monarch would be a despot. When a war is necessary for the benefit of the nation, the means of carrying it on are never denied. If any unjust requisition be made on Parliament, it will be, as it ought to be, refused. The same principle ought to be observed in our government. In times of real danger, the states will have the same enthusiasm in aiding the general government, and granting its demands, which is seen in England, when the king is engaged in a war apparently for the interest of the nation. This power is necessary; but we ought to guard against danger. If ever they attempt to harass and abuse the militia, they may abolish them, and raise a standing army in their stead. There are various ways of destroying the militia. A standing army may be perpetually established in their stead. I abominate and detest the idea of a government, where there is a standing army. The militia may be here destroyed by that method which has been practised in other parts of the world before; that is, by rendering them useless—by disarming them. Under various pretences, Congress may neglect to provide for arming and disciplining the militia; and the state governments cannot do it, for Congress has an exclusive right to arm them, &c. Here is a line of division drawn between them—the state and general governments. The power over the militia is divided between them. The national government has an exclusive right to provide for arming, organizing, and disciplining the militia, and for governing such part of them as may be employed in the service of the United States. The state governments have the power of appointing the officers, and of training the militia, according to the discipline prescribed by Congress, if they should think proper to prescribe any. Should the national government wish to render the militia useless, they may neglect them, and let them perish, in order to have a pretence of establishing a standing army.

14

HOUSE OF REPRESENTATIVES, MILITIA
16, 21 Dec. 1790
Annals 2:1811–12, 1817–18

[*16 Dec.*]

Mr. HARTLEY observed, that the Constitution declares that the persons of members shall be privileged from arrest during their attendance on Congress; in going to, and returning from the session; with a special reference to the independence of the Legislature. He conceived that it would counteract the spirit of the Constitution to render the members liable to be called on to discharge duties incompatible in their nature; on this principle also, it would be in the power of a designing President, should such a character ever be elected, to prevent the members assembling by calling out individuals to attend military duties at the moment when their attendance would be necessary in Congress. The States individually, as well as the Parliament of Great Britain, have set us a good example in this respect.

Mr. BOUDINOT agreed in sentiment with Mr. HARTLEY, that the independence of the members was an important object. The ideas of the gentlemen from Virginia (Messrs. MADISON and GILES) that legislators ought to participate in the burthens imposed on others, ought never to be lost sight of—but in the present instance, the doctrine would be carried into practice; for at the end of every two years, the members would revert to the mass of citizens, and feel in common with others the influence of the laws. The business of legislation is more arduous and momentous than any other; and ought not to be impeded, or rendered liable to be frustrated by any other. This he thought would be the case by adopting the amendment.

Mr. MADISON supposed nothing would be risked by the amendment, as the Constitution had sufficiently secured the independence of the members. He had not anticipated so much debate on the motion. He was satisfied in his own mind of its propriety. The possible cases which had been stated did not, in his opinion, justify the violation of the great principle he had mentioned; but, to simplify the question, he would withdraw his motion, so far as only to propose to strike out from the exemptions, "the members of Congress."

[*21 Dec.*]

Mr. MADISON said, he conceived it would be necessary to pass a law authorizing a President of the United States to call out the militia, as the Constitution only says that he shall be commander-in-chief of the militia when in the service of the United States, without giving him the power of ordering it out.

Mr. FITZSIMONS wished a clause inserted in the bill, granting to the President that power.

Mr. BOUDINOT conceived it was not the intention of the Constitution that he should be possessed of such a power. It could only be granted to him by a special act of Congress.

Mr. SMITH read a law passed last session, and still in force, giving him that authority.

The sixteenth section, providing penalties for those not performing militia duty, and pointing out exemptions, being read,

Mr. SHERMAN moved to have it struck out. It was, he said, an absolute poll-tax, and not levied according to the number of inhabitants, which was in violation of the Constitution.

Mr. BURKE said, it was contrary to the interest of the militia to establish so many exemptions as had been provided. He gave notice that when the report came before the House, he would move for their reduction, and gave his reasons fully. It was contrary to the Constitution, he also observed, to lay a tax upon certain classes of citizens; not being consonant with the principles of justice to make those conscientiously scrupulous of bearing arms pay for not acting against the voice of their conscience. This, he said, was called the land of liberty, in it, we boasted, that no one suffered on account of his conscientious scruples, and yet we are going to make a respectable class of citizens pay for a right to a free exercise of their religious principles; it was contrary to the Constitution; it was contrary to that sound policy which ought to direct the House in establishing the militia.

Mr. JACKSON said, he certainly should oppose the principle started by the gentleman last up. Who are to know, he asked, what persons were really conscientiously scrupulous? There is no tribunal erected to make them swear to their scruples. If the principle were adopted, he conceived very few would be found, if their own word was to be taken, not conscientiously scrupulous. There were other sects, he said, besides the Quakers averse to bearing arms. If the principle be adopted of requiring no compensation from the exempted, it will lay the axe to the root of the militia, and, in his opinion, the bill might as well be postponed altogether. He did not choose to enter into the subject fully at this time; he would wait until the bill came before the House.

15

GEORGE WASHINGTON, ORDER CALLING UP THE MILITIA
7 Aug. 1794

Richardson 1:158–60

Whereas, combinations to defeat the execution of the laws levying duties upon spirits distilled within the United States and upon stills, have from the time of the commencement of those laws existed in some of the western parts of Pennsylvania. And whereas, the said combinations, proceeding in a manner subversive equally of the just authority of government and of the right of individuals, have hitherto effected their dangerous and criminal purpose, by the influence of certain irregular meetings, whose proceedings have tended to encourage and uphold the spirit of opposition, by misrepresentations of the laws calculated to render them obnoxious, by endeavours to deter those who might be so disposed from accepting offices under them, through fear of public resentment and injury to person and property, and to compel those who had accepted such offices by actual violence to surrender or forbear the execution of them, by circulating vindictive menaces against all those who should otherwise directly or indirectly aid in the execution of the said laws, or who, yielding to the dictates of conscience and to a sense of obligation, should themselves comply therewith, by actually injuring and destroying the property of persons who were understood to have so complied, by inflicting cruel and humiliating punishments upon private citizens for no other cause than that of appearing to be the friends of the laws, by intercepting the public officers on the highways, abusing, assaulting and otherwise ill-treating them, by going to their houses in the night, gaining admittance by force, taking away their papers and committing other outrages, employing for their unwarrantable purposes the agency of armed banditti, disguised in such manner as for the most part to escape discovery. And whereas, the endeavours of the legislature to obviate objections to the said laws, by lowering the duties and by other alterations conducive to the convenience of those whom they immediately affect (though they have given satisfaction in other quarters), and the endeavours of the executive officers to conciliate a compliance with the laws, by explanations, by forbearance, and even by particular accommodations founded on the suggestion of local considerations, have been disappointed of their effect by the machinations of persons whose industry to excite resistance has increased with every appearance of a disposition among the people to relax in their opposition and to acquiesce in the laws, insomuch that many persons in the said western parts of Pennsylvania have at length been hardy enough to perpetrate acts which I am advised amount to treason, being overt acts of levying war against the United States, the said persons having on the sixteenth and seventeenth of July last, proceeded in arms (on the second day amounting to several hundreds) to the house of John Neville, inspector of the revenue for the Fourth survey of the district of Pennsylvania, having repeatedly attacked the said house with the persons therein, wounding some of them, having seized David Lennox, marshal of the district of Pennsylvania, who previous thereto had been fired upon, while in the execution of his duty, by a party of armed men, detaining him for some time prisoner, till, for the preservation of his life, and the obtaining of his liberty, he found it necessary to enter into stipulations to forbear the execution of certain official duties, touching processes issuing out of a court of the United States, and having finally obliged the said inspector of the revenue and the said marshal, from considerations of personal safety, to fly from that part of the country, in order by a circuitous route to proceed to the seat of government, avowing as the motives of these outrageous proceedings an intention to prevent by force of arms the execution of the said laws, to oblige the said inspector of the revenue to renounce his said office, to withstand by open violence the lawful authority of the government of the United States, and to compel thereby an alteration in the measures of the legislature, and a repeal of the laws aforesaid. And whereas, by a law of the United States, entitled, "An act to provide for calling forth the militia to execute the laws of the Union, suppress insurrections and repel invasions," it is enacted that whenever the laws of the United States shall be opposed, or the execution thereof obstructed, in any state by combinations too powerful to be suppressed by the ordinary course of judicial proceedings, or by the powers vested in the marshals by that act, the same being notified by an associate justice or the district judge, it shall be lawful for the president of the United States to call forth the militia of such state to suppress such combinations, and to cause the laws to be duly executed. And if the militia of a state where such combinations may happen, shall refuse or be insufficient to suppress the same, it shall be lawful for the president, if the legislature of the United States shall not be in session, to call forth and employ such numbers of the militia of any other state or states, most convenient thereto, as may be necessary, and the use of the militia so to be called forth, may be continued, if necessary, until the expiration of thirty days after the commencement of the ensuing session: Provided always, that wherever it may be necessary in the judgment of the president to use the military force hereby directed to be called forth, the president shall forthwith and previous thereto, by proclamation, command such insurgents "to disperse and retire peaceably to their respective abodes within a limited time." And whereas, James Wilson, as associate justice, on the fourth instant, by writing under his hand, did, from evidence which had been laid before him, notify to me, "that in the counties of Washington and Alleghany, in Pennsylvania, laws of the United States are opposed, and the execution thereof obstructed by combinations too powerful to be suppressed by the ordinary course of judicial proceedings, or by the powers vested in the marshal of that district." And whereas, it is in my judgment necessary, under the circumstances of the case, to take measures for calling forth the militia, in order to suppress the combinations aforesaid, and to cause the laws to be duly executed, and I have accordingly determined so to do, feeling the deepest regret for the occasion, but withal the most solemn conviction, that the essential interests of the Union demand it, that the very existence of government, and the fundamental principles of social order, are materially involved in the issue; and that the patriotism and firmness of all good citizens are seriously called upon, as occasion may require, to aid in the effectual suppression of so fatal a spirit. Wherefore, and in pursuance of the proviso above recited, I, George Washington, President of the United States, do hereby command all persons, being insurgents as aforesaid, and all others whom it may concern, on or before the first day of September next, to disperse and retire peaceably to their respective abodes. And I do moreover warn all persons whomsoever, against aiding, abetting, or comforting the perpetrators of the aforesaid treasonable acts, and do require all officers and other citizens, according to their respective duties and the laws of the land, to exert their utmost endeavours to prevent and suppress such dangerous proceedings.

16

George Washington, Sixth Annual Address
19 Nov. 1794
Richardson 1:162–67

During the session of the year 1790 it was expedient to exercise the legislative power granted by the Constitution of the United States "to lay and collect excises." In a majority of the States scarcely an objection was heard to this mode of taxation. In some, indeed, alarms were at first conceived, until they were banished by reason and patriotism. In the four western counties of Pennsylvania a prejudice, fostered and imbittered by the artifice of men who labored for an ascendency over the will of others by the guidance of their passions, produced symptoms of riot and violence. It is well known that Congress did not hesitate to examine the complaints which were presented, and to relieve them as far as justice dictated or general convenience would permit. But the impression which this moderation made on the discontented did not correspond with what it deserved. The arts of delusion were no longer confined to the efforts of designing individuals. The very forbearance to press prosecutions was misinterpreted into a fear of urging the execution of the laws, and associations of men began to denounce threats against the officers employed. From a belief that by a more formal concert their operation might be defeated, certain self-created societies assumed the tone of condemnation. Hence, while the greater part of Pennsylvania itself were conforming themselves to the acts of excise, a few counties were resolved to frustrate them. It was now perceived that every expectation from the tenderness which had been hitherto pursued was unavailing, and that further delay could only create an opinion of impotency or irresolution in the Government. Legal process was therefore delivered to the marshal against the rioters and delinquent distillers.

No sooner was he understood to be engaged in this duty than the vengeance of armed men was aimed at *his* person and the person and property of the inspector of the revenue. They fired upon the marshal, arrested him, and detained him for some time as a prisoner. He was obliged, by the jeopardy of his life, to renounce the service of other process on the west side of the Allegheny Mountain, and a deputation was afterwards sent to him to demand a surrender of that which he *had* served. A numerous body repeatedly attacked the house of the inspector, seized his papers of office, and finally destroyed by fire his buildings and whatsoever they contained. Both of these officers, from a just regard to their safety, fled to the seat of Government, it being avowed that the motives to such outrages were to compel the resignation of the inspector, to withstand by force of arms the authority of the United States, and thereby to extort a repeal of the laws of excise and an alteration in the conduct of Government.

Upon the testimony of these facts an associate justice of the Supreme Court of the United States notified to me that "in the counties of Washington and Allegheny, in Pennsylvania, laws of the United States were opposed, and the execution thereof obstructed, by combinations too powerful to be suppressed by the ordinary course of judicial proceedings or by the powers vested in the marshal of the district." On this call, momentous in the extreme, I sought and weighed what might best subdue the crisis. On the one hand the judiciary was pronounced to be stripped of its capacity to enforce the laws; crimes which reached the very existence of social order were perpetrated without control; the friends of Government were insulted, abused, and overawed into silence or an apparent acquiescence; and to yield to the treasonable fury of so small a portion of the United States would be to violate the fundamental principle of our constitution, which enjoins that the will of the majority shall prevail. On the other, to array citizen against citizen, to publish the dishonor of such excesses, to encounter the expense and other embarrassments of so distant an expedition, were steps too delicate, too closely interwoven with many affecting considerations, to be lightly adopted. I postponed, therefore, the summoning the militia immediately into the field, but I required them to be held in readiness, that if my anxious endeavors to reclaim the deluded and to convince the malignant of their danger should be fruitless, military force might be prepared to act before the season should be too far advanced.

My proclamation of the 7th of August last was accordingly issued, and accompanied by the appointment of commissioners, who were charged to repair to the scene of insurrection. They were authorized to confer with any bodies of men or individuals. They were instructed to be candid and explicit in stating the sensations which had been excited in the Executive, and his earnest wish to avoid a resort to coercion; to represent, however, that, without submission, coercion *must* be the resort; but to invite them, at the same time, to return to the demeanor of faithful citizens, by such accommodations as lay within the sphere of Executive power. Pardon, too, was tendered to them by the Government of the United States and that of Pennsylvania, upon no other condition than a satisfactory assurance of obedience to the laws.

Although the report of the commissioners marks their firmness and abilities, and must unite all virtuous men, by shewing that the means of conciliation have been exhausted, all of those who had committed or abetted the tumults did not subscribe the mild form which was proposed as the atonement, and the indications of a peaceable temper were neither sufficiently general nor conclusive to recommend or warrant the further suspension of the march of the militia.

Thus the painful alternative could not be discarded. I ordered the militia to march, after once more admonishing the insurgents in my proclamation of the 25th of September last.

It was a task too difficult to ascertain with precision the lowest degree of force competent to the quelling of the insurrection. From a respect, indeed, to economy and the ease of my fellow-citizens belonging to the militia, it would have gratified me to accomplish such an estimate. My very reluctance to ascribe too much importance to the opposition, had its extent been accurately seen, would have been a decided inducement to the smallest efficient numbers. In this uncertainty, therefore, I put into motion 15,000 men, as being an army which, according to all human calculation, would be prompt and adequate in every view, and might, perhaps, by rendering resistance desperate, prevent the effusion of blood. Quotas had been assigned to the States of New Jersey, Pennsylvania, Maryland, and Virginia, the governor of Pennsylvania having declared on this occasion an opinion which justified a requisition to the other States.

As commander in chief of the militia when called into the actual service of the United States, I have visited the places of general rendezvous to obtain more exact information and to direct a plan for ulterior movements. Had there been room for a persuasion that the laws were secure from obstruction; that the civil magistrate was able to bring to justice such of the most culpable as have not embraced the proffered terms of amnesty, and may be deemed fit objects of example; that the friends to peace and good government were not in need of that aid and countenance which they ought always to receive, and, I trust, ever will receive, against the vicious and turbulent, I should have caught with avidity the opportunity of restoring the militia to their families and homes. But succeeding intelligence has tended to manifest the necessity of what has been done, it being now confessed by those who were not inclined to exaggerate the ill conduct of the insurgents that their malevolence was not pointed merely to a particular law, but that a spirit inimical to all order has actuated many of the offenders. If the state of things had afforded reason for the continuance of my presence with the army, it would not have been withholden. But every appearance assuring such an issue as will redound to the reputation and strength of the United States, I have judged it most proper to resume my duties at the seat of Government, leaving the chief command with the governor of Virginia.

Still, however, as it is probable that in a commotion like the present, whatsoever may be the pretense, the purposes of mischief and revenge may not be laid aside, the stationing of a small force for a certain period in the four western counties of Pennsylvania will be indispensable, whether we contemplate the situation of those who are connected with the execution of the laws or of others who may have exposed themselves by an honorable attachment to them. Thirty days from the commencement of this session being the legal limitation of the employment of the militia, Congress can not be too early occupied with this subject.

Among the discussions which may arise from this aspect of our affairs, and from the documents which will be submitted to Congress, it will not escape their observation that not only the inspector of the revenue, but other officers of the United States in Pennsylvania have, from their fidelity in the discharge of their functions, sustained material injuries to their property. The obligation and policy of indemnifying them are strong and obvious. It may also merit attention whether policy will not enlarge this provision to the retribution of other citizens who, though not under the ties of office, may have suffered damage by their generous exertions for upholding the Constitution and the laws. The amount, even if all the injured were included, would not be great, and on future emergencies the Government would be amply repaid by the influence of an example that he who incurs a loss in its defense shall find a recompense in its liberality.

While there is cause to lament that occurrences of this nature should have disgraced the name or interrupted the tranquillity of any part of our community, or should have diverted to a new application any portion of the public resources, there are not wanting real and substantial consolations for the misfortune. It has demonstrated that our prosperity rests on solid foundations, by furnishing an additional proof that my fellow-citizens understand the true principles of government and liberty; that they feel their inseparable union; that notwithstanding all the devices which have been used to sway them from their interest and duty, they are now as ready to maintain the authority of the laws against licentious invasions as they were to defend their rights against usurpation. It has been a spectacle displaying to the highest advantage the value of republican government to behold the most and the least wealthy of our citizens standing in the same ranks as private soldiers, preeminently distinguished by being the army of the Constitution—undeterred by a march of 300 miles over rugged mountains, by the approach of an inclement season, or by any other discouragement. Nor ought I to omit to acknowledge the efficacious and patriotic cooperation which I have experienced from the chief magistrates of the States to which my requisitions have been addressed.

To every description of citizens, indeed, let praise be given. But let them persevere in their affectionate vigilance over that precious depository of American happiness, the Constitution of the United States. Let them cherish it, too, for the sake of those who, from every clime, are daily seeking a dwelling in our land. And when in the calm moments of reflection they shall have retraced the origin and progress of the insurrection, let them determine whether it has not been fomented by combinations of men who, careless of consequences and disregarding the unerring truth that those who rouse can not always appease a civil convulsion, have disseminated, from an ignorance or perversion of facts, suspicions, jealousies, and accusations of the whole Government.

Having thus fulfilled the engagement which I took when I entered into office, "to the best of my ability to preserve, protect, and defend the Constitution of the United States," on you, gentlemen, and the people by whom you are deputed, I rely for support.

In the arrangements to which the possibility of a similar contingency will naturally draw your attention it ought not to be forgotten that the militia laws have exhibited such striking defects as could not have been supplied but by the zeal of our citizens. Besides the extraordinary expense and waste, which are not the least of the defects, every appeal to those laws is attended with a doubt on its success.

The devising and establishing of a well-regulated militia would be a genuine source of legislative honor and a perfect title to public gratitude. I therefore entertain a hope that the present session will not pass without carrying to its full energy the power of organizing, arming, and disciplining the militia, and thus providing, in the language of the Constitution, for calling them forth to execute the laws of the Union, suppress insurrections, and repel invasions.

17

Governor Caleb Strong to Justices of the Supreme Judicial Court of Massachusetts, and Reply

8 Mass. 548–51 (1812)

The Honorable the Justices of the Supreme Judicial Court of the Commonwealth of Massachusetts.

BOSTON, *August* 1, 1812.

GENTLEMEN,

Having laid before the council of this state a letter from the secretary of war of the 12th of June last, and letters dated June 22d, and July 15th, which I received from Major Gen. *Dearborn,* and also a letter which I have received from the secretary of war of July 21, 1812, requesting their advice what measures ought to be adopted in consequence of the requisition expressed in the said letters:—The council thereupon advised that, as upon important questions of law, and upon solemn occasions, the governor and council have authority by the constitution to require the opinions of the justices of the Supreme Judicial Court, it is advisable to request the opinion of the justices of that court on the following questions, *to wit:*—

1. Whether the commanders in chief of the militia of the several states have a right to determine whether any of the exigencies contemplated by the constitution of the *United States* exist, so as to require them to place the militia, or any part of it, in the service of the *United States,* at the request of the president, to be commanded by him, pursuant to acts of congress.

2. Whether, when either of the exigencies exist authorizing the employing of the militia in the service of the *United States,* the militia thus employed can be lawfully commanded by any officers but of the militia, except by the president of the *United States.*

In conformity with the foregoing advice of the council, I request you, gentlemen, to state to me your opinions on the questions above mentioned, as soon as conveniently may be. The secretary will deliver you herewith the letters above mentioned.

I am, gentlemen, with great respect,
Your most obedient servant,
CALEB STRONG.

To his Excellency the Governor, and the Honorable Council of the Commonwealth of Massachusetts.

The undersigned, justices of the Supreme Judicial Court, have considered the several questions proposed by your Excellency and Honors for their opinion.

By the constitution of this state, the authority of commanding the militia of the commonwealth is vested exclusively in the governor, who has all the powers incident to the office of commander in chief, and is to exercise them personally, or by subordinate officers under his command, agreeably to the rules and regulations of the constitution and the laws of the land.

While the governor of the commonwealth remained in the exercise of these powers, the federal constitution was ratified, by which was vested in the congress a power to provide for calling forth the militia, *to execute the laws of the Union, suppress insurrection, and repel invasions;* and to provide for governing such part of them as may be employed in the service of the *United States,* reserving to the states respectively the appointment of the officers. The federal constitution further provides that the president shall be commander in chief of the army of the *United States,* and of the militia of the several states when called into the actual service of the *United States.*

On the construction of the federal and state constitutions must depend the answers to the several questions proposed. As the militia of the several states may be employed in the service of the *United States* for the three specific purposes of executing the laws of the Union, of suppressing insurrections, and repelling invasions, the opinion of the judges is requested, whether the commanders in chief of the militia of the several states have a right to determine whether any of the exigencies aforesaid exist, so as to require them to place the militia, or any part of it, in the service of the *United States,* at the request of the president, to be commanded by him pursuant to acts of congress.

It is the opinion of the undersigned, that this right is vested in the commanders in chief of the militia of the several states.

The federal constitution provides, that when either of these exigencies exist, the militia may be employed, pursuant to some act of congress, in the service of the *United States;* but no power is given, either to the president, or to the congress, to determine that either of the said exigencies does in fact exist. As this power is not delegated to the *United States* by the federal constitution, nor prohibited by it to the states, it is reserved to the states respectively; and from the nature of the power, it must be exercised by those, with whom the states have respectively entrusted the chief command of the militia.

It is the duty of these commanders to execute this important trust agreeably to the laws of their several states respectively, without reference to the laws or officers of the *United States,* in all cases, except those specially provided for in the federal constitution. They must, therefore, determine when either of the special cases exist, obliging them to relinquish the execution of this trust, and to render themselves and the militia subject to the command of the president.

A different construction, giving to congress the right to determine when those special cases exist, authorizing them to call forth the whole of the militia, and taking them from the commanders in chief of the several states, and subjecting them to the command of the president, would place all the militia in effect at the will of congress, and produce a military consolidation of the states, without any constitutional remedy, against the intentions of the people, when ratifying the federal constitution. Indeed, since the passing of the act of congress of February 28th, 1795, vesting in the president the power of calling forth the militia, when the exigencies mentioned in the constitution shall exist; if the president has the power of determining when those exigencies exist, the militia of the several states is in fact at his command, and subject to his control.

No inconveniences can reasonably be presumed to result from the construction, which vests in the commanders in chief of the militia in the several states the right of determining when the exigencies exist, obliging them to place the militia in the service of the *United States.* These exigencies are of such a nature, that the existence of them can be easily ascertained by, or made known to the commanders in chief of the militia; and when ascertained, the public interest will induce a prompt obedience to the acts of congress.

Another question proposed to the consideration of the justices, is, whether, when either of the exigencies exist, authorizing the employing of the militia in the service of the *United States,* the militia thus employed can be lawfully commanded by any officer but of the militia, except by the president of the *United States.*

The federal constitution declares, that the president shall be the commander in chief of the army of the *United States.* He may undoubtedly exercise this command by officers of the army of the *United States,* by him commissioned according to law. The president is also declared to be the commander in chief of the militia of the several states, when called into the actual service of the *United States.* The officers of the militia are to be appointed by the states; and the president may exercise his command of the militia by the officers of the militia duly appointed. But we know of no constitutional provision, authorizing any officer of the army of the *United States* to command the militia, or authorizing any officer of the militia to command the army of the *United States.* The congress may provide laws for the government of the militia, when in actual service; but to extend this power to the placing of them under the command of an officer, not of the militia, except the president, would render nugatory the provision, that the militia are to have officers appointed by the states.

The union of the militia in the actual service of the *United States,* with the troops of the *United States,* so as to form one army, seems to be a case not provided for or contemplated in the constitution. It is therefore not within our department to determine on whom the command would devolve on such an emergency, in the absence of the president. Whether one officer, either of the militia, or of the army of the *United States,* to be settled according to military rank, should command the whole; whether the corps must be commanded by their respective officers, acting in concert as allied forces; or what other expedient should be adopted, are questions to be answered by others.

The undersigned regret, that the distance of the other justices of the Supreme Judicial Court renders it impracticable to obtain their opinions seasonably upon the questions submitted.

(SIGNED) THEOP. PARSONS.
SAMUEL SEWALL.
ISAAC PARKER.

18

JAMES MONROE TO CHAIRMAN OF SENATE MILITARY COMMITTEE
Feb. 1815
Writings 5:308–18

D. is a copy of a correspondence between the Governor of New Jersey and the Department of War relating to the appointment of the Governor of New York to the command of the military district No. 3. A copy of this correspondence is presented to communicate to the committee every circumstance that has occurred relating to the command of the militia in the service of the United States.

It appears by these documents that the Governors of Massachusetts, Connecticut & Rhode Island have objected to the requisitions made on the several States for parts of their respective quotas of militia on the following grounds: 1st., That the President has no right to make a requisition for any portion of the militia for either of the purposes specified by the Constitution unless the Executive of the State on whose militia such call is made admits that the case alleged exists, and approves the call. 2ndly. That when the militia of a State should be called into the service of the United States no officers of the regular army had a right to command them, or other person not an officer of the militia, except the President of the United States in person. These being the only difficulties which have arisen between the Executive of the United States and the Executive of any of the individual States relative to the command of the militia, known to the Department, are, it is presumed, those respecting which the Committee has asked information.

By these documents it is also shewn that certain portions of the militia were called out by the Executives of these States, and a part of them put into the service of the United States. These doctrines were nevertheless adhered to. I do not go into a detail on these points, deeming it unnecessary, as all the facts will be found in the documents.

Respecting as I do and always have done the rights of the individual States, and believing that the preservation of those rights, in their full extent, according to a just construction of the principles of our Constitution, is necessary to the existence of our Union, and of free government in these States, I take a deep interest in every question which involves such high considerations. I have no hesitation however in declaring it as my opinion that the construction given to the Constitution by the Executives of these States is repugnant to its principles, and of dangerous tendency.

By the Constitution Congress has power to provide for calling forth the militia to execute the laws of the Union, suppress insurrections, and repel invasions. To provide for organizing, arming, and disciplining the militia, and for governing such part of them as may be employed in the service of the United States, reserving to the States respectively the appointment of the officers, and the authority of training the militia according to the discipline prescribed by Congress.

The President is likewise made Commander in Chief of the army and navy of the United States, and of the militia of the several States, when called into the actual service of the United States.

The power which is thus given to Congress by the people of the United States, to provide for calling forth the militia for the purposes specified in the Constitution, is unconditional. It is a complete power, vested in the National government, extending to all those purposes. If it was dependent on the assent of the Executives of the individual States it might be entirely frustrated. The character of the government would undergo an entire and radical change. The State Executives might deny that the case had occurred which justified the call, and withhold the militia from the service of the general government.

It was obviously the intention of the framers of the Constitution that these powers vested in the general government should be independent of the State authorities, and adequate to the end proposed. Terms more comprehensive than those which have been used cannot well be conceived. Congress shall have power to provide for calling forth the militia to execute the laws of the Union; what laws? All laws which may be constitutionally made. Whatever laws are adopted for that purpose within the great scope of that power, which do not violate the restraints provided in favor of the great fundamental principles of liberty, are constitutional, and ought to be obeyed. They have a right to provide for calling forth the militia to suppress insurrections. This right is also unqualified. It extends to every case of insurrection against the legitimate authority of the U. States. It may be said that the government may abuse its authority, and force the people into insurrection in defence of their rights. I do not think that this is a probable danger under our system, or that it is the mode of redress, even if such abuse should be practised, which a free people, zealous of their rights, ought to resort to. The right which they have to change their Representatives, in the legislative & executive branches of the government, at short intervals, and thereby the whole system of measures, if they should think proper, is an ample security against the abuse, and a remedy if it should occur.

Congress have also a right to provide for calling forth the militia to repel invasions. This right, by fair construction, is in my judgment, an exemplification of the power over the militia, to enable the government to prosecute the war with effect, and not a limitation of it, by strict construction, to the special case of the descent of the enemy on any particular part of our territory. War exists; the enemy is powerful; his preparations are extensive. We may expect his attacks in many quarters. Shall we remain inactive spectators of the dangers which surround us, without making the arrangements suggested by an ordinary instinctive foresight for our defence?

A regular army in sufficient extent may not exist. The militia is the principal resource. Is it possible that a free people would thus intentionally trammel a government which they had created for the purpose of sustaining them in their just rank, and in the enjoyment of all their rights as a nation, against the encroachments of other powers, more especially after they had experienced that reliance could not be placed on the States individually, and that without a general government thus endowed, their best interests would be sacrificed, and even their independence insecure?

A necessary consequence of so complete and absolute a restraint on the power of the general government over the militia would be to force the United States to resort to standing armies for all national purposes. A policy so fraught with mischief, and so absurd, ought not to be imputed to a free people in this enlightened age. It ought not, more especially, to be imputed to the good people of these States. Such a construction of the Constitution is, in my opinion, repugnant to their highest interests, to the unequivocal intention of its framers, and to the just and obvious import of the instrument itself.

The construction given to the Constitution by the Executive is sanctioned by legislative authority, by the practice of the government, and by the assent and acquiescence of all the States, since the adoption of the Constitution to the period of the late unhappy differences, respecting which the Committee has asked to be informed. By the law of 1795 the President is authorized to call forth the militia, for the purposes mentioned in the Constitution, by a direct application to the militia officers, without any communication with, or reference to the Executives of the individual States, and penalties are prescribed for carrying the law into effect, should resort to them be necessary. It merits attention, in regard to the question under consideration, that the power given to the President to call forth the militia, is not made dependent, by this law, on the fact of our invasion having actually occurred, but takes effect in case of an eminent danger of it. In the year 1795 the President of the United States, on the certificate of a Judge of the Supreme Court that an insurrection existed in the western parts of Pennsylvania, called out the militia of several of the States, including the militia of Pennsylvania, to suppress it, which call was obeyed. In this instance the assent of the governor of Pennsylvania to the existence of an insurrection was not asked. General Washington, who then held the office of Chief Magistrate, relied exclusively on the powers of the general government for the purpose. The opinion of the same Chief Magistrate of the power of the general government over the militia was also made known by another distinguished act of his administration. By a report from General Knox, the then Secretary of War to Congress, bearing date on the [blank] this doctrine is maintained to the utmost extent, and exemplifications of it insisted on, which prove that from the nature of our population the militia was the force which, in his judgment, ought principally to be relied on for all national purposes. See the instances under consideration. Powers are granted to Congress for specified purposes, in distinct terms. A right to carry powers thus granted into effect follows of course. The government to whom they are granted must judge of the means necessary for the purpose, subject to the checks provided by the system. It adopts a measure authorized, supervises its execution, & sees the impediments to it. It has a right to amend the laws to carry the power into effect. If any doubt existed on this point in any case, on general principles, and I see cause for none, it cannot in the present, a power having been explicitly granted to Congress by the Constitution to pass all necessary & proper laws for carrying into execution the powers which are vested in the general government. Equally unfounded, in my opinion, is the other objection of the Executives of the States above mentioned, that when the militia of a State is called into the service of the United States no officer of the regular army, or other person not a militia officer, except the President of the United States in person, has a right to command them.

When the militia are called into the service of the United States all State authority over them ceases. They constitute a part of the national force, for the time, as essentially as do the troops of the regular army. Like the regular troops, they are paid by the nation. Like them, their operations are directed by the same government. The circumstance that the officers of the militia are appointed by, and trained under the authority of the States individually (which must however be done according to the discipline prescribed by Congress) produces no effect on the great character of our political institutions, or on the character and duties of the militia, when called into the service of the United States.

That the President alone has a right to command the militia in person, when called into the service of the United States, and that no officer of the regular army can take the command in his absence, is a construction for which I can see nothing in the Constitution to afford the slightest pretext. Is it inferred from the circumstance that he is appointed Commander in Chief of the Militia when called into the service of the United States? The same clause appoints him Commander in Chief of the land & naval forces of the United States. Equally sound therefore would the inference be that no other person could command either the land or naval forces of the United States. In construction of law he is Commander in Chief tho' not present. His presence is not contemplated in either case. Equally necessary is it in the one as in the other. What has been the practice under the Constitution, commencing with the first Chief Magistrate, and pursuing it under his successors to the present time? Has any President ever commanded in person either the land or naval forces, or the militia? Is it not known that the power to do it is vested in him principally for the purpose of giving him control over militia & naval operations, being a necessary attribute of the Executive branch of the government? That altho' he might take the command of all the forces under it, no President has ever done it? That a provision for the actual command is an object of legislative regulation, and the selection of the person to whom committed, of Executive discretion?

Under the commander, all the officers of every species of service and corps, regular and militia, acting together take rank with common consent and perfect harmony according to an article of war sanctioned by the Constitution. By this the officers of the regular army take rank of those of the militia of the same grade, without regard to the dates of their commission, and officers of any and every grade of the militia take rank of all officers of inferior grade of the regular army. When these troops serve together they constitute but one national force. They are governed by the same articles of war. The details for detachment, guard, or any other service are made from them equally. They are in truth blended together as much as are the troops of the regular army when acting by themselves only.

The idea advanced by the Honble. Judges of Massachusetts that when the regular troops and militia act together, and are commanded by the President in person, who withdraws, there can be no chief commander of right, of either species of force, over the whole; but that the regulars and militia as implied may even be considered as allied forces, is a consequence of the construction for which they contend. It pushes the doctrine of State rights further than I have ever known it to be carried in any other instance. It is only in the case of powers who are completely independent of each other, and who maintain armies, and prosecute war against a common enemy for objects equally distinct, and independent, that this doctrine can apply. It does not apply to the case of one independent power, who takes into its service the troops of another, for then the command is always at the disposal of the power making War, and employing such troops, whether regular or militia. How much less does it apply to the case under consideration, where there is but one power, and one government, and the troops, whether regular or militia, tho' distinguished by shades of character, constitute but one people, and are in fact countrymen, friends & brethren.

The President is in himself no bond of union in that respect. He holds his station as Commander in Chief of the land and naval forces, and of the militia, under a constitution which binds together as one people, for that, and many other important purposes. His absence would not dissolve the bond. It would not revive discordant, latent claims, or become a signal for disorganization.

The judicious selection of the Chief Commander for any expedition, or important station, is an object of high interest to the nation. Success often depends on it. The right to do this appears to me to have been explicitly vested in the President, by the authority given to Congress to provide for calling forth the militia, organizing, arming, disciplining and governing them, when employed in the service of the United States, and by the powers vested in him as Chief Executive of the United States. The rights of that highly respectable and virtuous body of our fellow citizens are I am persuaded completely secured when the militia officers commanding corps are retained in their command, a Major-General over his division, a Brigadier over his brigade, a Colonel over his regiment and inferior officers in their respective stations.

These rights are not injured or affected by the exercise of the right of the Chief Magistrate, a right incident to the executive power, equally applicable to every species of force, and of high importance to the public, to appoint a commander over them of the regular army when employed in the service of the United States, if he should deem it expedient. The rights of the militia officers, and those of the general government, are strictly compatible with each other, there is no collision between them. To displace militia officers for the employment of regular, or to multiply commands of a separate character, especially of small bodies, for that purpose, would be improper.

19

MEADE v. DEPUTY MARSHAL

1 Marshall's C.C. 324 (C.C.D.Va. 1815)

The Constitution of the United States, gives power to congress, "to provide for calling forth the militia to execute the laws of the Union," &c.

In the execution of this power, it is not doubted, that congress may provide the means of punishing those who shall fail to obey the requisitions, made in pursuance of the laws of the Union, and may prescribe the mode of proceeding against such delinquents, and the tribunal before which such proceedings should be had. Indeed, it would seem reasonable to expect, that all the proceedings against delinquents, should rest on the authority of that power, which had been offended by the delinquency.

This idea must be retained, whilst considering the acts of congress. The first section of the act of 1795, authorizes the president, "whenever the United States shall be invaded, or be in imminent danger of invasion," &c., "to call forth such number of the militia of the state, or states, most convenient to the place of danger, or scene of action, as he may judge necessary, to repel such invasion, and to issue his orders for that purpose, to such officer, or officers of the militia, as he shall think proper."

The fifth section enacts, "That every officer, non-commissioned officer, or private of the militia, who shall fail to obey the order of the President of the United States, in any of the cases before recited, shall forfeit a sum, not exceeding one year's pay, and not less than one month's pay, to be determined and adjudged by a court martial."

The sixth section enacts, "That courts martial, for the trial of militia, shall be composed of militia officers only."

Upon these sections, depends the question, whether courts martial for the assessment of fines against delinquent militia-men, should be constituted under the authority of the United States, or of the state to which the delinquent belongs. The idea orginally suggested, that the tribunal for the trial of the offence, should be constituted by, or derive its authority from, the government against which the offence had been committed, would seem to require, that the court thus referred to in general terms, should be a court sitting under the authority of the United States. It would be reasonable to expect, if the power were to be devolved on the court of a state government, that more explicit terms would be used for conveying it. And it seems, also, to be a reasonable construction, that the legislature, when in the sixth section, providing a court martial for the trial of militia, held in mind the offences described in the preceding section, and to be submitted to a court martial. If the offences described in the fifth section, are to be tried by a court, constituted according to the provisions of the sixth section, then we should be led by the language of that section, to suppose, that congress had in contemplation a court formed of officers in actual service, since the provision that it should be composed "of militia officers only," would otherwise be nugatory.

This construction derives some aid from the act of 1814. By that act, courts martial for the trial of offences, such as that with which Mr. Meade is charged, are to be appointed according to the rules prescribed by the articles of war. The court in the present case, is not appointed according to those rules.

The only argument which occurs to me against this reasoning, grows out of the inconvenience arising from trying delinquent militia-men, who remain at home, by a court martial, composed of officers in actual service.

This inconvenience may be great, and well deserves the consideration of congress; but I doubt whether it is sufficient to justify a judge, in so construing a law, as to devolve on courts, sitting under the authority of the state, a power which, in its nature, belongs to the United States.

If, however, this should be the proper construction, then the court must be constituted according to the laws of the state.

On examining the laws of Virginia, it appears, that no court martial can be called for the assessment of fines, or for the trial of privates, not in actual service. This duty is performed by courts of inquiry, and a second court must sit to receive the excuses of those against whom a previous court may have assessed fines, before the sentence becomes final, or can be executed.

If it be supposed, that the act of congress has conferred the jurisdiction against delinquent militia privates on courts martial, constituted as those are for the trial of officers, still this court has proceeded in such a manner, that its sentence cannot be sustained.

It is a principle of natural justice, which courts are never at liberty to dispense with, unless under the mandate of positive law, that no person shall be condemned unheard, or without an opportunity of being heard. There is no law authorizing courts martial to proceed against any person, without notice. Consequently, such proceeding is entirely unlawful. In the case of the courts of inquiry, sitting under the authority of the state, the practice has, I believe, prevailed, to proceed in the first instance, without notice; but this inconvenience is, in some degree remedied, by a second court, and I am by no means prepared for such a construction of the act, as would justify rendering the sentence final, without substantial notice. But, be this as it may, this is a court martial, not a court of inquiry, and no law exists, authorizing a court martial to proceed without notice, as in this case, the court appears to have proceeded. For these reasons, I consider its sentences as entirely nugatory, and do, therefore, direct the petitioner to be discharged from the custody of the marshal.

20

HOUSTON V. MOORE

5 Wheat. 1 (1820)

February 16th, 1820. The judgment of the court was delivered at the present term, by WASHINGTON, Justice, who, after stating the facts of the case, proceeded as follows:—There is but one question in this cause, and it is, whether the act of the legislature of Pennsylvania, under the authority of which the plaintiff in error was tried, and sentenced to pay a fine, is repugnant to the constitution of the United States, or not? But before this question can be clearly understood, it will be necessary to inquire: 1. What are the powers granted to the general government, by the constitution of the United States, over the militia? and 2. To what extent they have been assumed and exercised?

1. The constitution declares, that congress shall have power to provide for calling forth the militia, in three specified cases: for organizing, arming and disciplining them; and for governing such part of them as may be employed in the service of the United States; reserving to the states, respectively, the appointment of the officers, and the authority of training the militia, according to the discipline prescribed by congress. It is further provided, that the president of the United States shall be commander of the militia, when called into the actual service of the United States.

2. After the constitution went into operation, congress proceeded, by many successive acts, to exercise these powers, and to provide for all the cases contemplated by the constitution. The act of the 2d of May 1792, which is reenacted almost *verbatim* by that of the 28th of February 1795, authorizes the president of the United States, in case of invasion, or of imminent danger of it, or when it may be necessary for executing the laws of the United States, or to suppress insurrections, to call forth such number of the militia of the states, most convenient to the scene of action, as he may judge necessary, and to issue his orders for that purpose, to such officer of the militia as he shall think proper. It prescribes the amount of pay and allowances of the militia so called forth, and employed in the

service of the United States, and subjects them to the rules and articles of war applicable to the regular troops. It then proceeds to prescribe the punishment to be inflicted upon delinquents, and the tribunal which is to try them, by declaring, that every officer or private who should fail to obey the orders of the president, in any of the cases before recited, should be liable to pay a certain fine, to be determined and adjudged by a court-martial, and to be imprisoned, by a like sentence, on failure of payment. The courts-martial for the trial of militia, are to be composed of militia officers only, and the fines to be certified by the presiding officer of the court, to the marshal of the district, and to be levied by him, and also to the supervisor, to whom the fines are to be paid over.

The act of the 18th of April 1814, provides, that courts-martial, to be composed of militia officers only, for the trial of militia, drafted, detached and called forth for the service of the United States, whether acting in conjunction with the regular forces or otherwise, shall, whenever necessary, be appointed, held and conducted in the manner prescribed by the rules and articles of war, for appointing, holding and conducting courts-martial for the trial of delinquents in the army of the United States. Where the punishment prescribed, is by stoppage of pay, or imposing a fine limited by the amount of pay, the same is to have relation to the monthly pay existing at the time the offence was committed. The residue of the act is employed in prescribing the manner of conducting the trial; the rules of evidence for the government of the court; the time of service, and other matters not so material to the present inquiry. The only remaining act of congress which it will be necessary to notice in this general summary of the laws, is that of the 8th of May 1792, for establishing an uniform militia in the United States. It declares who shall be subject to be enrolled in the militia, and who shall be exempt; what arms and accoutrements the officers and privates shall provide themselves with; arranges them into divisions, brigades, regiments, battalions and companies, in such manner as the state legislatures may direct; declares the rules of discipline by which the militia is to be governed, and makes provision for such as should be disabled whilst in the actual service of the United States. The pay and subsistence of the militia, whilst in service, are provided for by other acts of congress, and particularly by one passed on the third of January 1795.

The laws which I have referred to, amount to a full execution of the powers conferred upon congress by the constitution. They provide for calling forth the militia to execute the laws of the Union, suppress insurrections and repel invasion. They also provide for organizing, arming and disciplining the militia, and for governing such part of them as may be employed in the service of the United States; leaving to the states, respectively, the appointment of the officers, and the authority of training them according to the discipline prescribed by congress.

This system may not be formed with as much wisdom as, in the opinion of some, it might have been, or as time and experience may hereafter suggest. But to my apprehension, the whole ground of congressional legislation is covered by the laws referred to. The manner in which the militia is to be organized, armed, disciplined and governed, is fully prescribed; provisions are made for drafting, detaching and calling forth the state *quotas*, when required by the president. The president's orders may be given to the chief executive magistrate of the state, or to any militia officer he may think proper; neglect or refusal to obey orders, is declared to be an offence against the laws of the United States, and subjects the offender to trial, sentence and punishment, to be adjudged by a court-martial, to be summoned in the way pointed out by the articles and rules of war; and the mode of proceeding to be observed by these courts, is detailed with all necessary perspicuity.

If I am not mistaken in this view of the subject, the way is now open for the examination of the great question in the cause. Is it competent to a court-martial, deriving its jurisdiction under state authority, to try, and to punish militia men, drafted, detached and called forth by the president into the service of the United States, who have refused, or neglected to obey the call?

In support of the judgment of the court below, I understand the leading arguments to be the two following: 1. That militia-men, when called into the service of the United States by the president's orders, communicated either to the executive magistrate, or to any inferior militia officer of a state, are not to be considered as being in the service of the United States, until they are mustered at the place of rendezvous. If this be so, then, 2d. The state retains a right, concurrent with the government of the United States, to punish his delinquency. It is admitted on the one side, that so long as militia are acting under the military jurisdiction of the state to which they belong, the powers of legislation over them are concurrent in the general and state government. Congress has power to provide for organizing, arming and disciplining them; and this power being unlimited, except in the two particulars of officering and training them, according to the discipline to be prescribed by congress, it may be exercised to any extent that may be deemed necessary by congress. But as state militia, the power of the state governments to legislate on the same subjects, having existed prior to the formation of the constitution, and not having been prohibited by that instrument, it remains with the states, subordinate nevertheless to the paramount law of the general government, operating upon the same subject. On the other side, it is conceded, that after a detachment of the militia have been called forth, and have entered into the service of the United States, the authority of the general government over such detachment is exclusive. This is also obvious. Over the national militia, the state governments never had, or could have, jurisdiction. None such is conferred by the constitution of the United States; consequently, none such can exist.

The first question then is, at what time, and under what circumstances, does a portion of militia, drafted, detached, and called forth by the president, enter into the service of the United States, and change their character from state to national militia? That congress might by law have fixed the period, by confining it to the draft; the order given to the chief magistrate or other militia officer of the state; to the arrival of the men at the place of rendezvous; or to any other circumstance, I can entertain no doubt. This would certainly be included in the more extensive powers of calling forth the militia, organizing, arming, disciplining and governing them. But has congress made any declaration on this subject, and in what manner is the will of that body, as expressed in the before-mentioned laws, to be construed? It must be conceded, that there is no law of the United States which declares, in express terms, that the organizing, arming and equipping a detachment, on the order of the president to the state militia officers, or to the militia-men personally, places them in the service of the United States. It is true, that the refusal or neglect of the militia to obey the orders of the president, is declared to be an offence against the United States, and subjects the offender to a certain prescribed punishment. But this flows from the power bestowed upon the general government to call them forth; and, consequently, to punish disobedience to a legal order; and by no means proves, that the call of the president places the detachment in the service of the United States. But although congress has been less explicit on this subject than they might have been, and it could be wished they had been, I am, nevertheless, of opinion, that a fair construction of the different militia laws of the United States, will lead to a conclusion, that something more than organizing and equipping a detachment, and ordering it into service, was considered as necessary to place the militia in the service of the United States. That preparing a detachment for such service, does not place it in the service, is clearly to be collected from the various temporary laws which have been passed, authorizing the president to require of the state executives to organize, arm and equip their state *quotas* of militia for the service of the United States. Because they all provide that the requisition shall be to hold such *quotas* in readiness to march at a moment's warning; and some, if not all of them, authorize the president to call into actual service any part, or the whole of said *quotas* or detachments; clearly distinguishing between the orders of the president to organize, and hold the detachments in readiness for service, and their entering into service.

The act of the 28th of February 1795, declares, that the militia employed in the service of the United States, shall receive the same pay and allowance as the troops of the United States, and shall be subject to the same rules and articles of war. The provisions made for disabled militia-men, and for their families, in case of their death, are, by other laws, confined to such militia as are, or have been, in actual service. There are other laws which seem very strongly to indicate the time at which they are considered as being in service. Thus, the act of the 28th of February 1795, declares, that a militia-man called into the service of the United States, shall not be compelled to serve more than three months, after his arrival at the place of rendezvous, in any one year. The 8th section of the act of the 18th of April 1814, declares, that the militia, when called into the service of the United States, if, in the president's opinion, the public interest requires it, may be compelled to serve for a term not exceeding six months, after their arrival at the place of rendezvous, in any one year; and by the 10th section, provision is made for the expenses which may be incurred by marching the militia to their places of rendezvous, in pursuance of a requisition of the president, and they are to be adjusted and paid in like manner as those incurred after their arrival at the rendezvous. The 3d section of the act of the 2d of January 1795, provides, that whenever the militia shall be called into the actual service of the United States, their pay shall be deemed to commence, from the day of their appearing at the place of battalion, regimental or brigade rendezvous, allowing a day's pay and ration for every fifteen miles from their homes to said rendezvous.

From this brief summary of the laws, it would seem, that actual service was considered by congress as the criterion of national militia; and that the service did not commence, until the arrival of the militia at the place of rendezvous. That is the *terminus a quo,* the service, the pay and subjection to the articles of war, are to commence and continue. If the service, in particular, is to continue for a certain length of time, from a certain day, it would seem to follow, almost conclusively, that the service commenced on that, and not on some prior day. And, indeed, it would seem to border somewhat upon an absurdity, to say, that a militia-man was in the service of the United States, at any time, who, so far from entering into it, for a single moment, had refused to do so, and who never did any act to connect him with such service. It has already been admitted, that if congress had pleased so to declare, a militia-man, called into the service of the United States, might have been held and considered as being constructively in that service, though not actually so; and might have been treated in like manner as if he had appeared at the place of rendezvous. But congress has not so declared, nor have they made any provision applicable to such a case; on the contrary, it would appear, that a fine to be paid by the delinquent militia-man, was deemed an equivalent for his services, and an atonement for his disobedience.

If, then, a militia-man, called into the service of the United States, shall refuse to obey the order, and is, consequently, not to be considered as in the service of the United States, or removed from the military jurisdiction of the state to which he belongs, the next question is, is it competent to the state to provide for trying and punishing him for his disobedience, by a court-martial, deriving its authority under the state? It may be admitted, at once, that the militia belong to the states, respectively, in which they are enrolled, and that they are subject, both in their civil and military capacities, to the jurisdiction and laws of such state, except so far as those laws are controlled by acts of congress constitutionally made. Congress has power to provide for organizing, arming and disciplining the militia; and it is presumable, that the framers of the constitution contemplated a full exercise of all these powers. Nevertheless, if congress had declined to exercise them, it was competent to the state governments to provide for organizing, arming and disciplining their respective militia, in such manner as they might think proper. But congress has provided for all these subjects, in the way which that body must have supposed the best calculated to promote the general welfare, and to provide for the national defence. After this, can the state governments enter upon the same ground—provide for the same objects, as they may think proper, and punish in their own way violations of the laws they have so enacted? The affirmative of this question is asserted by the defendant's counsel, who, it is understood, contend, that unless such state laws are in direct contradiction to those of the United States, they are not repugnant to the constitution of the United States.

From this doctrine, I must, for one, be permitted to dissent. The two laws may not be in such absolute opposition to each other, as to render the one incapable of execution, without violating the injunctions of the other; and yet, the will of the one legislature may be in direct collision with that of the other. This will is to be discovered, as well by what the legislature has not declared, as by what they have expressed. Congress, for example, has declared, that the punishment for disobedience of the act of congress, shall be a certain fine; if that provided by the state legislature for the same offence be a similar fine, with the addition of imprisonment or death, the latter law would not prevent the former from being carried into execution, and may be said, therefore, not to be repugnant to it. But surely the will of congress is, nevertheless, thwarted and opposed.

This question does not so much involve a contest for power between the two governments, as the rights and privileges of the citizen, secured to him by the constitution of the United States, the benefit of which he may lawfully claim. If, in a specified case, the people have thought proper to bestow certain powers on congress, as the safest depositary of them, and congress has legislated within the scope of them, the people have reason to complain, that the same powers should be exercised at the same time by the state legislatures. To subject them to the operation of two laws upon the same subject, dictated by distinct wills, particularly in a case inflicting pains and penalties, is, to my apprehension, something very much like oppression, if not worse. In short, I am altogether incapable of comprehending how two distinct wills can, at the same time, be exercised in relation to the same subject, to be effectual, and at the same time, compatible with each other. If they correspond in every respect, then the latter is idle and inoperative; if they differ, they must, in the nature of things, oppose each other, so far as they do differ. If the one imposes a certain punishment, for a certain offence, the presumption is, that this was deemed sufficient, and, under all circumstances, the only proper one. If the other legislature impose a different punishment, in kind or degree, I am at a loss to conceive, how they can both consist harmoniously together.

I admit, that a legislative body may, by different laws, impose upon the same person, for the same offence, different and cumulative punishments; but then it is the will of the same body to do so, and the second, equally with the first law, is the will of that body; there is, therefore, and can be, no opposition of wills. But the case is altogether different, where the laws flow from the will of distinct co-ordinate bodies. This course of reasoning is intended as an answer to what I consider a novel and unconstitutional doctrine, that in cases where the state governments have a concurrent power of legislation with the national government, they may legislate upon any subject on which congress has acted, provided the two laws are not in terms, or in their operation, contradictory and repugnant to each other.

Upon the subject of the militia, congress has exercised the powers conferred on that body by the constitution, as fully as was thought right, and has thus excluded the power of legislation by the states on these subjects, except so far as it has been permitted by congress; although it should be conceded, that important provisions have been omitted, or that others which have been made might have been more extended, or more wisely devised.

There still remains another question to be considered, which more immediately involves the merits of this cause. Admit, that the legislature of Pennsylvania could not constitutionally legislate in respect to delinquent militia-men, and to prescribe the punishment to which they should be subject, had the state court-martial jurisdiction over the subject, so as to enforce the laws of congress against these delinquents? This, it will be seen, is a different question from that which has been just examined. That respects the power of a state legislature to legislate upon a subject, on which congress has declared its will. This concerns the jurisdiction of a state military tribunal to adjudicate in a case which depends on a law of congress, and to enforce it.

It has been already shown, that congress has prescribed the punishment to be inflicted on a militia-man, detached and called forth, but who has refused to march; and has also provided that courts-martial for the trial of such delinquents, to be composed of militia officers only, shall be held and conducted in the manner pointed out by the rules and articles of war. That congress might have vested the exclusive jurisdiction in courts-martial, to be held and conducted as the laws of the United States have prescribed, will, I presume, hardly be questioned. The offence to be punished grows out of the constitution and laws of the United States, and is, therefore, clearly a case which might have been withdrawn from the concurrent jurisdiction of the state tribunals. But an exclusive jurisdiction is not given to courts-martial, deriving their authority under the national government, by express words—the question, then (and I admit the difficulty of it), occurs, is this a case in which the state courts-martial could exercise jurisdiction?

Speaking upon the subject of the federal judiciary, the Federalist distinctly asserts the doctrine, that the United States, in the course of legislation upon the objects intrusted to their direction, may commit the decision of causes arising upon a particular regulation to the federal courts solely, if it should be deemed expedient; yet that in every case, in which the state tribunals should not be expressly excluded by the acts of the national legislature, they would, of course, take cognisance of the causes to which those acts might give birth. I can discover, I confess, nothing unreasonable in this doctrine; nor can I perceive any inconvenience which can grow out of it, so long as the power of congress to withdraw the whole, or any part of those cases, from the jurisdiction of the state courts, is, as I think it must be, admitted.

The practice of the general government seems strongly to confirm this doctrine; for at the first session of congress which commenced after the adoption of the constitution, the judicial system was formed; and the exclusive and concurrent jurisdiction conferred upon the courts created by that law, were clearly distinguished and marked; showing that, in the opinion of that body, it was not sufficient to vest an exclusive jurisdiction, where it was deemed proper, merely by a grant of jurisdiction generally. In particular, this law grants exclusive jurisdiction to the circuit courts of all crimes and offences cognisable under the authority of the United States, except where the laws of the United States should otherwise provide; and this will account for the proviso in the act of the 24th of February 1807, ch. 75, concerning the forgery of the notes of the Bank of the United States, "that nothing in that act contained should be construed to deprive the courts of the individual states of jurisdiction, under the laws of the several states, over offences made punishable by that act." A similar proviso is to be found in the act of the 21st of April 1806, ch. 49, concerning the counterfeiters of the current coin of the United States. It is clear, that, in the opinion of congress, this saving was necessary, in order to authorize the exercise of concurrent jurisdiction by the state courts over those offences; and there can be very little doubt, but that this opinion was well founded. The judiciary act had vested in the federal courts exclusive jurisdiction of all offences cognisable under the authority of the United States, unless where the laws of the United States should otherwise direct. The states could not, therefore, exercise a concurrent jurisdiction in those cases, without coming into direct collision with the laws of congress. But by these savings, congress did provide, that the jurisdiction of the federal courts, in the specified cases, should not be exclusive; and the concurrent jurisdiction of the state courts was instantly restored, so far as, under state authority, it could be exercised by them.

There are many other acts of congress which permit jurisdiction over the offences therein described, to be exercised by state magistrates and courts; not, I presume, because such permission was considered to be necessary, under the constitution, in order to vest a concurrent jurisdiction in those tribunals; but because, without it, the jurisdiction was exclusively vested in the national courts, by the judiciary act, and consequently, could not be otherwise exercised by the state courts. For I hold it to be perfectly clear, that congress cannot confer jurisdiction upon any courts, but such as exist under the constitution and laws of the United States, although the state courts may exercise jurisdiction on cases authorized by the laws of the state, and not prohibited by the exclusive jurisdiction of the federal courts.

What, then, is the real object of the law of Pennsylvania which we are considering? I answer, to confer authority upon a state court-martial to enforce the laws of the United States against delinquent militia-men, who had disobeyed the call of the president to enter into the service of the United States, for, except the provisions for vesting this jurisdiction in such a court, this act is, in substance, a re-enactment of the acts of congress, as to the description of the offence, the nature and extent of the punishment, and the collection and appropriation of the fines imposed.

Why might not this court-martial exercise the authority thus vested in it by this law? As to crimes and offences against the United States, the law of congress had vested the cognisance of them, exclusively in the federal courts. The state courts, therefore, could exercise no jurisdiction whatever over such offences, unless where, in particular cases, other laws of the United States had otherwise provided, and wherever such provision was made, the claim of exclusive jurisdiction to the particular cases was withdrawn by the United States, and the concurrent jurisdiction of the state courts was *eo instanti* restored, not by way of grant from the national government, but by the removal of a disability before imposed upon the state tribunals.

But military offences are not included in the act of congress, conferring jurisdiction upon the circuit and district courts; no person has ever contended that such offences are cognisable before the common-law courts. The militia laws have, therefore, provided, that the offence of disobedience to the president's call upon the militia, shall be cognisable by a court-martial of the United States; but an exclusive cognisance is not conferred upon that court, as it had been upon the common-law courts, as to other offences, by the judiciary act. It follows, then, as I conceive, that jurisdiction over this offence remains to be concurrently exercised by the national and state courts-martial, since it is authorized by the laws of the state, and not prohibited by those of the United States. Where is the repugnance of the one law to the other? The jurisdiction was clearly concurrent over militia-men, not engaged in the service of the United States; and the acts of congress have not disturbed this state of things, by asserting an exclusive jurisdiction. They certainly have not done so, in terms; and I do not think, that it can be made out, by any fair construction of them. The act of 1795 merely declares, that this offence shall be tried by a court-martial. This was clearly not exclusive; but on the contrary, it would seem to import, that such court might be held under national or state authority.

The act of 1814 does not render the jurisdiction necessarily exclusive. It provides, that courts-martial, for the trial of militia, drafted and called forth, shall, when necessary, be appointed, held and conducted, in the manner prescribed by the rules of war. If the mere assignment of jurisdiction to a particular court, does not necessarily render it exclusive, as I have already endeavored to prove, then it would follow, that this law can have no such effect; unless, indeed, there is a difference in this respect between the same language, when applied to military, and to civil courts; and if there be a difference, I have not been able to perceive it. But the law uses the expression "when necessary." How is this to be understood? It may mean, I acknowledge, whenever, there are delinquents to try; but, surely, if it import no more than this, it was very unnecessarily used, since it would have been sufficient, to say, that, courts-martial for the trial of militia called into service, should be formed and conducted in the manner prescribed by the law. The act of 1795 had declared who were liable to be tried, but had not said, with precision, before what court the trial should be had. This act describes the court; and the two laws being construed together, would seem to mean that every such delinquent as is described in the act of 1795, should pay a certain fine, to be determined and adjudged by a court-martial to be composed of militia officers, to be appointed and conducted in the manner prescribed by the articles of war. These words, when necessary, have no definite meaning, if they are confined to the existence of cases for trial before the court. But if they be construed (as I think they ought to be), to applied to trials rendered necessary by the omission of the states to provide for state courts-martial to exercise a jurisdiction in the case, or of such courts to take cognisance of them, when so authorized, they have an important, and a useful meaning. If the state court-martial proceeds to take cognisance of the cases, it may not appear necessary to the proper officer in the service of the United States, to summon a court to try the same cases; if they do not, or for want of authority cannot try them, then it may be deemed necessary to convene a court-martial, under the articles of war, to take and to exercise the jurisdiction.

There are two objections which were made by the plaintiff's counsel, to the exercise of jurisdiction in this case, by the state court-martial, which remain to be noticed.

1. It was contended, that if the exercise of this jurisdiction be admitted, that the sentence of the court would either oust the jurisdiction of the United States court-martial, or might subject the accused to be twice tried for the same offence. To this, I answer, that, if the jurisdiction of the two courts be concurrent, the sentence of either court, either of conviction or acquittal, might be pleaded in bar of the prosecution before the other, as much so as the judgment of a state court, in a civil case of concurrent jurisdiction, may be pleaded in bar of an action for the same cause, instituted in a circuit court of the United States.

Another objection is, that if the state court-martial had authority to try these men, the governor of that state, in case of conviction, might have pardoned them. I am by no means satisfied, that he could have done so; but if he could, this would only furnish a reason why congress should vest the jurisdiction in these cases, exclusively in a court martial acting under the authority of the United States.

Upon the whole, I am of opinion, after the most laborious examination of this delicate question, that the state court-martial had a concurrent jurisdiction with the tribunal pointed out by the acts of congress, to try a militia-man who had disobeyed the call of the president, and to enforce the laws of congress against such delinquent; and that this authority will remain to be so exercised, until it shall please congress to vest it exclusively elsewhere, or until the state of Pennsylvania shall withdraw from their court-martial the authority to take such jurisdiction. At all events, this is not one of those clear cases of repugnance to the constitution of the United States, where I shall feel myself at liberty to declare the law to be unconstitutional; the sentence of the court *coram non judice;* and the judgment of the supreme court of Pennsylvania erroneous on these grounds.

Two of the judges are of opinion, that the law in question is unconstitutional, and that the judgment below ought to be reversed. The other judges are of opinion, that the judgment ought to be affirmed; but they do not concur in all respects in the reasons which influence my opinion.

JOHNSON, Justice.—It is not very easy to form a distinct idea of what the question in this case really is. An individual, having offended against a law of his own state, has been cited before a court constituted under the laws of that state, and there convicted and fined. His complaint is that his offence was an offence against the laws of the United States, that he is liable to be punished under those laws, and cannot, therefore, be constitutionally punished under the laws of his own state.

If any right, secured to him under the state constitution, has been violated, it is not our affair. His complaint before this court must be either that some law, or some constitutional provision, of the United States, has been violated in this instance; or he must seek elsewhere for redress. This court can relieve him only upon the supposition, that the state law under which he has been fined, is inconsistent with some right secured to him, or secured to the United States, under the constitution. Now, the United States complain of nothing; the act of Pennsylvania was a candid, spontaneous, ancillary effort, in the service of the United States; and all the plaintiff in error has to complain of is, that he has been punished by a state law, when he ought to have been punished under a law of the United States, which he contends he has violated.

I really have not been able to satisfy myself that it is any case at all for the cognisance of this court; but from respect for the opinion of others, I will proceed to make some remarks on the questions which have been raised in the argument.

Why may not the same offence be made punishable both under the laws of the states, and of the United States? Every citizen of a state owes a double allegiance; he enjoys the protection and participates in the government of both the state and the United States. It is obvious, that in those cases in which the United States may exercise the right of exclusive legislation, it will rest with congress to determine whether the general government shall exercise the right of punishing exclusively, or leave the states at liberty to exercise their own discretion. But where the United States cannot assume, or where they have not assumed, this exclusive exercise of power, I cannot imagine a reason why the states may not also, if they feel themselves injured by the same offence, assert their right of inflicting punishment also. In cases affecting life or member, there is an express restraint upon the exercise of the punishing power. But it is a restriction which operates equally upon both governments; and according to a very familiar principle of construction, this exception would seem to establish the existence of the general right. The actual exercise of this concurrent right of punishing, is familiar to every day's practice. The laws of the United States have made many offences punishable in their courts, which were and still continue punishable under the laws of the states. Witness the case of counterfeiting the current coin of the United States, under the act of April 21st, 1806, in which the state right of punishing is expressly recognised and preserved. Witness also the crime of robbing the mail, on the highway, which is unquestionably cognisable as highway-robbery under the state laws, although made punishable under those of the United States.

With regard to militia-men ordered into service, there exists a peculiar propriety in leaving them subject to the coercive regulations of both governments. The safety of each is so worked up with that of all the states, and the honor and peculiar safety of a particular state may so often be dependent upon the alacrity with which her citizens repair to the field, that the most serious mortifications and evils might result, from refusing the right of lending the strength of the state authority to quicken their obedience to the calls of the United States.

But it is contended, if the states can at all legislate or adjudicate on the subject, they may affect to aid, when their real object is nothing less than to embarrass, the progress of the general government. I acknowledge myself at a loss to imagine how this could ever be successfully attempted. Opposition, whether disguised or real, is the same thing. It is true, if we could admit, that an acquittal in the state courts could be pleaded in bar to a prosecution in the courts of the United States, the evil might occur. But this is a doctrine which can only be maintained, on the ground, that an offence against the laws of the one government, is an offence against the other government; and can surely never be successfully asserted in any instances but those in which jurisdiction is vested in the state courts by statutory provisions of the United States. In contracts, the law is otherwise. The decision of any court of competent jurisdiction is final, whatever be the government that gives existence to the court. But crimes against a government are only cognisable in its own courts, or in those which derive their right of holding jurisdiction from the offended government.

Yet, were it otherwise, I cannot perceive with what correctness we can, from the possible abuse of a power, reason away the actual possession of it in the states. Such considerations were only proper for the ears of those who established the actual distribution of powers between the states and the United States. The absurdities that might grow out of an affected co-operation in the states, with a real view to produce embarrassment, furnish the best guarantee against the probability of its ever being attempted, and the surest means of detecting and defeating it. We may declare defects in the constitution, without being justly chargeable with creating them; but if they exist, it is not for us to correct them. In the present instance, I believe the danger imaginary, and if it is not, it must pass *ad aliud examen.*

But whatever be the views entertained on this question, I am perfectly satisfied, that the individual in this case was not amenable to any law of the United States. Both that there was no law of the United States that reached his case, and that there was nothing done or intended to be done by the government of the United States, to bring him within their laws, before he reached the place of rendezvous.

It is obvious, that there are two ways by which the militia may be called into service; the one is under state authority, the other under authority of the United States. The power of congress over the militia is limited but by two reservations in favor of the states, viz., the right of officering and that of training them. When distributed by the states, under their own officers, the general government have the right, if they choose to exercise it, of designating both the officer and private who shall serve, and to call him forth or punish him for not coming. But the possession of this power, or even the passing of laws in the exercise of it, does not preclude the general government from leaning upon the state authority, if they think proper, for the purpose of calling the militia into service. They may command or request; and in the case before us, they obviously confined themselves to the latter mode. Indeed, extensive as their power over the militia is, the United States are obviously intended to be made in some measure dependent upon the states for the aid of this species of force. For, if the states will not officer or train their men, there is no power given to congress to supply the deficiency.

The method of calling forth the militia, by requisition, is, it is believed, the only one hitherto resorted to in any instance. Being partially dependent upon the integrity of the states, the general government has hitherto been satisfied to rest wholly on that integrity, and, except in very few instances, has never been disappointed. The compulsory power has been, in its practice, held in reserve, as only intended for use when the other shall fail. Historically, it is known, that the act of 1795 was passed with a view to a state of things then existing in the interior of Pennsylvania, when it became probable that the president of the United States would have to exert the authority of the general government immediately on detached portions of the officers or militia of the Union, to aid in the execution of the laws of the United States. And instances may still occur, in which the exercise of that power may become necessary for the same purpose. But whenever bodies of militia have been called forth, for the purpose of general defence, it is believed, that in no instance has it been done otherwise than by requisition, the only mode practised towards the states from the commencement of the revolution to the present day. That it was the mode intended to be pursued in this case, is obvious from the perusal of the letter of the secretary of war to the governor of Pennsylvania.* The words made use of are: "The president has deemed it advisable to invite the executives of certain states to organize," &c.: Words which no military man would construe into a military command.

It is true, that this letter also refers to the acts of 1795 and 1814, as the authority under which the requisition is made, and the act of 1795 authorises the president to issue his order for that purpose: but this makes no difference in the case; it only leaves him the power of proceeding by order, if he thinks proper, without enjoining that mode, or depriving him of the option to pursue the other mode, so long as the principles upon which the states acted were such as to render it advisable. Or, if the construction be otherwise, the result only will be, that the president has not pursued the mode pointed out by that act, and therefore, has not brought the case within it.

But suppose the letter of the secretary of war was intended by him to operate as an order (although I cannot believe that congress ever intended an order should issue immediately to the governor of a state), how is this individual made punishable under the acts of 1795 and 1814?

The doctrine must be admitted, that congress might, if they thought proper, have authorized the issuing of the president's order, even to the governor. For when the constitution of Pennsylvania makes her governor commander-in-chief of the militia, it must subject him, in that capacity (at least, when in actual service), to the orders of him who is made commander-in-chief of all the militia of the Union. Yet if he is to be addressed in that capacity, and not as the general organ or representative of the state sovereignty, surely he has a right to be apprised of it. But is he, then, to be charged as a delinquent? Where is the law that has provided, or can provide, a court-martial for his trial? And where is the law that would oblige him to consider such a letter as this, a military order? It would then seem somewhat strange, if he, to whom this letter was immediately addressed, received no order from the president, that one to whom his order was transmitted through fifty grades, should yet be adjudged to have disobeyed the president's order.

But the situation of the private in this case, is still more favorable. It must be recollected, we are now construing a penal statute. And the criminality of the person charged, depends altogether on the 5th section of the act of 1795. The 1st section of the act of 1814, makes no difference in this particular, inasmuch as it does no more than create a tribunal for the trial of crimes, and supposes the commission of such crimes to be against the provisions of some existing law. The command of the president, then, I hold to have been indispensable to the creation of an offence, under the 5th section of this act. But how the president could, in the actual state of things, have issued such a command to the private, consistently with the provisions of this act, it is not easy to show. For, by the section immediately preceding the 5th, it is provided, "that no officer, non-commissioned officer or private of the militia, shall be compelled to serve more than three months, after his arrival at the place of rendezvous, in any one year, nor more than in due rotation with every other able-bodied man of the same rank in the battalion to which he belongs." Now, what was meant by due rotation? and how was the president's order to reach the individual, without previously establishing this due rotation? I admit, that this rotation may have been established, through the aid of a state law; but it became indispensable, that such law should have been authorized or adopted by some law of congress; and there exists no law, that I know of, either authorizing or requiring the designation or distribution by the states, which this law contemplates. On a call of the whole militia, there would have been no difficulty; but in the case of a partial call, some designation, legally known to the president, became indispensable, before he could issue his orders with that precision which may well be required in a criminal prosecution. And this probably operated as forcibly as considerations of comity, in determining the government to proceed by the ancient mode of requisition, instead of addressing the executive of Pennsylvania in the language of command and authority; if, indeed (what I will not readily admit), the act was ever intended to apply to the case of an immediate order to the executive.

Pursuing the same course of reasoning a little further, we shall also be led to the conclusion, that neither could there be a court constituted by a law of the United States for the trial of this offender. I hold it unquestionable, that whenever, in the statutes of any government, a general reference is made to law, either implicitly or expressly, that it can only relate to the laws of the government making this reference. Now, the only act which it is pretended vests any court with jurisdiction of offences created by the 5th section of the act of 1795, as to persons not yet mustered into service, is the 1st section of the act of 1814. The 4th and 6th sections of the act of 1795, taken together, furnish courts-martial for the trial of offences committed by militia employed by the United States; and the act of 1814, I admit, was intended to act upon the offences of

*Letter from the Secretary of War to the Governor of Pennsylvania.

"War Department, July 4, 1814.

"Sir:—The late pacification in Europe offers to the enemy a large disposable force, both naval and military, and with it the means of giving to the war here, a character of new and increased activity and extent. Without knowing, with certainty, that such will be its application, and still less, that any particular point or points will become objects of attack; the president has deemed it advisable, as a measure of precaution, to strengthen ourselves on the line of the Atlantic; and (as the principal means of doing this will be found in the militia) to invite the executives of certain states to organize and hold in readiness for immediate service, a corps of ninety-three thousand, five hundred men, under the laws of the 28th of February 1795, and the 18th of April 1814. The inclosed detail will show your Excellency what, under this requisition, will be the *quota* of Pennsylvania. As far as volunteer uniform companies can be found, they will be preferred. The expediency of regarding (as well in the designations of the militia, as of their places of rendezvous) the points, the importance or exposure of which will be most likely to attract the views of the enemy, need but be suggested. A report of the organization of your *quota*, when completed, and of its place or places of rendezvous, will be acceptable. I have the honor to be, &c.

(Signed) John Armstrong."

"P. S.—The points to be defended by the *quota* from Pennsylvania, will be the shores of the Delaware, Baltimore and this city."

those who were not yet in actual service, but had been called into service. Can it, on any legal principle, be so construed as to answer the end proposed? The words are, "that courts-martial for the trial of militia, drafted, detached and called forth for the service of the United States, shall be appointed," &c. But how drafted, detached and called forth? Under the laws of the United States, or of Russia? For the laws of the states, unless adopted by congress, are no more the laws of the United States than those of any foreign power. There is nothing in this act or any other act, that designates the drafting, and detaching or calling forth, there expressed as the grounds of jurisdiction, as a drafting, &c., under the laws of a state. Nor would it have had such a drafting, &c., in view, if it was intended to provide for punishing offences against the provisions of the act of 1795; for, in that act, it is required to be a calling forth by the president, not by state authority. And this suggests the only reasonable exposition that can be given it, consistent with the principle, that it must be a drafting, detaching and calling forth under laws of the United States. If we can find a sensible and consistent exposition, we are bound to adopt it, as the only one intended.

I have no doubt, that under the powers given the president by the act of 1795, and under the restriction contained in the 4th section of that act, it was in the power of the president, to have issued orders to the adjutant-general of Pennsylvania, to bring into the field this *quota* of militia, and to have prescribed the manner in which they should be drafted and detached; and had this been done, everything would have been sensible and consistent, and the exigencies of both these laws would have been satisfied. It is obvious, that the act of 1814 recognises the construction, which makes the drafting and detaching, as necessary to precede the calling forth; and if the power to call forth existed in the president alone, it would seem, that the other subordinate, but necessary ancillary powers to which this act has relation, must have existed in him also, and could be exercised by him, or under his authority only. Under this view of the subject, I am of opinion, that a court-martial constituted under this act of April 18th, 1814, could not legally have tried this individual, because he was not drafted and detached, under the meaning of that act, taken in connection with the act of 1795. Neither, in my opinion, was the calling forth such as was in the contemplation of that act. In addition to the reasons already given for this opinion, exists this obvious consideration. The calling forth authorized by that act is to be expressed by an order from the president. It is disobedience to such an order alone, that is made punishable by that act. Now, though it be unquestionable, that this order may be communicated through any proper organ, yet it must be communicated to the individual, as an order from the president, or he is not brought within the enactment of the law, nor put on his guard against incurring the penalty. But, from first to last, the whole case makes out an offence against the orders of the governor of Pennsylvania. It does not appear, that the order communicated to the individual was made to assume the form of an order from the president; and how, in that case, he could have been held guilty of having violated an order from the president, it is not easy to conceive.

For these reasons, I am very clearly of opinion, that neither the United States, nor the plaintiff in error, can complain of the infraction of any constitutional right, if the state did constitute a court for trying offences against the laws of the United States, or ingraft those laws into its own code, and make offences against the United States punishable in its courts; that if the individual has any cause of complaint, it is between him and his own state government: and that even were it otherwise, the plaintiff in error does not make out such a case here; inasmuch as the general government could not have had it in contemplation, to bring into operation the penal provisions of the act of 1795, and if they had, that they did not pursue the steps indispensable for that purpose; therefore, that the court-martial by which the plaintiff in error was tried, was really acting wholly under the authority of state laws, punishing state offences.

But it is contended, that if the states do possess this power over the militia, they may abuse it. This is a branch of the exploded doctrine, that within the scope in which congress may legislate, the states shall not legislate. That they cannot, when legislating within that ceded region of power, run counter to the laws of congress, is denied by no one; but, as I before observed, to reason against the exercise of this power, from the possible abuse of it, is not for a court of justice. When instances of this opposition occur, it will be time enough to meet them. The present was an instance of the most honorable and zealous co-operation with the general government. The legislature of Pennsylvania, influenced, no doubt, by views similar to those in which I have presented the subject, saw the defects in the means of coercing her citizens into the service; and unwilling to bear the imputation of lukewarmness in the common cause, legislated on the occasion, just so far as the laws of the United States were defective, or not brought into operation. And to vindicate her disinterestedness, she even gratuitously surrenders to the United States the fines to be inflicted. To have paused on legal subtleties, with the enemy at her door, or to have shrunk from duty, under shelter of pretexts which she could remove, would have been equally inconsistent with her character for wisdom and for candor.

I will make one further observation, in order to prevent myself from being misunderstood. I have observed, that the governors of states, as military commanders, must be considered as subordinate to the president: I do not mean to intimate, nor have I the least idea, that the act of 1795 gives authority to the president to issue an order to a governor, in that capacity. I hold the opinion to be absurd; for he comes not within the idea of a militia officer, in the language of that act. If he is so, what is his grade? He will not be included under any title of rank, known to the laws of the United States, from the highest to the lowest. And how is he to be tried? What is his pay? What his punishment? An act which authorizes an order for militia, obviously authorizes a requisition. And if the purposes of the general government could as well be subserved, by depending on the state authority for calling out the militia, there was no reason against resorting to that authority for the purpose. But the power of ordering out the militia is an alternative given to the president, when the other is too circuitous, or likely to fail. In that case, the president may address himself to the executive; and having obtained through him the necessary information relative to the distribution and organization of the militia, may proceed, under his own immediate orders, to draft and detach the numbers wanted. And thus everything in the act becomes sensible, consistent and adequate to the purposes in view, with the sole defect intended to have been remedied by the 1st section of the act of 1814.

In this case, it will be observed, that there is no point whatever decided, except that the fine was constitutionally imposed upon the plantiff in error. The course of reasoning by which the judges have reached this conclusion are various, coinciding in but one thing, viz., that there is no error in the judgment of the state court of Pennsylvania.

21

JAMES KENT, COMMENTARIES 1:244–50 1826

Congress have authority to provide for calling forth the militia to execute the laws of the union, suppress insurrections, and repel invasions; and to provide for organizing, arming, and disciplining the militia, and for governing such part of them as may be employed in the service of the United States; reserving to the states respectively, the appointment of the officers, and the authority of training the the militia, according to the discipline prescribed by congress. The president of the United States is to be the commander of the militia when called into actual service. The act of 28th of February, 1795, authorized the president, in case of invasion, or of imminent danger of it, to call forth such number of the militia most convenient to the scene of action as he might judge necessary. The militia so called out are made subject to the rules of war, and the law imposes a fine upon every delinquent, to be adjudged by a court martial composed of militia officers only. These militia court martials are to be held and conducted in the manner prescribed by the articles of war, and the act of 18th of April, 1814, prescribes the manner of holding them.

During the last war, the authority of the president of the United States over the militia, became a subject of doubt and difficulty, and of a collision of opinion between the general government and the governments of some of the states. It was the opinion of the government of Connecticut, that the militia could not be called out, upon the requisition of the general government, except in a case declared, and founded upon the existence of one of the specified exigencies; that when called out, they could not be taken from under the command of the officers duly appointed by the states, or placed under the immediate command of an officer of the army of the United States. Nor could the United States lawfully detach a portion of the privates from the body of the company to which they belonged, and which was organized with proper officers. This would, in the opinion of the government of Connecticut, impair, and eventually destroy, the state militia. When the militia are duly called into the service of the United States, they must be called as militia furnished with proper officers by the state.

Similar difficulties arose between the government of the United States and that of the state of Massachusetts, on the power of the national government over the militia. Both those states refused to furnish detachments of militia for the maritime frontier, on an exposition of the constitution, which they deemed sound and just.

In Connecticut, the claim of the governor to judge whether the exigency existed, authorizing a call of the militia of that state, or any portion of it, into the service of the union, and the claim on the part of that state to retain the command of the militia, when duly ordered out, as against any subordinate officer of the army of the United States, were submitted to and received the strong and decided sanction not only of the governor and council of that state, but of the legislature itself. In Massachusetts, the governor consulted the judges of the supreme judicial court, as to the true construction of the constitution on these very interesting points. The judges of the supreme court, who were consulted, were of opinion, that it belonged to the governors of the several states to determine when any of the exigencies contemplated by the constitution of the United States existed, so as to require them to place the militia, or any part of it, in the service of the union, and under the command of the president. It was observed, that the constitution of the United States did not give that right, by any express terms, to the president or congress, and that the power to determine when the exigency existed, was not prohibited to the states, and that it was, therefore, as of course, reserved to the states. A different construction would place all the militia in effect at the will of congress, and produce a military consolidation of these states. The act of 28th February, 1795, vested in the president the power of calling forth the militia when any one of the exigencies existed, and if to that be superadded the power of determining when the *casus foederis* occurred, the militia would in fact be under the president's control.

As to the question how the militia were to be commanded, when duly called out, the judges were of opinion, that the president alone, of all the officers acting under the United States, was authorized to command them, and that he must command them as they were organized, under officers appointed by the states. The militia could not be placed under the command of any officer not of the militia, except that officer be the president of the United States. But the judges did not determine how the militia were to be commanded, in case of the absence of the president, and of a union of militia with troops of the United States; and whether they were to act under their separate officers, but in concert as allied forces, or whether the officer present who was highest in rank, be he of the militia or of the federal troops, was to command the whole, was a difficult and perplexing question, which the judges did not undertake to decide.

The president of the United States declared that these constructions of the constitutional powers of the general government over the militia were novel and unfortunate, and he was evidently and decidedly of a different opinion. He observed, in his message to congress on the 4th November, 1812, that if the authority of the United States to call into service and to command the militia, could be thus frustrated, we were not one nation for the purpose most of all requiring it. These embarrassing questions, and the high authority by which each side of the argument is supported, have remained to this day unsettled by the proper and final decision of the tribunal that is competent to put them to rest. The case of *Houston* v. *Moore,* is the only one in which the national command of the militia seems to have been at all a subject of judicial discussion, and that case does not touch the points at issue between the United States and the states of Massachusetts and Connecticut, though the opinion of one of the judges went far towards destroying the claims advanced on the part of those states. I do not wish to interfere in this place with vexed and undecided questions. My object, in the course of these elementary lectures, is to confine myself to a comprehensive and just survey of the principles of our government as they have been discussed, or as they have been practically explained and settled by competent authority. It may, however, be truly observed, that since the year 1812, when those questions were raised, many great and deeply interesting questions arising on the powers of the union, have been investigated and decided, and the progress of opinion, and the course of those decisions, have been in favour of a pretty liberal and enlarged construction of the constitution of the United States. The principles of the government, as now understood, would be much more favourable than they were in 1812, to the claim of the President of the United States, to judge exclusively and authoritatively *when* the militia were to be called out into the service of the union.

The case of *Houston* v. *Moore* settled some important questions arising upon the national authority over the militia. The acts of congress already referred to, and the act of 8th March, 1792, for establishing a uniform militia, were considered as covering the whole ground of congressional legislation over the subject. The manner in which the militia were to be organized, armed, disciplined and governed, was fully prescribed; provision was made for drafting, detaching and calling forth the state quotas, when requested by the president. His orders were to be given to the chief executive magistrate, or to any militia officer he might think proper. Neglect or refusal to obey his orders was declared to be a public offence, and subjected the offender to trial and punishment, to be adjudged by a court martial, and the mode of proceeding was perspicuously detailed.

The question before the Supreme Court of the United States was, whether it was competent for a court martial, deriving its jurisdiction under state authority, to try and punish militia men drafted, detached and called forth by the president into the service of the United States, and who had refused or neglected to obey the call. The court decided, that the militia, when called into the service of the United States, were not to be considered as being in that service, or in the character of national militia, until they were mustered at the place of rendezvous, and that until then, the state retained a right, concurrent with the government of the United States, to punish their delinquency. But after the militia had been called forth, and had entered into the service of the United States, their character changed from state to national militia, and the authority of the general government over such detachments was exclusive. Actual service was considered by congress as the criterion of national militia, and the place of rendezvous was the *terminus a quo* the service, the pay, and subjection to the articles of war were to commence. And if the militia, when called into the service of the United States, refuse to obey the order, they remain within the military jurisdiction of the state, and it is competent for the state to provide for trying and punishing them by a state court martial, to the extent and in the manner prescribed by the act of congress. The act of Pennsylvania of 1814, provided for punishing, by a state court martial, delinquent militia men, who were called into the service of the United States, and neglected or refused to serve; and they were to be punished by the infliction of the penalties prescribed by the act of congress, and such an act was held not to be repugnant to the constitution and laws of the United States. It was the lawful exercise of concurrent power, and could be concurrently exercised by the national and state courts martial, as it was authorized by the laws of the state, and not prohibited by those of the United States. It would remain to be so exercised, until congress should vest the power exclusively elsewhere, or until the states should divest their courts martial of such a jurisdiction. This was the decision, in the first instance, of the supreme court of Pennsylvania; and it was affirmed, on appeal, by the majority of the Supreme Court of the United States.

22

MARTIN v. MOTT

12 Wheat. 19 (1827)

February 2d. STORY, Justice, delivered the opinion of the court.—This is a writ of error to the judgment of the court for the trial of impeachments and the correction of errors of the state of New York, being the highest court of that state, and is brought here in virtue of the 25th section of the judiciary act of 1789, ch. 20. The original action was a replevin for certain goods and chattels, to which the original defendant put in an avowry, and to that avowry there was a demurrer, assigning nineteen distinct and special causes of demurrer. Upon a joinder in demurrer, the supreme court of the state gave judgment against the avowant; and that judgment was affirmed by the high court to which the present writ of error is addressed.

The avowry, in substance, asserts a justification of the taking of the goods and chattels, to satisfy a fine and forfeiture imposed upon the original plaintiff, by a court-martial, for a failure to enter the service of the United States as a militia-man, when thereto required by the president of the United States, in pursuance of the act of the 28th of February 1795, c. 101. It is argued, that this avowry is defective, both in substance and form; and it will be our business to discuss the most material of these objections: and as to others, of which no particular notice is taken, it is to be understood that the court are of opinion, that they are either unfounded in fact or in law, and do not require any separate examination.

For the more clear and exact consideration of the subject, it may be necessary to refer to the constitution of the United States, and some of the provisions of the act of 1795. The constitution declares, that congress shall have power "to provide for calling forth the militia, to execute the laws of the Union, suppress insurrections, and repel invasions:" and also "to provide for organizing, arming and disciplining the militia, and for governing such part of them as may be employed in the service of the United States." In pursuance of this authority, the act of 1795 has provided, "that whenever the United States shall be invaded, or be in imminent danger of invasion from any foreign nation or Indian tribe, it shall be lawful for the president of the United States to call forth such number of the militia of the state or states most convenient to the place of danger, or scene of action, as he may judge necessary to repel such invasion, and to issue his order for that purpose to such officer or officers of the militia as he shall think proper." And like provisions are made for the other cases stated in the constitution. It has not been denied here, that the act of 1795 is within the constitutional authority of congress, or that congress may not lawfully provide for cases of imminent danger of invasion, as well as for cases where an invasion has actually taken place. In our opinion, there is no ground for a doubt on this point, even if it had been relied on, for the power to provide for repelling invasions includes the power to provide against the attempt and danger of invasion, as the necessary and proper means to effectuate the object. One of the best means to repel invasions is to provide the requisite force for action, before the invader himself has reached the soil.

The power thus confided by congress to the president, is, doubtless, of a very high and delicate nature. A free people are naturally jealous of the exercise of military power; and the power to call the militia into actual service, is certainly felt to be one of no ordinary magnitude. But it is not a power which can be executed without a correspondent responsibility. It is, in its terms, a limited power, confined to cases of actual invasion, or of imminent danger of invasion. If it be a limited power, the question arises, by whom is the exigency to be judged of and decided? Is the president the sole and exclusive judge whether the exigency has arisen, or is it to be considered as an open question, upon which every officer to whom the orders of the president are addressed, may decide for himself, and equally open to be contested by every militia-man who shall refuse to obey the orders of the president? We are all of opinion, that the authority to decide whether the exigency has arisen, belongs exclusively to the president, and that his decision is conclusive upon all other persons. We think that this construction necessarily results from the nature of the power itself, and from the manifest object contemplated by the act of congress. The power itself is to be exercised upon sudden emergencies, upon great occasions of state, and under circumstances which may be vital to the existence of the Union. A prompt and unhesitating obedience to orders is indispensable to the complete attainment of the object. The service is a military service, and the command, of a military nature; and in such cases, every delay, and every obstacle to an efficient and immediate compliance, necessarily tend to jeopard the public interests. While subordinate officers or soldiers are pausing to consider whether they ought to obey, or are scrupulously weighing the evidence of the facts upon which the commander-in-chief exercises the right to demand their services, the hostile enterprise may be accomplished, without the means of resistance. If "the power of regulating the militia, and of commanding its services in times of insurrection and invasion, are (as it has been emphatically said they are) natural incidents to the duties of superintending the common defence, and watching over the internal peace of the confederacy" (Federalist, No. 29), these powers must be so construed as to the modes of their exercise, as not to defeat the great end in view. If a superior officer has a right to contest the orders of the president, upon his own doubts as to the exigency having arisen, it must be equally the right of every inferior officer and soldier; and any act done by any person in furtherance of such orders, would subject him to responsibility in a civil suit, in which his defence must finally rest upon his ability to establish the facts by competent proofs. Such a course would be subversive of all discipline, and expose the best-disposed officers to the chances of ruinous litigation. Besides, in many instances, the evidence upon which the president might decide that there is imminent danger of invasion, might be of a nature not constituting strict technical proof, or the disclosure of the evidence might reveal important secrets of state, which the public interest, and even safety, might imperiously demand to be kept in concealment.

If we look at the language of the act of 1795, every conclusion drawn from the nature of the power itself, is strongly fortified. The words are, "whenever the United States shall be invaded, or be in imminent danger of invasion, &c., it shall be lawful for the president, &c., to call forth such number of the militia, &c., as he may judge necessary to repel such invasion." The power itself is confided to the executive of the Union, to him who is, by the constitution, "the commander-in-chief of the militia, when called into the actual service of the United States," whose duty it is to "take care that the laws be faithfully executed," and whose responsibility for an honest discharge of his official obligations is secured by the highest sanctions. He is necessarily constituted the judge of the existence of the exigency, in the first instance, and is bound to act according to his belief of the facts. If he does so act, and decides to call forth the militia, his orders for this purpose are in strict conformity with the provisions of the law; and it would seem to follow as a necessary consequence, that every act done by a subordinate officer, in obedience to such orders, is equally justifiable. The law contemplates that, under such circumstances, orders shall be given to carry the power into effect; and it cannot, therefore, be a correct inference, that any other person has a just right to disobey them. The law does not provide for any appeal from the judgment of the president, or for any right in subordinate officers to review his decision, and in effect defeat it. Whenever a statute gives a discretionary power to any person, to be exercised by him, upon his own opinion of certain facts, it is a sound rule of construction, that the statute constitutes him the sole and exclusive judge of the existence of those facts. And in the present case, we are all of opinion, that such is the true construction of the act of 1795. It is no answer, that such a power may be abused, for there is no power which is not susceptible of abuse. The remedy for this, as well as for all other official misconduct, if it should occur, is to be found in the constitution itself. In a free government, the danger must be remote, since, in addition to the high qualities which the executive must be presumed to possess, of public virtue, and honest devotion to the public interests, the frequency of elections, and the watchfulness of the representatives of the nation, carry with them all the checks which can be useful to guard against usurpation or wanton tyranny.

This doctrine has not been seriously contested upon the present occasion. It was, indeed, maintained and approved by the supreme court of New York, in the case of *Vanderheyden* v. *Young,* 11 Johns. 150, where the reasons in support of it were most ably expounded by Mr. Justice SPENCER, in delivering the opinion of the court. But it is now contended, as it was contended in that case, that notwithstanding the judgment of the president is conclusive as to the existence of the exigency, and may be given in evidence as conclusive proof thereof, yet that the avowry is fatally defective, because it omits to aver that the fact did exist. The argument is, that the power confided to the president is a limited power, and can be exercised only in the cases pointed out in the statute, and therefore, it is necessary to aver the facts which bring the exercise within the purview of the statute. In short, the same principles are sought to be applied to the delegation and exercise of this power intrusted to the executive of the nation for great political purposes, as might be applied to the humblest officer in the government, acting upon the most narrow and special authority. It is the opinion of the court, that this objection cannot be maintained. When the president exercises an authority confided to him by law, the presumption is, that it is exercised in pursuance of law. Every public officer is presumed to act in obedience to his duty, until the contrary is shown; and, *a fortiori,* this presumption ought to be favorably applied to the chief magistrate of the Union. It is not necessary to aver, that the act which he might rightfully do, was so done. If the fact of the existence of the exigency were averred, it would be traversable, and, of course, might be passed upon by a jury; and thus the legality of the orders of the president would depend, not on his own judgment of the facts, but upon the finding of those facts, upon the proofs submitted to a jury. This view of the objection is precisely the same which was acted upon by the supreme court of New York, in the case already referred to, and, in the opinion of this court, with entire legal correctness.

Another objection is, that the orders of the president are not set forth; nor is it averred, that he issued any orders, but only that the governor of New York called out the militia, upon the requisition of the president. The objection, so far as it proceeds upon a supposed difference between a requisition and an order, is untenable; for a requisition calling forth the militia is, in legal intendment, an order, and must be so interpreted in this avowry. The majority of the court understood and acted upon this sense, which is one of the acknowledged senses of the word, in *Houston* v. *Moore,* 5 Wheat. 1. It was unnecessary to set forth the orders of the president at large; it was quite sufficient to state that the call was in obedience to them. No private citizen is presumed to be conversant of the particulars of those orders; and if he were, he is not bound to set them forth *in haec verba.*

The next objection is, that it does not sufficiently appear in the avowry, that the court-martial was a lawfully constituted court-martial, having jurisdiction of the offence, at the time of passing its sentence against the original plaintiff. Various grounds have been assigned in support of this objection. In the first place, it is said, that the original plaintiff was never employed in the service of the United States, but refused to enter that service, and that, consequently, he was not liable to the rules and articles of war, or to be tried for the offence by any court-martial organized under the authority of the United States. The case of *Houston* v. *Moore,* 5 Wheat. 1, affords a conclusive answer to this suggestion. It was decided in that case, that although a militia-man, who refused to obey the orders of the president, calling him into the public service, was not, in the sense of the act of 1795, "employed in the service of the United States," so as to be subject to the rules and articles of war; yet that he was liable to be tried for the offence, under the 5th section of the same act, by a court martial called under the authority of the United States. The great doubt in that case was, whether the delinquent was liable to be tried for the offence, by a court-martial organized under state authority.

In the next place, it is said, the court-martial was not composed of the proper number of officers required by law. In order to understand the force of this objection, it is necessary to advert to the terms of the act of 1795, and the rules and articles of war. The act of 1795, § 5, provides, "that every officer, non-commissioned officer, or private of the militia, who shall fail to obey the orders of the president of the United States," &c., "shall forfeit a sum not exceeding one year's pay, and not less than one month's pay, to be determined and adjudged by a court martial." And it further provides (§ 6), "that courts-martial for the trial of militia shall be composed of militia officers only." These are the only provisions in the act on this subject. It is not stated by whom the courts-martial shall be called, nor in what manner, nor of what number, they shall be composed. But the court is referred to the 64th and 65th of the rules and articles of war, enacted by the act of 10th of April 1806, ch. 20, which provide, "that general courts-martial may consist of any number of commissioned officers from five to thirteen inclusively; but they shall not consist of less than thirteen, where that number can be convened without manifest injury to the service:" and that "any general officer commanding an army, or colonel commanding a separate department, may appoint general courts-martial when necessary." Supposing these clauses applicable to the court-martial in question, it is very clear, that the act is merely directory to the officer appointing the court, and that his decision as to the number which can be convened without manifest injury to the service, being in a matter submitted to his sound discretion, must be conclusive. But the present avowry goes further, and alleges, not only that the court-martial was appointed by a general officer commanding an army, that it was composed of militia officers, naming them, but it goes on to assign the reason why a number short of thirteen composed the court, in the very terms of the 64th article; and the truth of this allegation is admitted by the demurrer. Tried, therefore, by the very test which has been resorted to in support of the objection, it utterly fails.

But, in strictness of law, the propriety of this resort may admit of question. The rules and articles of war, by the very terms of the statute of 1806, are those "by which the armies of the United States shall be governed;" and the act of 1795 has only provided, "that the militia employed in the service of the United States (not the militia ordered into the service of the United States) shall be subject to the same rules and articles of war as the troops of the United States;" and this is, in substance, re-enacted by the 97th of the rules and articles of war. It is not, therefore, admitted, that any express authority is given by either statute, that such a court-martial as is contemplated for the trial of delinquents, under the 5th section of the act of 1795, is to be composed of the same number of officers, organized in the same manner, as these rules and articles contemplate for persons in actual service. If any resort is to be had to them, it can only be to guide the discretion of the officer ordering the court, as matter of usage, and not as matter of positive institution. If, then, there be no mode pointed out for the formation of the court-martial in these cases, it may be asked, in what manner is such court to be appointed? The answer is, according to the general usage of the military service, or what may not unfitly be called the customary military law. It is by the same law, that courts-martial, when duly organized, are bound to execute their duties, and regulate their modes of proceeding, in the absence of positive enactments. Upon any other principle, courts-martial would be left without any adequate means to exercise the authority confided to them; for there could scarcely be framed a positive code to provide for the infinite variety of incidents applicable to them.

The act of the 18th of April 1814, ch. 141, which expired at the end of the late war, was, in a great measure, intended to obviate difficulties arising from the imperfection of the provisions of the act of 1795, and especially to aid courts-martial in exercising jurisdiction over cases like the present. But whatever may have been the legislative intention, its terms do not extend to the declaration of the number of which such courts-martial shall be composed. The first section provides,"that courts-martial, to be composed of militia officers alone, for the trial of militia drafted, detached, *and* called forth (not *or* called forth) for the service of the United States, whether acting in conjunction with the regular forces or otherwise, shall, when necessary, be appointed, held and conducted, in the manner prescribed by the rules and articles of war, for appointing, holding and conducting courts-martial for the trial of delinquents in the army of the United States." This language is obviously confined to the militia in the actual service of the United States, and does not extend to such as are drafted and refuse to obey the call. So that the court are driven back to the act of 1795 as the legitimate source for the ascertainment of the organization and jurisdiction of the court-martial in the present case. And we are of opinion, that nothing appears on the face of the avowry, to lead to any doubt that it was a legal court-martial, organized according to military usage, and entitled to take cognisance of the delinquencies stated in the avowry.

This view of the case affords an answer to another objection which has been urged at the bar, viz., that the sentence has not been approved by the commanding officer, in the manner pointed out in the 65th of the rules and articles of war. That article cannot, for the reasons already stated, be drawn in aid of the argument; and the avowry itself shows that the sentence has been approved by the president of the United States, who is the commander-in-chief, and that there was not any other officer of equal grade with the major-generals by whom the court-martial had been organized and continued, within the military district, by whom the same could be approved. If, therefore, an approval of the sentence were necessary, that approval has been given by the highest, and indeed only, military authority competent to give it. But it is by no means clear, that the act of 1795 meant to require any approval of the sentences imposing fines for delinquencies of this nature. The act does not require it, either expressly or by necessary implication. It directs (§ 7) that the fines assessed shall be certified by the presiding officer of the court-martial to the marshal, for him to levy the same, without referring to any prior act to be done, to give validity to the sentences. The natural inference from such an omission is, that the legislature did not intend, in cases of this subordinate nature, to require any further sanction of the sentences. And if such an approval is to be deemed essential, it must be upon the general military usage, and not from positive institution. Either way, we think, that all has been done, which the act required.

Another objection to the proceedings of the court-martial is, that they took place, and the sentence was given, three years and more after the war was concluded, and in a time of profound peace. But the opinion of this court is, that a court-martial, regularly called under the act of 1795, does not expire with the end of a war then existing, nor is its jurisdiction to try these offences in any shape dependent upon the fact of war or peace. The act of 1795 is not confined in its operation to cases of refusal to obey the orders of the president, in times of public war. On the contrary, that act authorizes the president to call forth the militia to suppress insurrections, and to enforce the laws of the United States, in times of peace. And courts-martial are, under the 5th section of the act, entitled to take cognisance of, and to punish delinquencies, in such cases, as well as in cases where the object is to repel invasion in times of war. It would be a strained construction of the act, to limit the authority of the court to the mere time of the existence of the particular exigency, when it might be thereby unable to take cognisance of, and decide upon a single offence. It is sufficient for us to say, that there is no such limitation in the act itself.

The next objection to the avowry is, that the certificate of the president of the court-martial is materially variant from the sentence itself, as set forth in a prior allegation. The sentence as there set forth is, "and thereupon, the said general court-martial imposed the sum of $96 as a fine, on the said Jacob, for having thus failed, neglected and refused to rendezvous and enter in the service of the United States of America, when thereto required as aforesaid." The certificate adds, "and that the said Jacob E. Mott was sentenced by the said general court-martial, on failure of the payment of said fine imposed on him, to twelve months' imprisonment." It is material to state, that the averment does not purport to set forth the sentence *in haec verba;* nor was it necessary in this avowry to allege anything more than that part of the sentence which imposed the fine, since that was the sole ground of the justification of taking the goods and chattels in controversy. But there is nothing repugnant in this averment to that which relates to the certificate. The latter properly adds the fact which respects the imprisonment, because the certificate constitutes the warrant to the marshal for his proceedings. The act of 1795 expressly declares, that the delinquents "shall be liable to be imprisoned by a like sentence, on failure of payment of the fines adjudged against them, for one calendar month for every five dollars of such fine." If, indeed, it had been necessary to set forth the whole sentence at large, the first omission would be helped by the certainty of the subsequent averment. There is, then, no variance or repugnance in these allegations; but they may well stand together.

Of the remaining causes of special demurrer, some are properly matters of defence before the court-martial, and its sentence being upon a subject within its jurisdiction, is conclusive; and others turn upon niceties of pleading, to which no separate answers are deemed necessary. In general, it may be said of them, that the court do not deem them well-founded objections to the avowry.

Upon the whole, it is the opinion of the court, that the judgment of the court for the trial of impeachments and the correction of errors ought to be reversed, and that the cause be remanded to the same court, with directions to cause a judgment to be entered upon the pleadings in favor of the avowant.

23

JOSEPH STORY, COMMENTARIES ON THE CONSTITUTION 3:§§ 1195–97
1833

§ 1195. This clause seems, after a slight amendment, to have passed the convention without opposition. It cured a defect severely felt under the confederation, which contained no provision on the subject.

§ 1196. The power of regulating the militia, and of commanding its services to enforce the laws, and to suppress insurrections, and repel invasions, is a natural incident to the duty of superintending the common defence, and preserving the internal peace of the nation. In short, every argument, which is urged, or can be urged against standing armies in time of peace, applies forcibly to the propriety of vesting this power in the national government. There is but one of two alternatives, which can be resorted to in cases of insurrection, invasion, or violent opposition to the laws; either to employ regular troops, or to employ the militia to suppress them. In ordinary cases, indeed, the resistance to the laws may be put down by the *posse comitatus,* or the assistance of the common magistracy. But cases may occur, in which such a resort would be utterly vain, and even mischievous; since it might encourage the factious to more rash measures, and prevent the application of a force, which would at once destroy the hopes, and crush the efforts of the disaffected. The general power of the government to pass all laws necessary and proper to execute its declared powers, would doubtless authorize laws to call forth the *posse comitatus,* and employ the common magistracy, in cases, where such measures would suit the emergency. But if the militia could not be called in aid, it would be absolutely indispensable to the common safety to keep up a strong regular force in time of peace. The latter would certainly not be desirable, or economical; and therefore this power over the militia is highly salutary to the public repose, and at the same time an additional security to the public liberty. In times of insurrection or invasion, it would be natural and proper, that the militia of a neighbouring state should be marched into another to resist a common enemy, or guard the republic against the violence of a domestic faction or sedition. But it is scarcely possible, that in the exercise of the power the militia should ever be called to march great distances, since it would be at once the most expensive and the most inconvenient force, which the government could employ for distant expeditions. The regulation of the whole subject is always to be in the power of congress; and it may from time to time be moulded so, as to escape from all dangerous abuses.

§ 1197. Notwithstanding the reasonableness of these suggestions, the power was made the subject of the most warm appeals to the people, to alarm their fears, and surprise their judgment. At one time it was said, that the militia under the command of the national government might be dangerous to the public liberty; at another, that they might be ordered to the most distant places, and burthened with the most oppressive services; and at another, that the states might thus be robbed of their immediate means of defence. How these things could be accomplished with the consent of both houses of congress, in which the states and the people of the states are represented, it is difficult to conceive. But the highly coloured and impassioned addresses, used on this occasion, produced some propositions of amendment in the state conventions, which, however, were never duly ratified, and have long since ceased to be felt, as matters of general concern.

SEE ALSO:

Generally 1.8.12–14; 1.8.16; 4.4; Amends. II, III

Records of the Federal Convention, Farrand 1:21, 247; 2:135, 144, 159, 168, 182, 570, 595

James McHenry, Maryland House of Delegates, 29 Nov. 1787, Farrand 3:148

Thomas McKean, Pennsylvania Ratifying Convention, 11 Dec. 1787, Elliot 2:537

James Madison, Virginia Ratifying Convention, 6 June 1788, Elliot 3:90

William Lancaster, North Carolina Ratifying Convention, 30 July 1788, Elliot 4:214–15

An Act to Provide for Calling Forth the Militia to Execute the Laws of the Union, 1 Stat. 264 (1792)

An Act to Provide for Calling Forth the Militia to Execute the Laws of the Union, 1 Stat. 424 (1795)

Kentucky Constitution of 1799, art. 3, Thorpe 3:1283

Senate, Militia of the United States, 22 Nov. 1814, Annals 28:95–102

House of Representatives, Militia Draughts, 9, 13 Dec. 1814, Annals 28:821–22, 885–86, 887–88

Illinois Constitution of 1818, art. 8, secs. 1–2, Thorpe 2:1003–4

James Madison to John Tyler, 1833, Farrand 3:527–28

Article 1, Section 8, Clause 16

To provide for organizing, arming, and disciplining, the Militia, and for governing such Part of them as may be employed in the Service of the United States, reserving to the States respectively, the Appointment of the Officers, and the Authority of training the Militia according to the discipline prescribed by Congress;

1

Sir Matthew Hale, History of the Common Law
1713 (posthumous)

Gray 26–27

Touching the business of martial law, these things are to be observed, viz.:

First. That in truth and reality it is not a law, but something indulged rather than allowed as a law; the necessity of government, order, and discipline in an army, is that only which can give those laws a countenance: *quod enim necessitas cogit defendit.*

Secondly. This indulged law was only to extend to members of the army, or to those of the opposed army, and never was so much indulged as intended to be executed or exercised upon others, for others who had not listed under the army had no color or reason to be bound by military constitutions applicable only to the army, whereof they were not parts, but they were to be ordered and governed according to the laws to which they were subject, though it were a time of war.

Thirdly. That the exercises of martial law, whereby any person should lose his life, or member, or liberty, may not be permitted in time of peace, when the king's courts are open for all persons to receive justice according to the laws of the land. This is declared in the Petition of Right (3 Car. I), whereby such commissions and martial law were repealed and declared to be contrary to law.

2

William Blackstone, Commentaries 1:401–4
1765

To prevent the executive power from being able to oppress, says baron Montesquieu, it is requisite that the armies with which it is entrusted should consist of the people, and have the same spirit with the people; as was the case at Rome, till Marius new-modelled the legions by enlisting the rabble of Italy, and laid the foundation of all the military tyranny that ensued. Nothing then, according to these principles, ought to be more guarded against in a free state, than making the military power, when such a one is necessary to be kept on foot, a body too distinct from the people. Like ours therefore, it should wholly be composed of natural subjects; it ought only to be enlisted for a short and limited time; the soldiers also should live intermixed with the people; no separate camp, no barracks, no inland fortresses should be allowed. And perhaps it might be still better, if, by dismissing a stated number and enlisting others at every renewal of their term, a circulation could be kept up between the army and the people, and the citizen and the soldier be more intimately connected together.

To keep this body of troops in order, an annual act of parliament likewise passes, "to punish mutiny and desertion, and for the better payment of the army and their quarters." This regulates the manner in which they are to be dispersed among the several inn-keepers and victuallers throughout the kingdom; and establishes a law martial for their government. By this, among other things, it is enacted, that if any officer and soldier shall excite, or join any mutiny, or, knowing of it, shall not give notice to the commanding officer; or shall desert, or list in any other regiment, or sleep upon his post, or leave it before he is relieved, or hold correspondence with a rebel or enemy, or strike or use violence to his superior officer, or shall disobey his lawful commands; such offender shall suffer such punishment as a court martial shall inflict, though it extend to death itself.

However expedient the most strict regulations may be in time of actual war, yet, in times of profound peace, a little relaxation of military rigour would not, one should hope, be productive of much inconvenience. And, upon this principle, though by our standing laws (still remaining in force, though not attended to) desertion in time of war is made felony, without benefit of clergy, and the offence is triable by a jury and before the judges of the common law; yet, by our militia laws beforementioned, a much lighter punishment is inflicted for desertion in time of peace. So, by the Roman law also, desertion in time of war was punished with death, but more mildly in time of tranquillity. But our mutiny act makes no such distinction: for any of the faults therein mentioned are, equally at all times, punishable with death itself, if a court martial shall think proper. This discretionary power of the court martial is indeed to be guided by the directions of the crown; which, with regard to military offences, has almost an absolute legislative power. "His majesty, says the act, may form articles of war, and constitute courts martial, with power to try any crime by such articles, and inflict such penalties as the articles direct." A vast and most important trust! an unlimited power to create crimes, and annex to them any punishments, not extending to life or limb! These are indeed forbidden to be inflicted, except for crimes declared to be so punishable by this act; which crimes we have just enumerated, and, among which, we may observe that any disobedience to lawful commands is one. Perhaps in some future revision of this act, which is in many respects hastily penned, it may be thought worthy the wisdom of parliament to ascertain the limits of military subjection, and to enact express articles of war for the government of the army, as is done for the government of the navy: especially as, by our present constitution, the nobility and gentry of the kingdom, who serve their country as militia officers, are annually subjected to the same arbitrary rule, during their time of exercise.

One of the greatest advantages of our English law is, that not only the crimes themselves which it punishes, but also the penalties which it inflicts, are ascertained and notorious: nothing is left to arbitrary discretion: the king by his judges dispenses what the law has previously ordained;

but is not himself the legislator. How much therefore is it to be regretted that a set of men, whose bravery has so often preserved the liberties of their country, should be reduced to a state of servitude in the midst of a nation of freemen! for sir Edward Coke will inform us, that it is one of the genuine marks of servitude, to have the law, which is our rule of action, either concealed or precarious: *"misera est servitus, ubi jus est vagum aut incognitum."* Nor is this state of servitude quite consistent with the maxims of sound policy observed by other free nations. For, the greater the general liberty is which any state enjoys, the more cautious has it usually been of introducing slavery in any particular order or profession. These men, as baron Montesquieu observes, seeing the liberty which others possess, and which they themselves are excluded from, are apt (like eunuchs in the eastern seraglios) to live in a state of perpetual envy and hatred towards the rest of the community; and indulge a malignant pleasure in contributing to destroy those privileges, to which they can never be admitted. Hence have many free states, by departing from this rule, been endangered by the revolt of their slaves: while, in absolute and despotic governments where there no real liberty exists, and consequently no invidious comparisons can be formed, such incidents are extremely rare. Two precautions are therefore advised to be observed in all prudent and free governments; 1. To prevent the introduction of slavery at all: or, 2. If it be already introduced, not to intrust those slaves with arms; who will then find themselves an overmatch for the freemen. Much less ought the soldiery to be an exception to the people in general, and the only state of servitude in the nation.

3

Records of the Federal Convention

[*2:330; Madison, 18 Aug.*]

Mr. Mason moved as an additional power "to make laws for the regulation and discipline of the Militia of the several States reserving to the States the appointment of the Officers". He considered uniformity as necessary in the regulation of the Militia throughout the Union.

Genl Pinkney mentioned a case during the war in which a dissimilarity in the militia of different States had produced the most serious mischiefs. Uniformity was essential. The States would never keep up a proper discipline of their militia.

Mr. Elseworth was for going as far in submitting the militia to the Genl Government as might be necessary, but thought the motion of Mr. Mason went too far. He moved that the militia should have the same arms & exercise and be under rules established by the Genl Govt. when in actual service of the U. States and when States neglect to provide regulations for militia, it shd. be regulated & established by the Legislature of U. S. The whole authority over the Militia ought by no means to be taken away from the States whose consequence would pine away to nothing after such a sacrifice of power. He thought the Genl Authority could not sufficiently pervade the Union for such a purpose, nor could it accommodate itself to the local genius of the people. It must be vain to ask the States to give the Militia out of their hands.

Mr Sherman 2ds. the motion.

Mr Dickenson. We are come now to a most important matter, that of the sword. His opinion was that the States never would nor ought to give up all authority over the Militia. He proposed to restrain the general power to one fourth part at a time, which by rotation would discipline the whole Militia.

Mr. Butler urged the necessity of submitting the whole Militia to the general Authority, which had the care of the general defence.

Mr. Mason– had suggested the idea of a select militia. He was led to think that would be in fact as much as the Genl. Govt could advantageously be charged with. He was afraid of creating insuperable objections to the plan. He withdrew his original motion, and moved a power "to make laws for regulating and disciplining the militia; not exceeding one tenth part in any one year, and reserving the appointment of officers to the States."

Genl Pinkney, renewed Mr. Mason's original motion. For a part to be under the genl. and a part under the State Govts. wd be an incurable evil. he saw no room for such distrust of the Genl Govt.

Mr. Langdon 2ds. Genl. Pinkney's renewal. He saw no more reason to be afraid of the Genl. Govt than of the State Govts. He was more apprehensive of the confusion of the different authorities on this subject, than of either.

Mr Madison thought the regulation of the Militia naturally appertaining to the authority charged with the public defence. It did not seem in its nature to be divisible between two distinct authorities. If the States would trust the Genl. Govt. with a power over the public treasure, they would from the same consideration of necessity grant it the direction of the public force. Those who had a full view of the public situation wd. from a sense of the danger, guard agst. it: the States would not be separately impressed with the general situation, nor have the due confidence in the concurrent exertions of each other.

Mr. Elseworth– considered the idea of a select militia as impracticable; & if it were not it would be followed by a ruinous declension of the great body of the Militia. The States will never submit to the same militia laws. Three or four shilling's as a penalty will enforce obedience better in New England, than forty lashes in some other places.

Mr. Pinkney thought the power such an one as could not be abused, and that the States would see the necessity of surrendering it. He had however but a scanty faith in Militia. There must be also a real military force—This alone can effectually answer the purpose. The United States had been making an experiment without it, and we see the consequence in their rapid approaches toward anarchy.

Mr Sherman, took notice that the States might want their Militia for defence agst invasions and insurrections, and for enforcing obedience to their laws. They will not give up this point– In giving up that of taxation, they retain a concurrent power of raising money for their own use.

Mr. Gerry thought this the last point remaining to be surrendered. If it be agreed to by the Convention, the plan will have as black a mark as was set on Cain. He had no such confidence in the Genl. Govt. as some Gentlemen possessed, and believed it would be found that the States have not.

Col. Mason. thought there was great weight in the remarks of Mr. Sherman– and moved an exception to his motion "of such part of the Militia as might be required by the States for their own use."

Mr. Read doubted the propriety of leaving the appointment of the Militia officers in the States. In some States they are elected by the legislatures; in others by the people themselves. He thought at least an appointment by the State Executives ought to be insisted on.

On committing to the grand Committee last appointed, the latter motion of Col. Mason, & the original one revived by Gel Pinkney

N. H– ay. Mas. ay. Ct no. N– J. no. Pa ay. Del. ay. Md. divid. Va ay. N. C. ay– S. C. ay. Geo. ay. [Ayes—8; noes—2; divided—1.]

[*2:384; Madison, 23 Aug.*]

The Report of the committee of Eleven made Aug: 21. being taken up, and the following clause being under consideration to wit "To make laws for organizing, arming & disciplining the Militia, and for governing such parts of them as may be employed in the service of the U. S. reserving to the States respectively, the appointment of the officers, and authority of training the militia according to the discipline prescribed"—

Mr Sherman moved to strike out the last member—"and authority of training &c." He thought it unnecessary. The States will have this authority of course if not given up.

Mr. Elsworth doubted the propriety of striking out the sentence. The reason assigned applies as well to the other reservation of the appointment to offices. He remarked at the same time that the term discipline was of vast extent and might be so expounded as to include all power on the subject.

Mr. King, by way of explanation, said that by *organizing* the Committee meant, proportioning the officers & men—by *arming*, specifying the kind size and caliber of arms—& by *disciplining* prescribing the manual exercise evolutions &c.

Mr. Sherman withdrew his motion

Mr Gerry, This power in the U—S. as explained is making the States drill-sergeants. He had as lief let the Citizens of Massachusetts be disarmed, as to take the command from the States, and subject them to the Genl Legislature. It would be regarded as a system of Despotism.

Mr Madison observed that *"arming"* as explained did not did not extend to furnishing arms; nor the term "disciplining" to penalties & Courts martial for enforcing them.

Mr. King added, to his former explanation that *arming* meant not only to provide for uniformity of arms, but included authority to regulate the modes of furnishing, either by the militia themselves, the State Governments, or the National Treasury: that *laws* for disciplining, must involve penalties and every thing necessary for enforcing penalties.

Mr. Dayton moved to postpone the paragraph, in order to take up the following proposition

"To establish an uniform & general system of discipline for the Militia of these States, and to make laws for organizing, arming, disciplining & governing *such part of them as may be employed in the service of the U. S.*, reserving to the States respectively the appointment of the officers, and all authority over the Militia not herein given to the General Government"

On the question to postpone in favor of this proposition: it passed in the Negative

N. H. no. Mas— no. Ct no. N. J. ay. P. no. Del. no. Maryd ay. Va. no. N. C. no. S. C. no. Geo. ay. [Ayes—3; noes—8.]

Mr. Elsworth & Mr. Sherman moved to postpone the 2d. clause in favor of the following

"To establish an uniformity of arms, exercise & organization for the Militia, and to provide for the Government of them when called into the service of the U. States"

The object of this proposition was to refer the plan for the Militia to the General Govt. but leave the execution of it to the State Govts.

Mr Langdon said He could not understand the jealousy expressed by some Gentleman. The General & State Govts. were not enemies to each other, but different institutions for the good of the people of America. As one of the people he could say, the National Govt. is mine, the State Govt is mine—In transferring power from one to the other—I only take out of my left hand what it cannot so well use, and put it into my right hand where it can be better used.

Mr. Gerry thought it was rather taking out of the right hand & putting it into the left. Will any man say that liberty will be as safe in the hands of eighty or a hundred men taken from the whole continent, as in the hands of two or three hundred taken from a single State?

Mr. Dayton was against so absolute a uniformity. In some States there ought to be a greater proportion of cavalry than in others. In some places rifles would be most proper, in others muskets &c—

Genl Pinkney preferred the clause reported by the Committee, extending the meaning of it to the case of fines &c—

Mr. Madison. The primary object is to secure an effectual discipline of the Militia. This will no more be done if left to the States separately than the requisitions have been hitherto paid by them. The States neglect their Militia now, and the more they are consolidated into one nation, the less each will rely on its own interior provisions for its safety & the less prepare its Militia for that purpose; in like manner as the Militia of a State would have been still more neglected than it has been if each County had been independently charged with the care of its Militia. The Discipline of the Militia is evidently a *National* concern, and ought to be provided for in the *National* Constitution.

Mr L—Martin was confident that the States would never give up the power over the Militia; and that, if they were to do so, the militia would be less attended to by the Genl. than by the State Governments.

Mr Randolph asked what danger there could be that the Militia could be brought into the field and made to commit suicide on themselves. This is a power that cannot from its nature be abused, unless indeed the whole mass should be corrupted. He was for trammelling the Genl Govt. whenever there was danger. but here there could be none—He urged this as an essential point; observing that the Militia were every where neglected by the State Legislatures, the members of which courted popularity too much to enforce a proper discipline. Leaving the appointment of officers to the States protects the people agst. every apprehension that could produce murmur.

On Question on Mr. Elsworth's Motion

N. H. no. Mas— no— Ct. ay. N. J. no. Pa. no. Del. no. Md. no. Va no— N— C. no. S. C no. Geo. no. [Ayes—1; noes—10.]

A motion was then made to recommit the 2d clause which was negatived.

On the question to agree to the 1st. part of the clause, namely

"To make laws for organizing arming & disciplining the Militia, and for governing such part of them as may be employed in the service of the U. S.".

N. H ay. Mas. ay. Ct. no. N. J. ay. Pa. ay. Del. ay. Md no. Va ay. N— C— ay. S. C. ay. Geo. ay. [Ayes—9 noes—2.]

Mr. Madison moved to amend the next part of the clause so as to read "reserving to the States respectively, the appointment of the officers, *under the rank of General officers.*"

Mr. Sherman considered this as absolutely inadmissible. He said that if the people should be so far asleep as to allow the Most influential officers of the Militia to be appointed by the Genl. Government, every man of discernment would rouse them by sounding the alarm to them—

Mr. Gerry. Let us at once destroy the State Govts have an Executive for life or hereditary, and a proper Senate, and then there would be some consistency in giving full powers to the Genl Govt. but as the States are not to be abolished, he wondered at the attempts that were made to give powers inconsistent with their existence. He warned the Convention agst pushing the experiment too far. Some people will support a plan of vigorous Government at every risk. Others of a more democratic cast will oppose it with equal determination. And a Civil war may be produced by the conflict.

Mr. Madison. As the greatest danger is that of disunion of the States, it is necessary to guard agst. it by sufficient powers to the Common Govt. and as the greatest danger to liberty is from large standing armies, it is best to prevent them by an effectual provision for a good Militia—

On the Question to agree to Mr. Madison's motion

N— H—ay — Mas— no— Ct no— N— J— no— Pa no— Del— no— Md no— Va no— N— C— no— S— C— ay— Geo— ay. [Ayes—3; noes—8.]

On the question to agree to the "reserving to the States the appointment of the officers". It was agreed to nem: contrad:

On the question on the clause "and the authority of training the Militia according to the discipline prescribed by the U. S"—

N. H. ay. Mas. ay. Ct. ay— N—J— ay. Pa. ay— Del. no. Md. ay. Va. no— N— C. ay. S. C. no. Geo. no— [Ayes—7; noes—4.]

4

CHARLES PINCKNEY, OBSERVATIONS ON THE PLAN OF GOVERNMENT
1787

Farrand 3:118–19

The exclusive right of establishing regulations for the Government of the Militia of the United States, ought certainly to be ves[t]ed in the Federal Councils. As standing Armies are contrary to the Constitutions of most of the States, and the nature of our Government, the only immediate aid and support that we can look up to, in case of necessity, is the Militia. As the several States form one Government, united for their common benefit and security, they are to be considered as a Nation—their Militia therefore, should be as far as possible national—an uniformity in Discipline and Regulations should pervade the whole, otherwise, when the Militia of several States are required to act together, it will be difficult to combine their operations from the confusion a difference of Discipline and Military Habits will produce. Independent of our being obliged to rely on the Militia as a security against foreign Invasions or Domestic Convulsions, they are in fact the only adequate force the Union possess, if any should be requisite to coerce a refractory or negligent Member, and to carry the Ordinances and Decrees of Congress into execution. This, as well as the cases I have alluded to, will sometimes make it proper to order the Militia of one State into another. At present the United States possess no power of directing the Militia, and must depend upon the States to carry their Recommendations upon this subject into execution—while this dependence exists, like all their other reliances upon the States for measures they are not obliged to adopt, the Federal views and designs must ever be delayed and disappointed. To place therefore a necessary and Constitutional power of defence and coercion in the hands of the Federal authority, and to render our Militia uniform and national, I am decidedly in opinion they should have the exclusive right of establishing regulations for their Government and Discipline, which the States should be bound to comply with, as well as with their Requisitions for any number of Militia, whose march into another State, the Public safety or benefit should require.

In every Confederacy of States, formed for their general benefit and security, there ought to be a power to oblige the parties to furnish their respective quotas without the possibility of neglect or evasion;—there is no such clause in the present Confederation, and it is therefore *without this indispensable security*. Experience justifies me in asserting that we may detail as minutely as we can, the duties of the States, but unless they are assured that these duties will be required and enforced, the details will be regarded as nugatory. No Government has more severely felt the want of a coercive Power than the United States; for want of it the principles of the Confederation have been neglected with impunity in the hour of the most pressing necessity, and at the imminent hazard of its existence: Nor are we to expect they will be more attentive in future. Unless there is a compelling principle in the Confederacy, there must be an injustice in its tendency; It will expose an unequal proportion of the strength and resources of some of the States, to the hazard of war in defence of the rest—the first principles of Justice direct that this danger should be provided against—many of the States have certainly shewn a disposition to evade a performance of their Federal Duties, and throw the burden of Government upon their neighbors. It is against this shameful evasion in the delinquent, this forced assumption in the more attentive, I wish to provide, and they ought to be guarded against by every means in our power. Unless this power of coercion is infused, and exercised when necessary, the States will most assuredly neglect their duties. The consequence is either a dissolution of the Union, or an unreasonable sacrifice by those who are disposed to support and maintain it.

5

"John DeWitt," no. 5
Fall 1787
Storing 4.3.27–29

They have the power of "organizing, arming and disciplining the militia, and of governing them when in service of the United States, giving to the separate States the appointment of the officers, and the authority of training the militia according to the discipline prescribed by Congress." Let us enquire, why they have assumed this power, for if it is for the purpose of forming you into one uniform, solid body throughout the United States, making you respectable both at home and abroad—of arming you more compleatly and exercising you oftener—of strengthening the power which is now lodged in your hands, and relying upon you and you solely for aid and support to the civil power in the execution of all the laws of the New Congress, it certainly can be no where better placed under the restrictions therein mentioned, than in that body. But is this probable. Does the complection of the proceedings countenance such a supposition? When they unprecedently claim the power of raising and supporting standing armies, do they tell you for what purposes they are to be raised?—How they are to be employed?—How many they are to consist of, and where to be stationed?—Is this power fettered with any one of these necessary restrictions which will shew they depend upon the militia, and not upon this infernal engine of oppression to execute their civil laws. The nature of the demand in itself contradicts such a supposition, and forces you to believe that it is for none of these causes—but rather for the purpose of consolidating and finally destroying your strength, as your respective Governments are to be destroyed.

They well know the impolicy of putting or keeping arms in the hands of a nervous people, at a distance from the Seat of Government, upon whom they mean to exercise the powers granted in that Government.—They have no idea of calling upon the party aggrieved to support and enforce their own grievances. They are aware of the necessity of catching Samson asleep to trim him of his locks. It is asserted by the most respectable writers upon Government, that a well regulated militia, composed of the yeomanry of the country have ever been considered as the bulwark of a free people; and, says the celebrated Mr. HUME, "without it, it is folly to think any free government will have stability or security—When the sword is introduced, as in our constitution (speaking of the British) the person entrusted will always neglect to discipline the militia, in order to have a pretext for keeping up a standing army; and it is evident this is a mortal distemper in the British parliament, of which it must finally inevitably perish."—If they have not the same design, why do they wish a standing army unrestrained? It is universally agreed, that a militia and a standing body of troops never yet flourished in the same soil. Tyrants have uniformly depended upon the latter, at the expence of the former. Experience has taught them, that a standing body of regular forces, where ever they can be compleatly introduced, are always efficacious in enforcing their edicts, however arbitrary, and slaves by profession themselves, are "nothing loath" to break down the barriers of freedom with a *gout.*—No, my fellow-citizens, this plainly shews they do not mean to depend upon the citizens of the States alone to enforce their powers, wherefore it is their policy to neglect them, and lean upon something more substantial and summary. It is true, they have left the appointment of officers in the breast of the several States; but this to me, appears an insult, rather than a priveledge, for what avails this right, if they in their pleasure should choose to neglect to arm, organize and discipline the men over whom such Officers are to be appointed. It is a bait, that you might be led to suppose they did intend to apply to them in all cases, and to pay particular attention to making them the bulwark of this Continent.—And would they not be equal to such an undertaking? Are they not abundantly able to give security and stability to your government as long as it is free? Are they not the only proper persons to do it? Are they not the most respectable body of yeomanry in that character upon earth? Have they not been deeply engaged in some of the most brilliant actions in America, and more than once decided the fate of armies? In short, do they not preclude the necessity of any standing army whatsoever, unless in case of invasion; and in that case it would be time enough to raise them, for no free government under Heaven, with a well disciplined militia was ever yet subdued by mercenary troups.

The advocates at the present day, for a standing army in the New Congress pretend it is necessary for the respectability of government. I defy them to produce an instance in any country, in the Old or New World, where they have not finally done away the liberties of the people:—Every writer upon government,—Lock, Sidney, Hamden, and a list of others have uniformly asserted, that standing armies are a solecism in any government; that no nation ever supported them, that did not resort to, rely on, and finally become a prey to them.—No Western Historians have yet been hardy enough to advance principles that look a different way. What historians have asserted, all the Grecian Republicks have verified.—They are brought up to obedience and unconditional submission.—With arms in their hands, they are taught to feel the weight of rigid discipline:—They are excluded from the enjoyments which liberty gives to its votaries, they, in consequence, hate and envy the rest of the community in which they are placed, and indulge a malignant pleasure in destroying those privileges to which they never can be admitted.

6

Alexander Hamilton, Federalist, no. 29, 181–87
9 Jan. 1788

(See 1.8.15, no. 9)

7

Federal Farmer, no. 18
25 Jan. 1788

Storing 2.8.217

(See 1.8.15, no. 11)

8

Luther Martin, Genuine Information
1788

Storing 2.4.61–62

By the *next* paragraph, Congress is to have the power to provide for *organizing, arming,* and *disciplining* the *militia,* and for *governing* such part of them as may be *employed in the service* of the United States.

For this *extraordinary* provision, by which the *militia,* the *only defence* and *protection* which the *State* can have for the security of *their rights* against *arbitrary encroachments* of the *general government,* is taken entirely *out of the power* of their *respective States,* and placed under the *power of Congress,* it was speciously assigned as a reason, that the general government would cause the militia to be better regulated and better disciplined than the State governments, and that it would be proper for the whole militia of the union to have a uniformity in their arms and exercise. To this it was answered, that the reason, however *specious,* was *not just;* that it would be absurd the militia of the western settlements, who were exposed to an Indian enemy, should either be confined to the *same arms* or *exercise* as the militia of the eastern or middle States; that the same penalties which would be sufficient to enforce an obedience to militia laws in some States, would be totally disregarded in others—That leaving the power to the several States, they would respectively best know the situation and circumstances of their citizens, and the regulations that would be necessary and sufficient to effect a well regulated militia in each—That we were satisfied the militia had heretofore been as well disciplined, as if they had been under the regulations of Congress; and the States would now have an *additional* motive to keep their militia in proper order, and fit for service, as it would be the *only chance* to preserve their *existence* against a general government, armed with powers *sufficient* to destroy them. These observations, Sir, procured from some of the members an open avowal of those reasons, by which we believed before that they were actuated. They said, that as the States would be opposed to the general government, and at enmity with it, which, as I have already observed, they *assumed* as a *principle,* if the militia was under the controul and the authority of the respective States, it would *enable them* to *thwart* and *oppose* the general government:—They said the States ought to be at the mercy of the general government, and, therefore, that the militia ought to be put under its power, and not suffered to remain under the power of the respective States. In answer to these declarations, it was urged, that if after having obtained to the general government the great powers already granted, and among those, that of *raising and keeping up regular troops without limitation,* the *power* over the *militia* should be *taken away* from *the States,* and also given to the general government, it ought to be considered as the *last coup de grace* to the *State governments;* that it must be the most convincing proof, the advocates of this system design the *destruction* of the State governments, and that no *professions,* to the contrary, ought to be *trusted;* and that every State in the union ought to reject such a system with indignation, since, if the general government should attempt to oppress and enslave them, they could not have any possible means of self defence; because the proposed system, taking away from the States the right of organizing, arming and disciplining of the militia, the *first attempt* made by a *State* to put the militia in a situation to counteract the arbitrary measures of the general government, would be construed into an *act of rebellion,* or *treason;* and Congress would *instantly march* their *troops* into the State.—It was further observed, that when a government *wishes* to deprive their citizens of freedom, and reduce them to slavery, it *generally makes use of a standing army* for that purpose, and *leaves the militia in a situation as contemptible as possible,* [*lest*] *they might oppose its arbitrary designs*—That in *this* system, we give the general government every provision it could wish for, and even *invite* it to *sub-*

vert the *liberties* of the *States* and *their citizens,* since we give them the right to encrease and keep up a standing army as numerous as *it* would wish, and by placing the militia under *its* power, enable it to leave the militia *totally unorganized, undisciplined,* and *even to disarm them;* while the *citizens,* so far from complaining of this *neglect,* might even esteem it a favor in the general government, as thereby they would be freed from the burthen of militia duties, and left to their own private occupations or pleasures. However, *all* arguments, and every reason that could be urged on *this* subject, as well as on many others, were obliged to yield to *one* that was *unanswerable,* a *majority* upon the division.

9

A Native of Virginia, Observations upon the Proposed Plan of Federal Government
1788

Monroe Writings 1:371–72

By these clauses, the appointment of the militia officers, and training the militia, are reserved to the respective States; except that Congress have a right to direct in what manner they are to be disciplined, and the time when they are to be ordered out.

These clauses have been extremely misunderstood, or purposely misconstrued, by the enemies to the Constitution. Some have said, "the absolute unqualified command that Congress have over the militia may be instrumental to the destruction of all liberty, both public and private, whether of a personal, civil, or religious nature."

Is this the result of reason, or is it the dictate of resentment? How can the command of Congress over the militia be either absolute or unqualified, when its officers are appointed by the States, and consequently can by no possibility become its creatures?

They will generally be men of property and probity: And can any one for a moment suppose that such men will ever be so lost to a sense of liberty, the rights of their country, and their own dignity, as to become the instruments of arbitrary measures? Whenever that shall be the case, we may in vain contend for forms of government; the spirit of liberty will have taken its flight from America, and nothing but an arbitrary government will be fit for such a people, however accurately defined the powers of her Constitution may be. But so long as there shall be a militia so officered, or the majority of the people landholders, America will have little to fear for liberty. Congress have the power of organizing the militia; and can it be put into better hands? They can have no interest in destroying the personal liberty of any man, or raising his fortune in the mode of organization: They can make no law upon this, or any other subject, which will not affect themselves, their children, or their connexions.

Can any one seriously suppose, that Congress will ever think of drawing the militia of one State out, in order to destroy the liberties of another? Of Virginia, for instance, to destroy the liberties of Pennsylvania? Or should they be so wicked, that an American militia, officered by the States, would obey so odious a mandate? The supposition is monstrous.

10

Patrick Henry, Virginia Ratifying Convention
5 June 1788

Elliot 3:51–52

A standing army we shall have, also, to execute the execrable commands of tyranny; and how are you to punish them? Will you order them to be punished? Who shall obey these orders? Will your mace-bearer be a match for a disciplined regiment? In what situation are we to be? The clause before you gives a power of direct taxation, unbounded and unlimited, exclusive power of legislation, in all cases whatsoever, for ten miles square, and over all places purchased for the erection of forts, magazines, arsenals, dockyards, &c. What resistance could be made? The attempt would be madness. You will find all the strength of this country in the hands of your enemies; their garrisons will naturally be the strongest places in the country. Your militia is given up to Congress, also, in another part of this plan: they will therefore act as they think proper: all power will be in their own possession. You cannot force them to receive their punishment: of what service would militia be to you, when, most probably, you will not have a single musket in the state? for, as arms are to be provided by Congress, they may or may not furnish them.

Let me here call your attention to that part which gives the Congress power "to provide for organizing, arming, and disciplining the militia, and for governing such part of them as may be employed in the service of the United States—reserving to the states, respectively, the appointment of the officers, and the authority of training the militia according to the discipline prescribed by Congress." By this, sir, you see that their control over our last and best defence is unlimited. If they neglect or refuse to discipline or arm our militia, they will be useless: the states can do neither—this power being exclusively given to Congress. The power of appointing officers over men not disciplined or armed is ridiculous; so that this pretended little remains of power left to the states may, at the pleasure of Congress, be rendered nugatory. Our situation will be deplorable indeed: nor can we ever expect to get this government amended, since I have already shown that a very small minority may prevent it, and that small minority interested in the continuance of the oppression. Will the oppressor let go the oppressed? Was there ever an instance?

Can the annals of mankind exhibit one single example where rulers overcharged with power willingly let go the oppressed, though solicited and requested most earnestly? The application for amendments will therefore be fruitless. Sometimes, the oppressed have got loose by one of those bloody struggles that desolate a country; but a willing relinquishment of power is one of those things which human nature never was, nor ever will be, capable of.

11

MELANCTON SMITH, PROPOSED AMENDMENT, NEW YORK RATIFYING CONVENTION
2 July 1788
Elliot 2:406

Respecting the organization and arming the *militia,* &c.,—

> "*Provided,* That the militia of any state shall not be marched out of such state without the consent of the executive thereof, nor be continued in service out of the state, without the consent of the legislature thereof, for a longer term than six weeks; and *provided,* that the power to organize, arm, and discipline the militia, shall not be construed to extend further than to prescribe the mode of arming and disciplining the same."

Moved by Mr. SMITH.

12

JAMES IREDELL, PROPOSED AMENDMENT, NORTH CAROLINA RATIFYING CONVENTION
1 Aug. 1788
Elliot 4:249

3. Each state respectively shall have the power to provide for organizing, arming, and disciplining, its own militia, whensoever Congress shall omit or neglect to provide for the same. The militia shall not be subject to martial law, except when in actual service in time of war, invasion, or rebellion; and when they are not in the actual service of the United States, they shall be subject only to such fines, penalties, and punishments, as shall be directed or inflicted by the laws of its own state.

13

JAMES MADISON, FOURTH ANNUAL MESSAGE TO CONGRESS
4 Nov. 1812
Richardson 1:516

Among the incidents to the measures of the war I am constrained to advert to the refusal of the governors of Massachusetts and Connecticut to furnish the required detachments of militia toward the defense of the maritime frontier. The refusal was founded on a novel and unfortunate exposition of the provisions of the Constitution relating to the militia. The correspondences which will be laid before you contain the requisite information on the subject. It is obvious that if the authority of the United States to call into service and command the militia for the public defense can be thus frustrated, even in a state of declared war and of course under apprehensions of invasion preceding war, they are not one nation for the purpose most of all requiring it, and that the public safety may have no other resource than in those large and permanent military establishments which are forbidden by the principles of our free government, and against the necessity of which the militia were meant to be a constitutional bulwark.

14

VANDERHEYDEN V. YOUNG
11 Johns. R. 150 (N.Y. 1814)

SPENCER, J., delivered the opinion of the court. The first and second objections to the pleas are wholly untenable. It is not necessary to allege that a case had occurred which gave authority to the president of the *United States* to call forth the militia, under the act of the 28th of *February,* 1795. That act, after enumerating the cases, on the occurrence of which the militia may be called into the public service of the *United States,* vests in the president a high discretionary power: he, and he alone, is made the judge, as well of the happening of the events, on which the militia may be called forth, as of the number, time and destination of that species of force. In every case in which the president acts under that law, he acts upon his responsibility under the constitution.

If it was necessary to the validity of these pleas to state, either that the *United States* were invaded, or in imminent danger of invasion, or that the laws of the *United States* were opposed, or the execution thereof obstructed, the matter thus stated would be issuable, and the plaintiff might, in his replication, take issue on them, and oblige the defendant to prove the occurrence of a case specified in the act; and thus every subordinate officer, who should be called into service, would be put to the necessity, when he was sued for any act of discipline upon the privates, to prove to a jury that the president had acted correctly in making his requisitions; and if he failed in this proof, it would subject him to damages for an act otherwise lawful.

To countenance such a construction of the act would be monstrous. Every trial would either subject all the archives of state to an examination before the court and jury, or the defendant would inevitably be found guilty. No man would dare to obey the orders, either of the president, or of his superior officer, lest, peradventure, the president had either abused his authority, or misjudged, in relation to the occurrence of the fact, which authorized him to call forth the militia.

It is a general and sound principle, that whenever the law vests any person with a power to do an act, and constitutes him a judge of the evidence on which the act may be done, and, at the same time, contemplates that the act is to be carried into effect, through the instrumentality of agents, the person thus clothed with power is invested with discretion, and is, *quoad hoc,* a judge. His mandates to his legal agents, on his declaring the event to have happened, will be a protection to those agents; and it is not their duty or business to investigate the facts thus referred to their superior, and to rejudge his determination. In a military point of view, the contrary doctrine would be subversive of all discipline; and as it regards the safety and security of the *United States* and its citizens, the consequences would be deplorable and fatal. It was not necessary, therefore, to set forth the occurrence of these events in the pleas, as a justification of the defendant's conduct, because they were not, and could not, be matter of trial.

The objection that the governor's order does not mention which president gave the order to him, nor what number of militia was called out, is too refined and idle to require examination.

The third objection is also untenable. Courts-martial for the trial of militia officers or privates are to be composed of militia officers. (97th article of rules and articles of war.) It is not a superadded qualification that such officers shall have been in the service of the *United States.*

The objections that the pleas do not allege that General *Dearborn,* when he ordered the court-martial, commanded the army of the *United States,* or that he ordered the sentence to be executed, are not well taken. The plea states that General *Dearborn,* when he issued the order, was a major general of the army of the *United States;* and this imports that he then commanded the army; but, under the act of 1795, it is not required that courts-martial should be ordered by a general commanding an army. The 65th article gives to the officer ordering the court the power of confirming and executing the sentence; but it does not prescribe the manner of doing either; and from analogy to all other courts of criminal jurisdiction, it necessarily follows, that the court before whom the trial is had, has the power, after conviction, of keeping the person of the delinquent, until the will and pleasure of the superior officer be known.

It is also objected that the plaintiff was not subject to the rules and articles of war, because they were enacted in 1806, and posterior to the act authorizing the president to call out the militia.

The 4th section of the act of the 28th of *February,* 1795, provides that the militia employed in the service of the *United States* shall be subject to the same rules and articles of war as the troops of the *United States.* The act of the 10th of *April,* 1806, establishing the rules and articles of war, ordains, that from and after the passing that act, the rules and articles therein shall be the rules and articles by which the army of the *United States* shall be governed. It follows, necessarily, then, that these rules and articles attached to the militia which were called into the service of the *United States* thereafter, without reference to the time when the power to call them out was conferred; and this independently of the 97th article, which actually extends the rules to the militia. The act of 1795 is clearly prospective.

The only remaining objection is, that the pleas do not state that the plaintiff's term of service was unexpired when he was tried, and sentenced, and put under guard.

Without examining the question whether the plaintiff was liable to be tried, after the period for which he was called out had elapsed, we are clearly of opinion, that the defendant is not liable to this action.

The court-martial was constituted to try all the delinquent militia men in three counties, and the plaintiff was personally and regularly before the court, and charged with the offence of desertion. The defendant, and the other members of the court, were sitting as judges. It was competent to the plaintiff to have raised the objection under consideration, or any other; but he waived every objection by pleading guilty, and throwing himself on the mercy of the court. (*Cowp.* 172.) After this, can he be permitted to turn round upon the court, and pretend that he was not liable to their jurisdiction? Had he urged the objection, it might have availed him; but his plea admits their jurisdiction, and his own guilt. Besides, the court-martial had not power to carry any sentence into execution. Their proceedings were liable to the review of General *Dearborn,* and there he should have resorted with his exculpatory proof. (5 *Term Rep.* 182. 6 *Term Rep.* 248.)

The distinction taken by Justice *Wilson,* in *Drewy* v. *Coulton,* (1 *East,* 56. in the notes,) is a very sound one. "In very few instances," he says, "is an officer answerable for what he does to the best of his judgment, in cases where [he] is compellable to act; but the action lies where the officer has an option whether he will act or not." If the court-martial had jurisdiction over the person of the plaintiff, and over the subject matter, (his offence,) then, most clearly, the members of that court are not answerable. (1 Ld. *Raym.* 467.) The plaintiff admitted both facts, by submitting to the jurisdiction of the court, and pleading guilty. I will only add, that it would be most mischievous and pernicious, to subject men acting in a judicial capacity, to actions, where their conduct is fair and impartial, when they are uninfluenced by any corrupt or improper motives, for a mere mistake of judgment. In the present case, they are called in question by a person who, by acknowledging the jurisdiction of the court and his own guilt, never required them even to deliberate on any of these points or objections.

PLATT, J., not having heard the argument, gave no opinion

15

GOUVERNEUR MORRIS TO MOSS KENT
12 Jan. 1815
Life 3:328–29

When, in framing the Constitution, we restricted so closely the power of government over our fellow citizens of the militia, it was not because we supposed there would ever be a Congress so mad as to attempt tyrannizing over the people or militia, by the militia. The danger we meant chiefly to provide against was, the hazarding of the national safety by a reliance on that expensive and inefficient force. An overweening vanity leads the fond many, each man against the conviction of his own heart, to believe or affect to believe, that militia can beat veteran troops in the open field and even play of battle. This idle notion, fed by vaunting demagogues, alarmed us for our country, when in the course of that time and chance, which happen to all, she should be at war with a great power.

Those, who, during the Revolutionary storm, had confidential acquaintance with the conduct of affairs, knew well that to rely on militia was to lean on a broken reed. We knew, also, that to coop up in a camp those habituated to the freedom and comforts of social life, without subjecting them to the strict observation and severe control of officers regularly bred, would expose them to such fell disease, that pestilence would make more havoc than the sword. We knew that when militia were of necessity called out, and nothing but necessity can justify the call, mercy as well as policy requires, that they be led immediately to attack their foe. This gives them a tolerable chance; and when superior in number, possessing, as they must, a correct knowledge of the country, it is not improbable that their efforts may be crowned with success. To that end, nevertheless, it is proper to maintain in them a good opinion of themselves, for despondency is not the road to victory.

But to rely on undisciplined, ill-officered men, though each were individually as brave as Caesar, to resist the well-directed impulse of veterans, is to act in defiance of reason and experience. We flattered ourselves, that the constitutional restriction on the use of militia, combined with the just apprehension of danger to liberty from a standing army, would force those entrusted with the conduct of national affairs, to make seasonable provision for a naval force. We were not ignorant of the puerile notions entertained by some on that subject, but we hoped, alas! we vainly hoped, that our councils would not be swayed by chattering boys, nor become the sport of senseless declamation.

16

HOUSTON V. MOORE
5 Wheat. 1 (1820)

(See 1.8.15, no. 20)

17

WILLIAM WIRT, COURTS-MARTIAL—NEW YORK MILITIA
19 June 1821
1 Ops. Atty. Gen. 473

SIR: I am of the opinion that the court-martial which imposed the fine on Cyprian Elton had no jurisdiction of the case. The call was not made by the President on the militia of New York. The militiaman, therefore, disobeyed no order of the President, and, consequently, is not within the provisions of our act of Congress. By the circular from the War Department, of the 4th July, 1814, the executive of the State of New York was merely invited to organize and hold in readiness for immediate service that State's quota of ninety-three thousand men, under the laws of the 28th February, 1795, and the 18th April, 1814. The details of designating the portion of the State's militia which should be held in readiness, of appointing the place of rendezvous, and ordering them to this place, were all confided to the executive of New York; and the alleged offence of Elton was a disobedience, not of the orders of the President, but of the orders of the governor of the State, in refusing to march to the place of rendezvous, This was no violation of any existing law of the United States; and a court-martial of the United States had no jurisdiction over the offence, because our laws take cognizance of no other offence, in this respect, but a disobedience of the orders of the President of the United States issued to the officers of the militia. I am of the opinion, therefore, that the United States are not entitled to the fines imposed on the militia of New York by the court-martial which was convened under the authority of the United States. But the cause of Houston and Moore, (5 Wheaton, page 1,) leaves it very questionable whether the Supreme Court might not decide otherwise. For this reason, and with a view to the settlement of so delicate and important a question by a court of the last resort, I submit it to you whether it would not be advisable to have the avowry (which is confessedly defective) amended, and bring up the case to the Supreme Court of the United States. One case might, by consent, decide all the rest.

18

MARTIN V. MOTT
12 Wheat. 19 (1827)

(See 1.8.15, no. 22)

19

JOSEPH STORY, COMMENTARIES ON THE CONSTITUTION 3:§§ 1199–1210
1833

§ 1199. This power has a natural connexion with the preceding, and, if not indispensable to its exercise, furnishes the only adequate means of giving it promptitude and efficiency in its operations. It requires no skill in the science of war to discern, that uniformity in the organization and discipline of the militia will be attended with the most beneficial effects, whenever they are called into active service. It will enable them to discharge the duties of the camp and field with mutual intelligence and concert, an advantage of peculiar moment in the operations of an army; and it will enable them to acquire, in a much shorter period, that degree of proficiency in military functions, which is essential to their usefulness. Such an uniformity, it is evident, can be attained only through the superintending power of the national government.

§ 1200. This clause was not in the original draft of the constitution; but it was subsequently referred to a committee, who reported in favour of the power; and after considerable discussion it was adopted in its present shape by a decided majority. The first clause in regard to organizing, arming, disciplining, and governing the militia, was passed by a vote of nine states against two; the next, referring the appointment of officers to the states, after an ineffectual effort to amend it by confining the appointment to officers under the rank of general officers, was passed without a division; and the last, referring the authority to train the militia according to the discipline prescribed by congress, was passed by a vote of seven states against four.

§ 1201. It was conceived by the friends of the constitution, that the power thus given, with the guards, reserving the appointment of the officers, and the training of the militia to the states, made it not only wholly unexceptionable, but in reality an additional security to the public liberties. It was nevertheless made a topic of serious alarm and powerful objection. It was suggested, that it was indispensable to the states, that they should possess the control and discipline of the militia. Congress might, under pretence of organizing and disciplining them, inflict severe and ignominious punishments on them. The power might be construed to be exclusive in congress. Suppose, then, that congress should refuse to provide for arming or organizing them, the result would be, that the states would be utterly without the means of defence, and prostrate at the feet of the national government. It might also be said, that congress possessed the exclusive power to suppress insurrections, and repel invasions, which would take from the states all effective means of resistance. The militia might be put under martial law, when not under duty in the public service.

§ 1202. It is difficult fully to comprehend the influence of such objections, urged with much apparent sincerity and earnestness at such an eventful period. The answers then given seem to have been in their structure and reasoning satisfactory and conclusive. But the amendments proposed to the constitution (some of which have been since adopted) show, that the objections were extensively felt, and sedulously cherished. The power of congress over the militia (it was urged) was limited, and concurrent with that of the states. The right of governing them was confined to the single case of their being in the actual service of the United States, in some of the cases pointed out in the constitution. It was then, and then only, that they could be subjected by the general government to martial law. If congress did not choose to arm, organize, or discipline the militia, there would be an inherent right in the states to do it. All, that the constitution intended, was, to give a power to congress to ensure uniformity, and thereby efficiency. But, if congress refused, or neglected to perform the duty, the states had a perfect concurrent right, and might act upon it to the utmost extent of sovereignty. As little pretence was there to say, that congress possessed the exclusive power to suppress insurrections and repel invasions. Their power was merely competent to reach these objects; but did not, and could not, in regard to the militia, supersede the ordinary rights of the states. It was, indeed, made a duty of congress to provide for such cases; but this did not exclude the co-operation of the states. The idea of congress inflicting severe and ignominious punishments upon the militia in times of peace was absurd. It presupposed, that the representatives had an interest, and would intentionally take measures to oppress them, and alienate their affections. The appointment of the officers of the militia was exclusively in the states; and how could it be presumed, that such men would ever consent to the destruction of the rights or privileges of their fellow-citizens. The power to discipline and train the militia, except when in the actual service of the United States, was also exclusively vested in the states; and under such circumstances, it was secure against any serious abuses. It was added, that any project of disciplining the whole militia of the United States would be so utterly impracticable and mischievous, that it would probably never be attempted. The most, that could be done, would be to organize and discipline select corps; and these for all general purposes, either of the states, or of the Union, would be found to combine all, that was useful or desirable in militia services.

§ 1203. It is hardly necessary to say, how utterly without any practical justification have been the alarms, so industriously spread upon this subject at the time, when the constitution was put upon its trial. Upon two occasions only has it been found necessary on the part of the general government, to require the aid of the militia of the states, for the purpose of executing the laws of the Union, suppressing insurrections, or repelling invasions. The first was to suppress the insurrection in Pennsylvania in 1794; and the other, to repel the enemy in the recent war with Great Britain. On other occasions, the militia has indeed been called into service to repel the incursions of the Indians; but in all such cases, the injured states have led the way, and requested the co-operation of the national government. In regard to the other power of organizing, arming, and disciplining the militia, congress passed an act in 1792, more effectually to provide for the national defence, by establishing a uniform militia throughout the United States. The system provided by this act, with the exception of that portion, which established the rules of discipline and field service, has ever since remained in force. And the militia are now governed by the same general system of discipline and field exercise, which is observed by the regular army of the United States. No jealousy of military power, and no dread of severe punishments are now indulged. And the whole militia system has been as mild in its operation, as it has been satisfactory to the nation.

§ 1204. Several questions of great practical importance have arisen under the clauses of the constitution respecting the power over the militia, which deserve mention in this place. It is observable, that power is given to congress "to *provide* for calling forth the militia to execute the laws of the Union, suppress insurrections, and repel invasions." Accordingly, congress in 1795, in pursuance of this authority, and to give it a practical operation, provided by law, "that whenever the United States shall be invaded, or be in imminent danger of invasion from any foreign nation or Indian tribe, it shall be lawful for the president to call forth such number of the militia of the state, or states most convenient to the place of danger, or scene of action, as he may judge necessary, to repel such invasion, and to issue his order for that purpose to such officer or officers of the militia, as he shall think proper." Like provisions are made for the other cases stated in the constitution. The constitutionality of this act has not been questioned, although it provides for calling forth the militia, not only in cases of invasion, but of imminent danger of invasion; for the power to repel invasions must include the power to provide against any attempt and danger of invasion, as the necessary and proper means to effectuate the object. One of the best means to repel invasion is, to provide the requisite force for action, before the invader has reached the territory of the nation. Nor can there be a doubt, that the president, who is (as will be presently seen) by the constitution the commander-in-chief of the army and navy of the United States, and of the militia, when called into the actual service of the United States, is the proper functionary, to whom this high and delicate trust ought to be confided. A free people will naturally be jealous of the exercise of military power; and that of calling forth the militia is certainly one of no ordinary magnitude. It is, however, a power limited in its nature to certain exigencies; and by whomsoever it is to be executed, it carries with it a corresponding responsibility. Who is so fit to exercise the power, and to incur the responsibility, as the president?

§ 1205. But a most material question arises: By whom is the exigency (the *casus foederis,* if one may so say) to be decided? Is the president the sole and exclusive judge, whether the exigency has arisen, or is it to be considered, as an open question, which every officer, to whom the orders of the president are addressed, may decide for himself, and equally open to be contested by every militiaman, who shall refuse to obey the orders of the president? This question was much agitated during the late war with Great Britain, although it is well known, that it had been practically settled by the government, in the year 1794, to belong exclusively to the president; and no inconsiderable diversity of opinion was then manifested in the heat of the controversy, *pendente lite, et flagrante bello.* In Connecticut and Massachusetts, it was held, that the governors of the states, to whom orders were addressed by the president to call forth the militia on account of danger of invasion, were entitled to judge for themselves, whether the exigency had arisen; and were not bound by the opinion or orders of the president. This doctrine, however, was disapproved elsewhere It was contested by the government of the United States; and was renounced by other states.

§ 1206. At a very recent period, the question came before the Supreme Court of the United States for a judicial decision; and it was then unanimously determined, that the authority to decide, whether the exigency has arisen, belongs exclusively to the president and that his decision is conclusive upon all other persons. The court said, that this construction necessarily resulted from the nature of the power itself, and from the manifest objects contemplated by the act of congress. The power itself is to be exercised upon sudden emergencies, upon great occasions of state, and under circumstances, which may be vital to the existence of the Union. A prompt and unhesitating obedience to orders is indispensable to the complete attainment of the object. The service is a military service, and the command of a military nature; and in such cases, every delay and every obstacle to an efficient and immediate compliance would necessarily tend to jeopard the public interests. While subordinate officers or soldiers are pausing to consider, whether they ought to obey, or are scrupulously weighing the facts, upon which the commander-in-chief exercises the right to demand their services, the hostile enterprize may be accomplished, without the means of resistance. If the power of regulating the militia, and of commanding its services in times of insurrection and invasion, are, as it has been emphatically said, they are, natural incidents to the duties of superintending the common defence, and of watching over the internal peace of the confederacy, these powers must be so construed, as to the modes of their exercise, as not to defeat the great end in view. If a superior officer has a right to contest the orders of the president, upon his own doubts, as to the exigency having arisen, it must be equally the right of every inferior officer and soldier. And any act done by any person in furtherance of such orders would subject him to responsibility in a civil suit, in which his defence must finally rest upon his ability to establish the facts by competent proofs. Besides; in many instances the evidence, upon which the president might decide, that there was imminent danger of invasion, might be of a nature not constituting strict technical proof; or the disclosure of the evidence might reveal important state secrets, which the public interest, and even safety, might imperiously demand to be kept in concealment. The act of 1795 was manifestly framed upon this reasoning. The president is by it necessarily constituted, in the first instance, the judge of the existence of the exigency, and is bound to act according to his belief of the facts. If he does so act and decides to call out the militia, his orders for this purpose are in strict conformity to the law; and it would seem to follow, as a necessary consequence, that every act done by a subordinate officer in obedience to such orders is equally justifiable. The law contemplates, that under such circumstances orders shall be given to carry the power into effect; and it cannot be that it is a correct inference, that any other person has a right to disobey them. No provision is made for an appeal from, or review of the president's opinion. And whenever a statute gives a discretionary power to any person to be exercised by him upon his own opinion of certain facts, the general rule of construction is, that he is thereby constituted the sole and exclusive judge of the existence of those facts.

§ 1207. It seems to be admitted, that the power to call forth the militia may be exercised either by requisitions upon the executive of the states; or by order directed to such executive, or to any subordinate officers of the militia. It is not, however, to be understood, that the state executive is in any case bound to leave his executive duties, and go personally into the actual service of the United States.

§ 1208. The power to govern the militia, when in the actual service of the United States, is denied by no one to be an exclusive one. Indeed, from its very nature, it must be so construed; for the notion of distinct and independent orders from authorities wholly unconnected, would be utterly inconsistent with that unity of command and action, on which the success of all military operations must essentially depend. But there is nothing in the constitution, which prohibits a state from calling forth its own militia, not detached into the service of the Union, to aid the United States in executing the laws, in suppressing insurrections, and in repelling invasions. Such a concurrent exercise of power in no degree interferes with, or obstructs the exercise of the powers of the Union. Congress may, by suitable laws, provide for the calling forth of the militia, and annex suitable penalties to disobedience of their orders, and direct the manner, in which the delinquents may be tried. But the authority to call forth, and the authority exclusively to govern, are quite distinct in their nature. The question, when the authority of congress over the militia becomes exclusive, must essentially depend upon the fact, when they are to be deemed in the actual service of the United States. There is a clear distinction between calling forth the militia, and their being in actual service. These are not contemporaneous acts, nor necessarily identical in their constitutional bearings. The president is not commander-in-chief of the militia, except when in actual service; and not, when they are merely ordered into service. They are subjected to martial law only, when in actual service, and not merely when called forth, before they have obeyed the call. The act of 1795, and other acts on this subject, manifestly contemplate and recognise this distinction. To bring the militia within the meaning of being in actual service, there must be an obedience to the call, and some acts of organization, mustering, rendezvous, or marching, done in obedience to the call, in the public service.

§ 1209. But whether the power is exclusive in congress to punish delinquencies in not obeying the call on the militia, by their own courts-martial, has been a question much discussed, and upon which no inconsiderable contrariety of opinion has been expressed. That it may, by law, be made exclusive, is not denied. But if no such law be made, whether a state may not, by its own laws, constitute courts-martial to try and punish the delinquencies, and inflict the penalties prescribed by the act of congress, has been the point of controversy. It is now settled, that, under such circumstances, a state court-martial may constitutionally take cognizance of, and inflict the punishment. But a state cannot add to, or vary the punishments inflicted by the acts of congress upon the delinquents.

§ 1210. A question of another sort was also made during the late war with Great Britain; whether the militia, called into the actual service of the United States, were to be governed and commanded by any officer, but of the same militia, except the president of the United States; in other words, whether the president could delegate any other officer of the regular army, of equal or superior rank, to command the militia in his absence. It was held in several of the Eastern states, that the militia were exclusively under the command of their own officers, subject to the personal orders of the president; and that he could not authorize any officer of the army of the United States to command them in his absence, nor place them under the command of any such officer. This doctrine was deemed inadmissible by the functionaries of the United States. It has never yet been settled by any definitive judgment of any tribunal competent to decide it. If, however, the doctrine can be maintained, it is obvious, that the public service must be continually liable to very great embarrassments in all cases, where the militia are called into the public service in connexion with the regular troops.

SEE ALSO:

Generally 1.8.12; 1.8.15; Amend. VI
Matthew Hale, History of the Common Law, 42–43 (1713)
An Act for Regulating and Disciplining the Militia, 1777, Laws of Virginia, Hening 9:267–74
Records of the Federal Convention, Farrand 2:135, 136, 159, 168, 323, 352, 368, 380–81, 570, 595
Vermont Constitution of 1786, c. 1, art. 19, Thorpe 6:3754
Luther Martin, Defense of Elbridge Gerry, 18 Jan. 1788, Essays 342
An Act More Effectually to Provide for the National Defense, 1 Stat. 271 (1792)
Kentucky Constitution of 1792, art. 6, cl. 2–4, Thorpe 3:1271
House of Representatives, The Militia Bill, 21 Feb., 12 Apr. 1792, Annals 3:418–23, 553–55
House of Representatives, Organization of the Militia, 9 Jan. 1795, Annals 4:1067–70

Wise v. *Withers,* 3 Cranch 331 (1806)
House of Representatives, Classification of the Militia, 2 Jan. 1808, Annals 15:327–29
Caesar A. Rodney, Power of President to Nominate a Brigadier for Territorial Militia, 12 Apr. 1810, 1 Ops. Atty. Gen. 165
Commonwealth v. *Irish,* in *Moore* v. *Houston,* 3 Serg. & Rawle 176n (Pa. 1817)
Duffield v. *Smith,* 3 Serg. & Rawle 590 (Pa. 1818)
Mills v. *Martin,* 19 Johns. R. 7 (N.Y. 1821)

Article 1, Section 8, Clause 17

To exercise exclusive Legislation in all Cases whatsoever, over such District (not exceeding ten Miles square) as may, by Cession of Particular States, and the Acceptance of Congress, become the Seat of the Government of the United States, and to exercise like Authority over all Places purchased by the Consent of the Legislature of the State in which the Same shall be, for the Erection of Forts, Magazines, Arsenals, dock-Yards, and other needful Buildings;—

1

WILLIAM BLACKSTONE, COMMENTARIES 1:255
1765

This statute, it is obvious to observe, extends not only to fleets and armies, but also to forts, and other places of strength, within the realm; the sole prerogative as well of erecting, as manning and governing of which, belongs to the king in his capacity of general of the kingdom: and all lands were formerly subject to a tax, for building of castles wherever the king thought proper. This was one of the three things, from contributing to the performance of which no lands were exempted; and therefore called by our Saxon ancestors the *trinoda necessitas: sc. pontis reparatio, arcis constructio, et expeditio contra hostem.* And this they were called upon to do so often, that, as sir Edward Coke from M. Paris assures us, there were in the time of Henry II 1115 castles subsisting in England. The inconvenience of which, when granted out to private subjects, the lordly barons of those times, was severely felt by the whole kingdom; for, as William of Newbury remarks in the reign of king Stephen, *"erant in Anglia quodammodo tot reges vel potius tyranni, quot domini castellorum:"* but it was felt by none more sensibly than by two succeeding princes, king John and king Henry III. And therefore, the greatest part of them being demolished in the barons' wars, the kings of after times have been very cautious of suffering them to be rebuilt in a fortified manner: and sir Edward Coke lays it down, that no subject can build a castle, or house of strength imbatteled, or other fortress defensible, without the licence of the king; for the danger which might ensue, if every man at his pleasure might do it.

2

RECORDS OF THE FEDERAL CONVENTION

[*2:127; Madison, 26 July*]

Col. Mason. observed that it would be proper, as he thought, that some provision should be made in the Constitution agst. choosing for the seat of the Genl. Govt. the City or place at which the seat of any State Govt. might be fixt. There were 2 objections agst. having them at the same place, which without mentioning others, required some precaution on the subject. The 1st. was that it tended to produce disputes concerning jurisdiction—The 2d. & principal one was that the intermixture of the two Legislatures tended to give a provincial tincture to ye Natl. deliberations. He moved that the Come. be instructed to receive a clause to prevent the seat of the Natl. Govt. being in the same City or town with the seat of the Govt. of any State longer than untill the necessary public buildings could be erected.

Mr. Alex. Martin 2ded. the motion.

Mr. Govr. Morris did not dislike the idea, but was apprehensive that such a clause might make enemies of Philda. & N. York which had expectations of becoming the Seat of the Genl. Govt.

Mr. Langdon approved the idea also: but suggisted the case of a State moving its seat of Govt. to the natl. seat after the erection of the public buildings

Mr. Ghorum. the precaution may be evaded by the Natl. Legislre. by delaying to erect the public buildings

Mr. Gerry conceived it to be the genel. sense of America, that neither the Seat of a State Govt. nor any large commercial City should be the seat of the Genl. Govt.

Mr. Williamson liked the idea, but knowing how much the passions of men were agitated by this matter, was apprehensive of turning them agst. the system. He apprehended also that an evasion might be practiced in the way hinted by Mr. Ghorum.

Mr. Pinkney thought the seat of a State Govt. ought to be avoided; but that a large town or its vicinity would be proper for the seat of the Genl. Govt.

Col. Mason did not mean to press the motion at this time, nor to excite any hostile passions agst. the system. He was content to withdraw the motion for the present.

Mr. Butler was for fixing by the Constitution the place, & a central one, for the seat of the Natl Govt

[*2:261; Madison, 11 Aug.*]

Mr. King remarked that the section authorized the 2 Houses to adjourn to a new place. He thought this inconvenient. The mutability of place had dishonored the federal Govt. and would require as strong a cure as we could devise. He thought a law at least should be made necessary to a removal of the Seat of Govt.

Mr Madison viewed the subject in the same light, and joined with Mr. King in a motion requiring a law.

Mr. Governr. Morris proposed the additional alteration by inserting the words "during the Session" &c".

Mr. Spaight. this will fix the seat of Govt at N. Y. The present Congress will convene them there in the first instance, and they will never be able to remove; especially if the Presidt. should be Northern Man.

Mr Govr Morris. such a distrust is inconsistent with all Govt.

Mr. Madison supposed that a central place for the Seat of Govt. was so just and wd. be so much insisted on by the H. of Representatives, that though a law should be made requisite for the purpose, it could & would be obtained. The necessity of a central residence of the Govt wd be much greater under the new than old Govt The members of the new Govt wd. be more numerous. They would be taken more from the interior parts of the States: they wd. not, like members of ye present Congs. come so often from the distant States by water. As the powers & objects of the new Govt. would be far greater yn. heretofore, more private individuals wd. have business calling them to the seat of it, and it was more necessary that the Govt should be in that position from which it could contemplate with the most equal eye, and sympathize most equally with, every part of the nation. These considerations he supposed would extort a removal even if a law were made necessary. But in order to quiet suspicions both within & without doors, it might not be amiss to authorize the 2 Houses by a concurrent vote to adjourn at their first meeting to the most proper place, and to require thereafter, the sanction of a law to their removal. The motion was accordingly moulded into the following form: "the Legislature shall at their first assembling determine on a place at which their future sessions shall be held; neither House shall afterwards, during the session of the House of Reps. without the consent of the other, adjourn for more than three days, nor shall they adjourn to any other place than such as shall have been fixt by law"

Mr. Gerry thought it would be wrong to let the Presdt check the will of the 2 Houses on this subject at all.

Mr Williamson supported the ideas of Mr. Spaight

Mr Carrol was actuated by the same apprehensions

Mr. Mercer. it will serve no purpose to require the two Houses at their first Meeting to fix on a place. They will never agree.

After some further expressions from others denoting an apprehension that the seat of Govt. might be continued at an improper place if a law should be made necessary to a removal, and the motion above stated with another for recommitting the section had been negatived, the Section was left in the shape it which it was reported, as to this point. The words "during the session of the legislature" were prefixed to the 8th section—and the last sentence "But this regulation shall not extend to the Senate when it shall exercise the powers mentioned in the article" struck out. The 8th. section as amended was then agreed to.

[*2:510; Madison, 5 Sept.*]

So much of the (4) clause as related to the seat of Government was agreed to nem: con:

On the residue, to wit, "to exercise like authority over all places purchased for forts &c.

Mr Gerry contended that this power might be made use of to enslave any particular State by buying up its territory, and that the strongholds proposed would be a means of awing the State into an undue obedience to the Genl. Government—

Mr. King thought himself the provision unnecessary, the power being already involved: but would move to insert after the word "purchased" the words "by the consent of the Legislature of the State" This would certainly make the power safe.

Mr. Govr Morris 2ded. the motion, which was agreed to nem: con: as was then the residue of the clause as amended.

3

James Madison, Federalist, no. 43, 288–90
23 Jan. 1788

The indispensible necessity of compleat authority at the seat of Government carries its own evidence with it. It is a power exercised by every Legislature of the Union, I might say of the world, by virtue of its general supremacy. Without it, not only the public authority might be insulted and its proceedings be interrupted, with impunity; but a dependence of the members of the general Government, on the State comprehending the seat of the Government for protection in the exercise of their duty, might bring on the national councils an imputation of awe or influence, equally dishonorable to the Government, and dissatisfactory to the other members of the confederacy. This consideration has the more weight as the gradual accumulation of public improvements at the stationary residence of the Government, would be both too great a public pledge to be left in the hands of a single State; and would create so many obstacles to a removal of the Government, as still further to abridge its necessary independence. The extent of this federal district is sufficiently circumscribed to satisfy every jealousy of an opposite nature. And as it is to be appropriated to this use with the consent of the State ceding it; as the State will no doubt provide in the compact for the rights, and the consent of the citizens inhabiting it; as the inhabitants will find sufficient inducements of interest to become willing parties to the cession; as they will have had their voice in the election of the Government which is to exercise authority over them; as a municipal Legislature for local purposes, derived from their own suffrages, will of course be allowed them; and as the authority of the Legislature of the State, and of the inhabitants of the ceded part of it, to concur in the cession, will be derived from the whole people of the State, in their adoption of the Constitution, every imaginable objection seems to be obviated.

The necessity of a like authority over forts, magazines &c. established by the general Government is not less evident. The public money expended on such places, and the public property deposited in them, require that they should be exempt from the authority of the particular State. Nor would it be proper for the places on which the security of the entire Union may depend, to be in any degree dependent on a particular member of it. All objections and scruples are here also obviated by requiring the concurrence of the States concerned, in every such establishment.

4

Debate in Massachusetts Ratifying Convention
24 Jan. 1788
Elliot 2:99

Hon. Mr. Strong said, every gentleman must think that the erection of a federal town was necessary, wherein Congress might remain protected from insult. A few years ago, said the honorable gentleman, Congress had to remove, because they were not protected by the authority of the state in which they were then sitting. He asked whether this Convention, though convened for but a short period, did not think it was necessary that they should have power to protect themselves from insult; much more so must they think it necessary to provide for Congress, considering they are to be a permanent body.

Hon. Mr. Davis (of Boston) said it was necessary that Congress should have a permanent residence; and that it was the intention of Congress, under the Confederation, to erect a federal town. He asked, Would Massachusetts, or any other state, wish to give to New York, or the state in which Congress shall sit, the power to influence the proceedings of that body, which was to act for the benefit of the whole, by leaving them liable to the outrage of the citizens of such states?

Dr. Taylor asked, why it need be *ten miles square,* and whether one mile square would not be sufficient.

Hon. Mr. Strong said, Congress was not to exercise jurisdiction over a district of ten miles, but one not *exceeding* ten miles square.

Rev. Mr. Stillman said, that, whatever were the limits of the district, it would depend on the cession of the legislature of one of the states.

5

Federal Farmer, no. 18
25 Jan. 1788
Storing 2.8.222–28

The constitution provides, that congress shall have the sole and exclusive government of what is called the federal city, a place not exceeding ten miles square, and of all places ceded for forts, dock-yards. &c. I believe this is a novel kind of provision in a federal republic; it is repugnant to the spirit of such a government, and must be founded in an apprehension of a hostile disposition between the federal head and the state governments; and it is not improbable, that the sudden retreat of congress from Philadelphia, first gave rise to it.—With this apprehension, we provide, the government of the union shall have secluded places, cities, and castles of defence, which no state laws whatever shall invade. When we attentively examine this provision in all its consequences, it opens to view scenes almost without bounds. A federal, or rather a national city, ten miles square, containing a hundred square miles, is about four times as large as London; and for forts, magazines, arsenals, dock-yards, and other needful buildings, congress may possess a number of places or towns in each state. It is true, congress cannot have them unless the state legislatures cede them; but when once ceded, they never can be recovered, and though the general temper of the legislatures may be averse to such cessions, yet many opportunities and advantages may be taken of particular times and circumstances of complying assemblies, and of particular parties, to obtain them. It is not improbable, that some considerable towns or places, in some intemperate moments, or influenced by anti-republican principles, will petition to be ceded for the purposes mentioned in the provision. There are men, and even towns, in the best republics, which are often fond of withdrawing from the government of them, whenever occasion shall present. The case is still stronger: if the provision in question holds out allurements to attempt to withdraw, the people of a state must ever be subject to state as well as federal taxes; but the federal city and places will be subject only to the latter, and to them by no fixed proportion, nor of the taxes raised in them, can the separate states demand any account of congress.—These doors opened for withdrawing from the state governments entirely, may, on other accounts, be very alluring and pleasing to those anti-republican men who prefer a place under the wings of courts.

If a federal town be necessary for the residence of congress and the public officers, it ought to be a small one, and the government of it fixed on republican and common law principles, carefully enumerated and established by the constitution. It is true, the states, when they shall cede places, may stipulate, that the laws and government of congress in them, shall always be formed on such principlès; but it is easy to discern, that the stipulations of a state, or of the inhabitants of the place ceded, can be of but little avail against the power and gradual encroachments of the union. The principles ought to be established by the federal constitution, to which all the states are parties; but in no event can there be any need of so large a city and places for forts, &c. totally exempted from the laws and jurisdictions of the state governments. If I understand the constitution, the laws of congress, constitutionally made, will have complete and supreme jurisdiction to all federal purposes, on every inch of ground in the United States, and exclusive jurisdiction on the high seas, and this by the highest authority, the consent of the people. Suppose ten acres at West-Point shall be used as a fort of the union, or a sea port town as a dock-yard, the laws of the union in those places respecting the navy, forces of the union, and all federal objects, must prevail, be noticed by all judges and officers, and executed accordingly: and I can discern no one reason for excluding from these places, the operation of state laws, as to mere state purposes; for instance, for the collection of state taxes in them, recovering debts, deciding questions of property arising within them on state laws, punishing, by state laws, theft, trespasses, and offences committed in them by mere citizens against the state laws.

The city, and all the places in which the union shall have this exclusive jurisdiction, will be immediately under one entire government, that of the federal head; and be no part of any state, and consequently no part of the United States. The inhabitants of the federal city and places, will be as much exempt from the laws and controul of the state governments, as the people of Canada or Nova Scotia will be. Neither the laws of the states respecting taxes, the militia, crimes or property, will extend to them; nor is there a single stipulation in the constitution, that the inhabitants of this city, and these places, shall be governed by laws founded on principles of freedom. All questions, civil and criminal, arising on the laws of these places, which must be the laws of congress, must be decided in the federal courts; and also, all questions that may, by such judicial fictions as these courts may consider reasonable, be supposed to arise within this city, or any of these places, may be brought into these courts; and by a very common legal fiction, any personal contract may be supposed to have been made in any place. A contract made in Georgia may be supposed to have been made in the federal city, in Pennsylvania; the courts will admit the fiction, and not in these cases, make it a serious question, where it was in fact made. Every suit in which an inhabitant of a federal district may be a party, of course may be instituted in the federal courts—also, every suit in which it may be alledged, and not denied, that a party in it is an inhabitant of such a district—also, every suit to which a foreign state or subject, the union, a state, citizens of different states, in fact, or by reasonable legal fictions, may be a party or parties: And thus, by means of bankrupt laws, federal districts, &c. almost all judicial business, I apprehend may be carried into the federal courts, without essentially departing from the usual course of judicial proceedings. The courts in Great Britain have acquired their powers, and extended, very greatly, their jurisdictions by such fictions and suppositions as I have mentioned. The constitution, in these points, certainly involves in it principles, and almost hidden cases, which may unfold, and in time exhibit consequences we hardly think of. The power of naturalization, when viewed in connection with the judicial powers and cases, is, in my mind, of very doubtful extent. By the constitution itself, the citizens of each state will be naturalized citizens of every state, to the general purposes of instituting suits, claiming the benefits of the laws, &c. And in order to give the federal courts jurisdiction of an action, between citizens of the same state, in common acceptation, may not a court allow the plaintiff to say, he is a citizen of one state, and the defendant a citizen of another, without carrying legal fictions so far, by any means, as they have been carried by the courts of King's Bench and Exchequer, in order to bring causes within their cognizance—Further, the federal city and districts, will be totally distinct from any state, and a citizen of a state will not of course be a subject of any of them; and to avail himself of the privileges and immunities of them, must he not be naturalized by congress in them? and may not congress make any proportion of the citizens of the states naturalized subjects of the federal city and districts, and thereby entitle them to sue or defend, in all cases, in the federal courts? I have my doubts, and many sensible men, I find, have their doubts, on these points; and we ought to observe, they must be settled in the courts of law, by their rules, distinctions, and fictions. To avoid many of these intricacies and difficulties, and to avoid the undue and unnecessary extension of the federal judicial powers, it appears to me, that no federal districts ought to be allowed, and no federal city or town, except perhaps a small town, in which the government shall be republican, but in which congress shall have no jurisdiction over the inhabitants, but in common with the other inhabitants of the states. Can the union want, in such a town, any thing more than a right to the soil on which it may set its buildings, and extensive jurisdiction over the federal buildings, and property, its own members, officers, and servants in it? As to all federal objects, the union will have complete jurisdiction over them, of course any where, and every where. I still think, that no actions ought to be allowed to be brought in the federal courts, between citizens of different states, at least, unless the cause be of very considerable importance: that no action against a state government, by any citizen or foreigner, ought to be allowed; and no action, in which a foreign subject is party, at least, unless it be of very considerable importance, ought to be instituted in the federal courts—I confess, I can see no reason whatever, for a foreigner, or for citizens of different states, carrying sixpenny causes into the federal courts; I think the state courts will be found by experience, to be bottomed on better principles, and to administer justice better than the federal courts.

The difficulties and dangers I have supposed, will result from so large a federal city, and federal districts, from the extension of the federal judicial powers, &c. are not, I conceive, merely possible, but probable. I think, pernicious political consequences will follow from them, and from the federal city especially, for very obvious reasons, a few of which I will mention.

We must observe, that the citizens of a state will be subject to state as well as federal taxes, and the inhabitants of the federal city and districts, only to such taxes as congress may lay—We are not to suppose all our people are attached to free government, and the principles of the common law, but that many thousands of them will prefer a city governed, not on republican principles—This city, and the government of it, must indubitably take their tone from the characters of the men, who from the nature of its situation and institution, must collect there. This city will not be established for productive labour, for mercantile, or mechanic industry; but for the residence of government, its officers and attendants. If hereafter it should ever become a place of trade and industry, in the early periods of its existence, when its laws and government must receive their fixed tone, it must be a mere court, with its appendages, the executive, congress, the law courts, gentlemen of fortune and pleasure, with all the officers, attendants, suitors, expectants and dependants on the whole, however brilliant and honourable this collection may be. If we expect it will have any sincere attachments to simple and frugal republicanism, to that liberty and mild government, which is dear to the laborious part of a free people, we most assuredly deceive ourselves. This early collection will draw to it men from all parts of the country, of a like political description: we see them looking towards the place already.

Such a city, or town, containing a hundred square miles, must soon be the great, the visible, and dazzling centre, the mistress of fashions, and the fountain of politics. There may be a free or shackled press in this city, and the streams which may issue from it may overflow the country, and they will be poisonous or pure, as the fountain may be corrupt or not. But not to dwell on a subject that must give pain to the virtuous friends of freedom, I will only add, can a free and enlightened people create a common head so extensive, so prone to corruption and slavery, as this city probably will be, when they have it in their power to form one pure and chaste, frugal and republican.

Under the confederation congress has no power whereby to govern its own officers and servant[s]: a federal town, in which congress might have special jurisidiction, might be expedient; but under the new constitution, without a federal town, congress will have all necessary powers of course over its officers and servants; indeed it will have a complete system of powers to all the federal purposes mentioned in the constitution; so that the reason for a federal town under the confederation, will by no means exist under the constitution.—Even if a trial by jury should be admitted in the federal city, what man, with any state attachments or republican virtue about him, will submit to be tried by a jury of it.

6

DEBATE IN VIRGINIA RATIFYING CONVENTION 6, 16 June 1788

Elliot 3:89, 430–36, 439–42

[*6 June*]

[Mr. MADISON:] He [Patrick Henry] next objects to the exclusive legislation over the district where the seat of government may be fixed. Would he submit that the representatives of this state should carry on their deliberations under the control of any other member of the Union? If any state had the power of legislation over the place where Congress should fix the general government, this would impair the dignity, and hazard the safety, of Congress. If the safety of the Union were under the control of any particular state, would not foreign corruption probably prevail, in such a state, to induce it to exert its controlling influence over the members of the general government? Gentlemen cannot have forgotten the disgraceful insult which Congress received some years ago. When we also reflect that the previous cession of particular states is necessary before Congress can legislate exclusively any where, we must, instead of being alarmed at this part, heartily approve of it.

[*16 June*]

Mr. GRAYSON: . . . Adverting to the clause investing Congress with the power of exclusive legislation in a district not exceeding ten miles square, he said he had before expressed his doubts that this district would be the favorite of the generality, and that it would be possible for them to give exclusive privileges of commerce to those residing within it. He had illustrated what he said by European examples. It might be said to be impracticable to exercise this power in this manner. Among the various laws and customs which pervaded Europe, there were exclusive privileges and immunities enjoyed in many places. He thought that this ought to be guarded against; for should such exclusive privileges be granted to merchants residing within the ten miles square, it would be highly injurious to the inhabitants of other places.

Mr. GEORGE MASON thought that there were few clauses in the Constitution so dangerous as that which gave Congress exclusive power of legislation within ten miles square. Implication, he observed, was capable of any extension, and would probably be extended to augment the congressional powers. But here there was no need of implication. This clause gave them an unlimited authority, in every possible case, within that district. This ten miles square, says Mr. Mason, may set at defiance the laws of the surrounding states, and may, like the custom of the superstitious days of our ancestors, become the sanctuary of the blackest crimes. Here the federal courts are to sit. We have heard a good deal said of justice.

It has been doubted whether jury trial be secured in civil cases. But I will suppose that we shall have juries in civil cases. What sort of a jury shall we have within the ten miles square? The immediate creatures of the government. What chance will poor men get, where Congress have the power of legislating in all cases whatever, and where judges and juries may be under their influence, and bound to support their operations? Even with juries the chance of justice may here be very small, as Congress have unlimited authority, legislative, executive, and judicial. Lest this power should not be sufficient, they have it in every case. Now, sir, if an attempt should be made to establish tyranny over the people, here are ten miles square where the greatest offender may meet protection. If any of their officers, or creatures, should attempt to oppress the people, or should actually perpetrate the blackest deed, he has nothing to do but get into the ten miles square. Why was this dangerous power given? Felons may receive an asylum there and in their strongholds. Gentlemen have said that it was dangerous to argue against possible abuse, because there could be no power delegated but might be abused. It is an incontrovertible axiom, that, when the dangers that may arise from *abuse* are greater than the benefits that may result from the use, the power ought to be withheld. I do not conceive that this power is at all necessary, though capable of being greatly abused.

We are told by the honorable gentleman that Holland has its Hague. I confess I am at a loss to know what inference he could draw from that observation. This is the place where the deputies of the United Provinces meet to transact the public business. But I do not recollect that they have any exclusive jurisdiction whatever in that place, but are subject to the laws of the province in which the Hague is. To what purpose the gentleman mentioned that Holland has its Hague, I cannot see.

Mr. MASON then observed that he would willingly give them exclusive power, as far as respected the police and good government of the place; but he would give them no more, because he thought it unnecessary. He was very willing to give them, in this as well as in all other cases, those powers which he thought indispensably necessary.

Mr. MADISON. Mr. Chairman: I did conceive, sir, that the clause under consideration was one of those parts which would speak its own praise. It is hardly necessary to say any thing concerning it. Strike it out of the system, and let me ask whether there would not be much larger scope for those dangers. I cannot comprehend that the power of legislating over a small district, which cannot exceed ten miles square, and may not be more than one mile, will involve the dangers which he apprehends. If there be any knowledge in my mind of the nature of man, I should think it would be the last thing that would enter into the mind of any man to grant exclusive advantages, in a very circumscribed district, to the prejudice of the community at large. We make suppositions, and afterwards deduce conclusions from them, as if they were established axioms. But, after all, bring home this question to ourselves. Is it probable that the members from Georgia, New Hampshire, &c., will concur to sacrifice the privileges of their friends? I believe that, whatever state may become the seat of the general government, it will become the object of the jealousy and envy of the other states. Let me remark, if not already remarked, that there must be a cession, by particular states, of the district to Congress, and that the states may settle the terms of the cession. The states may make what stipulation they please in it, and, if they apprehend any danger, they may refuse it altogether. How could the general government be guarded from the undue influence of particular states, or from insults, without such exclusive power? If it were at the pleasure of a particular state to control the session and deliberations of Congress, would they be secure from insults, or the influence of such state? If this commonwealth depended, for the freedom of deliberation, on the laws of any state where it might be necessary to sit, would it not be liable to attacks of that nature (and with more indignity) which have been already offered to Congress? With respect to the government of Holland, I believe the States General have no jurisdiction over the Hague; but I have heard that mentioned as a circumstance which gave undue influence to Holland over the rest. We must limit our apprehensions to certain degrees of probability. The evils which they urge must result from this clause are extremely improbable; nay, almost impossible.

Mr. Grayson. Mr. Chairman, one answer which has been given is, the improbability of the evil—that it will never be attempted, and that it is almost impossible. This will not satisfy us, when we consider the great attachments men have to a great and magnificent capital. It would be the interest of the citizens of that district to aggrandize themselves by every possible means in their power, to the great injury of the other states. If we travel all over the world, we shall find that people have aggrandized their own capitals. Look at Russia and Prussia. Every step has been taken to aggrandize their capitals. In what light are we to consider the ten miles square? It is not to be a fourteenth state. The inhabitants will in no respect whatever be amenable to the laws of any state. A clause in the 4th article, highly extolled for its wisdom, will be rendered nugatory by this exclusive legislation. This clause runs thus: "No person held to service or labor in one state, under the laws thereof, escaping into another, shall, in consequence of any law or regulation therein, be discharged from such service or labor, but shall be delivered up on the claim of the party to whom such labor or service may be due." Unless you consider the ten miles square as a state, persons bound to labor, who shall escape thither, will not be given up; for they are only to be delivered up after they shall have escaped into a state. As my honorable friend mentioned, felons, who shall have fled from justice to the ten miles square, cannot be apprehended. The executive of a state is to apply to that of another for the delivery of a felon. He cannot apply to the ten miles square. It was often in contemplation of Congress to have power of regulating the police of the seat of government; but they never had an idea of exclusive legislation in all cases. The power of regulating the police and good government of it will secure Congress against insults. What originated the idea of the exclusive legislation was, some insurrection in Pennsylvania, whereby Congress was insulted,—on account of which, it is supposed, they left the state.

It is answered that the consent of the state must be required, or else they cannot have such a district, or places for the erecting of forts, &c. But how much is already given them! Look at the great country to the north-west of the Ohio, extending to and commanding the lakes.

Look at the other end of the Ohio, towards South Carolina, extending to the Mississippi. See what these, in process of time, may amount to. They may grant exclusive privileges to any particular part of which they have the possession. But it may be observed that those extensive countries will be formed into independent states, and that their consent will be necessary. To this I answer, that they may still grant such privileges as, in that country, are already granted to Congress by the states. The grants of Virginia, South Carolina, and other states, will be subservient to Congress in this respect. Of course, it results from the whole, that requiring the consent of the states will be no guard against this abuse of power.

[A desultory conversation ensued.]

Mr. Nicholas insisted that as the state, within which the ten miles square might be, could prescribe the terms on which Congress should hold it, no danger could arise, as no state would consent to injure itself: there was the same security with respect to the places purchased for the erection of forts, magazines, &c.; and as to the territory of the United States, the power of Congress only extended to make needful rules and regulations concerning it, without prejudicing the claim of any particular state, the right of territory not being given up; that the grant of those lands to the United States was for the general benefit of all the states, and not to be perverted to their prejudice; that, consequently, whether that country were formed into new states or not, the danger apprehended could not take place; that the seat of government was to be still a part of the state, and, as to general regulations, was to be considered as such.

Mr. Grayson, on the other hand, contended that the ten miles square could not be viewed as a state; that the state within which it might be would have no power of legislating over it; that, consequently, persons bound to labor, and felons, might receive protection there; that exclusive emoluments might be granted to those residing within it; that the territory of the United States, being a part of no state or states, might be appropriated to what use Congress pleased, without the consent of any state or states; and that, consequently, such exclusive privileges and exemptions might be granted, and such protection afforded to fugitives, within such places, as Congress should think proper; that, after mature consideration, he could not find that the ten miles square was to be looked upon even as a part of a state, but to be totally independent of all, and subject to the exclusive legislation of Congress.

Mr. Lee strongly expatiated on the impossibility of securing any human institution from possible abuse. He thought the powers conceded in the paper on the table not so liable to be abused as the powers of the state governments. Gentlemen had suggested that the seat of government would become a sanctuary for state villains, and that, in a short time, ten miles square would subjugate a country of eight hundred miles square. This appeared to him a most improbable possibility; nay, he might call it impossibility. Were the place crowded with rogues, he asked if it would be an agreeable place of residence for the members of the general government, who were freely chosen by the people and the state governments. Would the people be so lost to honor and virtue, as to select men who would willingly associate with the most abandoned characters? He thought the honorable gentleman's objections against remote possibility of abuse went to prove that government of no sort was eligible, but that a state of nature was preferable to a state of civilization. He apprehended no danger; and thought that persons bound to labor, and felons, could not take refuge in the ten miles square, or other places exclusively governed by Congress, because it would be contrary to the Constitution, and a palpable usurpation, to protect them.

. . . . .

Mr. HENRY replied that, if Congress were vested with supreme power of legislation, paramount to the constitution and laws of the states, the dangers he had described might happen; for that Congress would not be confined to the enumerated powers. This construction was warranted, in his opinion, by the addition of the word *department,* at the end of the clause, and that they could make any laws which they might think necessary to execute the powers of any department or officer of the government.

Mr. PENDLETON. Mr. Chairman, this clause does not give Congress power to impede the operation of any part of the Constitution, or to make any regulation that may affect the interests of the citizens of the Union at large. But it gives them power over the local police of the place, so as to be secured from any interruption in their proceedings. Notwithstanding the violent attack upon it, I believe, sir, this is the fair construction of the clause. It gives them power of exclusive legislation in any case within that district. What is the meaning of this? What is it opposed to? Is it opposed to the general powers of the federal legislature, or to those of the state legislatures? I understand it as opposed to the legislative power of that state where it shall be. What, then, is the power? It is, that Congress shall exclusively legislate there, in order to preserve the police of the place and their own personal independence, that they may not be overawed or insulted, and of course to preserve them in opposition to any attempt by the state where it shall be. This is the fair construction. Can we suppose that, in order to effect these salutary ends, Congress will make it an asylum for villains and the vilest characters from all parts of the world? Will it not degrade their own dignity to make it a sanctuary for villains? I hope that no man that will ever compose that Congress will associate with the most profligate characters.

Why oppose this power? Suppose it was contrary to the sense of their constituents to grant exclusive privileges to citizens residing within that place; the effect would be directly in opposition to what he says. It could have no operation without the limits of that district. Were Congress to make a law granting them an exclusive privilege of trading to the East Indies, it could have no effect the moment it would go without that place; for their exclusive power is confined to that district. Were they to pass such a law, it would be nugatory; and every member of the community at large could trade to the East Indies as well as the citizens of that district. This exclusive power is limited to that place solely, for their own preservation, which all gentlemen allow to be necessary.

Will you pardon me when I observe that their construction of the preceding clause does not appear to me to be natural, or warranted by the words.

. . . . .

With respect to the necessity of the ten miles square being superseded by the subsequent clause, which gives them power to make all laws which shall be necessary and proper for carrying into execution the foregoing powers, and all other powers vested by this Constitution in the government of the United States, or in any department or officer thereof, I understand that clause as not going a single step beyond the delegated powers. What can it act upon? Some power given by this Constitution. If they should be about to pass a law in consequence of this clause, they must pursue some of the delegated powers, but can by no means depart from them, or arrogate any new powers; for the plain language of the clause is, to give them power to pass laws in order to give effect to the delegated powers.

Mr. GEORGE MASON. Mr. Chairman, gentlemen say there is no new power given by this clause. Is there any thing in this Constitution which secures to the states the powers which are said to be retained? Will powers remain to the states which are not expressly guarded and reserved? I will suppose a case. Gentlemen may call it an impossible case, and suppose that Congress will act with wisdom and integrity. Among the enumerated powers, Congress are to lay and collect taxes, duties, imposts, and excises, and to pay the debts, and to provide for the general welfare and common defence; and by that clause (so often called the *sweeping clause*) they are to make all laws necessary to execute those laws. Now, suppose oppressions should arise under this government, and any writer should dare to stand forth, and expose to the community at large the abuses of those powers; could not Congress, under the idea of providing for the general welfare, and under their own construction, say that this was destroying the general peace, encouraging sedition, and poisoning the minds of the people? And could they not, in order to provide against this, lay a dangerous restriction on the press? Might they not even bring the trial of this restriction within the ten miles square, when there is no prohibition against it? Might they not thus destroy the trial by jury? Would they not extend their implication? It appears to me that they may and will. And shall the support of our rights depend on the bounty of men whose interest it may be to oppress us? That Congress should have power to provide for the general welfare of the Union, I grant. But I wish a clause in the Constitution, with respect to all powers which are not granted, that they are retained by the states. Otherwise, the power of providing for the general welfare may be perverted to its destruction.

Many gentlemen, whom I respect, take different sides of this question. We wish this amendment to be introduced, to remove our apprehensions. There was a clause in the Confederation reserving to the states respectively every power, jurisdiction, and right, not expressly delegated to the United States. This clause has never been complained of, but approved by all. Why not, then, have a similar clause in this Constitution, in which it is the more indispensably necessary than in the Confederation, because of the great augmentation of power vested in the former? In my humble apprehension, unless there be some such clear and finite expression, this clause now under consideration will go to any thing our rulers may think proper. Unless there be some express declaration that every thing not given is retained, it will be carried to any power Congress may please.

7

Thomas Tredwell, New York Ratifying Convention
2 July 1788
Elliot 2:402

The plan of the *federal city,* sir, departs from every principle of freedom, as far as the distance of the two polar stars from each other; for, subjecting the inhabitants of that district to the exclusive legislation of Congress, in whose appointment they have no share or vote, is laying a foundation on which may be erected as complete a tyranny as can be found in the Eastern world. Nor do I see how this evil can possibly be prevented, without razing the foundation of this happy place, where men are to live, without labor, upon the fruit of the labors of others; this political hive, where all the drones in the society are to be collected to feed on the honey of the land. How dangerous this city may be, and what its operation on the general liberties of this country, time alone must discover; but I pray God, it may not prove to this western world what the city of Rome, enjoying a similar constitution, did to the eastern.

8

Debate in North Carolina Ratifying Convention
30 July 1788
Elliot 4:209, 219–20

Mr. Spaight: He objects to giving the government exclusive legislation in a district not exceeding ten miles square, although the previous consent and cession of the state within which it may be, is required. Is it to be supposed that the representatives of the people will make regulations therein dangerous to liberty? Is there the least color or pretext for saying that the militia will be carried and kept there for life? Where is there any power to do this? The power of calling forth the militia is given for the common defence; and can we suppose that our own representatives, chosen for so short a period, will dare to pervert a power, given for the general protection, to an absolute oppression? But the gentleman has gone farther, and says, that any man who will complain of their oppressions, or write against their usurpation, may be deemed a traitor, and tried as such in the ten miles square, without a jury. What an astonishing misrepresentation! Why did not the gentleman look at the Constitution, and see their powers? Treason is there defined. It says, expressly, that treason against the United States shall consist only in levying war against them, or in adhering to their enemies, giving them aid and comfort. Complaining, therefore, or writing, cannot be treason. [Here Mr. Lenoir rose, and said he meant misprision of treason.] The same reasons hold against that too. The liberty of the press being secured, creates an additional security. Persons accused cannot be tried without a jury; for the same article provides that "the trial of all crimes shall be by jury." They cannot be carried to the ten miles square; for the same clause adds, "and such trial shall be held in the state where the said crimes shall have been committed."

. . . . .

[Mr. Iredell:] A gentleman who spoke some time ago (Mr. Lenoir) observed, that the government might make it treason to write against the most arbitrary proceedings. He corrected himself afterwards, by saying he meant *misprision of treason.* But in the correction he committed as great a mistake as he did at first. Where is the power given to them to do this? They have power to define and punish piracies and felonies committed on the high seas, and offences against the law of nations. They have no power to define any other crime whatever. This will show how apt gentlemen are to commit mistakes. I am convinced, on the part of the worthy member, it was not designed, but arose merely from inattention.

Mr. Lenoir arose, and declared, that he meant that those punishments might be inflicted by them within the ten miles square, where they would have exclusive powers of legislation.

Mr. Iredell continued: They are to have exclusive power of legislation,—but how? Wherever they may have this district, they must possess it from the authority of the state within which it lies; and that state may stipulate the conditions of the cession. Will not such state take care of the liberties of its own people? What would be the consequence if the seat of the government of the United States, with all the archives of America, was in the power of any one particular state? Would not this be most unsafe and humiliating? Do we not all remember that, in the year 1783, a band of soldiers went and insulted Congress? The sovereignty of the United States was treated with indignity. They applied for protection to the state they resided in, but could obtain none. It is to be hoped such a disgraceful scene will never happen again; but that, for the future, the national government will be able to protect itself.

9

Samuel Adams to Elbridge Gerry
22 Aug. 1789
Writings 4:330–32

I wrote to you hastily two days ago, & as hastily venturd an Opinion concerning the Right of Congress to controul a Light-house erected on Land belonging to this sovereign & independent State for its own Use & at its own Expence. I say *sovereign & independent,* because I think the State retains all the Rights of Sovereignty which it has not expressly parted with to the Congress of the United States—a federal Power instituted *solely* for the Support of the federal Union.

The Sovereignty of the State extends over every part of its Territory. The federal Constitution expresses the same Idea in Sec. 8, Art. 1. A Power is therein given to Congress "to exercise like Authority," that is to exercise exclusive Legislation in all Cases whatsoever, "over all places purchased by *the Consent of the Legislature* in which the same shall be, for the Erection of Forts, Magazines, and other needful Buildings," among which Light-houses may be included. Is it not the plain Conclusion from this Clause in the Compact, that Congress have not the Right to exercise exclusive Legislation in all Cases whatsoever, nor even to purchase or controul any part of the Territory within a State for the Erection of needful Buildings unless it has the Consent of its Legislature. If there are any such Buildings already erected, which operate to the General Welfare of the U S, and Congress by Virtue of the Power vested in them have taken from a State for the general Use, the necessary Means of supporting such Buildings it appears to be reasonable & just that the U S should maintain them; but I think that it follows not from hence, that Congress have a right to exercise any Authority over those buildings even to make Appointments of officers for the immediate Care of them or furnishing them with necessary Supplies. I wish to have your Opinion if you can find Leisure.

10

James Madison, Location of Capital, House of Representatives
4, 21 Sept. 1789
Papers 12:373–79, 416–18

[*4 Sept.*]

Mr. Madison Said, if this delay should not have produced any alteration in the sentiments of the gentlemen, it will at least soften that hard decision which seems to threaten the friends of the Potowmack. He hoped that all would concur in the great principle on which they ought to conduct, and decide this business: an equal attention to the rights of the community. No government, he said, not even the most despotic, could, beyond a certain point, violate that idea of justice, and equal right, which prevailed in the mind of the community. In republican governments, justice and equality form the basis of the system; and perhaps the structure can rest on no other that the wisdom of man can devise. In a federal republic, give me leave to say, it is even more necessary and proper, that a sacred regard should be paid to these considerations. For beyond the sense of the community at large, which has its full agency in such a system, no such government can act with safety. The federal ingredient involves local distinctions, which not only produce local jealousies, but, give at the same time, a greater local capacity to support, and insist upon equitable demands. In a confederacy of states, in which the people operate, in one respect as citizens, and in another as forming political communities, the local governments will ever possess a keener sense and capacity, to take advantages of those powers, on which the protection of local rights depend. If these great rights be the basis of republics, and if there be a double necessity of attending to them in a federal republic, it is further to be considered, that there is no one right, of which the people can judge with more ease and certainty, and of which they will judge with more jealousy, than of the establishment of the permanent seat of government; and I am persuaded, that however often this subject may be discussed in the representative body, or however the attention of the committee may be drawn to it, the observations I have made will be more and more verified. We see the operation of this sentiment fully exemplified in what has taken place in the several states. In every instance where, the seat of government has been placed in an eccentric position; we have seen the people struggling to place it where it ought to be. In some instances they have not yet succeeded, but I believe they will succeed in all. In many they have actually gained their point.

One of the first measures in the state of Virginia, after the commencement of the revolution, was the removal of the seat of government, from an eccentric position, to one which corresponds more with the sense of the state, and an equal regard to the general conveniency. In North-Carolina, we have seen the same principle operating, though in a different mode. In South-Carolina the same. In the state of Pennsylvania, powerful as the inducements are in favor of its capital, we have seen serious, and almost successful efforts already to translate it to a proper place. In the state of Delaware, where the government was as little removed from the centre, as it could be in any other state, we have seen the same spirit displaying itself. In the state of New-York, the same thing has happened with some fluctuations, arising from occasional motives of convenience. In Massachusetts, the same efforts have been made, and in all probability, when some temporary considerations cease, we shall find the same principle taking effect there also. It is not surprising, when we consider the nature of mankind, that this should be the case.

With respect, however, to the federal government, there is one consideration that shews, in a peculiar manner, the necessity and policy of paying a strict attention to this principle. One of the greatest objections, which have been made by the opponents of the system; which has been allowed most weight by its friends, is the extent of the United States. It has been asserted by some, and almost feared by others, that within so great a space, no free government can exist. I hope and trust, that the opinion is erroneous; but at the same time, I acknowledge it to have such a certain degree of force, that it is incumbent on those who wish well to the union, to diminish this inconvenience as much as possible. The way to diminish it, is to place the government in that spot which will be least removed from every part of the empire. Carry it to an eccentric position, and it will be equivalent to an extension of our limits. And if our limits are already extended so far as warrants, in any degree, the apprehension before mentioned, we ought to take care not to extend them farther.

The truth is, in every point of view in which we can contemplate this subject, we shall perceive its high importance. It is important, that every part of the community should have the power of sending, with equal facility, to the seat of government such representatives to take care of their interests, as they are disposed to confide in. If you place the government in an eccentric situation, the attendance of the members, and of all others who are to transact the public business, cannot be equally convenient. The members of the union, must be on an unequal footing. Thus you violate the principle of equality, where it ought most carefully to be ascertained, and wound the feelings of the component parts of the community, which can be least injured with impunity. If we consider the expence, that is an inconvenience not without its weight. In the compensations that have been lately voted, the eccentricity of our position has had a manifest influence. The more remote the government is, the greater will be the necessity of making liberal compensations, and holding out powerful inducements, in order to obtain the services of fit characters, from every part of the union; and as you can make no distinction, you must give to those who make the fewest sacrifices, the same as to those who make the most.

The seat of government is of great importance; if you consider the diffusion of wealth, that proceeds from this source. I presume that the expenditures which will take place, where the government will be established, by them who are immediately concerned in its administration, and by others who may resort to it, will not be less than a half a million of dollars a year. It is to be regretted, that those who may be most convenient to the centre, should enjoy this advantage in a higher degree than others; but the inequality is an evil imposed by necessity; we diminish it as we place the source from which those emanations of wealth are to proceed, as near the centre as possible.

If we consider, sir, the effects of legislative power on the aggregate community, we must feel equal inducements to look for the centre, in order to find the proper seat of government. Those who are most adjacent to the seat of legislation, will always possess advantages over others. An earlier knowledge of the laws; a greater influence in enacting them; better opportunities for anticipating them, and a thousand other circumstances, will give a superiority to those who are thus situated. If it were possible to promulge our laws, by some instantaneous operation, it would be of less consequence in that point of view where the government might be placed; but if, on the contrary, time is necessary for this purpose, we ought, as far as possible, to put every part of the community on a level.

If we consider the influence of the government in its executive department, there is no less reason to conclude, that it ought to be placed in the centre of the union. It ought to be in a situation to command information relative to every part of the union, to watch every conjuncture, to seize every circumstance that can be improved. The executive eye ought to be placed where it can best see the dangers which may threaten, and the executive arm, whence it may be extended most effectually to the protection of every part. Perhaps it is peculiarly necessary, that in looking for this position, we should keep our eye as much as possible towards our western borders; for a long time dangers will be most apt to assail that quarter of the union.

In the judiciary department, if it is not equally necessary, it is highly important that the government should be equally accessible to all.

Why should the citizens of one quarter of the union be subject to greater difficulties than others? Why should they be obliged to travel farther, to carry their witnesses at a greater expence, and be more subject to all the inconveniencies attending the administration of justice at a remote distance? In short, whether we consider the subject with regard to the executive, the legislative, or the judicial departments, we see the soundest reasons for fixing the government in that place, which may be the most permanent centre of territory and population.

With respect to the Western Territory, we are not to expect it, for it would be an affront to the understanding of our fellow citizens on the western waters, that they will be united with their Atlantic brethren, on any other principle than that of equality and justice. He would venture to say, that it was essentially necessary, therefore, that we should deal out the blessings of government with an impartial hand; and that, in placing the government from which these blessings are to flow, we should retire from the Atlantic as far as is consistent, and approach towards that point which will best accommodate the western country; in doing this, we shall still stop short of that geographical centre, whose circle would most commodiously embrace our *ultramontane* fellow-citizens. In his opinion, he said, the desire manifested by them, on this subject, was as reasonable as possible; they do not expect that we should lose sight of a proper and easy communication with the Atlantic, and will acquiesce, with cheerfulness, in a position necessary for that purpose, though it would still leave them subject to peculiar inconveniences. From the Atlantic to the Mississippi, according to the best computation, the distance is not less than 750 miles: If we go to that part of the Potowmack which is proposed, we carry the government 250 miles only west, it will still be 500 miles from the Mississippi.

He was sure, that if justice required us to take any one position in preference to another, we had every inducement, both of interest and of prudence, to fix on the Potowmack, as most satisfactory to our western brethren. It is impossible to reflect a moment on the possible severance of that branch of the union, without seeing the mischiefs which such an event must create. The area of the United States, divided into two equal parts, will leave, perhaps, one half on the west side of the Allegany mountains: From the fertility of soil, the fineness of climate, and every thing that can favor a growing population, we may suppose the settlement will go on with every degree of rapidity which our imagination can conceive. If the calculation be just, that we double in twenty-five years, we shall speedily behold an astonishing mass of people on the western waters. Whether this great mass shall form a permanent part of the confederacy, or whether it shall be separated into an alien, a jealous and a hostile people, may depend on the system of measures that is shortly to be taken. The difference, he observed, between considering them in the light of fellow-citizens, bound to us by a common affection, obeying common laws, pursuing a common good, and considering them in the other light, presents one of the most interesting questions that can occupy an American mind: Instead of peace and friendship, we shall have rivalship and enmity; instead of being a great people, invulnerable on all sides, and without the necessity of those military establishments which other nations require, we shall be driven into the same expensive and dangerous means of defence: We shall be obliged to lay burthens on the people, to support establishments which, sooner or later, may prove fatal to their liberties. It is incumbent on us, he said, if we wished to act the part of magnanimous legislators, or patriotic citizens, to consider well, when we are about to take a step of such vast importance, that it be directed by the views he had described; we must consider what is just, what is equal, and what is satisfactory.

It may be asked, why it was necessary to urge these principles, since they would not be denied? He apprehended, that in general, there would be a disagreement as to the principles which ought to govern: But, at the same time, principles were so connected with facts, in the present case, that it was not more necessary to collect all the light, than to fortify all the impressions that might be favorable to a just decision.

On a candid view of the two rivers, he flattered himself, that the seat, which would most correspond with the public interest, would be found on the banks of the Potowmack. It was proper that we should have some regard to the centre of territory; if that was to have weight, he begged leave to say, that there was no comparison between the two rivers. He defied any gentleman to cast his eye, in the most cursory manner, over a map, and say, that the Potowmack is not much nearer this centre than any part of the Susquehanna. If we measure from the banks of the Potowmack to the most eastern parts of the United States, it is less distant than to the most southern. If we measure this great area diagonally, the Potowmack will still have the advantage: If you draw a line perpendicular, to the direction of the Atlantic coast, we shall find that it will run more equally through the Potowmack than through any other part of the union; or, if there be any difference between one side and the other, there will be a greater space on the south-west than on the north-east: All the maps of the United States shew the truth of this. From the Atlantic coast to that line which separates the British possessions from the United States, the average distance is not more than 150 miles: If you take the average breadth of the other great division of the United States, it will be found to be six, seven, and eight hundred miles.

From this view of the subject, which is not easy to describe by words, but which will strike every eye that looks on a map, I am sure, that if the Potowmack is not the geographical centre, it is because the Susquehanna is less so.

He acknowledged that regard was also to be paid to the centre of population. But where shall we find this centre? He knew of no rule by which to be governed, except the proportion among the representatives of the different states; and he believed, if that criterion was taken, the present centre of population would be found somewhere in Pennsylvania, and not far from the Susquehanna. He granted that the present centre of population is nearer the Susquehanna than the Potowmack. But are we chusing a seat of government for the present moment only? He presumed not, we must look forward to those probable changes that may soon take place. He appealed to the judgment of every gentleman, if they had not reason to suppose, that these future changes, in the population of this country, would be particularly favorable to that part which lies south of the Potowmack. On what do the measures and extent of population depend? They depend on the climate, on the soil, and the vacancy to be filled. We find that population, like money, seeks those places where it least abounds, and has always the same tendency to equalize itself. We see the people moving from the more crouded to the less crouded parts. The swarms do not come from the southern, but from the northern and eastern hives. This will continue to be the case, until every part of America receives its due share of population. If there be any event, on which we may calculate with certainty, I take it that the centre of population will continually advance in a south-western direction. It must then travel from the Susquehanna; if it is now found there, it may even extend beyond the Potowmack. But the time would be long first, and as the Potowmack is the great highway of communication between the Atlantic and the western country, attempts to remove the seat farther south must be improbable. I have said that the communication with the Western Territory is more commodious through the Potowmack than through the Susquehanna; I wish all the facts connected with this subject could have been more fully ascertained, and more fully stated; but if we consider the facts that have been offered, by gentlemen who have spoken on the subject, we must conclude, that the communication through the Potowmack would be more facile and effectual than through any other channel. If we consider what was related by the gentleman from Pennsylvania, (Mr. Scott) whose judgment is the more to be relied on, as it is founded on his personal knowledge of that country. He tells you, that the communication by water, either to or from the western country, is next to impracticable by the Susquehanna.

[*21 Sept.*]

MR. MADISON Felt himself compelled to move for striking out that part of the bill, which provided, that the temporary residence of congress should continue at New-York; as he conceived it irreconcileable with the spirit of the constitution. If it was not from viewing it in this light, he should have given the bill no further opposition; and now he did not mean to enter on the merits of the main question.

From the constitution, it appeared, that the concurrence of the two houses of congress were sufficient to enable them to adjourn from one place to another; nay, the legal consent of the president was, in some degree, proscribed in the 7th sect. of art. 1. where it is declared, that every order, resolution, or vote, to which the concurrence of the senate and house of representatives may be necessary, (except on a question of adjournment) shall be presented to the president of the United States, and approved by him, before the same shall take effect. Any attempt, therefore, to adjourn by law, is a violation of that part of the constitution which gives the power, exclusively, to the two branches of the legislature. If gentlemen saw it in the same light, he flattered himself they would reject that part of [the] bill; and, however little they valued the reflection that this city was eccentrical, which had been so often urged, they would be guided by arguments, springing from a superior source.

He would proceed to state the reasons which induced him to be of this opinion: It is declared, in the constitution, that neither house, during the session of congress, shall, without the consent of the other, adjourn for more than three days, nor to any other place than that in which the two houses shall be sitting: From hence he inferred, that the two houses, by a concurrence, could adjourn for more than three days, and to any other place which they thought proper; by the other clause he had mentioned, the executive power is restrained from any interference with the legislative, on this subject; hence, he concluded, it would be dangerous to attempt to give to the president, a power the constitution expressly denied him. He did not suppose that the attempt to vest the executive with a power over the adjournment of the legislature would absolutely convey the power; but he conceived it wrong to make the experiment. He submitted it to those gentlemen who were attached to the success of the bill, how far an unconstitutional declaration may impede its passage through the other branch of the legislature.

It has been supposed, by some, that the seat of government may be at a place different from that where the congress sit; and, altho' the former may be established by law, the legislature might remove elsewhere; he could not subscribe to this doctrine. What is the government of the United States for which a seat is to be provided? Will not the government necessarily comprehend the congress as a part? In arbitrary governments, the residence of the monarch may be stiled the seat of government, because he is, within himself the supreme, legislative, executive, and judicial power; the same may be said of the residence of a limited monarchy, where the efficiency of the executive operates, in a great degree, to the exclusion of the legislative authority; but in such a government as ours, according to the legal and common acceptation of the term, government must include the legislative power; so, the term administration, which, in other countries, is specially appropriated to the executive branch of government, is used here for both the executive and legislative branches: We, in official communications, say, legislative administration, or executive administration, according as the one or the other is employed in the exercise of its constitutional powers. He mentioned these circumstances to shew, that they ought not to look for the meaning of terms used in the laws and constitution of the United States, into the acceptation of them in other countries, whose situation and government were different from that of United America. If his reasoning was just, he should conclude, that the seat of government would be at that place where both the executive and legislative bodies were fixed; and this depended upon the vote of the two branches of the legislature. There was another clause favorable to this opinion; it was, that giving congress authority to exercise exclusive legislation, in all cases whatsoever, over such district as may, by cession of particular states, and the acceptance of congress, become the seat of the government of the United States; this was the only place where any thing respecting the seat of government was mentioned; and would any gentlemen contend that congress might have a seat of government over which they are empowered to exercise exclusive legislation, and yet reside at the distance of 2 or 300 miles from it? Such a construction would contradict the plain and evident meaning of the constitution, and, as such, was inadmissible.

He hoped these observations would be attended to; and did not doubt but, if seen in their true light, they would induce the house to reject that part of the bill which he moved to have struck out.

11

ST. GEORGE TUCKER, BLACKSTONE'S COMMENTARIES 1:APP. 276–78 1803

---

14. Congress have power to exercise exclusive legislation, in all cases whatsoever, over such district, (not exceeding ten miles square) as may, by cession of particular states, and the acceptance of congress, become the seat of the government of the United States; and to exercise like authority over all places purchased by the consent of the legislature of the state; in which the same shall be, for the erection of forts, magazines, arsenals, dock-yards, and other needful buildings. C. U. S. Art. 1. §. 8.

The exclusive right of legislation granted to congress by this clause of the constitution, is a power, probably, more extensive than it was in the contemplation of the framers of the constitution to grant: such, at least, was the construction which the convention of Virginia gave to it.

They, therefore, proposed an article, as an amendment to the constitution, declaring, "that the powers granted by this clause, should extend only to such regulations as respect the police, and good government thereof." The states of New-York and North-Carolina proposed similar amendments; and one to the like effect was actually proposed in the senate of the United States, but shared the fate of many others, whose object was to limit the exercise of power in the federal government.

I agree with the author of the Federalist, that a complete authority at the seat of government was necessary to secure the public authority from insult, and it's proceedings from interruption. But the amendment proposed by Virginia, certainly, would not have abridged the federal government of such an authority. A system of laws incompatible with the nature and principles of a representative democracy, though not likely to be introduced at once, may be matured by degrees, and diffuse it's influence through the states, and finally lay the foundation of the most important changes in the nature of the federal government. Let foreigners be enabled to hold lands, and transmit them by inheritance or devise; let the preference to males, and the rights of primogeniture, be revived, together with the doctrine of entails, and aristocracy will neither want a ladder to climb by, nor a base for it's support. Many persons already possess an extent of territory in the United States, not inferior to many of the German principalities: if they can be retained for a few generations, without a division, our posterity may count upon the revival of feudal principles, with feudal tenures.

The permanent seat for the government of the United States has been established under the authority of an act passed 1 Cong. 2 Sess. c. 28, and 3 Sess. c. 17, upon the river Potowmac, including the towns of Alexandria in Virginia, and Georgetown in Maryland. And the laws of Virginia (with some exceptions) were declared in force in that part of the ten miles square, which was ceded by Virginia, and those of Maryland in the other part, ceded by Maryland; and several other regulations were likewise established by two several acts, 6 Cong. 2 Sess. c. 15 and 24. An amendatory act passed also at the first session of the seventh congress, but the system does not appear to be as yet completely organized. It has been said, that it was in contemplation to establish a subordinate legislature, with a governor to preside over the district. But it seems highly questionable whether such a substitution of legislative authority is compatible with the constitution; unless it be supposed that a power to exercise exclusive legislation in all cases whatsoever, comprehends an authority to delegate that power to another subordinate body. If the maxim be sound, that a delegated authority cannot be transferred to another to exercise, the project here spoken of will probably never take effect. At present that part of the union is neither represented in the congress, nor in any state legislature; a circumstance, of which there seems to be some disposition to complain. An amendment of the constitution seems to be the only means of remedying this oversight.

12

HEPBURN v. ELLZEY

2 Cranch 445 (1804)

MARSHALL, C. J., delivered the opinion of the court.

The question in this case is, whether the plaintiffs, as residents of the District of Columbia, can maintain an action in the circuit court of the United States for the district of Virginia.

This depends on the act of congress describing the jurisdiction of that court. That act gives jurisdiction to the circuit courts in cases between a citizen of the State in which the suit is brought, and a citizen of another State. To support the jurisdiction in this case, therefore, it must appear that Columbia is a State.

On the part of the plaintiffs it has been urged that Columbia is a distinct political society; and is, therefore, "a State," according to the definitions of writers on general law.

This is true. But as the act of congress obviously uses the word "State" in reference to that term as used in the constitution, it becomes necessary to inquire whether Columbia is a State in the sense of that instrument. The result of that examination is a conviction that the members of the American confederacy only are the States contemplated in the constitution.

The house of representatives is to be composed of members chosen by the people of the several States; and each State shall have at least one representative.

The senate of the United States shall be composed of two senators from each State.

Each State shall appoint, for the election of the executive, a number of electors equal to its whole number of senators and representatives.

These clauses show that the word State is used in the constitution as designating a member of the Union, and excludes from the term the signification attached to it by writers on the law of nations. When the same term which has been used plainly in this limited sense in the articles respecting the legislative and executive departments, is also employed in that which respects the judicial department, it must be understood as retaining the sense originally given to it.

Other passages from the constitution have been cited by the plaintiffs to show that the term State is sometimes used in its more enlarged sense. But on examining the passages quoted, they do not prove what was to be shown by them.

It is true that as citizens of the United States, and of that particular district which is subject to the jurisdiction of congress, it is extraordinary that the courts of the United States, which are open to aliens, and to the citizens of every State in the Union, should be closed upon them. But this is a subject for legislative, not for judicial consideration.

13

United States v. More
3 Cranch 159 (1805)

(See 3.2.2, no. 8)

14

Commonwealth v. Clary
8 Mass. 72 (1811)

[Sewall, C. J.:] The defendant was indicted at the Court of Common Pleas for this county, November term, 1809, for selling spirituous liquors within the town of *Springfield,* in this county, against the form of the statute, &c.

The indictment contained three counts, charging the defendant with three distinct offences in selling rum to three several persons.

Upon a trial had in the court below, he was convicted, and sentenced to pay a fine and costs. From that sentence he appealed to this Court, having agreed on record that, in any future stage of the proceedings, he would admit the selling of the rum, as charged in the first and third counts of the indictment; and the attorney prosecuting for the commonwealth having entered a *nolle prosequi* as to the second count,

The cause was submitted to the opinion of the Court upon the following facts, stated and agreed by the defendant and the counsel for the commonwealth.

"Before and at the time of the adoption of the constitution of the *United States,* there were standing in the town of *Springfield,* and on land owned by said town, divers buildings erected and occupied by the *U. S.* as arsenals, in which they then had, and always since have had, large quantities of guns and other military stores; and one building erected by the *U. S.* and occupied by them as a powder magazine. After the passing of the law of the *U.S.* of April 2d, 1794, providing for the erecting and maintaining of arsenals and magazines, and for other purposes, viz., on the 22d of June, 1795, one *N. Patten* conveyed certain land on *Mill River,* in said *Springfield,* to the then secretary of state, in trust for the *U. S.,* on which they erected, and have ever since maintained, buildings suitable for manufacturing small-arms; and have occupied the same for performing parts of the labor in making small-arms; and ever since the year 1794 have occupied other buildings, near to the said military stores and magazine, for performing other parts of the labor in making small-arms; said last-mentioned buildings having been erected by the *U. S.* before that time on land owned by the town of *Springfield.*—On the 14th of May, 1798, the *U. S.* by law authorized the president, in case he should think proper, to take by lease, or to purchase in fee, lands, and erect founderies for cannon, and armories for making small-arms. On the 25th of June, 1798, a law of this commonwealth passed, giving the consent thereof that the U. S. might purchase a tract of land in *Springfield,* not exceeding six hundred and forty acres, for the sole purpose of erecting forts, magazines, arsenals, and other needful buildings, the evidence of the purchases to be recorded in the registry of deeds for the county of *Hampshire.* On the 19th of September, 1798, *John Ashley,* by his deed duly recorded as aforesaid, conveyed to the *U. S.* in fee a parcel of land on *Mill River,* so called, in said *Springfield,* on which the *U. S.* the same year erected, and have ever since kept and occupied, large and suitable buildings and machinery for making small-arms. On the 24th of August, 1801, the said town of *Springfield,* by their deed duly recorded as aforesaid, conveyed to the *U. S.* a parcel of land in said town, on which the military stores before mentioned then stood, on which also then stood divers other buildings, some of which, ever since the year 1794, have been occupied by the *U. S.* for the manufacture of small-arms, and also another small piece of land, on which then stood and still stands the said powder magazine. On the 9th of January, 1809, *James Byers,* by his deed duly recorded, conveyed to the *U. S.* another parcel of land in said town, lying also on *Mill River* aforesaid, on which, before the time of committing the supposed offence alleged in the indictment, there were erected by the *U. S.* divers buildings suitable for the manufacture of small-arms, and several dwelling-houses occupied by the artificers employed in the said manufactures by the *U. S.* The said several parcels of land are separate and distant from each other, and do not contain in the whole 640 acres; and a line may be so drawn as to enclose the whole of them, and not to contain within the same more than 640 acres. The said parcels of land lying on *Mill River* have not been occupied by the *U. S.* as arsenals, but as parts of an armory; and the two pieces conveyed by the town of *Springfield* have, ever since the year 1794, been occupied by the *U. S.* as well for arsenals and magazines as for parts of an armory.

The said *Clary,* at the several times set forth in the first and third counts of the indictment, did sell, as therein mentioned, to the several persons therein named, the said spirituous liquors, without license therefor first had and obtained from the Court of Common Pleas for said county. But he was at the said several times employed as an overseer of one of the water-shops owned by the *U. S.,* and sold the said liquors in a dwelling-house erected by the *U. S.* on the said land purchased by them of *James Byers,* to the said persons, by the permission and approbation of *Benjamin Prescott,* superintendent of the armory of the *U. S.* in *Springfield.*"

If the Court, upon the whole matters aforesaid, are of opinion that the said *Clary* is guilty, as charged in the first and third counts of the indictment, judgment was to be rendered thereon against him; otherwise he was to be acquitted and discharged.

The defence relied on was, that the offence charged was

committed within a territory over which the laws of the *United States* had exclusive jurisdiction; that the laws of the commonwealth had no operation therein; and of consequence that the defendant was not bound to answer for the offence in the courts of the commonwealth.

. . . . .

On the facts agreed in this case we are of opinion, that the territory, on which the offence charged is agreed to have been committed, is the territory of the *United States*, over which the congress have the exclusive power of legislation. The assent of the commonwealth to the purchase of this territory by the *United States*, had this condition annexed to it—that civil and criminal process might be served therein by the officers of the commonwealth. This condition was made with a view to prevent the territory from becoming a sanctuary for debtors and criminals; and from the subsequent assent of the *United States* to the said condition, evidenced by their making the purchase, it results that the officers of the commonwealth, in executing such process, act under the authority of the *United States*. No offences committed within that territory, are committed against the laws of this commonwealth; nor can such offences be punishable by the courts of the commonwealth, unless the congress of the *United States* should give to the said courts jurisdiction thereof.

As a consequence of these positions, it is the opinion of the Court, that they have no cognizance of the offences charged in this indictment, and that the defendant must be discharged.

An objection occurred to the minds of some members of the Court, that if the laws of the commonwealth have no force within this territory, the inhabitants thereof cannot exercise any civil or political privileges, under the laws of *Massachusetts*, within the town of *Springfield*. We are agreed that such consequence necessarily follows; and we think that no hardship is thereby imposed on those inhabitants; because they are not interested in any elections made within the state, or held to pay any taxes imposed by its authority, nor bound by any of its laws.—And it might be very inconvenient to the *United States* to have their laborers, artificers, officers, and other persons employed in their service, subjected to the services required by the commonwealth of the inhabitants of the several towns.

It will be noticed, that in this decision we make a distinction between persons who actually dwell within the territory owned by the *United States*, and the laborers and artificers employed therein, who have their dwelling elsewhere.

15

Custis v. Lane

3 Munf. 579 (Va. 1813)

Saturday, February 13th, 1813, Judge Roane, (after stating the case) pronounced the following opinion of the Court:

If the pleas of the appellee should even be adjudged to be bad, yet, upon the principle of going up to the first fault, judgment would still be rendered against the appellant, if, on the case made by his declaration, he has no right to recover; and it is evident that his right may be much weaker under the declaration than under the pleas, as the latter do not exclude (as the former does) the idea of his having been still a citizen of this commonwealth, at the time he offered to vote. We infer this diversity, from its being stated in the declaration that the appellant was inhabiting within the district of Columbia at the time of its separation from this commonwealth; he was consequently expatriated thereby from the government of Virginia.

The act of Virginia, on the subject of expatriation, relates only to individual cases; it does not relate to those public and general acts of expatriation, by cession, or otherwise, which are more or less incident to all governments and countries. With respect to the particular cession now in question, it was contemplated and provided for by the constitution of the United States, agreed to by the commonwealth of Virginia, by its act tendering the territory to the general government, and also by the congress of the United States, who accepted the cession. To all these acts the appellant, by his representatives, was a party. He has therefore, no reason to complain that he has been cut off from the dominion of Virginia, in consideration of, perhaps, adequate advantages. That he is no longer within the jurisdiction of the commonwealth of Virginia, is manifest from this consideration, that congress are vested, by the constitution, with exclusive power of legislation over the territory in question; and it is only by the consent and courtesy of congress that any of the laws of Virginia have been permitted to operate therein. This last fact will be fully manifested by recurring to the several acts of congress on the subject. It follows, that the district of Columbia being without the jurisdiction of the laws of Virginia, is, as to it, another and distinct jurisdiction, and that the appellant is not merely a citizen of Virginia, abiding, or inhabiting therein, but passed, with that territory, from the jurisdiction of this commonwealth, by the act of cession, and owes no allegiance thereto. It might well, therefore, be true, that the case made by the pleas might be in favour of the appellant, and yet that he is prohibited from recovering, upon the weaker ground of claim admitted by his own declaration.

With respect to the right of a citizen, or subject, of a foreign government, to intermeddle with the civil polity of Virginia, and, especially, to exercise the all-important function of legislation, the matter cannot admit of a possible doubt. Such subjects, or citizens, cannot exercise this inestimable right, as they owe to the commonwealth no corresponding duties, and would not be amenable to the laws by them enacted. They cannot exercise this right in person, for their personal attendance may be necessary, at the same time, in their own country; and, besides, in time of war, they would be prohibited from coming here for the purpose. In some small democracies, the people have exercised the legislative power in person; and this principle is not lost sight of, when, owing to the extent of the territory, or the numbers of the people, they are compelled to exercise that power by means of deputies. This necessity of acting by agents does not change the principle; does not let in, to the appointment of such deputies, persons who, but for the necessity aforesaid, would be inhibited from acting in their primary and original character. In other words, none are competent to legislate mediately, by their representatives, but those who would be admitted, but for the impediments aforesaid, to exercise the right in person.

It follows, from these premises, that before this great principle shall be departed from, it ought, at least, manifestly to appear, from the act of government itself, that an exception has been explicitly assented to by the people; in a case in any degree equivocal, the general principle would undoubtedly turn the scale.

There is no such exception to be found in the constitution of this commonwealth. That instrument, and the declaration of rights on which it is based, has no eye towards the subjects of foreign powers. It only purports to declare the rights, and settle the duties of those who are parties to the compact. There is not only no such exception in that instrument, but, on the contrary, the converse is explicitly declared and expressed. The declaration of rights is stated to have been made by the representatives "of the good people of Virginia;" and it is declared, "that these rights do pertain to them, and their posterity, as the basis and foundation of government." This instrument, therefore, can never be construed to bestow the inestimable right of suffrage upon aliens and enemies, who have no "permanent common interest with, or attachment to," this community; who owe paramount and conflicting duties to other sovereigns; who have superior attachments in other countries; and who, from their residence elsewhere, cannot perform duties which imply the necessity of a residence within this commonwealth. On the case made by the declaration, therefore, the appellant is, clearly, not entitled to recover.

With respect to the ground supposed to be taken by the pleas as aforesaid; while we are free to admit that it is weaker for the appellee than that made by the declaration, which admits the appellant to be no citizen, and leaves a great discretion to the officer, as to the fact of a foreign residence; we are of opinion, that the provision of the act of 1808, in relation to it, is in consonance with the principles of the constitution. As the constitution is to be construed, as aforesaid, only in reference to our own citizens; so, such of them are not embraced by its provisions in favour of the right of suffrage, who, through absence, are disabled from performing the duties in question; whose other ties of allegiance, temporary or perpetual, are thrown into a scale conflicting with their duties and allegiance to this commonwealth, and whose foreign residence diminishes their former "common interest with, and attachment to," this commonwealth.

Persons standing in this predicament cannot be admitted to the right of suffrage, without running counter to all the principles on which that right is founded. As well might a resident citizen claim to vote, after he had parted with that freehold which guarantied his attachment to the community.

In thus deciding against the right of the appellant, upon the general principles just mentioned, the Court is, by no means, disposed to admit, that that result would be varied by any of the legislative provisions upon the subject. On the contrary, a recurrence to the various acts in our code, ancient and modern, will manifestly show that they are in strict conformity therewith. On every ground, therefore, the judgment of the Court below is correct, and ought to be affirmed.

16

UNITED STATES v. CORNELL

25 Fed. Cas. 646, no. 14,867 (C.C.D.R.I. 1819)

STORY, Circuit Justice, in summing up to the jury, said: The first question for the consideration of the jury, is, whether the offence is proved to be committed as alleged in the indictment, in a place within the sole and exclusive jurisdiction of the United States. If so, then the crime falls within the prohibitions of the third or seventh section of the act of 1790, c. 9 [1 Stat. 112], and is clearly cognizable by this court; if otherwise, then the jurisdiction entirely fails, and it is quite immaterial to us, what other court possesses jurisdiction. It is completely proved by the evidence, that Fort Adams, the place in which the offence was committed, is the property of the United States, having been duly purchased by the president more than nineteen years ago, under the authority of an act of congress (as we shall presently see), and ever since exclusively possessed by the United States. Copies of the deeds are now before us, and their sufficiency to pass the fee of the lands is not now disputed. But although the United States may well purchase and hold lands for public purposes, within the territorial limits of a state, this does not of itself oust the jurisdiction of sovereignty of such state over the lands so purchased. It remains until the state has relinquished its authority over the land either expressly or by necessary implication.

The constitution of the United States declares that congress shall have power to exercise "exclusive legislation" in all "cases whatsoever" over all places purchased by the consent of the legislature of the state in which the same shall be, for the erection of forts, magazines, arsenals, dockyards and other needful buildings. When therefore a purchase of land for any of these purposes is made by the national government, and the state legislature has given its consent to the purchase, the land so purchased by the very terms of the constitution ipso facto falls within the exclusive legislation of congress, and the state jurisdiction is completely ousted. This is the necessary result, for exclusive jurisdiction is the attendant upon exclusive legislation; and the consent of the state legislature is by the very terms of the constitution, by which all the states are bound, and to which all are parties, a virtual surrender and cession of its sovereignty over the place. Nor is there anything novel in this construction. It is under the like terms in the same clause of the constitution that exclusive jurisdiction is now exercised by congress in the District of Columbia; for if exclusive jurisdiction and exclusive legislation do not import the same thing, the states could not cede or the United States accept for the purposes enumerated in this clause, any exclusive jurisdiction. And such was manifestly the avowed intention of those wise and great men who framed the constitution.

We are then to consider whether the United States have authorized this purchase, and the legislature of Rhode Island has given its consent to it. By an act of congress of March 20, 1794, c. 9 [1 Stat. 345], several harbors and ports, and among them, that of Newport, were authorized to be fortified under the direction of the president; and he was authorized to receive from any state, in behalf of the United States, a cession of the lands on which any of the fortifications with the necessary buildings might be erected, or be intended to be erected; or where such cessions should not be made, to purchase such lands, not being the property of a state, on behalf of the United States. The legislature of Rhode Island, in furtherance of this object, by an act passed in the same year (Laws R. I. p. 551), authorized any town or person in the state, by and with the consent of the governor of the state, to sell and dispose of to the president, for the use of the United States, all such lands as should be deemed necessary to erect fortifications upon, for the defence of the port and harbor of Newport, and to execute deeds thereof in due form of law. The act contains a proviso that all civil and criminal processes issued under the authority of the state, or any officer thereof, may be executed on the lands so ceded, and within the fortifications which may be erected thereon, in the same way and manner as if such lands had not been ceded as aforesaid. The governor of Rhode Island gave his consent in writing to the purchase of the lands in question in due form, by a certificate on the original deeds. The argument of the prisoner's counsel is, in the first place, that the act of Rhode Island contains no cession of jurisdiction in terms, and the consent of the legislature through the governor to the purchase is not a virtual cession of its sovereignty over the place. That argument has been sufficiently considered already, and stands repudiated by the express terms of the constitution. The counsel for the prisoner next contend that the state has retained a concurrent jurisdiction over the place; and, if so, then the averment in the indictment is not supported in point of fact. This leads us to the consideration of the true intent and effect of the proviso already mentioned. In its terms it certainly does not contain any reservation of concurrent jurisdiction or legislation. It provides only that civil and criminal processes, issued under the authority of the state, which must of course be for acts done within, and cognizable by, the state, may be executed within the ceded lands, nothwithstanding the cession. Not a word is said from which we can infer that it was intended that the state should have a right to punish for acts done within the ceded lands. The whole apparent object is answered by considering the clause as meant to prevent these lands from becoming a sanctuary for fugitives from justice, for acts done within the acknowledged jurisdiction of the state. Now there is nothing incompatible with the exclusive sovereignty or jurisdiction of one state, that it should permit another state, in such cases, to execute its processes within its limits. And a cession, or exclusive jurisdiction, may well be made with a reservation of a right of this nature, which then operates only as a condition annexed to the cession, and as an agreement of the new sovereign to permit its free exercise as quoad hoc his own process. This is the light in which clauses of this nature, (which are very frequent in grants made by the states to the United States,) have been received by this court on various occasions, on which the subject has been heretofore brought before it for consideration; and it is the same light in which it has also been received by a very learned state court. Com. v. Clary, 8 Mass. 72. In our judgment it comports entirely with the apparent intention of the parties, and gives effect to acts which might otherwise perhaps be construed entirely nugatory. For it may well be doubted whether congress are by the terms of the constitution, at liberty to purchase lands for forts, dockyards, &c. with the consent of a state legislature, where such consent is so qualified that it will not justify the "exclusive legislation" of congress there. It may well be doubted if such consent be not utterly void. "Ut res magis valeat quam pereat," we are bound to give the present act a different construction, if it may reasonably be done; and we have not the least hesitation in declaring that the true interpretation of the present proviso leaves the sole and exclusive jurisdiction of Fort Adams in the United States.

17

PEOPLE V. GODFREY

17 Johns. R. 225 (1819)

[SPENCER, Ch. J.] . . . The jurisdiction of the courts of the *United States* must be derived under the eighth section of the first article and seventeenth paragraph of the constitution of the *United States,* which gives to the Congress *"exclusive legislation over all places purchased by the consent of the legislature of the state in which the same shall be, for the erection of forts, magazines, arsenals, dock-yards, and other needful buildings."*

The only evidence of a purchase by the *United States,* of fort *Niagara,* from this state, or of a cession of any kind by it to the *United States,* is contained in the act of the 6th of *April,* 1803. (1 *N. R. L.* 197.) That act authorizes the governor to agree with such person or persons as shall be authorized by the *United States* for that purpose, for the sale of such quantity of the lands adjoining the fort *Niagara,* as shall be necessary for the accommodation of that post, and to cede the right of the people of this state to the said lands to the *United States.*

It does not appear, nor is there the slightest ground to believe, that the powers conferred on the governor, by this act, have ever been executed, or that any cession has ever been made under it, of the fort itself, or of the adjoining lands, to the *United States.*

It has been argued, that this state, though they have made no cession, have tacitly consented, by a necessary implication from the act of 1803, that the *United States* should hold the fortress of *Niagara,* and that in such case, the second paragraph of the third section of the fourth article of the constitution of the *United States,* would give to the Congress the like exclusive power of legislation. That section declares, *"that the Congress shall have power to dispose of, and make all needful rules and regulations respecting the territory or other property belonging to the United States, and that nothing in the constitution shall be so construed as to prejudice any claims of the United States, or any particular state."*

The treaty of peace between the *United States* and *Great Britain,* in 1783, has also been brought into view, as containing provisions bearing on the question. That treaty contains a stipulation that his *Britannic* majesty should withdraw, with all convenient speed, all his garrisons from the *United States,* and from every post, place and harbor within the same; and the treaty of amity, commerce and navigation, concluded between *Great Britain* and the *United States,* in 1794, contains a stipulation, on the part of the former, to withdraw their troops and garrisons, from all posts and places within the boundary lines assigned by the treaty of peace, before the first of *June,* 1796. Fort *Niagara* was captured from the *French,* in 1759, and passed, by virtue of the treaty of peace of 1763, to the crown of *Great Britain;* and has continued to be held by that power, as a fortress, until it was surrendered under the treaty of 1794, since which it has been possessed and garrisoned by the *United States,* with a short interruption during the late war, to the present period. That fort *Niagara* is within the acknowledged boundaries and limits of this state is indisputable.

We consider it beyond all doubt, that the *United States* acquired no territorial rights to any portion of this state, in virtue of the treaties of 1783 and 1794. Neither of those treaties contain any words of grant to the *United States,* as such; nor should we have submitted to accept as a grant what had already been acquired by our arms, and established by the solemn declaration of independence. The Congress, under the articles of confederation, were the representatives of the several states; and, having the power to make war and peace, were a party to the treaty of peace, in behalf of the confederated states, and every stipulation in the treaty enured to the benefit of the states in their sovereign capacities. When, therefore, it was agreed, by the treaty of peace of 1783, that *Great Britain* should withdraw, with all convenient speed, its garrisons from the *United States,* and from every port, place and harbor within the same; that agreement was for the benefit of the several states within whose limits those garrisons were. The section of the articles of confederation removes every doubt upon this subject: it provides, that "each state should retain its sovereignty, freedom and independence, and every power, jurisdiction, and right, which was not thereby expressly delegated to the *United States* in Congress assembled:" and it is not within our knowledge or belief, that the *United States* have ever claimed, or set up any pretension of property, to any fort within the boundaries of a state, under these treaties.

The occupation of fort *Niagara,* by the troops of the *United States,* since its evacuation, in pursuance of the treaty of 1794, cannot be considered either as evidence of a right in the general government to the post itself, nor as an act hostile to the rights of this state. One of the great objects in the formation of a federal government was, that it should provide for the common defence. This post was considered an essential point to be garrisoned by the troops of the *United States,* as a security to our frontiers; and this state acquiesced tacitly in the propriety and necessity of the measure; under these circumstances to consider the occupation of the post as, *per se,* evidence of territorial right, in the *United States,* or as in hostility to the rights of this state, would be imputing to the federal government a disregard of its obligations and duties, and a spirit of violence and injustice, highly derogatory to its known justice and providence. Their possession of this post must be regarded, therefore, as a possession for the state, not against it; it was a friendly occupation, not in derogation of our rights; and we regard it as a fundamental principle, that the rights of sovereignty are never to be taken away by implication. In the case of the *United States* v. *Bevans,* (3 *Wheaton,* 388.) Chief Justice *Marshall* said, "the power of exclusive legislation under the 8th section of the first article of the constitution, which is jurisdiction, is united with cession of territory, which is to be the free act of the states." The correctness of this remark is fully admitted; and if the *United States* had the right of exclusive legislation over the fortress of *Niagara,* they would have also exclusive jurisdiction; but we are of opinion, that the right of exclusive legislation within the territorial limits of any state, can be acquired by the *United States* only in the mode pointed out in the constitution, *by purchase, by consent of the legislature of the state in which the same shall be, for the erection of forts, magazines, arsenals, dockyards, and other needful buildings.* The essence of that provision is, that the state shall freely cede the particular place to the *United States,* for one of the specific and enumerated objects. This jurisdiction cannot be acquired tortiously, or by disseisin of the state; much less, can it be acquired by mere occupancy, with the implied or tacit consent of the state, when such occupancy is for the purpose of protection.

The 3d section of the 4th article of the constitution of the *United States* is clearly adapted to the territorial rights of the *United States,* beyond the limits or boundaries of any of the states, and to their chattel interests, and it therefore drops the expression of exclusive legislation.

To oust this state of its jurisdiction to support and maintain its laws, and to punish crimes, it must be shown that an offence committed within the acknowledged limits of the state, is clearly and exclusively cognizable by the laws and courts of the *United States.* In the case already cited, Chief Justice *Marshall* observed, that to bring the offence within the jurisdiction of the courts of the union, it must have been committed out of the jurisdiction of any state; it is not, (he says,) the offence committed, but the place in which it is committed, which must be out of the jurisdiction of the state. It does not, therefore, enter into the consideration of this question, that the prisoner and the deceased were in the service of the *United States,* when the crime was perpetrated. On the whole, we are perfectly satisfied that the jurisdiction of this state attaches on the crime, and extends to the person of the prisoner, and nothing remains but that judgment be passed upon him according to law.

18

LOUGHBOROUGH V. BLAKE

5 Wheat. 317 (1820)

(See 1.9.4, no. 16)

19

COHENS V. VIRGINIA

6 Wheat. 264 (1821)

(See 3.2.1, no. 74)

20

WILLIAM WIRT, RIGHT TO TAX GOVERNMENT PROPERTY
8 Sept. 1823

1 Ops. Atty. Gen. 620

Sir: The constitution of the United States provides that Congress shall have exclusive legislation in all cases whatsoever over all places purchased, by the consent of the legislature of the State in which the same shall be, for the erection of forts, magazines, arsenals, dock-yards, and other needful buildings.

If, therefore, the ground in Philadelphia to which you allude in your letter of the 4th, was purchased with the consent of the legislature of the State of Pennsylvania for either of these purposes, and has been ceded for such purpose, my opinion is, that neither the State of Pennsylvania, nor the corporation, (whose powers are merely derivative from the State,) possess the power to impose and collect taxes from this property.

21

AMERICAN INSURANCE CO. V. CANTER

1 Pet. 511 (1828)

(See 1.8.9, no. 5)

22

JOSEPH STORY, COMMENTARIES ON THE CONSTITUTION 3:§§ 1212–22
1833

§ 1212. This clause was not in the original draft of the constitution; but was referred to a committee, who reported in its favour; and it was adopted into the constitution with a slight amendment without any apparent objection.

§ 1213. The indispensable necessity of complete and exclusive power, on the part of the congress, at the seat of government, carries its own evidence with it. It is a power exercised by every legislature of the Union, and one might say of the World, by virtue of its general supremacy. Without it not only the public authorities might be insulted, and their proceedings be interrupted with impunity; but the public archives might be in danger of violation, and destruction, and a dependence of the members of the national government on the state authorities for protection in the discharge of their functions be created, which would bring on the national councils the imputation of being subjected to undue awe and influence, and might, in times of high excitement, expose their lives to jeopardy. It never could be safe to leave in possession of any state the exclusive power to decide, whether the functionaries of the national government should have the moral or physical power to perform their duties. It might subject the favoured state to the most unrelenting jealousy of the other states, and introduce earnest controversies from time to time respecting the removal of the seat of government.

§ 1214. Nor can the cession be justly an object of jealousy to any state; or in the slightest degree impair its sovereignty. The ceded district is of a very narrow extent; and it rests in the option of the state, whether it shall be made or not. There can be little doubt, that the inhabitants composing it would receive with thankfulness such a blessing, since their own importance would be thereby increased, their interests be subserved, and their rights be under the immediate protection of the representatives of the whole Union. It is not improbable, that an occurrence, at the very close of the revolutionary war, had a great effect in introducing this provision into the constitution. At the period alluded to, the congress, then sitting at Philadelphia, was surrounded and insulted by a small, but insolent body of mutineers of the continental army. Congress applied to the executive authority of Pennsylvania for defence; but, under the ill-conceived constitution of the state at that time, the executive power was vested in a council consisting of thirteen members; and they possessed, or exhibited so little energy, and such apparent intimidation, that congress indignantly removed to New Jersey, whose inhabitants welcomed them with promises of defending them. Congress remained for some time at Princeton without being again insulted, till, for the sake of greater convenience, they adjourned to Annapolis. The general dissatisfaction with the proceedings of Pennsylvania, and the degrading spectacle of a fugitive congress, were sufficiently striking to produce this remedy. Indeed, if such a lesson could have been lost upon the people, it would have been as humiliating to their intelligence, as it would have been offensive to their honour.

§ 1215. And yet this clause did not escape the common fate of most of the powers of the national government. It was represented, as peculiarly dangerous. It may, it was said, become a sort of public sanctuary, with exclusive privileges and immunities of every sort. It may be the very spot for the establishment of tyranny, and of refuge of the oppressors of the people. The inhabitants will be answerable to no laws, except those of congress. A powerful army may be here kept on foot; and the most oppressive and sanguinary laws may be passed to govern the district. Nay, at the distance of fourteen years after the constitution had quietly gone into operation, and this power had been acted upon with a moderation, as commendable, as it ought to be satisfactory, a learned commentator expressed regret at the extent of the power, and intimated in no inexplicit terms his fears for the future. "A system of laws," says he, "incompatible with the nature and principles of a representative democracy, though not likely to be introduced at once, may be matured by degrees, and diffuse its influence through the states, and finally lay the foundation of the most important changes in the nature of the federal government. Let foreigners be enabled to hold lands, and transmit them by inheritance, or devise; let the preference to males, and the rights of primogeniture be revived with the doctrine of entails; and aristocracy will neither want a ladder to climb by, nor a base for its support."

§ 1216. What a superstructure to be erected on such a narrow foundation! Several of the states now permit foreigners to hold and transmit lands; and yet their liberties are not overwhelmed. The whole South, before the revolution, allowed and cherished the system of primogeniture; and yet they possessed, and transmitted to their children their colonial rights and privileges, and achieved under this very system the independence of the country. The system of entails is still the law of several of the states; and yet no danger has yet assailed them. They possess, and enjoy the fruits of republican industry and frugality, without any landed or other aristocracy. And yet the petty district of ten miles square is to overrule in its policy and legislation all, that is venerable and admirable in state legislation! The states, and the people of the states are represented in congress. The district has no representatives there; but is subjected to the exclusive legislation of the former. And yet congress, at home republican, will here nourish aristocracy. The states will here lay the foundation for the destruction of their own institutions, rights, and sovereignty. At home, they will follow the legislation of the district, instead of guiding it by their precept and example. They will choose to be the engines of tyranny and oppression in the district, that they may become enslaved within their own territorial sovereignty. What, but a disposition to indulge in all sorts of delusions and alarms, could create such extraordinary flights of imagination? Can such things be, and overcome us, like a summer's cloud, without our special wonder? At this distance of time, it seems wholly unnecessary to refute the suggestions, which have been so ingeniously urged. If they prove any thing, they prove, that there ought to be no government, because no persons can be found worthy of the trust.

§ 1217. The seat of government has now, for more than thirty years, been permanently fixed on the river Potomac, on a tract of ten miles square, ceded by the states of Virginia and Maryland. It was selected by that great man, the boast of all America, the first in war, the first in peace, and the first in the hearts of his countrymen. It bears his name; it is the monument of his fame and wisdom. May it be for ever consecrated to its present noble purpose, *capitolî immobile saxum!*

§ 1218. The inhabitants enjoy all their civil, religious, and political rights. They live substantially under the same laws, as at the time of the cession, such changes only having been made, as have been devised, and sought by themselves. They are not indeed citizens of any state, entitled to the privileges of such; but they are citizens of the United States. They have no immediate representatives in congress. But they may justly boast, that they live under a paternal government, attentive to their wants, and zealous for their welfare. They, as yet, possess no local legislature; and have, as yet, not desired to possess one. A learned commentator has doubted, whether congress can create such a legislature, because it is the delegation of a delegated authority. A very different opinion was expressed by the Federalist; for it was said, that "a municipal legislature for local purposes, derived from their own suffrages, will of course be allowed them."In point of fact, the corporations of the three cities within its limits possess and exercise a delegated power of legislation under their charters, granted by congress, to the full extent of their municipal wants, without any constitutional scruple, or surmise of doubt.

§ 1219. The other part of the power, giving exclusive legislation over places ceded for the erection of forts, magazines, &c., seems still more necessary for the public convenience and safety. The public money expended on such places, and the public property deposited in them, and the nature of the military duties, which may be required there, all demand, that they should be exempted from state authority. In truth, it would be wholly improper, that places, on which the security of the entire Union may depend, should be subjected to the control of any member of it. The power, indeed, is wholly unexceptionable; since it can only be exercised at the will of the state; and therefore it is placed beyond all reasonable scruple. Yet, it did not escape without the scrutinizing jealousy of the opponents of the constitution, and was denounced, as dangerous to state sovereignty.

§ 1220. A great variety of cessions have been made by the states under this power. And generally there has been a reservation of the right to serve all state process, civil and criminal, upon persons found therein. This reservation has not been thought at all inconsistent with the provision of the constitution; for the state process, *quoad hoc,* becomes the process of the United States, and the general power of exclusive legislation remains with congress.

Thus, these places are not capable of being made a sanctuary for fugitives, to exempt them from acts done within, and cognizable by, the states, to which the territory belonged; and at the same time congress is enabled to accomplish the great objects of the power.

§ 1221. The power of congress to exercise exclusive jurisdiction over these ceded places is conferred on that body, as the legislature of the Union; and cannot be exercised in any other character. A law passed in pursuance of it is the supreme law of the land, and binding on all the states, and cannot be defeated by them. The power to pass such a law carries with it all the incidental powers to give it complete and effectual execution; and such a law may be extended in its operation incidentally throughout the United States, if congress think it necessary so to do. But if intended to have efficiency beyond the district, language must be used in the act expressive of such an intention; otherwise it will be deemed purely local.

§ 1222. It follows from this review of the clause, that the states cannot take cognizance of any acts done in the ceded places after the cession; and, on the other hand, the inhabitants of those places cease to be inhabitants of the state, and can no longer exercise any civil or political rights under the laws of the state. But if there has been no cession by the state of the place, although it has been constantly occupied and used, under purchase, or otherwise, by the United States for a fort, arsenal, or other constitutional purpose, the state jurisdiction still remains complete and perfect.

SEE ALSO:

Records of the Federal Convention, Farrand 2:117, 321–22, 505, 506, 570
A Friend to the Rights of the People, 8 Feb. 1788, Storing 4.23.3
House of Representatives, Permanent Seat of Government, 3 Sept. 1789, Annals 1:836–42
An Act for Establishing the Temporary and Permanent Seat of the Government, 1 Stat. 130 (1790)
James Madison, Constitutionality of the Residence Bill, 14 July 1790, Papers 13:279
House of Representatives, The Territory of Columbia, 31 Dec. 1800, Annals 10:868–74
House of Representatives, District of Columbia, 7–8 Jan. 1805, Annals 14:874–75, 877–902, 906–10
William Wirt, Lotteries in Washington, 18 May 1825, 1 Ops. Atty. Gen. 721
James Kent, Commentaries 1:402–4 (1826)
United States v. *Watkins,* 28 Fed. Cas. 419, no. 16,649 (C.C.D.C. 1829)
Tayloe v. *Thomson,* 5 Pet. 358 (1831)

Article 1, Section 8, Clause 18

To make all Laws which shall be necessary and proper for carrying into Execution the foregoing Powers, and all other Powers vested by this Constitution in the Government of the United States, or in any Department or Officer thereof.

1

CENTINEL, NO. 5
Fall 1787
Storing 2.7.97

The words "pursuant to the constitution" will be no restriction to the authority of congress; for the foregoing section gives them unlimited legislation; their unbounded power of taxation does alone include all others, as whoever has the purse strings will have full dominion. But the convention has superadded another power, by which the congress may stamp with the sanction of the constitution every possible law; it is contained in the following clause—"To make all laws which shall be necessary and proper for carrying into execution the foregoing powers, and all other powers vested by this constitution in the government of the United States, or in any department or officer thereof." Whatever law congress may deem necessary and proper for carrying into execution any of the powers vested in them, may be enacted; and by virtue of this clause, they may controul and abrogate any and every of the laws of the state governments, on the allegation that they interfere with the execution of any of their powers, and yet these laws will "be made in pursuance of the constitution," and of course will "be the supreme law of the land, and the judges in every state shall be bound thereby, any thing in the *constitution* or *laws* of any state to the contrary notwithstanding."

2

AN OLD WHIG, NO. 2
Fall 1787
Storing 3.3.12–13

These powers are very extensive, but I shall not stay at present to inquire whether these *express* powers were necessary to be given to Congress? whether they are too great or too small? My object is to consider that *undefined, unbounded and immense power* which is comprised in the following clause;—"And, to make all laws which shall be necessary and proper for carrying into execution the *foregoing powers and all other powers* vested by this constitution in the government of the United States; or in any department or offices [officer] thereof." Under such a clause as this can any thing be said to be reserved and kept back from Congress? Can it be said that the Congress have no power but what *is expressed?* "To make all laws which shall be necessary and proper" is in other words to make all such laws which *the Congress shall think necessary and proper,*—for who shall judge for the legislature what is necessary and proper?—Who shall set themselves above the sovereign?—What inferior legislature shall set itself above the supreme legislature?—To me it appears that no other power on earth can dictate to them or controul them, unless by force; and force either internal or external is one of those calamities which every good man would wish his country at all times to be delivered from.—This generation in America have seen enough of war and its usual concomitants to prevent all of us from wishing to see any more of it;—all except those who make a trade of war. But to the question;—without force what can restrain the Congress from making such laws as they please? What limits are there to their authority?—I fear none at all; for surely it cannot justly be said that they have no power but what is expressly given to them, where by the very terms of their creation they are vested with the powers of making laws in all cases necessary and proper; when from the nature of their power they must necessarily be the judges, what laws are necessary and proper. The British act of Parliament, declaring the power of Parliament to make laws to bind America in all cases whatsoever, was not more extensive; for it is as true as a maxim, that even the British Parliament neither could nor would pass any law in any case in which they did not either deem it necessary and proper to make such law or pretend to deem it so. And in such cases it is not of a farthing consequence whether they really are of opinion that the law is necessary and proper, or only *pretend to think so;* for who can overrule their pretensions?—No one; unless we had a bill of rights to which we might appeal, and under which we might contend against any assumption of undue power and appeal to the judicial branch of the government to protect us by their judgements. This reasoning I fear Mr. Printer is but too just; and yet, if any man should doubt the truth of it; let me ask him one other question, what is the meaning of the latter part of the clause which vests the Congress with the authority of making all laws which shall be necessary and proper for carrying into execution ALL OTHER POWERS;—besides the foregoing powers vested, &c. &c. Was it thought that the foregoing powers might perhaps admit of some restraint in *their* construction as to what was necessary and proper to carry them into execution? Or was it deemed right to add still further that they should not be restrained to the powers already named?—besides the powers already mentioned, other powers may be assumed hereafter as contained by implication in this constitution. The Congress shall judge of what is necessary and proper in all these cases and in all other cases;—in short in all cases whatsoever.

Where then is the restraint? How are Congress bound down to the powers expressly given? what is reserved or can be reserved?

3

FEDERAL FARMER, NO. 4
12 Oct. 1787
Storing 2.8.49

The federal constitution, the laws of congress made in pursuance of the constitution, and all treaties must have full force and effect in all parts of the United States; and all other laws, rights and constitutions which stand in their way must yield: It is proper the national laws should be supreme, and superior to state or district laws: but then the national laws ought to yield to unalienable or fundamental rights—and national laws, made by a few men, should extend only to a few national objects. This will not be the case with the laws of congress: To have any proper idea of their extent, we must carefully examine the legislative, executive and judicial powers proposed to be lodged in the general government, and consider them in connection with a general clause in art. 1. sect. 8, in these words (after inumerating a number of powers) "To make all laws which shall be necessary and proper for carrying into execution the foregoing powers, and all other powers vested by this constitution in the government of the United States, or in any department or officer thereof."—The powers of this government as has been observed, extend to internal as well as external objects, and to those objects to which all others are subordinate; it is almost impossible to have a just conception of these powers, or of the extent and number of the laws which may be deemed necessary and proper to carry them into effect, till we shall come to exercise those powers and make the laws. In making laws to carry those powers into effect, it is to be expected, that a wise and prudent congress will pay respect to the opinions of a free people, and bottom their laws on those principles which have been considered as essential and fundamental in the British, and in our government. But a congress of a different character will not be bound by the constitution to pay respect to those principles.

4

BRUTUS, NO. 1
18 Oct. 1787
Storing 2.9.8–9

How far the clause in the 8th section of the 1st article may operate to do away all idea of confederated states, and to effect an entire consolidation of the whole into one general government, it is impossible to say. The powers given by this article are very general and comprehensive, and it may receive a construction to justify the passing almost any law. A power to make all laws, which shall be *necessary and proper,* for carrying into execution, all powers vested by the constitution in the government of the United States, or any department or officer thereof, is a power very comprehensive and definite [indefinite?], and may, for ought I know, be exercised in a such manner as entirely to abolish the state legislatures. Suppose the legislature of a state should pass a law to raise money to support their government and pay the state debt, may the Congress repeal this law, because it may prevent the collection of a tax which they may think proper and necessary to lay, to provide for the general welfare of the United States? For all laws made, in pursuance of this constitution, are the supreme law of the land, and the judges in every state shall be bound thereby, any thing in the constitution or laws of the different states to the contrary notwithstanding.—By such a law, the government of a particular state might be overturned at one stroke, and thereby be deprived of every means of its support.

It is not meant, by stating this case, to insinuate that the constitution would warrant a law of this kind; or unnecessarily to alarm the fears of the people, by suggesting, that the federal legislature would be more likely to pass the limits assigned them by the constitution, than that of an individual state, further than they are less responsible to the people. But what is meant is, that the legislature of the United States are vested with the great and uncontroulable powers, of laying and collecting taxes, duties, imposts, and excises; of regulating trade, raising and supporting armies, organizing, arming, and disciplining the militia, instituting courts, and other general powers. And are by this clause invested with the power of making all laws, *proper and necessary,* for carrying all these into execution; and they may so exercise this power as entirely to annihilate all the state governments, and reduce this country to one single government. And if they may do it, it is pretty certain they will; for it will be found that the power retained by individual states, small as it is, will be a clog upon the wheels of the government of the United States; the latter therefore will be naturally inclined to remove it out of the way. Besides, it is a truth confirmed by the unerring experience of ages, that every man, and every body of men, invested with power, are ever disposed to increase it, and to acquire a superiority over every thing that stands in their way. This disposition, which is implanted in human nature, will operate in the federal legislature to lessen and ultimately to subvert the state authority, and having such advantages, will most certainly succeed, if the federal government succeeds at all. It must be very evident then, that what this constitution wants of being a complete consolidation of the several parts of the union into one complete government, possessed of perfect legislative, judicial, and executive powers, to all intents and purposes, it will necessarily acquire in its exercise and operation.

5

JAMES WILSON, PENNSYLVANIA RATIFYING CONVENTION
1, 4 Dec. 1787
Elliot 2:448–49, 468

The gentleman in opposition strongly insists that the general clause at the end of the eighth section gives to Congress a power of legislating generally; but I cannot conceive by what means he will render the words susceptible of that expansion. Can the words, "The Congress shall have power to make all laws which shall be necessary and proper to carry into execution the foregoing powers," be capable of giving them general legislative power? I hope that it is not meant to give to Congress merely an illusive show of authority, to deceive themselves or constituents any longer. On the contrary, I trust it is meant that they shall have the power of carrying into effect the laws which they shall make under the powers vested in them by this Constitution.

. . . . .

Another objection is, "that Congress may borrow money, keep up standing armies, and command the militia." The present Congress possesses the power of borrowing money and of keeping up standing armies. Whether it will be proper at all times to keep up a body of troops, will be a question to be determined by Congress; but I hope the necessity will not subsist at all times. But if it should subsist, where is the gentleman that will say that they ought not to possess the necessary power of keeping them up?

It is urged, as a general objection to this system, that "the powers of Congress are unlimited and undefined, and that they will be the judges, in all cases, of what is necessary and proper for them to do." To bring this subject to your view, I need do no more than point to the words in the Constitution, beginning at the 8th sect. art. 1st. "The Congress (it says) shall have power," &c. I need not read over the words, but I leave it to every gentleman to say whether the powers are not as accurately and minutely defined, as can be well done on the same subject, in the same language. The old Constitution is as strongly marked on this subject; and even the concluding clause, with which so much fault has been found, gives no more or other powers; nor does it, in any degree, go beyond the particular enumeration; for, when it is said that Congress shall have power to make all laws which shall be necessary and proper, those words are limited and defined by the following, "for carrying into execution the foregoing powers." It is saying no more than that the powers we have already particularly given, shall be effectually carried into execution.

6

ALEXANDER HAMILTON, FEDERALIST, NO. 33, 203–208
2 Jan. 1788

The residue of the argument against the provisions in the constitution, in respect to taxation, is ingrafted upon the following clauses; the last clause of the eighth section of the first article of the plan under consideration, authorises the national legislature "to make all laws which shall be *necessary* and *proper,* for carrying into execution *the powers* by that Constitution vested in the government of the United States, or in any department or officer thereof"; and the second clause of the sixth article declares, that "the Constitution and the Laws of the United States made *in pursuance thereof,* and the treaties made by their authority shall be the *supreme law* of the land; any thing in the constitution or laws of any State to the contrary notwithstanding."

These two clauses have been the sources of much virulent invective and petulant declamation against the proposed constitution, they have been held up to the people, in all the exaggerated colours of misrepresentation, as the pernicious engines by which their local governments were to be destroyed and their liberties exterminated—as the hideous monster whose devouring jaws would spare neither sex nor age, nor high nor low, nor sacred nor profane; and yet strange as it may appear, after all this clamour, to those who may not have happened to contemplate them in the same light, it may be affirmed with perfect confidence, that the constitutional operation of the intended government would be precisely the same, if these clauses were entirely obliterated, as if they were repeated in every article. They are only declaratory of a truth, which would have resulted by necessary and unavoidable implication from the very act of constituting a Foederal Government, and vesting it with certain specified powers. This is so clear a proposition, that moderation itself can scarcely listen to the railings which have been so copiously vented against this part of the plan, without emotions that disturb its equanimity.

What is a power, but the ability or faculty of doing a thing? What is the ability to do a thing but the power of employing the *means* necessary to its execution? What is a LEGISLATIVE power but a power of making LAWS? What are the *means* to execute a LEGISLATIVE power but LAWS? What is the power of laying and collecting taxes but a *legislative power,* or a power of *making laws,* to lay and collect taxes? What are the proper means of executing such a power but *necessary* and *proper* laws?

This simple train of enquiry furnishes us at once with a test by which to judge of the true nature of the clause complained of. It conducts us to this palpable truth, that a power to lay and collect taxes must be a power to pass all laws *necessary* and *proper* for the execution of that power; and what does the unfortunate and calumniated provision in question do more than declare the same truth; to wit, that the national legislature to whom the power of laying and collecting taxes had been previously given, might in the execution of that power pass all laws *necessary* and *proper* to carry it into effect? I have applied these observations thus particularly to the power of taxation, because it is the immediate subject under consideration, and because it is the most important of the authorities proposed to be conferred upon the Union. But the same process will lead to the same result in relation to all other powers declared in the constitution. And it is *expressly* to execute these powers, that the sweeping clause, as it has been affectedly called, authorises the national legislature to pass all *necessary* and *proper* laws. If there is any thing exceptionable, it must be sought for in the specific powers, upon which this general declaration is predicated. The declaration itself, though it may be chargeable with tautology or redundancy, is at least perfectly harmless.

But SUSPICION may ask why then was it introduced? The answer is, that it could only have been done for greater caution, and to guard against all cavilling refinements in those who might hereafter feel a disposition to curtail and evade the legitimate authorities of the Union. The Convention probably foresaw what it has been a principal aim of these papers to inculcate that the danger which most threatens our political welfare, is, that the State Governments will finally sap the foundations of the Union; and might therefore think it necessary, in so cardinal a point, to leave nothing to construction. Whatever may have been the inducement to it, the wisdom of the precaution is evident from the cry which has been raised against it; as that very cry betrays a disposition to question the great and essential truth which it is manifestly the object of that provision to declare.

But it may be again asked, who is to judge of the *necessity* and *propriety* of the laws to be passed for executing the powers of the Union? I answer first that this question arises as well and as fully upon the simple grant of those powers, as upon the declaratory clause: And I answer in the second place, that the national government, like every other, must judge in the first instance of the proper exercise of its powers; and its constituents in the last. If the Foederal Government should overpass the just bounds of its authority, and make a tyrannical use of its powers; the people whose creature it is must appeal to the standard they have formed, and take such measures to redress the injury done to the constitution, as the exigency may suggest and prudence justify. The propriety of a law in a constitutional light, must always be determined by the nature of the powers upon which it is founded. Suppose by some forced constructions of its authority (which indeed cannot easily be imagined) the Foederal Legislature should attempt to vary the law of descent in any State; would it not be evident that in making such an attempt it had exceeded its jurisdiction and infringed upon that of the State? Suppose again that upon the pretence of an interference with its revenues, it should undertake to abrogate a land tax imposed by the authority of a State, would it not be equally evident that this was an invasion of that concurrent jurisdiction in respect to this species of tax which its constitution plainly supposes to exist in the State governments? If there ever should be a doubt on this head the credit of it will be intirely due to those reasoners, who, in the imprudent zeal of their animosity to the plan of the Convention, have laboured to invelope it in a cloud calculated to obscure the plainest and simplest truths.

But it is said, that the laws of the Union are to be the *supreme law* of the land. But what inference can be drawn from this or what would they amount to, if they were not to be supreme? It is evident they would amount to nothing. A LAW by the very meaning of the term includes supremacy. It is a rule which those to whom it is prescribed are bound to observe. This results from every political association. If individuals enter into a state of society the laws of that society must be the supreme regulator of their conduct. If a number of political societies enter into a larger political society, the laws which the latter may enact, pursuant to the powers entrusted to it by its constitution, must necessarily be supreme over those societies, and the individuals of whom they are composed. It would otherwise be a mere treaty, dependent on the good faith of the parties, and not a government; which is only another word for POLITICAL POWER AND SUPREMACY. But it will not follow from this doctrine that acts of the larger society which are *not pursuant* to its constitutional powers but which are invasions of the residuary authorities of the smaller societies will become the supreme law of the land. These will be merely acts of usurpation and will deserve to be treated as such. Hence we perceive that the clause which declares the supremacy of the laws of the Union, like the one we have just before considered, only declares a truth, which flows immediately and necessarily from the institution of a Foederal Government. It will not, I presume, have escaped observation that it *expressly* confines this supremacy to laws made *pursuant to the Constitution;* which I mention merely as an instance of caution in the Convention; since that limitation would have been to be understood though it had not been expressed.

Though a law therefore for laying a tax for the use of the United States would be supreme in its nature, and could not legally be opposed or controuled; yet a law for abrogating or preventing the collection of a tax laid by the authority of a State (unless upon imports and exports) would not be the supreme law of the land, but an usurpation of power not granted by the constitution. As far as an improper accumulation of taxes on the same object might tend to render the collection difficult or precarious, this would be a mutual inconvenience not arising from a superiority or defect of power on either side, but from an injudicious exercise of power by one or the other, in a manner equally disadvantageous to both. It is to be hoped and presumed however that mutual interest would dictate a concert in this respect which would avoid any material inconvenience. The inference from the whole is—that the individual States would, under the proposed constitution, retain an independent and uncontroulable authority to raise revenue to any extent of which they may stand in need by every kind of taxation except duties on imports and exports. It will be shewn in the next paper that this CONCURRENT JURISDICTION in the article of taxation was the only admissible substitute for an intire subordination, in respect to this branch of power, of the State authority to that of the Union.

7

JAMES MADISON, FEDERALIST, NO. 44, 303–5
25 Jan. 1788

Few parts of the Constitution have been assailed with more intemperance than this; yet on a fair investigation of it, no part can appear more compleatly invulnerable. Without the *substance* of this power, the whole Constitution would be a dead letter. Those who object to the article therefore as a part of the Constitution, can only mean that the *form* of the provision is improper. But have they considered whether a better form could have been substituted?

There are four other possible methods which the Convention might have taken on this subject. They might have copied the second article of the existing confederation which would have prohibited the exercise of any power not *expressly* delegated; they might have attempted a positive enumeration of the powers comprehended under the general terms "necessary and proper"; they might have attempted a negative enumeration of them, by specifying the powers excepted from the general definition: They might have been altogether silent on the subject; leaving these necessary and proper powers, to construction and inference.

Had the Convention taken the first method of adopting the second article of confederation; it is evident that the new Congress would be continually exposed as their predecessors have been, to the alternative of construing the term *"expressly"* with so much rigour as to disarm the government of all real authority whatever, or with so much latitude as to destroy altogether the force of the restriction. It would be easy to shew if it were necessary, that no important power, delegated by the articles of confederation, has been or can be executed by Congress, without recurring more or less to the doctrine of *construction* or *implication.* As the powers delegated under the new system are more extensive, the government which is to administer it would find itself still more distressed with the alternative of betraying the public interest by doing nothing; or of violating the Constitution by exercising powers, indispensably necessary and proper; but at the same time, not *expressly* granted.

Had the convention attempted a positive enumeration of the powers necessary and proper for carrying their other powers into effect; the attempt would have involved a complete digest of laws on every subject to which the Constitution relates; accommodated too not only to the existing state of things, but to all the possible changes which futurity may produce: For in every new application of a general power, the *particular powers,* which are the means of attaining the *object* of the general power, must always necessarily vary with that object; and be often properly varied whilst the object remains the same.

Had they attempted to enumerate the particular powers or means, not necessary or proper for carrying the general powers into execution, the task would have been no less chimerical; and would have been liable to this further objection; that every defect in the enumeration, would have been equivalent to a positive grant of authority. If to avoid this consequence they had attempted a partial enumeration of the exceptions, and described the residue by the general terms, *not necessary or proper:* It must have happened that the enumeration would comprehend a few of the excepted powers only; that these would be such as would be least likely to be assumed or tolerated, because the enumeration would of course select such as would be least necessary or proper, and that the unnecessary and improper powers included in the residuum, would be less forceably excepted, than if no partial enumeration had been made.

Had the Constitution been silent on this head, there can be no doubt that all the particular powers, requisite as means of executing the general powers, would have resulted to the government, by unavoidable implication. No axiom is more clearly established in law, or in reason, than that wherever the end is required, the means are authorised; wherever a general power to do a thing is given, every particular power necessary for doing it, is included. Had this last method therefore been pursued by the Convention, every objection now urged against their plan, would remain in all its plausibility; and the real inconveniency would be incurred, of not removing a pretext which may be seized on critical occasions for drawing into question the essential powers of the Union.

If it be asked, what is to be the consequence, in case the Congress shall misconstrue this part of the Constitution, and exercise powers not warranted by its true meaning? I answer the same as if they should misconstrue or enlarge any other power vested in them, as if the general power had been reduced to particulars, and any one of these were to be violated; the same in short, as if the State Legislatures should violate their respective constitutional authorities. In the first instance, the success of the usurpation will depend on the executive and judiciary departments, which are to expound and give effect to the legislative acts; and in the last resort, a remedy must be obtained from the people, who can by the election of more faithful representatives, annul the acts of the usurpers. The truth is, that this ultimate redress may be more confided in against unconstitutional acts of the foederal than of the State Legislatures, for this plain reason, that as every such act of the former, will be an invasion of the rights of the latter, these will be ever ready to mark the innovation, to sound the alarm to the people, and to exert their local influence in effecting a change of foederal representatives. There being no such intermediate body between the State Legislatures and the people, interested in watching the conduct of the former, violations of the State Constitutions are more likely to remain unnoticed and unredressed.

8

JOHN LANSING, PROPOSED AMENDMENT, NEW YORK RATIFYING CONVENTION
2 July 1788
Elliot 2:406

Respecting the power to make all *laws necessary* for the carrying the Constitution into execution,—

> "*Provided,* That no power shall be exercised by Congress, but such as is expressly given by this Constitution; and all others, not expressly given, shall be reserved to the respective states, to be by them exercised."

Moved by Mr. LANSING.

9

JAMES MADISON, THE BANK BILL, HOUSE OF REPRESENTATIVES
2 Feb. 1791
Papers 13:376–78

The *third* clause is that which gives the power to pass all laws necessary and proper to execute the specified powers.

Whatever meaning this clause may have, none can be admitted, that would give an unlimited discretion to Congress.

Its meaning must, according to the natural and obvious force of the terms and the context, be limited to means *necessary* to the *end,* and *incident* to the *nature* of the specified powers.

The clause is in fact merely declaratory of what would have resulted by unavoidable implication, as the appropriate, and as it were, technical means of executing those powers. In this sense it had been explained by the friends of the constitution, and ratified by the state conventions.

The essential characteristic of the government, as composed of limited and enumerated powers, would be destroyed: If instead of direct and incidental means, any means could be used, which in the language of the preamble to the bill, "might be conceived to be conducive to the successful conducting of the finances; or might be *conceived* to *tend* to give *facility* to the obtaining of loans." He urged an attention to the diffuse and ductile terms which had been found requisite to cover the stretch of power contained in the bill. He compared them with the terms *necessary* and *proper,* used in the Constitution, and asked whether it was possible to view the two descriptions as synonimous, or the one as a fair and safe commentary on the other.

If, proceeded he, Congress, by virtue of the power to borrow, can create the means of lending, and in pursuance of these means, can incorporate a Bank, they may do any thing whatever creative of like means.

The East-India company has been a lender to the British government, as well as the Bank, and the South-Sea company is a greater creditor than either. Congress then may incorporate similar companies in the United States, and that too not under the idea of regulating trade, but under that of borrowing money.

Private capitals are the chief resources for loans to the British government. Whatever then may be conceived to favor the accumulation of capitals may be done by Congress. They may incorporate manufacturers. They may give monopolies in every branch of domestic industry.

If, again, Congress by virtue of the power to borrow money, can create the ability to lend, they may by virtue of the power to levy money, create the ability to pay it. The ability to pay taxes depends on the general wealth of the society, and this, on the general prosperity of agriculture, manufactures and commerce. Congress then may give bounties and make regulations on all of these objects.

The States have, it is allowed on all hands, a concurrent right to lay and collect taxes. This power is secured to them not by its being expressly reserved, but by its not being ceded by the constitution. The reasons for the bill cannot be admitted, because they would invalidate that right; why may it not be *conceived* by Congress, that an uniform and exclusive imposition of taxes, would not less than the proposed Banks "be *conducive* to the successful conducting of the national finances, and *tend* to *give facility* to the obtaining of revenue, for the use of the government?"

The doctrine of implication is always a tender one. The danger of it has been felt in other governments. The delicacy was felt in the adoption of our own; the danger may also be felt, if we do not keep close to our chartered authorities.

Mark the reasoning on which the validity of the bill depends. To borrow money is made the *end* and the accumulation of capitals, *implied* as the *means.* The accumulation of capitals is then the *end,* and a bank *implied* as the *means.* The bank is then the *end,* and a charter of incorporation, a monopoly, capital punishments, &c. *implied* as the *means.*

If implications, thus remote and thus multiplied, can be linked together, a chain may be formed that will reach every object of legislation, every object within the whole compass of political economy.

The latitude of interpretation required by the bill is condemned by the rule furnished by the constitution itself.

Congress have power "to regulate the value of money"; yet it is expressly added not left to be implied, that counterfeitors may be punished.

They have the power "to declare war," to which armies are more incident, than incorporated Banks, to borrowing; yet is expressly added, the power "to raise and support armies"; and to this again, the express power "to make rules and regulations for the government of armies"; a like remark is applicable to the powers as to a navy.

The regulation and calling out of the militia are more appurtenant to war, than the proposed bank, to borrowing; yet the former is not left to construction.

The very power to borrow money is a less remote implication from the power of war, than an incorporated monopoly bank, from the power of borrowing—yet the power to borrow is not left to implication.

It is not pretended that every insertion or omission in the constitution is the effect of systematic attention. This is not the character of any human work, particularly the work of a body of men. The examples cited, with others that might be added, sufficiently inculcate nevertheless a rule of interpretation, very different from that on which the bill rests. They condemn the exercise of any power, particularly a great and important power, which is not evidently and necessarily involved in an express power.

It cannot be denied that the power proposed to be exercised is an important power.

As a charter of incorporation the bill creates an artificial person previously not existing in law. It confers important civil rights and attributes, which could not otherwise be claimed. It is, though not precisely similar, at least equivalent, to the naturalization of an alien, by which certain new civil characters are acquired by him. Would Congress have had the power to naturalize, if it had not been expressly given?

In the power to make bye laws, the bill delegated a sort of legislative power, which is unquestionably an act of a high and important nature. He took notice of the only restraint on the bye laws, that they were not to be contrary to the law and the constitution of the bank; and asked what law was intended; if the law of the United States, the scantiness of their code would give a power, never before given to a corporation—and obnoxious to the States, whose laws would then be superceded not only by the laws of Congress, but by the bye laws of a corporation within their own jurisdiction. If the law intended, was the law of the State, then the State might make laws that would destroy an institution of the United States.

The bill gives a power to purchase and hold lands; Congress themselves could not purchase lands within a State "without the consent of its legislature." How could they delegate a power to others which they did not possess themselves?

It takes from our successors, who have equal rights with ourselves, and with the aid of experience will be more capable of deciding on the subject, an opportunity of exercising that right, for an immoderate term.

It takes from our constituents the opportunity of deliberating on the untried measure, although their hands are also to be tied by it for the same term.

It involves a monopoly, which affects the equal rights of every citizen.

It leads to a penal regulation, perhaps capital punishments, one of the most solemn acts of sovereign authority.

From this view of the power of incorporation exercised in the bill, it could never be deemed an accessary or subaltern power, to be deduced by implication, as a means of executing another power; it was in its nature a distinct, an independent and substantive prerogative, which not being enumerated in the constitution could never have been meant to be included in it, and not being included could never be rightfully exercised.

He here adverted to a distinction, which he said had not been sufficiently kept in view, between a power necessary and proper for the government or union, and a power necessary and proper for executing the enumerated powers. In the latter case, the powers included in each of the enumerated powers were not expressed, but to be drawn from the nature of each. In the former, the powers composing the government were expressly enumerated. This constituted the peculiar nature of the government, no power therefore not enumerated, could be inferred from the general nature of government. Had the power of making treaties, for example, been omitted, however necessary it might have been, the defect could only have been lamented, or supplied by an amendment of the constitution.

But the proposed bank could not even be called necessary to the government; at most it could be but convenient. Its uses to the government could be supplied by keeping the taxes a little in advance—by loans from individuals—by the other banks, over which the government would have equal command; nay greater, as it may grant or refuse to these the privilege, made a free and irrevocable gift to the proposed bank, of using their notes in the federal revenue.

10

THOMAS JEFFERSON, OPINION ON THE CONSTITUTIONALITY OF THE BILL FOR ESTABLISHING A NATIONAL BANK
15 Feb. 1791
Papers 19:275–80

The bill for establishing a National Bank undertakes, among other things

1. to form the subscribers into a Corporation.
2. to enable them, in their corporate capacities to receive grants of land; and so far is against the laws of *Mortmain.**
3. to make *alien* subscribers capable of holding lands, and so far is against the laws of *Alienage.*
4. to transmit these lands, on the death of a proprietor, to a certain line of successors: and so far changes the course of *Descents.*
5. to put the lands out of the reach of forfeiture or escheat and so far is against the laws of *Forfeiture and Escheat.*
6. to transmit personal chattels to successors in a certain line: and so far is against the laws of *Distribution.*

*Though the constitution controuls the laws of Mortmain so far as to permit Congress itself to hold lands for certain purposes, yet not so far as to permit them to communicate a similar right to other corporate bodies.

7. to give them the sole and exclusive right of banking under the national authority: and so far is against the laws of *Monopoly.*
8. to communicate to them a power to make laws paramount to the laws of the states: for so they must be construed, to protect the institution from the controul of the state legislatures; and so, probably they will be construed.

I consider the foundation of the Constitution as laid on this ground that "all powers not delegated to the U.S. by the Constitution, not prohibited by it to the states, are reserved to the states or to the people" [XIIth. Amendmt.]. To take a single step beyond the boundaries thus specially drawn around the powers of Congress, is to take possession of a boundless feild of power, no longer susceptible of any definition.

The incorporation of a bank, and other powers assumed by this bill have not, in my opinion, been delegated to the U.S. by the Constitution.

I. They are not among the powers specially enumerated, for these are

1. A power to *lay taxes* for the purpose of paying the debts of the U.S. But no debt is paid by this bill, nor any tax laid. Were it a bill to raise money, it's origination in the Senate would condemn it by the constitution.

2. "to borrow money." But this bill neither borrows money, nor ensures the borrowing it. The proprietors of the bank will be just as free as any other money holders, to lend or not to lend their money to the public. The operation proposed in the bill, first to lend them two millions, and then borrow them back again, cannot change the nature of the latter act, which will still be a payment, and not a loan, call it by what name you please.

3. "to regulate commerce with foreign nations, and among the states, and with the Indian tribes." To erect a bank, and to regulate commerce, are very different acts. He who erects a bank creates a subject of commerce in it's bills: so does he who makes a bushel of wheat, or digs a dollar out of the mines. Yet neither of these persons regulates commerce thereby. To erect a thing which may be bought and sold, is not to prescribe regulations for buying and selling. Besides; if this was an exercise of the power of regulating commerce, it would be void, as extending as much to the internal commerce of every state, as to it's external. For the power given to Congress by the Constitution, does not extend to the internal regulation of the commerce of a state (that is to say of the commerce between citizen and citizen) which remains exclusively with it's own legislature; but to it's external commerce only, that is to say, it's commerce with another state, or with foreign nations or with the Indian tribes. Accordingly the bill does not propose the measure as a "regulation of trade," but as "productive of considerable advantage to trade."

Still less are these powers covered by any other of the special enumerations.

II. Nor are they within either of the general phrases, which are the two following.

1. "To lay taxes to provide for the general welfare of the U.S." that is to say "to lay taxes *for the purpose* of providing for the general welfare." For the laying of taxes is the *power* and the general welfare the *purpose* for which the power is to be exercised. They are not to lay taxes ad libitum *for any purpose they please;* but only to *pay the debts or provide for the welfare of the Union.* In like manner they are not *to do anything they please* to provide for the general welfare, but only *to lay taxes* for that purpose. To consider the latter phrase, not as describing the purpose of the first, but as giving a distinct and independent power to do any act they please, which might be for the good of the Union, would render all the preceding and subsequent enumerations of power completely useless. It would reduce the whole instrument to a single phrase, that of instituting a Congress with power to do whatever would be for the good of the U.S. and as they would be the sole judges of the good or evil, it would be also a power to do whatever evil they pleased. It is an established rule of construction, where a phrase will bear either of two meanings, to give it that which will allow some meaning to the other parts of the instrument, and not that which would render all the others useless. Certainly no such universal power was meant to be given them. It was intended to lace them up straitly within the enumerated powers, and those without which, as means, these powers could not be be carried into effect. It is known that the very power now proposed *as a means,* was rejected *as an end,* by the Convention which formed the constitution. A proposition was made to them to authorize Congress to open canals, and an amendatory one to empower them to incorporate. But the whole was rejected, and one of the reasons of rejection urged in debate was that then they would have a power to erect a bank, which would render the great cities, where there were prejudices and jealousies on that subject adverse to the reception of the constitution.

2. The second general phrase is "to make all laws *necessary* and proper for carrying into execution the enumerated powers." But they can all be carried into execution without a bank. A bank therefore is not *necessary,* and consequently not authorised by this phrase.

It has been much urged that a bank will give great facility, or convenience in the collection of taxes. Suppose this were true: yet the constitution allows only the means which are "necessary" not those which are merely "convenient" for effecting the enumerated powers. If such a latitude of construction be allowed to this phrase as to give any non-enumerated power, it will go to every one, for [there] is no one which ingenuity may not torture into a *convenience, in some way or other,* to *some one* of so long a list of enumerated powers. It would swallow up all the delegated powers, and reduce the whole to one phrase as before observed. Therefore it was that the constitution restrained them to the *necessary* means, that is to say, to those means without which the grant of the power would be nugatory.

But let us examine this *convenience,* and see what it is. The report on this subject, page 3. states the only *general* convenience to be the preventing the transportation and re-transportation of money between the states and the treasury. (For I pass over the increase of circulating medium ascribed to it as a merit, and which, according to my ideas of paper money is clearly a demerit.) Every state will have to pay a sum of tax-money into the treasury: and the treasury will have to pay, in every state, a part of the interest on the public debt, and salaries to the officers of government resident in that state. In most of the states there will still be a surplus of tax-money to come up to the seat of government for the officers residing there. The payments of interest and salary in each state may be made by treasury-orders on the state collector. This will take up the greater part of the money he has collected in his state, and consequently prevent the great mass of it from being drawn out of the state. If there be a balance of commerce in favour of that state against the one in which the government resides, the surplus of taxes will be remitted by the bills of exchange drawn for that commercial balance. And so it must be if there was a bank. But if there be no balance of commerce, either direct or circuitous, all the banks in the world could not bring up the surplus of taxes but in the form of money. Treasury orders then and bills of exchange may prevent the displacement of the main mass of the money collected, without the aid of any bank: and where these fail, it cannot be prevented even with that aid.

Perhaps indeed bank bills may be a more *convenient* vehicle than treasury orders. But a little *difference* in the degree of *convenience*, cannot constitute the necessity which the constitution makes the ground for assuming any non-enumerated power.

Besides; the existing banks will without a doubt, enter into arrangements for lending their agency: and the more favourable, as there will be a competition among them for it: whereas the bill delivers us up bound to the national bank, who are free to refuse all arrangement, but on their own terms, and the public not free, on such refusal, to employ any other bank. That of Philadelphia, I believe, now does this business, by their post-notes, which by an arrangement with the treasury, are paid by any state collector to whom they are presented. This expedient alone suffices to prevent the existence of that *necessity* which may justify the assumption of a non-enumerated power as a means for carrying into effect an enumerated one. The thing may be done, and has been done, and well done without this assumption; therefore it does not stand on that degree of *necessity* which can honestly justify it.

It may be said that a bank, whose bills would have a currency all over the states, would be more convenient than one whose currency is limited to a single state. So it would be still more convenient that there should be a bank whose bills should have a currency all over the world. But it does not follow from this superior conveniency that there exists anywhere a power to establish such a bank; or that the world may not go on very well without it.

Can it be thought that the Constitution intended that for a shade or two of *convenience*, more or less, Congress should be authorised to break down the most antient and fundamental laws of the several states, such as those against Mortmain, the laws of alienage, the rules of descent, the acts of distribution, the laws of escheat and forfeiture, the laws of monopoly? Nothing but a necessity invincible by any other means, can justify such a prostration of laws which constitute the pillars of our whole system of jurisprudence. Will Congress be too strait-laced to carry the constitution into honest effect, unless they may pass over the foundation-laws of the state-governments for the slightest convenience to theirs?

The Negative of the President is the shield provided by the constitution to protect against the invasions of the legislature 1. the rights of the Executive 2. of the Judiciary 3. of the states and state legislatures. The present is the case of a right remaining exclusively with the states and is consequently one of those intended by the constitution to be placed under his protection.

It must be added however, that unless the President's mind on a view of every thing which is urged for and against this bill, is tolerably clear that it is unauthorised by the constitution, if the pro and the con hang so even as to balance his judgment, a just respect for the wisdom of the legislature would naturally decide the balance in favour of their opinion. It is chiefly for cases where they are clearly misled by error, ambition, or interest, that the constitution has placed a check in the negative of the President.

11

Alexander Hamilton, Opinion on the Constitutionality of the Bank
23 Feb. 1791

Papers 8:97–106

The Secretary of the Treasury having perused with attention the papers containing the opinions of the Secretary of State and Attorney General concerning the constitutionality of the bill for establishing a National Bank proceeds according to the order of the President to submit the reasons which have induced him to entertain a different opinion.

It will naturally have been anticipated that, in performing this task he would feel uncommon solicitude. Personal considerations alone arising from the reflection that the measure originated with him would be sufficient to produce it. The sense which he has manifested of the great importance of such an institution to the successful administration of the department under his particular care, and an expectation of serious ill consequences to result from a failure of the measure, do not permit him to be without anxiety on public accounts. But the chief solicitude arises from a firm persuasion, that principles of construction like those espoused by the Secretary of State and the Attorney General would be fatal to the just and indispensable authority of the United States.

In entering upon the argument it ought to be premised, that the objections of the Secretary of State and Attorney General are founded on a general denial of the authority of the United States to erect corporations. The latter indeed expressly admits, that if there be anything in the bill which is not warranted by the constitution, it is the clause of incorporation.

Now it appears to the Secretary of the Treasury, that this *general principle* is *inherent* in the very *definition* of *Government* and *essential* to every step of the progress to be made by that of the United States, namely—that every power vested in a Government is in its nature *sovereign,* and includes by *force* of the *term,* a right to employ all the *means* requisite, and fairly *applicable* to the attainment of the *ends* of such power; and which are not precluded by restrictions and exceptions specified in the constitution, or not immoral, or not contrary to the essential ends of political society.

This principle in its application to Government in general would be admitted as an axiom. And it will be incumbent upon those, who may incline to deny it, to *prove* a distinction and to shew that a rule which in the general system of things is essential to the preservation of the social order, is inapplicable to the United States.

The circumstances that the powers of sovereignty are in this country divided between the National and State Governments, does not afford the distinction required. It does not follow from this, that each of the *portions* of powers delegated to the one or to the other is not sovereign *with regard to its proper objects.* It will only *follow* from it, that each has sovereign power as to *certain things,* and not as to *other things.* To deny that the Government of the United States has sovereign power as to its declared purposes and trusts, because its power does not extend to all cases, would be equally to deny, that the State Governments have sovereign power in any case; because their power does not extend to every case. The tenth section of the first article of the constitution exhibits a long list of very important things which they may not do. And thus the United States would furnish the singular spectacle of a *political society* without *sovereignty,* or of a people *governed* without *government.*

If it would be necessary to bring proof to a proposition so clear as that which affirms that the powers of the federal Government, *as to its objects,* are sovereign, there is a clause of its constitution which would be decisive. It is that which declares, that the constitution and the laws of the United States made in pursuance of it, and all treaties made or which shall be made under their authority shall be the supreme law of the land. The power which can create the *Supreme law* of the land, in any case, is doubtless sovereign *as to such case.*

This general and indisputable principle puts at once an end to the *abstract* question. Whether the United States have power to *erect a corporation?* that is to say, to give a *legal* or *artificial capacity* to one or more persons, distinct from the natural. For it is unquestionably incident to *sovereign power* to erect corporations, and consequently to *that* of the United States, in *relation to the objects* intrusted to the management of the government. The difference is this—where the authority of the government is general, it can create corporations in *all cases;* where it is confined to certain branches of legislation, it can create corporations only in those cases.

Here then as far as concerns the reasonings of the Secretary of State and the Attorney General, the affirmative of the constitutionality of the bill might be permitted to rest. It will occur to the President that the principle here advanced has been untouched by either of them.

For a more complete elucidation of the point nevertheless, the arguments which they had used against the power of the government to erect corporations, however foreign they are to the great and fundamental rule which has been stated, shall be particularly examined. And after shewing that they do not tend to impair its force, it shall also be shewn that the power of incorporation incident to the government in certain cases, does fairly extend to the particular case which is the object of the bill.

The first of these arguments is, that the foundation of the constitution is laid on this ground "that all powers not delegated to the United States by the Constitution, nor prohibited by it to the States are reserved to the States or to the people," whence it is meant to be inferred, that congress can in no case exercise any power not included in those enumerated in the constitution. And it is affirmed that the power of erecting a corporation is not included in any of the enumerated powers.

The main proposition here laid down, in its true signification is not to be questioned. It is nothing more than a consequence of this republican maxim, that all government is a delegation of power. But how much is delegated in each case, is a question of fact to be made out by fair reasoning and construction, upon the particular provisions of the constitution—taking as guides the general principles and general ends of government.

It is not denied, that there are *implied,* as well as *express powers,* and that the *former* are as effectually delegated as the latter. And for the sake of accuracy it shall be mentioned, that there is another class of powers, which may be properly denominated *resulting* powers. It will not be doubted that if the United States should make a conquest of any of the territories of its neighbours, they would possess sovereign jurisdiction over the conquered territory. This would rather be a result from the whole mass of the powers of the government and from the nature of political society, than a consequence of either of the powers specially enumerated.

But be this as it may, it furnishes a striking illustration of the general doctrine contended for. It shows an extensive case, in which a power of erecting corporations is either implied in, or would result from some or all of the powers, vested in the National Government. The jurisdiction acquired over such conquered territory would certainly be competent to every species of legislation.

To return—It is conceded, that implied powers are to be considered as delegated equally with express ones.

Then it follows, that as a power of erecting a corporation may as well be *implied* as any other thing; it may as well be employed as an *instrument* or *means* of carrying into execution any of the specified powers, as any other instrument or mean whatever. The only question must be, in this as in every other case, whether the mean to be employed, or in this instance the corporation to be erected, has a natural relation to any of the acknowledged objects or lawful ends of the government. Thus a corporation may not be erected by congress, for superintending the police of the city of Philadelphia because they are not authorized to *regulate* the *police* of that city; but one may be erected in relation to the collection of taxes, or to the trade with foreign countries, or to the trade between the States, or with the Indian Tribes, because it is the province of the federal government to *regulate those objects* and because it is incident to a general *sovereign* or *legislative power* to *regulate* a thing, to employ all the means which relate to its regulation to the *best* and *greatest advantage*.

A strange fallacy seems to have crept into the manner of thinking and reasoning upon this subject. Imagination appears to have been unusually busy concerning it. An incorporation seems to have been regarded as some great, independent, substantive thing—as a political end of peculiar magnitude and moment; whereas it is truly to be considered as a *quality, capacity, or means* to an end. Thus a mercantile company is formed with a certain capital for the purpose of carrying on a particular branch of business. Here the business to be prosecuted is the *end;* the association in order to form the requisite capital is the primary mean. Suppose than an incorporation were added to this; it would only be to add a new *quality* to that association; to give it an artificial capacity by which it would be enabled to prosecute the business with more safety and convenience.

That the importance of the power of incorporation has been exaggerated, leading to erroneous conclusions, will further appear from tracing it to its origin. The roman law is the source of it, according to which a *voluntary* association of individuals at *any time* or *for any purpose* was capable of producing it. In England, whence our notions of it are immediately borrowed, it forms a part of the executive authority, and the exercise of it has been often *delegated* by that authority. Whence therefore the ground of the supposition, that it lies beyond the reach of all those very important portions of sovereign power, legislative as well as executive, which belong to the government of the United States?

To this mode of reasoning respecting the right of employing all the means requisite to the execution of the specified powers of the Government, it is objected that none but *necessary* and proper means are to be employed, and the Secretary of State maintains, that no means are to be considered as *necessary,* but those without which the grant of the power would be *nugatory.* Nay so far does he go in his restrictive interpretation of the word, as even to make the case of *necessity* which shall warrant the constitutional exercise of the power to depend on *casual* and *temporary* circumstances; an idea which alone refutes the construction. The *expediency* of exercising a particular power, at a particular time, must indeed depend on *circumstances;* but the constitutional right of exercising it must be uniform and invariable—the same to day as to morrow.

All the arguments therefore against the constitutionality of the bill derived from the accidental existence of certain State banks—institutions which *happen* to exist today, and, for ought that concerns the government of the United States, may disappear tomorrow, must not only be rejected as falacious, but must be viewed as demonstrative, that there is a *radical* source of error in the reasoning.

It is essential to the being of the National government, that so erroneous a conception of the meaning of the word *necessary,* should be exploded.

It is certain, that neither the grammatical nor popular sense of the term requires that construction. According to both, *necessary* often means no more than *needful, requisite, incidental, useful,* or *conductive to.* It is a common mode of expression to say, that it is *necessary* for a government or a person to do this or that thing, when nothing more is intended or understood, than that the interests of the government or person require, or will be promoted, by the doing of this or that thing. The imagination can be at no loss for exemplifications of the use of the word in this sense.

And it is the true one in which it is to be understood as used in the constitution. The whole turn of the clause containing it indicates, that it was the intent of the convention, by that clause to give a liberal latitude to the exercise of the specified powers. The expressions have peculiar comprehensiveness. They are, "to make *all laws,* necessary and proper for *carrying into execution* the foregoing powers and *all other powers* vested by the constitution in the *government* of the United States, or in any *department* or *officer* thereof." To understand the word as the Secretary of State does, would be to depart from its obvious and popular sense, and to give it a *restrictive* operation; an idea never before entertained. It would be to give it the same force as if the word *absolutely* or *indispensably* had been prefixed to it.

Such a construction would beget endless uncertainty and embarrassment. The cases must be palpable and extreme in which it could be pronounced with certainty that a measure was absolutely necessary, or one without which the exercise of a given power would be nugatory. There are few measures of any government, which would stand so severe a test. To insist upon it, would be to make the criterion of the exercise of any implied power *a case of extreme necessity;* which is rather a rule to justify the overleaping of the bounds of constitutional authority, than to govern the ordinary exercise of it.

It may be truly said of every government, as well as of that of the United States, that it has only a right, to pass such laws as are necessary and proper to accomplish the objects intrusted to it. For no government has a right to do *merely what it pleases.* Hence by a process of reasoning similar to that of the Secretary of State, it might be proved, that neither of the State governments has the right to incorporate a bank. It might be shown, that all the public business of the State, could be performed without a bank, and inferring thence that it was unnecessary it might be argued that it could not be done, because it is against the rule which has been just mentioned. A like mode of reasoning would prove, that there was no power to incorporate the Inhabitants of a town, with a view to a more perfect police. For it is certain, that an incorporation may be dispensed with, though it is better to have one. It is to be remembered that there is no *express* power in any State constitution to erect corporations.

The *degree* in which a measure is necessary, can never be a test of the *legal* right to adopt it. That must be a matter of opinion; and can only be a test of expediency. The *relation* between the *measure* and the *end,* between the *nature* of *the mean* employed towards the execution of a power and the object of that power, must be the criterion of constitutionality not the more or less of *necessity* or *utility.*

The practice of the government is against the rule of construction advocated by the Secretary of State. Of this the act concerning light houses, beacons, buoys and public piers, is a decisive example. This doubtless must be referred to the power of regulating trade, and is fairly relative to it. But it cannot be affirmed, that the exercise of that power, in this instance, was strictly necessary, or that the power itself would be *nugatory* without that of regulating establishments of this nature.

This restrictive interpretation of the word *necessary* is also contrary to this sound maxim of construction; namely, that the powers contained in a constitution of government, especially those which concern the general administration of the affairs of a country, its finances, trade, defence etc. ought to be construed liberally, in advancement of the public good. This rule does not depend on the particular form of a government or on the particular demarkation of the boundaries of its powers, but on the nature and objects of government itself. The means by which national exigencies are to be provided for, national inconveniences obviated, national prosperity promoted, are of such infinite variety, extent and complexity that there must, of necessity be great latitude of discretion in the selection and application of those means. Hence consequently, the necessity and propriety of exercising the authorities intrusted to a government on principles of liberal construction.

The Attorney General admits the *rule,* but takes a distinction between a State, and the federal constitution. The latter, he thinks, ought to be construed with great strictness, because there is more danger of error in defining partial than general powers.

But the reason of the *rule* forbids such a distinction. This reason is—the variety and extent of public exigencies, a far greater proportion of which and of a far more critical kind are objects of national than of State administration. The greater danger of error, as far as it is supposable, may be a prudential reason for caution in practice, but it cannot be a rule of restrictive interpretation.

In regard to the clause of the constitution immediately under consideration, it is admitted by the Attorney General, that no *restrictive* effect can be ascribed to it. He defines the word necessary thus: "To be necessary is to be *incidental,* and may be denominated the natural means of executing a power."

But while on the one hand, the construction of the Secretary of State is deemed inadmissable, it will not be contended on the other, that the clause in question gives any *new* or *independent* power. But it gives an explicit sanction to the doctrine of *implied* powers, and is equivalent to an admission of the proposition, that the government, *as to its specified powers and objects,* has plenary and sovereign authority, in some cases paramount to that of the States in others co-ordinate with it. For such is the plain import of the declaration, that it may pass all *laws* necessary and proper to carry into execution those powers.

It is no valid objection to the doctrine to say, that it is calculated to extend the powers of the general government throughout the entire sphere of State legislation. The same thing has been said, and may be said with regard to every exercise of power by *implication* or *construction.* The moment the literal meaning is departed from there is a chance of error and abuse. And yet an adherence to the letter of its powers would at once arrest the motions of the government. It is not only agreed, on all hands, that the exercise of constructive powers is indispensable, but every act which has been passed is more or less an exemplification of it. One has been already mentioned, that relating to light houses etc. That which declares the power of the President to remove officers at pleasure, acknowledges the same truth in another, and a signal instance.

The truth is, that difficulties on this point are inherent in the nature of the federal constitution. They result inevitably from a division of the legislative power. The consequence of this division is, that there will be cases clearly within the power of the National Government; others clearly without its powers; and a third class, which will leave room for controversy and difference of opinion, and concerning which a reasonable latitude of judgment must be allowed.

But the doctrine which is contended for is not chargeable with the consequence imputed to it. It does not affirm that the National government is sovereign in all respects, but that it is sovereign to a certain extent: that is, to the *extent* of the objects of its specified powers.

It leaves therefore a criterion of what is constitutional, and of what is not so. This criterion is the *end,* to which the measure relates as a *mean.* If the end be clearly comprehended within any of the specified powers, and if the measure have an obvious relation to that end, and is not forbidden by any particular provision of the constitution—it may safely be deemed to come within the compass of the national authority. There is also this further criterion which may materially assist the decision: Does the proposed measure abridge a pre-existing right of any State, or of any individual? If it does not, there is a strong presumption in favour of its constitutionality; and slighter relations to any declared object of the constitution may be permitted to turn the scale.

12

St. George Tucker, Blackstone's Commentaries 1:App. 286–90 1803

After the satisfactory exposition of this article given in the Federalist, that if the constitution had been silent on this head, there could be no doubt, that all the particular powers requisite, as the proper means of executing the general powers specified in the constitution, would have resulted to the federal government, by unavoidable implication; and that if there be any thing exceptionable in this particular clause, it must be sought for in the specific powers, upon which this general declaration is predicated: and after the explicit declaration contained in the twelfth article of the amendments to the constitution, that the powers not delegated to the United States by the Constitution, nor prohibited by it to the states, are reserved to the states respectively, or to the people: we might have indulged a reasonable hope, that this clause would neither have continued to afford any ground of alarm, and apprehension, on the part of the people, or the individual states, nor any pretext for an assumption of any power not specified in the constitution, on the part of the federal government. But, notwithstanding this remarkable security against misconstruction, a design has been indicated to expound these phrases in the constitution, so as to destroy the effect of the particular enumeration of powers, by which it explains and limits them, which must have fallen under the observation of those who have attended to the course of public transactions.

The plain import of this clause is, that congress shall have all the incidental or instrumental powers, necessary and proper for carrying into execution all the express powers; whether they be vested in the government of the United States, more collectively, or in the several departments, or officers thereof. It neither enlarges any power specifically granted, nor is it a grant of new powers to congress, but merely a declaration, for the removal of all uncertainty, that the means of carrying into execution those otherwise granted, are included in the grant. A single example may illustrate this matter. The executive has power to make treaties, and by the treaty with Algiers, a certain tribute is to be paid annually to that regency. But the executive have no power to levy a tax for the payment of this tribute; congress, therefore, are authorised by this clause, to pass a law for that purpose: without which the treaty, although it be a supreme law of the land, in it's nature, and therefore binding upon congress, could not be executed with good faith. For the constitution expressly prohibits drawing any money from the treasury but in consequence of appropriations made by law.

Whenever, therefore, a question arises concerning the constitutionality of a particular power; the first question is, whether the power be expressed in the constitution? If it be, the question is decided. If it be not expressed, the next enquiry must be, whether it is properly an incident to an express power, and necessary to it's execution. If it be, it may be exercised by congress. If it be not, congress cannot exercise it. . . . And this construction of the words *"necessary and proper,"* is not only consonant with that which prevailed during the discussions and ratifications of the constitution, but is absolutely necessary to maintain their consistency with the peculiar character of the government, as possessed of particular and defined powers, only; not of the general and indefinite powers vested in ordinary governments.

Under this construction of the clause in question, it is calculated to operate as a powerful and immediate check upon the proceedings of the federal legislature, itself, so long as the sanction of an oath, and the obligations of conscience, are regarded, among men. For, as every member is bound by oath to support the constitution, if he were to bring every measure that is proposed to the test here mentioned, and reject whatsoever could not stand the scrutiny, we should probably cease to hear any questions respecting the constitutionality of the acts of the federal government. To which we may add, that this interpretation of the clause is indispensably necessary to support that principle of the constitution, which regards the judicial exposition of that instrument, as the bulwark provided against undue extension of the legislative power. If it be understood that the powers implied in the specified powers, have an immediate and appropriate relation to them, as means, necessary and proper for carrying them into execution, questions on the constitutionality of laws passed for this purpose, will be of a nature sufficiently precise and determinate, for judicial cognizance and control. If on the one hand congress are not limited in the choice of the means, by any such appropriate relation of them to the specified powers, but may use all such as they may deem capable of answering the end, without regard to the necessity, or propriety of them, all questions relating to means of this sort must be questions of mere policy, and expediency, and from which the judicial interposition and control are completely excluded. . . . If, for example, congress were to pass a law prohibiting any person from bearing arms, as a means of preventing insurrections, the judicial courts, under the construction of the words necessary and proper, here contended for, would be able to pronounce decidedly upon the constitutionality of these means. But if congress may use any means, which they choose to adopt, the provision in the constitution which secures to the people the right of bearing arms, is a mere nullity; and any man imprisoned for bearing arms under such an act, might be without relief; because in that case, no court could have any power to pronounce on the necessity or propriety of the means adopted by congress to carry any specified power into complete effect.

This finishes our view of the legislative powers granted to the federal government; great and extensive as they must appear, they are in general such as experience had evinced to be necessary, or as the principles of a federal government had recommended to experiment, at least. In many instances these powers have been guarded by wise provisions, and restraints; some of which have been already noticed; the remainder will soon pass under review. Experience has already evinced the benefit of these restraints; and had they been more numerous, and more effectual, there is little reason to doubt that it would have contributed largely to the peace and harmony of the union, both heretofore, and hereafter. All governments have a natural tendency towards an increase, and assumption of power; and the administration of the federal government, has too frequently demonstrated, that the people of America are not exempt from this vice in their constitution. We have seen that parchment chains are not sufficient to correct this unhappy propensity; they are, nevertheless, capable of producing the most salutary effects; for, when broken, they warn the people to change those perfidious agents, who dare to violate them.

13

Martin v. Hunter's Lessee

1 Wheat. 304 (1816)

(See 3.2.1, no. 65)

14

McCulloch v. Maryland

4 Wheat. 316 (1819)

February 22d–27th, and March 1st–3d. *Webster,* for the plaintiff in error, stated: 1. That the question whether congress constitutionally possesses the power to incorporate a bank, might be raised upon this record; and it was in the discretion of the defendant's counsel to agitate it. But it might have been hoped, that it was not now to be considered as an open question. It is a question of the utmost magnitude, deeply interesting to the government itself, as well as to individuals. The mere discussion of such a question may most essentially affect the value of a vast amount of private property. We are bound to suppose, that the defendant in error is well aware of these consequences, and would not have intimated an intention to agitate such a question, but with a real design to make it a topic of serious discussion, and with a view of demanding upon it the solemn judgment of this court. This question arose early after the adoption of the constitution, and was discussed and settled, so far as legislative decision could settle it, in the first congress. The arguments drawn from the constitution, in favor of this power, were stated and exhausted in that discussion. They were exhibited, with characteristic perspicuity and force, by the first secretary of the treasury, in his report to the president of the United States. The first congress created and incorporated a bank. Act of 5th February 1791, ch. 84. Nearly each succeeding congress, if not every one, has acted and legislated on the presumption of the legal existence of such a power in the government. Individuals, it is true, have doubted, or thought otherwise; but it cannot be shown, that either branch of the legislature has, at any time, expressed an opinion against the existence of the power. The executive government has acted upon it; and the courts of law have acted upon it. Many of those who doubted or denied the existence of the powers, when first attempted to be exercised, have yielded to the first decision, and acquiesced in it, as a settled question. When all branches of the government have thus been acting on the existence of this power, nearly thirty years, it would seem almost too late to call it in question, unless its repugnancy with the constitution were plain and manifest. Congress, by the constitution, is invested with certain powers; and as to the objects, and within the scope of these powers, it is sovereign. Even without the aid of the general clause in the constitution, empowering congress to pass all necessary and proper laws for carrying its powers into execution, the grant of powers itself necessarily implies the grant of all usual and suitable means for the execution of the powers granted. Congress may declare war; it may consequently carry on war, by armies and navies, and other suitable means and methods of warfare. So, it has power to raise a revenue, and to apply it in the support of the government, and defence of the country; it may, of course, use all proper and suitable means, not specially prohibited, in the raising and disbursement of the revenue. And if, in the progress of society and the arts, new means arise, either of carrying on war, or of raising revenue, these new means doubtless would be properly considered as within the grant. Steam-frigates, for example, were not in the minds of those who framed the constitution, as among the means of naval warfare; but no one doubts the power of congress to use them, as means to an authorized end. It is not enough to say, that it does not appear that a bank was not in the contemplation of the framers of the constitution. It was not their intention, in these cases, to enumerate particulars. The true view of the subject is, that if it be a fit instrument to an authorized purpose, it may be used, not being specially prohibited. Congress is authorized to pass all laws "necessary and proper" to carry into execution the powers conferred on it. These words, "necessary and proper," in such an instrument, are probably to be considered as synonymous. Necessarily, powers must here intend such powers as are suitable and fitted to the object; such as are best and most useful in relation to the end proposed. If this be not so, and if congress could use no means but such as were absolutely indispensable to the existence of a granted power, the government would hardly exist; at least, it would be wholly inadequate to the purposes of its formation. A bank is a proper and suitable instrument to assist the operations of the government, in the collection and disbursement of the revenue; in the occasional anticipations of taxes and imposts; and in the regulation of the actual currency, as being a part of the trade and exchange between the states. It is not for this court to decide, whether a bank, or such a bank as this, be the best possible means to aid these purposes of government. Such topics must be left to that discussion which belongs to them, in the two houses of congress. Here, the only question is, whether a bank, in its known and ordinary operations, is capable of being so connected with the finances and revenues of the government, as to be fairly within the discretion of congress, when selecting means and instruments to execute its powers and perform its duties. A bank is not less the proper subject for the choice of congress, nor the less constitutional, because it requires to be executed by granting a charter of incorporation. It is not, of itself, unconstitutional in congress to create a corporation. Corporations are but means. They are not ends and objects of government. No government exists for the purpose of creating corporations as one of the ends of its being. They are institutions established to effect certain beneficial purposes; and, as means, take their character generally from their end and object. They are civil or eleemosynary, public or private, according to the object intended by their creation. They are common means, such as all governments use. The state governments create corporations to execute powers confided to their trust, without any specific authority in the state constitutions for that purpose. There is the same reason that congress should exercise its discretion as to the means by which it must execute the powers conferred upon it. Congress has duties to perform and powers to execute. It has a right to the means by which these duties can be properly and most usefully performed, and these powers executed. Among other means, it has established a bank; and before the act establishing it can be pronounced unconstitutional and void, it must be shown, that a bank has no fair connection with the execution of any power or duty of the national government, and that its creation is consequently a manifest usurpation.

Martin, Attorney-General of Maryland.—1. Read several extracts from the Federalist, and the debates of the Virginia and New York conventions, to show that the contemporary exposition of the constitution, by its authors, and by those who supported its adoption, was wholly repugnant to that now contended for by the counsel for the plaintiff in error. That it was then maintained, by the enemies of the constitution, that it contained a vast variety of powers, lurking under the generality of its phraseology, which would prove highly dangerous to the liberties of the people, and the rights of the states, unless controlled by some declaratory amendment, which should negative their existence. This apprehension was treated as a dream of distempered jealousy. The danger was denied to exist; but to provide an assurance against the possibility of its occurrence, the 10th amendment was added to the constitution. This, however, could be considered as nothing more than declaratory of the sense of the people as to the extent of the powers conferred on the new government. We are now called upon to apply that theory of interpretation, which was then rejected by the friends of the new constitution, and we are asked to engraft upon it powers of vast extent, which were disclaimed by them, and which if they had been fairly avowed at the time, would have prevented its adoption. Before we do this, they must, at least, be proved to exist, upon a candid examination of this instrument, as if it were now, for the first time, submitted to interpretation. Although we cannot, perhaps, be allowed to say, that the states have been "deceived in their grant;" yet we may justly claim something like a rigorous demonstration of this power, which nowhere appears upon the face of the constitution, but which is supposed to be tacitly inculcated in its general object and spirit. That the scheme of the framers of the constitution, intended to leave nothing to implication, will be evident, from the consideration, that many of the powers expressly given are only means to accomplish other powers expressly given. For example, the power to declare war involves, by necessary implication, if anything was to be implied, the powers of raising and supporting armies, and providing and maintaining a navy, to prosecute the war then declared. So also, as money is the sinew of war, the powers of laying and collecting taxes, and of borrowing money, are involved in that of declaring war. Yet all these powers are specifically enumerated. If, then, the convention has specified some powers, which being only means to accomplish the ends of government, might have been taken by implication; by what just rule of construction, are other sovereign powers, equally vast and important, to be assumed by implication? We insist, that the only safe rule is, the plain letter of the constitution; the rule which the constitutional legislators themselves have prescribed in the 10th amendment, which is merely declaratory; that the powers not delegated to the United States, nor prohibited to the states, are reserved to the states respectively, or to the people. The power of establishing corporations is not delegated to the United States, nor prohibited to the individual states. It is, therefore, reserved to the states, or to the people. It is not expressly delegated, either as an end, or a means, of national government. It is not to be taken by implication, as a means of executing any or all of the powers expressly granted; because other means, not more important or more sovereign in their character, are expressly enumerated. We still insist, that the authority of establishing corporations is one of the great sovereign powers of government. It may well exist in the state governments, without being expressly conferred in the state constitutions; because those governments have all the usual powers which belong to every political society, unless expressly forbidden, by the letter of the state constitutions, from exercising them. The power of establishing corporations has been constantly exercised by the state governments, and no portion of it has been ceded by them to the government of the United States.

March 7th, 1819. MARSHALL, Ch. J., delivered the opinion of the court.—In the case now to be determined, the defendant, a sovereign state, denies the obligation of a law enacted by the legislature of the Union, and the plaintiff, on his part, contests the validity of an act which has been passed by the legislature of that state. The constitution of our country, in its most interesting and vital parts, is to be considered; the conflicting powers of the government of the Union and of its members, as marked in that constitution, are to be discussed; and an opinion given, which may essentially influence the great operations of the government. No tribunal can approach such a question without a deep sense of its importance, and of the awful responsibility involved in its decision. But it must be decided peacefully, or remain a source of hostile legislation, perhaps, of hostility of a still more serious nature; and if it is to be so decided, by this tribunal alone can the decision be made. On the supreme court of the United States has the constitution of our country devolved this important duty.

The first question made in the cause is—has congress power to incorporate a bank? It has been truly said, that this can scarcely be considered as an open question, entirely unprejudiced by the former proceedings of the nation respecting it. The principle now contested was introduced at a very early period of our history, has been recognised by many successive legislatures, and has been acted upon by the judicial department, in cases of peculiar delicacy, as a law of undoubted obligation.

It will not be denied, that a bold and daring usurpation might be resisted, after an acquiescence still longer and more complete than this. But it is conceived, that a doubtful question, one on which human reason may pause, and the human judgment be suspended, in the decision of which the great principles of liberty are not concerned, but the respective powers of those who are equally the representatives of the people, are to be adjusted; if not put at rest by the practice of the government, ought to receive a considerable impression from that practice. An exposition of the constitution, deliberately established by legislative acts, on the faith of which an immense property has been advanced, ought not to be lightly disregarded.

The power now contested was exercised by the first congress elected under the present constitution. The bill for incorporating the Bank of the United States did not steal upon an unsuspecting legislature, and pass unobserved. Its principle was completely understood, and was opposed with equal zeal and ability. After being resisted, first, in the fair and open field of debate, and afterwards, in the executive cabinet, with as much persevering talent as any measure has ever experienced, and being supported by arguments which convinced minds as pure and as intelligent as this country can boast, it became a law. The original act was permitted to expire; but a short experience of the embarrassments to which the refusal to revive it exposed the government, convinced those who were most prejudiced against the measure of its necessity, and induced the passage of the present law. It would require no ordinary share of intrepidity, to assert that a measure adopted under these circumstances, was a bold and plain usurpation, to which the constitution gave no countenance. These observations belong to the cause; but they are not made under the impression, that, were the question entirely new, the law would be found irreconcilable with the constitution.

In discussing this question, the counsel for the state of Maryland have deemed it of some importance, in the construction of the constitution, to consider that instrument, not as emanating from the people, but as the act of sovereign and independent states. The powers of the general government, it has been said, are delegated by the states, who alone are truly sovereign; and must be exercised in subordination to the states, who alone possess supreme dominion. It would be difficult to sustain this proposition. The convention which framed the constitution was indeed elected by the state legislatures. But the instrument, when it came from their hands, was a mere proposal, without obligation, or pretensions to it. It was reported to the then existing congress of the United States, with a request that it might "be submitted to a convention of delegates, chosen in each state by the people thereof, under the recommendation of its legislature, for their assent and ratification." This mode of proceeding was adopted; and by the convention, by congress, and by the state legislatures, the instrument was submitted to the *people.* They acted upon it in the only manner in which they can act safely, effectively and wisely, on such a subject, by assembling in convention. It is true, they assembled in their several states—and where else should they have assembled? No political dreamer was ever wild enough to think of breaking down the lines which separate the states, and of compounding the American people into one common mass. Of consequence, when they act, they act in their states. But the measures they adopt do not, on that account, cease to be the measures of the people themselves, or become the measures of the state governments.

From these conventions, the constitution derives its whole authority. The government proceeds directly from the people; is "ordained and established," in the name of the people; and is declared to be ordained, "in order to form a more perfect union, establish justice, insure domestic tranquillity, and secure the blessings of liberty to themselves and to their posterity." The assent of the states, in their sovereign capacity, is implied, in calling a convention, and thus submitting that instrument to the people. But the people were at perfect liberty to accept or reject it; and their act was final. It required not the affirmance, and could not be negatived, by the state governments. The constitution, when thus adopted, was of complete obligation, and bound the state sovereignties.

It has been said, that the people had already surrendered all their powers to the state sovereignties, and had nothing more to give. But, surely, the question whether they may resume and modify the powers granted to government, does not remain to be settled in this country. Much more might the legitimacy of the general government be doubted, had it been created by the states. The powers delegated to the state sovereignties were to be exercised by themselves, not by a distinct and independent sovereignty, created by themselves. To the formation of a league, such as was the confederation, the state sovereignties were certainly competent. But when, "in order to form a more perfect union," it was deemed necessary to change this alliance into an effective government, possessing great and sovereign powers, and acting directly on the people, the necessity of referring it to the people, and of deriving its powers directly from them, was felt and acknowledged by all. The government of the Union, then (whatever may be the influence of this fact on the case), is, emphatically and truly, a government of the people. In form, and in substance, it emanates from them. Its powers are granted by them, and are to be exercised directly on them, and for their benefit.

This government is acknowledged by all, to be one of enumerated powers. The principle, that it can exercise only the powers granted to it, would seem too apparent, to have required to be enforced by all those arguments, which its enlightened friends, while it was depending before the people, found it necessary to urge; that principle is now universally admitted. But the question respecting the extent of the powers actually granted, is perpetually arising, and will probably continue to arise, so long as our system shall exist. In discussing these questions, the conflicting powers of the general and state governments must be brought into view, and the supremacy of their respective laws, when they are in opposition, must be settled.

If any one proposition could command the universal assent of mankind, we might expect it would be this—that the government of the Union, though limited in its powers, is supreme within its sphere of action. This would seem to result, necessarily, from its nature. It is the government of all; its powers are delegated by all; it represents all, and acts for all. Though any one state may be willing to control its operations, no state is willing to allow others to control them. The nation, on those subjects on which it can act, must necessarily bind its component parts. But this question is not left to mere reason: the people have, in express terms, decided it, by saying, "this constitution, and the laws of the United States, which shall be made in pursuance thereof," "shall be the supreme law of the land," and by requiring that the members of the state legislatures, and the officers of the executive and judicial departments of the states, shall take the oath of fidelity to it. The government of the United States, then, though limited in its powers, is supreme; and its laws, when made in pursuance of the constitution, form the supreme law of the land, "anything in the constitution or laws of any state to the contrary notwithstanding."

Among the enumerated powers, we do not find that of establishing a bank or creating a corporation. But there is no phrase in the instrument which, like the articles of confederation, excludes incidental or implied powers; and which requires that everything granted shall be expressly and minutely described. Even the 10th amendment, which was framed for the purpose of quieting the excessive jealousies which had been excited, omits the word "expressly," and declares only, that the powers "not delegated to the United States, nor prohibited to the states, are reserved to the states or to the people;" thus leaving the question, whether the particular power which may become the subject of contest, has been delegated to the one government, or prohibited to the other, to depend on a fair construction of the whole instrument. The men who drew and adopted this amendment had experienced the embarrassments resulting from the insertion of this word in the articles of confederation, and probably omitted it, to avoid those embarrassments. A constitution, to contain an accurate detail of all the subdivisions of which its great powers will admit, and of all the means by which they may be carried into execution, would partake of the prolixity of a legal code, and could scarcely be embraced by the human mind. It would, probably, never be understood by the public. Its nature, therefore, requires, that only its great outlines should be marked, its important objects designated, and the minor ingredients which compose those objects, be deduced from the nature of the objects themselves. That this idea was entertained by the framers of the American constitution, is not only to be inferred from the nature of the instrument, but from the language. Why else were some of the limitations, found in the 9th section of the 1st article, introduced? It is also, in some degree, warranted, by their having omitted to use any restrictive term which might prevent its receiving a fair and just interpretation. In considering this question, then, we must never forget that it is a *constitution* we are expounding.

Although, among the enumerated powers of government, we do not find the word "bank" or "incorporation," we find the great powers, to lay and collect taxes; to borrow money; to regulate commerce; to declare and conduct a war; and to raise and support armies and navies. The sword and the purse, all the external relations, and no inconsiderable portion of the industry of the nation, are intrusted to its government. It can never be pretended, that these vast powers draw after them others of inferior importance, merely because they are inferior. Such an idea can never be advanced. But it may with great reason be contended, that a government, intrusted with such ample powers, on the due execution of which the happiness and prosperity of the nation so vitally depends, must also be intrusted with ample means for their execution. The power being given, it is the interest of the nation to facilitate its execution. It can never be their interest, and cannot be presumed to have been their intention, to clog and embarrass its execution, by withholding the most appropriate means. Throughout this vast republic, from the St. Croix to the Gulf of Mexico, from the Atlantic to the Pacific, revenue is to be collected and expended, armies are to be marched and supported. The exigencies of the nation may require, that the treasure raised in the north should be transported to the south, that raised in the east, conveyed to the west, or that this order should be reversed. Is that construction of the constitution to be preferred, which would render these operations difficult, hazardous and expensive? Can we adopt that construction (unless the words imperiously require it), which would impute to the framers of that instrument, when granting these powers for the public good, the intention of impeding their exercise, by withholding a choice of means? If, indeed, such be the mandate of the constitution, we have only to obey; but that instrument does not profess to enumerate the means by which the powers it confers may be executed; nor does it prohibit the creation of a corporation, if the existence of such a being be essential, to the beneficial exercise of those powers. It is, then, the subject of fair inquiry, how far such means may be employed.

It is not denied, that the powers given to the government imply the ordinary means of execution. That, for example, of raising revenue, and applying it to national purposes, is admitted to imply the power of conveying money from place to place, as the exigencies of the nation may require, and of employing the usual means of conveyance. But it is denied, that the government has its choice of means; or, that it may employ the most convenient means, if, to employ them, it be necessary to erect a corporation. On what foundation does this argument rest? On this alone: the power of creating a corporation, is one appertaining to sovereignty, and is not expressly conferred on congress. This is true. But all legislative powers appertain to sovereignty. The original power of giving the law on any subject whatever, is a sovereign power; and if the government of the Union is restrained from creating a corporation, as a means for performing its functions, on the single reason that the creation of a corporation is an act of sovereignty; if the sufficiency of this reason be acknowledged, there would be some difficulty in sustaining the authority of congress to pass other laws for the accomplishment of the same objects. The government which has a right to do an act, and has imposed on it, the duty of performing that act, must, according to the dictates of reason, be allowed to select the means; and those who contend that it may not select any appropriate means, that one particular mode of effecting the object is excepted, take upon themselves the burden of establishing that exception.

The creation of a corporation, it is said, appertains to sovereignty. This is admitted. But to what portion of sovereignty does it appertain? Does it belong to one more than to another? In America, the powers of sovereignty are divided between the government of the Union, and those of the states. They are each sovereign, with respect to the objects committed to it, and neither sovereign, with respect to the objects committed to the other. We cannot comprehend that train of reasoning, which would maintain, that the extent of power granted by the people is to be ascertained, not by the nature and terms of the grant, but by its date. Some state constitutions were formed before, some since that of the United States. We cannot believe, that their relation to each other is in any degree dependent upon this circumstance. Their respective powers must, we think, be precisely the same, as if they had been formed at the same time. Had they been formed at the same time, and had the people conferred on the general government the power contained in the constitution, and on the states the whole residuum of power, would it have been asserted, that the government of the Union was not sovereign, with respect to those objects which were intrusted to it, in relation to which its laws were declared to be supreme? If this could not have been asserted, we cannot well comprehend the process of reasoning which maintains, that a power appertaining to sovereignty cannot be connected with that vast portion of it which is granted to the general government, so far as it is calculated to subserve the legitimate objects of that government. The power of creating a corporation, though appertaining to sovereignty, is not, like the power of making war, or levying taxes, or of regulating commerce, a great substantive and independent power, which cannot be implied as incidental to other powers, or used as a means of executing them. It is never the end for which other powers are exercised, but a means by which other objects are accomplished. No contributions are made to charity, for the sake of an incorporation, but a corporation is created to administer the charity; no seminary of learning is instituted, in order to be incorporated, but the corporate character is conferred to subserve the purposes of education. No city was ever built, with the sole object of being incorporated, but is incorporated as affording the best means of being well governed. The power of creating a corporation is never used for its own sake, but for the purpose of effecting something else. No sufficient reason is, therefore, perceived, why it may not pass as incidental to those powers which are expressly given, if it be a direct mode of executing them.

But the constitution of the United States has not left the right of congress to employ the necessary means, for the execution of the powers conferred on the government, to general reasoning. To its enumeration of powers is added, that of making "all laws which shall be necessary and proper, for carrying into execution the foregoing powers, and all other powers vested by this constitution, in the government of the United States, or in any department thereof." The counsel for the state of Maryland have urged various arguments, to prove that this clause, though, in terms, a grant of power, is not so, in effect; but is really restrictive of the general right, which might otherwise be implied, of selecting means for executing the enumerated powers. In support of this proposition, they have found it necessary to contend, that this clause was inserted for the purpose of conferring on congress the power of making laws. That, without it, doubts might be entertained, whether congress could exercise its powers in the form of legislation.

But could this be the object for which it was inserted? A government is created by the people, having legislative, executive and judicial powers. Its legislative powers are vested in a congress, which is to consist of a senate and house of representatives. Each house may determine the rule of its proceedings; and it is declared, that every bill which shall have passed both houses, shall, before it becomes a law, be presented to the president of the United States. The 7th section describes the course of proceedings, by which a bill shall become a law; and, then, the 8th section enumerates the powers of congress. Could it be necessary to say, that a legislature should exercise legislative powers, in the shape of legislation? After allowing each house to prescribe its own course of proceeding, after describing the manner in which a bill should become a law, would it have entered into the mind of a single member of the convention, that an express power to make laws was necessary, to enable the legislature to make them? That a legislature, endowed with legislative powers, can legislate, is a proposition too self-evident to have been questioned.

But the argument on which most reliance is placed, is drawn from that peculiar language of this clause. Congress is not empowered by it to make all laws, which may have relation to the powers confered on the government, but such only as may be *"necessary and proper"* for carrying them into execution. The word *"necessary"* is considered as controlling the whole sentence, and as limiting the right to pass laws for the execution of the granted powers, to such as are indispensable, and without which the power would be nugatory. That it excludes the choice of means, and leaves to congress, in each case, that only which is most direct and simple.

Is it true, that this is the sense in which the word "necessary" is always used? Does it always import an absolute physical necessity, so strong, that one thing to which another may be termed necessary, cannot exist without that other? We think it does not. If reference be had to its use, in the common affairs of the world, or in approved authors, we find that it frequently imports no more than that one thing is convenient, or useful, or essential to another. To employ the means necessary to an end, is generally understood as employing any means calculated to produce the end, and not as being confined to those single means, without which the end would be entirely unattainable. Such is the character of human language, that no word conveys to the mind, in all situations, one single definite idea; and nothing is more common than to use words in a figurative sense. Almost all compositions contain words, which, taken in their rigorous sense, would convey a meaning different from that which is obviously intended. It is essential to just construction, that many words which import something excessive, should be understood in a more mitigated sense—in that sense which common usage justifies. The word "necessary" is of this description. It has not a fixed character, peculiar to itself. It admits of all degrees of comparison; and is often connected with other words, which increase or diminish the impression the mind receives of the urgency it imports. A thing may be necessary, very necessary, absolutely or indispensably necessary. To no mind would the same idea be conveyed by these several phrases. The comment on the word is well illustrated by the passage cited at the bar, from the 10th section of the 1st article of the constitution. It is, we think, impossible to compare the sentence which prohibits a state from laying "imposts, or duties on imports or exports, except what may be *absolutely* necessary for executing its inspection laws," with that which authorizes congress "to make all laws which shall be necessary and proper for carrying into execution" the powers of the general government, without feeling a conviction, that the convention understood itself to change materially the meaning of the word "necessary," by prefixing the word "absolutely." This word, then, like others, is used in various senses; and, in its construction, the subject, the context, the intention of the person using them, are all to be taken into view.

Let this be done in the case under consideration. The subject is the execution of those great powers on which the welfare of a nation essentially depends. It must have been the intention of those who gave these powers, to insure, so far as human prudence could insure, their beneficial execution. This could not be done, by confiding the choice of means to such narrow limits as not to leave it in the power of congress to adopt any which might be appropriate, and which were conducive to the end. This provision is made in a constitution, intended to endure for ages to come, and consequently, to be adapted to the various *crises* of human affairs. To have prescribed the means by which government should, in all future time, execute its powers, would have been to change, entirely, the character of the instrument, and give it the properties of a legal code. It would have been an unwise attempt to provide, by immutable rules, for exigencies which, if foreseen at all, must have been seen dimly, and which can be best provided for as they occur. To have declared, that the best means shall not be used, but those alone, without which the power given would be nugatory, would have been to deprive the legislature of the capacity to avail itself of experience, to exercise its reason, and to accommodate its legislation to circumstances. If we apply this principle of construction to any of the powers of the government, we shall find it so pernicious in its operation that we shall be compelled to discard it. The powers vested in congress may certainly be carried into execution, without prescribing an oath of office. The power to exact this security for the faithful performance of duty, is not given, nor is it indispensably necessary. The different departments may be established; taxes may be imposed and collected; armies and navies may be raised and maintained; and money may be borrowed, without requiring an oath of office. It might be argued, with as much plausibility as other incidental powers have been assailed, that the convention was not unmindful of this subject. The oath which might be exacted—that of fidelity to the constitution—is prescribed, and no other can be required. Yet, he would be charged with insanity, who should contend, that the legislature might not superadd, to the oath directed by the constitution, such other oath of office as its wisdom might suggest.

So, with respect to the whole penal code of the United States: whence arises the power to punish, in cases not prescribed by the constitution? All admit, that the government may, legitimately, punish any violation of its laws; and yet, this is not among the enumerated powers of congress. The right to enforce the observance of law, by punishing its infraction, might be denied, with the more plausibility, because it is expressly given in some cases. Congress is empowered "to provide for the punishment of counterfeiting the securities and current coin of the United States," and "to define and punish piracies and felonies committed on the high seas, and offences against the law of nations." The several powers of congress may exist, in a very imperfect state, to be sure, but they may exist and be carried into execution, although no punishment should be inflicted, in cases where the right to punish is not expressly given.

Take, for example, the power "to establish post-offices and post-roads." This power is executed, by the single act of making the establishment. But, from this has been inferred the power and duty of carrying the mail along the post-road, from one post-office to another. And from this implied power, has again been inferred the right to punish those who steal letters from the post-office, or rob the mail. It may be said, with some plausibility, that the right to carry the mail, and to punish those who rob it, is not indispensably necessary to the establishment of a post-office and post-road. This right is indeed essential to the beneficial exercise of the power, but not indispensably necessary to its existence. So, of the punishment of the crimes of stealing or falsifying a record or process of a court of the United States, or of perjury in such court. To punish these offences, is certainly conducive to the due administration of justice. But courts may exist, and may decide the causes brought before them, though such crimes escape punishment.

The baneful influence of this narrow construction on all the operations of the government, and the absolute impracticability of maintaining it, without rendering the government incompetent to its great objects, might be illustrated by numerous examples drawn from the constitution, and from our laws. The good sense of the public has pronounced, without hesitation, that the power of punishment appertains to sovereignty, and may be exercised, whenever the sovereign has a right to act, as incidental to his constitutional powers. It is a means for carrying into execution all sovereign powers, and may be used, although not indispensably necessary. It is a right incidental to the power, and conducive to its beneficial exercise.

If this limited construction of the word "necessary" must be abandoned, in order to punish, whence is derived the rule which would reinstate it, when the government would carry its powers into execution, by means not vindictive in their nature? If the word "necessary" means "needful," "requisite," "essential," "conducive to," in order to let in the power of punishment for the infraction of law; why is it not equally comprehensive, when required to authorize the use of means which facilitate the execution of the powers of government, without the infliction of punishment?

In ascertaining the sense in which the word "necessary" is used in this clause of the constitution, we may derive some aid from that with which it is associated. Congress shall have power "to make all laws which shall be necessary and proper to carry into execution" the powers of the government. If the word "necessary" was used in that strict and rigorous sense for which the counsel for the state of Maryland contend, it would be an extraordinary departure from the usual course of the human mind, as exhibited in composition, to add a word, the only possible effect of which is, to qualify that strict and rigorous meaning; to present to the mind the idea of some choice of means of legislation, not strained and compressed within the narrow limits for which gentlemen contend.

But the argument which most conclusively demonstrates the error of the construction contended for by the counsel for the state of Maryland, is founded on the intention of the convention, as manifested in the whole clause. To waste time and argument in proving that, without it, congress might carry its powers into execution, would be not much less idle, than to hold a lighted taper to the sun. As little can it be required to prove, that in the absence of this clause, congress would have some choice of means. That it might employ those which, in its judgment, would most advantageously effect the object to be accomplished. That any means adapted to the end, any means which tended directly to the execution of the constitutional powers of the government, were in themselves constitutional. This clause, as construed by the state of Maryland, would abridge, and almost annihilate, this useful and necessary right of the legislature to select its means. That this could not be intended, is, we should think, had it not been already controverted, too apparent for controversy.

We think so for the following reasons: 1st. The clause is placed among the powers of congress, not among the limitations on those powers. 2d. Its terms purport to enlarge, not to diminish the powers vested in the government. It purports to be an additional power, not a restriction on those already granted. No reason has been, or can be assigned, for thus concealing an intention to narrow the discretion of the national legislature, under words which purport to enlarge it. The framers of the constitution wished its adoption, and well knew that it would be endangered by its strength, not by its weakness. Had they been capable of using language which would convey to the eye one idea, and, after deep reflection, impress on the mind, another, they would rather have disguised the grant of power, than its limitation. If, then, their intention had been, by this clause, to restrain the free use of means which might otherwise have been implied, that intention would have been inserted in another place, and would have been expressed in terms resembling these. "In carrying into execution the foregoing powers, and all others," &c., "no laws shall be passed but such as are necessary and proper." Had the intention been to make this clause restrictive, it would unquestionably have been so in form as well as in effect.

The result of the most careful and attentive consideration bestowed upon this clause is, that if it does not enlarge, it cannot be construed to restrain the powers of congress, or to impair the right of the legislature to exercise its best judgment in the selection of measures to carry into execution the constitutional powers of the government. If no other motive for its insertion can be suggested, a sufficient one is found in the desire to remove all doubts respecting the right to legislate on that vast mass of incidental powers which must be involved in the constitution, if that instrument be not a splendid bauble.

We admit, as all must admit, that the powers of the government are limited, and that its limits are not to be transcended. But we think the sound construction of the constitution must allow to the national legislature that discretion, with respect to the means by which the powers it confers are to be carried into execution, which will enable that body to perform the high duties assigned to it, in the manner most beneficial to the people. Let the end be legitimate, let it be within the scope of the constitution, and all means which are appropriate, which are plainly adapted to that end, which are not prohibited, but consist with the letter and spirit of the constitution, are constitutional.

That a corporation must be considered as a means not less usual, not of higher dignity, not more requiring a particular specification than other means, has been sufficiently proved. If we look to the origin of corporations, to the manner in which they have been framed in that government from which we have derived most of our legal principles and ideas, or to the uses to which they have been applied, we find no reason to suppose, that a constitution, omitting, and wisely omitting, to enumerate all the means for carrying into execution the great powers vested in government, ought to have specified this. Had it been intended to grant this power, as one which should be distinct and independent, to be exercised in any case whatever, it would have found a place among the enumerated powers of the government. But being considered merely as a means, to be employed only for the purpose of carrying into execution the given powers, there could be no motive for particularly mentioning it.

The propriety of this remark would seem to be generally acknowledged, by the universal acquiescence in the construction which has been uniformly put on the 3d section of the 4th article of the constitution. The power to "make all needful rules and regulations respecting the territory or other property belonging to the United States," is not more comprehensive, than the power "to make all laws which shall be necessary and proper for carrying into execution" the powers of the government. Yet all admit the constitutionality of a territorial government, which is a corporate body.

If a corporation may be employed, indiscriminately with other means, to carry into execution the powers of the government, no particular reason can be assigned for excluding the use of a bank, if required for its fiscal operations. To use one, must be within the discretion of congress, if it be an appropriate mode of executing the powers of government. That it is a convenient, a useful, and essential instrument in the prosecution of its fiscal operations, is not now a subject of controversy. All those who have been concerned in the administration of our finances, have concurred in representing its importance and necessity; and so strongly have they been felt, that statesmen of the first class, whose previous opinions against it had been confirmed by every circumstance which can fix the human judgment, have yielded those opinions to the exigencies of the nation. Under the confederation, congress, justifying the measure by its necessity, transcended, perhaps, its powers, to obtain the advantage of a bank; and our own legislation attests the universal conviction of the utility of this measure. The time has passed away, when it can be necessary to enter into any discussion, in order to prove the importance of this instrument, as a means to effect the legitimate objects of the government.

But were its necessity less apparent, none can deny its being an appropriate measure; and if it is, the degree of its necessity, as has been very justly observed, is to be discussed in another place. Should congress, in the execution of its powers, adopt measures which are prohibited by the constitution; or should congress, under the pretext of executing its powers, pass laws for the accomplishment of objects not intrusted to the government; it would become the painful duty of this tribunal, should a case requiring such a decision come before it, to say, that such an act was not the law of the land. But where the law is not prohibited, and is really calculated to effect any of the objects intrusted to the government, to undertake here to inquire into the degree of its necessity, would be to pass the line which circumscribes the judicial department, and to tread on legislative ground. This court disclaims all pretensions to such a power.

After this declaration, it can scarcely be necessary to say, that the existence of state banks can have no possible influence on the question. No trace is to be found in the constitution, of an intention to create a dependence of the government of the Union on those of the states, for the execution of the great powers assigned to it. Its means are adequate to its ends; and on those means alone was it expected to rely for the accomplishment of its ends. To impose on it the necessity of resorting to means which it cannot control, which another government may furnish or withhold, would render its course precarious, the result of its measures uncertain, and create a dependence on other governments, which might disappoint its most important designs, and is incompatible with the language of the constitution. But were it otherwise, the choice of means implies a right to choose a national bank in preference to state banks, and congress alone can make the election.

After the most deliberate consideration, it is the unanimous and decided opinion of this court, that the act to incorporate the Bank of the United States is a law made in pursuance of the constitution, and is a part of the supreme law of the land.

The branches, proceeding from the same stock, and being conducive to the complete accomplishment of the object, are equally constitutional. It would have been unwise, to locate them in the charter, and it would be unnecessarily inconvenient, to employ the legislative power in making those subordinate arrangements. The great duties of the bank are prescribed; those duties require branches; and the bank itself may, we think, be safely trusted with the selection of places where those branches shall be fixed; reserving always to the government the right to require that a branch shall be located where it may be deemed necessary.

15

James Madison to Spencer Roane
2 Sept. 1819
Writings 8:447–53

I have recd. your favor of the 22d Ult inclosing a copy of your observations on the Judgment of the Supreme Court of the U. S. in the case of M'Culloch agst. the State of Maryland; and I have found their latitudinary mode of expounding the Constitution, combated in them with the ability and the force which were to be expected.

It appears to me as it does to you that the occasion did not call for the general and abstract doctrine interwoven with the decision of the particular case. I have always supposed that the meaning of a law, and for a like reason, of a Constitution, so far as it depends on Judicial interpretation, was to result from a course of particular decisions, and not these from a previous and abstract comment on the subject. The example in this instance tends to reverse the rule and to forego the illustration to be derived from a series of cases actually occurring for adjudication.

I could have wished also that the Judges had delivered their opinions seriatim. The case was of such magnitude, in the scope given to it, as to call, if any case could do so, for the views of the subject separately taken by them. This might either by the harmony of their reasoning have produced a greater conviction in the Public mind; or by its discordance have impaired the force of the precedent now ostensibly supported by a unanimous & perfect concurrence in every argument & dictum in the judgment pronounced.

But what is of most importance is the high sanction given to a latitude in expounding the Constitution which seems to break down the landmarks intended by a specification of the Powers of Congress, and to substitute for a definite connection between means and ends, a Legislative discretion as to the former to which no practical limit can be assigned. In the great system of Political Economy having for its general object the national welfare, everything is related immediately or remotely to every other thing; and consequently a Power over any one thing, if not limited by some obvious and precise affinity, may amount to a Power over every other. Ends & means may shift their character at the will & according to the ingenuity of the Legislative Body. What is an end in one case may be a means in another; nay in the same case, may be either an end or a means at the Legislative option. The British Parliament in collecting a revenue from the commerce of America found no difficulty in calling it either a tax for the regulation of trade, or a regulation of trade with a view to the tax, as it suited the argument or the policy of the moment.

Is there a Legislative power in fact, not expressly prohibited by the Constitution, which might not, according to the doctrine of the Court, be exercised as a means of carrying into effect some specified Power?

Does not the Court also relinquish by their doctrine, all controul on the Legislative exercise of unconstitutional powers? According to that doctrine, the expediency & constitutionality of means for carrying into effect a specified Power are convertible terms; and Congress are admitted to be Judges of the expediency. The Court certainly cannot be so; a question, the moment it assumes the character of mere expediency or policy, being evidently beyond the reach of Judicial cognizance.

It is true, the Court are disposed to retain a guardianship of the Constitution against legislative encroachments. "Should Congress," say they, "under the pretext of executing its Powers, pass laws for the accomplishment of objects not entrusted to the Government, it would become the painful duty of this Tribunal to say that such an act was not the law of the land." But suppose Congress should, as would doubtless happen, pass unconstitutional laws not to accomplish objects not specified in the Constitution, but the same laws as means expedient, convenient or conducive to the accomplishment of objects entrusted to the Government; by what handle could the Court take hold of the case? We are told that it was the policy of the old Government of France to grant monopolies, such as that of Tobacco, in order to create funds in particular hands from which loans could be made to the Public, adequate capitalists not being formed in that Country in the ordinary course of commerce. Were Congress to grant a like monopoly merely to aggrandize those enjoying it, the Court might consistently say, that this not being an object entrusted to the Governt. the grant was unconstitutional and void. Should Congress however grant the monopoly according to the French policy as a means judged by them to be necessary, expedient or conducive to the borrowing of money, which is an object entrusted to them by the Constitution, it seems clear that the Court, adhering to its doctrine, could not interfere without stepping on Legislative ground, to do which they justly disclaim all pretension.

It could not but happen, and was foreseen at the birth of the Constitution, that difficulties and differences of opinion might occasionally arise in expounding terms & phrases necessarily used in such a charter; more especially those which divide legislation between the General & local Governments; and that it might require a regular course of practice to liquidate & settle the meaning of some of them. But it was anticipated I believe by few if any of the friends of the Constitution, that a rule of construction would be introduced as broad & as pliant as what has occurred. And those who recollect, and still more those who shared in what passed in the State Conventions, thro' which the people ratified the Constitution, with respect to the extent of the powers vested in Congress, cannot easily be persuaded that the avowal of such a rule would not have prevented its ratification. It has been the misfortune, if not the reproach, of other nations, that their Govts. have not been freely and deliberately established by themselves. It is the boast of ours that such has been its source and that it can be altered by the same authority only which established it. It is a further boast that a regular mode of making proper alterations has been providently inserted in the Constitution itself. It is anxiously to be wished therefore, that no innovations may take place in other modes, one of which would be a constructive assumption of powers never meant to be granted. If the powers be deficient, the legitimate source of additional ones is always open, and ought to be resorted to.

Much of the error in expounding the Constitution has its origin in the use made of the species of sovereignty implied in the nature of Govt. The specified powers vested in Congress, it is said, are sovereign powers, and that as such they carry with them an unlimited discretion as to the means of executing them. It may surely be remarked that a limited Govt. may be limited in its sovereignty as well with respect to the means as to the objects of his powers; and that to give an extent to the former, superseding the limits to the latter, is in effect to convert a limited into an unlimited Govt. There is certainly a reasonable medium between expounding the Constitution with the strictness of a penal law, or other ordinary statute, and expounding it with a laxity which may vary its essential character, and encroach on the local sovereignties with wch. it was meant to be reconcilable.

The very existence of these local sovereignties is a controul on the pleas for a constructive amplification of the powers of the General Govt. Within a single State possessing the entire sovereignty, the powers given to the Govt. by the People are understood to extend to all the Acts whether as means or ends required for the welfare of the Community, and falling within the range of just Govt. To withhold from such a Govt. any particular power necessary or useful in itself, would be to deprive the people of the good dependent on its exercise; since the power must be there or not exist at all. In the Govt. of the U. S. the case is obviously different. In establishing that Govt. the people retained other Govts. capable of exercising such necessary and useful powers as were not to be exercised by the General Govt. No necessary presumption therefore arises from the importance of any particular power in itself, that it has been vested in that Govt. because tho' not vested there, it may exist elsewhere, and the exercise of it elsewhere might be preferred by those who alone had a right to make the distribution. The presumption which ought to be indulged is that any improvement of this distribution sufficiently pointed out by experience would not be withheld.

Altho' I have confined myself to the single question concerning the rule of interpreting the Constitution, I find that my pen has carried me to a length which would not have been permitted by a recollection that my remarks are merely for an eye to which no aspect of the subject is likely to be new. I hasten therefore to conclude with assurances &c &c.

16

THOMAS JEFFERSON TO SPENCER ROANE
6 Sept. 1819
Works 12:135–38

I had read in the Enquirer, and with great approbation, the pieces signed Hampden, and have read them again with redoubled approbation, in the copies you have been so kind as to send me. I subscribe to every tittle of them. They contain the true principles of the revolution of 1800, for that was as real a revolution in the principles of our government as that of 1776 was in its form; not effected indeed by the sword, as that, but by the rational and peaceable instrument of reform, the suffrage of the people. The nation declared its will by dismissing functionaries of one principle, and electing those of another, in the two branches, executive and legislative, submitted to their election. Over the judiciary department, the constitution had deprived them of their control. That, therefore, has continued the reprobated system, and although new matter has been occasionally incorporated into the old, yet the leaven of the old mass seems to assimilate to itself the new, and after twenty years' confirmation of the federal system by the voice of the nation, declared through the medium of elections, we find the judiciary on every occasion, still driving us into consolidation.

In denying the right they usurp of exclusively explaining the constitution, I go further than you do, if I understand rightly your quotation from the *Federalist,* of an opinion that "the judiciary is the last resort in relation *to the other departments* of the government, but not in relation to the rights of the parties to the compact under which the judiciary is derived." If this opinion be sound, then indeed is our constitution a complete *felo de se.* For intending to establish three departments, co-ordinate and independent, that they might check and balance one another, it has given, according to this opinion, to one of them alone, the right to prescribe rules for the government of the others, and to that one too, which is unelected by, and independent of the nation. For experience has already shown that the impeachment it has provided is not even a scarecrow; that such opinions as the one you combat, sent cautiously out, as you observe also, by detachment, not belonging to the case often, but sought for out of it, as if to rally the public opinion beforehand to their views, and to indicate the line they are to walk in, have been so quietly passed over as never to have excited animadversion, even in a speech of any one of the body entrusted with impeachment. The constitution, on this hypothesis, is a mere thing of wax in the hands of the judiciary, which they may twist, and shape into any form they please. It should be remembered, as an axiom of eternal truth in politics, that whatever power in any government is independent, is absolute also; in theory only, at first, while the spirit of the people is up, but in practice, as fast as that relaxes. Independence can be trusted nowhere but with the people in mass. They are inherently independent of all but moral law. My construction of the constitution is very different from that you quote. It is that each department is truly independent of the others, and has an equal right to decide for itself what is the meaning of the constitution in the cases submitted to its action; and especially, where it is to act ultimately and without appeal. I will explain myself by examples, which, having occurred while I was in office, are better known to me, and the principles which governed them.

A legislature had passed the sedition law. The federal courts had subjected certain individuals to its penalties of fine and imprisonment. On coming into office, I released these individuals by the power of pardon committed to executive discretion, which could never be more properly exercised than where citizens were suffering without the authority of law, or, which was equivalent, under a law unauthorized by the constitution, and therefore null. In the case of Marbury and Madison, the federal judges declared that commissions, signed and sealed by the President, were valid, although not delivered. I deemed delivery essential to complete a deed, which, as long as it remains in the hands of the party, is as yet no deed, it is in *posse* only, but not in *esse,* and I withheld delivery of the commissions. They cannot issue a mandamus to the President or legislature, or to any of their officers.[1] When the British treaty of——— arrived, without any provision against the impressment of our seamen, I determined not to ratify it. The Senate thought I should ask their advice. I thought that would be a mockery of them, when I was predetermined against following it, should they advise its ratification. The constitution had made their advice necessary to confirm a treaty, but not to reject it. This has been blamed by some; but I have never doubted its soundness.

[1]The constitution controlling the common law in this particular,—T. J.

17

GIBBONS V. OGDEN
9 Wheat. 1 (1824)

(See 1.8.3 [commerce], no. 16)

18

American Insurance Co. v. Canter
1 Pet. 511 (1828)

(See 1.8.9, no. 5)

19

James Madison to Reynolds Chapman
6 Jan. 1831
Writings 9:433–37

For my general opinion on the question of Internal Improvements, I may refer to the veto message agst. the "Bonus Bill," at the close of the session of Congs. in March 1817. The message denies the constitutionality as well of the appropriating as of the Executing and Jurisdictional branches of the power. And my opinion remains the same, subject, as heretofore, to the exception of particular cases, where a reading of the Constitution, different from mine may have derived from a continued course of practical sanctions an authority sufficient to overrule individual constructions.

It is not to be wondered that doubts & difficulties should occur in expounding the Constitution of the U. States. Hitherto the aim, in well-organized Governments, has been to discriminate & distribute the Legislative, Executive, and Judiciary powers; and these sometimes touch so closely or rather run the one so much into the other, as to make the task difficult, and leave the lines of division obscure. A settled practice, enlightened by occurring cases, and obviously conformable to the public good, can alone remove the obscurity. The case is parallel in new statutes on complex subjects.

In the Constitution of the U. S. where each of these powers is divided, and portions alloted to different Governments, and where a language technically appropriate may be deficient, the wonder wd. be far greater if different rules of exposition were not applied to the text by different commentators.

Thus it is found that in the case of the Legislative department particularly, where a division & definition of the powers according to their specific objects is most difficult, the Instrument is read by some as if it were a Constitution for a single Govt. with powers co-extensive with the general welfare, and by others interpreted as if it were an ordinary statute, and with the strictness almost of a penal one.

Between these adverse constructions an intermediate course must be the true one, and it is hoped that it will finally if not otherwise settled be prescribed by an amendment of the Constitution. In no case is a satisfactory one more desirable than in that of internal improvements, embracing Roads, Canals, Light Houses, Harbours, Rivers, and other lesser objects.

With respect to Post Roads, the general view taken of them in the manuscript, shows a way of thinking on the subject with which mine substantially accords. Roads, when plainly necessary for the march of troops and for military transportations, must speak for themselves, as occasions arise.

Canals as an Item in the general improvement of the Country have always appeared to me not to be embraced by the authority of Congs. It may be remarked that Mr. Hamilton, in his Report on the Bank, when enlarging the range of construction to the utmost of his ingenuity, admitted that Canals were beyond the sphere of Federal Legislation.

Light Houses having a close and obvious relation to navigation and external commerce, and to the safety of public as well as private ships, and having recd. a positive sanction and general acquiescence from the commencement of the Federal Government, the constitutionality of them is I presume not now to be shaken if it were ever much contested. It seems, however, that the power is liable to great abuse, and to call for the most careful & responsible scrutiny into every particular case before an application be complied with.

Harbours, within the above character, seem to have a like claim on the Federal authority. But what an interval between such a Harbour as that of N. York or N. Orleans and the mouth of a creek forming an outlet for the trade of a single State or part of a State into a navigable stream; and the principle of which would authorize the improvement of every road leading out of the State towards a destined market.

What again the interval between clearing of its sawyers &c. the Mississippi the commercial highway for half the nation, and removing obstructions by which the navigation of an inconsiderable stream may be extended a few miles only within a single State.

The navigation of the Mississippi is so important in a national view, so essentially belongs to the foreign commerce of many States, and the task of freeing it from obstructions is so much beyond the means of a single State, and beyond a feasible concert of all who are interested in it, that claims on the authority and resources of the nation will continue to be, as they have been irresistible. Those who regard it as a case not brought by these features within the legitimate powers of Congress, must of course oppose the claim, and with it every inferior claim. Those who admit the power as applicable to a case of that description, but disown it in every case not marked by adequate peculiarities, must find, as they can, a line separating this admissible class from the others; a necessity but too often to be encountered in a legislative career.

Perhaps I ought not to omit the remark that altho' I concur in the defect of powers in Congress on the subject of internal improvements, my abstract opinion has been that in the case of Canals particularly, the power would have been properly vested in Congress. It was more than once proposed in the Convention of 1787, & rejected from an apprehension, chiefly that it might prove an obstacle to the adoption of the Constitution. Such an addition to the Federal powers was thought to be strongly recommended by several considerations. 1. As Congress would possess, exclusively, the sources of Revenue most productive and least unpopular, that body ought to provide & apply the means for the greatest & most costly works. 2. There would be cases where Canals would be highly important in a national view, and not so in a local view. 3. Cases where, tho' highly important in a national view, they might violate the interest real or supposed of the State through which they would pass; of which an example might now be cited in the Chesapeake & Delaware canal, known to have been viewed in an unfavourable light by the State of Delaware. 4. There might be cases where Canals, or a chain of Canals, would pass through sundry States, and create a channel and outlet for their foreign commerce, forming at the same time a ligament for the Union, and extending the profitable intercourse of its members, and yet be of hopeless attainment if left to the limited faculties and joint exertions of the States possessing the authority.

It cannot be denied, that the abuse to which the exercise of the power in question has appeared to be liable in the hands of Congress, is a heavy weight in the scale opposed to it. But may not the evil have grown, in a great degree, out of a casual redundancy of revenue, and a temporary apathy to a burden bearing indirectly on the people, and mingled, moreover, with the discharge of debts of peculiar sanctity. It might not happen, under ordinary circumstances, that taxes even of the most disguised kind, would escape a wakeful controul on the imposition & application of them. The late reduction of duties on certain imports and the calculated approach of an extinguishment of the public debt, have evidently turned the popular attention to the subject of taxes, in a degree quite new; and it is more likely to increase than to relax. In the event of an amendment of the Constitution, guards might be devised against a misuse of the power without defeating an important exercise of it. If I err or am too sanguine in the views I indulge it must be ascribed to my conviction that canals, railroads, and turnpikes are at once the criteria of a wise policy and causes of national prosperity; that the want of them will be a reproach to our Republican system, if excluding them, and that the exclusion, to a mortifying extent will ensue if the power be not lodged where alone it can have its due effect.

20

ANDREW JACKSON, VETO MESSAGE
10 July 1832
Richardson 2:581–91

It is maintained by the advocates of the bank that its constitutionality in all its features ought to be considered as settled by precedent and by the decision of the Supreme Court. To this conclusion I can not assent. Mere precedent is a dangerous source of authority, and should not be regarded as deciding questions of constitutional power except where the acquiescence of the people and the States can be considered as well settled. So far from this being the case on this subject, an argument against the bank might be based on precedent. One Congress, in 1791, decided in favor of a bank; another, in 1811, decided against it. One Congress, in 1815, decided against a bank; another, in 1816, decided in its favor. Prior to the present Congress, therefore, the precedents drawn from that source were equal. If we resort to the States, the expressions of legislative, judicial, and executive opinions against the bank have been probably to those in its favor as 4 to 1. There is nothing in precedent, therefore, which, if its authority were admitted, ought to weigh in favor of the act before me.

If the opinion of the Supreme Court covered the whole ground of this act, it ought not to control the coordinate authorities of this Government. The Congress, the Executive, and the Court must each for itself be guided by its own opinion of the Constitution. Each public officer who takes an oath to support the Constitution swears that he will support it as he understands it, and not as it is understood by others. It is as much the duty of the House of Representatives, of the Senate, and of the President to decide upon the constitutionality of any bill or resolution which may be presented to them for passage or approval as it is of the supreme judges when it may be brought before them for judicial decision. The opinion of the judges has no more authority over Congress than the opinion of Congress has over the judges, and on that point the President is independent of both. The authority of the Supreme Court must not, therefore, be permitted to control the Congress or the Executive when acting in their legislative capacities, but to have only such influence as the force of their reasoning may deserve.

But in the case relied upon the Supreme Court have not decided that all the features of this corporation are compatible with the Constitution. It is true that the court have said that the law incorporating the bank is a constitutional exercise of power by Congress; but taking into view the whole opinion of the court and the reasoning by which they have come to that conclusion, I understand them to have decided that inasmuch as a bank is an appropriate means for carrying into effect the enumerated powers of the General Government, therefore the law incorporating it is in accordance with that provision of the Constitution which declares that Congress shall have power "to make all laws which shall be necessary and proper for carrying those powers into execution." Having satisfied themselves that the word *"necessary"* in the Constitution means *"needful," "requisite," "essential," "conducive to,"* and that "a bank" is a convenient, a useful, and essential instrument in the prosecution of the Government's "fiscal operations," they conclude that to "use one must be within the discretion of Congress" and that "the act to incorporate the Bank of the United States is a law made in pursuance of the Constitution;" "but," say they, *"where the law is not prohibited and is really calculated to effect any of the objects intrusted to the Government, to undertake here to inquire into the degree of its necessity would be to pass the line which circumscribes the judicial department and to tread on legislative ground."*

The principle here affirmed is that the "degree of its necessity," involving all the details of a banking institution, is a question exclusively for legislative consideration. A bank is constitutional, but it is the province of the Legislature to determine whether this or that particular power, privilege, or exemption is "necessary and proper" to enable the bank to discharge its duties to the Government, and from their decision there is no appeal to the courts of justice. Under the decision of the Supreme Court, therefore, it is the exclusive province of Congress and the President to decide whether the particular features of this act are *necessary* and *proper* in order to enable the bank to perform conveniently and efficiently the public duties assigned to it as a fiscal agent, and therefore constitutional, or *unnecessary* and *improper,* and therefore unconstitutional.

Without commenting on the general principle affirmed by the Supreme Court, let us examine the details of this act in accordance with the rule of legislative action which they have laid down. It will be found that many of the powers and privileges conferred on it can not be supposed necessary for the purpose for which it is proposed to be created, and are not, therefore, means necessary to attain the end in view, and consequently not justified by the Constitution.

The original act of incorporation, section 21, enacts "that no other bank shall be established by any future law of the United States during the continuance of the corporation hereby created, for which the faith of the United States is hereby pledged: *Provided,* Congress may renew existing charters for banks within the District of Columbia not increasing the capital thereof, and may also establish any other bank or banks in said District with capitals not exceeding in the whole $6,000,000 if they shall deem it expedient." This provision is continued in force by the act before me fifteen years from the 3d of March, 1836.

If Congress possessed the power to establish one bank, they had power to establish more than one if in their opinion two or more banks had been "necessary" to facilitate the execution of the powers delegated to them in the Constitution. If they possessed the power to establish a second bank, it was a power derived from the Constitution to be exercised from time to time, and at any time when the interests of the country or the emergencies of the Government might make it expedient. It was possessed by one Congress as well as another, and by all Congresses alike, and alike at every session. But the Congress of 1816 have taken it away from their successors for twenty years, and the Congress of 1832 proposes to abolish it for fifteen years more. It can not be *"necessary"* or *"proper"* for Congress to barter away or divest themselves of any of the powers vested in them by the Constitution to be exercised for the public good. It is not *"necessary"* to the efficiency of the bank, nor is it *"proper"* in relation to themselves and their successors. They may *properly* use the discretion vested in them, but they may not limit the discretion of their successors. This restriction on themselves and grant of a monopoly to the bank is therefore unconstitutional.

In another point of view this provision is a palpable attempt to amend the Constitution by an act of legislation. The Constitution declares that "the Congress shall have power to exercise exclusive legislation in all cases whatsoever" over the District of Columbia. Its constitutional power, therefore, to establish banks in the District of Columbia and increase their capital at will is unlimited and uncontrollable by any other power than that which gave authority to the Constitution. Yet this act declares that Congress shall *not* increase the capital of existing banks, nor create other banks with capitals exceeding in the whole $6,000,000. The Constitution declares that Congress *shall* have power to exercise exclusive legislation over this District *"in all cases whatsoever,"* and this act declares they shall not. Which is the supreme law of the land? This provision can not be *"necessary"* or *"proper"* or *constitutional* unless the absurdity be admitted that whenever it be "necessary and proper" in the opinion of Congress they have a right to barter away one portion of the powers vested in them by the Constitution as a means of executing the rest.

On two subjects only does the Constitution recognize in Congress the power to grant exclusive privileges or monopolies. It declares that "Congress shall have power to promote the progress of science and useful arts by securing for limited times to authors and inventors the exclusive right to their respective writings and discoveries." Out of this express delegation of power have grown our laws of patents and copyrights. As the Constitution expressly delegates to Congress the power to grant exclusive privileges in these cases as the means of executing the substantive power "to promote the progress of science and useful arts," it is consistent with the fair rules of construction to conclude that such a power was not intended to be granted as a means of accomplishing any other end. On every other subject which comes within the scope of Congressional power there is an ever-living discretion in the use of proper means, which can not be restricted or abolished without an amendment of the Constitution. Every act of Congress, therefore, which attempts by grants of monopolies or sale of exclusive privileges for a limited time, or a time without limit, to restrict or extinguish its own discretion in the choice of means to execute its delegated powers is equivalent to a legislative amendment of the Constitution, and palpably unconstitutional.

This act authorizes and encourages transfers of its stock to foreigners and grants them an exemption from all State and national taxation. So far from being *"necessary and proper"* that the bank should possess this power to make it a safe and efficient agent of the Government in its fiscal operations, it is calculated to convert the Bank of the United States into a foreign bank, to impoverish our people in time of peace, to disseminate a foreign influence through every section of the Republic, and in war to endanger our independence.

The several States reserved the power at the formation of the Constitution to regulate and control titles and transfers of real property, and most, if not all, of them have laws disqualifying aliens from acquiring or holding lands within their limits. But this act, in disregard of the undoubted right of the States to prescribe such disqualifications, gives to aliens stockholders in this bank an interest and title, as members of the corporation, to all the real property it may acquire within any of the States of this Union. This privilege granted to aliens is not *"necessary"* to enable the bank to perform its public duties, nor in any sense *"proper,"* because it is vitally subversive of the rights of the States.

The Government of the United States have no constitutional power to purchase lands within the States except "for the erection of forts, magazines, arsenals, dockyards, and other needful buildings," and even for these objects only "by the consent of the legislature of the State in which the same shall be." By making themselves stockholders in the bank and granting to the corporation the power to purchase lands for other purposes they assume a power not granted in the Constitution and grant to others what they do not themselves possess. It is not *necessary* to the receiving, safe-keeping, or transmission of the funds of the Government that the bank should possess this power, and it is not *proper* that Congress should thus enlarge the powers delegated to them in the Constitution.

The old Bank of the United States possessed a capital of only $11,000,000, which was found fully sufficient to enable it with dispatch and safety to perform all the functions required of it by the Government. The capital of the present bank is $35,000,000—at least twenty-four more than experience has proved to be *necessary* to enable a bank to perform its public functions. The public debt which existed during the period of the old bank and on the establishment of the new has been nearly paid off, and our revenue will soon be reduced. This increase of capital is therefore not for public but for private purposes.

The Government is the only *"proper"* judge where its agents should reside and keep their offices, because it best knows where their presence will be *"necessary."* It can not, therefore, be *"necessary"* or *"proper"* to authorize the bank to locate branches where it pleases to perform the public service, without consulting the Government, and contrary to its will. The principle laid down by the Supreme Court concedes that Congress can not establish a bank for purposes of private speculation and gain, but only as a means of executing the delegated powers of the General Government. By the same principle a branch bank can not constitutionally be established for other than public purposes. The power which this act gives to establish two branches in any State, without the injunction or request of the Government and for other than public purposes, is not *"necessary"* to the due *execution* of the powers delegated to Congress.

The bonus which is exacted from the bank is a confession upon the face of the act that the powers granted by it are greater than are *"necessary"* to its character of a fiscal agent. The Government does not tax its officers and agents for the privilege of serving it. The bonus of a million and a half required by the original charter and that of three millions proposed by this act are not exacted for the privilege of giving "the necessary facilities for transferring the public funds from place to place within the United States or the Territories thereof, and for distributing the same in payment of the public creditors without charging commission or claiming allowance on account of the difference of exchange," as required by the act of incorporation, but for something more beneficial to the stockholders. The original act declares that it (the bonus) is granted "in consideration of the exclusive privileges and benefits conferred by this act upon the said bank," and the act before me declares it to be "in consideration of the exclusive benefits and privileges continued by this act to the said corporation for fifteen years, as aforesaid." It is therefore for "exclusive privileges and benefits" conferred for their own use and emolument, and not for the advantage of the Government, that a bonus is exacted. These surplus powers for which the bank is required to pay can not surely be *"necessary"* to make it the fiscal agent of the Treasury. If they were, the exaction of a bonus for them would not be *"proper."*

It is maintained by some that the bank is a means of executing the constitutional power "to coin money and regulate the value thereof." Congress have established a mint to coin money and passed laws to regulate the value thereof. The money so coined, with its value so regulated, and such foreign coins as Congress may adopt are the only currency known to the Constitution. But if they have other power to regulate the currency, it was conferred to be exercised by themselves, and not to be transferred to a corporation. If the bank be established for that purpose, with a charter unalterable without its consent, Congress have parted with their power for a term of years, during which the Constitution is a dead letter. It is neither necessary nor proper to transfer its legislative power to such a bank, and therefore unconstitutional.

By its silence, considered in connection with the decision of the Supreme Court in the case of McCulloch against the State of Maryland, this act takes from the States the power to tax a portion of the banking business carried on within their limits, in subversion of one of the strongest barriers which secured them against Federal encroachments. Banking, like farming, manufacturing, or any other occupation or profession, is a *business,* the right to follow which is not originally derived from the laws. Every citizen and every company of citizens in all of our States possessed the right until the State legislatures deemed it good policy to prohibit private banking by law. If the prohibitory State laws were now repealed, every citizen would again possess the right. The State banks are a qualified restoration of the right which has been taken away by the laws against banking, guarded by such provisions and limitations as in the opinion of the State legislatures the public interest requires. These corporations, unless there be an exemption in their charter, are, like private bankers and banking companies, subject to State taxation. The manner in which these taxes shall be laid depends wholly on legislative discretion. It may be upon the bank, upon the stock, upon the profits, or in any other mode which the sovereign power shall will.

Upon the formation of the Constitution the States guarded their taxing power with peculiar jealousy. They surrendered it only as it regards imports and exports. In relation to every other object within their jurisdiction, whether persons, property, business, or professions, it was secured in as ample a manner as it was before possessed. All persons, though United States officers, are liable to a poll tax by the States within which they reside. The lands of the United States are liable to the usual land tax, except in the new States, from whom agreements that they will not tax unsold lands are exacted when they are admitted into the Union. Horses, wagons, any beasts or vehicles, tools, or property belonging to private citizens, though employed in the service of the United States, are subject to State taxation. Every private business, whether carried on by an officer of the General Government or not, whether it be mixed with public concerns or not, even if it be carried on by the Government of the United States itself, separately or in partnership, falls within the scope of the taxing power of the State. Nothing comes more fully within it than banks and the business of banking, by whomsoever instituted and carried on. Over this whole subject-matter it is just as absolute, unlimited, and uncontrollable as if the Constitution had never been adopted, because in the formation of that instrument it was reserved without qualification.

The principle is conceded that the States can not rightfully tax the operations of the General Government. They can not tax the money of the Government deposited in the State banks, nor the agency of those banks in remitting it; but will any man maintain that their mere selection to perform this public service for the General Government would exempt the State banks and their ordinary business from State taxation? Had the United States, instead of establishing a bank at Philadelphia, employed a private banker to keep and transmit their funds, would it have deprived Pennsylvania of the right to tax his bank and his usual banking operations? It will not be pretended. Upon what principle, then, are the banking establishments of the Bank of the United States and their usual banking operations to be exempted from taxation? It is not their public agency or the deposits of the Government which the States claim a right to tax, but their banks and their banking powers, instituted and exercised within State jurisdiction for their private emolument—those powers and privileges for which they pay a bonus, and which the States tax in their own banks. The exercise of these powers within a State, no matter by whom or under what authority, whether by private citizens in their original right, by corporate bodies created by the States, by foreigners or the agents of foreign governments located within their limits, forms a legitimate object of State taxation. From this and like sources, from the persons, property, and business that are found residing, located, or carried on under their jurisdiction, must the States, since the surrender of their right to raise a revenue from imports and exports, draw all the money necessary for the support of their governments and the maintenance of their independence. There is no more appropriate subject of taxation than banks, banking, and bank stocks, and none to which the States ought more pertinaciously to cling.

It can not be *necessary* to the character of the bank as a fiscal agent of the Government that its private business should be exempted from that taxation to which all the State banks are liable, nor can I conceive it *"proper"* that the substantive and most essential powers reserved by the States shall be thus attacked and annihilated as a means of executing the powers delegated to the General Government. It may be safely assumed that none of those sages who had an agency in forming or adopting our Constitution ever imagined that any portion of the taxing power of the States not prohibited to them nor delegated to Congress was to be swept away and annihilated as a means of executing certain powers delegated to Congress.

If our power over means is so absolute that the Supreme Court will not call in question the constitutionality of an act of Congress the subject of which "is not prohibited, and is really calculated to effect any of the objects intrusted to the Government," although, as in the case before me, it takes away powers expressly granted to Congress and rights scrupulously reserved to the States, it becomes us to proceed in our legislation with the utmost caution. Though not directly, our own powers and the rights of the States may be indirectly legislated away in the use of means to execute substantive powers. We may not enact that Congress shall not have the power of exclusive legislation over the District of Columbia, but we may pledge the faith of the United States that as a means of executing other powers it shall not be exercised for twenty years or forever. We may not pass an act prohibiting the States to tax the banking business carried on within their limits, but we may, as a means of executing our powers over other objects, place that business in the hands of our agents and then declare it exempt from State taxation in their hands. Thus may our own powers and the rights of the States, which we can not directly curtail or invade, be frittered away and extinguished in the use of means employed by us to execute other powers. That a bank of the United States, competent to all the duties which may be required by the Government, might be so organized as not to infringe on our own delegated powers or the reserved rights of the States I do not entertain a doubt. Had the Executive been called upon to furnish the project of such an institution, the duty would have been cheerfully performed. In the absence of such a call it was obviously proper that he should confine himself to pointing out those prominent features in the act presented which in his opinion make it incompatible with the Constitution and sound policy. A general discussion will now take place, eliciting new light and settling important principles; and a new Congress, elected in the midst of such discussion, and furnishing an equal representation of the people according to the last census, will bear to the Capitol the verdict of public opinion, and, I doubt not, bring this important question to a satisfactory result.

Under such circumstances the bank comes forward and asks a renewal of its charter for a term of fifteen years upon conditions which not only operate as a gratuity to the stockholders of many millions of dollars, but will sanction any abuses and legalize any encroachments.

Suspicions are entertained and charges are made of gross abuse and violation of its charter. An investigation unwillingly conceded and so restricted in time as necessarily to make it incomplete and unsatisfactory discloses enough to excite suspicion and alarm. In the practices of the principal bank partially unveiled, in the absence of important witnesses, and in numerous charges confidently made and as yet wholly uninvestigated there was enough to induce a majority of the committee of investigation—a committee which was selected from the most able and honorable members of the House of Representatives—to recommend a suspension of further action upon the bill and a prosecution of the inquiry. As the charter had yet four years to run, and as a renewal now was not necessary to the successful prosecution of its business, it was to have been expected that the bank itself, conscious of its purity and proud of its character, would have withdrawn its application for the present, and demanded the severest scrutiny into all its transactions. In their declining to do so there seems to be an additional reason why the functionaries of the Government should proceed with less haste and more caution in the renewal of their monopoly.

The bank is professedly established as an agent of the executive branch of the Government, and its constitutionality is maintained on that ground. Neither upon the propriety of present action nor upon the provisions of this act was the Executive consulted. It has had no opportunity to say that it neither needs nor wants an agent clothed with such powers and favored by such exemptions. There is nothing in its legitimate functions which makes it necessary or proper. Whatever interest or influence, whether public or private, has given birth to this act, it can not be found either in the wishes or necessities of the executive department, by which present action is deemed premature, and the powers conferred upon its agent not only unnecessary, but dangerous to the Government and country.

It is to be regretted that the rich and powerful too often bend the acts of government to their selfish purposes. Distinctions in society will always exist under every just government. Equality of talents, of education, or of wealth can not be produced by human institutions. In the full enjoyment of the gifts of Heaven and the fruits of superior industry, economy, and virtue, every man is equally entitled to protection by law; but when the laws undertake to add to these natural and just advantages artificial distinctions, to grant titles, gratuities, and exclusive privileges, to make the rich richer and the potent more powerful, the humble members of society—the farmers, mechanics, and laborers—who have neither the time nor the means of securing like favors to themselves, have a right to complain of the injustice of their Government. There are no necessary evils in government. Its evils exist only in its abuses. If it would confine itself to equal protection, and, as Heaven does its rains, shower its favors alike on the high and the low, the rich and the poor, it would be an unqualified blessing. In the act before me there seems to be a wide and unnecessary departure from these just principles.

Nor is our Government to be maintained or our Union preserved by invasions of the rights and powers of the several States. In thus attempting to make our General Government strong we make it weak. Its true strength consists in leaving individuals and States as much as possible to themselves—in making itself felt, not in its power, but in its beneficence; not in its control, but in its protection; not in binding the States more closely to the center, but leaving each to move unobstructed in its proper orbit.

Experience should teach us wisdom. Most of the difficulties our Government now encounters and most of the dangers which impend over our Union have sprung from an abandonment of the legitimate objects of Government by our national legislation, and the adoption of such principles as are embodied in this act. Many of our rich men have not been content with equal protection and equal benefits, but have besought us to make them richer by act of Congress. By attempting to gratify their desires we have in the results of our legislation arrayed section against section, interest against interest, and man against man, in a fearful commotion which threatens to shake the foundations of our Union. It is time to pause in our career to review our principles, and if possible revive that devoted patriotism and spirit of compromise which distinguished the sages of the Revolution and the fathers of our Union. If we can not at once, in justice to interests vested under improvident legislation, make our Government what it ought to be, we can at least take a stand against all new grants of monopolies and exclusive privileges, against any prostitution of our Government to the advancement of the few at the expense of the many, and in favor of compromise and gradual reform in our code of laws and system of political economy.

21

Joseph Story, Commentaries on the Constitution 3:§§ 1238–89
1833

---

§ 1238. The plain import of the clause is, that congress shall have all the incidental and instrumental powers, necessary and proper to carry into execution all the express powers. It neither enlarges any power specifically granted; nor is it a grant of any new power to congress. But it is merely a declaration for the removal of all uncertainty, that the means of carrying into execution those, otherwise granted, are included in the grant. Whenever, therefore, a question arises concerning the constitutionality of a particular power, the first question is, whether the power be *expressed* in the constitution. If it be, the question is decided. If it be not *expressed,* the next inquiry must be, whether it is properly an incident to an express power, and necessary to its execution. If it be, then it may be exercised by congress. If not, congress cannot exercise it.

§ 1239. But still a ground of controversy remains open, as to the true interpretation of the terms of the clause; and it has been contested with no small share of earnestness and vigour. What, then, is the true constitutional sense of the words "necessary and proper" in this clause? It has been insisted by the advocates of a rigid interpretation, that the word "necessary" is here used in its close and most intense meaning; so that it is equivalent to *absolutely and indispensably necessary.* It has been said, that the constitution allows only the means, which are *necessary;* not those, which are merely *convenient* for effecting the enumerated powers. If such a latitude of construction be given to this phrase, as to give any non-enumerated power, it will go far to give every one; for there is no one, which ingenuity might not torture into a convenience in some way or other to some one of so long a list of enumerated powers. It would swallow up all the delegated powers, and reduce the whole to one phrase. Therefore it is, that the constitution has restrained them to the *necessary* means; that is to say, to those means, *without which the grant of the power would be nugatory.* A little difference in the degree of convenience cannot constitute the necessity, which the constitution refers to.

§ 1240. The effect of this mode of interpretation is to exclude all choice of means; or, at most, to leave to congress in each case those only, which are most direct and simple. If, indeed, such implied powers, and such only, as can be shown to be indispensably necessary, are within the purview of the clause, there will be no end to difficulties, and the express powers must practically become a mere nullity. It will be found, that the operations of the government, upon any of its powers, will rarely admit of a rigid demonstration of the necessity (in this strict sense) of the particular means. In most cases, various systems or means may be resorted to, to attain the same end; and yet, with respect to each, it may be argued, that it is not constitutional, because it is not indispensable; and the end may be obtained by other means. The consequence of such reasoning would be, that, as no means could be shown to be constitutional, none could be adopted. For instance, congress possess the power to make war, and to raise armies, and incidentally to erect fortifications, and purchase cannon and ammunition, and other munitions of war. But war may be carried on without fortifications, cannon, and ammunition. No particular kind of arms can be shown to be absolutely necessary; because various sorts of arms of different convenience, power, and utility are, or may be resorted to by different nations. What then becomes of the power? Congress has power to borrow money, and to provide for the payment of the public debt; yet no particular method is indispensable to these ends. They may be attained by various means. Congress has power to provide a navy; but no particular size, or form, or equipment of ships is indispensable. The means of providing a naval establishment are very various; and the applications of them admit of infinite shades of opinion, as to their convenience, utility, and necessity. What then is to be done? Are the powers to remain dormant? Would it not be absurd to say, that congress did not possess the choice of means under such circumstances, and ought not to be empowered to select, and use any means, which are in fact conducive to the exercise of the powers granted by the constitution? Take another example; congress has, doubtless, the authority, under the power to regulate commerce, to erect light-houses, beacons, buoys, and public piers, and authorize the employment of pilots. But it cannot be affirmed, that the exercise of these powers is in a strict sense necessary; or that the power to regulate commerce would be nugatory without establishments of this nature. In truth, no particular regulation of commerce can ever be shown to be exclusively and indispensably necessary; and thus we should be driven to admit, that all regulations are within the scope of the power, or that none are. If there be any general principle, which is inherent in the very definition of government, and essential to every step of the progress to be made by that of the United States, it is, that every power, vested in a government, is in its nature sovereign, and includes, by force of the term, a right to employ all the means requisite, and fairly applicable to the attainment of the end of such power; unless they are excepted in the constitution, or are immoral, or are contrary to the essential objects of political society.

§ 1241. There is another difficulty in the strict construction above alluded to, that it makes the constitutional authority depend upon casual and temporary circumstances, which may produce a necessity to-day, and change it to-morrow. This alone shows the fallacy of the reasoning. The expediency of exercising a particular power at a particular time must, indeed, depend on circumstances; but the constitutional right of exercising it must be uniform and invariable; the same to-day as to-morrow.

§ 1242. Neither can the degree, in which a measure is necessary, ever be a test of the legal right to adopt it. That must be a matter of opinion, (upon which different men, and different bodies may form opposite judgments,) and can only be a test of expediency. The relation between the measure and the end, between the nature of the means employed towards the execution of a power, and the object of that power, must be the criterion of constitutionality; and not the greater or less of necessity or expediency. If the legislature possesses a right of choice as to the means, who can limit that choice? Who is appointed an umpire, or arbiter in cases, where a discretion is confided to a government? The very idea of such a controlling authority in the exercise of its powers is a virtual denial of the supremacy of the government in regard to its powers. It repeals the supremacy of the national government, proclaimed in the constitution.

§ 1243. It is equally certain, that neither the grammatical, nor the popular sense of the word, "necessary," requires any such construction. According to both, "necessary" often means no more than *needful, requisite, incidental, useful,* or *conducive to.* It is a common mode of expression to say, that it is necessary for a government, or a person to do this or that thing, when nothing more is intended or understood, than that the interest of the government or person requires, or will be promoted by the doing of this or that thing. Every one's mind will at once suggest to him many illustrations of the use of the word in this sense. To employ the means, necessary to an end, is generally understood, as employing any means calculated to produce the end, and not as being confined to those single means, without which the end would be entirely unattainable.

§ 1244. Such is the character of human language, that no word conveys to the mind in all situations one single definite idea; and nothing is more common, than to use words in a figurative sense. Almost all compositions contain words, which, taken in their rigorous sense, would convey a meaning, different from that, which is obviously intended. It is essential to just interpretation, that many words, which import something excessive, should be understood in a more mitigated sense; in a sense, which common usage justifies. The word "necessary" is of this description. It has not a fixed character peculiar to itself. It admits of all degrees of comparison; and is often connected with other words, which increase or diminish the impression, which the mind receives of the urgency it imports. A thing may be necessary, very necessary, absolutely or indispensably necessary. It may be little necessary, less necessary, or least necessary. To no mind would the same idea be conveyed by any two of these several phrases. The tenth section of the first article of the constitution furnishes a strong illustration of this very use of the word. It contains a prohibition upon any state to "lay any imposts or duties, &c. except what may be *absolutely necessary* for executing its inspection laws." No one can compare this clause with the other, on which we are commenting, without being struck with the conviction, that the word "*absolutely,*" here prefixed to "necessary," was intended to distinguish it from the sense, in which, standing alone, it is used in the other.

§ 1245. That the restrictive interpretation must be abandoned, in regard to certain powers of the government, cannot be reasonably doubted. It is universally conceded, that the power of punishment appertains to sovereignty, and may be exercised, whenever the sovereign has a right to act, as incidental to his constitutional powers. It is a means for carrying into execution all sovereign powers, and may be used, although not indispensably necessary. If, then, the restrictive interpretation must be abandoned, in order to justify the constitutional exercise of the power to punish; whence is the rule derived, which would reinstate it, when the government would carry its powers into operation, by means not vindictive in their nature? If the word, "necessary" means *needful, requisite, essential, conducive to,* to let in the power of punishment, why is it not equally comprehensive, when applied to other means used to facilitate the execution of the powers of the government?

§ 1246. The restrictive interpretation is also contrary to a sound maxim of construction, generally admitted, namely, that the powers contained in a constitution of government, especially those, which concern the general administration of the affairs of the country, such as its finances, its trade, and its defence, ought to be liberally expounded in advancement of the public good. This rule does not depend on the particular form of a government, or on the particular demarcations of the boundaries of its powers; but on the nature and objects of government itself. The means, by which national exigencies are provided for, national inconveniences obviated, and national prosperity promoted, are of such infinite variety, extent, and complexity, that there must of necessity be great latitude of discretion in the selection, and application of those means. Hence, consequently, the necessity and propriety of exercising the authorities, entrusted to a government, on principles of liberal construction.

§ 1247. It is no valid objection to this doctrine to say, that it is calculated to extend the powers of the government throughout the entire sphere of state legislation. The same thing may be said, and has been said, in regard to every exercise of power by implication and construction. There is always some chance of error, or abuse of every power; but this furnishes no ground of objection against the power; and certainly no reason for an adherence to the most rigid construction of its terms, which would at once arrest the whole movements of the government. The remedy for any abuse, or misconstruction of the power, is the same, as in similar abuses and misconstructions of the state governments. It is by an appeal to the other departments of the government; and finally to the people, in the exercise of their elective franchises.

§ 1248. There are yet other grounds against the restrictive interpretation derived from the language, and the character of the provision. The language is, that congress shall have power "to make all laws, which shall be *necessary* and *proper.*" If the word "necessary" were used in the strict and rigorous sense contended for, it would be an extraordinary departure from the usual course of the human mind, as exhibited in solemn instruments, to add another word "proper;" the only possible effect of which is to qualify that strict and rigorous meaning, and to present clearly the idea of a choice of means in the course of legislation. If no means can be resorted to, but such as are indispensably necessary, there can be neither sense, nor utility in adding the other word; for the necessity shuts out from view all consideration of the propriety of the means, as contradistinguished from the former. But if the intention was to use the word "necessary" in its more liberal sense, then there is a peculiar fitness in the other word. It has a sense at once admonitory, and directory. It requires, that the means should be, *bonâ fide,* appropriate to the end.

§ 1249. The character of the clause equally forbids any presumption of an intention to use the restrictive interpretation. In the first place, the clause is placed among the powers of congress, and not among the limitations on those powers. In the next place, its terms purport to enlarge, and not to diminish, the powers vested in the government. It purports, on its face, to be an additional power, not a restriction on those already granted. If it does not, in fact, (as seems the true construction,) give any new powers, it affirms the right to use all necessary and proper means to carry into execution the other powers; and thus makes an *express* power, what would otherwise be merely an *implied* power. In either aspect, it is impossible to construe it to be a restriction. If it have any effect, it is to remove the implication of any restriction. If a restriction had been intended, it is impossible, that the framers of the constitution should have concealed it under phraseology, which purports to enlarge, or at least give the most ample scope to the other powers. There was every motive on their part to give point and clearness to every restriction of national power; for they well knew, that the national government would be more endangered in its adoption by its supposed strength, than by its weakness. It is inconceivable, that they should have disguised a restriction upon its powers under the form of a grant of power. They would have sought other terms, and have imposed the restraint by negatives. And what is equally strong, no one, in or out of the state conventions, at the time when the constitution was put upon its deliverance before the people, ever dreamed of, or suggested, that it contained a restriction of power. The whole argument on each side, of attack and of defence, gave it the positive form of an express power, and not of an express restriction.

§ 1250. Upon the whole, the result of the most careful examination of this clause is, that, if it does not enlarge, it cannot be construed to restrain the powers of congress, or to impair the right of the legislature to exercise its best judgment, in the selection of measures to carry into execution the constitutional powers of the national government. The motive for its insertion doubtless was, the desire to remove all possible doubt respecting the right to legislate on that vast mass of incidental powers, which must be involved in the constitution, if that instrument be not a splendid pageant, or a delusive phantom of sovereignty. Let the end be legitimate; let it be within the scope of the constitution; and all means, which are appropriate, which are plainly adapted to the end, and which are not prohibited, but are consistent with the letter and spirit of the instrument, are constitutional.

§ 1251. It may be well, in this connexion, to mention another sort of implied power, which has been called with great propriety a resulting power, arising from the aggregate powers of the national government. It will not be doubted, for instance, that, if the United States should make a conquest of any of the territories of its neighbours, the national government would possess sovereign jurisdiction over the conquered territory. This would, perhaps, rather be a result from the whole mass of the powers of the national government, and from the nature of political society, than a consequence or incident of the powers specially enumerated. It may, however, be deemed, if an incident to any, an incident to the power to make war. Other instances of resulting powers will easily suggest themselves. The United States are nowhere declared in the constitution to be a sovereignty entitled to sue, though jurisdiction is given to the national courts over controversies, to which the United States shall be a party. It is a natural incident, resulting from the sovereignty and character of the national government. So the United States, in their political capacity, have a right to enter into a contract, (although it is not expressly provided for by the constitution,) for it is an incident to their general right of sovereignty, so far as it is appropriate to any of the ends of the government, and within the constitutional range of its powers. So congress possess power to punish offences committed on board of the public ships of war of the government by persons not in the military or naval service of the United States, whether they are in port, or at sea; for the jurisdiction on board of public ships is every where deemed exclusively to belong to the sovereign.

§ 1252. And not only may implied powers, but implied exemptions from state authority, exist, although not expressly provided for by law. The collectors of the revenue, the carriers of the mail, the mint establishment, and all those institutions, which are public in their nature, are examples in point. It has never been doubted, that all, who are employed in them, are protected, while in the line of their duty, from state control; and yet this protection is not expressed in any act of congress. It is incidental to, and is implied in, the several acts, by which those institutions are created; and is preserved to them by the judicial department, as a part of its functions. A contractor for supplying a military post with provisions cannot be restrained from making purchases within a state, or from transporting provisions to the place, at which troops are stationed. He could not be taxed, or fined, or lawfully obstructed, in so doing. These incidents necessarily flow from the supremacy of the powers of the Union, within their legitimate sphere of action.

§ 1253. It would be almost impracticable, if it were not useless, to enumerate the various instances, in which congress, in the progress of the government, have made use of incidental and implied means to execute its powers. They are almost infinitely varied in their ramifications and details. It is proposed, however, to take notice of the principal measures, which have been contested, as not within the scope of the powers of congress, and which may be distinctly traced in the operations of the government, and in leading party divisions.

§ 1254. One of the earliest and most important measures, which gave rise to a question of constitutional power, was the act chartering the bank of the United States in 1791. That question has often since been discussed; and though the measure has been repeatedly sanctioned by congress, by the executive, and by the judiciary, and has obtained the like favour in a great majority of the states, yet it is, up to this very hour, still debated upon constitutional grounds, as if it were still new, and untried. It is impossible, at this time, to treat it, as an open question, unless the constitution is for ever to remain an unsettled text, possessing no permanent attributes, and incapable of having any ascertained sense; varying with every change of doctrine, and of party; and delivered over to interminable doubts. If the constitution is to be only, what the administration of the day may wish it to be; and is to assume any, and all shapes, which may suit the opinions and theories of public men, as they successively direct the public councils, it will be difficult, indeed, to ascertain, what its real value is. It cannot possess either certainty, or uniformity, or safety. It will be one thing to-day, and another thing to-morrow, and again another thing on each succeeding day. The past will furnish no guide, and the future no security. It will be the reverse of a law; and entail upon the country the curse of that miserable servitude, so much abhorred and denounced, where all is vague and uncertain in the fundamentals of government.

§ 1255. The reasoning, upon which the constitutionality of a national bank is denied, has been already in some degree stated in the preceding remarks. It turns upon the strict interpretation of the clause, giving the auxiliary powers necessary, and proper to execute the other enumerated powers. It is to the following effect: The power to incorporate a bank is not among those enumerated in the constitution. It is known, that the very power, thus proposed, as a means, was rejected, as an end, by the convention, which formed the constitution. A proposition was made in that body, to authorize congress to open canals, and an amendatory one to empower them to create corporations. But the whole was rejected; and one of the reasons of the rejection urged in debate was, that they then would have a power to create a bank, which would render the great cities, where there were prejudices and jealousies on that subject, adverse to the adoption of the constitution. In the next place, all the enumerated powers can be carried into execution without a bank. A bank, therefore, is not *necessary*, and consequently not authorized by this clause of the constitution. It is urged, that a bank will give great facility, or convenience to the collection of taxes. If this were true, yet the constitution allows only the means, which are *necessary*, and not merely those, which are *convenient* for effecting the enumerated powers. If such a latitude of construction were allowed, as to consider convenience, as justifying the use of such means, it would swallow up all the enumerated powers. Therefore, the constitution restrains congress to those means, without which the power would be nugatory.

§ 1256. Nor can its convenience be satisfactorily established. Bank-bills may be a more convenient vehicle, than treasury orders, for the purposes of that department. But a little difference in the degree of convenience cannot constitute the necessity contemplated by the constitution. Besides; the local and state banks now in existence are competent, and would be willing to undertake all the agency required for those very purposes by the government. And if they are able and willing, this establishes clearly, that there can be no necessity for establishing a national bank. If there would ever be a superior conveniency in a national bank, it does not follow, that there exists a power to establish it, or that the business of the country cannot go on very well without it. Can it be thought, that the constitution intended, that for a shade or two of convenience, more or less, congress should be authorized to break down the most ancient and fundamental laws of the states, such as those against mortmain, the laws of alienage, the rules of descent, the acts of distribution, the laws of escheat and forfeiture, and the laws of monopoly? Nothing but a necessity, invincible by any other means, can justify such a prostration of laws, which constitute the pillars of our whole system of jurisprudence. If congress have the power to create one corporation, they may create all sorts; for the power is no where limited; and may even establish monopolies. Indeed this very charter is a monopoly.

§ 1257. The reasoning, by which the constitutionality of the national bank has been sustained, is contained in the following summary. The powers confided to the national government are unquestionably, so far as they exist, sovereign and supreme. It is not, and cannot be disputed, that the power of creating a corporation is one belonging to sovereignty. But so are all other legislative powers; for the original power of giving the law on any subject whatever is a sovereign power. If the national government cannot create a corporation, because it is an exercise of sovereign power, neither can it, for the same reason, exercise any other legislative power. This consideration alone ought to put an end to the abstract inquiry, whether the national government has power to erect a corporation, that is, to give a legal or artificial capacity to one or more persons, distinct from the natural capacity. For, if it be an incident to sovereignty, and it is not prohibited, it must belong to the national government in relation to the objects entrusted to it. The true difference is this; where the authority of a government is general, it can create corporations in all cases; where it is confined to certain branches of legislation, it can create corporations only as to those cases. It cannot be denied, that implied powers may be delegated, as well as express. It follows, that a power to erect corporations may as well be implied, as any other thing, if it be an instrument or means of carrying into execution any specified power. The only question in any case must be, whether it be such an instrument or means, and have a natural relation to any of the acknowledged objects of government. Thus, congress may not erect a corporation for superintending the police of the city of Philadelphia, because they have no authority to regulate the police of that city. But if they possessed the authority to regulate the police of such city, they might, unquestionably, create a corporation for that purpose; because it is incident to the sovereign legislative power to regulate a thing, to employ all the means, which relate to its regulation, to the best and greatest advantage.

§ 1258. A strange fallacy has crept into the reasoning on this subject. It has been supposed, that a corporation is some great, independent thing; and that the power to erect it is a great, substantive, independent power; whereas, in truth, a corporation is but a legal capacity, quality, or means to an end; and the power to erect it is, or may be, an implied and incidental power. A corporation is never the end, for which other powers are exercised; but a means, by which other objects are accomplished. No contributions are made to charity for the sake of an incorporation; but a corporation is created to administer the charity. No seminary of learning is instituted in order to be incorporated; but the corporate character is conferred to subserve the purposes of education. No city was ever built with the sole object of being incorporated; but it is incorporated as affording the best means of being well governed. So a mercantile company is formed with a certain capital for carrying on a particular branch of business. Here, the business to be prosecuted is the end. The association, in order to form the requisite capital, is the primary means. If an incorporation is added to the association, it only gives it a new quality, an artificial capacity, by which it is enabled to prosecute the business with more convenience and safety. In truth, the power of creating a corporation is never used for its own sake; but for the purpose of effecting something else. So that there is not a shadow of reason to say, that it may not pass as an incident to powers expressly given, as a mode of executing them.

§ 1259. It is true, that among the enumerated powers we do not find that of establishing a bank, or creating a corporation. But we do find there the great powers to lay and collect taxes; to borrow money; to regulate commerce; to declare and conduct war; and to raise and support armies and navies. Now, if a bank be a fit means to execute any or all of these powers, it is just as much implied, as any other means. If it be "necessary and proper" for any of them, how is it possible to deny the authority to create it for such purposes? There is no more propriety in giving this power in *express* terms, than in giving any other incidental powers or means in express terms. If it had been intended to grant this power generally, and to make it a distinct and independent power, having no relation to, but reaching beyond the other enumerated powers, there would then have been a propriety in giving it in express terms, for otherwise it would not exist. Thus, it was proposed in the convention, to give a general power "to grant charters of incorporation;"—to "grant charters of incorporation in cases, where the public good may require them, and the authority of a single state may be incompetent;"—and "to grant letters of incorporation for canals, &c." If either of these propositions had been adopted, there would have been an obvious propriety in giving the power in express terms; because, as to the two former, the power was general and unlimited, and reaching far beyond any of the other enumerated powers; and as to the latter, it might be far more extensive than any incident to the other enumerated powers. But the rejection of these propositions does not prove, that congress in no case, as an incident to the enumerated powers, should erect a corporation; but only, that they should not have a substantive, independent power to erect corporations beyond those powers.

§ 1260. Indeed, it is most manifest, that it never could have been contemplated by the convention, that congress should, in no case, possess the power to erect a corporation. What otherwise would become of the territorial governments, all of which are corporations created by congress? There is no where an express power given to congress to erect them. But under the confederation, congress did provide for their erection, as a resulting and implied right of sovereignty, by the celebrated ordinance of 1787; and congress, under the constitution, have ever since, without question, and with the universal approbation of the nation, from time to time created territorial governments. Yet congress derive this power only by implication, or as necessary and proper, to carry into effect the express power to regulate the territories of the United States. In the convention, two propositions were made and referred to a committee at the same time with the propositions already stated respecting granting of charters, "to dispose of the unappropriated lands of the United States," and "to institute temporary governments for new states arising therein." Both these propositions shared the same fate, as those respecting charters of incorporation. But what would be thought of the argument, built upon this foundation, that congress did not possess the power to erect territorial governments, because these propositions were silently abandoned, or annulled in the convention?

§ 1261. This is not the only case, in which congress may erect corporations. Under the power to accept a cession of territory for the seat of government, and to exercise exclusive legislation therein; no one can doubt, that congress may erect corporations therein, not only public, but private corporations. They have constantly exercised the power; and it has never yet been breathed, that it was unconstitutional. Yet it can be exercised only as an incident to the power of general legislation. And if so, why may it not be exercised, as an incident to any specific power of legislation, if it be a means to attain the objects of such power?

§ 1262. That a national bank is an appropriate means to carry into effect some of the enumerated powers of the government, and that this can be best done by erecting it into a corporation, may be established by the most satisfactory reasoning. It has a relation, more or less direct, to the power of collecting taxes, to that of borrowing money, to that of regulating trade between the states, and to those of raising and maintaining fleets and armies. And it may be added, that it has a most important bearing upon the regulation of currency between the states. It is an instrument, which has been usually applied by governments in the administration of their fiscal and financial operations. And in the present times it can hardly require argument to prove, that it is a convenient, a useful, and an essential instrument in the fiscal operations of the government of the United States. This is so generally admitted by sound and intelligent statesmen, that it would be a waste of time to endeavour to establish the truth by an elaborate survey of the mode, in which it touches the administration of all the various branches of the powers of the government.

§ 1263. In regard to the suggestion, that a proposition was made, and rejected in the convention to confer this very power, what was the precise nature or extent of this proposition, or what were the reasons for refusing it, cannot now be ascertained by any authentic document, or even by any accurate recollection of the members. As far as any document exists, it specifies only canals. If this proves any thing, it proves no more, than that it was thought inexpedient to give a power to incorporate for the purpose of opening canals generally. But very different accounts are given of the import of the proposition, and of the motives for rejecting it. Some affirm, that it was confined to the opening of canals and obstructions of rivers; others, that it embraced banks; and others, that it extended to the power of incorporations generally. Some, again, allege, that it was disagreed to, because it was thought improper to vest in congress a power of erecting corporations; others, because they thought it unnecessary to specify the power; and inexpedient to furnish an additional topic of objection to the constitution. In this state of the matter, no inference whatever can be drawn from it. But, whatever may have been the private intentions of the framers of the constitution, which can rarely be established by the mere fact of their votes, it is certain, that the true rule of interpretation is to ascertain the public and just intention from the language of the instrument itself, according to the common rules applied to all laws. The people, who adopted the constitution, could know nothing of the private intentions of the framers. They adopted it upon its own clear import, upon its own naked text. Nothing is more common, than for a law to effect more or less, the intention of the persons, who framed it; and it must be judged of by its words and sense, and not by any private intentions of members of the legislature.

§ 1264. In regard to the faculties of the bank, if congress could constitutionally create it, they might confer on it such faculties and powers, as were fit to make it an appropriate means for fiscal operations. They had a right to adapt it in the best manner to its end. No one can pretend, that its having the faculty of holding a capital; of lending and dealing in money; of issuing bank notes; of receiving deposits; and of appointing suitable officers to manage its affairs; are not highly useful and expedient, and appropriate to the purposes of a bank. They are just such, as are usually granted to state banks; and just such, as give increased facilities to all its operations. To say, that the bank might have gone on without this or that faculty, is nothing. Who, but congress, shall say, how few, or how many it shall have, if all are still appropriate to it, as an instrument of government, and may make it more convenient, and more useful in its operations? No man can say, that a single faculty in any national charter is useless, or irrelevant, or strictly improper, that is conducive to its end, as a national instrument. Deprive a bank of its trade and business, and its vital principles are destroyed. Its form may remain, but its substance is gone. All the powers given to the bank are to give efficacy to its functions of trade and business.

§ 1265. As to another suggestion, that the same objects might have been accomplished through the state banks, it is sufficient to say, that no trace can be found in the constitution of any intention to create a dependence on the states, or state institutions, for the execution of its great powers. Its own means are adequate to its end; and on those means it was expected to rely for their accomplishment. It would be utterly absurd to make the powers of the constitution wholly dependent on state institutions. But if state banks might be employed, as congress have a choice of means, they had a right to choose a national bank, in preference to state banks, for the financial operations of the government. Proof, that they might use one means, is no proof, that they cannot constitutionally use another means.

§ 1266. After all, the subject has been settled repeatedly by every department of the government, legislative, executive, and judicial. The states have acquiesced; and a majority have constantly sustained the power. If it is not now settled, it never can be. If it is settled, it would be too much to expect a re-argument, whenever any person may choose to question it.

§ 1267. Another question, which has for a long time agitated the public councils of the nation, is, as to the authority of congress to make roads, canals, and other internal improvements.

§ 1268. So far, as regards the right to appropriate money to internal improvements generally, the subject has already passed under review in considering the power to lay and collect taxes. The doctrine there contended for, which has been in a great measure borne out by the actual practice of the government, is, that congress may appropriate money, not only to clear obstructions to navigable rivers; to improve harbours; to build breakwaters; to assist navigation; to erect forts, light-houses, and piers; and for other purposes allied to some of the enumerated powers; but may also appropriate it in aid of canals, roads, and other institutions of a similar nature, existing under state authority. The only limitations upon the power are those prescribed by the terms of the constitution, that the objects shall be for the common defence, or the general welfare of the Union. The true test is, whether the object be of a local character, and local use; or, whether it be of general benefit to the states. If it be purely local, congress cannot constitutionally appropriate money for the object. But, if the benefit be general, it matters not, whether in point of locality it be in one state, or several; whether it be of large, or of small extent; its nature and character determine the right, and congress may appropriate money in aid of it; for it is then in a just sense for the general welfare.

§ 1269. But it has been contended, that the constitution is not confined to mere appropriations of money; but authorizes congress directly to undertake and carry on a system of internal improvements for the general welfare; wherever such improvements fall within the scope of any of the enumerated powers. Congress may not, indeed, engage in such undertakings merely because they are internal improvements for the general welfare, unless they fall within the scope of the enumerated powers. The distinction between this power, and the power of appropriation is, that in the latter, congress may appropriate to any purpose, which is for the common defence or general welfare; but in the former, they can engage in such undertakings only, as are means, or incidents to its enumerated powers. Congress may, therefore, authorize the making of a canal, as incident to the power to regulate commerce, where such canal may facilitate the intercourse between state and state. They may authorize light-houses, piers, buoys, and beacons to be built for the purposes of navigation. They may authorize the purchase and building of custom-houses, and revenue cutters, and public ware-houses, as incidents to the power to lay and collect taxes. They may purchase places for public uses; and erect forts, arsenals, dock-yards, navy-yards, and magazines, as incidents to the power to make war.

§ 1270. For the same reason congress may authorize the laying out and making of a military road, and acquire a right over the soil for such purposes; and as incident thereto they have a power to keep the road in repair, and prevent all obstructions thereto. But in these, and the like cases, the general jurisdiction of the state over the soil, subject only to the rights of the United States, is not excluded. As, for example, in case of a military road; although a state cannot prevent repairs on the part of the United States, or authorize any obstructions of the road, its general jurisdiction remains untouched. It may punish all crimes committed on the road; and it retains in other respects its territorial sovereignty over it. The right of soil may still remain in the state, or in individuals, and the right to the easement only in the national government. There is a great distinction between the exercise of a power, excluding altogether state jurisdiction, and the exercise of a power, which leaves the state jurisdiction generally in force, and yet includes, on the part of the national government, a power to preserve, what it has created.

§ 1271. In all these, and other cases, in which the power of congress is asserted, it is so upon the general ground of its being an incidental power; and the course of reasoning, by which it is supported, is precisely the same, as that adopted in relation to other cases already considered. It is, for instance, admitted, that congress cannot authorize the making of a canal, except for some purpose of commerce among the states, or for some other purpose belonging to the Union; and it cannot make a military road, unless it be necessary and proper for purposes of war. To go over the reasoning at large would, therefore, be little more, than a repetition of what has been already fully expounded. The Journal of the Convention is not supposed to furnish any additional lights on the subject, beyond what have been already stated.

§ 1272. The resistance to this extended reach of the national powers turns also upon the same general reasoning, by which a strict construction of the constitution has been constantly maintained. It is said, that such a power is not among those enumerated in the constitution; nor is it implied, as a means of executing any of them. The power to regulate commerce cannot include a power to construct roads and canals, and improve the navigation of water-courses in order to facilitate, promote, and secure such commerce, without a latitude of construction departing from the ordinary import of the terms, and incompatible with the nature of the constitution. The liberal interpretation has been very uniformly asserted by congress; the strict interpretation has not uniformly, but has upon several important occasions been insisted upon by the executive. In the present state of the controversy, the duty of forbearance seems inculcated upon the commentator; and the reader must decide for himself upon his own views of the subject.

§ 1273. Another question has been made, how far congress could make a law giving to the United States a preference and priority of payment of their debts, in cases of the death, or insolvency, or bankruptcy of their debtors, out of their estates. It has been settled, upon deliberate argument, that congress possess such a constitutional power. It is a necessary and proper power to carry into effect the other powers of the government. The government is to pay the debts of the Union; and must be authorized to use the means, which appear to itself most eligible to effect that object. It may purchase, and remit bills for this object; and it may take all those precautions, and make all those regulations, which will render the transmission safe. It may, in like manner, pass all laws to render effectual the collection of its debts. It is no objection to this right of priority, that it will interfere with the rights of the state sovereignties respecting the dignity of debts, and will defeat the measures, which they have a right to adopt to secure themselves against delinquencies on the part of their own revenue or other officers. This objection, if of any avail, is an objection to the powers given by the constitution. The mischief suggested, so far as it can really happen, is the necessary consequence of the supremacy of the laws of the United States on all subjects, to which the legislative power of congress extends.

§ 1274. It is under the same implied authority, that the United States have any right even to sue in their own courts; for an express power is no where given in the constitution, though it is clearly implied in that part respecting the judicial power. And congress may not only authorize suits to be brought in the name of the United States, but in the name of any artificial person, (such as the Postmaster-General,) or natural person for their benefit. Indeed, all the usual incidents appertaining to a *personal* sovereign, in relation to contracts, and suing, and enforcing rights, so far as they are within the scope of the powers of the government, belong to the United States, as they do to other sovereigns. The right of making contracts and instituting suits is an incident to the general right of sovereignty; and the United States, being a body politic, may, within the sphere of the constitutional powers confided to it, and through the instrumentality of the proper department, to which those powers are confided, enter into contracts not prohibited by law, and appropriate to the just exercise of those powers; and enforce the observance of them by suits and judicial process.

§ 1275. There are almost innumerable cases, in which the auxiliary and implied powers belonging to congress have been put into operation. But the object of these Commentaries is, rather to take notice of those, which have been the subject of animadversion, than of those, which have hitherto escaped reproof, or have been silently approved.

§ 1276. Upon the ground of a strict interpretation, some extraordinary objections have been taken in the course of the practical operations of the government. The very first act, passed under the government, which regulated the time, form, and manner, of administering the oaths prescribed by the constitution, was denied to be constitutional. But the objection has long since been abandoned. It has been doubted, whether it is constitutional to permit the secretaries to draft bills on subjects connected with their departments, to be presented to the house of representatives for their consideration. It has been doubted, whether an act authorizing the president to lay, regulate, and revoke, embargoes was constitutional. It has been doubted, whether congress have authority to establish a military academy. But these objections have been silently, or practically abandoned.

§ 1277. But the most remarkable powers, which have been exercised by the government, as auxiliary and implied powers, and which, if any, go to the utmost verge of liberal construction, are the laying of an unlimited embargo in 1807, and the purchase of Louisiana in 1803, and its subsequent admission into the Union, as a state. These measures were brought forward, and supported, and carried, by the known and avowed friends of a strict construction of the constitution; and they were justified at the time, and can be now justified, only upon the doctrines of those, who support a liberal construction of the constitution. The subject has been already hinted at; but it deserves a more deliberate review.

§ 1278. In regard to the acquisition of Louisiana:—The treaty of 1803 contains a cession of the whole of that vast territory by France to the United States, for a sum exceeding eleven millions of dollars. There is a stipulation in the treaty on the part of the United States, that the inhabitants of the ceded territory shall be incorporated into the Union, and admitted, as soon as possible, according to the principles of the federal constitution, to the enjoyment of all the rights, advantages, and immunities of citizens of the United States.

§ 1279. It is obvious, that the treaty embraced several very important questions, each of them upon the grounds of a strict construction full of difficulty and delicacy. In the first place, had the United States a constitutional authority to accept the cession and pay for it? In the next place, if they had, was the stipulation for the admission of the inhabitants into the Union, as a state, constitutional, or within the power of congress to give it effect?

§ 1280. There is no pretence, that the purchase, or cession of any foreign territory is within any of the powers expressly enumerated in the constitution. It is no where in that instrument said, that congress, or any other department of the national government, shall have a right to purchase, or accept of any cession of foreign territory. The power itself (it has been said) could scarcely have been in the contemplation of the framers of it. It is, in its own nature, as dangerous to liberty, as susceptible of abuse in its actual application, and as likely as any, which could be imagined, to lead to a dissolution of the Union. If congress have the power, it may unite any foreign territory whatsoever to our own, however distant, however populous, and however powerful. Under the form of a cession, we may become united to a more powerful neighbour or rival; and be involved in European, or other foreign interests, and contests, to an interminable extent. And if there may be a stipulation for the admission of foreign states into the Union, the whole balance of the constitution may be destroyed, and the old states sunk into utter insignificance. It is incredible, that it should have been contemplated, that any such overwhelming authority should be confided to the national government with the consent of the people of the old states. If it exists at all, it is unforeseen, and the result of a sovereignty, intended to be limited, and yet not sufficiently guarded. The very case of the cession of Louisiana is a striking illustration of the doctrine. It admits, by consequence, into the Union an immense territory, equal to, if not greater, than that of all the United States under the peace of 1783. In the natural progress of events, it must, within a short period, change the whole balance of power in the Union, and transfer to the West all the important attributes of the sovereignty of the whole. If, as is well known, one of the strong objections urged against the constitution was, that the original territory of the United States was too large for a national government; it is inconceivable, that it could have been within the intention of the people, that any additions of foreign territory should be made, which should thus double every danger from this source. The treaty-making power must be construed, as confined to objects within the scope of the constitution. And, although congress have authority to admit new states into the firm, yet it is demonstrable, that this clause had sole reference to the territory then belonging to the United States; and was designed for the admission of the states, which, under the ordinance of 1787, were contemplated to be formed within its old boundaries. In regard to the appropriation of money for the purposes of the cession the case is still stronger. If no appropriation of money can be made, except for cases within the enumerated powers, (and this clearly is not one,) how can the enormous sum of eleven millions be justified for this object? If it be said, that it will be "for the common defence, and general welfare" to purchase the territory, how is this reconcileable with the strict construction of the constitution? If congress can appropriate money for one object, because it is deemed for the common defence and general welfare, why may they not appropriate it for all objects of the same sort? If the territory can be purchased, it must be governed; and a territorial government must be created. But where can congress find authority in the constitution to erect a territorial government, since it does not possess the power to erect corporations?

§ 1281. Such were the objections, which have been, and in fact may be, urged against the cession, and the appropriations made to carry the treaty into effect. The friends of the measure were driven to the adoption of the doctrine, that the right to acquire territory was incident to national sovereignty; that it was a resulting power, growing necessarily out of the aggregate powers confided by the federal constitution; that the appropriation might justly be vindicated upon this ground, and also upon the ground, that it was for the common defence and general welfare. In short, there is no possibility of defending the constitutionality of this measure, but upon the principles of the liberal construction, which has been, upon other occasions, so earnestly resisted.

§ 1282. As an incidental power, the constitutional right of the United States to acquire territory would seem so naturally to flow from the sovereignty confided to it, as not to admit of very serious question. The constitution confers on the government of the Union the power of making war, and of making treaties; and it seems consequently to possess the power of acquiring territory either by conquest or treaty. If the cession be by treaty, the terms of that treaty must be obligatory; for it is the law of the land. And if it stipulates for the enjoyment by the inhabitants of the rights, privileges, and immunities of citizens of the United States, and for the admission of the territory into the Union, as a state, these stipulations must be equally obligatory. They are within the scope of the constitutional authority of the government, which has the right to acquire territory, to make treaties, and to admit new states into the Union.

§ 1283. The more recent acquisition of Florida, which has been universally approved, or acquiesced in by all the states, can be maintained only on the same principles; and furnishes a striking illustration of the truth, that constitutions of government require a liberal construction to effect their objects, and that a narrow interpretation of their powers, however it may suit the views of speculative philosophers, or the accidental interests of political parties, is incompatible with the permanent interests of the state, and subversive of the great ends of all government, the safety and independence of the people.

§ 1284. The other instance of an extraordinary application of the implied powers of the government, above alluded to, is the embargo laid in the year 1807, by the special recommendation of President Jefferson. It was avowedly recommended, as a measure of safety for our vessels, our seamen, and our merchandise from the then threatening dangers from the belligerents of Europe; and it was explicitly stated "to be a measure of precaution called for by the occasion;" and "neither hostile in its character, nor as justifying, or inciting, or leading to hostility with any nation whatever." It was in no sense, then, a war measure. If it could be classed at all, as flowing from, or as an incident to, any of the enumerated powers, it was that of regulating commerce. In its terms, the act provided, that an embargo be, and hereby is, laid on all ships and vessels in the ports, or within the limits or jurisdiction, of the United States, &c. bound to any foreign port or place. It was in its terms unlimited in duration; and could be removed only by a subsequent act of congress, having the assent of all the constitutional branches of the legislature.

§ 1285. No one can reasonably doubt, that the laying of an embargo, suspending commerce for a limited period, is within the scope of the constitution. But the question of difficulty was, whether congress, under the power to regulate commerce with foreign nations, could constitutionally suspend and interdict it wholly for an unlimited period, that is, by a permanent act, having no limitation as to duration, either of the act, or of the embargo. It was most seriously controverted, and its constitutionality denied in the Eastern states of the Union, during its existence. An appeal was made to the judiciary upon the question; and it having been settled to be constitutional by that department of the government, the decision was acquiesced in, though the measure bore with almost unexampled severity, upon the Eastern states; and its ruinous effects can still be traced along their extensive seaboard. The argument was, that the power to regulate did not include the power to annihilate commerce, by interdicting it permanently and entirely with foreign nations. The decision was, that the power of congress was sovereign, relative to commercial intercourse, qualified by the limitations and restrictions contained in the constitution itself. Non-intercourse and Embargo laws are within the range of legislative discretion; and if congress have the power, for purposes of safety, of preparation, or counteraction, to suspend commercial intercourse with foreign nations, they are not limited, as to the duration, any more, than as to the manner and extent of the measure.

§ 1286. That this measure went to the utmost verge of constitutional power, and especially of implied power, has never been denied. That it could not be justified by any, but the most liberal construction of the constitution, is equally undeniable. It was the favourite measure of those, who were generally the advocates of the strictest construction. It was sustained by the people from a belief, that it was promotive of the interests, and important to the safety of the Union.

§ 1287. At the present day, few statesmen are to be found, who seriously contest the constitutionality of the acts respecting either the embargo, or the purchase and admission of Louisiana into the Union. The general voice of the nation has sustained, and supported them. Why, then, should not that general voice be equally respected in relation to other measures of vast public importance, and by many deemed of still more vital interest to the country, such as the tariff laws, and the national bank charter? Can any measures furnish a more instructive lesson, or a more salutary admonition, in the whole history of parties, at once to moderate our zeal, and awaken our vigilance, than those, which stand upon principles repudiated at one time upon constitutional scruples, and solemnly adopted at another time, to subserve a present good, or foster the particular policy of an administration? While the principles of the constitution should be preserved with a most guarded caution, and a most sacred regard to the rights of the states; it is at once the dictate of wisdom, and enlightened patriotism to avoid that narrowness of interpretation, which would dry up all its vital powers, or compel the government (as was done under the confederation,) to break down all constitutional barriers, and trust for its vindication to the people, upon the dangerous political maxim, that the safety of the people is the supreme law, *(salus populi suprema lex;)* a maxim, which might be used to justify the appointment of a dictator, or any other usurpation.

§ 1288. There remain one or two other measures of a political nature, whose constitutionality has been denied; but which, being of a transient character, have left no permanent traces in the constitutional jurisprudence of the country. Reference is here made to the Alien and Sedition laws, passed in 1798, both of which were limited to a short duration, and expired by their own limitation. One (the Alien act) authorized the president to order out of the country such aliens, as he should deem dangerous to the peace and safety of the United States; or should have reasonable grounds to suspect to be concerned in any treasonable, or secret machinations against the government of the United States, under severe penalties for disobedience. The other declared it a public crime, punishable with fine and imprisonment, for any persons unlawfully to combine, and conspire together, with intent to oppose any measure or measures of the United States, &c.; or with such intent, to counsel, advise, or attempt to procure any insurrection, unlawful assembly, or combination; or to write, print, utter, or publish, or cause, or procure to be written, &c., or willingly to assist in writing, &c., any false, scandalous, and malicious writing or writings against the government of the United States, or either house of congress, or the president, with intent to defame them, or to bring them into contempt, or disrepute, or to excite against them the hatred of the people, or to stir up sedition; or to excite any unlawful combination for opposing, or resisting any law, or any lawful act of the president, or to resist, oppose, or defeat any such law or act; or to aid, encourage, or abet any hostile designs of any foreign nations against the United States. It provided, however, that the truth of the writing or libel might be given in evidence; and that the jury, who tried the cause, should have a right to determine the law and the fact, under the direction of the court, as in other cases.

§ 1289. The constitutionality of both the acts was assailed with great earnestness and ability at the time; and was defended with equal masculine vigour. The ground of the advocates, in favour of these laws, was, that they resulted from the right and duty in the government of self-preservation, and the like duty and protection of its functionaries in the proper discharge of their official duties. They were impugned, as not conformable to the letter or spirit of the constitution; and as inconsistent in their principles with the rights of citizens, and the liberty of the press. The Alien act was denounced, as exercising a power not delegated by the constitution; as uniting legislative and judicial functions, with that of the executive; and by this Union as subverting the general principles of free government, and the particular organization and positive provisions of the constitution. It was added, that the Sedition act was open to the same objection, and was expressly forbidden by one of the amendments of the constitution, on which there will be occasion hereafter to comment. At present it does not seem necessary to present more than this general outline, as the measures are not likely to be renewed; and as the doctrines, on which they are maintained, and denounced, are not materially different from those, which have been already considered.

SEE ALSO:

Generally 1.8.1–17; Amend. X

Records of the Federal Convention, Farrand 2:144, 168, 344–45, 570, 596, 640; 4:56–57

Thomas McKean, Pennsylvania Ratifying Convention, 11 Dec. 1787, Elliot 2:537–38

James Iredell, Marcus, Answers to Mr. Mason's Objections to the New Constitution, 1788, Pamphlets 356–66

Federal Farmer, no. 16, 20 Jan. 1788, Storing 2.8.196–98

Edmund Randolph, Virginia Ratifying Convention, 10 June 1788, Elliot 3:206–7

John Williams, New York Ratifying Convention, 27 June 1788, Elliot 2:338–39

Alexander Contee Hanson, Remarks, 1788, Pamphlets 233–34

A Native of Virginia, Some Observations upon the Proposed Constitution, June 1788, Monroe Writings 1:App. 333

House of Representatives, Bank of the United States, 2–5, 7–8 Feb. 1791, Annals 2:1896–1912, 1914–27, 1927, 1931–60

An Act to Incorporate the Subscribers to the Bank of the United States, 1 Stat. 191 (1791)

James Iredell, Charge to Grand Jury (C.C.D.Md. 1793), Life 2:393–94

James Iredell, Charge to Grand Jury, 9 Fed. Cas. 826, no. 5,126 (C.C.D.Pa. 1799)

House of Representatives, Amendment to the Constitution, 11 Dec. 1806, Annals 16:131–48

Senate, Bank of the United States, 8, 14–15, 18–20 Feb. 1811, Annals 22:134–47, 178–93, 211–19, 272–84, 295–96, 297, 346–47

House of Representatives, Bank of the United States, 16–19, 21–24 Jan. 1811, Annals 22:581–85, 604–6, 620–24, 627–38, 640–44, 646, 651–52, 659–66, 668–72, 675–78, 696–97, 701–2, 712–16, 717–21, 735–40, 762–65, 767–72, 820–22

House of Representatives, Internal Improvements, 6 Feb. 1817, Annals 30:886–90, 895–900

Senate, Internal Improvements, 26 Feb. 1817, Annals 30:165–74

James Madison, Veto Message on Internal Improvements Bill, 3 Mar. 1817, Annals 30:211–13

House of Representatives, Internal Improvements, 6–7, 9 Mar. 1818, Annals 31:1114, 1119–24, 1129–35, 1140–46, 1159–60, 1167–72, 1175–79, 1195–96

John Marshall's Defense of *McCulloch* v. *Maryland*, Mar.–June 1819 (G. Gunther ed. 1969)

James Monroe, Veto Message, 4 May 1822, Richardson 2:142–43

James Monroe, Views of the President of the United States on the Subject of Internal Improvements, 4 May 1822, Richardson 2:155–80

Osborn v. *Bank of United States*, 9 Wheat. 738 (1824)

James Kent, Commentaries 1:233–39 (1826)

William Rawle, A View of the Constitution of the United States 114 (2d ed. 1829)

United States v. *Tingey*, 5 Pet. 115 (1831)

Article 1, Section 9, Clause 1

The Migration or Importation of such Persons as any of the States now existing shall think proper to admit, shall not be prohibited by the Congress prior to the Year one thousand eight hundred and eight, but a Tax or duty may be imposed on such Importation, not exceeding ten dollars for each Person.

1

Thomas Jefferson, Bill to Prevent the Importation of Slaves
16 June 1777

Papers 2:22–23

To prevent more effectually the practice of holding persons in Slavery and importing them into this State Be it enacted by the General Assembly that all persons who shall be hereafter imported into this Commonwealth by Sea or by Land whether they were bond or free in their native Country upon their taking the Oath of Fidelity to this Commonwealth shall from thenceforth become free and absolutely exempted from all Slavery or Bondage to which they had been subjected in any other State or Country whatsoever. That it shall and may be lawful for any person by Deed duly executed in the presence of two or more Witnesses and acknowledged or proved and recorded in the General Court or Court of the County where he or she resides within eight Months from the making thereof or by their last Will and Testament in writing fully and absolutely to manumit and set at Liberty any Slave or Slaves to which they are entitled, But no Slave absconding from the owner who resides in any of the thirteen united States of America, or any other state in amity with them, and coming into this commonwealth, or coming with the owner to dwell here, or attending him as a Servant, or falling to any Inhabitant of this Commonwealth by Marriage Will or Inheritance and not brought to be sold, shall not become free, And if any Slave manumitted shall, within years thereafter, become chargeable to a Parish, the former owner, or his Executors or Administrators shall be compelled to reimburse the expenses of his or her maintenance, And so much of the Act of general Assembly made in the year of our Lord one thousand seven hundred and fifty three intitled "an act for the better government of Servants and Slaves" as is contrary to this act, is hereby declared to be repealed.

2

PIRATE v. DALBY

1 Dall. 167 (Pa. 1786)

The Chief Justice delivered the following sentiments, in the course of an elaborate charge to the jury:

MCKEAN, Chief Justice.—The issue is, whether the plaintiff is a freeman or a slave. If the jury think, from the evidence, that the plaintiff's mother was a slave at the time of his birth, according to the laws of Virginia, where he was born, we will point out the legal consequence that flows from the establishment of this fact.

Slavery is of a very ancient origin. By the sacred books of Leviticus and Deuteronomy, it appears to have existed in the first ages of the world; and we know it was established among the Greeks, the Romans, and the Germans. In England, there was formerly a species of slavery, distinct from that which was termed *villenage.* Swinb. p. 84, 6th edit., is the only authority I remember on this point, though I have before had occasion to look into it with attention. But from this distinction has arisen the rule, that the issue follows the condition of the father; and its consequence, that the bastard is always free; because, in contemplation of law, his father is altogether unknown, and that, therefore, his slavery shall not be presumed, must be confined implicitly to the case of villeins. It would, perhaps, be difficult to account for this singular deviation in the law of England, from the law of every other country upon the same subject. But it is enough for the present occasion, to know, that as *villenage* never existed in America, no part of the doctrine founded upon that condition can be applicable here. The contrary practice has, indeed, been universal, in America; and our practice is so strongly authorized by the civil law, from which this sort of domestic slavery is derived, and is, in itself, so consistent with the precepts of nature, that we must now consider it as the law of the land.

There is a case in 2 Salk. 666 *(Smith* v. *Browne),* which has not been mentioned at the bar, though it bears considerable relation to the present controversy. It was an action of *indebitatus assumpsit,* for a negro sold; and it was said by HOLT, Chief Justice, that a negro, by entering England, becomes free; but that a sale in Virginia, if properly laid, will support the action. Hence, we perceive, how solicitous the courts of that kingdom have been, on the one hand, to discountenance slavery in England; but, on the other hand, to do full justice to the sale, which, by the *lex loci,* was lawful in Virginia, where it was made.

It only remains to observe, that property in a negro may be obtained by a *bonâ fide* purchase, without deed.

Verdict for the defendant.

3

RECORDS OF THE FEDERAL CONVENTION

[*2:95; Madison, 23 July*]

Genl. Pinkney reminded the Convention that if the Committee should fail to insert some security to the Southern States agst. an emancipation of slaves, and taxes on exports, he shd. be bound by duty to his State to vote agst. their Report.—The appt. of a Come. as moved by Mr. Gerry. Agd. to nem. con.

[*2:220; Madison, 8 Aug.*]

Mr. King wished to know what influence the vote just passed was meant have on the succeeding part of the Report, concerning the admission of slaves into the rule of Representation. He could not reconcile his mind to the article if it was to prevent objections to the latter part. The admission of slaves was a most grating circumstance to his mind, & he believed would be so to a great part of the people of America. He had not made a strenuous opposition to it heretofore because he had hoped that this concession would have produced a readiness which had not been manifested, to strengthen the Genl. Govt. and to mark a full confidence in it. The Report under consideration had by the tenor of it, put an end to all these hopes. In two great points the hands of the Legislature were absolutely tied. The importation of slaves could not be prohibited—exports could not be taxed. Is this reasonable? What are the great objects of the Genl. System? 1. difence agst. foreign invasion. 2. agst. internal sedition. Shall all the States then be bound to defend each; & shall each be at liberty to introduce a weakness which will render defence more difficult? Shall one part of the U.S. be bound to defend another part, and that other part be at liberty not only to increase its own danger, but to withhold the compensation for the burden? If slaves are to be imported shall not the exports produced by their labor, supply a revenue the better to enable the Genl. Govt. to defend their Masters?—There was so much inequality & unreasonableness in all this, that the people of the Northern States could never be reconciled to it. No candid man could undertake to justify it to them. He had hoped that some accommodation wd. have taken place on this subject; that at least a time wd. have been limited for the importation of slaves. He never could agree to let them be imported without limitation & then be represented in the Natl. Legislature. Indeed he could so little persuade himself of the rectitude of such a practice, that he was not sure he could assent to it under any circumstances. At all events, either slaves should not be represented, or exports should be taxable.

Mr. Sherman regarded the slave-trade as iniquitous; but the point of representation having been Settled after much difficulty & deliberation, he did not think himself bound to make opposition; especially as the present article as amended did not preclude any arrangement whatever on that point in another place of the Report.

[*2:364; Madison, 21 Aug.*]

Mr L—Martin, proposed to vary the sect: 4. art VII so as to allow a prohibition or tax on the importation of slaves. 1. As five slaves are to be counted as 3 free men in the apportionment of Representatives; such a clause wd. leave an encouragement to this trafic. 2 slaves weakened one part of the Union which the other parts were bound to protect: the privilege of importing them was therefore unreasonable—3. it was inconsistent with the principles of the revolution and dishonorable to the American character to have such a feature in the Constitution.

Mr. Rutlidge did not see how the importation of slaves could be encouraged by this section. He was not apprehensive of insurrections and would readily exempt the other States from the obligation to protect the Southern against them.—Religion & humanity had nothing to do with this question—Interest alone is the governing principle with Nations—The true question at present is whether the Southn. States shall or shall not be parties to the Union. If the Northern States consult their interest, they will not oppose the increase of Slaves which will increase the commodities of which they will become the carriers.

Mr. Elseworth was for leaving the clause as it stands. let every State import what it pleases. The morality or wisdom of slavery are considerations belonging to the States themselves—What enriches a part enriches the whole, and the States are the best judges of their particular interest. The old confederation had not meddled with this point, and he did not see any greater necessity for bringing it within the policy of the new one:

Mr Pinkney. South Carolina can never receive the plan if it prohibits the slave trade. In every proposed extension of the powers of Congress, that State has expressly & watchfully excepted that of meddling with the importation of negroes. If the States be all left at liberty on this subject, S. Carolina may perhaps by degrees do of herself what is wished, as Virginia & Maryland have already done.

[*2:369; Madison, 22 Aug.*]

Art. VII sect 4. resumed. Mr. Sherman was for leaving the clause as it stands. He disapproved of the slave trade: yet as the States were now possessed of the right to import slaves, as the public good did not require it to be taken from them, & as it was expedient to have as few objections as possible to the proposed scheme of Government, he thought it best to leave the matter as we find it. He observed that the abolition of slavery seemed to be going on in the U. S. & that the good sense of the several States would probably by degrees compleat it. He urged on the Convention the necessity of despatching its business.

Col. Mason. This infernal trafic originated in the avarice of British Merchants. The British Govt. constantly checked the attempts of Virginia to put a stop to it. The present question concerns not the importing States alone but the whole Union. The evil of having slaves was experienced during the late war. Had slaves been treated as they might have been by the Enemy, they would have proved dangerous instruments in their hands. But their folly dealt by the slaves, as it did by the Tories. He mentioned the dangerous insurrections of the slaves in Greece and Sicily; and the instructions given by Cromwell to the Commissioners sent to Virginia, to arm the servants & slaves, in case other means of obtaining its submission should fail. Maryland & Virginia he said had already prohibited the importation of slaves expressly. N. Carolina had done the same in substance. All this would be in vain if S. Carolina & Georgia be at liberty to import. The Western people are already calling out for slaves for their new lands; and will fill that Country with slaves if they can be got thro' S. Carolina & Georgia. Slavery discourages arts & manufactures. The poor despise labor when performed by slaves. They prevent the immigration of Whites, who really enrich & strengthen a Country. They produce the most pernicious effect on manners. Every master of slaves is born a petty tyrant. They bring the judgment of heaven on a Country. As nations can not be rewarded or punished in the next world they must be in this. By an inevitable chain of causes & effects providence punishes national sins, by national calamities. He lamented that some of our Eastern brethren had from a lust of gain embarked in this nefarious traffic. As to the States being in possession of the Right to import, this was the case with many other rights, now to be properly given up. He held it essential in every point of view, that the Genl. Govt. should have power to prevent the increase of slavery.

Mr. Elsworth. As he had never owned a slave could not judge of the effects of slavery on character. He said however that if it was to be considered in a moral light we ought to go farther and free those already in the Country.—As slaves also multiply so fast in Virginia & Maryland that it is cheaper to raise than import them, whilst in the sickly rice swamps foreign supplies are necessary, if we go no farther than is urged, we shall be unjust towards S. Carolina & Georgia—Let us not intermeddle. As population increases; poor laborers will be so plenty as to render slaves useless. Slavery in time will not be a speck in our Country. Provision is already made in Connecticut for abolishing it. And the abolition has already taken place in Massachusetts. As to the danger of insurrections from foreign influence, that will become a motive to kind treatment of the slaves.

Mr. Pinkney—If slavery be wrong, it is justified by the example of all the world. He cited the case of Greece Rome & other antient States; the sanction given by France England, Holland & other modern States. In all ages one half of mankind have been slaves. If the S. States were let alone they will probably of themselves stop importations. He wd. himself as a Citizen of S. Carolina vote for it. An attempt to take away the right as proposed will produce serious objections to the Constitution which he wished to see adopted.

General Pinkney declared it to be his firm opinion that if himself & all his colleagues were to sign the Constitution & use their personal influence, it would be of no avail towards obtaining the assent of their Constituents. S. Carolina & Georgia cannot do without slaves. As to Virginia she will gain by stopping the importations. Her slaves will rise in value, & she has more than she wants. It would be unequal to require S. C. & Georgia to confederate on such unequal terms. He said the Royal assent before the Revolution had never been refused to S. Carolina as to Virginia. He contended that the importation of slaves would be for the interest of the whole Union. The more slaves, the more produce to employ the carrying trade; The more consumption also, and the more of this, the more of revenue for the common treasury. He admitted it to be reasonable that slaves should be dutied like other imports, but should consider a rejection of the clause as an exclusion of S. Carola from the Union.

Mr. Baldwin had conceived national objects alone to be before the Convention, not such as like the present were of a local nature. Georgia was decided on this point. That State has always hitherto supposed a Genl Governmt to be the pursuit of the central States who wished to have a vortex for every thing—that her distance would preclude her from equal advantage—& that she could not prudently purchase it by yielding national powers. From this it might be understood in what light she would view an attempt to abridge one of her favorite prerogatives. If left to herself, she may probably put a stop to the evil. As one ground for this conjecture, he took notice of the sect of which he said was a respectable class of people, who carryed their ethics beyond the mere *equality of men*, extending their humanity to the claims of the whole animal creation.

Mr. Wilson observed that if S. C. & Georgia were themselves disposed to get rid of the importation of slaves in a short time as had been suggested, they would never refuse to Unite because the importation might be prohibited. As the Section now stands all articles imported are to be taxed. Slaves alone are exempt. This is in fact a bounty on that article.

Mr. Gerry thought we had nothing to do with the conduct of the States as to Slaves, but ought to be careful not to give any sanction to it.

Mr. Dickenson considered it as inadmissible on every principle of honor & safety that the importation of slaves should be authorized to the States by the Constitution. The true question was whether the national happiness would be promoted or impeded by the importation, and this question ought to be left to the National Govt. not to the States particularly interested. If Engd. & France permit slavery, slaves are at the same time excluded from both those Kingdoms. Greece and Rome were made unhappy by their slaves. He could not believe that the Southn. States would refuse to confederate on the account apprehended; especially as the power was not likely to be immediately exercised by the Genl. Government.

Mr Williamson stated the law of N. Carolina on the subject, to wit that it did not directly prohibit the importation of slaves. It imposed a duty of £5. on each slave imported from Africa. £10. on each from elsewhere, & £50 on each from a State licensing manumission. He thought the S. States could not be members of the Union if the clause should be rejected, and that it was wrong to force any thing down, not absolutely necessary, and which any State must disagree to.

Mr. King thought the subject should be considered in a political light only. If two States will not agree to the Constitution as stated on one side, he could affirm with equal belief on the other, that great & equal opposition would be experienced from the other States. He remarked on the exemption of slaves from duty whilst every other import was subjected to it, as an inequality that could not fail to strike the commercial sagacity of the Northn. & middle States.

Mr. Langdon was strenuous for giving the power to the Genl. Govt. He cd. not with a good conscience leave it with the States who could then go on with the traffic, without being restrained by the opinions here given that they will themselves cease to import slaves.

Genl. Pinkney thought himself bound to declare candidly that he did not think S. Carolina would stop her importations of slaves in any short time, but only stop them occasionally as she now does. He moved to commit the clause that slaves might be made liable to an equal tax with other imports which he he thought right & wch. wd. remove one difficulty that had been started.

Mr. Rutlidge. If the Convention thinks that N. C; S. C. & Georgia will ever agree to the plan, unless their right to import slaves be untouched, the expectation is vain. The people of those States will never be such fools as to give up so important an interest. He was strenuous agst. striking out the Section, and seconded the motion of Genl. Pinkney for a commitment.

Mr Govr. Morris wished the whole subject to be committed including the clauses relating to taxes on exports & to a navigation act. These things may form a bargain among the Northern & Southern States.

Mr. Butler declared that he never would agree to the power of taxing exports.

Mr. Sherman said it was better to let the S. States import slaves than to part with them, if they made that a sine qua non. He was opposed to a tax on slaves imported as making the matter worse, because it implied they were *property*. He acknowledged that if the power of prohibiting the importation should be given to the Genl. Government that it would be exercised. He thought it would be its duty to exercise the power.

Mr. Read was for the commitment provided the clause concerning taxes on exports should also be committed.

Mr. Sherman observed that that clause had been agreed to & therefore could not committed.

Mr. Randolph was for committing in order that some middle ground might, if possible, be found. He could never agree to the clause as it stands. He wd. sooner risk the constitution—He dwelt on the dilemma to which the Convention was exposed. By agreeing to the clause, it would revolt the Quakers, the Methodists, and many others in the States having no slaves. On the other hand, two States might be lost to the Union. Let us then, he said, try the chance of a commitment.

On the question for committing the remaining part of Sect 4 & 5. of art: 7. N. H. no. Mas. abst. Cont. ay N. J. ay Pa. no. Del. no Maryd ay. Va ay. N. C. ay S. C. ay. Geo. ay. [Ayes—7; noes—3; absent—1.]

[*2:415; Madison, 25 Aug.*]

Genl Pinkney moved to strike out the words "the year eighteen hundred" as the year limiting the importation of slaves, and to insert the words "the year eighteen hundred and eight"

Mr. Ghorum 2ded. the motion

Mr. Madison. Twenty years will produce all the mischief that can be apprehended from the liberty to import slaves. So long a term will be more dishonorable to the National character than to say nothing about it in the Constitution.

On the motion; which passed in the affirmative.

N—H—ay. Mas. ay—Ct. ay. N. J. no. Pa. no. Del—no. Md. ay. Va. no. N—C. ay. S—C. ay. Geo. ay. [Ayes—7; noes—4.]

Mr. Govr. Morris was for making the clause read at once, "importation of slaves into N. Carolina, S—Carolina & Georgia". shall not be prohibited &c. This he said would be most fair and would avoid the ambiguity by which, under the power with regard to naturalization, the liberty reserved to the States might be defeated. He wished it to be known also that this part of the Constitution was a compliance with those States. If the change of language however should be objected to by the members from those States, he should not urge it.

Col: Mason was not against using the term "slaves" but agst naming N—C—S—C. & Georgia, lest it should give offence to the people of those States.

Mr Sherman liked a description better than the terms proposed, which had been declined by the old Congs & were not pleasing to some people. Mr. Clymer concurred with Mr. Sherman

Mr. Williamson said that both in opinion & practice he was, against slavery; but thought it more in favor of humanity, from a view of all circumstances, to let in S—C & Georgia on those terms, than to exclude them from the Union—

Mr. Govr. Morris withdrew his motion.

Mr. Dickenson wished the clause to be confined to the States which had not themselves prohibited the importation of slaves, and for that purpose moved to amend the clause so as to read "The importation of slaves into such of the States as shall permit the same shall not be prohibited by the Legislature of the U—S—until the year 1808".—which was disagreed to nem: cont:

The first part of the report was then agreed to, amended as follows. "The migration or importation of such persons as the several States now existing shall think proper to admit, shall not be prohibited by the Legislature prior to the year 1808."

N. H. Mas. Con. Md. N. C. S. C: Geo: . . . . . ay
N. J. Pa. Del. Virga . . . . no
[Ayes—7; noes—4.]

Mr. Baldwin in order to restrain & more explicitly define "the average duty" moved to strike out of the 2d. part the words "average of the duties laid on imports" and insert "common impost on articles not enumerated" which was agreed to nem: cont:

Mr. Sherman was agst. this 2d part, as acknowledging men to be property, by taxing them as such under the character of slaves,

Mr. King & Mr. Langdon considered this as the price of the 1st part.

Genl. Pinkney admitted that it was so.

Col: Mason. Not to tax, will be equivalent to a bounty on the importation of slaves.

Mr. Ghorum thought that Mr Sherman should consider the duty, not as implying that slaves are property, but as a discouragement to the importation of them.

Mr Govr, Morris remarked that as the clause now stands it implies that the Legislature may tax freemen imported.

Mr. Sherman in answer to Mr. Ghorum observed that the smallness of the duty shewed revenue to be the object, not the discouragement of the importation.

Mr. Madison thought it wrong to admit in the Constitution the idea that there could be property in men. The reason of duties did not hold, as slaves are not like merchandise, consumed. &c

Col. Mason (in answr. to Govr. Morris) the provision as it stands was necessary for the case of Convicts in order to prevent the introduction of them.

It was finally agreed nem: contrad: to make the clause read "but a tax or duty may be imposed on such importation not exceeding ten dollars for each person", and then the 2d. part as amended was agreed to.

4

Tench Coxe, An Examination of the Constitution
Fall 1787
Pamphlets 146

The importation of slaves from any foreign country is, by a clear implication, held up to the world as equally inconsistent with the dispositions and the duties of the people of America. A solid foundation is laid for exploding the principles of negro slavery, in which many good men of all parties in Pennsylvania, and throughout the union, have already concurred. The temporary reservation of any particular matter must ever be deemed an admission that it should be done away. This appears to have been well understood. In addition to the arguments drawn from liberty, justice and religion, opinions against this practice, founded in sound policy, have no doubt been urged. Regard was necessarily paid to the peculiar situation of our southern fellow-citizens; but they on the other hand, have not been insensible of the delicate situation of our national character on this subject.

5

A Federal Republican
28 Oct. 1787
Storing 3.6.22

The next thing which we proceed to, is the importation of slaves, contained in the ninth section of the first article. It says, that "the migration or importation of such persons as any of the states now existing shall think proper to admit, shall not be prohibited by Congress prior to the year 1808, but a tax or duty may be imposed upon such importation, not exceeding ten dollars for each person." ["]The truth is, (says a citizen of America) Congress cannot prohibit the importation of slaves during that period; but the laws against the importation of them into any particular state stand unrepealed. An immediate abolition of slavery would be ruin upon the whites and misery upon the blacks in the southern states. The constitution therefore hath wisely left each state to pursue its own measures with respect to this article of legislation during the period of twenty one years." That the importation of slaves shall not be forbidden till that time may be very wise—but what hath that to do with the abolition of slavery? To prohibit the importation of slaves is not to abolish slavery. For all that is contained in this constitution, this country may remain degraded by this impious custom till the end of time.

6

James Wilson, Pennsylvania Ratifying Convention
3–4 Dec. 1787
Elliot 2:451–53, 484–86

[*3 Dec.*]

Much fault has been found with the mode of expression used in the 1st clause of the 9th section of the 1st article. I believe I can assign a reason why that mode of expression was used, and why the term *slave* was *not* admitted in this *Constitution;* and as to the manner of laying taxes, this is not the first time that the subject has come into the view of the United States, and of the legislatures of the several states. The gentleman, (Mr. Findley) will recollect that, in the present Congress, the quota of the federal debt, and general expenses, was to be in proportion to the value of land, and other enumerated property, within states. After trying this for a number of years, it was found, on all hands, to be a mode that could not be carried into execution. Congress were satisfied of this; and, in the year 1783, recommended, in conformity with the powers they possessed under the Articles of Confederation, that the quota should be according to the number of free people, including those bound to servitude, and excluding Indians not taxed. These were the expressions used in 1783; and the fate of this recommendation was similar to all their other resolutions. It was not carried into effect, but it was adopted by no fewer than eleven out of thirteen states; and it cannot but be matter of surprise to hear gentlemen, who agreed to this very mode of expression at that time, come forward and state it as an objection on the present occasion. It was natural, sir, for the late Convention to adopt the mode after it had been agreed to by eleven states, and to use the expression which they found had been received as unexceptionable before.

With respect to the clause restricting Congress from prohibiting the *migration or importation of such persons* as any of the states now existing shall think proper to admit, prior to the year 1808, the honorable gentleman says that this clause is not only dark, but intended to grant to Congress, for that time, the power to admit the importation of *slaves.* No such thing was intended. But I will tell you what was done, and it gives me high pleasure that so much was done. Under the present Confederation, the states may admit the importation of slaves as long as they please; but by this article, after the year 1808, the Congress will have power to prohibit such importation, notwithstanding the disposition of any state to the contrary. I consider this as laying the foundation for banishing slavery out of this country; and though the period is more distant than I could wish, yet it will produce the same kind, gradual change, which was pursued in Pennsylvania. It is with much satisfaction I view this power in the general government, whereby they may lay an interdiction on this reproachful trade: but an immediate advantage is also obtained; for a tax or duty may be imposed on such importation, not exceeding ten dollars for each person; and this, sir, operates as a partial prohibition; it was all that could be obtained. I am sorry it was no more; but from this I think there is reason to hope, that yet a few years, and it will be prohibited altogether; and in the mean time, the *new* states which are to be formed will be under *the control* of Congress in this particular, and slaves will never be introduced amongst them. The gentleman says that it is unfortunate in another point of view: it means to prohibit the introduction of white people from Europe, as this tax may deter them from coming amongst us. A little impartiality and attention will discover the care that the Convention took in selecting their language. The words are, "the migration or importation of such persons, &c., shall not be prohibited by Congress prior to the year 1808, but a tax or duty may be imposed on such importation." It is observable here that the term *migration* is dropped, when a tax or duty is mentioned, so that Congress have power to impose the tax only on those imported.

[*4 Dec.*]

I recollect, on a former day, the honorable gentleman from Westmoreland, (Mr. Findley,) and the honorable gentleman from Cumberland, (Mr. Whitehill,) took exceptions against the 1st clause of the 9th sect., art. 1, arguing, very unfairly, that, because Congress might impose a tax or duty of ten dollars on the importation of slaves, within any of the United States, Congress might therefore permit slaves to be imported within this state, contrary to its laws. I confess, I little thought that this part of the system would be excepted to.

I am sorry that it could be extended no farther; but so far as it operates, it presents us with the pleasing prospect that the rights of mankind will be acknowledged and established throughout the Union.

If there was no other lovely feature in the Constitution but this one, it would diffuse a beauty over its whole countenance. Yet the lapse of a few years, and Congress will have power to exterminate slavery from within our borders.

How would such a delightful prospect expand the breast of a benevolent and philanthropic European! Would he cavil at an expression? catch at a phrase? No, sir, that is only reserved for the gentleman on the other side of your chair to do. What would be the exultation of that great man [Necker], whose name I have just now mentioned, we may learn from the following sentiments on this subject; they cannot be expressed so well as in his own words (vol. 1, page 329.)

> "The colonies of France contain, as we have seen, near five hundred thousand slaves; and it is from the number of these wretches the inhabitants set a value on their plantations. What a fatal prospect, and how profound a subject for reflection! Alas! how inconsequent we are, both in our morality and our principles! We preach up humanity, and yet go every year to bind in chains twenty thousand natives of Africa. We call the Moors barbarians and ruffians, because they attack the liberty of Europeans at the risk of their own; yet these Europeans go, without danger, and as mere speculators, to purchase slaves, by gratifying the cupidity of their masters, and excite all those bloody scenes which are the usual preliminaries of this traffic! In short, we pride ourselves on the superiority of man, and it is with reason that we discover this superiority in the wonderful and mysterious unfolding of the intellectual faculties; and yet the trifling difference in the hair of the head, or in the color of the epidermis, is sufficient to change our respect into contempt, and to engage us to place beings like ourselves in the rank of those animals devoid of reason, whom we subject to the yoke, that we may make use of their strength and of their instinct at command.
>
> "I am sensible, and I grieve at it, that these reflections, which others have made much better than I, are unfortunately of very little use! The necessity of supporting sovereign power has its peculiar laws, and the wealth of nations is one of the foundations of this power: thus the sovereign who should be the most thoroughly convinced of what is due to humanity, would not singly renounce the service of slaves in his colonies: time alone could furnish a population of free people to replace them, and the great difference that would exist in the price of labor would give so great an advantage to the nation that should adhere to the old custom, that the others would soon be discouraged in wishing to be more virtuous. And yet, would it be a chimerical project to propose a general compact, by which all the European nations should unanimously agree to abandon the traffic of African slaves! they would, in that case, find themselves exactly in the same proportion, relative to each other, as at present; for it is only on comparative riches that the calculations of power are founded.
>
> "We cannot as yet indulge such hopes; statesmen in general think that every common idea must be a low one; and since the morals of private people stand in need of being curbed and maintained by the laws, we ought not to wonder if those of sovereigns conform to their independence.
>
> "The time may nevertheless arrive, when, fatigued of that ambition which agitates them, and of the continual rotation of the same anxieties and the same plans, they may turn their views to the great principles of humanity; and if the present generation is to be witness of this happy revolution, they may at least be allowed to be unanimous in offering up their vows for the perfection of the social virtues, and for the progress of public beneficial institutions."

These are the enlarged sentiments of that great man.

7

A Countryman
13 Dec. 1787

Storing 6.7.5–6

There is another thing, in this new constitution, that my neighbour and me, have talked a good deal about; it is what is called in the writings you sent me, article 9th, section 1st. Indeed, we hardly know what they will be at by this; for fear you should mistake me, I believe I had better write it down; they say, "the migration, or importation of such persons, as any of the states now existing shall think proper to admit, shall not be prohibited by the congress, prior to the year 1808, but a tax, or duty may be imposed on such importation, not exceeding ten dollars for each person."

Now we think it very hard, if that is their meaning, that they should make every man, that comes from the old countries here, pay ten dollars to the new government. A great many of us, have our relations in the North of Ireland, and other places, that were very good friends to us all the war, and gave a great deal of trouble to the British, and I believe, partly upon our accounts, who might wish to come and settle here, among us; and I am sure they would be of great service to us, but do not you think it would be a hard matter for them to pay for their passages, besides their other expences, ten hard dollars for themselves, and each person in their families, when they get to this country. But our old neighbour from Pennsylvania, says, that it is thought among them, to mean worse than this, that its true meaning, is to give leave to import negroes from Guinea, for slaves, to work upon the rich men's plantations, to the southward; but that it is not mentioned plainly on purpose, because the quakers, and a great many other good religious people, are very much against making slaves of our fellow-creatures, and especially, against suffering any more to be brought into the country, and this, if it was known, might make them all against the new government: now, if this is really the case, it is to be sure, much worse than my neighbour and me first thought it to be; for all good christians must agree, that this trade is an abomination to the Lord, and must, if continued, bring down a heavy judgment upon our land. It does not seem to be justice, that one man should take another from his own country, and make a slave of him; and yet we are told by this new constitution, that one of its great ends, is to establish justice; alas! my worthy friend, it is a serious thing to trifle with the great God; his punishments are slow, but always sure; and the cunning of men, however deep, cannot escape them. I well remember, that our congress (and I believe, as I mentioned before, that they were honest, good men who meant as they said) when they declared independence, solemnly said, that "all men were created equal; and that they were endowed by their creator with certain unalienable rights; and that among them, are these, life, liberty, and the pursuit of happiness." They also talked much about the sacredness of a trial by jury; and complained loudly, that the old government tried to hinder the peopleing of this country, by discourageing people to come here from the old countries; and for these, and other causes, they went to war, after making a solemn appeal to God, for the rectitude of their intentions; and even the infidel must confess, that God was remarkably with us, watched over us in the hour of danger, fought our battles, and subdued our enemies, and finally gave us success. Alas! my good friend, it is a terrible thing to mock the almighty, for how can we expect to merit his favor, or escape his vengeance; if it should appear, that we were not serious in our professions, and that they were mere devices to gratify our pride and ambition, we ought to remember, he sees into the secret recesses of our hearts, and knows what is passing there. It becomes us then to bear testimony against every thing which may be displeasing in his sight, and be careful that we incur not the charge mentioned by the prophet Hosea, "ye have plowed wickedness, ye have reaped iniquity; ye have eaten the fruit of lies, because thou didst trust in thy ways, in the multitude of thy mighty men."

8

LUTHER MARTIN, GENUINE INFORMATION
1788

Storing 2.4.63–71

By the *ninth* section of this article, the importation of such persons as any of the States now existing, shall think proper to admit, shall not be prohibited prior to the year one thousand eight hundred and eight, but a duty may be imposed on such importation not exceeding ten dollars for each person.

The design of this clause is to prevent the general government from prohibiting the importation of slaves, but the same reasons which caused them to strike out the word *"national,"* and not admit the word *"stamps,"* influenced them here to guard against the word *"slaves."* They anxiously sought to avoid the admission of expressions which might be odious in the ears of Americans, although they were willing to admit into their system those *things* which the *expressions* signified: And hence it is, that the clause is so worded, as really to authorise the general government to impose a duty of ten dollars on every foreigner who comes into a State to become a citizen, whether he comes *absolutely free,* or *qualifiedly* so as a servant; although this is contrary to the design of the framers, and the duty was only meant to extend to the importation of *slaves.*

This clause was the subject of a great diversity of sentiment in the convention;—as the system was reported by the committee of detail, the provision was general, that such importation should not be prohibited, without confining it to any particular period. This was rejected by eight States—Georgia, South-Carolina, and I think North-Carolina voting for it.

We were then told by the delegates of the two first of those States, that their States would never agree to a system which put it in the power of the general government to prevent the importation of slaves, and that they, as delegates from those States, must withhold their assent from such a system.

A committee of one member from each State was chosen by ballot, to take this part of the system under their consideration, and to endeavour to agree upon some report, which should reconcile those States; to this committee also was referred the following proposition, which had been reported by the committee of detail, to wit, "No *navigation act* shall be passed without the assent of *two thirds* of the members present in each house;" a proposition which the *staple* and *commercial* States were solicitous to *retain,* lest their *commerce* should be placed too much under the power of the *eastern* States, but which these last States were as anxious to *reject.*—This committee, of which also I had the honour to be a member, met and took under their consideration the subjects committed to them; I found the *eastern* States, notwithstanding their *aversion to slavery,* were very willing to indulge the southern States, at least with a temporary liberty to prosecute the *slave trade,* provided the southern States would in their turn gratify them, by laying no *restriction* on *navigation acts;* and after a very little time, the committee by a great majority, agreed on a report, by which the general government was to be prohibited from preventing the importation of slaves for a limited time, and the restrictive clause relative to navigation acts was to be omitted.

This report was adopted by a majority of the convention, but not without considerable opposition.—It was said, that we had but just assumed a place among independent nations, in consequence of our opposition to the attempts of Great-Britain to *enslave us;* that this opposition was grounded upon the *preservation* of *those rights,* to which God and Nature had entitled *us,* not in *particular,* but in *common* with *all the rest of mankind*—That we had *appealed* to the *Supreme being* for his *assistance,* as the *God of freedom,* who could not but *approve* our efforts to preserve the *rights* which he had thus *imparted to his creatures;* that now, when we scarcely had risen from our *knees,* from *supplicating* his *aid* and *protection*—in *forming our government* over *a free peo-*

ple, a government formed pretendedly on the *principles* of *liberty* and for *its preservation,*—in *that* government to have a provision, not only putting it out *of its power* to *restrain* and *prevent* the *slave trade,* but *even encouraging that most infamous traffic,* by giving the *States power* and *influence* in the *union, in proportion* as they *cruelly and wantonly sport with the rights of their fellow creatures,* ought to be considered as a *solemn mockery of,* and *insult to, that God* whose protection we had then implored, and could not fail to hold us up in *detestation,* and render us *contemptible* to every *true friend* of liberty in the world. It was said, it ought to be considered that *national* crimes can *only be,* and *frequently are, punished* in this world by *national punishments,* and that the *continuance* of the slave trade, and thus giving it a *national sanction* and *encouragement,* ought to be considered as *justly exposing* us to the *displeasure* and *vengeance* of *Him,* who is equal Lord of all, and who views with equal eye, the poor *African slave* and his *American master!*

It was urged, that by this system, we were giving the general government full and absolute power to regulate commerce, under which general power it would have a right to *restrain, or totally prohibit* the *slave trade:* it must therefore, appear to the world absurd and disgraceful to the last degree, that we should *except* from the exercise of that power, the *only branch* of *commerce* which is *unjustifiable in its nature,* and *contrary* to the *rights* of *mankind*—That on the contrary, we ought *rather to prohibit expressly* in our *constitution,* the *further importation* of *slaves;* and to *authorise* the general government from time to time, to make such regulations as should be thought most advantageous for the *gradual abolition* of *slavery,* and the *emancipation* of the *slaves* which are already in the States.

That *slavery* is *inconsistent* with the *genius* of *republicanism,* and has a tendency to *destroy* those *principles* on which it is *supported,* as it *lessens the sense* of the *equal rights* of *mankind,* and habituates us to *tyranny* and *oppression.* It was further urged, that by this system of government, every State is to be protected both from *foreign invasion* and from *domestic insurrections;* that from this consideration, it was of the *utmost importance* it should have a power to restrain the importation of slaves, since in proportion as the number of slaves were increased in any State, in the same proportion the State is *weakened* and *exposed* to foreign invasion, or domestic insurrection, and by *so much the less* will it be able to protect itself against *either;* and therefore will by so much the more, want aid from, and be a burthen to, the union. It was further said, that as in this system we were giving the general government a power under the idea of national character, or national interest, to regulate even our *weights* and *measures,* and have prohibited all possibility of *emitting paper money,* and *passing instalment laws, &c.* It must appear still more extraordinary, that we should prohibit the government from interfering with the slave trade, than which *nothing* could so *materially affect* both our *national honour* and *interest.*—These reasons influenced me both on the committee and in convention, most decidedly to oppose and vote against the clause, as it now makes a part of the system.

You will perceive, Sir, not only that the general government is prohibited from interfering in the slave trade *before* the year eighteen hundred and eight, but that there is no provision in the constitution that it shall *afterwards* be prohibited, nor any security that such prohibition will ever take place; and I think there is great reason to believe, that if the importation of slaves is permitted until the year eighteen hundred and eight, it will not be prohibited afterwards: At *this time* we do not generally hold this commerce in so *great* abhorrence as we have done—When our liberties were at stake, we *warmly* felt for the *common rights of men*—The danger being thought to be past, which threatened ourselves, we are daily growing *more insensible* to those rights—In those States who have restrained or prohibited the importation of slaves, it is only done by legislative acts which may be repealed—When those States find that they must in their *national character* and *connexion* suffer in the *disgrace,* and share in the *inconveniencies* attendant upon that detestable and iniquitous traffic, they may be desirous also to share in the *benefits* arising from it, and the odium attending it will be greatly effaced by the sanction which is given to it in the general government.

9

JOSHUA ATHERTON, NEW HAMPSHIRE RATIFYING CONVENTION
1788
Elliot 2:203–4

Mr. President, I cannot be of the opinion of the honorable gentlemen who last spoke, that this paragraph is either so useful or so inoffensive as they seem to imagine, or that the objections to it are so totally void of foundation. The idea that strikes those, who are opposed to this clause, so disagreeably and so forcibly, is, hereby it is conceived (if we ratify the Constitution) that we become *consenters to,* and *partakers in,* the sin and guilt of this abominable traffic, at least for a certain period, without any positive stipulation that it should even then be brought to an end. We do not behold in it that valuable acquisition so much boasted of by the honorable member from Portsmouth, *"that an end is then to be put to slavery."* Congress may be as much, or more, puzzled to put a stop to it then, than we are now. The clause has not secured its abolition.

We do not think ourselves under any obligation to perform works of supererogation in the reformation of mankind; we do not esteem ourselves under any necessity to go to Spain or Italy to suppress the inquisition of those countries; or of making a journey to the Carolinas to abolish the detestable custom of enslaving the Africans; but, sir, we will not lend the aid of our ratification to this cruel and inhuman merchandise, not even for a day. There is a great distinction in not taking a part in the most barbarous violation of the sacred laws of God and humanity, and our becoming guaranties for its exercise for a term of years. Yes, sir, it is our full purpose to wash our hands clear of it; and, however unconcerned spectators we may remain of such predatory infractions of the laws of our nature, however unfeelingly we may subscribe to the ratification of manstealing, with all its baneful consequences, yet I cannot but believe, in justice to human nature, that, if we reserve the consideration, and bring this claimed power somewhat nearer to our own doors, we shall form a more equitable opinion of its claim to this ratification. Let us figure to ourselves a company of these manstealers, well equipped for the enterprise, arriving on our coast. They seize and carry off the whole or a part of the inhabitants of the town of Exeter. Parents are taken, and children left; or possibly they may be so fortunate as to have a whole family taken and carried off together by these relentless robbers. What must be their feelings in the hands of their new and arbitrary masters? Dragged at once from every thing they held dear to them—stripped of every comfort of life, like beasts of prey—they are hurried on a loathsome and distressing voyage to the coast of Africa, or some other quarter of the globe, where the greatest price may await them; and here, if any thing can be added to their miseries, comes on the heart-breaking scene! A parent is sold to one, a son to another, and a daughter to a third! Brother is cleft from brother, sister from sister, and parents from their darling offspring! Broken with every distress that human nature can feel, and bedewed with tears of anguish, they are dragged into the last stage of depression and slavery, never, never to behold the faces of one another again! The scene is too affecting. I have not fortitude to pursue the subject!

10

DEBATE IN SOUTH CAROLINA HOUSE OF REPRESENTATIVES
16–17 Jan. 1788
Elliot 4:272–73, 285–86

[*16 Jan.*]

[Mr. LOWNDES . . .] In the first place, what cause was there for jealousy of our importing negroes? Why confine us to twenty years, or rather why limit us at all? For his part, he thought this trade could be justified on the principles of religion, humanity, and justice; for certainly to translate a set of human beings from a bad country to a better, was fulfilling every part of these principles. But they don't like our slaves, because they have none themselves, and therefore want to exclude us from this great advantage. Why should the Southern States allow of this, without the consent of nine states?

Judge PENDLETON observed, that only three states, Georgia, South Carolina, and North Carolina, allowed the importation of negroes. Virginia had a clause in her Constitution for this purpose, and Maryland, he believed, even before the war, prohibited them.

Mr. LOWNDES continued—that we had a law prohibiting the importation of negroes for three years, a law he greatly approved of; but there was no reason offered why the Southern States might not find it necessary to alter their conduct, and open their ports. Without negroes, this state would degenerate into one of the most contemptible in the Union: and he cited an expression that fell from General Pinckney on a former debate, that whilst there remained one acre of swamp-land in South Carolina, he should raise his voice against restricting the importation of negroes. Even in granting the importation for twenty years, care had been taken to make us pay for this indulgence, each negro being liable, on importation, to pay a duty not exceeding ten dollars; and, in addition to this, they were liable to a capitation tax. Negroes were our wealth, our only natural resource; yet behold how our kind friends in the north were determined soon to tie up our hands, and drain us of what we had! The Eastern States drew their means of subsistence, in a great measure, from their shipping; and, on that head, they had been particularly careful not to allow of any burdens: they were not to pay tonnage or duties; no, not even the form of clearing out: all ports were free and open to them! Why, then, call this a reciprocal bargain, which took all from one party, to bestow it on the other!

Major BUTLER observed, that they were to pay five per cent. impost.

This, Mr. LOWNDES proved, must fall upon the consumer. They are to be the carriers; and, we being the consumers, therefore all expenses would fall upon us. A great number of gentlemen were captivated with this new Constitution, because those who were in debt would be compelled to pay; others pleased themselves with the reflection that no more confiscation laws would be passed; but those were small advantages, in proportion to the evils that might be apprehended from the laws that might be passed by Congress, whenever there was a majority of representatives from the Eastern States, who were governed by prejudices and ideas extremely different from ours.

[*17 Jan.*]

Gen. C. C. PINCKNEY: . . . The general then said he would make a few observations on the objections which the gentleman had thrown out on the restrictions that might be laid on the African trade after the year 1808. On this point your delegates had to contend with the religious and political prejudices of the Eastern and Middle States, and with the interested and inconsistent opinion of Virginia, who was warmly opposed to our importing more slaves. I am of the same opinion now as I was two years ago, when I used the expressions the gentleman has quoted—that, while there remained one acre of swamp-land uncleared of South Carolina, I would raise my voice against restricting the importation of negroes. I am as thoroughly convinced as that gentleman is, that the nature of our climate, and the flat, swampy situation of our country, obliges us to cultivate our lands with negroes, and that without them South Carolina would soon be a desert waste.

You have so frequently heard my sentiments on this subject, that I need not now repeat them. It was alleged, by some of the members who opposed an unlimited importation, that slaves increased the weakness of any state who admitted them; that they were a dangerous species of property, which an invading enemy could easily turn against ourselves and the neighboring states; and that, as we were allowed a representation for them in the House of Representatives, our influence in government would be increased in proportion as we were less able to defend ourselves. "Show some period," said the members from the Eastern States, "when it may be in our power to put a stop, if we please, to the importation of this weakness, and we will endeavor, for your convenience, to restrain the religious and political prejudices of our people on this subject." The Middle States and Virginia made us no such proposition; they were for an immediate and total prohibition. We endeavored to obviate the objections that were made in the best manner we could, and assigned reasons for our insisting on the importation, which there is no occasion to repeat, as they must occur to every gentleman in the house: a committee of the states was appointed in order to accommodate this matter, and, after a great deal of difficulty, it was settled on the footing recited in the Constitution.

By this settlement we have secured an unlimited importation of negroes for twenty years. Nor is it declared that the importation shall be then stopped; it may be continued. We have a security that the general government can never emancipate them, for no such authority is granted; and it is admitted, on all hands, that the general government has no powers but what are expressly granted by the Constitution, and that all rights not expressed were reserved by the several states. We have obtained a right to recover our slaves in whatever part of America they may take refuge, which is a right we had not before. In short, considering all circumstances, we have made the best terms for the security of this species of property it was in our power to make. We would have made better if we could; but, on the whole, I do not think them bad.

11

DEBATE IN MASSACHUSETTS RATIFYING CONVENTION
18, 25–26, 30 Jan. 1788
Elliot 2:40–41, 107–8, 115–16

[*18 Jan.*]

MR. DAWES said, he was very sorry to hear so many objections raised against the paragraph under consideration. He thought them wholly unfounded; that the *black inhabitants* of the Southern States must be considered either as slaves, and as so much *property*, or in the character of so many freemen; if the former, why should they not be wholly represented? Our own state laws and constitution would lead us to consider these blacks as freemen, and so indeed would our own ideas of natural justice. If, then, they are freemen, they might form an equal basis for representation as though they were all white inhabitants. In either view, therefore, he could not see that the Northern States would suffer, but directly to the contrary. He thought, however, that gentlemen would do well to connect the passage in dispute with another article in the Constitution, that permits Congress, in the year 1808, wholly to prohibit the importation of slaves, and in the mean time to impose a duty of ten dollars a head on such blacks as should be imported before that period. Besides, by the new Constitution, every particular state is left to its own option totally to prohibit the introduction of slaves into its own territories. What could the Convention do more? The members of the Southern States, like ourselves, have *their* prejudices. It would not do to abolish slavery, by an act of Congress, in a moment, and so destroy what our southern brethren consider as property. But we may say, that, although slavery is not smitten by an apoplexy, yet it has received a mortal wound, and will die of a consumption.

[*25 Jan.*]

MR. NEAL (from Kittery) went over the ground of objection to this section, on the idea that the slave trade was allowed to be continued for twenty years. His profession, he said, obliged him to bear witness against any thing that should favor the making merchandise of the bodies of men, and, unless his objection was removed, he could not put his hand to the Constitution. Other gentlemen said, in addition to this idea, that there was not even a proposition that the negroes ever shall be free; and Gen. THOMPSON exclaimed, Mr. President, shall it be said that, after we have established our own independence and freedom, we make *slaves* of others? O! Washington, what a name has he had! How he has immortalized himself! But he holds those in slavery who have as good a right to be free as he has. He is still for self; and, in my opinion, his character has sunk fifty per cent.

On the other side, gentlemen said, that the step taken in this article towards the abolition of slavery was one of the beauties of the Constitution. They observed, that in the Confederation there was no provision whatever for its being abolished; but this Constitution provides that Congress may, after twenty years, totally annihilate the slave trade; and that, as all the states, except two, have passed laws to this effect, it might reasonably be expected that it would then be done. In the interim, all the states were at liberty to prohibit it.

[*26 Jan.*]

[The debate on the 9th section still continued desultory, and consisted of similar objections, and answers thereto, as had before been used. Both sides deprecated the slave trade in the most pointed terms; on one side, it was most pathetically lamented by Mr. Nason, Major Lusk, Mr. Neal, and others, that this Constitution provided for the continuation of the slave trade for twenty years; and on the other, the Hon. Judge Dana, Mr. Adams, and others, rejoiced that a door was now to be opened for the annihilation of this odious, abhorrent practice, in a certain time.]

[*30 Jan.*]

Gen. HEATH . . . The paragraph respecting the migration or importation of such persons as any of the states now existing shall think proper to admit, &c., is one of those considered during my absence, and I have heard nothing on the subject, save what has been mentioned this morning; but I think the gentlemen who have spoken have carried the matter rather too far on both sides. I apprehend that it is not in our power to do any thing for or against those who are in slavery in the Southern States. No gentleman, within these walls, detests every idea of slavery more than I do: it is generally detested by the people of this commonwealth; and I ardently hope that the time will soon come when our brethren in the Southern States will view it as we do, and put a stop to it; but to this we have no right to compel them. Two questions naturally arise: If we ratify the Constitution, shall we do any thing by our act to hold the blacks in slavery? or shall we become the partakers of other men's sins? I think, neither of them. Each state is sovereign and independent to a certain degree, and the states have a right, and they will regulate their own internal affairs as to themselves appears proper; and shall we refuse to eat, or to drink, or to be united, with those who do not think, or act, just as we do? Surely not. We are not, in this case, partakers of other men's sins; for in nothing do we voluntarily encourage the slavery of our fellowmen. A restriction is laid on the federal government, which could not be avoided, and a union take place. The federal Convention went as far as they could. The migration or importation, &c., is confined to the states now *existing only;* new states cannot claim it. Congress, by their ordinance for erecting new states, some time since, declared that the new states shall be republican, and that there shall be no slavery in them. But whether those in slavery in the Southern States will be emancipated after the year 1808, I do not pretend to determine. I rather doubt it.

12

JAMES MADISON, FEDERALIST, NO. 42, 281–82
22 Jan. 1788

It were doubtless to be wished that the power of prohibiting the importation of slaves, had not been postponed until the year 1808, or rather that it had been suffered to have immediate operation. But it is not difficult to account either for this restriction on the general government, or for the manner in which the whole clause is expressed. It ought to be considered as a great point gained in favor of humanity, that a period of twenty years may terminate for ever within these States, a traffic which has so long and so loudly upbraided the barbarism of modern policy; that within that period it will receive a considerable discouragement from the foederal Government, and may be totally abolished by a concurrence of the few States which continue the unnatural traffic, in the prohibitory example which has been given by so great a majority of the Union. Happy would it be for the unfortunate Africans, if an equal prospect lay before them, of being redeemed from the oppressions of their European brethren! Attempts have been made to pervert this clause into an objection against the Constitution, by representing it on one side as a criminal toleration of an illicit practice, and on another, as calculated to prevent voluntary and beneficial emigrations from Europe to America. I mention these misconstructions, not with a view to give them an answer, for they deserve none; but as specimens of the manner and spirit in which some have thought fit to conduct their opposition to the proposed government.

13

CONSIDER ARMS, MALICHI MAYNARD, AND SAMUEL FIELD, REASONS FOR DISSENT
16 Apr. 1788

Storing 4.26.8–14

But we pass on to another thing, which (aside from every other consideration) was, and still is an insuperable objection in the way of our assent. This we find in the 9th section under the head of restrictions upon Congress, viz. "The migration or importation of such persons as any of the states now existing shall think proper to admit, shall not be prohibited by the Congress, prior to the year one thousand eight hundred and eight," &c. It was not controverted in the Convention, but owned that this provision was made purely that the southern states might not be deprived of their profits arising from that most *nefarious* trade of enslaving the Africans. The hon. Mr. King himself, who was an assistant in forming this constitution, in discoursing upon the slave trade, in the late Convention at Boston, was pleased to design it by this epithet, *nefarious,* which carries with it the idea of something peculiarly wicked and abominable: and indeed we think it deserving of this and every odious epithet which our language affords, descriptive of the iniquity of it. This being the case, we were naturally led to enquire why we should establish a constitution, which gives licence to a measure of this sort—How is it possible we could do it consistent with our ideas of government consistent with the principles and documents we endeavour to inculcate upon others? It is a standing law in the kingdom of Heaven. "Do unto others as ye would have others do unto you." This is the royal law—this we often hear inculcated upon others. But had we given our affirmative voice in this case, could we have claimed to ourselves that consistent line of conduct, which marks the path of every honest man? Should we not rather have been guilty of a contumelious repugnancy, to what we profess to believe is equitable and just? Let us for once bring the matter home to ourselves, and summon up our own feelings upon the occasion, and hear the simple sober verdict of our own hearts, were we in the place of those unhappy Africans—this is the test, the proper *touch-stone* by which to try the matter before us. Where is the man, who under the influence of sober dispassionate reasoning, and not void of natural affection, can lay his hand upon his heart and say, I am willing my sons and my daughters should be torn from me and doomed to perpetual slavery? We presume that man is not to be found amongst us: And yet we think the consequence is fairly drawn, that this is what every man ought so be able to say, who voted for this constitution. But we dare say this will never be the case here, so long as the country has power to repel force by force. Notwithstanding this we will practice this upon those who are destitute of the power of repulsion: from whence we conclude it is not the tincture of a skin, or any disparity of features that are necessarily connected with slavery, and possibly may therefore fall to the lot of some who voted it, to have the same measure measured unto them which they have measured unto others. If we could once make it our own case, we should soon discover what distress & anxiety, what poignant feelings it would produce in our own breasts, to have our infants torn from the bosoms of their tender mothers—indeed our children of all ages, from infancy to manhood, arrested from us by a banditti of lawless ruffians, in defiance of all the laws of humanity, and carried to a country far distant, without any hopes of their return—attended likewise with the curring reflection, that they were likely to undergo all those indignities, those miseries, which are the usual concomitants of slavery. Indeed when we consider the depredations committed in Africa, the cruelties exercised towards the poor captivated inhabitants of that country on their passage to this—crowded by droves into the holds of ships, suffering what might naturally be expected would result from scanty provisions, and inelastic infectious air, and after their arrival, drove like brutes from market to market, *branded* on their naked *bodies* with *hot irons*, with the initial letters of their masters names—fed upon the entrails of beasts like swine in the slaughter-yard of a butcher; and many other barbarities, of which we have documents well authenticated: then put to the hardest of labour, and to perform the vilest of drudges—their master (or rather *usurpers*) by far less kind and benevolent to them, than to their horses and their hounds. We say, when we consider these things (the recollection of which gives us pain) conscience applauds the dicision we have made, and we feel that satisfaction which arises from acting agreeable to its dictates. When we hear those barbarities pled for—When we see them voted for, (as in the late Convention at Boston) when we see them practised by those who denominate themselves Christians, we are presented with something truely *heterogeneous*—something *monstrous* indeed! Can we suppose this line of conduct keeps pace with the rule of right? Do such practices coincide with the plain and simple ideas of government before-mentioned? By no means. We could wish it might be kept in mind, that the very notion of government is to protect men in the enjoyment of those privileges to which they have a natural, therefore an indefeasible right; and not to be made an engine of rapine, robbery and murder. This is but establishing inequity, by law founded on usurpation. Establishing this constitution is, in our opinion establishing the most ignominious kind of theft, man-stealing, and so heinous and agrivated was this crime considered, by ONE who cannot err, that under the Jewish theocracy it was punished with death. Indeed what can shew men scarcely more hardened, than being guilty of this crime? For there is *nothing else* they will stick at in order to perpetrate this.

The question therefore—Why should we vote for the establishment of this system? recoils upon us armed with treple force—force which sets at defiance, the whole power of sophistry, employed for the defence of those, who by a "cursed thirst for gold," are prompted on to actions, which cast an indelible stain upon the character of the human species—actions at which certain quadrupeds, were they possessed of Organs for the purpose, would discover a BLUSH.

But we were told by an honourable gentleman who was one of the framers of this Constitution, that the two southernmost states, absolutely refused to confederate at all, except they might be gratified in this article. What then? Was this an argument sufficient to induce us to give energy to this article, thus fraught with iniquity? By no means. But we were informed by that gentleman, further that those two states pled, that they had lost much of their property during the late war. Their slaves being either taken from them by the British troops, or they themselves taking the liberty of absconding from them, and therefore they must import more, in order to make up their losses. To this we say they lost no property, because they never had any in them, however much money they might have paid for them. For we look upon it, every man is the sole proprietor of his own liberty, and no one but himself hath a right to convey it unless by some crime adequate to the punishment, it should be made forfeit, and so by that means becomes the property of government: But this is by no means the case in the present instance. And we cannot suppose a vendee, can acquire property in any thing, which at the time of purchase, he knew the vendor had no right to convey. This is an acknowledgment, we are constrained to make as a tribute due to justice and equity. But suppose they had lost real property; so have we; and indeed where is the man, but will tell us he has been a great looser by means of the war? And shall we from thence argue that we have a right to make inroads upon another nation, pilfer and rob them, in order to compensate ourselves for the losses we have sustained by means of a war, in which they had been utterly neutral? Truly upon this plan of reasoning it is lawful thus to do, and had we voted the constitution as it stands, we must have given countenance to conduct equally criminal, and more so, if possible. Such arguments as the above seem to be calculated and designed for idiotcy. We however acknowledge, we think them rather an affront, even upon that.

The Hon. Gentleman above named, was asked the question—What would be the consequence, suppose one or two states, upon any principle, should refuse confederating? His answer was—"The consequence is plain and easy—they would be compelled to it; not by force of arms; but all commerce with them would be interdicted; their property would be seized in every port they should enter, and by law made forfeit: and this line of conduct would soon reduce them to order." This method of procedure perhaps no one would be disposed to reprehend; and if eleven, or even nine states were agreed, could they not, ought they not to take this method, rather than to make a compact with them, by which they give countenance, nay even bind themselves (as the case may be) to aid and assist them in spo[r]ting with the liberties of others, and accumulating to themselves fortunes, by making thousands of their fellow creatures miserable. To animadvert upon the British manoe[u]vres at that time, would not fall within the compass of our present design. But that the Africans had a right to depart, we must assert, and are able to prove it from the highest authority perhaps that this Commonwealth does or ever did afford. In a printed pamphlet, published in Boston in the year 1772, said to be the report of a Committee, and unanimously voted by said town, and ordered to be sent to the several towns in the state for their consideration. In said pamphlet we find the following *axiom,* which we will quote verbatim,—page 2d—"All men have a right to remain in a state of nature as long as they please, and in case of intolerable oppression, civil or religious, to leave the society they belong to, and enter into another." If it can by any kind of reasoning be made to appear, that this authority is not pertinently adduced in the case before us, then we think it can by the same reasoning be investigated, that black is white and white is black—that oppression and freedom are exactly similar, and benevolence and malignity synonymous terms.

The advocates for the constitution seemed to suppose, that this restriction being laid upon Congress only for a term of time, is the "fair dawning of liberty." That "it was a glorious acquisition towards the final abolition of slavery." But how much more glorious would the acquisition have been, was such abolition to take place the first moment the constitution should be established. If we had said that after the expiration of a certain term the practice should cease, it would have appeared with a better grace; but this is not the case, for even after that, it is wholly optional with the Congress, whether they abolish it or not. And by that time we presume that enslaving the Africans will be accounted by far less an inconsiderable affair than it is at present; therefore conclude from good reasons, that the *"nefarious practice"* will be continued and increased as the inhabitants of the country shall be found to increase.

This practice of enslaving mankind is in direct opposition to a fundamental maxim of truth, on which our state constitution is founded, viz. "All men are born free and equal." This is our motto. We have said it—we cannot go back. Indeed no man can justify himself in enslaving another, unless he can produce a commission under the broad seal of Heaven, purporting a licence therefor from him who created all men, and can therefore dispose of them at his pleasure.

We would not be thought to detract from the character of any person, but to us it is somewhat nearly paradoxical, that some of our leading characters in the law department (especially in the western counties) after having (to their honour be it spoken) exerted themselves to promote, and finally to effect the emancipation of slaves, should now turn directly about, and exhibit to the world principles diametrically opposite thereto: that they should now appear such strenuous advocates for the establishment of that diabolical trade of importing the Africans. But said some, it is not we who do it—and compared it to entering into an alliance with another nation, for some particular purpose; but we think this by no means a parallel. We are one nation, forming a constitution for the whole, and suppose the states are under obligation, whenever this constitution shall be established, reciprocally to aid each other in defence and support of every thing to which they are entitled thereby, right or wrong. Perhaps we may never be called upon to take up arms for the defence of the southern states, in prosecuting this abominable traffick.

It is true at present there is not much danger to be apprehended, and for this plain reason are those innocent Africans (as to us) pitched upon to drag out their lives in misery and chains. Such is their local situation—their unpolished manner—their inexperience in the art of war, that those invaders of the rights of mankind knew they can, at present, perpetrate those enormities with impunity. But let us suppose for once, a thing which is by no means impossible, viz. that those Africans should rise superior to all their local and other disadvantages, and attempt to avenge themselves for the wrongs done them? Or suppose some potent nation should interfere in their behalf, as France in the cause of America, must we not rise and resist them? Would not the Congress immediately call forth the whole force of the country, if needed, to oppose them, and so attempt more closely to rivet their manacles upon them, and in that way perpetuate the miseries of those unhappy people? This we think the natural consequence which will flow from the establishment of this constitution, and that it is not a forced, but a very liberal construction of it. It was said that "the adoption of this Constitution, would be ominous of much good, and betoken the smiles of Heaven upon the country." But we view the matter in a very different light; we think this latch for unjust gains, this lust for slavery, portentous of much evil in America, for the cry of innocent blood, which hath been shed in carrying on this execrable commerce, hath undoubtedly reached to the Heavens, to which that cry is always directed, and will draw down upon them vengeance adequate to the enormity of the crime. To what other cause, than a full conviction, of the moral evil in this practice, together with some fearful forebodings of punishment therefor arising in the minds of the Congress in the year 1774, can it be imputed, that drew from them at that time, (at least an implied) confession of guilt, and a solemn, explicit promise of reformation? This is a fact, but lest it should be disputed, we think it most safe for ourselves to lay before our readers, an extract from a certain pamphlet, entitled "Extracts from the votes and proceedings of the American Continental Congress, held at Philadelphia, on the 5th of September, 1774, &c." In the 22d page of this same pamphlet, we find the following paragraph, viz. "Second. That we will neither import, nor purchase any slave imported, after the first day of December next; after which time we will wholly discontinue the slave-trade, and will neither be concerned in it ourselves, nor will we hire our vessels nor sell our commodities or manufactures to those who are concerned in it." The inconsistency of opposing slavery, which they thought designed for themselves, and by clandestine means, procuring others to enslave at the same time—it is very natural to suppose would stare them in the face, and at all times guard them against breaking their resolution. Hence it appears to us unaccountably strange, that any person who signed the above resolve, should sign the federal constitution. For do they not hold up to view principles diametrically opposite? Can we suppose that what was morally evil in the year 1774, has become in the year 1788, morally good? Or shall we change evil into good and good into evil, as often as we find it will serve a turn? We cannot but say the conduct of those who associated in the year 1774 in the manner above, and now appear advocates for this new constitution, is highly inconsistent, although we find such conduct has the celebrated names of a *Washington* and an *Adams* to grace it. And this may serve as a reason why we could not be wrought upon by another argument, which was made use of in the Convention in favour of the constitution, viz. the *weight of names*—a solid argument with some people who belonged to the Convention, and would have induced them to comply with measures of almost any kind. It was urged that the gentlemen who composed the federal Convention, were men of the greatest abilities, integrity and erudition, and had been the greatest contenders for freedom. We suppose it to be true, and that they have exemplified it, by the manner in which they have earnestly dogmatized for liberty—But notwithstanding we could not view this argument, as advancing any where towards infallibility—because long before we entered upon the business of the Convention, we were by some means or other possessed with a notion (and we think from good authority) that *"great men are not always wise."* And to be sure the weight of the name adduced to give efficacy to a measure where liberty is in dispute, cannot be so likely to have its intended effect, when the person designed by that name, at the same time he is brandishing his sword, in the behalf of freedom for himself—is likewise tyranizing over two or three hundred miserable Africans, as free born as himself.

In fine we view this constitution as a curious piece of political mechanism, fabricated in such manner as may finally despoil the people of all their privileges; and we are fully satisfied, that had the same system been offered to the people in the time of the contest with Great-Britain, the person offering the same would not have met the approbation of those who now appear the most strenuous advocates for it. We cannot slip this opportunity of manifesting our disgust at the unfair methods which were taken in order to obtain a vote in this state, which perhaps was the means of producing the *small* majority of *nineteen,* out of nearly three hundred and sixty members. What those methods were is well known. It is past dispute that the opposers of the constitution were, in sundry instances, treated in a manner utterly inconsistent with that respect which is due to every freeborn citizen of the commonwealth, especially when acting in the capacity of a representative.

Notwithstanding what has been said, we would not have it understood, that we mean to be disturbers of the peace, should the states receive the constitution; but on the contrary, declare it our intention, as we think it our duty, to be subject to "the powers that be," wherever our lot may be cast.

14

DEBATE IN VIRGINIA RATIFYING CONVENTION
15 June 1788
Elliot 3:452–54, 456–59

MR. GEORGE MASON. Mr. Chairman, this is a fatal section, which has created more dangers than any other. The first clause allows the importation of slaves for twenty years. Under the royal government, this evil was looked upon as a great oppression, and many attempts were made to prevent it; but the interest of the African merchants prevented its prohibition. No sooner did the revolution take place, than it was thought of. It was one of the great causes of our separation from Great Britain. Its exclusion has been a principal object of this state, and most of the states in the Union. The augmentation of slaves weakens the states; and such a trade is diabolical in itself, and disgraceful to mankind; yet, by this Constitution, it is continued for twenty years. As much as I value a union of all the states, I would not admit the Southern States into the Union unless they agree to the discontinuance of this disgraceful trade, because it would bring weakness, and not strength, to the Union. And, though this infamous traffic be continued, we have no security for the property of that kind which we have already. There is no clause in this Constitution to secure it; for they may lay such a tax as will amount to manumission. And should the government be amended, still this detestable kind of commerce cannot be discontinued till after the expiration of twenty years; for the 5th article, which provides for amendments, expressly excepts this clause. I have ever looked upon this as a most disgraceful thing to America. I cannot express my detestation of it. Yet they have not secured us the property of the slaves we have already. So that "they have done what they ought not to have done, and have left undone what they ought to have done."

MR. MADISON. Mr. Chairman, I should conceive this clause to be impolitic, if it were one of those things which could be excluded without encountering greater evils. The Southern States would not have entered into the Union of America without the temporary permission of that trade; and if they were excluded from the Union, the consequences might be dreadful to them and to us. We are not in a worse situation than before. That traffic is prohibited by our laws, and we may continue the prohibition. The Union in general is not in a worse situation. Under the Articles of Confederation, it might be continued forever; but, by this clause, an end may be put to it after twenty years. There is, therefore, an amelioration of our circumstances. A tax may be laid in the mean time; but it is limited; otherwise Congress might lay such a tax as would amount to a prohibition. From the mode of representation and taxation, Congress cannot lay such a tax on slaves as will amount to manumission. Another clause secures us that property which we now possess. At present, if any slave elopes to any of those states where slaves are free, he becomes emancipated by their laws; for the laws of the states are uncharitable to one another in this respect. But in this Constitution, "no person held to service or labor in one state, under the laws thereof, escaping into another, shall, in consequence of any law or regulation therein, be discharged from such service or labor; but shall be delivered up on claim of the party to whom such service or labor shall be due." This clause was expressly inserted, to enable owners of slaves to reclaim them.

This is a better security than any that now exists. No power is given to the general government to interpose with respect to the property in slaves now held by the states. The taxation of this state being equal only to its representation, such a tax cannot be laid as he supposes. They cannot prevent the importation of slaves for twenty years; but after that period, they can. The gentlemen from South Carolina and Georgia argued in this manner: "We have now liberty to import this species of property, and much of the property now possessed had been purchased, or otherwise acquired, in contemplation of improving it by the assistance of imported slaves. What would be the consequence of hindering us from it? The slaves of Virginia would rise in value, and we should be obliged to go to your markets." I need not expatiate on this subject. Great as the evil is, a dismemberment of the Union would be worse. If those states should disunite from the other states for not indulging them in the temporary continuance of this traffic, they might solicit and obtain aid from foreign powers.

Mr. Tyler warmly enlarged on the impolicy, iniquity, and disgracefulness of this wicked traffic. He thought the reasons urged by gentlemen in defence of it were inconclusive and ill founded. It was one cause of the complaints against British tyranny, that this trade was permitted. The revolution had put a period to it; but now it was to be revived. He thought nothing could justify it. This temporary restriction on Congress militated, in his opinion, against the arguments of gentlemen on the other side, that what was not given up was retained by the states; for that, if this restriction had not been inserted, Congress could have prohibited the African trade. The power of prohibiting it was not expressly delegated to them; yet they would have had it by implication, if this restraint had not been provided. This seemed to him to demonstrate most clearly the necessity of restraining them, by a bill of rights, from infringing our unalienable rights. It was immaterial whether the bill of rights was by itself, or included in the Constitution. But he contended for it one way or the other. It would be justified by our own example and that of England. His earnest desire was, that it should be handed down to posterity that he had opposed this wicked clause.

. . . . .

Mr. George Nicholas wondered that gentlemen who were against slavery should be opposed to this clause; as, after that period, the slave trade would be done away. He asked if gentlemen did not see the inconsistency of their arguments. They object, says he, to the Constitution, because the slave trade is laid open for twenty odd years; and yet they tell you that, by some latent operation of it, the slaves who are so now will be manumitted. At the same moment it is opposed for being promotive and destructive of slavery. He contended that it was advantageous to Virginia that it should be in the power of Congress to prevent the importation of slaves after twenty years, as it would then put a period to the evil complained of.

As the Southern States would not confederate without this clause, he asked if gentlemen would rather dissolve the confederacy than to suffer this temporary inconvenience, admitting it to be such. Virginia might continue the prohibition of such importation during the intermediate period, and would be benefited by it, as a tax of ten dollars on each slave might be laid, of which she would receive a share. He endeavored to obviate the objection of gentlemen, that the restriction on Congress was a proof that they would have powers not given them, by remarking, that they would only have had a general superintendency of trade, if the restriction had not been inserted. But the Southern States insisted on this exception to that general superintendency for twenty years. It could not, therefore, have been a power by implication, as the restriction was an exception from a delegated power. The taxes could not, as had been suggested, be laid so high on negroes as to amount to emancipation because taxation and representation were fixed according to the census established in the Constitution. The exception of taxes from the uniformity annexed to duties and excises could not have the operation contended for by the gentleman, because other clauses had clearly and positively fixed the census. Had taxes been uniform, it would have been universally objected to; for no one object could be selected without involving great inconveniences and oppressions. But, says Mr. Nicholas, is it from the general government we are to fear emancipation? Gentlemen will recollect what I said in another house, and what other gentlemen have said, that advocated emancipation. Give me leave to say, that clause is a great security for our slave tax. I can tell the committee that the people of our country are reduced to beggary by the taxes on negroes. Had this Constitution been adopted, it would not have been the case. The taxes were laid on all our negroes. By this system, two fifths are exempted. He then added, that he had not imagined gentlemen would support here what they had opposed in another place.

Mr. Henry replied that, though the proportion of each was to be fixed by the census, and three fifths of the slaves only were included in the enumeration, yet the proportion of Virginia, being once fixed, might be laid on blacks and blacks only; for, the mode of raising the proportion of each state being to be directed by Congress, they might make slaves the sole object to raise it of. Personalities he wished to take leave of: they had nothing to do with the question, which was solely whether that paper was wrong or not.

Mr. NICHOLAS replied, that negroes must be considered as persons or property. If as property, the proportion of taxes to be laid on them was fixed in the Constitution. If he apprehended a poll tax on negroes, the Constitution had prevented it; for, by the census, where a white man paid ten shillings, a negro paid but six shillings; for the exemption of two fifths of them reduced it to that proportion.

Mr. GEORGE MASON said, that gentlemen might think themselves secured by the restriction, in the 4th clause, that no capitation or other direct tax should be laid but in proportion to the census before directed to be taken; but that, when maturely considered, it would be found to be no security whatsoever. It was nothing but a direct assertion, or mere confirmation of the clause which fixed the ratio of taxes and representation. It only meant that the quantum to be raised of each state should be in proportion to their numbers, in the manner therein directed. But the general government was not precluded from laying the proportion of any particular state on any one species of property they might think proper.

For instance, if five hundred thousand dollars were to be raised, they might lay the whole of the proportion of the Southern States on the blacks, or any one species of property; so that, by laying taxes too heavily on slaves, they might totally annihilate that kind of property. No real security could arise from the clause which provides that persons held to labor in one state, escaping into another, shall be delivered up. This only meant that runaway slaves should not be protected in other states. As to the exclusion of *ex post facto* laws, it could not be said to create any security in this case; for laying a tax on slaves would not be *ex post facto*.

Mr. MADISON replied, that even the Southern States, which were most affected, were perfectly satisfied with this provision, and dreaded no danger to the property they now hold. It appeared to him that the general government would not intermeddle with that property for twenty years, but to lay a tax on every slave imported not exceeding ten dollars; and that, after the expiration of that period, they might prohibit the traffic altogether. The census in the Constitution was intended to introduce equality in the burdens to be laid on the community. No gentleman objected to laying duties, imposts, and excises, uniformly. But uniformity of taxes would be subversive of the principles of equality; for it was not possible to select any article which would be easy for one state but what would be heavy for another; that, the proportion of each state being ascertained, it would be raised by the general government in the most convenient manner for the people, and not by the selection of any one particular object; that there must be some degree of confidence put in agents, or else we must reject a state of civil society altogether. Another great security to this property, which he mentioned, was, that five states were greatly interested in that species of property, and there were other states which had some slaves, and had made no attempt, or taken any step, to take them from the people. There were a few slaves in New York, New Jersey, and Connecticut: these states would, probably, oppose any attempts to annihilate this species of property. He concluded by observing that he should be glad to leave the decision of this to the committee.

15

DEBATE IN NORTH CAROLINA RATIFYING CONVENTION
26 July 1788
Elliot 4:100–102

Mr. J. M'DOWALL wished to hear the reasons of this restriction.

Mr. SPAIGHT answered, that there was a contest between the Northern and Southern States; that the Southern States, whose principal support depended on the labor of slaves, would not consent to the desire of the Northern States to exclude the importation of slaves absolutely; that South Carolina and Georgia insisted on this clause, as they were now in want of hands to cultivate their lands; that in the course of twenty years they would be fully supplied; that the trade would be abolished then, and that, in the mean time, some tax or duty might be laid on.

Mr. M'DOWALL replied, that the explanation was just such as he expected, and by no means satisfactory to him, and that he looked upon it as a very objectionable part of the system.

Mr. IREDELL. Mr. Chairman, I rise to express sentiments similar to those of the gentleman from Craven. For my part, were it practicable to put an end to the importation of slaves immediately, it would give me the greatest pleasure; for it certainly is a trade utterly inconsistent with the rights of humanity, and under which great cruelties have been exercised. When the entire abolition of slavery takes place, it will be an event which must be pleasing to every generous mind, and every friend of human nature; but we often wish for things which are not attainable. It was the wish of a great majority of the Convention to put an end to the trade immediately; but the states of South Carolina and Georgia would not agree to it. Consider, then, what would be the difference between our present situation in this respect, if we do not agree to the Constitution, and what it will be if we do agree to it. If we do not agree to it, do we remedy the evil? No, sir, we do not. For if the Constitution be not adopted, it will be in the power of every state to continue it forever. They may or may not abolish it, at their discretion. But if we adopt the Constitution, the trade must cease after twenty years, if Congress declare so, whether particular states please so or not; surely, then, we can gain by it. This was the utmost that could be obtained. I heartily wish more could have been done. But as it is, this government is nobly distinguished above others by that very provision. Where is there another country in which such a restriction prevails? We, therefore, sir, set an example of humanity, by providing for the abolition of this inhuman traffic, though at a distant period. I hope, therefore, that this part of the Constitution will not be condemned because it has not stipulated for what was impracticable to obtain.

Mr. SPAIGHT further explained the clause. That the limitation of this trade to the term of twenty years was a compromise between the Eastern States and the Southern States. South Carolina and Georgia wished to extend the term. The Eastern States insisted on the entire abolition of the trade. That the state of North Carolina had not thought proper to pass any law prohibiting the importation of slaves, and therefore its delegation in the Convention did not think themselves authorized to contend for an immediate prohibition of it.

Mr. IREDELL added to what he had said before, that the states of Georgia and South Carolina had lost a great many slaves during the war, and that they wished to supply the loss.

Mr. GALLOWAY. Mr. Chairman, the explanation given to this clause does not satisfy my mind. I wish to see this abominable trade put an end to. But in case it be thought proper to continue this abominable traffic for twenty years, yet I do not wish to see the tax on the importation extended to all persons whatsoever. Our situation is different from the people to the north. We want citizens; they do not. Instead of laying a tax, we ought to give a bounty to encourage foreigners to come among us. With respect to the abolition of slavery, it requires the utmost consideration. The property of the Southern States consists principally of slaves. If they mean to do away slavery altogether, this property will be destroyed. I apprehend it means to bring forward manumission. If we must manumit our slaves, what country shall we send them to? It is impossible for us to be happy, if, after manumission, they are to stay among us.

Mr. IREDELL. Mr. Chairman, the worthy gentleman, I believe, has misunderstood this clause, which runs in the following words: "The migration or importation of such persons as any of the states now existing shall think proper to admit, shall not be prohibited by the Congress prior to the year 1808; but a tax or duty may be imposed on such importation, not exceeding ten dollars for each person." Now, sir, observe that the Eastern States, who long ago have abolished slaves, did not approve of the expression *slaves;* they therefore used another, that answered the same purpose. The committee will observe the distinction between the two words *migration* and *importation.* The first part of the clause will extend to persons who come into this country as free people, or are brought as slaves. But the last part extends to slaves only. The word *migration* refers to free persons; but the word *importation* refers to slaves, because free people cannot be said to be imported. The tax, therefore, is only to be laid on slaves who are imported, and not on free persons who migrate. I further beg leave to say that the gentleman is mistaken in another thing. He seems to say that this extends to the abolition of slavery. Is there any thing in this Constitution which says that Congress shall have it in their power to abolish the slavery of those slaves who are now in the country? Is it not the plain meaning of it, that after twenty years they may prevent the future importation of slaves? It does not extend to those now in the country. There is another circumstance to be observed. There is no authority vested in Congress to restrain the states, in the interval of twenty years, from doing what they please. If they wish to prohibit such importation, they may do so. Our next Assembly may put an entire end to the importation of slaves.

16

JAMES MADISON, IMPORT DUTY ON SLAVES, HOUSE OF REPRESENTATIVES
13 May 1789
Papers 12:160–63

MR. MADISON. I cannot concur with gentlemen who think the present an improper time or place to enter into a discussion of the proposed motion; if it is taken up in a separate view, we shall do the same thing at a greater expence of time. But the gentleman says that it is improper to connect the two objects, because they do not come within the title of the bill; but this objection may be obviated by accomodating the title to the contents; there may be some inconsistency in combining the ideas which gentlemen have expressed, that is, considering the human race as a species of property; but the evil does not arise from adopting the clause now proposed; it is from the importation to which it relates. Our object in enumerating persons on paper with merchandize, is to prevent the practice of actually treating them as such, by having them in future, forming part of the cargoes of goods, wares, and merchandize to be imported into the United States, the motion is calculated to avoid the very evil intimated by the gentleman.

It has been said that this tax will be partial and oppressive; but suppose a fair view is taken of this subject, I think we may form a different conclusion. But if it be partial or oppressive, are there not many instances in which we have laid taxes of this nature? Yet are they not thought to be justified by national policy? If any article is warranted on this account, how much more are we authorised to proceed on this occasion? The dictates of humanity, the principles of the people, the national safety and happiness, and prudent policy requires it of us; the constitution has particularly called our attention to it—and of all the articles contained in the bill before us, this is one of the last I should be willing to make a concession upon so far as I was at liberty to go, according to the terms of the constitution or principles of justice—I would not have it understood that my zeal would carry me to disobey the inviolable commands of either.

I understood it had been intimated, that the motion was inconsistent or unconstitutional. I believe, sir, my worthy colleague has formed the words with a particular reference to the constitution; any how, so far as the duty is expressed, it perfectly accords with that instrument; if there are any inconsistencies in it, they may be rectified; I believe the intention is well understood, but I am far from supposing the diction improper. If the description of the persons does not accord with the ideas of the gentleman from Georgia (Mr. Jackson) and his idea is a proper one for the committee to adopt, I see no difficulty in changing the phraseology.

I conceive the constitution in this particular, was formed in order that the government, whilst it was restrained from laying a total prohibition, might be able to give some testimony of the sense of America, with respect to the African trade. We have liberty to impose a tax or duty upon the importation of such persons as any of the states now existing shall think proper to admit; and this liberty was granted, I presume, upon two considerations—the first was, that until the time arrived when they might abolish the importation of slaves, they might have an opportunity of evidencing their sentiments, on the policy and humanity of such a trade; the other was that they might be taxed in due proportion with other articles imported; for if the possessor will consider them as property, of course they are of value, and ought to be paid for. If gentlemen are apprehensive of oppression from the weight of the tax, let them make an estimate of its proportion, and they will find that it very little exceeds five per cent. ad valorem, so that they will gain very little by having them thrown into that mass of articles, whilst by selecting them in the manner proposed, we shall fulfil the prevailing expectation of our fellow citizens, and perform our duty in executing the purposes of the constitution. It is to be hoped, that by expressing a national disapprobation of this trade, we may destroy it, and save ourselves from reproaches, and our posterity the imbecility ever attendant on a country filled with slaves.

I do not wish to say any thing harsh, to the hearing of gentlemen who entertain different sentiments from me, or different sentiments from those I represent; but if there is any one point in which it is clearly the policy of this nation, so far as we constitutionally can, to vary the practice obtaining under some of the state governments it is this; but it is certain a majority of the states are opposed to this practice; therefore, upon principle, we ought to discountenance it as far as is in our power.

If I was not afraid of being told that the representatives of the several states, are the best able to judge of what is proper and conducive to their particular prosperity, I should venture to say that it is as much the interest of Georgia and South Carolina, as of any in the union. Every addition they receive to their number of slaves, tends to weaken them and renders them less capable of self defence; in case of hostilities with foreign nations, they will be the means of inviting attack instead of repelling invasion. It is a necessary duty of the general government to protect every part of the empire against danger, as well internal as external; every thing therefore which tends to encrease this danger, though it may be a local affair, yet if it involves national expence or safety, becomes of concern to every part of the union, and is a proper subject for the consideration of those charged with the general administration of the government. I hope in making these observations, I shall not be understood to mean that a proper attention ought not to be paid to the local opinions and circumstances of any part of the United States, or that the particular representatives are not best able to judge of the sense of their immediate constituents.

If we examine the proposed measure, by the agreement there is between it, and the existing state laws, it will shew us that it is patronized by a very respectable part of the union. I am informed that South-Carolina has prohibited the importation of slaves, for several years yet to come; we have the satisfaction then of reflecting that we do nothing more than their own laws do at this moment. This is not the case with one state. I am sorry that her situation is such as to seem to require a population of this nature, but it is impossible in the nature of things, to consult the national good without doing what we do not wish to do, to some particular part.

Perhaps gentlemen contend against the introduction of the clause, on too slight grounds. If it does not comport with the title of the bill, alter the latter. If it does not conform to the precise terms of the constitution amend it. But if it will tend to delay the whole bill, that perhaps will be the best reason for making it the object of a separate one. If this is the sense of the committee I shall submit.

17

HOUSE OF REPRESENTATIVES, SLAVE TRADE
23 Mar. 1790
Annals 2:1472–74

Report of the Special Committee.

The Committee to whom were referred sundry memorials from the people called Quakers; and also a memorial from the Pennsylvania Society for promoting the Abolition of Slavery, submit the following report:

That from the nature of the matters contained in these memorials, they were induced to examine the powers vested in Congress, under the present Constitution, relating to the Abolition of Slavery, and are clearly of opinion,

First. That the General Government is expressly restrained from prohibiting the importation of such persons "as any of the States now existing shall think proper to admit, until the year one thousand eight hundred and eight."

Secondly. That Congress, by a fair construction of the Constitution, are equally restrained from interfering in the emancipation of slaves, who already are, or who may, within the period mentioned, be imported into, or born within, any of the said States.

Thirdly. That Congress have no authority to interfere in the internal regulations of particular States, relative to the instructions of slaves in the principles of morality and religion; to their comfortable clothing, accommodations and subsistence; to the regulation of their marriages, and the prevention of the violation of the rights thereof, or to the separation of children from their parents; to a comfortable provision in cases of sickness, age, or infirmity; or to the seizure, transportation, or sale of free negroes; but have the fullest confidence in the wisdom and humanity of the Legislatures of the several States, that they will revise their laws from time to time, when necessary, and promote the objects mentioned in the memorials, and every other measure that may tend to the happiness of slaves.

Fourthly. That, nevertheless, Congress have authority, if they shall think it necessary, to lay at any time a tax or duty, not exceeding ten dollars for each person of any description, the importation of whom shall be by any of the States admitted as aforesaid.

Fifthly. That Congress have authority to interdict, or (so far as it is or may be carried on by citizens of the United States, for supplying foreigners) to regulate the African trade, and to make provision for the humane treatment of slaves, in all cases while on their passage to the United States, or to foreign ports, so far as it respects the citizens of the United States.

Sixthly. That Congress have also authority to prohibit foreigners from fitting out vessels, in any port of the United States, for transporting persons from Africa to any foreign port.

Seventhly. That the memorialist[s] be informed, that in all cases to which the authority of Congress extends, they will exercise it for the humane objects of the memorialists, so far as they can be promoted on the principles of justice, humanity, and good policy."

Report of the Committee of the whole House.

The Committee of the whole House, to whom was committed the report of the committee on memorials of the people called Quakers, and of the Pennsylvania Society for promoting the Abolition of Slavery, report the following amendments:

Strike out the first clause, together with the recital thereto, and in lieu thereof insert, "That the migration or importation of such persons as any of the States now existing shall think proper to admit, cannot be prohibited by Congress, prior to the year one thousand eight hundred and eight."

Strike out the second and third clauses, and in lieu thereof insert "That Congress have no authority to interfere in the emancipation of slaves, or in the treatment of them within any of the States; it remaining with the several States alone to provide any regulations therein, which humanity and true policy may require."

Strike out the fourth and fifth clauses, and in lieu thereof insert, "That Congress have authority to restrain the citizens of the United States from carrying on the African trade, for the purpose of supplying foreigners with slaves, and of providing, by proper regulations, for the humane treatment, during their passage, of slaves imported by the said citizens into the States admitting such importation."

Strike out the seventh clause.

18

St. George Tucker, Blackstone's Commentaries 1:App. 290 1803

This article, at the time the constitution was framed, was deemed necessary to prevent an opposition, on that ground, to it's adoption in those states which still permitted the importation of slaves from Africa, and other foreign parts. A more liberal policy has since prevailed, so far as to render it probable that congress will never have occasion to exert the right of prohibiting the importation of slaves, such importation being now prohibited by the laws of all the states in the union. But should any of them shew an inclination to rescind the present prohibitions, congress, after the year 1808, will be able to interpose it's authority to prevent it, and impose some partial restraint upon the farther extension of the miseries of mankind. How to remove the calamities of slavery from among us, is left to the wisdom of the state government; the federal government can only prevent the further importation of slaves after the period limited.

19

John Jay to Elias Boudinot 17 Nov. 1819 *Correspondence 4:430–31*

I have received the copy of a circular letter which, as chairman of the committee appointed by the late public meeting at Trenton respecting slavery, you were pleased to direct to me on the 5th instant. Little can be added to what has been said and written on the subject of slavery. I concur in the opinion that it ought not to be introduced nor permitted in any of the new States; and that it ought to be gradually diminished and finally abolished in all of them.

To me the constitutional authority of the Congress to prohibit the migration and importation of slaves into any of the States, does not appear questionable. The first article of the constitution specifies the legislative powers committed to the Congress. The ninth section of that article has these words:

"The *migration* or *importation* of such *persons* as any of the *now existing* States shall think proper to admit, shall not be prohibited by the Congress prior to the year 1808. But a tax or duty may be imposed on such importations, not exceeding ten dollars for each person."

I understand the sense and meaning of this clause to be,

that the power of the Congress, although competent to prohibit such migration and importation, was not to be exercised with respect to the *then existing* States (and them only) until the year 1808; but that the Congress were at liberty to make such prohibition as to any new State, which might, in the *mean* time, be established, and further, that from and after *that period,* they were authorized to make such prohibition, as to all the States, whether new or old.

It will, I presume, be admitted, that *slaves* were the *persons* intended. The word *slaves* was avoided, probably on account of the existing toleration of slavery, and of its discordancy with the principles of the Revolution; and from a consciousness of its being repugnant to the following positions in the Declaration of Independence, viz.:

"We hold these truths to be self-evident: that all men are created equal; that they are endowed by their Creator with certain unalienable rights; that among them are life, liberty, and the pursuit of happiness."

20

James Madison to Robert Walsh
27 Nov. 1819
Writings 9:1–13

Your letter of the 11th was duly recd. and I should have given it a less tardy answer, but for a succession of particular demands on my attention, and a wish to assist my recollections, by consulting both Manuscript & printed sources of information on the subjects of your enquiry. Of these, however, I have not been able to avail myself but very partially.

As to the intention of the framers of the Constitution in the clause relating to "the migration and importation of persons, &c" the best key may perhaps be found in the case which produced it. The African trade in slaves had long been odious to most of the States, and the importation of slaves into them had been prohibited. Particular States however continued the importation, and were extremely averse to any restriction on their power to do so. In the convention the former States were anxious, in framing a new constitution, to insert a provision for an immediate and absolute stop to the trade. The latter were not only averse to any interference on the subject; but solemnly declared that their constituents would never accede to a Constitution containing such an article. Out of this conflict grew the middle measure providing that Congress should not interfere until the year 1808; with an implication, that after that date, they might prohibit the importation of slaves into the States then existing, & previous thereto, into the States not then existing. Such was the tone of opposition in the States of S. Carolina & Georgia, & such the desire to gain their acquiescence in a prohibitory power, that on a question between the epochs of 1800 & 1808, the States of N. Hampshire, Masstts. & Connecticut, (all the eastern States in the Convention,) joined in the vote for the latter, influenced however by the collateral motive of reconciling those particular States to the power over commerce & navigation; against which they felt, as did some other States, a very strong repugnance. The earnestness of S. Carolina & Georgia was farther maniested by their insisting on the security in the V article, against any amendment to the Constitution affecting the right reserved to them, & their uniting with the small states, who insisted on a like security for their equality in the Senate.

But some of the States were not only anxious for a Constitutional provision against the introduction of slaves. They had scruples against admitting the term "slaves" into the Instrument. Hence the descriptive phrase, "migration or importation of persons;" the term migration allowing those who were scrupulous of acknowledging expressly a property in human beings, to view *imported* persons as a species of emigrants, while others might apply the term to foreign malefactors sent or coming into the country. It is possible tho' not recollected, that some might have had an eye to the case of freed blacks, as well as malefactors.

But whatever may have been intended by the term "migration" or the term "persons," it is most certain, that they referred exclusively to a migration or importation from other countries into the U. States; and not to a removal, voluntary or involuntary, of slaves or freemen, from one to another part of the U. States. Nothing appears or is recollected that warrants this latter intention. Nothing in the proceedings of the State conventions indicates such a construction there.* Had such been the construction it is easy to imagine the figure it would have made in many of the states, among the objections to the constitution, and among the numerous amendments to it proposed by the

*The debates of the Pennsylvania Convention contain a speech of Mr. Willson, (Decr. 3, 1787) who had been a member of the general convention, in which, alluding to the clause tolerating for a time, the farther importation of slaves, he consoles himself with the hope that, in a few years it would be prohibited altogether; observing that in the mean time, the new States which were to be formed would be under the controul of Congress *in this particular,* and slaves would never be introduced among them. In another speech on the day following and alluding to the same clause, his words are "yet the lapse of a few years & Congress will have power to *exterminate* slavery within our borders." How far the language of Mr. W. may have been accurately reported is not known. The expressions used, are more vague & less consistent than would be readily ascribed to him. But as they stand, the fairest construction would be, that he considered the power given to Congress, to arrest the importation of slaves as "laying a foundation for banishing slavery out of the country; & tho' at a period more distant than might be wished; producing the same kind of gradual change which was pursued in Pennsylvania." (See his speech, page 90 of the Debates.) By this "change," after the example of Pennsylvania, he must have meant a change by the other States influenced by that example, & yielding to the general way of thinking & feeling, produced by the policy of putting an end to the importation of slaves. He could not mean by "banishing slavery," more than by a power "to exterminate it," that Congress were authorized to do what is literally expressed.

State conventions* not one of which amendments refers to the clause in question. Neither is there any indication that Congress have heretofore considered themselves as deriving from this Clause a power over the migration of removal of individuals, whether freemen or slaves, from one State to another, whether new or old: For it must be kept in view that if the power was given at all, it has been in force eleven years over all the States existing in 1808, and at all times over the States not then existing. Every indication is against such a construction by Congress of their constitutional powers. Their alacrity in exercising their powers relating to slaves, is a proof that they did not claim what they did not exercise. They punctually and unanimously put in force the power accruing in 1808 against the further importation of slaves from abroad. They had previously directed their power over American vessels on the high seas, against the African trade. They lost no time in applying the prohibitory power to Louisiana, which having maritime ports, might be an inlet for slaves from abroad. But they forebore to extend the prohibition to the introduction of slaves from other parts of the Union. They had even prohibited the importation of slaves into the Mississippi Territory from *without the limits of the U. S.* in the year 1798, without extending the prohibition to the introduction of slaves from *within those limits;* altho' at the time the ports of Georgia and S. Carolina were open for the importation of slaves from abroad, and increasing the mass of slavery within the U. States.

If these views of the subject be just, a power in Congress to controul the interior migration or removals of persons, must be derived from some other source than Sect 9, Art. 1; either from the clause giving power "to make all needful rules and regulations respecting the Territory or other property belonging to the U. S. or from that providing for the admission of New States into the Union."

The terms in which the 1st. of these powers is expressed, tho' of a ductile character, cannot well be extended beyond a power over the Territory as property, & a power to make the provisions really needful or necessary for the Govt. of settlers until ripe for admission as States into the Union. It may be inferred that Congress did not regard the interdict of slavery among the needful regulations contemplated by the constitution; since in none of the Territorial Governments created by them, is such an interdict found. The power, however be its import what it may, is obviously limited to a Territory whilst remaining in that character as distinct from that of a State.

*In the convention of Virga. the opposition to the Constitution comprised a number of the ablest men in the State. Among them were Mr. Henry & Col. Mason, both of them distinguished by their acuteness, and anxious to display unpopular constructions. One of them Col. Mason, had been a member of the general convention and entered freely into accounts of what passed within it. Yet neither of them, nor indeed any of the other opponents, among the multitude of their objections, and farfetched interpretations, ever hinted, in the debates on the 9th Sect. of Ar. 1, at a power given by it to prohibit an interior migration of any sort. The meaning of the Secn. as levelled against migrations or importations from abroad, was not contested.

As to the power of admitting new States into the federal compact, the questions offering themselves are; whether congress can attach conditions, or the new States concur in conditions, which after admission, would abridge or *enlarge* the constitutional rights of legislation common to the other States; whether Congress can by a compact with a new member take power either to or from itself, or place the new member above or below the equal rank & rights possessed by the others; whether all such stipulations, expressed or implied would not be nullities, and so pronounced when brought to a practical test. It falls within the Scope of your enquiry, to state the fact, that there was a proposition in the convention to discriminate between the old and new States, by an Article in the Constitution declaring that the aggregate number of representatives from the States thereafter to be admitted should never exceed that of the States originally adopting the Constitution. The proposition happily was rejected. The effect of such a discrimination, is sufficiently evident.

In the case of Louisiana, there is a circumstance which may deserve notice. In the Treaty ceding it, a privilege was retained by the ceding party, which distinguishes between its ports & others of the U. S. for a special purpose & a short period. This privilege however was the result not of an ordinary legislative power in Congress; nor was it the result of an arrangement between Congress & the people of Louisiana. It rests on the ground that the same entire power, even in the nation, over that territory, as over the original territory of the U. S. never existed; the privilege alluded to being in the deed of cession carved by the foreign owner, out of the title conveyed to the purchaser. A sort of necessity therefore was thought to belong to so peculiar & extraordinary a case. Notwithstanding this plea it is presumable that if the privilege had materially affected the rights of other ports, or had been of a permanent or durable character, the occurrence would not have been so little regarded. Congress would not be allowed to effect through the medium of a Treaty, obnoxious discriminations between new and old States, more than among the latter.

With respect to what has taken place in the N. W. Territory, it may be observed, that the ordinance giving its distinctive character on the Subject of Slaveholding proceeded from the old Congress, acting, with the best intentions, but under a charter which contains no shadow of the authority exercised. And it remains to be decided how far the States formed within that Territory & admitted into the Union, are on a different footing from its other members, as to their legislative sovereignty.

For the grounds on which 3/5 of the slaves were admitted into the ratio of representation, I will with your permission, save trouble by referring to No. 54 of the Federalist. In addition, it may be stated that this feature in the Constitution was combined with that relating to the power over Commerce & navigation. In truth these two powers, with those relating to the importation of slaves, & the Articles establishing the equality of representation in the Senate & the rule of taxation, had a complicated influence on each other which alone would have justified the remark, that the Constitution was "the result of mutual deference & Concession."

It was evident that the large States holding slaves, and those not large which felt themselves so by anticipation, would not have concurred in a constitution, allowing them no more Representation in one legislative branch than the smallest States, and in the other less than their proportional contributions to the Common Treasury.

The considerations which led to this mixed ratio which had been very deliberately agreed on in Apl., 1783, by the old Congress, make it probable that the Convention could not have looked to a departure from it, in any instance where slaves made a part of the local population.

Whether the Convention could have looked to the existence of slavery at all in the new States is a point on which I can add little to what has been already stated. The great object of the Convention seemed to be to prohibit the increase by the *importation* of slaves. A power to emancipate slaves was disclaimed; Nor is anything recollected that denoted a view to controul the distribution of those within the Country. The case of the N. Western Territory was probably superseded by the provision agst. the importation of slaves by S. Carolina & Georgia, which had not then passed laws prohibiting it. When the existence of slavery in that territory was precluded, the importation of slaves was rapidly going on, and the only mode of checking it was by narrowing the space open to them. It is not an unfair inference that the expedient would not have been undertaken, if the power afterward given to terminate the importation everywhere, had existed or been even anticipated. It has appeared that the present Congress never followed the example during the twenty years preceding the prohibitory epoch.

The *expediency* of exercising a supposed power in Congress, to prevent a diffusion of the slaves actually in the Country, as far as the local authorities may admit them, resolves itself into the probable effects of such a diffusion on the interests of the slaves and of the Nation.

Will it or will it not better the condition of the slaves, by lessening the number belonging to individual masters, and intermixing both with greater masses of free people? Will partial manumissions be more or less likely to take place, and a general emancipation be accelerated or retarded? Will the moral & physical condition of slaves, in the mean time, be improved or deteriorated? What do experiences and appearances decide as to the comparative rates of generative increase, in their present, and, in a dispersed situation?

Will the aggregate strength security tranquillity and harmony of the whole nation be advanced or impaired by lessening the proportion of slaves to the free people in particular sections of it?

How far an occlusion of the space now vacant, agst. the introduction of slaves may be essential to prevent compleatly a smuggled importation of them from abroad, ought to influence the question of expediency, must be decided by a reasonable estimate of the degree in which the importation would take place in spight of the spirit of the times, the increasing co-operation of foreign powers agst the slave trade, the increasing rigor of the Acts of Congress and the vigilant enforcement of them by the Executive; and by a fair comparison of this estimate with the considerations opposed to such an occlusion.

Will a multiplication of States holding slaves, multiply advocates of the importation of foreign slaves, so as to endanger the continuance of the prohibitory Acts of Congress? To such an apprehension seem to be opposed the facts, that the States holding fewest slaves are those which most readily abolished slavery altogether; that of the 13 primitive States, Eleven had prohibited the importation before the power was given to Congs., that all of them, with the newly added States, unanimously concurred in exerting that power; that most of the present slaveholding States cannot be tempted by motives of interest to favor the reopening of the ports to foreign slaves; and that these, with the States which have even abolished slavery within themselves, could never be outnumbered in the National Councils by new States wishing for slaves, and not satisfied with the supply attainable within the U. S.

On the whole, the Missouri question, as a constitutional one, amounts to the question whether the condition proposed to be annexed to the admission of Missouri would or would not be void in itself, or become void the moment the territory should enter as a State within the pale of the Constitution. And as a question of expediency & humanity, it depends essentially on the probable influence of such restrictions on the quantity & duration of slavery, and on the general condition of slaves in the U. S.

The question raised with regard to the tenor of the stipulation in the Louisiana Treaty, on the subject of its admission, is one which I have not examined, and on which I could probably throw no light if I had.

Under one aspect of the general subject, I cannot avoid saying, that apart from its merits under others, the tendency of what has passed and is passing, fills me with no slight anxiety. Parties under some denominations or other must always be expected in a Govt. as free as ours. When the individuals belonging to them are intermingled in every part of the whole Country, they strengthen the Union of the Whole, while they divide every part. Should a State of parties arise, founded on geographical boundaries and other Physical & permanent distinctions which happen to coincide with them, what is to controul those great repulsive Masses from awful shocks agst. each other?

The delay in answering your letter made me fear you might doubt my readiness to comply with its requests. I now fear you will think I have done more than these justified. I have been the less reserved because you are so ready to conform to my inclination formerly expressed, not to be drawn from my sequestered position into public view.

Since I thanked you for the copy of your late volume I have had the pleasure of going thro' it; and I should have been much disappointed, if it had been recd. by the public with less favor than is everywhere manifested. According to all accounts from the Continent of Europe, the American character has suffered much there by libels conveyed by British Prints, or circulated by itinerant Calumniators. It is to be hoped the truths in your book may find their way thither. Good translations of the Preface alone could not but open many eyes which have been blinded by prejudices against this Country.

21

Walter Lowrie, Senate
20 Jan. 1820
Annals 35:202–3

In the Constitution it is provided that "the migration or importation of such persons as any of the States now existing shall think proper to admit, shall not be prohibited by the Congress prior to the year 1808, but a tax," etc. In this debate it seems generally to be admitted, by gentlemen on the opposite side, that these two words are not synonomous; but what their meaning is, they are not so well agreed. One gentleman tells us, it was intended to prevent slaves from being brought in by land; another gentleman says, it was intended to restrain Congress from interfering with emigration from Europe.

These constructions cannot both be right. The gentlemen who have preceded me on the same side, have advanced a number of pertinent arguments to settle the proper meaning of these words. I, sir, shall not repeat them. Indeed, to me, there is nothing more dry and uninteresting, than discussions to explain the meaning of single words. In the present case, I will only refer to the authority of Mr. Madison and Judge Wilson, who were both members of the Convention, and who gave their construction to these words, long before this question was agitated. Mr. Madison observes, that, to say this clause was intended to prevent emigration does not deserve an answer. And Judge Wilson says, expressly, it was intended to place the new States under the control of Congress, as to the introduction of slaves. The opinion of this latter gentleman is entitled to peculiar weight. After the Convention had labored for weeks on the subject of representation and direct taxes—when those great men were like to separate without obtaining their object, Judge Wilson submitted the provision on this subject, which now stands as a part of your Constitution. Sir, there is no man, from any part of the nation, who understood the system of our Government better than him; not even excepting Virginia, from whence the gentleman from Georgia (Mr. Walker) tells us we have all our great men.

22

James Madison to James Monroe
10 Feb. 1820
Writings 9:22

I have been truly astonished at some of the doctrines and deliberations to which the Missouri question has led; and particularly so at the interpretations put on the terms "migration or importation &c." Judging from my own impressions I shd. deem it impossible that the memory of any one who was a member of the Genl. Convention, could favor an opinion that the terms did not *exclusively* refer to Migration & importation *into the U. S.* Had they been understood in that Body in the sense now put on them, it is easy to conceive the alienation they would have there created in certain States; And no one can decide better than yourself the effect they would have had in the State Conventions, if such a meaning had been avowed by the Advocates of the Constitution. If a suspicion had existed of such a construction, it wd. at least have made a conspicuous figure among the amendments proposed to the Instrument.

23

Charles Pinckney, House of Representatives
14 Feb. 1820
Annals 36:1315–17

The supporters of the amendment contend that Congress have the right to insist on the prevention of involuntary servitude in Missouri; and found the right on the ninth section of the first article, which says, "the migration or importation of such persons as the States now existing may think proper to admit, shall not be prohibited by the Congress prior to the year 1808, but a tax or duty may be imposed on such importation not exceeding ten dollars."

In considering this article, I will detail, as far as at this distant period is possible, what was the intention of the Convention that formed the Constitution in this article. The intention was, to give Congress a power, after the year 1808, to prevent the importation of slaves either by land or water from other countries. The word *import,* includes both, and applies wholly to slaves. Without this limitation, Congress might have stopped it sooner under their general power to regulate commerce; and it was an agreed point, a solemnly understood compact, that, on the Southern States consenting to shut their ports against the importation of Africans, no power was to be delegated to Congress, nor were they ever to be authorized to touch the question of slavery; that the property of the Southern States in slaves was to be as sacredly preserved, and protected to them, as that of land, or any other kind of property in the Eastern States were to be to their citizens.

The term, or word, migration, applies wholly to free whites; in its Constitutional sense, as intended by the Convention, it means "voluntary change of servitude", from one country to another. The reasons of its being adopted and used in the Constitution, as far as I can recollect, were these; that the Constitution being a frame of government, consisting wholly of delegated powers, all power, not expressly delegated, being reserved to the people or the States, it was supposed, that, without some express grant to them of power on the subject, Congress would not be authorized ever to touch the question of migration hither, or emigration to this country, however pressing or urgent the necessity for such a measure might be; that they could derive no such power from the usages of nations, or even the laws of war; that the latter would only enable them to make prisoners of alien enemies, which would not be sufficient, as spies or other dangerous emigrants, who were not alien enemies, might enter the country for treasonable purposes, and do great injury; that, as all governments possessed this power, it was necessary to give it to our own, which could alone exercise it, and where, on other and much greater points, we had placed unlimited confidence; it was, therefore, agreed that, in the same article, the word migration should be placed; and that, from the year 1808, Congress should possess the complete power to stop either or both, as they might suppose the public interest required; the article, therefore, is a *negative pregnant,* restraining for twenty years, and giving the power after.

The reasons for restraining the power to prevent migration hither for twenty years, were, to the best of my recollection, these: That, as at this time, we had immense and almost immeasurable territory, peopled by not more than two millions and a half of inhabitants, it was of very great consequence to encourage the emigration of able, skilful, and industrious Europeans. The wise conduct of William Penn, and the unexampled growth of Pennsylvania, were cited. It was said, that the portals of the only temple of true freedom now existing on earth should be thrown open to all mankind; that all foreigners of industrious habits should be welcome, and none more so than men of science, and such as may bring to us arts we are unacquainted with, or the means of perfecting those in which we are not yet sufficiently skilled—capitalists whose wealth may add to our commerce or domestic improvements; let the door be ever and most affectionately open to illustrious exiles and sufferers in the cause of liberty; in short, open it liberally to science, to merit, and talents, wherever found, and receive and make them your own. That the safest mode would be to pursue the course for twenty years, and not, before that period, put it at all into the power of Congress to shut it; that, by that time, the Union would be so settled, and our population would be so much increased, we could proceed on our own stock, without the farther accession of foreigners; that, as Congress were to be prohibited from stopping the importation of slaves to settle the Southern States, as no obstacle was to be thrown in the way of their increase and settlement for that period, let it be so with the Northern and Eastern, to which, particularly New York and Philadelphia, it was expected most of the emigrants would go from Europe: and it so happened, for, previous to the year 1808, more than double as many Europeans emigrated to these States, as of Africans were imported into the Southern States.

24

Gibbons v. Ogden

9 Wheat. 1 (1824)

(See 1.8.3 [commerce], no. 16)

25

The Antelope

10 Wheat. 66 (1825)

Mr. Chief Justice MARSHALL delivered the opinion of the court, and after stating the case, proceeded as follows:

In prosecuting this appeal, the United States assert no property in themselves. They appear in the character of guardians, or next friends, of these Africans, who are brought, without any act of their own, into the bosom of our country, insist on their right to freedom, and submit their claim to the laws of the land, and to the tribunals of the nation.

The consuls of Spain and Portugal, respectively, demand these Africans as slaves, who have, in the regular course of legitimate commerce, been acquired as property by the subjects of their respective sovereigns, and claim their restitution under the laws of the United States.

In examining claims of this momentous importance; claims in which the sacred rights of liberty and of property come in conflict with each other; which have drawn from the bar a degree of talent and of eloquence worthy of the questions that have been discussed; this court must not yield to feelings which might seduce it from the path of duty, and must obey the mandate of the law.

That the course of opinion on the slave trade should be unsettled, ought to excite no surprise. The Christian and civilized nations of the world, with whom we have most intercourse, have all been engaged in it. However abhorrent this traffic may be to a mind whose original feelings are not blunted by familiarity with the practice, it has been sanctioned in modern times by the laws of all nations who possess distant colonies, each of whom has engaged in it as a common commercial business which no other could rightfully interrupt. It has claimed all the sanction which could be derived from long usage, and general acquiescence. That trade could not be considered as contrary to the law of nations which was authorized and protected by the laws of all commercial nations; the right to carry on which was claimed by each, and allowed by each.

The course of unexamined opinion, which was founded on this inveterate usage, received its first check in America; and, as soon as these states acquired the right of self-government, the traffic was forbidden by most of them. In the beginning of this century, several humane and enlightened individuals of Great Britain devoted themselves to the cause of the Africans; and, by frequent appeals to the nation, in which the enormity of this commerce was unveiled and exposed to the public eye, the general sentiment was at length roused against it, and the feelings of justice and humanity, regaining their long lost ascendency, prevailed so far in the British Parliament as to obtain an act for its abolition. The utmost efforts of the British government, as well as of that of the United States, have since been assiduously employed in its suppression. It has been denounced by both in terms of great severity, and those concerned in it are subjected to the heaviest penalties which law can inflict. In addition to these measures operating on their own people, they have used all their influence to bring other nations into the same system, and to interdict this trade by the consent of all.

Public sentiment has, in both countries, kept pace with the measures of government; and the opinion is extensively, if not universally entertained, that this unnatural traffic ought to be suppressed. While its illegality is asserted by some governments, but not admitted by all; while the detestation in which it is held is growing daily, and even those nations who tolerate it in fact, almost disavow their own conduct, and rather connive at, than legalize, the acts of their subjects; it is not wonderful that public feeling should march somewhat in advance of strict law, and that opposite opinions should be entertained on the precise cases in which our own laws may control and limit the practice of others. Indeed, we ought not to be surprised, if, on this novel series of cases, even courts of justice should, in some instances, have carried the principle of suppression farther than a more deliberate consideration of the subject would justify.

The Amedie (1 Acton's Rep., 240), which was an American vessel employed in the African trade, was captured by a British cruiser, and condemned in the Vice-Admiralty Court of Tortola. An appeal was prayed; and Sir William Grant, in delivering the opinion of the court, said, that the trade being then declared unjust and unlawful by Great Britain, "a claimant could have no right, upon principles of universal law, to claim restitution in a prize court, of human beings carried as his slaves. He must show some right that has been violated by the capture, some property of which he has been dispossessed, and to which he ought to be restored. In this case, the laws of the claimant's country allow of no right of property such as he claims. There can, therefore, be no right of restitution. The consequence is, that the judgment must be affirmed."

The Fortuna (1 Dodson's Rep., 81), was condemned on the authority of *The Amedie,* and the same principle was again affirmed.

The Diana (1 Dodson's Rep., 95), was a Swedish vessel, captured with a cargo of slaves, by a British cruiser, and condemned in the Court of Vice-Admiralty at Sierra Leone. This sentence was reversed on appeal, and Sir William Scott, in pronouncing the sentence of reversal, said, "the condemnation also took place on a principle which this court cannot in any manner recognize, inasmuch as the sentence affirms, 'that the slave trade, from motives of humanity, hath been abolished by most civilized nations, and is not, at the present time, legally authorized by any.' This appears to me to be an assertion by no means sustainable." The ship and cargo were restored, on the principle that the trade was allowed by the laws of Sweden.

The principle common to these cases is, that the legality of the capture of a vessel engaged in the slave trade, depends on the law of the country to which the vessel belongs. If that law gives its sanction to the trade, restitution will be decreed; if that law prohibits it, the vessel and cargo will be condemned as good prize.

This whole subject came on afterwards to be considered in *The Louis* (2 Dodson's Rep., 238). The opinion of Sir William Scott, in that case, demonstrates the attention he had bestowed upon it, and gives full assurance that it may be considered as settling the law in the British courts of admiralty as far as it goes.

The Louis was a French vessel, captured on a slaving voyage, before she had purchased any slaves, brought into Sierra Leone, and condemned by the Vice-Admiralty Court at that place. On an appeal to the Court of Admiralty in England, the sentence was reversed.

In the very full and elaborate opinion given on this case, Sir William Scott, in explicit terms, lays down the broad principle that the right of search is confined to a state of war. It is a right strictly belligerent in its character, which can never be exercised by a nation at peace, except against professed pirates, who are the enemies of the human race. The act of trading in slaves, however detestable, was not, he said, "the act of freebooters, enemies of the human race, renouncing every country, and ravaging every country, in its coasts and vessels, indiscriminately." It was not piracy.

He also said that this trade could not be pronounced contrary to the law of nations. "A court, in the administration of law, cannot attribute criminality to an act where the law imputes none. It must look to the legal standard of morality; and, upon a question of this nature, that standard must be found in the law of nations, as fixed and evidenced by general, and ancient, and admitted practice, by treaties, and by the general tenor of the laws and ordinances, and the formal transactions of civilized states; and, looking to those authorities, he found a difficulty in maintaining that the transaction was legally criminal."

The right of visitation and search being strictly a belligerent right, and the slave trade being neither piratical nor contrary to the law of nations, the principle is asserted and maintained with great strength of reasoning, that it cannot be exercised on the vessels of a foreign power, unless permitted by treaty. France had refused to assent to the insertion of such an article in her treaty with Great Britain, and, consequently, the right could not be exercised on the high seas by a British cruiser on a French vessel.

"It is pressed as a a difficulty," says the judge, "what is to be done, if a French ship, laden with slaves, is brought in? I answer, without hesitation, restore the possession which has been unlawfully devested; rescind the illegal act done by your own subject, and leave the foreigner to the justice of his own country."

This reasoning goes far in support of the proposition that, in the British courts of admiralty, the vessel even of a nation which had forbidden the slave trade, but had not conceded the right of search, must, if wrongfully brought in, be restored to the original owner. But the judge goes farther, and shows that no evidence existed to prove that France had, by law, forbidden that trade. Consequently, for this reason, as well as for that previously assigned, the sentence of condemnation was reversed, and restitution awarded.

In the United States, different opinions have been entertained in the different circuits and districts; and the subject is now, for the first time, before this court.

The question whether the slave trade is prohibited by the law of nations has been seriously propounded, and both the affirmative and negative of the proposition have been maintained with equal earnestness.

That it is contrary to the law of nature will scarcely be denied. That every man has a natural right to the fruits of his own labor, is generally admitted; and that no other person can rightfully deprive him of those fruits, and appropriate them against his will, seems to be the necessary result of this admission. But from the earliest times war has existed, and war confers rights in which all have acquiesced. Among the most enlightened nations of antiquity, one of these was, that the victor might enslave the vanquished. This, which was the usage of all, could not be pronounced repugnant to the law of nations, which is certainly to be tried by the test of general usage. That which has received the assent of all, must be the law of all.

Slavery, then, has its origin in force; but as the world has agreed that it is a legitimate result of force, the state of things which is thus produced by general consent, cannot be pronounced unlawful.

Throughout Christendom, this harsh rule has been exploded, and war is no longer considered as giving a right to enslave captives. But this triumph of humanity has not been universal. The parties to the modern law of nations do not propagate their principles by force; and Africa has not yet adopted them. Throughout the whole extent of that immense continent, so far as we know its history, it is still the law of nations that prisoners are slaves. Can those who have themselves renounced this law, be permitted to participate in its effects by purchasing the beings who are its victims?

Whatever might be the answer of a moralist to this question, a jurist must search for its legal solution in those principles of action which are sanctioned by the usages, the national acts, and the general assent of that portion of the world of which he considers himself as a part, and to whose law the appeal is made. If we resort to this standard as the test of international law, the question, as has already been observed, is decided in favor of the legality of the trade. Both Europe and America embarked in it; and for nearly two centuries it was carried on without opposition, and without censure. A jurist could not say that a practice thus supported was illegal, and that those engaged in it might be punished, either personally, or by deprivation of property.

In this commerce, thus sanctioned by universal assent, every nation had an equal right to engage. How is this right to be lost? Each may renounce it for its own people; but can this renunciation affect others?

No principle of general law is more universally acknowledged than the perfect equality of nations. Russia and Geneva have equal rights. It results from this equality, that no one can rightfully impose a rule on another. Each legislates for itself, but its legislation can operate on itself alone. A right, then, which is vested in all by the consent of all, can be devested only by consent; and this trade, in which all have participated, must remain lawful to those who cannot be induced to relinquish it. As no nation can prescribe a rule for others, none can make a law of nations; and this traffic remains lawful to those whose governments have not forbidden it.

If it is consistent with the law of nations, it cannot in itself be piracy. It can be made so only by statute; and the obligation of the statute cannot transcend the legislative power of the state which may enact it.

If it be neither repugnant to the law of nations, nor piracy, it is almost superfluous to say in this court that the right of bringing in for adjudication in time of peace, even where the vessel belongs to a nation which has prohibited the trade, cannot exist. The courts of no country execute the penal laws of another; and the course of the American government on the subject of visitation and search, would decide any case in which that right had been exercised by an American cruiser, on the vessel of a foreign nation, not violating our municipal laws, against the captors.

It follows, that a foreign vessel engaged in the African slave trade, captured on the high seas in time of peace, by an American cruiser, and brought in for adjudication, would be restored.

26

James Kent, Commentaries 1:179–87
1826

The African slave trade is an offence against the municipal laws of most nations in Europe, and it is declared to be piracy by the statute laws of England and the United States. Whether it is to be considered as an offence against the law of nations, independent of compact, has been a grave question, much litigated in the courts charged with the administration of public law; and it will be useful to take a short view of the progress and present state of the sense and practice of nations on this subject.

Personal slavery, arising out of forcible captivity, has existed in every age of the world, and among the most refined and civilized people. The possession of persons so acquired, has been invested with the character of property. The slave trade was a regular branch of commerce among the ancients; and a great object of Athenian traffic with the Greek settlements on the Euxine, was procuring slaves from the barbarians for the Greek market. In modern times, treaties have been framed, and national monopolies sought, to facilitate and extend commerce in this species of property. It has been interwoven into the municipal institutions of all the European colonies in America, and with the approbation and sanction of the parent states. It forms to this day the foundation of large masses of property in the southern parts of these United States. But, for half a century past, the African slave trade began to awaken a spirit of remorse and sympathy in the breasts of men, and a conviction that the traffic was repugnant to the principles of Christian duty, and the maxims of justice and humanity.

Montesquieu, who has disclosed so many admirable truths, and so much profound reflection, in his Spirit of Laws, not only condemned all slavery as useless and unjust, but he animadverted upon the African slave trade by the most pungent reproaches. It was impossible, he observed, that we could admit the negroes to be human beings, because, if we were once to admit them to be men, we should soon come to believe that we ourselves were not Christians. Why has it not, says he, entered into the heads of the European princes, who make so many useless conventions, to make one general stipulation in favour of humanity. We shall see presently that this suggestion was, in some degree, carried into practice by a modern European congress.

The constitution of the United States laid the foundation of a series of provisions, to put a final stop to the progress of this great moral pestilence, by admitting a power in Congress to prohibit the importation of slaves, *after* the expiration of the year 1807. The constitution evidently looked forward to the year 1808 as the commencement of an epoch in the history of human improvement. Prior to that time, Congress did all on this subject that it was within their competence to do. By the acts of March 22d, 1794, and May 10th, 1800, the citizens of the United States, and residents within them, were prohibited from engaging in the transportation of slaves from the United States to any foreign place or country, or from one foreign country or place to another. These provisions prohibited our citizens from all concern in the slave trade, with the exception of direct importation into the United States; and the most prompt and early steps were taken, within the limits of the constitution, to interdict that part of the traffic also. By the act of 2d March, 1807, it was prohibited, under severe penalties, to import slaves into the United States, after the 1st January, 1808; and, on the 20th April, 1818, the penalties and punishments were increased, and the prohibition extended not only to importation, but generally against any citizen of the United States being concerned in the slave trade. It has been decided, that these statute prohibitions extend as well to the carrying slaves on freight, as to cases where they were the property of American citizens, and to carrying them from one port to another of the same foreign empire, as well as from one foreign country to another. The object was to prevent, on the part of our citizens, all concern whatever in such a trade.

The act of March 3d, 1819, went a step further, and authorized national armed vessels to be sent to the coast of Africa, to stop the slave trade, so far as citizens or residents of the United States were engaged in that trade; and their vessels and effects were made liable to seizure and confiscation. The act of 15th May, 1820, went still further, and declared, that if any citizen of the United States, being of the crew of any foreign vessel engaged in the slave trade, or any person whatever, being of the crew of any vessel armed in whole or in part, or navigated for or on behalf of any citizen of the United States, should land on any foreign shore, and seize any negro or mulatto, with intent to make him a slave, or should decoy, or forcibly bring, or receive such negro on board such vessel, with like intent, such citizen or person should be adjudged a pirate, and, on conviction, should suffer death.

It is to be observed, that the statute operates only where our municipal jurisdiction might be applied consistently with the general theory of public law, to the persons of our citizens, or to foreigners on board of American vessels. Declaring the crime piracy, does not make it so, within the purview of the law of nations, if it were not so without the statute; and the legislature intended to legislate only where they had a right to legislate, over their own citizens and vessels. The question, notwithstanding these expressions in the statute, still remained to be discussed and settled, whether the African slave trade could be adjudged piracy, or any other crime within the contemplation of the code of international law. It has been attempted, by negotiation between this country and Great Britain, to agree that both nations should consider the slave trade piratical; but the convention for that purpose between the two nations has not, as yet, been ratified, though the British nation have carried their statute denunciation of the trade as far as the law of the United States.

The first British statute that declared the slave trade unlawful, was in March, 1807. This was a great triumph of British justice. It was called for by the sense of the British nation, which had become deeply convinced of the impolicy and injustice of the slave trade; and by the subsequent statute of 51 Geo. III. the trade was declared to be contrary to the principles of justice, humanity, and sound policy; and lastly, by the act of Parliament of 31st March, 1824, the trade is declared to be piracy. England is thus, equally with the United States, honestly and zealously engaged in promoting the universal abolition of the trade, and in holding out to the world their sense of its extreme criminality. Almost every maritime nation in Europe has also deliberately and solemnly, either by legislative acts, or by treaties and other formal engagements, acknowledged the injustice and inhumanity of the trade, and pledged itself to promote its abolition. By the treaty of Paris of the 30th May, 1814, between Great Britain and France, Lewis XVIII. agreed that the traffic was repugnant to the principles of natural justice, and he engaged to unite his efforts at the ensuing congress, to induce all the powers of christendom to decree the abolition of the trade, and that it should cease definitively, on the part of the French government, in the course of five years. The ministers of the principal European powers who met at the congress at Vienna, on the 8th February, 1815, solemnly declared, in the face of Europe and the world, that the African slave trade had been regarded by just and enlightened men, in all ages, as repugnant to the principles of humanity and of universal morality, and that the public voice in all civilized countries demanded that it should be suppressed; and that the universal abolition of it was conformable to the spirit of the age, and the generous principles of the allied powers. In March, 1815, the Emperor Napoleon decreed that the slave trade should be abolished; but this effort of ephemeral power was afterwards held to be null and void, as being the act of an usurper; and in July following, Lewis XVIII. gave directions that this odious and wicked traffic should from that present time cease. The first French decree, however, that was made public, abolishing the trade, was of the date of the 8th January, 1817, and that was only a partial and modified decree. In December, 1817, the Spanish government prohibited the purchase of slaves on any part of the coast of Africa, after the 31st May, 1820; and in January, 1818, the Portuguese government made the like prohibition as to the purchase of slaves on any part of the coast of Africa north of the equator. In 1821, there was not a flag of any European state which could legally cover this traffic, to the north of the equator; and yet, in 1825, the importation of slaves covertly continued, if it was not openly countenanced, from the Rio de la Plata to the Amazon, and through the whole American archipelago.

The case of the *Amedie* was the earliest decision in the English courts on the great question touching the legality of the slave trade, on general principles of international law. That was the case of an American vessel, employed in carrying slaves from the coast of Africa to a Spanish colony. She was captured by an English cruiser, and the vessel and cargo were condemned to the captors, in a vice-admiralty court in the West Indies, and, on appeal to the Court of Appeals in England, the judgment was affirmed. Sir Wm. Grant, who pronounced the opinion of the court, observed, that the slave trade being abolished by both England and the United States, the court was authorized to assert, that the trade, abstractedly speaking, could not have a legitimate existence, and was, *prima facie,* illegal, upon principles of universal law. The claimant, to entitle him to restitution, must show affirmatively a right of property under the municipal laws of his own country; for, if it be unprotected by his own municipal law, he can have no right of property in human beings carried as his slaves, for such a claim is contrary to the principles of justice and humanity. The *Fortuna* was condemned on the authority of the *Amedie,* and the same principle was again affirmed. But, in the subsequent case of the *Diana,* the doctrine was not carried so far as to hold the trade itself to be piracy, or a crime against the law of nations. A Swedish vessel was taken by a British cruiser on the coast of Africa, engaged in carrying slaves from Africa to a Swedish island in the West Indies, and she was restored to the owner, on the ground that Sweden had not then prohibited the trade, and had tolerated it in practice. England had abolished the trade as unjust and criminal, but she claimed no right of enforcing that prohibition against the subjects of those states which had not adopted the same opinion; and England did not mean to set herself up as the legislator, and *custos morum,* for the whole world, or presume to interfere with the commercial regulations of other states. The principle of the case of the *Amedie* was, that where the municipal law of the country to which the parties belonged had prohibited the trade, English tribunals would hold it to be illegal, upon general principles of justice and humanity, but they would respect the property of persons engaged in it, under the sanction of the laws of their own country.

The doctrine of these cases is, that the slave trade is, abstractedly speaking, immoral and unjust, and it is illegal, when declared so by treaty, or municipal law; but that it is not piratical or illegal by the common law of nations, because, if it were so, every claim founded on the trade would at once be rejected every where, and in every court, on that ground alone.

The whole subject underwent further, and a most full, elaborate, and profound discussion, in the case of the *Le Louis.* A French vessel, owned and documented as a French vessel, was captured by a British armed force on the coast of Africa, after resistance made to a demand to visit and search. She was carried into Sierra Leone, and condemned by a court of vice-admiralty, for being concerned in the slave trade contrary to the French law. On appeal to the British High Court of Admiralty, the question respecting the legality of the capture and condemnation, was argued, and it was judicially decided, that the right of visitation and search, on the high seas, did not exist in time of peace. If it belonged to one nation, it equally belonged to all, and would lead to gigantic mischief, and universal war. Other nations had refused to accede to the English proposal of a reciprocal right of search in the African seas, and it would require an express convention to give the right of search in time of peace. The slave trade, though unjust and condemned by the statute law of England, was not piracy, nor was it a crime by the universal law of nations. To make it piracy, or such a crime, it must have been so considered and treated in practice by all civilized states, or made so by virtue of a general convention. On the contrary, it had been carried on by all nations, even by Great Britain herself, until within a few years, and was then carried on by Spain and Portugal, and not absolutely prohibited by France. It was, therefore, not a criminal traffic by the law of nations; and every nation, independent of treaty, retained a legal right to carry it on. No one nation had a right to force the way to the liberation of Africa, by trampling on the independence of other states; or to procure an eminent good by means that were unlawful; or to press forward to a great principle, by breaking through other great principles that stood in the way. The condemnation of the French vessel at Sierra Leone was, therefore, reversed, and the penalties imposed by the French law, (if any there were,) were left to be enforced, not in an English, but in a French court.

The same subject was brought into discussion in the K. B. in 1820, in *Madrazo* v. *Willes.* The Court held, that the British statutes against the slave trade, were only applicable to British subjects, and only rendered the slave trade unlawful when carried on by them. The British parliament could not prevent the subjects of other states from carrying on the trade out of the limits of the British dominions. If a ship be acting contrary to the general law of nations, she is thereby subject to condemnation; but it is impossible to say that the slave trade was contrary to the general law of nations. It was, until lately, carried on by all the nations of Europe; and a practice so sanctioned can only be rendered illegal, on the principles of international law, by the consent of all the powers. Many states had so consented, but others had not, and the cases had gone no further than to establish the rule, that ships belonging to countries that had prohibited the trade, were liable to capture and condemnation, if found engaged in it.

The final decision of the question, in this country, has been the same as in the case of the *Le Louis.* In the case of the *La Jeune Eugenie,* it was decided in the Circuit Court of the United States, in Massachusetts, after a masterly discussion, that the slave trade was prohibited by universal law. But, subsequently, in the case of the *Antelope,* the Supreme Court of the United States declared that the slave trade had been sanctioned, in modern times, by the laws of all nations who possessed distant colonies; and a trade could not be considered as contrary to the law of nations, which had been authorized and protected by the usages and laws of all commercial nations. It was not piracy, except so far as it was made so by the treaties or statutes of the nation to which the party belonged. It might still be lawfully carried on by the subjects of those nations who have not prohibited it by municipal acts or treaties.

27

Hunter v. Fulcher

1 Leigh 172 (Va. 1829)

Green, J. The decision of this case in favour of the appellant, does not appear to me to involve the proposition, that in all cases and under all circumstances (except that of persons bound to service in one state, escaping to another, provided for by the constitution of the U. States), a slave born and owned in Virginia, and found in another state, may be emancipated by the laws of that state, so as to enable him to assert that right in our courts. If it did, I should wish the cause to be submitted to the consideration of a full court. My strong impression is, that such a proposition cannot be supported, and was rightly denied by this court in Lewis v. Fullerton, where it was held, that a slave temporarily employed in Ohio, for the benefit of her master, a resident citizen of Virginia, was not thereby entitled to be considered as free in the courts of Virginia, although she might be so considered in those of Ohio.

In this case, a slave born and owned in Virginia, was carried to Maryland to reside there, and he was kept there for twelve years, by one who acquired a title to him by marriage, then being a resident citizen of Maryland, or soon afterwards removing and domiciliating himself there; thus voluntarily becoming a permanent member of that community, and submitting himself and his property to the full force of the laws of Maryland, by which the slave was declared to be free; and thereby also (according to the opinion of judge Cabell, in Murray v. M'Carty, 2 Munf. 393, in which I concur) becoming, upon the principles of natural law, and the spirit of our institutions, a citizen of that state. We are, therefore, called upon in this case, to enforce rights acquired in Maryland, under the laws of that state, against one claiming under a citizen of that state, after those rights were vested. And I see no objection, in principle, to giving full effect here, to those laws, operating on the rights of persons, who were to all intents and purposes justly subjected to them, and touching the rights of no others: in this respect, the case is like that of Griffith v. Fanny, where a citizen of Virginia carried a slave to Ohio, and there sold and delivered her to a resident citizen of that state, who, in fraud of the laws of Ohio, took a bill of sale to a resident citizen of Virginia, in trust for himself, and retained possession of the slave in Ohio for two years. The court there, enforced the laws of Ohio against a resident citizen of that state, without affecting the rights or interests of any other.

The english cases cited do not touch this, in any point. They were all collated and examined by lord Stowell in the case of The mongrel woman Grace, decided by him in 1827. And he declared their effect to be, that the laws of England did not emancipate slaves brought there, or annihilate the master's rights, but afforded no remedy for enforcing them, the relation of master and slave not being known to the common law; and that, upon the return of the slave to the country from whence he was brought, the subsisting rights of the master might be there enforced, according to the laws of that country.

Carr, J. Agreeing, as I do, with the general view taken of this case by my brother Green, I should not add a word, but to mark the exact extent to which I mean to go. The law of Maryland, having enacted, that slaves carried into that state for sale or to reside, shall be free; and the owner of the slave here, having carried him to Maryland, and resided there with him for twelve years, thus becoming himself a citizen of Maryland, and voluntarily subjecting himself and the slave to the operation of her laws; I think the right to freedom vested, and could not be divested, by the bringing him back afterwards to Virginia.

Cabell, J., concurred in the opinion, that the judgment should be reversed, and judgment entered for the appellant.

28

Joseph Story, Commentaries on the Constitution 3:§§ 1327–31
1833

§ 1327. The corresponding clause of the first draft of the constitution was in these words: "No tax, or duty, shall be laid, &c. on the migration, or importation of such persons, as the several states shall think proper to admit; nor shall such migration, or importation be prohibited." In this form it is obvious, that the migration and importation of slaves, which was the sole object of the clause, was in effect perpetuated, so long, as any state should choose to allow the traffic. The subject was afterwards referred to a committee, who reported the clause substantially in its present shape; except that the limitation was the year one thousand eight hundred, instead of one thousand eight hundred and eight. The latter amendment was substituted by the vote of seven states against four; and as thus amended, the clause was adopted by the like vote of the same states.

§ 1328. It is to the honour of America, that she should have set the first example of interdicting and abolishing the slave-trade, in modern times. It is well known, that it constituted a grievance, of which some of the colonies complained before the revolution, that the introduction of slaves was encouraged by the crown, and that prohibitory laws were negatived. It was doubtless to have been wished, that the power of prohibiting the importation of slaves had been allowed to be put into immediate operation, and had not been postponed for twenty years. But it is not difficult to account, either for this restriction, or for the manner, in which it is expressed. It ought to be considered, as a great point gained in favour of humanity, that a period of twenty years might for ever terminate, within the United States, a traffic, which has so long, and so loudly upbraided the barbarism of modern policy. Even within this period, it might receive a very considerable discouragement, by curtailing the traffic between foreign countries; and it might even be totally abolished by the concurrence of a few states. "Happy," it was then added by the Federalist, "would it be for the unfortunate Africans, if an equal prospect lay before them of being redeemed from the oppressions of their European brethren." Let it be remembered, that at this period this horrible traffic was carried on with the encouragement and support of every civilized nation of Europe; and by none with more eagerness and enterprize, than by the parent country. America stood forth alone, uncheered and unaided, in stamping ignominy upon this traffic on the very face of her constitution of government, although there were strong temptations of interest to draw her aside from the performance of this great moral duty.

§ 1329. Yet attempts were made to pervert this clause into an objection against the constitution, by representing it on one side, as a criminal toleration of an illicit practice; and on another, as calculated to prevent voluntary and beneficial emigrations to America. Nothing, perhaps, can better exemplify the spirit and manner, in which the opposition to the constitution was conducted, than this fact. It was notorious, that the postponement of an immediate abolition was indispensable to secure the adoption of the constitution. It was a necessary sacrifice to the prejudices and interests of a portion of the Southern states. The glory of the achievement is scarcely lessened by its having been gradual, and by steps silent, but irresistible.

§ 1330. Congress lost no time in interdicting the traffic, as far as their power extended, by a prohibition of American citizens carrying it on between foreign countries. And as soon, as the stipulated period of twenty years had expired, congress, by a prospective legislation to meet the exigency, abolished the whole traffic in every direction to citizens and residents. Mild and moderate laws were, however, found insufficient for the purpose of putting an end to the practice; and at length congress found it necessary to declare the slave-trade to be a piracy, and to punish it with death. Thus it has been elevated in the catalogue of crimes to this "bad eminence" of guilt; and has now annexed to it the infamy, as well as the retributive justice, which belongs to an offence equally against the laws of God and man, the dictates of humanity, and the solemn precepts of religion. Other civilized nations are now alive to this great duty; and by the noble exertions of the British government, there is now every reason to believe, that the African slave-trade will soon become extinct; and thus another triumph of virtue would be obtained over brutal violence and unfeeling cruelty.

§ 1331. This clause of the constitution, respecting the importation of slaves, is manifestly an exception from the power of regulating commerce. Migration seems appropriately to apply to voluntary arrivals, as importation does to involuntary arrivals; and so far, as an exception from a power proves its existence, this proves, that the power to regulate commerce applies equally to the regulation of vessels employed in transporting men, who pass from place to place voluntarily, as to those, who pass involuntarily.

SEE ALSO:

Generally 1.2.3; 4.2.3; 4.3.1
Continental Congress, Agreement to Abolish Slave Trade, 20 Oct. 1774, Journals 1:32
Records of the Federal Convention, Farrand 2:378, 396, 408–9, 446, 449–50, 571, 596, 640
Centinel, no. 3, 5 Nov. 1787, Storing, 2.7.76
James McHenry, Maryland House of Representatives, 29 Nov. 1787, Farrand 3:149
A Friend of the Rights of the People, 8 Feb. 1788, Storing 4.23.3
Republicus, 1 Mar. 1788, Storing 5.13.14
James Iredell, Marcus, Answers to Mr. Mason's Objections to the New Constitution, 1788, Pamphlets 367
Phileleutheros, 21 May 1788, Storing 4.27.5
Respublica v. *Betsey*, 1 Dall. 469 (Pa. 1789)
House of Representatives, Slave Trade, 11–12 Feb., 17, 22–23 Mar. 1790, Annals 2:1184–91, 1198–1205, 1451–64, 1466–71
Tench Coxe to James Madison, 31 Mar. 1790, Farrand 3:361
George Mason, Deficiencies of the Constitution, 30 Sept. 1792, Farrand 3:367
Edmund Randolph, Abduction and Restitution of Slaves, 1 Nov. 1792, 1 Ops. Atty. Gen. 29
Kentucky Constitution of 1792, art. 9, Thorpe 3:1272–73
An Act to Prohibit the Carrying On the Slave Trade from the United States to Any Foreign Place or Country, 1 Stat. 347 (1794)
Respublica v. *Richards*, 2 Dall. 224 (Pa. 1795)
House of Representatives, Alien Enemies, June 1798, Annals 8:1968–69, 1992–93, 2003–5
Kentucky Constitution of 1799, art. 7, secs. 1 & 2, Thorpe 1287–88
Wilson v. *Isbell*, 5 Call 425 (Va. 1805)
Scott v. *London*, 3 Cranch 324 (1806)
Butler v. *Hopper*, 4 Fed. Cas. 904, no. 2,241 (C.C.D.Pa. 1806)
Indiana Constitution of 1816, art. 11, sec. 7, Thorpe 2:1070
Mississippi Constitution of 1817, art. 6, secs. 1 and 2, Thorpe 4:2045

Senate, The African Slave Trade, 12 Jan. 1818, Annals 31:94–108
Harry v. *Decker,* 1 Walker 36 (Miss. 1818)
William Wirt, Duties of Collectors Concerning the Slave Trade, 8 Oct. 1819, 1 Ops. Atty. Gen. 312
William Wirt, Suppression of Slave Trade, 14, 16 Oct. 1819, 1 Ops. Atty. Gen. 315, 317
Alabama Constitution of 1819, art. 6, secs. 1–3, Thorpe 1:111–12
William Wirt, The Slave Trade, 2 Jan. 1820, 1 Ops. Atty. Gen. 334
James Madison to Robert Walsh, 11 Jan. 1820, Farrand 3:438
The Josefa Segunda, 5 Wheat. 338 (1820)
William Wirt, Importation of Slaves, 20 Jan. 1821, 1 Ops. Atty. Gen. 447
Lewis v. *Fullerton,* 1 Rand. 15 (Va. 1821)
William Wirt, Concerning the Importation of Slaves, 5 Nov. 1821, 1 Ops. Atty. Gen. 503
Winny v. *Whitesides,* 1 Mo. 472 (1824)
Documents Relating to the Slave Trade Referred to in the Case of the Antelope, 10 Wheat. App. 3 (1825)
LaGrange v. *Chouteau,* 2 Mo. 20 (1828)
John Macpherson Berrien, The Grampus and the Slave Trade, 18 Aug. 1830, 2 Ops. Atty. Gen. 365
James Macpherson Berrien, Validity of the South Carolina Police Bill, 25 Mar. 1831, 2 Ops. Atty. Gen. 427
Roger B. Taney, Slaves on British Vessels Trading with the United States, 6 Dec. 1831, 2 Ops. Atty. Gen. 475
Roger B. Taney, Importation of Slaves, 20 Dec. 1831, 2 Ops. Atty. Gen. 479
Mississippi Constitution of 1832, art. 7, secs. 1–3, Thorpe 4:2062
Julia v. *McKinney,* 3 Mo. 270 (1833)
Betty v. *Horton,* 5 Leigh 615 (Va. 1833)
Lee v. *Lee,* 8 Pet. 44 (1834)

Article 1, Section 9, Clause 2

The Privilege of the Writ of Habeas Corpus shall not be suspended, unless when in Cases of Rebellion or Invasion the public Safety may require it.

1

CHAMBERS'S CASE

79 Eng. Rep. 746 (K.B. 1629)

Chambers was brought by a *habeas corpus* out of the Fleet, and returned, that he was "committed to the Fleet by virtue of a decree in the Star Chamber, by reason of certain words he used at the council table, viz. that the merchants of England were screwed up here in England more than in Turkey." And for these and other words of defamation of the Government, he was censured to be committed to the Fleet, and to be there imprisoned until he made his submission at the council table, and to pay a fine of two thousand pounds.

And now at the Bar he prayed to be delivered, because this sentence is not warranted by any law or statute; for the statute of 3 Hen. 7. c. 1. which is the foundation of the Court of Star Chamber, doth not give them any authority to punish for words only.

But all the Court informed him, that the Court of Star Chamber was not erected by the 3 Hen. 7. c. 1. but was a Court many years before, and one of the most high and honourable Courts of Justice; and to deliver one who was committed by the decree of one of the Courts of Justice, was not the usage of this Court. And therefore he was remanded. *Vide* 3 Ass. pl. 38. 28 Ass. pl. 34. 21 Hen. 8. c. 20.

2

HABEAS CORPUS ACT
31 Car. 2, c. 2, 27 May 1679

WHEREAS *great delays have been used by sheriffs, gaolers and other officers, to whose custody any of the King's subjects have been committed for criminal or supposed criminal matters, in making returns of writs of* habeas corpus *to them directed, by standing out an* alias *and* pluries habeas corpus, *and sometimes more, and by other shifts to avoid their yielding obedience to such writs, contrary to their duty and the known laws of the land, whereby many of the King's subjects have been and hereafter may be long detained in prison, in such cases where by law they are bailable, to their great charges and vexation:*

II. For the prevention whereof, and the more speedy relief of all persons imprisoned for any such criminal or supposed criminal matters; (2) be it enacted by the King's most excellent majesty, by and with the advice and consent of the lords spiritual and temporal, and commons, in this present parliament assembled, and by the authority thereof, That whensoever any person or persons shall bring any *habeas corpus* directed unto any sheriff or sheriffs, gaoler, minister or other person whatsoever, for any person in his or her custody, and the said writ shall be served upon the said officer, or left at the gaol or prison with any of the under-officers, under-keepers or deputy of the said officers or keepers, that the said officer or officers, his or their under-officers, under-keepers or deputies, shall within three days after the service thereof as aforesaid (unless the commitment aforesaid were for treason or felony, plainly and specially expressed in the warrant of commitment) upon payment or tender of the charges of bringing the said prisoner, to be ascertained by the judge or court that awarded the same, and endorsed upon the said writ, not exceeding twelve pence *per* mile, and upon security given by his own bond to pay the charges of carrying back the prisoner, if he shall be remanded by the court or judge to which he shall be brought according to the true intent of this present act, and that he will not make any escape by the way, make return of such writ; (3) and bring or cause to be brought the body of the party so committed or restrained, unto or before the lord chancellor, or lord keeper of the great seal of *England* for the time being, or the judges or barons of the said court from whence the said writ shall issue, or unto and before such other person or persons before whom the said writ is made returnable, according to the command thereof; (4) and shall then likewise certify the true causes of his detainer or imprisonment, unless the commitment of the said party be in any place beyond the distance of twenty miles from the place or places where such court or person is or shall be residing; and if beyond the distance of twenty miles, and not above one hundred miles, then within the space of ten days, and if beyond the distance of one hundred miles, then within the space of twenty days, after such delivery aforesaid, and not longer.

III. And to the intent that no sheriff, gaoler or other officer may pretend ignorance of the import of any such writ; (2) be it enacted by the authority aforesaid, That all such writs shall be marked in this manner, *Per statutum tricesimo primo Caroli secundi Regis,* and shall be signed by the person that awards the same; (3) and if any person or persons shall be or stand committed or detained as aforesaid, for any crime, unless for felony or treason plainly expressed in the warrant of commitment, in the vacation-time, and out of term, it shall and may be lawful to and for the person or persons so committed or detained (other than persons convict or in execution by legal process) or any one on his or their behalf, to appeal or complain to the lord chancellor or lord keeper, or any one of his Majesty's justices, either of the one bench or of the other, or the barons of the exchequer of the degree of the coif; (4) and the said lord chancellor, lord keeper, justices or barons or any of them, upon view of the copy or copies of the warrant or warrants of commitment and detainer, or otherwise upon oath made that such copy or copies were denied to be given by such person or persons in whose custody the prisoner or prisoners is or are detained, are hereby authorized and required, upon request made in writing by such person or persons, or any on his, her or their behalf, attested and subscribed by two witnesses who were present at the delivery of the same, to award and grant an *habeas corpus* under the seal of such court whereof he shall then be one of the judges, (5) to be directed to the officer or officers in whose custody the party so committed or detained shall be, returnable *immediate* before the said lord chancellor or lord keeper, or such justice, baron or any other justice or baron of the degree of the coif of any of the said courts; (6) and upon service thereof as aforesaid, the officer or officers, his or their under-officer or under-officers, under-keeper or under-keepers, or their deputy, in whose custody the party is so committed or detained, shall within the times respectively before limited, bring such prisoner or prisoners before the said lord chancellor or lord keeper, or such justices, barons or one of them, before whom the said writ is made returnable, and in case of his absence before any other of them, with the return of such writ, and the true causes of the commitment and detainer; (7) and thereupon within two days after the party shall be brought before them, the said lord chancellor or lord keeper, or such justice or baron before whom the prisoner shall be brought as aforesaid, shall discharge the said prisoner from his imprisonment, taking his or their recognizance, with one or more surety or sureties, in any sum according to their discretions, having regard to the quality of the prisoner and nature of the offence, for his or their appearance in the court of King's bench the term following, or at the next assizes, sessions or general gaol-delivery of and for such county, city or place where the commitment was, or where the offence was committed, or in such other court where the said offence is properly cognizable, as the case shall require, and then shall certify the said writ with the return thereof, and the said recognizance or recognizances into the said court where such appearance is to be made; (8) unless it shall appear unto the said lord chancellor or lord keeper, or justice or justices, or baron or barons, that the party so committed is detained upon a legal process, order or warrant, out of some court that hath jurisdiction of criminal matters, or by some warrant signed and sealed with the hand and seal of any of the said justices or barons, or some justice or justices of the peace, for such matters or offences for the which by the law the prisoner is not bailable.

IV. Provided always, and be it enacted, That if any person shall have wilfully neglected by the space of two whole terms after his imprisonment, to pray a *habeas corpus* for his enlargement, such person so wilfully neglecting shall not have any *habeas corpus* to be granted in vacation-time, in pursuance of this act.

V. And be it further enacted by the authority aforesaid, That if any officer or officers, his or their under-officer or under-officers, under-keeper or under-keepers, or deputy, shall neglect or refuse to make the returns aforesaid, or to bring the body or bodies of the prisoner or prisoners according to the command of the said writ, within the respective times aforesaid, or upon demand made by the prisoner or person in his behalf, shall refuse to deliver, or within the space of six hours after demand shall not deliver, to the person so demanding, a true copy of the warrant or warrants of commitment and detainer of such prisoner, which he and they are hereby required to deliver accordingly, all and every the head gaolers and keepers of such prisons, and such other person in whose custody the prisoner shall be detained, shall for the first offence forfeit to the prisoner or party grieved the sum of one hundred pounds; (2) and for the second offence the sum of two hundred pounds, and shall and is hereby made incapable to hold or execute his said office; (3) the said penalties to be recovered by the prisoner or party grieved, his executors or administrators, against such offender, his executors or administrators, by any action of debt, suit, bill, plaint or information, in any of the King's courts at *Westminster*, wherein no essoin, protection, privilege, injunction, wager of law, or stay of prosecution by *Non vult ulterius prosequi*, or otherwise, shall be admitted or allowed, or any more than one imparlance; (4) and any recovery or judgment at the suit of any party grieved, shall be a sufficient conviction for the first offence; and any after recovery or judgment at the suit of a party grieved for any offence after the first judgment, shall be a sufficient conviction to bring the officers or person within the said penalty for the second offence.

VI. And for the prevention of unjust vexation by reiterated commitments for the same offence; (2) be it enacted by the authority aforesaid, That no person or persons which shall be delivered or set at large upon any *habeas corpus*, shall at any time hereafter be again imprisoned or committed for the same offence by any person or persons whatsoever, other than by the legal order and process of such court wherein he or they shall be bound by recognizance to appear, or other court having jurisdiction of the cause; (3) and if any other person or persons shall knowingly contrary to this act recommit or imprison, or knowingly procure or cause to be recommitted or imprisoned, for the same offence or pretended offence, any person or persons delivered or set at large as aforesaid, or be knowingly aiding or assisting therein, then he or they shall forfeit to the prisoner or party grieved the sum of five hundred pounds; any colourable pretence or variation in the warrant or warrants of commitment notwithstanding, to be recovered as aforesaid.

VII. Provided always, and be it further enacted, That if any person or persons shall be committed for high treason or felony, plainly and specially expressed in the warrant of commitment, upon his prayer or petition in open court the first week of the term, or first day of the sessions of *oyer* and *terminer* or general gaol-delivery, to be brought to his trial, shall not be indicted some time in the next term, sessions of *oyer* and *terminer* or general gaol-delivery, after such commitment; it shall and may be lawful to and for the judges of the court of King's bench and justices of *oyer* and *terminer* or general gaol-delivery, and they are hereby required, upon motion to them made in open court the last day of the term, sessions or gaol-delivery, either by the prisoner or any one in his behalf, to set at liberty the prisoner upon bail, unless it appear to the judges and justices upon oath made, that the witnesses for the King could not be produced the same term, sessions or general gaol-delivery; (2) and if any person or persons committed as aforesaid, upon his prayer or petition in open court the first week of the term or first day of the sessions of *oyer* and *terminer* and general gaol-delivery, to be brought to his trial, shall not be indicted and tried the second term, sessions of *oyer* and *terminer* or general gaol-delivery, after his commitment, or upon his trial shall be acquitted, he shall be discharged from his imprisonment.

VIII. Provided always, That nothing in this act shall extend to discharge out of prison any person charged in debt, or other action, or with process in any civil cause, but that after he shall be discharged of his imprisonment for such his criminal offence, he shall be kept in custody according to the law, for such other suit.

IX. Provided always, and be it enacted by the authority aforesaid, That if any person or persons, subjects of this realm, shall be committed to any prison or in custody of any officer or officers whatsoever, for any criminal or supposed criminal matter, that the said person shall not be removed from the said prison and custody into the custody of any other officer or officers; (2) unless it be by *habeas corpus* or some other legal writ; or where the prisoner is delivered to the constable or other inferior officer to carry such prisoner to some common gaol; (3) or where any person is sent by order of any judge or assize or justice of the peace, to any common workhouse or house of correction; (4) or where the prisoner is removed from one prison or place to another within the same county, in order to his or her trial or discharge in due course of law; (5) or in case of sudden fire or infection, or other necessity; (6) and if any person or persons shall after such commitment aforesaid make out and sign, or countersign any warrant or warrants for such removal aforesaid, contrary to this act; as well he that makes or signs, or countersigns such warrant or warrants, as the officer or officers that obey or execute the same, shall suffer and incur the pains and forfeitures in this act before mentioned, both for the first and second offence respectively, to be recovered in manner aforesaid by the party grieved.

X. Provided also, and be it further enacted by the authority aforesaid, That it shall and may be lawful to and for any prisoner and prisoners as aforesaid, to move and obtain his or their *habeas corpus* as well out of the high court of chancery or court of exchequer, as out of the courts of King's bench or common pleas, or either of them; (2) and if the said lord chancellor or lord keeper, or any judge or judges, baron or barons for the time being, of the degree of the coif, of any of the courts aforesaid, in the vacation time, upon view of the copy or copies of the warrant or warrants of commitment or detainer, or upon oath made that such copy or copies were denied as aforesaid, shall deny any writ of *habeas corpus* by this act required to be granted, being moved for as aforesaid, they shall severally forfeit to the prisoner or party grieved the sum of five hundred pounds, to be recovered in manner aforesaid.

XI. And be it declared and enacted by the authority aforesaid, That an *habeas corpus* according to the true intent and meaning of this act, may be directed and run into any county palatine, the cinque-ports, or other privileged places within the kingdom of *England,* dominion of *Wales,* or town of *Berwick* upon *Tweed,* and the islands of *Jersey* or *Guernsey;* any law or usage to the contrary notwithstanding.

XII. And for preventing illegal imprisonments in prisons beyond the seas; (2) be it further enacted by the authority aforesaid, That no subject of this realm that now is, or hereafter shall be an inhabitant or resiant of this kingdom of *England,* dominion of *Wales,* or town of *Berwick* upon *Tweed,* shall or may be sent prisoner into *Scotland, Ireland, Jersey, Guernsey, Tangier,* or into parts, garrisons, islands or places beyond the seas, which are or at any time hereafter shall be within or without the dominions of his Majesty, his heirs or successors; (3) and that every such imprisonment is hereby enacted and adjudged to be illegal; (4) and that if any of the said subjects now is or hereafter shall be so imprisoned, every such person and persons so imprisoned, shall and may for every such imprisonment maintain by virtue of this act an action or actions of false imprisonment, in any of his Majesty's courts of record, against the person or persons by whom he or she shall be so committed, detained, imprisoned, sent prisoner or transported, contrary to the true meaning of this act, and against all or any person or persons that shall frame, contrive, write, seal or countersign any warrant or writing for such commitment, detainer, imprisonment or transportation, or shall be advising, aiding or assisting, in the same, or any of them; (5) and the plaintiff in every such action shall have judgment to recover his treble costs, besides damages, which damages so to be given, shall not be less than five hundred pounds; (6) in which action no delay stay or stop of proceeding by rule, order or command, nor no injunction, protection or privilege whatsoever, nor any more than one imparlance shall be allowed, excepting such rule of the court wherein the action shall depend, made in open court, as shall be thought in justice necessary, for special cause to be expressed in the said rule; (7) and the person or persons who shall knowingly frame, contrive, write, seal or countersign any warant for such commitment, detainer or transportation, or shall so commit, detain, imprison or transport any person or persons contrary to this act, or be any ways advising, aiding or assisting therein, being lawfully convicted thereof, shall be disabled from thenceforth to bear any office of trust or profit within the said realm of *England,* dominion of *Wales,* or town of *Berwick* upon *Tweed,* or any of the islands, territories or dominions thereunto belonging; (8) and shall incur and sustain the pains, penalties and forfeitures limited, ordained and provided in and by the statute of provision and praemunire made in the sixteenth year of King *Richard* the Second; (9) and be incapable of any pardon from the King, his heirs or successors, of the said forfeitures, losses or disabilities, or any of them.

XIII. Provided always, That nothing in this act shall extend to give benefit to any person who shall by contract in writing agree with any merchant or owner of any plantation, or other person whatsoever, to be transported to any parts beyond the seas, and receive earnest upon such agreement, although that afterwards such person shall renounce such contract.

XIV. Provided always, and be it enacted, That if any person or persons lawfully convicted of any felony, shall in open court pray to be transported beyond the seas, and the court shall think fit to leave him or them in prison for that purpose, such person or persons may be transported into any parts beyond the seas, this act or any thing therein contained to the contrary notwithstanding.

XV. Provided also, and be it enacted, That nothing herein contained shall be deemed, construed or taken, to extend to the imprisonment of any person before the first day of *June* one thousand six hundred seventy and nine, or to any thing advised, procured, or otherwise done, relating to such imprisonment; any thing herein contained to the contrary notwithstanding.

XVI. Provided also, That if any person or persons at any time resiant in this realm, shall have committed any capital offence in *Scotland* or *Ireland,* or any of the islands, or foreign plantations of the King, his heirs or successors, where he or she ought to be tried for such offence, such person or persons may be sent to such place, there to receive such trial, in such manner as the same might have been used before the making of this act; any thing herein contained to the contrary notwithstanding.

XVII. Provided also, and be it enacted, That no person or persons shall be sued, impleaded, molested, or troubled for any offence against this act, unless the party offending be sued or impleaded for the same within two years at the most after such time wherein the offence shall be committed, in case the party grieved shall not be then in prison; and if he shall be in prison, then within the space of two years after the decease of the person imprisoned, or his or her delivery out of prison, which shall first happen.

XVIII. And to the intent no person may avoid his trial at the assizes or general gaol-delivery, by procuring his removal before the assizes, at such time as he cannot be brought back to receive his trial there; (2) be it enacted, That after the assizes proclaimed for that county where the prisoner is detained, no person shall be removed from the common gaol upon any *habeas corpus* granted in pursuance of this act, but upon any such *habeas corpus* shall be brought before the judge of assize in open court, who is thereupon to do what to justice shall appertain.

XIX. Provided nevertheless, That after the assizes are ended, any person or persons detained, may have his or her *habeas corpus* according to the direction and intention of this act.

XX. And be it also enacted by the authority aforesaid, That if any information, suit or action shall be brought or exhibited against any person or persons for any offence committed or to be committed against the form of this law, it shall be lawful for such defendants to plead the general issue, that they are not guilty, or that they owe nothing, and to give such special matter in evidence to the jury that shall try the same, which matter being pleaded had been good and sufficient matter in law to have discharged the said defendant or defendants against the said information, suit or action, and the said matter shall be then as available to him or them, to all intents and purposes, as if he or they had sufficiently pleaded, set forth or alledged the same matter in bar or discharge of such information suit or action.

XXI. *And because many times persons charged with petty treason or felony, or as accessaries thereunto, are committed upon suspicion only, whereupon they are bailable, or not, according as the circumstances making out that suspicion are more or less weighty, which are best known to the justices of peace that committed the persons, and have the examinations before them, or to other justices of the peace in the county;* (2) be it therefore enacted, That where any person shall appear to be committed by any judge or justice of the peace and charged as accessary before the fact, to any petty treason or felony, or upon suspicion thereof, or with suspicion of petty treason or felony, which petty treason or felony shall be plainly and specially expressed in the warrant of commitment, that such person shall not be removed or bailed by virtue of this act, or in any other manner than they might have been before the making of this act.

3

OPINION ON THE WRIT OF HABEAS CORPUS
97 Eng. Rep. 29, 31–51 (H.L. 1758)

Answer of Mr. Justice Wilmot to the questions proposed to the Judges by the House of Lords, on the second reading of the bill, intituled, "An Act for giving a more Speedy Remedy to the Subject, upon the Writ of Habeas Corpus."

. . . . .

1st Question. "Whether in cases, not within the Act 31 Car. II. writs of habeas corpus ad subjiciendum, by the law as it now stands, ought to issue of course, or upon probable cause verified by affidavit?"

Answer. I am of opinion, that in cases not within the Act of the 31 Car. II. writs of habeas corpus ad subjiciendum, by the law as it now stands, ought not to issue of course, but upon probable cause verified by affidavit.

A writ which issues upon a probable cause, verified by affidavit, is as much a writ of right, as a writ which issues of course.

There are many other writs, besides the writ of habeas corpus, which fall exactly under the same circumstances: writs of mandamus, prohibition, 1 Syd. 65. Sir R. Raymond, 4. Supplicavit, ne exeat regnum, the writ of homine replegiando;—are all writs of right; but a proper case must be laid before the Court by affidavit, before the parties, praying such writs, may be entitled to them. They are the birthright of the people, subject to such provisions as the law has established for granting them. Those provisions are not a check upon justice, but a wise and provident direction of it.

The very learned and able men who framed the 31 Car. II. could not avoid taking these writs of habeas corpus for private custody, into their consideration. Three or four years before that Act passed, there had been two very great cases, extremely agitated in Westminster Hall, upon writs of habeas corpus for private custody, viz. the cases of *Lord Leigh,* 2 Lev. 128, and *Sir Robert Viner, Lord Mayor of London,* 3 Keb. 434, 447, 470, 504. 2 Lev. 128. Freem. 389. But they wisely drew the line betweeen civil constitutional liberty, as opposed to the power of the Crown, and liberty as opposed to the violence and power of private persons. They thought this power of judging might be abused in favour of the Crown, but they saw no danger of an abuse of it as between one subject and another; and therefore they applied the remedy to the evil they had seen and experienced, and left the law as they found it in respect of private persons.

There is no such thing in the law, as writs of grace and favour issuing from the Judges: they are all writs of right; but they are not all writs of course.

Writs of course, are those writs which lie between party and party, for the commencement of civil suits: and if they are sued without a good foundation, the common law punishes the plaintiff for suing out the writ vexatiously, by amercing him "pro falso clamore." And by the statute law, he is to pay the costs of the suit.

But the writ of habeas corpus is not the commencement of a civil suit, where the party proceeds at the peril of costs, if his complaint is a groundless one: it is a remedial mandatory writ, by which the King's Supreme Court of Justice, and the Judges of that Court, at the instance of a subject aggrieved, commands the production of that subject, and inquires after the cause of his imprisonment; and it is a writ of such a sovereign and transcendent authority, that no privilege of person or place can stand against it. It runs, at the common law, to all dominions held of the Crown. It is accommodated to all persons and places. 2 Cro. 543. Palmer, 54. And, as all these remedial mandatory writs were, originally, rather the suits of the King than of the subject, the King's Courts of Justice would not suffer them to issue upon a mere suggestion; but upon some proof of a wrong and injury done to a subject.

Writs of habeas corpus, upon imprisonment for criminal matters, were never writs of course: they always issued upon a motion, grafted on a copy of the commitment; and cases may be put in which they ought not to be granted. 1 Lev. 1. Comber. 74. Habeas corpus was denied to one committed to Bridewell for lewdness. 3 Bul. 27. 2 Mod. 306. If malefactors, under sentence of death in all the gaols in the kingdom, could have these writs of course, the sentence of the law might be suspended, and perhaps totally eluded by them.

The 31 Car. II. makes no alteration in the practice of the Courts in granting them: they are still moved for, in term time, upon the same foundation as they were before: and when a single Judge in vacation grants them under the 31 Car. II. in criminal cases, a copy of the commitment, or an affidavit of the refusal of it, must be laid before him. He must judge, even in that case, whether treason or felony is specially expressed in the warrant of commitment: and there have been a great number of cases where a doubt has arisen on the frame and wording of the warrant; so that even upon the Act, the probable cause of bailing is really disclosed to the Judge, unless the copy of the commitment is refused, and then the law will presume every thing against it; and in cases out of the Act, which take in all kinds of confinement and restraint, not for criminal, or supposed criminal matter, and to which this question relates, it has been the uniform uninterrupted practice, both of the Court of King's Bench, and of the Judges of that Court, that the foundation, upon which the writ is prayed, should be laid before the Court or Judge who awards it.

The reasons of guarding the writ in this manner, I take to be these: there are many kinds of private restraint that are lawful. There was a much greater number formerly. The Reformation opened the doors of religious prisons; and the abolition of military tenures unfettered an unhappy class of men, called villeins, who lived in a state of captivity under their masters.

There are many kinds of restraint that exist at this day; some in the nature of punishments. In domestic government, which takes in the case of husbands, fathers, guardians, and masters, the law authorizes restraints, in order to enforce a performance of those natural, moral, and civil duties, which wives, children, wards, and apprentices, owe to their superiors, in their several relative capacities. These domestic governments could not subsist without such authorities; and therefore all States have endeavoured most anxiously, some in a greater degree, and others in a less degree, to preserve the greatest reverence for them.

The wisdom of our ancestors would not suffer this kind of authorities to be broken in upon wantonly, upon mere suggestion, and without seeing some reason for an interposition; because they saw it would have encouraged disobedience and rebellion in private families; and, at all events, must have abated that awe and respect which act so materially in the support of those authorities. They may be abused: if they are, the law says, let it be shewn, and the party shall have relief; but if he cannot shew they are abused, he is entitled to none. The legal presumption is certainly in favour of these authorities; the law will not presume they are unduly or irregularly executed.

But if these writs were to have issued without any case made, they must have issued indiscriminately, in the cases of lawful restraints, as well as unlawful ones; which would have been levelling all distinction between them, and have been subjecting the authority of fathers, husbands, guardians, and masters, to be canvassed and questioned in the same manner, and upon the same suggestions, as the extravagant outrages of persons acting without any authority at all.

It would have been proceeding upon an inversion of the legal presumption, and would thereby have destroyed all that order, discipline, and subordination in private families, which lead men into a habit of obedience, and dispose them early to obey the laws of their country.

When a Judge is called upon for a habeas corpus, in order to bail a man for a bailable offence, the injustice of the imprisonment is obvious and self-evident: for imprisonment before trial, being only to secure his being amenable to justice; if that security can be obtained by bail, in bailable offences, it is unjust that he should be kept in prison. The authority which committed him ought to have bailed him.

The authorities I have mentioned are equally legal, and therefore within the spirit and reason of the Habeas Corpus Act itself. The injustice of the imprisonment ought to appear in the first instance, before the party has a right to demand the remedy.

The law laid this check, to prevent that scene of disorder and confusion which must arise, if wives, children, wards, and apprentices, or any other person in their name, and on their behalf, were to be at liberty, without any foundation or cause shewn, to force a production of them in Westminster Hall, or before a Judge, where-ever he should happen to be, whenever they pleased, and as often as they pleased, at a risk of having them rescued out of their hands, "in transitu," and without a possibility of a satisfaction from any body.

There are many other lawful restraints besides those arising under the authorities I have mentioned:—All persons who are in custody upon civil process, or under special authorities, created by Act of Parliament, proceeding "civiliter," and not "criminaliter," against the persons who are the objects of them:—Persons who are bailed, paupers in hospitals or workhouses, madmen under commissions of lunacy, or confined by parish officers, under the Vagrant Act of 17 Geo. II. are all under a lawful confinement.

If all these persons were to have had these writs of habeas corpus of course, without shewing any cause or foundation for granting them, it would have been suffering this great remedial mandatory writ to have been used as an instrument of vexation and oppression; it would have become a weapon in the hands of madmen, and of dissolute, profligate and licentious people, to harrass and disturb persons acting under the powers which the law had given them.—One most frightful instance occurs: the case of a crew performing quarantine.—If this writ were to issue of course, it might bring back pestilence and death along with it.

The check upon the writ, by requiring a probable cause to be shewn before it issues, is only saying, "shew you want redress, and you shall have it:" and if a person cannot disclose such a case himself, as to shew he is aggrieved when he tells his own story, and is not opposed or contradicted by any body; it is decisive against his being in such a condition as to want relief.

Besides the practice, which is a decisive evidence of the law, it appears from a case, Hilary, 8th King William, called *Griffiths's case,* that the Court would not grant this writ, until a probable cause was laid before the Court that the party was entitled to it.

When this writ was first applied to relieve against private restraints, does not appear; but whenever it was, the manner of issuing it seems to have been adopted from that of the writ of homine replegiando, which was the true common law remedy for the assertion of liberty against a private person: and that writ never issued of course, but was applied for by petition to the Great Seal, and an affidavit made, disclosing the foundation on which it was prayed. State Trials, 3 vol. 632. 2 Lill. Pr. Reg. 23. 2 Freeman, 27, *Jennings's case,* upon affidavit made, that Jennings had got a young heiress into his custody without the consent of the guardian, upon the motion of the Attorney-General, a homine replegiando was granted. And as the law checked that writ of homine replegiando; the habeas corpus, which seems by practice to have been substituted in its place, took the check along with it.

Careful as the law is to prevent this writ from being abused, it cannot always prevent it: for if a man does not disclose the whole case, it may issue sometimes where it would not have issued, if the case had been fairly stated.

I will mention one case, which happened last term, and which shews the reason of the law, in expecting to see a full state of the case before the writ issues.

A gentleman applied to a Judge of the Court of King's Bench in vacation time, for a habeas corpus to his wife's mother, to bring up his wife, upon an affidavit of detention of her from him. As it was near term, the writ was returnable first day of term.

The fact was, that they had entered into articles of separation, which had determined his right to the custody of his wife; the mother brought the wife into Court, and returned the articles of separation. The return was of great length, and the mother was put to a very great expence in the making it, and if she had brought her daughter from the remotest part of the Kingdom, she could have had no satisfaction at all.

If the affidavit had disclosed the articles of separation, as it ought to have done, the Court, or Judge, would have said, "You have no right to the relief you pray, and therefore must not put the parties to costs and vexation, in a case which is remediless of your own shewing."

2d Question. Whether in cases, not within the said Act, such writs of habeas corpus, by the law as it now stands, may issue in the vacation by fiat from a Judge of the Court of King's Bench, returnable before himself?

Answer. I am of opinion that in cases, not within the Act of the 31st Car. II. writs of habeas corpus ad subjiciendum, by the law as it now stands, may issue in the vacation by fiat from a Judge of the Court of King's Bench, returnable before himself.

From the best inquiry I can make, writs of habeas corpus, in criminal cases, have been awarded by the Chief Justice of the King's Bench, and the Judges of that Court, long before the 31st Car. II.

The files of the fiats for writs made out in the Crown Office before the reign of Car. II. are not to be found there, except for four or five terms in Queen Elizabeth's time, one or two in James I. and for six or seven terms in Car. I.

No information is to be had from the records; but there are traces from cases in print, and from fiats since the Restoration, and before the 31st Car. II. that there had been a kind of unsettled practice for the Chief Justice, and Judges of the Court of King's Bench, granting them in vacation; and as the Judges of that Court are justices of peace all over the kingdom, they have a power of bailing, as incident to that authority; and I don't see how that power of bailing could well be exercised, without removing the person to be bailed before them by habeas corpus.

Catesby's case in vacation, is in Hilary, 43 Eliz. in the 7th vol. of the State Trials, 175.

I have a list of fiats for habeas corpus, since the Restoration, and before the 31 Car. II. Thirty of them appear to have been granted and made returnable before the Judges in vacation. Since the 31 Car. II. these writs have issued, in criminal cases, under that Act, when granted at the instance of a subject.

As to writs of habeas corpus in cases of private custody, I cannot ascertain the commencement of their being first issued by the Court.

By the common law, the liberty of a man's person against private persons, acting without any legal authority, was protected in this manner:

1st. First, the law gave every man a right to repel force by force, and to defend his liberty in the same manner as he might his life.

2d. As every unlawful imprisonment was a breach of the peace, it must be proceeded against as such, by justices of peace; and the delivery of the party perhaps enforced by a rigorous execution of that authority. It might also be punished by indictment. Satisfaction might likewise be recovered for the injury, by an action of false imprisonment.

The writ of homine replegiando, as mentioned before, was the only specific remedy provided by the common law, for the protection and defence of his liberty, against any private invasion of it.

Though there is an "obiter" saying by Justice Wild, in Carter, 222, of a case where the Court sent a habeas corpus to Dr. Prujean, beyond sea, for Sir Robert Carr's brother, yet it is so loosely stated, I lay no stress upon it.

The first case is the case of *Sir Philip Howard,* mentioned in *Lord Leigh's case,* and therefore must have been before that time. *Lord Leigh's case* was in the 27 Car. II. where habeas corpus was granted to bring up his wife. And the case of *Viner and Emmerton* was in the 27th year of Car. II. where a habeas corpus was granted to Viner to bring up his daughter-in-law, viz. his wife's daughter by a first husband. From that time to this, the Court has constantly granted them.

When the practice of the Chief Justice, and the Judges of the Court of King's Bench, granting these writs in vacation, in cases of private custody, first began, does not appear; but in all probability, it was either coeval with what the Court did, or very soon followed it; because the principle which supports the one, concludes as forcibly to the supporting the other: and the principle is this; if the writ is applicable to one species of unlawful imprisonment, it is in reason equally applicable to another. They are cases "ejusdem generis;" and therefore let the usage of issuing this writ have begun sooner or later, it was in the first instance a warrantable extension of a legal remedy in one case, to another case of the same nature; and I consider the usage in this case as the voice and testimony of the Judges, for near eighty years together, to the legality of the very first application of it.

The principle upon which the usage was founded, lay in the law; and the usage is nothing but a drawing that principle out into action, and a legal application of it to attain the ends of justice. It is upon this foundation only, that an infinite variety of forms, rules, regulations, and modes of practice in all Courts of Justice must stand, and can only be supported.

In many instances, an usage for some time is considered as an evidence of an antecedent immemorial usage, and therefore may be called the common law. 2 Co. 16 b., *Lane's case.* "The customs and courses of the King's Courts are as a law. The course of a Court makes a law."

But when the commencement of an usage can be fixed and ascertained, it cannot be supported by a presumption, and the legality of the usage must then depend upon some other principle; and that principle is this, "ubi eadem est ratio, ibi idem est jus;" a writ applicable to one kind of imprisonment, is in reason equally applicable to another.

It would be endless to enumerate instances where the King's Supreme Courts of Justice in Westminster Hall have, for the ease and benefit of the suitors of the Court, reformed, amended, and new moulded and modified their practice, as from experience and observation they found it would best advance, improve, and accelerate the administration of justice; and all acts done by Judges at their chambers, and by officers of the Court, either in term or out of term, are under a delegated authority from the Court. They are controulable by the Court, and obedience to them must be enforced by the Court. And the acts done in Court and out of Court, taken together, form that system of practice by which the benefit of the law is dealt out to the people.

I will mention an instance where a writ has been extended by usage to a purpose much beyond the original intention of it, viz. "ne exeat regnum;" which is a State writ to restrain people from going abroad; first used to hinder the clergy from going to Rome; then extended to laymen, machinating and concerting measures against the State; now applied to prevent a subterfuge from the justice of the nation, though in matters of private concernment, in order to get bail for an equitable demand, upon affidavit of intention to go abroad.

The legality of that application was settled in Car. II.'s time, upon an usage first begun in the time of James I. 1 Ch. Ca. 115. *Read* against *Read,* 2 Ch. Ca. 245. If usage, where the commencement of it was known, could legitimate a process which is to take away a man's liberty, surely usage, founded upon a legal principle, will legitimate a process which is applied to protect it.

I will mention a case in the Year Book 13 Hen. VII. fol. 17, where the mode of proceeding, in one kind of action, was translated to another, in favour of liberty. Action of trespass.—Plaintiff sets forth that he was a freeman, and that the defendant claimed him to be a villein, so that he durst not go about his business, and that the defendant had taken some of his goods; and he prayed that the defendant might give security to deliver them, and not take any more of them, or his body, pending the writ. This was the practice in a "homine replegiando;" and in a "homine replegiando," the plaintiff was to give security to deliver his body in case the action was against him.

It was resolved they should find security to one another, as if it had been a "homine replegiando;" and the Court said, "it was good discretion to favour liberty as much as might be by reason." They applied the provisions applicable to one writ, to another writ, because it fell under the same reason, and was to favour liberty.

It has been lately said, that the practice of issuing these writs by the Judges in vacation, was taken up under an apprehension of their being within the 31 Car. II. and that they have been marked in the Crown Office by that statute. How such an apprehension or practice could have prevailed, is to me inexplicable! No man could ever have such an apprehension who had ever read the Act: it is confined in words, and by the nature almost of every provision in it, to criminal, or supposed criminal, matter.

As to marking them by the statute, as there were fifty writs in criminal cases, for one writ in the case of private custody, the mistake might easily be made; if observed, could do no harm: it might quicken the returns; or be an inaccuracy in the office: I lay no stress upon it; because we see some few writs of habeas corpus, issued by the Court, marked by the statute, and yet the Act gives the Court of King's Bench no power of awarding these writs, but leaves that power exactly as it found it; and therefore it might as well be inferred, that the Court thought their power was by the statute, when their writ was marked by the statute, as that a single Judge thought his power was by the statute, because the writ was marked so.

I will never offer such an indignity to the very great and eminent men who have presided in that Court, and to the succession of Judges who have sat in it for near eighty years, as to say, that they founded this practice upon a mistake which could not have infected the meanest capacity.

I must say they never read the Act if they thought so. And *Griffiths cases,* already cited, shews that these kinds of habeas corpus were understood not to be within the Act.

Lord Chief Justice Hale does say, in second volume of Pleas of the Crown, 145, that this writ is not regularly to issue but in the term time, when the Court may judge of the return, or bail or discharge the prisoner; and in page 147, he says, it seems, "regularly," this writ should issue out of the Court of Chancery in vacation time, and out of the King's Bench in term time.

That word "regularly," alludes to some unsettled practice of the Judges issuing that writ in vacation.

This was a noble, but a posthumous, work, not fitted by him for the press, nor corrected; and, I have heard, a collection of notes made by him before the Restoration.

If it was, then the precedents and practice since the Restoration, were not taken into his consideration; and yet the practice after the Restoration, and even his own practice, varied the law extremely from what he asserted it to be in his book: for he says, that this writ issues for matter only of crime; and that assertion is confuted by his own practice, because he was Chief Justice when the writs were awarded in *Lady Leigh's case,* and *Viner's case,* in the 27 Car. II. which were not for matters of crime, but for private custodies; and *Viner's case* seems to have been as much agitated as any case could be, and there never was the least objection to the Court's right of awarding the writ. That circumstance is decisive against his authority upon the nature of this writ; or rather a declaration that he changed his opinion, and thought it might issue for other matters.

In 2 Ins. 53, and 4 Ins. 81, 182, Lord Coke says, "It ought to issue out of the Court of King's Bench in term time, and out of Chancery either in term time or vacation." All writs, in supposition of law, do issue in the term; and he might mean no more, than that Judges could not grant them by their own proper authority, as separate and detached from the Court, as they issue warrants.

First, this was no judicial determination; a mere "prolatum," which, as to the Court of Chancery, is very doubtful. For no writ of habeas corpus can be found to have ever issued out of the Court of Chancery, except some returnable in the House of Lords. The 16 Car. I. takes no notice of the Court of Chancery, which it is most probable it would have done, if it had been thought that the writ had issued out of that Court in vacation. And the 31 Car. II. seems to proceed upon a supposition, that it could not issue out of the Court of Chancery, because the 10th section expressly empowers the Court of Chancery to grant it, which would have been unnecessary, if it could have granted the writ before; and it only shews, what I really take to be the truth of the case, that there was no settled fixed practice, then established, of their issuing in vacation; but if they could not, nor ever did issue out of the Court of Chancery, it is the strongest reason that can be urged in support of the practice of issuing these writs by the Judges of the Court of King's Bench, in vacation, before the statute, because there could not otherwise have been a perfect and complete remedy at all times for the subject against imprisonment, for a bailable offence at the common law, and before the Statute of 31 Car. II.

That Act proceeds upon a supposition of a practice of that kind then prevailing. To what purpose is the writ to be marked by the statute, if the Judges, in vacation, could issue no writ of habeas corpus ad subjiciendum, but under this statute? That direction was to distinguish this writ, when issued at the suit of a subject to be bailed, from every other writ of this nature, which the Judges in vacation might issue: not meant to give a power which they did not exercise before, but to reduce an unsettled, informal, vague practice, into a formal regular system, as to the bailing for bailable offences, and to correct the abuse of any power which they had in fact exercised.

But upon Lord Coke's own principles, suppose no such practice when he wrote, yet a subsequent practice, founded upon legal principles, and an experience of its utility, has made the law; "per varios actus legem experientia fecit." Lord Coke's averment has not the weight it would have had, if made after 31 Car. II.; according to his own principles, the practice would have made it law; and as it appears by the fiats between the Restoration and the 31 Car. II. that three Chief Justices, Foster, Hyde, Keyling, and four Judges of the Court, Morton, Twisden, Mallet, and Wyld, granted these writs in vacation, and the practice is warranted by legal principles, and it is admitted they were always grantable "pro Rege," (which establishes the vacation right) the opinion both of Lord Hale and Lord Coke may be true; and, upon Lord Coke's own principle, if he had written twenty years after the Restoration, instead of thirty years before it, he must have been of the opinion I now give.

As to the 4th and 5th questions upon your Lordships paper, viz.

4th question. Whether, at the common law, and before the Statute of Habeas Corpus in the 31 King Car. II. any, and which, of the Judges could regularly issue a writ of habeas corpus ad subjiciendum, in time of vacation, in all or in what cases particularly?

5th question. Whether the Judges at the common law, and before the said statute, were bound to issue such writs of habeas corpus subjiciendum, in time of vacation, upon the demand of any person under restraint, or might they refuse to award such writ if they thought proper?

Answer. I think the Chief Justice of the Court of King's Bench, and the other Judges of that Court, did in fact issue them in vacation, before 31 Car. II. in criminal cases, and might do so on principles of law; possibly it might be done at first for the King only, and afterwards for the subject; but I do not think there was any settled course of practice observed in granting them before the statute, and that such unsettled manner of practice produced the statute in the cases of bailable offences: and, in cases out of the Act, usage has now fixed a regular course or manner of granting them; but I desire to be understood, that the present usage of granting them must be supported upon such principles of law, as would have supported the granting them when such usage first began. And I think they were not bound to grant them upon the demand of any person under restraint, at the common law, and before the statute, any more than they are bound to grant them now upon demand. There must have been some case made, before they could be bound to grant them at any time.

6th question. Whether the Judges, at the common law,

and before the said statute, were bound to make such writs, so issued in time of vacation, returnable "immediate;" and could they enforce obedience to such writ so issued in time of vacation, if the party served therewith, should neglect or refuse to obey the same, and by what means?

Answer. I am of opinion, that the Judges at the common law, and before the said statute, were not bound to make writs of habeas corpus ad subjiciendum, issued in vacation time, returnable "immediate;" because I find by the files of fiats for these writs before the statute, that they were sometimes made returnable "immediate," and sometimes in term time; and I think the Judges cannot enforce obedience to any writs of habeas corpus, issued in time of vacation, (whether they issue in cases within the 31 Car. II. or in cases out of that Act) if the party served therewith, should neglect or refuse to obey the same, by any means but by attachment for a contempt, which can only issue out of Court in term time.

7th question. Whether, if a Judge, before the said statute, should have refused to grant the said writ upon the demand of any person under any restraint, had the subject any remedy at law, by action or otherwise, against the Judge for such refusal?

Answer. I think that the subject had no remedy at law, by action or otherwise, against the Judge for such refusal. The denying a writ stands upon the same ground as any other breach of duty.

8th question. Whether, in case a writ of habeas corpus ad subjiciendum, at the common law, be directed to any person returnable "immediate," such person may not stand out an alias and pluries habeas corpus, before due obedience thereto can be regularly enforced by the course of the common law?

Answer. I am of opinion, that in case a writ of habeas corpus ad subjiciendum, at the common law, be directed to any person returnable "immediate," the Court, upon the affidavit of the service of the writ, will grant a rule for an attachment.

By the course of the common law, he might have stood out an alias and pluries; but by practice the course is now altered, and in many cases the Court has enforced obedience to a writ for private restraints, in the first instance, by attachment, for the furtherance of justice. The method of proceeding by alias and pluries, is gone into disuse, in almost all cases, and the process by attachment substituted in its stead; and that practice stands upon this legal principle;—that disobeying the King's writ is a contempt, and equally a contempt to disobey the first writ as the last.

9th question. Whether the said Statute of the 31 Car. II. and the several provisions therein made for the immediate awarding and returning the writ of habeas corpus, extend to the case of any man compelled, against his will, in time of peace, either into the land or sea service, without any colour of legal authority; or to any cases of imprisonment, detainer, or restraint whatsoever, except cases of commitment for criminal, or supposed criminal, matters?

Answer. I think they do not extend to the case of a man so compelled; because the person who compels a man against his will, in time of peace, either into the land or sea service, without any colour of legal authority, is the criminal, and not the man impressed. And I think that Act doth not extend to any cases of imprisonment, detainer, or restraint whatsoever, except cases of commitment for criminal, or supposed criminal, matters.

10th question. Whether, in all cases whatsoever, the Judges are so bound by the facts set forth in the return to the writ of habeas corpus, that they cannot discharge the person brought up before them, although it should appear most manifestly to the Judges, by the clearest and most undoubted proof, that such return is false in fact, that the person so brought up is restrained of his liberty by the most unwarrantable means, and in direct violation of law and justice?

Answer. I am of opinion, that no cases whatsoever, the Judges are so bound by the facts set forth in the return to the writ of habeas corpus, that they cannot discharge the person brought up before them, if it shall most manifestly appear to the Judges, by the clearest and most undoubted proof, that such return is false in fact, and that the person so brought up is restrained of his liberty by the most unwarrantable means, and in direct violation of law and justice. But by the clearest and most undoubted proof, I mean the verdict of a jury, or judgment on demurrer, or otherwise in an action for a false return: and in case the facts averred in the return to a writ of habeas corpus, are sufficient in point of law to justify the restraint, I am of opinion, that the Court or Judge, before whom such writ is returnable, cannot try the facts averred in such return, by affidavits, in any proceeding grafted upon the return to such writ of habeas corpus.

The clearest and most undoubted proof in the law, is the verdict of a jury; and if the facts, set forth in a return, are disproved by a verdict, I think the Judges are not bound by those facts in any case whatsoever, from discharging the person brought up before them; but as I presume the question means, "proof by affidavit," in order to examine the truth or falsity of a return; I shall consider the question in that view.

To get at the bottom of it, the nature of this writ must first be considered: it is a demand by the King's Supreme Court of Justice to produce a person under confinement, and to signify the reason of his confinement.

In imprisonment for criminal offences, the Court can act upon it only in one of these three manners:

1st. If it appears clearly that the fact, for which the party is committed, is no crime; or that it is a crime, but he is committed for it by a person who has no jurisdiction, the Court discharges.

2d. If doubtful whether a crime or not, or whether the party be committed by a competent jurisdiction; or it appears to be a crime, but a bailable one, the Court bails him.

3d. If an offence not bailable, and committed by a competent jurisdiction, the Court remands or commits.

The nature and quality of the fact with which the party is charged, and the jurisdiction which has taken cognizance of it, are to be considered on the return; but the existence of the fact, that is, whether such a fact was committed, or whether there is such a warrant of commitment as the gaoler has returned, is a matter which belongs "ad aliud examen." The Court says, "Tell the reason why you confine him." The Court will determine whether it is a good or bad reason; but not whether it is a true or a false one. The Judges are not competent to this inquiry; it is not their province, but the province of a jury, to determine it: "ad questionem juris, non facti, judices respondent." The writ is not framed or adapted to litigating facts: it is a summary short way of taking the opinion of the Court upon a matter of law, where the facts are disclosed and admitted; it puts the case exactly in the same situation as if an action of false imprisonment had been brought, and the defendant had set forth a series of facts to justify the imprisonment, and the plaintiff had demurred to the plea. A return is the same as the justification demurred to; but, in both cases, if the facts are controverted, they must go to a jury; and when the return to a habeas corpus is made and filed, there is an end of the whole proceeding, and the parties have "no day" in Court; and therefore it is impossible that a proceeding, by way of trial, should be grafted upon it.

All the arguments upon the habeas corpus, in the seventh volume of the State Trials, 123, 156, take it for granted that it is impossible to go out of the return; and Mr. Calthorp, who was recorder of London, a very ingenious man, and argued for the subject, lays it down, "that it ought to be precise and direct, so as to be able to judge of the cause, whether sufficient or not. For there may not any doubt be taken to the return, be it true or false; but the Court is to accept the same as true; and if it be false, the party must take his remedy by action upon the case."

Mr. Selden likewise in his argument in the same book, page 156, says, "The keeper of the prison returns by what warrant he detains the prisoner, and with his return fixed to his writ, brings the prisoner to the Bar at the time appointed: when the return is thus made, the Court judgeth of the sufficiency or insufficiency of it, only out of the body of it, without having respect to any other thing whatsoever, that is, they suppose the return to be true, whatever it be; if it be false, the prisoner may have his action on the case against the gaoler that brought him." And it is for this reason the law requires such exact critical certainty in returns, because the party can have no answer to it upon the return. Nothing can be pleaded to it. It must be taken to be true, until twelve men, upon their oaths, have said that it is false.

To enter into a disquisition of this sort upon affidavits, would be confounding the offices of judge and jury, and introducing a mode of trial where no issue is or can be joined. The parties, in such a summary way of trial, must lose the benefit of a "viva voce" examination, where the looks, the manner, and deportment of the witness, are extremely material to confirm or discredit his testimony: it is found by the experience of ages, that nothing does so effectually explore the truth as a cross-examination, which strikes so suddenly that fiction can never endure it.

Another decisive reason against this mode of trial, is, that there is no compulsory method of forcing men to swear affidavits; so that if a person were obliged to prove the truth of his return by affidavit, he is totally destitute of any means of obliging men to make affidavits to prove them.

Another reason is, that the parties are entitled to no costs upon the return to a habeas corpus; and if the Court pronounces a wrong judgment upon the facts, there is no method of controverting it. But in an action for a false return, witnesses may be compelled to appear, and must be examined "viva voce." Costs will follow the event of the trial. If the verdict is false, or contrary to evidence, the law has established a legal method of controuling it.

Writs of mandamus stood exactly upon the same foundation. They are both the King's mandatory writs, issued at the instance and for the relief of the subject. The answer to them shall be taken to be true, till it has undergone that examination which the wisdom of our ancestors has established for the decision of facts. And the law gave such credit to returns of these writs, that they would not even suffer the facts to be denied and brought to trial before a jury in that course of proceeding. "You have asked a question; you shall take the answer as it is given you: if it is insufficient in point of law, the Judges will give instantaneous relief; if it is false in fact, you have received an injury; vindicate yourself against that injury by an action, and when you have proved the fact to be false, you will be entitled to a complete relief."

This rule was adhered to so strictly, that even in the case of annual offices in corporations, where the offices would expire before the truth or falsity of a return to a mandamus could be tried in an action for a false return, the law would not suffer the return to be traversed.

In 9th Queen Anne, an Act of Parliament was obtained, to permit the traversing returns to mandamus's for such offices as are within that Act; and all offices, not within that Act, stand as they did at the common law; and the facts, though ever so false, cannot be disproved but in an action for a false return, or in some cases by an information.

This is a strong Parliamentary declaration of what the law is, upon returns to writs of mandamus, which are always considered as standing upon the same foundation as returns to writs of habeas corpus.

I have looked through the books as carefully as I can, and so far from finding an instance of their being controverted by affidavit, where a person has been in custody of an officer under a legal authority, there is not an instance where the party is let in upon the record of the return to traverse any of the facts contained in it; but if that might have been done, yet it does not contradict my assertion, because a traverse carries it to its proper manner of trial, a trial by jury.

There are two cases, *King and Gardiner,* Cro. Eliz. 821. Trem. 354. *Swallow and The City of London,* 1 Syd. 287, where facts, consistent with the return, have been let in to be averred: I will cite them, because they shew that even facts, confessing the truth of the return, and avoiding it, must go to the jury.

A bailiff going to arrest a justice of the peace, he carried with him a hand gun: the 33 Hen. VIII. prohibits all persons from carrying such weapons. The justice sends out his servant and apprehends him for carrying this hand-gun; the justice convicts him upon the statute for the penalty, and sends him to gaol till he paid the penalty. Gardiner brings a habeas corpus, and removes himself into Court. The return was the warrant of execution, where the fact of his being a sheriff's officer did not appear; but the matter being disclosed to the Court, it was thought to be no offence, and that a minister of justice might carry a hand-gun. How was it to be come at? This was a fact which did not contradict the return, but confessed and avoided it; and yet the Court would not interpose by affidavit: they ordered a plea to be put in, comprising the whole matter, and upon the King's coroner and attorney confessing the plea, the man was discharged. But if it had been controverted, the plea put it into such a method, as would bring the fact to that form of trial, which the law has established as the best for investigating truth.

In the other case, Swallow was committed by the Court of Aldermen to Newgate, for refusing to accept the office of alderman, to which he had been elected by the ward where he lived; he was brought up by habeas corpus; after the return filed, it was moved for him to have leave to plead to the return, that he was an officer of the Mint, and by charter exempt from all offices—not a hint at an affidavit, and they put him to a writ of privilege, besides the plea; and as facts confessed and avoided the return, it was admitted: but still it brought the point to trial by jury; and it was agreed in that case, that matter, contrary to the return, could not be pleaded, but the party is put to his action for the false return.

It appears by Sir G. Treby's report, February 1688, that the House of Commons came to twenty-eight resolutions, to be carried into the Bill of Rights. Many of them were afterwards dropped, and amongst the rest, the twenty-fifth, which was, "that the subject should have liberty to traverse returns to writs of habeas corpus and mandamus."

This doctrine is echoed through all the books for three or four hundred years together. Y. B. 9 Hen. VI. fol. 44. Babington, who was then Chief Justice; "If the cause appear to us sufficient in itself, notwithstanding it be false, it is enough for us upon the return, which the whole Court agreed. And if he had returned that he was his villein, this shall not make an issue here, whether he be his villein or not: wherefore, if you cannot prove but that the cause is sufficient in itself, he shall be sent back again." 11 Coke 99, *Bagges's case.* 12 Coke 129, *Hawkeridges case:* "that upon an insufficient return, the party must be bailed or discharged; otherwise, if return shall be sufficient, when it is false." Godbolt, 129. If the return is false, the party cannot be delivered. 8 Co. 127 b.

I find no authority which warrants a difference between returns, when filed to writs of habeas corpus in cases of private custody, and of public custody, where the facts justifying the imprisonment have been set forth; that is, where there has been a full, complete, sufficient return.

For as to returns of process, which are to bring parties into Court, in order to have the right tried and examined, when the Court is proceeding not "legem dicere," but only "sistere in judicio," the Court often proceeds in a summary way upon such returns for the expedition of justice; the Court will not see their process disobeyed and eluded by tricks and falsities; and the case of *Emerton and Viner,* which was in Hilary term, 26 and 27 Car. II. and Easter and Trinity terms, 27 Car. II. seems to have proceeded upon this principle. It is reported in 3 Keb. 434, 447, 470, and 504. 2 Lev. 128. Freeman, 389, 401, 522.

I will state the case particularly, as it appears upon the record. In Hilary term, 26 and 27 Car. II. a habeas corpus issued to Sir Robert Viner, Lord Mayor of London, for the body of Bridget, the only daughter and heir of Sir Thomas Hyde. (Note, Sir Robert Viner had married Lady Hyde, the mother of Bridget, who was then dead.) In the same Hilary term, an "alias" habeas corpus issued under the penalty of £40; and afterwards in the same term, a "pluries" habeas corpus issued under the penalty of £500.

Sir Robert Viner to the "pluries" returned, that Bridget, the only daughter and heir of Sir Thomas Hyde, Knight, mentioned in the writ, at the time of the receipt of the aforesaid writ, or ever afterwards to that time, was not in his custody, as by the said writ is supposed; and for that reason he could not have the said Bridget before the King at the day and place mentioned in the writ, as by the said writ he was commanded.

A rule was then made that the return should be filed, and counsel be heard thereupon the next day. Upon that next day, the day after was given to Sir Robert Viner's counsel to speak to the return, and upon that next day, which was Saturday, this rule was made. "Upon the undertaking of Mr. Jefferys, as counsel for Sir Robert Viner, upon the writ of habeas corpus for the body of Bridget Hyde, that the said Robert Viner should bring the said Bridget into Court on Wednesday next, it is ordered, that no process in the mean time should be made out thereupon against the said Sir Robert Viner."

Upon the Wednesday, the following entry was made: "Bridget the only daughter and heir of Sir Thomas Hyde, Knight, being brought here into Court, in the custody of Sir Robert Viner, Knight, desired to remain in the custody of the said Sir Robert Viner." Upon the Friday afterwards, which was either the last day of the term, or very near the last day of the term, the following rule appears to have been made: "It is ordered, that Sir Robert Viner, before the end of next week, shall bind himself before the justices of this Court, or one of them, in a recognizance of £40,000 upon condition that the said Sir Robert Viner, before the end of the next week, between the entering into that recognizance, and one month next after Easter then next ensuing, should not, directly or indirectly, cause or procure, or knowingly consent, that the said Bridget, then being in the house of the said Sir Robert Viner, should be married or contracted in marriage with or to any person whatsoever, or should be solicited in order to marry with any person whatsoever, or should be delivered into the hands or custody of any person whatsoever, out of the custody of the said Sir Robert Viner; and if the said Sir Robert Viner shall not enter into such recognizance before the end of the next week, then let a writ of attachment issue against him for a contempt: and it is further ordered, that the said Sir Robert Viner shall permit Lady Acheson, the godmother, and the uncles and aunts of the said Bridget, and the sons and daughters of the said uncles and aunts (except John Emerton, one of her cousins) to have access to her, in order only to visit her, every Monday, Wednesday, and Friday, in every week, between the time of entering into the said recognizance and one month next after Easter, between the hours of four and seven in the afternoon: and it is further ordered" by the consent of counsel on both sides, "that the several affidavits now delivered here into Court, of and concerning the said Bridget, should be filed here in Court upon record." No affidavits are mentioned or taken notice of in any of the subsequent rules.

These are all the rules which appear to have been made in Hilary term; but Emerton brought an ejectment in that Hilary term, upon the demise of himself and Bridget his wife, for a messuage and some lands in North Mymms, in the county of Hertford, in order to establish his marriage, and that ejectment appears by the record to have been tried upon Tuesday next after five weeks from the Feast of Easter; and after this trial at Bar, by which Mr. Emerton established his marriage with Bridget Hyde, and upon the very same day of the trial, a habeas corpus issued to Sir Robert Viner, tested 11th May, to bring up the body of Bridget, the wife of John Emerton, lately called Bridget Hyde, the only daughter and heir of Sir Thomas Hyde, returnable on Friday next after the morrow of the Ascension; then an "alias" issued, tested 14th of May, and then a "pluries" issued, tested 15th May; and to all these writs of habeas corpus Sir Robert Viner made the same return, which was, "that Bridget, the wife of John Emerton, lately called Bridget Hyde, the only daughter and heir of Sir Thomas Hyde, in the said writ mentioned, at the time of the receipt of the aforesaid writ, or of any other writ of the King to him directed, or ever afterward to this time, was not, nor yet is, in his custody, as by the said writ is supposed, and for that reason he could not have the said Bridget at the day and place mentioned in the said writ, as by the said writ he was commanded." And upon the same day that these writs were returned, it was ordered, that the returns should be filed; and it does not appear that there were any other proceedings on those returns in that term.

But in the beginning of Trinity term, there appears to have been a rule made in the following words: "It is ordered, that unless Sir Robert Viner shall immediately permit William Emerton and Owen Davies to see Bridget, the wife of John Emerton, the son of the said William Emerton, or shall give notice to the said William Emerton and Owen Davies, where the said Bridget now is, that the said Robert Viner should attend the Court to-morrow;" and the next day, which was Saturday, a rule was made, "that the said Sir Robert Viner do attend the Court on Tuesday next without any further notice." But upon the Monday a rule was made, whereby "it was ordered, that the said Sir Robert Viner should attend the Court on Wednesday next peremptorily."

Upon the Thursday afterwards, "it was ordered, that Sir Robert Viner should attend the Court the next day, and that Mr. Francis Woodward, one of the officers of the Court, should give him notice of the order." Upon that next day, which was Friday, a rule was made, "that Sir Robert Viner should attend the Court upon the day after, to inform the Court where Bridget Emerton, wife of John Emerton, then was; otherwise a tipstaff should take him up and bring him into Court; and it was ordered, that Mr. Barrington should attend the Court the same day." Upon the Wednesday afterward a rule was made, "that the marshal should take up Sir Robert Viner upon the 30th day of October then next ensuing (the day after Lord Mayor's Day, when he would have been out of office) or as soon afterwards as he could take him, and bring him into Court." Early in Michaelmas term, to wit on Wednesday after one month of St. Michael, a rule was made, "that the marshal should take up Sir Robert Viner on the 13th November then next ensuing, or so soon afterward as he could take him; and that Mr. Emerton and his wife, and the other relations of the said Bridget, should, in the mean time, have free access to her at all convenient times."

By these proceedings it appears, that the Court was proceeding against him for a contempt in disobeying the writ; and as Sir Robert Viner had returned, that the said Bridget was not in his possession at the receipt of any writ, which was disproved by the record of their own Court, (for the rules I have stated shew she was in his possession) the fact, averred by the return upon the record, was falsified by evidence of equal dignity, viz. the records of the Court, grafted upon Sir Robert Viner's own acts and admissions.

In the next place, it does not appear by any acts of the Court, that any affidavits were read; for though the last rule of Court in Hilary term mentions, that the several affidavits delivered into Court concerning the said Bridget Emerton, should be filed; yet it does not appear from the records that they were ever read; and it is observable, that they were filed by consent of both parties; and if any affidavits were read, it could only be the affidavits mentioned in that rule; because no notice is taken of any affidavit in the subsequent rules, and consequently none could have been read to contradict the return to the second habeas corpus, because they were made two months before the second habeas corpus issued.

But suppose there had been no such proceedings upon the record, and affidavits had been read to shew that Bridget was in the custody of Sir Robert Viner, it would not encounter the doctrine I lay down; for it was not a return, averring facts justifying the cause of imprisonment, but only an excuse for not obeying the writ; and if it be false, the Court proceeds for a contempt in a summary way in this case as they would in all others. In Godbolt, 219, Smith, one of the officers of the Court of Admiralty, was committed by the Court of Common Pleas to the prison of the Fleet, because he had made return of a writ, contrary to what he had said in the same Court the day before. And to bring it home to my point, I would suppose there had been no verdict, evidencing the marriage of Bridget with Emerton, and that Sir Robert Viner had returned, that Bridget was not the wife of Emerton, but his own wife: in case there had been no legal disability, would the Court, upon affidavits, have tried the fact of that marriage?—If it were a case of that nature, it had been in point—I apprehend clearly they could not, without usurping a power which the law has not given them.

And it is further observable in that case, that there never was any rule made upon Sir Robert Viner to produce her. The compulsory rule was, that unless he should permit William Emerton and Owen Davies to see her, or give them notice where she was, he should attend the Court.

The next compulsory rule is, "that he should attend to inform the Court where she was, or otherwise that a tipstaff should take him up and bring him into Court;" and the two subsequent rules, for the marshal to take him up, and to bring him into Court, were in consequence of his non-attendance.

If they had considered the return as duly falsified by affidavit, and had proceeded upon that principle, they would have issued an attachment for the contempt in the first instance, as they had ordered in Hilary term upon the insufficiency of the first writ. And as Sir Robert Viner was indictable for making a false return, the affidavits might be properly read, as a foundation for the apprehending him; and the rather, because the marriage was established, and the Court saw he was guilty of a great offence in secreting and withholding a wife from her husband.

Affidavits may be read to collateral purposes; as in order to bail, or adjust the sum for which bail is to be given; and in the cases of madmen, when they have been brought up without any formal return at all, or only a return, "that I have the body ready according to the command of the writ." 22 Ass. pl. 56, battery and false imprisonment: defendant says plaintiff was in a rage, and did great mischief, whereupon the defendant and his other relations took him and bound him, and put him into a house, and chastised and beat him with a stick or rod.

As there was no return of a fact justifying the cause of imprisonment, the Judges were at liberty to look into it, and read affidavits, to direct them what to do upon it. For as the facts do not appear upon every return, the Court, or Judge, can be enabled only from affidavits to know whether they should interpose or not;—if satisfied the party was mad; though under no legal custody—they would not interpose. If doubtful,—they would direct an application for a commission, or put it into some way of inquiry; if quite satisfied it was a scene of oppression,—they would set the party at liberty.

So in cases of wives, children, and wards—all the Court, or Judge, does, is to see that the party is under no illegal restraint. The law so laid down, 1 Str. 445. 2 Str. 982, *The King and Smith.*

In the case of *The King and Smith,* habeas corpus was brought by the father against an aunt, for a child near fourteen; the return was only "ready in Court." She made an affidavit that the uncle had devised an estate to trustees, upon trust to pay her a yearly sum for the child's maintenance, and directed the money should be paid only to her; that the child had lived with her from its birth; that it was the uncle's desire it might so continue, the father being a very extravagant person.

The noble Lord, who then presided in the Court, said, "The detention being undefended, we must set the child at liberty: we can take no notice of the justification in the affidavit; we can determine nothing about the possession of the child: all the Court can do is to see that persons are not unlawfully confined."

In all these cases, the parties have opportunities of asserting their title at law, and may have the benefit of a writ of error. If we should take upon us the summary determination of this question, it would debar the parties of their writ of error, and such other privilege as the law has given.

The remedies, which the law has provided in different cases, should not be confounded. If there are any cases where facts have been entered into by affidavit, upon habeas corpus, yet unless there have been returns to such writs filed, and those returns have set forth a sufficient cause of the imprisonment, and affidavits have been read to contradict that cause in point of fact, such cases will not encounter the position I am now advancing.

A difference is made between the case of an officer and a mere private person—a difference in favour of interposing upon the return of an officer, rather than of a private person, because an officer is a minister of justice, and more under the controul of the Court than a mere stranger. If said to be a wrong-doer—that is begging the question; for it depends upon the truth or falsity of the return, whether he is a wrong-doer.

If a lawful cause of restraint is not returned, the party will be discharged for the insufficiency of it; but the facts, evidencing the legality, must not be presumed to be false, in order to warrant an examination whether they be false or not.

But suppose there was a distinction between custody by a public officer, and a private person acting without any authority whatsoever; yet, in regard to pressed men, they are in the custody of public officers, acting under an authority given by Act of Parliament; they are under a necessity of receiving them; they take them as persons within the description of the Act; and if they return them to be so, they have a right to have that fact tried by a jury as well as any other person. But it is not the privilege of an officer, but of an Englishman, to have a fact, justifying his conduct, and which he has averred upon record, tried by a jury.

It is said, that it is a very hard case, and that a man may be sent to the West Indies before the falsity of the return is proved in an action.—If there be any particular hardship, the Act which produces the case, must provide for it.

Judges will construe the law as liberally as possible in favour of liberty, but they cannot make laws; they are only to expound them: particular cases must yield to the law, and not the law to particular cases.

There is no difference between facts in a return, and any other facts averred upon record.

Suppose an action brought upon a bond for any given sum of money, and the party is arrested upon it, and he pleads that he never executed the bond; suppose he could shew by affidavits ever so clearly, that he did not execute the bond, or, by a copy of the register, that he was not born when it is dated. The Court could not interpose; why? Because the law says, the fact must be tried by a jury:

the Judges have no more cognizance or power to try it than if they were not Judges.

If they were to do it where there was the clearest and most undoubted proof, they must do it in every case: for the degree of proof cannot alter or vary the mode of trial, and translate the examination of the fact from the jury to the Judge.

If a man is arrested and in custody, in a civil action, upon an affidavit made by the plaintiff of the debt, the Court will not, even for the purpose of discharging him out of custody, enter into any examination of the reality of the debt, though there is the most clear and undoubted proof laid before the Court of the falsity of the demand; it must be tried by a jury. The Court cannot look at it. We must administer justice, not as we wish the law to be, but as it is.

Laws are framed upon principles of general utility, and adapted to such cases as most frequently happen. Judges cannot set up natural reason against the reason of the law—cannot dispense with the law, for the sake of a particular case, arising upon an act which will expire with the session, and perhaps may never be enacted again; and in a case, where the hardship may be prevented by making a rule upon all the parties concerned in supporting the right to the recruit, that he shall not be carried away till the merits are tried in an action; or by letting him out, on security to return, if the merits are against him: and if the case was ever so remediless, I think we are not warranted to impeach, by affidavits, the truth of the return of an officer, acting under an Act of Parliament, which the law says ought to be impeached by a verdict.

But the case is not a remediless one: by the common law, the writ of "homine replegiando" will clearly relieve him. That writ, which is obtained out of the Court of Chancery upon an affidavit, goes to the sheriff, and commands him to replevy the man. If he cannot replevy him, he returns it, and a process goes out instantly to seize the body of the person who is supposed to have him in custody, and he is imprisoned himself till he produces the body. Fitzherbert, Nat. Bre. 67 b. (edition 1616), 5 Hen. 7, 3.

If a person is seized by virtue of the first writ, and the party, who has him in custody, claims any right to the detention of him, still he is to be delivered, upon giving security for his appearance, and to try the right in a Court of Justice; and if the point is determined against him, to deliver himself up to the person in whose custody he was: so that, by this writ, the party may be instantly set at liberty, without violating any rule of law whatsoever; and where a person is in actual custody, the sheriff will be sure to find him and deliver him; and it is a more sure and certain remedy in that case, than where a man is imprisoned by a mere private person, and may be shifted about so secretly, that the sheriff cannot find him.

There is another method by which a man impressed may get at his liberty, laying the gaoler and the return quite out of the case: and that is, by appealing to that summary jurisdiction, which the Court of King's Bench exercises over all inferior jurisdictions, powers, and authorities whatsoever.

The authority given to the commissioners, being a particular, special authority, if it is abused, they are answerable to the Court for it; and the Court will relieve the party oppressed by it in a summary way, by affidavits. But in that case, the complaint is founded on affidavits, and therefore must be answered by affidavits; and the fact is tried, between the persons who did the wrong, and the person who sustained it.

The Crown, being interested in the recruit, is likewise heard "pro interesse." The gaoler is no party to that complaint or inquiry; and as to him, the fact, which he has averred upon record, stands unimpeached; and if it is false, he must and can only be answerable for it in an action: and by this mode of proceeding, the party acquires such a discharge as will completely work a manumission of him from his condition of a soldier.

For if a gaoler should let a man go, or return only that he had his body ready, without shewing any cause of his imprisonment, or should make an insufficient return, or a false return; no man can say that an act of the gaoler can affect the right which the public have in the recruit. That must and can only be determined between the commissioners and the Crown on the one side, and the party imprisoned on the other.

The distinction, between a proceeding by habeas corpus and upon motion, I take to be this: In a proceeding by motion, the Court goes upon affidavits; and it may take its rise collaterally, various ways, out of disputes which come before the Court upon record. For instance, the return to a habeas corpus cannot be tried and set aside by affidavits; but the Court may take the matter up "diverso intuitu," in order to grant an information against a man who has seized another by outrage and violence, and detains him without any colour of authority; or perhaps to proceed against such person by way of information for a false return, which Hale says is an indictable offence; or in order to commit him for an outrageous breach of the peace.

Suppose habeas corpus for a maid taken away, according to the Statute of Philip and Mary, or of 3 Henry VII.; by the one, a great misdemeanor,—by the other a felony; and the party returns that he is married, that she is his wife. The fact, or validity of the marriage, cannot be controverted upon the return; but upon affidavits the Court might commit him for a misdemeanor in one case, and for a felony in the other. And in cases where the Court has a discretion as to bailing, the Court might put such terms upon him as would force the immediate relief of the person imprisoned and agreeable to these principles, is *The King and White,* Trin. 1745, where the Court would not discharge the impressed man, T. Reynolds, upon the affidavits contradicting the return; but being brought up on a Monday, and the writ and return, which was full and sufficient, being filed, the Court ordered him to be brought up again on Wednesday; and upon reading the several affidavits of Reynolds and others on his behalf, made a rule upon the commissioners and the Master, to shew cause the next day, why he should not be discharged out of the custody of the said Richard White. The rule was as follows:

Monday, 1st July 1745. "The defendant being brought here into Court, in custody of Richard White, Esquire, Major of the Tower of London, by virtue of His Majesty's writ of habeas corpus, it is ordered, by consent of counsel on both sides, that the name Thomas White, mentioned in the said writ, be made Richard White: and it is further ordered, that the said writ and returns thereto be filed, and that the said Richard White bring into this Court the body of the said defendant Thomas Reynolds on Wednesday next; and upon reading the several affidavits of Thomas Kell and others, George Stewart and others, Thomas Reynolds and John Mangaar, it is further ordered, that Thomas Bedwell, Francis Bedwell, Charles Scriven, John West, and John Robinson (commissioners under the Act) do to-morrow shew cause why the said defendant should not be discharged out of the custody of the said Richard White, upon notice of this rule to be given to them respectively in the mean time."

There is a decisive mark upon this rule, which shews the Court industriously avoided twisting the complaint against the commissioners with the return; because they ordered the rule on the commissioners to come on at a different day: whereas, if the affidavits had been levelled and pointed at the return, the Court would have directed them to have come on together; and it is extremely material, that Major White is not so much as a party to that part of the rule which is upon the commissioners; the Court considered the return with regard to him as sacred, and not to be litigated by affidavits against him.

If the Court had meant to have impeached the truth of the return by affidavits, as between Reynolds the man impressed, and White the gaoler, they would have certainly given White an opportunity of supporting the truth of his return by affidavits.

Wednesday. Sir John Strange for Major White, said, the question was of great consequence to the liberty of the subject on the one hand, and to the service of the public on the other, and that there had not been time for him to be sufficiently prepared: he proposed therefore, without prejudice to the question, to admit him to bail. The rule upon the commissioners was discharged; and it appears that the defendant's recognizance was afterwards discharged.

I have searched for writs of habeas corpus and returns to them, in Queen Anne's time. There are many; eight of the persons are remanded, seven are discharged; as to some, it does not appear what was done. And in every case where the party was remanded, the return appears to be good upon the face of it; where discharged, insufficient upon the face of it.

I directed a search to be made for affidavits, or for any rules that might have been made upon the discharge or remanding of the parties. The affidavits were stolen many years ago out of the office; and there are no rules to be found in the rule-book except one, in *Bolton's case,* which I will mention by and by, and submit to your Lordships, as the most decisive instance which can be produced, that the return was sacred, and could not be touched but by consent.

As no more light could be got from that inquiry, I then examined the returns where the parties were remanded and where they were discharged; and if I could have found two returns in the same words, one where the person was remanded, and another where he was discharged, it would have afforded a very strong reason to have believed that some extrinsic collateral evidence had been received, which had produced a remand in the one case, and a discharge in the other; but as all the returns where the parties were remanded are sufficient, and all the discharges are in cases where the returns are insufficient, it demonstrates most clearly to my satisfaction, that the Court proceeded only upon the sufficiency or insufficiency of the return, on the face of it.

There is one return of an enlisted soldier, Alexander James, committed by the captain to the Savoy, plainly insufficient. The captain is not stated to have had any authority to commit, and no offence is stated for which the soldier was committed; he is not so much as said to be a captain of the regiment in which he was enlisted.

The case of *Bolton* is in Hil. 3d of Queen Anne. A rule was made by consent to refer it to arbitrators, to determine whether he was such a person as was within the description of the Act. If the Court could have discharged upon reading affidavits, why put it into any other mode of enquiry? They saw it could be done only by action for a false return; but upon consent, they might have directed an issue to try, or fixed upon referees, who are a jury of the party's own choosing, to try whether he was within the Act or not: it is nothing more than if the parties, upon a return to a mandamus, should agree to refer the fact to referees, instead of going to trial by a jury: it is so far from proving, that the Court could try the question by affidavits, it proves that they could not; and that inference is strengthened by seeing no traces of such an examination. There is no mention of it in any books of that time; and it is not to be conceived that it should by accident have happened, that all the men, remanded upon good returns, had no evidence, and that all the persons discharged, had.

I am clearly of opinion that Judges are not bound down by any fact set forth on a return, if disproved by a verdict; but that the Court can look at no other proof, as to any facts averred on a return, admitting and justifying the imprisonment.

The other Judges delivered their opinions "seriatim" on the same questions, the 25th, 26th, and 30th May 1758; and on the 2d June,

It was ordered, that the bill, intituled, "An Act for giving a more Speedy Remedy to the Subject upon the Writ of Habeas Corpus," be

Rejected.

4

WILLIAM BLACKSTONE, COMMENTARIES 3:129–37 1768

---

3. The writ *de homine replegiando* lies to replevy a man out of prison, or out of the custody of any private person, (in the same manner that chattels taken in distress may be replevied, of which in the next chapter) upon giving security

to the sheriff that the man shall be forthcoming to answer any charge against him. And, if the person be conveyed out of the sheriff's jurisdiction, the sheriff may return that he is eloigned, *elongatus;* upon which a process issues (called a *capias in withernam*) to imprison the defendant himself, without bail or mainprize, till he produces the party. But this writ is guarded with so many exceptions, that it is not an effectual remedy in numerous instances, especially where the crown is concerned. The incapacity therefore of these three remedies to give complete relief in every case hath almost intirely antiquated them, and hath caused a general recourse to be had, in behalf of persons aggrieved by illegal imprisonment, to

4. The writ of *habeas corpus,* the most celebrated writ in the English law. Of this there are various kinds made use of by the courts at Westminster, for removing prisoners from one court into another for the more easy administration of justice. Such is the *habeas corpus ad respondendum,* when a man hath a cause of action against one who is confined by the process of some inferior court; in order to remove the prisoner, and charge him with this new action in the courts above. Such is that *ad satisfaciendum,* when a prisoner hath had judgment against him in an action, and the plaintiff is desirous to bring him up to some superior court to charge him with process of execution. Such also are those *ad prosequendum, testificandum, deliberandum, &c;* which issue when it is necessary to remove a prisoner, in order to prosecute or bear testimony in any court, or to be tried in the proper jurisdiction wherein the fact was committed. Such is, lastly the common writ *ad faciendum et recipiendum,* which issues out of any of the courts of Westminster-hall, when a person is sued in some inferior jurisdiction, and is desirous to remove the action into the superior court; commanding the inferior judges to produce the body of the defendant, together with the day and cause of his caption and detainer (whence the writ is frequently denominated an *habeas corpus cum causa*) to *do and receive* whatsoever the king's court shall consider in that behalf. This is a writ grantable of common right, without any motion in court; and it instantly supersedes all proceedings in the court below. But, in order to prevent the surreptitious discharge of prisoners, it is ordered by statute 1 & 2 P.&M. c. 13. that no *habeas corpus* shall issue to remove any prisoner out of any gaol, unless signed by some judge of the court out of which it is awarded. And, to avoid vexatious delays by removal of frivolous causes, it is enacted by statute 21 Jac. I. c. 23. that, where the judge of an inferior court of record is a barrister of three years standing, no cause shall be removed from thence by *habeas corpus* or other writ, after issue or demurrer deliberately joined: that no cause, if once remanded to the inferior court by writ of *procedendo* or otherwise, shall ever afterwards be again removed: and that no cause shall be removed at all, if the debt or damages laid in the declaration do not amount to the sum of five pounds. But an *expedient* having been found out to elude the latter branch of the statute, by procuring a nominal plaintiff to bring another action for five pounds or upwards, (and then by the course of the court the *habeas corpus* removed both actions together) it is therefore enacted by statute 12 Geo. I. c. 29. that the inferior court may proceed in such actions as are under the value of five pounds, notwithstanding other actions may be brought against the same defendant to a greater amount.

But the great and efficacious writ in all manner of illegal confinement, is that of *habeas corpus ad subjiciendum;* directed to the person detaining another, and commanding him to produce the body of the prisoner with the day and cause of his caption and detention, *ad faciendum, subjiciendum, et recipiendum,* to do, submit to, and receive, whatsoever the judge or court awarding such writ shall consider in that behalf. This is a high prerogative writ, and therefore by the common law issuing out of the court of king's bench not only in term-time, but also during the vacation, by a *fiat* from the chief justice or any other of the judges, and running into all parts of the king's dominions: for the king is at all times intitled to have an account, why the liberty of any of his subjects is restrained, wherever that restraint may be inflicted. If it issues in vacation, it is usually returnable before the judge himself who awarded it, and he proceeds by himself thereon; unless the term should intervene, and then it may be returned in court. Indeed, if the party were privileged in the courts of common pleas and exchequer, as being an officer or suitor of the court, an *habeas corpus ad subjiciendum* might also have been awarded from thence: and, if the cause of imprisonment were palpably illegal, they might have discharged him; but, if he were committed for any criminal matter, they could only have remanded him, or taken bail for his appearance in the court of king's bench; which occasioned the common pleas to discountenance such applications. It hath also been said, and by very respectable authorities, that the like *habeas corpus* may issue out of the court of chancery in vacation: but, upon the famous application to lord Nottingham by Jenks, notwithstanding the most diligent searches, no precedent could be found where the chancellor had issued such a writ in vacation, and therefore his lordship refused it.

In the court of king's bench it was, and is still, necessary to apply for it by motion to the court, as in the case of all other prerogative writs (*certiorari,* prohibition, *mandamus, &c*) which do not issue as of mere course, without shewing some probable cause why the extraordinary power of the crown is called in to the party's assistance. For, as was argued by lord chief justice Vaughan, "it is granted on motion, because it cannot be had of course; and there is therefore no *necessity* to grant it: for the court ought to be satisfied that the party hath a probable cause to be delivered." And this seems the more reasonable, because (when once granted) the person to whom it is directed can return no satisfactory excuse for not bringing up the body of the prisoner. So that, if it issued of mere course, without shewing to the court or judge some reasonable ground for awarding it, a traitor or felon under sentence of death, a soldier or mariner in the king's service, a wife, a child, a relation, or a domestic, confined for insanity or other prudential reasons, might obtain a temporary enlargement by suing out an *habeas corpus,* though sure to be remanded as soon as brought up to the court. And therefore Edward Coke, when chief justice, did not scruple in 13 Jac. I. to deny a *habeas corpus* to one confined by the court of admiralty for piracy; there appearing, upon his own shewing, sufficient grounds to confine him. On the other hand, if a probable ground be shewn, that the party is imprisoned without just cause, and therefore hath a right to be delivered, the writ of *habeas corpus* is then a writ of right, which "may not be denied, but ought to be granted to every man that is committed, or detained in prison, or otherwise restrained, though it be by the command of the king, the privy council, or any other."

In a former part of these commentaries we expatiated at large on the personal liberty of the subject. It was shewn to be a natural inherent right, which could not be surrendered or forfeited unless by the commission of some great and atrocious crime, nor ought to be abridged in any case without the special permission of law. A doctrine co-eval with the first rudiments of the English constitution; and handed down to us from our Saxon ancestors, notwithstanding all their struggles with the Danes, and the violence of the Norman conquest: asserted afterwards and confirmed by the conqueror himself and his descendants: and though sometimes a little impaired by the ferocity of the times, and the occasional despotism of jealous or usurping princes, yet established on the firmest basis by the provisions of *magna carta*, and a long succession of statutes enacted under Edward III. To assert an absolute exemption from imprisonment in all cases, is inconsistent with every idea of law and political society; and in the end would destroy all civil liberty, by rendering it's protection impossible: but the glory of the English law consists in clearly defining the times, the causes, and the extent, when, wherefore, and to what degree, the imprisonment of the subject may be lawful. This induces an absolute necessity of expressing upon every commitment the reason for which it is made; that the court upon an *habeas corpus* may examine into it's validity; and according to the circumstances of the case may discharge, admit to bail, or remand the prisoner.

And yet, early in the reign of Charles I, the court of king's bench, relying on some arbitrary precedents (and those perhaps misunderstood) determined that they could not upon an *habeas corpus* either bail or deliver a prisoner, though committed without any cause assigned, in case he was committed by the special command of the king, or by the lords of the privy council. This drew on a parliamentary enquiry, and produced the *petition of right*, 3 Car. I. which recites this illegal judgment, and enacts that no freeman hereafter shall be so imprisoned or detained. But when, in the following year, Mr Selden and others were committed by the lords of the council, in pursuance of his majesty's special command, under a general charge of "notable contempts and stirring up sedition against the king and government," the judges delayed for two terms (including also the long vacation) to deliver an opinion how far such a charge was bailable. And, when at length they agreed that it was, they however annexed a condition of finding sureties for the good behaviour, which still protracted their imprisonment; the chief justice, sir Nicholas Hyde, at the same time declaring, that "if they were again remanded for that cause, perhaps the court would not afterwards grant a *habeas corpus*, being already made acquainted with the cause of the imprisonment." But this was heard with indignation and astonishment by every lawyer present; according to Mr Selden's own account of the matter, whose resentment was not cooled at the distance of four and twenty years.

These pitiful evasions gave rise to the statute 16 Car. I. c. 10. §. 8. whereby it was enacted, that if any person be committed by the king himself in person, or by his privy council, or by any of the members thereof, he shall have granted unto him, without any delay upon any pretence whatsoever, a writ of *habeas corpus*, upon demand or motion made to the court of king's bench *or common pleas;* who shall thereupon, within three court days after the return is made, examine and determine the legality of such commitment, and do what to justice shall appertain, in delivering, bailing, or remanding such prisoner. Yet still in the case of Jenks, before alluded to, who in 1676 was committed by the king in council for a turbulent speech at Guildhall, new shifts and devices were made use of to prevent his enlargement by law; the chief justice (as well as the chancellor) declining to award a writ of *habeas corpus ad subjiciendum* in vacation, though at last he thought proper to award the usual writs *ad deliberandum, &c,* whereby the prisoner was discharged at the Old Bailey. Other abuses had also crept into daily practice, which had in some measure defeated the benefit of this great constitutional remedy. The party imprisoning was at liberty to delay his obedience to the first writ, and might wait till a second and a third, called an *alias* and a *pluries,* were issued, before he produced the party: and many other vexatious shifts were practiced to detain state-prisoners in custody. But whoever will attentively consider the English history may observe, that the flagrant abuse of any power, by the crown or it's ministers, has always been productive of a struggle; which either discovers the exercise of that power to be contrary to law, or (if legal) restrains it for the future. This was the case in the present instance. The oppression of an obscure individual gave birth to the famous *habeas corpus* act, 31 Car. II. c. 2. which is frequently considered as another *magna carta* of the kingdom; and by consequence has also in subsequent times reduced the method of proceeding on these writs (though not within the reach of that statute, but issuing merely at the common law) to the true standard of law and liberty.

The statute itself enacts, 1. That the writ shall be returned and the prisoner brought up within a limited time according to the distance, not exceeding in any case twenty days. 2. That such writs shall be endorsed as granted in pursuance of this act, and signed by the person awarding them. 3. That on complaint and request in writing by or on behalf of any person committed and charged with any crime (unless committed for treason or felony expressed in the warrant, or for suspicion of the same, or as accessory thereto before the fact, or convicted or charged in execution by legal process) the lord chancellor or any of the twelve judges, in vacation, upon viewing a copy of the warrant or affidavit that a copy is denied, shall (unless the party has neglected for two terms to apply to any court for his enlargement) award a *habeas corpus* for such prisoner, returnable immediately before himself or any other of the judges; and upon the return made shall discharge the party, if bailable, upon giving security to appear and answer to the accusation in the proper court of judicature. 4. That officers and keepers neglecting to make due returns, or not delivering to the prisoner or his agent within six hours after demand a copy of the warrant of commitment, or shifting the custody of a prisoner from one to another, without sufficient reason or authority (specified in the act) shall for the first offence forfeit 100*l.* and for the second offence 200*l.* to the party grieved, and be disabled to hold his office. 5. That no person, once delivered by *habeas corpus,* shall be recommitted for the same offence on penalty of 500*l.* 6. That every person committed for treason or felony shall, if he requires it the first week of the next term or the first day of the next session of *oyer* and *terminer,* be indicted in that term or session, or else admitted to bail; unless the king's witnesses cannot be produced at that time: and if acquitted, or if not indicted and tried in the second term of session, he shall be discharged from his imprisonment for such imputed offence: but that no person, after the assises shall be opened for the county in which he is detained, shall be removed by *habeas corpus,* till after the assises are ended; but shall be left to the justice of the judges of assise. 7. That any such prisoner may move for and obtain his *habeas corpus,* as well out of the chancery or exchequer, as out of the king's bench or common pleas; and the lord chancellor or judges denying the same, on sight of the warrant or oath that the same is refused, forfeit severally to the party grieved the sum of 500*l.* 8. That this writ of *habeas corpus* shall run into the counties palatine, cinque ports, and other privileged places, and the islands of Jersey and Guernsey. 9. That no inhabitant of England (except persons contracting, or convicts praying, to be transported; or having committed some capital offence in the place to which they are sent) shall be sent prisoner to Scotland, Ireland, Jersey, Guernsey, or any places beyond the seas, within or without the king's dominions: on pain that the party committing, his advisors, aiders, and assistants shall forfeit to the party grieved a sum not less than 500*l.* to be recovered with treble costs; shall be disabled to bear any office of trust or profit; shall incur the penalties of *praemunire;* and shall be incapable of the king's pardon.

This is the substance of that great and important statute: which extends (we may observe) only to the case of commitments for such criminal charge, as can produce no inconvenience to public justice by a temporary enlargement of the prisoner: all other cases of unjust imprisonment being left to the *habeas corpus* at common law. But even upon writs at the common law it is now expected by the court, agreeable to antient precedents and the spirit of the act of parliament, that the writ should be immediately obeyed, without waiting for any *alias* or *pluries;* otherwise an attachment will issue. By which admirable regulations, judicial as well as parliamentary, the remedy is now complete for *removing* the injury of unjust and illegal confinement. A remedy the more necessary, because the oppression does not always arise from the ill-nature, but sometimes from the mere inattention, of government.

5

BRASS CROSBY'S CASE

95 Eng. Rep. 1005 (C.P. 1771)

(See 1.5, no. 2)

6

MASSACHUSETTS CONSTITUTION OF 1780, PT. 2, CH. 6, ART. 7

VII. The privilege and benefit of the writ of *habeas corpus* shall be enjoyed in this commonwealth, in the most free, easy, cheap, expeditious, and ample manner; and shall not be suspended by the legislature, except upon the most urgent and pressing occasions, and for a limited time, not exceeding twelve months.

7

NEW HAMPSHIRE CONSTITUTION OF 1784

Thorpe 4:2469

The privilege and benefit of the habeas corpus, shall be enjoyed in this state, in the most free, easy, cheap, expeditious, and ample manner, and shall not be suspended by the legislature, except upon the most urgent and pressing occasions, and for a time not exceeding three months.

8

RECORDS OF THE FEDERAL CONVENTION

[*2:334; Journal, 20 Aug.*]

The privileges and benefit of the writ of habeas corpus shall be enjoyed in this government in the most expeditious and ample manner: and shall not be suspended by the Legislature except upon the most urgent and pressing occasions, and for a limited time not exceeding months.

[*2:435; Journal, 28 Aug.*]

It was moved and seconded to add the following amendment to the 4 sect. II article

"The privilege of the writ of Habeas Corpus shall not be suspended; unless where in cases of rebellion or invasion the public safety may require it."

which passed in the affirmative [Ayes—7; noes—3.]

[*2:438; Madison, 28 Aug.*]

Mr. Pinkney, urging the propriety of securing the benefit of the Habeas corpus in the most ample manner, moved "that it should not be suspended but on the most urgent occasions, & then only for a limited time not exceeding twelve months"

Mr. Rutlidge was for declaring the Habeas Corpus inviolable—He did not conceive that a suspension could ever be necessary at the same time through all the States—

Mr. Govr Morris moved that "The privilege of the writ of Habeas Corpus shall not be suspended, unless where in cases of Rebellion or invasion the public safety may require it".

Mr. Wilson doubted whether in any case a suspension could be necessary, as the discretion now exists with Judges, in most important cases to keep in Gaol or admit to Bail.

The first part of Mr. Govr. Morris' motion, to the word "unless" was agreed to nem: con:—on the remaining part;

N. H. ay. Mas. ay. Ct. ay. Pa. ay. Del. ay. Md. ay. Va. ay. N. C. no. S. C. no. Geo. no. [Ayes—7; noes—3.]

[*2:576, 596; Committee of Style*]

The privilege of the writ of Habeas Corpus shall not be suspended; unless where in cases of rebellion or invasion the public safety may require it.

9

LUTHER MARTIN, GENUINE INFORMATION 1788

Storing 2.4.72

By the next paragraph, the general government is to have a *power* of *suspending* the *habeas corpus act,* in cases of *rebellion* or *invasion.*

As the State governments have a power of suspending the habeas corpus act in those cases, it was said, there could be no reason for giving such a power to the general government, since, whenever the *State* which is invaded, or in which an insurrection takes place, finds its safety requires it, *it* will make use of that power—*And* it was urged, that if we gave this power to the general government, it would be an engine of oppression in its hands, since whenever a State should oppose its views, however arbitrary and unconstitutional, and refuse submission to them, the general government may declare it to be *an act of rebellion,* and suspending the habeas corpus act, may *seize* upon the persons of those *advocates of freedom,* who have had *virtue* and *resolution* enough to excite the opposition, and may *imprison* them during its pleasure in the *remotest* part of the union, so that a citizen of Georgia might be *bastiled* in the furthest part of New-Hampshire; or a citizen of New-Hampshire in the furthest extreme to the south, cut off from their family, their friends, and their every connexion—These considerations induced me, Sir, to give my negative also to this clause.

10

DEBATE IN MASSACHUSETTS RATIFYING CONVENTION 26 Jan. 1788

Elliot 2:108–9

Gen. THOMPSON asked the president to please to proceed. We have, said he, read the book often enough; it is a consistent piece of inconsistency.

Hon. Mr. ADAMS, in answer to an inquiry of the Hon. Mr. Taylor, said, that this power given to the general government to suspend this privilege in cases of rebellion and invasion, did not take away the power of the several states to suspend it, if they shall see fit.

Dr. TAYLOR asked, why this darling privilege was not expressed in the same manner it was in the Constitution of Massachusetts. [Here the honorable gentleman read the paragraph respecting it, in the constitution of that state, and then the one in the proposed Constitution.] He remarked on the difference of expression, and asked why the time was not limited.

Judge DANA said, the answer, in part, to the honorable gentleman, must be, that the same men did not make both Constitutions; that he did not see the necessity or great benefit of limiting the *time.* Supposing it had been, as in our constitution, "not exceeding twelve months," yet, as our legislature can, so might the Congress, continue the suspension of the writ from time to time, or from year to year. The safest and best restriction, therefore, arises from the nature of the cases in which Congress are authorized to exercise that power at all, namely, in those of rebellion or invasion. These are clear and certain terms, facts of public notoriety, and whenever these shall cease to exist, the suspension of the writ must necessarily cease also. He thought, the citizen had a better security for his privilege of the writ of *habeas corpus* under the federal than under the state constitution; for our legislature may suspend the writ as often as they judge *"the most urgent and pressing occasions"* call for it. He hoped these short observations would satisfy the honorable gentleman's inquiries; otherwise, he should be happy in endeavoring to do it by going more at large into the subject.

Judge SUMNER said, that this was a restriction on Congress, that the writ of *habeas corpus* should not be suspended, except in cases of rebellion or invasion. The learned judge then explained the nature of this writ. When a person, said he, is imprisoned, he applies to a judge of the Supreme Court; the judge issues his writ to the jailer, calling upon him to have the body of the person imprisoned before him, with the crime on which he was committed. If it then appears that the person was legally committed, and that he was not bailable, he is remanded to prison; if illegally confined, he is enlarged. This privilege, he said, is essential to freedom, and therefore the power to suspend it is restricted. On the other hand, the state, he said, might be involved in danger; the worst enemy may lay plans to destroy us, and so artfully as to prevent any evidence against him, and might ruin the country, without the power to suspend the writ was thus given. Congress have only power to suspend the privilege to persons committed by their authority. A person committed under the authority of the states will still have a right to this writ.

11

Thomas Jefferson to James Madison
31 July 1788
Papers 13:442

(See vol. 1, ch. 14, no. 46)

12

St. George Tucker,
Blackstone's Commentaries
1:App. 290–92
1803

The writ of *habeas corpus,* is the great and efficacious remedy provided for all cases of illegal confinement; and is directed to the person detaining another, commanding him to produce the body of the prisoner, with the day and cause of his caption and detention, to do, submit to, and receive whatsoever the judge or court awarding such writ shall consider in that behalf. In England this is a high prerogative writ, and issues out of the court of king's-bench, not only in term time, but during the vacation, by a *fiat* from the chief justice, or any other of the judges, and running into all parts of the king's dominions. In Virginia it may issue out of the high court of chancery, the general court, or the court of the district in which the person is confined, and may be awarded by any judge of either of those courts in vacation: and if any judge in vacation, upon view of the copy of the warrant of commitment or detainer, or upon affidavit made, that such copy was denied, shall refuse any writ of *habeas corpus,* required to be granted by law, such judge shall be liable to the action of the party aggrieved. And by the laws of the United States, all the courts of the United States, and either of the justices of the supreme court, as well as judges of the district courts, have power to grant writs of *habeas corpus* for the purpose of an enquiry into the cause of commitment. . . . Provided that writs of *habeas corpus* shall in no case extend to prisoners in gaol, unless they are in custody under, or by colour of the authority of the United States, or are committed for trial before some court of the same, or are necessary to be brought into court to testify.

Here a question naturally occurs: if a person be illegally committed to prison in any state, under, or by colour of the authority of the United States, can any judge, or court of the state in which he is confined, award a writ of *habeas corpus,* for the purpose of an enquiry into the cause of his commitment? To which, I answer, that if he be committed or detained for any crime, unless it be for treason or felony, plainly expressed in the warrant of commitment, and be neither convicted thereof, nor in execution by legal process, the writ (due requisites being observed) can not be refused him: for the act is imperative, as to awarding the writ. The court or judge, before whom the prisoner is brought, must judge from the return made to the writ, what course he ought to pursue: whether, to discharge him from his imprisonment, or bail him, or remand him again to the custody of the person from whom he may be brought.

In England the benefit of this important writ can only be suspended by authority of parliament. It has been done several times of late years, both in England and in Ireland, to the great oppression of the subject, as hath been said. In the United States, it can be suspended, only, by the authority of congress; but not whenever congress may think proper; for it cannot be suspended, unless in cases of actual rebellion, or invasion. A suspension under any other circumstances, whatever might be the pretext, would be unconstitutional, and consequently must be disregarded by those whose duty it is to grant the writ. The legislatures of the respective states are left, I presume, to judge of the causes which may induce a suspension within any particular state. This is the case, at least, in Virginia.

13

House of Representatives, Suspension of the Habeas Corpus
26 Jan. 1807
Annals 16:402, 403–15, 422–24

A message was received from the Senate, by Mr. Samuel Smith, as follows:

> Mr. Speaker: I am directed by the Senate of the United States to deliver to this House a confidential message, in writing.

The House being cleared of all persons except the members and the Clerk, Mr. Smith delivered to the Speaker the following communication in writing:

> *Gentlemen of the House of Representatives:*
>
> The Senate have passed a bill suspending for three months the privilege of the writ of habeas corpus, in certain cases, which they think expedient to communicate to you in confidence, and to request your concurrence therein, as speedily as the emergency of the case shall in your judgment require.

Mr. SMITH, also delivered in the bill referred to in the said communication, and then withdrew.

The bill was read as follows:

> A Bill suspending the writ of Habeas Corpus for three months, in certain cases.
>
> *Be it enacted, by the Senate and House of Representatives of the United States of America, in Congress assembled,* That in all cases, where any person or persons, charged on oath with treason, misprision of treason, or other high crime or misdemeanor, endangering the peace, safety, or neutrality of the United States, have been or shall be arrested or imprisoned, by virtue of any warrant or authority of the President of the United States, or from the Chief Executive Magistrate of any State or Territorial Government, or from any person acting under the direction or authority of the President of the United States, the privilege of the writ of *habeas corpus* shall be, and the same hereby is suspended, for and during the term of three months from and after the passage of this act, and no longer.

. . . . .

Mr. EPPES moved that the bill be rejected. This motion was afterwards withdrawn to give place to another motion, but with the idea of renewing it again.

Mr. BURWELL said, he was unacquainted with the particular reasons which had induced the Senate to pass this bill. None had been assigned when the bill was communicated, and no additional documents presented. He could, therefore, only be governed by that information which the House had received; and he believed that it would justify the motion before the House. The President, in his Message of the 22d, says, "on the whole the fugitives from Ohio and their associates from Cumberland, or other places in that quarter, cannot threaten serious danger to the city of New Orleans." If that be the case, upon what ground shall we suspend the writ of habeas corpus? Can any person imagine the United States are in danger, after this declaration of the President, who unquestionably possesses more correct information than any other person can be supposed to have. In another part of the Message, we are informed—

> "That the persons arrested at New Orleans have been embarked for some of the Atlantic ports, probably on the consideration that an impartial trial could not be expected during the present agitations of New Orleans, and that that city was not as yet a safe place of confinement. As soon as these persons shall arrive, they will be delivered to the custody of the law, and left to such course of trial, both as to place and process, as its functionaries may direct; the presence of the highest judicial authorities to be assembled at this place within a few days, the means of pursuing a sounder course of proceedings here than elsewhere, and the Executive means, should the judges have occasion to use them, render it equally desirable, for the criminals as for the public, that being already removed from the place where they were apprehended, the first regular arrest should take place here, and the course of proceedings receive here its proper direction."

The President evidently holds out the idea, that the correct and proper mode of proceeding can be had under the existing laws of the United States. These persons may be transferred from the military to the civil authority, and be proceeded against according to law. Those, therefore, who fear the escape of the traitors already apprehended, and would, by this measure, obviate the difficulty, must perceive that consequence would not ensue. Mr. B. said, he should consider the suspension of the habeas corpus as holding out an idea of danger and alarm, which was highly improper, inasmuch as it did not exist. It is true, this conspiracy was once formidable, extensive, and threatening; but it has been dissipated by the vigilance of Government. He would ask gentlemen, if they seriously believed the danger sufficiently great to justify the suspension of this most important right of the citizen, to proclaim the country in peril, and to adopt a measure so pregnant with mischief, by which the innocent and guilty will be involved in one common destruction? He said this was not the first instance of the kind since the formation of the Federal Government; there had been already two insurrections in the United States, both of which had defied the authority of Congress, and menaced the Union with dissolution. Notwithstanding one of them justified the calling out of fifteen thousand men, and the expenditure of one million of dollars, he had not heard of a proposition to suspend the writ of habeas corpus. What, then, will be said of us, if now, when the danger is over, firm in the attachment of the people to the Union, with ample resources to encounter any difficulties which may occur, we resort to a measure so harsh in its nature, oppressive in its operation, and ruinous as a precedent? While, in former times, it was thought unsafe to suspend this most important and valuable part of the Constitution, he would ask, whether the necessity at the present time could be considered greater? With regard to those persons who may be implicated in the conspiracy, if the writ of habeas corpus be not suspended, what will be the consequence? When apprehended, they will be brought before a court of justice, who will decide whether there is any evidence that will justify their commitment for farther prosecution. From the communication of the Executive, it appeared there was sufficient evidence to authorize their commitment. Several months would elapse before their final trial, which would give time to collect evidence, and if this shall be sufficient, they will not fail to receive the punishment merited by their crimes, and inflicted by the laws of their country.

Mr. B. said, he could conceive no injury that would result on this score; and, indeed, if some persons should elude justice, it would not endanger society so materially as to come within the terms of the Constitution. He observed, it appeared to him the commencement of an insurrection was the only time when the writ of habeas corpus ought to be suspended; when the seizure of the ringleaders, by dismaying the inferior agents, would enable the Government, without the effusion of blood, to suppress it. But it was manifest that, at this moment, everything intended by the conspirators was effected, or they were in the hands of the civil authority; there was, therefore, no good reason to take this precautionary step with that view; while on the one hand, it would unavoidably produce unnecessary alarm, and much inconvenience to the citizens of the United States. Nothing but the most imperious necessity would excuse us in confining to the Executive, or any person under him, the power of seizing and confining a citizen, upon bare suspicion, for three months, without responsibility, for the abuse of such unlimited discretion. Mr. B. said, he could judge from what he had already seen, that men, who are perfectly innocent, would be doomed to feel the severity of confinement, and undergo the infamy of the dungeon. What reparation can be made to those who shall thus suffer? The people of the United States would have just reason to reproach their representatives with wantonly sacrificing their dearest interests, when, from the facts presented to this House, it seems the country was perfectly safe, and the conspiracy nearly annihilated. Under these circumstances, there can be no apology for suspending the privilege of the writ of habeas corpus, and violating the Constitution, which declares "the writ of habeas corpus shall not be suspended, unless when, in cases of invasion or rebellion, the public safety may require it."

Mr. B. said he hoped he had shown that, admitting the two cases specified in the Constitution existed, they were not accompanied with such symptoms of calamity as rendered the passage of the bill expedient.

What, in another point of light, would be the effect of passing such a law? Would it not establish a dangerous precedent? A corrupt and vicious Administration, under the sanction and example of this law, might harass and destroy the best men of the country. It would only be necessary to excite artificial commotions, circulate exaggerated rumors of danger, and then follows the repetition of this law, by which every obnoxious person, however honest, is surrendered to the vindictive resentment of the Government. It will not be a sufficient answer, that this power will not be abused by the President of the United States. He, Mr. B. believed, would not abuse it, but it would be impossible to restrain all those who are under him. Besides, he would not consent to advocate a principle, bad, in itself, because it will not, probably, be abused. For these reasons, Mr. B. said, he should vote to reject the bill.

Mr. ELLIOT said, that he regretted the motion to reject the bill had been made, because, considering the subject of very great importance, he thought it most proper that it should take the usual course of business, that the bill should be read a second time, and referred to a Committee of the Whole, for the purposes of deliberation and discussion.

Called upon, however, said Mr. E., to answer to the question, Shall the bill be rejected? I must answer that question in the affirmative, as I should deem it my duty to advocate its rejection, in any form which it might assume, and in any stage of its progress; and I deem it equally my duty, on the present occasion, to express my sentiments upon the subject. It is, indeed, difficult for me, consistently, with the sincere and high respect which I entertain for the source from whence this measure originated, to express, in decorous terms, the hostility which I feel to the proposition. I am therefore disposed to consider it as an original proposition here; as a motion in this body to suspend, for a limited time, the privileges attached to the writ of habeas corpus. And, in this point of view, I am prepared to say that it is the most extraordinary proposition that has ever been presented for our consideration and adoption. Sir, what is the language of our Constitution upon this subject? "The privilege of the writ of habeas corpus shall not be suspended, except when, in cases of invasion or rebellion, the public safety shall require it." Have we a right to suspend it in any and every case of invasion and rebellion? So far from it, that we are under a Constitutional interdiction to act, unless the existing invasion or rebellion, in our sober judgment, threatens the first principles of the national compact, and the Constitution itself. In other words, we can only act, in this case, with a view to national self-preservation. We can suspend the writ of habeas corpus only in a case of extreme emergency; that alone is *salus populi* which will justify this *lex suprema.* And is this a crisis of such awful moment? Is it necessary, at this time, to constitute a dictatorship, to save the people from themselves, and to take care that the Republic shall receive no detriment? What is the proposition? To create a single Dictator, as in ancient Rome, in whom all power shall be vested for a time? No; to create one great Dictator, and a multitude, an army of subaltern and petty despots; to invest, not only the President of the United States, but the Governors of States and Territories, and, indeed, all persons deriving civil or military authority from the supreme Executive, with unlimited and irresponsible power over the personal liberty of your citizens. Is this one of those great crises that require a suspension, a temporary prostration of the Constitution itself? Does the stately superstructure of our Republic thus tremble to its centre, and totter towards its fall? Common sense must give a negative answer to these questions. What are the facts? Is it, indeed, a case of rebellion? We are officially informed that rebellion has reared its hydra front in the peaceful valleys of the West. But we are also informed by the Executive that treason has no prospect of success; that "the fugitives from the Ohio, and their associates from Cumberland, cannot threaten serious danger even to the city of New Orleans." Not a single city, still less a Territory or a State, is considered in danger; and the Executve, not only possesses all the information which has been communicated to us, but much more, for we are informed that the communication has been made under the reservation contained in the resolution requesting it, and of course all the facts in the knowledge of the Executive, which are decided to be improper for disclosure at this time, have been kept back. And the Executive, possessing all this information, assures us that the public safety is not endangered. Can we, under these circumstances, consent to the investiture of dictatorial powers in that department of the Government which thus assures us that all is safe? It would be contrary to the spirit of the Constitution.

But we shall be told that the Constitution has contemplated cases of this kind, and, in reference to them, invested us with unlimited discretion. When any gentleman shall advance such a position, we, who advocate the rejection of the bill, will meet him upon that ground, and put the point at issue. We contend that the framers of the Constitution never contemplated the exercise of such a power, under circumstances like the present; and that the Constitution itself, instead of authorizing, has prohibited such discretion, unless in an extreme case. And can any member lay his hand upon his heart and say, that the present is a case of that description? He who cannot do this must, with us, consider the proposed measure as unconstitutional.

Let us pay a little attention to the nature and character of the writ of habeas corpus. It has its origin in Great Britain, and is there considered in two great points of view, as it respects the Monarch, and as it respects the subject. As it respects the Monarch, it is one of the *jura prerogativa,* a writ of prerogative; but it is not considered as calculated to increase the power of the King, or the splendor of the throne; in its origin and true character it is viewed as a prerogative, exercised by the King, or those authorities to whom his judicial powers are supposed to be delegated, only for the purpose of securing the Constitutional rights of the subject, and restraining the invasion of those rights. As it respects the subject, it is a writ of right, and is emphatically called, by English writers, a writ of liberty.

By the provisions of the famous statute of Charles II., which has even been called a second *magna charta,* its privileges are guarantied to all British subjects at all times. An eminent English author, and the most popular writer upon subjects of legal science, considers its suspension as the suspension of liberty itself; declares that the measure ought never to be resorted to but in cases of extreme emergency; and says that the nation then parts with its freedom for a short and limited time, only to resume and secure it forever. Hence, he compares the suspension of the habeas corpus act in Great Britain to the dictatorship of the Roman Republic.

But objectionable as the bill upon the table is in point of principle, it is, if possible, still more objectionable in point of detail. It invests with the power of violating the first principles of civil and political liberty, not only the supreme Executive, and the Executives of individual States and Territories, but all civil and military officers who may derive any authority whatever from the Chief Magistrate. And it extends the operation of the suspension of the privileges of the habeas corpus, not only to persons guilty or suspected of treason, or misprision of treason, but, to those who may be accused of any other crime or misdemeanor, tending to endanger the "peace, safety, or neutrality," of the United States! What a vast and almost illimitable field of power is here opened, in which Executive discretion may wander at large and uncontrolled! A vast and dangerous scene of power, indeed! It gives the power of dispensing with the ordinary operation of the laws to a host of those *little great men,* who are attached to every Government under heaven. I wish not to reflect upon any of those subordinate officers who may be employed by the Government of my country.

But no one will doubt that, in times of alarm and danger, many men will be clothed with the functions of office, who are incompetent to the discreet exercise of such boundless discretion. I can never wish to see such persons invested with the means of aiming at the heads of their private enemies, or other innocent and unoffending citizens, the thunderbolts of public indignation, or scorching them with the lightning of public suspicion—says the poet:

> "Could great men thunder, Jove would ne'er be
> quiet,
> For every petty pelting officer
> Would use his heaven for thunder."

Let us again ask for evidence of the necessity of this measure? Certainly none can be produced, for we are informed, from the first authority, that if the present be not a time of profound peace, it is far from being a period of public danger. The leader of this petty rebellion has been called the modern Catiline. Undoubtedly, he possesses many of the qualities which a celebrated ancient historian ascribes to the Catiline of Rome: his genius, his address, his activity, his profligacy; but he is destitute of his means and resources. He wants that power of doing mischief, which the Roman conspirator possessed. So far is he from being able to make war upon his country, that he cannot take possession of a single city. He is rapidly hastening to the same fate, although he may not meet it in the same manner. Already is he "damn'd to everlasting fame," or rather, damned to everlasting infamy. Already is he a fugitive. Already a price is set upon his head. In the papers of this morning, we see that the Governor of Orleans has offered a reward for his apprehension. We cannot but detest the traitor, but we can have no fears of the consequences of the treason.

Mr. E. concluded, by expressing a hope that the bill would meet a decided vote of rejection.

Mr. EPPES.—When I feel a decided hostility to a principle, it is not material to me in what form I meet it. Decidedly opposed to the principle of this bill, I shall vote against it in all its stages, and cannot but hope that the motion of my colleague to reject it will prevail. By this bill, we are called upon to exercise one of the most important powers vested in Congress by the Constitution of the United States. A power which suspends the personal rights of your citizens, which places their liberty wholly under the will, not of the Executive Magistrate only, but of his inferior officers. Of the importance of this power, of the caution which ought to be employed in its exercise, the words of the Constitution afford irresistible evidence. The words of the Constitution are: "The privilege of the writ of habeas corpus shall not be suspended, unless when, in cases of rebellion or invasion, the public safety may require it." The wording of this clause of the Constitution deserves peculiar attention. It is not in every case of invasion, nor in every case of rebellion, that the exercise of this power by Congress can be justified under the words of the Constitution. The words of the Constitution confine the exercise of this power exclusively to cases of rebellion or invasion, where the public safety requires it. In carrying into effect most of the important powers of Congress, something is left for the exercise of its discretion. We raise armies when, in our opinion, armies are necessary. We may call forth the militia to suppress insurrection or repel invasion, when we consider this measure necessary. But we can only suspend the privilege of the habeas corpus, "when, in cases of rebellion or invasion, the public safety requires it." Well, indeed, may this caution have been used as to the exercise of this important power. It is in a free country the most tremendous power which can be placed in the hands of a legislative body. It suspends, at once, the chartered rights of the community, and places even those who pass the act under military despotism. The Constitution, however, having vested this power in Congress, and a branch of the Legislature having thought its exercise necessary, it remains for us to inquire whether the present situation of our country authorizes, on our part, a resort to this extraordinary measure.

The inquiry is confined within very narrow limits. The power can only be exercised under the Constitution, "when, in cases of rebellion or invasion, the public safety may require it." Our country is not invaded. We have only, therefore, to inquire whether there exists in this country a rebellion, and whether the public safety requires a suspension of the habeas corpus. Of the existence of the rebellion or combination against the authority of the United States there can be no doubt, as we have on our table a detailed account of its origin and progress. I shall confine my observations solely to the latter part; whether the public safety requires a suspension of the habeas corpus for its suppression. In the communication now on our table, from the Executive, we have been informed that the militia of Ohio, Kentucky, and Tennessee, and of the Mississippi and Orleans Territories, have been ordered out. That General Wilkinson was at Orleans, on the 10th of December, with his troops from the Sabine, which from other information we know to consist of one thousand effective men. These are resources of the nation now in active operation. What is the force of the conspirators? By the same documents, we are informed that "some boats, accounts vary from five to double or treble that number, and persons, differently estimated from one to three hundred, had passed the falls of the Ohio to rendezvous at the mouth of Cumberland river, with others expected down that river." From the same document it appears that the force which comes down Cumberland river amounts to two boats, in one of which is Aaron Burr. From this statement, it appears that the largest calculation as to the actual force of the conspirators, is three hundred. But when we know the propensity of human nature to magnify accounts of this kind, we may fairly infer that the whole force does not exceed one hundred and fifty men. To oppose which, we have one thousand regular troops, and the militia of Ohio, Kentucky, and Tennessee, and of the Mississippi and Orleans Territories. Is there a man present who believes, on this statement, that the public safety requires a suspension of the habeas corpus? This Government has now been in operation thirty years; during this whole period, our political charter, whatever it may have sustained, has never been suspended. Never, under this Government, has personal liberty been held at the will of a single individual. Shall we, in the full tide of prosperity, possessed of the confidence of the nation, with a revenue of fifteen millions of dollars, and six hundred thousand freemen, able and ready to bear arms in defence of their country, believe its safety endangered by a collection of men which the militia of any one county in our country would be amply sufficient to subdue? Shall we, sir, suspend the chartered rights of the community for the suppression of a few desperadoes; of a small banditti already surrounded by your troops; pressed from above by your militia; met below by your regulars, and without a chance of escape, but by abandoning their boats, and seeking safety in the woods? I consider the means at present in operation amply sufficient for the suppression of this combination. If additional means were necessary, I should be willing to vote as many additional bayonets as shall be necessary for every traitor. I cannot, however bring myself to believe that this country is placed in such a dreadful situation as to authorize me to suspend the personal rights of the citizen, and to give him, in lieu of a free Constitution, the Executive will for his charter. I consider the provision in the Constitution for suspending the habeas corpus as designed only for occasions of great national danger. Like the power of creating a Dictator in ancient Rome, it prostrates the rights of your citizens and endangers public liberty. Like that it may, on some very extraordinary occasions, prove salutary, but like that, it ought never to be resorted to, but in cases of absolute necessity; or, to use the emphatic language of the Constitution, "when the public safety requires it." Believing that the public safety is not endangered, and that the discussion of this question is calculated to alarm the public mind at a time when no real danger exists, I shall vote for the rejection of the bill in its present stage.

Mr. VARNUM said, if he was of opinion with the gentlemen from Vermont and Virginia, he should vote for the rejection of this bill; but he entertained a different opinion, and, unless he heard something to change it, he should vote differently from them. He did not believe the Constitution restricted the power of the Government to suspend the privilege of the habeas corpus in cases where the country was shaken to its centre. There were no expressions in it to justify this inference. Its terms are: "The privilege of the writ of habeas corpus shall not be suspended, except when, in cases of invasion or rebellion, the public safety shall require it." Will gentlemen deny that there exists in the United States at present a rebellion? I presume not, said Mr. V., it is too notorious to admit of doubt. Will they deny that the conspiracy has been formed with deliberation, and has existed for a long time? Is it not evident that it has become very extensive? If, then, this is the case, and the head of the conspiracy has said that he is aided by a foreign Power; if this is true, are we justified in considering the country in a perfect state of safety, until it is brought to a close? I conceive not. I consider the country, in a degree, in a state of insecurity; and if so, the power is vested in the Congress of the United States, under the Constitution, to suspend the writ of habeas corpus. I am also apprehensive that we shall not be able to trace the conspiracy to its source without such a suspension. We have had an instance in which the head of the conspiracy has been brought before a court of justice, and where nothing has been brought against him. It is not my wish to insinuate that any court or public functionary is contemplated by this conspiracy; yet it is possible that this may be the case, and the very existence of the country may depend on tracing it to its source. I am not disposed to advocate sanguinary punishments, but I think they ought to be exemplary in regard to the chiefs of the conspiracy; for which purpose we ought to adopt those measures which will lead to a full discovery of those concerned in it. I am sensible that the Government of the United States has not hitherto resorted to this measure; but I know a particular State of the Union who did consider the measure necessary, in the case of an insurrection which occurred within her limits; and I think it very doubtful whether that insurrection would have so happily closed, if it had not been for her suspension of the writ of habeas corpus. Have we had any insurrection or rebellion in the United States like this? We have had one insurrection in Massachusetts, but whence did it arise? Not from a design to subvert the Government, but from the burden of taxes; taxes which, perhaps, exceeded those laid in any country since the formation of society. I do not mean, by these observations, by any means to justify that insurrection, and, I believe, from the circumstances with which I am acquainted, that the insurrection which took place in Pennsylvania did not go to the subversion of the Government. But let us look at this conspiracy. While the nation, from one extreme to the other, enjoys a degree of prosperity and happiness unparalleled in any other nation, and not a single individual within our limits has any reason to complain of oppression, an insurrection is fomented, subversive of the Government and destructive of the rights of the people. It appears to me that this insurrection is the most aggravating of all insurrections which history gives us an account of. There is not the least oppression or the least pressure of circumstances to induce any individual to rise up against the Government of this country; and it consequently betrays the greatest turpitude of mind in those who either lead or unite in it. For these reasons, I think it ought to be traced to its source, and I think it very doubtful whether this can be effected without, in the first instance, suspending the habeas corpus. Will gentlemen say that any innocent man will have a finger laid upon him, should this law pass? No; there is no probability of it; it is scarcely possible. But, even if it be possible, if the public good requires the suspension of the privilege, every man attached to the Government and to the liberty he enjoys, will be surely willing to submit to this inconvenience for a time, in order to secure the public happiness. The suspension only applies to particular crimes, the liberties of the people will not therefore be touched. I do think a great responsibility will rest on this branch of the Legislature, in case they refuse to pass this act. Suppose the head of this conspiracy shall be taken in a district of country where no evidence exists of the crime charged to him, and he shall consequently be set at liberty by the tribunals of justice; where will the responsibility rest, but upon this branch of the Legislature? It is too great for me, as an individual member, to bear. I shall, therefore, vote for this bill, under the impression that it will not have the injurious effects that some gentlemen seem to apprehend; and that it will only more effectually consign the guilty into the hands of justice.

Mr. R. Nelson.—As the motion to reject the bill meets my most hearty approbation, and as I consider it involving a great national question, I cannot reconcile it to my duty to give a silent vote on it. I shall, however, in order to avoid an unnecessary consumption of the time of the House, offer my remarks in as concise a compass as possible. I shall first consider the nature of the writ of habeas corpus; afterwards examine its effects, not only on the individual, but on the community at large; taking into view the mode of proceeding under it, to show, as I conceive, that no danger can ensue, on the refusal to pass this bill.

What is a writ of habeas corpus? It is a writ directing a certain person in custody to be brought before a tribunal of justice, to inquire into the legality of his confinement. If the judge is of opinion that the confinement is illegal, the person will of course be discharged; if, on the contrary, from the evidence, he shall be of opinion that there is sufficient grounds to suspect that he is guilty of offence, he will not be discharged. Now, to me, it appears that this is a proper and necessary power to be vested in our judges, and that a suspension of the writ of habeas corpus is, in all cases, improper. If a man is taken up, and is denied an examination before a judge or a court, he may, although innocent, in this case, continue to suffer confinement. This, in my opinion, is dangerous to the liberty of the citizen. He may be taken up on vague suspicion, and may not have his case examined for months, or even for years. Would not this bear hard upon the rights of the citizen?

Let us turn over a leaf, and see how the Government stands. If the person accused is legally committed, or if it shall be proved that he has committed any offence, the judge will say that he shall not be released. If he has committed an offence, there can be no grounds for this suspicion, because, without such suspension, he will not be discharged, because it does not follow that, inasmuch as a man has a right to demand that he be brought before a judge by a writ of habeas corpus, he shall therefore be discharged. He is only bound to examine him, and if he finds there is strong reason to believe he has committed a crime, he may remand him to confinement.

This is a writ of right, which ought to exist under all Governments on earth. What right? The right of being examined by the tribunals of his country, to determine whether there is any ground for the deprivation of his liberty. Is this a right which ought to be suspended merely to gratify the apprehensions of gentlemen? I think not. The framers of the Constitution have said, "the privilege of the writ of habeas corpus shall not be suspended, except when, in cases of invasion or rebellion, the public safety shall require it." Well, but, says the gentleman from Massachusetts, can any one deny that this is a rebellion? It may perhaps be, but I think it does not deserve the name of a rebellion; it is a little, petty, trifling, contemptible thing, led on by a desperate man, at the head of a few desperate followers: a thing which might have been dangerous, if the virtue of the people had not arrested and destroyed it. But admit that it is a rebellion; will every rebellion justify a suspension of the writ of habeas corpus? The Constitution says, "the privilege of the writ of habeas corpus shall not be suspended, except when, in cases of invasion or rebellion, the public safety shall require it." Does, then, the public safety require this suspension? Does the Constitution justify it? And, under present circumstances, confining a man in prison without a cause. There is no danger, the enemy is not at our door; there is no invasion; and yet we are called upon to suspend the writ of habeas corpus. This precedent, let me tell gentlemen, may be a ruinous, may be a most damnable precedent—a precedent which, hereafter, may be most flagrantly abused. The Executive may wish to make use of more energetic measures than the established laws of the land enable him to do; he will resort to this as a precedent, and this important privilege will be suspended at the smallest appearance of danger. The effect will be, that whenever a man is at the head of our affairs, who wishes to oppress or wreak his vengeance on those who are opposed to him, he will fly to this as a precedent; it will truly be a precedent fraught with the greatest danger; a precedent which ought not to be set, except in a case of the greatest necessity; indeed, I can hardly contemplate a case in which, in my opinion, it can be necessary.

In my opinion, this is a measure which ought never to be proposed, unless when the country is so corrupt that we cannot even trust the judges themselves. This, I consider the cause of the frequent suspension of this privilege in England. Whenever the whole mass of society becomes contaminated, and the officers of the judicial court are so far corrupted as to countenance rebellion, and release rebels from their confinement, it may be then time to say, they shall no longer remain in your hands; we will take them from you. But I apprehend there is no such danger here, and I repeat it, we are at once creating one of the most dangerous precedents, and passing one of the most unjust acts that was ever proposed.

Mr. Sloan.—At the same time that I express my purpose to vote on the same side with the gentleman from Maryland, I shall take the liberty of assigning very different reasons for my vote from those offered by him. The gentleman from Virginia has mentioned two preceding insurrections, which he considers of much greater magnitude than this. I am of a different opinion. Compared to this, I consider them as only a drop to the bucket. For a moment, let me ask the attention of gentlemen to those insurrections, or as I think they might, with more correctness, be termed, oppositions to Government. In consequence of certain citizens thinking themselves aggrieved by certain acts, in which they have been, in some measure, justified by their subequent repeal, a handful of people raised in opposition to their execution. What analogy do those oppositions bear to this rebellion? I consider the late or present conspiracy to be of greater magnitude than any we know of in history. Under what authority has it been created? Under that of a man of great abilities and experience, who states that he expects encouragement from foreign nations. I do not pretend to say that this is a fact; but what has he done? Has he not drawn resources from every part of the Union? I, therefore, consider it of great magnitude, and it is certainly excited against the best Government on earth, under which the people enjoy the greatest happiness. I shall, however, vote against the bill, under the belief that we may confidently rely on the love and affection of the people for their Government, to which we are already probably indebted for its suppression. Had this measure been brought forward a month or six weeks ago, I should have voted for it.

. . . . .

Mr. Smilie.—I shall not detain the House long by the remarks which I propose to make on this subject. I shall waive all observations on the mode of proceeding on this occasion—whether we shall reject the bill on its first, or suffer it to go to a second reading. The question is now put, and I am called upon to give my vote, either in the affirmative or negative. I, therefore, feel under a necessity to put my negative upon it. I consider this one of the most important subjects upon which we have been called to act. It is a question which is neither more nor less than, whether we shall exercise the only power with which we are clothed, to repeal an important part of the Constitution? It is in this case only, that we have power to repeal that instrument. A suspension of the privilege of the writ of habeas corpus is, in all respects, equivalent to repealing that essential part of the Constitution which secures that principle which has been called, in the country where it originated, the "palladium of personal liberty." If we recur to England, we shall find that the writ of habeas corpus in that country has been frequently suspended. But, under what circumstances? We find it was suspended in the year 1715, but what was the situation of the country at that time? It was invaded by the son of James II. There was a rebellion within the kingdom, and an army was organized. The same thing happened in the year 1745. On this occasion it was found necessary to suspend it. In latter times, when the Government had grown more corrupt, we have seen it suspended for an infinitely less cause. We have taken from the statute book of this country, this most valuable part of our Constitution. The convention who framed that instrument, believing that there might be cases when it would be necessary to vest a discretionary power in the Executive, have constituted the Legislature the judges of this necessity, and the only question now to be determined is, Does this necessity exist? There must either be in the country a rebellion or an invasion, before such an act can be passed. I really doubt whether a single law of the United States has been, as yet, violated. I will not say this is the fact; but I do not know anything to prove the contrary. But, supposing that a rebellion does exist, we are then left at liberty to decide whether it is such an one as to endanger the peace of society to such a degree that no ordinary remedy will answer. If an ordinary remedy will not, it may be our duty to apply an extraordinary one. What is this mighty business? What is the opinion of the Executive as to its danger? Does he consider it dangerous? It is a little remarkable that, in every instance under the British Government, the proposition of such a measure originated with the Executive, while here, without any intimation of danger from the Executive, we propose, on our own suggestion, to suspend one of the most valuable privileges that is secured to the citizen. Let us attend to the communication of the President on this subject. He states that, according to his information, the persons concerned in the conspiracy depend on receiving two kinds of aid; foreign aid, and aid derived in their own country. After giving his opinion of the foreign aid expected, he says:

> "On the whole, the fugitives from the Ohio, with their associates from Cumberland, or any other place in that quarter, cannot threaten serious danger to the city of New Orleans."

The President declares that, in his opinion, there is no danger to be apprehended. With regard to foreign force, he states his reasons for thinking there is no danger. As the Message is in the hands of every gentleman, there can be no necessity for me to read it. But, he explicitly declares, from the state of our relations with other nations, there can be no danger from that quarter. This being the deliberate opinion of the Executive Magistrate, who is more deeply responsible on this occasion than any other member of the Government, is it not most extraordinary that we should attempt to take steps which can only be justified in the last resort? Are gentlemen aware of the danger of this precedent? This is the first attempt ever made under the Government to suspend this law. If we suspend it when the Executive tells us there is no danger, on what occasion may it not be suspended? Let us suppose that it shall be suspended on this occasion, what will be its effect? Parties will probably forever continue to exist in this country. Let us suppose a predominant party to conjure up a plot to avenge themselves. Do not gentlemen see that the personal liberty of all their enemies would be endangered? I mention this to forewarn gentlemen of the dangerous ground before them. I do not say that our country may not, at some future day, be in such a situation as to justify such a suspension, but I have never yet seen her in such a situation, and, at this moment, I think it does not exist. When we see the great body of the people so firmly attached to their Government, ought we to be thus alarmed on beholding a few desperate and unprincipled men attempting to stir up an insurrection? There is another consideration which will induce me to give my hearty negative to this bill. If foreign nations see that we are obliged, under such circumstances, to suspend the writ of habeas corpus, will it not show that the Constitution is incapable of supporting itself, without the application of the most dangerous and extraordinary remedies?

Mr. DANA.—I understand that the question is, whether the bill shall be rejected on its first reading, without passing through the ordinary forms of proceeding. In such cases, the ordinary question is, Is there anything in the bill proper for the House to deliberate upon? If they are of opinion that it can be modified in such a way as to insure its passage, it ought to go to a Committee of the Whole. This was my opinion when the motion was first made to reject the bill. I was disposed to vote against the question, although the bill went to repeal the Constitution. I have been accustomed to view the privilege of the writ of habeas corpus as the most glorious invention of man. I was notwithstanding, however, from a respect to the other branch of the Legislature, disposed to investigate the subject—to examine whether there was any necessity for it. As, on the one hand, I was inclined to believe that the judgment of the Senate had, on this occasion, been tinged by a strong abhorrence of rebellion; so I was willing, on the other, to take time to guard myself against an equally strong feeling of abhorrence of dictators. But, on one principle, I cannot agree to consider this bill as a proper subject of investigation, for one moment. I perceive, on further examination of the bill, that the Senate have provided for its suspension, in cases where persons have been already presented. Had it been confined to future arrests, I might have agreed to deliberate on it, but viewing it in the light of an *ex post facto* law, I must give it my instantaneous negative. There is another principle, which appears to me highly objectionable. It authorizes the arrest of persons, not merely by the President, or other high officers, but by any person acting under him. I imagine this to be wholly without precedent. If treason was marching to force us from our seats, I would not agree to do this. I would not agree thus to destroy the fundamental principles of the Constitution, or to commit such an act, either of despotism or pusillanimity. Under this view of the subject, I am disposed to reject the bill, as containing a proposition on which I cannot deliberate.

The yeas and nays were then taken on the question, "Shall the bill be rejected?"—yeas 113, nays 19.

14

EX PARTE BOLLMAN & SWARTWOUT

4 Cranch 75 (1807)

MARSHALL, Ch. J. delivered the opinion of the court, as follows:

As preliminary to any investigation of the merits of this motion, this court deems it proper to declare that it disclaims all jurisdiction not given by the constitution, or by the laws of the United States.

Courts which originate in the common law possess a jurisdiction which must be regulated by their common law, until some statute shall change their established principles; but courts which are created by written law, and whose jurisdiction is defined by written law, cannot transcend that jurisdiction. It is unnecessary to state the reasoning on which this opinion is founded, because it has been repeatedly given by this court; and with the decisions heretofore rendered on this point, no member of the bench has, even for an instant, been dissatisfied. The reasoning from the bar, in relation to it, may be answered by the single observation, that for the meaning of the term *habeas corpus,* resort may unquestionably be had to the common law; but the power to award the writ by any of the courts of the United States, must be given by written law.

This opinion is not to be considered as abridging the power of courts over their own officers, or to protect themselves, and their members, from being disturbed in the exercise of their functions. It extends only to the power of taking cognizance of any question between individuals, or between the government and individuals.

To enable the court to decide on such question, the power to determine it must be given by written law.

The inquiry therefore on this motion will be, whether by any statute, compatible with the constitution of the United States, the power to award a writ of *habeas corpus,* in such a case as that of Erick Bollman and Samuel Swartwout, has been given to this court.

The 14th section of the judicial act *(Laws U. S. vol. 1. p. 58.)* has been considered as containing a substantive grant of this power.

It is in these words: "That all the before mentioned courts of the United States shall have power to issue writs of *scire facias, habeas corpus,* and all other writs, not specially provided for by statute, which may be necessary for the exercise of their respective jurisdictions, and agreeable to the principles and usages of law. And that either of the justices of the supreme court, as well as judges of the district courts, shall have power to grant writs of *habeas corpus,* for the purpose of an inquiry into the cause of commitment. *Provided,* that writs of *habeas corpus* shall in no case extend to prisoners in gaol, unless where they are in custody under or by colour of the authority of the United States, or are committed for trial before some court of the same, or are necessary to be brought into court to testify."

The only doubt of which this section can be susceptible is, whether the restrictive words of the first sentence limit the power to the award of such writs of *habeas corpus* as are necessary to enable the courts of the United States to exercise their respective jurisdictions in some cause which they are capable of finally deciding.

It has been urged, that in strict grammatical construction, these words refer to the last antecedent, which is, "all other writs not specially provided for by statute."

This criticism may be correct, and is not entirely without its influence; but the sound construction which the court thinks it safer to adopt, is, that the true sense of the words is to be determined by the nature of the provision, and by the context.

It may be worthy of remark, that this act was passed by the first congress of the United States, sitting under a constitution which had declared "that the privilege of the writ of *habeas corpus* should not be suspended, unless when, in cases of rebellion or invasion, the public safety might require it."

Acting under the immediate influence of this injunction, they must have felt, with peculiar force, the obligation of providing efficient means by which this great constitutional privilege should receive life and activity; for if the means be not in existence, the privilege itself would be lost, although no law for its suspension should be enacted. Under the impression of this obligation, they give, to all the courts, the power of awarding writs of *habeas corpus.*

It has been truly said, that this is a generic term, and includes every species of that writ. To this it may be added, that when used singly—when we say *the writ of habeas corpus,* without addition, we most generally mean that great writ which is now applied for; and in that sense it is used in the constitution.

The section proceeds to say, that "either of the justices of the supreme court, as well as judges of the district courts, shall have power to grant writs of *habeas corpus* for the purpose of an inquiry into the cause of commitment."

It has been argued that congress could never intend to give a power of this kind to one of the judges of this court, which is refused to all of them when assembled.

There is certainly much force in this argument, and it receives additional strength from the consideration, that if the power be denied to this court, it is denied to every other court of the United States, the right to grant this important writ is given, in this sentence, to every judge of the circuit, or district court, but can neither be exercised by the circuit nor district court. It would be strange if the judge, sitting on the bench, should be unable to hear a motion for this writ where it might be openly made, and openly discussed, and might yet retire to his chamber, and in private receive and decide upon the motion. This is not consistent with the genius of our legislation, nor with the course of our judicial proceedings. It would be much more consonant with both, that the power of the judge at his chambers should be suspended during his term, than that it should be exercised only in secret.

Whatever motives might induce the legislature to withhold from the *supreme* court the power to award the great writ of *habeas corpus,* there could be none which would induce them to withhold it from *every* court in the United States: and as it is granted to *all* in the *same sentence* and by the *same words,* the sound construction would seem to be, that the first sentence vests this power in all the courts of the United States; but as those courts are not always in session, the second sentence vests it in every justice or judge of the United States.

The doubt which has been raised on this subject may be further explained by examining the character of the various writs of *habeas corpus,* and selecting those to which this general grant of power must be restricted, if taken in the limited sense of being merely used to enable the court to exercise its jurisdiction in causes which it is enabled to decide finally.

The various writs of *habeas corpus,* as stated and accurately defined by judge Blackstone, (3 *Bl. Com.* 129.) are, 1st. The writ of *habeas corpus ad respondendum,* "when a man hath a cause of action against one who is confined by the process of some inferior court; in order to remove the prisoner and charge him with this new action in the court above."

This case may occur when a party having a right to sue in this court, (as a state at the time of the passage of this act, or a foreign minister,) wishes to institute a suit against a person who is already confined by the process of an inferior court. This confinement may be either by the process of a court of the *United States,* or of a *state* court. If it be in a court of the United States, this writ would be inapplicable, because perfectly useless, and consequently could not be contemplated by the legislature. It would not be required, in such case, to bring the body of the defendant actually into court, as he would already be in the charge of the person who, under an original writ from this court, would be directed to take him into custody, and would already be confined in the same jail in which he would be confined under the process of this court, if he should be unable to give bail.

If the party should be confined by process from a state court, there are many additional reasons against the use of this writ in such a case.

The state courts are not, in any sense of the word, *inferior* courts, except in the particular cases in which an appeal lies from their judgment to this court; and in these cases the mode of proceeding is particularly prescribed, and is not by *habeas corpus.* They are not inferior courts because they emanate from a different authority, and are the creatures of a distinct government.

2d. The writ of *habeas corpus ad satisfaciendum,* "when a prisoner hath had judgment against him in an action, and the plaintiff is desirous to bring him up to some superior court to charge him with process of execution."

This case can never occur in the courts of the United States. One court never awards execution on the judgment of another. Our whole juridical system forbids it.

3d. *Ad prosequendum, testificandum, deliberandum,* &c. "which issue when it is necessary to remove a prisoner, in order to prosecute, or bear testimony, in any court, or to be tried in the proper jurisdiction wherein the fact was committed."

This writ might unquestionably be employed to bring up a prisoner to bear testimony in a court, consistently with the most limited construction of the words in the act of congress; but the power to bring a person up that he may be tried in the proper jurisdiction is understood to be the very question now before the court.

4th, and last. The common writ *ad faciendum et recipiendum,* "which issues out of any of the courts of Westminster-hall, when a person is sued in some inferior jurisdiction, and is desirous to remove the action into the superior court, commanding the inferior judges to produce the body of the defendant, together with the day and cause of his caption and detainer, (whence the writ is frequently denominated an *habeas corpus cum causa,*) to *do and receive* whatever the king's court shall consider in that behalf. This writ is grantable of common right, without any motion in court, and it instantly supersedes all proceedings in the court below."

Can a solemn grant of power to a court to award a writ be considered as applicable to a case in which that writ, if issuable at all, issues by law without the leave of the court?

It would not be difficult to demonstrate that the writ of *habeas corpus cum causa* cannot be the particular writ contemplated by the legislature in the section under consideration; but it will be sufficient to observe generally that the same act prescribes a different mode for bringing into the courts of the United States suits brought in a state court against a person having a right to claim the jurisdiction of the courts of the United States. He may, on his first appearance, file his petition and authenticate the fact, upon which the cause is *ipso facto* removed into the courts of the United States.

The only power then, which on this limited construction would be granted by the section under consideration, would be that of issuing writs of *habeas corpus ad testificandum.* The section itself proves that this was not the intention of the legislature. It concludes with the following *proviso,* "That writs of *habeas corpus* shall in no case extend to prisoners in jail, unless where they are in custody under or by colour of the authority of the United States, or are committed for trial before some court of the same, or are necessary to be brought into court to testify."

This proviso extends to the whole section. It limits the powers previously granted to the courts, because it specifies a case in which it is particularly applicable to the use of the power by courts:—where the person is necessary to be brought into court to testify. That construction cannot be a fair one which would make the legislature except from the operation of a proviso, limiting the express grant of a power, the whole power intended to be granted.

From this review of the extent of the power of awarding writs of *habeas corpus,* if the section be construed in its restricted sense; from a comparison of the nature of the writ which the courts of the United States would, on that view of the subject, be enabled to issue; from a comparison of the power so granted with the other parts of the section, it is apparent that this limited sense of the term cannot be that which was contemplated by the legislature.

But the 33d section throws much light upon this question. It contains these words: "And upon all arrests in criminal cases, bail shall be admitted, except where the punishment may be death; in which cases it shall not be admitted *but by the supreme* or a circuit *court,* or by a justice of the supreme court, or a judge of a district court, who shall exercise their discretion therein, regarding the nature and circumstances of the offence, and of the evidence, and of the usages of law."

The appropriate process of bringing up a prisoner, not committed by the court itself, to be bailed, is by the writ now applied for. Of consequence, a court possessing the power to bail prisoners not committed by itself, may award a writ of *habeas corpus* for the exercise of that power. The clause under consideration obviously proceeds on the supposition that this power was previously given, and is explanatory of the 14th section.

If, by the sound construction of the act of congress, the power to award writs of *habeas corpus* in order to examine into the cause of commitment is given to this court, it remains to inquire whether this be a case in which the writ ought to be granted.

The only objection is, that the commitment has been made by a court having power to commit and to bail.

Against this objection the argument from the bar has been so conclusive that nothing can be added to it.

If then this were *res integra,* the court would decide in favour of the motion. But the question is considered as long since decided. The case of Hamilton is expressly in point in all its parts; and although the question of jurisdiction was not made at the bar, the case was several days under advisement, and this question could not have escaped the attention of the court. From that decision the court would not lightly depart. (*United States* v. *Hamilton*, 3 *Dall.* 17.)

If the act of congress gives this court the power to award a writ of *habeas corpus* in the present case, it remains to inquire whether that act be compatible with the constitution.

In the *mandamus* case, (*ante, vol.* 1. *p.* 175. *Marbury* v. *Madison,*) it was decided that this court would not exercise original jurisdiction except so far as that jurisdiction was given by the constitution. But so far as that case has distinguished between original and appellate jurisdiction, that which the court is now asked to exercise is clearly *appellate.* It is the revision of a decision of an inferior court, by which a citizen has been committed to jail.

It has been demonstrated at the bar, that the question brought forward on a *habeas corpus,* is always distinct from that which is involved in the cause itself. The question whether the individual shall be imprisoned is always distinct from the question whether he shall be convicted or acquitted of the charge on which he is to be tried, and therefore these questions are separated, and may be decided in different courts.

The decision that the individual shall be imprisoned must always precede the application for a writ of *habeas corpus,* and this writ must always be for the purpose of revising that decision, and therefore appellate in its nature.

But this point also is decided in Hamilton's case and in Burford's case.

If at any time the public safety should require the suspension of the powers vested by this act in the courts of the United States, it is for the legislature to say so.

That question depends on political considerations, on which the legislature is to decide. Until the legislative will be expressed, this court can only see its duty, and must obey the laws.

The motion, therefore, must be granted.

JOHNSON, J. In this case I have the misfortune to dissent from the majority of my brethren. As it is a case of much interest, I feel it incumbent upon me to assign the reasons upon which I adopt the opinion, that this court has not authority to issue the writ of *habeas corpus* now moved for. The prisoners are in confinement under a commitment ordered by the superior court of the district of Columbia, upon a charge of high treason. This motion has for its object their discharge or admission to bail, under an order of this court, as circumstances upon investigation shall appear to require. The attorney general having submitted the case without opposition, I will briefly notice such objections as occur to my mind against the arguments urged by the counsel for the prisoners.

Two questions were presented to the consideration of the court.

1st. Does this court possess the power generally of issuing the writ of *habeas corpus?*

2d. Does it retain that power in this case after the commitment by the district court of Columbia?

In support of the affirmative of the first of these questions, two grounds were assumed.

1st. That the power to issue this writ was necessarily incident to this court, as the supreme tribunal of the union.

2dly. That it is given by statute, and the right to it has been recognized by precedent.

On the first of these questions it is not necessary to ponder long; this court has uniformly maintained that it possesses no other jurisdiction or power than what is given it by the constitution and laws of the United States, or is necessarily incident to the exercise of those expressly given.

Our decision must then rest wholly on the due construction of the constitution and laws of the union, and the effect of precedent, a subject which certainly presents much scope for close legal inquiry, but very little for the play of a chastened imagination.

The first section of the third article of the constitution vests the judicial power of the United States in one supreme court, and in such inferior courts as the congress may from time to time establish. The second section declares the extent of that power, and distinguishes its jurisdiction into original and appellate.

The *original jurisdiction* of this court is restricted to cases affecting ambassadors or other public ministers, and consuls, and those in which a state shall be a party. In all other cases within the judicial powers of the union, it can exercise only an appellate jurisdiction. The former it possesses independently of the will of any other constituent branch of the general government. Without a violation of the constitution, that division of our jurisdiction can neither be restricted or extended. In the latter its powers are subjected to the will of the legislature of the union, and it can exercise appellate jurisdiction in no case, unless expressly authorised to do so by the laws of congress. If I understand the case of *Marbury* v. *Madison,* it maintains this doctrine in its full extent. I cannot see how it could ever have been controverted.

It is incumbent, then, I presume, on the counsel, in order to maintain their motion, to prove that the issuing of this writ is an act within the power of this court in its original jurisdiction, or that, in its appellate capacity, the power is expressly given by the laws of congress.

This it is attempted to do, by the fourteenth and thirty-third sections of the judiciary act, and the cases of *Hamilton* and *Burford,* which occurred in this court, the former in 1795, the latter in 1806.

How far their position is supported by that act and those cases, will now be the subject of my inquiry.

With a very unnecessary display of energy and pathos, this court has been imperatively called upon to extend to the prisoners the benefit of precedent. I am far, very far, from denying the general authority of adjudications. Uniformity in decisions is often as important as their abstract justice. But I deny that a court is precluded from the right or exempted from the necessity of examining into the correctness or consistency of its own decisions, or those of any other tribunal. If I need precedent to support me in this doctrine, I will cite the example of this court, which, in the case of the *United States* v. *Moore,* February, 1805, acknowledged that in the case of the *United States* v. *Sims,*

February, 1803, it had exercised a jurisdiction it did not possess. Strange indeed would be the doctrine, that an inadvertency once committed by a court shall ever after impose on it the necessity of persisting in its error. A case that cannot be tested by principle is not *law,* and in a thousand instances have such cases been declared so by courts of justice.

The claim of the prisoners, as founded on precedent, stands thus. The case of Hamilton was strikingly similar to the present. The prisoner had been committed by order of the district judge on a charge of high treason. A writ of *habeas corpus* was issued by the supreme court, and the prisoner bailed by their order. The case of Burford was also strictly parallel to the present; but the writ in the latter case having been issued expressly on the authority of the former, it is presumed that it gives no additional force to the claim of the prisoners, but must rest on the strength of the case upon which the court acted.

It appears to my mind that the case of Hamilton bears upon the face of it evidence of its being entitled to little consideration, and that the authority of it was annihilated by the very able decision in *Marbury* v. *Madison.* In this case it was decided that congress could not vest in the supreme court any original powers beyond those to which this court is restricted by the constitution. That an act of congress vesting in this court the power to issue a writ of *mandamus* in a case not within their original jurisdiction, and in which they were not called upon to exercise an appellate jurisdiction, was unconstitutional and void. In the case of Hamilton the court does not assign the reasons on which it founds its decisions, but it is fair to presume that they adopted the idea which appears to have been admitted by the district attorney in his argument, to wit, that this court possessed a concurrent power with the district court in admitting to bail. Now a concurrent power in such a case must be an original power, and the principle in *Marbury* v. *Madison* applies as much to the issuing of a *habeas corpus* in a case of treason, as to the issuing of a *mandamus* in a case not more remote from the original jurisdiction of this court. Having thus disembarrassed the question from the effect of precedent, I proceed to consider the construction of the two sections of the judiciary act above referred to.

It is necessary to premise that the case of *treason* is one in which this court possesses neither original nor appellate jurisdiction. The 14th section of the judiciary act, so far as it has relation to this case, is in these words:—"All the beforementioned courts (of which this is one) of the United States shall have power to issue writs of *scire facias, habeas corpus,* and all other writs not specially provided for by statute, which may be necessary for the exercise of their respective jurisdictions, and agreeable to the principles and usages of law." I do not think it material to the opinion I entertain what construction is given to this sentence. If the power to issue the writs of *scire facias* and *habeas corpus* be not restricted to the cases within the original or appellate jurisdiction of this court, the case of Marbury and Madison rejects the clauses as unavailing; and if it relate only to cases within their jurisdiction, it does not extend to the case which is now moved for. But it is impossible to give a sensible construction to that clause without taking the whole together; it consists of but one sentence, intimately connected throughout, and has for its object the creation of those powers which probably would have vested in the respective courts without statutory provision, as incident to the exercise of their jurisdiction. To give to this clause the construction contended for by counsel, would be to suppose that the legislature would commit the absurd act of granting the power of issuing the writs of *scire facias* and *habeas corpus,* without an object or end to be answered by them. This idea is not a little supported by the next succeeding clause, in which a power is vested in the individual judges to issue the writ of *habeas corpus,* expressly for the purpose of inquiring into the cause of commitment. That part of the thirty-third section of the judiciary act which relates to this subject is in the following words:—"And upon all arrests in criminal cases, bail shall be admitted, except where the punishment is death, in which cases it shall not be admitted but by the supreme or a circuit court, or by a justice of the supreme court, or a judge of a district court, who shall exercise their discretion therein, regarding the nature and circumstances of the offence, and of the evidence, and usage of law."

On considering this act it cannot be denied that if it vests any power at all, it is an original power. "It is the essential criterion of appellate jurisdiction, that it revises and corrects the proceedings in a cause already instituted." I quote the words of the court in the case of *Marbury* v. *Madison.*

And so far is this clause from giving a power to revise and correct, that it actually vests in the district judge the same latitude of discretion by the same words that it communicates to this court. And without derogating from a respectability which I must feel as deep an interest in maintaining as any member of this court, I must believe that the district court, or any individual district judge, possesses the same power to revise our decision, that we do to revise theirs; nay, more, for the powers with which they may be vested are not so particularly limited and divided by the constitution as ours are. Should we perform an act which according to our own principle we cannot be vested with power to perform, what obligation would any other court or judge be under to respect that act? There is one mode of construing this clause, which appears to me to remove all ambiguity, and to render every part of it sensible and operative. By the consent of his sovereign, a foreign minister may be subjected to the laws of the state near which he resides. This court may then be called upon to exercise an original criminal jurisdiction. If the power of this court to bail be confined to that one case, *reddendo singula singulis,* if the power of the several courts and individual judges be referred to their respective jurisdictions, all clashing and interference of power ceases, and sufficient means of redress are still held out to the citizen, if deprived of his liberty; and this surely must have been the intention of the legislature. It never could have been contemplated that the mandates of this court should be borne to the extremities of the states, to convene before them every prisoner who may be committed under the authority of the general government. Let it be remembered that I am not disputing the power of the individual judges who compose this court to issue the writ of *habeas corpus*. This application is not made to us as at chambers, but to us as holding the supreme court of the United States—a creature of the constitution, and possessing no greater capacity to receive jurisdiction or power than the constitution gives it. We may in our individual capacities, or in our circuits courts, be susceptible of powers merely ministerial, and not inconsistent with out judicial characters, for on that point the constitution has left much to construction; and on such an application the only doubt that could be entertained would be, whether we can exercise any power beyond the limits of our respective circuits. On this question I will not now give an opinion. One more observation, and I dismiss the subject.

In the case of Burford I was one of the members who constituted the court. I owe it to my own consistency to declare that the court were then apprized of my objections to the issuing of the writ of *habeas corpus*. I did not then comment at large on the reasons which influenced my opinion, and the cause was this: The gentleman who argued that cause confined himself strictly to those considerations which ought alone to influence the decisions of this court. No popular observations on the necessity of protecting the citizen from executive oppression, no animated address calculated to enlist the passions or prejudices of an audience in defence of his motion, imposed on me the necessity of vindicating my opinion. I submitted in silent deference to the decision of my brethren.

In this case I feel myself much relieved from the painful sensation resulting from the necessity of dissenting from the majority of the court, in being supported by the opinion of one of my brethren, who is prevented by indisposition from attending.

15

William Rawle, A View of the Constitution of the United States 117–19
1829 (2d ed.)

Reasons will be given hereafter for considering many of the restrictions, contained in the amendments to the Constitution, as extending to the states as well as to the United States, but the nature of the writ of *habeas corpus* seems peculiarly to call for this construction. It is the great remedy of the citizen or subject against arbitrary or illegal imprisonment; it is the mode by which the judicial power speedily and effectually protects the personal liberty of every individual, and repels the injustice of unconstitutional laws or despotic governors. After erecting the distinct government which we are considering, and after declaring what should constitute the supreme law in every state in the Union, fearful minds might entertain jealousies of this great and all-controlling power, if some protection against its energies when misdirected, was not provided by itself.

The national code in which the writ of *habeas corpus* was originally found, is not expressly or directly incorporated into the Constitution.

If this provision had been omitted, the existing powers under the state governments, none of whom are without it, might be questioned, and a person imprisoned on a mandate of the president or other officer, under colour of lawful authority derived from the United States, might be denied relief. But the judicial authority, whether vested in a state judge, or a judge of the United States, is an integral and identified capacity; and if congress never made any provision for issuing writs of *habeas corpus*, either the state judges must issue them, or the individual be without redress. The Constitution seems to have secured this benefit to the citizen by the description of the writ, and in an unqualified manner admitting its efficacy, while it declares that *it shall not be suspended unless when, in case of rebellion or invasion, the public safety shall require it.* This writ is believed to be known only in countries governed by the common law, as it is established in England; but in that country the benefit of it may at any time be withheld by the authority of parliament, whereas we see that in this country it cannot be suspended even in cases of rebellion or invasion, unless the public safety shall require it. Of this necessity the Constitution probably intends, that the legislature of the United States shall be the judges. Charged as they are with the preservation of the United States from both those evils, and superseding the powers of the several states in the prosecution of the measures they may find it expedient to adopt, it seems not unreasonable that this control over the writ of *habeas corpus*, which ought only to be exercised on extraordinary occasions, should rest with them. It is at any rate certain, that congress, which has authorized the courts and judges of the United States to issue writs of *habeas corpus* in cases within their jurisdiction, can alone suspend their power, and that no state can prevent those courts and judges from exercising their regular functions, which are, however, confined to cases of imprisonment professed to be under the authority of the United States. But the state courts and judges possess the right of determining on the legality of imprisonment under either authority.

16

Joseph Story, Commentaries on the Constitution 3:§§ 1333–36
1833

§ 1333. In order to understand the meaning of the terms here used, it will be necessary to have recourse to the common law; for in no other way can we arrive at the true definition of the writ of habeas corpus. At the common law there are various writs, called writs of habeas corpus. But the particular one here spoken of is that great and celebrated writ, used in all cases of illegal confinement, known by the name of the writ of *habeas corpus ad subjiciendum*, directed to the person detaining another, and commanding him to produce the body of the prisoner, with the day and cause of his caption and detention, *ad faciendum, subjiciendum, et recipiendum,* to do, submit to, and receive, whatsoever the judge or court, awarding such writ, shall consider in that behalf. It is, therefore, justly esteemed the great bulwark of personal liberty; since it is the appropriate remedy to ascertain, whether any person is rightfully in confinement or not, and the cause of his confinement; and if no sufficient ground of detention appears, the party is entitled to his immediate discharge. This writ is most beneficially construed; and is applied to every case of illegal restraint, whatever it may be; for every restraint upon a man's liberty is, in the eye of the law, an imprisonment, wherever may be the place, or whatever may be the manner, in which the restraint is effected.

§ 1334. Mr. Justice Blackstone has remarked with great force, that "to bereave a man of life, or by violence to confiscate his estate without accusation or trial, would be so gross and notorious an act of despotism, as must at once convey the alarm of tyranny throughout the whole kingdom. But confinement of the person by secretly hurrying him to gaol, where his sufferings are unknown or forgotten, is a less public, a less striking, and therefore a more dangerous engine of arbitrary force." While the justice of the remark must be felt by all, let it be remembered, that the right to pass bills of attainder in the British parliament still enables that body to exercise the summary and awful power of taking a man's life, and confiscating his estate, without accusation or trial. The learned commentator, however, has slid over this subject with surprising delicacy.

§ 1335. In England this is a high prerogative writ, issuing out of the Court of King's Bench, not only in term time, but in vacation, and running into all parts of the king's dominions; for it is said, that the king is entitled, at all times, to have an account, why the liberty of any of his subjects is restrained. It is grantable, however, as a matter of right, *ex merito justitiae,* upon the application of the subject. In England, however, the benefit of it was often eluded prior to the reign of Charles the Second; and especially during the reign of Charles the First. These pitiful evasions gave rise to the famous Habeas Corpus Act of 31 Car. 2, c. 2, which has been frequently considered, as another magna charta in that kingdom; and has reduced the general method of proceedings on these writs to the true standard of law and liberty. That statute has been, in substance, incorporated into the jurisprudence of every state in the Union; and the right to it has been secured in most, if not in all, of the state constitutions by a provision, similar to that existing in the constitution of the United States. It is not without reason, therefore, that the common law was deemed by our ancestors a part of the law of the land, brought with them upon their emigration, so far, as it was suited to their circumstances; since it affords the amplest protection for their rights and personal liberty. Congress have vested in the courts of the United States full authority to issue this great writ, in cases falling properly within the jurisdiction of the national government.

§ 1336. It is obvious, that cases of a peculiar emergency may arise, which may justify, nay even require, the temporary suspension of any right to the writ. But as it has frequently happened in foreign countries, and even in England, that the writ has, upon various pretexts and occasions, been suspended, whereby persons apprehended upon suspicion have suffered a long imprisonment, sometimes from design, and sometimes, because they were forgotten, the right to suspend it is expressly confined to cases of rebellion or invasion, where the public safety may require it. A very just and wholesome restraint, which cuts down at a blow a fruitful means of oppression, capable of being abused in bad times to the worst of purposes. Hitherto no suspension of the writ has ever been authorized by congress since the establishment of the constitution. It would seem, as the power is given to congress to suspend the writ of habeas corpus in cases of rebellion or invasion, that the right to judge, whether exigency had arisen, must exclusively belong to that body.

SEE ALSO:

Generally 3.2.1–2; 3.3.1–2
The King v. *Orrery,* 88 Eng. Rep. 75 (K.B. 1722)
Georgia Constitution of 1777, art. 60, Thorpe 2:785
James McHenry, Maryland House of Delegates, 29 Nov. 1787, Farrand 3:149
Luther Martin, Maryland House of Delegates, 29 Nov. 1787, Farrand 3:157
Luther Martin, Reply to Landholder, 14 Mar. 1788, Farrand 3:290
Georgia Constitution of 1789, art. 4, sec. 4, Thorpe 2:789
Vermont Constitution of 1793, art. of amendment [12], Thorpe 6:3774
James Iredell, Charge to the Grand Jury (C.C.D.Md., 1793), Life 2:388–89
William Bradford, Habeas Corpus, 24 June 1794, 1 Ops. Atty. Gen. 47
Respublica v. *Arnold,* 3 Yeates 263 (Pa. 1801)
Ex parte Cabrera, 4 Fed. Cas. 964, no. 2,278 (C.C.D.Pa. 1805)
Ex parte Burford, 3 Cranch 448 (1806)
House of Representatives, The Writ of Habeas Corpus, 17–19 Feb. 1807, Annals 16A:502–27, 528–54, 555–87
Case of Yates, 4 Johns. R. 317 (N.Y. 1809)
Ex parte Wilson, 6 Cranch 52 (1810)
United States v. *Anderson,* 24 Fed. Cas. 813, no. 14,449 (C.C.D.Tenn. 1812)
United States v. *French,* 25 Fed. Cas. 1217, no. 15,165 (C.C.D.N.H. 1812)
Matter of Ferguson, 9 Johns. R. 239 (N.Y. 1812)
Matter of Stacy, 10 Johns. 328 (N.Y. 1813)
Illinois Constitution of 1818, art. 8, sec. 16, Thorpe 2:982
State v. *Brearly,* 2 Southard 653 (N.J. 1819)
Bank of United States v. *Jenkins,* 18 Johns. R. 305 (N.Y. 1820)
Ex parte Kearney, 7 Wheat. 38 (1822)
Commonwealth v. *Deacon,* 8 Serg. & Rawle 72 (Pa. 1822)
Elkison v. *Deliesseline,* 8 Fed. Cas. 493, no. 4,366 (C.C.D.S.C. 1823)
United States v. *Green,* 26 Fed. Cas. 30, no. 15,256 (C.C.D.R.I. 1824)
James Kent, Commentaries 2:22–30 (1827)
In the Matter of Carlton, 7 Cow. 471 (N.Y. 1827)
Ex parte Watkins, 3 Pet. 193 (1829)
State v. *Philpot,* Dudley 46 (Ga. 1831)
Commonwealth ex rel. Davis v. *Lecky,* 1 Watt. 66 (Pa. 1832)

An Act Further to Provide for the Collection of Duties, secs. 7 and 8, 4 Stat. 632 (1833)
Ex parte Watkins, 7 Pet. 568 (1833)
Ex parte Randolph, 20 Fed. Cas. 242, no. 11,558 (C.C.D.Va. 1833)
Commonwealth v. *Briggs,* 16 Pick. 203 (Mass. 1834)
Peltier v. *Pennington,* 2 Green 312 (N.J. 1834)
Ex parte Kellogg, 6 Vt. 509 (1834)
Ex parte Milburn, 9 Pet. 704 (1835)
State v. *Sheriff of Middlesex,* 3 Green 68 (N.J. 1835)

Article 1, Section 9, Clause 3

No Bill of Attainder or ex post facto Law shall be passed.

1

MONTESQUIEU, SPIRIT OF LAWS, BK. 12, CH. 19
1748

19.—In what Manner the Use of Liberty is suspended in a Republic

In countries where liberty is most esteemed, there are laws by which a single person is deprived of it, in order to preserve it for the whole community. Such are in England what they call Bills of Attainder. These are in relation to those Athenian laws by which a private person was condemned, provided they were made by the unanimous suffrage of six thousand citizens. They are in relation also to those laws which were made at Rome against private citizens, and were called privileges. These were never passed except in the great meetings of the people. But in what manner soever they were enacted, Cicero was for having them abolished, because the force of a law consists in its being made for the whole community. I must own, notwithstanding, that the practice of the freest nation that ever existed induces me to think that there are cases in which a veil should be drawn for a while over liberty, as it was customary to cover the statues of the gods.

2

WILLIAM BLACKSTONE, COMMENTARIES
4:373–79
1769

When sentence of death, the most terrible and highest judgment in the laws of England, is pronounced, the immediate inseparable consequence by the common law is *attainder.* For when it is now clear beyond all dispute, that the criminal is no longer fit to live upon the earth, but is to be exterminated as a monster and a bane to human society, the law sets a note of infamy upon him, puts him out of it's protection, and takes no farther care of him than barely to see him executed. He is then called attaint, *attinctus,* stained, or blackened. He is no longer of any credit or reputation; he cannot be a witness in any court; neither is he capable of performing the functions of another man: for, by an anticipation of his punishment, he is already dead in law. This is after *judgment:* for there is great difference between a man *convicted,* and *attainted;* though they are frequently through inaccuracy confounded together. After conviction only, a man is liable to none of these disabilities: for there is still in contemplation of law a possibility of his innocence. Something may be offered in arrest of judgment: the indictment may be erroneous, which will render his guilt uncertain, and thereupon the present conviction may be quashed: he may obtain a pardon, or be allowed the benefit of clergy; both which suppose some latent sparks of merit, which plead in extenuation of his fault. But when judgment is once pronounced, both law and fact conspire to prove him completely guilty; and there is not the remotest possibility left of any thing to be said in his favour. Upon judgment therefore of death, and not before, the attainder of a criminal commences: or upon such circumstances as are equivalent to judgment of death; as judgment of outlawry on a capital crime, pronounced for absconding or fleeing from justice, which tacitly confesses the guilt. And therefore either upon judgment of outlawry, or of death, for treason or felony, a man shall be said to be attainted.

The consequences of attainder are forfeiture, and corruption of blood.

I. Forfeiture is twofold; of real, and personal, estates. First, as to real estates: by attainder in high treason a man forfeits to the king all his lands and tenements of inheritance, whether fee-simple or fee-tail, and all his rights of entry on lands and tenements, which he held at the time of the offence committed, or at any time afterwards, to be for ever vested in the crown: and also the profits of all lands and tenements, which he had in his own right for life or years, so long as such interest shall subsist. This forfeiture relates backwards to the time of the treason committed; so as to avoid all intermediate sales and incumbrances, but not those before the fact: and therefore a wife's jointure is not forfeitable for the treason of the husband; because settled upon her previous to the treason committed. But her dower is forfeited, by the express provision of statute 5 & 6 Edw. VI. c. 11. And yet the husband shall be tenant by the curtesy of the wife's lands, if the wife be attainted of treason: for that is not prohibited by the statute. But, though after attainder the forfeiture relates back to the time of the treason committed, yet it does not take effect unless an attainder be had, of which it is one of the fruits: and therefore, if a traitor dies before judgment pronounced, or is killed in open rebellion, or is hanged by martial law, it works no forfeiture of his lands; for he never was attainted of treason.

The natural justice of forfeiture or confiscation of property, for treason, is founded in this consideration: that he who hath thus violated the fundamental principles of government, and broken his part of the original contract between king and people, hath abandoned his connexions with society; and hath no longer any right to those advantages, which before belonged to him purely as a member of the community: among which *social* advantages the right of transferring or transmitting property to others is one of the chief. Such forfeitures moreover, whereby his posterity must suffer as well as himself, will help to restrain a man, not only by the sense of his duty, and dread of personal punishment, but also by his passions and natural affections; and will interest every dependent and relation he has, to keep him from offending: according to that beautiful sentiment of Cicero, "*nec vero me fugit quam sit acerbum, parentum scelera filiorum poenis lui: sed hoc praeclare legibus comparatum est, ut caritas liberorum amiciores parentes reipublicae redderet.*" And therefore Aulus Cascellius, a Roman lawyer in the time of the triumvirate, used to boast that he had two reasons for despising the power of the tyrants; his old age, and his want of children: for children are pledges to the prince of the father's obedience. Yet many nations have thought, that this posthumous punishment favours of hardship to the innocent; especially for crimes that do not strike at the very root and foundation of society, as treason against the government expressly does. And therefore, though confiscations were very frequent in the times of the earlier emperors, yet Arcadius and Honorius in every other instance but that of treason thought it more just, "*ibi esse poenam, ubi et noxa est;*" and ordered that "*peccata suos teneant auctores, nec ulterius progrediatur metus, quam reperiatur delictum:*" and Justinian also made a law to restrain the punishment of relations; which directs the forfeiture to go, except in the case of *crimen majestatis,* to the next of kin to the delinquent. On the other hand the Macedonian laws extended even the capital punishment of treason, not only to the children but to all the relations of the delinquent: and of course their estates must be also forfeited, as no man was left to inherit them. And in Germany, by the famous golden bulle, (copied almost *verbatim* from Justinian's code) the lives of the sons of such as conspire to kill an elector are spared, as it is expressed, by the emperor's *particular bounty.* But they are deprived of all their effects and rights of succession, and are rendered incapable of any honour ecclesiastical or civil: "to the end that, being always poor and necessitous, they may for ever be accompanied by the infamy of their father; may languish in continual indigence; and may find (says this merciless edict) their punishment in living, and their relief in dying."

With us in England, forfeiture of lands and tenements to the crown for treason is by no means derived from the feodal policy, (as has been already observed) but was antecedent to the establishment of that system in this island; being transmitted from our Saxon ancestors, and forming a part of the antient Scandinavian constitution. But in some treasons relating to the coin, (which, as we formerly observed, seem rather a species of the *crimen falsi,* than the *crimen laesae majestatis*) it is provided by the several modern statutes which constitute the offence, that it shall work no forfeiture of lands. And, in order to abolish such hereditary punishment intirely, it was enacted by statute 7 Ann. c. 21. that, after the decease of the late pretender, no attainder for treason should extend to the disinheriting of any heir, nor to the prejudice of any person, other than the traitor himself. By which, the law of forfeitures for high treason would by this time have been at an end, had not a subsequent statute intervened to give them a longer duration. The history of this matter is somewhat singular and worthy observation. At the time of the union, the crime of treason in Scotland was, by the Scots law, in many respects different from that of treason in England; and particularly in it's consequence of forfeitures of intailed estates, which was more peculiarly English: yet it seemed necessary, that a crime so nearly affecting government should, both in it's essence and consequences, be put upon the same footing in both parts of the united kingdoms. In new-modelling these laws, the Scotch nation and the English house of commons struggled hard, partly to maintain, and partly to acquire, a total immunity from forfeiture and corruption of blood: which the house of lords as firmly resisted. At length a compromise was agreed to, which is established by this statute, *viz.* that the same crimes, and no other, should be treason in Scotland that are so in England; and that the English forfeitures and corruption of blood, should take place in Scotland, till the death of the then pretender; and then cease throughout the whole of Great Britain: the lords artfully proposing this temporary clause, in hopes (it is said) that the prudence of succeeding parliaments would make it perpetual. This has partly been done by the statute 17 Geo. II. c. 39. (made in the year preceding the late rebellion) the operation of these indemnifying clauses being thereby still farther suspended, till the death of the sons of the pretender.

In petit treason and felony, the offender also forfeits all his chattel interests absolutely, and the profits of all estates of freehold during life; and, after his death, all his lands and tenements in fee-simple (but not those in tail) to the crown, for a very short period of time: for the king shall have them for a year and a day, and may commit therein what waste he pleases; which is called the king's *year, day,* and *waste.* Formerly the king had only a liberty of committing waste on the lands of felons, by pulling down their houses, extirpating their gardens, ploughing their meadows, and cutting down their woods. And a punishment of a similar spirit appears to have obtained in the oriental countries, from the decrees of Nebuchadnezzar and Cyrus in the books of Daniel and Ezra; which, besides the pain of death inflicted on the delinquents there specified, ordain, "that their houses shall be made a dunghill." But this tending greatly to the prejudice of the public, it was agreed in the reign of Henry the first, in this kingdom, that the king should have the profits of the land for one year and a day, in lieu of the destruction he was otherwise at liberty to commit: and therefore *magna carta* provides, that the king shall only hold such lands for a year and day, and then restore them to the lord of the fee; without any mention made of waste. But the statute 17 Edw. II. *de praerogativa regis,* seems to suppose, that the king shall have his year, day, *and* waste; and not the year and day *instead of* waste. Which sir Edward Coke (and the author of the mirror, before him) very justly look upon as an encroachment, though a very antient one, of the royal prerogative. This year, day, and waste are now usually compounded for; but otherwise they regularly belong to the crown: and, after their expiration, the land would naturally have descended to the heir, (as in gavelkind tenure it still does) did not it's feodal quality intercept such descent, and give it by way of escheat to the lord. These forfeitures for felony do also arise only upon attainder; and therefore a *felo de se* forfeits no lands of inheritance or freehold, for he never is attainted as a felon. They likewise relate back to the time of the offence committed, as well as forfeitures for treason; so as to avoid all intermediate charges and conveyances. This may be hard upon such as have unwarily engaged with the offender: but the cruelty and reproach must lie on the part, not of the law, but of the criminal; who has thus knowingly and dishonestly involved others in his own calamities.

3

Delaware Declaration of Rights and Fundamental Rules
11 Sept. 1776

11. That retrospective Laws, punishing Offenses committed before the Existence of such Laws, are oppressive and unjust and ought not to be made.

4

Thomas Jefferson, Bill to Attaint Josiah Phillips
28 May 1778

Papers 2:189–91

Whereas a certain Josiah Philips labourer of the parish of Lynhaven and county of Princess Anne together with divers others inhabitants of the counties of Princess Anne and Norfolk and citizens of this commonwealth contrary to their fidelity associating and confederating together have levied war against this Commonwealth, within the same, committing murders, burning houses, wasting farms and doing other acts of hostility in the said counties of Princess Anne, and Norfolk, and still continue to exercise the same enormities on the good people of this commonwealth: and whereas the delays which would attend the proceeding to outlaw the said offenders according to the usual forms and procedures of the courts of law would leave the said good people for a long time exposed to murder and devastation. Be it therefore enacted by the General assembly that if the said Josiah Philips his associates and confederates shall not on or before the   day of June in this present year render themselves to the Governor or to some member of the privy council, judge of the General court, justice of the peace or commissioned officer of the regular troops, navy, or militia of this commonwealth in order to their trials for the treasons, murders and other felonies by them committed, that then such of them the said Josiah Philips his associates and confederates as shall not so render him or themselves, shall stand and be convicted and attainted of high treason, and shall suffer the pains of death, and incur all forfeitures, penalties and disabilities prescribed by the law against those convicted and attainted of High-treason: and that execution of this sentence of attainder shall be done by order of the General court to be entered as soon as may be conveniently after notice that any of the said offenders are in custody of the keeper of the public gaol. And if any person committed to the custody of the keeper of the public gaol as an associate or confederate of the said Josiah Philips shall alledge that he hath not been of his associates or confederates at any time after the day of in the year of our lord at which time the said murders and devastations were begun, a petty jury shall be summoned and charged according to the forms of the law to try in presence of the said court the fact so alledged; and if it be found against the defendant, execution of this act shall be done as before directed.

And that the good people of this commonwealth may not in the mean time be subject to the unrestrained hostilities of the said insurgents, be it further enacted that from and after the passing of this act it shall be lawful for any person with or without orders, to pursue and slay the said Josiah Philips and any others who have been of his associates or confederates at any time after the said day of aforesaid and shall not have previously rendered him or themselves to any of the officers civil or military before described, or otherwise to take and deliver them to justice to be dealt with according to law provided that the person so slain be in arms at the time or endeavoring to escape being taken.

5

Alexander Hamilton, Letter from Phocion
1–27 Jan. 1784

Papers 3:485–86

Nothing is more common than for a free people, in times of heat and violence, to gratify momentary passions, by letting into the government, principles and precedents which afterwards prove fatal to themselves. Of this kind is the doctrine of disqualification, disfranchisement and banishment by acts of legislature. The dangerous consequences of this power are manifest. If the legislature can disfranchise any number of citizens at pleasure by general descriptions, it may soon confine all the votes to a small number of partizans, and establish an aristocracy or an oligarchy; if it may banish at discretion all those whom particular circumstances render obnoxious, without hearing or trial, no man can be safe, nor know when he may be the innocent victim of a prevailing faction. The name of liberty applied to such a government would be a mockery of common sense.

6

Alexander Hamilton, A Second Letter from Phocion
April 1784

Papers 3:543–45

If we examine it with an unprejudiced eye, we must acknowledge not only that it was an evasion of the treaty, but a subversion of one great principle of social security, to wit, that every man shall be presumed innocent until he is proved guilty: This was to invert the order of things; and instead of obliging the state to prove the guilt, in order to inflict the penalty, it was to oblige the citizen to establish his own innocence, to avoid the penalty. It was to excite scruples in the honest and conscientious, and to hold out a bribe to perjury.

That this was an evasion of the treaty, the fourth proposition already laid down will illustrate. It was a mode of inquiry who had committed any of those crimes to which the penalty of disqualification was annexed, with this aggravation, that it deprived the citizen of the benefit of that advantage which he would have enjoyed by leaving, as in all other cases, the burthen of the proof upon the prosecutor.

To place this matter in a still clearer light, let it be supposed, that instead of the mode of indictment and trial by jury, the legislature was to declare that every citizen who did not swear he had never adhered to the King of Great-Britain, should incur all the penalties which our treason laws prescribe. Would this not be a palpable evasion of the treaty, and a direct infringement of the constitution? The principle is the same in both cases, with only this difference in the consequences; that in the instance already acted upon, the citizen forfeits a part of his rights,—in the one supposed he would forfeit the whole. The degree of punishment is all that distinguishes the cases. In either justly considered, it is substituting a new and arbitrary mode of prosecution to that antient and highly esteemed one, recognized by laws and the constitution of the state; I mean the trial by jury.

Let us not forget that the constitution declares that trial by jury in all cases in which it has been formerly used, should remain inviolate forever, and that the legislature should at no time, erect any new jurisdiction which should not proceed, according to the course of the common law. Nothing can be more repugnant to the true genius of the common law, than such an inquisition as has been mentioned into the consciences of men.

A share in the sovereignty of the state, which is exercised by the citizens at large, in voting at elections is one of the most important rights of the subject, and in a republic ought to stand foremost in the estimation of the law. It is that right, by which we exist a free people; and it certainly therefore will never be admitted, that less ceremony ought to be used in divesting any citizen of that right, than in depriving him of his property. Such a doctrine would ill suit the principles of the revolution, which taught the inhabitants of this country to risk their lives and fortunes in asserting their *liberty;* or in other words, their *right* to a *share* in the government. That portion of the sovereignty, to which each individual is entitled, can never be too highly prized. It is that for which we have fought and bled; and we should cautiously guard against any precedents, however they may be immediately directed against those we hate, which may in their consequences render our title to this great privilege, precarious. Here we may find the criterion to distinguish the genuine from the pretended whig. The man that would attack that right, in whatever shape, is an enemy to whiggism.

If any oath, with retrospect to past conduct, were to be made the condition, on which individuals, who have resided within the British lines, should hold their estates; we should immediately see, that this proceeding would be tyrannical, and a violation of the treaty, and yet when the same mode is employed to divest that right, which ought to be deemed still more sacred, many of us are so infatuated as to overlook the mischief.

To say that the persons, who will be affected by it, have previously forfeited that right, and that therefore nothing is taken away from them, is a begging of the question. How do we know who are the persons in this situation? If it be answered, this is the mode taken to ascertain it, the objection returns, 'tis an improper mode, because it puts the most essential interests of the citizen upon a worse footing, than we should be willing to tolerate where inferior interests were concerned; and because to elude the treaty it substitutes to the established and legal mode of investigating crimes, and inflicting forfeitures, on[e] that is unknown to the constitution, and repugnant to the genius of our law.

7

Vermont Constitution of 1786, ch. 2, sec. 17

Thorpe 6:3757

XVII. No person ought, in any case, or in any time, to be declared guilty of treason or felony by the Legislature.

8

Records of the Federal Convention

[*2:375; Madison, 22 Aug.*]

Mr. Gerry & Mr. McHenry moved to insert after the 2d. sect. art: 7. the clause following, to wit, "The Legislature shall pass no bill of attainder nor any ex post facto law"

Mr. Gerry urged the necessity of this prohibition, which he said was greater in the National than the State Legislature, because the number of members in the former being fewer, they were on that account the more to be feared.

Mr. Govr. Morris thought the precaution as to ex post facto laws unnecessary; but essential as to bills of attainder

Mr Elseworth contended that there was no lawyer, no civilian who would not say that ex post facto laws were void of themselves. It cannot then be necessary to prohibit them.

Mr. Wilson was against inserting anything in the Constitution as to ex post facto laws. It will bring reflexions on the Constitution—and proclaim that we are ignorant of the first principles of Legislation, or are constituting a Government which will be so.

The question being divided, The first part of the motion relating to bills of attainder was agreed to nem. contradicente.

On the second part relating to ex post facto laws—

Mr Carrol remarked that experience overruled all other calculations. It had proved that in whatever light they might be viewed by civilians or others, the State Legislatures had passed them, and they had taken effect.

Mr. Wilson. If these prohibitions in the State Constitutions have no effect, it will be useless to insert them in this Constitution. Besides, both sides will agree to the principle & will differ as to its application.

Mr. Williamson. Such a prohibitory clause is in the Constitution of N. Carolina, and tho it has been violated, it has done good there & may do good here, because the Judges can take hold of it

Docr. Johnson thought the clause unnecessary, and implying an improper suspicion of the National Legislature.

Mr. Rutlidge was in favor of the clause.

On the question for inserting the prohibition of ex post facto laws.

N— H— ay— Mas. ay. Cont. no. N. J— no. Pa. no. Del—ay. Md. ay. Virga. ay N— C. divd. S. C. ay— Geo. ay. [Ayes—7; noes—3; divided—1.]

[*2:448; Madison, 29 Aug.*]

Mr. Dickenson mentioned to the House that on examining Blackstone's Commentaries, he found that the terms "ex post facto" related to criminal cases only; that they would not consequently restrain the States from retrospective laws in civil cases, and that some further provision for this purpose would be requisite.

[*2:571, 596; Committee of Style*]

The Legislature shall pass no bill of attainder nor any ex post facto laws.

. . . . .

(*b*) No bill of attainder shall be passed, nor any ex post facto law.

[*2:617; Madison, 14 Sept.*]

Col: Mason moved to strike out from the clause (art I sect 9.) "No bill of attainder nor any expost facto law shall be passed" the words "nor any ex post facto law". He thought it not sufficiently clear that the prohibition meant by this phrase was limited to cases of a criminal nature—and no Legislature ever did or can altogether avoid them in Civil cases.

Mr. Gerry 2ded. the motion but with a view to extend the prohibition to "Civil cases", which he thought ought to be done.

On the question; all the States were—no

[*2:640; Mason, 15 Sept.*]

Both the general legislature and the State legislature are expressly prohibited making *ex post facto* laws; though there never was nor can be a legislature but must and will make such laws, when necessity and the public safety require them; which will hereafter be a breach of all the constitutions in the Union, and afford precedents for other innovations.

9

Oliver Ellsworth, Landholder, no. 6
10 Dec. 1787
Essays 163

There is to be no ex post facto laws. This was moved by Mr. Gerry and supported by Mr. Mason, and is exceptional only as being unnecessary; for it ought not to be presumed that government will be so tyrannical, and opposed to the sense of all modern civilians, as to pass such laws: if they should, they would be void.

10

James Iredell, Marcus, Answers to Mr. Mason's Objections to the New Constitution
1788
Pamphlets 368

My ideas of liberty are so different from those of Mr. Mason, that in my opinion this very prohibition is one of the most valuable parts of the new constitution. *Ex post facto* laws may sometimes be convenient, but that they are ever absolutely necessary I shall take the liberty to doubt, till that necessity can be made apparent. Sure I am, they have been the instrument of some of the grossest acts of tyranny that were ever exercised, and have this never failing consequence, to put the minority in the power of a passionate and unprincipled majority, as to the most sacred things, and the plea of necessity is never wanting where it can be of any avail. This very clause, I think, is worth ten thousand declarations of rights, if this, the most essential right of all, was omitted in them. A man may feel some pride in his security, when he knows that what he does innocently and safely to-day in accordance with the laws of his country, cannot be tortured into guilt and danger to-morrow. But if it should happen, that a great and overruling necessity, acknowledged and felt by all, should make a deviation from this prohibition excusable, shall we not be more safe in leaving the excuse for an extraordinary exercise of power to rest upon the apparent equity of it alone, than to leave the door open to a tyranny it would be intolerable to bear? In the one case, every one must be sensible of its justice, and therefore excuse it; in the other, whether its exercise was just or unjust, its being lawful would be sufficient to command obedience. Nor would a case like that, resting entirely on its own bottom, from a conviction of invincible necessity, warrant an avowed abuse of another authority, where no such necessity existed or could be pretended.

11

Calder v. Bull
3 Dall. 386 (1798)

(See 1.10.1, no. 10)

12

St. George Tucker, Blackstone's Commentaries
1:App. 292–93
1803

Bills of attainder are legislative acts passed for the special purpose of attainting particular individuals of treason, or felony, or to inflict pains and penalties beyond, or contrary to the common law. They are state-engines of oppression in the last resort, and of the most powerful and extensive operation, reaching to the absent and the dead, as well as to the present and the living. They supply the want of legal forms, legal evidence, and of every other barrier which the laws provide against tyranny and injustice in ordinary cases: being a legislative declaration of the guilt of the party, without trial, without a hearing, and often without the examination of witnesses, and subjecting his person to condign punishment, and his estate to confiscation and forfeiture. Instances of their application to these nefarious purposes occur in almost every page of the English history for a very considerable period: and very few reigns have passed in which the power has not been exercised, though, to the honour of the nation, I believe, no instance of the kind has occurred for more than half a century.

In May, 1778, an act passed in Virginia, to attaint one Josiah Philips, unless he should render himself to justice, within a limited time: he was taken, after the time had expired, and was brought before the general court to receive sentence of execution pursuant to the directions of the act. But the court refused to pass the sentence, and he was put upon his trial, according to the ordinary course of law. . . . This is a decisive proof of the importance of the separation of the powers of government, and of the independence of the judiciary; a dependent judiciary might have executed the law, whilst they execrated the principles upon which it was founded.

If any thing yet more formidable, or more odious than a bill of attainder can be found in the catalogue of state-enginery, it is what the constitution prohibits in the same clause, by the name of *ex post facto* laws: whereby an action indifferent in itself, and not prohibited by any law at the time it is committed, is declared by the legislature to have been a crime, and punishment in consequence thereof, is inflicted on the person committing it. Happily, for the people of Virginia, I can not cite any case of an *ex post facto* law, (according to this definition, which I have borrowed from Judge Blackstone,) that has been made in this commonwealth, nor have I heard of any such, in any other of the United States, that I recollect.

13

THOMAS JEFFERSON TO L. H. GIRARDIN
12 Mar. 1815
Writings 14:272–73

That case [of Josiah Phillips] is personally known to me, because I was of the legislature at the time, was one of those consulted by Mr. Henry, and had my share in the passage of the bill. I never before saw the observations of those gentlemen, which you quote on this case, and will now therefore briefly make some strictures on them.

Judge Tucker, instead of a definition of the functions of bills of attainder, has given a diatribe against their abuse. The occasion and proper office of a bill of attainder is this: When a person charged with a crime withdraws from justice, or resists it by force, either in his own or a foreign country, no other means of bringing him to trial or punishment being practicable, a special act is passed by the legislature adapted to the particular case. This prescribes to him a sufficient time to appear and submit to a trial by his peers; declares that his refusal to appear shall be taken as a confession of guilt, as in the ordinary case of an offender at the bar refusing to plead, and pronounces the sentence which would have been rendered on his confession or conviction in a court of law. No doubt that these acts of attainder have been abused in England as instruments of vengeance by a successful over a defeated party. But what institution is insusceptible of abuse in wicked hands?

Again, the judge says "the court refused to pass sentence of execution pursuant to the directions of the act." The court could not refuse this, because it was never proposed to them; and my authority for this assertion shall be presently given.

For the perversion of a fact so intimately known to himself, Mr. Randolph can be excused only by our indulgence for orators who, pressed by a powerful adversary, lose sight, in the ardor of conflict of the rigorous accuracies of fact, and permit their imagination to distort and color them to the views of the moment. He was Attorney General at the time, and told me himself, the first time I saw him after the trial of Philips, that when taken and delivered up to justice, he had thought it best to make no use of the act of attainder, and to take no measure under it; that he had indicted him at the common law either for murder or robbery (I forgot which and whether for both); that he was tried on this indictment in the ordinary way, found guilty by the jury, sentenced and executed under the common law; a course which every one approves, because the first object of the act of attainder was to bring him to fair trial. Whether Mr. Randolph was right in this information to me, or when in the debate with Mr. Henry, he represents this atrocious offender as sentenced and executed under the act of attainder, let the record of the case decide.

14

WILLIAM JOHNSON, NOTE TO SATTERLEE V. MATHEWSON
2 Pet. 380, 416n (1829)

The case in which the meaning of the phrase *"ex post facto,"* in the constitution came first to be considered, was that of Calder and wife *v.* Bull and wife, 3 Dall. 386. Mrs. Calder claimed as heiress to one Morrison, Bull and wife claimed by devise, and the question was *devisavit vel non.* The court of probate in Connecticut, having jurisdiction of the question, decided against the will; but there was a right to appeal from that decision to the supreme court of errors, provided it was prosecuted within eighteen months. It was not prosecuted within the limited time, and thereby it was contended, the decision of the court of probate became final against the will, and ought to have quieted Calder and wife in possession of the property. But Bull and wife made application to the legislature of Connecticut for relief, and obtained from them a resolution or law, setting aside the decree of the court of probate, and granting Bull a new hearing in that court. On that new hearing, the decision was in favor of the will; and Calder and wife were, of course, evicted of an interest, which they contended had been finally affirmed in them by the previous decision, and the effect of the limitation barring the right of appeal. The argument of counsel is not reported; but it is obvious, from the opinions ascribed to the judges, that, in behalf of Calder, it was contended, that the act of the Connecticut legislature was an *ex post facto* law, in the sense of the constitution, and void; and in behalf of Bull, that the legislature had exercised a power, constitutional in Connecticut, and therefore, not *ex post facto,* in the sense of the constitution. This appears distinctly the ground upon which CUSHING, the presiding judge, places his opinion: "The case," he says "appears to me to be clear of all difficulties, taken either way; if the act is a judicial act, it is not touched by the federal constitution; and if it is a legislative act, it is maintained and justified by the ancient and uniform practice of the State of Connecticut." That state, it must be observed, had at that time no written constitution; and as in Rhode Island at the present day, what it could constitutionally do, could only be decided by what it did habitually. The decision, therefore, rendered at this term, in the case of Wilkinson *v.* Leland *et al.*, was precisely that in the case of Calder *v.* Bull.

That the cause did not go off on the ground, that the phrase *"ex post facto,"* in the constitution, was inapplicable to civil acts, is distinctly expressed also by Judge Iredell. "Upon the whole," says he, "though there cannot be a case in which an *ex post facto* law in criminal matters is requisite, or justifiable yet in the present instance, the objection does not arise; because, 1. If the act of the legislature of Connecticut was a judicial act, it is not within the words of the constitution; and 2. Even if it was a legislative act, it is not within the meaning of the prohibition." In the commencement of the opinion, he expresses himself thus: "From the best information to be collected, relative to the constitution of Connecticut, it appears, that the legislature of that state has been in the uniform and uninterrupted exercise of a general superintending power over its courts of law, by granting new trials." And again, "When Connecticut was settled, the right of empowering her legislature to superintend the courts of justice was, I presume, early assumed; and its expediency, as applied to the local circumstances, and municipal policy of the state, is sanctioned by a long and uniform practice. The power, however, is judicial in its nature, and whenever it is exercised, as in the present instance, it is an exercise of judicial not legislative authority." Here, then, is a positive opinion as to the judicial character of this transaction, and it shows, that his vote upon the decision rendered, must rest upon the first of the alternatives stated in his conclusion. And the mode in which he enters upon the examination of the second alternative, shows that he attaches no importance to it. He enters upon it hypothetically, commencing with the words "But let us for a moment suppose." Judge Paterson also says, "True it is, that the awarding of new trials falls properly within the province of the judiciary; but if the legislature of Connecticut have been in the uninterrupted exercise of this authority, in certain cases, we must, in such cases, respect their decisions, as flowing from a competent jurisdiction or constitutional organ; and therefore, we may, in the present instance, consider the legislature of the state as having acted in their customary judicial capacity." Judge Chase express himself thus: "Whether the legislature of any state can revise and correct by law, a decision of its courts of justice, although not prohibited by the constitution of the state, is a question of very great importance, and not necessary to be now considered; because the resolution or law in question does not go so far." And again, "It does not appear to me, that the resolution or law in question is contrary to the charter of Connecticut, or its constitution, which is said by counsel to be composed of its charter, acts of assembly, and usages and customs. I should think, that the courts of Connecticut are the proper tribunals to decide whether laws contrary to the constitution thereof are void. In the present case, they have, both in the inferior and superior courts, decided, that the resolution or law in question was not contrary to either the state or the federal constitution."

Thus it appears, that all the judges who sat in the case of Calder *v.* Bull, concurred in the opinion, that the decision of the court of probate, and the lapse of the time given for an appeal to their court of errors, were not final upon the rights of the parties; that there still existed in the legislature, a controlling and revising power over the controversy; and that this was duly exercised in the reversal of the first decree of the court of probate. And who can doubt, that the legislature of a state may be vested by the state constitution with such a power? And what invasion of private right can result from the exercise of such power, when so delegated? All the rights claimed or exercised in a state, which thus modify the administration of justice, are held and exercised under the restrictions which such a constitution imposes. How, then, could the question, whether the phrase *ex post facto* was confined to criminal law, arise in this cause? the law complained of was equally free from that characteristic; though the phrase be held to extend to laws of a civil character.

I then have a right to deny that the construction intimated by three of the judges in the case of Calder *v.* Bull, is entitled to the weight of an adjudication. Nor is it immaterial, to observe, that an adjudication upon a fundamental law, ought never to be irrevocably settled by a decision that is not necessary and explicit. It is laid down indeed, as a principle of the Roman civil law, "that in cases which depend upon fundamental principles, from which demonstrations may be drawn, millions of precedents are of no value." Ayliffe, 5. And the English law concurs with the Roman in this, "that an extra-judicial opinion, given in or out of court, is no good precedent for it is not more than the *prolatum,* or saying of him who gives it." "An opinion given in court, if not necessary to the judgment given of record, is, according to Vaughan, no judicial opinion at all, and consequently, no precedent; for the same judgment might as well have been given, if no such, or a contrary, opinion had been brought; nor is such an opinion any more than a *gratis-dictum.*" Ayliffe, 9.

That the phrase *"ex post facto"* is not confined, in its ordinary signification, to criminal law, or criminal statutes, admits of positive demonstration; and with great respect for my learned predecessors, but a due regard to what I owe to the discharge of my own duties, I will endeavor to show that they have not proved the contrary. I think it will not be doubted by any one, who has considered the remarks made by the learned judges on the translation and construction of the phrase *ex post facto,* that some misapprehension must have prevailed, as to the parts of speech of which it is composed. By applying the English preposition after, so often, to the translation of *post,* in the sentence, I am warranted in believing, that the latter word was mistaken for the Latin preposition *post;* whereas, it is unquestionably an abbreviation of the adjective *postremo,* as will appear by reference to the maxims of Sir Francis Bacon. and comparing the 8th in the table, with the 8th maxim in the text; in the latter of which *post* is extended to *postremo;* and such must be the fact, to comport with the sense attached to the phrase in its common use and application. But the phrase is of such antiquity, and so generally used in its abridged form, that its origin and derivation, as is the case with a vast proportion of every language, has been nearly forgotten. I am indebted to a friend for a quotation from the Pandects, in which it appears, even in Justinian's time, to have been used as a quaint phrase; just as a *ca. sa.*, or writ in the *pone*, or *quo minus*, is used at the present day. (L. 34, tit. 4, law 15.) The antiquity of its use among the English jurists may be fairly inferred, from its being ingrafted into the maxims of the law constituting its fundamental rules; as we see, in Elements of the Com. Law, by Lord Verulam, Max. 8 and 21.

But my present purpose is, to fix its signification and legal import, and this is best done by reference to an adjudged case. At the time of the great speculation in England in south-sea stock, it was thought necessary, for the peace of the nation, to pass the stat. 7 Geo. I., c. 8, § 2, which required a registry of contracts for south-sea stock, to be made by the 29th of September 1721, and if not so registered, they were declared void. W. bought of M., stock to a large amount, for which an assignment was duly executed, dated 19th August 1720 (which was prior to the passing of the act); but exception was taken, on the ground of defect in the form of registration, on which the defendant insisted that the contract was avoided by the statute. RAYMOND, Justice:—"This acts being *ex post facto*, the construction of the words ought not to be strained, in order to defeat a contract, to the benefit whereof the party was well entitled, at the time the contract was made." Wilkinson *v.* Meyer, 2 Ld. Raym. 1350–52. This case is authority to three points: 1st, To show that the phrase is used in a sense equally applicable to contracts and to crimes. 2d, That it was applied to statutes affecting contracts. And 3d, That as late as Lord Raymond's time, it had not received a practical or technical construction, which confined it to criminal cases.

The learned judges, in the case of Calder *v.* Bull, rely on Blackstone and Woddeson for a contrary doctrine; but on examining these writers, the latter will be found to be anything but an authority to their purpose; and that in the former, there is nothing furnished that can be held conclusive on the subject. The passage in Wooddeson will be found in vol. 2, p. 641. The author is animadverting upon bills of attainder, bills of pains and penalties, and other laws of that class; and his words are these: "It must be admitted, that in all penal statutes, passed *ex post facto*, except where the innovation mollifies the rigor of the criminal code, justice wears her sternest aspect." Penal statutes, passed *ex post facto;* but why say *penal* statutes, and not simply statutes passed *ex post facto*, if the use of the phrase was exclusively limited to penal statutes? And with what propriety could the phrase be applied to statutes mollifying the rigor of the criminal law, if it had the fixed restriction, since attached to it, which they propose to assign to it, in their reasoning upon that cause?

Judge Blackstone is by no means conclusive, if any authority at all upon the subject. Arch. & Christ. Black. 41, old edit. 46. He is commenting upon the definition of a law generally; and that member of the definition which designates it as "a rule prescribed." And when illustrating the nature and necessity of this attribute of a law, he illustrates it by referring to the laws of Caligula, written in small characters, and hung up out of view, to ensnare the people; and then remarks, "There is still a more unreasonable method than this, which is called making of laws *ex post facto;* where, after an action, indifferent in itself, has been committed, the legislator then, for the first time, declares it to have been a crime, and inflicts a punishment upon the person who has committed it."

This is precisely what Wooddeson calls a penal statute, passed *ex post facto;* but it by no means follows, that because a penal statute may be *ex post facto*, that none other can be affected with that character; and certainly, his commentator, Mr. Christian, in his note upon the phase *"ex post facto,"* seems to have had no idea of this restrictive application of it. His words are: "an *ex post facto* law may be either of a public or private nature; and when we speak generally of an *ex post facto* law, we, perhaps, always, mean a law which comprehends the whole community. The Roman *privilegia* seem to correspond to our bills of attainder, and bills of pains and penalties, which, though in their nature they are *ex post facto* laws, yet are seldom called so." Here he speaks of a *law*, not of a *penal* law, which comprehends the whole community; and of certain penal laws, in their nature *ex post facto;* that is, of the description of *ex post facto* laws; which they certainly are, without being exclusively so.

The "Federalist" also is referred to, for an exposition of the phrase. The passage is found in the 44th number, and is from the pen of Mr. Madison. But the writer has made no attempt at giving a distinct exposition of the phrase, as used in the constitution. Bills of attainder, *ex post facto* laws, and laws impairing the obligation of contracts, are all considered together; and regarded, as they really are, as forming together "a bulwark, in favor of personal security and private rights;" but on the separate office of each, in the work of defence, he makes no remark, and attempts no definition or distribution.

Some of the state constitutions are also referred to, as furnishing an exposition of the words *ex post facto*, which confine its application to criminal cases. But of the four that have been cited, it will be found, that those of Massachusetts and Delaware do not contain the phrase; and, as if sensible of the general application of its meaning to all laws, giving effects and consequences to past actions, which were not attached to them when they occurred, simply give a description of the laws they mean to prohibit, without resorting to the aid of a quaint phrase which can only be explained by an extended periphrasis. The constitutions of Maryland and North Carolina would seem to have applied the phrase in the restricted sense. And yet there is good reason to think, that in the application of those articles to questions arising in their courts of justice; before the provision in the constitution of the United States superseded the necessity of resorting to their own constitutions in the defence of private rights, when invaded by *ex post facto* laws; a general application of the phrase, as well to civil as to criminal cases, would have been justified by the generality of the prohibition to pass *ex post facto* laws, as used in both those constitutions. But if otherwise, why should the erroneous use of language in two instances only, control the meaning of it everywhere? or anywhere, but in the construction of the particular instrument in which it is so used?

It is obvious, in the case of Calder *v.* Bull, that the great reason which influenced the opinion of the three judges who gave an exposition of the phrase *"ex post facto,"* was, that they considered its application to civil cases as unnecessary, and fully supplied by the prohibition to pass laws impairing the obligation of contracts. Judge Chase says, "if the prohibition against making *'ex post facto'* laws was intended to secure personal rights from being affected or injured by such laws, and the prohibition is sufficiently extensive for that object; the other restraints I have enumerated were unnecessary, and therefore improper; for both of them are retrospective." Judge Paterson says, "where is the necessity or use of the latter words, if a law impairing the obligation of contracts be comprehended within the terms *ex post facto* law? It is obvious from the specification of contracts in the last member of the clause, that the framers of the constitution did not understand or use the words in the sense contended for on the part of the plaintiffs in error. They understood and used the words in their known and appropriate signification, as referring to crimes, pains and penalties, and no further. The arrangement of the distinct members of this section necessarily points to this meaning." Judge Iredell considers the extended construction of the phrase as unnecessary for another reason. "The policy, the reason and humanity of the prohibition do not, I repeat," says the judge, "extend to civil cases, to cases that merely affect the private property of citizens."

On these opinions, a variety of remarks may be made. And the first is, that the learned judges could not then have foreseen the great variety of forms in which the violations of private right have since been presented to this court. The case of a legislature declaring a void deed to be a valid deed, is a striking one to show, both that the prohibition to pass laws violating the obligation of contracts, is not a sufficient protection to private rights; and that the policy and reason of the prohibition to pass *ex post facto* laws, does extend to civil as well as criminal cases. This court has had more than once to toil up hill, in order to bring within the restriction on the states to pass laws violating the obligation of contracts, the most obvious cases to which the constitution was intended to extend its protection; a difficulty, which it is obvious, might often be avoided, by giving to the phrase *ex post facto* its original and natural application. It is then due to the venerable men whose opinions I am combating, to believe, that had this and the many other similar cases which may occur and will occur, been presented to their minds, they would have seen that, in civil cases, the restriction not to pass *ex post facto* laws could not be limited to criminal statutes, without restricting the protection of the constitution to bounds that would import a positive absurdity.

2. High and respectable as is the authority of these distinguished men, it is not unpermitted to say, that when they speak of the known and settled and technical meaning of words, they submit their opinions to that arbiter of truth, to whose jurisdiction all men have an equal right to appeal. I think, I have gone far to show, that their quotations do not fix the meaning of the phrase under consideration, with immovable firmness. Maryland first used it in this restricted sense, and North Carolina copied from Maryland; and if the evidence of contemporaries may be relied on, Mr. Chase was one of the committee who reported the constitution of Maryland; and thus stands the authority for the restricted use. Very many instances of the more general use of the phrase may be added to the authority of Lord Raymond, some of which I will mention. Certainly, in Lord Raymond's time, it had not received this technical established signification; and how it can be proved to have acquired it since, is not very easy to perceive.

The following instances of its ancient general use will show, that if acquired, it must be in modern times, and therefore the proof ought to be the more accessible.

In Sir F. Bacon's Maxims, Max. 8: *Estimatio pretereti delicti ex post facto nunquam crescit.* And all the cases given to illustrate the maxim, are cases at common law, such as "slander of one who after becomes noble; this is not *scandalum magnatum.*" Thus showing that it has no peculiar connection with statute law. Max. 21. *Clausula vel dispositio inutilis per praesumptionem vel causam remotam ex post facto non fulcitur.* And all the examples furnished on this maxim, are cases of civil rights and liberties.

1 Sheppard's Touchstone, 63. "It is a rule, that if a contract be not in its inception usurious, no matter *ex post facto* shall make it so." Ibid. 68. "Where a deed good in its creation shall become void *ex post facto;* by razure, &c." Ibid. 20. "Where a deed is void *ab initio,* and where it doth become void by matter *ex post facto.*"

Godolphin's View of the Admiralty, 109. "And the performance of something *ex post facto* within the realm, in pursuance of a preceding contract, &c., doth not make it cease to be maritime." The same, in his Law of Executors, table D. "How a devise originally void may become good *ex post facto.*"

Bulstrode, 17, 5, B, a, p. 416. "Where the first contract is not usurious, it shall never be made so by matter *ex post facto.*"

3. It is a remark of Judge Paterson, that the arrangement of the distinct members of this section in the constitution, necessarily points to the restrictive meaning which he assigns to this phrase. But with all deference, I must contend, that if anything is to be deduced from the arrangement of the three instances of restriction, the argument will be against him. For by placing *"ex post facto* laws" between bills of attainder, which are exclusively criminal, and laws violating the obligation of contracts which are exclusively civil, it would rather seem that *ex post facto* laws partook of both characters, was common to both purposes.

4. There is one view in which the consistency and comprehensiveness of the views of the learned judges, whose opinions I have ventured to examine, may be well de-

fended. And it presents an alternative to which I have no doubt that this court will sooner or later be compelled to resort, in order to maintain its own consistency, and yet give to the constitution the scope which is necessary to attain its general purposes in this section, and to rescue it from the imputation of absurdity, in guarding against the minor evil, and making no provision against a greater; in leaving uncontrolled the exercise of a power to create the contracts of parties, while they restrict the exercise of a power to violate those contracts, when made by parties themselves. That is, to bring cases similar to the present within what the law terms the equity of a statute. According to my construction, this is unnecessary, and I shall never be compelled to resort to this application of a principle so exceptionable in its influence upon a fundamental law. But I see not how those who think differently from me will be able to advocate it, unless by an amendment of the constitution.

If the correct exposition of "the equity of a statute," be "a construction made by the judges, that cases out of the letter of the statute, which are within the same mischief, or cause of making the statute, shall be within the remedy thereby given," 1 Inst. 24; or as another author defines it, "*verborum legis directio effeciem cum una res solumnodo legis cavetur verbis, ut omnis alia in aequali genere eisdem caveatur verbis,*" Plowd. 407; there could be no objection to bringing the case of making a void deed valid within the provision of the constitution against violating the obligation of contracts, if we were construing a statute. And then, the protection which is lost to the constitution by the restricted construction of "*ex post facto* laws" would be, I believe, wholly restored. But whether this latitude of construction can be safely and on principle applied to the constitution, is with me a serious doubt; and hence I have felt an interest in endeavoring to avoid the necessity of resorting to it, by showing that the case of Calder *v.* Bull cannot claim the pre-eminence of an adjudged case upon this point, and if adjudged, was certainly not sustained by reason of authorities.

15

JOSEPH STORY, COMMENTARIES ON THE CONSTITUTION 3:§§ 1338–39
1833

§ 1338. Bills of attainder, as they are technically called, are such special acts of the legislature, as inflict capital punishments upon persons supposed to be guilty of high offences, such as treason and felony, without any conviction in the ordinary course of judicial proceedings. If an act inflicts a milder degree of punishment than death, it is called a bill of pains and penalties. But in the sense of the constitution, it seems, that bills of attainder include bills of pains and penalties; for the Supreme Court have said, "A bill of attainder may affect the life of an individual, or may confiscate his property, or both." In such cases, the legislature assumes judicial magistracy, pronouncing upon the guilt of the party without any of the common forms and guards of trial, and satisfying itself with proofs, when such proofs are within its reach, whether they are conformable to the rules of evidence, or not. In short, in all such cases, the legislature exercises the highest power of sovereignty, and what may be properly deemed an irresponsible despotic discretion, being governed solely by what it deems political necessity or expediency, and too often under the influence of unreasonable fears, or unfounded suspicions. Such acts have been often resorted to in foreign governments, as a common engine of state; and even in England they have been pushed to the most extravagant extent in bad times, reaching, as well to the absent and the dead, as to the living. Sir Edward Coke has mentioned it to be among the transcendent powers of parliament, that an act may be passed to attaint a man, after he is dead. And the reigning monarch, who was slain at Bosworth, is said to have been attainted by an act of parliament a few months after his death, notwithstanding the absurdity of deeming him at once in possession of the throne and a traitor. The punishment has often been inflicted without calling upon the party accused to answer, or without even the formality of proof; and sometimes, because the law, in its ordinary course of proceedings, would acquit the offender. The injustice and iniquity of such acts, in general, constitute an irresistible argument against the existence of the power. In a free government it would be intolerable; and in the hands of a reigning faction, it might be, and probably would be, abused to the ruin and death of the most virtuous citizens. Bills of this sort have been most usually passed in England in times of rebellion, or of gross subserviency to the crown, or of violent political excitements; periods, in which all nations are most liable (as well the free, as the enslaved) to forget their duties, and to trample upon the rights and liberties of others.

§ 1339. Of the same class are *ex post facto* laws, that is to say, (in a literal sense,) laws passed after the act done. The terms, *ex post facto* laws, in a comprehensive sense, embrace all retrospective laws, or laws governing, or controlling past transactions, whether they are of a civil, or a criminal nature. And there have not been wanting learned minds, that have contended with no small force of authority and reasoning, that such ought to be the interpretation of the terms in the constitution of the United States. As an original question, the argument would be entitled to grave consideration; but the current of opinion and authority has been so generally one way, as to the meaning of this phrase in the state constitutions, as well as in that of the United States, ever since their adoption, that it is difficult to feel, that it is now an open question. The general interpretation has been, and is, that the phrase applies to acts of a criminal nature only; and, that the prohibition reaches every law, whereby an act is declared a crime, and made punishable as such, when it was not a crime, when done; or whereby the act, if a crime, is aggravated in enormity, or punishment; or whereby different, or less evidence, is required to convict an offender, than was required, when the act was committed. The Supreme Court have given the following definition. "An *ex post facto* law is one, which renders an act punishable in a manner, in which it was not punishable, when it was committed." Such a law may inflict penalties on the person, or may inflict pecuniary penalties, which swell the public treasury. Laws, however, which mitigate the character, or punishment of a crime already committed, may not fall within the prohibition, for they are in favour of the citizen.

SEE ALSO:

Generally 1.10.1; 3.2.3; 3.3.2
Debates in Virginia Ratifying Convention, 17 June 1788, Elliot 3:66, 140, 153, 223, 236, 274, 290, 400
Ricup v. *Baxter,* 2 Dall. 132 (Pa. 1791)
James Iredell, Charge to Grand Jury (C.C.D.Md. 1793), Life 2:389–90
United States v. *Hall,* 26 Fed. Cas. 84, no. 15,285 (C.C.D.Pa. 1809), aff'd 6 Cranch 171

Article 1, Section 9, Clause 4

No Capitation, or other direct, Tax shall be laid, unless in Proportion to the Census of Enumeration herein before directed to be taken.

1. Continental Congress, Taxation and Representation, 12 July 1776, in 1.2.3, no. 1
2. James Madison, Bill Authorizing Amendment in Articles of Confederation, 21 June 1784
3. Records of the Federal Convention
4. William Blount, Richard D. Spaight, Hugh Williamson to Governor Caswell, 18 Sept. 1787
5. James McHenry, Maryland House of Delegates, 29 Nov. 1787
6. Alexander Hamilton, Federalist, no. 36, 8 Jan. 1788, in 1.2.3, no. 10
7. Thomas Davies, Massachusetts Ratifying Convention, 18 Jan. 1788
8. James Madison, Federalist, nos. 54–58, 12–20 Feb. 1788, in 1.2.3, nos. 13–17
9. George Mason, Virginia Ratifying Convention, 17 June 1788
10. Richard D. Spaight, North Carolina Ratifying Convention, 30 July 1788
11. Hugh Williamson, Cod Fisheries, House of Representatives, 3 Feb. 1792
12. House of Representatives, Tax on Carriages, 29 May 1794
13. *Hylton* v. *United States,* 3 Dall. 171 (1796)
14. St. George Tucker, Blackstone's Commentaries (1803)
15. Rufus King, Senate, ca. Mar. 1819
16. *Loughborough* v. *Blake,* 5 Wheat. 317 (1820)

1

Continental Congress, Taxation and Representation
12 July 1776

(See 1.2.3, no. 1)

2

James Madison, Bill Authorizing Amendment in Articles of Confederation
21 June 1784

Papers 8:84

For the purpose of introducing a more convenient and certain rule of ascertaining the proportions to be supplied to the common Treasury of the United States recommended by Congress in their act of the 18 of April 1783. Be it enacted by the General Assembly that so much of the 8th. of the articles of Confederation & perpetual Union between the 13 States of America, as is contained in the words following, to wit, "all charges of war, and all other expences that shall be incurred for the common defence, or General welfare, and allowed by the U. S. in Congs.

assembd. shall be defrayed out of a Common Treasury, which shall be supplied by the several States in proportion to the value of all land within each State granted to or surveyed for any person, as such land and the buildings & improvement thereon, shall be estimated according to such mode as the U. S. in Congress assembd. shall from time to time direct and appoint," shall be revoked & made void on the part of this Commonwealth; and in place thereof it is declared & concluded, the same having been agreed to in a Congress of the U. States, that all charges of war & all other expences that have been or shall be incurred for the common defence or general welfare, and allowed by the U. S. in Congress assembled, except so far as shall be otherwise provided for, shall be defrayed out of a Common Treasury, which shall be supplied by the several states in proportion to the whole number of white & other free Citizens & inhabitants of every age, sex and condition, including those bound to servitude for a term of years, and three fifths of all other persons not comprehended in the foregoing description, except Indians not paying taxes, in each State; which number shall be biennially taken & transmitted to the U. S. in Congress assembled, in such mode as they shall direct and appoint: And the Delegates representing this State in Congress, or any two of them, are hereby authorised & required to subscribe & ratify the said alteration of the Articles of Confederation & perpetual Union; and the same when subscribed & ratified by the said Delegates, and by the Delegates of each of the other Confoederated States duly authorised therefor, shall be valid & binding as to this Commonwealth.

3

Records of the Federal Convention

[*2:142, 169; Committee of Detail, IV, IX*]

1. direct taxation proportioned to representation 2. No (headpost) capitation-tax which does not apply to all inhabitants under the above limitation (& to be levied uniform) 3. no (other) indirect tax which is not common to all 4. (Delinquencies shall be distress—[illegible words])*

. . . . .

No Capitation Tax shall be laid, unless in Proportion to the Census herein before directed to be taken.

[*2:572, 596; Committee of Style*]

Sect. 5. No capitation tax shall be laid, unless in proportion to the census herein before directed to be taken.

[*2:618; Madison, 14 Sept.*]

Art. I. Sect. 9. "no capitation tax shall be laid, unless &c"

Mr Read moved to insert after "capitation" the words. "or other direct tax" He was afraid that some liberty might otherwise be taken to saddle the States with a readjustment by this rule, of past Requisitions of Congs—and that his amendment by giving another cast to the meaning would take away the pretext. Mr Williamson 2ded. the motion, which was agreed to,

On motion of Col: Mason "or enumeration" inserted after, as explanatory of "Census" Con. & S. C. only. no.

*[Editors' note—Words in parentheses were crossed out in the original.]

4

William Blount, Richard D. Spaight, Hugh Williamson to Governor Caswell
18 Sept. 1787
Farrand 3:83

We had many things to hope from a National Government and the chief thing we had to fear from such a Government was the Risque of unequal or heavy Taxation, but we hope you will believe as we do that the Southern States in general and North Carolina in particular are well secured on that head by the proposed system. It is provided in the 9th Section of Article the first that no Capitation or other direct Tax shall be laid except in proportion to the number of Inhabitants, in which number five blacks are only Counted as three. If a land tax is laid we are to pay the same rate, for Example: fifty Citizens of North Carolina can be taxed no more for all their Lands than fifty Citizens in one of the Eastern States. This must be greatly in our favour for as most of their Farms are small & many of them live in Towns we certainly have, one with another, land of twice the value that they Possess. When it is also considered that five Negroes are only to be charged the Same Poll Tax as three whites the advantage must be considerably increased under the proposed Form of Government.

5

James McHenry, Maryland House of Delegates
29 Nov. 1787
Farrand 3:149

Convention have also provided against any direct or Capitation Tax but according to an equal proportion among the respective States: This was thought a necessary precaution though it was the idea of every one that government would seldom have recourse to direct Taxation, and that the objects of Commerce would be more than Sufficient to answer the common exigencies of State and should further supplies be necessary, the power of Congress would not be exercised while the respective States would raise those supplies in any other manner more suitable to their own inclinations.

6

ALEXANDER HAMILTON, FEDERALIST, NO. 36, 226, 229–30
8 Jan. 1788

(See 1.2.3, no. 10)

7

THOMAS DAVIES, MASSACHUSETTS RATIFYING CONVENTION
18 Jan. 1788

Elliot 2:42

Some gentlemen have said, that Congress may draw their revenue wholly by direct taxes; but they cannot be induced so to do; it is easier for them to have resort to the impost and excise; but as it will not do to overburden the impost, (because that would promote smuggling, and be dangerous to the revenue,) therefore Congress should have the power of applying, in extraordinary cases, to direct taxation. War may take place, in which case it would not be proper to alter those appropriations of impost which may be made for peace establishments. It is inexpedient to divert the public funds; the power of direct taxation would, in such circumstances, be a very necessary power. As to the rule of apportioning such taxes, it must be by the quantity of lands, or else in the manner laid down in the paragraph under debate. But the quantity of lands is an uncertain rule of wealth. Compare the lands of different nations of Europe, some of them have great comparative wealth and less quantities of lands, whilst others have more land and less wealth. Compare Holland with Germany. The rule laid down in the paragraph is the best that can be obtained for the apportionment of the little direct taxes which Congress will want.

8

JAMES MADISON, FEDERALIST, NOS. 54–58, 366–97
12–20 Feb. 1788

(See 1.2.3, nos. 13–17)

9

GEORGE MASON, VIRGINIA RATIFYING CONVENTION
17 June 1788

Papers 3:1087

MR. GEORGE MASON said, that gentlemen might think themselves secured by the restriction in the fourth clause, that no capitation or other direct tax should be laid but in proportion to the census before directed to be taken. But that when maturely considered it would be found to be no security whatsoever. It was nothing but a direct assertion, or mere confirmation of the clause which fixed the ratio of taxes and representation. It only meant that the quantum to be raised of each state, should be in proportion to their numbers in the manner therein directed. But the general government was not precluded from laying the proportion of any particular state on any one species of property they might think proper. For instance, if 500,000 dollars were to be raised, they might lay the whole of the proportion of the southern states on the blacks, or any one species of property: So that by laying taxes too heavily on slaves, they might totally annihilate that kind of property. No real security could arise from the clause which provides, that persons held to labour in one state, escaping into another, shall be delivered up. This only meant, that run-away slaves should not be protected in other states. As to the exclusion of *ex post facto* laws, it could not be said to create any security in this case. For laying a tax on slaves would not be *ex post facto.*

10

RICHARD D. SPAIGHT, NORTH CAROLINA RATIFYING CONVENTION
30 July 1788

Elliot 4:209–10

He has made another objection, that land might not be taxed, and the other taxes might fall heavily on the poor people. Congress has a power to lay taxes, and no article is exempted or excluded. The proportion of each state may be raised in the most convenient manner. The census or enumeration provided is meant for the salvation and benefit of the Southern States. It was mentioned that land ought to be the only object of taxation. As an acre of land in the Northern States is worth many acres in the Southern States, this would have greatly oppressed the latter. It was then judged that the number of people, as therein provided, was the best criterion for fixing the proportion of each state, and that proportion in each state to be raised in the most easy manner for the people.

11

HUGH WILLIAMSON, COD FISHERIES, HOUSE OF REPRESENTATIVES
3 Feb. 1792
Annals 3:378–80

In the Constitution of this Government there are two or three remarkable provisions, which seem to be in point. It is provided, that direct taxes shall be apportioned among the several States according to their respective numbers. It is also provided, that all duties, imposts, and excises, shall be uniform throughout the United States; and it is provided, that no preference shall be given, by any regulation of commerce or revenue, to the ports of one State over those of another. The clear and obvious intention of the articles mentioned was, that Congress might not have the power of imposing unequal burdens; that it might not be in their power to gratify one part of the Union by oppressing another. It appeared possible, and not very improbable, that the time might come, when, by greater cohesion, by more unanimity, by more address, the Representatives of one part of the Union might attempt to impose unequal taxes, or to relieve their constituents at the expense of other people. To prevent the possibility of such a combination, the articles that I have mentioned were inserted in the Constitution.

. . . . .

Perhaps the case I have put is too strong—Congress can never do a thing that is so palpably unjust—but this, sir, is the very mark at which the theory of bounties seems to point. The certain operation of that measure is the oppression of the Southern States, by superior numbers in the Northern interest. This was to be feared at the formation of this Government, and you find many articles in the Constitution, besides those I have quoted, which were certainly intended to guard us against the dangerous bias of interest, and the power of numbers. Wherefore was it provided that no duty should be laid on exports? Was it not to defend the great staples of the Southern States—tobacco, rice and indigo—from the operation of unequal regulations of commerce, or unequal indirect taxes, as another article had defended us from unequal direct taxes?

I do not hazard much in saying, that the present Constitution had never been adopted without those preliminary guards in it.

12

HOUSE OF REPRESENTATIVES, TAX ON CARRIAGES
29 May 1794
Annals 4:729–30

An engrossed bill, laying duties upon carriages for the conveyance of persons, was read the third time, and,

Ordered, That the first section thereof be committed to a Committee of the Whole House immediately.

The House accordingly resolved itself into a Committee of the Whole House, on the said section; and, after some time spent therein, the Chairman reported that the Committee had had the section committed to them under consideration, and made an amendment thereto; which was twice read, and agreed to by the House.

Ordered, That the said section, as amended, be presently engrossed; and, the said section being accordingly brought in engrossed,

Mr. MADISON objected to this tax on carriages as an unconstitutional tax; and, as an unconstitutional measure, he would vote against it.

Mr. AMES said, that it was not to be wondered at if he, coming from so different a part of the country, should have a different idea of this tax from the gentleman who spoke last. In Massachusetts, this tax had been long known; and there it was called an excise. It was difficult to define whether a tax is direct or not. He had satisfied himself that this was not so. The duty falls not on the possession, but the use; and it is very easy to insert a clause to that purpose, which will satisfy the gentleman himself. Mr. MADISON had said that the introduction of this tax would break down one of the safeguards of the Constitution. Mr. A. really saw very little danger to the Constitution from it.

Mr. MADISON explained.

The said bill was then read the third time; and, on the question that the same do pass, it was resolved in the affirmative—yeas 49, nays 22.

13

HYLTON v. UNITED STATES
3 Dall. 171 (1796)

The court delivered their opinions *seriatim,* in the following terms:

CHASE, Justice.—By the case stated, only one question is submitted to the opinion of this court—whether the law of congress of the 5th of June 1794, entitled, "An act to lay duties upon carriages for the conveyance of persons," is unconstitutional and void?

The principles laid down, to prove the above law void,

are these: that a tax on carriages is a direct tax, and, therefore, by the constitution, must be laid according to the census, directed by the constitution to be taken, to ascertain the number of representatives from each state. And that the tax in question on carriages is not laid by that rule of apportionment, but by the rule of uniformity, prescribed by the constitution in the case of duties, imposts and excises; and a tax on carriages is not within either of those descriptions.

By the 2d section of the 1st article of the constitution, it is provided, that direct taxes shall be apportioned among the several states, according to their numbers, to be determined by the rule prescribed.

By the 9th section of the same article, it is further provided, that no capitation, or other direct tax, shall be laid, unless in proportion to the census or enumeration before directed.

By the 8th section of the same article, it was declared, that congress shall have power to lay and collect taxes, duties, imposts and excises; but all duties, imposts and excises shall be uniform throughout the United States.

As it was incumbent on the plaintiff's counsel in error, so they took great pains to prove that the tax on carriages was a direct tax; but they did not satisfy my mind. I think, at least, it may be doubted; and if I only doubted, I should affirm the judgment of the circuit court. The deliberate decision of the national legislature (who did not consider a tax on carriages a direct tax, but thought it was within the description of a duty), would determine me, if the case was doubtful, to receive the construction of the legislature; but I am inclined to think, that a tax on carriages is not a direct tax, within the letter or meaning of the constitution.

The great object of the constitution was, to give congress a power to lay taxes adequate to the exigencies of government; but they were to observe two rules in imposing them, namely, the rule of uniformity, when they laid duties, imposts or excise; and the rule of apportionment, according to the *census,* when they laid any direct tax.

If there are any other species of taxes that are not direct, and not included within the words duties, imposts or excises, they may be laid by the rule of uniformity or not; as congress shall think proper and reasonable. If the framers of the constitution did not contemplate other taxes than direct taxes, and duties, imposts and excises, there is great inaccuracy in their language. If these four species of taxes were all that were meditated, the general power to lay taxes was unnecessary. If it was intended, that congress should have authority to lay only one of the four above enumerated, to wit, direct taxes, by the rule of apportionment, and the other three by the rule of uniformity, the expressions would have run thus: "Congress shall have power to lay and collect direct taxes, and duties, imposts and excises; the first shall be laid according to the *census;* and the last three shall be uniform throughout the United States." The power, in the 8th section of the 1st article, to lay and collect taxes, included a power to lay direct taxes (whether capitation or any other), and also duties, imposts and excises; and every other species or kind of tax whatsoever, and called by any other name. Duties, imposts and excises were enumerated, after the general term taxes, only for the purpose of declaring, that they were to be laid by the rule of uniformity. I consider the constitution to stand in this manner. A general power is given to congress, to lay and collect taxes, of every kind or nature, without any restraint, except only on exports; but two rules are prescribed for their government, namely, uniformity and apportionment: Three kinds of taxes, to wit, duties, imposts and excises by the first rule, and capitation or other direct taxes, by the second rule.

I believe some taxes may be both direct and indirect, at the same time. If so, would congress be prohibited from laying such a tax, because it is partly a direct tax? The constitution evidently contemplated no taxes as direct taxes, but only such as congress could lay in proportion to the *census.* The rule of apportionment is only to be adopted in such cases, where it can reasonably apply; and the subject taxed, must ever determine the application of the rule. If it is proposed to tax any specific article by the rule of apportionment, and it would evidently create great inequality and injustice, it is unreasonable to say, that the constitution intended such tax should be laid by that rule.

It appears to me, that a tax on carriages cannot be laid by the rule of apportionment, without very great inequality and injustice. For example: suppose, two states, equal in *census,* to pay $80,000 each, by a tax on carriages, of eight dollars on every carriage; and in one state, there are 100 carriages, and in the other 1000. The owners of carriages in one state, would pay ten times the tax of owners in the other. A. in one state, would pay for his carriage eight dollars, but B. in the other state, would pay for his carriage, eighty dollars.

It was argued, that a tax on carriages was a direct tax, and might be laid according to the rule of apportionment, and (as I understood) in this manner: Congress, after determining on the gross sum to be raised, was to apportion it, according to the *census,* and then lay it in one state on carriages, in another on horses, in a third on tobacco, in a fourth on rice; and so on. I admit, that this mode might be adopted, to raise a certain sum in each state, according to the *census,* but it would not be a tax on carriages, but on a number of specific articles; and it seems to me, that it would be liable to the same objection of abuse and oppression, as a selection of any one article in all the states.

I think, an annual tax on carriages for the conveyance of persons, may be considered as within the power granted to congress to lay duties. The term *duty,* is the most comprehensive, next to the generi[c]al term *tax;* and practically, in Great Britain (whence we take our general ideas of taxes, duties, imposts, excises, customs, &c.), embraces taxes on stamps, tolls for passage, &c., and is not confined to taxes on importation only. It seems to me, that a tax on expense is an indirect tax; and I think, an annual tax on a carriage for the conveyance of persons, is of that kind; because a carriage is a consumable commodity; and such annual tax on it, is on the expense of the owner.

I am inclined to think, but of this I do not give a judicial opinion, that the direct taxes contemplated by the constitution, are only two, to wit, a capitation or poll tax, simply, without regard to property, profession or any other circumstance; and a tax on land. I doubt, whether a tax, by a general assessment of personal property, within the United States, is included within the term direct tax.

As I do not think the tax on carriages is a direct tax, it is unnecessary, at this time, for me to determine, whether this court, constitutionally possesses the power to declare an act of congress void, on the ground of its being made contrary to, and in violation of, the constitution; but if the court have such power, I am free to declare, that I will never exercise it, but in a very clear case. I am for affirming the judgment of the circuit court.

PATERSON, Justice.—By the second section of the first article of the constitution of the United States, it is ordained, that representatives and direct taxes shall be apportioned among the states, according to their respective numbers, which shall be determined by adding to the whole number of free persons, including those bound to service for a term of years, and including Indians not taxed, three-fifths of all other persons. The eighth section of the said article, declares, that congress shall have power to lay and collect taxes, duties, imposts and excises; but all duties, imposts and excises shall be uniform throughout the United States. The ninth section of the same article provides, that no capitation or other direct tax shall be laid, unless in proportion to the census or enumeration before directed to be taken.

Congress passed a law, on the 5th of June 1794, entitled, "An act laying duties upon carriages for the conveyance of persons." Daniel Lawrence Hilton, on the 5th of June 1794, and therefrom to the last day of September next following, owned, possessed and kept one hundred and twenty-five chariots for the conveyance of persons, but exclusively for his own separate use, and not to let out to hire, or for the conveyance of persons for hire.

The question is, whether a tax upon carriages be a direct tax? If it be a direct tax, it is unconstitutional, because it has been laid pursuant to the rule of uniformity, and not to the rule of apportionment. In behalf of the plaintiff in error, it has been urged, that a tax on carriages does not come within the description of a duty, impost or excise, and therefore, is a direct tax. It has, on the other hand, been contended, that as a tax on carriages is not a direct tax, it must fall within one of the classifications just enumerated, and particularly, must be a duty or excise. The argument on both sides turns in a circle; it is not a duty, impost or excise, and therefore, must be a direct tax; it is not tax, and therefore, must be a duty or excise. What is the natural and common, or technical and appropriate, meaning of the words, duty and excise, it is not easy to ascertain; they present no clear and precise idea to the mind; different persons will annex different significations to the terms. It was, however, obviously the intention of the framers of the constitution, that congress should possess full power over every species of taxable property, except exports. The term taxes, is generical, and was made use of, to vest in congress plenary authority in all cases of taxation. The general division of taxes is into direct and indirect; although the latter term is not to be found in the constitution, yet the former necessarily implies it; indirect stands opposed to direct. There may, perhaps, be an indirect tax on a particular article, that cannot be comprehended within the description of duties, or imposts or excises; in such case, it will be comprised under the general denomination of taxes. For the term tax is the *genus,* and includes: 1. Direct taxes. 2. Duties, imposts and excises. 3. All other classes of an indirect kind, and not within any of the classifications enumerated under the preceding heads.

The question occurs, how is such tax to be laid, uniformly or apportionately? The rule of uniformity will apply, because it is an indirect tax, and direct taxes only are to be apportioned. What are direct taxes, within the meaning of the constitution? The constitution declares, that a capitation tax is a direct tax; and both in theory and practice, a tax on land is deemed to be a direct tax. In this way, the terms direct taxes, and capitation and other direct tax, are satisfied. It is not necessary to determine, whether a tax on the product of land be a direct or indirect tax. Perhaps, the immediate product of land, in its original and crude state, ought to be considered as the land itself; it makes part of it; or else the provision made against taxing exports would be easily eluded. Land, independently of its produce, is of no value. When the produce is converted into a manufacture, it assumes a new shape; its nature is altered; its original state is changed; it becomes quite another subject, and will be differently considered. Whether direct taxes, in the sense of the constitution, comprehend any other tax than a capitation tax, and tax on land, is a questionable point. If congress, for instance, should tax, in the aggregate or mass, things that generally pervade all the states in the Union, then, perhaps, the rule of apportionment would be the most proper, especially, if an assessment was to intervene. This appears by the practice of some of the states, to have been considered as a direct tax. Whether it be so, under the constitution of the United States, is a matter of some difficulty; but as it is not before the court, it would be improper to give any decisive opinion upon it. I never entertained a doubt, that the principal, I will not say, the only, objects, that the framers of the constitution contemplated, as falling within the rule of apportionment, were a capitation tax and a tax on land. Local considerations, and the particular circumstances, and relative situation of the states, naturally lead to this view of the subject. The provision was made in favor of the southern states; they possessed a large number of slaves; they had extensive tracts of territory, thinly settled, and not very productive. A majority of the states had but few slaves, and several of them a limited territory, well settled, and in a high state of cultivation. The southern states, if no provision had been introduced in the constitution, would have been wholly at the mercy of the other states. Congress in such case, might tax slaves, at discretion or arbitrarily, and land in every part of the Union, after the same rate or measure: so much a head, in the first instance, and so much an acre, in the second. To guard them against imposition, in these particulars, was the reason of introducing the clause in the constitution, which directs that representatives and direct taxes shall be apportioned among the states, according to their respective numbers.

On the part of the plaintiff in error, it has been contended, that the rule of apportionment is to be favored, rather than the rule of uniformity; and, of course, that the instrument is to receive such a construction, as will extend the former, and restrict the latter. I am not of that opinion. The constitution has been considered as an accommodating system; it was the effect of mutual sacrifices and concessions; it was the work of compromise. The rule of apportionment is of this nature; it is radically wrong; it cannot be supported by any solid reasoning. Why should slaves, who are a species of property, be represented more than any other property? The rule, therefore, ought not to be extended by construction.

Again, numbers do not afford a just estimate or rule of wealth. It is, indeed, a very uncertain and incompetent sign of opulence. This is another reason against the extension of the principle laid down in the constitution.

The counsel on the part of the plaintiff in error, have further urged, that an equal participation of the expense or burden by the several states in the Union, was the primary object, which the framers of the constitution had in view; and that this object will be effected by the principle of apportionment, which is an operation upon states, and not on individuals; for each state will be debited for the amount of its *quota* of the tax, and credited for its payments. This brings it to the old system of requisitions. An equal rule is doubtless the best: but how is this to be applied to states or to individuals? The latter are the objects of taxation, without reference to states, except in the case of direct taxes. The fiscal power is exerted certainly, equally, and effectually on individuals; it cannot be exerted on states. The history of the United Netherlands, and of our own country, will evince the truth of this position. The government of the United States could not go on, under the confederation, because congress were obliged to proceed in the line of requisition. Congress could not, under the old confederation, raise money by taxes, be the public exigencies ever so pressing and great; they had no coercive authority—if they had, it must have been exercised against the delinquent states, which would be ineffectual, or terminate in a separation. Requisitions were a dead letter, unless the state legislatures could be brought into action; and when they were, the sums raised were very disproportional. Unequal contributions or payments engendered discontent, and fomented state jealousy. Whenever it shall be thought necessary or expedient to lay a direct tax on land, where the object is one and the same, it is to be apprehended, that it will be a fund not much more productive than that of requisition under the former government. Let us put the case. A given sum is to be raised from the landed property in the United States. It is easy to apportion this sum, or to assign to each state its *quota.* The constitution gives the rule. Suppose the proportion of North Carolina to be $80,000. This sum is to be laid on the landed property in the state, but by what rule, and by whom? Shall every acre pay the same sum, without regard to its quality, value, situation or productiveness? This would be manifestly unjust. Do the laws of the different states furnish sufficient *data* for the purpose of forming one common rule, comprehending the quality, situation and value of the lands? In some of the states, there has been no land-tax for several years, and where there has been, the mode of laying the tax is so various, and the diversity in the land is so great, that no common principle can be deduced, and carried into practice. Do the laws of each state furnish *data* from whence to extract a rule, whose operation shall be equal and certain in the same state? Even this is doubtful. Besides, sub-divisions will be necessary; the apportionment of the state, and perhaps, of a particular part of the state, is again to be apportioned among counties, townships, parishes or districts. If the lands be classed, then a specific value must be annexed to each class. And there a question arises, how often are classifications and assessments to be made? Annually, triennally, septennially? The oftener they are made, the greater will be the expense; and the seldomer they are made, the greater will be the inequality and injustice. In the process of the operation, a number of persons will be necessary to class, to value and assess the land; and after all the guards and provisions that can be devised, we must ultimately rely upon the discretion of the officers in the exercise of their functions. Tribunals of appeal must also be instituted, to hear and decide upon unjust valuations, or the assessors will act *ad libitum,* without check or control. The work, it is to be feared, will be operose and unproductive, and full of inequality, injustice and oppression. Let us, however, hope, that a system of land taxation may be so corrected and matured by practice, as to become easy and equal in its operation, and productive and beneficial in its effects.

But to return. A tax on carriages, if apportioned, would be oppressive and pernicious. How would it work? In some states, there are many carriages, and in others, but few. Shall the whole sum fall on one or two individuals in a state, who may happen to own and possess carriages? The thing would be absurd and inequitable. In answer to this objection, it has been observed, that the sum, and not the tax is to be apportioned; and that congress may select, in the different states, different articles or objects from whence to raise the apportioned sum. The idea is novel. What? shall land be taxed in one state, slaves in another, carriages in a third, and horses in a fourth? or shall several of these be thrown together, in order to levy and make the quotated sum? The scheme is fanciful. It would not work well, and perhaps is utterly impracticable. It is easy to discern, that great, and perhaps insurmountable, obstacles must arise in forming the subordinate arrangements necessary to carry the system into effect; when formed, the operation would be slow and expensive, unequal and unjust. If a tax upon land, where the object is simple and uniform throughout the states, is scarcely practicable, what shall we say of a tax attempted to be apportioned among, and raised and collected from, a number of dissimilar objects. The difficulty will increase with the number and variety of the things proposed for taxation. We shall be obliged to resort to intricate and endless valuations and assessments, in which everything will be arbitrary, and nothing certain. There will be no rule to walk by. The rule of uniformity, on the contrary, implies certainty, and leaves nothing to the will and pleasure of the assessor. In such case, the object and the sum coincide, the rule and the thing unite, and, of course, there can be no imposition. The truth is, that the articles taxed in one state should be taxed in another; in this way, the spirit of jealousy is appeased, and tranquillity preserved; in this way, the pressure on industry will be equal in the several states, and the relation between the different objects of taxation duly preserved. Apportionment is an operation on states, and involves valuations and assessments, which are arbitrary, and should not be resorted to but in case of necessity. Uniformity is an instant operation on individuals, without the intervention of assessments, or any regard to states, and is at once easy, certain and efficacious. All taxes on expenses or consumption are indirect taxes; a tax on carriages is of this kind, and of course, is not a direct tax. Indirect taxes are circuitous modes of reaching the revenue of individuals, who generally live according to their income. In many cases of this nature, the individual may be said to tax himself. I shall close the discourse, with reading a passage or two from Smith's Wealth of Nations.

"The impossibility of taxing people in proportion to their revenue, by any capitation, seems to have given occasion to the invention of taxes upon consumable commodities; the state, not knowing how to tax directly and proportionably the revenue of its subjects, endeavors to tax it indirectly, by taxing their expense, which it is supposed, in most cases, will be nearly in proportion to their revenue. Their expense is taxed, by taxing the consumable commodities upon which it is laid out." 3 Vol. page 331.

"Consumable commodities, whether necessaries or luxuries, may be taxed in two different ways; the consumer may either pay an annual sum, on account of his using or consuming goods of a certain kind, or the goods may be taxed, while they remain in the hands of the dealer, and before they are delivered to the consumer. The consumable goods, which last a considerable time before they are consumed altogether, are most properly taxed in the one way; those of which the consumption is immediate, or more speedy, in the other: the coach-tax and plate-tax are examples of the former method of imposing; the greater part of the other duties of excise and customs of the latter." 3 Vol. page 341.

I am, therefore, of opinion, that the judgment rendered in the circuit court of Virginia ought to be affirmed.

IREDELL, Justice.—I agree in opinion with my brothers, who have already expressed theirs, that the tax in question is agreeable to the constitution; and the reasons which have satisfied me, can be delivered in a very few words, since I think the constitution itself affords a clear guide to decide the controversy.

The congress possess the power of taxing all taxable objects, without limitation, with the particular exception of a duty on exports. There are two restrictions only on the exercise of this authority. 1. All direct taxes must be apportioned. 2. All duties, imposts and excises must be uniform.

If the carriage-tax be a direct tax, within the meaning of the constitution, it must be apportioned. If it be a duty, impost or excise, within the meaning of the constitution, it must be uniform.

If it can be considered as a tax, neither direct, within the meaning of the constitution, nor comprehended within the term duty, impost or excise; there is no provision in the constitution, one way or another, and then it must be left to such an operation of the power, as if the authority to lay taxes had been given generally, in all instances, without saying whether they should be apportioned or uniform; and in that case, I should presume, the tax ought to be uniform; because the present constitution was particularly intended to affect individuals, and not states, except in particular cases specified: and this is the leading distinction between the articles of confederation and the present constitution.

As all direct taxes must be apportioned, it is evident, that the constitution contemplated none as direct, but such as could be apportioned. If this cannot be apportioned, it is, therefore, not a direct tax in the sense of the constitution.

That this tax cannot be apportioned, is evident. Suppose, ten dollars contemplated as a tax on each chariot, or post-chaise, in the United States, and the number of both in all the United States be computed at 105, the number of representatives in congress.

This would produce in the whole,..............................		$1050.00
The share of Virginia being $^{19}/_{105}$ parts, would be	$190.00	
The share of Connecticut being $^{7}/_{105}$ parts, would be	70.00	
Then suppose Virginia had 50 carriages, Connecticut 2,		
The share of Virginia being $190, this must, of course, Be collected from the owners of carriages, and there would, therefore, be collected from each carriage,.................		3.80
The share of Connecticut being $70, each carriage would pay		35.00

If any state had no carriages, there could be no apportionment at all. This mode is too manifestly absurd to be supported, and has not even been attempted in debate.

But two expedients have been proposed, of a very extraordinary nature, to evade the difficulty.

I. To raise the money a tax on carriage would produce, not by laying a tax on each carriage uniformly, but by selecting different articles in different states, so that the amount paid in each state may be equal to the sum due on a principle of apportionment. One state might pay by a tax on carriages, another, by a tax on slaves, &c. I should have thought this merely an exercise of ingenuity, if it had not been pressed with some earnestness; and as this was done by gentlemen of high respectability in their profession, it deserves a serious answer, though it is very difficult to give such a one.

1. This is not an apportionment of a tax on carriages, but of the money a tax on carriages might be supposed to produce, which is quite a different thing.

2. It admits, that congress cannot lay an uniform tax on all carriages in the Union, in any mode, but that they may

on carriages in one or more states. They may, therefore, lay a tax on carriages in 14 states, but not in the 15th.

3. If congress, according to this new decree, may select carriages as a proper object, in one or more states, but omit them in others, I presume, they may omit them in all and select other articles.

Suppose, then, a tax on carriages would produce $100,000, and a tax on horses a like sum of $100,000, and $100,000 were to be apportioned according to that mode. Gentlemen might amuse themselves with calling this a tax on carriages, or a tax on horses, while not a single carriage, nor a single horse, was taxed throughout the Union.

4. Such an arbitrary method of taxing different states differently, is a suggestion altogether new, and would lead, if practised, to such dangerous consequences, that it will require very powerful arguments to show, that that method of taxing would be in any manner compatible with the constitution, with which, at present, I deem it utterly irreconcilable, it being altogether destructive of the notion of a common interest, upon which the very principles of the constitution are founded, so far as the condition of the United States will admit.

II. The second expedient proposed was, that of taxing carriages, among other things, in a general assessment. This amounts to saying, that congress may lay a tax on carriages, but that they may not do it, unless they blend it with other subjects of taxation. For this, no reason or authority has been given, and in addition to other suggestions offered by the counsel on that side, affords an irrefragable proof, that when positions, plainly so untenable, are offered to counteract the principle contended for by the opposite counsel, the principle itself is a right one; for no one can doubt, that if better reasons could have been offered, they would not have escaped the sagacity and learning of the gentlemen who offered them.

There is no necessity or propriety, in determining what is or is not, a direct or indirect tax, in all cases. Some difficulties may occur, which we do not at present foresee. Perhaps, a direct tax, in the sense of the constitution, can mean nothing but a tax on something inseparably annexed to the soil: something capable of apportionment, under all such circumstances. A land or a poll tax may be considered of this description. The latter is to be considered so particularly, under the present constitution, on account of the slaves in the southern states, who give a *ratio* in the representation in the proportion of 3 to 5. Either of these is capable of apportionment. In regard to other articles, there may possibly be considerable doubt. It is sufficient, on the present occasion, for the court to be satisfied, that this is not a direct tax contemplated by the constitution, in order to affirm the present judgment; since, if it cannot be apportioned, it must necessarily be uniform.

I am clearly of opinion, this is not a direct tax in the sense of the constitution, and therefore, that the judgment ought to be affirmed.

WILSON, Justice.—As there were only four judges, including myself, who attended the argument of this cause, I should have thought it proper to join in the decision, though I had before expressed a judicial opinion on the subject, in the circuit court of Virginia, did not the unanimity of the other three judges relieve me from the necessity. I shall now, however, only add, that my sentiments, in favor of the constitutionality of the tax in question, have not been changed.

CUSHING, Justice.—As I have been prevented, by indisposition, from attending to the argument, it would be improper to give an opinion on the merits of the cause.

BY THE COURT.—Let the judgment of the circuit court be affirmed.

14

ST. GEORGE TUCKER, BLACKSTONE'S COMMENTARIES 1:APP. 292–94 1803

4. To check any possible disposition in congress towards partiality in the imposition of burthens, it is further provided, that no capitation or other direct tax shall be laid, unless in proportion to the census, or enumeration, by the constitution directed to be taken. And the fifth article of the constitution declares, that no amendment made prior to the year 1808, shall in any manner affect this, and the first clause of the ninth section, above noticed.

The acts of 3 Cong. c. 45, and 4 Cong. c. 37, laying duties upon carriages for the conveyance of persons, were thought to be infringements of this article, it being supposed, that such a tax was a direct tax, and ought to have been apportioned among the states. The question was tried in this state, in the case of the United States, against Hylton, and the court being divided in opinion, was carried to the supreme court of the United States, by consent. It was there argued by the proposer of it, (the first secretary of the treasury,) on behalf of the United States, and by the present chief justice of the United States, on behalf of the defendant. Each of those gentlemen was supposed to have defended his own private opinion. That of the secretary of the treasury prevailed, and the tax was afterwards submitted to, universally, in Virginia.

15

RUFUS KING, SENATE ca. Mar. 1819 *Life 6:697–700*

By the articles of confederation the common treasury was to be supplied by the several states, according to the value of the lands, with the houses and improvements thereon, within the respective states. From the difficulty in making this valuation, the old congress were unable to apportion the requisitions for the supply of the general treasury, and were obliged to propose to the states an alteration of the articles of confederation, by which the whole number of free persons, with three-fifths of the slaves contained in the respective states, should become the rule of such apportionment of the taxes. A majority of the states approved of this alteration, but some of them disagreed to the same; and for want of a practicable rule of apportionment, the whole of the requisitions of taxes made by congress during the revolutionary war, and afterwards, up to the establishment of the constitution of the United States, were merely provisional, and subject to the revision and correction as soon as such rules should be adopted. The several states were credited for their supplies, and charged for the advances made to them by congress; but no settlement of their accounts could be made for the want of a rule of [apportionment], until the establishment of the constitution.

When the general convention that formed the constitution took this subject into their consideration, the whole question was once more examined, and while it was agreed that all contributions to the common treasury should be made according to the ability of the several states, to furnish the same, the old difficulty recurred in agreeing upon a rule whereby such ability should be ascertained, there being no simple standard by which the ability of individuals to pay taxes, can be ascertained. A diversity in the selection of taxes has been deemed requisite to their equalization: between communities, this difficulty is less considerable, and although the rule of relative numbers would not accurately measure the relative wealth of nations, in states, in the circumstances of the United States, whose institutions, laws and employments are so much alike, the rule of number is probably as nearly equal as any other simple and practical rule can be expected to be, (though between the old and new states its equity is defective,) these considerations, added to the approbation which had already been given to the rule, by a majority of the states, induced the convention to agree, that direct taxes should be apportioned among the states, according to the whole number of free persons, and three-fifths of the slaves which they might respectively contain.

. . . The present House of Representatives consists of 181 members, which are apportioned among the states in a ratio of one representative for every thirty-five thousand federal numbers, which are ascertained by adding to the whole number of free persons, three-fifths of the slaves. . . . Thus while 35,000 free persons are requisite to elect one representative in a state where slavery is prohibited, 25,559 free persons in Virginia may and do elect a representative—so that five free persons in Virginia have as much power in the choice of representatives to Congress, and in the appointment of presidential electors, as seven free persons in any of the states in which slavery does not exist.

This inequality in the appointment of representatives was not misunderstood at the adoption of the constitution; but as no one anticipated the fact that the whole of the revenue of the United States would be derived from indirect taxes (which cannot be supposed to spread themselves over the several states according to the rule for the apportionment of direct taxes), but it was believed that a part of the contribution to the common treasury would be apportioned among the states by the rule for the apportionment of representatives—the states in which slavery is prohibited, ultimately, though with reluctance, acquiesced in the disproportionate number of representatives and electors that was secured to the slave-holding states. The concession was, at the time, believed to be a great one, and has proved to have been the greatest which was made to secure the adoption of the constitution.

Great, however, as this concession was, it was definite, and its full extent was comprehended. It was a settlement between the original thirteen states. The considerations arising out of their actual condition, their past connection, and the obligation which all felt to promote a reformation in the federal government, were peculiar to the time and to the parties; and are not applicable to the new states which congress may now be willing to admit into the Union.

The equality of rights, which includes an equality of burdens, is a vital principle in our theory of government, and its jealous preservation is the best security of public and individual freedom; the departure from this principle in the disproportionate power and influence allowed to the slave-holding states, was a necessary sacrifice to the establishment of the constitution. The effect of this concession has been obvious in the preponderance which it has given to the slave-holding states, over the other states. Nevertheless, it is an ancient settlement, and faith and honor stand pledged not to disturb it. But the extension of this disproportionate power to the new states would be unjust and odious. The states whose power would be abridged, and whose burdens would be increased by the measure, cannot be expected to consent to it; and we may hope that the other states are too magnanimous to insist on it.

16

LOUGHBOROUGH V. BLAKE

5 Wheat. 317 (1820)

Mr. Chief Justice MARSHALL delivered the opinion of the court: This case presents to the consideration of the court a single question. It is this: Has Congress a right to impose a direct tax on the District of Columbia?

The counsel who maintains the negative has contended, that Congress must be considered in two distinct characters. In one character as legislating for the states; in the other, as a local legislature for the district. In the latter character, it is admitted, the power of levying direct taxes may be exercised; but, it is contended, for district purposes only, in like manner as the legislature of a state may tax the people of a state for state purposes.

Without inquiring at present into the soundness of this distinction, its possible influence on the application in this district of the first article of the constitution, and of several of the amendments, may not be altogether unworthy of consideration. It will readily suggest itself to the gentlemen who press this argument, that those articles which, in general terms, restrain the power of Congress, may be applied to the laws enacted by that body for the district, if it be considered as governing the district in its character as the national legislature, with less difficulty than if it be considered a mere local legislature.

But we deem it unnecessary to pursue this investigation, because we think the right of Congress to tax the district does not depend solely on the grant of exclusive legislation.

The 8th section of the 1st article gives to Congress the "power to lay and collect taxes, duties, imposts and excises," for the purposes thereinafter mentioned. This grant is general, without limitation as to place. It consequently extends to all places over which the government extends. If this could be doubted, the doubt is removed by the subsequent words which modify the grant. These words are, "but all duties, imposts, and excises, shall be uniform throughout the United States." It will not be contended that the modification of the power extends to places to which the power itself does not extend. The power, then, to lay and collect duties, imposts, and excises, may be exercised, and must be exercised throughout the United States. Does this term designate the whole, or any particular portion of the American empire? Certainly this question can admit of but one answer. It is the name given to our great republic, which is composed of states and territories. The District of Columbia, or the territory west of the Missouri, is not less within the United States than Maryland or Pennsylvania; and it is not less necessary, on the principles of our constitution, that uniformity in the imposition of imposts, duties, and excises, should be observed in the one than in the other. Since, then, the power to lay and collect taxes, which includes direct taxes, is obviously coextensive with the power to lay and collect duties, imposts and excises, and since the latter extends throughout the United States, it follows that the power to impose direct taxes also extends throughout the United States.

The extent of the grant being ascertained, how far is it abridged by any part of the constitution?

The 20th section of the first article declares, that "representatives and direct taxes shall be apportioned among the several states which may be included within this Union, according to their respective numbers."

The object of this regulation is, we think, to furnish a standard by which taxes are to be apportioned, not to exempt from their operation any part of our country. Had the intention been to exempt from taxation those who were not represented in Congress, that intention would have been expressed in direct terms. The power having been expressly granted, the exception would have been expressly made. But a limitation can scarcely be said to be insinuated. The words used do not mean that direct taxes shall be imposed on states only which are represented, or shall be apportioned to representatives; but that direct taxation, in its application to states, shall be apportioned to numbers. Representation is not made the foundation of taxation. If, under the enumeration of a representative for every 30,000 souls, one state had been found to contain 59,000, and another 60,000, the first would have been entitled to only one representative, and the last to two. Their taxes, however, would not have been as one to two, but as fifty-nine to sixty. This clause was obviously not intended to create any exemption from taxation, or to make taxation dependent on representation, but to furnish a standard for the apportionment of each on the states.

The 4th paragraph of the 9th section of the same article will next be considered. It is in these words: "No capitation, or other direct tax, shall be laid, unless in proportion to the census, or enumeration hereinbefore directed to be taken."

The census referred to is in that clause of the constitution which has just been considered, which makes numbers the standard by which both representatives and direct taxes shall be apportioned among the states. The actual enumeration is to be made "within three years after the first meeting of the Congress of the United States, and within every subsequent term of ten years, in such manner as they shall by law direct."

As the direct and declared object of this census is, to furnish a standard by which "representatives, and direct taxes, may be apportioned among the several states which may be included within this Union," it will be admitted that the omission to extend it to the district or the territories would not render it defective. The census referred to is admitted to be a census exhibiting the numbers of the respective states. It cannot, however, be admitted, that the argument which limits the application of the power of direct taxation to the population contained in this census is a just one. The language of the clause does not imply this restriction. It is not that "no capitation or other direct tax shall be laid, unless on those comprehended within the census hereinbefore directed to be taken," but "unless in proportion to" that census. Now, this proportion may be applied to the district or territories. If an enumeration be taken of the population in the district and territories, on the same principles on which the enumeration of the respective States is made, then the information is acquired by which a direct tax may be imposed on the district and territories, "in proportion to the census or enumeration" which the constitution directs to be taken.

The standard, then, by which direct taxes must be laid, is applicable to this district, and will enable Congress to apportion on it its just and equal share of the burthen, with the same accuracy as on the respective states. If the tax be laid in this proportion, it is within the very words of the restriction. It is a tax in proportion to the census or enumeration referred to.

But the argument is presented in another form, in which its refutation is more difficult. It is urged against this construction, that it would produce the necessity of extending direct taxation to the district and territories, which would not only be inconvenient, but contrary to the understanding and practice of the whole government. If the power of imposing direct taxes be co-extensive with the United States, then it is contended, that the restrictive clause, if applicable to the district and territories, requires that the tax should be extended to them, since to omit them would be to violate the rule of proportion.

We think a satisfactory answer to this argument may be drawn from a fair comparative view of the different clauses of the constitution which have been recited.

That the general grant of power to lay and collect taxes is made in terms which comprehend the district and territories as well as the states, is, we think, incontrovertible. The subsequent clauses are intended to regulate the exercise of this power, not to withdraw from it any portion of the community. The words in which those clauses are expressed import this intention. In thus regulating its exercise, a rule is given in the 2d section of the first article for its application to the respective states. That rule declares how direct taxes upon the states shall be imposed. They shall be apportioned upon the several states according to their numbers. If, then, a direct tax be laid at all, it must be laid on every state, conformably to the rule provided in the constitution. Congress has clearly no power to exempt any state from its due share of the burden. But this regulation is expressly confined to the states, and creates no necessity for extending the tax to the district or territories. The words of the 9th section do not in terms require that the system of direct taxation, when resorted to, shall be extended to the territories, as the words of the 2d section require that it shall be extended to all the states. They, therefore, may, without violence, be understood to give a rule when the territories shall be taxed, without imposing the necessity of taxing them. It could scarcely escape the members of the convention that the expense of executing the law in a territory might exceed the amount of the tax. But be this as it may, the doubt created by the words of the 9th section relates to the obligation to apportion a direct tax on the territories as well as the states, rather than to the power to do so.

If, then, the language of the constitution be construed to comprehend the territories and District of Columbia, as well as the states, that language confers on Congress the power of taxing the district and territories as well as the states. If the general language of the constitution should be confined to the states, still the 16th paragraph of the 8th section gives to Congress the power of exercising "exclusive legislation in all cases whatsoever within this district."

On the extent of these terms, according to the common understanding of mankind, there can be no difference of opinion; but it is contended that they must be limited by that great principle which was asserted in our revolution—that representation is inseparable from taxation.

The difference between requiring a continent, with an immense population, to submit to be taxed by a government having no common interest with it, separated from it by a vast ocean, restrained by no principle of apportionment, and associated with it by no common feelings; and permitting the representatives of the American people, under the restrictions of our constitution, to tax a part of the society, which is either in a state of infancy advancing to manhood, looking forward to complete equality so soon as that state of manhood shall be attained, as is the case with the territories; or which has voluntarily relinquished the right of representation, and has adopted the whole body of Congress for its legitimate government, as is the case with the district, is too obvious not to present itself to the minds of all. Although in theory it might be more congenial to the spirit of our institutions to admit a representative from the district, it may be doubted whether, in fact, its interests would be rendered thereby the more secure; and certainly the constitution does not consider their want of a representative in Congress as exempting it from equal taxation.

If it were true that, according to the spirit of our constitution, the power of taxation must be limited by the right of representation, whence is derived the right to lay and collect duties, imposts and excises, within this district? If the principles of liberty, and of our constitution, forbid the raising of revenue from those who are not represented, do not these principles forbid the raising it by duties, imposts, and excises, as well as by a direct tax? If the principles of our revolution give a rule applicable to this case, we cannot have forgotten that neither the stamp act nor the duty on tea were direct taxes.

Yet it is admitted that the constitution not only allows, but enjoins the government to extend the ordinary revenue system to this district.

If it be said that the principle of uniformity, established in the constitution, secures the district from oppression in the imposition of indirect taxes, it is not less true that the principle of apportionment, also established in the constitution, secures the district from any oppressive exercise of the power to lay and collect direct taxes.

After giving this subject its serious attention, the court is unanimously of opinion that Congress possesses, under the constitution, the power to lay and collect direct taxes within the District of Columbia, in proportion to the census directed to be taken by the constitution, and that there is no error in the judgment of the Circuit Court.

SEE ALSO:

Generally 1.2.3; 1.8.1

Continental Congress, Amendment to Share Expenses according to Population, 18 Apr. 1783, Jensen 1:149–50

James Kent, Commentaries 1:239–42 (1826)

Article 1, Section 9, Clause 5

No Tax or Duty shall be laid on Articles exported from any State.

1

Records of the Federal Convention

[*1:286; Madison, 18 June*]

Mr Hamilton: . . . Whence then is the national revenue to be drawn? from Commerce, even from exports which notwithstanding the common opinion are fit objects of moderate taxation, from excise, &c &c. These tho' not equal, are less unequal than quotas.

[*1:592; Madison, 12 July*]

Mr. Govr. Morris, admitted that some objections lay agst. his motion, but supposed they would be removed by restraining the rule to *direct* taxation. With regard to indirect taxes on *exports* & imports & on consumption, the rule would be inapplicable. Notwithstanding what had been said to the contrary he was persuaded that the imports & consumption were pretty nearly equal throughout the Union.

General Pinkney liked the idea. He thought it so just that it could not be objected to. But foresaw that if the revision of the census was left to the discretion of the Legislature, it would never be carried into execution. The rule must be fixed, and the execution of it enforced by the Constitution. He was alarmed at what was said yesterday, concerning the Negroes. He was now again alarmed at what had been thrown out concerning the taxing of exports. S. Carola. has in one year exported to the amount of £600,000 Sterling all which was the fruit of the labor of her blacks. Will she be represented in proportion to this amount? She will not. Neither ought she then to be subject to a tax on it. He hoped a clause would be inserted in the system restraining the Legislature from a taxing Exports.

Mr. Wilson approved the principle, but could not see how it could be carried into execution; unless restrained to direct taxation.

Mr. Govr. Morris having so varied his motion by inserting the word "direct". It passd.

[*2:95; Madison, 23 July*]

Genl. Pinkney reminded the Convention that if the Committee should fail to insert some security to the Southern States agst. an emancipation of slaves, and taxes on exports, he shd. be bound by duty to his State to vote agst. their Report.—

[*2:142, 168; Committee of Detail, IV, IX*]

agrd. No Taxes on exports.—

. . . . .

No Tax or Duty shall be laid by the Legislature, on Articles exported from any State;

[*2:305; Madison, 16 Aug.*]

Art: VII. Sect. 1. taken up.

Mr. L. Martin asked what was meant by the Committee of detail in the expression *"duties"* and *"imposts"*. If the meaning were the same, the former was unnecessary; if different, the matter ought to be made clear.

Mr Wilson, *duties* are applicable to many objects to which the word *imposts* does not relate. The latter are appropriated to commerce; the former extend to a variety of objects, as stamp duties &c.

Mr. Carroll reminded the Convention of the great difference of interests among the States, and doubts the propriety in that point of view of letting a majority be a quorum.

Mr. Mason urged the necessity of connecting with the power of levying taxes duties &c, the prohibition in Sect 4 of art VI that no tax should be laid on exports. He was unwilling to trust to its being done in a future article. He hoped the Northn. States did not mean to deny the Southern this security. It would hereafter be as desirable to the former when the latter should become the most populous. He professed his jealousy for the productions of the Southern or as he called them, the staple States. He moved to insert the following amendment: "provided that no tax duty or imposition, shall be laid by the Legislature of the U. States on articles exported from any State"

Mr Sherman had no objection to the proviso here, other than it would derange the parts of the report as made by the Committee, to take them in such an order.

Mr. Rutlidge. It being of no consequence in what order

points are decided, he should vote for the clause as it stood, but on condition that the subsequent part relating to negroes should also be agreed to.

Mr. Governeur Morris considered such a proviso as inadmissible any where. It was so radically objectionable, that it might cost the whole system the support of some members. He contended that it would not in some cases be equitable to tax imports without taxing exports; and that taxes on exports would be often the most easy and proper of the two.

Mr. Madison. 1. the power of taxing exports is proper in itself, and as the States cannot with propriety exercise it separately, it ought to be vested in them collectively. 2. it might with particular advantage be exercised with regard to articles in which America was not rivalled in foreign markets, as Tobo. &c. The contract between the French Farmers Genl. and Mr. Morris stipulating that if taxes sd. be laid in America on the export of Tobo. they sd. be paid by the Farmers, shewed that it was understood by them, that the price would be thereby raised in America, and consequently the taxes be paid by the European Consumer. 3. it would be unjust to the States whose produce was exported by their neighbours, to leave it subject to be taxed by the latter. This was a grievance which had already filled N. H. Cont. N. Jery. Del. and N. Carolina with loud complaints, as it related to imports, and they would be equally authorized by taxes by the States on exports. 4. The Southn. States being most in danger and most needing naval protection, could the less complain if the burden should be somewhat heaviest on them. 5. we are not providing for the present moment only, and time will equalize the situation of the States in this matter. He was for these reasons, agst the motion

Mr. Williamson considered the clause proposed agst taxes on exports as reasonable and necessary.

Mr. Elseworth was agst. Taxing exports; but thought the prohibition stood in the most proper place, and was agst. deranging the order reported by the Committee

Mr. Wilson was decidedly agst prohibiting general taxes on exports. He dwelt on the injustice and impolicy of leaving N. Jersey Connecticut &c any longer subject to the exactions of their commercial neighbours.

Mr Gerry thought the legislature could not be trusted with such a power. It might ruin the Country. It might be exercised partially, raising one and depressing another part of it.

Mr Govr Morris. However the legislative power may be formed, it will if disposed be able to ruin the Country— He considered the taxing of exports to be in many cases highly politic. Virginia has found her account in taxing Tobacco. All Countries having peculiar articles tax the exportation of them; as France her wines and brandies. A tax here on lumber, would fall on the W. Indies & punish their restrictions on our trade. The same is true of livestock and in some degree of flour. In case of a dearth in the West Indies, we may extort what we please. Taxes on exports are a necessary source of revenue. For a long time the people of America will not have money to pay direct taxes. Seize and sell their effects and you push them into Revolts—

Mr. Mercer was strenous against giving Congress power to tax exports. Such taxes were impolitic, as encouraging the raising of articles not meant for exportation. The States had now a right where their situation permitted, to tax both the imports and exports of their uncommercial neighbours. It was enough for them to sacrifice one half of it. It had been said the Southern States had most need of naval protection. The reverse was the case. Were it not for promoting the carrying trade of the Northn States, the Southn States could let their trade go into foreign bottoms, where it would not need our protection. Virginia by taxing her tobacco had given an advantage to that of Maryland.

Mr. Sherman. To examine and compare the States in relation to imports and exports will be opening a boundless field. He thought the matter had been adjusted, and that imports were to be subject, and exports not, to be taxed. He thought it wrong to tax exports except it might be such articles as ought not to be exported. The complexity of the business in America would render an equal tax on exports impracticable. The oppression of the uncommercial States was guarded agst. by the power to regulate trade between the States. As to compelling foreigners, that might be done by regulating trade in general. The Government would not be trusted with such a power. Objections are most likely to be excited by considerations relating to taxes & money. A power to tax exports would shipwreck the whole.

Mr. Carrol was surprised that any objection should be made to an exception of exports from the power of taxation.

It was finally agreed that the question concerning exports shd. lie over for the place in which the exception stood in the report. Maryd. alone voting agst it

[*2:359; Madison, 21 Aug.*]

Art. VII. sect. 4.—Mr. Langdon. by this section the States are left at liberty to tax exports. N. H. therefore with other non-exporting States, will be subject to be taxed by the States exporting its produce. This could not be admitted. It seems to be feared that the Northern States will oppress the trade of the Southn. This may be guarded agst by requiring the concurrence of ⅔ or ¾ of the legislature in such cases.

Mr Elseworth—It is best as it stands—The power of regulating trade between the States will protect them agst each other—Should this not be the case, the attempts of one to tax the produce of another passing through its hands, will force a direct exportation and defeat themselves—There are solid reasons agst. Congs taxing exports. 1. it will discourage industry, as taxes on imports discourage luxury. 2. The produce of different States is such as to prevent uniformity in such taxes. there are indeed but a few articles that could be taxed at all; as Tobo. rice & indigo, and a tax on these alone would be partial & unjust. 3. The taxing of exports would engender incurable jealousies.

Mr Williamson. Tho' N—C. has been taxed by Virga by a duty on 12,000 Hhs of her Tobo. exported thro' Virga yet he would never agree to this power. Should it take take place, it would destroy the last hope of an adoption of the plan.

Mr. Govr Morris. These local considerations ought not to impede the general interest. There is great weight in the argument, that the exporting States will tax the produce of their uncommercial neighbours. The power of regulating the trade between Pa & N. Jersey will never prevent the former from taxing the latter. Nor will such a tax force a direct exportation from N—Jersey—The advantages possessed by a large trading City, outweigh the disadvantage of a moderate duty; and will retain the trade in that channel—If no tax can be laid on exports, an embargo cannot be laid, though in time of war such a measure may be of critical importance—Tobacco, lumber, and live-stock are three objects belonging to different States, of which great advantage might be made by a power to tax exports—To these may be added Ginseng and Masts for Ships by which a tax might be thrown on other nations. The idea of supplying the West Indies with lumber from Nova Scotia, is one of the many follies of lord Sheffield's pamphlets. The State of the Country also, will change, and render duties on exports, as skins, beaver & other peculiar raw materials, politic in the view of encouraging American Manufactures.

Mr. Butler was strenuously opposed to a power over exports; as unjust and alarming to the staple States.

Mr. Langdon suggested a prohibition on the States from taxing the produce of other States exported from their harbours.

Mr. Dickenson. The power of taxing exports may be inconvenient at present; but it must be of dangerous consequence to prohibit it with respect to all articles and for ever. He thought it would be better to except particular articles from the power.

Mr. Sherman—It is best to prohibit the National legislature in all cases. The States will never give up all power over trade. An enumeration of particular articles would be difficult invidious and improper.

Mr Madison As we ought to be governed by national and permanent views, it is a sufficient argument for giving ye power over exports that a tax, tho' it may not be expedient at present, may be so hereafter. A proper regulation of exports may & probably will be necessary hereafter, and for the same purposes as the regulation of—imports; viz, for revenue—domestic manufactures—and procuring equitable regulations from other nations. An Embargo may be of absolute necessity, and can alone be effectuated by the Genl. authority. The regulation of trade between State and State can not effect more than indirectly to hinder a State from taxing its own exports; by authorizing its Citizens to carry their commodities freely into a neighbouring State which might decline taxing exports in order to draw into its channel the trade of its neighbours—As to the fear of disproportionate burdens on the more exporting States, it might be remarked that it was agreed on all hands that the revenue wd. principally be drawn from trade, and as only a given revenue would be needed, it was not material whether all should be drawn wholly from imports—or half from those, and half from exports—The imports and exports must be pretty nearly equal in every State—and relatively the same among the different States.

Mr Elseworth did not conceive an embargo by the Congress interdicted by this section.

Mr. McHenry conceived that power to be included in the power of war.

Mr. Wilson. Pennsylvania exports the produce of Maryd. N. Jersey, Deleware & will by & by when the River Delaware is opened, export for N—York. In favoring the general power over exports therefore, he opposed the particular interest of his State. He remarked that the power had been attacked by reasoning which could only have held good in case the Genl Govt. had been *compelled,* instead of *authorized,* to lay duties on exports. To deny this power is to take from the Common Govt. half the regulation of trade—It was his opinion that a power over exports might be more effectual than that over imports in obtaining beneficial treaties of commerce.

Mr. Gerry was strenuously opposed to the power over exports. It might be made use of to compel the States to comply with the will of the Genl Government, and to grant it any new powers which might be demanded—We have given it more power already than we know how will be exercised—It will enable the Genl Govt to oppress the States, as much as Ireland is oppressed by Great Britain.

Mr. Fitzimmons would be agst. a tax on exports to be laid immediately; but was for giving a power of laying the tax when a proper time may call for it—This would certainly be the case when America should become a manufacturing country—He illustrated his argument by the duties in G—Britain on wool &c.

Col. Mason—If he were for reducing the States to mere corporations as seemed to be the tendency of some arguments, he should be for subjecting their exports as well as imports to a power of general taxation—He went on a principle often advanced & in which he concurred, that "a majority when interested will oppress the minority". This maxim had been verified by our own Legislature (of Virginia). If we compare the States in this point of view the 8 Northern States have an interest different from the five Southn. States,—and have in one branch of the legislature 36 votes agst 29. and in the other, in the proportion of 8 agst 5. The Southern States had therefore good ground for their suspicions. The case of Exports was not the same with that of imports. The latter were the same throughout the States: the former very different. As to Tobacco other nations do raise it, and are capable of raising it as well as Virga. &c. The impolicy of taxing that article had been demonstrated by the experiment of Virginia—

Mr Clymer remarked that every State might reason with regard to its particular productions, in the same manner as the Southern States. The middle States may apprehend an oppression of their wheat flour, provisions, &c. and with more reason, as these articles were exposed to a competition in foreign markets not incident to Tobo. rice &c—They may apprehend also combinations agst. them between the Eastern & Southern States as much as the latter can apprehend them between the Eastern & middle—He moved as a qualification of the power of taxing Exports that it should be restrained to regulations of trade, by inserting after the word "duty" Sect 4 art VII the words "for the purpose of revenue."

On Question on Mr. Clymer's motion

N. H— no— Mas. no. Ct. no. N. J— ay. Pa ay. Del. ay. Md. no. Va. no. N—C. no. Geo. no. [Ayes—3; noes—7.]

Mr. Madison, In order to require ⅔ of each House to tax exports—as a lesser evil than a total prohibition moved to insert the words "unless by consent of two thirds of the Legislature", Mr Wilson 2ds. and on this question, it passed in the Negative.

N. H. ay. Mas— ay. Ct. no. N. J. ay. Pa. ay. Del. ay. Md. no. Va. no. (Col. Mason, Mr. Randolph Mr. Blair no. Genl Washington & J. M. ay.) N. C. no. S—C. no. Geo. no. [Ayes—5; noes—6.]

Question on sect: 4. art VII. as far as to "no tax shl. be laid on exports—It passed in the affirmative—

N. H. no. Mas. ay. Ct. ay. N—J. no. Pa. no—Del. no. Md ay. Va. ay (Genl W. & J. M. no.) N. C. ay. S. C. ay. Geo—ay. [Ayes—7; noes—4.]

[*2:374; Madison, 22 Aug.*]

Mr Govr. Morris wished the whole subject to be committed including the clauses relating to taxes on exports & to a navigation act. These things may form a bargain among the Northern & Southern States.

Mr. Butler declared that he never would agree to the power of taxing exports.

Mr. Sherman said it was better to let the S. States import slaves than to part with them, if they made that a sine qua non. He was opposed to a tax on slaves imported as making the matter worse, because it implied they were *property*. He acknowledged that if the power of prohibiting the importation should be given to the Genl. Government that it would be exercised. He thought it would be its duty to exercise the power.

Mr. Read was for the commitment provided the clause concerning taxes on exports should also be committed.

Mr. Sherman observed that that clause had been agreed to & therefore could not committed.

Mr. Randolph was for committing in order that some middle ground might, if possible, be found. He could never agree to the clause as it stands. He wd. sooner risk the constitution—He dwelt on the dilemma to which the Convention was exposed. By agreeing to the clause, it would revolt the Quakers, the Methodists, and many others in the States having no slaves. On the other hand, two States might be lost to the Union. Let us then, he said, try the chance of a commitment.

On the question for committing the remaining part of Sect 4 & 5. of art: 7. N. H. no. Mas. abst. Cont. ay N. J. ay Pa. no. Del. no Maryd ay. Va ay. N. C. ay S. C. ay. Geo. ay. [Ayes—7; noes—3; absent—1.]

[*2:571, 596; Committee of Style*]

Sect. 4. No tax or duty shall be laid by the Legislature on articles exported from any State.

2

JAMES MADISON TO THOMAS JEFFERSON
24 Oct. 1787
Papers 10:214

Begging pardon for this immoderate digression I return to the third object above mentioned, the adjustments of the different interests of different parts of the Continent. Some contended for an unlimited power over trade including exports as well as imports, and over slaves as well as other imports; some for such a power, provided the concurrence of two thirds of both Houses were required; Some for such a qualification of the power, with an exemption of exports and slaves, others for an exemption of exports only. The result is seen in the Constitution. S. Carolina & Georgia were inflexible on the point of the slaves.

3

JAMES MCHENRY, MARYLAND HOUSE OF DELEGATES
29 Nov. 1787
Farrand 3:149

That no Duties shall be laid on Exports or Tonage, on Vessells bound from one State to another is the effect of that attention to general Equality that governed the deliberations of Convention. Hence unproductive States cannot draw a revenue from productive States into the Public Treasury, nor unproductive States be hampered in their Manufactures to the emolument of others.

4

JOSEPH STORY, COMMENTARIES ON THE CONSTITUTION 2:§§ 1011–12
1833

§ 1011. The obvious object of these provisions is, to prevent any possibility of applying the power to lay taxes, or regulate commerce, injuriously to the interests of any one state, so as to favour or aid another. If congress were allowed to lay a duty on exports from any one state it might unreasonably injure, or even destroy, the staple productions, or common articles of that state. The inequality of such a tax would be extreme. In some of the states, the whole of their means result from agricultural exports. In others, a great portion is derived from other sources; from external fisheries; from freights; and from the profits of commerce in its largest extent. The burthen of such a tax would, of course, be very unequally distributed. The power is, therefore, wholly taken away to intermeddle with the subject of exports. On the other hand, preferences might be given to the ports of one state by regulations, either of commerce or revenue, which might confer on them local facilities or privileges in regard to commerce, or revenue. And such preferences might be equally fatal, if individually given under the milder form of requiring an entry, clearance, or payment of duties in the ports of any state, other than the ports of the state, to or from which the vessel was bound. The last clause, therefore, does not prohibit congress from requiring an entry or clearance, or payment of duties at the custom-house on importations in any port of a state, to or from which the vessel is bound; but cuts off the right to require such acts to be done in other states, to which the vessel is not bound. In other words, it cuts off the power to require, that circuity of voyage, which, under the British colonial system, was employed to interrupt the American commerce before the revolution. No American vessel could then trade with Europe, unless through a circuitous voyage to and from a British port.

§ 1012. The first part of the clause was reported in the first draft of the constitution. But it did not pass without opposition; and several attempts were made to amend it; as by inserting after the word "duty" the words, "for the purpose of revenue," and by inserting at the end of it, "unless by consent of two thirds of the legislature;" both of which propositions were negatived. It then passed by a vote of seven states against four. Subsequently, the remaining parts of the clause were proposed by a report of a committee, and they appear to have been adopted without objection. Upon the whole, the wisdom and sound policy of this restriction cannot admit of reasonable doubt; not so much that the powers of the general government were likely to be abused, as that the constitutional prohibition would allay jealousies, and confirm confidence. The prohibition extends not only to exports, but to the exporter. Congress can no more rightfully tax the one, than the other.

SEE ALSO:

Generally 1.2.3; 1.8.1; 1.10.2
Continental Congress, Amendment to Share Expenses according to Population, 18 Apr. 1783, Jensen 1:149–50
James Kent, Commentaries 1:239–42 (1826)

Article 1, Section 9, Clause 6

No Preference shall be given by any Regulation of Commerce or Revenue to the Ports of one State over those of another; nor shall Vessels bound to, or from, one State, be obliged to enter, clear or pay Duties in another.

1

Records of the Federal Convention

[*2:410; Journal, 25 Aug.*]

It was moved and seconded to agree to the following propositions

"The Legislature of the United States shall not oblige Vessels belonging to Citizens thereof, or to foreigners, to enter or pay duties, or imposts in any other State than in that to which they may be bound, or to clear out in any other than the State in which their cargoes may be laden on board—Nor shall any privilege, or immunity, be granted to any vessels on entering, clearing out, or paying duties or imposts in one State in preference to another"

"Should it be judged expedient by the Legislature of the United States that one or more ports for collecting duties or imposts other than those ports of entrance and clearance already established by the respective States should be established, the Legislature of the U. S. shall signify the same to the Executive of the respective States ascertaining the number of such ports judged necessary; to be laid by the said Executives before the Legislatures of the States at their next session; and the legislature of the U. S. shall not have the power of fixing or establishing the particular ports for collecting duties or imposts in any State except the Legislature of such State shall neglect to fix and establish the same during their first session to be held after such notification by the legislature of the U. S. to the executive of such State.

"all duties, imposts, and excises, prohibitions or restraints laid or made by the Legislature of the U. S. shall be uniform and equal throughout the United States"

It was moved and seconded to refer the above propositions to a Committee of a Member from each State

which passed in the affirmative

[*2:417; Madison, 25 Aug.*]

Mr. Carrol & Mr. L. Martin expressed their apprehensions, and the probable apprehensions of their constituents, that under the power of regulating trade the General Legislature, might favor the ports of particular States, by requiring vessels destined to or from other States to enter & clear thereat, as vessels belonging or bound to Baltimore, to enter & clear at Norfolk &c They moved the following proposition

"The Legislature of the U— S. shall not oblige vessels belonging to citizens thereof, or to foreigners, to enter or pay duties or imposts in any other State than in that to which they may be bound, or to clear out in any other than the State in which their cargoes may be laden on board; nor shall any privilege or immunity be granted to any vessels on entering or clearing out or paying duties or imposts in one state in preference to another"

Mr Ghorum thought such a precaution unnecessary; & that the revenue might be defeated, if vessels could run up long rivers, through the jurisdiction of different States without being required to enter, with the opportunity of landing & selling their cargoes by the way.

Mr McHenry & Genl Pinkney made the following propositions

"Should it be judged expedient by the Legislature of the U— S— that one or more ports for collecting duties or imposts other than those ports of entrance & clearance already established by the respective States, should be established, the Legislature of the U— S— shall signify the same to the Executives of the respective States, ascertaining the number of such ports judged necessary; to be laid by the said Executives before the Legislatures of the States at their next Session; and the Legislature of the U— S— shall not have the power of fixing or establishing the particular ports for collecting duties or imposts in any State, except the Legislature of such State shall neglect to fix and establish the same during their first Session to be held after such notification by the Legislature of the U— S— to the Executive of such State"

"All duties imposts & excises, prohibitions or restraints laid or made by the Legislature of the U— S— shall be uniform and equal throughout the U— S—"

These several propositions were referred, nem: con: to a committee composed of a member from each State, The committee appointed by ballot were Mr. Langdon, Mr. Ghorum, Mr. Sherman, Mr Dayton, Mr. Fitzimmons, Mr. Read, Mr. Carrol, Mr. Mason, Mr. Williamson, Mr. Butler, Mr. Few.

[*2:420; McHenry, 25 Aug.*]

Moved several propositions to restrict the legislature from giving any preference in duties, or from obliging duties to be collected in a manner injurious to any State, and from establishing new ports of entrance and clerance, unless neglected to be established by the States after application—Opposed by Massachusetts—Mr. Gorahm said it might be very proper to oblige vessels, for example, to stop at Norfolk on account of the better collection of the revenue.

Mr. King thought it improper to deliberate long on such propositions but to take the sense of the house immediately upon them.

I moved to have them committed to a committee consisting of a member from each State. Committed.

[*2:434; Journal, 28 Aug.*]

The honorable Mr Sherman from the Committee to whom were referred several propositions entered on the Journal of the 25 instant informed the House that the Committee were prepared to report—The report was then delivered in at the Secretary's table, was read, and is as follows.

The Committee report that the following be inserted after the 4 clause of the 7 section

"Nor shall any regulation of commerce or revenue give preference to the ports of one State over those of another or oblige Vessels bound to or from any State to enter, clear, or pay duties in another.

And all tonnage, duties, imposts, and excises, laid by the Legislature shall be uniform throughout the United States"

[*2:470; McHenry, 30 Aug.*]

Endeavoured to recall the house to the reported propositions from maryland, to prevent the U. S. from giving preferences to one State above another or to the shipping of one State above another, in collecting or laying duties.—The house averse to taking any thing up till this system is got through. XXI. adjourned on this article.

[*2:480; Madison, 31 Aug.*]

The report of the grand Committee of eleven made by Mr. Sherman was then taken up (see Aug: 28).

On the question to agree to the following clause, to be inserted after sect— 4. art: VII. "nor shall any regulation of commerce or revenue give preference to the ports of one State over those of another". Agreed to nem: con:

On the clause "or oblige vessels bound to or from any State to enter clear or pay duties in another"

Mr. Madison thought the restriction wd. be inconvenient, as in the River Delaware, if a vessel cannot be required to make entry below the jurisdiction of Pennsylvania.

Mr. Fitzimmons admitted that it might be inconvenient,

but thought it would be a greater inconveniency to require vessels bound to Philada. to enter below the jurisdiction of the State.

Mr. Gorham & Mr. Langdon, contended that the Govt would be so fettered by this clause, as to defeat the good purpose of the plan. They mentioned the situation of the trade of Mas. & N. Hampshire, the case of Sandy Hook which is in the State of N. Jersey, but where precautions agst smuggling into N. York, ought to be established by the Genl. Government.

Mr. McHenry said the clause would not shreen a vessel from being obliged to take an officer on board as a security for due entry &c—.

Mr Carrol was anxious that the clause should be agreed to. He assured the House, that this was a tender point in Maryland.

Mr Jenifer urged the necessity of the clause in the same point of view

On the question for agreeing to it

N. H. no. Ct ay. N. J. ay. Pa. ay. Del. ay. Md ay. Va. ay. N— C— ay. S— C. no. Geo. ay, [Ayes—8; noes—2.]

The word "tonnage" was struck out, nem: con: as comprehended in "duties"

[*2:571, 596; Committee of Style*]

Nor shall any regulation of commerce or revenue give preference to the ports of one State over those of another, or oblige Vessels bound to or from any State to enter, clear, or pay duties in another.

. . . . .

No preference shall be given by any regulation of commerce or revenue to the ports of one State over those of another—nor shall vessels bound to or from one State be obliged to enter, clear or pay duties in another.

2

LUTHER MARTIN, MARYLAND HOUSE OF DELEGATES
29 Nov. 1787

Farrand 3:157–58

S: 9. By this Article Congress will obtain unlimitted power over all the Ports in the Union and consequently acquire an influence that may be prejudicial to general Liberty. It was sufficient for all the purposes of General Government that Congress might lay what Duties they thought proper, and those who did not approve the extended power here given, contended that the Establishment of the Particular ports ought to remain with the Government of the respective States; for if Maryland for instance should have occasion to oppose the Encroachments of the General Government—Congress might direct that all Vessels coming into this Bay, to enter and clear at Norfolk, and thereby become as formidable to this State by an exercise of this power, as they could be by the Military arrangements or Civil Judiciaries. That the same reason would not apply in prohibiting the respective States from laying a Duty on Exports, as applied to that regulation being exercised by Congress: in the latter case a revenue would be drawn from the productive States to the General Treasury, to t[?] ease of the unproductive, but particular States might be desirous by this method to contribute to the support of their Local Government or for the Encouragement of their Manufactures.

3

LUTHER MARTIN, GENUINE INFORMATION
1788

Storing 2.4.73–74

In this same section there is a provision that no preference shall be given to the ports of one State over another, and that vessels bound to or from one State shall not be obliged to enter, clear, or pay duties in another. This provision, as well as that which relates to the uniformity of impost duties and excises, was introduced, Sir, by the delegation of this State.—Without such a provision, it would have been in the power of the general government to have compelled all ships sailing into, or out of the Cheseapeak, to clear and enter at Norfolk, or some port in Virginia—a regulation which would be extremely injurious to our commerce, but which would if considered merely as to the interest of the union, perhaps not be thought unreasonable, since it would render the collection of the revenue arising from commerce more certain and less expensive.

But, Sir, as the system is now reported, the general government have a *power* to *establish what ports they please in each State,* and to ascertain at what ports in every State ships shall clear and enter in such State, a power which *may* be so used as to *destroy* the *effect* of that provision, since by it may be established a port in such a place, as shall be so *inconvenient* to the State, as to render it *more eligible* for their shipping to clear and enter in *another* than in their *own State;* suppose, for instance, the general government should determine that all ships which cleared or entered in Maryland, should clear and enter at George-Town, on Potowmack, it would oblige all the ships which sailed from, or were bound to, any other port of Maryland, to clear or enter in some port in *Virginia.* To prevent such a use of the power which the general government now has of *limiting the number of ports* in a State, and *fixing the place or places where they shall be,* we endeavoured to obtain a provision, that the general government should only, in the first instance, have authority to ascertain the *number* of ports proper to be established in each State, and transmit information thereof to the several States, the legislatures of which, respectively, should have the power to fix the *places* where those ports should be, according to their idea of what would be most advantageous to the *commerce* of their State, and most for the *ease* and *convenience* of their *citizens;* and that the general government should not interfere in the establishment of the *places,* unless the legislature of the State should neglect or refuse so to do; but we could not obtain this alteration.

4

James Iredell, Proposed Amendment to the Constitution, North Carolina Ratifying Convention
1 Aug. 1788
Elliot 4:249

6. Instead of the following words in the 9th section of the 1st article, viz., "Nor shall vessels bound to or from one state be obliged to enter, clear, or pay duties, in another," [the meaning of which is by many deemed not sufficiently explicit,] it is proposed that the following shall be substituted: "No vessel bound to one state shall be obliged to enter or pay duties, to which such vessel may be liable at any port of entry, in any other state than that to which such vessel is bound; nor shall any vessel bound from one state be obliged to clear, or pay duties to which such vessel shall be liable at any port of clearance, in any other state than that from which such vessel is bound."

Article 1, Section 9, Clause 7

No Money shall be drawn from the Treasury, but in Consequence of Appropriations made by Law; and a regular Statement and Account of the Receipts and Expenditures of all public Money shall be published from time to time.

1

Records of the Federal Convention

[*1:524; Journal, 5 July*]

. . . and that no money shall be drawn from the public Treasury but in pursuance of appropriations to be originated by the first Branch.

[*1:538; Journal, 6 July*]

. . . and that no money shall be drawn from the Public Treasury but in pursuance of appropriations to be originated by the first Branch.

it passed in the affirmative [Ayes—5; noes—3; divided—3.]

[*2:14; Journal, 16 July*]

. . . and that no money shall be drawn from the Public Treasury but in pursuance of appropriations to be originated by the first Branch.

[*2:154, 164; Committee of Detail, VI, IX*]

. . . No money shall be drawn from the public Treasury, but in Pursuance of Appropriations that shall originate in the House of Representatives.

[*2:200; Madison, 13 Aug.*]

Question on the last clause of sect: 5—Art: IV—viz "No money shall be drawn from the Public Treasury, but in pursuance of *appropriations* that shall originate in the House of Reps. It passed in the negative

N. H. no. Mas. ay Con. no N. J no. Pa. no Del no. Md no Va no. N. C. no. S. C. no. Geo. no. [Ayes—1; noes—10.]

[*2:545; Journal, 8 Sept.*]

no money shall be drawn from the Treasury but in consequence of appropriations made by law.

which passed in the affirmative.

[*2:568, 596; Committee of Style*]

No money shall be drawn from the Treasury but in consequence of appropriations made by law.

[*2:618; Madison, 14 Sept.*]

Col. Mason moved a clause requiring "that an Account of the public expenditures should be annually published" Mr Gerry 2ded. the motion

Mr Govr. Morris urged that this wd. be impossible in many cases.

Mr. King remarked, that the term expenditures went to every minute shilling. This would be impracticable. Congs. might indeed make a monthly publication, but it would be in such general Statements as would afford no satisfactory information.

Mr. Madison proposed to strike out "annually" from the motion & insert "from time to time". which would enjoin the duty of frequent publications and leave enough to the discretion of the Legislature. Require too much and the difficulty will beget a habit of doing nothing. The articles of Confederation require half-yearly publications on this subject—A punctual compliance being often impossible, the practice has ceased altogether—

Mr Wilson 2ded. & supported the motion—Many operations of finance cannot be properly published at certain times.

Mr, Pinkney was in favor of the motion.

Mr. Fitzimmons—It is absolutely impossible to publish expenditures in the full extent of the term.

Mr. Sherman thought "from time to time" the best rule to be given.

"Annual" was struck out—& those words—inserted nem: con:

The motion of Col. Mason so amended was then agreed to nem: con: and added after—"appropriations by law as follows—"And a regular statement and account of the receipts & expenditures of all public money shall be published from time to time."

2

HOUSE OF REPRESENTATIVES, OFFICIAL CONDUCT OF THE SECRETARY OF THE TREASURY
28 Feb.–1 Mar. 1793

Annals 3:900–904, 911, 938–39, 963

[*28 Feb.*]

1. *Resolved,* That it is essential to the due administration of the Government of the United States, that laws making specific appropriations of money should be strictly observed by the administrator of the finances thereof.

2. *Resolved,* That a violation of a law making appropriations of money, is a violation of that section of the Constitution of the United States which requires that no money shall be drawn from the Treasury but in consequence of appropriations made by law.

3. *Resolved,* That the Secretary of the Treasury has violated the law passed the 4th of August, 1790, making appropriations of certain moneys authorized to be borrowed by the same law, in the following particulars, viz: *First,* By applying a certain portion of the principal borrowed to the payment of interest falling due upon that principal, which was not authorized by that or any other law. *Secondly,* By drawing part of the same moneys into the United States, without the instructions of the President of the United States.

4. *Resolved,* That the Secretary of the Treasury has deviated from the instructions given by the President of the United States, in exceeding the authorities for making loans under the acts of the 4th and 12th of August, 1790.

5. *Resolved,* That the Secretary of the Treasury has omitted to discharge an essential duty of his office, in failing to give Congress official information in due time, of the moneys drawn by him from Europe into the United States; which drawing commenced December, 1790, and continued till January, 1793; and of the causes of making such drafts.

6. *Resolved,* That the Secretary of the Treasury has, without the instructions of the President of the United States, drawn more moneys borrowed in Holland into the United States than the President of the United States was authorized to draw, under the act of the 12th of August, 1790: which act appropriated two millions of dollars only, when borrowed, to the purchase of the Public Debt: And that he has omitted to discharge an essential duty of his office, in failing to give official information to the Commissioners for purchasing the Public Debt, of the various sums drawn from time to time, suggested by him to have been intended for the purchase of the Public Debt.

7. *Resolved,* That the Secretary of the Treasury did not consult the public interest in negotiating a Loan with the Bank of the United States, and drawing therefrom four hundred thousand dollars, at five per cent. per annum, when a greater sum of public money was deposited in various banks at the respective periods of making the respective drafts.

8. *Resolved,* That the Secretary of the Treasury has been guilty of an indecorum to this House, in undertaking to judge of its motives in calling for information which was demandable of him, from the constitution of his office; and in failing to give all the necessary information within his knowledge, relatively to the subjects of the reference made to him of the 19th January, 1792, and of the 22d November, 1792, during the present session.

9. *Resolved,* That a copy of the foregoing resolutions be transmitted to the President of the United States.

Mr. GILES then moved that they should be referred to a Committee of the Whole House.

Mr. W. SMITH was decidedly opposed to referring those resolutions to the consideration of the Committee of the Whole House, because he neither viewed a discussion of them as necessary on the present occasion nor warranted by the nature of the inquiry into the Secretary's conduct. It was trifling with the precious time of the House to lavish it on abstract propositions, when the object of the inquiry ought to be into the facts. He was satisfied that should the House once involve itself in an investigation of theoretic principles of Government the short residue of the session would be exhausted, and no opportunity remain for examining the charges themselves. Those charges being made, it became the House from a sense of duty to the public and justice to the accused to proceed immediately to consider them. If the mover intended to apply the principles of the two first resolutions to the facts contained in the subsequent ones, it was unquestionably proper first to substantiate the facts, and then establish the principles which were applicable to them; but it was surely a reversal of order to spend much time in establishing principles, when it might happen that the charges themselves would be totally unsupported. He did not like this mode of proceeding, because it might tend to mislead the House; it was sometimes a parliamentary practice to endeavor to lead the mind to vague and uncertain results, by first laying down theorems from which no one could dissent, and then proceeding by imperceptible shades to move unsettled positions, in order ultimately to entrap the House in a vote which in the first instance it would have rejected. This mode of conducting public business, he considered as inconsistent with fair inquiry. The question was, had the Secretary violated a law? If so, let it be shown; every member was competent to decide so plain a question. He could examine the proofs, read the law, and pronounce him guilty or innocent without the aid of these preliminary metaphysical discussions.

If it were urged that the propositions are so plain and obvious that no time would be lost in considering them, he then begged leave to observe that all antecedent discussions of constitutional questions had never failed to occupy a large portion of their time, and that however self-evident the resolutions might at the first glance appear, a more critical attention would satisfy a mind not much given to doubt that they were by no means so conclusive as to be free from objections.

Though the position contained in the first resolution, as a general rule, was not to be denied; yet it must be admitted, that there may be cases of a sufficient urgency to justify a departure from it, and to make it the duty of the Legislature to indemnify an officer; as if an adherence would in particular cases, and under particular circumstances, prove ruinous to the public credit, or prevent the taking measures essential to the public safety, against invasion or insurrection. In cases of that nature, and which cannot be foreseen by the Legislature nor guarded against, a discretionary authority must be deemed to reside in the PRESIDENT, or some other Executive officer, to be exercised for the public good; such exercise instead of being construed into a crime, would always meet the approbation of the National Legislature. If there be any weight in these remarks, it does not then follow as a general rule, that it is essential to the due administration of the Government, that laws making specific appropriations should in all cases whatsoever, and under every public circumstance, be strictly observed. Before the Committee could come to a vote on such a proposition, it would be proper to examine into the exceptions out of the rule, to state all the circumstances which would warrant any departure from it, to whom the exercise of the discretion should be entrusted, and to what extent. Did any member wish at this period to attempt this inquiry? He supposed not. Let every deviation from law be tested by its own merits or demerits.

The second resolution was liable to stronger objections. It might with propriety be questioned whether, as a general rule, the position was well founded. A law making appropriations may be violated in various particulars without infringing the Constitution, which only enjoins that no moneys shall be drawn from the Treasury but in consequence of the appropriations made by law. This is only to say, that every disbursement must be authorized by some appropriation. Where a sum of money is paid out of the Treasury, the payment of which is authorized by law, the Constitution is not violated, yet there may have been a violation of the law in some collateral particulars. There may even have been a shifting of funds, and however exceptionable this may be on other accounts, it would not amount to that species of offence which is created by the Constitution. The Comptroller of the Treasurer must countersign every warrant, and is responsible that it be authorized by a legal appropriation; yet it cannot be supposed that he is to investigate the source of the fund.

One of the alleged infractions stated in the subsequent resolution, namely, the drawing part of the loans into the United States without the instructions of the PRESIDENT, evinces that the opposite construction is not a sound one. For, suppose the fact proved, and suppose it a violation of the law, it certainly would be a very different thing from drawing money out of the Treasury without an appropriation by law, for, in this case, there would be no drawing money from the Treasury at all, the money never having been in the Treasury.

Mr. S. Then said, he should also object to referring the last resolution, which is in these words,

> "*Resolved,* That a copy of the foregoing resolutions be transmitted to the PRESIDENT."

The object of this resolution went clearly to direct the PRESIDENT to remove the Secretary from office; the foregoing were to determine the guilt, the last to inflict the punishment, and both the one and other without the accused being heard in his defence. When the violation of the Constitution was so uppermost in our minds, it would be indeed astonishing that we should be so hoodwinked as to commit such a palpable violation of it in this instance. The principles of that Constitution, careful of the lives and liberties of the citizens, and what is dearer to every man of honor, his reputation, secure to every individual in every class of society, the precious advantage of being heard before he is condemned.

That Constitution, peculiarly careful of the reputation of great public functionaries, directs that when accused of a breach of duty, the impeachment must be voted by a majority of the House of Representatives, and tried by the Senate, who are to be on oath, and two thirds of whom must concur before a sentence can pass, by which the officer is to be deemed guilty. The officer is to be furnished with a copy of the charge, and is heard by himself or his counsel in vindication of his conduct. Such are the solemnities and guards by which they are protected, and which precede a sentence, the only effect of which is a removal from office. But if the House proceed in the manner contemplated by this resolution; if they first vote the charges, and send a copy of them to the PRESIDENT, as an instruction to him to remove the officer, they will violate the sacred and fundamental principles of this, and every free Government. They will condemn a man unheard, nay, without his having even been furnished with the charges against him; they will condemn to infamy a high and responsible officer convicted by the Representatives of the people, of a violation of the important trusts committed to him, without affording him one opportunity of vindicating his character and justifying his conduct.

Mr. MURRAY said he was opposed to the reference of the resolutions to the Committee of the Whole. He had, as far as the time permitted, examined the several reports on which the examination depended, and was then ready to vote on them, though he confessed, from the intricacy which was inherent in such a subject, as well as from the vast variety of the detail involved, he had not had sufficient time for a complete investigation. Nor did he imagine that any man who had not previously mediated on the subject for a length of time, and made choice of his ground of attack, could say he was completely master of the subject. Some vote, however, was now rendered essential to the character, not only of Government, but of the gentleman who presided over the finances of the country. But three days were left for this inquiry, and to finish a great deal of other business; and he thought that despatch which was usual in the House ought to be used in preference to the indulgence which a Committee afforded. As to the abstract propositions, if it were necessary now to go into them, he thought it would be proper to decide on them first. He thought it most logical to lay down principles of reasoning before facts were developed. Were they agreed to by the House, it would be under provisions and restrictions. They could not have the implicit force of axioms, but at most must be yielded to as wholesome maxims, the application of which must be frequently modified by a certain degree of discretion. With respect to all the other resolutions, he imagined they would, on examination, be found to be unwarranted by facts. He hoped the movers and supporters of the resolutions would not be gratified at so late a season by the House in resolving itself into a Committee of the Whole. The mode in which they were brought forward did not entitle them to much confidence. He said a more unhandsome proceeding he had never seen in Congress. It had been a practice, derived from the lights of common liberty, common right, and the first principles of justice, that whoever was charged with a violation of law on which a punishment ensued, should have some mode of answering to the charge. It had, in a recent instance, been the practice of Congress, when an officer's conduct was even in the first instance inquired into, to afford the officer an opportunity of attending upon the examination on which his offence or his freedom from blame was to appear. He alluded to the conduct of the House when an examination took place relatively to the failure of General St. Clair's expedition. Suspicions were entertained that blame lay somewhere. A committee was appointed to examine. The three officers particularly concerned were, he understood, invited, as it were, to come before the committee, to explain, to interrogate, and to give information. Though the Secretary of War was not permitted to explain on this floor, justice and delicacy, and the most common principles of jurisprudence, to which we attempted to hold some analogy, demanded that he should be heard somewhere, and the committee was renewed for this purpose. The Quartermaster General asked to be heard on this floor. Though refused, he was permitted to attend that committee, on whose examination his character as a Quartermaster depended. Were any man responsible as an officer to this House to fall under the suspicion of its members, a regard to decency and to the established rights of citizenship, would teach gentlemen to inquire formally before they hastily laid a charge on the table, to which they might move the assent of the House. But in this proceeding a Legislative charge was gone into before inquiry had been instituted. Every rule of justice, and all that delicacy which ought ever to attend her progress, had been disregarded, and in the very first instance, a number of charges are brought forward, not for inquiry, but conviction, which, if sanctioned by a majority of the House, are to be followed by the dismission of one of the highest officers in the Government. This mode was as tyrannical as it was new, and, if any thing could throw a bias against the resolutions, independent of inquiry, it was the partial and unjust form in which the proceeding had commenced. Resolutions of conviction might rise out of the report of a committee of inquiry, who would act as a Grand Jury to the House, but could never precede it. He hoped the House would not refer to a Committee of the Whole what might be decided in the House with more despatch.

[*1 Mar.*]

Mr. W. SMITH: . . . With respect to discretion, Mr. S. observed that, though in the present inquiry it was not necessary to say much on that topic, being firmly persuaded the Secretary had strictly pursued the injunctions of law, yet, while on the subject, he took occasion to insist that in all Governments a discretionary latitude was implied in Executive officers, where that discretion resulted from the nature of the office, or was in pursuance of general authority delegated by law. This principle was so obvious that it required no illustration; were it contradicted, he would appeal to the conduct of the Secretary of State, who, though directed to report to the House on the commerical intercourse with foreign nations, had, in the exercise of a warrantable discretion, judiciously withheld his Report. He would appeal to the Report of the Committee on the failure of St. Clair's expedition, wherein that failure was in part attributed to the Commanding General's not being invested with a discretion to act according to circumstances.

. . . . .

Mr. MADISON: . . . It was unnecessary to repeat the emphatic remarks on this subject, which had fallen from the member from Pennsylvania, [Mr. FINDLEY.] It was sufficiently understood. He concluded that appropriations of money were of a high and sacred character; that they were the great bulwark which our Constitution had carefully and jealously established against Executive usurpations. He meant only to take notice of the different plans into which appropriations might be moulded, and of the particular operation which ought to be given to them.

One the the plans was that of appropriating specified funds to specified objects, in which the supposed certainty of the funds was adjusted to the supposed importance of the objects.

The other plan formed all the branches of revenue into an aggregate fund, on which the several objects should have a priority of claim according to their superiority of importance. It was evident that in both these cases, the Legislature alone possessed the competent authority. The exclusive right of that Department of the Government to make the proper regulations, was the basis of the utility and efficacy of appropriations.

There was a third question incident to the doctrine of appropriations, viz: Whether, under specific appropriations, such as had been adopted by Congress, the Executive authority could, without special permission of the law, apply the excess of one fund to the aid of a deficient one, or borrow from one fund for the object of another. On this question, there might perhaps be a difference of opinion. He would only remark, that, admitting such a discretion to be implied in the trust of executing the laws, it would still be requisite that the due sanction of the Executive should be given, that a regular account should be kept between the different funds, and that all advances from one to the other should be replaced as soon as possible. This was equally necessary to the preservation of order in the public finances, and to the proper respect for the authority of the laws.

In the present case, it did not appear that the moneys taken at different times from the Loans designated by the PRESIDENT, and thereby placed under the appropriation of the act of August 4, 1790, to the Foreign Debt, had ever been replaced. It did not appear that any such replacement was regularly planned or provided for. It was particularly worthy of observation, moreover, that the only use within the United States for which any loan in Europe could be assigned, was that of the Sinking Fund; that the Trustees of this Fund had never been even informed of the drafts; that if the moneys drawn had been carried to the Sinking Fund, the limited sum of $2,000,000 would have been exceeded; and that the statements and accounts had, in fact, been so wound up, as mentioned by the Secretary, that not a single dollar of the money laid out in purchasing the Public Debt had been charged on loans drawn into the United States, although such was the only purpose to which they were legally applicable, and such the principal reason assigned for making the drafts.

He did not go into a particular proof that the sum drawn into the United States, after subtracting the whole sum placed to a foreign account, exceeded the sum of $2,000,000, because the fact had been conceded on the other side, particularly by the statement of the member from Connecticut, [Mr. HILLHOUSE.]

Thus it appeared clearly, in confirmation of the first point, that the application of a certain portion of the principal borrowed in Europe, to payment of the interest, was not a mere transposition of moneys, to prevent the sending them backwards or forwards, nor an advance of money from an overflowing fund in favor of a deficient one; but an absolute diversion of appropriated money, and consequently a violation of the law making the appropriation.

. . . . .

Mr. FINDLEY said: Since these resolutions were laid on the table, I have, upon reflection, been convinced of the impropriety of connecting it with the others, or of treating this part of the Secretary's conduct in this manner. It is solely in the power of this House to punish all contemptuous or indecent treatment of its authority or orders; for this purpose, it is not necessary to lay our opinions in this way before the public, report them to the PRESIDENT, or make them a foundation of impeachment. We might have ordered him to the bar of this House, and obliged him to make proper acknowledgments. I have known some high in office treated in this manner for infinitely less impropriety. It is true, in the case to which I allude, I thought the affair was carried too far; the offence was only a letter to the House respecting the conduct of a member, whom the officer charged with making free with his character in an insidious manner among the members. I would be sorry to see this House pursue such trifles. Though the indecorum of the Secretary to this House is of a higher nature, I think it is best to treat it with silent contempt; I will vote against this resolution, lest it should be interpreted as a relinquishment of our authority to punish contempts.

3

ST. GEORGE TUCKER, BLACKSTONE'S COMMENTARIES 1:APP. 362–64 1803

All the expenses of government being paid by the people, it is the right of the people, not only, not to be taxed without their own consent, or that of their representatives freely chosen, but also to be actually consulted upon the disposal of the money which they have brought into the treasury; it is therefore stipulated that no money shall be drawn from the treasury, but in consequence of appropriations, previously made by law: and, that the people may have an opportunity of judging not only of the propriety of such appropriations, but of seeing whether their money has been actually expended only, in pursuance of the same; it is further provided, that a regular statement and account of the receipts and expenditures of all public money shall be published from time to time. These provisions form a salutary check, not only upon the extravagance, and profusion, in which the executive department might otherwise indulge itself, and its adherents and dependents; but also against any misappropriation, which a rapacious, ambitious, or otherwise unfaithful executive might be disposed to make. In those governments where the people are taxed by the executive, no such check can be interposed. The prince levies whatever sums he thinks proper; disposes of them as he thinks proper; and would deem it sedition against him and his government, if any account were required of him, in what manner he had disposed of any part of them. Such is the difference between governments, where there is responsibility, and where there is none.

Yet even this excellent regulation has an inconvenience attending it, which was formerly hinted at. According to the theory of the American constitutions, the judiciary ought to be enabled to afford complete redress in all cases, where a man may have a just claim for compensation for any injury done him, or for any service which he may have rendered another, in expectation of a just recompence. According to the laws of Virginia, if a claim against the commonwealth be disallowed or abated by the auditor of public accounts, any person who may think himself aggrieved thereby may petition the high court of chancery, or the district court held at Richmond, according to the nature of his case, for redress; and such court shall proceed to do right thereon; and a like petition shall be allowed in all other cases to any person who is entitled to demand against the commonwealth any right in law or equity. But although redress is thus intended to be afforded in such cases, yet it seems to be held, that the treasurer can not pay the money for which the claiment may have obtained a judgment, or decree, until the general assembly have passed a law making an appropriation, for that purpose, if no law authorising such payment be previously passed. But whatever doubt there may be upon the subject, under the laws of the state, it seems to be altogether without a question, that no claim against the United States (by whatever authority it may be established,) can be paid, but in consequence of a previous appropriation made by law; unless, perhaps, it might be considered as falling properly under the head of contingent charges against the government. An interpretation which may be somewhat strained, and which the executive department of the government, to which the management of the fund appropriated for contingent charges is committed, might be as little disposed to admit, as congress might be to pass a law making a specific appropriation.

Both the constitution and laws of the United States appear, then, to be defective upon this subject; inasmuch, as they neither provide in what manner a just claim against the United States, which may happen to be disallowed by the auditor and comptroller of the treasury, shall be judicially examined; nor for the payment of any just claim which might be judicially established, without submitting it to the discretion of congress, whether they will make an appropriation for that purpose. As the congress are supposed, in all pecuniary cases, to have the same common interest with their constituents, they can hardly be considered in any other light than as parties, whenever a demand is made against the public. They cannot then be presumed to be altogether as impartial judges in such cases, as those who are sworn to do equal right to all persons, without distinction: and although the practice has been to petition them for any disputed claim against the United States, cases may arise where such a petition might be highly improper, and yet the nature of the case be such, as to entitle the party to obtain redress according to the dictates of moral obligation. A judicial court is, according to the true spirit of the constitution, the proper place in which such a right should be enquired into, and from which redress might be finally obtained: and that, without impediment from any other department of the government. This might be effected by an amendment, declaring, that no money shall be drawn from the treasury but in consequence of appropriations made by law; or, of a judicial sentence of a court of [the] United States.

4

Joseph Story, Commentaries on the Constitution 3:§§ 1341–43
1833

§ 1341. This clause was not in the original draft of the constitution; but the first part was subsequently introduced, upon a report of a committee; and the latter part was added at the very close of the convention.

§ 1342. The object is apparent upon the slightest examination. It is to secure regularity, punctuality, and fidelity, in the disbursements of the public money. As all the taxes raised from the people, as well as the revenues arising from other sources, are to be applied to the discharge of the expenses, and debts, and other engagements of the government, it is highly proper, that congress should possess the power to decide, how and when any money should be applied for these purposes. If it were otherwise, the executive would possess an unbounded power over the public purse of the nation; and might apply all its monied resources at his pleasure. The power to control, and direct the appropriations, constitutes a most useful and salutary check upon profusion and extravagance, as well as upon corrupt influence and public peculation. In arbitrary governments the prince levies what money he pleases from his subjects, disposes of it, as he thinks proper, and is beyond responsibility or reproof. It is wise to interpose, in a republic, every restraint, by which the public treasure, the common fund of all, should be applied, with unshrinking honesty to such objects, as legitimately belong to the common defence, and the general welfare. Congress is made the guardian of this treasure; and to make their responsibility complete and perfect, a regular account of the receipts and expenditures is required to be published, that the people may know, what money is expended, for what purposes, and by what authority.

§ 1343. A learned commentator has, however, thought, that the provision, though generally excellent, is defective in not having enabled the creditors of the government, and other persons having vested claims against it, to recover, and to be paid the amount judicially ascertained to be due to them out of the public treasury, without any appropriation. Perhaps it is a defect. And yet it is by no means certain, that evils of an opposite nature might not arise, if the debts, judicially ascertained to be due to an individual by a regular judgment, were to be paid, of course, out of the public treasury. It might give an opportunity for collusion and corruption in the management of suits between the claimant, and the officers of the government, entrusted with the performance of this duty. Undoubtedly, when a judgment has been fairly obtained, by which a debt against the government is clearly made out, it becomes the duty of congress to provide for its payment; and, generally though certainly with a tardiness, which has become, in some sort, a national reproach, this duty is discharged by congress in a spirit of just liberality. But still, the known fact, that the subject must pass in review before congress, induces a caution and integrity in making and substantiating claims, which would in a great measure be done away, if the claim were subject to no restraint, and no revision.

Article 1, Section 9, Clause 8

No Title of Nobility shall be granted by the United States: And no Person holding any Office of Profit or Trust under them, shall, without the Consent of the Congress, accept of any present, Emolument, Office, or Title, of any kind whatever, from any King, Prince or foreign State.

1

William Blackstone, Commentaries 1:153–54, 261–62 1765

The distinction of rank and honours is necessary in every well-governed state; in order to reward such as are eminent for their services to the public, in a manner the most desirable to individuals, and yet without burthen to the community; exciting thereby an ambitious yet laudable ardor, and generous emulation in others. And emulation, or virtuous ambition, is a spring of action which, however dangerous or invidious in a mere republic or under a despotic sway, will certainly be attended with good effects under a free monarchy; where, without destroying it's existence, it's excesses may be continually restrained by that superior power, from which all honour is derived. Such a spirit, when nationally diffused, gives life and vigour to the community; it sets all the wheels of government in motion, which under a wise regulator, may be directed to any beneficial purpose; and thereby every individual may be made subservient to the public good, while he principally means to promote his own particular views. A body of nobility is also more peculiarly necessary in our mixed and compounded constitution, in order to support the rights of both the crown and the people, by forming a barrier to withstand the encroachments of both. It creates and preserves that gradual scale of dignity, which proceeds from the peasant to the prince; rising like a pyramid from a broad foundation, and diminishing to a point as it rises. It is this ascending and contracting proportion that adds stability to any government; for when the departure is sudden from one extreme to another, we may pronounce that state to be precarious. The nobility therefore are the pillars, which are reared from among the people, more immediately to support the throne; and if that falls, they must also be buried under it's ruins. Accordingly, when in the last century the commons had determined to extirpate monarchy, they also voted the house of lords to be useless and dangerous. And since titles of nobility are thus expedient in the state, it is also expedient that their owners should form an independent and separate branch of the legislature. If they were confounded with the mass of the people, and like them had only a vote in electing representatives, their privileges would soon be borne down and overwhelmed by the popular torrent, which would effectually level all distinctions. It is therefore highly necessary that the body of nobles should have a distinct assembly, distinct deliberations, and distinct powers from the commons.

. . . . .

IV. The king is likewise the fountain of honour, of office, and of privilege: and this in a different sense from that wherein he is stiled the fountain of justice; for here he is really the parent of them. It is impossible that government can be maintained without a due subordination of rank; that the people may know and distinguish such as are set over them, in order to yield them their due respect and obedience; and also that the officers themselves, being encouraged by emulation and the hopes of superiority, may the better discharge their functions: and the law supposes, that no one can be so good a judge of their several merits and services, as the king himself who employs them. It has therefore intrusted with him the sole power of conferring dignities and honours, in confidence that he will bestow them upon none, but such as deserve them. And therefore all degrees of nobility, of knighthood, and other titles, are received by immediate grant from the crown: either expressed in writing, by writs or letters patent, as in the creations of peers and baronets; or by corporeal investiture, as in the creation of a simple knight.

2

Thomas Paine, Reflections on Titles
May 1775
Life 2:65–67

When I reflect on the pompous titles bestowed on unworthy men, I feel an indignity that instructs me to despise the absurdity. The *Honorable* plunderer of his country, or the *Right Honorable* murderer of mankind, create such a contrast of ideas as exhibit a monster rather than a man. Virtue is inflamed at the violation, and sober reason calls it nonsense.

Dignities and high sounding names have different effects on different beholders. The lustre of the *Star* and the title of *My Lord,* over-awe the superstitious vulgar, and forbid them to inquire into the character of the possessor: Nay more, they are, as it were, bewitched to admire in the great, the vices they would honestly condemn in themselves. This sacrifice of common sense is the certain badge which distinguishes slavery from freedom; for when men yield up the privilege of thinking, the last shadow of liberty quits the horizon.

But the reasonable freeman sees through the magic of a title, and examines the man before he approves him. To him the honors of the worthless serve to write their masters' vices in capitals, and their stars shine to no other end than to read them by. The possessors of undue honors are themselves sensible of this; for when their repeated guilt renders their persons unsafe, they disown their rank, and, like glow-worms, extinguish themselves into common reptiles, to avoid discovery. Thus Jeffries sunk into a fisherman, and his master escaped in the habit of a peasant.

Modesty forbids men, separately or collectively, to assume titles. But as all honors, even that of kings, originated from the public, the public may justly be called the fountain of true honor. And it is with much pleasure I have heard the title of *Honorable* applied to a body of men, who nobly disregarding private ease and interest for public welfare, have justly merited the address of The Honorable Continental Congress.

3

Virginia Declaration of Rights, sec. 4
12 June 1776

4. That no man, or set of men, are entitled to exclusive or separate emoluments or privileges from the community, but in consideration of publick services; which, not being descendible, neither ought the offices of magistrate, legislator, or judge, to be hereditary.

4

Benjamin Franklin to Sarah Bache
26 Jan. 1784
Writings 9:161–63, 165–66

Your Care in sending me the Newspapers is very agreable to me. I received by Capt. Barney those relating to the *Cincinnati.* My Opinion of the Institution cannot be of much Importance; I only wonder that, when the united Wisdom of our Nation had, in the Articles of Confederation, manifested their Dislike of establishing Ranks of Nobility, by Authority either of the Congress or of any particular State, a Number of private Persons should think proper to distinguish themselves and their Posterity, from their fellow Citizens, and form an Order of *hereditary Knights,* in direct Opposition to the solemnly declared Sense of their Country! I imagine it must be likewise contrary to the Good Sense of most of those drawn into it by the Persuasion of its Projectors, who have been too much struck with the Ribbands and Crosses they have seen among them hanging to the Buttonholes of Foreign Officers. And I suppose those, who disapprove of it, have not hitherto given it much Opposition, from a Principle somewhat like that of your good Mother, relating to punctilious Persons, who are always exacting little Observances of Respect; that, *"if People can be pleased with small Matters, it is a pity but they should have them."*

In this View, perhaps, I should not myself, if my Advice had been ask'd, have objected to their wearing their Ribband and Badge according to their Fancy, tho' I certainly should to the entailing it as an Honour on their Posterity. For Honour, worthily obtain'd (as for Example that of our Officers), is in its Nature a *personal* Thing, and incommunicable to any but those who had some Share in obtaining it. Thus among the Chinese, the most ancient, and from long Experience the wisest of Nations, honour does not *descend,* but *ascends.* If a man from his Learning, his Wisdom, or his Valour, is promoted by the Emperor to the Rank of Mandarin, his Parents are immediately entitled to all the same Ceremonies of Respect from the People, that are establish'd as due to the Mandarin himself; on the supposition that it must have been owing to the Education, Instruction, and good Example afforded him by his Parents, that he was rendered capable of serving the Publick.

This *ascending* Honour is therefore useful to the State, as it encourages Parents to give their Children a good and virtuous Education. But the *descending Honour,* to Posterity who could have no Share in obtaining it, is not only groundless and absurd, but often hurtful to that Posterity, since it is apt to make them proud, disdaining to be employ'd in useful Arts, and thence falling into Poverty, and all the Meannesses, Servility, and Wretchedness attending it; which is the present case with much of what is called the *Noblesse* in Europe. Or if, to keep up the Dignity of the Family, Estates are entailed entire on the Eldest male heir, another Pest to Industry and Improvement of the Country is introduc'd, which will be followed by all the odious mixture of pride and Beggary, and idleness, that have half depopulated [and *decultivated*] Spain; occasioning continual Extinction of Families by the Discouragements of Marriage [and neglect in the improvement of estates].

. . . . .

. . . I hope, therefore, that the Order will drop this part of their project, and content themselves, as the Knights of the Garter, Bath, Thistle, St. Louis, and other Orders of Europe do, with a Life Enjoyment of their little Badge and Ribband, and let the Distinction die with those who have merited it. This I imagine will give no offence. For my own part, I shall think it a Convenience, when I go into a Company where there may be Faces unknown to me, if I discover, by this Badge, the Persons who merit some particular Expression of my Respect; and it will save modest Virtue the Trouble of calling for our Regard, by awkward roundabout Intimations of having been heretofore employ'd in the Continental Service.

5

Thomas Jefferson to George Washington
16 Apr. 1784
Papers 7:105–8

I received your favor of the 8th. inst. by Colo. Harrison. The subject of it is interesting, and, so far as you have stood connected with it, has been matter of anxiety to me: because whatever may be the ultimate fate of the institution of the Cincinnati, as in it's course it draws to it some degree of disapprobation, I have wished to see you stand on ground separated from it; and that the character which will be handed to future ages at the head of our revolution may in no instance be compromitted in subordinate altercations. The subject has been at the point of my pen in every letter I have written to you; but has been still restrained by a reflection that you had among your friends more able counsellors, and in yourself one abler than them all. Your letter has now rendered a duty what was before a desire, and I cannot better merit your confidence than by a full and free communication of facts and sentiments as far as they have come within my observation.

When the army was about to be disbanded, and the officers to take final leave, perhaps never again to meet, it was natural for men who had accompanied each other through so many scenes of hardship, of difficulty and danger, who in a variety of instances must have been rendered mutually dear by those aids and good offices to which their situations had given occasion, it was natural I say for these to seize with fondness any propositions which promised to bring them together again at certain and regular periods. And this I take for granted was the origin and object of this institution: and I have no suspicion that they foresaw, much less intended those mischeifs which exist perhaps in the forebodings of politicians only. I doubt however whether in it's execution it would be found to answer the wishes of those who framed it, and to foster those friendships it was intended to preserve. The members would be brought together at their annual assemblies no longer to encounter a common enemy, but to encounter one another in debate and sentiment. Something I suppose is to be done at those meetings, and however unimportant, it will suffice to produce difference of opinion, contradiction and irritation. The way to make friends quarrel is to pit them in disputation under the public eye. An experience of near twenty years has taught me that few friendships stand this test; and that public assemblies where every one is free to speak and to act, are the most powerful looseners of the bands of private friendship. I think therefore that this institution would fail of it's principal object, the perpetuation of the personal friendships contracted thro' the war.

The objections of those opposed to the institution shall be briefly sketched; you will readily fill them up. They urge that it is against the Confederation; against the letter of some of our constitutions; against the spirit of them all, that the foundation, on which all these are built, is the natural equality of man, the denial of every preeminence but that annexed to legal office, and particularly the denial of a preeminence by birth;—that however, in their present dispositions, citizens might decline accepting honorary instalments into the order, a time may come when a change of dispositions would render these flattering; when a well directed distribution of them might draw into the order all the men of talents, of office and wealth; and in this case would probably procure an ingraftment into the government; that in this they will be supported by their foreign members, and the wishes and influence of foreign courts; that experience has shewn that the hereditary branches of modern governments are the patrons of privilege and prerogative, and not of the natural rights of the people, whose oppressors they generally are; that besides these evils which are remote, others may take place more immediately; that a distinction is kept up between the civil and military which it is for the happiness of both to obliterate; that when the members assemble they will be proposing to do something, and what that something may be will depend on actual circumstances; that being an organized body, under habits of subordination, the first obstructions to enterprize will be already surmounted; that the moderation and virtue of a single character has probably prevented this revolution from being closed as most others have been by a subversion of that liberty it was intended to establish; that he is not immortal, and his successor or some one of his successors at the head of this institution may adopt a more mistaken road to glory.

What are the sentiments of Congress on this subject, and what line they will pursue can only be stated conjecturally. Congress as a body, if left to themselves, will in my opinion say nothing on the subject. They may however be forced into a declaration by instructions from some of the states or by other incidents. Their sentiments, if forced from them, will be unfriendly to the institution. If permitted to pursue their own tract, they will check it by side blows whenever it comes in their way, and in competitions for office on equal or nearly equal ground will give silent preferences to those who are not of the fraternity. My reasons for thinking this are: 1. The grounds on which they lately declined the foreign order proposed to be conferred on some of our citizens. 2. The fourth of the fundamental articles of constitution for the new states. I inclose you the report. It has been considered by Congress, recommitted and reformed by a Committee according to the sentiments expressed on other parts of it, but the principle referred to having not been controverted at all, stands in this as in the original report. It is not yet confirmed by Congress. 3. Private conversations on this subject with the members. Since the receipt of your letter I have taken occasion to extend these; not indeed to the military members, because being of the order delicacy forbade it; but to the others pretty generally; and among these I have found but one who is not opposed to the institution, and that with an anguish of mind, tho' covered under a guarded silence, which I have not seen produced by any circumstance before. I arrived at Philadelphia before the separation of the last Congress, and saw there and at Princeton some of it's members not now in delegation. Burke's peice happened to come out at that time which occasioned this institution to be the subject of conversation. I found the same impression made on them which their successors have received. I hear from other quarters that it is disagreeable generally to such citizens as have attended to it, and therefore will probably be so to all when any circumstance shall present it to the notice of all.

This Sir is as faithful an account of sentiments and facts as I am able to give you. You know the extent of the circle within which my observations are at present circumscribed; and can estimate how far, as forming a part of the general opinion, it may merit notice, or ought to influence your particular conduct. It remains now to pay obedience to that part of your letter which requests sentiments on the most eligible measures to be pursued by the society at their next meeting. I must be far from pretending to be a judge of what would *in fact* be the most eligible measures for the society. I can only give you the opinions of those with whom I have conversed, and who, as I have before observed, are unfriendly to it. They lead to these conclusions. 1. If the society proceeds according to it's institution, it will be better to make no applications to Congress on that subject, or on any other in their associated character. 2. If they should propose to modify it so as to render it unobjectionable, I think this would not be effected without such a modification as would amount almost to annihilation; for such would it be to part with it's inheritability, it's organisation and it's assemblies. 3. If they should be disposed to discontinue the whole it would remain with them to determine whether they would chuse it to be done by their own act only, or by a reference of the matter to Congress, which would infallibly produce a recommendation of total discontinuance.

You will be sensible, Sir, that these communications are without all reserve. I supposed such to be your wish, and mean them but as materials, with such others as you may collect, for your better judgment to work on. I consider the whole matter as between ourselves alone, having determined to take no active part in this or any thing else which may lead to altercation, or disturb that quiet and tranquillity of mind to which I consign the remaining portion of my life. I have been thrown back by events on a stage where I had never more thought to appear. It is but for a time however, and as a day labourer, free to withdraw or be withdrawn at will. While I remain I shall pursue in silence the path of right; but in every situation public or private shall be gratified by all occasions of rendering you service and of convincing you there is no one to whom your reputation and happiness are dearer than to, Sir, Your most obedient & most humble servt. . . .

6

RECORDS OF THE FEDERAL CONVENTION

[*2:183; Madison, 6 Aug.*]

Sect. 7. The United States shall not grant any title of nobility.

[*2:389; Madison, 23 Aug.*]

On the question to agree to Art. VII—sect. 7. as reported It passed nem: contrad:

Mr Pinkney urged the necessity of preserving foreign Ministers & other officers of the U. S. independent of external influence and moved to insert—after Art VII sect 7. the clause following—"No person holding any office of profit or trust under the U. S. shall without the consent of the Legislature, accept of any present, emolument, office or title of any kind whatever, from any King, Prince or foreign State which passed nem: contrad.

[*2:572, 596; Committee of Style*]

Sect. 7. The United States shall not grant any title of nobility. No person holding any office of profit or trust under the United States, shall without the consent of the Legislature accept of any present, emolument, office, or title of any kind whatever, from any king, prince or foreign State.

. . . . .

(*f*) No title of nobility shall be granted by the United States. And no person holding any office of profit or trust under them, shall, without the consent of the Congress, accept of any present, emolument, office, or title, of any kind whatever, from any king, prince, or foreign state.

7

CATO, NO. 2
10 Dec. 1787
Storing 5.10.4

It is denied, and that *boldly* by my opponent, that the President would be cloathed with the robes of Royalty—Well may he deny, what has never been asserted—If Cato said that he would be possessed of Royalty, he afterwards informed the Public how he would be understood. He pointed out regal qualities with which the President would be invested, and so far he would be cloathed with Royalty. But in order to give some colour to his assertions, Maecenas has quoted Montesquieu, and shewn the shallowness of his reasoning. Truth is ever apparent, it requires no borrowed garb, no authorities to support her intrinsick grandeur; but falsehood ever resorts to what she thinks will protect, and which in the end, like an ungrateful friend, will desert her when she has most need of assistance. The proper definition of Royalty is "the administration of certain powers appertaining to the most exalted station," and whoever possesses any of these, is possessed in a greater or less degree of Royalty. But my oppugner says "that no title of nobility shall be granted by the Congress, and no person holding any office under Congress shall accept any title from any foreign King, State, or Empire." As he has given me permission, I will refer, and beg him to do so likewise, to the 9th Sect. of the 1st Art. of the resolves of the convention: where he will find there is still an opening for dignities and titles *with the consent of Congress,* which he has artfully skipped over, and forgotten to mention. When a writer of this sort steps forth, giving one half of the Text he comments upon, and suppressing the other if it be not for his purpose; are we not to conclude that his intent is more to puzzle with opposition, than to convince with fair reasoning? Are we not to imagine that his desire is more to thwart public measures, than to be actuated by generous motives to the public weal? With regard to what Cato advanced in a former paper, what was the end he had in view? Was it not proving the dangers attending the re-election of a President? Has Maecenas by his false conclusions, and badly applied arguments, weakened his reasons tending to that point? No. As waves following waves are nevertheless broken, and turned aside by the opposing rock; so have all Maecenas's arguments been foiled by truths, and his every effort rendered feeble, and ineffectual. His writing is half filled up with quotations, which prove nothing even in his own favor: And his conclusion takes away even what ground he might have gained: for it shews that he did not know what he intended to confute. And he finishes with saying, "that from what he has said, the President will have no powers, but which are essentially necessary for the executory department." Is it not distressing that I must inform this new warrior in the lists of opposition, that Cato never opposed any of the President's powers; for he saw that an officer without power, would be *corpus sine capite.* His only endeavours were to set forth those powers, in such a light: as to persuade his countrymen of the necessity of restricting the President in the enjoyment of his office. It was to that point his whole attention was bent, and there he hopes now to come off victorious. So that notwithstanding his opponents thoughtful motto, and asserting style; his solecisms and his sophistical reasoning, he has wandered from his mark, and *Parturient montes, nascetur—ridiculus mus.*

8

James Madison to Thomas Jefferson
9 May 1789
Papers 12:143

Inclosed is the Speech of the President with the Address of the House of Reps. & his reply. You will see in the caption of the address that we have pruned the ordinary stile of the degrading appendages of Excellency, Esqr. &c. and restored it to its naked dignity. *Titles* to both the President & vice President were formally & unanimously condemned by a vote of the H. of Reps. This I hope will shew to the friends of Republicanism that our new Government was not meant to substitute either Monarchy or Aristocracy, and that the genius of the people is as yet adverse to both.

9

James Madison, Title for the President, House of Representatives
11 May 1789
Papers 12:155–56

I may be well disposed to concur in opinion with gentlemen that we ought not to recede from our former vote on this subject, yet at the same time I may wish to proceed with due respect to the Senate, and give dignity and weight to our own opinion so far as it contradicts theirs by the deliberate and decent manner in which we decide. For my part, Mr. Speaker, I do not conceive titles to be so pregnant with danger as some gentlemen apprehend. I believe a President of the United States cloathed with all the powers given in the constitution would not be a dangerous person to the liberties of America, if you were to load him with all the titles of Europe or Asia. We have seen superb and august titles given without conferring power and influence or without even obtaining respect; one of the most impotent sovereigns in Europe has assumed a title as high as human invention can devise; for example, what words can imply a greater magnitude of power and strength than that of high mightiness; this title seems to border almost upon impiety; it is assuming the pre-eminence and omnipotency of the deity; yet this title and many others cast in the same mould have obtained a long time in Europe, but have they conferred power? Does experience sanctify such opinion? Look at the republic I have alluded to and say if their present state warrants the idea.

I am not afraid of titles because I fear the danger of any power they could confer, but I am against them because they are not very reconcilable with the nature of our government, or the genius of the people; even if they were proper in themselves, they are not so at this juncture of time. But my strongest objection is founded in principle; instead of encreasing they diminish the true dignity and importance of a republic, and would in particular, on this occasion, diminish the true dignity of the first magistrate himself. If we give titles, we must either borrow or invent them—if we have recourse to the fertile fields of luxuriant fancy, and deck out an airy being of our own creation, it is a great chance but its fantastic properties renders the empty fantom ridiculous and absurd. If we borrow, the servile imitation will be odious, not to say ridiculous also—we must copy from the pompous sovereigns of the east, or follow the inferior potentates of Europe; in either case, the splendid tinsel or gorgeous robe would disgrace the manly shoulders of our Chief. The more truly honorable shall we be, by shewing a total neglect and disregard to things of this nature; the more simple, the more republican we are in our manners, the more rational dignity we acquire; therefore I am better pleased with the report adopted by the house, than I should have been with any other whatsoever.

The Senate, no doubt, entertain different sentiments on this subject. I would wish therefore to treat their opinion with respect and attention. I would desire to justify the reasonable and republican decision of this house to the other branch of Congress, in order to prevent a misunderstanding. But that the motion of my worthy colleague, (Mr. Parker) has possession of the house, I would move a more temperate proposition, and I think it deserves some pains to bring about that good will and urbanity, which for the dispatch of public business, ought to be kept up between the two houses. I do not think it would be a sacrifice of dignity to appoint a committee of conference, but imagine it would tend to cement that harmony which has hitherto been preserved between the Senate and this House—therefore, while I concur with the gentlemen who express in such decided terms, their disapprobation of bestowing titles, I concur also, with those who are for the appointment of a committee of conference, not apprehending they will depart from the principles adopted and acted upon by the House.

10

Thomas Jefferson to William Temple Franklin
20 Apr. 1790
Papers 16:363

We are now about making up our minds as to the presents which it would be proper for us to give to diplomatic characters which take leave of us. For this purpose it is important to know what are given by other nations. Not foreseeing that I might ever have any thing to do with the decision of such a question, I did not inform myself of the usage even in the court with which I resided. Perhaps you may have had occasion to learn their practice, and particularly I presume you can inform me of the estimated value and the form of the present they gave Dr. Franklin on his departure. This, and any other information you can give me as to the distinction they make between different grades in their farewell presents will much oblige me.

11

William Temple Franklin to Thomas Jefferson
27 Apr. 1790
Jefferson Papers 16:364–66

I duly received the Letter Your Excellency did me the honor of writing to me the 20th Inst. The Scene of Distress in which I have been engaged, has prevented my answering it sooner: you will I know excuse it. In the Loss I have lately sustained of a valuable and dear Relation, you, Sir, have likewise lost a Friend, who held your Virtues and Talents in the highest Estimation.

You mention, as being now under Consideration, the Subject of Presents, to be given by the United States to diplomatic Characters on their taking Leave; and are desirous of knowing what is the Custom of other Nations in this respect?—In compliance with your Request I shall with Pleasure give you what Information I can on this Subject, and shall be happy if it contributes to facilitate your Determination.

The Custom of Courts in this matter formerly differ'd much, and may now in some Degree. Originally Public Ministers on their taking Leave, were conducted out of the Country, and their Expences paid, by the Sovereign at whose Court they had resided: but the Usage of making Presents has succeeded that, and is now so well establish'd, that it constitutes in a manner Part of the Law of Nations.

It is now, as far as I could learn when in Europe, an establish'd Custom, that when an Ambassador or other public Minister leaves a Court, where he has given Satisfaction by his Conduct, he receives a Testimony thereof at his Departure. And after he has had his Audience of Leave, he is presented, according to the Estimation he is in, or the Consideration entertained for his Sovereign, and sometimes also according to the Importance of the Business that has been the Object of his Embassy.

These Presents vary as to their Nature, consisting either of Jewels, Plate, Tapestry, Porcelain, and sometimes Money.—A distinction is likewise made as to the Grade of the diplomatic Character, but there is nothing absolutely fix'd as to this; for frequently the personal Respect entertained for the Negotiator, or the Importance of his Negotiations, will wave the usual Regulation that may be made as to the different Grades. This I have understood was the Case with regard to the Present made to my Grandfather on his Departure, which was more valuable than those generally given to Ministers Plenipotentiary; and was so, in consequence of the Kings saying to Count de Vergennes, who was taking his Orders on the Subject,—*"Je desire que Monsieur Franklin soit bien traité."*

I do not recollect what is the Value of the Present usually given by the Court of France, to an Ambassador taking leave, but, if I remember right that given to Ministers Plenipotentiary is about one thousand Louis d'ors. Mr. Lee and Mr. Deane, when they left the Court of France, where they had resided as *Commissioners,* received each of them a Present, estimated at about three hundred Louis d'ors.

The Present to my Grandfather was supposed to be worth fifteen hundred Louis d'ors, and consisted in a large Miniature of the King, set with four hundred and eight Diamonds, of a beautiful Water, forming a Wreath round the Picture and a Crown on the Top. This is the form of the Presents usually given to Ambassadors and Ministers Plenipotentiary, tho' of more or less value.—I had an Opportunity of seeing several given by the King of France, and some by other Princes, and they were generally in the form above mentioned. The Presents to our Commissioners Lee and Dean, consisted, if I am not mistaken, in a Gold Snuff-Box, curiously enamell'd, with a Miniature of the King or Queen, set round with Diamonds.

It is the Custom when a diplomatic Character, has received his Present, to make a Present to the Introductor, and his Assistant, and he is guided therein by the Value of the Present he receives. My Grandfather I think, gave the Introductor a gold enamel'd Snuff-Box of about one hundred and fifty Louis d'ors value: and understanding that it would be more agreable to his Assistant, M. de Sequeville, to receive his Present in Money, he sent him a *Rouleau* of Fifty Louis d'ors.

Thus I have, I believe, answer'd the different Queries your Excellency has been pleas'd to put to me: what Conduct it may be proper for the United States to adopt in this Business you are the best Judge: as we do not deal much in Jewels or Gold, perhaps a Tract of Land, or a present of valuable Furrs might answer the Purpose.

Tho it does not come immediately under this Subject, permit me to suggest, that in the Bill, about to be pass'd, providing for Persons the United States may employ abroad; some additional Allowance ought to be made them, in order to commence their Establishment, otherwise, Furniture, Plate, Table Linnen, Carriages, Horses and Liveries, will entirely consume their first Year's Salary. This Allowance is usual in other Countries. . . .

Dr. Franklin, Silas Deane, Dr. Lee } Recieved each a gold snuff box with the king's pictures set in briliants in the lid. On signing the treaty with France. Dr. Lee on his return consulted Congress whether he should return the present. They decided negatively and this formed the subsequent rule.

Dr. Franklin recieved a present on taking leave as Minister Plenipotiary in France.

Mr. Jay recieved a present as Minister Plenipotiary to Spain.

Mr. Adams recieved a gold medal and chain from the United Netherlands on taking leave.

Mr. Adams recieved the accustomary present on taking leave of the court of St. James.

Th: J. recieved on taking leave as Minister Plenipotiary to France a miniature picture of the king set in brilliants estimated at about 360. Louis. He gave presents according to usage to certain officers of the court of about 80. Louis.

The above appointments were all under the old Congress, and comprehended every instance of resident appointments under them. No present was recieved on the Prussian treaty. I never heard whether there was on the Swedish and Dutch treaties.

12

St. George Tucker, Blackstone's Commentaries 1:App. 216–22, 295–96 1803

---

1. As to the necessity of a distinct order of men in a state, with exclusive privileges annexed to the individual capacity, the author of the commentaries observes, "That the distinction of rank and honours is necessary in every well governed state, in order to reward such as are eminent for their public services, in a manner the most desirable to individuals, and yet without burthen to the community; exciting thereby an ambitious, yet laudable ardor, and generous emulation, in others. A spring of action, which however dangerous or invidious in a mere republic, will certainly be attended with good effects under a monarchy. And since titles of nobility are thus expedient in the state, it is also expedient that their owners should form an independent and separate branch of the legislature. If they were confounded with the mass of the people, and like them only had a vote in electing representatives their privileges would soon be borne down and overwhelmed by the popular torrent, which would effectually level all distinctions."

The conclusion which evidently arises from the former part of this quotation, "that no mere republic can ever be a well governed state," inasmuch as honours and titles, the necessity of which, is here so pointedly urged, are dangerous and invidious in such a government, may be proved to be false, both from reasoning and example. But it will be time enough to controvert our author's conclusion, when the truth of the principle upon which it is founded is established. The British constitution, with him, is somewhat like the bed of *Procrustes;* principles must be limited, extended, narrowed, or enlarged, to fit it. If they are not susceptible of so convenient a modification, they are to be wholly rejected. . . . But to return:

The vital principle of mixt governments is the distinction of orders, possessing, both collectively and individually, different rights, privileges or prerogatives. In an absolute monarchy, a confirmed aristocracy, or a pure democracy, this distinction cannot be found. There being no distinction of orders, there can be no contention about rights, in either of these forms of government, so long as the government remains in the full vigour of its constitution. When either of these three forms of government departs from its intrinsic nature, unless it assumes one of the other instead thereof, it becomes a mixt government. . . . And this mixture may consist in the combination of monarchy with aristocracy, as in Poland; or with democracy, as in France, under it's late constitution, as modelled by the national assembly, and ratified by the king; or, in the blending of the aristocratic and democratic forms, as was the case with the Roman republic after the establishment of the tribunes; or of all three, as in the British constitution. The existence of either of these combinations are said to form the constitution of the state, in all the governments of the world, except those of America, and France under it's late constitution; in these the constitution creates the powers that exist: In all others, the existing powers determine the nature of the constitution. To preserve those existing powers in their full tone and vigour, respectively, it may be necessary that each should possess an independent share in the supreme legislature, for the reasons assigned by the author of the commentaries; but this no more proves the necessity of the order, in a well governed state, than the necessity of wings to the human body would be proved, by a critical dissertation, on the structure, size, and position, of those of the fabulous deities of antiquity.

Our author considers those rewards which constitute a separate order of men, as attended with no burthen to the community; nothing can be more false than such a supposition. If the distinction be personal, only, it must be created at the expence of the personal degradation of the rest of the community, during the life of the distinguished person. If hereditary, this degradation is entailed upon the people: personal distinctions cannot be supported without power, or without wealth; these are the true supporters of the arms of nobility; take them away, the shield falls to the ground, and the pageantry of heraldry is trodden under foot. What character is less respected in England, than a poor Scotch lord, who is not one of the sixteen peers of that kingdom? That lord in his own clan, possesses comparative wealth and power sufficient among his humble dependents, to be looked up to as a Craesus in wealth, and a Caesar in authority.

"A titled nobility," says a late distinguished English writer [Mackintosh], "is the most undisputed progeny of feudal barbarism. Titles had in all nations denoted offices; it was reserved for Gothic Europe, to attach them to ranks. Yet this conduct admits explanation, for with them offices were hereditary, and hence the titles denoting them became hereditary too. These distinctions only serve to unfit the nobility for obedience, and the people for freedom; to keep alive the discontent of the one and to perpetuate the servility of the other; to deprive the one of the moderation that sinks them into citizens, and to rob the other of the spirit that exalts them into freemen. The possession of honours by the multitude, who have inherited, but not acquired them, engrosses and depreciates these incentives and rewards of virtue." If these are the genuine fruits of that laudable ardour, and generous emulation, which give life and vigour to the community, and sets all the wheels of government in motion, heaven protect those whom it encounters in it's progress.

But is there no stimulous to that laudable ardour and generous emulation which the commentator speaks of, to be found in a pure democracy, which may compensate for the absence of ranks and honors? Yes. Virtue; that principle which actuated the Bruti, a Camillus, and a Cato in the Roman republic, a Timoleon, an Aristides, and an Epaminondas among the Greeks, with thousands of their fellow citizens whose names are scarcely yet lost in the wreck of time. That principle whose operation we have seen in our own days and in our own country, and of which, examples will be quoted by posterity so long as the remembrance of American liberty shall continue among men. . . . "Virtue," says Montesquieu, "in a republic is a most simple thing; it is a love of the republic. Love of the republic in a democracy is a love of the democracy: love of the democracy is that of equality. The love of equality in a democracy limits ambition to the sole desire, to the sole happiness, of doing greater services to our own country than the rest of our fellow citizens. . . . But all cannot render equal services: hence distinctions arise here from the principle of equality, even when it seems to be removed, by signal services, or superior abilities."

This distinction, the only one which is reconcileable to the genius and principle of a pure republic, is, if we may reason from effect to cause, the most powerful incentive to good government that can animate the human heart, with this advantage over those hereditary honors for which the commentator is so zealous an advocate, that the ambition excited by the former must of necessity be directed to the public good, whilst the latter springing from self love, alone, may exist in the breast of a Caesar or a Cataline. A Franklin, or a Washington, need not the pageantry of honours, the glare of titles, nor the pre-eminence of station to distinguish them. Their heads like the mountain pine are seen above the surrounding trees of the forest, but their roots engross not a larger portion of the soil.

Equality of rights, in like manner, precludes not that distinction which superiority in virtue introduces among the citizens of a republic. Washington in retirement was equal, and only equal, in rights, to the poorest citizen of the state. Yet in the midst of that retirement the elevation of his character was superior to that of any prince in the universe, and the lustre of it far transcended the brightest diadem.

But even where it conceded that distinctions of rank and honours were necessary to good government, it would by no means follow that they should be hereditary; the same laudable ardour which leads to the acquisition of honor, is not necessary to the preservation of its badges; and these are all which it's hereditary possessors, in general, regard. Had nature in her operations shewn that the same vigour of mind and activity of virtue which manifests itself in a father, descends unimpaired to his son, and from him to latest posterity, in the same order of succession, that his estate may be limited to, some appearance of reason in favour of hereditary rank and honors might have been offered. But nature in every place, and in every age, has contradicted, and still contradicts this theory. The sons of Junius Brutus were traitors to the republic; the emperor Commodus was the son of Antoninus the philosopher; and Domitian was at once the son of Vespasian, and the brother of Titus.

If what has been said be a sufficient answer to the necessity of the distinction of ranks and honours to the well government of a state, the commentator himself hath afforded an unanswerable argument against their expedience in a republic, by acknowledging them to be both dangerous and invidious in such a government. And herewith agrees the author of the Spirit of Laws, who informs us, that the principle of a democracy is corrupted, when the spirit of equality is extinct. The same admirable writer gives us a further reason why so heterogeneous a mixture ought not to have a place in any government where the freedom and happiness of the people is thought an object worthy the attention of the government. "A nobility," says he, "think it an honour to obey a king, but consider it as the lowest infamy to share the power with the people."

We are indebted to the same author, for the following distinguished features of aristocracy: "If the reigning families observe the laws, aristocracy is a monarchy with several monarchs: but when they do not observe them, it is a despotic state governed by a great many despotic princes. In this case, the republic consists only in respect to the nobles, and among them only. It is in the governing body; and the despotic state is in the body governed. The extremity of corruption is when the power of the nobles becomes hereditary; they can hardly then have any moderation." Such is the picture of that order of men who are elevated above the people by the distinctions of rank and honours. When the subjects of a monarchy, they are the pillars of the throne, as the commentator stiles them; or, according to Montesquieu, the tools of the monarch. . . . When rulers, as in an aristocracy, they are the despots of the people. . . . In a mixed government, they are the political Janizaries of the state, supporting and insulting the throne by turns, but still threatening and enslaving the people.

In America the senate are not a distinct order of individuals, but, the second branch of the national legislature, taken collectively. They have no privileges, but such as are common to the members of the house of representatives, and of the several state legislatures: we have seen that these privileges extend only to an exemption from personal arrests, in certain cases, and that it is utterly lost, in cases of treason, felony, or breach of the peace. They are more properly the privileges of the constituents, than of the members, since it is possible that a state might have no representative, and the United States no legislature, if the members might be restrained from attending their duty, by process issued at the suit of a creditor, or other person who might suppose he had cause of action against them. In England the privileges of the peerage are in some instances an insult to the morals of the people, the honour of a peer, on several occasions, being equipollent with the oath of a commoner. The exemption from personal arrests in civil cases is extended as well to his servant, as to the lord of parliament; to the injury of creditors, and the no small encouragement of fraud and knavery. And the statutes of *scandalum magnatum* hang *in terrorem* over the heads of those who dare to scrutinize, or to question the reality of those superior endowments which the law ascribes, to the immaculate character of a peer or peeress of the realm. Happy for America that her constitution and the genius of her people, equally secure her against the introduction of such a pernicious and destructive class of men.

. . . . .

The first of these prohibitions was indispensably necessary to preserve the several states in their democratic form, tone, and vigour. Distinctions between the citizens of the same state, are utterly incompatible with the principles of such governments. Their admission, therefore, can not be too cautiously guarded against: and their total exclusion seems to be the only mode by which this caution can operated effectually. We have already noticed, that the several acts passed for establishing an uniform rule of naturalization, require of every alien becoming a citizen, of the United States, an absolute renunciation, on oath, of any title of nobility, which he might have borne under any other prince or state. Without this wise provision, this clause of the constitution might have failed of some of those salutary effects which it was intended to produce. The second prohibition is not less important. Corruption is too subtle a poison to be approached, without injury. Nothing can be more dangerous to any state, than influence from without, because it must be invariably bottomed upon corruption within. Presents, pensions, titles and offices are alluring things. In the reign of Charles the second of England, that prince, and almost all his officers of state were either actual pensioners of the court of France, or supposed to be under its influence, directly, or indirectly, from that cause. The reign of that monarch has been, accordingly, proverbially disgraceful to his memory. The economy which ought to prevail in republican governments, with respects to salaries and other emoluments of office, might encourage the offer of presents from abroad, if the constitution and laws did not reprobate their acceptance. Congress, with great propriety, refused their assent to one of their ministers to a foreign court, accepting, what was called the usual presents, upon taking his leave: a precedent which we may reasonably hope will be remembered by all *future* ministers, and ensure a proper respect to this clause of the constitution, which on a former occasion is said to have been overlooked.

13

Thomas Jefferson to John Adams
28 Oct. 1813

Cappon 2:389–92

It is probable that our difference of opinion may in some measure be produced by a difference of character in those among whom we live. From what I have seen of Massachusets and Connecticut myself, and still more from what I have heard, and the character given of the former by yourself, who know them so much better, there seems to be in those two states a traditionary reverence for certain families, which has rendered the offices of the government nearly hereditary in those families. I presume that from an early period of your history, members of these families happening to possess virtue and talents, have honestly exercised them for the good of the people, and by their services have endeared their names to them.

In coupling Connecticut with you, I mean it politically only, not morally. For having made the Bible the Common law of their land they seem to have modelled their morality on the story of Jacob and Laban. But altho' this hereditary succession to office with you may in some degree be founded in real family merit, yet in a much higher degree it has proceeded from your strict alliance of church and state. These families are canonised in the eyes of the people on the common principle 'you tickle me, and I will tickle you.' In Virginia we have nothing of this. Our clergy, before the revolution, having been secured against rivalship by fixed salaries, did not give themselves the trouble of acquiring influence over the people. Of wealth, there were great accumulations in particular families, handed down from generation to generation under the English law of entails. But the only object of ambition for the wealthy was a seat in the king's council. All their court then was paid to the crown and it's creatures; and they Philipised in all collisions between the king and people. Hence they were unpopular; and that unpopularity continues attached to their names. A Randolph, a Carter, or a Burwell must have great personal superiority over a common competitor to be elected by the people, even at this day.

At the first session of our legislature after the Declaration of Independance, we passed a law abolishing entails. And this was followed by one abolishing the privilege of Primogeniture, and dividing the lands of intestates equally among all their children, or other representatives. These laws, drawn by myself, laid the axe to the root of Pseudo-aristocracy. And had another which I prepared been adopted by the legislature, our work would have been compleat. It was a Bill for the more general diffusion of learning. This proposed to divide every county into wards of 5. or 6. miles square, like your townships; to establish in each ward a free school for reading, writing and common arithmetic; to provide for the annual selection of the best subjects from these schools who might receive at the public expence a higher degree of education at a district school; and from these district schools to select a certain number of the most promising subjects to be compleated at an University, where all the useful sciences should be taught. Worth and genius would thus have been sought out from every condition of life, and compleatly prepared by education for defeating the competition of wealth and birth for public trusts.

My proposition had for a further object to impart to these wards those portions of self-government for which they are best qualitifed, by confiding to them the care of their poor, their roads, police, elections, the nomination of jurors, administration of justice in small cases, elementary exercises of militia, in short, to have made them little republics, with a Warden at the head of each, for all those concerns which, being under their eye, they would better manage than the larger republics of the county or state. A general call of ward-meetings by their Wardens on the same day thro' the state would at any time produce the genuine sense of the people on any required point, and would enable the state to act in mass, as your people have so often done, and with so much effect, by their town meetings. The law for religious freedom, which made a part of this system, having put down the aristocracy of the clergy, and restored to the citizen the freedom of the mind, and those of entails and descents nurturing an equality of condition among them, this on Education would have raised the mass of the people to the high ground of moral respectability necessary to their own safety, and to orderly government; and would have compleated the great object of qualifying them to select the veritable aristoi, for the trusts of government, to the exclusion of the Pseudalists: and the same Theognis who has furnished the epigraphs of your two letters assures us that ουδεμιαν πω, Κυρν' ἀγαθοι πολιν ὤλεσαν ἀνδρες ["Curnis, good men have never harmed any city"]. Altho' this law has not yet been acted on but in a small and inefficient degree, it is still considered as before the legislature, with other bills of the revised code, not yet taken up, and I have great hope that some patriotic spirit will, at a favorable moment, call it up, and make it the key-stone of the arch of our government.

With respect to Aristocracy, we should further consider that, before the establishment of the American states, nothing was known to History but the Man of the old world, crouded within limits either small or overcharged, and steeped in the vices which that situation generates. A government adapted to such men would be one thing; but a very different one that for the Man of these states. Here every one may have land to labor for himself if he chuses; or, preferring the exercise of any other industry, may exact for it such compensation as not only to afford a comfortable subsistence, but wherewith to provide for a cessation from labor in old age. Every one, by his property, or by his satisfactory situation, is interested in the support of law and order. And such men may safely and advantageously reserve to themselves a wholsome controul over their public affairs, and a degree of freedom, which in the hands of the Canaille of the cities of Europe, would be instantly perverted to the demolition and destruction of every thing public and private. The history of the last 25. years of France, and of the last 40. years in America, nay of it's last 200. years, proves the truth of both parts of this observation.

But even in Europe a change has sensibly taken place in the mind of Man. Science had liberated the ideas of those who read and reflect, and the American example had kindled feelings of right in the people. An insurrection has consequently begun, of science, talents and courage against rank and birth, which have fallen into contempt. It has failed in it's first effort, because the mobs of the cities, the instrument used for it's accomplishment, debased by ignorance, poverty and vice, could not be restrained to rational action. But the world will recover from the panic of this first catastrophe. Science is progressive, and talents and enterprize on the alert. Resort may be had to the people of the country, a more governable power from their principles and subordination; and rank, and birth, and tinsel-aristocracy will finally shrink into insignificance, even there. This however we have no right to meddle with. It suffices for us, if the moral and physical condition of our own citizens qualifies them to select the able and good for the direction of their government, with a recurrence of elections at such short periods as will enable them to displace an unfaithful servant before the mischief he meditates may be irremediable.

I have thus stated my opinion on a point on which we differ, not with a view to controversy, for we are both too old to change opinions which are the result of a long life of inquiry and reflection; but on the suggestion of a former letter of yours, that we ought not to die before we have explained ourselves to each other. . . .

Of the pamphlet on aristocracy which has been sent to you, or who may be it's author, I have heard nothing but thro' your letter. If the person you suspect it may be known from the quaint, mystical and hyperbolical ideas, involved in affected, new-fangled and pedantic terms, which stamp his writings. Whatever it be, I hope your quiet is not to be affected at this day by the rudeness of intemperance of scribblers; but that you may continue in tranquility to live and to rejoice in the prosperity of our country until it shall be your own wish to take your seat among the Aristoi who have gone before you. Ever and affectionately yours.

14

WILLIAM RAWLE, A VIEW OF THE CONSTITUTION OF THE UNITED STATES 119–20 1829 (2d ed.)

No title of nobility shall be granted by the United States, or by any individual state. Of this there could have been but little danger. The independent spirit of republicans leads them to contemn the vanity of hereditary distinctions, but the residue of the clause is more important. *No person holding any office of trust or profit under the United States shall, without the consent of congress, accept of any present, emolument, office, or title of any kind whatever, from any king, prince, or foreign state.*

There cannot be too much jealousy in respect to foreign influence. The treasures of Persia were successfully distributed in Athens; and it is now known that in England a profligate prince and many of his venal courtiers were bribed into measures injurious to the nation by the gold of Louis XIV.

A salutary amendment, extending the prohibition to all citizens of the United States, and disfranchising those who infringe it, has been adopted by some of the states; but not yet by a sufficient number. The clause in the text is defective in not providing a specific penalty for a breach of it. Disfranchisement, or a deprivation of all the rights of a citizen, seems the most appropriate punishment that could be applied, since it renders the seduction useless to those who were the authors of it, and disgraceful to the person seduced.

15

Joseph Story, Commentaries on the Constitution 3:§§ 1345–46 1833

§ 1345. This clause seems scarcely to require even a passing notice. As a perfect equality is the basis of all our institutions, state and national, the prohibition against the creation of any titles of nobility seems proper, if not indispensable, to keep perpetually alive a just sense of this important truth. Distinctions between citizens, in regard to rank, would soon lay the foundation of odious claims and privileges, and silently subvert the spirit of independence and personal dignity, which are so often proclaimed to be the best security of a republican government.

§ 1346. The other clause, as to the acceptance of any emoluments, title, or office, from foreign governments, is founded in a just jealousy of foreign influence of every sort. Whether, in a practical sense, it can produce much effect, has been thought doubtful. A patriot will not be likely to be seduced from his duties to his country by the acceptance of any title, or present, from a foreign power. An intriguing, or corrupt agent, will not be restrained from guilty machinations in the service of a foreign state by such constitutional restrictions. Still, however, the provision is highly important, as it puts it out of the power of any officer of the government to wear borrowed honours, which shall enhance his supposed importance abroad by a titular dignity at home. It is singular, that there should not have been, for the same object, a general prohibition against any citizen whatever, whether in private or public life, accepting any foreign title of nobility. An amendment for this purpose has been recommended by congress; but, as yet, it has not received the ratification of the constitutional number of states to make it obligatory, probably from a growing sense, that it is wholly unnecessary.

SEE ALSO:

A Letter, 24 Oct. 1787, Storing 4.2.10
Federal Farmer, no. 16, 20 Jan. 1787, Storing 2.8.198
House of Representatives, Titles for President and Vice-President, 5 May 1789, Annals 1:247
Benjamin Rush to John Adams, 4 June 1789, Letters 1:514
Benjamin Rush to John Adams, 21 July 1789, Letters 1:523–24
Walter Jones to James Madison, 25 July 1789, Madison Papers 12:307–8
John Adams to Benjamin Rush, 5 July 1789, Old Family Letters 1:41–43; 24 July 1789, 1:44–47; 28 July 1789, 1:47–49

Article 1, Section 10, Clause 1

No State shall enter into any Treaty, Alliance, or Confederation; grant Letters of Marque and Reprisal; coin Money; emit Bills of Credit; make any Thing but gold and silver Coin a Tender in Payment of Debts; pass any Bill of Attainder, ex post facto Law, or Law impairing the Obligation of Contracts, or grant any Title of Nobility.

1

Deering v. Parker

4 Dall. App. xxiii (P.C. 1760)

This was an appeal from New Hampshire, heard before a Committee of the Privy Council (Lord Mansfield being one of them), on the 10th of July 1760. The facts were these: One Parker had given a bond to Deering, payable the 30th of July 1735, conditioned for the payment of 2460*l.*, "in good public bills of the province of Massachusetts Bay, or current lawful money of New England, with interest." There had been many payments made and indorsed. About the year 1752, the defendant tendered a large sum, in the bills of credit then current in New Hampshire, which the plaintiff refused, brought his action, and recovered judgment for the penalty in the bond, upon the verdict of a jury, in December 1758. After which, the cause was heard in the Chancery of New Hampshire, and the court decreed for the sum of 354*l.* 6*s.* 9*d.*, in bills of credit of New Hampshire, new tenor, being the nominal sum due at the time of the tender, deducting the sums paid and indorsed. So that the court went upon the principle, that the plaintiff should take the bills as tendered, and that the debtor was not bound to make good their depreciation, nor to pay in silver, or real money.

On the side of the *appellant,* or creditor, it was insisted, that the payment ought either to have been in bills of Massachusetts Bay (which, it seems, were all called in, and sunk, before the tender), or in silver money, agreeable to queen Anne's proclamation, which, they insisted, was the true meaning of that clause or part of the condition, to wit, current lawful money of New England. It was also claimed by him to have all the sums indorsed, reduced in nominal sums down to the value of silver at the time of giving the bond, to wit, 27*s.* per ounce.

On the side of the *respondent,* or debtor, it was urged, that current money of New England then meant, and was understood to be, indifferently, the bills of credit of any or either of the New England colonies, received in that colony in payments. That, therefore, the tender was in the specie contracted for, and that the sums indorsed were not only, of course, upon that supposition, equal to the sums expressed; but that the creditor, by indorsing, had agreed to and accepted of so much as the same expressed, in real as well as nominal sums.

The LORD PRESIDENT and LORD MANSFIELD expressed themselves fully in favor of the creditor's construction of the words, "current lawful money of New England;" to wit, that it did not mean bills of credit of any colony, but the words were put in contradistinction thereto. Lord MANSFIELD further added, that he was clear, on the one hand, that the sums indorsed ought to be allowed according to the nominal sums so indorsed, equal to the same sums of money mentioned in the bond, and that the plaintiff had no right to have the same any way reduced or altered. On the other hand, his lordship thought that the tender was not good in any respect; for not only because it was made in a species of currency, different from that contracted for; but also because it was out of time, being many years after the time of payment was lapsed, and also without notice. "What (said his lordship), shall a man meet his creditor in the street unawares, and tender a debt to him? The chancery allows six months' notice of time and place to be given. The law of the province enabling the court to turn itself into a court of equity, and to reduce the bond to the sum due by the *auditem,* was a very good thing; and what Sir Thomas Moore, in his time, labored so hard to obtain an act of parliament for here. And because the judges (with whom he had several conferences about the matter) were for retaining the old artificial way, he declared, that he would always grant injunctions in such cases. In the present case (his lordship continued), he was at no loss to determine, that the judgment ought to be reversed: but he was at a loss what rule to go by, in determining the *quantum* of the debt. Since the province bills contracted for were called in and gone; with a desire to know the usage, he had inquired of Mr. I., a New England gentleman (who had practised the law), and was informed, that "when old tenor had been contracted for, it had been allowed to be tendered, although depreciated in value, if the tender was made in season. That towards the close of existence of old tenor, and after it had been called in and sunk, when judgment was given for real money, this matter (of how much to give) was greatly agitated. Some were for giving the value of the old tenor, or bills contracted for, as it stood when the obligation was out, or the debt became due. Others would have it settled, as it was when at the last and worst period; and others again, were for taking a medium. But the more general method was, to take the value of the bills, when they should have been paid by the contract." Lord MANSFIELD observed, that from this information, he had received much light, and was relieved from his difficulty. That much might be said, for taking as a rule the value of the old tenor, at the time set by the bond for payment. That, upon the mention of it, it struck him as the rule of right in general: but that, in the present case, the bond had been outstanding so very long, the bills of credit, which were the currency of the country, had, in the meantime, sunk gradually, and became, in some measure, every one's loss: and that, therefore, in this case, he thought the loss ought to be divided between them.

The Board, upon the whole, instead of taking the price of silver at the time of the contract, and time set for the payment (which was about 27*s.* per ounce), fixed it at 37*s.* per ounce, and computed the debt accordingly. This made about 100*l.* sterling in favor of the appellant, by which he got the opinion of the court in his favor; but as no costs are allowed upon appeal, he could not be much a gainer by the general result.

2

JAMES MADISON, NOTES FOR SPEECH OPPOSING PAPER MONEY 1 Nov. 1786

Papers 9:158–59

Agst. Paper money. Novr. 1786 Virg: Assy.

Unequal to specie. 1. being redemble at future day and not bearing interest. 2. illustrated by tax of Bank notes—Stock in funds—paper of Spain issued during late war [see Neckar on finance] Navy bills—tallies. 3. being of less *use* than specie which answers externally as well as internally—must be of less *value,* which depends on the use.

Unjust. 1. to Creditors if a legal tender. 2 to debtors if not legal tender, by increasing difficulty of getting specie. This it does by increasing extravagance & unfavorable balance of trade—& by destroying that confidence between man & man, by which resources of one may be commanded by another—3 illustrated 1. by raising denomination of coin 2. increasing alloy of do. brass made as silver by the Romans according to Sallust—3 by changing weights & measures. 4. by case of Creditors within who are dbtors without the State

Unconstitutional 1. affects Rights of property as much as taking away equal value in land: illustrd. by case of land pd. for down & to be conveyd. in future, & of a law permitting conveyance to be satisfied by conveying a part only—or other land of inferior quality—2. affects property without trial by Jury.

Antifederal. Right of regulating coin given to Congs. for two reasons. 1. for sake of uniformity. 2. to prevent fraud in States towards each other or foreigners. Both these reasons hold equally as to paper money.

Unnecessary. 1. Produce of Country will bring in specie, if not laid out in superfluities., 2. of paper, if necessary, eno' already in Tobo. notes, & public securities—3. the true mode of giving value to these, and bringing in specie is to enforce Justice & taxes.

Pernicious. 1. by fostering luxury, extends instead of curing scarcity of specie—2. by disabling compliance with requisition of Congs. 3. serving dissentions between States. 4. destroyg. confidence between individuals. 5. discouraging commerce—6 enrichg collectors & sharpers—7 vitiating morals—8 reversing end of Govt. which is to reward best & punish worst. 9. conspiring with the examples of other States to disgrace Republican Govts. in the eyes of mankind.

Objection. paper money good before the War.

Answr. 1. not true in N. Engd. nor in Va. where exchange rose to 60 per Ct. nor in Maryd. see Franklyn on paper money 2. confidence then not now—3. principles of paper credit not then understood—Such wd. not then, nor now succeed in Great Britain &c.

3

Records of the Federal Convention

[*2:439; Madison, 28 Aug.*]

Art: XII being taken up.

Mr. Wilson & Mr. Sherman moved to insert after the words "coin money" the words "nor emit bills of credit, nor make any thing but gold & silver coin a tender in payment of debts" making these prohibitions absolute, instead of making the measures allowable (as in the XIII art:) *with the consent of the Legislature of the U. S.*

Mr. Ghorum thought the purpose would be as well secured by the provision of art: XIII which makes the consent of the Genl. Legislature necessary, and that in that mode, no opposition would be excited; whereas an absolute prohibition of paper money would rouse the most desperate opposition from its partizans—

Mr. Sherman thought this a favorable crisis for crushing paper money. If the consent of the Legislature could authorize emissions of it, the friends of paper money would make every exertion to get into the Legislature in order to license it.

The question being divided; on the 1st part—"nor emit bills of credit"

N. H. ay. Mas. ay. Ct. ay. Pa. ay— Del. ay. Md divd. Va. no. N— C— ay— S— C. ay. Geo. ay. [Ayes—8; noes—1; divided—1.]

The remaining part of Mr. Wilson's & Sherman's motion, was agreed to nem: con:

Mr King moved to add, in the words used in the Ordinance of Congs establishing new States, a prohibition on the States to interfere in private contracts.

Mr. Govr. Morris. This would be going too far. There are a thousand laws relating to bringing actions—limitations of actions & which affect contracts— The Judicial power of the U— S— will be a protection in cases within their jurisdiction; and within the State itself a majority must rule, whatever may be the mischief done among themselves.

Mr. Sherman. Why then prohibit bills of credit?

Mr. Wilson was in favor of Mr. King's motion.

Mr. Madison admitted that inconveniences might arise from such a prohibition but thought on the whole it would be overbalanced by the utility of it. He conceived however that a negative on the State laws could alone secure the effect. Evasions might and would be devised by the ingenuity of the Legislatures—

Col: Mason. This is carrying the restraint too far. Cases will happen that can not be foreseen, where some kind of interference will be proper, & essential— He mentioned the case of limiting the period for bringing actions on open account—that of bonds after a certain lapse of time,—asking whether it was proper to tie the hands of the States from making provision in such cases?

Mr. Wilson. The answer to these objections is that *retrospective* interferences only are to be prohibited.

Mr. Madison. Is not that already done by the prohibition of ex post facto laws, which will oblige the Judges to declare such interferences null & void.

Mr. Rutlidge moved instead of Mr. King's Motion to insert—"nor pass bills of attainder nor retrospective laws" on which motion

N. H. ay— Ct. no. N. J. ay. Pa. ay. Del. ay. Md. no. Virga. no. N— C. ay. S. C. ay. Geo. ay. [Ayes—7; noes—3.]

[*2:448; Madison, 29 Aug.*]

Mr. Dickenson mentioned to the House that on examining Blackstone's Commentaries, he found that the terms "ex post facto" related to criminal cases only; that they would not consequently restrain the States from retrospective laws in civil cases, and that some further provision for this purpose would be requisite.

[*2:619; Madison, 14 Sept.*]

The first clause of Art I. sect 10—was altered so as to read—"No State shall enter into any Treaty alliance or confederation; grant letters of marque and reprisal; coin money; emit bills of credit; make any thing but gold & silver coin a tender in payment of debts; pass any bill of attainder, ex post law, or law impairing the obligation of contracts, or grant any title of nobility."

Mr Gerry entered into observations inculcating the importance of public faith, and the propriety of the restraint put on the States from impairing the obligation of contracts—Alledging that Congress ought to be laid under the like prohibitions. he made a motion to that effect. He was not 2ded

[*2:640; Mason, 15 Sept.*]

Both the general legislature and the State legislature are expressly prohibited making *ex post facto* laws; though there never was nor can be a legislature but must and will make such laws, when necessity and the public safety require them; which will hereafter be a breach of all the constitutions in the Union, and afford precedents for other innovations.

4

Luther Martin, Genuine Information 1788

Storing 2.4.75–78

By the tenth section every State is *prohibited* from *emitting bills of credit*—As it was reported by the committee of detail, the States were *only* prohibited from emitting them *without the consent of Congress;* but the convention was so *smitten* with the *paper money dread,* that they insisted the prohibition should be *absolute.* It was my opinion, Sir, that the States ought not to be *totally deprived of the right to emit bills of credit,* and that as we had *not given* an *authority* to the *general government* for that purpose, it was the *more necessary* to *retain* it in the *States*—I considered that *this State,* and *some others,* have *formerly received great benefit* from paper emissions, and that if public and private credit should once more be restored, such emissions may *hereafter be equally advantageous;* and further, that it is impossible to foresee that events may not take place which shall render paper money of *absolute necessity;* and it was my opinion, if this power was not to be exercised by a State without the permission of the general government, it ought to be satisfactory even to those who were the *most haunted* by the apprehensions of paper money; I therefore, thought it my duty to vote against this part of the system.

The same section also, puts it out of the power of the States, to make any thing but gold and silver coin a tender in payment of debts, or to pass any law impairing the obligation of contracts.

I considered, Sir, that there might be times of such *great public calamities* and *distress,* and of such *extreme scarcity* of *specie* as should render it the *duty* of a government, for the *preservation* of even the *most valuable part* of its citizens in some measure to interfere in their favour, by passing laws *totally* or *partially stopping* the courts of justice, or authorising the debtor to pay by *instalments,* or by delivering up his property to his creditors at a *reasonable* and *honest* valuation. The times have been such as to render regulations of this kind necessary in most, or all of the States, to prevent the *wealthy creditor* and the *monied man* from *totally* destroying the *poor* though even *industrious* debtor—*Such times* may *again* arrive. I therefore, voted against depriving the States of this power, a power which I am decided they ought to possess, but which I admit ought only to be exercised on very important and urgent occasions. I apprehend, Sir, the principal cause of complaint among the people at large is, the public and private debt with which they are oppressed, and which, in the present scarcity of cash, threatens them with destruction, unless they can obtain so much indulgence in point of time that by industry and frugality they may extricate themselves.

This *government proposed,* I apprehend, so *far from removing* will greatly *encrease* those complaints, since grasping in its all powerful hand the citizens of the respective States, it will by the imposition of the variety of *taxes, imposts, stamps, excises,* and *other duties, squeeze* from them the little money they acquire, the hard earnings of their industry, as you would squeeze the juice from an orange, till not a drop more can be extracted, and then let *loose* upon them their *private creditors,* to whose *mercy* it *consigns* them, by *whom* their property is to be *seized upon* and *sold* in this *scarcity* of *specie* at a *sheriff's sale,* where nothing but *ready cash* can be received, for a *tenth part* of its *value,* and *themselves* and their *families* to be consigned to *indigence* and *distress,* without *their governments* having a *power* to *give them a moment's indulgence,* however *necessary* it might be, and however *desirous* to grant them aid.

5

James Madison, Federalist, no. 44, 299–302 25 Jan. 1788

The prohibition against treaties, alliances and confederations, makes a part of the existing articles of Union; and for reasons which need no explanation, is copied into the new Constitution. The prohibition of letters of marque is another part of the old system, but is somewhat extended in the new. According to the former, letters of marque could be granted by the States after a declaration of war. According to the latter, these licenses must be obtained as well during war as previous to its declaration, from the government of the United States. This alteration is fully justified by the advantage of uniformity in all points which relate to foreign powers; and of immediate responsibility to the nation in all those, for whose conduct the nation itself is to be responsible.

The right of coining money, which is here taken from the States, was left in their hands by the confederation as a concurrent right with that of Congress, under an exception in favor of the exclusive right of Congress to regulate the alloy and value. In this instance also the new provision is an improvement on the old. Whilst the alloy and value depended on the general authority, a right of coinage in the particular States could have no other effect than to multiply expensive mints, and diversify the forms and weights of the circulating pieces. The latter inconveniency defeats one purpose for which the power was originally submitted to the foederal head. And as far as the former might prevent an inconvenient remittance of gold and silver to the central mint for recoinage, the end can be as well attained, by local mints established under the general authority.

The extension of the prohibition to bills of credit must give pleasure to every citizen in proportion to his love of justice, and his knowledge of the true springs of public prosperity. The loss which America has sustained since the peace, from the pestilent effects of paper money, on the necessary confidence between man and man; on the necessary confidence in the public councils; on the industry and morals of the people, and on the character of Republican Government, constitutes an enormous debt against the States chargeable with this unadvised measure, which must long remain unsatisfied; or rather an accumulation of guilt, which can be expiated no otherwise than by a voluntary sacrifice on the altar of justice, of the power which has been the instrument of it. In addition to these persuasive considerations, it may be observed that the same reasons which shew the necessity of denying to the States the power of regulating coin, prove with equal force that they ought not to be at liberty to substitute a paper medium in the place of coin. Had every State a right to regulate the value of its coin, there might be as many different currencies as States; and thus the intercourse among them would be impeded; retrospective alterations in its value might be made, and thus the citizens of other States be injured; and animosities be kindled among the States themselves. The subjects of foreign powers might suffer from the same cause, and hence the Union be discredited and embroiled by the indiscretion of a single member. No one of these mischiefs is less incident to a power in the States to emit paper money than to coin gold or silver. The power to make any thing but gold and silver a tender in payment of debts, is withdrawn from the States, on the same principle with that of striking of paper currency.

Bills of attainder, ex post facto laws, and laws impairing the obligation of contracts, are contrary to the first principles of the social compact, and to every principle of sound legislation. The two former are expressly prohibited by the declarations prefixed to some of the State Constitutions, and all of them are prohibited by the spirit and scope of these fundamental charters. Our own experience has taught us nevertheless, that additional fences against these dangers ought not to be omitted. Very properly therefore have the Convention added this constitutional bulwark in favor of personal security and private rights; and I am much deceived if they have not in so doing as faithfully consulted the genuine sentiments, as the undoubted interests of their constituents. The sober people of America are weary of the fluctuating policy which has directed the public councils. They have seen with regret and with indignation, that sudden changes and legislative interferences in cases affecting personal rights, become jobs in the hands of enterprizing and influential speculators; and snares to the more industrious and less informed part of the community. They have seen, too, that legislative interference, is but the first link of a long chain of repetitions; every subsequent interference being naturally produced by the effects of the preceding. They very rightly infer, therefore, that some thorough reform is wanting which will banish speculations on public measures, inspire a general prudence and industry, and give a regular course to the business of society. The prohibition with respect to titles of nobility, is copied from the articles of confederation, and needs no comment.

6

Charles Pinckney, South Carolina Ratifying Convention
20 May 1788
Elliot 4:333–36

This section I consider as the soul of the Constitution,—as containing, in a few words, those restraints upon the states, which, while they keep them from interfering with the powers of the Union, will leave them always in a situation to comply with their federal duties—will teach them to cultivate those principles of public honor and private honesty which are the sure road to national character and happiness

The only parts of this section that are objected to are those which relate to the emission of paper money, and its consequences, tender-laws, and the impairing the obligation of contracts.

The other parts are supposed as exclusively belonging to, and such as ought to be vested in, the Union.

If we consider the situation of the United States as they are at present, either individually or as the members of a general confederacy, we shall find it extremely improper they should ever be intrusted with the power of emitting money, or interfering in private contracts; or, by means of tender-laws, impairing the obligation of contracts.

I apprehend these general reasonings will be found true with respect to paper money: That experience has shown that, in every state where it has been practised since the revolution, it always carries the gold and silver out of the country, and impoverishes it—that, while it remains, all the foreign merchants, trading in America, must suffer and lose by it; therefore, that it must ever be a discouragement to commerce—that every medium of trade should have an intrinsic value, which paper money has not; gold and silver are therefore the fittest for this medium, as they are an equivalent, which paper can never be—that debtors in the assemblies will, whenever they can, make paper money with fraudulent views—that in those states where the credit of the paper money has been best supported, the bills have never kept to their nominal value in circulation, but have constantly depreciated to a certain degree.

I consider it as a granted position that, while the productions of a state are useful to other countries, and can find a ready sale at foreign markets, there can be no doubt of their always being able to command a sufficient sum in specie to answer as a medium for the purposes of carrying on this commerce; provided there is no paper money, or other means of conducting it. This, I think, will be the case even in instances where the balance of trade is against a state; but where the balance is in favor, or where there is nearly as much exported as imported, there can be no doubt that the products will be the means of always introducing a sufficient quantity of specie.

If we were to be governed by partial views, and each

state was only to consider how far a general regulation suited her own interests, I think it can be proved there is no state in the Union which ought to be so anxious to have this part of the Constitution passed as ourselves.

We are to reflect that this Constitution is not framed to answer temporary purposes. We hope it will last for ages—that it will be the perpetual protector of our rights and properties.

This state is, perhaps, of all others, more blessed in point of soil and productions than any in the Union. Notwithstanding all her sufferings by the war, the great quantity of lands still uncultivated, and the little attention she pays to the improvement of agriculture, she already exports more than any state in the Union, (except Virginia,) and in a little time must exceed her.

Exports are a surer mode of determining the productive wealth of a country than any other, and particularly when these products are in great demand in foreign countries.

Thus circumstanced, where can be the necessity of paper money? Will you not have specie in sufficient quantities? Will you not have more money in circulation without paper money than with it?—I mean, without having only paper in such quantities as you are able to maintain the credit of, as at present. I aver you may, and appeal only to the experience of the last five or six years. Will it not be confessed that, in 1783 and 1784, we had more money than we have at present, and that the emission of your present paper banished double the amount out of circulation? Besides, if paper should become necessary, the general government still possess the power of emitting it, and Continental paper, well funded, must ever answer the purpose better than state paper.

How extremely useful and advantageous must this restraint be to those states which mean to be honest, and not to defraud their neighbors! Henceforth, the citizens of the states may trade with each other without fear of tender-laws or laws impairing the nature of contracts. The citizen of South Carolina will then be able to trade with those of Rhode Island, North Carolina, and Georgia, and be sure of receiving the value of his commodities. Can this be done at present? It cannot! However just the demand may be, yet still your honest, suffering citizen must be content to receive their depreciated paper, or give up the debt.

But above all, how much will this section tend to restore your credit with foreigners—to rescue your national character from that contempt which must ever follow the most flagrant violations of public faith and private honesty! No more shall paper money, no more shall tender-laws, drive their commerce from our shores, and darken the American name in every country where it is known. No more shall our citizens conceal in their coffers those treasures which the weakness and dishonesty of our government have long hidden from the public eye. The firmness of a just and even system shall bring them into circulation, and honor and virtue shall be again known and countenanced among us. No more shall the widow, the orphan, and the stranger, become the miserable victims of unjust rulers. Your government shall now, indeed, be a government of laws. The arm of Justice shall be lifted on high; and the poor and the rich, the strong and the weak, shall be equally protected in their rights. Public as well as private confidence shall again be established; industry shall return among us; and the blessings of our government shall verify that old, but useful maxim, that with states, as well as individuals, honesty is the best policy.

7

EDMUND RANDOLPH, VIRGINIA RATIFYING CONVENTION
6 June 1788
Elliot 3:66–67

There is one example of this violation in Virginia, of a most striking and shocking nature—an example so horrid, that, if I conceived my country would passively permit a repetition of it, dear as it is to me, I would seek means of expatriating myself from it. A man, who was then a citizen, was deprived of his life thus: from a mere reliance on general reports, a gentleman in the House of Delegates informed the house, that a certain man (Josiah Philips) had committed several crimes, and was running at large, perpetrating other crimes. He therefore moved for leave to attaint him; he obtained that leave instantly; no sooner did he obtain it, than he drew from his pocket a bill ready written for that effect; it was read three times in one day, and carried to the Senate. I will not say that it passed the same day through the Senate; but he was attainted very speedily and precipitately, without any proof better than vague reports. Without being confronted with his accusers and witnesses, without the privilege of calling for evidence in his behalf, he was sentenced to death, and was afterwards actually executed. Was this arbitrary deprivation of life, the dearest gift of God to man, consistent with the genius of a republican government? Is this compatible with the spirit of freedom? This, sir, has made the deepest impression on my heart, and I cannot contemplate it without horror.

8

DEBATE IN VIRGINIA RATIFYING CONVENTION
15 June 1788
Elliot 3:471–81

Mr. HENRY apologized for repeatedly troubling the committee with his fears. But he apprehended the most serious consequences from these restrictions on the states. As they could not emit bills of credit, make any thing but gold and silver coin a tender in payment of debts, pass *ex post facto* laws, or impair the obligation of contracts,—though these restrictions were founded on good principles, yet he feared they would have this effect; that this state would be obliged to pay for her share of the Continental money, shilling for shilling. He asked gentlemen who had been in high authority, whether there were not some state speculations on this matter. He had been informed that some states had acquired vast quantites of that money, which they would be able to recover in its nominal value of the other states.

Mr. MADISON admitted there might be some speculations on the subject. He believed the old Continental money was settled in a very disproportionate manner. It appeared to him, however, that it was unnecessary to say any thing on this point, for there was a clause in the Constitution which cleared it up. The first clause of the 6th article provides that "all debts contracted, and engagements entered into, before the adoption of this Constitution, shall be as valid against the United States, under this Constitution, as under the Confederation." He affirmed that it was meant there should be no change with respect to claims by this political alteration; and that the public would stand, with respect to their creditors, as before. He thought that the validity of claims ought not to diminish by the adoption of the Constitution. But, however, it could not increase the demands on the public.

Mr. GEORGE MASON declared he had been informed that some states had speculated most enormously in this matter. Many individuals had speculated so as to make great fortunes on the ruin of their fellow-citizens. The clause which has been read, as a sufficient security, seemed to him to be satisfactory as far as it went; that is, that the Continental money ought to stand on the same ground as it did previously, or that the claim should not be impaired. Under the Confederation, there were means of settling the old paper money, either in Congress or in the state legislatures. The money had at last depreciated to a thousand for one. The intention of state speculation, as well as individual speculation, was to get as much as possible of that money, in order to recover its nominal value. The means, says he, of settling this money, were in the hands of the old Congress. They could discharge it at its depreciated value. Is there that means here? No, sir, we must pay it shilling for shilling, or at least at the rate of one for forty. The amount will surpass the value of the property of the United States. Neither the state legislatures nor Congress can make an *ex post facto* law. The nominal value must therefore be paid. Where is the power in the new government to settle this money so as to prevent the country from being ruined? When they prohibit the making *ex post facto* laws, they will have no authority to prevent our being ruined by paying that money at its nominal value.

Without some security against it, we shall be compelled to pay it to the last particle of our property. Shall we ruin our people by taxation, from generation to generation, to pay that money? Should any *ex post facto* law be made to relieve us from such payments, it would not be regarded, because *ex post facto* laws are interdicted in the Constitution. We may be taxed for centuries, to give advantage to a few particular states in the Union, and a number of rapacious speculators. If there be any real security against this misfortune, let gentlemen show it. I can see none. The clause under consideration does away the pretended security in the clause which was adduced by the honorable gentleman. This enormous mass of worthless money, which has been offered at a thousand for one, must be paid in actual gold and silver at the nominal value.

Mr. MADISON. Mr. Chairman, it appears to me immaterial who holds those great quantities of paper money which were in circulation before the peace, or at what value they acquired it; for it will not be affected by this Constitution. What would satisfy gentlemen more than that the new Constitution would place us in the same situation with the old? In this respect, it has done so. The claims against the United States are declared to be as *valid* as they were, but *not more so.* Would they have a particular specification of these matters? Where can there be any danger? Is there any reason to believe that the new rulers, one branch of which will be drawn from the mass of the people, will neglect or violate our interests more than the old? It rests on the obligation of public faith only, in the Articles of Confederation. It will be so in this Constitution, should it be adopted. If the new rulers should wish to enhance its value, in order to gratify its holders, how can they compel the states to pay it if the letter of the Constitution be observed? Do gentlemen wish the public creditors should be put in a worse situation? Would the people at large wish to satisfy creditors in such a manner as to ruin them? There cannot be a majority of the people of America that would wish to defraud their public creditors. I consider this as well guarded as possible. It rests on plain and honest principles. I cannot conceive how it could be more honorable or safe. [Mr. Madison made some other observations, which could not be heard.]

Mr. HENRY. Mr. Chairman, I am convinced, and I see clearly, that this paper money must be discharged, shilling for shilling. The honorable gentleman must see better than I can, from his particular situation and judgment; but this has certainly escaped his attention. The question arising on the clause before you is, whether an act of the legislature of this state, for scaling money, will be of sufficient validity to exonerate you from paying the nominal value, when such a law, called *ex post facto,* and impairing the obligation of contracts, is expressly interdicted by it. Your hands are tied up by this clause, and you must pay shilling for shilling; and, in the last section, there is a clause that prohibits the general legislature from passing any *ex post facto* law; so that the hands of Congress are tied up, as well as the hands of the state legislatures.

How will this thing operate, when ten or twenty millions are demanded as the quota of this state? You will cry out that speculators have got it at one for a thousand, and that they ought to be paid so. Will you then have recourse, for relief, to legislative interference? They cannot relieve you, because of that clause. The expression includes public contracts, as well as private contracts between individuals. Notwithstanding the sagacity of the gentleman, he cannot prove its exclusive relation to private contracts. Here is an enormous demand, which your children, to the tenth generation, will not be able to pay. Should we ask if there be any obligation in justice to pay more than the depreciated value, we shall be told that contracts must not be impaired.

Justice may make a demand of millions, but the people cannot pay them.

I remember the clamors and public uneasiness concerning the payments of British debts put into the treasury. Was not the alarm great and general lest these payments should be laid on the people at large? Did not the legislature interfere, and pass a law to prevent it? Was it not reechoed every where, that the people of this country ought not to pay the debts of their great ones? And though some urged their patriotism and merits in putting money, on the faith of the public, into the treasury, yet the outcry was so great that it required legislative interference. Should those enormous demands be made upon us, would not legislative interference be more necessary than it was in that case? Let us not run the risk of being charged with carelessness, and neglect of the interests of our constituents and posterity. I would ask the number of millions. It is, without exaggeration, immense. I ask gentlemen if they can pay one hundred millions, or two hundred millions? Where have they the means of paying it? Still they would make us proceed to tie the hands of the states and of Congress.

A gentleman has said, with great force, that there is a contest for empire. There is also a contest for money. The states of the north wish to secure a superiority of interest and influence. In one part their deliberation is marked with wisdom, and in the other with the most liberal generosity. When we have paid all the gold and silver we could to replenish the congressional coffers, here they ask for confidence. Their hands will be tied up. They cannot merit confidence. Here is a transfer from the old to the new government, without the means of relieving the greatest distresses which can befall the people. This money might be scaled, sir; but the exclusion of *ex post facto* laws, and laws impairing the obligation of contracts, steps in and prevents it. These were admitted by the old Confederation. There is a contest for money as well as empire, as I have said before. The Eastern States have speculated chiefly in this money. As there can be no congressional scale, their speculations will be extremely profitable. Not satisfied with a majority in the legislative councils, they must have all our property. I wish the southern genius of America had been more watchful.

This state may be sued in the federal court for those enormous demands, and judgment may be obtained, unless *ex post facto* laws be passed. To benefit whom are we to run this risk? I have heard there were vast quantities of that money packed up in barrels: those formidable millions are deposited in the Northern States, and whether in public or private hands makes no odds. They have acquired it for the most inconsiderable trifle. If you accord to this part, you are bound hand and foot. Judgment must be rendered against you for the whole. Throw all pride out of the question, this is a most nefarious business. Your property will be taken from you to satisfy this most infamous speculation. It will destroy your public peace, and establish the ruin of your citizens. Only general resistance will remedy. You will shut the door against every ray of hope, if you allow the holders of this money, by this clause, to recover their formidable demands. I hope gentlemen will see the absolute necessity of amending it, by enabling the state legislatures to relieve their people from such nefarious oppressions.

Mr. George Nicholas. Mr. Chairman, I beg gentlemen to consider most attentively the clause under consideration, and the objections against it. He says there exists the most dangerous prospect. Has the legislature of Virginia any right to make a law or regulation to interfere with the Continental Debts? Have they a right to make *ex post facto* laws, and laws impairing the obligation of contracts, for that purpose? No, sir. If his fears proceed from this clause, they are without foundation. This clause does not hinder them from from doing it, because the state never could do it; the jurisdiction of such general objects being exclusively vested in Congress.

But, says he, this clause will hinder the general government from preventing the nominal value of those millions from being paid. On what footing does this business stand, if the Constitution be adopted? By it all contracts will be as valid, and only as valid, as under the old Confederation. The new government will give the holders the same power of recovery as the old one. There is no law under the existing system which gives power to any tribunal to enforce the payment of such claims. On the will of Congress alone the payment depends. The Constitution expressly says that they shall be only as binding as under the present Confederation. Cannot they decide according to real equity? Those who have this money must make application to Congress for payment. Some positive regulation must be made to redeem it. It cannot be said that they have power of passing a law to enhance its value. They cannot make a law that that money shall no longer be but one for one; for, though they have power to pay the debts of the United States, they can only pay the real debts; and this is no further a debt than it was before. Application must, therefore, be made by the holders of that money to Congress, who will make the most proper regulation to discharge its real and equitable, and not its nominal, value.

We are told of the act passed to exonerate the public from the payments of the British debts put into the treasury. That has no analogy to this: those payments were opposed because they were unjust. But he supposes that Congress may be sued by those speculators. Where is the clause that gives that power? It gives no such power. This, according to my idea, is inconsistent. Can the supreme legislature be sued in their own subordinate courts, by their own citizens, in cases where they are not a party? They may be plaintiffs, but not defendants. But the individual states, perhaps, may be sued. Pennsylvania or Virginia may be sued. How is this? Do I owe the man in New England any thing? Does Virginia owe any thing to the Pennsylvanian holder of such money? Who promised to pay it? Congress, sir. Congress are answerable to the individual holders of this money, and individuals are answerable over to Congress. Therefore, no individual can call on any state.

But the Northern States struggle for money as well as for empire. Congress cannot make such a regulation as they please at present. If the Northern States wish to injure us, why do they not do it now? What greater dangers are there to be dreaded from the new government, since there is no alteration? It they have a majority in the one case, they have in the other. The interests of those states would be as dangerous for us under the old as under the new government, which leaves this business where it stands, because the conclusion says that all debts contracted, or engagements entered into, shall be only as valid in the one case as the other.

GOV. RANDOLPH. Mr. Chairman, this clause, in spite of the invective of the gentleman, is a great favorite of mine, because it is essential to justice. I shall reserve my answer respecting the safety of the people till the objection be urged; but I must make a few observations. He says this clause will be injurious, and that no scale can be made, because there is a prohibition on Congress of passing *ex post facto* laws. If the gentleman did not make such strong objections to logical reasoning, I could prove, by such reasoning, that there is no danger. *Ex post facto* laws, if taken technically, relate solely to criminal cases; and my honorable colleague tells you it was so interpreted in Convention. What greater security can we have against arbitrary proceedings in criminal jurisprudence than this? In addition to the interpretation of the Convention, let me show him still greater authority. The same clause provides that no bill of attainder shall be passed. It shows that the attention of the Convention was drawn to criminal matters alone. Shall it be complained, against this government, that it prohibits the passing of a law annexing a punishment to an act which was lawful at the time of committing it? With regard to retrospective laws, there is no restraint.

Let us examine the cause of the clamors which are made with regard to the Continental money. A friend has mentioned a clause which shows there is no danger from the new Congress. Does it not manifestly appear that they are precisely in the same predicament as under the old Confederation? And do gentlemen wish that this should be put in a worse condition? If they have equity under the old Confederation, they have equity still. There is no tribunal to recur to by the old government. There is none in the new for that purpose. If the old Congress can scale that money, they have this power still. But he says not, because the states cannot impair the obligation of contracts. What is to be done by the states with regard to it? Congress, and not they, have contracted to pay it. It is not affected by this clause at all. I am still a warm friend to the prohibition, because it must be promotive of virtue and justice, and preventive of injustice and fraud. If we take a review of the calamities which have befallen our reputation as a people, we shall find they have been produced by frequent interferences of the state legislatures with private contracts. If you inspect the greater corner-stone of republicanism, you will find it to be justice and honor.

I come now to what will be agitated by the judiciary. They are to enforce the performance of private contracts. The British debts, which are withheld contrary to treaty, ought to be paid. Not only the law of nations, but justice and honor, require that they be punctually discharged. I fear their payment may press on my country; but we must retrench our superfluities, and profuse and idle extravagance, and become more economical and industrious. Let me not be suspected of being interested in this respect; for, without a sad reverse of my fortune, I shall never be in a situation to be benefited by it. I am confident the honest Convention of Virginia will not oppose it. Can any society exist without a firm adherence to justice and virtue? The federal judiciary cannot intermeddle with those public claims without violating the letter of the Constitution. Why, then, such opposition to the clause? His excellency then concluded that he would, if necessary, display his feelings more fully on the subject another time.

MR. GEORGE MASON. Mr. Chairman, the debt is transferred to Congress, but not the means of paying it. They cannot pay it any other way than according to the nominal value; for they are prohibited from making *ex post facto* laws; and it would be *ex post facto,* to all intents and purposes, to pay off creditors with less than the nominal sum which they were originally promised. But the honorable gentleman has called to his aid technical definitions. He says, that *ex post facto* laws relate solely to criminal matters. I beg leave to differ from him. Whatever it may be at the bar, or in a professional line, I conceive that, according to the common acceptation of the words, *ex post facto* laws and retrospective laws are synonymous terms. Are we to trust business of this sort to technical definition? The contrary is the plain meaning of the words. Congress has no power to scale this money. The states are equally precluded. The debt is transferred without the means of discharging it. Implication will not do. The means of paying it are expressly withheld. When this matter comes before the federal judiciary, they must determine according to this Constitution. It says, expressly, that they shall not make *ex post facto* laws. Whatever may be the professional meaning, yet the general meaning of *ex post facto* laws is an act having a retrospective operation. This construction is agreeable to its primary etymology. Will it not be the duty of the federal court to say that such laws are prohibited? This goes to the destruction and annihilation of all the citizens of the United States, to enrich a few. Are we to part with every shilling of our property, and be reduced to the lowest insignificancy, to aggrandize a few speculators? Let me mention a remarkable effect this Constitution will have. How stood our taxes before this Constitution was introduced? Requisitions were made on the state legislatures, and, if they were unjust, they could be refused. If we were called upon to pay twenty millions, shilling for shilling, or at the rate of one for forty, our legislature could refuse it, and remonstrate against the injustice of the demand. But now this could not be done; for direct taxation is brought home to us. The federal officer collects immediately of the planters. When it withholds the only possible means of discharging those debts, and by direct taxation prevents any opposition to the most enormous and unjust demand, where are you? Is there a ray of hope? As the law has never been my profession, if I err, I hope to be excused. I spoke from the general sense of the words. The worthy gentleman has told you that the United States can be plaintiffs, but never defendants. If so, it stands on very unjust grounds. The United States cannot be come at for any thing they may owe, but may get what is due to them. There is therefore no reciprocity. The thing is so incomprehensible that it cannot be explained. As an express power is given to the federal court to take cognizance of such controversies, and to declare null all *ex post facto* laws, I think gentlemen must see there is danger, and that it ought to be guarded against.

Mr. MADISON. Mr. Chairman, I did expect, from the earnestness he has expressed, that he would cast some light upon it; but the ingenuity of the honorable member could make nothing of this objection. He argues from a supposition that the state legislatures, individually, might have passed laws to affect the value of the Continental debt. I believe he did not well consider this, before he hazarded his observations. He says that the United States, being restrained in this case, will be obliged to pay at an unjust rate. It has been so clearly explained by the honorable gentleman over the way that there could be no danger, that it is unnecessary to say more on the subject. The validity of these claims will neither be increased nor diminished by this change. There must be a law made by Congress respecting their redemption. The states cannot interfere. Congress will make such a regulation as will be just. There is, in my opinion, but one way of scaling improperly and unjustly; and that is, by acceding to the favorite mode of the honorable gentleman—by requisitions. Is it to be presumed any change can be made in the system inconsistent with reason or equity? Strike the clause out of the Constitution—what will it be then? The debt will be as valid only as it was before the adoption. Gentlemen will not say that obligations are varied. This is merely a declaratory clause, that things are to exist in the same manner as before.

But I fear the very extensive assertions of the gentleman may have misled the committee. The whole of that Continental money amounted to but little more than one hundred millions. A considerable quantity of it has been destroyed. At the time when no share of it had been destroyed, the quota of this state did not amount to more than twenty-six millions. At forty for one, this is but five hundred thousand dollars at most. In every point of view it appears to me that it cannot be on a more reasonable, equitable, or honorable footing than it is. Do gentlemen suppose that they will agree to any system or alteration that will place them in a worse situation than before? Let us suppose this commonwealth was possessed of the same money that the Northern States have; and suppose an objection was made by them to its redemption at its real value—what would be the consequence? We should pronounce them to be unreasonable, and on good grounds. This case is so extremely plain, that it was unecessary to say as much as has been said.

Mr. MASON was still convinced of the rectitude of his former opinion. He thought it might be put on a safer footing by three words. By continuing the restriction of *ex post facto* laws to crimes, it would then stand under the new government as it did under the old.

Gov. RANDOLPH could not coincide with the construction put by the honorable gentleman on *ex post facto* laws. The technical meaning which confined such laws solely to criminal cases was followed in the interpretation of treaties between nations, and was concurred in by all civilians. The prohibition of bills of attainder he thought a sufficient proof that *ex post facto* laws related to criminal cases only, and that such was the idea of the Convention.

9

DEBATE IN NORTH CAROLINA RATIFYING CONVENTION 29 July 1788

Elliot 4:183–85, 190–91

[Mr. DAVIE.] The Federal Convention knew that several states had large sums of paper money in circulation, and that it was an interesting property, and they were sensible that those states would never consent to its immediate destruction, or ratify any system that would have that operation. The mischief already done could not be repaired: all that could be done was, to form some limitation to this great political evil. As the paper money had become private property, and the object of numberless contracts, it could not be destroyed or intermeddled with in that situation, although its baneful tendency was obvious and undeniable. It was, however, effecting an important object to put bounds to this growing mischief. If the states had been compelled to sink the paper money instantly, the remedy might be worse than the disease. As we could not put an immediate end to it, we were content with prohibiting its future increase, looking forward to its entire extinguishment when the states that had an emission circulating should be able to call it in by a gradual redemption.

In Pennsylvania, their paper money was not a tender in discharge of private contracts. In South Carolina, their bills became eventually a tender; and in Rhode Island, New York, New Jersey, and North Carolina, the paper money was made a legal tender in all cases whatsoever. The other states were sensible that the destruction of the circulating paper would be a violation of the rights of private property, and that such a measure would render the accession of those states to the system absolutely impracticable. The injustice and pernicious tendency of this disgraceful policy were viewed with great indignation by the states which adhered to the principles of justice. In Rhode Island, the paper money had depreciated to eight for one, and a hundred per cent. with us. The people of Massachusetts and Connecticut had been great sufferers by the dishonesty of Rhode Island, and similar complaints existed against this state. This clause became in some measure a preliminary with the gentlemen who represented the other states. "You have," said they, "by your iniquitous laws and paper emissions shamefully defrauded our citizens. The Confederation prevented our compelling you to do them justice; but before we confederate with you again, you must not only agree to be honest, but put it out of your power to be otherwise." Sir, a member from Rhode Island itself could not have set his face against such language. The clause was, I believe, unanimously assented to: it has only a future aspect, and can by no means have a retrospective operation; and I trust the principles upon which the Convention proceeded will meet the approbation of every honest man.

Mr. Cabarrus. Mr. Chairman, I contend that the clause which prohibits the states from emitting bills of credit will not affect our present paper money. The clause has no retrospective view. This Constitution declares, in the most positive terms, that no *ex post facto* law shall be passed by the general government. Were this clause to operate retrospectively, it would clearly be *ex post facto,* and repugnant to the express provision of the Constitution. How, then, in the name of God, can the Constitution take our paper money away? If we have contracted for a sum of money, we ought to pay according to the nature of our contract. Every honest man will pay in specie who engaged to pay it. But if we have contracted for a sum of paper money, it must be clear to every man in this committee, that we shall pay in paper money. This is a Constitution for the *future* government of the United States. It does not look back. Every gentleman must be satisfied, on the least reflection, that our paper money will not be destroyed. To say that it will be destroyed, is a popular argument, but not founded in fact, in my opinion. I had my doubts, but on consideration, I am satisfied.

Mr. Bloodworth. Mr. Chairman, I beg leave to ask if the payment of sums now due be *ex post facto.* Will it be an *ex post facto* law to compel the payment of money now due in silver coin? If suit be brought in the federal court against one of our citizens, for a sum of money, will paper money be received to satisfy the judgment? I inquire for information; my mind is not yet satisfied. It has been said that we are to send our own gentlemen to represent us, and that there is not the least doubt they will put that construction on it which will be most agreeable to the people they represent. But it behoves us to consider whether they can do so if they would, when they mix with the body of Congress. The Northern States are much more populous than the Southern ones. To the north of the Susquehannah there are thirty-six representatives, and to the south of it only twenty-nine. They will always outvote us. Sir, we ought to be particular in adopting a Constitution which may destroy our currency, when it is to be the supreme law of the land, and prohibits the emission of paper money. I am not, for my own part, for giving an indefinite power. Gentlemen of the best abilities differ in the construction of the Constitution. The members of Congress will differ too. Human nature is fallible. I am not for throwing ourselves out of the Union; but we ought to be cautious by proposing amendments. The majority in several great adopting states was very trifling. Several of them have proposed amendments, but not in the mode most satisfactory to my mind. I hope this Convention never will adopt it till the amendments are actually obtained.

Mr. Iredell. Mr. Chairman, with respect to this clause, it cannot have the operation contended for. There is nothing in the Constitution which affects our present paper money. It prohibits, for the future, the emitting of any, but it does not interfere with the paper money now actually in circulation in several states. There is an express clause which protects it. It provides that there shall be no *ex post facto* law. This would be *ex post facto,* if the construction contended for were right, as has been observed by another gentleman. If a suit were brought against a man in the federal court, and execution should go against his property, I apprehend he would, under this Constitution, have a right to pay our paper money, there being nothing in the Constitution taking away the validity of it. Every individual in the United States will keep his eye watchfully over those who administer the general government, and no usurpation of power will be acquiesced in. The possibility of usurping powers ought not to be objected against it. Abuse may happen in any government. The only resource against usurpation is the inherent right of the people to prevent its exercise. This is the case in all free governments in the world. The people will resist if the government usurp powers not delegated to it. We must run the risk of abuse. We must take care to give no more power than is necessary.

. . . . .

Mr. J. Galloway. Mr. Chairman, I should make no objection to this clause were the powers granted by the Constitution sufficiently defined; for I am clearly of opinion that it is absolutely necessary for every government, and especially for a general government, that its laws should be the supreme law of the land. But I hope the gentlemen of the committee will advert to the 10th section of the 1st article. This is a negative which the Constitution of our own state does not impose upon us. I wish the committee to attend to that part of it which provides that no state shall pass any law which will impair the obligation of contracts. Our public securities are at a low ebb, and have been so for many years. We well know that this country has taken those securities as specie. This hangs over our heads as a contract. There is a million and a half in circulation at least. That clause of the Constitution may compel us to make good the nominal value of these securities. I trust this country never will leave it to the hands of the general government to redeem the securities which they have already given. Should this be the case, the consequence will be, that they will be purchased by speculators, when the citizens will part with them, perhaps for a very trifling consideration. Those speculators will look at the Constitution, and see that they will be paid in gold and silver. They will buy them at a half-crown in the pound, and get the full nominal value for them in gold and silver. I therefore wish the committee to consider whether North Carolina can redeem those securities in the manner most agreeable to her citizens, and justifiable to the world, if this Constitution be adopted.

Mr. Davie. Mr. Chairman, I believe neither the 10th section, cited by the gentleman, nor any other part of the Constitution, has vested the general government with power to interfere with the public securities of any state. I will venture to say that the last thing which the general government will attempt to do will be this. They have nothing to do with it. The clause refers merely to contracts between individuals. That section is the best in the Constitution. It is founded on the strongest principles of justice. It is a section, in short, which I thought would have endeared the Constitution to this country. When the worthy gentleman comes to consider, he will find that the general government cannot possibly interfere with such securities. How can it? It has no negative clause to that effect. Where is there a negative clause, operating negatively on the states themselves? It cannot operate retrospectively, for this would be repugnant to its own express provisions. It will be left to ourselves to redeem them as we please. We wished we could put it on the shoulders of Congress, but could not. Securities may be higher, but never less. I conceive, sir, that this is a very plain case, and that it must appear perfectly clear to the committee that the gentleman's alarms are groundless.

10

Calder v. Bull

3 Dall. 386 (1798)

Chase, Justice.—The decision of one question determines (in my opinion) the present dispute. I shall, therefore, state from the record no more of the case, than I think necessary for the consideration of that question only.

The legislature of Connecticut, on the 2d Thursday of May 1795, passed a resolution or law, which, for the reasons assigned, set aside a decree of the Court of Probate for Hartford, on the 21st of March 1793, which decree disapproved of the will of Normand Morrison (the grandson), made the 21st of August 1779, and refused to record the said will; and granted a new hearing by the said court of probate, with liberty of appeal therefrom, in six months. A new hearing was had, in virtue of this resolution or law, before the said court of probate, who, on the 27th of July 1795, approved the said will, and ordered it to be recorded. At August 1795, appeal was then had to the superior court at Hartford, who, at February term 1796, affirmed the decree of the court of probate. Appeal was had to the supreme court of errors of Connecticut, who, in June 1796, adjudged that there were no errors. More than eighteen months elapsed from the decree of the court of probate (on the 1st of March 1793), and thereby Caleb Bull and wife were barred of all right of appeal, by a statute of Connecticut. There was no law of that state whereby a new hearing or trial, before the said court of probate, might be obtained. Calder and wife claimed the premises in question, in right of the wife, as heiress of N. Morrison, physician; Bull and wife claimed under the will of N. Morrison, the grandson.

The counsel for the plaintiffs in error contend, that the said resolution or law of the legislature of Connecticut, granting a new hearing, in the above case, is an *ex post facto* law, prohibited by the constitution of the United States; that any law of the federal government, or of any of the state governments, contrary to the constitution of the United States, is void; and that this court possesses the power to declare such law void.

It appears to me a self-evident proposition, that the several state legislatures retain all the powers of legislation, delegated to them by the state constitutions; which are not expressly taken away by the constitution of the United States. The establishing courts of justice, the appointment of judges, and the making regulations for the administration of justice within each state, according to its laws, on all subjects not intrusted to the federal government, appears to me to be the peculiar and exclusive province and duty of the state legislatures. All the powers delegated by the people of the United States to the federal government are defined, and no *constructive* powers can be exercised by it, and all the powers that remain in the state governments are indefinite; except only in the constitution of Massachusetts.

The effect of the resolution or law of Connecticut, above stated, is to revise a decision of one of its inferior courts, called the court of probate for Hartford, and to direct a new hearing of the case by the same court of probate, that passed the decree against the will of Normand Morrison. By the existing law of Connecticut, a right to recover certain property had vested in Calder and wife (the appellants), in consequence of a decision of a court of justice, but in virtue of a subsequent resolution or law, and the new hearing thereof, and the decision in consequence, this right to recover certain property was divested, and the right to the property declared to be in Bull and wife, the appellees. The sole inquiry is, whether this resolution or law of Connecticut, having such operation, is an *ex post facto* law, within the prohibition of the federal constitution?

Whether the legislature of any of the states can revise and correct by law, a decision of any of its courts of justice, although not prohibited by the constitution of the state, is a question of very great importance, and not necessary now to be determined; because the resolution or law in question does not go so far. I cannot subscribe to the omnipotence of a state legislature, or that it is absolute and without control; although its authority should not be expressly restrained by the constitution, or fundamental law of the state. The people of the United States erected their constitutions or forms of government, to establish justice, to promote the general welfare, to secure the blessings of liberty, and to protect their persons and property from violence. The purposes for which men enter into society will determine the nature and terms of the social compact; and as they are the foundation of the legislative power, they will decide what are the proper objects of it. The nature, and ends of legislative power will limit the exercise of it. This fundamental principle flows from the very nature of our free republican governments, that no man should be compelled to do what the laws do not require; nor to refrain from acts which the laws permit. There are acts which the federal, or state legislature cannot do, without exceeding their authority. There are certain vital principles in our free republican governments, which will determine and overrule an apparent and flagrant abuse of legislative power; as to authorize manifest injustice by positive law; or to take away that security for personal liberty, or private property, for the protection whereof the government was established. An act of the legislature (for I cannot call it a law), contrary to the great first principles of the social compact, cannot be considered a righful exercise of legislative authority. The obligation of a law, in governments established on express compact, and on republican principles, must be determined by the nature of the power on which it is founded.

A few instances will suffice to explain what I mean. A law that punished a citizen for an innocent action, or, in other words, for an act, which, when done, was in violation of no existing law; a law that destroys or impairs the lawful private contracts of citizens; a law that makes a man a judge in his own cause; or a law that takes property from A. and gives it to B.: it is against all reason and justice, for a people to intrust a legislature with such powers; and therefore, it cannot be presumed that they have done it. The genius, the nature and the spirit of our state governments, amount to a prohibition of such acts of legislation; and the general principles of law and reason forbid them. The legislature may enjoin, permit, forbid and punish; they may declare new crimes; and establish rules of conduct for all its citizens in future cases; they may command what is right, and prohibit what is wrong; but they cannot change innocence into guilt; or punish innocence as a crime; or violate the right of an antecedent lawful private contract; or the right of private property. To maintain that our federal, or state legislature possesses such powers, if they had not been expressly restrained; would, in my opinion, be a political heresy, altogether inadmissible in our free republican governments.

All the restrictions contained in the constitution of the United States on the power of the state legislatures, were provided in favor of the authority of the federal government. The prohibition against their making any *ex post facto* laws was introduced for greater caution, and very probably arose from the knowledge, that the parliament of Great Britain claimed and exercised a power to pass such laws, under the denomination of bills of attainder, or bills of pains and penalties; the first inflicting capital, and the other less punishment. These acts were legislative judgments; and an exercise of judicial power. Sometimes, they respected the crime, by declaring acts to be treason, which were not treason, when committed; at other times, they violated the rules of evidence (to supply a deficiency of legal proof) by admitting one witness, when the existing law required two; by receiving evidence without oath; or the oath of the wife against the husband; or other testimony, which the courts of justice would not admit; at other times, they inflicted punishments, where the party was not, by law, liable to any punishment; and in other cases, they inflicted greater punishment, than the law annexed to the offence. The ground for the exercise of such legislative power was this, that the safety of the kingdom depended on the death, or other punishment, of the offender: as if traitors, when discovered, could be so formidable, or the government so insecure! With very few exceptions, the advocates of such laws were stimulated by ambition, or personal resentment and vindictive malice. To prevent such and similar acts of violence and injustice, I believe, the federal and state legislatures were prohibited from passing any bill of attainder, or any *ex post facto* law.

The constitution of the United States, article I., section 9, prohibits the legislature of the United States from passing any *ex post facto* law; and, in § 10, lays several restrictions on the authority of the legislatures of the several states; and, among them, "that no state shall pass any *ex post facto* law."

It may be remembered, that the legislatures of several of the states, to wit, Massachusetts, Pennsylvania, Delaware, Maryland, and North and South Carolina, are expressly prohibited, by their state constitutions, from passing any *ex post facto* law.

I shall endeavor to show what law is to be considered, an *ex post facto* law, within the words and meaning of the prohibition in the federal constitution. The prohibition, "that no state shall pass any *ex post facto* law," necessarily requires some explanation; for, naked and without explanation, it is unintelligible, and means nothing. Literally, it is only, that a law shall not be passed concerning, and after the fact, or thing done, or action committed. I would ask, what fact; of what nature or kind; and by whom done? That Charles I., king of England, was beheaded; that Oliver Cromwell was protector of England; that Louis XVI., late king of France, was guillotined; are all facts that have happened; but it would be nonsense to suppose, that the states were prohibited from making any law, after either of these events, and with reference thereto. The prohibition, in the letter, is not to pass any law concerning, and after the fact; but the plain and obvious meaning and intention of the prohibition is this: that the legislatures of the several states, shall not pass laws, after a fact done by a subject or citizen, which shall have relation to such fact, and shall punish him for having done it. The prohibition, considered in this light, is an additional bulwark in favor of the personal security of the subject, to protect his person from punishment by legislative acts, having a retrospective operation. I do not think it was inserted, to secure the citizen in his private rights of either property or contracts. The prohibitions not to make anything but gold and silver coin a tender in payment of debts, and not to pass any law impairing the obligation of contracts, were inserted to secure private rights; but the restriction not to pass any *ex post facto* law, was to secure the person of the subject from injury or punishment, in consequence of such law. If the prohibition against making *ex post facto* laws was intended to secure personal rights from being affected or injured by such laws, and the prohibition is sufficiently extensive for that object, the other restraints I have enumerated, were unnecessary, and therefore, improper; for both of them are retrospective.

I will state what laws I consider *ex post facto* laws, within the words and the intent of the prohibition. 1st. Every law that makes an action done before the passing of the law, and which was innocent when done, criminal; and punishes such action. 2d. Every law that aggravates a crime, or makes it greater than it was, when committed. 3d. Every law that changes the punishment, and inflicts a greater punishment, than the law annexed to the crime, when committed. 4th. Every law that alters the legal rules of evidence, and receives less, or different testimony, than the law required at the time of the commission of the offence, in order to convict the offender. All these, and similar laws, are manifestly unjust and oppressive. In my opinion, the true distinction is between *ex post facto* laws, and retrospective laws. Every *ex post facto* law must necessarily be retrospective; but every retrospective law is not an *ex post facto* law: the former only are prohibited. Every law that takes away or impairs rights vested, agreeable to existing laws, is retrospective, and is generally unjust, and may be oppressive; and it is a good general rule, that a law should have no retrospect: but there are cases in which laws may justly, and for the benefit of the community, and also of individuals, relate to a time antecedent to their commencement; as statutes of oblivion or of pardon. They are certainly retrospective, and literally both concerning and after the facts committed. But I do not consider any law *ex post facto,* within the prohibition, that mollifies the rigor of the criminal law: but only those that create or aggravate the crime; or increase the punishment, or change the rules of evidence, for the purpose of conviction. Every law that is to have an operation before the making thereof, as to commence at an antecedent time; or to save time from the statute of limitations; or to excuse acts which were unlawful, and before committed, and the like, is retrospective. But such laws may be proper or necessary, as the case may be. There is a great and apparent difference between making an unlawful act lawful; and the making an innocent action criminal, and punishing it as a crime. The expressions "*ex post facto* laws," are technical, they had been in use long before the revolution, and had acquired an appropriate meaning, by legislators, lawyers and authors. The celebrated and judicious Sir William Blackstone, in his commentaries, considers an *ex post facto* law precisely in the same light as I have done. His opinion is confirmed by his successor, Mr. Wooddeson; and by the author of the *Federalist,* who I esteem superior to both, for his extensive and accurate knowledge of the true principles of government.

I also rely greatly on the definition or explanation of *ex post facto* laws, as given by the conventions of Massachusetts, Maryland and North Carolina, in their several constitutions or forms of government. In the declaration of rights, by the convention of Massachusetts, part 1st, § 24, "Laws made to punish actions done before the existence of such laws, and which have not been declared crimes by preceding laws, are unjust, &c." In the declaration of rights, by the convention of Maryland, art. 15th, "Retrospective laws punishing facts committed before the existence of such laws, and by them only declared criminal, are oppressive, &c." In the declaration of rights, by the convention of North Carolina, art. 24th, I find the same definition, precisely in the same words, as in the Maryland constitution. In the declaration of rights, by the convention of Delaware, art. 11th, the same definition was clearly intended, but inaccurately expressed: by saying "laws punishing offences (instead of actions or facts) committed before the existence of such laws, are oppressive, &c."

I am of opinion, that the fact, contemplated by the prohibition, and not to be affected by a subsequent law, was some fact to be done by a citizen or subject. In 2 Lord Raymond 1352 Raymond, Justice, called the stat. 7 Geo. I., stat. 2, par. 8, about registering contracts for South Sea stock, an *ex post facto* law; because it affected contracts made before the statute.

In the present case, there is no fact done by Bull and wife, plaintiffs in error, that is in any manner affected by the law or resolution of Connecticut: it does not concern, or relate to, any act done by them. The decree of the court of probate of Hartford (on the 21st March), in consequence of which Calder and wife claim a right to the property in question, was given before the said law or resolution, and in that sense, was affected and set aside by it; and in consequence of the law allowing a hearing and the decision in favor of the will, they have lost what they would have been entitled to, if the law or resolution, and the decision in consequence thereof, had not been made. The decree of the court of probate is the only fact, on which the law or resolution operates. In my judgment, the case of the plaintiffs in error, is not within the letter of the prohibition; and for the reasons assigned, I am clearly of opinion, that it is not within the intention of the prohibition; and if within the intention, but out of the letter, I should not, therefore, consider myself justified to construe it within the prohibition, and therefore, that the whole was void.

It was argued by the counsel for the plaintiffs in error, that the legislature of Connecticut had no constitutional power to make the resolution (or law) in question, granting a new hearing, &c. Without giving an opinion, at this time, whether this court has jurisdiction to decide that any law made by congress, contrary to the constitution of the United States, is void: I am fully satisfied, that this court has no jurisdiction to determine that any law of any state legislature, contrary to the constitution of such state, is void. Further, if this court had such jurisdiction, yet it does not appear to me, that the resolution (or law) in question, is contrary to the charter of Connecticut, or its constitution, which is said by counsel to be composed of its acts of assembly, and usages and customs. I should think, that the courts of Connecticut are the proper tribunals to decide, whether laws contrary to the constitution thereof, are void. In the present case, they have, both in the inferior and superior courts, determined that the resolution (or law) in question was not contrary to either their state, or the federal constitution.

To show that the resolution was contrary to the constitution of the United States, it was contended, that the words, *ex post facto* law have a precise and accurate meaning, and convey but one idea to professional men, which is, "by matter of after fact; by something after the fact." And Co. Litt. 241; Fearne's Cont. Rem. (Old Ed.) 175 and 203; Powell on Devises 113, 133, 134, were cited; and the table to Coke's Reports (by Wilson), title *ex post facto,* was referred to. There is no doubt, that a man may be a trespasser from the beginning, by matter of *after fact;* as where an entry is given by law, and the party abuses it; or where the law gives a distress, and the party kills or works the distress.

I admit, an act unlawful in the beginning may, in some

cases, become lawful by matter of *after fact.* I also agree, that the words *"ex post facto"* have the meaning contended for, and no other, in the cases cited, and in all similar cases, where they are used unconnected with, and without relation to, legislative acts or laws. There appears to me a manifest distinction between the case where one fact relates to, and affects, another fact, as where an after fact, by operation of law, makes a former fact either lawful or unlawful; and the case where a law made after a fact done, is to operate on, and to affect, such fact. In the first case, both the acts are done by private persons; in the second case, the first act is done by a private person, and the second act is done by the legislature, to affect the first act.

I believe, that but one instance can be found in which a British judge called a statute, that affected contracts made before the statute, an *ex post facto* law; but the judges of Great Britain always considered penal statutes, that created crimes, or increased the punishment of them, as *ex post facto* laws. If the term *ex post facto* law is to be construed to include and to prohibit the enacting any law, after a fact, it will greatly restrict the power of the federal and state legislatures; and the consequences of such a construction may not be foreseen. If the prohibition to make no *ex post facto* law extends to all laws made after the fact, the two prohibitions, not to make anything but gold and silver coin a tender in payment of debts; and not to pass any law impairing the obligation of contracts, were improper and unnecessary.

It was further urged, that if the provision does not extend to prohibit the making any law, after a fact, then all *choses in action;* all lands by devise; all personal property by bequest, or distribution; by *elegit;* by execution; by judgments, particularly on *torts;* will be unprotected from the legislative power of the states; rights vested may be divested at the will and pleasure of the state legislatures; and therefore, that the true construction and meaning of the prohibition is, that the states pass no law to deprive a citizen of any right vested in him by existing laws.

It is not to be presumed, that the federal or state legislatures will pass laws to deprive citizens of rights vested in them by existing laws; unless for the benefit of the whole community; and on making full satisfaction. The restraint against making any *ex post facto* laws was not considered by the framers of the constitution, as extending to prohibit the depriving a citizen even of a vested right to property; or the provision, "that private property should not be taken for public use, without just compensation," was unnecessary.

It seems to me, that the right of property, in its origin, could only arise from compact, express or implied, and I think it the better opinion, that the right, as well as the mode, or manner of acquiring property, and of alienating or transferring, inheriting or transmitting it, is conferred by society; is regulated by civil institution, and is always subject to the rules prescribed by positive law. When I say, that a right is vested in a citizen, I mean, that he has the power to do certain actions; or to possess certain things, according to the law of the land.

If any one has a right to property, such a right is perfect and exclusive right; but no one can have such right, before he has acquired a better right to the property, than any other person in the world; a right, therefore, only to recover property, cannot be called a perfect and exclusive right. I cannot agree, that a right to property vested in Calder and wife, in consequence of the decree (of the 21st of March 1783) disapproving of the will of Morrison, the grandson. If the will was valid, Mrs. Calder could have no right, as heiress of Morrison, the physician; but if the will was set aside, she had an undoubted title. The resolution (or law) alone had no manner of effect on any right whatever vested in Calder and wife. The resolution (or law), combined with the new hearing, and the decision in virtue of it, took away their right to recover the property in question. But when combined, they took away no right of property vested in Calder and wife; because, the decree against the will (21st March 1783) did not vest in or transfer any property to them.

I am under a necessity to give a construction or explanation of the words, "*ex post facto* law," because they have not any certain meaning attached to them. But I will not go further than I feel myself bound to do; and if I ever exercise the jurisdiction, I will not decide any law to be void, but in a very clear case.

I am of opinion, that the decree of the supreme court of errors of Connecticut be affirmed, with costs.

Paterson, Justice.—The constitution of Connecticut is made up of usages, and it appears, that its legislature have, from the beginning, exercised the power of granting new trials. This has been uniformly the case, until the year 1762, when this power was, by a legislative act, imparted to the superior and county courts. But the act does not remove or annihilate the pre-existing power of the legislature, in this particular; it only communicates to other authorities a concurrence of jurisdiction, as to the awarding of new trials. And the fact is, that the legislature have, in two instances, exercised this power, since the passing of the law in 1762. They acted in a double capacity, as a house of legislation, with undefined authority, and also as a court of judicature, in certain exigencies. Whether the latter arose from the indefinite nature of their legislative powers, or in some other way, it is not necessary to discuss. From the best information, however, which I have been able to collect on this subject, it appears, that the legislature, or general court of Connecticut, originally possessed and exercised all legislative, executive and judicial authority; and that, from time to time, they distributed the two latter in such manner as they thought proper; but without parting with the general superintending power, or the right of exercising the same, whenever they should judge it expedient. But be this as it may, it is sufficient for the present, to observe, that they have, on certain occasions, exercised judicial authority, from the commencement of their civil polity. This usage makes up part of the constitution of Connecticut, and we are bound to consider it as such, unless it be inconsistent with the constitution of the United States. True it is, that the awarding of new trials falls properly within the province of the judiciary; but if the legislature of Connecticut have been in the uninterrupted exercise of this authority, in certain cases, we must, in such cases, respect their decisions, as flowing from a competent jurisdiction or constitutional organ. And therefore, we may, in the present instance, consider the legislature of the state as having acted in their customary judicial capacity. if so, there is an end of the question. For if the power, thus exercised, comes more properly within the description of a judicial than of a legislative power; and if by usage or the constitution, which, in Connecticut, are synonymous terms, the legislature of that state acted in both capacities; then, in the case now before us, it would be fair to consider the awarding of a new trial, as an act emanating from the judiciary side of the department.

But as this view of the subject militates against the plaintiffs in error, their counsel has contended for a reversal of the judgment, on the ground, that the awarding of a new trial was the effect of a legislative act, and that it is unconstitutional, because an *ex post facto* law. For the sake of ascertaining the meaning of these terms, I will consider the resolution of the general court of Connecticut, as the exercise of a legislative and not a judicial authority. The question, then, which arises on the pleadings in this cause, is, whether the resolution of the legislature of Connecticut, be an *ex post facto* law, within the meaning of the constitution of the United States? I am of opinion, that it is not. The words, *ex post facto,* when applied to a law, have a technical meaning, and, in legal phraseology, refer to crimes, pains and penalties. Judge Blackstone's description of the terms is clear and accurate. "There is," says he, "a still more unreasonable method than this, which is called making of laws, *ex post facto,* when, after an action, indifferent in itself, is committed, the legislature, then, for the first time, declares it to have been a crime, and inflicts a punishment upon the person who has committed it. Here, it is impossible, that the party could foresee, that an action, innocent when it was done, should be afterwards converted to guilt, by a subsequent law; he had, therefore, no cause to abstain from it; and all punishment for not abstaining, must, of consequence, be cruel and unjust." 1 Bl. Com. 46. Here, the meaning annexed to the terms *ex post facto* laws, unquestionably refers to crimes, and nothing else. The historic page abundantly evinces, that the power of passing such laws should be withheld from legislators; as it is a dangerous instrument in the hands of bold, unprincipled, aspiring and party men, and has been too often used to effect the most detestable purposes.

On inspecting such of our state constitutions, as take notice of laws made *ex post facto,* we shall find, that they are understood in the same sense. The constitution of Massachusetts, article 24th of the declaration of rights: "Laws made to punish for actions done before the existence of such laws, and which have not been declared crimes by preceding laws, are unjust, oppressive, and inconsistent with the fundamental principles of a free government." The constitution of Delaware, article 11th of the declaration of rights: "That retrospective laws punishing offences committed before the existence of such laws, are oppressive and unjust, and ought not to be made." The constitution of Maryland, article 15th of the declaration of rights: "That retrospective laws, punishing facts committed before the existence of such laws, and by them only declared criminal, are oppressive, unjust and incompatible with liberty; wherefore, no *ex post facto* law ought to be made." The constitution of North Carolina, article 24th of the declaration of rights: "That retrospective laws, punishing facts committed before the existence of such laws, and by them only declared criminal, are oppressive, unjust and incompatible with liberty; wherefore, no *ex post facto* law ought to be made."

From the above passages, it appears, that *ex post facto* laws have an appropriate signification; they extend to penal statutes and no further; they are restricted, in legal estimation, to the creation, and, perhaps, enhancement of crimes, pains and penalties. The enhancement of a crime or penalty seems to come within the same mischief as the creation of a crime or penalty; and therefore, they may be classed together.

Again, the words of the constitution of the United States are, "That no state shall pass any bill of attainder, *ex post facto* law, or law impairing the obligation of contracts." Article I., § 10. Where is the necessity or use of the latter words, if a law impairing the obligation of contracts, be comprehended within the terms *ex post facto* law? It is obvious, from the specification of contracts in the last member of the clause, that the framers of the constitution did not understand or use the words in the sense contended for on the part of the plaintiffs in error. They understood and used the words in their known and appropriate signification, as referring to crimes, pains and penalties, and no further. The arrangement of the distinct members of this section, necessarily points to this meaning.

I had an ardent desire to have extended the provision in the constitution to retrospective laws in general. There is neither policy or safety in such laws; and therefore, I have always had a strong aversion against them. It may, in general, be truly observed of retrospective laws of every description, that they neither accord with sound legislation, nor the fundamental principles of the social compact. But on full consideration, I am convinced, that *ex post facto* laws must be limited in the manner already expressed; they must be taken in their technical, which is also their common and general, acceptation, and are not to be understood in their literal sense.

IREDELL, Justice.—Though I concur in the general result of the opinions which have been delivered, I cannot entirely adopt the reasons that are assigned upon the occasion.

From the best information to be collected, relative to the constitution of Connecticut, it appears, that the legislature of that state has been in the uniform, uninterrupted habit of exercising a general superintending power over its courts of law, by granting new trials. It may, indeed, appear strange to some of us, that in any form, there should exist a power to grant, with respect to suits depending or adjudged, new rights of trial, new privileges of proceeding, not previously recognised and regulated by positive institutions; but such is the established usage of Connecticut, and it is obviously consistent with the general superintending authority of her legislature. Nor is it altogether without some sanction, for a legislature to act as a court of justice. In England, we know that one branch of the parliament, the House of Lords, not only exercises a judicial power, in cases of impeachment, and for the trial of its own members, but as the court of dernier resort, takes cognisance of many suits of law and in equity; and that in construction of law, the jurisdiction there exercised is by the king in full parliament; which shows that, in its origin, the causes were probably heard before the whole parliament. When Connecticut was settled, the right of empowering the legislature to superintend the courts of justice, was, I presume, early assumed; and its expediency, as applied to the local circumstances and municipal policy of the state, is sanctioned by a long and uniform practice. The power, however, is judicial in its nature; and whenever it is exercised, as in the present instance, it is an exercise of judicial, not of legislative, authority.

But let us, for a moment, suppose, that the resolution, granting a new trial, was a legislative act, it will by no means follow, that it is an act affected by the constitutional prohibition, that "no state shall pass any *ex post facto* law." I will endeavor to state the general principles which influence me, on this point, succinctly and clearly, though I have not had an opportunity to reduce my opinion to writing.

If, then, a government, composed of legislative, executive and judicial departments, were established, by a constitution which imposed no limits on the legislative power, the consequence would inevitably be, that whatever the legislative power chose to enact, would be lawfully enacted, and the judicial power could never interpose to pronounce it void. It is true, that some speculative jurists have held, that a legislative act against natural justice must, in itself, be void; but I cannot think that, under such a government any court of justice would possess a power to declare it so. Sir William Blackstone, having put the strong case of an act of parliament, which authorize a man to try his own cause, explicitly adds, that even in that case, "there is no court that has power to defeat the intent of the legislature, when couched in such evident and express words, as leave no doubt whether it was the intent of the legislature, or no." 1 Bl. Com. 91.

In order, therefore, to guard against so great an evil, it has been the policy of all the American states, which have, individually, framed their state constitutions, since the revolution, and of the people of the United States, when they framed the federal constitution, to define with precision the objects of the legislative power, and to restrain its exercise within marked and settled boundaries. If any act of congress, or of the legislature of a state, violates those constitutional provisions, it is unquestionably void; though, I admit, that as the authority to declare it void is of a delicate and awful nature, the court will never resort to that authority, but in a clear and urgent case. If, on the other hand, the legislature of the Union, or the legislature of any member of the Union, shall pass a law, within the general scope of their constitutional power, the court cannot pronounce it to be void, merely because it is, in their judgment, contrary to the principles of natural justice. The ideas of natural justice are regulated by no fixed standard: the ablest and the purest men have differed upon the subject; and all that the court could properly say, in such an event, would be, that the legislature (possessed of an equal right of opinion) had passed an act which, in the opinion of the judges, was inconsistent with the abstract principles of natural justice. There are then but two lights, in which the subject can be viewed: 1st. If the legislature pursue the authority delegated to them, their acts are valid. 2d. If they transgress the boundaries of that authority, their acts are invalid. In the former case, they exercise the discretion vested in them by the people, to whom alone they are responsible for the faithful discharge of their trust: but in the latter case, they violate a fundamental law, which must be our guide, whenever we are called upon, as judges, to determine the validity of a legislative act.

Still, however, in the present instance, the act or resolution of the legislature of Connecticut, cannot be regarded as an *ex post facto* law; for the true construction of the prohibition extends to criminal, not to civil cases. It is only in criminal cases, indeed, in which the danger to be guarded against, is greatly to be apprehended. The history of every country in Europe will furnish flagrant instances of tyranny exercised under the pretext of penal dispensations. Rival factions, in their efforts to crush each other, have superseded all the forms, and suppressed all the sentiments of justice; while attainders, on the principle of retaliation and proscription, have marked all the vicissitudes of party triumph. The temptation to such abuses of power is unfortunately too alluring for human virtue; and therefore, the framers of the American constitutions have wisely denied to the respective legislatures, federal as well as state, the possession of the power itself: they shall not pass any *ex post facto* law; or, in other words, they shall not inflict a punishment for any act, which was innocent at the time it was committed; nor increase the degree of punishment previously denounced for any specific offence.

The policy, the reason and humanity of the prohibition, do not, I repeat, extend to civil cases, to cases that merely affect the private property of citizens. Some of the most necessary and important acts of legislation are, on the contrary, founded upon the principle, that private rights must yield to public exigencies. Highways are run through private grounds; fortifications, light-houses, and other public edifices, are necessarily sometimes built upon the soil owned by individuals. In such, and similar cases, if the owners should refuse voluntarily to accommodate the public, they must be constrained, so far as the public necessities require; and justice is done, by allowing them a reasonable equivalent. Without the possession of this power, the operations of government would often be obstructed, and society itself would be endangered. It is not sufficient to urge, that the power may be abused, for such is the nature of all power—such is the tendency of every human institution: and, it might as fairly be said, that the power of taxation, which is only circumscribed by the discretion of the body in which it is vested, ought not to be granted, because the legislature, disregarding its true objects, might, for visionary and useless projects, impose a tax to the amount of nineteen shillings in the pound. We must be content to limit power, where we can, and where we cannot, consistently with its use, we must be content to repose a salutary confidence. It is our consolation, that there never existed a government, in ancient or modern times, more free from danger in this respect, than the governments of America.

Upon the whole, though there cannot be a case, in which an *ex post facto* law in criminal matters is requisite or justifiable (for providence never can intend to promote the prosperity of any country by bad means), yet, in the present instance, the objection does not arise: because, 1st, if the act of the legislature of Connecticut was a judicial act, it is not within the words of the constitution; and 2d, even if it was a legislative act, it is not within the meaning of the prohibition.

CUSHING, Justice.—The case appears to me to be clear of all difficulty, taken either way. If the act is a judicial act, it is not touched by the federal constitution: and if it is a legislative act, it is maintained and justified by the ancient and uniform practice of the state of Connecticut.

11

UNIVERSITY OF NORTH CAROLINA V. FOX
1 Mur. 58 (N.C. 1805)

(See Amend. V [due process and taking], no. 19)

12

FLETCHER V. PECK
6 Cranch 87 (1810)

March 16, 1810. MARSHALL, *Ch. J.*, delivered the opinion of the court as follows:

The pleadings being now amended, this cause comes on again to be heard on sundry demurrers, and on a special verdict.

The suit was instituted on several covenants contained in a deed made by John Peck, the defendant in error, conveying to Robert Fletcher, the plaintiff in error, certain lands which were part of a large purchase made by James Gunn and others, in the year 1795, from the state of Georgia, the contract for which was made in the form of a bill passed by the legislature of that state.

The first count in the declaration set forth a breach in the second covenant contained in the deed. The covenant is, "that the legislature of the state of Georgia, at the time of passing the act of sale aforesaid, had good right to sell and dispose of the same in the manner pointed out by the said act." The breach assigned is, that the legislature had no power to sell.

The plea in bar sets forth the constitution of the state of Georgia, and avers that the lands sold by the defendant to the plaintiff, were within that state. It then sets forth the granting act, and avers the power of the legislature to sell and dispose of the premises as pointed out by the act.

To this plea the plaintiff below demurred, and the defendant joined in demurrer.

That the legislature of Georgia, unless restrained by its own constitution, possesses the power of disposing of the unappropriated lands within its own limits, in such manner as its own judgment shall dictate, is a proposition not to be controverted. The only question, then, presented by this demurrer, for the consideration of the court, is this, did the then constitution of the state of Georgia prohibit the legislature to dispose of the lands, which were the subject of this contract, in the manner stipulated by the contract?

The question, whether a law be void for its repugnancy to the constitution, is, at all times, a question of much delicacy, which ought seldom, if ever, to be decided in the affirmative in a doubtful case. The court, when impelled by duty to render such a judgment, would be unworthy of its station, could it be unmindful of the solemn obligations which that station imposes. But it is not on slight implication and vague conjecture that the legislature is to be pronounced to have transcended its powers, and its acts to be considered as void. The opposition between the constitution and the law should be such that the judge feels a clear and strong conviction of their incompatibility with each other.

In this case the court can perceive no such opposition. In the constitution of Georgia, adopted in the year 1789, the court can perceive no restriction on the legislative power, which inhibits the passage of the act of 1795. The court cannot say that, in passing that act, the legislature has transcended its powers and violated the constitution.

In overruling the demurrer, therefore, to the first plea, the Circuit Court committed no error.

The 3d convenant is, that all the title which the state of Georgia ever had in the premises had been legally conveyed to John Peck, the grantor.

The 2d count assigns, in substance, as a breach of this covenant, that the original grantees from the state of Georgia promised and assured divers members of the legislature, then sitting in general assembly, that if the said members would assent to, and vote for, the passing of the act, and if the said bill should pass, such members should have a share of, and be interested in, all the lands purchased from the said state by virtue of such law. And that divers of the said members, to whom the said promises were made, were unduly influenced thereby, and, under such influence, did vote for the passing of the said bill; by reason whereof the said law was a nullity, &c., and so the title of the state of Georgia did not pass to the said Peck, &c.

The plea to this count, after protesting that the promises it alleges were not made, avers, that until after the purchase made from the original grantees by James Greenleaf, under whom the said Peck claims, neither the said James Greenleaf, nor the said Peck, nor any of the mesne vendors between the said Greenleaf and Peck, had any notice or knowledge that any such promises or assurances were made by the said original grantees, or either of them, to any of the members of the legislature of the state of Georgia.

To this plea the plaintiff demurred generally, and the defendant joined in the demurrer.

That corruption should find its way into the governments of our infant republics, and contaminate the very source of legislation, or that impure motives should contribute to the passage of a law, or the formation of a legislative contract, are circumstances most deeply to be deplored. How far a court of justice would, in any case, be competent, on proceedings instituted by the state itself, to vacate a contract thus formed, and to annul rights acquired, under that contract, by third persons having no notice of the improper means by which it was obtained, is a question which the court would approach with much circumspection. It may well be doubted how far the validity of a law depends upon the motives of its framers, and how far the particular inducements, operating on members of the supreme soverign power of a state, to the formation of a contract by that power, are examinable in a court of justice. If the principle be conceded, that an act of the supreme sovereign power might be declared null by a court, in consequence of the means which procured it, still would there be much difficulty in saying to what extent those means must be applied to produce this effect. Must it be direct corruption, or would interest or undue influence of any kind be sufficient? Must the vitiating cause operate on a majority, or on what number of the members? Would the act be null, whatever might be the wish of the nation, or would its obligation or nullity depend upon the public sentiment?

If the majority of the legislature be corrupted, it may well be doubted, whether it be within the province of the judiciary to control their conduct, and, if less than a majority act from impure motives, the principle by which judicial interference would be regulated, is not clearly discerned.

Whatever difficulties this subject might present, when viewed under aspects of which it may be susceptible, this court can perceive none in the particular pleadings now under consideration.

This is not a bill brought by the state of Georgia, to annul the contract, nor does it appear to the court, by this count, that the state of Georgia is dissatisfied with the sale that has been made. The case, as made out in the pleadings, is simply this: One individual who holds lands in the state of Georgia, under a deed covenanting that the title of Georgia was in the grantor, brings an action of covenant upon this deed, and assigns, as a breach, that some of the members of the legislature were induced to vote in favor of the law, which constituted the contract, by being promised an interest in it, and that therefore the act is a mere nullity.

This solemn question cannot be brought thus collaterally and incidentally before the court. It would be indecent in the extreme, upon a private contract between two individuals, to enter into an inquiry respecting the corruption of the sovereign power of a state. If the title be plainly deduced from a legislative act, which the legislature might constitutionally pass, if the act be clothed with all the requisite forms of a law, a court, sitting as a court of law, cannot sustain a suit brought by one individual against another founded on the allegation that the act is a nullity, in consequence of the impure motives which influenced certain members of the legislature which passed the law.

The Circuit Court, therefore, did right in overruling this demurrer.

The 4th covenant in the deed is, that the title to the premises has been in no way, constitutionally or legally, impaired by virtue of any subsequent act of any subsequent legislature of the state of Georgia.

The third count recites the undue means practiced on certain members of the legislature, as stated in the second count, and then alleges that, in consequence of these practices, and of other causes, a subsequent legislature passed an act annulling and rescinding the law under which the conveyance to the original grantees was made, declaring that conveyance void, and asserting the title of the state to the lands it contained. The court proceeds to recite at large, this rescinding act, and concludes with averring that, by reason of this act the title of the said Peck in the premises was constitutionally and legally impaired, and rendered null and void.

After protesting, as before, that no such promises were made as stated in this count, the defendant again pleads that himself and the first purchaser under the original grantees, and all intermediate holders of the property, were purchasers without notice.

To this plea there is a demurrer and joinder.

The importance and the difficulty of the questions, presented by these pleadings, are deeply felt by the court.

The lands in controversy vested absolutely in James Gunn and others, the original grantees, by the conveyance of the governor, made in pursuance of an act of assembly to which the legislature was fully competent. Being thus in full possession of the legal estate, they, for a valuable consideration, conveyed portions of the land to those who were willing to purchase. If the original transaction was infected with fraud, these purchasers did not participate in it, and had no notice of it. They were innocent. Yet the legislature of Georgia has involved them in the fate of the first parties to the transaction, and, if the act be valid, has annihilated their rights also.

The legislature of Georgia was a party to this transaction; and for a party to pronounce its own deed invalid, whatever cause may be assigned for its invalidity, must be considered as a mere act of power which must find its vindication in a train of reasoning not often heard in courts of justice.

But the real party, it is said, are the people, and when their agents are unfaithful, the acts of those agents cease to be obligatory.

It is, however, to be recollected that the people can act only by these agents, and that, while within the powers conferred on them, their acts must be considered as the acts of the people. If the agents be corrupt, others may be chosen, and, if their contracts be examinable, the common sentiment, as well as common usage of mankind, points out a mode by which this examination may be made, and their validity determined.

If the legislature of Georgia was not bound to submit its pretensions to those tribunals which are established for the security of property, and to decide on human rights, if it might claim to itself the power of judging in its own case, yet there are certain great principles of justice, whose authority is universally acknowledged, that ought not to be entirely disregarded.

If the legislature be its own judge in its own case, it would seem equitable that its decision should be regulated by those rules which would have regulated the decision of a judicial tribunal. The question was, in its nature, a question of title, and the tribunal which decided it was either acting in the character of a court of justice, and performing a duty usually assigned to a court, or it was exerting a mere act of power in which it was controlled only by its own will.

If a suit be brought to set aside a conveyance obtained by fraud, and the fraud be clearly proved, the conveyance will be set aside, as between the parties; but the rights of third persons, who are purchasers without notice, for a valuable consideration, cannot be disregarded. Titles which, according to every legal test, are perfect, are acquired with that confidence which is inspired by the opinion that the purchaser is safe. If there be any concealed defect, arising from the conduct of those who had held the property long before he acquired it, of which he had no notice, that concealed defect cannot be set up against him. He has paid his money for a title good at law, he is innocent, whatever may be the guilt of others, and equity will not subject him to the penalties attached to that guilt. All titles would be insecure, and the intercourse between man and man would be very seriously obstructed, if this principle be overturned.

A court of chancery, therefore, had a bill been brought to set aside the conveyance made to James Gunn and others, as being obtained by improper practices with the legislature, whatever might have been its decision as respected the original grantees, would have been bound, by its own rules, and by the clearest principles of equity, to leave unmolested those who were purchasers, without notice, for a valuable consideration.

If the legislature felt itself absolved from those rules of property which are common to all the citizens of the United States, and from those principles of equity which are acknowledged in all our courts, its act is to be supported by its power alone, and the same power may devest any other individual of his lands, if it shall be the will of the legislature so to exert it.

It is not intended to speak with disrespect of the legislature of Georgia, or of its acts. Far from it. The question is a general question, and is treated as one. For although such powerful objections to a legislative grant, as are alleged against this, may not again exist, yet the principle, on which alone this rescinding act is to be supported, may be applied to every case to which it shall be the will of any legislature to apply it. The principle is this: that a legislature may, by its own act, devest the vested estate of any man whatever, for reasons which shall, by itself, be deemed sufficient.

In this case the legislature may have had ample proof that the original grant was obtained by practices which can never be too much reprobated, and which would have justified its abrogation so far as respected those to whom crime was imputable. But the grant, when issued, conveyed an estate in fee-simple to the grantee, clothed with all the solemnities which law can bestow. This estate was transferable; and those who purchased parts of it were not stained by that guilt which infected the original transaction. Their case is not distinguishable from the ordinary case of purchasers of a legal estate without knowledge of any secret fraud which might have led to the emanation of the original grant. According to the well known course of equity, their rights could not be affected by such fraud. Their situation was the same, their title was the same, with that of every other member of the community who holds land by regular conveyances from the original patentee.

Is the power of the legislature competent to the annihilation of such title, and to a resumption of the property thus held?

The principle asserted is, that one legislature is competent to repeal any act which a former legislature was competent to pass; and that one legislature cannot abridge the powers of a succeeding legislature.

The correctness of this principle, so far as respects general legislation, can never be controverted. But, if an act be done under a law, a succeeding legislature cannot undo it. The past cannot be recalled by the most absolute power. Conveyances have been made; those conveyances have vested legal estates, and, if those estates may be seized by the sovereign authority, still, that they originally vested is a fact, and cannot cease to be a fact.

When, then, a law is in its nature a contract, when absolute rights have vested under that contract, a repeal of the law cannot devest those rights; and the act of annulling them, if legitimate, is rendered so by a power applicable to the case of every individual in the community.

It may well be doubted whether the nature of society and of government does not prescribe some limits to the legislative power; and, if any be prescribed, where are they to be found, if the property of an individual, fairly and honestly acquired, may be seized without compensation?

To the legislature all legislative power is granted; but the question, whether the act of transferring the property of an individual to the public, be in the nature of the legislative power, is well worthy of serious reflection.

It is the peculiar province of the legislature to prescribe general rules for the government of society; the application of those rules to individuals in society would seem to be the duty of other departments. How far the power of giving the law may involve every other power, in cases where the constitution is silent, never has been, and perhaps never can be, definitely stated.

The validity of this rescinding act, then, might well be doubted, were Georgia a single sovereign power. But Georgia cannot be viewed as a single, unconnected, sovereign power, on whose legislature no other restrictions are imposed than may be found in its own constitution. She is a part of a large empire; she is a member of the American Union; and that Union has a constitution the supremacy of which all acknowledge, and which imposes limits to the legislatures of the several states, which none claim a right to pass. The constitution of the United States declares that no state shall pass any bill of attainder, *ex post facto* law, or law impairing the obligation of contracts.

Does the case now under consideration come within this prohibitory section of the constitution?

In considering this very interesting question, we immediately ask ourselves what is a contract? Is a grant a contract?

A contract is a compact between two or more parties, and is either executory or executed. An executory contract is one in which a party binds himself to do, or not to do, a particular thing; such was the law under which the conveyance was made by the governor. A contract executed is one in which the object of contract is performed: and this, says Blackstone, differs in nothing from a grant. The contract between Georgia and the purchasers was executed by the grant. A contract executed, as well as one which is executory, contains obligations binding on the parties. A grant, in its own nature, amounts to an extinguishment of the right of the grantor, and implies a contract not to reassert that right. A party is, therefore, always estopped by his own grant.

Since, then, in fact, a grant is a contract executed, the obligation of which still continues, and since the constitution uses the general term contract, without distinguishing between those which are executory and those which are executed, it must be construed to comprehend the latter as well as the former. A law annulling conveyances between individuals, and declaring that the grantors should stand seized of their former estates, notwithstanding those grants, would be as repugnant to the constitution as a law discharging the vendors of property from the obligation of executing their contracts by conveyances. It would be strange if a contract to convey was secured by the constitution, while an absolute conveyance remained unprotected.

If, under a fair construction of the constitution, grants are comprehended under the term contracts, is a grant from the state excluded from the operation of the provision? Is the clause to be considered as inhibiting the state from impairing the obligation of contracts between two individuals, but as excluding from that inhibition contracts made with itself?

The words themselves contain no such distinction. They are general, and are applicable to contracts of every description. If contracts made with the state are to be exempted from their operation, the exception must arise from the character of the contracting party, not from the words which are employed.

Whatever respect might have been felt for the state sovereignties, it is not to be disguised that the framers of the constitution viewed, with some apprehension, the violent acts which might grow out of the feelings of the moment; and that the people of the United States, in adopting that instrument, have manifested a determination to shield themselves and their property from the effects of those sudden and strong passions to which men are exposed. The restrictions on the legislative power of the states are obviously founded in this sentiment: and the constitution of the United States contains what may be deemed a bill of rights for the people of each state.

No state shall pass any bill of attainder, *ex post facto* law, or law impairing the obligation of contracts.

A bill of attainder may affect the life of an individual, or may confiscate his property, or may do both.

In this form the power of the legislature over the lives and fortunes of individuals is expressly restrained. What motive, then, for implying, in words which import a general prohibition to impair the obligation of contracts, an exception in favor of the right to impair the obligation of those contracts into which the state may enter?

The state legislatures can pass no *ex post facto* law. An *ex post facto* law is one which renders an act punishable in a manner in which it was not punishable when it was committed. Such a law may inflict penalties on the person, or may inflict pecuniary penalties which swell the public treasury. The legislature is then prohibited from passing a law by which a man's estate, or any part of it, shall be seized for a crime which was not declared, by some previous law, to render him liable to that punishment. Why, then, should violence be done to the natural meaning of words for the purpose of leaving to the legislature the power of seizing, for public use, the estate of an individual in the form of a law annulling the title by which he holds that estate? The court can perceive no sufficient grounds for making this distinction. This rescinding act would have the effect of an *ex post facto* law. It forfeits the estate of Fletcher for a crime not committed by himself, but by those from whom he purchased. This cannot be effected in the form of an *ex post facto* law, or bill of attainder; why, then, is it allowable in the form of a law annulling the original grant?

The argument in favor of presuming an intention to except a case, not excepted by the words of the constitution, is susceptible of some illustration from a principle originally ingrafted in that instrument, though no longer a part of it. The constitution, as passed, gave the courts of the United States jurisdiction in suits brought against individual states. A state, then, which violated its own contract was suable in the courts of the United States for that violation. Would it have been a defense in such a suit to say that the state had passed a law absolving itself from the contract? It is scarcely to be conceived that such a defense could be set up. And yet, if a state is neither restrained by the general principles of our political institutions, nor by the words of the constitution, from impairing the obligation of its own contracts, such a defense would be a valid one. This feature is no longer found in the constitution; but it aids in the construction of those clauses with which it was originally associated.

It is, then, the unanimous opinion of the court, that, in this case, the estate having passed into the hands of a purchaser for a valuable consideration, without notice, the state of Georgia was restrained, either by general principles, which are common to our free institutions, or by the particular provisions of the constitution of the United

States, from passing a law whereby the estate of the plaintiff in the premises so purchased could be constitutionally and legally impaired and rendered null and void.

In overruling the demurrer to the 3d plea, therefore, there is no error.

The first covenant in the deed is, that the state of Georgia, at the time of the act of the legislature thereof, entitled as aforesaid, was legally seized in fee of the soil thereof subject only to the extinguishment of part of the Indian title thereon.

The 4th count assigns, as a breach of this covenant, that the right to the soil was in the United States, and not in Georgia.

To this count the defendant pleads, that the state of Georgia was seized; and tenders an issue on the fact in which the plaintiff joins. On this issue a special verdict is found.

The jury find the grant of Carolina by Charles second to the Earl of Clarendon and others, comprehending the whole country from 36 deg. 30 min. north lat. to 29 deg. north lat., and from the Atlantic to the South Sea.

They find that the northern part of this territory was afterwards erected into a separate colony, and that the most northern part of the 35 deg. of north lat. was the boundary line between North and South Carolina.

That seven of the eight proprietors of the Carolinas surrendered to George second in the year 1729, who appointed a governor of South Carolina.

That, in 1732, George the second granted, to the Lord Viscount Percival and others, seven-eighths of the territory between the Savannah and the Alatamaha, and extending west to the South Sea, and that the remaining eighth part, which was still the property of the heir of Lord Carteret, one of the original grantees of Carolina, was afterwards conveyed to them. This territory was constituted a colony and called Georgia.

That the governor of South Carolina continued to exercise jurisdiction south of Georgia.

That, in 1752, the grantees surrendered to the crown.

That, in 1754, a governor was appointed by the crown, with a commission describing the boundaries of the colony.

That a treaty of peace was concluded between Great Britain and Spain, in 1763, in which the latter ceded to the former Florida, with fort St. Augustine and the bay of Pensacola.

That, in October, 1763, the King of Great Britain issued a proclamation, creating four new colonies, Quebec, East Florida, West Florida, and Grenada; and prescribing the bounds of each, and further declaring that all the lands between the Alatamaha and St. Mary's should be annexed to Georgia. The same proclamation contained a clause reserving, under the dominion and protection of the crown, for the use of the Indians, all the lands on the western waters, and forbidding a settlement on them, or a purchase of them from the Indians. The lands conveyed to the plaintiff lie on the western waters.

That, in November, 1763, a commission was issued to the governor of Georgia, in which the boundaries of that province are described as extending westward to the Mississippi. A commission, describing boundaries of the same extent, was afterwards granted in 1764.

That a war broke out between Great Britain and her colonies, which terminated in a treaty of peace acknowledging them as sovereign and independent states.

That in April, 1787, a convention was entered into between the states of South Carolina and Georgia settling the boundary line between them.

The jury afterwards describe the situation of the lands mentioned in the plaintiff's declaration, in such manner that their lying within the limits of Georgia, as defined in the proclamation of 1763, in the treaty of peace, and in the convention between that state and South Carolina, has not been questioned.

The counsel for the plaintiff rest their argument on a single proposition. They contend that the reservation for the use of the Indians, contained in the proclamation of 1763, excepts the lands on the western waters from the colonies within whose bounds they would otherwise have been, and that they were acquired by the revolutionary war. All acquisitions during the war, it is contended, were made by the joint arms, for the joint benefit of the United States, and not for the benefit of any particular state.

The court does not understand the proclamation as it is understood by the counsel for the plaintiff. The reservation for the use of the Indians appears to be a temporary arrangement suspending, for a time, the settlement of the country reserved, and the powers of the royal governor within the territory reserved, but is not conceived to amount to an alteration of the boundaries of the colony. If the language of the proclamation be, in itself, doubtful, the commissions subsequent thereto, which were given to the governors of Georgia, entirely remove the doubt.

The question, whether the vacant lands within the United States became a joint property, or belonged to the separate states, was a momentous question which, at one time, threatened to shake the American confederacy to its foundation. This important and dangerous contest has been compromised, and the compromise is not now to be disturbed.

It is the opinion of the court, that the particular land stated in the declaration appears, from this special verdict, to lie within the state of Georgia, and that the state of Georgia had power to grant it.

Some difficulty was produced by the language of the covenant, and of the pleadings. It was doubted whether a state can be seized in fee of lands, subject to the Indian title, and whether a decision that they were seized in fee, might not be construed to amount to a decision that their grantee might maintain an ejectment for them, notwithstanding that title.

The majority of the court is of opinion that the nature of the Indian title, which is certainly to be respected by all courts, until it be legitimately extinguished, is not such as to be absolutely repugnant to seizin in fee on the part of the state.

Judgment affirmed with costs.

JOHNSON, *J.* In this case I entertain, on two points, an

opinion different from that which has been delivered by the court.

I do not hesitate to declare that a state does not possess the power of revoking its own grants. But I do it on a general principle, on the reason and nature of things: a principle which will impose laws even on the Deity.

A contrary opinion can only be maintained upon the ground that no existing legislature can abridge the powers of those which will succeed it. To a certain extent this is certainly correct; but the distinction lies between power and interest, the right of jurisdiction and the right of soil.

The right of jurisdiction is essentially connected to, or rather identified with, the national sovereignty. To part with it is to commit a species of political suicide. In fact, a power to produce its own annihilation is an absurdity in terms. It is a power as utterly incommunicable to a political as to a natural person. But it is not so with the interests or property of a nation. Its possessions nationally are in nowise necessary to its political existence; they are entirely accidental, and may be parted with in every respect similarly to those of the individuals who compose the community. When the legislature have once conveyed their interest or property in any subject to the individual, they have lost all control over it; have nothing to act upon; it has passed from them; is vested in the individual; becomes intimately blended with his existence, as essentially so as the blood that circulates through his system. The government may indeed demand of him the one or the other, not because they are not his, but because whatever is his is his country's.

As to the idea, that the grants of a legislature may be void because the legislature are corrupt, it appears to me to be subject to insuperable difficulties. The acts of the supreme power of a country must be considered pure for the same reason that all sovereign acts must be considered just; because there is no power that can declare them otherwise. The absurdity in this case would have been strikingly perceived, could the party who passed the act of cession have got again into power, and declared themselves pure, and the intermediate legislature corrupt.

The security of a people against the misconduct of their rulers, must lie in the frequent recurrence to first principles, and the imposition of adequate constitutional restrictions. Nor would it be difficult, with the same view, for laws to be framed which would bring the conduct of individuals under the review of adequate tribunals, and make them suffer under the consequences of their own immoral conduct.

I have thrown out these ideas that I may have it distinctly understood that my opinion on this point is not founded on the provision in the constitution of the United States, relative to laws impairing the obligation of contracts. It is much to be regretted that words of less equivocal signification had not been adopted in that article of the constitution. There is reason to believe, from the letters of Publius, which are well known to be entitled to the highest respect, that the object of the convention was to afford a general protection to individual rights against the acts of the state legislatures. Whether the words, "acts impairing the obligation of contracts," can be construed to have the same force as must have been given to the words "obligation and effect of contracts," is the difficulty in my mind.

There can be no solid objection to adopting the technical definition of the word "contract," given by Blackstone. The etymology, the classical signification, and the civil law idea of the word, will all support it. But the difficulty arises on the word "obligation," which certainly imports an existing moral or physical necessity. Now, a grant or conveyance by no means necessarily implies the continuance of an obligation beyond the moment of executing it. It is most generally but the consummation of a contract, is *functus officio* the moment it is executed, and continues afterwards to be nothing more than the evidence that a certain act was done.

I enter with great hesitation upon this question, because it involves a subject of the greatest delicacy and much difficulty. The states and the United States are continually legislating on the subject of contracts, prescribing the mode of authentication, the time within which suits shall be prosecuted for them, in many cases affecting existing contracts by the laws which they pass, and declaring them to cease or lose their effect for want of compliance, in the parties, with such statutory provisions. All these acts appear to be within the most correct limits of legislative powers, and most beneficially exercised, and certainly could not have been intended to be affected by this constitutional provision; yet where to draw the line, or how to define or limit the words, "obligation of contracts," will be found a subject of extreme difficulty.

To give it the general effect of a restriction of the state powers in favor of private rights, is certainly going very far beyond the obvious and necessary import of the words, and would operate to restrict the states in the exercise of that right which every community must exercise, of possessing itself of the property of the individual, when necessary for public uses; a right which a magnanimous and just government will never exercise without amply indemnifying the individual, and which perhaps amounts to nothing more than a power to oblige him to sell and convey, when the public necessities require it.

13

Thomas Jefferson to W. H. Torrance
11 June 1815
Works 11:471–75

I received a few days ago your favor of May 5th, stating a question on a law of the State of Georgia which suspends judgments for a limited time, and asking my opinion whether it may be valid under the inhibition of our Constitution to pass laws impairing the obligations of contracts. It is more than forty years since I have quitted the practice of the law, and been engaged in vocations which furnished little occasion of preserving a familiarity with that science. I am far, therefore, from being qualified to decide on the problems it presents, and certainly not disposed to obtrude in a case where gentlemen have been consulted of the first qualifications, and of actual and daily familiarity with the subject, especially, too, in a question on the law of another State. We have in this State a law resembling in some degree that you quote, suspending executions until a year after the treaty of peace; but no question under it has been raised before the courts. It is also, I believe, expected that when this shall expire, in consideration of the absolute impossibility of procuring coin to satisfy judgments, a law will be passed, similar to that passed in England, on suspending the cash payments of their bank, that provided that on refusal by a party to receive notes of the Bank of England in any case either of past or future contracts, the judgment should be suspended during the continuance of that act, bearing, however, legal interest. They seemed to consider that it was not this law which changed the conditions of the contract, but the circumstances which had arisen, and had rendered its literal execution impossible; by the disappearance of the metallic medium stipulated by the contract, that the parties not concurring in a reasonable and just accommodation, it became the duty of the legislature to arbitrate between them; and that less restrained than the Duke of Venice by the letter of decree, they were free to adjudge to Shylock a reasonable equivalent. And I believe that in our States this umpirage of the legislatures has been generally interposed in cases where a literal execution of contract has, by a change of circumstances, become impossible, or, if enforced, would produce a disproportion between the subject of the contract and its price, which the parties did not contemplate at the time of the contract.

The second question, whether the judges are invested with exclusive authority to decide on the constitutionality of a law, has been heretofore a subject of consideration with me in the exercise of official duties. Certainly there is not a word in the Constitution which has given that power to them more than to the executive or legislative branches. Questions of property, of character and of crime being ascribed to the judges, through a definite course of legal proceeding, laws involving such questions belong, of course, to them; and as they decide on them ultimately and without appeal, they of course decide *for themselves.* The constitutional validity of the law or laws again prescribing executive action, and to be administered by that branch ultimately and without appeal, the executive must decide for *themselves* also, whether, under the Constitution, they are valid or not. So also as to laws governing the proceedings of the legislature, that body must judge *for itself* the constitutionality of the law, and equally without appeal or control from its co-ordinate branches. And, in general, that branch which is to act ultimately, and without appeal, on any law, is the rightful expositor of the validity of the law, uncontrolled by the opinions of the other co-ordinate authorities. It may be said that contradictory decisions may arise in such case, and produce inconvenience. This is possible, and is a necessary failing in all human proceedings. Yet the prudence of the public functionaries, and authority of public opinion, will generally produce accommodation. Such an instance of difference occurred between the judges of England (in the time of Lord Holt) and the House of Commons, but the prudence of those bodies prevented inconvenience from it. So in the cases of Duane and of William Smith of South Carolina, whose characters of citizenship stood precisely on the same ground, the judges in a question of meum and tuum which came before them, decided that Duane was not a citizen; and in a question of membership, the House of Representatives, under the same words of the same provision, adjudged William Smith to be a citizen. Yet no inconvenience has ensued from these contradictory decisions. This is what I believe myself to be sound. But there is another opinion entertained by some men of such judgment and information as to lessen my confidence in my own. That is, that the legislature alone is the exclusive expounder of the sense of the Constitution, in every part of it whatever. And they allege in its support, that this branch has authority to impeach and punish a member of either of the others acting contrary to its declaration of the sense of the Constitution. It may indeed be answered, that an act may still be valid although the party is punished for it, right or wrong. However, this opinion which ascribes exclusive exposition to the legislature, merits respect for its safety, there being in the body of the nation a control over them, which, if expressed by rejection on the subsequent exercise of their elective franchise, enlists public opinion against their exposition, and encourages a judge or executive on a future occasion to adhere to their former opinion. Between these two doctrines, every one has a right to choose, and I know of no third meriting any respect.

I have thus, Sir, frankly, without the honor of your acquaintance, confided to you my opinion; trusting assuredly that no use will be made of it which shall commit me to the contentions of the newspapers. From that field of disquietude my age asks exemption, and permission to enjoy the privileged tranquillity of a private and unmeddling citizen. In this confidence accept the assurances of my respect and consideration.

14

Gill v. Jacobs

10 Fed. Cas. 373, no. 5,426 (C.C.D.S.C. 1816)

(See 1.8.4 [bankruptcy], no. 7)

15

Farmers & Mechanics' Bank v. Smith

3 Serg. & Rawle 63 (Pa. 1816)

(See 1.8.4 [bankruptcy], no. 8)

16

STURGES V. CROWNINSHIELD
4 Wheat. 122 (1819)

(See 1.8.4. [bankruptcy], no. 10)

17

TRUSTEES OF DARTMOUTH COLLEGE V. WOODWARD
4 Wheat. 518 (1819)

The opinion of the court was delivered by MARSHALL, *Ch. J.*:

This is an action of trover, brought by the trustees of Dartmouth College against William H. Woodward, in the State Court of New Hampshire, for the book of records, corporate seal, and other corporate property, to which the plaintiffs allege themselves to be entitled.

A special verdict, after setting out the rights of the parties, finds for the defendant, if certain acts of the legislature of New Hampshire, passed on the 27th of June, and on the 18th of December, 1816, be valid, and binding on the trustees without their assent, and not repugnant to the constitution of the United States; otherwise, it finds for the plaintiffs.

The Superior Court of Judicature of New Hampshire rendered a judgment upon this verdict for the defendant, which judgment has been brought before this court by writ of error. The single question now to be considered is, do the acts to which the verdict refers violate the constitution of the United States?

This court can be insensible neither to the magnitude nor delicacy of this question. The validity of a legislative act is to be examined; and the opinion of the highest law tribunal of a state is to be revised: an opinion which carries with it intrinsic evidence of the diligence, of the ability, and the integrity, with which it was formed. On more than one occasion this court has expressed the cautious circumspection with which it approaches the consideration of such questions; and has declared that, in no doubtful case would it pronounce a legislative act to be contrary to the constitution. But the American people have said, in the constitution of the United States, that "no state shall pass any bill of attainder, *ex post facto* law, or law impairing the obligation of contracts." In the same instrument they have also said, "that the judicial power shall extend to all cases in law and equity arising under the constitution." On the judges of this court, then, is imposed the high and solemn duty of protecting, from even legislative violation, those contracts which the constitution of our country has placed beyond legislative control; and, however irksome the task may be, this is a duty from which we dare not shrink.

The title of the plaintiffs originates in a charter dated the 13th day of December, in the year 1769, incorporating twelve persons therein mentioned, by the name of "The Trustees of Dartmouth College," granting to them and their successors the usual corporate privileges and powers, and authorizing the trustees, who are to govern the college, to fill up all vacancies which may be created in their own body.

The defendant claims under three acts of the legislature of New Hampshire, the most material of which was passed on the 27th of June, 1816, and is entitled, "an act to amend the charter, and enlarge and improve the corporation of Dartmouth College." Among other alterations in the charter, this act increases the number of trustees to twenty-one, gives the appointment of the additional members to the executive of the state, and creates a board of overseers, with power to inspect and control the most important acts of the trustees. This board consists of twenty-five persons. The president of the senate, the speaker of the house of representatives, of New Hampshire, and the Governor and Lieutenant-Governor of Vermont, for the time being, are to be members *ex officio*. The board is to be completed by the Governor and council of New Hampshire, who are also empowered to fill all vacancies which may occur. The acts of the 18th and 26th of December are supplemental to that of the 27th of June, and are principally intended to carry that act into effect.

The majority of the trustees of the college have refused to accept this amended charter. and have brought this suit for the corporate property, which is in possession of a person holding by virtue of the acts which have been stated.

It can require no argument to prove that the circumstances of this case constitute a contract. An application is made to the crown for a charter to incorporate a religious and literary institution. In the application, it is stated that large contributions have been made for the object, which will be conferred on the corporation as soon as it shall be created. The charter is granted, and on its faith the property is conveyed. Surely in this transaction every ingredient of a complete and legitimate contract is to be found.

The points for consideration are:

1. Is this contract protected by the constitution of the United States?

2. Is it impaired by the acts under which the defendant holds?

1. On the first point it has been argued, that the word "contract," in its broadest sense, would comprehend the political relations between the government and its citizens, would extend to offices held within a state for state purposes, and to many of those laws concerning civil institutions, which must change with circumstances, and be modified by ordinary legislation; which deeply concern the public, and which, to preserve good government, the public judgment must control. That even marriage is a contract, and its obligations are affected by the laws respecting divorces. That the clause in the constitution, if construed in its greatest latitude, would prohibit these laws. Taken in its broad unlimited sense, the clause would be an unprofitable and vexatious interference with the internal concerns of a state, would unnecessarily and unwisely embarrass its legislation, and render immutable those civil institutions which are established for purposes of internal

government, and which, to subserve those purposes, ought to vary with varying circumstances. That as the framers of the constitution could never have intended to insert in that instrument a provision so unnecessary, so mischievous, and so repugnant to its general spirit, the term "contract" must be understood in a more limited sense. That it must be understood as intended to guard against a power of at least doubtful utility, the abuse of which had been extensively felt; and to restrain the legislature in future from violating the right to property. That anterior to the formation of the constitution, a course of legislation had prevailed in many, if not in all, of the states, which weakened the confidence of man in man, and embarrassed all transactions between individuals, by dispensing with a faithful performance of engagements. To correct this mischief, by restraining the power which produced it, the state legislatures were forbidden "to pass any law impairing the obligation of contracts," that is, of contracts respecting property, under which some individual could claim a right to something beneficial to himself; and that since the clause in the constitution must in construction receive some limitation, it may be confined, and ought to be confined, to cases of this description; to cases within the mischief it was intended to remedy.

The general correctness of these observations cannot be controverted. That the framers of the constitution did not intend to restrain the states in the regulation of their civil institutions, adopted for internal government, and that the instrument they have given us is not to be so construed, may be admitted. The provision of the constitution never has been understood to embrace other contracts than those which respect property, or some object of value, and confer rights which may be asserted in a court of justice. It never has been understood to restrict the general right of the legislature to legislate on the subject of divorces. Those acts enable some tribunal, not to impair a marriage contract, but to liberate one of the parties because it has been broken by the other. When any state legislature shall pass an act annulling all marriage contracts, or allowing either party to annul it without the consent of the other, it will be time enough to inquire whether such an act be constitutional.

The parties in this case differ less on general principles, less on the true construction of the constitution in the abstract, than on the application of those principles to this case, and on the true construction of the charter of 1769. This is the point on which the cause essentially depends. If the act of incorporation be a grant of political power, if it create a civil institution to be employed in the administration of the government. or if the funds of the college be public property, or if the state of New Hampshire, as a government, be alone interested in its transactions, the subject is one in which the legislature of the state may act according to its own judgment, unrestrained by any limitation of its power imposed by the constitution of the United States.

But if this be a private eleemosynary institution, endowed with a capacity to take property for objects unconnected with government, whose funds are bestowed by individuals on the faith of the charter; if the donors have stipulated for the future disposition and management of those funds in the manner prescribed by themselves, there may be more difficulty in the case, although neither the persons who have made these stipulations nor those for whose benefit they were made, should be parties to the cause. Those who are no longer interested in the property, may yet retain such an interest in the preservation of their own arrangements as to have a right to insist that those arrangements shall be held sacred. Or, if they have themselves disappeared, it becomes a subject of serious and anxious inquiry, whether those whom they have legally empowered to represent them forever may not assert all the rights which they possessed, while in being; whether, if they be without personal representatives who may feel injured by a violation of the compact, the trustees be not so completely their representatives, in the eye of the law, as to stand in their place, not only as respects the government of the college, but also as respects the maintenance of the college charter.

It becomes, then, the duty of the court most seriously to examine this charter, and to ascertain its true character.

From the instrument itself, it appears that about the year 1754, the Rev. Eleazar Wheelock established at his own expense, and on his own estate, a charity-school for the instruction of Indians in the Christian religion. The success of this institution inspired him with the design of soliciting contributions in England for carrying on, and extending, his undertaking. In this pious work he employed the Rev. Nathaniel Whitaker, who, by virtue of a power of attorney from Dr. Wheelock, appointed the Earl of Dartmouth and others, trustees of the money which had been, and should be, contributed; which appointment Dr. Wheelock confirmed by a deed of trust authorizing the trustees to fix on a site for the college. They determined to establish the school on Connecticut River, in the western part of New Hampshire; that situation being supposed favorable for carrying on the original design among the Indians, and also for promoting learning among the English; and the proprietors in the neighborhood having made large offers of land, on condition that the college should there be placed. Dr. Wheelock then applied to the crown for an act of incorporation, and represented the expediency of appointing those whom he had, by his last will, named as trustees in America, to be members of the proposed corporation. "In consideration of the premises," "for the education and instruction of the youth of the Indian tribes," &c., "and also of English youth, and any others," the charter was granted, and the trustees of Dartmouth college were by that name created a body corporate, with power, for the use of the said college, to acquire real and personal property, and to pay the president, tutors, and other officers of the college, such salaries as they shall allow.

The charter proceeds to appoint Eleazer Wheelock, "the founder of said college," president thereof, with power by his last will to appoint a successor, who is to continue in office until disapproved by the trustees. In case of vacancy, the trustees may appoint a president, and in case of the ceasing of a president, the senior professor or tutor, being one of the trustees, shall exercise the office, until an appointment shall be made. The trustees have power to appoint and displace professors, tutors, and other officers, and to supply any vacancies which may be created in their own body, by death, resignation, removal, or disability; and also to make orders, ordinances, and laws, for the government of the college, the same not being repugnant to the laws of Great Britain, or of New Hampshire, and not excluding any person on account of his speculative sentiments in religion, or his being of a religious profession different from that of the trustees.

This charter was accepted, and the property, both real and personal, which had been contributed for the benefit of the college, was conveyed to, and vested in, the corporate body.

From this brief review of the most essential parts of the charter, it is apparent that the funds of the college consisted entirely of private donations. It is, perhaps, not very important who were the donors. The probability is, that the Earl of Dartmouth, and the other trustees in England, were, in fact, the largest contributors. Yet the legal conclusion, from the facts recited in the charter, would probably be, that Dr. Wheelock was the founder of the college.

The origin of the institution was, undoubtedly, the Indian charity-school, established by Dr. Wheelock, at his own expense. It was at his instance, and to enlarge this school, that contributions were solicited in England. The person soliciting these contributions was his agent; and the trustees, who received the money, were appointed by, and act under, his authority. It is not too much to say that the funds were obtained by him, in trust, to be applied by him to the purposes of his enlarged school. The charter of incorporation was granted at his instance. The persons named by him in his last will, as the trustees of his charity school, compose a part of the corporation, and he is declared to be the founder of the college, and its president for life. Were the inquiry material, we should feel some hesitation in saying that Dr. Wheelock was not, in law, to be considered as the founder of this institution, and as possessing all the rights appertaining to that character. But be this as it may, Dartmouth College is really endowed by private individuals, who have bestowed their funds for the propagation of the Christian religion among the Indians, and for the promotion of piety and learning generally. From these funds the salaries of the tutors are drawn; and these salaries lessen the expense of education to the students. It is, then, an eleemosynary, and, as far as respects its funds, a private corporation.

Do its objects stamp on it a different character? Are the trustees and professors public officers, invested with any portion of political power, partaking in any degree in the administration of civil government, and performing duties which flow from the sovereign authority?

That education is an object of national concern, and a proper subject of legislation, all admit. That there may be an institution founded by government, and placed entirely under its immediate control, the officers of which would be public officers, amenable exclusively to government, none will deny. But is Dartmouth College such an institution? Is education altogether in the hands of government? Does every teacher of youth become a public officer, and do donations for the purpose of education necessarily become public property, so far that the will of the legislature, not the will of the donor, becomes the law of the donation? These questions are of serious moment to society, and deserve to be well considered.

Doctor Wheelock, as the keeper of his charity-school, instructing the Indians in the art of reading, and in our holy religion; sustaining them at his own expense, and on the voluntary contributions of the charitable, could scarcely be considered as a public officer, exercising any portion of those duties which belong to government; nor could the legislature have supposed that his private funds, or those given by others, were subject to legislative management, because they were applied to the purposes of education. When, afterwards, his school was enlarged, and the liberal contributions made in England, and in America, enabled him to extend his cares to the education of the youth of his own country, no change was wrought in his own character, or in the nature of his duties. Had he employed assistant tutors with the funds contributed by others, or had the trustees in England established a school with Dr. Wheelock at its head, and paid salaries to him and his assistants, they would still have been private tutors; and the fact that they were employed in the education of youth could not have converted them into public officers, concerned in the administration of public duties, or have given the legislature a right to interfere in the management of the fund. The trustees, in whose care that fund was placed by the contributors, would have been permitted to execute their trust uncontrolled by legislative authority.

Whence, then, can be derived the idea that Dartmouth College has become a public institution, and its trustees public officers, exercising powers conferred by the public for public objects? Not from the source whence its funds were drawn; for its foundation is purely private and eleemosynary. Not from the application of those funds; for money may be given for education, and the persons receiving it do not, by being employed in the education of youth, become members of the civil government. Is it from the act of incorporation? Let this subject be considered.

A corporation is an artificial being, invisible, intangible, and existing only in contemplation of law. Being the mere creature of law, it possesses only those properties which the charter of its creation confers upon it, either expressly or as incidental to its very existence. These are such as are supposed best calculated to effect the object for which it was created. Among the most important are immortality, and, if the expression may be allowed, individuality; properties by which a perpetual succession of many persons are considered as the same, and may act as a single individual. They enable a corporation to manage its own affairs, and to hold property without the perplexing intricacies, the hazardous and endless necessity, of perpetual conveyances for the purpose of transmitting it from hand to hand. It is chiefly for the purpose of clothing bodies of men, in succession, with these qualities and capacities, that corporations were invented, and are in use. By these means, a perpetual succession of individuals are capable of acting for the promotion of the particular object, like one immortal being. But this being does not share in the civil government of the country, unless that be the purpose for which it was created. Its immortality no more confers on it political power, or a political character, than immortality would confer such power or character on a natural person. It is no more a state instrument than a natural person exercising the same powers would be. If, then, a natural person, employed by individuals in the education of youth, or for the government of a seminary in which youth is educated, would not become a public officer, or be considered as a member of the civil government, how is it that this artificial being, created by law, for the purpose of being employed by the same individuals for the same purposes, should become a part of the civil government of the country? Is it because its existence, its capacities, its powers, are given by law? Because the government has given it the power to take and to hold property in a particular form, and for particular purposes, has the government a consequent right substantially to change that form, or to vary the purposes to which the property is to be applied? This principle has never been asserted or recognized, and is supported by no authority. Can it derive aid from reason?

The objects for which a corporation is created are universally such as the government wishes to promote. They are deemed beneficial to the country; and this benefit constitutes the consideration, and, in most cases, the sole consideration of the grant. In most eleemosynary institutions, the object would be difficult, perhaps unattainable, without the aid of a charter of incorporation. Charitable, or public-spirited individuals, desirous of making permanent appropriations for charitable or other useful purposes, find it impossible to effect their design securely, and certainly, without an incorporating act. They apply to the government, state their beneficient object, and offer to advance the money necessary for its accomplishment, provided the government will confer on the instrument which is to execute their designs the capacity to execute them. The proposition is considered and approved. The benefit to the public is considered as an ample compensation for the faculty it confers, and the corporation is created. If the advantages to the public constitute a full compensation for the faculty it gives, there can be no reason for exacting a further compensation, by claiming a right to exercise over this artificial being a power which changes its nature, and touches the fund, for the security and application of which it was created. There can be no reason for implying in a charter, given for a valuable consideration, a power which is not only not expressed, but is in direct contradiction to its express stipulations.

From the fact, then, that a charter of incorporation has been granted, nothing can be inferred which changes the character of the institution, or transfers to the government any new power over it. The character of civil institutions does not grow out of their incorporation, but out of the manner in which they are formed, and the objects for which they are created. The right to change them is not founded on their being incorporated, but on their being the instruments of government, created for its purposes. The same institutions, created for the same objects, though not incorporated, would be public institutions, and, of course, be controllable by the legislature. The incorporating act neither gives nor prevents this control. Neither, in reason, can the incorporating act change the character of a private eleemosynary institution.

We are next led to the inquiry, for whose benefit the property given to Dartmouth College was secured. The counsel for the defendant have insisted that the beneficial interest is in the people of New Hampshire. The charter, after reciting the preliminary measures which had been taken, and the application for an act of incorporation, proceeds thus: "Know ye, therefore, that we, considering the premises, and being willing to encourage the laudable and charitable design of spreading Christian knowledge among the savages of our American wilderness, and, also, that the best means of education be established, in our province of New Hampshire, for the benefit of said province, do, of our special grace," &c. Do these expressions bestow on New Hampshire any exclusive right to the property of the college, any exclusive interest in the labors of the professors? Or do they merely indicate a willingness that New Hampshire should enjoy those advantages which result to all from the establishment of a seminary of learning in the neighborhood? On this point we think it impossible to entertain a serious doubt. The words themselves, unexplained by the context, indicate that the "benefit intended for the province" is that which is derived from "establishing the best means of education therein;" that is, from establishing in the province Dartmouth College, as constituted by the charter. But, if these words, considered alone, could admit of doubt, that doubt is completely removed by an inspection of the entire instrument.

The particular interests of New Hampshire never entered into the mind of the donors, never constituted a motive for their donation. The propagation of the Christian religion among the savages, and the dissemination of useful knowledge among the youth of the country, were the avowed and the sole objects of their contributions. In these, New Hampshire would participate; but nothing particular or exclusive was intended for her. Even the site of the college was selected, not for the sake of New Hampshire, but because it was "most subservient to the great ends in view," and because liberal donations of land were offered by the proprietors, on condition that the institution should be there established. The real advantage from the location of the college, are, perhaps, not less considerable to those on the west than to those on the east side of Connecticut River. The clause which constitutes the incorporation, and expresses the objects for which it was made, declares those objects to be the instruction of the Indians, "and also of English youth, and any others." So that the objects of the contributors, and the incorporating act, were the same: the promotion of Christianity, and of education generally, not the interests of New Hampshire particularly.

From this review of the charter, it appears that Dartmouth College is an eleemosynary institution, incorporated for the purpose of perpetuating the application of the bounty of the donors, to the specified objects of that bounty; that its trustees or governors were originally named by the founder, and invested with the power of perpetuating themselves; that they are not public officers, nor is it a civil institution, participating in the administration of government; but a charity school, or a seminary of education, incorporated for the preservation of its property, and the perpetual application of that property to the objects of its creation.

Yet a question remains to be considered, of more real difficulty, on which more doubt has been entertained than on all that have been discussed. The founders of the college, at least those whose contributions were in money, have parted with the property bestowed upon it, and their representatives have no interest in that property. The donors of land are equally without interest, so long as the corporation shall exist. Could they be found, they are unaffected by any alteration in its constitution, and probably regardless of its form, or even of its existence. The students are fluctuating, and no individual among our youth has a vested interest in the institution, which can be asserted in a court of justice. Neither the founders of the college nor the youth for whose benefit it was founded complain of the alteration made in its charter, or think themselves injured by it. The trustees alone complain, and the trustees have no beneficial interest to be protected. Can this be such a contract as the constitution intended to withdraw from the power of state legislation? Contracts, the parties to which have a vested beneficial interest, and those only, it has been said, are the objects about which the constitution is solicitous, and to which its protection is extended.

The court has bestowed on this argument the most deliberate consideration, and the result will be stated. Dr. Wheelock, acting for himself, and for those who, at his solicitation, had made contributions to his school, applied for this charter, as the instrument which should enable him, and them, to perpetuate their beneficent intention. It was granted. An artificial, immortal being, was created by the crown, capable of receiving and distributing forever, according to the will of the donors, the donations which should be made to it. On this being, the contributions which had been collected were immediately bestowed. These gifts were made, not, indeed, to make a profit for the donors, or their posterity, but for something in their opinion of inestimable value; for something which they deemed a full equivalent for the money with which it was purchased. The consideration for which they stipulated, is the perpetual application of the fund to its object, in the mode prescribed by themselves. Their descendants may take no interest in the preservation of this consideration. But in this respect their descendants are not their representatives. They are represented by the corporation. The corporation is the assignee of their rights, stands in their place, and distributes their bounty, as they would themselves have distributed it, had they been immortal. So with respect to the students who are to derive learning from this source. The corporation is a trustee for them also. Their potential rights, which, taken distributively, are imperceptible, amount collectively to a most important interest. These are, in the aggregate, to be exercised, asserted and protected, by the corporation. They were as completely out of the donors, at the instant of their being vested in the corporation, and as incapable of being asserted by the students, as at present.

According to the theory of the British constitution, their parliament is omnipotent. To annul corporate rights might give a shock to public opinion, which that government has chosen to avoid; but its power is not questioned. Had parliament, immediately after the emanation of this charter, and the execution of those conveyances which followed it, annulled the instrument, so that the living donors would have witnessed the disappointment of their hopes, the perfidy of the transaction would have been universally acknowledged. Yet then, as now, the donors would have had no interest in the property; then, as now, those who might be students would have had no rights to be violated; then, as now, it might be said, that the trustees, in whom the rights of all were combined, possessed no private, individual, beneficial interest in the property confided to their protection. Yet the contract would at that time have been deemed sacred by all. What has since occurred to strip it of its inviolability? Circumstances have not changed it. In reason, in justice, and in law, it is now what it was in 1769.

This is plainly a contract to which the donors, the trustees, and the crown (to whose rights and obligations New Hampshire succeeds), were the original parties. It is a contract made on a valuable consideration. It is a contract for the security and disposition of property. It is a contract, on the faith of which real and personal estate has been conveyed to the corporation. It is then a contract within the letter of the constitution, and within its spirit also, unless the fact that the property is invested by the donors in trustees for the promotion of religion and education, for the benefit of persons who are perpetually changing, though the objects remain the same, shall create a particular exception, taking this case out of the prohibition contained in the constitution.

It is more than possible that the preservation of rights of this description was not particularly in the view of the framers of the constitution when the clause under consideration was introduced into that instrument. It is probable that interferences of more frequent recurrence, to which the temptation was stronger, and of which the mischief was more extensive, constituted the great motive for imposing this restriction on the state legislatures. But although a particular and a rare case may not, in itself, be of sufficient magnitude to induce a rule, yet it must be governed by the rule, when established, unless some plain and strong reason for excluding it can be given. It is not enough to say that this particular case was not in the mind of the convention when the article was framed, nor of the American people when it was adopted. It is necessary to go farther, and to say that, had this particular case been suggested, the language would have been so varied, as to exclude it, or it would have been made a special exception. The case being within the words of the rule, must be within its operation likewise, unless there be something in the literal construction so obviously absurd, or mischievous, or repugnant to the general spirit of the instrument, as to justify those who expound the constitution in making it an exception.

On what safe and intelligible ground can this exception stand. There is no exception in the constitution, no sentiment delivered by its contemporaneous expounders, which would justify us in making it. In the absence of all authority of this kind, is there, in the nature and reason of the case itself, that which would sustain a construction of the constitution, not warranted by its words? Are contracts of this description of a character to excite so little interest that we must exclude them from the provisions of the constitution, as being unworthy of the attention of those who framed the instrument? Or does public policy so imperiously demand their remaining exposed to legislative alteration, as to compel us, or rather permit us to say that these words, which were introduced to give stability to contracts, and which in their plain import comprehend this contract, must yet be so construed as to exclude it?

Almost all eleemosynary corporations, those which are created for the promotion of religion, of charity, or of education, are of the same character. The law of this case is the law of all. In every literary or charitable institution, unless the objects of the bounty be themselves incorporated, the whole legal interest is in trustees, and can be asserted only by them. The donors, or claimants of the bounty, if they can appear in court at all, can appear only to complain of the trustees. In all other situations, they are identified with, and personated by, the trustees; and their rights are to be defended and maintained by them. Religion, Charity, and Education, are, in the law of England, legatees or donees, capable of receiving bequests or donations in this form. They appear in court, and claim or defend by the corporation. Are they of so little estimation in the United States that contracts for their benefit must be excluded from the protection of words which, in their natural import, include them? Or do such contracts so necessarily require new-modeling by the authority of the legislature that the ordinary rules of construction must be disregarded in order to leave them exposed to legislative alteration?

All feel that these objects are not deemed unimportant in the United States. The interest which this case has excited proves that they are not. The framers of the constitution did not deem them unworthy of its care and protection. They have, though in a different mode, manifested their respect for science, by reserving to the government of the Union the power "to promote the progress of science and useful arts, by securing for limited times to authors and inventors the exclusive right to their respective writings and discoveries." They have so far withdrawn science, and the useful arts, from the action of the state governments. Why, then, should they be supposed so regardless of contracts made for the advancement of literature as to intend to exclude them from provisions made for the security of ordinary contracts between man and man? No reason for making this supposition is perceived.

If the insignificance of the object does not require that we should exclude contracts respecting it from the protection of the constitution, neither, as we conceive, is the policy of leaving them subject to legislative alteration so apparent as to require a forced construction of that instrument in order to effect it. These eleemosynary institutions do not fill the place, which would otherwise be occupied by government, but that which would otherwise remain vacant. They are complete acquisitions to literature. They are donations to education; donations which any government must be disposed rather to encourage than to discountenance. It requires no very critical examination of the human mind to enable us to determine that one great inducement to these gifts is the conviction felt by the giver, that the disposition he makes of them is immutable. It is probable that no man ever was, and that no man ever will be, the founder of a college, believing at the time that an act of incorporation constitutes no security for the institution; believing that it is immediately to be deemed a public institution, whose funds are to be governed and applied, not by the will of the donor, but by the will of the legislature. All such gifts are made in the pleasing, perhaps delusive hope, that the charity will flow forever in the channel which the givers have marked out for it. If every man finds in his own bosom strong evidence of the universality of this sentiment, there can be but little reason to imagine that the framers of our constitution were strangers to it, and that, feeling the necessity and policy of giving permanence and security to contracts, of withdrawing them from the influence of legislative bodies, whose fluctuating policy, and repeated interferences, produced the most perplexing and injurious embarrassments, they still deemed it necessary to leave these contracts subject to those interferences. The motives for such an exception must be very powerful, to justify the construction which makes it.

The motives suggested at the bar grow out of the original appointment of the trustees, which is supposed to have been in a spirit hostile to the genius of our government, and the presumption that, if allowed to continue themselves, they now are, and must remain forever, what they originally were. Hence is inferred the necessity of applying to this corporation, and to other similar corporations, the correcting and improving hand of the legislature.

It has been urged repeatedly, and certainly with a degree of earnestness which attracted attention, that the trustees deriving their power from a regal source, must necessarily partake of the spirit of their origin; and that their first principles, unimproved by that resplendent light which has been shed around them, must continue to govern the college, and to guide the students. Before we inquire into the influence which this argument ought to have on the constitutional question, it may not be amiss to examine the fact on which it rests. The first trustees were undoubtedly named in the charter by the crown; but at whose suggestion were they named? By whom were they selected? The charter informs us. Dr. Wheelock had represented "that, for many weighty reasons, it would be expedient that the gentlemen whom he had already nominated in his last will, to be trustees in America, should be of the corporation now proposed." When, afterwards, the trustees are named in the charter, can it be doubted that the persons mentioned by Dr. Wheelock in his will were appointed? Some were probably added by the crown, with the approbation of Dr. Wheelock. Among these is the doctor himself. If any others were appointed at the instance of the crown, they are the governor, three members of the council, and the speaker of the house of representatives of the colony of New Hampshire. The stations filled by these persons ought to rescue them from any other imputation than too great a dependence on the crown. If, in the revolution that followed, they acted under the influence of this sentiment, they must have ceased to be trustees; if they took part with their countrymen, the imputation which suspicion might excite would no longer attach to them. The original trustees, then, or most of them, were named by Dr. Wheelock, and those who were added to his nomination, most probably with his approbation, were among the most eminent and respectable individuals in New Hampshire.

The only evidence which we possess of the character of Dr. Wheelock is furnished by this charter. The judicious means employed for the accomplishment of his object, and the success which attended his endeavors, would lead to the opinion that he united a sound understanding to that humanity and benevolence which suggested his undertaking. It surely cannot be assumed that his trustees were selected without judgment. With as little probability can it be assumed, that, while the light of science, and of liberal principles, pervades the whole community these originally benighted trustees remain in utter darkness, incapable of participating in the general improvement; that, while the human race is rapidly advancing, they are stationary. Reasoning *a priori,* we should believe that learned and intelligent men, selected by its patrons for the government of a literary institution, would select learned and intelligent men for their successors; men as well fitted for the government of a college as those who might be chosen by other means. Should this reasoning ever prove erroneous in a particular case, public opinion, as has been stated at the bar, would correct the institution. The mere possibility of the contrary would not justify a construction of the constitution which should exclude these contracts from the protection of a provision whose terms comprehend them.

The opinion of the court, after mature deliberation, is, that this is a contract, the obligation of which cannot be impaired without violating the constitution of the United States. This opinion appears to us to be equally supported by reason, and by the former decisions of this court.

2. We next proceed to the inquiry whether its obligations has been impaired by those acts of the legislature of New Hampshire to which the special verdict refers.

From the review of this charter, which has been taken, it appears that the whole power of governing the college, of appointing and removing tutors, of fixing their salaries, of directing the course of study to be pursued by the students, and of filling up vacancies created in their own body, was vested in the trustees. On the part of the crown it was expressly stipulated that this corporation, thus constituted, should continue forever; and that the number of trustees should forever consist of twelve, and no more. By this contract the crown was bound, and could have made no violent alteration in its essential terms, without impairing its obligation.

By the revolution, the duties, as well as the powers, of government devolved on the people of New Hampshire. It is admitted, that among the latter was comprehended the transcendent power of parliament, as well as that of the executive department. It is too clear to require the support of argument, that all contracts, and rights, respecting property, remained unchanged by the revolution. The obligations, then, which were created by the charter to Dartmouth College, were the same in the new that they had been in the old government. The power of the government was also the same. A repeal of this charter at any time prior to the adoption of the present constitution of the United States, would have been an extraordinary and unprecedented act of power, but one which could have been contested only by the restrictions upon the legislature, to be found in the constitution of the state. But the constitution of the United States has imposed this additional limitation, that the legislature of a state shall pass no act "impairing the obligation of contracts."

It has been already stated that the act "to amend the charter, and enlarge and improve the corporation of Dartmouth College," increases the number of trustees to twenty-one, gives the appointment of the additional members to the executive of the state, and creates a board of overseers, to consist of twenty-five persons, of whom twenty-one are also appointed by the executive of New Hampshire, who have power to inspect and control the most important acts of the trustees.

On the effect of this law, two opinions cannot be entertained. Between acting directly, and acting through the agency of trustees and overseers, no essential difference is perceived. The whole power of governing the college is transferred from trustees appointed according to the will of the founder, expressed in the charter, to the executive of New Hampshire. The management and application of the funds of this eleemosynary institution, which are placed by the donors in the hands of trustees named in the charter, and empowered to perpetuate themselves, are placed by this act under the control of the government of the state. The will of the state is substituted for the will of the donors, in every essential operation of the college. This is not an immaterial change. The founders of the college contracted, not merely for the perpetual application of the funds which they gave, to the objects for which those funds were given; they contracted also to secure that application by the constitution of the corporation. They contracted for a system which should, as far as human foresight can provide, retain forever the government of the literary institution they had informed, in the hands of persons approved by themselves. This system is totally changed. The charter of 1769 exists no longer. It is reorganized; and re-organized in such a manner as to convert a literary institution, moulded according to the will of its founders, and placed under the control of private literary men, into a machine entirely subservient to the will of government. This may be for the advantage of this college in particular, and may be for the advantage of literature in general, but it is not according to the will of the donors, and is subversive of that contract, on the faith of which their property was given.

In the view which has been taken of this interesting case, the court has confined itself to the right possessed by the trustees, as the assignees and representatives of the donors and founders, for the benefit of religion and literature. Yet it is not clear that the trustees ought to be considered as destitute of such beneficial interest in themselves as the law may respect. In addition to their being the legal owners of the property, and to their having a freehold right in the powers confided to them, the charter itself countenances the idea that trustees may also be tutors with salaries. The first president was one of the original trustees; and the charter provides, that in case of vacancy in that office, "the senior professor or tutor, being one of the trustees, shall exercise the office of president, until the trustees shall make choice of, and appoint a president." According to the tenor of the charter, then, the trustees might, without impropriety, appoint a president and other professors from their own body. This is a power not entirely unconnected with an interest. Even if the proposition of the counsel for the defendant were sustained; if it were admitted that those contracts only are protected by the constitution, a beneficial interest in which is vested in the party, who appears in court to assert that interest; yet it is by no means clear that the trustees of Dartmouth College have no beneficial interest in themselves.

But the court has deemed it unnecessary to investigate this particular point, being of opinion, on general principles, that in these private eleemosynary institutions, the body corporate, as possessing the whole legal and equitable interest, and completely representing the donors, for the purpose of executing the trust, has rights which are protected by the constitution.

It results from this opinion, that the acts of the legislature of New Hampshire, which are stated in the special verdict found in this cause, are repugnant to the constitution of the United States; and that the judgment on this special verdict ought to have been for the plaintiffs. The judgment of the State Court must therefore be reversed.

WASHINGTON, *J.* This cause turns upon the validity of certain laws of the state of New Hampshire, which have been stated in the case, and which, it is contended by the counsel for the plaintiffs in error, are void, being repugnant to the constitution of that state, and also to the constitution of the United States. Whether the first objection to these laws be well founded or not, is a question with which this court, in this case, has nothing to do; because it has no jurisdiction, as an appellate court, over the decisions of a state court, except in cases where is drawn in question the validity of a treaty, or statute of, or an authority exercised under, the United States, and the decision is against their validity; or where is drawn in question the validity of a statute of, or an authority exercised under, any state, on the ground of their being repugnant to the constitution, treaties, or laws of the United States, and the decision is in favor of their validity; or where is drawn in question the construction of any clause of the constitution, or of a treaty, or statute of, or commission held under, the United States, and the decision is against the title, right, privilege, or exemption specially set up or claimed by either party, under such clause of the said constitution, treaty, statute, or commission.

The clause in the constitution of the United States which was drawn in question in the court from whence this transcript has been sent, is that part of the tenth section of the first article which declares that "no state shall pass any bill of attainder, *ex post facto* law, or any law impairing the obligation of contracts." The decision of the State Court is against the title specially claimed by the plaintiffs in error, under the above clause, because they contend that the laws of New Hampshire, above referred to, impair the obligation of a contract, and are, consequently, repugnant to the above clause of the constitution of the United States, and void.

There are, then, two questions for this court to decide:

1st. Is the charter granted to Dartmouth College on the 13th of December, 1769, to be considered as a contract? If it be, then, 2d. Do the laws in question impair its obligation?

1. What is a contract? It may be defined to be a transaction between two or more persons, in which each party comes under an obligation to the other, and each reciprocally acquires a right to whatever is promised by the other. Under this definition, says Mr. Powell, it is obvious that every feoffment, gift, grant, agreement, promise, &c., may be included, because in all there is a mutual consent of the minds of the parties concerned in them, upon an agreement between them respecting some property or right that is the object of the stipulation. He adds, that the ingredients requisite to form a contract, are, parties, consent, and an obligation to be created or dissolved; these must all concur, because the regular effect of all contracts is on one side to acquire, and on the other to part with, some property or rights; or to abridge, or to restrain natural liberty, by binding the parties to do, or restraining them from doing, something which before they might have done, or omitted. If a doubt could exist that a grant is a contract, the point was decided in the case of *Fletcher* v. *Peck,* in which it was laid down that a contract is either executory or executed; by the former, a party binds himself to do or not to do a particular thing; the latter is one in which the object of the contract is performed, and this differs in nothing from a grant; but whether executed or executory, they both contain obligations binding on the parties, and both are equally within the provisions of the constitution of the United States, which forbids the state governments to pass laws impairing the obligation of contracts.

If, then, a grant be a contract, within the meaning of the constitution of the United States, the next inquiry is, whether the creation of a corporation by charter be such a grant as includes an obligation of the nature of a contract, which no state legislature can pass laws to impair.

A corporation is defined by Mr. Justice Blackstone to be a franchise. "It is," says he, "a franchise for a number of persons, to be incorporated and exist as a body politic, with a power to maintain perpetual succession, and to do corporate acts, and each individual of such corporation is also said to have a franchise, or freedom." This franchise, like other franchises, is an incorporeal hereditament, issuing out of something real or personal or concerning or annexed to, and exercisable within a thing corporate. To this grant, or this franchise, the parties are, the king, and the persons for whose benefit it is created, or trustees for them. The assent of both is necessary. The subjects of the grant are not only privileges and immunities, but property, or, which is the same thing, a capacity to acquire and to hold property in perpetuity. Certain obligations are created, binding both on the grantor and the grantees. On the part of the former, it amounts to an extinguishment of the king's prerogative to bestow the same identical franchise on another corporate body, because it would prejudice his prior grant. It implies, therefore, a contract not to re-assert the right to grant the franchise to another, or to impair it. There is also an implied contract, that the founder of a private charity, or his heirs, or other persons appointed by him for that purpose, shall have the right to visit, and to govern the corporation, of which he is the acknowledged founder and patron, and also, that in case of its dissolution, the reversionary right of the founder to the property, with which he had endowed it, should be preserved inviolate.

The rights acquired by the other contracting party are those of having perpetual succession, of suing and being sued, of purchasing lands for the benefit of themselves and their successors, and of having a common seal, and of making by-laws. The obligation imposed upon them, and which forms the consideration of the grant, is that of acting up to the end or design for which they were created by their founder. Mr. Justice Buller, in the case of the *King* v. *Passmore,* says, that the grant of a corporation is a compact between the crown and a number of persons, the latter of whom undertake, in consideration of the privileges bestowed, to exert themselves for the good government of the place. If they fail to perform their part of it, there is an end of the compact. The charter of a corporation, says Mr. Justice Blackstone, may be forfeited through negligence, or abuse of its franchises, in which case the law judges that the body politic has broken the condition upon which it was incorporated, and thereupon the corporation is void.

It appears to me, upon the whole, that these principles and authorities prove, incontrovertibly, that a charter of incorporation is a contract.

2. The next question is, do the acts of the legislature of New Hampshire of the 27th of June, and 18th and 26th of December, 1816, impair this contract, within the true intent and meaning of the constitution of the United States?

Previous to the examination of this question, it will be proper clearly to mark the distinction between the different kinds of lay aggregate corporations, in order to prevent any implied decision by this court of any other case than the one immediately before it.

We are informed by the case of *Philips* v. *Bury,* which contains all the doctrine of corporations connected with this point, that there are two kinds of corporations aggregate, viz., such as are for public government, and such as are for private charity. The first are those for the government of a town, city, or the like; and being for public advantage, are to be governed according to the law of the land. The validity and justice of their private laws and constitutions are examinable in the king's courts. Of these there are no particular founders, and consequently no particular visitor. There are no patrons of these corporations. But private and particular corporations for charity, founded and endowed by private persons, are subject to the private government of those who erect them, and are to be visited by them or their heirs, or such other persons as they may appoint. The only rules for the government of these private corporations are the laws and constitutions assigned by the founder. This right of government and visitation arises from the property which the founder had in the lands assigned to support the charity; and, as he is the author of the charity, the law invests him with the necessary power of inspecting and regulating it. The authorities are full to prove that a college is a private charity, as well as a hospital, and that there is, in reality, no difference between them, except in degree; but they are within the same reason, and both eleemosynary.

These corporations, civil and eleemosynary, which differ from each other so especially in their nature and constituion, may very well differ in matters which concern their rights and privileges, and their existence and subjection to public control. The one is the mere creature of public institution, created exclusively for the public advantage, without other endowments than such as the king or government may bestow upon it, and having no other founder or visitor than the king or government, the *fundator incipiens.* The validity and justice of its laws and constitution are examinable by the courts having jurisdiction over them; and they are subject to the general law of the land. It would seem reasonable that such a corporation may be controlled, and its constitution altered and amended by the government, in such manner as the public interest may require. Such legislative interferences cannot be said to impair the contract by which the corporation was formed, because there is in reality but one party to it, the trustees or governors of the corporation being merely the trustees for the public, the *cestui que trust* of the foundation. These trustees or governors have no interest, no privileges or immunities, which are violated by such interference, and can have no more right to complain of them than an ordinary trustee, who is called upon in a court of equity to execute the trust. They accepted the charter for the public benefit alone, and there would seem to be no reason why the government, under proper limitations, should not alter or modify such a grant at pleasure. But the case of a private corporation is entirely different. That is the creature of private benefaction for a charity or private purpose. It is endowed and founded by private persons, and subject to their control, laws, and visitation, and not to the general control of the government; and all these powers, rights and privileges, flow from the property of the founder in the funds assigned for the support of the charity. Although the king, by the grant of the charter, is in some sense the founder of all eleemosynary corporations, because, without his grant they cannot exist; yet the patron or endower is the perficient founder, to whom belongs, as of right, all the powers and privilege, which have been described. With such a corporation, it is not competent for the legislature to interfere. It is a franchise, or incorporeal hereditament, founded upon private property, devoted by its patron to a private charity of a peculiar kind, the offspring of his own will and pleasure, to be managed and visited by persons of his own appointment, according to such laws and regulations as he, or the persons so selected, may ordain.

It has been shown that the charter is a contract on the part of the government, that the property with which the charity is endowed shall be forever vested in a certain number of persons, and their successors, to subserve the particular purposes designated by the founder, and to be managed in a particular way. If a law increases or diminishes the number of the trustees, they are not the persons which the grantor agreed should be the managers of the fund. If it appropriate the fund intended for the support of a particular charity to that of some other charity, or to an entirely different charity, the grant is in effect set aside, and a new contract substituted in its place; thus disappointing completely the intentions of the founder, by changing the objects of his bounty. And can it be seriously contended that a law which changes so materially the terms of a contract does not impair it? In short, does not every alteration of a contract, however unimportant, even though it be manifestly for the interest of the party objecting to it, impair its obligation? If the assent of all the parties to be bound by a contract be of its essence, how is it possible that a new contract, substituted for, or engrafted on another, without such assent, should not violate the old charter?

This course of reasoning, which appears to be perfectly manifest, is not without authority to support it. Mr. Justice Blackstone, lays it down, that the same identical franchise, that has been before granted to one, cannot be bestowed on another; and the reason assigned is, that it would prejudice the former grant. In *The King* v. *Passmore,* Lord Kenyon says, that an existing corporation cannot have another charter obtruded upon it by the crown. It may reject it, or accept the whole, or any part of the new charter. The reason is obvious. A charter is a contract, the validity of which the consent of both parties is essential, and, therefore, it cannot be altered or added to without such consent.

But the case of *Terrett* v. *Taylor*, fully supports the distinction above stated, between civil and private corporations, and is entirely in point. It was decided in that case, that a private corporation, created by the legislature, may lose its franchises by misuser, or non-user, and may be resumed by the government under a judicial judgment of forfeiture. In respect to public corporations which exist only for public purposes, such as town, cities, &c., the legislature may, under proper limitations, change, modify, enlarge, or restrain them, securing, however, the property for the use of those for whom, and at whose expense, it was purchased. But it is denied that it has power to repeal statutes creating private corporations, or confirming to them property already acquired under the faith of previous laws; and that it can, by such repeal, vest the property of such corporations in the state, or dispose of the same to such purposes as it may please, without the consent or default of the corporators. Such a law, it is declared, would be repugnant both to the spirit and the letter of the constitution of the United States.

If these principles, before laid down, be correct, it cannot be denied that the obligations of the charter to Dartmouth College are impaired by the laws under consideration. The name of the corporation, its constitution and government, and the objects of the founder, and of the grantor of the charter, are totally changed. By the charter, the property of this founder was vested in twelve trustees, and no more, to be disposed of by them, or a majority, for the support of a college, for the education and instruction of the Indians, also of English youths, and others. Under the late acts, the trustees and visitors are different; and the property and franchises of the college are transferred to different and new uses, not comtemplated by the founder. In short, it is most obvious that the effect of these laws is to abolish the old corporation, and to create a new one in its stead. The laws of Virginia, referred to in the case of *Terrett* v. *Taylor,* authorized the overseers of the poor to sell the glebes belonging to the Protestant Episcopal Church, and to appropriate the proceeds to other uses. The laws in question devest the trustees of Dartmouth College of the property vested in them by the founder, and vest it in the other trustees, for the support of a different institution, called Dartmouth University. In what respects do they differ? Would the difference have been greater in principle if the law had appropriated the funds of the college to the making of turnpike roads, or to any other purpose of a public nature? In all respects in which the contract has been altered without the assent of the corporation its obligations have been impaired; and the degree can make no difference in the construction of the above provision of the constitution.

It has been insisted, in the argument at the bar, that Dartmouth College was a mere civil corporation, created for a public purpose, the public being deeply interested in the education of its youth; and that, consequently, the charter was as much under the control of the government of New Hampshire as if the corporation had concerned the government of a town or city. But it has been shown that the authorities are all the other way. There is not a case to be found which contradicts the doctrine laid down in the case of *Phillips* v. *Bury*, viz., that a college founded by an individual, or individuals, is a private charity, subject to the government and visitation of the founder, and not to the unlimited control of the government.

It is objected, in this case, that Dr. Wheelock is not the founder of Dartmouth College. Admit he is not. How would this alter the case? Neither the king nor the province of New Hampshire was the founder; and if the contributions made by the Governor of New Hampshire, by those persons who granted lands for the college, in order to induce its location in a particular part of the state, by the other liberal contributors in England and America, bestow upon them claims equal with Dr. Wheelock, still it would not alter the nature of the corporation, and convert it into one for public government. It would still be a private eleemosynary corporation, a private charity endowed by a number of persons, instead of a single individual. But the fact is, that whoever may mediately have contributed to swell the funds of this charity, they were bestowed at the solicitation of Dr. Wheelock, and vested in persons appointed by him, for the use of a charity, of which he was the immediate founder, and is so styled in the charter.

Upon the whole, I am of opinion that the above acts of New Hampshire, not having received the assent of the corporate body of Dartmouth College, are not binding on them, and, consequently, that the judgment of the state court ought to be reversed.

JOHNSON, *J.*, concurred, for the reasons stated by the Chief Justice.

LIVINGSTON, *J.*, concurred, for the reasons stated by the Chief Justice, and Justices Washington and Story.

STORY, *J.* This is a cause of great importance, and, as the very learned discussions, as well here as in the State Court, show, of no inconsiderable difficulty. There are two questions to which the appellate jurisdiction of this court properly applies: 1. Whether the original charter of Dartmouth College is a contract within the prohibitory clause of the constitution of the United States, which declares that no state shall pass "any law impairing the obligation of contracts." 2. If so, whether the legislative acts of New Hampshire of the 27th of June, and of the 18th and 27th of December, 1816, or any of them, impair the obligations of that charter.

It will be necessary, however, before we proceed to discuss these questions, to institute an inquiry into the nature, rights, and duties of aggregate corporations at common law; that we may apply the principles, drawn from this source, to the exposition of this charter, which was granted emphatically with reference to that law.

An aggregate corporation at common law is a collection of individuals united into one collective body, under a special name, and possessing certain immunities, privileges, and capacities in its collective character which do not belong to the natural persons composing it. Among other things it possesses the capacity of perpetual succession, and of acting by the collected vote or will of its component members, and of suing and being sued in all things touching its corporate rights and duties. It is, in short, an artificial person, existing in contemplation of law, and endowed with certain powers and franchises which, though they must be exercised through the medium of its natural members, are yet considered as subsisting in the corporation itself, as distinctly as if it were a real personage. Hence, such a corporation may sue and be sued by its own members; and may contract with them in the same manner as with any strangers. A great variety of these corporations exist in every country governed by the common law; in some of which the corporate existence is perpetuated by new elections, made from time to time; and in others by a continual accession of new members, without any corporate act. Some of these corporations are, from the particular purposes to which they are devoted, denominated spiritual, and some lay; and the latter are again divided into civil and eleemosynary corporations. It is unnecessary, in this place, to enter into any examination of civil corporations. Eleemosynary corporations are such as are constituted for the perpetual distribution of the free alms and bounty of the founder, in such manner as he has directed; and in this class are ranked hospitals for the relief of poor and impotent persons, and colleges for the promotion of learning and piety, and the support of persons engaged in literary pursuits.

Another division of corporations is into public and private. Public corporations are generally esteemed such as exist for public political purposes only, such as towns, cities, parishes, and counties; and in many respects they are so, although they involve some private interests; but strictly speaking, public corporations are such only as are founded by the government for public purposes, where the whole interests belong also to the government. If, therefore, the foundation be private, though under the charter of the government, the corporation is private, however extensive the uses may be to which it is devoted, either by the bounty of the founder or the nature and objects of the institution. For instance, a bank created by the government for its own uses, whose stock is exclusively owned by the government, is, in the strictest sense, a public corporation. So a hospital created and endowed by the government for general charity. But a bank, whose stock is owned by private persons, is a private corporation, although it is erected by the government, and its objects and operations partake of a public nature. The same doctrine may be affirmed of insurance, canal, bridge, and turnpike companies. In all these cases, the uses may, in a certain sense, be called public, but the corporations are private; as much so, indeed, as if the franchises were vested in a single person.

This reasoning applies in its full force to eleemosynary corporations. A hospital founded by a private benefactor is, in point of law, a private corporation, although dedicated by its charter to general charity. So a college, founded and endowed in the same manner, although, being for the promotion of learning and piety, it may extend its charity to scholars from every class in the community, and thus acquire the character of a public institution. This is the unequivocal doctrine of the authorities, and cannot be shaken but by undermining the most solid foundations of the common law.

It was indeed supposed at the argument, that if the uses of an eleemosynary corporation be for general charity, this alone would constitute it a public corporation. But the law is certainly not so. To be sure, in a certain sense, every charity, which is extensive in its reach, may be called a public charity, in contradistinction to a charity embracing but a few definite objects. In this sense the language was unquestionably used by Lord Hardwicke in the case cited at the argument; and, in this sense, a private corporation may well enough be denominated a public charity. So it would be if the endowment, instead of being vested in a corporation, were assigned to a private trustee; yet in such a case no one would imagine that the trust ceased to be private, or the funds became public property. That the mere act of incorporation will not change the charity from a private to a public one, is most distinctly asserted in the authorities. Lord Hardwicke, in the case already alluded to, says, "the charter of the crown cannot make a charity more or less public, but only more permanent than it would otherwise be; but it is the extensiveness which will constitute it a public one. A devise to the poor of the parish is a public charity. Where testators leave it to the discretion of a trustee to choose out the objects, though each particular object may be said to be private, yet in the extensiveness of the benefit accruing from them, they may properly be called public charities. A sum to be disposed of by A. B. and his executors, at their discretion, among poor housekeepers, is of this kind." The charity, then, may, in this sense, be public, although it may be administered by private trustees; and, for the same reason, it may thus be public, though administered by a private corporation. The fact, then, that the charity is public, affords no proof that the corporation is also public; and, consequently, the argument, so far as it is built on this foundation, falls to the ground. If, indeed, the argument were correct, it would follow that almost every hospital and college would be a public corporation; a doctrine utterly irreconcilable with the whole current of decisions since the time of Lord Coke.

When, then, the argument assumes, that because the charity is public the corporation is public, it manifestly confounds the popular with the strictly legal sense of the terms. And if it stopped here, it would not be very material to correct the error. But it is on this foundation that a superstructure is erected which is to compel a surrender of the cause. When the corporation is said at the bar to be public, it is not merely meant that the whole community may be the proper objects of the bounty, but that the government have the sole right, as trustees of the public interests, to regulate, control, and direct the corporation, and its funds and its franchises, at its own good will and pleasure. Now, such an authority does not exist in the government, except where the corporation is in the strictest sense public; that is, where its whole interests and franchises are the exclusive property and domain of the government itself. If it had been otherwise, courts of law would have been spared many laborious adjudications in respect to eleemosynary corporations, and the visitatorial powers over them, from the time of Lord Holt down to the present day. Nay, more, private trustees for charitable purposes would have been liable to have the property confided to their care taken away from them without any assent or default on their part, and the administration submitted, not to the control of law and equity, but to the arbitrary discretion of the government. Yet, who ever thought before, that the munificent gifts of private donors for general charity became instantaneously the property of the government; and that the trustees appointed by the donors, whether corporate or unincorporated, might be compelled to yield up their rights to whomsoever the government might appoint to administer them? If we were to establish such a principle, it would extinguish all future eleemosynary endowments; and we should find as little of public policy as we now find of law to sustain it.

An eleemosynary corporation, then, upon a private foundation, being a private corporation, it is next to be considered, what is deemed a foundation, and who is the founder. This cannot be stated with more brevity and exactness than in the language of the elegant commentator upon the laws of England. "The founder of all corporations (says Sir William Blackstone), in the strictest and original sense, is the king alone, for he only can incorporate a society; and in civil corporations, such as mayor, commonalty, &c., where there are no possessions or endowments given to the body, there is no other founder but the king; but in eleemosynary foundations, such as colleges and hospitals, where there is an endowment of lands, the law distinguishes and makes two species of foundation, the one *fundatio incipiens,* or the incorporation, in which sense the king is the general founder of all colleges and hospitals; the other *fundatio perficiens,* or the dotation of it, in which sense the first gift of the revenues is the foundation, and he who gives them is, in the law, the founder; and it is in this last sense we generally call a man the founder of a college or hospital."

To all eleemosynary corporations a visitatorial power attaches, as a necessary incident; for these corporations being composed of individuals, subject to human infirmities, are liable, as well as private persons, to deviate from the end of their institution. The law, therefore, has provided, that there shall somewhere exist a power to visit, inquire into, and correct all irregularities and abuses in such corporations, and to compel the original purposes of the charity to be faithfully fulfilled. The nature and extent of this visitatorial power has been expounded with admirable fullness and accuracy by Lord Holt in one of his most celebrated judgments. And of common right by the dotation the founder and his heirs are the legal visitors, unless the founder has appointed and assigned another person to be visitor. For the founder may, if he please, at the time of the endowment, part with his visitatorial power, and the person to whom it is assigned will, in that case, possess it in exclusion of the founder's heirs. This visitatorial power is, therefore, an hereditament founded in property, and valuable in intendment of law; and stands upon the maxim that he who gives his property has a right to regulate it in future. It includes also the legal right of patronage, for as Lord Holt justly observes, "patronage and visitation are necessary consequents one upon another." No technical terms are necessary to assign or vest the visitatorial power; it is sufficient if, from the nature of the duties to be performed by particular persons under the charter, it can be inferred that the founder meant to part with it in their favor; and he may divide it among various persons, or subject it to any modifications or control, by the fundamental statutes of the corporation. But where the appointment is given in general terms, the whole power vests in the appointee. In the construction of charter, too, it is a general rule that if the objects of the charity are incorporated, as for instance, the master and fellows of a college, or the master and poor of a hospital, the visitatorial power, in the absence of any special appointment, silently vests in the founder and his heirs. But where trustees or governors are incorporated to manage the charity, the visitatorial power is deemed to belong to them in their corporate character.

When a private eleemosynary corporation is thus created by the charter of the crown, it is subject to no other control on the part of the crown than what is expressly or implicitly reserved by the charter itself. Unless a power be reserved for this purpose, the crown cannot, in virtue of its prerogative, without the consent of the corporation, alter or amend the charter, or devest the corporation of any of its franchises, or add to them, or add to, or diminish, the number of the trustees, or remove any of the members, or change, or control the administration of the charity, or compel the corporation to receive a new charter. This is the uniform language of the authorities, and forms one of the most stubborn, and well-settled doctrines of the common law.

But an eleemosynary, like every other corporation, is subject to the general law of the land. It may forfeit its corporate franchises, by misuser or non-user of them. It is subject to the controlling authority of its legal visitor, who, unless restrained by the terms of the charter, may amend and repeal its statutes, remove its officers, correct abuses and generally superintend the management of the trusts. Where, indeed, the visitatorial power is vested in the trustees of the charity in virtue of their incorporation, there can be no amotion of them from their corporate capacity. But they are not, therefore, placed beyond the reach of the law. As managers of the revenues of the corporation, they are subject to the general superintending power of the court of chancery, not as itself possessing a visitatorial power, or a right to control the charity, but as possessing a general jurisdiction in all cases of an abuse of trusts to redress grievances, and suppress frauds. And where a corporation is a mere trustee of a charity, a court of equity will go yet farther; and though it cannot appoint or remove a corporator, it will yet, in a case of gross fraud, or abuse of trust, take away the trust from the corporation, and vest it in other hands.

Thus much it has been thought proper to premise respecting the nature, rights and duties of eleemosynary corporations, growing out of the common law. We may now proceed to an examination of the original charter of Dartmouth College.

It begins by a recital, among other things, that the Rev. Eleazar Wheelock. of Lebanon, in Connecticut, about the year 1754, at his own expense, on his own estate, set on foot an Indian Charity-School; and by the assistance of other persons, educated a number of the children of the Indians, and employed them as missionaries and schoolmasters among the savage tribes; that the design became reputable among the Indians, so that more desired the education of their children at the school than the contributions in the American colonies would support; that the said Wheelock thought it expedient to endeavor to procure contributions in England, and requested the Rev. Nathaniel Whitaker to go to England as his attorney, to solicit contribution, and also solicited the Earl of Dartmouth and others to receive the contributions and become trustees thereof, which they cheerfully agreed to, and he constituted them trustees, accordingly, by a power of attorney, and they testified their acceptance by a sealed instrument. That the said Wheelock also authorized the trustees to fix and determine upon the place for the said school; and, to enable them understandingly to give the preference, laid before them the several offers of the governments in America, inviting the settlement of the school among them; that a large number of the proprietors of lands, in the western part of New Hampshire, to aid the design, and considering that the same school might be enlarged and improved to promote learning among the English, and to supply the churches there with an orthodox ministry, promised large tracts of land for the uses aforesaid, provided the school should be settled in the western part of said province; that the trustees thereupon gave a preference to the western part of said province, lying on Connecticut River, as a situation most convenient for said school. That the said Wheelock further represented the necessity for a legal incorporation, in order to the safety and well-being of said seminary, and its being capable of the tenure and disposal of lands and bequests for the use of the same; that in the infancy of said institution, certain gentlemen whom he had already nominated in his last will (which he had transmitted to the trustees in England) to be trustees in America, should be the corporation now proposed; and lastly, that there were already large contributions for said school in the hands of the trustees in England, and further success might be expected; for which reason the said Wheelock desired they might be invested with all that power therein which could consist with their distance from the same. The charter, after these recitals, declares, that the king, considering the premises, and being willing to encourage the charitable design, and that the best means of education might be established in New Hampshire for the benefit thereof, does, of his special grace, certain knowledge, and mere motion, ordain and grant, that there be a college erected in New Hampshire, by the name of Dartmouth College, for the education and instruction of youth of the Indian tribes, and also of English youth and others; that the trustees of said college shall be a corporation forever, by the name of the Trustees of Dartmouth College; that the then Governor of New Hampshire, the said Wheelock, and ten other persons, specially named in the charter, shall be trustees of the said college, and that the whole number of trustees shall forever thereafter consist of twelve, and no more; that the said corporation shall have power to sue and to be sued by their corporate name, and to acquire and hold for the use of the said Dartmouth College, lands, tenements, hereditaments, and franchises; to receive, purchase, and build any houses for the use of said college, in such town in the western part of New Hampshire as the trustees, or a major part of them, shall by a written instrument agree on; and to receive, accept, and dispose of any lands, goods, chattels, rents, gifts, legacies, &c., &c., not exceeding the yearly value of £6,000. It further declares, that the trustees, or a major part of them, regularly convened (for which purpose seven shall form a quorum), shall have authority to appoint and remove the professors, tutors and other officers of the college, and to pay them and also such missionaries and schoolmasters as shall be employed by the trustees for instructing the Indians, salaries and allowances, as well as other corporate expenses, out of the corporate funds. It further declares, that the said trustees, as often as one or more of the trustees shall die, or, by removal or otherwise, shall, according to their judgment, become unfit or incapable to serve the interests of the college, shall have power to elect and appoint other trustees in their stead, so that when the whole number shall be complete of twelve trustees, eight shall be resident freeholders of New Hampshire, and seven of the whole number laymen. It further declares that the trustees shall have power from time to time to make and establish rules, ordinances, and laws for the government of the college not repugnant to the laws of the land, and to confer collegiate degrees. It further appoints the said Wheelock, whom it denominates "the founder of the college," to be president of the college, with authority to appoint his successor, who shall be president until disapproved of by the trustees. It then concludes with a direction that it shall be the duty of the president to transmit to the trustees in England, so long as they should perpetuate their board, and as there should be Indian natives remaining to be proper objects of the bounty, an annual account of all the disbursements from the donations in England, and of the general plans and prosperity of the institution.

Such are the most material clauses of the charter. It is observable, in the first place, that no endowment whatever is given by the crown; and no power is reserved to the crown or government in any manner to alter, amend, or control the charter. It is also apparent, from the very terms of the charter, that Dr. Wheelock is recognized as the founder of the college, and that the charter is granted upon his application, and that the trustees were in fact nominated by him. In the next place, it is apparent that the objects of the institution are purely charitable, for the distribution of the private contributions of private benefactors. The charity was, in the sense already explained, a public charity, that is, for the general promotion of learning and piety; but in this respect it was just as much public before as after the incorporation. The only effect of the charter was to give permanency to the design, by enlarging the sphere of its action, and granting a perpetuity of corporate powers and franchises the better to secure the administration of the benevolent donations. As founder, too, Dr. Wheelock and his heirs would have been completely clothed with the visitatorial power; but the whole government and control, as well of the officers as of the revenues of the college, being with his consent assigned to the trustees in their corporate character, the visitatorial power, which is included in this authority, rightfully devolved on the trustees. As managers of the property and revenues of the corporation, they were amenable to the jurisdiction of the judicial tribunals of the state; but as visitors, their discretion was limited only by the charter, and liable to no supervision or control, at least, unless it was fraudulently misapplied.

From this summary examination it follows that Dartmouth College was, under its original charter, a private eleemosynary corporation, endowed with the usual privileges and franchises of such corporations, and, among others, with a legal perpetuity, and was exclusively under the government and control of twelve trustees, who were to be elected and appointed, from time to time, by the existing board, as vacancies or removals should occur.

We are now led to the consideration of the first question in the cause, whether this charter is a contract, within the clause of the constitution prohibiting the states from passing any law impairing the obligation of contracts. In the case of *Fletcher* v. *Peck,* this court laid down its exposition of the word "contract" in this clause, in the following manner: "A contract is a compact between two or more persons, and is either executory or executed. An executory contract is one in which a party binds himself to do or not to do a particular thing. A contract executed is one in which the object of the contract is performed; and this, says Blackstone, differs in nothing from a grant. A contract executed, as well as one that is executory, contains obligations binding on the parties. A grant in its own nature amounts to an extinguishment of the right of the grantor, and implies a contract not to re-assert that right. A party is always estopped by his own grant." This language is perfectly unambiguous, and was used in reference to a grant of land by the governor of a state under a legislative act. It determines, in the most unequivocal manner, that the grant of a state is a contract within the clause of the constitution now in question, and that it implies a contract not to re-assume the rights granted. *A fortiori,* the doctrine applies to a charter or grant from the king.

But it is objected that the charter of Dartmouth College is not a contract contemplated by the constitution, because no valuable consideration passed to the king as an equivalent for the grant, it purporting to be granted *ex mero motu,* and further, that no contracts merely voluntary are within the prohibitory clause. It must be admitted that mere executory contracts cannot be enforced at law, unless there be a valuable consideration to sustain them; and the constitution certainly did not mean to create any new obligations, or give any new efficacy to nude pacts. But it must, on the other hand, be also admitted, that the constitution did intend to preserve all the obligatory force of contracts, which they have by the general principles of law. Now, when a contract has once passed, *bona fide,* into grant, neither the king or any private person, who may be the grantor, can recall the grant of the property, although the conveyance may have been purely voluntary. A gift, completely executed, is irrevocable. The property conveyed by it becomes, as against the donor, the absolute property of the donee; and no such subsequent change of intention of the donor can change the rights of the donee. And a gift by the crown of incorporeal hereditaments, such as corporate franchises, when executed, comes completely within the principle, and is, in the strictest sense of the terms, a grant. Was it ever imagined that land, voluntarily granted to any person by a state, was liable to be resumed at its own good pleasure? Such a pretension would, under any circumstances, be truly alarming; but in a country like ours, where thousands of land titles had their origin in gratuitous grants of the states, it would go far to shake the foundations of the best settled estates. And a grant of franchises is not, in point of principle, distinguishable from a grant of any other property. If, therefore, this charter were a pure donation, when the grant was complete, and accepted by the grantees, it involved a contract that the grantees should hold, and the grantor should not re-assume the grant, as much as if it had been founded on the most valuable consideration.

But it is not admitted that this charter was not granted for what the law deems a valuable consideration. For this purpose it matters not how trifling the consideration may be; a pepper corn is as good as a thousand dollars. Nor is it necessary that the consideration should be a benefit to the grantor. It is sufficient if it import damage or loss, or forbearance of benefit, or any act done, or to be done, on the part of the grantee. It is unnecessary to state cases; they are familiar to the mind of every lawyer.

With these principles in view, let us now examine the terms of this charter. It purports, indeed, on its face, to be granted "of the special grace, certain knowledge, and mere motion" of the king; but these words were introduced for a very different purpose from that now contended for. It is a general rule of the common law (the reverse of that applied in ordinary cases), that a grant of the king, at the suit of the grantee, is to be construed most beneficially for the king, and most strictly against the grantee. Wherefore, it is usual to insert in the king's grants a clause, that they are made, not at the suit of the grantee, but of the special grace, certain knowledge, and mere motion of the king; and then they receive a more liberal construction. This is the true object of the clause in question, as we are informed by the most accurate authorities. But the charter also on its face purports to be granted in consideration of the premises in the introductory recitals. Now, among these recitals it appears that Dr. Wheelock had founded a charity-school at his own expense, on his own estate; that divers contributions had been made in the colonies, by others, for its support; that new contributions had been made and were making in England for this purpose, and were in the hands of trustees appointed by Dr. Wheelock to act in his behalf; that Dr. Wheelock had consented to have the school established at such other place as the trustees should select; that offers had been made by several of the governments in America, inviting the establishment of the school among them; that offers of land had also been made by divers proprietors of lands in the western parts of New Hampshire, if the school should be established there; that the trustees had finally consented to establish it in New Hampshire; and that Dr. Wheelock represented that, to effectuate the purposes of all parties, an incorporation was necessary. Can it be truly said that these recitals contain no legal consideration of benefit to the crown, or of forbearance of benefit on the other side? Is there not an implied contract by Dr. Wheelock, if a charter is granted, that the school shall be removed from his estate to New Hampshire? and that he will relinquish all his control over the funds collected, and to be collected, in England under his auspices, and subject to his authority? that he will yield up the management of his charity school to the trustees of the college? that he will relinquish all the offers made by other American governments, and devote his patronage to this institution? It will scarcely be denied that he gave up the right any longer to maintain the charity school already established on his own estate; and that the funds collected for its use, and subject to his management, were yielded up by him as an endowment of the college. The very language of the charter supposes him to be the legal owner of the funds of the charity-school, and, in virtue of this endowment, declares him the founder of the college. It matters not whether the funds were great or small: Dr. Wheelock had procured them by his own influence, and they were under his control, to be applied to the support of his charity-school; and when he relinquished this control he relinquished a right founded in property acquired by his labors. Besides, Dr. Wheelock impliedly agreed to devote his future services to the college, when erected, by becoming president thereof at a period when sacrifices must necessarily be made to accomplish the great design in view. If, indeed, a pepper corn be, in the eye of the law, of sufficient value to found a contract, as upon a valuable consideration, are these implied agreements, and these relinquishments of right and benefit, to be deemed wholly worthless? It has never been doubted that an agreement not to exercise a trade in a particular place was a sufficient consideration to sustain a contract for the payment of money. *A fortiori,* the relinquishment of property which a person holds, or controls the use of, as a trust, is a sufficient consideration; for it is parting with a legal right. Even a right of patronage *(jus patronatus)* is of great value in intendment of law. Nobody doubts that an advowson is a valuable hereditament; and yet, in fact, it is but a mere trust, or right of nomination to a benefice, which cannot be legally sold to the intended incumbent.

In respect to Dr. Wheelock, then, if a consideration be necessary to support the charter as a contract, it is to be found in the implied stipulations on his part in the charter itself. He relinquished valuable rights, and undertook a laborious office in consideration of the grant of the incorporation.

This is not all. A charter may be granted upon an executory, as well as an executed or present consideration. When it is granted to persons who have not made application for it, until their acceptance thereof, the grant is yet *in fieri.* Upon the acceptance there is an implied contract on the part of the grantees, in consideration of the charter, that they will perform the duties, and exercise the authorities conferred by it. This was the doctrine, asserted by the late learned Mr. Justice Buller, in a modern case. He there said: "I do not know how to reason on this point better than in the manner urged by one of the relator's counsel, who considered the grant of incorporation to be a compact between the crown and a certain number of the subjects, the latter of whom undertake, in consideration of the privileges which are bestowed, to exert themselves for the good government of the place," (*i. e.,* the place incorporated). It will not be pretended, that if a charter be granted for a bank, and the stockholders pay in their own funds, the charter is to be deemed a grant without consideration, and, therefore, revocable at the pleasure of the grantor. Yet here the funds are to be managed, and the services performed exclusively for the use and benefit of the stockholders themselves. And where the grantees are mere trustees to perform services without reward, exclusively for the benefit of others, for public charity, can it be reasonably argued that these services are less valuable to the government than if performed for the private emolument of the trustees themselves? In respect, then, to the trustees also, there was a valuable consideration for the charter, the consideration of services agreed to be rendered by them in execution of a charity, from which they could receive no private remuneration.

There is yet another view of this part of the case, which deserves the most weighty consideration. The corporation was expressly created for the purpose of distributing in perpetuity the charitable donations of private benefactors. By the terms of the charter, the trustees, and their successors, in their corporate capacity, were to receive, hold, and exclusively manage, all the funds so contributed. The crown, then, upon the face of the charter, pledged its faith that the donations of private benefactors should be perpetually devoted to their original purposes, without any interference on its own part, and should be forever administered by the trustees of the corporation, unless its corporate franchises should be taken away by due process of law. From the very nature of the case, therefore, there was an implied contract on the part of the crown with every benefactor, that if he would give his money, it should be deemed a charity protected by the charter, and be administered by the corporation according to the general law of the land. As soon, then, as a donation was made to the corporation, there was an implied contract springing up, and founded on a valuable consideration, that the crown would not revoke or alter the charter, or change its administration, without the consent of the corporation. There was also an implied contract between the corporation itself, and every benefactor upon a like consideration, that it would administer his bounty according to the terms, and for the objects stipulated in the charter.

In every view of the case, if a consideration were necessary (which I utterly deny) to make the charter a valid contract, a valuable consideration did exist, as to the founder, the trustees, and the benefactors. And upon the soundest legal principles, the charter may be properly deemed, according to the various aspects, in which it is viewed, as a several contract with each of these parties, in virtue of the foundation, or the endowment of the college, or the acceptance of the charter, or the donations to the charity.

And here we might pause; but there is yet remaining another view of the subject, which cannot consistently be passed over without notice. It seems to be assumed by the argument of the defendant's counsel, that there is no contract whatsoever, in virtue of the charter, between the crown and the corporation itself. But it deserves consideration, whether this assumption can be sustained upon a solid foundation.

If this had been a new charter granted to an existing corporation, or a grant of lands to an existing corporation, there could not have been a doubt that the grant would have been an executed contract with the corporation; as much so, as if it had been to any private person. But it is supposed, that as this corporation was not then in existence, but was created and its franchises bestowed, *uno flatu,* the charter cannot be construed a contract, because there was no person *in rerum natura,* with whom it might be made. Is this, however, a just and legal view of the subject? If the corporation had no existence so as to become a contracting party, neither had it for the purpose of receiving a grant of the franchises. The truth is, that there may be a priority of operation of things in the same grant; and the law distinguishes and gives such priority wherever it is necessary to effectuate the objects of the grant. From the nature of things, the artificial person called a corporation must be created before it can be capable of taking anything. When, therefore, a charter is granted, and it brings the corporation into existence without any act of the natural persons who compose it, and gives such corporation any privileges, franchises, or property, the law deems the corporation to be first brought into existence, and then clothes it with the granted liberties and property. When, on the other hand, the corporation is to be brought into existence by some future acts of the corporators, the franchises remain in abeyance, until such acts are done, and when the corporation is brought into life the franchises instantaneously attach to it. There may be, in intendment of law, a priority of time, even in an instant, for this purpose. And if the corporation have an existence before the grant of its other franchises attaches, what more difficulty is there in deeming the grant of these franchises a contract with it, than if granted by another instrument at a subsequent period? It behooves those also, who hold that a grant to a corporation, not then in existence, is incapable of being deemed a contract on that account, to consider, whether they do not at the same time establish that the grant itself is nullity for precisely the same reason. Yet such a doctrine would strike us all as pregnant with absurdity, since it would prove that an act of incorporation could never confer any authorities, or rights, or property, on the corporation it created. It may be admitted that two parties are necessary to form a perfect contract, but it is denied that it is necessary that the assent of both parties must be at the same time. If the legislature were voluntarily to grant land in fee to the first child of A to be hereafter born; as soon as such child should be born the estate would vest in it. Would it be contended that such grant, when it took effect, was revocable, and not an executed contract, upon the acceptance of the estate? The same question might be asked in a case of a gratuitous grant by the king or the legislature to A, for life, and afterwards to the heirs of B, who is then living. Take the case of a bank, incorporated for a limited period, upon the express condition that it shall pay out of its corporate funds a certain sum, as the consideration for the charter, and after the corporation is organized a payment duly made of the sum out of the corporate funds; will it be contended that there is not a subsisting contract between the government and the corporation, by the matters thus arising *ex post facto,* that the charter shall not be revoked during the stipulated period? Suppose an act declaring that all persons, who should thereafter pay into the public treasury a stipulated sum, should be tenants in common of certain lands belonging to the state in certain proportions; if a person afterwards born pays the stipulated sum into the treasury, it is less a contract with him than it would be with a person *in esse* at the time the act passed? We must admit that there may be future springing contracts in respect to persons not now *in esse,* or we shall involve ourselves in inextricable difficulties. And if there may be in respect to natural persons, why not also in respect to artificial persons, created by the law, for the very purpose of being clothed with corporate powers? I am unable to distinguish between the case of a grant of land or of franchises to an existing corporation, and a like grant to a corporation brought into life for the very purpose of receiving the grant. As soon as it is *in esse,* and the franchises and property become vested and executed in it, the grant is just as much an executed contract as if its prior existence had been established for a century.

Supposing, however, that in either of the views which have been suggested, the charter of Dartmouth College is to be deemed a contract, we are yet met with several objections of another nature.

It is, in the first place, contended that it is not a contract within the prohibitory clause of the constitution, because that clause was never intended to apply to mere contracts of civil institution, such as the contract of marriage, or to grants of power to state officers, or to contracts relative to their offices, or to grants of trust to be exercised for purposes merely public, where the grantees take no beneficial interest.

It is admitted that the state legislatures have power to enlarge, repeal, and limit the authorities of public officers in their official capacities, in all cases, where the constitutions of the states respectively do not prohibit them; and this, among others, for the very reason that there is no express or implied contract, that they shall always, during their continuance in office, exercise such authorities. They are to exercise them only during the good pleasure of the legislature. But when the legislature makes a contract with a public officer, as in the case of a stipulated salary for his services, during a limited period, this, during the limited period, is just as much a contract, within the purview of the constitutional prohibition as a like contract would be between two private citizens. Will it be contended that the legislature of a state can diminish the salary of a judge holding his office during good behavior? Such an authority has never yet been asserted to our knowledge. It may also be admitted that corporations for mere public government, such as towns, cities, and counties, may in many respects be subject to legislative control. But it will hardly be contended that, even in respect to such corporations, the legislative power is so transcendent that it may at its will take away the private property of the corporation, or change the uses of its private funds acquired under the public faith. Can the legislature confiscate to its own use the private funds which a municipal corporation holds under its charter, without any default or consent of the corporators? If a municipal corporation be capable of holding devises and legacies to charitable uses (as many municipal corporations are), does the legislature, under our forms of limited government, possess the authority to seize upon those funds, and appropriate them to other uses, at its own arbitrary pleasure, against the will of the donors and donees? From the very nature of our governments, the public faith is pledged the other way; and that pledge constitutes a valid compact; and that compact is subject only to judicial inquiry, construction, and abrogation. This court have already had occasion, in other causes, to express their opinion on this subject; and there is not the slightest inclination to retract it.

As to the case of the contract of marriage, which the argument supposes not to be within the reach of the prohibitory clause, because it is matter of civil institution, I profess not to feel the weight of the reason assigned for the exception. In a legal sense, all contracts, recognized as valid in any country, may be properly said to be matters of civil institution, since they obtain their obligation and construction *jure loci contractus.* Titles to land, constituting part of the public domain, acquired by grants under the provisions of existing laws by private persons, are certainly contracts of civil institution. Yet no one ever supposed that when acquired, *bona fide,* they were not beyond the reach of legislative revocation. And so, certainly, is the established doctrine of this court. A general law regulating divorces from the contract of marriage, like a law regulating remedies in other cases of breaches of contracts, is not necessarily a law impairing the obligation of such a contract. It may be the only effectual mode of enforcing the obligations of the contract on both sides. A law punishing a breach of a contract, by imposing a forfeiture of the rights acquired under it, or dissolving it because the mutual obligations were no longer observed, is in no correct sense a law impairing the obligations of the contract. Could a law, compelling a specific performance, by giving a new remedy, be justly deemed an excess of legislative power? Thus far the contract of marriage has been considered with reference to general laws regulating divorces upon breaches of that contract. But if the argument means to assert that the legislative power to dissolve such a contract, without any breach on either side, against the wishes of the parties, and without any judicial inquiry to ascertain a breach, I certainly am not prepared to admit such a power, or that its exercise would not entrench upon the prohibition of the constitution. If under the faith of existing laws a contract of marriage be duly solemnized, or a marriage settlement be made (and marriage is always in law a valuable consideration for a contract), it is not easy to perceive why a dissolution of its obligations, without any default or assent of the parties, may not as well fall within the prohibition as any other contract for a valuable consideration. A man has just as good a right to his wife as to the property acquired under a marriage contract. He has a legal right to her society and her fortune; and to devest such right without his default, and against his will, would be as flagrant a violation of the principles of justice as the confiscation of his own estate. I leave this case, however, to be settled when it shall arise. I have gone into it, because it was urged with great earnestness upon us, and required a reply. It is sufficient now to say, that as at present advised, the argument, derived from this source, does not press my mind with any new and insurmountable difficulty.

In respect also to grants and contracts, it would be far

too narrow a construction of the constitution to limit the prohibitory clause to such only where the parties take for their own private benefit. A grant to a private trustee for the benefit of a particular *cestui que trust,* or for any special, private or public charity, cannot be the less a contract because the trustee takes nothing for his own benefit. A grant of the next presentation to a church is still a contract, although it limit the grantee to a mere right of nomination or patronage. The fallacy of the argument consists in assuming the very ground in controversy. It is not admitted that a contract with a trustee is in its own nature revocable, whether it be for special or general purposes, for public charity or particular beneficence. A private donation, vested in a trustee for objects of a general nature, does not thereby become a public trust, which the government may, at its pleasure, take from the trustee, and administer in its own way. The truth is, that the government has no power to revoke a grant, even of its own funds, when given to a private person, or a corporation for special uses. It cannot recall its own endowments granted to any hospital, or college, or city, or town, for the use of such corporations. The only authority remaining to the government is judicial, to ascertain the validity of the grant, to enforce its proper uses, to suppress frauds, and, if the uses are charitable, to secure their regular administration through the means of equitable tribunals, in cases where there would otherwise be a failure of justice.

Another objection growing out of, and connected with that which we have been considering, is, that no grants are within the constitutional prohibition, except such as respect property in the strict sense of the term; that is to say, beneficial interests in lands, tenements, and hereditaments, &c., &c., which may be sold by the grantees for their own benefit; and that grants of franchises, immunities, and authorities not valuable to the parties as property, are excluded from its purview. No authority has been cited to sustain this distinction, and no reason is perceived to justify its adoption. There are many rights, franchises, and authorities, which are valuable in contemplation of law, where no beneficial interest can accrue to the possessor. A grant of the next presentation to a church, limited to the grantee alone, has been already mentioned. A power of appointment, reserved in a marriage settlement, either to a party or a stranger, to appoint uses in favor of third persons, without compensation, is another instance. A grant of lands to a trustee to raise portions or pay debts, is, in law, a valuable grant, and conveys a legal estate. Even a power given by will to executors to sell an estate for payment of debt is, by the better opinions and authority, coupled with a trust, and capable of survivorship. Many dignities and offices, existing at common law, are merely honorary, and without profit, and sometimes are onerous. Yet a grant of them has never been supposed the less a contract on that account. In respect to franchises, whether corporate or not, which include a pernancy of profits, such as a right of fishery, or to hold a ferry, a market, or a fair, or to erect a turnpike, bank, or bridge, there is no pretense to say that grants of them are not within the constitution. Yet they may, in point of fact, be of no exchangeable value to the owners. They may be worthless in the market. The truth, however, is, that all incorporeal hereditaments, whether they be immunities, dignities, offices, or franchises, or other rights, are deemed valuable in law. The owners have a legal estate and property in them, and legal remedies to support and recover them in case of any injury, obstruction, or disseizin of them. Whenever they are the subjects of a contract or grant, they are just as much within the reach of the constitution as any other grant. Nor is there any solid reason why a contract for the exercise of a mere authority should not be just as much guarded as a contract for the use and dominion of property. Mere naked powers, which are to be exercised for the exclusive benefit of the grantor, are revocable by him for that very reason. But it is otherwise where a power is to be exercised in aid of a right vested in the grantee. We all know that a power of attorney, forming a part of a security upon the assignment of a chose in action, is not revocable by the grantor. For it then sounds in contract and is coupled with an interest. So, if an estate be conveyed in trust for the grantor, the estate is irrevocable in the grantee, although he can take no beneficial interest for himself. Many of the best settled estates stand upon conveyances of this nature; and there can be no doubt that such grants are contracts within the prohibition in question.

In respect to corporate franchises, they are, properly speaking, legal estates vested in the corporation itself as soon as it is *in esse.* They are not mere naked powers granted to the corporation, but powers coupled with an interest. The property of the corporation vests upon the possession of its franchises; and whatever may be thought as to the corporators, it cannot be denied that the corporation itself has a legal interest in them. It may sue and be sued for them. Nay, more, this very right is one of its ordinary franchises. "It is likewise a franchise," says Justice Blackstone, "for a number of persons to be incorporated and subsist as a body politic, with power to maintain perpetual succession, and do other corporate acts; and each individual member of such corporation is also said to have a franchise or freedom." In order to get rid of the legal difficulty of these franchises being considered as valuable hereditaments or property, the counsel for the defendant are driven to contend that the corporators or trustees are mere agents of the corporation, in whom no beneficial interest subsists; and so nothing but a naked power is touched by removing them from the trust; and then to hold the corporation itself a mere ideal being, capable indeed of holding property or franchises, but having no interest in them which can be the subject of contract. Neither of these positions is admissible. The former has been already sufficiently considered, and the latter may be disposed of in a few words. The corporators are not mere agents, but have vested rights in their character, as corporators. The right to be a freeman of a corporation is a valuable temporal right. It is a right of voting and acting in the corporate concerns, which the law recognizes and enforces, and for a violation of which it provides a remedy. It is founded on the same basis as the right of voting in public elections; it is as sacred a right; and whatever might have been the prevalence of former doubts, since the time of Lord Holt, such a right has always been deemed a valuable franchise or privilege.

This reasoning, which has been thus far urged, applies with full force to the case of Dartmouth College. The franchises granted by the charter were vested in the trustees in their corporate character. The lands and other property, subsequently acquired, were held by them in the same manner. They were the private demesnes of the corporation held by it, not, as the argument supposes, for the use and benefit of the people of New Hampshire, but, as the charter itself declares, "for the use of Dartmouth College." There were not, and in the nature of things could not be, any other *cestui que use* entitled to claim those funds. They were indeed to be devoted to the promotion of piety and learning, not at large, but in that college, and the establishments connected with it; and the mode in which the charity was to be applied, and the objects of it, were left solely to the trustees, who were the legal governors and administrators of it. No particular person in New Hampshire possessed a vested right in the bounty; nor could he force himself upon the trustees as a proper object. The legislature itself could not deprive the trustees of the corporate funds, or annul their discretion in the application of them, or distribute them among its own favorites. Could the legislature of New Hampshire have seized the land given by the state of Vermont to the corporation, and appropriated it to uses distinct from those intended by the charity, against the will of the trustees? This question cannot be answered in the affirmative, until it is established, that the legislature may lawfully take the property of A and give it to B; and if it could not take away or restrain the corporate funds, upon what pretense can it take away or restrain the corporate franchises? Without the franchises, the funds could not be used for corporate purposes; but without the funds, the possession of the franchises might still be of inestimable value to the college and to the cause of religion and learning.

Thus far, the rights of the corporation itself, in respect to its property and franchises, have been more immediately considered. But there are other rights and privileges belonging to the trustees collectively, and severally, which are deserving of notice. They are entrusted with the exclusive power to manage the funds, to choose the officers, and to regulate the corporate concerns, according to their own discretion. The *jus patronatus* is vested in them. The visitatorial power, in its most enlarged extent, also belongs to them. When this power devolves upon the founder of a charity, it is an hereditament, descendible in perpetuity to his heirs, and in default of heirs, it escheats to the government. It is a valuable right founded in property, as much so as the right of patronage in any other case. It is a right which partakes of a judicial nature. May not the founder as justly contract for the possession of this right in return for his endowment as for any other equivalent? And, if instead of holding it as an hereditament, he assigns it in perpetuity to the trustees of the corporation, is it less a valuable hereditament in their hands? The right is not merely a collective right in all the trustees: each of them also has a franchise in it. Lord Holt says, "it is agreeable to reason, and the rules of law, that a franchise should be vested in the corporation aggregate, and yet the benefit redound to the particular members, and be enjoyed by them in their private capacities. Where the privilege of election is used by particular persons, it is a particular right vested in each particular man." Each of the trustees had a right to vote in all elections. If obstructed in the exercise of it, the law furnished him with an adequate recompense in damages. If ousted unlawfully from his office, the law would, by a *mandamus,* compel a restoration.

It is attempted, however, to establish, that the trustees have no interest in the corporate franchises, because it is said that they may be witnesses in a suit brought against the corporation. The case cited at the bar certainly goes the length of asserting, that in a suit brought against a charitable corporation for a recompense for services performed for the corporation, the governors, constituting the corporation (but whether entrusted with its funds or not by the act of incorporation does not appear), are competent witnesses against the plaintiff. But assuming this case to have been rightly decided (as to which, upon the authorities, there may be room to doubt), the corporators being technically parties to the record, it does not establish that in a suit for the corporate property vested in the trustees in their corporate capacity, the trustees are competent witnesses. At all events, it does not establish, that in a suit for the corporate franchises to be exercised by the trustees, or to enforce their visitatorial power, the trustees would be competent witnesses. On a *mandamus* to restore a trustee to his corporate or visitatorial power, it will not be contended that the trustee is himself a competent witness to establish his own rights, or the corporate rights. Yet why not, if the law deems that a trustee has no interest in the franchise? The test of interest assumed in the argument proves nothing in this case. It is not enough to establish that the trustees are sometimes competent witnesses; it is necessary to show that they are always so in respect to the corporate franchises, and their own. It will not be pretended, that in a suit for damages for obstruction in the exercise of his official powers, a trustee is a disinterested witness. Such an obstruction is not a *damnum absque injuria.* Each trustee has a vested right and legal interest in his office, and it cannot be devested but by due course of law. The illustration, therefore, lends no new force to the argument, for it does not establish that when their own rights are in controversy the trustees have no legal interest in their offices.

The principal objections having been thus answered satisfactorily, at least to my own mind, it remains only to declare that my opinion, after the most mature deliberation, is, that the charter of Dartmouth College, granted in 1769, is a contract within the purview of the constitutional prohibition.

I might now proceed to the discussion of the second question, but it is necessary previously to dispose of a doctrine which has been very seriously urged at the bar, viz., that the charter of Dartmouth College was dissolved at the revolution, and is, therefore, a mere nullity. A case before Lord Thurlow has been cited in support of this doctrine. The principal question in that case was, whether the corporation of William and Mary's College in Virginia (which had received its charter from King William, and Queen Mary) should still be permitted to administer the charity under Mr. Boyle's will, no interest having passed to the college under the will, but it acting as an agent or trustee under a decree in chancery, or whether a new scheme for the administration of the charity should be laid before the court. Lord Thurlow directed a new scheme, because the college belonging to an independent government, was no longer within the reach of the court. And he very unnecessarily added, that he could not now consider the college as a corporation, or as another report states, that he could not take notice of it as a corporation, it not having proved its existence as a corporation at all. If, by this, Lord Thurlow meant to declare that all charters acquired in America from the crown were destroyed by the revolution, his doctrine is not law; and if it had been true, it would equally apply to all other grants from the crown, which would be monstrous. It is a principal of the common law, which has been recognized as well in this as in other courts, that the division of an empire works no forfeiture of previously-vested rights of property. And this maxim is equally consonant with the common sense of mankind, and the maxims of eternal justice. This objection, therefore, may be safely dismissed without further comment.

The remaining inquiry is, whether the acts of the legislature of New Hampshire now in question, or any of them, impair the obligations of the charter of Dartmouth College. The attempt certainly is to force upon the corporation a new charter against the will of the corporators. Nothing seems better settled at the common law than the doctrine that the crown cannot force upon a private corporation a new charter, or compel the old members to give up their own franchises, or to admit new members into the corporation. Neither can the crown compel a man to become a member of such corporation against his will. As little has it been supposed, that under our limited governments, the legislature possessed such transcendent authority. On one occasion, a very able court held that the state legislature had no authority to compel a person to become a member of a mere private corporation created for the promotion of a private enterprise, because every man had a right to refuse a grant. On another occasion, the same learned court declared, that they were all satisfied that the rights legally vested in a corporation cannot be controlled or destroyed by any subsequent statute unless a power for that purpose be reserved to the legislature in the act of incorporation. These principles are so consonant with justice, sound policy, and legal reasoning, that it is difficult to resist the impression of their perfect correctness. The application of them, however, does not, from our limited authority, properly belong to the appellate jurisdiction of this court in this case.

A very summary examination of the acts of New Hampshire will abundantly show, that in many material respects they change the charter of Dartmouth College. The act of the 27th of June, 1816, declares that the corporation known by the name of the Trustees of Dartmouth College shall be called the Trustees of Dartmouth University. That the whole number of trustees shall be twenty-one, a majority of whom shall form a quorum; that they and their successors shall hold, use, and enjoy forever, all the powers, authorities, rights, property, liberties, privileges, and immunities, heretofore held, &c., by the trustees of Dartmouth College, except where the act otherwise provides; that they shall also have power to determine the times and places of their meetings and manner of notifying the same; to organize colleges in the university; to establish an institute, and elect fellows and members thereof; to appoint and displace officers, and determine their duties and compensation; to delegate the power of supplying vacancies in any of the offices of the university for a limited term; to pass ordinances for the government of the students; to prescribe the course of education; and to arrange, invest, and employ the funds of the university. The act then provides for the appointment of a board of twenty-five overseers, fifteen of whom shall form a quorum, of whom five are to be such *ex officio,* and the residue of the overseers, as well as the new trustees, are to be appointed by the governor and council. The board of overseers are, among other things, to have power "to inspect and confirm, or disapprove and negative, such votes and proceedings of the board of trustees as shall relate to the appointment and removal of president, professors and other permanent officers of the university, and determine their salaries; to the establishment of colleges and professorships, and the erection of new college buildings." The act then provides that the president and professors shall be nominated by the trustees, and appointed by the overseers, and shall be liable to be suspended and removed in the same manner; and that each of the two boards of trustees and overseers shall have power to suspend and remove any member of their respective boards. The supplementary act of the 18th of December, 1816, declares that nine trustees shall form a quorum, and that six votes at least shall be necessary for the passage of any act or resolution. The act of the 26th of December, 1816, contains other provisions, not very material to the question before us.

From this short analysis it is apparent that, in substance, a new corporation is created including the old corporators, with new powers, and subject to a new control; or that the old corporation is newly organized and enlarged, and placed under an authority hitherto unknown to it. The board of trustees are increased from twelve to twenty-one. The college becomes a university. The property vested in the old trustees is transferred to the new board of trustees in their corporate capacities. The quorum is no longer seven, but nine. The old trustees have no longer the sole right to perpetuate their succession by electing other trustees, but the nine new trustees are in the first instance to be appointed by the governor and council, and the new board are then to elect other trustees from time to time as vacancies occur. The new board, too, have the power to suspend or remove any member, so that a minority of the old board, co-operating with the new trustees, possess the unlimited power to remove the majority of the old board. The powers, too, of the corporation are varied. It has authority to organize new colleges in "the university, and to establish an institute, and elect fellows and members thereof." A board of overseers is created (a board utterly unknown to the old charter), and is invested with a general supervision and negative upon all the most important acts and proceedings of the trustees. And to give complete effect to this new authority, instead of the right to appoint, the trustees are in future only to nominate, and the overseers are to approve the president and professors of the university.

If these are not essential changes, impairing the rights and authorities of the trustees, and vitally affecting the interests and organization of Dartmouth College under its old charter, it is difficult to conceive what acts, short of an unconditional repeal of the charter, could have that effect. If a grant of land or franchises be made to A, in trust for special purposes, can the grant be revoked, and a new grant thereof be made to A, B and C, in trust for the same purposes, without violating the obligation of the first grant? If property be vested by grant in A and B, for the use of a college, or a hospital, of private foundation, is not the obligation of that grant impaired when the estate is taken from their exclusive management, and vested in them in common with ten other persons? If a power of appointment be given to A and B, is it no violation of their right to annul the appointment, unless it be assented to by five other persons, and then confirmed by a distinct body? If a bank, or insurance company, by the terms of its charter, be under the management of directors, elected by the stockholders, would not the rights acquired by the charter be impaired if the legislature should take the right of election from the stockholders, and appoint directors unconnected with the corporation? These questions carry their own answers along with them. The common sense of mankind will teach us that all these cases would be direct infringements of the legal obligations of the grants to which they refer; and yet they are, with no essential distinction, the same as the case now at the bar.

In my judgment it is perfectly clear that any act of a legislature which takes away any powers or franchises vested by its charter in a private corporation or its corporate officers, or which restrains or controls the legitimate exercise of them, or transfers them to other persons, without its assent, is a violation of the obligations of that charter. If the legislature mean to claim such an authority, it must be reserved in the grant. The charter of Dartmouth College contains no such reservation; and I am therefore bound to declare that the acts of the legislature of New Hampshire, now in question, do impair the obligations of that charter, and are, consequently, unconstitutional and void.

In pronouncing this judgment, it has not for one moment escaped me how delicate, difficult, and ungracious is the task devolved upon us. The predicament in which this court stands in relation to the nation at large is full of perplexities and embarrassments. It is called to decide on causes between citizens of different states, between a state and its citizens, and between different states. It stands, therefore, in the midst of jealousies and rivalries of conflicting parties, with the most momentous interests confided to its care. Under such circumstances, it never can have a motive to do more than its duty; and, I trust, it will always be found to possess firmness enough to do that.

Under these impressions I have pondered on the case before us with the most anxious deliberation. I entertain great respect for the legislature, whose acts are in question. I entertain no less respect for the enlightened tribunal whose decision we are called upon to review. In the examination, I have endeavored to keep my steps *super antiquas vias* of the law, under the guidance of authority and principle. It is not for judges to listen to the voice of persuasive eloquence or popular appeal. We have nothing to do but to pronounce the law as we find it; and having done this, our justification must be left to the impartial judgment of our country.

DUVALL, *J.*, dissented.

18

KING v. DEDHAM BANK

15 Mass. 447 (1819)

[Per curiam:] Having ascertained the nature and legal effect of the contract when made, we cannot give it a different construction, in consequence of the statute, which was afterwards passed. The contract remains the same, and the present action is founded on that contract. No act of the legislature would authorize this court to render a judgment in any particular case, which should be contrary to law: and most certainly the Act in question was not so intended. If intended as *declaratory* merely, as suggested in the argument for the plaintiff, it was founded on a misapprehension of the pre-existing laws: and if it should have the effect contended for, it would make a new law applicable to the case at bar, instead of ascertaining what the law was before its enactment.

If the defendants have been in the habit of drawing bills of this description, and have thereby exceeded their lawful powers, and violated their charter; they may be prosecuted in a regular manner, and subjected to the legal consequences of the abuse of their charter.—So if their proceedings have been contrary to the spirit and design of the institution, and injurious to the people, the legislature may restrain and prevent such proceedings for the future. But no Act of the legislature can alter the nature and legal effect of an existing contract, to the prejudice of either party; nor give to such a contract a judicial construction, which shall be binding on the parties, or on the courts of law.

19

OGDEN v. SAUNDERS

12 Wheat. 213 (1827)

The learned judges delivered their opinions as follows:

Mr. Justice WASHINGTON. The first and most important

point to be decided in this cause turns essentially upon the question, whether the obligation of a contract is impaired by a state bankrupt or insolvent law, which discharges the person and the future acquisitions of the debtor from his liability under a contract entered into in that state after the passage of the act.

This question has never before been distinctly presented to the consideration of this court and decided, although it has been supposed by the judges of highly respectable state court, that it was decided in the case of *M'Millan* v. *M'Neill* (4 Wheat. Rep., 209). That was the case of a debt contracted by two citizens of South Carolina, in that state, the discharge of which had a view to no other state. The debtor afterwards removed to the territory of Louisiana, where he was regularly discharged, as an insolvent, from all his debts, under an act of the legislature of that state, passed prior to the time when the debt in question was contracted. To an action brought by the creditor in the District Court of Louisiana, the defendant plead in bar his discharge under the law of that territory, and it was contended by the counsel for the debtor in this court, that the law under which the debtor was discharged having passed before the contract was made, it could not be said to impair its obligation. The cause was argued on one side only, and it would seem from the report of the case that no written opinion was prepared by the court. The Chief Justice stated that the circumstance of the state law under which the debt was attempted to be discharged having been passed before the debt was contracted, made no difference in the application of the principle, which had been asserted by the court in the case of *Sturges* v. *Crowninshield.* The correctness of this position is believed to be incontrovertible. The principle alluded to was, that a state bankrupt law which impairs the obligation of a contract, is unconstitutional in its application to such contract. In that case, it is true, the contract preceded in order of time the act of assembly, under which the debtor was discharged, although it was not thought necessary to notice that circumstance in the opinion which was pronounced. The principle, however, remained in the opinion of the court, delivered in *M'Millan* v. *M'Neill,* unaffected by the circumstance that the law of Louisiana preceded a contract made in another state, since that law having no extraterritorial force, never did at any time govern or affect the obligation of such contract. It could not, therefore, be correctly said to be prior to the contract in reference to its obligation, since, if upon legal principles it could affect the contract, that could not happen until the debtor became a citizen of Louisiana, and that was subsequent to the contract. But I hold the principle to be well established, that a discharge under the bankrupt laws of one government does not affect contracts made or to be executed under another, whether the law be prior or subsequent in the date to that of the contract; and this I take to be the only point really decided in the case alluded to. Whether the Chief Justice was correctly understood by the reporter when he is supposed to have said "that this case was not distinguishable in principle from the preceding case of *Sturges* v. *Crowninshield,*" it is not material at this time to inquire, because I understand the meaning of these expressions to go no farther than to intimate that there was no distinction between the cases as to the constitutional objection, since it professed to discharge a debt contracted in another state, which, at the time it was contracted, was not within its operation, nor subject to be discharged by it. The case now to be decided is that of a debt contracted in the state of New York by a citizen of that state, from which he was discharged so far as he constitutionally could be under a bankrupt law of that state, in force at the time when the debt was contracted. It is a case, therefore, that bears no resemblance to the one just noticed.

I come now to the consideration of the question, which for the first time has been directly brought before this court for judgment. I approach it with more than ordinary sensibility, not only on account of its importance, which must be acknowledged by all, but of its intrinsic difficulty, which every step I have taken in arriving at a conclusion with which my judgment could in any way be satisfied, has convinced me attends it. I have examined both sides of this great question with the most sedulous care, and the most anxious desire to discover which of them, when adopted, would be most likely to fulfil the intentions of those who framed the constitution of the United States. I am far from asserting that my labors have resulted in entire success. They have lead me to the only conclusion by which I can stand with any degree of confidence; and yet, I should be disingenuous were I to declare, from this place, that I embrace it without hesitation, and without a doubt of its correctness. The most that candor will permit me to say upon the subject, is that I see, or think I see, my way more clear on the side which my judgment leads me to adopt than on the other, and it must remain for others to decide whether the guide I have chosen has been a safe one or not.

It has constantly appeared to me throughout the different investigations of this question, to which it has been my duty to attend, that the error of those who controvert the constitutionality of the bankrupt law under consideration in its application to this case, if they be in error at all, has arisen from not distinguishing accurately between a law which impairs a contract, and one which impairs its obligation. A contract is defined by all to be an agreement to do, or not to do, some particular act; and in the construction of this agreement, depending essentially upon the will of the parties between whom it is formed, we seek for their intention with a view to fulfil it. Any law, then, which enlarges, abridges, or in any manner changes this intention when it is discovered, necessarily impairs the contract itself, which is but the evidence of that intention. The manner, or the degree, in which this change is effected, can in no respect influence this conclusion; for whether the law affect the validity, the construction, the duration, the mode of discharge, or the evidence of the agreement, it impairs the contract, though it may not do so to the same extent in all the supposed cases. Thus, a law which declares that no action shall be brought whereby to charge a person upon his agreement to pay the debt of another, or upon an agreement relating to lands, unless the same be reduced to writing, impairs a contract made by parol whether the law precede or follow the making of such contract; and if the argument that this law also impairs, in the former case, the obligation of the contract, be sound, it must follow that the statute of frauds and all other statutes which in any manner meddle with contracts, impair their obligation, and are consequently within the operation of this section and article of the constitution. It will not do to answer that in the particular case put, and in others of the same nature, there is no contract to impair, since the pre-existing law denies all remedy for its enforcement, or forbids the making of it, since it is impossible to deny that the parties have expressed their will in the form of a contract, notwithstanding the law denies to it any valid obligation.

This leads us to a critical examination of the particular phraseology of that part of the above section which relates to contracts. It is a law which impairs the obligation of contracts, and not the contracts themselves, which is interdicted. It is not to be doubted, that this term, obligation, when applied to contracts, was well considered and weighed by those who framed the constitution, and was intended to convey a different meaning from what the prohibition would have imported without it. It is this meaning of which we are all in search.

What is it, then, which constitutes the obligation of a contract? The answer is given by the Chief Justice, in the case of *Sturges* v. *Crowinshield,* to which I readily assent now, as I did then; it is the law which binds the parties to perform their agreement. The law, then, which has this binding obligation, must govern and control the contract in every shape in which it is intended to bear upon it, whether it affect its validity, construction, or discharge.

But the question, which law is referred to in the above definition, still remains to be solved. It cannot for a moment be conceded that the mere moral law is intended, since the obligation which that imposes is altogether of the imperfect kind, which the parties to it are free to obey, or not, as they please. It cannot be supposed, that it was with this law the grave authors of this instrument were dealing.

The universal law of all civilized nations, which declares that men shall perform that to which they have agreed, has been supposed by the counsel who have argued this cause for the defendant in error, to be the law which is alluded to; and I have no objection to acknowledging its obligation, whilst I must deny that it is that which exclusively governs the contract. It is upon this law that the obligation which nations acknowledge to perform their compacts with each other is founded, and I therefore feel no objection to answer the question asked by the same counsel—what law it is which constitutes the obligation of the compact between Virginia and Kentucky?—by admitting that it is this common law of nations which requires them to perform it. I admit further, that it is this law which creates the obligation of a contract made upon a desert spot, where no municipal law exists, and (which was another case put by the same counsel) which contract, by the tacit assent of all nations, their tribunals are authorized to enforce.

But can it be seriously insisted, that this, any more than the moral law upon which it is founded, was exclusively in the contemplation of those who framed this constitution? What is the language of this universal law? It is simply that all men are bound to perform their contracts. The injunction is as absolute as the contracts to which it applies. It admits of no qualification, and no restraint, either as to its validity, construction, or discharge, further than may be necessary to develop the intention of the parties to the contract. And if it be true, that this is exclusively the law to which the constitution refers us, it is very apparent that the sphere of state legislation upon subjects connected with the contracts of individuals, would be abridged beyond what it can for a moment be believed the sovereign states of this Union would have consented to; for it will be found, upon examination, that there are few laws which concern the general police of a state, or the government of its citizens, in their intercourse with each other, or with strangers, which may not in some way or other affect the contracts which they have entered into, or may thereafter form. For what are laws of evidence, or which concern remedies—frauds and perjuries—laws of registration, and those which affect landlord and tenant, sales at auction, acts of limitation, and those which limit the fees of professional men, and the charges of tavern-keepers, and a multitude of others which crowd the codes of every state, but laws which may affect the validity, construction or duration, or discharge of contracts? Whilst I admit, then, that this common law of nations, which has been mentioned, may form in part the obligation of a contract, I must unhesitatingly insist, that this law is to be taken in strict subordination to the municipal laws of the land where the contract is made, or is to be executed. The former can be satisfied by nothing short of performance; the latter may affect and control the validity, construction, evidence, remedy, performance and discharge of the contract. The former is the common law of all civilized nations, and of each of them; the latter is the peculiar law of each, and is paramount to the former whenever they come in collision with each other.

It is, then, the municipal law of the state, whether that be written or unwritten, which is emphatically the law of the contract made within the state, and must govern it throughout, wherever its performance is sought to be enforced.

It forms, in my humble opinion, a part of the contract, and travels with it wherever the parties to it may be found. It is so regarded by all the civilized nations of the world, and is enforced by the tribunals of those nations according to its own forms, unless the parties to it have otherwise agreed, as where the contract is to be executed in, or refers to the laws of, some other country than that in which it is formed, or where it is of an immoral character, or contravenes the policy of the nation to whose tribunals the appeal is made; in which latter cases, the remedy which the comity of nations affords for enforcing the obligation of contracts wherever formed, is denied. Free from these objections, this law, which accompanies the contract, as forming a part of it, is regarded and enforced everywhere, whether it affect the validity, construction, or discharge of the contract. It is upon this principle of universal law, that the discharge of the contract, or of one of the parties to it, by the bankrupt laws of the country where it was made, operates as a discharge everywhere.

If, then, it be true that the law of the country where the contract is made, or to be executed, forms a part of that contract, and of its obligation, it would seem to be somewhat of a solecism to say that it does at the same time impair that obligation.

But, it is contended, that if the municipal law of the state where the contract is so made, form a part of it, so does that clause of the constitution which prohibits the states from passing laws to impair the obligation of contracts; and, consequently, that the law is rendered inoperative by force of its controlling associate. All this I admit, provided it be first proved that the law so incorporated with, and forming a part of the contract, does, in effect, impair its obligation; and before this can be proved, it must be affirmed, and satisfactorily made out, that if, by the terms of the contract, it is agreed that, on the happening of a certain event, as, upon the future insolvency of one of the parties, and his surrender of all his property for the benefit of his creditors, the contract shall be considered as performed and at an end, this stipulation would impair the obligation of the contract. If this proposition can be successfully affirmed, I can only say that the soundness of it is beyond the reach of my mind to understand.

Again, it is insisted that if the law of the contract forms a part of it, the law itself cannot be repealed without impairing the obligation of the contract. This proposition I must be permitted to deny. It may be repealed at any time at the will of the legislature, and then it ceases to form any part of those contracts which may afterwards be entered into. The repeal is no more void than a new law would be which operates upon contracts to affect their validity, construction, or duration. Both are valid, (if the view which I take of this case be correct) as they may affect contracts afterwards formed; but neither are so, if they bear upon existing contracts; and, in the former case, in which the repeal contains no enactment, the constitution would forbid the application of the repealing law to past contracts, and to those only.

To illustrate this argument, let us take four laws, which, either by new enactments, or by the repeal of former laws, may affect contracts as to their validity, construction, evidence or remedy.

Laws against usury are of the first description.

A law which converts a penalty, stipulated for by the parties, as the only atonement for a breach of the contract, into a mere agreement for a just compensation, to be measured by the legal rate of interest, is of the second.

The statute of frauds, and the statute of limitations, may be cited as examples of the two last.

The validity of these laws can never be questioned by those who accompany me in the view which I take of the question under consideration, unless they operate, by their express provisions, upon contracts previously entered into; and even then they are void only so far as they do so operate, because, in that case, and in that case only, do they impair the obligation of those contracts. But if they equally impair the obligation of contracts subsequently made, which they must do if this be the operation of a bankrupt law upon such contracts, it would seem to follow, that all such laws, whether in the form of new enactments, or of repealing laws, producing the same legal consequences, are made void by the constitution; and yet the counsel for the defendants in error have not ventured to maintain so alarming a proposition.

If it be conceded that those laws are not repugnant to the constitution, so far as they apply to subsequent contracts, I am yet to be instructed how to distinguish between those laws, and the one now under consideration. How has this been attempted by the learned counsel who have argued this cause upon the ground of such a distinction?

They have insisted that the effect of the law first supposed, is to annihilate the contract in its birth, or rather to prevent it from having a legal existence, and, consequently, that there is no obligation to be impaired. But this is clearly not so, since it may legitimately avoid all contracts afterwards entered into, which reserve to the lender a higher rate of interest than this law permits.

The validity of the second law is admitted, and yet this can only be in its application to subsequent contracts; for it has not, and I think it cannot, for a moment, be maintained, that a law which, in express terms, varies the construction of an existing contract, or which, repealing a former law, is made to produce the same effect, does not impair the obligation of that contract.

The statute of frauds, and the statute of limitations, which have been put as examples of the third and fourth classes of laws, are also admitted to be valid, because they merely concern the modes of proceeding in the trial of causes. The former, supplying a rule of evidence, and the latter, forming a part of the remedy given by the legislature to enforce the obligation, and likewise providing a rule of evidence.

All this I admit. But how does it happen that these laws, like those which affect the validity and construction of contracts, are valid as to subsequent, and yet void as to prior and subsisting contracts? For we are informed by the learned judge who delivered the opinion of this court in the case of *Sturges* v. *Crowninshield,* that, "if, in a state where six years may be pleaded in bar to an action of *assumpsit,* a law should pass, declaring that contracts already in existence, not barred by the statute, should be construed within it, there could be little doubt of its unconstitutionality."

It is thus most apparent that, whichever way we turn, whether to laws affecting the validity, construction, or discharges of contracts, or the evidence or remedy to be employed in enforcing them, we are met by this overruling and admitted distinction, between those which operate retrospectively, and those which operate prospectively. In all of them the law is pronounced to be void in the first class of cases, and not so in the second.

Let us stop, then, to make a more critical examination of the act of limitations, which, although it concerns the remedy, or, if it must be conceded, the evidence, is yet void or otherwise, as it is made to apply retroactively, or prospectively, and see if it can, upon any intelligible principle, be distinguished from a bankrupt law, when applied in the same manner. What is the effect of the former? The answer is, to discharge the debtor and all his future acquisitions from his contract; because he is permitted to plead it in bar of any remedy which can be instituted against him, and consequently in bar or destruction of the obligation which his contract imposed upon him. What is the effect of a discharge under a bankrupt law? I can answer this question in no other terms than those which are given to the former question. If there be a difference, it is one which, in the eye of justice at least, is more favorable to the validity of the latter than of the former; for in the one, the debtor surrenders everything which he possesses towards the discharge of his obligation, and in the other, he surrenders nothing, and sullenly shelters himself behind a legal objection with which the law has provided him, for the purpose of protecting his person, and his present, as well as his future acquisitions, against the performance of his contract.

It is said that the former does not discharge him absolutely from his contract, because it leaves a shadow sufficiently substantial to raise a consideration for a new promise to pay. And is not this equally the case with a certificated bankrupt, who afterwards promises to pay a debt from which his certificate had discharged him? In the former case, it is said, the defendant must plead the statute in order to bar the remedy, and to exempt him from his obligation. And so, I answer, he must plead his discharge under the bankrupt law, and his conformity to it, in order to bar the remedy of his creditor, and to secure to himself a like exemption. I have, in short, sought in vain for some other grounds on which to distinguish the two laws from each other, than those which were suggested at the bar. I can imagine no other, and I confidently believe that none exist which will bear the test of a critical examination.

To the decision of this court, made in the case of *Sturges* v. *Crowninshield,* and to the reasoning of the learned judge who delivered that opinion, I entirely submit; although I did not then, nor can I now bring my mind to concur in that part of it which admits the constitutional power of the state legislatures to pass bankrupt laws, by which I understand, those laws which discharge the person and the future acquisitions of the bankrupt from his debts. I have always thought that the power to pass such a law was exclusively vested by the constitution in the legislature of the United States. But it becomes me to believe that this opinion was, and is incorrect, since it stands condemned by the decision of a majority of this court, solemnly pronounced.

After making this acknowledgment, I refer again to the above decision with some degree of confidence, in support of the opinion to which I am now inclined to come, that a bankrupt law, which operates prospectively, or in so far as it does so operate, does not violate the constitution of the United States. It is there stated, "that, until the power to pass uniform laws on the subject of bankruptcies be exercised by Congress, the states are not forbidden to pass a bankrupt law, provided it contain no principle which violates the tenth section of the first article of the constitution of the United States." The question in that case was, whether the law of New York, passed on the third of April, 1811, which liberates, not only the person of the debtor, but discharges him from all liability for any debt contracted previous, as well as subsequent to his discharge, on his surrendering his property for the use of his creditors, was a valid law under the constitution in its application to a debt contracted prior to its passage? The court decided that it was not, upon the single ground that it impaired the obligation of that contract. And if it be true, that the states cannot pass a similar law to operate upon contracts subsequently entered into, it follows inevitably, either that they cannot pass such laws at all, contrary to express declaration of the court, as before quoted, or that such laws do not impair the obligation of contracts subsequently entered into; in fine, it is a self-evident proposition, that every contract that can be formed, must either precede, or follow, any law by which it may be affected.

I have, throughout the preceding part of this opinion, considered the municipal law of the country where the contract is made, as incorporated with the contract, whether it affects its validity, construction, or discharge. But I think it quite immaterial to stickle for this position, if it be conceded to me, what can scarcely be denied, that this municipal law constitutes the law of the contract so formed, and must govern it throughout. I hold the legal consequences to be the same, in which every view the law, as it affects the contract, is considered.

I come now to a more particular examination and construction of the section under which this question arises; and I am free to acknowledge that the collocation of the subjects for which it provides has made an irresistible impression upon my mind, much stronger, I am persuaded, than I can find language to communicate to the minds of others.

It declares, that "no state shall coin money, emit bills of credit, make anything but gold and silver coin a tender in payment of debts." These prohibitions, associated with the powers granted to Congress "to coin money, and to regulate the value thereof, and of foreign coin," most obviously constitute members of the same family, being upon the same subject, and governed by the same policy.

This policy was to provide a fixed and uniform standard of value throughout the United States, by which the commercial and other dealings between the citizens thereof, or between them and foreigners, as well as the moneyed transactions of the government, should be regulated. For it might well be asked, why vest in Congress the power to establish a uniform standard of value by the means pointed out, if the states might use the same means, and thus defeat the uniformity of the standard, and, consequently, the standard itself? And why establish a standard at all, for the government of the various contracts might afterwards be discharged by a different standard, or by that which is not money, under the authority of state tender laws? It is obvious, therefore, that these prohibitions, in the 10th section, are entirely homogeneous, and are essential to the establishment of a uniform standard of value, in the formation and discharge of contracts. It is for this reason, independent of the general phraseology which is employed, that the prohibition, in regard to state tender laws, will admit of no construction which would confine it to state laws which have a restrospective operation.

The next class of prohibitions contained in this section consists of bills of attainder, *ex post facto* laws, and laws impairing the obligation of contracts.

Here, too, we observe, as I think, members of the same family brought together in the most intimate connection with each other. The states are forbidden to pass any bill of attainder or *ex post facto* law, by which a man shall be punished criminally or penally, by loss of life, of his liberty, property, or reputation, for an act which, at the time of its commission, violated no existing law of the land. Why did the authors of the constitution turn their attention to this subject, which, at the first blush, would appear to be peculiarly fit to be left to the discretion of those who have the police and good government of the state under their management and control? The only answer to be given is, because laws of this character are oppressive, unjust, and tyrannical; and, as such, are condemned by the universal sentence of civilized man. The injustice and tyranny which characterizes *ex post facto* laws, consists altogether in their retrospective operation, which applies with equal force, although not exclusively, to bills of attainder.

But if it was deemed wise and proper to prohibit state legislation as to retrospective laws, which concern, almost exclusively, the citizens and inhabitants of the particular state in which this legislation takes place, how much more did it concern the private and political interests of the citizens of all the states, in their commercial and ordinary intercourse with each other, that the same prohibition should be extended civilly to the contracts which they might enter into?

If it were proper to prohibit a state legislature to pass a retrospective law which should take from the pocket of one of its own citizens a single dollar, as a punishment for an act which was innocent at the time it was committed, how much more proper was it to prohibit laws of the same character precisely which might deprive the citizens of other states, and foreigners, as well as citizens of the same state, of thousands to which, by their contracts, they were justly entitled, and which they might possibly have realized but for such state interference? How natural, then, was it, under the influence of these considerations, to interdict similar legislation in regard to contracts, by providing that no state shall pass laws impairing the obligation of past contracts? It is true that the two first of these prohibitions apply to laws of a criminal, and the last to laws of a civil character; but if I am correct in my view of the spirit and motives of these prohibitions, they agree in the principle which suggested them. They are founded upon the same reason, and the application of it is at least as strong to the last as it is to the two first prohibitions.

But these reasons are altogether inapplicable to laws of a prospective character. There is nothing unjust or tyrannical in punishing offenses prohibited by law, and committed in violation of that law. Nor can it be unjust or oppressive to declare by law that contracts subsequently entered into may be discharged in a way different from that which the parties have provided, but which they know, or may know, are liable, under certain circumstances, to be discharged in a manner contrary to the provisions of their contract.

Thinking, as I have always done, that the power to pass bankrupt laws was intended by the authors of the constitution to be exclusive in Congress, or, at least, that they expected the power vested in that body would be exercised so as effectually to prevent its exercise by the states, it is the more probable that, in reference to all other interferences of the state legislatures upon the subject of contracts, retrospective laws were alone in the contemplation of the convention.

In the construction of this clause of the tenth section of the constitution, one of the counsel for the defendant supposed himself at liberty so to transpose the provisions contained in it as to place the prohibition to pass laws impairing the obligation of contracts in juxtaposition with the other prohibition to pass laws making anything but gold and silver coin a tender in payment of debts, inasmuch as the two provisions relate to the subject of contracts.

That the derangement of the words, and even sentences of a law, may sometimes be tolerated, in order to arrive at the apparent meaning of the legislature, to be gathered from other parts, or from the entire scope of the law, I shall not deny. But I should deem it a very hazardous rule to adopt in the construction of an instrument so maturely considered as this constitution was by the enlightened statesmen who framed it, and so severely examined and criticised by its opponents in the numerous state conventions which finally adopted it. And if, by the construction of this sentence, arranged as it is, or as the learned counsel would have it to be, it could have been made out that the power to pass prospective laws, affecting contracts, was denied to the states, it is most wonderful that not one voice was raised against the provision, in any of those conventions, by the jealous advocates of state rights, nor even an amendment proposed, to explain the clause, and to exclude a construction which trenches so extensively upon the sphere of state legislation.

But, although the transposition which is contended for may be tolerated in cases where the obvious intention of the legislature can in no other way be fulfilled, it can never be admitted in those where consistent meaning can be given to the whole clause as its authors thought proper to arrange it, and where the only doubt is, whether the construction which the transposition countenances, or that which results from the reading which the legislature has thought proper to adopt, is most likely to fulfil the supposed intention of the legislature. Now, although it is true that the prohibition to pass tender laws of a particular description, and laws impairing the obligation of contracts, relate, both of them, to contracts, yet the principle which governs each of them, clearly to be inferred from the subjects with which they stand associated, is altogether different; that of the first forming part of a system for fixing a uniform standard of value, and, of the last, being founded on a denunciation of retrospective laws. It is, therefore, the safest course, in my humble opinion, to construe this clause of the section according to the arrangement which the convention has thought proper to make of its different provisions. To insist upon a transposition, with a view to warrant one construction rather than the other, falls little short, in my opinion, of a begging of the whole question in controversy.

But why, it has been asked, forbid the states to pass laws making anything but gold and silver coin a tender in payment of debts, contracted subsequent, as well as prior, to the law which authorizes it; and yet confine the prohibition to pass laws impairing the obligation of contracts to past contracts, or in other words, to future bankrupt laws, when the consequence resulting from each is the same, the latter being considered by the counsel as being, in truth, nothing less than tender laws in disguise.

An answer to this question has, in part, been anticipated by some of the preceding observations. The power to pass bankrupt laws having been vested in Congress, either as an exclusive power, or under the belief that it would certainly be exercised, it is highly probable that state legislation upon that subject was not within the contemplation of the convention; or, if it was, it is quite unlikely that the exercise of the power by the state legislatures would have been prohibited by the use of terms which, I have endeavored to show, are inapplicable to laws intended to operate prospectively. For had the prohibition been to pass laws impairing contracts, instead of the obligation of contracts, I admit that it would have borne the construction which is contended for, since it is clear that the agreement of the parties in the first case, would be impaired as much by a prior as it would be by a subsequent bankrupt law. It has, besides, been attempted to be shown, that the limited restriction upon state legislation, imposed by the former prohibition, might be submitted to by the states, whilst the extensive operation of the latter would have hazarded, to say the least of it, the adoption of the constitution by the state conventions.

But an answer, still more satisfactory to my mind, is this: Tender laws, of the description stated in this section, are always unjust; and, where there is an existing bankrupt law at the time the contract is made, they can seldom be useful to the honest debtor. They violate the agreement of the parties to it, without the semblance of an apology for the measure, since they operate to discharge the debtor from his undertaking, upon terms variant from those by which he bound himself, to the injury of the creditor, and unsupported, in many cases, by the plea of necessity. They extend relief to the opulent debtor, who does not stand in need of it; as well as to the one who is, by misfortunes, often unavoidable, reduced to poverty, and disabled from complying with his engagements. In relation to subsequent contracts, they are unjust when extended to the former class of debtors, and useless to the second, since they may be relieved by conforming to the requisitions of the state bankrupt law, where there is one. Being discharged by this law from all his antecedent debts, and having his future acquisitions secured to him, an opportunity is afforded him to become once more a useful member of society.

If this view of the subject be correct, it will be difficult to prove that a prospective bankrupt law resembles in any of its features, a law which should make anything but gold and silver coin a tender in payment of debts.

I shall now conclude this opinion, by repeating the acknowledgment which candor compelled me to make in its commencement, that the question which I have been examining is involved in difficulty and doubt. But if I could rest my opinion in favor of the constitutionality of the law on which the question arises, on no other ground than this doubt so felt and acknowledged, that alone would, in my estimation, be a satisfactory vindication of it. It is but a decent respect due to the wisdom, the integrity, and the patriotism of the legislative body, by which any law is passed, to presume in favor of its validity, until its violation of the constitution is proved beyond all reasonable doubt. This has always been the language of this court, when that subject has called for its decision; and I know that it expresses the honest sentiments of each and every member of this bench. I am perfectly satisfied that it is entertained by those of them from whom it is the misfortune of the majority of the court to differ on the present occasion, and that they feel no reasonable doubt of the correctness of the conclusion to which their best judgment has conducted them.

My opinion is, that the judgment of the court below ought to be reversed, and judgment given for the plaintiff in error.

Mr. Justice JOHNSON. This suit was instituted in Louisiana, in the Circuit Court of the United States, by Saunders, the defendant here, against Ogden, upon certain bills of exchange. Ogden, the defendant there, pleads, in bar to the action, a discharge obtained, in due form of law, from the Courts of the State of New-York, which discharge purports to release him from all debts and demands existing against him on a specified day. This demand is one of that description, and the act under which the discharge was obtained, was the act of New-York of 1801, a date long prior to that of the cause of action on which this suit was instituted. The discharge is set forth in the plea, and represents Ogden as "an insolvent debtor, being, on the day and year therein after mentioned, in prison, in the city and county of New-York, on execution issued against him on some civil action," &c. It does not appear that any suit had ever been instituted against him by this party, or on this cause of action, prior to the present. The cause below was decided upon a special verdict, in which the jury find,

1st. That the acceptance of the bills on which the action was instituted, was made by Ogden, in the city of New-York, on the days they severally bear date, the said defendant then residing in the city of New-York, and continuing to reside there until a day not specified.

2nd. That under the laws of the State of New-York, in such case provided, and referred to in the discharge, (which laws are specially found, &c. meaning the State law of 1801,) application was made for, and the defendant obtained, the discharge hereunto annexed.

3d. That, by the laws of New-York, actions on bills of exchange, and acceptances thereof, are limited to the term of six years; and,

4th. That at the time the said bills were drawn and accepted, the drawee and the drawer of the same, were residents and citizens of the State of Kentucky.

On this state of facts the Court below gave judgment against Ogden, the discharged debtor.

We are not in possession of the grounds of the decision below; and it has been argued here, as having been given upon the general nullity of the discharge, on the ground of its unconstitutionality. But, it is obvious, that it might also have proceeded upon the ground of its nullity as to citizens of other States, who have never, by any act of their own, submitted themselves to the *lex fori* of the State that gives the discharge—considering the right given by the constitution to go into the Courts of the United States upon any contracts, whatever be their *lex loci,* as modifying and limiting the general power which States are acknowledged to possess over contracts formed under control of their peculiar laws.

This question, however, has not been argued, and must not now be considered as disposed of by this decision.

The abstract question of the general power of the States to pass laws for the relief of insolvent debtors, will be alone considered. And here, in order to ascertain with precision what we are to decide, it is first proper to consider what this Court has already decided on this subject. And this brings under review the two cases of *Sturges* v. *Crowninshield,* and *M'Millan* v. *M'Neal,* adjudged in the year 1819, and contained in the 4th vol. of the Reports. If the marginal note to the report, or summary of the effect of the case of *M'Millan* v. *M'Neal,* presented a correct view of the report of that decision, it is obvious, that there would remain very little, if any thing, for this Court to decide. But by comparing the note of the Reporter with the facts of the case, it will be found that there is a generality of expression admitted into the former, which the case itself does not justify. The principle recognised and affirmed in *M'Millan* v. *M'Neal,* is one of universal law, and so obvious and incontestible that it need be only understood to be assented to. It is nothing more than this, "*that insolvent laws have no extra-territorial operation upon the contracts of other States; that the principle is applicable as well to the discharges given under the laws of the States, as of foreign countries; and that the anterior or posterior character of the law under which the discharge is given, with reference to the date of the contract, makes no discrimination in the application of that principle.*"

The report of the case of *Sturges* v. *Crowninshield* needs also some explanation. The Court was, in that case, greatly divided in their views of the doctrine, and the judgment partakes as much of a compromise, as of a legal adjudication. The minority thought it better to yield something than risk the whole. And, although their course of reasoning led them to the general maintenance of the State power over the subject, controlled and limited alone by the oath administered to all their public functionaries to maintain the constitution of the United States, yet, as denying the power to act upon anterior contracts, could do no harm, but, in fact, imposed a restriction conceived in the true spirit of the constitution, they were satisfied to acquiesce in it, provided the decision were so guarded as to secure the power over posterior contracts, as well from the positive terms of the adjudication, as from inferences deducible from the reasoning of the Court.

The case of *Sturges* v. *Crowninshield,* then, must, in its authority, be limited to the terms of the certificate, and that certificate affirms two propositions.

1. That a State has authority to pass a bankrupt law, provided such law does not impair the obligation of contracts within the meaning of the constitution, and provided there be no act of Congress in force to establish an uniform system of bankruptcy, conflicting with such law.

2. That a law of this description, acting upon prior contracts, is a law impairing the obligation of contracts within the meaning of the constitution.

Whatever inferences or whatever doctrines the opinion of the Court in that case may seem to support, the concluding words of that opinion were intended to control and to confine the authority of the adjudication to the limits of the certificate.

I should, therefore, have supposed, that the question of exclusive power in Congress to pass a bankrupt law was not now open; but it has been often glanced at in argument, and I have no objection to express my individual opinion upon it. Not having recorded my views on this point in the case of *Crowninshield,* I avail myself of this occasion to do so.

So far, then, am I from admitting that the constitution affords any ground for this doctrine, that I never had a doubt, that the leading object of the constitution was to bring in aid of the States a power over this subject, which their individual powers never could attain to; so far from limiting, modifying, and attenuating legislative power in its known and ordinary exercise in favour of unfortunate debtors, that its sole object was to extend and perfect it, as far as the combined powers of the States, represented by the general government, could extend it. Without that provision, no power would have existed that could extend a discharge beyond the limits of the State in which it was given, but with that provision it might be made co-extensive with the United States. This was conducing to one of the great ends of the constitution, one which it never loses sight of in any of its provisions, that of making an American citizen as free in one State as he was in another. And when we are told that this instrument is to be construed with a view to its federative objects, I reply that this view alone of the subject is in accordance with its federative character.

Another object in perfect accordance with this, may have been that of exercising a salutary control over the power of the States, whenever that power should be exercised without due regard to the fair exercise of distributive justice. The general tendency of the legislation of the States at that time to favour the debtor, was a consideration which entered deeply into many of the provisions of the constitution. And as the power of the States over the law of their respective forums remained untouched by any other provision of the constitution; when vesting in Congress the power to pass a bankrupt law, it was worthy of the wisdom of the Convention to add to it the power to make that system uniform and universal. Yet, on this subject, the use of the term *uniform,* instead of *general,* may well raise a doubt whether it meant more than that such a law should not be *partial,* but have an equal and *uniform* application in every part of the Union. This is in perfect accordance with the spirit in which various other provisions of the constitution are conceived.

For these two objects there appears to have been much reason for vesting this power in Congress; but for extending to the grant the effect of *exclusiveness* over the power of the States, appears to me not only without reason, but to be repelled by weighty considerations.

1. There is nothing which, on the face of the constitution, bears the semblance of direct prohibition on the States to exercise this power; and it would seem strange that, if such a prohibition had been in the contemplation of the Convention, when appropriating an entire section to the enumeration of prohibitions on the States, they had forgotten this, if they had intended to enact it.

The antithetical language adopted in that section, as to every other subject to which the power of Congress had been previously extended, affords a strong reason to conclude, that some direct and express allusion to the power to pass a bankrupt law would have been here inserted also, if they had not intended that this power should be concurrently, or, at least, subordinately exercised by the States. It cannot be correct reasoning, to rely upon this fact as a ground to infer that the prohibition must be found in some provision not having that antithetical character, since this supposes an intention to insert the prohibition, which intention can only be assumed. Its omission is a just reason for forming no other conclusion than that it was purposely omitted. But,

2. It is insisted, that, though not express, the prohibition is to be inferred from the grant to Congress to establish uniform laws on the subject of bankruptcies throughout the United States; and that this grant, standing in connexion with that to establish an uniform rule of naturalization, which is, in its nature, exclusive, must receive a similar construction.

There are many answers to be given to this argument; and the first is, that a mere grant of a State power does not, in itself, necessarily imply an abandonment or relinquishment of the power granted, or we should be involved in the absurdity of denying to the States the power of taxation, and sundry other powers ceded to the general government. But much less can such a consequence follow from vesting in the general government *a power which no State possessed,* and which, all of them combined, could not exercise to meet the end proposed in the constitution. For, if every State in the Union were to pass a bankrupt law in the same unvarying words, although this would, undoubtedly, be an *uniform* system of bankruptcy in its literal sense, it would be very far from answering the grant to Congress. There would still need some act of Congress, or some treaty under sanction of an act of Congress, to give discharges in one State a full operation in the other. Thus, then, the inference which we are called upon to make, will be found not to rest upon any actual cession of State power, but upon the creation of a new power which no State ever pretended to possess; a power which, so far from necessarily diminishing, or imparing the State power over the subject, might find its full exercise in simply recognising as valid, in every State, all discharges which shall be honestly obtained under the existing laws of any State.

Again; the inference proposed to be deduced from this grant to Congress, will be found much broader than the principle in which the deduction is claimed. For, in this, as in many other instances in the constitution, the grant implies only *the right to assume and exercise a power over the subject.* Why, then, should the State powers cease before Congress shall have acted upon the subject? or why should that be converted into a present and absolute relinquishment of power, which is, in its nature, merely potential, and dependent on the discretion of Congress whether, and when, to enter on the exercise of a power that may supersede it?

Let any one turn his eye back to the time when this grant was made, and say if the situation of the people admitted of an abandonment of a power so familiar to the jurisprudence of every State; so universally sustained in its reasonable exercise, by the opinion and practice of mankind, and so vitally important to a people overwhelmed in debt, and urged to enterprise by the activity of mind that is generated by revolutions and free governments.

I will with confidence affirm, that the constitution had never been adopted, had it then been imagined that this question would ever have been made, or that the exercise of this power in the States should ever have depended upon the views of the tribunals to which that constitution was about to give existence. The argument proposed to be drawn from a comparison of this power with that of Congress over naturalization, is not a fair one, for the cases are not parallel; and if they were, it is by no means settled that the States would have been precluded from this power, if Congress had not assumed it. But, admitting, *argumenti gratia,* that they would, still there are considerations bearing upon the one power, which have no application to the other. Our foreign intercourse being exclusively committed to the general government, it is peculiarly their province to determine who are entitled to the privileges of American citizens, and the protection of the American government. And the citizens of any one State being entitled by the constitution to enjoy the rights of citizenship in every other State, that fact creates an interest in this particular in each other's acts, which does not exist with regard to their bankrupt laws; since State acts of naturalization would thus be *extra-territorial* in their operation, and have an influence on the most vital interests of other States.

On these grounds, State laws of naturalization may be brought under one of the four heads or classes of powers precluded to the States, to wit: that of incompatibility; and on this ground alone, if any, could the States be debarred from exercising this power, had Congress not proceeded to assume it. There is, therefore, nothing in that argument.

The argument deduced from the commercial character of bankrupt laws is still more unfortunate. It is but necessary to follow it out, and the inference, if any, deducible from it, will be found to be direct and conclusive in favour of the State rights over this subject. For if, in consideration of the power vested in Congress over foreign commerce, and the commerce between the States, it was proper to vest a power over bankruptcies that should pervade the States; it would seem, that by leaving the regulation of internal commerce in the power of the States, it became equally proper to leave the exercise of this power within their own limits unimpaired.

With regard to the universal understanding of the American people on this subject, there cannot be two opinions. If ever contemporaneous exposition, and the clear understanding of the contracting parties, or of the legislating power, (it is no matter in which light it be considered,) could be resorted to as the means of expounding an instrument, the continuing and unimpaired existence of this power in the States ought never to have been controverted. Nor was it controverted until the repeal of the bankrupt act of 1800, or until a state of things arose in which the means of compelling a resort to the exercise of this power by the United States became a subject of much interest. Previously to that period, the States remained in the peaceable exercise of this power, under circumstances entitled to great consideration. In every State in the Union was the adoption of the constitution resisted by men of the keenest and most comprehensive minds; and if an argument, such as this, so calculated to fasten on the minds of a people, jealous of State rights, and deeply involved in debt, could have been imagined, it never would have escaped them. Yet no where does it appear to have been thought of; and, after adopting the constitution, in every part of the Union, we find the very framers of it every where among the leading men in public life, and legislating or adjudicating under the most solemn oath to maintain the constitution of the United States, yet no where imagining that, in the exercise of this power, they violated their oaths, or transcended their rights. Every where, too, the principle was practically acquiesced in, *that taking away the power to pass a law on a particular subject was equivalent to a repeal of existing laws on that subject.* Yet in no instance was it contended that the bankrupt laws of the States were repealed, while those on navigation, commerce, the admiralty jurisdiction, and various others, were at once abandoned without the formality of a repeal. With regard to their bankrupt or insolvent laws, they went on carrying them into effect and abrogating, and re-enacting them, without a doubt of their full and unimpaired power over the subject. Finally, when the bankrupt law of 1800 was enacted, the only power that seemed interested in denying the right to the States, formally pronounced a full and absolute recognition of that right. It is impossible for language to be more full and explicit on the subject, than is the sixth section of this act of Congress. It acknowledges both the validity of existing laws, and the right of passing future laws. The practical construction given by that act to the constitution is precisely this, *that it amounts only to a right to assume the power to legislate on the subject, and, therefore, abrogates or suspends the existing laws, only so far as they may clash with the provisions of the act of Congress.* This construction was universally acquiesced in, for it was that on which there had previously prevailed but one opinion from the date of the constitution.

Much alarm has been expressed respecting the inharmonious operation of so many systems, all operating at the same time. But I must say that I cannot discover any real ground for these apprehensions. Nothing but a future operation is here contended for, and nothing is easier than to avoid those rocks and quicksands which are visible to all. Most of the dangers are imaginary, for the interests of each community, its respect for the opinion of mankind, and a remnant of moral feeling which will not cease to operate in the worst of times, will always present important barriers against the gross violation of principle. How is the general government itself made up, but of the same materials which separately make up the governments of the States?

It is a very important fact, and calculated to dissipate the fears of those who seriously apprehend danger from this quarter, that the powers assumed and exercised by the States over this subject, did not compose any part of the grounds of complaint by Great Britain, when negotiating with our government on the subject of violations of the treaty of peace. Nor is it immaterial as an historical fact, to show the evils against which the constitution really intended to provide a remedy. Indeed, it is a solecism to suppose, that the permanent laws of any government, particularly those which relate to the administration of justice between individuals, can be radically unequal or even unwise. It is scarcely ever so in despotic governments; much less in those in which the good of the whole is the predominating principle. The danger to be apprehended, is from temporary provisions and desultory legislation; and this seldom has a view to future contracts.

At all events, whatever be the degree of evil to be produced by such laws, the limits of its action are necessarily confined to the territory of those who inflict it. The ultimate object in denying to the States this power, would seem to be, to give the evil a wider range, if it be one, by extending the benefit of discharges over the whole of the Union. But it is impossible to suppose, that the framers of the constitution could have regarded the exercise of this power as an evil in the abstract, else they would hardly have engrafted it upon that instrument which was to become the great safeguard of public justice and public morals.

And had they been so jealous of the exercise of this power in the States, it is not credible that they would have left unimpaired those unquestionable powers over the administration of justice which the States do exercise, and which, in their immoral exercise, might leave to the creditor the mere shadow of justice. The debtor's person, no one doubts, may be exempted from execution. But there is high precedent for exempting his lands; and public feeling would fully sustain an exemption of his slaves. What is to prevent the extension of exemption, until nothing is left but the mere mockery of a judgment, without the means of enforcing its satisfaction?

But it is not only in their execution laws, that the creditor has been left to the justice and honour of the States for his security. Every judiciary in the Union owes its existence to some legislative act; what is to prevent a repeal of that act? and then, what becomes of his remedy, if he has not access to the Courts of the Union? Or what is to prevent the extension of the right to imparl? of the time to plead? of the interval between the sittings of the State Courts? Where is the remedy against all this? and why were not these powers taken also from the States, if they could not be trusted with the subordinate and incidental power here denied them? The truth is, the Convention saw all this, and saw the impossibility of providing an adequate remedy for such mischiefs, if it was not to be found ultimately in the wisdom and virtue of the State rulers, under the salutary control of that republican form of government which it guarantees to every State. For the *foreigner* and the *citizens of other States,* it provides the safeguard of a tribunal which cannot be controlled by State laws in the application of the remedy; and for the protection of all, was interposed that oath which it requires to be administered to all the public functionaries, as well of the States as the United States. It may be called the ruling principle of the constitution, to interfere as little as possible between the citizen and his own State government; and hence, with a few safeguards of a very general nature, the executive, legislative and judicial functions of the States are left as they were, as to their own citizens, and as to all internal concerns. It is not pretended that this discharge could operate upon the rights of the citizen of any other State, unless his contract was entered into in the State that gave it, or unless he had voluntarily submitted himself to the *lex fori* of the State before the discharge, in both which instances he is subjected to its effects by his own voluntary act.

For these considerations, I pronounce the exclusive power of Congress over the relief of insolvents untenable, and the dangers apprehended from the contrary doctrine unreal.

We will next inquire whether the States are precluded from the exercise of this power by that clause in the constitution, which declares that no State shall "pass any bill of attainder, *ex post facto* law, or law impairing the obligation of contracts."

This law of the State of New-York is supposed to have violated the obligation of a contract, by releasing Ogden from a debt which he had not satisfied; and the decision turns upon the question, first, in what consists the obligation of a contract? and, secondly, whether the act of New-York will amount to a violation of that obligation, in the sense of the constitution.

The first of these questions has been so often examined and considered in this and other Courts of the United States, and so little progress has yet been made in fixing the precise meaning of the words "obligation of a contract," that I should turn in despair from the inquiry, were I not convinced that the difficulties the question presents are mostly factitious, and the result of refinement and technicality; or of attempts at definition made in terms defective both in precision and comprehensiveness. Right or wrong, I come to my conclusion on their meaning, as applied to executory contracts, the subject now before us, by a simple and short-handed exposition.

Right and obligation are considered by all ethical writers as correlative terms: Whatever I by my contract give another a right to require of me, I by that act lay myself under an obligation to yield or bestow. The obligation of every contract will then consist of that right or power over my will or actions, which I, by my contract, confer on another. And that right and power will be found to be measured neither by moral law alone, nor universal law alone, nor by the laws of society alone, but by a combination of the three,—an operation in which the moral law is explained and applied by the law of nature, and both modified and adapted to the exigencies of society by positive law. The constitution was framed for society, and an advanced state of society, in which I will undertake to say that *all* the contracts of men receive a relative, and not a positive interpretation: for the rights of all must be held and enjoyed in subserviency to the good of the whole. The State construes them, the State applies them, the State controls them, and the State decides how far the social exercise of the rights they give us over each other can be justly asserted. I say the social exercise of these rights, because in a state of nature, they are asserted over a fellow creature, but in a state of society, over a fellow citizen. Yet, it is worthy of observation, how closely the analogy is preserved between the assertion of these rights in a state of nature and a state of society, in their application to the class of contracts under consideration.

Two men, A. and B., having no previous connexion with each other, (we may suppose them even of hostile nations,) are thrown upon a desert island. The first, having had the good fortune to procure food, bestows a part of it upon the other, and he contracts to return an equivalent in kind. It is obvious here, that B. subjects himself to something more than the moral obligation of his contract, and that the law of nature, and the sense of mankind, would justify A. in resorting to any means in his power to compel a compliance with this contract. But if it should appear that B., by sickness, by accident, or circumstances beyond human control, however superinduced, could not possibly comply with his contract, the decision would be otherwise, and the exercise of compulsory power over B. would be followed with the indignation of mankind. He has carried the power conferred on him over the will or actions of another beyond their legitimate extent, and done injustice in his turn. *"Summum jus est summa injuria."*

The progress of parties, from the initiation to the consummation of their rights, is exactly parallel to this in a state of society. With this difference, that in the concoction of their contracts, they are controlled by the laws of the society of which they are members; and for the construction and enforcement of their contracts, they rest upon the functionaries of its government. They can enter into no contract which the laws of that community forbid, and the validity and effect of their contracts is what the existing laws give to them. The remedy is no longer retained in their own hands, but surrendered to the community, to a power competent to do justice, and bound to discharge towards them the acknowledged duties of government to society, according to received principles of equal justice. The public duty, in this respect, is the substitute for that right which they possessed in a state of nature, to enforce the fulfilment of contracts; and if, even in a state of nature, limits were prescribed by the reason and nature of things, to the exercise of individual power in enacting the fulfilment of contracts, much more will they be in a state of society. For it is among the duties of society to enforce the rights of humanity; and both the debtor and the society have their interests in the administration of justice, and in the general good; interests which must not be swallowed up and lost sight of while yielding attention to the claim of the creditor. The debtor may plead the visitations of Providence, and the society has an interest in preserving every member of the community from despondency—in relieving him from a hopeless state of prostration, in which he would be useless to himself, his family, and the community. When that state of things has arrived in which the community has fairly and fully discharged its duties to the creditor, and in which, pursuing the debtor any longer would destroy the one, without benefitting the other, must always be a question to be determined by the common guardian of the rights of both; and in this originates the power exercised by governments in favour of insolvents. It grows out of the administration of justice, and is a necessary appendage to it.

There was a time when a different idea prevailed, and then it was supposed that the rights of the creditor required the sale of the debtor, and his family. A similar notion now prevails on the coast of Africa, and is often exercised there by brute force. It is worthy only of the country in which it now exists, and of that state of society in which it once originated and prevailed.

"Lex non cogit ad impossibilia," is a maxim applied by law to the contracts of parties in a hundred ways. And where is the objection, in a moral or political view, to applying it to the exercise of the power to relieve insolvents? It is in analogy with this maxim, that the power to relieve them is exercised; and if it never was imagined, that, in other cases, this maxim violated the obligation of contracts, I see no reason why the fair, ordinary, and reasonable exercise of it in this instance, should be subjected to that imputation.

If it be objected to these views of the subject, that they are as applicable to contracts prior to the law, as to those posterior to it, and, therefore, inconsistent with the decision in the case of *Sturges* v. *Crowninshield,* my reply is, that I think this no objection to its correctness. I entertained this opinion then, and have seen no reason to doubt it since. But if applicable to the case of prior debts, *multo fortiori,* will it be so to those contracted subsequent to such a law; the posterior date of the contract removes all doubt of its being in the fair and unexceptionable administration of justice that the discharge is awarded.

I must not be understood here, as reasoning upon the assumption that the remedy is grafted into the contract. I hold the doctrine untenable, and infinitely more restrictive on State power than the doctrine contended for by the opposite party. Since, if the remedy enters into the contract, then the States lose all power to alter their laws for the administration of justice. Yet, I freely admit, that the remedy enters into the views of the parties when contracting; that the constitution pledges the States to every creditor for the full, and fair, and candid exercise of State power to the ends of justice, according to its ordinary administration, uninfluenced by views to lighten, or lessen, or defer the obligation to which each contract fairly and legally subjects the individual who enters into it. Whenever an individual enters into a contract, I think his assent is to be inferred, to abide by those rules in the administration of justice which belong to the jurisprudence of the country of the contract. And when compelled to pursue his debtor in other States, he is equally bound to acquiesce in the law of the forum to which he subjects himself. The law of the contract remains the same every where, and it will be the same in every tribunal; but the remedy necessarily varies, and with it the effect of the constitutional pledge, which can only have relation to the laws of distributive justice known to the policy of each State severally. It is very true, that inconveniences may occasionally grow out of irregularities in the administration of justice by the States. But the citizen of the same State is referred to his influence over his own institutions for his security, and the citizens of the other States have the institutions and powers of the general government to resort to. And this is all the security the constitution ever intended to hold out against the undue exercise of the power of the States over their own contracts, and their own jurisprudence.

But, since a knowledge of the laws, policy, and jurisprudence of a State, is necessarily imputed to every one entering into contracts within its jurisdiction, of what surprise can he complain, or what violation of public faith, who still enters into contracts under that knowledge? It is no reply to urge, that, at the same time knowing of the constitution, he had a right to suppose the discharge void and inoperative, since this would be but speculating on a legal opinion, in which, if he proves mistaken, he has still nothing to complain of but his own temerity, and concerning which, all that come after this decision, at least, cannot complain of being misled by their ignorance or misapprehensions. Their knowledge of the existing laws of the State will henceforward be unqualified, and was so, in the view of the law, before this decision was made.

It is now about twelve or fourteen years since I was called upon, on my circuit, in the case of *Gell, Canonge & Co.* v. *L. Jacobs,* to review all this doctrine. The cause was ably argued by gentlemen whose talents are well known in this capitol, and the opinions which I then formed, I have seen no reason since to distrust.

It appears to me, that a great part of the difficulties of the cause, arise from not giving sufficient weight to the general intent of this clause in the constitution, and subjecting it to a severe literal construction, which would be better adapted to special pleadings.

By classing bills of attainder, *ex post facto* laws, and laws impairing the obligation of contracts together, the general intent becomes very apparent; it is a general provision against arbitrary and tyrannical legislation over existing rights, whether of person or property. It is true, that some confusion has arisen from an opinion, which seems early, and without due examination, to have found its way into this Court; that the phrase *"ex post facto,"* was confined to laws affecting criminal acts alone. The fact, upon examination, will be found otherwise; for neither in its signification or uses is it thus restricted. It applies to civil as well as to criminal acts, (1 *Shep. Touch.* 68. 70, 73.) and with this enlarged signification attached to that phrase, the purport of the clause would be, *"that the States shall pass no law, attaching to the acts of individuals other effects or consequences than those attached to them by the laws existing at their date; and all contracts thus construed, shall be enforced according to their just and reasonable purport.*"

But to assign to contracts, universally, a literal purport, and to exact for them a rigid literal fulfilment, could not have been the intent of the constitution. It is repelled by a hundred examples. Societies exercise a positive control as well over the inception, construction, and fulfilment of contracts, as over the form and measure of the remedy to enforce them.

As instances of the first, take the contract imputed to the drawer of a bill, or endorser of a note, with its modifications; the deviations of the law from the literal contract of the parties to a penal bond, a mortgage, a policy of insurance, bottomry bond, and various others that might be enumerated. And for instances of discretion exercised in applying the remedy, take the time for which executors are exempted from suit; the exemption of members of legislatures; of judges; of persons attending Courts, or going to elections; the preferences given in the marshalling of assets; sales on credit for a present debt; shutting of Courts altogether against gaming debts and usurious contracts, and above all, *acts of limitation.* I hold it impossible to maintain the constitutionality of an act of limitation, if the modification of the remedy against debtors, implied in the discharge of insolvents, is unconstitutional. I have seen no distinction between the cases that can bear examination.

It is in vain to say that acts of limitation appertain to the remedy only: both descriptions of laws appertain to the remedy, and exactly in the same way; they put a period to the remedy, and upon the same terms, by what has been called, a *tender of paper money in the form of a plea,* and to the advantage of the insolvent laws, since if the debtor can pay, he has been made to pay. But the door of justice is shut in the face of the creditor in the other instance, without an inquiry on the subject of the debtor's capacity to pay. And it is equally vain to say, that the act of limitation raises a presumption of payment, since it cannot be taken advantage of on the general issue, without provision by statute; and the only legal form of a plea implies an acknowledgment that the debt has not been paid.

Yet so universal is the assent of mankind in favour of limitation acts, that it is the opinion of profound politicians, that no nation could subsist without one.

The right, then, of the creditor, to the aid of the public arm for the recovery of contracts, is not absolute and unlimited, but may be modified by the necessities or policy of societies. And this, together with the contract itself, must be taken by the individual, subject to such restrictions and conditions as are imposed by the laws of the country. The right to pass bankrupt laws is asserted by every civilized nation in the world. And in no writer, I will venture to say, has it ever been suggested, that the power of annulling such contracts, universally exercised under their bankrupt or insolvent systems, involves a violation of the obligation of contracts. In international law, the subject is perfectly understood, and the right generally acquiesced in; and yet the denial of justice is, by the same code, an acknowledged cause of war.

But it is contended, that if the obligation of a contract has relation at all to the laws which give or modify the remedy, then the obligation of a contract is ambulatory, and uncertain, and will mean a different thing in every State in which it may be necessary to enforce the contract.

There is no question that this effect follows; and yet, after this concession, it will still remain to be shown how any violation of the obligation of the contract can arise from that cause. It is a casualty well known to the creditor when he enters into the contract; and if obliged to prosecute his rights in another State, what more can he claim of that State, than that its Courts shall be open to him on the same terms on which they are open to other individuals? It is only by voluntarily subjecting himself to the *lex fori* of a State, that he can be brought within the provisions of its statutes in favour of debtors, since, in no other instance, does any State pretend to a right to discharge the contracts entered into in another State. He who enters into a pecuniary contract, knowing that he may have to pursue his debtor, if he flees from justice, casts himself, in fact, upon the justice of nations.

It has also been urged, with an earnestness that could only proceed from deep conviction, that insolvent laws were tender laws of the worst description, and that it is impossible to maintain the constitutionality of insolvent laws that have a future operation, without asserting the right of the States to pass tender laws, provided such laws are confined to a future operation.

Yet to all this there appears to be a simple and conclusive answer. The prohibition in the constitution to make any thing but gold or silver coin a tender in payment of debts is express and universal. The framers of the constitution regarded it as an evil to be repelled without modification; they have, therefore, left nothing to be inferred or deduced from construction on this subject. But the contrary is the fact with regard to insolvent laws; it contains no express prohibition to pass such laws, and we are called upon here to deduce such a prohibition from a clause, which is any thing but explicit, and which already has been judicially declared to embrace a great variety of other subjects. The inquiry, then, is open and indispensable in relation to insolvent laws, prospective or retrospective, whether they do, in the sense of the constitution, violate the obligation of contracts? There would be much in the argument, if there was no express prohibition against passing tender laws; but with such express prohibition, the cases have no analogy. And, independent of the different provisions in the constitution, there is a distinction existing between tender laws and insolvent laws in their object and policy, which sufficiently points out the principle upon which the constitution acts upon them as several and distinct; a tender law supposes a capacity in the debtor to pay and satisfy the debt in some way, but the discharge of an insolvent is founded in his incapacity ever to pay, which incapacity is judicially determined according to the laws of the State that passes it. The one imports a positive violation of the contract, since all contracts to pay, not expressed otherwise, have relation to payment in the current coin of the country; the other imports an impossibility that the creditor ever can fulfil the contract.

If it be urged, that to assume this impossibility is itself an arbitrary act, that parties have in view something more than present possessions, that they look to future acquisitions, that industry, talents and integrity are as confidently trusted as property itself; and, to release them from this liability, impairs the obligation of contracts; plausible as the argument may seem, I think the answer is obvious and incontrovertible.

Why may not the community set bounds to the will of the contracting parties in this as in every other instance? That will is controlled in the instances of gaming debts, usurious contracts, marriage, brokage bonds, and various others; and why may not the community also declare that, "look to what you will, no contract formed within the territory which we govern shall be valid as against future acquisitions;" "we have an interest in the happiness, and services, and families of this community, which shall not be superseded by individual views?" Who can doubt the power of the State to prohibit her citizens from running in debt altogether? A measure a thousand times wiser than that impulse to speculation and ruin, which has hitherto been communicated to individuals by our public policy. And if to be prohibited altogether, where is the limit which may not be set both to the acts and the views of the contracting parties?

When considering the first question in this cause, I took occasion to remark on the evidence of contemporaneous exposition deducible from well known facts. Every candid mind will admit that this is a very different thing from contending that the frequent repetition of wrong will create a right. It proceeds upon the presumption, that the contemporaries of the constitution have claims to our deference on the question of right, because they had the best opportunities of informing themselves of the understanding of the framers of the constitution, and of the sense put upon it by the people when it was adopted by them; and in this point of view it is obvious that the consideration bears as strongly upon the second point in the cause as on the first. For, had there been any possible ground to think otherwise, who could suppose that such men, and so many of them, acting under the most solemn oath, and generally acting rather under a feeling of jealousy of the power of the general government than otherwise, would universally have acted upon the conviction, that the power to relieve insolvents by a discharge from the debt had not been taken from the States by the article prohibiting the violation of contracts? The whole history of the times, up to a time subsequent to the repeal of the bankrupt law, indicates a settled knowledge of the contrary.

If it be objected to the views which I have taken of this subject, that they imply a departure from the direct and literal meaning of terms, in order to substitute an artificial or complicated exposition; my reply is, that the error is on the other side; *qui haeret in literâ, haeret in cortice*. All the notions of society, particularly in their jurisprudence, are more or less artificial; our constitution no where speaks the language of men in a state of nature; let any one attempt a literal exposition of the phrase which immediately precedes the one under consideration, I mean "*ex post facto*," and he will soon acknowledge a failure. Or let him reflect on the mysteries that hang around the little slip of paper which lawyers know by the title of a bail-piece. The truth is, that even compared with the principles of natural law, scarcely any contract imposes an obligation conformable to the literal meaning of terms. He who enters into a contract to follow the plough for the year, is not held to its literal performance, since many casualties may intervene which would release him from the obligation without actual performance. There is a very striking illustration of this principle to be found in many instances in the books; I mean those cases in which parties are released from their contracts by a declaration of war, or where laws are passed rendering that unlawful, even incidentally, which was lawful at the time of the contract. Now, in both these instances, it is the government that puts an end to the contract, and yet no one ever imagined that it thereby violates the obligation of a contract.

It is, therefore, far from being true, as a general proposition, "that a government necessarily violates the obligation of a contract, which it puts an end to without performance." It is the motive, the policy, the object, that must characterize the legislative act, to affect it with imputation of violating the obligation of contracts.

In the effort to get rid of the universal vote of mankind in favour of limitation acts, and laws against gaming, usury, marriage, brokage, buying and selling of offices, and many of the same description, we have heard it argued, that, as to limitation acts, the creditor has nothing to complain of, because time is allowed him, of which, if he does not avail himself, it is his own neglect; and as to all others, there is no contract violated, because there was none ever incurred. But it is obvious that this mode of answering the argument involves a surrender to us of our whole ground. It admits the right of the government to limit and define the power of contracting, and the extent of the creditor's remedy against his debtor; to regard other rights besides his, and to modify his rights so as not to let them override entirely the general interests of society, the interests of the community itself in the talents and services of the debtor, the regard due to his happiness, and to the claims of his family upon him and upon the government.

No one questions the duty of the government to protect and enforce the just rights of every individual over all within its control. What we contend for is no more than this, that it is equally the duty and right of governments to impose limits to the avarice and tyranny of individuals, so as not to suffer oppression to be exercised under the semblance of right and justice. It is true, that in the exercise of this power, governments themselves may sometimes be the authors of oppression and injustice; but, wherever the constitution could impose limits to such power, it has done so; and if it has not been able to impose effectual and universal restraints, it arises only from the extreme difficulty of regulating the movements of sovereign power; and the absolute necessity, after every effort that can be made to govern effectually, that will, still exist to leave some space for the exercise of discretion, and the influence of justice and wisdom.

Mr. Justice THOMPSON. . . .

Mr. Chief Justice MARSHALL. It is well known that the Court has been divided in opinion on this case. Three Judges, Mr. Justice DUVALL, Mr. Justice STORY, and myself, do not concur in the judgment which has been pronounced. We have taken a different view of the very interesting question which has been discussed with so much talent, as well as labour, at the bar, and I am directed to state the course of reasoning on which we have formed the opinion that the discharge pleaded by the defendant is no bar to the action.

The single question for consideration, is, whether the act of the State of New-York is consistent with or repugnant to the constitution of the United States?

This Court has so often expressed the sentiments of profound and respectful reverence with which it approaches questions of this character, as to make it unnecessary now to say more than that, if it be right that the power of preserving the constitution from legislative infraction, should reside any where, it cannot be wrong, it must be right, that those whom the delicate and important duty is conferred should perform it according to their best judgment.

Much, too, has been said concerning the principles of construction which ought to be applied to the constitution of the United States.

On this subject, also, the Court has taken such frequent occasion to declare its opinion, as to make it unnecessary, at least, to enter again into an elaborate discussion of it. To say that the intention of the instrument must prevail; that this intention must be collected from its words; that its words are to be understood in that sense in which they are generally used by those for whom the instrument was intended; that its provisions are neither to be restricted into insignificance, nor extended to objects not comprehended in them, nor contemplated by its framers;—is to repeat what has been already said more at large, and is all that can be necessary.

As preliminary to a more particular investigation of the clause in the constitution, on which the case now under consideration is supposed to depend, it may be proper to inquire how far it is affected by the former decisions of this Court.

In *Sturges* v. *Crowninshield*, it was determined, that an act which discharged the debtor from a contract entered into previous to its passage, was repugnant to the constitution. The reasoning which conducted the Court to that conclusion might, perhaps, conduct it farther; and with that reasoning, (for myself alone this expression is used,) I have never yet seen cause to be dissatisfied. But that decision is not supposed to be a precedent for *Ogden* v. *Saunders*, because the two cases differ from each other in a material fact; and it is a general rule, expressly recognised by the Court in *Sturges* v. *Crowninshield*, that the positive authority of a decision is co-extensive only with the facts on which it is made. In *Sturges* v. *Crowninshield*, the law acted on a contract which was made before its passage; in this case, the contract was entered into after the passage of the law.

In *M'Neil* v. *M'Millan*, the contract, though subsequent to the passage of the act, was made in a different State, by persons residing in that State, and, consequently, without any view to the law, the benefit of which was claimed by the debtor.

The *Farmers' and Mechanics' Bank of Pennsylvania* v. *Smith* differed from *Sturges* v. *Crowninshield* only in this, that the plaintiff and defendant were both residents of the State in which the law was enacted, and in which it was applied. The Court was of opinion that this difference was unimportant.

It has then been decided, that an act which discharges the debtor from pre-existing contracts is void; and that an act which operates on future contracts is inapplicable to a contract made in a different State, at whatever time it may have been entered into.

Neither of these decisions comprehends the question now presented to the Court. It is, consequently, open for discussion.

The provision of the constitution is, that "no State shall pass any law" "impairing the obligation of contracts." The plaintiff in error contends that this provision inhibits the passage of retrospective laws only—of such as act on contracts in existence at their passage. The defendant in error maintains that it comprehends all future laws, whether prospective or retrospective, and withdraws every contract from State legislation, the obligation of which has become complete.

That there is an essential difference in principle between laws which act on past, and those which act on future contracts; that those of the first description can seldom be justified, while those of the last are proper subjects of ordinary legislative discretion, must be admitted. A constitutional restriction, therefore, on the power to pass laws of the one class, may very well consist with entire legislative freedom respecting those of the other. Yet, when we consider the nature of our Union; that it is intended to make us, in a great measure, one people, as to commercial objects; that, so far as respects the intercommunication of individuals, the lines of separation between States are, in many respects, obliterated; it would not be matter of surprise, if, on the delicate subject of contracts once formed, the interference of State legislation should be greatly abridged, or entirely forbidden. In the nature of the provision, then, there seems to be nothing which ought to influence our construction of the words; and, in making that construction, the whole clause, which consists of a single sentence, is to be taken together, and the intention is to be collected from the whole.

The first paragraph of the tenth section of the first article, which comprehends the provision under consideration, contains an enumeration of those cases in which the action of the State legislature is entirely prohibited. The second enumerates those in which the prohibition is modified. The first paragraph, consisting of total prohibitions, comprehends two classes of powers. Those of the first are political and general in their nature, being an exercise of sovereignty without affecting the rights of individuals. These are, the powers "to enter into any treaty, alliance, or confederation; grant letters of marque or reprisal, coin money, emit bills of credit."

The second class of prohibited laws comprehends those whose operation consists in their action on individuals. These are, laws which make any thing but gold and silver coin a tender in payment of debts, bills of attainder, *ex post facto* laws, or laws impairing the obligation of contracts, or which grant any title of nobility.

In all these cases, whether the thing prohibited be the exercise of mere political power, or legislative action on individuals, the prohibition is complete and total. There is no exception from it. Legislation of every description is comprehended within it. A State is as entirely forbidden to pass laws impairing the obligation of contracts, as to make treaties, or coin money. The question recurs, what is a law impairing the obligation of contracts?

In solving this question, all the acumen which controversy can give to the human mind, has been employed in scanning the whole sentence, and every word of it. Arguments have been drawn from the context, and from the particular terms in which the prohibition is expressed, for the purpose, on the one part, of showing its application to all laws which act upon contracts, whether prospectively or retrospectively; and, on the other, of limiting it to laws which act on contracts previously formed.

The first impression which the words make on the mind, would probably be, that the prohibition was intended to be general. A contract is commonly understood to be the agreement of the parties; and, if it be not illegal, to bind them to the extent of their stipulations. It requires reflection, it requires some intellectual effort, to efface this impression, and to come to the conclusion, that the words contract and obligation, as used in the constitution, are not used in this sense. If, however, the result of this mental effort, fairly made, be the correction of this impression, it ought to be corrected.

So much of this prohibition as restrains the power of the States to punish offenders in criminal cases, the prohibition to pass bills of attainder and *ex post facto* laws, is, in its very terms, confined to pre-existing cases. A bill of attainder can be only for crimes already committed; and a law is not *ex post facto,* unless it looks back to an act done before its passage. Language is incapable of expressing, in plainer terms, that the mind of the Convention was directed to retroactive legislation. The thing forbidden is retroaction. But that part of the clause which relates to the civil transactions of individuals, is expressed in more general terms; in terms which comprehend, in their ordinary signification, cases which occur after, as well as those which occur before, the passage of the act. It forbids a State to make any thing but gold and silver coin a tender in payment of debts, or to pass any law impairing the obligation of contracts. These prohibitions relate to kindred subjects. They contemplate legislative interference with private rights, and restrain that interference. In construing that part of the clause which respects tender laws, a distinction has never been attempted between debts existing at the time the law may be passed, and debts afterwards created. The prohibition has been considered as total; and yet the difference in principle between making property a tender in payment of debts, contracted after the passage of the act, and discharging those debts without payment, or by the surrender of property, between an absolute right to tender in payment, and a contingent right to tender in payment, or in discharge of the debt, is not clearly discernible. Nor is the difference in language so obvious, as to denote plainly a difference of intention in the framers of the instrument. "No State shall make any thing but gold and silver coin a tender in payment of debts." Does the word "debts" mean, generally, those due when the law applies to the case, or is it limited to debts due at the passage of the act? The same train of reasoning which would confine the subsequent words to contracts existing at the passage of the law, would go far in confining these words to debts existing at that time. Yet, this distinction has never, we believe, occurred to any person. How soon it may occur is not for us to determine. We think it would, unquestionably, defeat the object of the clause.

The counsel for the plaintiff insist, that the word "impairing," in the present tense, limits the signification of the provision to the operation of the act at the time of its passage; that no law can be accurately said to impair the obligation of contracts, unless the contracts exist at the time. The law cannot impair what does not exist. It cannot act on nonentities.

There might be weight in this argument, if the prohibited laws were such only as operated of themselves, and immediately on the contract. But insolvent laws are to operate on a future, contingent, unforeseen event. The time to which the word "impairing" applies, is not the time of the passage of the act, but of its action on the contract. That is, the time present in contemplation of the prohibition. The law, at its passage, has no effect whatever on the contract. Thus, if a note be given in New-York for the payment of money, and the debtor removes out of that State into Connecticut, and becomes insolvent, it is not pretended that his debt can be discharged by the law of New-York. Consequently, that law did not operate on the contract at its formation. When, then, does its operation commence? We answer, when it is applied to the contract. Then, if ever, and not till then, it acts on the contract, and becomes a law impairing its obligation. Were its constitutionality, with respect to previous contracts, to be admitted, it would not impair their obligation until an insolvency should take place, and a certificate of discharge be granted. Till these events occur, its impairing faculty is suspended. A law, then, of this description, if it derogates from the obligation of a contract, when applied to it, is grammatically speaking, as much a law impairing that obligation, though made previous to its formation, as if made subsequently.

A question of more difficulty has been pressed with great earnestness. It is, what is the original obligation of a contract, made after the passage of such an act as the insolvent law of New-York? Is it unconditional to perform the very thing stipulated, or is the condition implied, that, in the event of insolvency, the contract shall be satisfied by the surrender of property? The original obligation, whatever that may be, must be preserved by the constitution. Any law which lessens, must impair it.

All admit, that the constitution refers to, and preserves, the legal, not the moral obligation of a contract. Obligations purely moral, are to be enforced by the operation of internal and invisible agents, not by the agency of human laws. The restraints imposed on States by the constitution, are intended for those objects which would, if not restrained, be the subject of State legislation. What, then, was the original legal obligation of the contract now under the consideration of the Court?

The plaintiff insists, that the law enters into the contract so completely as to become a constituent part of it. That it is to be construed as if it contained an express stipulation to be discharged, should the debtor become insolvent, by the surrender of all his property for the benefit of his creditors, in pursuance of the act of the legislature.

This is, unquestionably, pressing the argument very far; and the establishment of the principle leads inevitably to consequences which would affect society deeply and seriously.

Had an express condition been inserted in the contract, declaring that the debtor might be discharged from it at any time by surrendering all his property to his creditors, this condition would have bound the creditor. It would have constituted the obligation of his contract; and a legislative act annulling the condition would impair the contract. Such an act would, as is admitted by all, be unconstitutional, because it operates on pre-existing agreements. If a law authorizing debtors to discharge themselves from their debts by surrendering their property, enters into the contract, and forms a part of it, if it is equivalent to a stipulation between the parties, no repeal of the law can affect contracts made during its existence. The effort to give it that effect would impair their obligation. The counsel for the plaintiff perceive, and avow this consequence, in effect, when they contend, that to deny the operation of the law on the contract under consideration, is to impair its obligation. Are gentlemen prepared to say, that an insolvent law, once enacted, must, to a considerable extent, be permanent? That the legislature is incapable of varying it so far as respects existing contracts?

So, too, if one of the conditions of an obligation for the payment of money be, that on the insolvency of the obligor, or on any event agreed on by the parties, he should be at liberty to discharge it by the tender of all, or part of his property, no question could exist respecting the validity of the contract, or respecting its security from legislative interference. If it should be determined, that a law authorizing the same tender, on the same contingency, enters into, and forms a part of the contract, then, a tender law, though expressly forbidden, with an obvious view to its prospective, as well as retrospective operation, would, by becoming the contract of the parties, subject all contracts made after its passage to its control. If it be said, that such a law would be obviously unconstitutional and void, and, therefore, could not be a constituent part of the contract, we answer, that if the insolvent law be unconstitutional, it is equally void, and equally incapable of becoming, by mere implication, a part of the the contract. The plainness of the repugnancy does not change the question. That may be very clear to one intellect, which is far from being so to another. The law now under consideration is, in the opinion of one party, clearly consistent with the constitution, and, in the opinion of the other, as clearly repugnant to it. We do not admit the correctness of that reasoning which would settle this question by introducing into the contract a stipulation not admitted by the parties.

This idea admits of being pressed still farther. If one law enters into all subsequent contracts, so does every other law which relates to the subject. A legislative act, then, declaring that all contracts should be subject to legislative control, and should be discharged as the legislature might prescribe, would become a component part of every contract, and be one of its conditions. Thus, one of the most important features in the constitution of the United States, one which the state of the times most urgently required, one on which the good and the wise reposed confidently for securing the prosperity and harmony of our citizens, would lie prostrate, and be construed into an inanimate, inoperative, unmeaning clause.

Gentlemen are struck with the enormity of this result, and deny that their principle leads to it. They distinguish, or attempt to distinguish, between the incorporation of a general law, such as has been stated, and the incorporation of a particular law, such as the insolvent law of New-York, into the contract. But will reason sustain this distinction? They say, that men cannot be supposed to agree to so indefinite an article as such a general law would be, but may well be supposed to agree to an article, reasonable in itself, and the full extent of which is understood.

But the principle contended for does not make the insertion of this new term or condition into the contract, to depend upon its reasonableness. It is inserted because the legislature has so enacted. If the enactment of the legislature becomes a condition of the contract because it is an enactment, then it is a high prerogative, indeed, to decide, that one enactment shall enter the contract, while another, proceeding from the same authority, shall be excluded from it.

The counsel for the plaintiff illustrates and supports this position by several legal principles, and by some decisions of this Court, which have been relied on as being applicable to it.

The first case put is, interest on a bond payable on demand, which does not stipulate interest. This, he says, is not a part of the remedy, but a new term in the contract.

Let the correctness of this averment be tried by the course of proceeding in such cases.

The failure to pay, according to stipulation, is a breach of the contract, and the means used to enforce it constitute the remedy which society affords the injured party. If the obligation contains a penalty, this remedy is universally so regulated that the judgment shall be entered for the penalty, to be discharged by the payment of the principal and interest. But the case on which counsel has reasoned is a single bill. In this case, the party who has broken his contract is liable for damages. The proceeding to obtain those damages is as much a part of the remedy as the proceeding to obtain the debt. They are claimed in the same declaration, and as being distinct from each other. The damages must be assessed by a jury; whereas, if interest formed a part of the debt, it would be recovered as part of it. The declaration would claim it as a part of the debt; and yet, if a suitor were to declare on such a bond as containing this new term for the payment of interest, he would not be permitted to give a bond in evidence in which this supposed term was not written. Any law regulating the proceedings of Courts on this subject, would be a law regulating the remedy.

The liability of the drawer of a bill of exchange, stands upon the same principle with every other implied contract. He has received the money of the person in whose favour the bill is drawn, and promises that it shall be returned by the drawee. If the drawee fail to pay the bill, then the promise of the drawer is broken, and for this breach of contract he is liable. The same principle applies to the endorser. His contract is not written, but his name is evidence of his promise that the bill shall be paid, and of his having received value for it. He is, in effect, a new drawer, and has made a new contract. The law does not require that this contract shall be in writing; and, in determining what evidence shall be sufficient to prove it, does not introduce new conditions not actually made by the parties. The same reasoning applies to the principle which requires notice. The original contract is not written at large. It is founded on the acts of the parties, and its extent is measured by those acts. A. draws on B. in favour of C., for value received. The bill is evidence that he has received value, and has promised that it shall be paid. He has funds in the hands of the drawer, and has a right to expect that his promise will be performed. He has, also, a right to expect notice of its non-performance, because his conduct may be materially influenced by this failure of the drawee. He ought to have notice that *his* bill is disgraced, because this notice enables him to take measures for his own security. It is reasonable that he should stipulate for this notice, and the law presumes that he did stipulate for it.

A great mass of human transactions depends upon implied contracts; upon contracts which are not written, but which grow out of the acts of the parties. In such cases, the parties are supposed to have made those stipulations, which, as honest, fair, and just men, they ought to have made. When the law assumes that they have made these stipulations, it does not vary their contract, or introduce new terms into it, but declares that certain acts, unexplained by compact, impose certain duties, and that the parties had stipulated for their performance. The difference is obvious between this and the introduction of a new condition into a contract drawn out in writing, in which the parties have expressed every thing that is to be done by either.

The usage of banks, by which days of grace are allowed on notes payable and negotiable in bank, is of the same character. Days of grace, from their very term, originate partly in convenience, and partly in the indulgence of the creditor. By the terms of the note, the debtor has to the last hour of the day on which it becomes payable, to comply with it; and it would often be inconvenient to take any steps after the close of day. It is often convenient to postpone subsequent proceedings till the next day. Usage has extended this time of grace generally to three days, and in some banks to four. This usage is made a part of the contract, not by the interference of the legislature, but by the act of the parties. The case cited from 9 *Wheat. Rep.* 581. is a note discounted in bank. In all such cases the bank receives, and the maker of the note pays, interest for the days of grace. This would be illegal and usurious, if the money was not lent for these additional days. The extent of the loan, therefore, is regulated by the act of the parties, and this part of the contract is founded on their act. Since, by contract, the maker is not liable for his note until the days of grace are expired, he has not broken his contract until they expire. The duty of giving notice to the endorser of his failure, does not arise, until the failure has taken place; and, consequently, the promise of the bank to give such notice is performed, if it be given when the event has happened.

The case of the *Bank of Columbia* v. *Oakley*, (4 *Wheat. Rep.* 235.) was one in which the legislature had given a summary remedy to the bank for a broken contract, and had placed that remedy in the hands of the bank itself. The case did not turn on the question whether the law of Maryland was introduced into the contract, but whether a party might not, by his own conduct, renounce his claim to the trial by jury in a particular case. The Court likened it to submissions to arbitration, and to stipulation and forthcoming bonds. The principle settled in that case is, that a party may renounce a benefit, and that *Oakley* had exercised this right.

The cases from *Strange* and *East* turn upon a principle, which is generally recognised, but which is entirely distinct from that which they are cited to support. It is, that a man who is discharged by the tribunals of his own country, acting under its laws, may plead that discharge in any other country. The principle is, that laws act upon a contract, not that they enter into it, and become a stipulation of the parties. Society affords a remedy for breaches of contract. If that remedy has been applied, the claim to it is extinguished. The external action of law upon contracts, by administering the remedy for their breach, or otherwise, is the usual exercise of legislative power. The interference with those contracts, by introducing conditions into them not agreed to by the parties, would be a very unusual and a very extraordinary exercise of the legislative power, which ought not to be gratuitously attributed to laws that do not profess to claim it. If the law becomes a part of the contract, change of place would not expunge the condition. A contract made in New-York would be the same in any other State as in New-York, and would still retain the stipulation originally introduced into it, that the debtor should be discharged by the surrender of his estate.

It is not, we think, true, that contracts are entered into in contemplation of the insolvency of the obligor. They are framed with the expectation that they will be literally performed. Insolvency is undoubtedly a casualty which is possible, but is never expected. In the ordinary course of human transactions, if even suspected, provision is made for it, by taking security against it. When it comes unlooked for, it would be entirely contrary to reason to consider it as a part of the contract.

We have, then, no hesitation in saying that, however law

may act upon contracts, it does not enter into them, and become a part of the agreement. The effect of such a principle would be a mischievous abridgment of legislative power over subjects within the proper jurisdiction of States, by arresting their power to repeal or modify such laws with respect to existing contracts.

But, although the argument is not sustainable in this form, it assumes another, in which it is more plausible. Contract, it is said, being the creature of society, derives its obligation from the law; and, although the law may not enter into the agreement so as to form a constituent part of it, still it acts externally upon the contract, and determines how far the principle of coercion shall be applied to it; and this being universally understood, no individual can complain justly of its application to himself, in a case where it was known when the contract was formed.

This argument has been illustrated by references to the statutes of frauds, of usury, and of limitations. The construction of the words in the constitution, respecting contracts, for which the defendants contend, would, it has been said, withdraw all these subjects from State legislation. The acknowledgment, that they remain within it, is urged as an admission, that contract is not withdrawn by the constitution, but remains under State control, subject to this restriction only, that no law shall be passed impairing the obligation of contracts in existence at its passage.

The defendants maintain that an error lies at the very foundation of this argument. It assumes that contract is the mere creature of society, and derives all its obligation from human legislation. That it is not the stipulation an individual makes which binds him, but some declaration of the supreme power of a State to which he belongs, that he shall perform what he has undertaken to perform. That though this original declaration may be lost in remote antiquity, it must be presumed as the origin of the obligation of contracts. This postulate the defendants deny, and, we think, with great reason.

It is an argument of no inconsiderable weight against it, that we find no trace of such an enactment. So far back as human research carries us, we find the judicial power as a part of the executive, administering justice by the application of remedies to violated rights, or broken contracts. We find that power applying these remedies on the idea of a pre-existing obligation on every man to do what he has promised on consideration to do; that the breach of this obligation is an injury for which the injured party has a just claim to compensation, and that society ought to afford him a remedy for that injury. We find allusions to the mode of acquiring property, but we find no allusion, from the earliest time, to any supposed act of the governing power giving obligation to contracts. On the contrary, the proceedings respecting them of which we know any thing, evince the idea of a pre-existing intrinsic obligation which human law enforces. If, on tracing the right to contract, and the obligations created by contract, to their source, we find them to exist anterior to, and independent of society, we may reasonably conclude that those original and pre-existing principles are, like many other natural rights, brought with man into society; and, although they may be controlled, are not given by human legislation.

In the rudest state of nature a man governs himself, and labours for his own purposes. That which he acquires is his own, at least while in his possession, and he may transfer it to another. This transfer passes his right to that other. Hence the right to barter. One man may have acquired more skins than are necessary for his protection from the cold; another more food than is necessary for his immediate use. They agree each to supply the wants of the other from his surplus. Is this contract without obligation? If one of them, having received and eaten the food he needed, refuses to deliver the skin, may not the other rightfully compel him to deliver it? Or two persons agree to unite their strength and skill to hunt together for their mutual advantage, engaging to divide the animal they shall master. Can one of them rightfully take the whole? or, should he attempt it, may not the other force him to a division? If the answer to these questions must affirm the duty of keeping faith between these parties, and the right to enforce it if violated, the answer admits the obligation of contracts, because, upon that obligation depends the right to enforce them. Superior strength may give the power, but cannot give the right. The rightfulness of coercion must depend on the pre-existing obligation to do that for which compulsion is used. It is no objection to the principle, that the injured party may be the weakest. In society, the wrong-doer may be too powerful for the law. He may deride its coercive power, yet his contracts are obligatory; and, if society acquire the power of coercion, that power will be applied without previously enacting that his contract is obligatory.

Independent nations are individuals in a state of nature. Whence is derived the obligation of their contracts? They admit the existence of no superior legislative power which is to give them validity, yet their validity is acknowledged by all. If one of these contracts be broken, all admit the right of the injured party to demand reparation for the injury, and to enforce that reparation if it be withheld. He may not have the power to enforce it, but the whole civilized world concurs in saying, that the power, if possessed, is rightfully used.

In a state of nature, these individuals may contract, their contracts are obligatory, and force may rightfully be employed to coerce the party who has broken his engagement.

What is the effect of society upon these rights? When men unite together and form a government, do they surrender their right to contract, as well as their right to enforce the observance of contracts? For what purpose should they make this surrender? Government cannot exercise this power for individuals. It is better that they should exercise it for themselves. For what purpose, then, should the surrender be made? It can only be, that government may give it back again. As we have no evidence of the surrender, or of the restoration of the right; as this operation of surrender and restoration would be an idle and useless ceremony, the rational inference seems to be, that neither has ever been made; that individuals do not derive from government their right to contract, but bring that right with them into society; that obligation is not conferred on contracts by positive law, but is intrinsic, and is conferred by the act of the parties. This results from the right which every man retains to acquire property, to dispose of that property according to his own judgment, and to pledge himself for a future act. These rights are not given by society, but are brought into it. The right of coercion is necessarily surrendered to government, and this surrender imposes on government the correlative duty of furnishing a remedy. The right to regulate contracts, to prescribe rules by which they shall be evidenced, to prohibit such as may be deemed mischievous, is unquestionable, and has been universally exercised. So far as this power has restrained the original right of individuals to bind themselves by contract, it is restrained; but beyond these actual restraints the original power remains unimpaired.

This reasoning is, undoubtedly, much strengthened by the authority of those writers on natural and national law, whose opinions have been viewed with profound respect by the wisest men of the present, and of past ages.

Supposing the obligation of the contract to be derived from the agreement of the parties, we will inquire how far law acts externally on it, and may control that obligation. That law may have, on future contracts, all the effect which the counsel for the plaintiff in error claim, will not be denied. That it is capable of discharging the debtor under the circumstances, and on the conditions prescribed in the statute which has been pleaded in this case, will not be controverted. But as this is an operation which was not intended by the parties, nor contemplated by them, the particular act can be entitled to this operation only when it has the full force of law. A law may determine the obligation of a contract on the happening of a contingency, because it is the law. If it be not the law, it cannot have this effect. When its existence as law is denied, that existence cannot be proved by showing what are the qualities of a law. Law has been defined by a writer, whose definitions especially have been the theme of almost universal panegyric, "to be a rule of civil conduct prescribed by the supreme power in a State." In our system, the legislature of a State is the supreme power, in all cases where its action is not restrained by the constitution of the United States. Where it is so restrained, the legislature ceases to be the supreme power, and its acts are not law. It is, then, begging the question to say, that, because contracts may be discharged by a law previously enacted, this contract may be discharged by this act of the legislature of New-York; for the question returns upon us, is this act a law? Is it consistent with, or repugnant to, the constitution of the United States? This question is to be solved only by the constitution itself.

In examining it, we readily admit, that the whole subject of contracts is under the control of society, and that all the power of society over it resides in the State legislatures, except in those special cases where restraint is imposed by the constitution of the United States. The particular restraint now under consideration is on the power to impair the obligation of contracts. The extent of this restraint cannot be ascertained by showing that the legislature may prescribe the circumstances, on which the original validity of a contract shall be made to depend. If the legislative will be, that certain agreements shall be in writing, that they shall be sealed, that they shall be attested by a certain number of witnesses, that they shall be recorded, or that they shall assume any prescribed form before they become obligatory, all these are regulations which society may rightfully make, and which do not come within the restrictions of the constitution, because they do not *impair* the obligation of the contract. The obligation must exist before it can be impaired; and a prohibition to impair it, when made, does not imply an inability to prescribe those circumstances which shall create its obligation. The statutes of frauds, therefore, which have been enacted in the several States, and which are acknowledged to flow from the proper exercise of State sovereignty, prescribe regulations which must precede the obligation of the contract, and, consequently, cannot impair that obligation. Acts of this description, therefore, are most clearly not within the prohibition of the constitution.

The acts against usury are of the same character. They declare the contract to be void in the beginning. They deny that the instrument ever became a contract. They deny it all original obligation; and cannot impair that which never came into existence.

Acts of limitations approach more nearly to the subject of consideration, but are not identified with it. They defeat a contract once obligatory, and may, therefore, be supposed to partake of the character of laws which impair its obligation. But a practical view of the subject will show us that the two laws stand upon distinct principles.

In the case of *Sturges* v. *Crowninshield,* it was observed by the Court, that these statutes relate only to the remedies which are furnished in the Courts; and their language is generally confined to the remedy. They do not purport to dispense with the performance of a contract, but proceed on the presumption that a certain length of time, unexplained by circumstances, is reasonable evidence of a performance. It is on this idea alone that it is possible to sustain the decision, that a bare acknowledgment of the debt, unaccompanied with any new promise, shall remove the bar created by the act. It would be a mischief not to be tolerated, if contracts might be set up at any distance of time, when the evidence of payment might be lost, and the estates of the dead, or even of the living, be subjected to these stale obligations. The principle is, without the aid of a statute, adopted by the Courts as a rule of justice. The legislature has enacted no statute of limitations as a bar to suits on sealed instruments. Yet twenty years of unexplained silence on the part of the creditor is evidence of payment. On parol contracts, or on written contracts not under seal, which are considered in a less solemn point of view than sealed instruments, the legislature has supposed that a shorter time might amount to evidence of performance, and has so enacted. All have acquiesced in these enactments, but have never considered them as being of that class of laws which impair the obligation of contracts. In prescribing the evidence which shall be received in its Courts, and the effect of that evidence, the State is exercising its acknowledged powers. It is likewise in the exercise of its legitimate powers, when it is regulating the remedy and mode of proceeding in its Courts.

The counsel for the plaintiff in error insist, that the right to regulate the remedy and to modify the obligation of the contract are the same; that obligation and remedy are identical, that they are synonymous—two words conveying the same idea.

The answer given to this proposition by the defendant's counsel seems to be conclusive. They originate at different times. The obligation to perform is coeval with the undertaking to perform; it originates with the contract itself, and operates anterior to the time of performance. The remedy acts upon a broken contract, and enforces a pre-existing obligation.

If there be any thing in the observations made in a preceding part of this opinion respecting the source from which contracts derive their obligation, the proposition we are now considering cannot be true. It was shown, we think, satisfactorily, that the right to contract is the attribute of a free agent, and that he may rightfully coerce performance from another free agent who violates his faith. Contracts have, consequently, an intrinsic obligation. When men come into society, they can no longer exercise this original and natural right of coercion. It would be incompatible with general peace, and is, therefore, surrendered. Society prohibits the use of private individual coercion, and gives in its place a more safe and more certain remedy. But the right to contract is not surrendered with the right to coerce performance. It is still incident to that degree of free agency which the laws leave to every individual, and the obligation of the contract is a necessary consequence of the right to make it. Laws regulate this right, but, where not regulated, it is retained in its original extent. Obligation and remedy, then, are not identical; they originate at different times, and are derived from different sources.

But, although the identity of obligation and remedy be disproved, it may be, and has been urged, that they are precisely commensurate with each other, and are such sympathetic essences, if the expression may be allowed, that the action of law upon the remedy is immediately felt by the obligation—that they live, languish, and die together. The use made of this argument is to show the absurdity and self-contradiction of the construction which maintains the inviolability of obligation, while it leaves the remedy to the State governments.

We do not perceive this absurdity or self-contradiction.

Our country exhibits the extraordinary spectacle of distinct, and, in many respects, independent governments over the same territory and the same people. The local governments are restrained from impairing the obligation of contracts, but they furnish the remedy to enforce them, and administer that remedy in tribunals constituted by themselves. It has been shown that the obligation is distinct from the remedy, and, it would seem to follow, that law might act on the remedy without acting on the obligation. To afford a remedy is certainly the high duty of those who govern to those who are governed. A failure in the performance of this duty subjects the government to the just reproach of the world. But the constitution has not undertaken to enforce its performance. That instrument treats the States with the respect which is due to intelligent beings, understanding their duties, and willing to perform them; not as insane beings, who must be compelled to act for self-preservation. Its language is the language of restraint, not of coercion. It prohibits the States from passing any law impairing the obligation of contracts; it does not enjoin them to enforce contracts. Should a State be sufficiently insane to shut up or abolish its Courts, and thereby withhold all remedy, would this annihilation of remedy annihilate the obligation also of contracts? We know it would not. If the debtor should come within the jurisdiction of any Court of another State, the remedy would be immediately applied, and the inherent obligation of the contract enforced. This cannot be ascribed to a renewal of the obligation; for passing the line of a State cannot re-create an obligation which was extinguished. It must be the original obligation derived from the agreement of the parties, and which exists unimpaired though the remedy was withdrawn.

But, we are told, that the power of the State over the remedy may be used to the destruction of all beneficial results from the right; and hence it is inferred, that the construction which maintains the inviolability of the obligation, must be extended to the power of regulating the remedy.

The difficulty which this view of the subject presents, does not proceed from the identity or connexion of right and remedy, but from the existence of distinct governments acting on kindred subjects. The constitution contemplates restraint as to the obligation of contracts, not as to the application of remedy. If this restraint affects a power which the constitution did not mean to touch, it can only be when that power is used as an instrument of hostility to invade the inviolability of contract, which is placed beyond its reach. A State may use many of its acknowledged powers in such manner as to come in conflict with the provisions of the constitution. Thus the power over its domestic police, the power to regulate commerce purely internal, may be so exercised as to interfere with regulations of commerce with foreign nations, or between the States. In such cases, the power which is supreme must control that which is not supreme, when they come in conflict. But this principle does not involve any self-contradiction, or deny the existence of the several powers in the respective governments. So, if a State shall not merely modify, or withhold a particular remedy, but shall apply it in such manner as to extinguish the obligation without performance, it would be an abuse of power which could scarcely be misunderstood, but which would not prove that remedy could not be regulated without regulating obligation.

The counsel for the plaintiff in error put a case of more difficulty, and urge it as a conclusive argument against the existence of a distinct line dividing obligation from remedy. It is this. The law affords remedy by giving execution against the person, or the property, or both. The same power which can withdraw the remedy against the person, can withdraw that against the property, or that against both, and thus effectually defeat the obligation. The constitution, we are told, deals not with form, but with substance; and cannot be presumed, if it designed to protect the obligation of contracts from State legislation, to have left it thus obviously exposed to destruction.

The answer is, that if the law goes farther, and annuls the obligation without affording the remedy which satisfies it, if its action on the remedy be such as palpably to impair the obligation of the contract, the very case arises which we suppose to be within the constitution. If it leaves the obligation untouched, but withholds the remedy, or affords one which is merely nominal, it is like all other cases of misgovernment, and leaves the debtor still liable to his creditor, should he be found, or should his property be found, where the laws afford a remedy. If that high sense of duty which men selected for the government of their fellow citizens must be supposed to feel, furnishes no security against a course of legislation which must end in self-destruction; if the solemn oath taken by every member, to support the constitution of the United States, furnishes no security against intentional attempts to violate its spirit while evading its letter;—the question how far the constitution interposes a shield for the protection of an injured individual, who demands from a Court of justice that remedy which every government ought to afford, will depend on the law itself which shall be brought under consideration. The anticipation of such a case would be unnecessarily disrespectful, and an opinion on it would be, at least, premature. But, however the question might be decided, should it be even determined that such a law would be a successful evasion of the constitution, it does not follow, that an act which operates directly on the contract after it is made, is not within the restriction imposed on the States by that instrument. The validity of a law acting directly on the obligation, is not proved by showing that the constitution has provided no means for compelling the States to enforce it.

We perceive, then, no reason for the opinion, that the prohibition "to pass any law impairing the obligation of contracts," is incompatible with the fair exercise of that discretion, which the State legislatures possess in common with all governments, to regulate the remedies afforded by their own Courts. We think, that obligation and remedy are distinguishable from each other. That the first is created by the act of the parties, the last is afforded by government. The words of the restriction we have been considering, countenance, we think, this idea. No State shall "pass any law impairing the obligation of contracts." These words seems to us to import, that the obligation is intrinsic, that it is created by the contract itself, not that it is dependent on the laws made to enforce it. When we advert to the course of reading generally pursued by American statesmen in early life, we must suppose, that the framers of our constitution were intimately acquainted with the writings of those wise and learned men, whose treatises on the laws of nature and nations have guided public opinion on the subjects of obligation and contract. If we turn to those treatises, we find them to concur in the declaration, that contracts possess an original intrinsic obligation, derived from the acts of free agents, and not given by government. We must suppose, that the framers of our constitution took the same view of the subject, and the language they have used confirms this opinion.

The propositions we have endeavoured to maintain, of the truth of which we are ourselves convinced, are these:

That the words of the clause in the constitution which we are considering, taken in their natural and obvious sense, admit of a prospective, as well as of a retrospective, operation.

That an act of the legislature does not enter into the contract, and become one of the conditions stipulated by the parties; nor does it act externally on the agreement, unless it have the full force of law.

That contracts derive their obligation from the act of the parties, not from the grant of government; and that the right of government to regulate the manner in which they shall be formed, or to prohibit such as may be against the policy of the State, is entirely consistent with their inviolability after they have been formed.

That the obligation of a contract is not identified with the means which government may furnish to enforce it; and that a prohibition to pass any law impairing it, does not imply a prohibition to vary the remedy; nor does a power to vary the remedy, imply a power to impair the obligation derived from the act of the parties.

We cannot look back to the history of the times when the august spectacle was exhibited of the assemblage of a whole people by their representatives in Convention, in order to unite thirteen independent sovereignties under one government, so far as might be necessary for the purposes of union, without being sensible of the great importance which was at that time attached to the tenth section of the first article. The power of changing the relative situation of debtor and creditor, of interfering with contracts, a power which comes home to every man, touches the interest of all, and controls the conduct of every individual in those things which he supposes to be proper for his own exclusive management, had been used to such an excess by the State legislatures, as to break in upon the ordinary intercourse of society, and destroy all confidence between man and man. The mischief had become so great, so alarming, as not only to impair commercial intercourse, and threaten the existence of credit, but to sap the morals of the people, and destroy the sanctity of private faith. To guard against the continuance of the evil was an object of deep interest with all the truly wise, as well as the virtuous, of this great community, and was one of the important benefits expected from a reform of the government.

To impose restraints on State legislation as respected this delicate and interesting subject, was thought necessary by all those patriots who could take an enlightened and comprehensive view of our situation; and the principle obtained an early admission into the various schemes of government which were submitted to the Convention. In framing an instrument, which was intended to be perpetual, the presumption is strong, that every important principle introduced into it is intended to be perpetual also;

that a principle expressed in terms to operate in all future time, is intended so to operate. But if the construction for which the plaintiff's counsel contend be the true one, the constitution will have imposed a restriction in language indicating perpetuity, which every State in the Union may elude at pleasure. The obligation of contracts in force, at any given time, is but of short duration; and, if the inhibition be of retrospective laws only, a very short lapse of time will remove every subject on which the act is forbidden to operate, and make this provision of the constitution so far useless. Instead of introducing a great principle, prohibiting all laws of this obnoxious character, the constitution will only suspend their operation for a moment, or except from it pre-existing cases. The object would scarcely seem to be of sufficient importance to have found a place in that instrument.

This construction would change the character of the provision, and convert an inhibition to pass laws impairing the obligation of contracts, into an inhibition to pass retrospective laws. Had this been the intention of the Convention, is it not reasonable to believe that it would have been so expressed? Had the intention been to confine the restriction to laws which were retrospective in their operation, language could have been found, and would have been used, to convey this idea. The very word would have occurred to the framers of the instrument, and we should have probably found it in the clause. Instead of the general prohibition to pass any "law impairing the obligation of contracts," the prohibition would have been to the passage of any retrospective law. Or, if the intention had been not to embrace all retrospective laws, but those only which related to contracts, still the word would have been introduced, and the State legislatures would have been forbidden "to pass any *retrospective* law impairing the obligation of contracts," or "to pass any law impairing the obligation of contracts previously made." Words which directly and plainly express the cardinal intent, always present themselves to those who are preparing an important instrument, and will always be used by them. Undoubtedly there is an imperfection in human language, which often exposes the same sentence to different constructions. But it is rare, indeed, for a person of clear and distinct perceptions, intending to convey one principal idea, so to express himself as to leave any doubt respecting that idea. It may be uncertain whether his words comprehend other things not immediately in his mind; but it can seldom be uncertain whether he intends the particular thing to which his mind is specially directed. If the mind of the Convention, in framing this prohibition, had been directed, not generally to the operation of laws upon the obligation of contracts, but particularly to their retrospective operation, it is scarcely conceivable that some word would not have been used indicating this idea. In instruments prepared on great consideration, general terms, comprehending a whole subject, are seldom employed to designate a particular, we might say, a minute portion of that subject. The general language of the clause is such as might be suggested by a general intent to prohibit State legislation on the subject to which that language is applied—the obligation of contracts; not such as would be suggested by a particular intent to prohibit retrospective legislation.

It is also worthy of consideration, that those laws which had effected all that mischief the constitution intended to prevent, were prospective as well as retrospective, in their operation. They embraced future contracts, as well as those previously formed. There is the less reason for imputing to the Convention an intention, not manifested by their language, to confine a restriction intended to guard against the recurrence of those mischiefs, to retrospective legislation. For these reasons, we are of opinion, that, on this point, the District Court of Louisiana has decided rightly.

20

Mason v. Haile

12 Wheat. 370 (1827)

Thompson, Justice, delivered the opinion of the court— . . . Can it be doubted, but the legislatures of the states, so far as relates to their own process, have a right to abolish imprisonment for debt altogether and that such law might extend to present, as well as future imprisonment? We are not aware, that such a power in the states has ever been questioned. And if such a general law would be valid, under the constitution of the United States, where is the prohibition to be found, that denies to the state of Rhode Island the right of applying the same remedy to individual cases? This is a measure which must be regulated by the views of policy and expediency entertained by the state legislatures. Such laws act merely upon the remedy, and that in part only. They do not take away the entire remedy, but only so far as imprisonment forms a part of such remedy. The doctrine of this court in the case of *Sturges* v. *Crowninshield,* 4 Wheat. 200, applies with full force to the present case. "Imprisonment of the debtor," say the court, "may be a punishment for not performing his contract, or may be allowed as a means for inducing him to perform it. But a state may refuse to inflict this punishment, or may withhold it altogether, and leave the contract in full force. Imprisonment is no part of the contract, and simply to release the prisoner, does not impair its obligation."

In whatever light, therefore, the question is viewed, no breach of the condition of the bond, according to its true sense and interpretation, has been committed. The liberation of the defendant from confinement, on his giving bond to the sheriff, to return to jail, in case his petition for a discharge should not be granted, was sanctioned by the due exercise of legislative power, and was analogous to extending to him more enlarged jail limits, and would not be considered an escape. And both this and the final discharge, so far, at all events, as it related to the imprisonment of the defendant, affected the remedy in part only, and was in the due and ordinary exercise of the powers vested in the legislature of Rhode Island, and was a lawful discharge, and no escape, and of course, no breach of the condition of the bond in question.

It must, accordingly, be certified to the circuit court, that the matters set forth in the defendant's amended pleas, are sufficient to bar the plaintiff's action.

WASHINGTON, Justice. *(Dissenting.)*—It has never been my habit to deliver dissenting opinions, in cases where it has been my misfortune to differ from those which have been pronounced by a majority of this court. Nor should I do so upon the present occasion, did I not believe, that the opinion just delivered is at variance with the fundamental principles upon which the cases of *Sturges* v. *Crowninshield,* and *Ogden* v. *Saunders,* have been decided. A regard for my own consistency, and that, too, upon a great constitutional question, compels me to record the reasons upon which my dissent is founded.

The great, the intelligent principle, upon which those cases were decided, is, that a retrospective state law, so far as it operates to discharge, or to vary the terms of, an existing contract, impairs its obligations, and is, for that reason, a violation of the tenth section of the first article of the constitution of the United States; but that a law, which is prospective in its operation, has not this effect, and, consequently, is not forbidden by that instrument. But, if I rightly understand the opinion pronounced in this case, and the facts upon which it is founded, this principle is subverted, and the distinction between retrospective and prospective laws, in their application to contracts, is altogether disregarded. The facts are, that the bond upon which this action is brought, bears date the 14th of March 1814, and the condition is, that the defendant, then a prisoner in the state's jail, in Providence, at the suit of the plaintiff, shall continue to be a true prisoner, in the custody and safe-keeping of the keeper of the said jail, within the limits of the said prison, until he shall be lawfully discharged. Upon the petition of the defendant to the legislature of Rhode Island, to extend to him the benefit of a certain act passed in the year 1756, an act was passed in February 1815, which liberated him from his confinement in the jail aforesaid, on his giving a bond to return to the said jail, in case his petition should not be granted; and, by a subsequent act, passed in the following year, he was discharged from his debts, upon a surrender previously made of all his estate, for the benefit of his creditors. The plea admits, that the defendant did depart from the limits of the jail, and justifies the alleged escape, under the above acts of the legislature. The opinion considers those acts as constitutional, and decides, that the defendant was lawfully discharged within the terms of his bond.

The case of *Sturges* v. *Crowninshield* arose upon a contract for the payment of money, from which the debtor was discharged under a subsequent state insolvent law, and this discharge was pleaded in bar of the action upon the contract. This court decided the plea to be insufficient, upon the ground, that the law upon which it was founded impaired the obligation of the contract, which was entered into previous to his discharge. The obligation of the contract upon which the present suit was brought, is not to pay money, but to continue a true prisoner within the limits of the jail in which he was then confined. A subsequent act of the legislature discharges him from his confinement, and authorizes him to go at large, of which law he availed himself, and under which he justifies the alleged breach of the condition of his bond.

A contract, we are informed by the above case, is an agreement by one or more persons to do, or not to do, a particular thing; and the law which compels a performance of such contract, constitutes its obligation. The thing to be done in that case was, to pay money; and in this it is to continue a true prisoner; and at the time it was concluded, the existing law of Rhode Island required him to perform this engagement. A discharge from his debts, in the former case, by a subsequent law of the state, impaired that obligation; but this obligation, it is said, is not impaired by a subsequent law, which discharges him from confinement, as well as from all his debts. If the principle which governs the two cases can be reconciled with each other, the course of reasoning by which it is to be effected is quite too subtle for my mind to comprehend it.

It was stated in the case alluded to, that imprisonment of the debtor forms no part of the contract, and, consequently, that a law which discharges his person from confinement, does not impair its obligation. This I admit, and the principle was strictly applicable to a contract for the payment of money. But can it possibly apply to a case where the restraint of the person is the sole object of the contract, and continuing within the limits of the prison, the thing contracted to be done. I admit the right of a state to put an end to imprisonment for debt altogether, and even to discharge insolvent debtors from their debts, by the enactment of a bankrupt law for that purpose. I am compelled, by the case of *Sturges* v. *Crowninshield,* to make this latter admission, and I voluntarily make the former. But what I insist upon is, that if a law, in either case, is made to operate retroactively upon contracts, to do what the law discharges the party from doing, it impairs the obligation of the contract, and is so far invalid.

I will now briefly consider the reasons which are assigned for distinguishing this case from that of *Sturges* v. *Crowninshield.* It is said, that the bond in this case is not, in point of law, a contract, since there is but one voluntary party to it, and a contract cannot exist, unless there be at least two parties to it. My answer is, that the law of Rhode Island which authorized the giving of the bond, made the creditor the other party, as much so as creditors and legatees are made parties to a bond, which the law requires an executor to give. If this answer be not considered as satisfactory, I will add another, which is, that the creditor has adopted it as his contract by putting it in suit.

Again, it is said, that the acts which discharged this defendant from his imprisonment, and even from the debt altogether, are not retrospective in their operation, and are not so considered in the state where they were passed. How they are considered in that state, is more than this court can judicially know, and, consequently, that circumstance cannot here form the basis of a judicial determination. All that we do judicially know is, that the act of 1756 was a temporary law, and expired nearly half a century ago. It was, then, in the year 1815, as if it had never existed. An act in this year to revive it, either as a general law, or for the purpose of benefiting a particular individual, is the enactment of a new law, which derives all its force from the will of the legislature which enacts it, and not from that of the legislature to which the expired law owed its temporary existence. Is it possible, that argument, or authorities, can be required to prove this proposition? Would the argument upon which the contrary proposition is founded have been adopted in the case of *Sturges* v. *Crowninshield,* if the discharge had been under an act passed subsequent to the contract, which revived an old expired insolvent or bankrupt law? And am I to understand, that contracts for the payment of money, as well as for the restraint of the person of the debtor, may now be discharged in the state of Rhode Island, at any time, by an act to revive the act of 1756 in favor of debtors for whose benefit it may be revived? If this be the effect of the present decision (and I confess I cannot perceive how it can be otherwise), the decision in the case of *Sturges* v. *Crowninshield* will avail nothing in that state, nor in any other of the states in whose code an old deceased insolvent law can be found, which, in the days of its existence, authorized a legislative discharge of a debtor from his debts, or from his prison bounds bond.

Lastly, it is said, that this law does no more than enlarge the limits of the prison-rules, within which the defendant bound himself to continue. And can it be contended, that a law which has this effect, does not vary (and if it does so, it impairs) the terms of the contract entered into by the defendant? For what object, was he restricted to certain limits, if not to coerce him to pay the debt for which the plaintiff had a judgment and execution against him? And is not this object defeated, and the whole value of his prison-bounds contract destroyed, by enlarging the limits to those of the state, of the United States, or of the four quarters of the globe? I shall add nothing further. I have prepared no written opinion; my object in declaring my dissent from that which has been delivered, being not so much to prove that opinion to be wrong, as to vindicate my own consistency.

21

Craig v. Missouri

4 Pet. 410 (1830)

Marshall, C. J. . . . This brings us to the great question in the cause: Is the act of the legislature of Missouri repugnant to the constitution of the United States?

The counsel for the plaintiffs in error maintain, that it is repugnant to the constitution, because its object is the emission of bills of credit contrary to the express prohibition contained in the tenth section of the first article.

The act under the authority of which the certificates loaned to the plaintiffs in error were issued, was passed on the 26th of June, 1821, and is entitled "an act for the establishment of loan offices." The provisions that are material to the present inquiry, are comprehended in the third, thirteenth, fifteenth, sixteenth, twenty-third and twenty-fourth sections of the act, which are in these words:

Section the third enacts: "that the auditor of public accounts and treasurer, under the direction of the governor, shall, and they are hereby required to issue certificates, signed by the said auditor and treasurer, to the amount of two hundred thousand dollars, of denominations not exceeding ten dollars, nor less than fifty cents (to bear such devices as they may deem the most safe), in the following form, to wit: "This certificate shall be receivable at the treasury, or any of the loan offices of the state of Missouri, in the discharge of taxes or debts due to the state, for the sum of $———, with interest for the same, at the rate of two per centum per annum from this date, the ——— day of ——— 182 ."

The thirteenth section declares: "that the certificates of the said loan office shall be receivable at the treasury of the state, and by all tax gatherers and other public officers, in payment of taxes or other moneys now due to the state or to any county or town therein, and the said certificates shall also be received by all officers civil and military in the state, in the discharge of salaries and fees of office."

The fifteenth section provides: "that the commissioners of the said loan offices shall have power to make loans of the said certificates, to citizens of this state, residing within their respective districts only, and in each district a proportion shall be loaned to the citizens of each county therein, according to the number thereof," &c.

Section sixteenth. "That the said commissioners of each of the said offices are further authorised to make loans on personal securities by them deemed good and sufficient, for sums less than two hundred dollars; which securities shall be jointly and severally bound for the payment of the amount so loaned, with interest thereon," &c.

Section twenty-third. "That the general assembly shall, as soon as may be, cause the salt springs and lands attached thereto, given by Congress to this state, to be leased out, and it shall always be the fundamental condition in such leases, that the lessee or lessees shall receive the certificates hereby required to be issued, in payment for salt, at a price not exceeding that which may be prescribed by law: and all the proceeds of the said salt springs, the interest accruing to the state, and all estates purchased by officers of the said several offices under the provisions of this act, and all the debts now due or hereafter to be due to this state; are hereby pledged and constituted a fund for the redemption of the certificates hereby required to be issued, and the faith of the state is hereby also pledged for the same purpose."

Section twenty-fourth. "That it shall be the duty of the said auditor and treasurer to withdraw annually from circulation, one-tenth part of the certificates which are hereby required to be issued," &c.

The clause in the constitution which this act is supposed to violate is in these words: "No state shall" "emit bills of credit."

What is a bill of credit? What did the constitution mean to forbid?

In its enlarged, and perhaps its literal sense, the term

"bill of credit" may comprehend any instrument by which a state engages to pay money at a future day; thus including a certificate given for money borrowed. But the language of the constitution itself, and the mischief to be prevented, which we know from the history of our country, equally limit the interpretation of the terms. The word "emit" is never employed in describing those contracts by which a state binds itself to pay money at a future day for services actually received, or for money borrowed for present use; nor are instruments executed for such purposes, in common language, denominated "bills of credit." To "emit bills of credit," conveys to the mind the idea of issuing paper intended to circulate through the community for its ordinary purposes, as money, which paper is redeemable at a future day. This is the sense in which the terms have been always understood.

At a very early period of our colonial history, the attempt to supply the want of the precious metals by a paper medium was made to a considerable extent; and the bills emitted for this purpose have been frequently denominated bills of credit. During the war of our revolution, we were driven to this expedient; and necessity compelled us to use it to a most fearful extent. The term has acquired an appropriate meaning; and "bills of credit" signify a paper medium, intended to circulate between individuals, and between government and individuals, for the ordinary purposes of society. Such a medium has been always liable to considerable fluctuation. Its value is continually changing; and these changes, often great and sudden, expose individuals to immense loss, are the sources of ruinous speculations, and destroy all confidence between man and man. To cut up this mischief by the roots, a mischief which was felt through the United States, and which deeply affected the interest and prosperity of all; the people declared in their constitution, that no state should emit bills of credit. If the prohibition means any thing, if the words are not empty sounds, it must comprehend the emission of any paper medium, by a state government, for the purpose of common circulation.

What is the character of the certificates issued by authority of the act under consideration? What office are they to perform? Certificates signed by the auditor and treasurer of the state, are to be issued by those officers to the amount of two hundred thousand dollars, of denominations not exceeding ten dollars, nor less than fifty cents. The paper purports on its face to be receivable at the treasury, or at any loan office of the state of Missouri, in discharge of taxes or debts due to the state.

The law makes them receivable in discharge of all taxes, or debts due to the state, or any county or town therein; and of all salaries and fees of office, to all officers civil and military within the state; and for salt sold by the lessees of the public salt works. It also pledges the faith and funds of the state for their redemption.

It seems impossible to doubt the intention of the legislature in passing this act, or to mistake the character of these certificates, or the office they were to perform. The denominations of the bills, from ten dollars to fifty cents, fitted them for the purpose of ordinary circulation; and their reception in payment of taxes, and debts to the government and to corporations, and of salaries and fees, would give them currency. They were to be put into circulation, that is, emitted by the government. In addition to all these evidences of an intention to make these certificates the ordinary circulating medium of the country, the law speaks of them in this character; and directs the auditor and treasurer to withdraw annually one-tenth of them from circulation. Had they been termed "bills of credit," instead of "certificates," nothing would have been wanting to bring them within the prohibitory words of the constitution.

And can this make any real difference? Is the proposition to be maintained, that the constitution meant to prohibit names and not things? That a very important act, big with great and ruinous mischief which is expressly forbidden by words most appropriate for its description; may be performed by the substitution of a name? That the constitution, in one of its most important provisions, may be openly evaded by giving a new name to an old thing? We cannot think so. We think the certificates emitted under the authority of this act, are as entirely bills of credit, as if they had been so denominated in the act itself.

But it is contended, that though these certificates should be deemed bills of credit, according to the common acceptation of the term, they are not so in the sense of the constitution; because they are not made a legal tender.

The constitution itself furnishes no countenance to this distinction. The prohibition is general. It extends to all bills of credit, not to bills of a particular description. That tribunal must be bold indeed, which, without the aid of other explanatory words, could venture on this construction. It is the less admissible in this case, because the same clause of the constitution contains a substantive prohibition to the enactment of tender laws. The constitution, therefore, considers the emission of bills of credit, and the enactment of tender laws, as distinct operations, independent of each other, which may be separately performed. Both are forbidden. To sustain the one, because it is not also the other; to say that bills of credit may be emitted, if they be not made a tender in payment of debts; is, in effect, to expunge that distinct independent prohibition, and to read the clause as if it had been entirely omitted. We are not at liberty to do this.

The history of paper money has been referred to, for the purpose of showing that its great mischief consists in being made a tender; and that therefore the general words of the constitution may be restrained to a particular intent.

Was it even true, that the evils of paper money resulted solely from the quality of its being made a tender, this Court would not feel itself authorized to disregard the plain meaning of words, in search of a conjectured intent to which we are not conducted by the language of any part of the instrument. But we do not think that the history of our country proves either, that being made a tender in payment of debts, is an essential quality of bills of credit, or the only mischief resulting from them. It may, indeed, be the most pernicious; but that will not authorise a Court to convert a general into a particular prohibition.

We learn from Hutchinson's History of Massachusetts, vol. 1, p. 402, that bills of credit were emitted for the first time in that colony in 1690. An army returning unexpectedly from an expedition against Canada, which had proved as disastrous as the plan was magnificent, found the government totally unprepared to meet their claims. Bills of credit were resorted to, for relief from this embarrassment. They do not appear to have been made a tender; but they were not on that account the less bills of credit, nor were they absolutely harmless. The emission, however, not being considerable, and the bills being soon redeemed, the experiment would have been productive of not much mischief, had it not been followed by repeated emissions to a much larger amount. The subsequent history of Massachusetts abounds with proofs of the evils with which paper money is fraught, whether it be or be not a legal tender.

Paper money was also issued in other colonies, both in the north and south; and whether made a tender or not, was productive of evils in proportion to the quantity emitted. In the war which commenced in America in 1755, Virginia issued paper money at several successive sessions, under the appellation of treasury notes. This was made a tender. Emissions were afterwards made in 1769, in 1771, and in 1773. These were not made a tender; but they circulated together; were equally bills of credit; and were productive of the same effects. In 1775 a considerable emission was made for the purposes of the war. The bills were declared to be current, but were not made a tender. In 1776, an additional emission was made, and the bills were declared to be a tender. The bills of 1775 and 1776 circulated together; were equally bills of credit; and were productive of the same consequences.

Congress emitted bills of credit to a large amount, and did not, perhaps could not, make them a legal tender. This power resided in the states. In May, 1777, the legislature of Virginia passed an act for the first time making the bills of credit issued under the authority of Congress a tender so far as to extinguish interest. It was not until March, 1781, that Virginia passed an act making all the bills of credit which had been emitted by Congress, and all which had been emitted by the state, a legal tender in payment of debts. Yet they were in every sense of the word bills of credit, previous to that time; and were productive of all the consequences of paper money. We cannot then assent to the proposition, that the history of our country furnishes any just argument in favour of that restricted construction of the constitution for which the counsel for the defendant in error contends.

The certificates for which this note was given, being in truth "bills of credit" in the sense of the constitution, we are brought to the inquiry:

Is the note valid of which they form the consideration?

It has been long settled, that a promise made in consideration of an act which is forbidden by law is void. It will not be questioned, that an act forbidden by the constitution of the United States, which is the supreme law, is against law. Now the constitution forbids a state to "emit bills of credit." The loan of these certificates is the very act which is forbidden. It is not the making of them while they lie in the loan offices; but the issuing of them, the putting them into circulation, which is the act of emission; the act that is forbidden by the constitution. The consideration of this note is the emission of bills of credit by the state. The very act which constitutes the consideration, is the act of emitting bills of credit, in the mode prescribed by the law of Missouri; which act is prohibited by the constitution of the United States.

Cases which we cannot distinguish from this in principle, have been decided in State Courts of great respectability; and in this Court. In the case of the Springfield Bank *vs.* Merrick et al., 14 Mass. Rep. 322, a note was made payable in certain bills, the loaning or negotiating of which was prohibited by statute, inflicting a penalty for its violation. The note was held to be void. Had this note been made in consideration of these bills, instead of being made payable in them, it would not have been less repugnant to the statute; and would consequently have been equally void.

In Hunt *vs.* Knickerbocker, 5 Johns. Rep. 327, it was decided that an agreement for the sale of tickets in a lottery, not authorised by the legislature of the state, although instituted under the authority of the government of another state, is contrary to the spirit and policy of the law, and void. The consideration on which the agreement was founded being illegal, the agreement was void. The books, both of Massachusetts and New York, abound with cases to the same effect. They turn upon the question whether the particular case is within the principle, not on the principle itself. It has never been doubted, that a note given on a consideration which is prohibited by law, is void. Had the issuing or circulation of certificates of this or of any other description been prohibited by a statute of Missouri, could a suit have been sustained in the Courts of that state, on a note given in consideration of the prohibited certificates? If it could not, are the prohibitions of the constitution to be held less sacred than those of a state law?

It had been determined, independently of the acts of Congress on that subject, that sailing under the license of an enemy is illegal. Patton *vs.* Nicholson, 3 Wheat. 204, was a suit brought in one of the Courts of this district on a note given by Nicholson to Patton, both citizens of the United States, for a British license. The United States were then at war with Great Britain; but the license was procured without any intercourse with the enemy. The judgment of the Circuit Court was in favour of the defendant; and the plaintiff sued out a writ of error. The counsel for the defendant in error was stopped, the Court declaring that the use of a license from the enemy being unlawful, one citizen had no right to purchase from or sell to another such a license, to be used on board an American vessel. The consideration for which the note was given being unlawful, it followed of course that the note was void.

A majority of the Court feels constrained to say that the consideration on which the note in this case was given, is against the highest law of the land, and that the note itself is utterly void. In rendering judgment for the plaintiff, the Court for the state of Missouri decided in favour of the validity of a law which is repugnant to the constitution of the United States.

In the argument, we have been reminded by one side of

the dignity of a sovereign state; of the humiliation of her submitting herself to this tribunal; of the dangers which may result from inflicting a wound on that dignity: by the other, of the still superior dignity of the people of the United States; who have spoken their will, in terms which we cannot misunderstand.

To these admonitions, we can only answer: that if the exercise of that jurisdiction which has been imposed upon us by the constitution and laws of the United States, shall be calculated to bring on those dangers which have been indicated: or if it shall be indispensable to the preservation of the union, and consequently of the independence and liberty of these states: these are considerations which address themselves to those departments which may with perfect propriety be influenced by them. This department can listen only to the mandates of law; and can tread only that path which is marked out by duty.

The judgment of the Supreme Court of the state of Missouri for the first judicial district is reversed; and the cause remanded, with directions to enter judgment for the defendants.

Mr. Justice JOHNSON. . . . This leads us to the main question: "Was this an emission of bills of credit in the sense of the constitution?" And here the difficulty which presents itself is to determine whether it was a loan or an emission of paper money; or, perhaps, whether it was not an emission of paper money, under the disguise of a loan. There cannot be a doubt that this latter view of the subject must always be examined; for that which it is not permitted to do directly, cannot be legalized by any change of names or forms. Acts done "in fraudem legis," are acts in violation of law.

The great difficulty, as it is here, must ever be to determine, in each case, whether it be a loan, or an emission of bills of credit. That the states have an unlimited power to effect the one, and are divested of power to do the other, are propositions equally unquestionable; but where to draw the discriminating line is the great difficulty. I fear it is an insuperable difficulty.

The terms, "bills of credit," are in themselves vague and general, and, at the present day, almost dismissed from our language. It is then only by resorting to the nomenclature of the day of the constitution, that we can hope to get at the idea which the framers of the constitution attached to it. The quotation from Hutchinson's History of Massachusetts, therefore, was a proper one for this purpose; inasmuch as the sense in which a word is used, by a distinguished historian, and a man in public life in our own country, not long before the revolution, furnishes a satisfactory criterion for a definition. It is there used as synonymous with paper money; and we will find it distinctly used in the same sense by the first Congress which met under the present constitution.

The whole history and legislation of the time prove that, by bills of credit, the framers of the constitution meant paper money, with reference to that which had been used in the states from the commencement of the century, down to the time when it ceased to pass, before reduced to its innate worthlessness.

It was contended, in argument, for the defendant in error, that it was essential to the description of bills of credit in the sense of the constitution, that they should be made a lawful tender. But his own quotations negative that idea; and the constitution does the same, in the general prohibition in the states to make any thing but gold or silver a lengal tender. If, however, it were otherwise, it would hardly avail him here, since these certificates were, as to their officers' salaries, declared a legal tender.

The great end and object of this restriction on the power of the states, will furnish the best definition of the terms under consideration. The whole was intended to exclude every thing from use, as a circulating medium, except gold and silver; and to give to the United States the exclusive control over the coining and valuing of the metallic medium. That the real dollar may represent property, and not the shadow of it.

Now, if a state were to pass a law declaring that this representative of money shall be issued by its officers, this would be a palpable and tangible case; and we could not hesitate to declare such a law, and every contract entered into on the issue of such paper, purporting a promise to return the sum borrowed, to be a mere nullity. But suppose a state enacts a law authorising her officers to borrow a hundred thousand dollars, and to give in lieu thereof certificates of one hundred dollars, each expressing an acknowledgement of the debt; it is presumed there could be no objection to this. Then suppose that the next year she authorises these certificates to be broken up into ten, five, and even one dollar bills. Where can be the objection to this? And if, at the institution of the loan, the individual had given for the script his note at twelve months, instead of paying the cash; it would be but doing in another form what was here done in Missouri; and what is often done, in principle, where the loan is not required to be paid immediately in cash.

Pursuing the scrutiny farther, and with a view to bringing it as close home to the present case as possible: a state having exhausted its treasury, proposes to anticipate its taxes for one, two or three years; its citizens, or others, being willing to aid it, give their notes payable at sixty days, and receive the script of the state at a premium, for the advance of their credit, which enables the state, by discounting these notes, to realise the cash. There could be no objection to this negotiation; and their script being by contract to be receivable in taxes, nothing would be more natural than to break it up into small parcels in order to adapt it to the payment of taxes. And if in this state it should be thrown into circulation, by passing into the hands of those who would want it to meet their taxes, I see nothing in this that could amount to a violation of the constitution. Thus far the transaction partakes of the distinctive features of a loan; and yet it cannot be denied that its adaptation to the payment of taxes does give it one characteristic of a circulating medium. And another point of similitude, if not of identity, is the provision for forcing the receipt of it upon those to whom the state had incurred the obligation to pay money.

The result is, that these certificates are of a truly amphibious character; but what then should be the course of this Court? My conclusion is, that, as it is a doubtful case, for that reason we are bound to pronounce it innocent. It does indeed approach as near to a violation of the constitution as it can well go, without violating its prohibition; but it is in the exercise of an unquestionable right, although in rather a questionable form; and I am bound to believe that it was done in good faith, until the contrary shall more clearly appear.

Believing it then a candid exercise of the power of borrowing, I feel myself at liberty to go further, and briefly to suggest two points, on which these bills vary from the distinctive features of the paper money of the revolution.

1. On the face of them they bear an interest, and for that reason vary in value every moment of their existence: this disqualifies them for the uses and purposes of a circulating medium; which the universal consent of mankind declares should be of an uniform and unchanging value, otherwise it must be the subject of exchange, and not the medium.

2. All the paper medium of the revolution consisted of promises to pay. This is a promise to receive, and to receive in payment of debts and taxes due the state. This is not an immaterial distinction; for the objection to a mere paper medium is, that its value depends upon mere national faith. But this certainly has a better dependence; the public debtor who purchases it may tender it in payment; and upon a suit brought to recover against him, the constitution contains another provision to which he may have recourse. As far as the feeble powers of this Court extend, he would be secured (if he could ever need security) from a violation of his contracts. This approximates them to bills on a fund; and a fund not to be withdrawn by a law of the state.

Upon the whole, I am of opinion that the judgment of the State Court should be affirmed.

22

James Madison to Charles J. Ingersoll
2 Feb. 1831

Writings 9:437–38

The evil which produced the prohibitory clause in the Constitution of the U. S. was the practice of the States in making bills of credit, and in some instances appraised property, "a legal tender." If the notes of the State Banks therefore, whether chartered or unchartered be made a legal tender, they are prohibited; if not made a legal tender, they do not fall within the prohibitory clause. The No. of the "Federalist" [no. 44] referred to was written with that view of the subject; and this, with probably other contemporary expositions, and the uninterrupted practice of the States in creating and permitting Banks, without making their notes a legal tender, would seem to be a bar to the question, if it were not inexpedient now to agitate it.

A virtual and incidental enforcement of the depreciated notes of the State Banks, by their crowding out a sound medium, tho' a great evil, was not foreseen; and if it had been apprehended, it is questionable whether the Constitution of the U. S. which had so many obstacles to encounter would have ventured to guard against it by an additional obstacle. A virtual and it is hoped an adequate remedy, may hereafter be found in the refusal of State paper, when debased, in any of the Federal transactions; and in the controul of the Federal Bank, this being itself controuled from suspending its specie payments by the public authority.

23

Joseph Story, Commentaries on the Constitution 3:§§ 1351, 1353–57, 1365–66, 1370–94
1833

§ 1351. The next prohibition is to coin money. We have already seen, that the power to coin money, and regulate the value thereof, is confided to the general government. Under the confederation a concurrent power was left in the states, with a restriction, that congress should have the exclusive power to regulate the alloy and value of the coin struck by the states. In this, as in many other cases, the constitution has made a great improvement upon the existing system. Whilst the alloy and value depended on the general government, a right of coinage in the several states could have no other effect, than to multiply expensive mints, and diversify the forms and weights of the circulating coins. The latter inconvenience would defeat one main purpose, for which the power is given to the general government, viz. uniformity of the currency; and the former might be as well accomplished by local mints established by the national government, if it should ever be found inconvenient to send bullion, or old coin for re-coinage to the central mint. Such an event could scarcely occur, since the common course of commerce throughout the United States is so rapid and so free, that bullion can with a very slight expense be transported from one extremity of the Union to another. A single mint only has been established, which has hitherto been found quite adequate to all our wants. The truth is, that the prohibition had a higher motive, the danger of the circulation of base and spurious coin connived at for local purposes, or easily accomplished by the ingenuity of artificers, where the coins are very various in value and denomination, and issued from so many independent and unaccountable authorities. This subject has, however, been already enlarged on in another place.

. . . . .

§ 1353. The evils attendant upon the issue of paper money by the states after the peace of 1783, here spoken of, are equally applicable, and perhaps apply with even increased force to the paper issues of the states and the Union during the revolutionary war. Public, as well as private credit, was utterly prostrated. The fortunes of many individuals were destroyed; and those of all persons were greatly impaired by the rapid and unparalleled depreciation of the paper currency during this period. In truth, the history of the paper currency, which during the revolution was issued by congress alone, is full of melancholy instruction. It is at once humiliating to our pride, and disreputable to our national justice. Congress at an early period (November, 1775,) directed an emission of bills of credit to the amount of three millions of dollars; and declared on the face of them, that "this bill entitles the bearer to receive ——— Spanish milled dollars, or the value thereof in gold or silver, according to a resolution of congress, passed at Philadelphia, November 29th, 1775." And they apportioned a tax of three millions on the states, in order to pay these bills, to be raised by the states according to their quotas at future designated periods. The bills were directed to be receivable in payment of the taxes; and the thirteen colonies were pledged for their redemption. Other emissions were subsequently made. The depreciation was a natural, and indeed a necessary consequence of the fact, that there was no fund to redeem them. Congress endeavoured to give them additional credit by declaring, that they ought to be a tender in payment of all private and public debts; and that a refusal to receive the tender ought to be an extinguishment of the debt, and recommending the states to pass such tender laws. They went even farther, and thought proper to declare, that whoever should refuse to receive this paper in exchange for any property, *as gold and silver, should be deemed "an enemy to the liberties of these United States."* This course of violence and terror, so far from aiding the circulation of the paper, led on to still farther depreciation. New issues continued to be made, until in September, 1779, the whole emission exceeded one hundred and sixty millions of dollars. At this time congress thought it necessary to declare, that the issues on no account should exceed two hundred millions; and still held out to the public the delusive hope of an ultimate redemption of the whole at par. They indignantly repelled the idea, in a circular address, that there could be any violation of the public faith, pledged for their redemption; or that there did not exist ample funds to redeem them. They indulged in still more extraordinary delusions, and ventured to recommend paper money, as of peculiar value. "Let it be remembered," said they, "that paper money is the only kind of money, which cannot make to itself wings and fly away."

§ 1354. The states still continued to fail in complying with the requisitions of congress to pay taxes; and congress, notwithstanding their solemn declaration to the contrary, increased the issue of paper money, until it amounted to the enormous sum of upwards of three hundred millions. The idea was then abandoned of any redemption at par. In March, 1780, the states were required to bring in the bills at *forty for one;* and new bills were then to be issued in lieu of them, bearing an interest of five per cent., redeemable in six years, to be issued on the credit of the individual states, and guaranteed by the United States. This new scheme of finance was equally unavailing. Few of the old bills were brought in; and of course few of the new were issued. At last the continental bills became of so little value, that they ceased to circulate; and in the course of the year 1780, they quietly died in the hands of their possessors. Thus were redeemed the solemn pledges of the national government! Thus, was a paper currency, which was declared to be equal to gold and silver, suffered to perish in the hands of persons compelled to take it; and the very enormity of the wrong made the ground of an abandonment of every attempt to redress it!

§ 1355. Without doubt the melancholy shades of this picture were deepened by the urgent distresses of the revolutionary war, and the reluctance of the states to perform their proper duty. And some apology, if not some justification of the proceedings, may be found in the eventful transactions and sufferings of those times. But the history of paper money, without any adequate funds pledged to redeem it, and resting merely upon the pledge of the national faith, has been in all ages and in all nations the same. It has constantly become more and more depreciated; and in some instances has ceased from this cause to have any circulation whatsoever, whether issued by the irresistible edict of a despot, or by the more alluring order of a republican congress. There is an abundance of illustrative facts scattered over the history of those of the American colonies, who ventured upon this pernicious scheme of raising money to supply the public wants, during their subjection to the British crown; and in the several states, from the declaration of independence down to the present times. Even the United States, with almost inexhaustible resources, and with a population of 9,000,000 of inhabitants, exhibited during the late war with Great-Britain the humiliating spectacle of treasury notes, issued and payable in a year, remaining unredeemed, and sunk by depreciation to about half of their nominal value!

§ 1356. It has been stated by a very intelligent historian, that the first case of any issue of bills of credit in any of the American colonies, as a substitute for money, was by Massachusetts to pay the soldiers, who returned unexpectedly from an unsuccessful expedition against Canada, in 1690. The debt, thus due to the soldiers, was paid by paper notes from two shillings to ten pounds denomination, which notes were to be received for payment of the tax, which was to be levied, and all other payments into the treasury. It is added, that they had better credit than King James's leather money in Ireland about the same time. But the notes could not command money, nor any commodities at money price. Being of small amount, they were soon absorbed in the discharge of taxes. At subsequent periods the government resorted to similar expedients. In 1714, there being a cry of a scarcity of money, the government caused £50,000 to be issued in bills of credit, and in 1716, £100,000 to be lent to the inhabitants for a limited period, upon lands mortgaged by them, as security, and in the mean time to pass as money. These bills were receivable into the treasury in discharge of taxes, and also of the mortgage debts so contracted. Other bills were afterwards issued; and, indeed, we are informed, that, for about forty years, the currency of the province was in much the same state, as if £100,000 sterling had been stamped on pieces of leather or paper, of various denominations, and declared to be the money of the government, receivable in payment of taxes, and in discharge of private debts. The consequence was a very great depreciation, so that an ounce of silver, which, in 1702, was worth six shillings and eight pence, was, in 1749, equal to fifty shillings of this paper currency. It seems, that all the other colonies, except Nova Scotia, at different times and for various purposes, authorized the issue of paper money. There was a uniform tendency to depreciation, wherever it was persisted in.

§ 1357. It would seem to be obvious, that, as the states are expressly prohibited from coining money, the prohibition would be wholly ineffectual, if they might create a paper currency, and circulate it as money. But, as it might become necessary for the states to borrow money, the prohibition could not be intended to prevent such an exercise of power, on giving to the lender a certificate of the amount borrowed, and a promise to repay it.

. . . . .

§ 1365. The next prohibition is, that no state shall "make any thing but gold and silver coin, a tender in payment of debts." This clause was manifestly founded in the same general policy, which procured the adoption of the preceding clause. The history, indeed, of the various laws, which were passed by the states in their colonial and independent character upon this subject, is startling at once to our morals, to our patriotism, and to our sense of justice. Not only was paper money issued, and declared to be a tender in payment of debts; but laws of another character, well known under the appellation of tender laws, appraisement laws, instalment laws, and suspension laws, were from time to time enacted, which prostrated all private credit, and all private morals. By some of these laws, the due payment of debts was suspended; debts were, in violation of the very terms of the contract, authorized to be paid by instalments at different periods; property of any sort, however worthless, either real or personal, might be tendered by the debtor in payment of his debts; and the creditor was compelled to take the property of the debtor, which he might seize on execution, at an appraisement wholly disproportionate to its known value. Such grievances, and oppressions, and others of a like nature, were the ordinary results of legislation during the revolutionary war, and the intermediate period down to the formation of the constitution. They entailed the most enormous evils on the country; and introduced a system of fraud, chicanery, and profligacy, which destroyed all private confidence, and all industry and enterprise.

§ 1366. It is manifest, that all these prohibitory clauses, as to coining money, emitting bills of credit, and tendering any thing, but gold and silver, in payment of debts, are founded upon the same general policy, and result from the same general considerations. The policy is, to provide a fixed and uniform value throughout the United States, by which commercial and other dealings of the citizens, as well as the monied transactions of the government, might be regulated. For it may well be asked, why vest in congress the power to establish a uniform standard of value, if the states might use the same means, and thus defeat the uniformity of the standard, and consequently the standard itself? And why establish a standard at all for the government of the various contracts, which might be entered into, if those contracts might afterwards be discharged by a different standard, or by that, which is not money, under the authority of state tender laws? All these prohibitions are, therefore, entirely homogeneous, and are essential to the establishment of a uniform standard of value in the formation and discharge of contracts. For this reason, as well as others derived from the phraseology employed, the prohibition of state tender laws will admit of no construction confining it to state laws, which have a retrospective operation. Accordingly, it has been uniformly held, that the prohibition applies to all future laws on the subject of tender; and therefore no state legislature can provide, that future pecuniary contracts may be discharged by any thing, but gold and silver coin.

. . . . .

§ 1370. In the first place, what is to be deemed a contract, in the constitutional sense of this clause? A contract is an agreement to do, or not to do, a particular thing; or (as was said on another occasion) a contract is a compact between two or more persons. A contract is either executory, or executed. An executory contract is one, in which a party binds himself to do, or not to do a particular thing. An executed contract is one, in which the object of the contract is performed. This differs in nothing from a grant; for a contract executed conveys a chose in possession; a contract executory conveys only a chose in action. Since, then, a grant is in fact a contract executed, the obligation of which continues; and since the constitution uses the general term, *contract,* without distinguishing between those, which are executory and those, which are executed; it must be construed to comprehend the former, as well as the latter. A state law, therefore, annulling conveyances between individuals, and declaring, that the grantors should stand seized of their former estates, notwithstanding those grants, would be as repugnant to the constitution, as a state law discharging the vendors from the obligation of executing their contracts of sale by conveyances. It would be strange, indeed, if a contract to convey were secured by the constitution, while an absolute conveyance remained unprotected. That the contract, while executory, was obligatory; but when executed, might be avoided.

§ 1371. Contracts, too, are express, or implied. Express contracts are, where the terms of the agreement are openly avowed, and uttered at the time of the making of it. Implied contracts are such, as reason and justice dictate from the nature of the transaction, and which therefore the law presumes, that every man undertakes to perform. The constitution makes no distinction between the one class of contracts and the other. It then equally embraces, and applies to both. Indeed, as by far the largest class of contracts in civil society, in the ordinary transactions of life, are implied, there would be very little object in securing the inviolability of express contracts, if those, which are implied, might be impaired by state legislation. The constitution is not chargeable with such folly, or inconsistency. Every grant in its own nature amounts to an extinguishment of the right of the grantor, and implies a contract not to re-assert it. A party is, therefore, always estopped by his own grant. How absurd would it be to provide, that an express covenant by him, as a muniment attendant upon the estate, should bind him for ever, because executory, and resting in action; and yet, that he might re-assert his title to the estate, and dispossess his grantee, because there was only an implied covenant not to re-assert it.

§ 1372. In the next place, what is the obligation of a contract? It would seem difficult to substitute words more intelligible, or less liable to misconstruction, than these. And yet they have given rise to much acute disquisition, as to their real meaning in the constitution. It has been said, that right and obligation are correlative terms. Whatever I, by my contract, give another a right to require of me, I, by that act, lay myself under an obligation to yield or bestow. The obligation of every contract, then, will consist of that right, or power over my will or actions, which I, by my contract, confer on another. And that right and power will be found to be measured, neither by moral law alone, nor by universal law alone, nor by the laws of society alone; but by a combination of the three; an operation, in which the moral law is explained, and applied by the law of nature, and both modified and adapted to the exigencies of society by positive law. In an advanced state of society, all contracts of men receive a relative, and not a positive interpretation. The state construes them, the state applies them, the state controls them, and the state decides, how far the social exercise of the rights, they give over each other, can be justly asserted. Again, it has been said, that the constitution distinguishes between a contract, and the obligation of a contract. The latter is the law, which binds the parties to perform their agreement. The law, then, which has this binding obligation, must govern and control the contract in every shape, in which it is intended to bear upon it. Again, it has been said, that the obligation of a contract consists in the power and efficacy of the law, which applies to, and enforces performance of it, or an equivalent for non-performance. The obligation does not inhere, and subsist in the contract itself, *proprio vigore,* but in the law applicable to the contract. And again, it has been said, that a contract is an agreement of the parties; and if it be not illegal, it binds them to the extent of their stipulations. Thus, if a party contracts to pay a certain sum on a certain day, the contract binds him to perform it on that day, and this is its obligation.

§ 1373. Without attempting to enter into a minute examination of these various definitions, and explanations of the obligation of contracts, or of the reasoning, by which they are supported and illustrated; there are some considerations, which are pre-supposed by all of them; and others, which enter into some, and are excluded in others.

§ 1374. It seems agreed, that, when the obligation of contracts is spoken of in the constitution, we are to understand, not the mere moral, but the legal obligation of contracts. The moral obligation of contracts is, so far as human society is concerned, of an imperfect kind, which the parties are left free to obey or not, as they please. It is addressed to the conscience of the parties, under the solemn admonitions of accountability to the Supreme Being. No human lawgiver can either impair, or reach it. The constitution has not in contemplation any such obligations, but such only, as might be impaired by a state, if not prohibited. It is the civil obligation of contracts, which it is designed to reach, that is, the obligation, which is recognized by, and results from the law of the state, in which it is made. If, therefore, a contract, when made, is by the law of the place declared to be illegal, or deemed to be a nullity, or a *nude pact,* it has no civil obligation, because the law in such cases forbids its having any binding efficacy, or force. It confers no legal right on the one party, and no correspondent legal duty on the other. There is no means allowed, or recognised to enforce it; for the maxim is, *ex nudo pacto non oritur actio.* But when it does not fall within the predicament of being either illegal, or void, its obligatory force is coextensive with its stipulations.

§ 1375. Nor is this obligatory force so much the result of the positive declarations of the municipal law, as of the general principles of natural, or (as it is sometimes called) universal law. In a state of nature, independent of the obligations of positive law; contracts may be formed, and their obligatory force be complete. Between independent nations, treaties and compacts are formed, which are deemed universally obligatory; and yet in no just sense can they be deemed dependent on municipal law. Nay, there may exist (abstractly speaking) a perfect obligation in contracts, where there is no known and adequate means to enforce them. As, for instance, between independent nations, where their relative strength and power preclude the possibility, on the side of the weaker party, of enforcing them. So in the same government, where a contract is made by a state with one of its own citizens, which yet its laws do not permit to be enforced by any action or suit. In this predicament are the United States, who are not suable on any contracts made by themselves; but no one doubts, that these are still obligatory on the United States. Yet their obligation is not recognised by any positive municipal law in a great variety of cases. It depends altogether upon principles of public or universal law. Still, in these cases there is a right in the one party to have the contract performed, and a duty on the other side to perform it. But, generally speaking, when we speak of the obligation of a contract, we include in the idea some known means acknowledged by the municipal law to enforce it. Where all such means are absolutely denied, the obligation of the contract is understood to be impaired, though it may not be completely annihilated. Rights may, indeed, exist without any present adequate correspondent remedies between private persons. Thus, a state may refuse to allow imprisonment for debt; and the debtor may have no property. But still the right of the creditor remains; and he may enforce it against the future property of the debtor. So a debtor may die without leaving any known estate, or without any known representative. In such cases we should not say, that the right of the creditor was gone; but only, that there was nothing, on which it could presently operate. But suppose an administrator should be appointed, and property in contingency should fall in, the right might then be enforced to the extent of the existing means.

§ 1376. The civil obligation of a contract, then, though

it can never arise, or exist contrary to positive law, may arise or exist independently of it; and it may be, exist, notwithstanding there may be no present adequate remedy to enforce it. Wherever the municipal law recognises an absolute duty to perform a contract, there the obligation to perform it is complete, although there may not be a perfect remedy.

§ 1377. But much diversity of opinion has been exhibited upon another point; how far the existing law enters into, and forms a part of the contract. It has been contended by some learned minds, that the municipal law of the place, where a contract is made, forms a part of it, and travels with it, wherever the parties to it may be found. If this were admitted to be true, the consequence would be, that all the existing laws of a state, being incorporated into the contract, would constitute a part of its stipulations, so that a legislative repeal of such laws would not in any manner affect it. Thus, if there existed at the time a statute of limitations, operating on such contracts, or an insolvent act, under which they might be discharged, no subsequent repeal of either could vary the rights of the parties, as to using them, as a bar to a suit upon such contracts. If, therefore, the legislature should provide by a law, that all contracts thereafter made should be subject to the entire control of the legislature, as to their obligation, validity, and execution, whatever might be their terms, they would be completely within the legislative power, and might be impaired, or extinguished by future laws; thus having a complete *ex post facto* operation. Nay, if the legislature should pass a law declaring, that all future contracts might be discharged by a tender of any thing, or things, besides gold and silver, there would be great difficulty in affirming them to be unconstitutional; since it would become a part of the stipulations of the contract. And yet it is obvious, that it would annihilate the whole prohibition of the constitution upon the subject of tender laws.

§ 1378. It has, therefore, been judicially held by a majority of the Supreme Court, that such a doctrine is untenable. Although the law of the place acts upon a contract, and governs its construction, validity, and obligation, it constitutes no part of it. The effect of such a principle would be a mischievous abridgment of legislative power over subjects within the proper jurisdiction of states, by arresting their power to repeal, or modify such laws with respect to existing contracts. The law necessarily steps in to explain, and construe the stipulations of parties, but never to supersede, or vary them. A great mass of human transactions depends upon implied contracts, upon contracts, not written, which grow out of the acts of the parties. In such cases the parties are supposed to have made those stipulations, which, as honest, fair, and just men, they ought to have made. When the law assumes, that the parties have made these stipulations, it does not vary their contract, or introduce new terms into it; but it declares, that certain acts, unexplained by compact, impose certain duties, and that the parties had stipulated for their performance. The difference is obvious between this, and the introduction of a new condition into a contract drawn out in writing, in which the parties have expressed every thing, that is to be done by either. So, if there be a written contract, which does not include every term, which is ordinarily and fairly to be implied, as accompanying what is stated, the law performs the office only of expressing, what is thus tacitly admitted by the parties to be a part of their intention. To such an extent the law acts upon contracts. It performs the office of interpretation. But this is very different from supposing, that every law, applicable to the subject matter, as a statute of limitations, or a statute of insolvency, enters into the contract, and becomes a part of the contract. Such a supposition is neither called for by the terms of the contract, nor can be fairly presumed to be contemplated by the parties, as matters *ex contractu*. The parties know, that they must obey the laws; and that the laws act upon their contracts, whatever may be their intention.

§ 1379. In the next place, what may properly be deemed impairing the obligation of contracts in the sense of the constitution? It is perfectly clear, that any law, which enlarges, abridges, or in any manner changes the intention of the parties, resulting from the stipulations in the contract, necessarily impairs it. The manner or degree, in which this change is effected, can in no respect influence the conclusion; for whether the law affect the validity, the construction, the duration, the discharge, or the evidence of the contract, it impairs its obligation, though it may not do so to the same extent in all the supposed cases. Any deviation from its terms by postponing, or accelerating the period of performance, which it prescribes; imposing conditions not expressed in the contract; or dispensing with the performance of those, which are a part of the contract; however minute or apparently immaterial in their effect upon it, impair its obligation. *A fortiori*, a law, which makes the contract wholly invalid, or extinguishes, or releases it, is a law impairing it. Nor is this all. Although there is a distinction between the obligation of a contract, and a remedy upon it; yet if there are certain remedies existing at the time, when it is made, all of which are afterwards wholly extinguished by new laws, so that there remain no means of enforcing its obligation, and no redress; such an abolition of all remedies, operating *in presenti*, is also an impairing of the obligation of such contract. But every change and modification of the remedy does not involve such a consequence. No one will doubt, that the legislature may vary the nature and extent of remedies, so always, that some substantive remedy be in fact left. Nor can it be doubted, that the legislature may prescribe the times and modes, in which remedies may be pursued; and bar suits not brought within such periods, and not pursued in such modes. Statutes of limitations are of this nature; and have never been supposed to destroy the obligation of contracts, but to prescribe the times, within which that obligation shall be enforced by a suit; and in default to deem it either satisfied, or abandoned. The obligation to perform a contract is coeval with the undertaking to perform it. It originates with the contract itself, and operates anterior to the time of performance. The remedy acts upon the broken contract, and enforces a pre-existing obligation. And a state legislature may discharge a party from imprisonment upon a judgment in a civil case of contract, without infringing the constitution; for this is but a modification of the remedy, and does not impair the obligation of the contract. So, if a party should be in gaol, and give a bond for the prison liberties, and to remain a true prisoner, until lawfully discharged, a subsequent discharge by an act of the legislature would not impair the contract; for it would be a lawful discharge in the sense of the bond.

§ 1380. These general considerations naturally conduct us to some more difficult inquiries growing out of them; and upon which there has been a very great diversity of judicial opinion. The great object of the framers of the constitution undoubtedly was, to secure the inviolability of contracts. This principle was to be protected in whatever form it might be assailed. No enumeration was attempted to be made of the modes, by which contracts might be impaired. It would have been unwise to have made such an enumeration, since it might have been defective; and the intention was to prohibit every mode or device for such purpose. The prohibition was universal.

§ 1381. The question has arisen, and has been most elaborately discussed, how far the states may constitutionally pass an insolvent law, which shall discharge the obligation of contracts. It is not doubted, that the states may pass insolvent laws, which shall discharge the person, or operate in the nature of a *cessio bonorum,* provided such laws do not discharge, or intermeddle with the obligation of contracts. Nor is it denied, that insolvent laws, which discharge the obligation of contracts, made antecedently to their passage, are unconstitutional. But the question is, how far the states may constitutionally pass insolvent laws, which shall operate upon, and discharge contracts, which are made subsequently to their passage. After the most ample argument it has at length been settled by a majority of the Supreme Court, that the states may constitutionally pass such laws operating upon future contracts.

§ 1382. The learned judges, who held the affirmative, were not all agreed, as to the grounds of their opinions. But their judgment rests on some one of the following grounds: (1.) Some of the judges held, that the law of the place, where a contract is made, not only regulates, and governs it, but constitutes a part of the contract itself; and, consequently, that an insolvent law, which, in the event of insolvency of the party, authorizes a discharge of the contract is obligatory as a part [of] the contract. (2.) Others held, that, though the law of the place formed no part of the contract, yet the latter derived its whole obligation from that law, and was controlled by its provisions; and, consequently, that its obligation could extend no further, than the law, which caused the obligation; and if it was subject to be discharged in case of insolvency, the law so far controlled, and limited its obligation. (3.) That the connexion with the other parts of the clause, (bills of attainder and *ex post facto* laws,) as they applied to retrospective legislation, fortified the conclusion, that the intention in this part was only to prohibit the like legislation. (4.) That the known history of the country, as to insolvent laws, and their having constituted a part of the acknowledged jurisprudence of several of the states for a long period, forbade the supposition, that under such a general phrase, as laws impairing the obligation of contracts, insolvent laws, in the ordinary administration of justice, could have been intentionally included. (5.) That, whenever any person enters into a contract, his assent may be properly inferred to abide by those rules in the administration of justice, which belong to the jurisprudence of the country of the contract. And, when he is compelled to pursue his debtor in other states, he is equally bound to acquiesce in the law of the latter, to which he subjects himself. (6.) That the law of the contract remains the same every where, and will be the same in every tribunal. But the remedy necessarily varies, and with it the effect of the constitutional pledge, which can only have relation to the laws of distributive justice, known to the policy of each state severally. These and other auxiliary grounds, which were illustrated by a great variety of arguments, which scarcely admit of abridgment, were deemed satisfactory to the majority of the court.

§ 1383. The minority of the judges maintained their opinions upon the following grounds: (1.) That the words of the clause in the constitution, taken in their natural and obvious sense, admit of a prospective, as well as of a retrospective operation. (2.) That an act of the legislature does not enter into the contract, and become one of the conditions stipulated by the parties; nor does it act externally on the agreement, unless it have the full force of law. (3.) That contracts derive their obligation from the act of the parties, and not from the grant of the government. And the right of the government to regulate the manner, in which they shall be formed, or to prohibit such as may be against the policy of the state, is entirely consistent with their inviolability, after they have been formed. (4.) That the obligation of a contract is not identified with the means, which government may furnish to enforce it. And that a prohibition to pass any law impairing it does not imply a prohibition to vary the remedy. Nor does a power to vary the remedy imply a power to impair the obligation derived from the act of the parties. (5.) That the history of the times justified this interpretation of the clause. The power of changing the relative situation of debtor and creditor, and of interfering with contracts, had been carried to such an excess by the state legislature, as to break in upon all the ordinary intercourse of society, and to destroy all private confidence. It was a great object to prevent for the future such mischievous measures. (6.) That the clause, in its terms, purports to be perpetual; and the principle, to be of any value, must be perpetual. It is expressed in terms sufficiently broad to operate in all future times; and the just inference, therefore, is, that it was so intended. But if the other interpretation of it be adopted, the clause will become of little effect; and the constitution will have imposed a restriction, in language indicating perpetuity, which every state in the Union may elude at pleasure. The obligation of contracts in force at any given time is but of short duration; and if the prohibition be of retrospective laws only, a very short lapse of time will remove every subject, upon which state laws are forbidden to operate, and make this provision of the constitution so far useless. Instead of introducing a great principle, prohibiting all laws of this noxious character, the constitution will suspend their operation only for a moment, or except preexisting cases from it. The nature of the provision is thus essentially changed. Instead of being a prohibition to pass laws impairing the obligation of contracts, it is only a prohibition to pass retrospective laws. (7.) That there is the less reason for adopting such a construction, since the state laws, which produced the mischief, were prospective, as well as retrospective.

§ 1384. The question is now understood to be finally at rest; and state insolvent laws, discharging the obligation of future contracts, are to be deemed constitutional. Still a very important point remains to be examined; and that is, to what contracts such laws can rightfully apply. The result of the various decisions on this subject is, (1.) That they apply to all contracts made within the state between citizens of the state. (2.) That they do not apply to contracts made within the state between a citizen of a state, and a citizen of another state. (3.) That they do not apply to contracts not made within the state. In all these cases it is considered, that the state does not possess a jurisdiction, coextensive with the contract, over the parties; and therefore, that the constitution of the United States protects them from prospective, as well as retrospective legislation. Still, however, if a creditor voluntarily makes himself a party to the proceedings under an insolvent law of a state, which discharges the contract, and accepts a dividend declared under such law, he will be bound by his own act, and be deemed to have abandoned his extra-territorial immunity. Of course, the constitutional prohibition does not apply to insolvent, or other laws passed before the adoption of the constitution, operating upon contracts and rights of property vested, and in *esse* before that time. And it may be added, that state insolvent laws have no operation whatsoever on contracts made with the United States; for such contracts are in no manner whatsoever subject to state jurisdiction.

§ 1385. It has been already stated, that a grant is a contract within the meaning of the constitution, as much as an unexecuted agreement. The prohibition, therefore, equally reaches all interferences with private grants and private conveyances, of whatever nature they may be. But it has been made a question, whether it applies, in the same extent, to contracts and grants of a state created directly by a law, or made by some authorized agent in pursuance of a law. It has been suggested, that, in such cases, it is to be deemed an act of the legislative power; and that all laws are repealable by the same authority, which enacted them. But it has been decided upon solemn argument, that contracts and grants made by a state are not less within the reach of the prohibition, than contracts and grants of private persons; that the question is not, whether such contracts or grants are made directly by law in the form of legislation, or in any other form, but whether they exist at all. The legislature may, by a law, directly make a grant; and such grant, when once made, becomes irrevocable, and cannot be constitutionally impaired. So the legislature may make a contract with individuals directly by a law, pledging the state to a performance of it; and then, when it is accepted, it is equally under the protection of the constitution. Thus, where a state authorized a sale of its public lands, and the sale was accordingly made, and conveyances given, it was held, that those conveyances could not be rescinded, or revoked by the state. So where a state, by a law, entered into a contract with certain Indians to exempt their lands from taxation for a valuable consideration, it was held, that the exemption could not be revoked. And grants of land, once voluntarily made by a state, by a special law, or under general laws, when once perfected, are equally as incapable of being resumed by a subsequent law, as those founded on a valuable consideration. Thus, if a state grant glebe lands, or other lands to parishes, towns, or private persons gratuitously, they constitute irrevocable executed contracts. And it may be laid down, as a general principle, that, whenever a law is in its own nature a contract, and absolute rights have vested under it, a repeal of that law cannot divest those rights, or annihilate or impair the title so acquired. A grant (as has been already stated) amounts to an extinguishment of the right of the grantor, and implies a contract not to reassert it.

§ 1386. The cases above spoken of are cases, in which rights of property are concerned, and are, manifestly, within the scope of the prohibition. But a question, of a more nice and delicate nature, has been also litigated; and that is, how far charters, granted by a state, are contracts within the meaning of the constitution. That the framers of the constitution did not intend to restrain the states in the regulation of their civil institutions, adopted for internal government, is admitted; and it has never been so construed. It has always been understood, that the contracts spoken of in the constitution were those, which respected property, or some other object of value, and which conferred rights capable of being asserted in a court of justice. A charter is certainly in form and substance a contract; it is a grant of powers, rights, and privileges; and it usually gives a capacity to take and to hold property. Where a charter creates a corporation, it emphatically confers this capacity; for it is an incident to a corporation, (unless prohibited,) to take and to hold property. A charter granted to private persons, for private purposes, is within the terms, and the reason of the prohibition. It confers rights and privileges, upon the faith of which it is accepted. It imparts obligations and duties on their part, which they are not at liberty to disregard; and it implies a contract on the part of the legislature, that the rights and privileges, so granted, shall be enjoyed. It is wholly immaterial, in such cases, whether the corporation take for their own private benefit, or for the benefit of other persons. A grant to a private trustee, for the benefit of a particular *cestui que trust*, is not less a contract, than if the trustee should take for his own benefit. A charter to a bank, or insurance, or turnpike company, is certainly a contract, founded in a valuable consideration. But it is not more so, than a charter incorporating persons for the erection and support of a hospital for the aged, the sick, or the infirm, which is to be supported by private contributions, or is founded upon private charity. It the state should make a grant of funds, in aid of such a corporation, it has never been supposed, that it could revoke them at its pleasure. It would have no remaining authority over the corporation, but that, which is judicial, to enforce the proper administration of the trust. Neither is a grant less a contract, though no beneficial interest accrues to the possessor.

Many a purchase, whether corporate or not, may, in point of fact, be of no exchangeable value to the owners; and yet the grants confirming them are not less within the protection of the constitution. All incorporeal hereditaments, such as immunities, dignities, offices, and franchises, are in law deemed valuable rights, and wherever they are subjects of a contract or grant, they are just as much within the reach of the constituion, as any other grants; for the constitution makes no account of the greater, or less value of any thing granted. All corporate franchises are legal estates. They are powers coupled with an interest; and the corporators have vested rights in their character as corporators.

§ 1387. A charter, then, being a contract within the scope of the constitution, the next consideration, which has arisen upon this important subject, is, whether the principle applies to all charters, public as well as private. Corporations are divisible into two sorts, such as are strictly public, and such as are private. Within the former denomination are included all corporations, created for public purposes only, such as cities, towns, parishes, and other public bodies. Within the latter denomination all corporations are included, which do not strictly belong to the former. There is no doubt, as to public corporations, which exist only for public purposes, that the legislature may change, modify, enlarge, and restrain them; with this limitation, however, that property, held by such corporation, shall still be secured for the use of those, for whom, and at whose expense it has been acquired. The principle may be stated in a more general form. If a charter be a mere grant of political power, if it create a civil institution, to be employed in the administration of the government, or, if the funds be public property alone, and the government alone be interested in the management of them, the legislative power over such charter is not restrained by the constitution, but remains unlimited. The reason is, that it is only a mode of exercising public rights and public powers, for the promotion of the general interest; and, therefore, it must, from its very nature, remain subject to the legislative will, so always that private rights are not infringed, or trenched upon.

§ 1388. But an attempt has been made to press this principle much farther, and to exempt from the constitutional prohibition all charters, which, though granted to private persons, are in reality trusts for purposes and objects, which may, in a certain sense, be deemed public and general. The first great case, in which this doctrine became the subject of judicial examination and decision, was the case of Dartmouth College. The legislature of New-Hampshire had, without the consent of the corporation, passed an act changing the organization of the original provincial charter of the college, and transferring all the rights, privileges, and franchises from the old charter trustees to new trustees, appointed under the act. The constitutionality of the act was contested, and after solemn argument, it was deliberately held by the Supreme Court, that the provincial charter was a contract within the meaning of the constitution, and that the amendatory act was utterly void, as impairing the obligation of that charter. The college was deemed, like other colleges of private foundation, to be a private eleemosynary institution, endowed, by its charter, with a capacity to take property unconnected with the government. Its funds were bestowed upon the faith of the charter, and those funds consisted entirely of private donations. It is true, that the uses were in some sense public; that is, for the general benefit, and not for the mere benefit of the corporators; but this did not make the corporation a public corporation. It was a private institution for general charity. It was not distinguishable in principle from a private donation, vested in private trustees, for a public charity, or for a particular purpose of beneficence. And the state itself, if it had bestowed funds upon a charity of the same nature, could not resume those funds. In short, the charter was deemed a contract, to which the government, and the donors, and the trustees of the corporation, were all parties. It was for a valuable consideration, for the security and disposition of property, which was entrusted to the corporation upon the faith of its terms; and the trustees acquired rights under it, which could not be taken away; for they came to them clothed with trusts, which they were obliged to perform, and could not constitutionally disregard. The reasoning in the case, of which this is a very faint and imperfect outline, should receive a diligent perusal; and it is difficult to present it in an abridged form, without impairing its force, or breaking its connexion. The doctrine is held to be equally applicable to grants of additional rights and privileges to an existing corporation, and to the original charter, by which a corporation is first brought into existence, and established. As soon as the latter become organized and in *esse,* the charter becomes a contract with the corporators.

§ 1389. It has not been thought any objection to this interpretation, that the preservation of charters, and other corporate rights, might not have been primarily, or even secondarily, within the contemplation of the framers of the constitution, when this clause was introduced. It is probable, that the other great evils, already alluded to, constituted the main inducement to insert it, where the temptations were more strong, and the interest more immediate and striking, to induce a violation of contracts. But though the motive may thus have been to reach other more pressing mischiefs, the prohibition itself is made general. It is applicable to all contracts, and not confined to the forms then most known, and most divided. Although a rare or particular case may not of itself be of sufficient magnitude to induce the establishment of a constitutional rule; yet it must be governed by that rule, when established, unless some plain and strong reason for excluding it can be given. It is not sufficient to show, that it may not have been foreseen, or intentionally provided for. To exclude it, it is necessary to go farther, and show, that if the case had been suggested, the language of the convention would have been varied so as to exclude and except it. Where a case falls within the words of a rule or prohibition, it must be held within its operation, unless there is something obviously absurd, or mischievous, or repugnant to the general spirit of the instrument, arising from such a construction. No such absurdity, mischief, or repugnancy, can be pretended in the present case. On the contrary, every reason of justice, convenience, and policy unite to prove the wisdom of embracing it in the prohibition. An impregnable barrier is thus thrown around all rights and franchises derived from the states, and solidity and inviolability are given to the literary, charitable, religious, and commercial institutions of the country.

§ 1390. It has also been made a question, whether a compact between two states, is within the scope of the prohibition. And this also has been decided in the affirmative. The terms, compact and contract, are synonymous; and, when propositions are offered by one state, and agreed to and accepted by another, they necessarily constitute a contract between them. There is no difference, in reason or in law, to distinguish between contracts made by a state with individuals, and contracts made between states. Each ought to be equally inviolable. Thus, where, upon the separation of Kentucky from Virginia, it was agreed by compact between them, that all private rights and interests in lands in Kentucky, derived from the laws of Virginia, should remain valid and secure under the laws of Kentucky, and should be determined by the laws then existing in Virginia; it was held by the Supreme Court, that certain laws of Kentucky, (commonly called the occupying claimant laws,) which varied and restricted the rights and remedies of the owners of such lands, were void, because they impaired the obligation of the contract. Nothing (said the court) can be more clear upon principles of law and reason, than that a law, which denies to the owner of the land a remedy to secure the possession of it, when withheld by any person, however innocently he may have obtained it; or to recover the profits received from it by the occupant; or which clogs his recovery of such possession and profits, by conditions and restrictions, tending to diminish the value and amount of the thing recovered; impairs his right to, and interest in, the property. If there be no remedy to recover the possession, the law necessarily presumes a want of right to it. If the remedy afforded be qualified and restrained by conditions of any kind, the right of the owner may indeed subsist, and be acknowledged; but it is impaired, and rendered insecure, according to the nature and extent of such restrictions. But statutes and limitations, which are mere regulations of the remedy, for the purposes of general repose and quieting titles, are not supposed to impair the right; but merely to provide for the prosecution of it within a reasonable period; and to deem the non-prosecution within the period an abandonment of it.

§ 1391. Whether a state legislature has authority to pass a law declaring a marriage void, or to award a divorce, has, incidentally, been made a question, but has never yet come directly in judgment. Marriage, though it be a civil institution, is understood to constitute a solemn, obligatory contract between the parties. And it has been, *arguendo*, denied, that a state legislature constitutionally possesses authority to dissolve that contract against the will, and without the default of either party. This point, however, may well be left for more exact consideration, until it becomes the very ground of the *lis mota*.

§ 1392. Before quitting this subject it may be proper to remark, that as the prohibition, respecting *ex post facto* laws, applies only to criminal cases; and the other is confined to impairing the obligation of contracts; there are many laws of a retrospective character, which may yet be constitutionally passed by the state legislatures, however unjust, oppressive, or impolitic they may be. Retrospective laws are, indeed, generally unjust; and, as has been forcibly said, neither accord with sound legislation, nor with the fundamental principles of the social compact. Still they are, with the exceptions above stated, left open to the states, according to their own constitutions of government; and become obligatory, if not prohibited by the latter. Thus, for instance, where the legislature of Connecticut, in 1795, passed a resolve, setting aside a decree of a court of probate disapproving of a will, and granted a new hearing; it was held, that the resolve, not being against any constitutional principle in that state, was valid; and that the will, which was approved upon the new hearing, was conclusive, as to the rights obtained under it. There is nothing in the constitution of the United States, which forbids a state legislature from exercising judicial functions; nor from divesting rights, vested by law in an individual; provided its effect be not to impair the obligation of a contract. If such a law be void, it is upon principles derived from the general nature of free governments, and the necessary limitations created thereby, or from the state restrictions upon the legislative authority, and not from the prohibitions of the constitution of the United States. If a state statute should, contrary to the general principles of law, declare, that contracts founded upon an illegal or immoral consideration, or otherwise void, should nevertheless be valid, and binding between the parties; its retrospective character could not be denied; for the effect would be to create a contract between the parties, where none had previously existed. Yet it would not be reached by the constitution of the United States; for to create a contract, and to impair or destroy one, can never be construed to mean the same thing. It may be within the same mischief, and equally unjust, and ruinous; but it does not fall within the terms of the prohibition. So, if a state court should decide, that the relation of landlord and tenant did not legally subsist between certain persons; and the legislature should pass a declaratory act; declaring, that it did subsist; the act, so far as the constitution of the United States is concerned, would be valid. So, if a state legislature should confirm a void sale, if it did not divest the settled rights of property, it would be valid. Nor (as has been already seen) would a state law, discharging a party from imprisonment under a judgment upon a contract, though passed subsequently to the imprisonment, be an unconstitutional exercise of power; for it would leave the obligation of the contract undisturbed. The states still possess the rightful authority to abolish imprisonment for debt; and may apply it to present, as well as to future imprisonment.

§ 1393. Whether, indeed, independently of the constitution of the United States, the nature of republican and free governments does not necessarily impose some restraints upon the legislative power, has been much discussed. It seems to be the general opinion, fortified by a strong current of judicial opinion, that since the American revolution no state government can be presumed to possess the transcendental sovereignty, to take away vested rights of property; to take the property of A. and transfer it to B. by a mere legislative act. That government can scarcely be deemed to be free, where the rights of property are left solely dependent upon a legislative body, without any restraint. The fundamental maxims of a free government seem to require, that the rights of personal liberty, and private property, should be held sacred. At least, no court of justice, in this country, would be warranted in assuming, that any state legislature possessed a power to violate and disregard them; or that such a power, so repugnant to the common principles of justice and civil liberty, lurked under any general grant of legislative authority, or ought to be implied from any general expression of the will of the people, in the usual forms of the constitutional delegation of power. The people ought not to be presumed to part with rights, so vital to their security and well-being, without very strong, and positive declarations to that effect.

§ 1394. The remaining prohibition in this clause is, that no state shall "grant any title of nobility." The reason of this prohibition is the same, as that, upon which the like prohibition to the government of the nation is founded. Indeed, it would be almost absurd to provide sedulously against such a power in the latter, if the states were still left free to exercise it. It has been emphatically said, that this is the corner-stone of a republican government; for there can be little danger, while a nobility is excluded, that the government will ever cease to be that of the people.

SEE ALSO:

Generally 1.8.4 (bankruptcy); 1.9.3; 3.2.1; Amend. X
Brason v. *Dean,* 87 Eng. Rep. 24 (K.B. 1684)
Thomas Paine, Dissertation on Government, 1786, Life 4:221
Noah Webster, The Devil Is in You, 1786, Collection 130
Roger Sherman and Oliver Ellsworth to Governor of Connecticut, 26 Sept. 1787, Farrand 3:100
James Madison, Preface to the Debates in the Convention of 1787, Farrand 3:548
Roger Sherman, Constitutional Proposals, 1787, Farrand 3:616
Records of the Federal Convention, Farrand 1:26; 2:135, 144, 169, 187, 435, 577, 596–97
James McHenry, Maryland House of Delegates, 29 Nov. 1787, Farrand 3:150
Noah Webster, Principles of Government and Commerce, 1788, Collection 40–41
Patrick Henry, Virginia Ratifying Convention, 9 June 1788, Storing 5.16.9
Kentucky Constitution of 1792, art. 12, chs. 18, 26, Thorpe 3:1275, 1276
Turner v. *Turner,* 4 Call. 234 (Va. 1792)
Minge v. *Gilmour,* 17 Fed. Cas. 440, no. 9,631 (C.C.D.N.C. 1798)
Holmes v. *Lansing,* 3 Johns. Cas. 73 (N.Y. 1802)
Beach v. *Woodhull,* 2 Fed. Cas. 1104, no. 1,154 (C.C.D.N.J. 1803)
Dash v. *Van Kleeck,* 7 Johns. R. 477 (N.Y. 1811), rev'd *Barry* v. *Mandell,* 10 Johns. 563
Louisiana Constitution of 1812, art. 6, ch. 20, Thorpe 3:1390
New Jersey v. *Wilson,* 7 Cranch 164 (1812)
Locke v. *Dane,* 9 Mass. 360 (1812)
Starr v. *Robinson,* 1 Chip. 257 (Vt. 1814)
Society for the Propagation of the Gospel v. *Wheeler,* 22 Fed. Cas. 756, no. 13,156 (C.C.D.N.H. 1814)
Myers v. *Irwin,* 2 Serg. & Rawle 367 (Pa. 1816)
Bedford v. *Shilling,* 4 Serg. & Rawle 401 (Pa. 1818)
Miller v. *Miller,* 16 Mass. 59 (1819)
Mather v. *Bush,* 16 Johns. R. 233 (N.Y. 1819)
Owings v. *Speed,* 5 Wheat. 420 (1820)
Matter of Wendell, 19 Johns. R. 153 (1821)
Hicks v. *Hotchkiss,* 7 Johns. Ch. 297 (N.Y. 1823)
Ross's Case, 2 Pick. 165 (Mass. 1824)
Barker v. *Jackson,* 2 Fed. Cas. 811, no. 989 (C.C.D.N.Y. 1826)
Presbyterian Church v. *City of New York,* 5 Cowan 538 (N.Y. 1826)
James Kent, Commentaries 1:381–82, 387–96 (1826)
Bradford v. *Brooks,* 2 Aiken 284 (Vt. 1827)
State v. *Stooltzfoos,* 16 Serg. & Rawle 35 (Pa. 1827)
Wilkinson v. *Leland,* 1 Pet. 627 (1829)
Saterlee v. *Matthewson,* 2 Pet. 380 (1829)
Bank of the United States v. *Longworth,* 2 Fed. Cas. 707, no. 923 (C.C.D.Ohio 1829)
VanZant v. *Waddel,* 2 Yerger 260 (Tenn. 1829)
William Rawle, A View of the Constitution of the United States 136–37 (2d ed. 1829)
Jackson v. *Lamphire,* 3 Pet. 280 (1830)
Providence Bank v. *Billings,* 4 Pet. 514 (1830)
Bennett v. *Boggs,* 3 Fed. Cas. 221, no. 1,319 (C.C.D.N.J. 1830)
Indiana & Edinsburg Turnpike Co. v. *Phillips,* 2 Pen. & W. 184 (Pa. 1830)
Commonwealth v. *Phillips,* 11 Pick. 28 (Mass. 1831)
Joseph Story, Commentaries on the Constitution 3:§§ 1349–50, 1367 (1833)
Watson v. *Mercer,* 8 Pet. 88 (1834)
Albee v. *May,* 1 Fed. Cas. 296, no. 134 (C.C.D.Vt. 1834)

Article 1, Section 10, Clause 2

No State shall, without the Consent of the Congress, lay any Imposts or Duties on Imports or Exports, except what may be absolutely necessary for executing it's inspection Laws: and the net Produce of all Duties and Imposts, laid by any State on Imports or Exports, shall be for the Use of the Treasury of the United States; and all such Laws shall be subject to the Revision and Controul of the Congress.

1. Articles of Confederation, art. 6, 1 Mar. 1781
2. Tench Coxe to Virginia Commissioners, 13 Sept. 1786
3. James Madison, Preface to Debates in the Convention of 1787
4. Records of the Federal Convention
5. Luther Martin, Genuine Information, 1788
6. Alexander Hamilton, Federalist, no. 32, 2 Jan. 1788
7. Debate in Virginia Ratifying Convention, 15 June 1788
8. *Gibbons* v. *Ogden,* 9 Wheat. 1 (1824), in 1.8.3 (commerce), no. 16
9. *Brown* v. *Maryland,* 12 Wheat. 419 (1827), in 1.8.3 (commerce), no. 17
10. James Madison to Professor Davis, 1832, in 1.8.3 (commerce), no. 21
11. Joseph Story, Commentaries on the Constitution (1833)

1

Articles of Confederation, art. 6
1 Mar. 1781

No state shall lay any imposts or duties, which may interfere with any stipulations in treaties, entered into by the united states in congress assembled, with any king, prince or state, in pursuance of any treaties already proposed by congress, to the courts of France and Spain.

2

Tench Coxe to Virginia Commissioners
13 Sept. 1786

Madison Papers 9:124–26

Prior to the receipt of the Act of Virginia leading to a general Convention of the States, the Governmt. of Pennsylvania had in contemplation the Assimilation of those Commercial Systems, which have been adopted for a time by the several States.

Tho difference of Circumstances has led to dissimilar regulations, it was thought that none should be adopted, which might be found to militate against the fundamental and essential principles of the Union. In examining the laws of Trade in several of the States, the following facts were found to exist.

1st. That the duty of Tonnage on Vessels built in, or belonging to the Citizens of the Other States was greater than that imposed on Vessels belonging to the Citizens of the State enacting the law; and equal in some instances to the Tonnage laid upon most of the foreign Nations, that have a Commercial intercourse with America.

2dly. That the Duties imposed upon Goods imported in Vessels built in, or belonging to other parts of the Union were greater than those laid on Goods imported in Vessels belonging to the enacting State.

3dly. That Goods of the growth product and manufacture of the Other States in Union were charged with high Duties upon importation into the enacting State—as great in many instances as those imposed on foreign Articles of the same Kinds.

To procure an alteration of these matters, evidently opposed to the great principles and Spirit of the Union, the State of Pennsylvania empowered her Commissioners to the general Convention to treat with Certain Commissioners appointed by the Legislature of Maryland, and with others, who, it was understood, would be appointed by the State of Virginia. As you do not conceive yourselves authorized to enter upon any discussion of this Business, I have thought it my Duty to make this Communication, and to request that you will do me the honor of reporting it to your Legislature.

Having pointed Out the Circumstances in the Commercial laws of the other States which appear to Our Government to require Reconsideration, it will be necessary to inform you how the laws of Pennsylvania Stand in these particulars—They declare as follows:

1st. That all Vessels belonging to the Citizens of the United States, whether Pennsylvanians or others, Shall pay *the same* Duty of Tonnage, and they do not discriminate against *Ships* belonging to the Citizens of the other States in any *charge* whatever. 2dly. They impose the *same* Duties on *Goods* imported in Ships belonging to the Citizens of Pennsylvania as are laid upon Goods imported in Ships belonging to Citizens of the other States in the Union. 3dly. They exempt intirely from impost all Goods Wares or Merchandise of the growth, product or Manufacture of the United States.

It is easy to see that the Legislature of Pennsylvania was influenced to this Kind of Conduct by a regard for the general Commerce of the Nation, and that Foederal considerations have led them to extend their care to that great object without any Discrimination in favour of their Own Citizens.

The Communication of these Circumstances not heretofore Sufficiently Known, and a due consideration of them, will it is hoped, be attended with the best consequences; and as the proceedings of the general Convention must necessarily require considerable time, Pennsylvania, I trust may confidently expect that a State of so much Wisdom and of Views so enlarged as the Commonwealth of Virginia will concur without delay in Measures which by blending the interests, must cement the Union of the States. I have the honor of being with the most respectful Consideration, Gentlemen Your Mo' Obedt Servt.

3

JAMES MADISON, PREFACE TO DEBATES IN THE CONVENTION OF 1787

Farrand 3:546–47

The act of Virga. providing for the Convention at Philada, was succeeded by appointments from other States as their Legislatures were assembled, the appointments being selections from the most experienced & highest standing Citizens. Rh. I. was the only exception to a compliance with the recommendation from Annapolis, well known to have been swayed by an obdurate adherence to an advantage which her position gave her of taxing her neighbors thro' their consumption of imported supplies, an advantage which it was foreseen would be taken from her by a revisal of the Articles of Confederation.

4

RECORDS OF THE FEDERAL CONVENTION

[*2:441; Madison, 28 Aug.*]

Mr. Madison moved that the words "nor lay imposts or duties on imports" be transferred from art: XIII where the consent of the Genl. Legislature may license the act—into art. XII which will make the prohibition on the States absolute. He observed that as the States interested in this power by which they could tax the imports of their neighbours passing thro' their markets, were a majority, they could give the consent of the Legislature, to the injury of N. Jersey, N. Carolina &c—

Mr. Williamson 2ded. the motion

Mr. Sherman thought the power might safely be left to the Legislature of the U. States.

Col: Mason, observed that particular States might wish to encourage by impost duties certain manufactures for which they enjoy natural advantages, as Virginia, the manufacture of Hemp &c.

Mr. Madison— The encouragement of Manufacture in that mode requires duties not only on imports directly from foreign Countries, but from the other States in the Union, which would revive all the mischiefs experienced from the want of a Genl. Government over commerce.

On the question

N. H. ay. Mas. no. Ct. no. N. J—ay. Pa. no. Del: ay. Md. no. Va. no N. C. ay. S. C. no. Geo. no. [Ayes—4; noes—7.]

Art: XII as amended agreed to nem: con:

Art: XIII being taken up. Mr. King moved to insert after the word "imports" the words "or exports" so as to prohibit the States from taxing either.—& on this question it passed in the affirmative.

N. H—ay. Mas. ay. Ct no. N. J. ay. P. ay. Del. ay. Md no. Va. no. N. C. ay. S. C. no. Geo. no. [Ayes—6; noes—5.]

Mr. Sherman moved to add, after the word "exports"—the words "nor with such consent but for the use of the U. S."—so as to carry the proceeds of all State duties on imports & exports, into the common Treasury.

Mr. Madison liked the motion as preventing all State imposts—but lamented the complexity we were giving to the commercial system.

Mr. Govr. Morris thought the regulation necessary to prevent the Atlantic States from endeavouring to tax the Western States—& promote their interest by opposing the navigation of the Mississippi which would drive the Western people into the arms of G. Britain.

Mr. Clymer thought the encouragement of the Western Country was suicide on the old States— If the States have such different interests that they can not be left to regulate their own manufactures without encountering the interests of other States, it is a proof that they are not fit to compose one nation.

Mr. King was afraid that the regulation moved by Mr. Sherman would too much interfere with a policy of States respecting their manufactures, which may be necessary. Revenue he reminded the House was the object of the general Legislature.

On Mr. Sherman's motion

N. H. ay. Mas. no. Ct. ay. N. J. ay. Pa. ay. Del. ay. Md. no. Va. ay. N. C. ay. S. C. ay. Geo. ay. [Ayes—9; noes—2.]

[*2:444; McHenry, 28 Aug.*]

XIII amended so [th]at all duties laid by a State shall accrue to the use of the U. S.

[*2:588; Madison, 12 Sept.*]

The Clause relating to exports being reconsidered, at the instance of Col: Mason, Who urged that the restriction on the States would prevent the incidental duties necessary for the inspection & safe-keeping of their produce, and be ruinous to the Staple States, as he called the five Southern States, he moved as follows—"provided nothing herein contained shall be construed to restrain any State from laying duties upon exports for the sole purpose of defraying the Charges of inspecting, packing, storing and indemnifying the losses, in keeping the commodities in the care of public officers, before exportation," In answer to a remark which he anticipated, to wit, that the States could provide for these expences, by a tax in some other way, he stated the inconveniency of requiring the Planters to pay a tax before the actual delivery for exportation.

Mr. Madison 2ded the motion— It would at least be harmless; and might have the good effect of restraining the States to bona fide duties for the purpose, as well as of authorizing explicitly such duties; tho' perhaps the best guard against an abuse of the power of the States on this subject, was the right in the Genl. Government to regulate trade between State & State.

Mr Govr Morris saw no objection to the motion. He did not consider the dollar per Hhd laid on Tobo in Virga. as a duty on exportation, as no drawback would be allowed on Tobo. taken out of the Warehouse for internal consumption,

Mr. Dayton was afraid the proviso wd. enable Pennsylva. to tax N. Jersey under the idea of Inspection duties of which Pena. would Judge.

Mr. Gorham & Mr. Langdon, though there would be no security if the proviso shd. be agreed to, for the States exporting thro' other States, agst. oppressions of the latter. How was redress to be obtained in case duties should be laid beyond the purpose expressed?

Mr. Madison— There will be the same security as in other cases— The jurisdiction of the supreme Court must be the source of redress. So far only had provision been made by the plan agst. injurious acts of the States. His own opinion was, that this was insufficient,— A negative on the State laws alone. could meet all the shapes which these could assume. But this had been overruled.

Mr. Fitzimons. Incidental duties on Tobo. & flour. never have been & never can be considered as duties on exports—

Mr. Dickinson. Nothing will save States in the situation of N. Hampshire N Jersey Delaware &c. from being oppressed by their Neighbors, but requiring the assent of Congs to inspection duties, He moved that this assent shd accordingly be required

Mr. Butler 2ded the motion.

[*2:624; Madison, 15 Sept.*]

Art. 1. sect. 10. (paragraph) 2) "No State shall, without the consent of Congress lay imposts or duties on imports or exports; nor with such consent, but to the use of the Treasury of the U. States"—

In consequence of the proviso moved by Col: Mason: and agreed to on the 13 Sepr, this part of the section was laid aside in favor of the following substitute viz. "No State shall, without the consent of Congress, lay any imposts or duties on imports or exports, except what may be absolutely necessary for executing its Inspection laws; and the nett produce of all duties and imposts, laid by any State on imports or exports, shall be for the use of the Treasury of the U— S—; and all such laws shall be subject to the revision and controul of the Congress"

On a motion to strike out the last part "and all such laws shall be subject to the revision and controul of the Congress" it passed in the Negative.

N. H. no. Mas. no. Ct no— N. J. no. Pa divd. Del. no. Md. no Va ay— N— C— ay. S. C. no Geo. ay. [Ayes—3; noes—7; divided—1.]

The substitute was then agreed to: Virga. alone being in the Negative.

[*2:640; Mason, 15 Sept.*]

The State legislatures are restrained from laying export duties on their own produce.

5

Luther Martin, Genuine Information 1788

Storing 2.4.79

By this same section, every State is also prohibited from laying any imposts, or duties on imports or exports, without the permission of the general government. It was urged, that as almost all sources of taxation were given to Congress, it would be but reasonable to leave the States the power of bringing revenue into their treasuries, by laying a duty on exports, if they should think proper, which might be so *light* as not to injure or discourage industry, and yet might be productive of considerable revenue— Also, that there might be cases in which it would be proper, for the purpose of encouraging manufactures, to lay duties to prohibit the exportation of raw materials, and even in addition to the duties laid by Congress on *imports* for the sake of *revenue,* to lay a duty to discourage the importation of particular articles into a State, or to enable the *manufacturer here* to supply us on as *good terms* as they could be obtained from a *foreign market;* however, the most we could obtain was, that this power might be exercised by the States with, and *only* with the consent of Congress, and subject to its controul—And so anxious were they to seize on *every shilling* of our money for the general government, that they insisted *even* the *little revenue* that might thus arise, should not be appropriated to the use of the respective States where it was collected, but should be paid into the treasury of the United States; and accordingly it is so determined.

6

Alexander Hamilton, Federalist, no. 32, 199–203
2 Jan. 1788

Although I am of opinion that there would be no real danger of the consequences, which seem to be apprehended to the State Governments, from a power in the Union to controul them in the levies of money; because I am persuaded that the sense of the people, the extreme hazard of provoking the resentments of the State Governments, and a conviction of the utility and necessity of local administrations, for local purposes, would be a complete barrier against the oppressive use of such a power: Yet I am willing here to allow in its full extent the justness of the reasoning, which requires that the individual States should possess an independent and uncontrolable authority to raise their own revenues for the supply of their own wants. And making this concession I affirm that (with the sole exception of duties on imports and exports) they would under the plan of the Convention retain that authority in the most absolute and unqualified sense; and that an attempt on the part of the national Government to abridge them in the exercise of it would be a violent assumption of power unwarranted by any article or clause of its Constitution.

An intire consolidation of the States into one complete national sovereignty would imply an intire subordination of the parts; and whatever powers might remain in them would be altogether dependent on the general will. But as the plan of the Convention aims only at a partial Union or consolidation, the State Governments would clearly retain all the rights of sovereignty which they before had and which were not by that act *exclusively* delegated to the United States. This exclusive delegation or rather this alienation of State sovereignty would only exist in three cases; where the Constitution in express terms granted an exclusive authority to the Union; where it granted in one instance an authority to the Union and in another prohibited the States from exercising the like authority; and where it granted an authority to the Union, to which a similar authority in the States would be absolutely and totally *contradictory* and *repugnant.* I use these terms to distinguish this last case from another which might appear to resemble it; but which would in fact be essentially different; I mean where the exercise of a concurrent jurisdiction might be productive of occasional interferences in the *policy* of any branch of administration, but would not imply any direct contradiction or repugnancy in point of constitutional authority. These three cases of exclusive jurisdiction in the Foederal Government may be exemplified by the following instances: The last clause but one in the 8th section of the 1st. article provides expressly that Congress shall exercise *"exclusive legislation"* over the district to be appropriated as the seat of government. This answers to the first case. The first clause of the same section impowers Congress *"to lay and collect taxes, duties, imposts and excises"* and the 2d. clause of the 10th. section of the same article declares that *"no State shall* without the consent of Congress, *lay any imposts or duties on imports or exports* except for the purpose of executing its inspection laws." Hence would result an exclusive power in the Union to lay duties on imports and exports with the particular exception mentioned; but this power is abriged by another clause which declares that no tax or duty shall be laid on articles exported from any State; in consequence of which qualification it now only extends to the *duties on imports.* This answers to the second case. The third will be found in that clause, which declares that Congress shall have power "to establish an UNIFORM RULE of naturalization throughout the United States." This must necessarily be exclusive; because if each State had power to prescribe a DISTINCT RULE there could be no UNIFORM RULE.

A case which may perhaps be thought to resemble the latter, but which is in fact widely different, affects the question immediately under consideration. I mean the power of imposing taxes on all articles other than exports and imports. This, I contend, is manifestly a concurrent and coequal authority in the United States and in the individual States. There is plainly no expression in the granting clause which makes that power *exclusive* in the Union. There is no independent clause or sentence which prohibits the States from exercising it. So far is this from being the case, that a plain and conclusive argument to the contrary is to be deduced from the restraint laid upon the States in relation to duties on imports and exports. This restriction implies an admission, that if it were not inserted the States would possess the power it excludes, and it implies a further admission, that as to all other taxes the authority of the States remains undiminished. In any other view it would be both unnecessary and dangerous; it would be unnecessary because if the grant to the Union of the power of laying such duties implied the exclusion of the States, or even their subordination in this particular there could be no need of such a restriction; it would be dangerous because the introduction of it leads directly to the conclusion which has been mentioned and which if the reasoning of the objectors be just, could not have been intended; I mean that the States in all cases to which the restriction did not apply would have a concurrent power of taxation with the Union. The restriction in question amounts to what lawyers call a NEGATIVE PREGNANT; that is a *negation* of one thing and an *affirmance* of another; a negation of the authority of the States to impose taxes on imports and exports, and an affirmance of their authority to impose them on all other articles. It would be mere sophistry to argue that it was meant to exclude them *absolutely* from the imposition of taxes of the former kind, and to leave them at liberty to lay others *subject to the controul* of the national Legislature. The restraining or prohibitory clause only says, that they shall not *without the consent of Congress* lay such duties; and if we are to understand this in the sense last mentioned, the Constitution would then be made to introduce a formal provision for the sake of a very absurd conclusion; which is that the States *with the consent* of the national Legislature might tax imports and exports; and that they might tax every other article *unless controuled* by the same body. If this was the intention why not leave it in the first instance to what is alleged to be the natural operation of the original clause conferring a general power of taxation upon the Union? It is evident that this could not have been the intention and that it will not bear a construction of the kind.

As to a supposition of repugnancy between the power of taxation in the States and in the Union, it cannot be supported in that sense which would be requisite to work an exclusion of the States. It is indeed possible that a tax might be laid on a particular article by a State which might render it *inexpedient* that thus a further tax should be laid on the same article by the Union; but it would not imply a constitutional inability to impose a further tax. The quantity of the imposition, the expediency or inexpediency of an increase on either side, would be mutually questions of prudence; but there would be involved no direct contradiction of power. The particular policy of the national and of the State systems of finance might now and then not exactly coincide, and might require reciprocal forbearances. It is not however a mere possibility of inconvenience in the exercise of powers, but an immediate constitutional repugnancy, that can by implication alienate and extinguish a pre-existing right of sovereignty.

The necessity of a concurrent jurisdiction in certain cases results from the division of the sovereign power; and the rule that all authorities of which the States are not explicitly divested in favour of the Union remain with them in full vigour, is not only a theoretical consequence of that division, but is clearly admitted by the whole tenor of the instrument which contains the articles of the proposed constitution. We there find that notwithstanding the affirmative grants of general authorities, there has been the most pointed care in those cases where it was deemed improper that the like authorities should reside in the States, to insert negative clauses prohibiting the exercise of them by the States. The tenth section of the first article consists altogether of such provisions. This circumstance is a clear indication of the sense of the Convention, and furnishes a rule of interpretation out of the body of the act which justifies the position I have advanced, and refutes every hypothesis to the contrary.

7

DEBATE IN VIRGINIA RATIFYING CONVENTION
15 June 1788
Elliot 3:481–83

MR. GEORGE MASON. Mr. Chairman, if gentlemen attend to this clause, they will see we cannot make any inspection law but what is subject to the control and revision of Congress. Hence gentlemen who know nothing of the business will make rules concerning it which may be detrimental to our interests. For forty years we have laid duties on tobacco, to defray the expenses of the inspection, and to raise an incidental revenue for the state. Under this clause, that incidental *revenue* which is calculated to pay for the inspection, and to defray contingent charges, is to be put into the federal treasury. But if any tobacco-house is burnt we cannot make up the loss. I conceive this to be unjust and unreasonable. When any profit arises from it, it goes into the federal treasury. But when there is any loss or deficiency from damage, it cannot be made up. Congress are to make regulations for our tobacco. Are men, in the states where no tobacco is made, proper judges of this business? They may perhaps judge as well, but surely no better than our own immediate legislature, who are accustomed and familiar with this business. This is one of the most wanton powers of the general government. I would concede any power that was essentially necessary for the interests of the Union; but this, instead of being necessary, will be extremely oppressive.

MR. GEORGE NICHOLAS. Mr. Chairman, I consider this clause as a good regulation. It will be agreed to that they will impose duties in the most impartial manner, and not throw the burdens on a part of the community. Every man who is acquainted with our laws must know that the duties on tobacco were as high as sixteen shillings a hogshead. The consequence was, that the tobacco-makers have paid upwards of twenty thousand pounds, annually, more than the other citizens; because they paid every other kind of tax, as well as the rest of the community. We have every reason to believe that this clause will prevent injustice and partiality. Tobacco-makers will be benefited by it. But the gentleman says that our tobacco regulations willl be subject to the control of Congress, who will be unacquainted with the subject. The clause says that all such laws shall be subject to the revision and control of Congress. What laws are meant by this? It means laws imposing duties on the exports of tobacco. But it does not follow that laws made for the regulation of the inspection shall be subject to the revision of Congress. He may say that the laws for imposing duties on the exports of tobacco, and laws regulating the inspection, must be blended in the same acts. Give me leave to say that they need not be so; for the duties on exports might be in one law, and the regulation of the inspection in another. The states may easily make them separately. But, he says, we shall lose the profit. We shall, then, find equity in our legislature which we have not found heretofore; for, as they will lay it not for their own exclusive advantages, but partly for the benefit of others, they will not be interested in laying it partially. As to the effect of warehouses being burnt, I differ from him. A tax may be laid to make up this loss. Though the amount of the duties go into the federal treasury, yet a tax may be laid for that purpose. Is it not necessary and just, if the inspection law obliges the planter to carry his tobacco to a certain place, that he should receive a compensation for the loss, if it be destroyed? The legislature must defray the expenses and contingent charges by laying a tax for that purpose; for such a tax is not prohibited. The net amounts only go into the federal treasury after paying the expenses. Gentlemen must be pleased with this part, especially those who are tobacco-makers.

Mr. GEORGE MASON replied, that the state legislatures could make no law but what would come within the general control given to Congress; and that the regulation of the inspection, and the imposition of duties, must be inseparably blended together.

Mr. MADISON. Mr. Chairman, let us take a view of the relative situation of the states. Some states export the produce of other states. Virginia exports the produce of North Carolina; Pennsylvania, that of New Jersey and Delaware; and Rhode Island, that of Connecticut and Massachusetts. The exporting states wished to retain the power of laying duties on exports, to enable them to pay the expenses incurred. The states whose produce is exported by other states were extremely jealous, lest a contribution should be raised of them by the exporting states, by laying heavy duties on their commodities. If this clause be fully considered, it will be found to be more consistent with justice and equity than any other practicable mode; for, if the states had the exclusive imposition of duties on exports, they might raise a heavy contribution from other states, for their own exclusive emolument. The honorable member who spoke in defence of the clause had fairly represented it. As to the reimbursement of the loss that may be sustained by individuals, a tax may be laid on tobacco, when brought to the warehouses, for that purpose. The sum arising therefrom may be appropriated to it consistently with the clause; for it only says that "the *net* produce of all duties and imposts, laid by any state on imports or exports, shall be for the use of the treasury of the United States," which necessarily implies that all contingent charges shall have been previously paid.

8

GIBBONS V. OGDEN
9 Wheat 1 (1824)

(See 1.8.3 [commerce], no. 16)

9

BROWN V. MARYLAND
12 Wheat. 419 (1827)

(See 1.8.3 [commerce], no. 17)

10

JAMES MADISON TO PROFESSOR DAVIS
1832
Letters 4:251–54

(See 1.8.3 [commerce], no. 21)

11

JOSEPH STORY, COMMENTARIES ON THE CONSTITUTION: 2:§§ 1013–15, 1029–30, 1049
1833

§ 1013. . . . In the first draft of the constitution, the clause stood, "no state, without the consent," &c. "shall lay imposts or duties on imports." The clause was then amended by adding, "or exports," not however without opposition, six states voting in the affirmative, and five in the negative; and again by adding, "nor with such consent, but for the use of the treasury of the United States," by a vote of nine states against two. In the revised draft, the clause was reported as thus amended. The clause was then altered to its present shape by a vote of ten states against one; and the clause, which respects the duty on tonnage, was then added by a vote of six states against four, one being divided. So, that it seems, that a struggle for state powers was constantly maintained with zeal and pertinacity throughout the whole discussion. If there is wisdom and sound policy in restraining the United States from exercising the power of taxation unequally in the states, there is, at least, equal wisdom and policy in restraining the states themselves from the exercise of the same power injuriously to the interests of each other. A petty warfare of regulation is thus prevented, which would rouse resentments, and create dissensions, to the ruin of the harmony and amity of the states. The power to enforce their respective laws is still retained, subject to the revision and control of congress; so, that sufficient provision is made for the convenient arrangement of their domestic and internal trade, whenever it is not injurious to the general interests.

§ 1014. Inspection laws are not, strictly speaking, regulations of commerce, though they may have a remote and considerable influence on commerce. The object of inspection laws is to improve the quality of articles produced by the labour of a country; to fit them for exportation, or for domestic use. These laws act upon the subject, before it becomes an article of commerce, foreign or domestic, and prepare it for the purpose. They form a portion of that immense mass of legislation, which embrace every thing in the territory of a state not surrendered to the general government. Inspection laws, quarantine laws, and health laws, as well as laws for regulating the internal commerce of a state, and others, which respect roads, fences, &c. are component parts of state legislation, resulting from the residuary powers of state sovereignty. No direct power over these is given to congress, and consequently they remain subject to state legislation, though they may be controlled by congress, when they interfere with their acknowledged powers. Under the confederation, there was a provision, that "no state shall lay any imposts or duties, which may interfere with any stipulations of treaties entered into by the United States," &c. &c. This prohibition was notoriously (as has been already stated) disregarded by the states; and in the exercise by the states of their general authority to lay imposts and duties, it is equally notorious, that the most mischievous restraints, preferences, and inequalities existed; so, that very serious irritations and feuds were constantly generated, which threatened the peace of the Union, and indeed must have inevitably led to a dissolution of it. The power to lay duties and imposts on imports and exports, and to lay a tonnage duty, are doubtless properly considered a part of the taxing power; but they may also be applied, as a regulation of commerce.

§ 1015. Until a recent period, no difficulty occurred in regard to the prohibitions of this clause. Congress, with a just liberality, gave full effect to the inspection laws of the states, and required them to be observed by the revenue officers of the United States. In the year 1821, the state of Maryland passed an act requiring, that all importers of foreign articles or commodities, &c. by bale or package, or of wine, rum, &c. &c., and other persons selling the same by wholesale, bale, or package, hogshead, barrel, or tierce, should, before they were authorized to sell, take out a license, for which they were to pay *fifty* dollars, under certain penalties. Upon this act a question arose, whether it was, or not a violation of the constitution of the United States, and especially of the prohibitory clause now under consideration. Upon solemn argument, the Supreme Court decided, that it was.

. . . . .

§ 1029. As the power of taxation exists in the states concurrently with the United States, subject only to the restrictions imposed by the constitution, several questions have from time to time arisen in regard to the nature and extent of the state power of taxation.

§ 1030. In the year 1818, the state of Maryland passed an act, laying a tax on all banks, and branches thereof, not chartered by the legislature of that state; and a question was made, whether the state had a right under the act, to lay a tax on the Branch Bank of the United States in that state. This gave rise to a most animated discussion in the Supreme Court of the United States; where it was finally decided, that the tax was, as to the Bank of the United States, unconstitutional.

. . . . .

§ 1049. It is observable, that these decisions turn upon the point, that no state can have authority to tax an instrument of the United States, or thereby to diminish the means of the United States, used in the exercise of powers confided to it. But there is no prohibition upon any state to tax any bank or other corporation created by its own authority, unless it has restrained itself, by the charter of incorporation, from the power of taxation. This subject, however will more properly fall under notice in some future discussions. It may be added, that congress may, without doubt, tax state banks; for it is clearly within the taxing power confided to the general government. When congress tax the chartered institutions of the states, they tax their own constituents; and such taxes must be uniform. But when a state taxes an institution created by congress, it taxes an instrument of a superior and independent sovereignty, not represented in the state legislature.

SEE ALSO:

Generally 1.8.3 (commerce); 1.8.4 (bankruptcy)

Records of the Federal Convention, Farrand 2:135, 143, 158–59, 169, 437, 577, 583, 597, 605

James Iredell, Marcus, Answers to Mr. Mason's Objections to the Constitution, 1788, Pamphlets 366–67

Article 1, Section 10, Clause 3

No State shall, without the Consent of Congress, lay any Duty of Tonnage, keep Troops, or Ships of War in time of Peace, enter into any Agreement or Compact with another State, or with a foreign Power, or engage in War, unless actually invaded, or in such imminent Danger as will not admit of delay.

1. Articles of Confederation, arts. 6, 9, 1 Mar. 1781
2. Records of the Federal Convention
3. *Green* v. *Biddle,* 8 Wheat. 1 (1823)
4. *Hawkins* v. *Barney's Lessee,* 5 Pet. 457 (1831)
5. Joseph Story, Commentaries on the Constitution (1833)

1

Articles of Confederation, arts. 6, 9
1 Mar. 1781

Article VI. No vessels of war shall be kept up in time of peace by any state, except such number only, as shall be deemed necessary by the united states in congress assembled, for the defence of such state, or its trade; nor shall any body of forces be kept up by any state, in time of peace, except such number only, as in the judgment of the united states, in congress assembled, shall be deemed requisite to garrison the forts necessary for the defence of such state; but every state shall always keep up a well regulated and disciplined militia, sufficiently armed and accoutred, and shall provide and constantly have ready for use, in public stores, a due number of field pieces and tents, and a proper quantity of arms, ammunition and camp equipage.

No state shall engage in any war without the consent of the united states in congress assembled, unless such state be actually invaded by enemies, or shall have received certain advice of a resolution being formed by some nation of Indians to invade such state, and the danger is so imminent as not to admit of a delay till the united states in congress assembled can be consulted: nor shall any state grant commissions to any ships or vessels of war, nor letters of marque or reprisal, except it be after a declaration of war by the united states in congress assembled, and then only against the kingdom or state and the subjects thereof, against which war has been so declared, and under such regulations as shall be established by the united states in congress assembled, unless such state be infested by pirates, in which case vessels of war may be fitted out for that occasion, and kept so long as the danger shall continue, or until the united states in congress assembled, shall determine otherwise.

. . . . .

tinue, or until the united states in congress assembled, shall determine otherwise.

Article IX. The united states in congress assembled, shall have the sole and exclusive right and power of determining on peace and war, except in the cases mentioned in the sixth article—of sending and receiving ambassadors—entering into treaties and alliances, provided that no treaty of commerce shall be made whereby the legislative power of the respective states shall be restrained from imposing such imposts and duties on foreigners as their own people are subjected to, or from prohibiting the exportation or importation of any species of goods or commodities whatsoever—of establishing rules for deciding in all cases, what captures on land or water shall be legal, and in what manner prizes taken by land or naval forces in the service of the united states shall be divided or appropriated—of granting letters of marque and reprisal in times of peace—appointing courts for the trial of piracies and felonies committed on the high seas and establishing courts for receiving and determining finally appeals in all cases of captures, provided that no member of congress shall be appointed a judge of any of the said courts.

2

Records of the Federal Convention

[*2:135, 169; Committee of Detail, III, IX*]

9 No State to make Treaties—lay interfering Duties—keep a naval or land Force (Militia excepted to be disciplined &c according to the Regulations of the U.S.

. . . . .

10

No State shall enter into any (Al) Treaty, Alliance (or) Confederation with any foreign Power nor witht. Const. of U. S. into any agreemt. or compact wh (any other) another State or Power; nor lay any Imposts or Duties on Imports; nor keep Troops or Ships of War in Time of Peace; nor grant Letters of Marque and Reprisal; nor coin Money; nor (emit Bills of Credit), without the Consent of the Legislature of the United States, emit Bills of Credit. No State shall, without such Consent engage in any War, unless it shall be actually invaded by Enemies, or the Danger of Invasion be so imminent as not to admit of a Delay, until the Legislature of the United States can be consulted. No State shall grant any Title of Nobility.*

[*2:187; Madison, 6 Aug.*]

XIII

No State, without the consent of the Legislature of the United States, shall emit bills of credit, or make any thing but specie a tender in payment of debts; nor lay imposts or duties on imports; nor keep troops or ships of war in time of peace; nor enter into any agreement or compact with another State, or with any foreign power; nor engage in any war, unless it shall be actually invaded by enemies, or the danger of invasion be so imminent, as not to admit of delay, until the Legislature of the United States can be consulted.

[*2:504; McHenry, 4 Sept.*]

Is it proper to declare all the navigable waters or rivers and within the U. S. common high ways? Perhaps a power to restrain any State from demanding tribute from citizens of another State in such cases is comprehended in the power to regulate trade between State and State.

[*2:577; Committee of Style*]

XIII.

No State, without the consent of the Legislature of the United States shall lay imposts or duties on imports or exports, nor with such consent but for the use of the treasury of the United States; nor keep troops or ships of war in time of peace; nor enter into any agreement or compact with another State, or with any foreign power; nor engage in any war, unless it shall be actually invaded by enemies, or the danger of invasion be so imminent, as not to admit of a delay, until the Legislature of the United States can be consulted.

. . . . .

(a) No state shall, without the consent of Congress, lay imposts or duties on imports or exports, nor with such consent, but to the use of the treasury of the United States. Nor keep troops nor ships of war in time of peace, nor enter into any agreement or compact with another state, nor with any foreign power; nor engage in any war, unless it shall be actually invaded by enemies, or the danger of invasion be so imminent, as not to admit of delay until the Congress can be consulted.

*[EDITORS' NOTE.—Words in parentheses were crossed out in the original.]

[*2:625; Madison, 15 Sept.*]

The remainder of the paragraph being under consideration—viz—"nor keep troops nor ships of war in time of peace, nor enter into any agreement or compact with another State, nor with any foreign power. Nor engage in any war, unless it shall be actually invaded by enemies, or the danger of invasion be so imminent as not to admit of delay, until Congress can be consulted"

Mr. Mc.Henry & Mr. Carrol moved that "no State shall be restrained from laying duties of tonnage for the purpose of clearing harbours and erecting light-houses".

Col. Mason in support of this explained and urged the situation of the Chesapeak which peculiarly required expences of this sort.

Mr. Govr. Morris. The States are not restrained from laying tonnage as the Constitution now Stands. The exception proposed will imply the Contrary, and will put the States in a worse condition than the gentleman (Col Mason) wishes.

Mr. Madison. Whether the States are now restrained from laying tonnage duties depends on the extent of the power "to regulate commerce". These terms are vague but seem to exclude this power of the States— They may certainly be restrained by Treaty. He observed that there were other objects for tonnage Duties as the support of Seamen &c. He was more & more convinced that the regulation of Commerce was in its nature indivisible and ought to be wholly under one authority.

Mr. Sherman. The power of the U. States to regulate trade being supreme can controul interferences of the State regulations when such interferences happen; so that there is no danger to be apprehended from a concurrent jurisdiction.

Mr. Langdon insisted that the regulation of tonnage was an essential part of the regulation of trade, and that the States ought to have nothing to do with it. On motion "that no State shall lay any duty on tonnage without the Consent of Congress"

N. H— ay— Mas. ay. Ct. divd. N. J. ay. Pa. no. Del. ay. Md. ay. Va. no. N— C. no. S— C. ay. Geo. no. [Ayes—6; noes—4; divided—1.]

The remainder of the paragraph was then remoulded and passed as follows viz— "No State shall without the consent of Congress, lay any duty of tonnage, keep troops or ships of war in time of peace, enter into any agreement or compact with another State, or with a foreign power, or engage in war, unless actually invaded, or in such imminent danger as will not admit of delay"

[*2:633; McHenry, 15 Sept.*]

Maryland moved.

> No State shall be prohibited from laying such duties of tonnage as may be sufficient for improving their harbors and keeping up lights, but all acts laying such duties shall be subject to the approbation or repeal of Congress.

Moved to amend it viz. No State without the consent of Congress shall lay a duty of tonnage. Carryed in the affirmative

6 ays 4 Noes, 1 divided.

3

Green v. Biddle
8 Wheat. 1 (1823)

Story, J. . . . 1. The first objection is founded upon the allegation that the compact was made without the consent of Congress, contrary to the tenth section of the first article, which declares that "no state shall, without the consent of Congress, enter into any agreement or compact with another state, or with a foreign power." Let it be observed, in the first place, that the constitution makes no provision respecting the mode or form in which the consent of Congress is to be signified, very properly leaving that matter to the wisdom of that body, to be decided upon according to the ordinary rules of law and of right reason. The only question in cases which involve that point is, has Congress, by some positive act in relation to such agreement, signified the consent of that body to its validity? Now, how stands the present case? The compact was entered into between Virginia and the people of Kentucky, upon the express condition that the general government should, prior to a certain day, assent to the erection of the district of Kentucky into an independent state, and agree that the proposed state should immediately, after a certain day, or at some convenient time future thereto, be admitted into the federal Union. On the 28th of July, 1790, the convention of that district assembled, under the provisions of the law of Virginia, and declared its assent to the terms and conditions prescribed by the proposed compact; and that the same was accepted as a solemn compact, and that the said district should become a separate state on the 1st of June, 1792. These resolutions, accompanied by a memorial from the convention, being communicated by the President of the United States to Congress, a report was made by a committee to whom the subject was referred, setting forth the agreement of Virginia, that Kentucky should be erected into a state upon certain terms and conditions, and the acceptance by Kentucky upon the terms and conditions so prescribed; and, on the 4th of February, 1791, Congress passed an act which, after referring to the compact, and the acceptance of it by Kentucky, declares the consent of that body to the erecting of the said district into a separate and independent state, upon a certain day, and receiving her into the Union.

Now, it is perfectly clear, that although Congress might have refused their consent to the proposed separation, yet they had no authority to declare Kentucky a separate and independent state without the assent of Virginia, or upon terms variant from those which Virginia had prescribed. But Congress, after recognizing the conditions upon which alone Virginia agreed to the separation, expressed, by a solemn act, the consent of that body to the separation. The terms and conditions, then, on which alone the separation could take place, or the act of Congress become a valid one, were necessarily assented to; not by a mere tacit acquiescence, but by an express declaration of the legislative mind, resulting from the manifest construction of the act itself. To deny this is to deny the validity of the act of Congress, without which Kentucky could not have become an independent state; and then it would follow that she is at this moment a part of the state of Virginia, and all her laws are acts of usurpation. The counsel who urged this argument would not, we are persuaded, consent to this conclusion; and yet it would seem to be inevitable if the premises insisted upon be true.

4

Hawkins v. Barney's Lessee
5 Pet. 457 (1831)

Mr. Justice Johnson delivered the opinion of the Court.

This is a writ of error to a judgment of the Circuit Court of Kentucky, brought to reverse the decision of that Court on a bill of exceptions.

The suit was ejectment, by Barney, brought to recover a part of a tract of fifty thousand acres of land, in possession of Mr. Hawkins, within the limits of his patent. Both parties claimed under Virginia patents, of which Barney's was the eldest. The plaintiff below proved a grant to Barbour, and a conveyance from the patentee to himself. The defendant below proved a grant to one May, a conveyance from May to Creemer, and from Creemer to himself. He then proved that Creemer entered into possession under May, in 1796, and resided on the land so conveyed to him, until he sold to defendant below; who has had peaceable possession of the premises ever since, until the present suit was brought, which was May 4th, 1817.

This state of facts brings out the principal question in the cause, which was on the constitutionality of the present limitation act of that state, commonly known by the epithet of the seven years law. The Court charged the jury in favor of Barney, and the verdict was rendered accordingly.

It is now argued that, by the seventh article of the compact with Virginia, Kentucky was precluded from passing such a law. And that this Court has, in fact, established this principle, in their decision against the validity of the occupying claimant laws.

I am instructed by the Court to say that such is not their idea of the bearing of that decision.

On the subject so often and so ably discussed in this Court and elsewhere, and on which the public mind has so long pondered, it would be an useless waste of time to amplify. A very few remarks only will be bestowed upon it.

The article reads thus: "All private rights and interests of lands within the said district, derived from the laws of Virginia prior to such separation, shall remain valid and secure under the laws of the proposed state, and shall be determined by the laws now existing in this state."

Taken in its literal sense, it is not very easy to ascribe to this article any more than a confirmation of present existing rights and interests, as derived under the laws of Virginia. And this, in ordinary cases of transfer of jurisdiction, is exactly what would have taken place upon a known principle of international and political law, without the protection of such an article. We have an analogous case in the thirty-fourth section of the judiciary act of the United States; in which it is enacted that the laws of the several states shall be rules of decision in the Courts of the United States; and which has been uniformly held to be no more than a declaration of what the law would have been without it: to wit, that the lex loci must be the governing rule of private right, under whatever jurisdiction private right comes to be examined.

And yet, when considered in relation to the actual subject to which this article was to be applied, and the peculiar phraseology of it; there will be found no little reason for inquiring whether it does not mean something more than would be implied without it; or, why it was introduced if not intended to mean something more. It had an almost anomalous subject to operate upon.

I perceive that in the copy of Littell's laws, which has been sent to our chambers, some one has had the perseverance to go over the legislation of Virginia, relating to the lands of Kentucky whilst under her jurisdiction, and to mark the various senses to which the word rights has been applied, in the course of her legislation. It is curious to observe how numerous they are. Her land system was altogether peculiar, and presented so many aspects in which it was necessary to consider it, in order to afford protection to the interests imparted by it, that it might, with much apparent reason, have been supposed to require something more than the general principle to secure those interests. So much remained yet to be done to impart to individuals the actual fruition of the sales or bounties of that state, that there must have been, unavoidably, left a wide range for the legislative and judicial action of the newly created commonwealth. When about then to surrender the care and preservation of rights and interests, so novel and so complex, into other hands, it was not unreasonably supposed by many, that the provisions of the compact of separation were intended to embrace something beyond the general assertion of the principles of international law, in behalf of the persons whose rights were implicated in, or jeoparded by the transfer.

Such appears to have been the view in which the majority of this Court regarded the subject in the case of Green *vs.* Biddle; when upon examining the practical operation of the occupying claimant laws of Kentucky, upon the rights of land-holders, they were thought to be like a disease planted in the vitals of men's estate, and a disease against which no human prudence could have guarded them, or at least no practical prudence, considering the state of the country, and the nature of their interests. And when again upon looking through the course of legislation in Virginia, there was found no principle or precedent to support such laws, the Court was induced to pass upon them as laws calculated in effect to annihilate the rights secured by the compact, while they avoided an avowed collision with its literal meaning. But in all their reasoning on the subject, they will be found to acknowledge, that whatever course of legislation could be sanctioned by the principles and practice of Virginia, would be regarded as an unaffected compliance with the compact.

Such, we conceive, are all reasonable quieting statutes. From as early a date as the year 1705, Virginia has never been without an act of limitation. And no class of laws is more universally sanctioned by the practice of nations, and the consent of mankind, than laws which give peace and confidence to the actual possessor and tiller of the soil. Such laws have frequently passed in review before this Court; and occasions have occurred, in which they have been particularly noticed as laws not to be impeached on the ground of violating private right. What right has any one to complain, when a reasonable time has been given him, if he has not been vigilant in asserting his rights? All the reasonable purposes of justice are subserved, if the Courts of a state have been left open to the prosecution of suits for such a time as may reasonably raise a presumption in the occupyer of the soil that the fruits of his labour are effectually secured beyond the chance of litigation. Interest reipublicae ut finis sit litium;—and vigilantibus non dormientibus succurrit lex; are not among the least favoured of the maxims of the law.

It is impossible to take any reasonable exception to the course of legislation pursued by Kentucky on this subject. She has in fact literally complied with the compact in its most rigid construction: for she adopted the very statute of Virginia in the first instance, and literally gave to her citizens the full benefit of twenty years to prosecute their suits, before she enacted the law now under consideration. As to the exceptions and provisos and savings in such statutes, they must necessarily be left in all cases to the wisdom or discretion of the legislative power.

It is not to be questioned that laws, limiting the time of bringing suit, constitute a part of the lex fori of every country: they are laws for administering justice; one of the most sacred and important of sovereign rights and duties: and a restriction upon which must materially affect both legislative and judicial independence. It can scarcely be supposed that Kentucky would have consented to accept a limited and crippled sovereignty; nor is it doing justice to Virginia to believe that she would have wished to reduce Kentucky to a state of vassalage. Yet it would be difficult if the literal and rigid construction necessary to exclude her from passing this law were to be adopted; it would be difficult, I say, to assign her a position higher than that of a dependant on Virginia. Let the language of the compact be literally applied, and we have the anomaly presented of a sovereign state governed by the laws of another sovereign; of one half the territory of a sovereign state hopelessly and forever subjected to the laws of another state. Or a motley multiform administration of laws, under which A would be subject to one class of laws, because holding under a Virginia grant; while B., his next door neighbour, claiming from Kentucky, would hardly be conscious of living under the same government.

If the seventh article of the compact can be construed so as to make the limitation act of Virginia perpetual and unrepealable in Kentucky; then I know not on what principle the same rule can be precluded from applying to laws of descent, conveyance, devise, dower, courtesy, and in fact every law applicable to real estate.

It is argued, that limitation laws, although belonging to the lex fori, and applying immediately to the remedy, yet indirectly they effect a complete divesture and even transfer of right. This is unquestionably true, and yet in no wise fatal to the validity of this law. The right to appropriate a derelict is one of universal law, well known to the civil law, the common law, and to all law: it existed in a state of nature, and is only modified by society, according to the discretion of each community. What is the evidence of an individual having abandoned his rights or property? It is clear that the subject is one over which every community is at liberty to make a rule for itself; and if the state of Kentucky has established the rule of seven years negligence to pursue a remedy, there can be but one question made upon the right to do so: which is, whether, after abstaining from the exercise of this right for twenty years, it is possible now to impute to her the want of good faith in the execution of this compact.

Virginia has always exercised an analogous right, not only in the form of an act of limitation, but in requiring actual seating and cultivation.

In the early settlement of the country, the man who received a grant of land and failed, at first in three, and afterwards in five years, to seat and improve it, was held to have abandoned it: it received the denomination of lapsed land, was declared to be forfeited (Mercer's Abr.;) and any one might take out a grant for it. The last member of the eighth article of this compact, distinctly recognises the existence of the power in Kentucky to pass similar laws; notwithstanding the restrictions of the seventh article, and also the probability of her resorting to the policy of such laws. It restricts her from passing them for six years: and what is remarkable, the protection of this restriction is expressly confined to the citizens of the two states; leaving the plaintiff below, and all others, not citizens of Virginia, to an uncontrolled exercise of such a power. Forfeiture is the word used in the old laws, and forfeiture is that used in the compact, and the term is correctly applied; since it supposes a revesting in the commonwealth: and it is remarkable how scrupulously Kentucky has adhered to the Virginian principle in her seven years law, since the benefit of it is confined to such only as claim under a grant from the commonwealth; thus literally applying the Virginian principle, of a revesting in the commonwealth and a regranting to the individual.

Upon the whole, we are unanimously of opinion that the Court below charged the jury incorrectly on this point; and if it stood alone in the cause, the judgment would be reversed. But as it must go back, there are two other points raised in the bill of exceptions which it is necessary to consider here.

The one is upon the sufficiency of the power of attorney executed by John to Robert Oliver, and under which the latter executed a deed to Barney to revest in him the fee simple of the land. Upon looking into that instrument, we are satisfied that although not professional in its style and form, it contains sufficient words to support the deed; and there was no error in the decision of the Court as to this point.

The other question is one of more difficulty. Upon the face of the deed from Barney to Oliver, and the reconveyance from Oliver to Barney, there are recited several conveyances of parcels of the tract granted to Barbour, to several individuals, and particularly to one of eleven thousand acres to one Berryman. The case on which the instruction was prayed makes out that Barney proved Hawkins to have trespassed within the limits of the fifty thousand acres; but it was insisted that he ought also to have proved the trespass to be without the limits of the tract shown to have been conveyed away by himself. On the other side it was insisted that the onus lay on Hawkins, to prove that his trespass was within the limits of one of those tracts, and the Court charged in favour of Barney.

This we conceive to be no longer an open question; it has been solemnly decided in a series of cases in Kentucky, that the party, offering in evidence a conveyance containing such exceptions, is bound to show that the trespass proved is without the limits of the land so sold or excepted. 3 Marshall, 20. 6 Littell, 281. 1 Monroe, 142.

The only doubt in this case was as to which of the two parties this rule applies, since both, and Hawkins first in order, produced in evidence a deed containing the exceptions. But, whether by the exceptions or by the deed, Hawkins's purpose was answered if he proved the whole land out of Barney. Not so with Barney; for in the act of proving the reinvestment of the estate in himself, he proved it to be with the exceptions mentioned, and therefore the rule unquestionably applied to him.

From these observations it results, that the Court below erred in refusing to instruct the jury according to the prayer of Hawkins; to wit, "that if they believed the evidence, the plaintiff, Barney, had no right of entry when this suit was instituted, and that unless he showed that the eleven thousand acres recited to be conveyed to Berryman by Barney did not cover the land in question, he was not entitled to recover in that suit."

The judgment is reversed, and the cause remanded for a venire facias de novo.

5

Joseph Story, Commentaries on the Constitution 3:§§ 1396–99
1833

§ 1396. The first part of this clause, respecting laying a duty on tonnage, has been already considered. The remaining clauses have their origin in the same general policy and reasoning, which forbid any state from entering into any treaty, alliance, or confederation; and from granting letters of marque and reprisal. In regard to treaties, alliances, and confederations, they are wholly prohibited. But a state may, *with the consent of congress,* enter into an agreement, or compact with another state, or with a foreign power. What precise distinction is here intended to be taken between *treaties,* and *agreements,* and *compacts* is nowhere explained; and has never as yet been subjected to any exact judicial, or other examination. A learned commentator, however, supposes, that the former ordinarily relate to subjects of great national magnitude and importance, and are often perpetual, or for a great length of time; but that the latter relate to transitory, or local concerns, or such, as cannot possibly affect any other interests, but those of the parties. But this is at best a very loose, and unsatisfactory exposition, leaving the whole matter open to the most latitudinarian construction. What are subjects of great national magnitude and importance? Why may not a compact, or agreement between states, be perpetual? If it may not, what shall be its duration? Are not treaties often made for short periods, and upon questions of local interest, and for temporary objects?

§ 1397. Perhaps the language of the former clause may be more plausibly interpreted from the terms used, "treaty, alliance, or confederation," and upon the ground, that the sense of each is best known by its association *(noscitur a sociis)* to apply to treaties of a political character; such as treaties of alliance for purposes of peace and war; and treaties of confederation, in which the parties are leagued for mutual government, political co-operation, and the exercise of political sovereignty; and treaties of cession of sovereignty, or conferring internal political jurisdiction, or external political dependence, or general commercial privileges. The latter clause, "compacts and agreements," might then very properly apply to such, as regarded what might be deemed mere private rights of sovereignty; such as questions of boundary; interests in land, situate in the territory of each other; and other internal regulations for the mutual comfort, and convenience of states, bordering on each other. Such compacts have been made since the adoption of the constitution. The compact between Virginia and Kentucky, already alluded to, is of this number. Compacts, settling the boundaries between states, are, or may be, of the same character. In such cases, the consent of congress may be properly required, in order to check any infringement of the rights of the national government; and at the same time a total prohibition, to enter into any compact or agreement, might be attended with permanent inconvenience, or public mischief.

§ 1398. The other prohibitions in the clause respect the power of making war, which is appropriately confided to the national government. The setting on foot of an army, or navy, by a state in times of peace, might be a cause of jealousy between neighbouring states, and provoke the hostilities of foreign bordering nations. In other cases, as the protection of the whole Union is confided to the national arm, and the national power, it is not fit, that any state should possess military means to overawe the Union, or to endanger the general safety. Still, a state may be so situated, that it may become indispensable to possess military forces, to resist an expected invasion, or insurrection. The danger may be too imminent for delay; and under such circumstances, a state will have a right to raise troops for its own safety, even without the consent of congress. After war is once begun, there is no doubt, that a state may, and indeed it ought to possess the power, to raise forces for its own defence; and its co-operation with the national forces may often be of great importance, to secure success and vigour in the operation of war. The prohibition is, therefore, wisely guarded by exceptions sufficient for the safety of the states, and not justly open to the objection of being dangerous to the Union.

§ 1399. In what manner the consent of congress is to be given to such acts of the state, is not positively provided for. Where an express consent is given, no possible doubt can arise. But the consent of congress may also be implied; and, indeed, is always to be implied, when congress adopts the particular act by sanctioning its objects, and aiding in enforcing them. Thus, where a state is admitted into the Union, notoriously upon a compact made between it and the state, of which it previously composed a part; there the act of congress, admitting such state into the Union, is an implied consent to the terms of the compact. This was true, as to the compact between Virginia and Kentucky, upon the admission of the latter into the Union; and the like rule will apply to other states, such as Maine, more recently admitted into the Union.

SEE ALSO:

Generally 1.8.3; 1.8.10–16; 1.10.1–2

James Madison, Preface to Debates in the Convention of 1787, Documentary History 3:796

Federal Farmer, no. 18, 25 Jan. 1788, Storing 2.8.220

An Act Granting Consent to South Carolina to Levy Duty on Tonnage, 2 Stat. 357 (1806)

Fleeger v. *Pool,* 9 Fed. Cas. 257, no. 4,860 (C.C.W.D.Tenn. 1832), aff'd 11 Pet. 185

Article 2, Section 1, Clause 1

The executive Power shall be vested in a President of the United States of America. He shall hold his Office during the Term of four Years, and, together with the Vice President, chosen for the same Term, be elected, as follows

1

John Locke, Second Treatise, §§ 144–48, 155–68 1689

144. But because the Laws, that are at once, and in a short time made, have a constant and lasting force, and need a *perpetual Execution,* or an attendance thereunto: Therefore 'tis necessary there should be a *Power always in being,* which should see to the *Execution* of the *Laws* that are made, and remain in force. And thus the *Legislative* and *Executive Power* come often to be separated.

145. There is another *Power* in every Commonwealth, which one may call *natural,* because it is that which answers to the Power every Man naturally had before he entered into Society. For though in a Commonwealth the Members of it are distinct Persons still in reference to one another, and as such are governed by the Laws of the Society; yet in reference to the rest of Mankind, they make one Body, which is, as every Member of it before was, still in the State of Nature with the rest of Mankind. Hence it is, that the Controversies that happen between any Man of the Society with those that are out of it, are managed by the publick; and an injury done to a Member of their Body, engages the whole in the reparation of it. So that under this Consideration, the whole Community is one Body in the State of Nature, in respect of all other States or Persons out of its Community.

146. This therefore contains the Power of War and Peace, Leagues and Alliances, and all the Transactions, with all Persons and Communities without the Commonwealth, and may be called *Federative,* if any one pleases. So the thing be understood, I am indifferent as to the name.

147. These two Powers, *Executive* and *Federative,* though they be really distinct in themselves, yet one comprehending the *Execution* of the Municipal Laws of the Society *within* its self, upon all that are parts of it; the other the management of the *security and interest of the publick without,* with all those that it may receive benefit or damage from,

yet they are always almost united. And though this *federative Power* in the well or ill management of it be of great moment to the commonwealth, yet it is much less capable to be directed by antecedent, standing, positive Laws, than the *Executive;* and so must necessarily be left to the Prudence and Wisdom of those whose hands it is in, to be managed for the publick good. For the *Laws* that concern Subjects one amongst another, being to direct their actions, may well enough *precede* them. But what is to be done in reference to *Foreigners,* depending much upon their actions, and the variation of designs and interests, must be *left* in great part *to* the *Prudence* of those who have this Power committed to them, to be managed by the best of their Skill, for the advantage of the Commonwealth.

148. Though, as I said, the *Executive* and *Federative Power* of every Community be really distinct in themselves, yet they are hardly to be separated, and placed, at the same time, in the hands of distinct Persons. For both of them requiring the force of the Society for their exercise, it is almost impracticable to place the Force of the Commonwealth in distinct, and not subordinate hands; or that the *Executive* and *Federative Power* should be *placed* in Persons that might act separately, whereby the Force of the Publick would be under different Commands: which would be apt sometime or other to cause disorder and ruine.

. . . . .

155. It may be demanded here, What if the Executive Power being possessed of the Force of the Commonwealth, shall make use of that force to hinder the *meeting* and *acting of the Legislative,* when the Original Constitution, or the publick Exigencies require it? I say using Force upon the People without Authority, and contrary to the Trust put in him, that does so, is a state of War with the People, who have a right to *reinstate* their *Legislative in the Exercise* of their Power. For having erected a Legislative, with an intent they should exercise the Power of making Laws, either at certain set times, or when there is need of it; when they are hindr'd by any force from, what is so necessary to the Society, and wherein in Safety and preservation of the People consists, the People have a right to remove it by force. In all States and Conditions the true remedy of *Force* without Authority, is to oppose *Force* to it. The use of *force* without Authority, always puts him that uses it into a *state of War,* as the Aggressor, and renders him liable to be treated accordingly.

156. The Power of *Assembling and dismissing the Legislative,* placed in the Executive, gives not the Executive a superiority over it, but is a Fiduciary Trust, placed in him, for the safety of the People, in a Case where the uncertainty, and variableness of humane affairs could not bear a steady fixed rule. For it not being possible, that the first Framers of the Government should, by any foresight, be so much Masters of future Events, as to be able to prefix so just periods of return and duration to the *Assemblies of the Legislative,* in all times to come, that might exactly answer all the Exigencies of the Commonwealth; the best remedy could be found for this defect, was to trust this to the prudence of one, who was always to be present, and whose business it was to watch over the publick good. Constant *frequent meetings of the Legislative,* and long Continuations of their Assemblies, without necessary occasion, could not but be burthensome to the People, and must necessarily in time produce more dangerous inconveniences, and yet the quick turn of affairs might be sometimes such as to need their present help: Any delay of their *Convening* might endanger the publick; and sometimes too their business might be so great, that the limited time of their sitting might be too short for their work, and rob the publick of that benefit, which could be had only from their mature deliberation. What then could be done, in this Case, to prevent the Community, from being exposed sometime or other to eminent hazard, on one side, or the other, by fixed intervals and periods, set to the prudence of some, who being present, and acquainted with the state of publick affairs, might make use of this Prerogative for the publick good? And where else could this be so well placed as in his hands, who was intrusted with the Execution of the Laws, for the same end? Thus supposing the regulation of times for the *Assembling and Sitting of the Legislative,* not settled by the original Constitution, it naturally fell into the hands of the Executive, not as an Arbitrary Power depending on his good pleasure, but with this trust always to have it exercised only for the publick Weal, as the Occurrences of times and change of affairs might require. Whether *settled periods of their Convening,* or a *liberty* left to the Prince *for Convoking the Legislative,* or perhaps a mixture of both, hath the least inconvenience attending it, 'tis not my business here to inquire, but only to shew, that though the Executive Power may have the Prerogative of *Convoking* and *dissolving* such *Conventions of the Legislative,* yet it is not thereby superior to it.

157. Things of this World are in so constant a Flux, that nothing remains long in the same State. Thus People, Riches, Trade, Power, change their Stations; flourishing mighty Cities come to ruine, and prove in time neglected desolate Corners, whilst other unfrequented places grow into populous Countries, fill'd with Wealth and Inhabitants. But things not always changing equally, and private interest often keeping up Customs and Priviledges, when the reasons of them are ceased, it often comes to pass, that in Governments, where part of the Legislative consists of *Representatives* chosen by the People, that in tract of time this *Representation* becomes very *unequal* and disproportionate to the reasons it was at first establish'd upon. To what gross absurdities the following of Custom, when Reason has left it, may lead, we may be satisfied when we see the bare Name of a Town, of which there remains not so much as the ruines, where scarce so much Housing as a Sheep-coat; or more inhabitants than a Shepherd is to be found, sends *as many Representatives* to the grand Assembly of Law-makers, as a whole County numerous in People, and powerful in riches. This Strangers stand amazed at, and every one must confess needs a remedy. Though most think it hard to find one, because the Constitution of the Legislative being the original and supream act of the Society, antecedent to all positive Laws in it, and depending wholly on the People, no inferiour Power can alter it. And therefore the *People,* when the *Legislative* is once Consti-

tuted, *having* in such a Government as we have been speaking of, *no Power* to act as long as the Government stands; this inconvenience is thought incapable of a remedy.

158. *Salus Populi Suprema Lex,* is certainly so just and fundamental a Rule, that he, who sincerely follows it, cannot dangerously err. If therefore the Executive, who has the power of Convoking the Legislative, observing rather the true proportion, than fashion of *Representation,* regulates, not by old custom, but true reason, the *number of Members,* in all places, that have a right to be distinctly represented, which no part of the People however incorporated can pretend to, but in proportion to the assistance, which it affords to the publick, it cannot be judg'd, to have set up a new Legislative, but to have restored the old and true one, and to have rectified the disorders, which succession of time had insensibly, as well as inevitably introduced. For it being the interest, as well as intention of the People, to have a fair and *equal Representative;* whoever brings it nearest to that, is an undoubted Friend, to, and Establisher of the Government, and cannot miss the Consent and Approbation of the Community. *Prerogative* being nothing, but a Power in the hands of the Prince to provide for the publick good, in such Cases, which depending upon unforeseen and uncertain Occurrences, certain and unalterable Laws could not safely direct, whatsoever shall be done manifestly for the good of the People, and the establishing the Government upon its true Foundations, is, and always will be just *Prerogative.* The Power of Erecting new Corporations, and therewith *new Representatives,* carries with it a supposition, that in time the *measures of representation* might vary, and those places have a just right to be represented which before had none; and by the same reason, those cease to have a right, and be too inconsiderable for such a Priviledge, which before had it. 'Tis not a change from the present State, which perhaps Corruption, or decay has introduced, that makes an Inroad upon the Government, but the tendency of it to injure or oppress the People, and to set up one part, or Party, with a distinction from, and an unequal subjection of the rest. Whatsoever cannot but be acknowledged to be of the Society, and People in general, upon just and lasting measures, will always, when done, justifie it self; and whenever the People shall chuse their *Representatives upon* just and undeniably *equal measures* suitable to the original Frame of the Government, it cannot be doubted to be the will and act of the Society, whoever permitted, or caused them, so to do.

159. Where the Legislative and Executive Power are in distinct hands, (as they are in all moderated Monarchies, and well-framed Governments) there the good of the Society requires, that several things should be left to the discretion of him, that has the Executive Power. For the Legislators not being able to foresee, and provide, by Laws, for all, that may be useful to the Community, the Executor of the Laws, having the power in his hands, has by the common Law of Nature, a right to make use of it, for the good of the Society, in many Cases, where the municipal Law has given no direction, till the Legislative can conveniently be Assembled to provide for it. Many things there are, which the Law can by no means provide for, and those must necessarily be left to the discretion of him that has the Executive Power in his hands, to be ordered by him, as the publick good and advantage shall require: nay, 'tis fit that the Laws themselves should in some Cases give way to the Executive Power, or rather to this Fundamental Law of Nature and Government, *viz.* That as much as may be, *all* the Members of the Society are to be *preserved.* For since many accidents may happen, wherein a strict and rigid observation of the Laws may do harm; (as not to pull down an innocent Man's House to stop the Fire, when the next to it is burning) and a Man may come sometimes within the reach of the Law, which makes no distinction of Persons, by an action, that may deserve reward and pardon; 'tis fit, the Ruler should have a Power, in many Cases, to mitigate the severity of the Law, and pardon some Offenders: For the *end of Government* being the *preservation of all,* as much as may be, even the guilty are to be spared, where it can prove no prejudice to the innocent.

160. This Power to act according to discretion, for the publick good, without the prescription of the Law, and sometimes even against it, *is* that which is called *Prerogative.* For since in some Governments the Law-making Power is not always in being, and is usually too numerous, and so too slow, for the dispatch requisite to Execution: and because also it is impossible to foresee, and so by laws to provide for, all Accidents and Necessities, that may concern the publick; or to make such Laws, as will do no harm, if they are Executed with an inflexible rigour, on all occasions, and upon all Persons, that may come in their way, therefore there is a latitude left to the Executive power, to do many things of choice, which the Laws do not prescribe.

161. This power whilst imployed for the benefit of the Community, and suitably to the trust and ends of the Government, is *undoubted Prerogative,* and never is questioned. For the People are very seldom, or never scrupulous, or nice in the point; they are far from examining *Prerogative,* whilst it is in any tolerable degree imploy'd for the use it was meant; that is, for the good of the People, and not manifestly against it. But if there comes to be a *question* between the Executive Power and the People, *about* a thing claimed as a *Prerogative;* the tendency of the exercise of such *Prerogative* to the good or hurt of the People, will easily decide the Question.

162. It is easie to conceive, that in the Infancy of Governments, when Commonwealths differed little from Families in number of People, they differ'd from them too but little in number of Laws: And the Governours, being as the Fathers of them, watching over them for their good, the Government was almost all *Prerogative.* A few establish'd Laws served the turn, and the discretion and care of the Ruler supply'd the rest. But when mistake, or flattery prevailed with weak Princes to make use of this Power, for private ends of their own, and not for the publick good, the People were fain by express Laws to get Prerogative determin'd, in those points, wherein they found disadvan-

tage from it: And thus declared *limitations of Prerogative* were by the People found necessary in Cases, which they and their Ancestors had left, in the utmost latitude, to the Wisdom of those Princes, who made no other but a right use of it, that is, for the good of their People.

163. And therefore they have a very wrong Notion of Government, who say, that the People have *incroach'd upon the Prerogative,* when they have got any part of it to be defined by positive Laws. For in so doing, they have not pulled from the Prince any thing, that of right belong'd to him, but only declared, that that Power which they indefinitely left in his, or his Ancestors, hands, to be exercised for their good, was not a thing, which they intended him, when he used it otherwise. For the end of government being the good of the Community, whatsoever alterations are made in it, tending to that end, cannot be an *incroachment* upon any body; since no body in Government can have a right tending to any other end. And those only are *incroachments* which prejudice or hinder the publick good. Those who say otherwise, speak as if the Prince had a distinct and separate Interest from the good of the Community, and was not made for it, the Root and Source, from which spring almost all those Evils, and Disorders, which happen in Kingly Government. And indeed if that be so, the People under his Government are not a Society of Rational Creatures entred into a Community for their mutual good; they are not such as have set Rulers over themselves, to guard, and promote that good; but are to be looked on as an Herd of inferiour Creatures, under the Dominion of a Master, who keeps them, and works them for his own Pleasure or Profit. If men were so void of Reason, and brutish, as to enter into Society upon such Terms, *Prerogative* might indeed be, what some Men would have it, an Arbitrary Power to do things hurtful to the People.

164. But since a Rational Creature cannot be supposed when free, to put himself into Subjection to another, for his own harm: (Though where he finds a good and wise Ruler, he may not perhaps think it either necessary, or useful to set precise Bounds to his Power in all things) *Prerogative* can be nothing, but the Peoples permitting their Rulers, to do several things of their own free choice, where the Law was silent, and sometimes too against the direct Letter of the Law, for the publick good; and their acquiescing in it when so done. For as a good Prince, who is mindful of the trust put into his hands, and careful of the good of his People, cannot have too much *Prerogative,* that is, Power to do good: So a weak and ill Prince, who would claim that Power, which his Predecessors exercised without the direction of the Law, as a Prerogative belonging to him by Right of his Office, which he may exercise at his pleasure, to make or promote an Interest distinct from that of the publick, gives the People an occasion, to claim their Right, and limit that Power, which, whilst it was exercised for their good, they were content should be tacitly allowed.

165. And therefore he, that will look into the *History of England,* will find, that Prerogative was always *largest* in the hands of our wisest and best Princes: because the People observing the whole tendency of their Actions to be the publick good, contested not what was done without Law to that end; or if any humane frailty or mistake (for Princes are but Men, made as others) appear'd in some small declinations from that end; yet 'twas visible, the main of their Conduct tended to nothing but the care of the publick. The People therefore finding reason to be satisfied with these Princes, whenever they acted without or contrary to the Letter of the Law, acquiesced in what they did, and, without the least complaint, let them inlarge their *Prerogative* as they pleased, judging rightly, that they did nothing herein to the prejudice of their Laws, since they acted conformable to the Foundation and End of all Laws, the publick good.

166. Such God-like Princes indeed had some Title to Arbitrary Power, by that Argument, that would prove Absolute Monarchy the best Government, as that which God himself governs the Universe by: because such Kings partake of his Wisdom and Goodness. Upon this is founded that saying, That the Reigns of good Princes have been always most dangerous to the Liberties of their People. For when their Successors, managing the Government with different Thoughts, would draw the Actions of those good Rulers into Precedent, and make them the Standard of their *Prerogative,* as if what had been done only for the good of the People, was a right in them to do, for the harm of the People, if they so pleased; it has often occasioned Contest, and sometimes publick Disorders, before the People could recover their original Right, and get that to be declared not to be *Prerogative,* which truly was never so: Since it is impossible, that any body in the Society should ever have a right to do the People harm; though it be very possible, and reasonable, that the People should not go about to set any Bounds to the *Prerogative* of those Kings or Rulers, who themselves transgressed not the Bounds of the publick good. For *Prerogative is nothing but the Power of doing publick good without a Rule.*

167. The Power of *calling Parliaments* in *England,* as to precise time, place, and duration, is certainly a *Prerogative* of the King, but still with this trust, that it shall be made use of for the good of the Nation, as the Exigencies of the Times, and variety of Occasions shall require. For it being impossible to foresee, which should always be the fittest place for them to assemble in, and what the best Season; the choice of these was left with the Executive Power, as might be most subservient to the publick good, and best suit the ends of Parliaments.

168. The old Question will be asked in this matter of *Prerogative,* But *who shall be Judge* when this Power is made a right use of? I Answer: Between an Executive Power in being, with such a Prerogative, and a Legislative that depends upon his will for their convening, there can be no *Judge on Earth:* As there can be none, between the Legislative, and the People, should either the Executive, or the Legislative, when they have got the Power in their hands, design, or go about to enslave, or destroy them. The People have no other remedy in this, as in all other cases where they have no Judge on Earth, but to *appeal to Heaven.* For the Rulers, in such attempts, exercising a

Power the People never put into their hands (who can never be supposed to consent, that any body should rule over them for their harm) do that, which they have not a right to do. And where the Body of the People, or any single Man, is deprived of their Right, or is under the Exercise of a power without right, and have no Appeal on Earth, there they have a liberty to appeal to Heaven, whenever they judge the Cause of sufficient moment. And therefore, tho' the *People* cannot be *Judge,* so as to have by the Constitution of that Society any Superiour power, to determine and give effective Sentence in the case; yet they have, by a Law antecedent and paramount to all positive Laws of men, reserv'd that ultimate Determination to themselves, which belongs to all Mankind, where there lies no Appeal on Earth, *viz.* to judge whether they have just Cause to make their Appeal to Heaven. And this judgment they cannot part with, it being out of a Man's power so to submit himself to another, as to give him a liberty to destroy him; God and Nature never allowing a Man so to abandon himself, as to neglect his own preservation: And since he cannot take away his own Life, neither can he give another power to take it. Nor let any one think, this lays a perpetual foundation for Disorder: for this operates not, till the Inconvenience is so great, that the Majority feel it, and are weary of it, and find a necessity to have it amended. But this the Executive Power, or wise Princes, never need come in the danger of: And 'tis the thing of all others, they have most need to avoid, as of all others the most perilous.

2

WILLIAM BLACKSTONE, COMMENTARIES 1:243–44 1765

It was observed in a former chapter, that one of the principal bulwarks of civil liberty, or (in other words) of the British constitution, was the limitation of the king's prerogative by bounds so certain and notorious, that it is impossible he should ever exceed them, without the consent of the people, on the one hand; or without, on the other, a violation of that original contract, which in all states impliedly, and in ours most expressly, subsists between the prince and the subject. It will now be our business to consider this prerogative minutely; to demonstrate it's necessity in general; and to mark out in the most important instances it's particular extent and restrictions: from which considerations this conclusion will evidently follow, that the powers which are vested in the crown by the laws of England, are necessary for the support of society; and do not intrench any farther on our *natural* liberties, than is expedient for the maintenance of our *civil.*

By the word prerogative we usually understand that special pre-eminence, which the king hath, over and above all other persons, and out of the ordinary course of the common law, in right of his regal dignity. It signifies, in it's etymology, (from *prae* and *rogo*) something that is required or demanded before, or in preference to, all others. And hence it follows, that it must be in it's nature singular and eccentrical; that it can only be applied to those rights and capacities which the king enjoys alone, in contradistinction to others, and not to those which he enjoys in common with any of his subjects: for if once any one prerogative of the crown could be held in common with the subject, it would cease to be prerogative any longer. And therefore Finch lays it down as maxim, that the prerogative is that law in case of the king, which is law in no case of the subject.

After what has been premised in this chapter, I shall not (I trust) be considered as an advocate for arbitrary power, when I lay it down as a principle, that in the exertion of lawful prerogative, the king is and ought to be absolute; that is, so far absolute, that there is no legal authority that can either delay or resist him. He may reject what bills, may make what treaties, may coin what money, may create what peers, may pardon what offences he pleases: unless where the constitution hath expressly, or by evident consequence, laid down some exception or boundary; declaring, that thus far the prerogative shall go and no farther. For otherwise the power of the crown would indeed be but a name and a shadow, insufficient for the ends of government, if, where it's jurisdiction is clearly established and allowed, any man or body of men were permitted to disobey it, in the ordinary course of law: I say, in the *ordinary* course of law; for I do not now speak of those *extraordinary* recourses to first principles, which are necessary when the contracts of society are in danger of dissolution, and the law proves too weak a defence against the violence of fraud or oppression. And yet the want of attending to this obvious distinction has occasioned these doctrines, of absolute power in the prince and of national resistance by the people, to be much misunderstood and perverted by the advocates for slavery on the one hand, and the demagogues of faction on the other. The former, observing the absolute sovereignty and transcendent dominion of the crown laid down (as it certainly is) most strongly and emphatically in our lawbooks, as well as our homilies, have denied that any case can be excepted from so general and positive a rule; forgetting how impossible it is, in any practical system of laws, to point out beforehand those eccentrical remedies, which the sudden emergence of national distress may dictate, and which that alone can justify. On the other hand, over-zealous republicans, feeling the absurdity of unlimited passive obedience, have fancifully (or sometimes factiously) gone over to the other extreme: and, because resistance is justifiable to the person of the prince when the being of the state is endangered, and the public voice proclaims such resistance necessary, they have therefore allowed to every individual the right of determining this expedience, and of employing private force to resist even private oppression. A doctrine productive of anarchy, and (in consequence) equally fatal to civil liberty as tyranny itself. For civil liberty, rightly understood, consists in protecting the rights of individuals by the united force of society: society cannot be maintained, and of course can exert no protection, without obedience to some sovereign power: and obedience is an empty name, if every individual has a right to decide how far he himself shall obey.

In the exertion therefore of those prerogatives, which the law has given him, the king is irresistible and absolute, according to the forms of the constitution. And yet, if the consequence of that exertion be manifestly to the grievance or dishonour of the kingdom, the parliament will call his advisers to a just and severe account. For prerogative consisting (as Mr. Locke has well defined it) in the discretionary power of acting for the public good, where the positive laws are silent, if the discretionary power be abused to the public detriment, such prerogative is exerted in an unconstitutional manner. Thus the king may make a treaty with a foreign state, which shall irrevocably bind the nation; and yet, when such treaties have been judged pernicious, impeachments have pursued those ministers, by whose agency or advice they were concluded.

3

Virginia Declaration of Rights, sec. 5
12 June 1776

5. That the legislative and executive powers of the state should be separate and distinct from the judicative; and that the members of the two first may be restrained from oppression, by feeling and participating the burthens of the people, they should, at fixed periods, be reduced to a private station, return into that body from which they were originally taken, and the vacancies be supplied by frequent, certain, and regular elections, in which all, or any part of the former members, to be again eligible, or ineligible, as the laws shall direct.

4

Records of the Federal Convention

[*1:21; Madison, 29 May*]

7. Resd. that a National Executive be instituted; to be chosen by the National Legislature for the term of years, to receive punctually at stated times, a fixed compensation for the services rendered, in which no increase or diminution shall be made so as to affect the Magistracy, existing at the time of increase or diminution, and to be ineligible a second time; and that besides a general authority to execute the National laws, it ought to enjoy the Executive rights vested in Congress by the Confederation.

[*1:64, 68; Madison, 1 June*]

The Committee of the whole proceeded to Resolution 7. "that a national Executive be instituted, to be chosen by the national Legislature——for the term of years &c to be ineligible thereafter, to possess the executive powers of Congress &c"—

Mr. Pinkney was for a vigorous Executive but was afraid the Executive powers of the existing Congress might extend to peace & war &c which would render the Executive a Monarchy, of the worst kind, towit an elective one.

Mr. Wilson moved that the Executive consist of a single person. Mr. C Pinkney seconded the motion so as to read "that a national Ex. to consist of a single person, be instituted—

A considerable pause ensuing and the Chairman asking if he should put the question, Docr. Franklin observed that it was a point of great importance and wished that the gentlemen would deliver their sentiments on it before the question was put.

Mr. Rutlidge animadverted on the shyness of gentlemen on this and other subjects. He said it looked as if they supposed themselves precluded by having frankly disclosed their opinions from afterwards changing them, which he did not take to be at all the case. He said he was for vesting the Executive power in a single person, tho' he was not for giving him the power of war and peace. A single man would feel the greatest responsibility and administer the public affairs best.

Mr. Sherman said he considered the Executive magistracy as nothing more than an institution for carrying the will of the Legislature into effect, that the person or persons ought to be appointed by and accountable to the Legislature only, which was the despositary of the supreme will of the Society. As they were the best judges of the business which ought to be done by the Executive department, and consequently of the number necessary from time to time for doing it, he wished the number might not be fixed, but that the legislature should be at liberty to appoint one or more as experience might dictate.

Mr. Wilson preferred a single magistrate, as giving most energy dispatch and responsibility to the office. He did not consider the Prerogatives of the British Monarch as a proper guide in defining the Executive powers. Some of these prerogatives were of a Legislative nature. Among others that of war & peace, etc. The only powers he conceived strictly Executive were those of executing the laws, and appointing officers, not appertaining to and appointed by the Legislature.

Mr. Gerry favored the policy of annexing a Council to the Executive in order to give weight & inspire confidence.

Mr. Randolph strenuously opposed a unity in the Executive magistracy. He regarded it as the foetus of monarchy. We had he said no motive to be governed by the British Governmt. as our prototype. He did not mean however to throw censure on that Excellent fabric. If we were in a situation to copy it he did not know that he should be opposed to it; but the fixt genius of the people of America required a different form of Government. He could not see why the great requisites for the Executive department, vigor, despatch & responsibility could not be found in three men, as well as in one man. The Executive ought to be independent. It ought therefore in order to support its independence to consist of more than one.

Mr. Wilson said that Unity in the Executive instead of

being the fetus of Monarchy would be the best safeguard against tyranny. He repeated that he was not governed by the British Model which was inapplicable to the situation of this Country; the extent of which was so great, and the manners so republican, that nothing but a great confederated Republic would do for it.

Mr. Wilson's motion for a single magistrate was postponed by common consent, the Committee seeming unprepared for any decision on it; and the first part of the clause agreed to, viz. "that a National Executive be instituted."

. . . . .

Mr. Wilson moves that the blank for the term of duration should be filled with three years, observing at the same time that he preferred this short period, on the supposition that a re-eligibility would be provided for.

Mr. Pinkney moves for seven years.

Mr. Sherman was for three years, and agst. the doctrine of rotation as throwing out of office the men best qualified to execute its duties.

Mr. Mason was for seven years at least, and for prohibiting a re-eligibility as the best expedient both for preventing the effect of a false complaisance on the side of the Legislature towards unfit characters; and a temptation on the side of the Executive to intrigue with the Legislature for a re-appointment.

Mr. Bedford was strongly opposed to so long a term as seven years. He begged the committee to consider what the situation of the Country would be, in case the first magistrate should be saddled on it for such period and it should be found on trial that he did not possess the qualifications ascribed to him, or should lose them after his appointment. An impeachment he said would be no cure for this evil, as an impeachment would reach misfeasance only, not incapacity. He was for a triennial election, and for an ineligibility after a period of nine years.

On the question for seven years,

Massts. dividd. Cont. no. N. J. ay. Pena. ay. Del. ay. Virga., ay. N. C. no. S. C. no. Georg. no [Ayes—5; noes—4; divided—1.]

There being 5. ays, 4 noes, 1 divd. a question was asked whether a majority had voted in the affirmative? The President decided that it was an affirmative vote.

[1:70; King, 1 June]

This amend. moved by Wilson & secd. by Cs. Pinck.

Rutledge in favor of it. Sherman proposes to leave the number wth. the Legislature—

Wilson—an extive. ought to possess the powers of secresy, vigour & Dispatch—and to be so constituted as to be responsible—Extive. powers are designed for the execution of Laws, and appointing Officers not otherwise to be appointed—If appointments of Officers are made by a sing. Ex he is responsible for the propriety of the same. not so where the Executive is numerous.

Mad: agrees wth. Wilson in his difinition of executive powers—executive powers ex vi termini, do not include the Rights of war & peace &c. but the powers shd. be confined and defined—if large we shall have the Evils of elective Monarchies—probably the best plan will be a single Executive of long duration wth. a Council, with liberty to depart from their Opinion at his peril—

Gerry—I am in favr. of a council to advise the Ex—they will be the organs of information of the persons proper for offices—their opinions may be recorded—they may be called to acct. for yr. Opinions. & impeached—if so their Responsibility will be certain, and in Case of misconduct their punishment certain—

Randolph—Danger of Monarchy, or Tyranny, if the ex. consists of three persons they may execute yr. Functions without Danger—if one he can not be impeached until the expiration of his Office, or he will be dependent on the Legislature—such an Unity wd. be agt. the fixed Genius of America &c &c—

Wilson

We must consider two points of Importance existing in our Country—the extent & manners of the United States—the former seems to require the vigour of Monarchy, the manners are agt. a King and are purely republican—Montesquieu is in favor of confederated Republicks—I am for such a confedn. if we can take for its basis liberty, and can ensure a vigourous execution of the laws.

A single ex. will not so soon introduce a Mony. or Despotism, as a complex one.

The people of Amer. did not oppose the British King but the parliament—the opposition was not agt. an Unity but a corrupt multitude—

Wmson—There is no true difference between a complex executive, formed by a single person with a Council, or by three or more persons as the executive—

The Question of the unity or plurality of the Exve. postponed—and the Come. proceeded to examine the powers—these points being discussed—the Come took into consideration the Duration of the Office of the Ex—

Wilson for 3 Yrs and no exclusion or rotation—

Mad. 7 years and an exclusion for ever after—or during good behavior—

Mason—in Favor of 7 years and an exclusion afterwards—thereby he is made independent of the Legislature, who are proposed as his Electors—if he is capable of reelection by the Leg: the Ex. will be complaisant, & reelect—the Executive will be subservient and court a reelection—on the Quest to fill the Blank for seven yrs.

Mass. divd.	Con	no	NY.	ay	
Gor. & K. ay }	NC.	no	NJ.	ay	
Ger. & Sg. no }	SC.	no	Pen.	ay	} filled
	G.	no	Del.	ay	
			Vir	ay	

[1:74; Pierce, 2 June]

Mr. Maddison was of opinion that an Executive formed of one Man would answer the purpose when aided by a Council, who should have the right to advise and record their proceedings, but not to control his authority.

Mr. Gerry was of opinion that a Council ought to be the medium through which the feelings of the people ought to be communicated to the Executive.

Mr. Randolph advanced a variety of arguments opposed to a unity of the Executive, and doubted whether even a

Council would be sufficient to check the improper views of an ambitious Man. A unity of the Executive he observed would savor too much of a monarchy.

Mr. Wilson said that in his opinion so far from a unity of the Executive tending to progress towards a monarchy it would be the circumstance to prevent it. A plurality in the Executive of Government would probably produce a tyranny as bad as the thirty Tyrants of Athens, or as the Decemvirs of Rome.

A confederated republic joins the happiest kind of Government with the most certain security to liberty.

(A CONSIDERATION.)

Every Government has certain moral and physical qualities engrafted in their very nature,—one operates on the sentiments of men, the other on their fears.

Mr. Dickinson was of opinion that the powers of the Executive ought to be defined before we say in whom the power shall vest.

Mr. Bedford said he was for appointing the Executive Officer for three years, and that he should be eligible for nine years only.

Mr. Maddison observed that to prevent a Man from holding an Office longer than he ought, he may for malpractice be impeached and removed;—he is not for any ineligibility.

[*1:88; Madison, 2 June*]

The Question for making ye. Executive ineligible after seven years, was next next taken, and agreed to:

Massts. ay. Cont. no. NY—ay Pa. divd. Del. ay. Maryd. ay. Va. ay. N. C. ay. S. C. ay. Geo. no: [Ayes—7; noes—2; divided—1.]

Mr. Williamson 2ded. by Mr. Davie moved to add to the last Clause, the words—"and to be removeable on impeachment & conviction of mal-practice or neglect of duty"—which was agreed to.

Mr. Rutlidge & Mr. C. Pinkney moved that the blank for the no. of persons in the Executive be filled with the words "one person". He supposed the reasons to be so obvious & conclusive in favor of one that no member would oppose the motion.

Mr. Randolph opposed it with great earnestness, declaring that he should not do justice to the Country which sent him if he were silently to suffer the establishmt. of a Unity in the Executive department. He felt an opposition to it which he believed he should continue to feel as long as he lived. He urged 1. that the permanent temper of the people was adverse to the very semblance of Monarchy. 2. that a unity was unnecessary a plurality being equally competent to all the objects of the department. 3. that the necessary confidence would never be reposed in a single Magistrate. 4. that the appointments would generally be in favor of some inhabitant near the center of the Community, and consequently the remote parts would not be on an equal footing. He was in favor of three members of the Executive to be drawn from different portions of the Country.

Mr. Butler contended strongly for a single magistrate as most likely to answer the purpose of the remote parts. If one man should be appointed he would be responsible to the whole, and would be impartial to its interests. If three or more should be taken from as many districts, there would be a constant struggle for local advantages. In Military matters this would be particularly mischievous. He said his opinion on this point had been formed under the opportunity he had had of seeing the manner in which a plurality of military heads distracted Holland when threatened with invasion by the imperial troops. One man was for directing the force to the defence of this part, another to that part of the Country, just as he happened to be swayed by prejudice or interest.

[*1:90; Yates, 2 June*]

Mr. Butler moved to fill the number of which the executive should consist.

Mr. Randolph.—The sentiments of the people ought to be consulted—they will not hear of the semblance of monarchy—He preferred three divisions of the states, and an executive to be taken from each. If a single executive, those remote from him would be neglected—local views would be attributed to him, frequently well founded, often without reason. This would excite disaffection. He was therefore for an executive of three.

Mr. Butler.—Delays, divisions and dissentions arise from an executive consisting of many. Instanced Holland's distracted state, occasioned by her many counsellors. Further consideration postponed.

[*1:90; King, 2 June*]

Dickinson

A vigs. executive with checks &c can not be republican, it is peculiar to monarchy—

The monarchl. Ex is vigour—not alone from power but attachment or respect—

The Repub. plan may have an equivalent to the attachmt. that is the 3d Br. of the Legis:

We cannot have a limited monarchy instanter—our situation will not allow it—Repubs. are for a while industrious but finally destroy ymselves—they were badly constituted—I dread a Consolidation of the States

[*1:96; Madison, 4 June*]

The Question was resumed on motion of Mr. Pinkney 2ded. by Wilson "shall the blank for the number of the Executive be filled with "a single person"?

Mr. Wilson was in favor of the motion. It had been opposed by the gentleman from Virga. (Mr. Randolph) but the arguments used had not convinced him. He observed that the objections of Mr. R. were levelled not so much agst. the measure itself, as agst. its unpopularity. If he could suppose that it would occasion a rejection of the plan of which it should form a part, though the part was an important one, yet he would give it up rather than lose the whole. On examination he could see no evidence of the alledged antipathy of the people. On the contrary he was persuaded that it does not exist. All know that a single magistrate is not a King. one fact has great weight with him. All the 13 States tho' agreeing in scarce any other instance, agree in placing a single magistrate at the head of the Government. The idea of three heads has taken place in none. The degree of power is indeed different: but there are no co-ordinate heads. In addition to his former reasons for preferring a Unity, he would mention another. The *tranquility* not less than the vigor of the Govt, he thought would be favored by it. Among three equal members, he foresaw nothing but uncontrouled, continued, & violent animosities; which would not only interrupt the public administration; but diffuse their poison thro' the other branches of Govt., thro' the States, and at length thro' the people at large. If the members were to be unequal in power the principle of the opposition to the Unity was given up. If equal, the making them an odd number would not be a remedy. In Courts of Justice there are two sides only to a question. In the Legislative & Executive departmts. questions have commonly many sides. Each member therefore might espouse a separate one & no two agree.

Mr. Sherman. This matter is of great importance and ought to be well considered before it is determined. Mr. Wilson he said had observed that in each State a single magistrate was placed at the head of the Govt. It was so he admitted, and properly so, and he wished the same policy to prevail in the federal Govt. But then it should be also remarked that in a all the States there was a Council of advice, without which the first magistrate could not act. A Council he thought necessary to make the establishment acceptable to the people. Even in G. B. the King has a council; and though he appoints it himself, its advice has its weight with him, and attracts the Confidence of the people.

Mr. Williamson asks Mr. Wilson whether he means to annex a Council

Mr. Wilson means to have no Council, which oftener serves to cover, than prevent malpractices.

Mr. Gerry. was at a loss to discover the policy of three members for the Executive. It wd. be extremely inconvenient in many instances, particularly in military matters, whether relating to the militia, an army, or a navy. It would be a general with three heads.

On the question for a single Executive it was agreed to Massts. ay. Cont. ay. N.Y. no. Pena. ay. Del. no. Maryd. no. Virg. ay. (Mr. R & Mr. Blair no—Docr. Mc.Cg. Mr.M. & Gen. W. ay. Col. Mason being no, but not in house, Mr. Wythe ay but gone home). N. C. ay. S. C. ay. Georga. ay. [Ayes—7; noes—3.]

[*1:109; Pierce, 4 June*]

Mr. Wilson said that all the Constitutions of America from New Hampshire to Georgia have their Executive in a single Person. A single Person will produce vigor and activity. Suppose the Executive to be in the hands of a number they will probably be divided in opinion.

[*4:17; Mason, 4 June*]

[Mr. Mason:] . . . by placing the Executive Power in three Persons, instead of one, we shall not only increase the Number of the Council of Revision (which I have endeavoured to show will want increasing), but by giving to each of the three a Vote in the Council of Revision, we shall increase the Strength of the Executive, in that particular Circumstance, in which it will most want Strength—in the Power of defending itself against the Encroachments of the Legislature.—These, I must acknowledge, are with me, weighty Considerations for vesting the Executive rather in three than in one Person.

The chief Advantages which have been urged in favour of Unity in the Executive, are the Secrecy, the Dispatch, the Vigour and Energy which the Government will derive from it; especially in time of war.—That these are great Advantages, I shall most readily allow—They have been strongly insisted on by all monarchical Writers—they have been acknowledged by the ablest and most candid Defenders of Republican Government; and it can not be denyed that a Monarchy possesses them in a much greater Degree than a Republic.—Yet perhaps a little Reflection may incline us to doubt whether these Advantages are not greater in Theory than in Practice—or lead us to enquire whether there is not some pervading Principle in Republican Governments which sets at Naught, and tramples upon this boasted Superiority—as hath been experienced, to their cost, by most Monarchys, which have been imprudent enough to invade or attack their republican Neighbors. This invincible Principle is to be found in the Love the Affection the Attachment of the Citizens to their Laws, to their Freedom, and to their Country—Every Husbandman will be quickly converted into a Soldier, when he knows and feels that he is to fight not in Defence of the Rights of a particular Family, or a Prince; but for his own. This is the true Construction of the pro Aris & focis which has, in all Ages, performed such Wonders—It was this which, in ancient times, enabled the little Cluster of Grecian Republics to resist, and almost constantly to defeat the Persian Monarch—It was this which supported the States of Holland against a Body of veteran Troops thro' a thirty Years War with Spain, then the greatest Monarchy in Europe, and finally rendered them victorious.—It is this which preserves the Freedom and Independence of the Swiss Cantons in the midst of the most powerful Nations—And who that reflects seriously upon the Situation of America, in the Beginning of the late War—without Arms—without Soldiers—without Trade, Money, or Credit—in a Manner destitute of all Resources, but must ascribe our Success to this pervading, all-powerful Principle?

We have not yet been able to define the Powers of the Executive; and however moderately some Gentlemen may talk or think upon the Subject, I believe there is a general Tendency to a strong Executive and I am inclined to think a strong Executive necessary—If strong and extensive Powers are vested in the Executive, and that Executive consists only of one Person; the Government will of course degenerate (for I will call it degeneracy) into a Monarchy—a Government so contrary to the Genius of the People that they will reject even the Appearance of it—I consider the federal Government as in some Measure dissolved by the Meeting of this Convention—Are there no Dangers to be apprehended from proscrastinating the time between the breaking up of this Assembly and the adoption of a new System of Government—I dread the

Interval—If it should not be brought to an Issue in the Course of the first Year the Consequences may be fatal—Has not the different Parts of this extensive Government, the several States of which it is composed a Right to expect an equal Participation in the Executive, as the best means of securing an equal Attention to their Interests? Should an Insurrection, a Rebellion or Invasion happen in New Hampshire when the single supreme Magistrate is a Citizen of Georgia, would not the People of New Hampshire naturally ascribe any Delay in defending them to such a Circumstance and so vice versa—If the Executive is vested in three Persons, one chosen from the northern, one from the middle, and one from the Southern States, will it not contribute to quiet the Minds of the People, and convince them that there will be proper attention paid to their respective Concerns? Will not three Men so chosen bring with them, into Office, a more perfect and extensive Knowledge of the real Interests of this great Union? Will not such a mode of Appointment be the most effectual means of preventing Cabals and Intrigues between the Legislature and the Candidates for this Office, especially with those Candidates who from their local Situation, near the Seat of the federal Government, will have the greatest Temptations and the greatest Opportunitys? Will it not be the most effectual means of checking and counteracting the aspiring Views of dangerous and ambitious Men, and consequently the best Security for the Stability and Duration of our Government upon the invaluable Principles of Liberty? These, Sir, are some of my motives for preferring an Executive consisting of three Persons rather than of one.

[*2:33; Madison, 17 July*]

"to be ineligible a second time"—Mr. Houston moved to strike out this clause.

Mr. Sherman 2ds. the motion.

Mr. Govr. Morris espoused the motion. The ineligibility proposed by the clause as it stood tended to destroy the great motive to good behavior, the hope of being rewarded by a re-appointment. It was saying to him, make hay while the sun shines.

On the question for striking out as moved by Mr. Houston, it passed in the affirmative.

Mas. ay. Cont. ay. N. J. ay. Pa. ay. Del. no. Md. ay. Va. no. N. C. no. S. C. no. Geo. ay. [Ayes—6; noes—4.]

"For the term of 7 years" resumed

Mr. Broom was for a shorter term since the Executive Magistrate was now to be re-eligible. Had he remained ineligible a 2d. time, he should have preferred a longer term.

Docr. McClurg moved to strike out 7 years, and insert "during good behavior". By striking out the words declaring him not re-eligible, he was put into a situation that would keep him dependent for ever on the Legislature; and he conceived the independence of the Executive to be equally essential with that of the Judiciary department.

Mr. Govr. Morris 2ded. the motion. He expressed great pleasure in hearing it. This was the way to get a good Government. His fear that so valuable an ingredient would not be attained had led him to take the part he had done. He was indifferent how the Executive should be chosen, provided he held his place by this tenure.

Mr. Broome highly approved the motion. It obviated all his difficulties.

Mr. Sherman considered such a tenure as by no means safe or admissible. As the Executive Magistrate is now re-eligible, he will be on good behavior as far as will be necessary. If he behaves well he will be continued; if otherwise, displaced on a succeeding election.

Mr. Madison. If it be essential to the preservation of liberty that the Legisl: Execut: & Judiciary powers be separate, it is essential to a maintenance of the separation, that they should be independent of each other. The Executive could not be independent of the Legislure, if dependent on the pleasure of that branch for a re-appointment. Why was it determined that the Judges should not hold their places by such a tenure? Because they might be tempted to cultivate the Legislature, by an undue complaisance, and thus render the Legislature the virtual expositor, as well the maker of the laws. In like manner a dependence of the Executive on the Legislature, would render it the Executor as well as the maker of laws; & then according to the observation of Montesquieu, tyrannical laws may be made that they may be executed in a tyrannical manner. There was an analogy between the Executive & Judiciary departments in several respects. The latter executed the laws in certain cases as the former did in others. The former expounded & applied them for certain purposes, as the latter did for others. The difference between them seemed to consist chiefly in two circumstances—1. the collective interest & security were much more in the power belonging to the Executive than to the Judiciary department. 2. in the administration of the former much greater latitude is left to opinion and discretion than in the administration of the latter. But if the 2d. consideration proves that it will be more difficult to establish a rule sufficiently precise for trying the Execut: than the Judges, & forms an objection to the same tenure of office, both considerations prove that it might be more dangerous to suffer a Union between the Executive & Legisl: powers, than between the Judiciary & Legislative powers. He conceived it to be absolutely necessary to a well constituted Republic that the two first shd. be kept distinct & independent of each other. Whether the plan proposed by the motion was a proper one was another question, as it depended on the practicability of instituting a tribunal for impeachmts. as certain & as adequate in the one case as in the other. On the other hand, respect for the mover entitled his proposition to a fair hearing & discussion, until a less objectionable expedient should be applied for guarding agst. a dangerous union of the Legislative & Executive departments.

Col. Mason. This motion was made some time ago, & negatived by a very large majority. He trusted that it wd. be again negatived. It wd. be impossible to define the misbehaviour in such a manner as to subject it to a proper trial; and perhaps still more impossible to compel so high an offender holding his office by such a tenure to submit to a trial. He considered an Executive during good behavior as a softer name only for an Executive for life. And that the next would be an easy step to hereditary Monarchy. If the motion should finally succeed, he might himself live to see such a Revolution. If he did not it was probable his children or grandchildren would. He trusted there were few men in that House who wished for it. No state he was sure had so far revolted from Republican principles as to have the least bias in its favor.

Mr. Madison, was not apprehensive of being thought to favor any step towards monarchy. The real object with him was to prevent its introduction. Experience had proved a tendency in our governments to throw all power into the Legislative vortex. The Executives of the States are in general little more than Cyphers; the legislatures omnipotent. If no effectual check be devised for restraining the instability & encroachments of the latter, a revolution of some kind or other would be inevitable. The preservation of Republican Govt. therefore required some expedient for the purpose, but required evidently at the same time that in devising it, the genuine principles of that form should be kept in view.

Mr. Govr. Morris was as little a friend to monarchy as any gentleman. He concurred in the opinion that the way to keep out monarchial Govt. was to establish such a Repub. Govt. as wd. make the people happy and prevent a desire of change.

Docr. McClurg was not so much afraid of the shadow of monarchy as to be unwilling to approach it; nor so wedded to Republican Govt. as not to be sensible of the tyrannies that had been & may be exercised under that form. It was an essential object with him to make the Executive independent of the Legislature; and the only mode left for effecting it, after the vote destroying his ineligibility a second time, was to appoint him during good behavior.

On the question for inserting "during good behavior" in place of 7 years (with a re-eligibility) it passed in the negative.

Mas. no. Ct. no. N. J. ay. Pa. ay. Del. ay. Md. no. Va. ay. N. C. no. S. C. no. Geo. no. [Ayes—4; noes—6.]

On the motion "to strike out seven years" it passed in the negative.

Mas. ay. Ct. no. N. J. no. Pa. ay. Del. ay. Md. no. Va. no. N. C. ay. S. C. no. Geo. no. [Ayes—4; noes—6.]

It was now unanimously agreed that the vote which had struck out the words "to be ineligible a second time" should be reconsidered tomorrow.

[*2:52; Madison, 19 July*]

Mr. Martin moved to reinstate the words "to be ineligible a 2d. time".

Mr. Governeur Morris. It is necessary to take into one view all that relates to the establishment of the Executive; on the due formation of which must depend the efficacy & utility of the Union among the present and future States. It has been a maxim in political Science that Republican Government is not adapted to a large extent of Country, because the energy of the Executive Magistracy can not reach the extreme parts of it. Our Country is an extensive one. We must either then renounce the blessings of the Union, or provide an Executive with sufficient vigor to pervade every part of it. This subject was of so much importance that he hoped to be indulged in an extensive view of it. One great object of the Executive is to controul the Legislature. The Legislature will continually seek to aggrandize & perpetuate themselves; and will seize those critical moments produced by war, invasion or convulsion for that purpose. It is necessary then that the Executive Magistrate should be the guardian of the people, even of the lower classes, agst. Legislative tyranny, against the Great & the wealthy who in the course of things will necessarily compose—the Legislative body. Wealth tends to corrupt the mind & to nourish its love of power, and to stimulate it to oppression. History proves this to be the spirit of the opulent. The check provided in the 2d. branch was not meant as a check on Legislative usurpations of power, but on the abuse of lawful powers, on the propensity in the 1st. branch to legislate too much to run into projects of paper money & similar expedients. It is no check on Legislative tyranny. On the contrary it may favor it, and if the 1st. branch can be seduced may find the means of success. The Executive therefore ought to be so constituted as to be the great protector of the Mass of the people.—It is the duty of the Executive to appoint the officers & to command the forces of the Republic: to appoint 1. ministerial officers for the administration of public affairs. 2. Officers for the dispensation of Justice—Who will be the best Judges whether these appointments be well made? The people at large, who will know, will see, will feel the effects of them—Again who can judge so well of the discharge of military duties for the protection & security of the people, as the people themselves who are to be protected & secured? He finds too that the Executive is not to be re-eligible. What effect will this have? 1. it will destroy the great incitement to merit public esteem by taking away the hope of being rewarded with a reappointment. It may give a dangerous turn to one of the strongest passions in the human breast. The love of fame is the great spring to noble & illustrious actions. Shut the Civil road to Glory & he may be compelled to seek it by the sword. 2. It will tempt him to make the most of the Short space of time allotted him, to accumulate wealth and provide for his friends. 3. It will produce violations of the very constitution it is meant to secure. In moments of pressing danger the tried abilities and established character of a favorite Magistrate will prevail over respect for the forms of the Constitution. The Executive is also to be impeachable. This is a dangerous part of the plan. It will hold him in such dependence that he will be no check on the Legislature, will not be a firm guardian of the people and of the public interest. He will be the tool of a faction, of some leading demagogue in the Legislature. These then are the faults of the Executive establishment as now proposed. Can no better establishmt. be devised? If he is to be the Guardian of the people let him be appointed by the people? If he is to be a check on the Legislature let him not be impeachable. Let him be of short duration, that he may with propriety be re-eligible.—It has been said that the candidates for this office will not be known to the people. If they be known to the Legislature, they must have such a notoriety and eminence of Character, that they cannot possibly be unknown to the people at large. It cannot be possible that a man shall have sufficiently distinguished himself to merit this high trust without having his character proclaimed by fame throughout the Empire. As to the danger from an unimpeachable magistrate he could not regard it as formidable. There must be certain great officers of State; a minister of finance, of war, of foreign affairs &c. These he presumes will exercise their functions in subordination to the Executive, and will be amenable by impeachment to the public Justice. Without these ministers the Executive can do nothing of consequence. He suggested a biennial election of the Executive at the time of electing the 1st. branch, and the Executive to hold over, so as to prevent any interregnum in the Administration. An election by the people at large throughout so great an extent of country could not be influenced, by those little combinations and those momentary lies which often decide popular elections within a narrow sphere. It will probably, be objected that the election will be influenced by the members of the Legislature; particularly of the the 1st. branch, and that it will be nearly the same thing with an election by the Legislature itself. It could not be denied that such an influence would exist. But it might be answered that as the Legislature or the candidates for it would be divided, the enmity of one part would counteract the friendship of another; that if the administration of the Executive were good, it would be unpopular to oppose his re-election, if bad it ought to be opposed & a reappointmt. prevented; and lastly that in every view this indirect dependence on the favor of the Legislature could not be so mischievous as a direct dependence for his appointment. He saw no alternative for making the Executive independent of the Legislature but either to give him his office for life, or make him eligible by the people.—Again, it might be objected that two years would be too short a duration. But he believes that as long as he should behave himself well, he would be continued in his place. The extent of the Country would secure his re-election agst the factions & discontents of particular States. It deserved consideration also that such an ingredient in the plan would render it extremely palatable to the people. These were the general ideas which occurred to him on the subject, and which led him to wish & move that the whole constitution of the Executive might undergo reconsideration.

Mr. Randolph urged the motion of Mr. L. Martin for restoring the words making the Executive ineligible a 2d. time. If he ought to be independent, he should not be left under a temptation to court a re-appointment. If he should be re-appointable by the Legislature, he will be no check on it. His revisionary power will be of no avail. He had always thought & contended as he still did that the danger apprehended by the little States was chimerical, but those who thought otherwise ought to be peculiarly anxious for the motion. If the Executive be appointed, as has been determined, by the Legislature, he will probably be appointed either by joint ballot of both houses, or be nominated by the 1st. and appointed by the 2d. branch. In either case the large States will preponderate. If he is to court the same influence for his re-appointment, will he not make his revisionary power. and all the other functions of his administration subservient to the views of the large States. Besides—is there not great reason to apprehend that in case he should be re-eligible, a false complaisance in the Legislature might lead them to continue an unfit man in office in preference to a fit one. It has been said that a constitutional bar to reappointment will inspire unconstitutional endeavours to perpetuate himself. It may be answered that his endeavours can have no effect unless the people be corrupt to such a degree as to render all precautions hopeless: to which may be added that this argument supposes him to be more powerful & dangerous, than other arguments which have been used, admit, and consequently calls for stronger fetters on his authority. He thought an election by the Legislature with an incapacity to be elected a second time would be more acceptable to the people tha[n] the plan suggested by Mr. Govr. Morris.

Mr. King. did not like the ineligibility. He thought there was great force in the remark of Mr. Sherman, that he who has proved himself to be most fit for an Office, ought not to be excluded by the constitution from holding it. He would therefore prefer any other reasonable plan that could be substituted. He was much disposed to think that in such cases the people at large would chuse wisely. There was indeed some difficulty arising from the improbability of a general concurrence of the people in favor of any one man. On the whole he was of opinion that an appointment by electors chosen by the people for the purpose, would be liable to fewest objections.

Mr. Patterson's ideas nearly coincided he said with those of Mr. King. He proposed that the Executive should be appointed by Electors to be chosen by the States in a ratio that would allow one elector to the smallest and three to the largest States.

Mr. Wilson. It seems to be the unanimous sense that the Executive should not be appointed by the Legislature, unless he be rendered in-eligible a 2d. time: he preceived with pleasure that the idea was gaining ground, of an election mediately or immediately by the people.

Mr. Madison If it be a fundamental principle of free Govt. that the Legislative, Executive & Judiciary powers should be *separately* exercised; it is equally so that they be *independently* exercised. There is the same & perhaps greater reason why the Executive shd. be independent of the Legislature, than why the Judiciary should: A coalition of the two former powers would be more immediately & certainly dangerous to public liberty. It is essential then that the appointment of the Executive should either be drawn from some source, or held by some tenure, that will give him a free agency with regard to the Legislature. This could not be if he was to be appointable from time to time by the Legislature. It was not clear that an appointment in the 1st. instance even with an ineligibility afterwards would not establish an improper connection between the two departments. Certain it was that the appointment would be attended with intrigues and contentions that ought not to be unnecessarily admitted. He was disposed for these reasons to refer the appointment to some other Source. The people at large was in his opinion the fittest in itself. It would be as likely as any that could be devised to produce an Executive Magistrate of distinguished Character. The people generally could only know & vote for some Citizen whose merits had rendered him an object of general attention & esteem. There was one difficulty however of a serious nature attending an immediate choice by the people. The right of suffrage was much more diffusive in the Northern than the Southern States; and the latter could have no influence in the election on the score of the Negroes. The substitution of electors obviated this difficulty and seemed on the whole to be liable to the fewest objections.

Mr. Gerry. If the Executive is to be elected by the Legislature he certainly ought not to be re-eligible. This would make him absolutely dependent. He was agst. a popular election. The people are uninformed, and would be misled by a few designing men. He urged the expediency of an appointment of the Executive by Electors to be chosen by the State Executives. The people of the States will then choose the 1st. branch: The legislatures of the States the 2nd. branch of the National Legislature, and the Executives of the States, the National Executive—This he thought would form a strong attachnt. in the States to the National System. The popular mode of electing the chief magistrate would certainly be the worst of all. If he should be so elected & should do his duty, he will be turned out for it like Govr Bowdoin in Masssts & President Sullivan in N. Hamshire.

[*2:102; Madison, 24 July*]

Mr. Gerry. That the Executive shd. be independent of the Legislature is a clear point. The longer the duration of his appointment the more will his dependence be diminished—It will be better then for him to continue 10, 15, or even 20—years and be ineligible afterwards.

Mr. King was for making him re-eligible. This is too great an advantage to be given up for the small effect it will have on his dependence, if impeachments are to lie. He considered these as rendering the tenure during pleasure.

Mr. L. Martin, suspending his motion as to the ineligibility, moved "that the appointment. of the Executive shall continue for Eleven years.

Mr. Gerry suggested fifteen years.

Mr. King twenty years. This is the medium life of princes.

Mr. Davie Eight years

Mr. Wilson. The difficulties & perplexities into which the House is thrown proceed from the election by the Legislature which he was sorry had been reinstated. The inconveniency of this mode was such that he would agree to almost any length of time in order to get rid of the dependence which must result from it. He was persuaded that the longest term would not be equivalent to a proper mode of election, unless indeed it should be during good behaviour. It seemed to be supposed that at a certain advance of life, a continuance in office would cease to be agreeable to the officer, as well as desirable to the public. Experience had shewn in a variety of instances that both a capacity & inclination for public service existed—in very advanced stages. He mentioned the instance of a Doge of Venice who was elected after he was 80 years of age. The popes have generally been elected at very advanced periods, and yet in no case has a more steady or a better concerted policy been pursued than in the Court of Rome. If the Executive should come into office at 35. years of age, which he presumes may happen & his continuance should be fixt at 15 years. at the age of 50. in the very prime of life, and with all the aid of experience, he must be cast aside like a useless hulk. What an irreparable loss would the British Jurisprudence have sustained, had the age of 50. been fixt there as the ultimate limit of capacity or readiness to serve the public. The great luminary (Ld. Mansfield) held his seat for thirty years after his arrival at that age. Notwithstanding what had been done he could not but hope that a better mode of election would yet be adopted; and one that would be more agreeable to the general sense of the House. That time might be given for further deliberation he wd. move that the present question be postponed till tomorrow.

Mr. Broom seconded the motion to postpone.

Mr. Gerry. We seem to be entirely at a loss on this head. He would suggest whether it would not be advisable to refer the clause relating to the Executive to the Committee of detail to be appointed. Perhaps they will be able to hit on something that may unite the various opinions which have been thrown out.

Mr. Wilson. As the great difficulty seems to spring from the mode of election, he wd. suggest a mode which had not been mentioned. It was that the Executive be elected for 6 years by a small number, not more than 15 of the Natl Legislature, to be drawn from it, not by ballot, but by lot and who should retire immediately and make the election without separating. By this mode intrigue would be avoided in the first instance, and the dependence would be diminished. This was not he said a digested idea and might be liable to strong objections.

Mr. Govr. Morris. Of all possible modes of appointment that by the Legislature is the worst. If the Legislature is to appoint, and to impeach or to influence the impeachment, the Executive will be the mere creature of it. He has been opposed to the impeachment, but was now convinced that impeachments must be provided for, if the appt. was to be of any duration. No man wd. say, that an Executive known to be in the pay of an Enemy, should not be removable in some way or other. He had been charged heretofore (by Col. Mason) with inconsistency in pleading for confidence in the Legislature on some occasions, & urging a distrust on others. The charge was not well founded. The Legislature is worthy of unbounded confidence in some respects, and liable to equal distrust in others. When their interest coincides precisely with that of their Constituents, as happens in many of their Acts, no abuse of trust is to be apprehended. When a strong personal interest happens to be opposed to the general interest, the Legislature can not be too much distrusted. In all public bodies there are two parties. The Executive will necessarily be more connected with one than with the other. There will be a personal interest therefore in one of the parties to oppose as well as in the other to support him. Much had been said of the intrigues that will be practiced by the Executive to get into office. Nothing had been said on the other side of the intrigues to get him out of office. Some leader of party will always covet his seat, will perplex his administration, will cabal with the Legislature, till he succeeds in supplanting him. This was the way in which the King of England was got out, he meant the real King, the Minister. This was the way in which Pitt (Ld. Chatham) forced himself into place. Fox was for pushing the matter still farther. If he had carried his India bill, which he was very near doing, he would have made the Minister, the King in form almost as well as in substance. Our President will be the British Minister, yet we are about to make him appointable by the Legislature. Something had been said of the danger of Monarchy—If a good government should not now be formed, if a good organization of the Execuve should not be provided, he doubted whether we should not have something worse than a limited Monarchy. In order to get rid of the dependence of the Executive on the Legislature, the expedient of making him ineligible a 2d. time had been devised. This was as much as to say we shd. give him the benefit of experience, and then deprive ourselves of the use of it. But make him ineligible a 2d. time-and prolong his duration even to 15-years, will he by any wonderful interposition of providence at that period cease to be a man? No he will be unwilling to quit his exaltation, the road to his object thro' the Constitution will be shut; he will be in possession of the sword, a civil war will ensue, and the Commander of the victorious army on which ever side, will be the despot of America. This consideration renders him particularly anxious that the Executive should be properly constituted. The vice here would not, as in some other parts of the system be curable- It is the most difficult of all rightly to balance the Executive. Make him too weak: The Legislature will usurp his powers: Make him too strong. He will usurp on the Legislature. He preferred a short period, a re-eligibility, but a different mode of election. A long period would prevent an adoption of the plan: it ought to do so. He shd. himself be afraid to trust it. He was not prepared to decide on Mr. Wilson's mode of election just hinted by him. He thought it deserved consideration. It would be better that chance sd. decide than intrigue.

On A question to postpone the consideration of the Resolution on the subject of the Executive

N. H. no. Mas. no. Ct. ay. N. J. no. Pa. ay. Del. divd. Md. ay. Va. ay. N. C. no. S. C. no. Geo. no. [Ayes—4; noes—6; divided—1.]

Mr. Wilson then moved "that the Executive be chosen every years by Electors to be taken by lot from the Natl Legislature who shall proceed immediately to the choice of the Executive and not separate until it be made"

Mr. Carrol 2ds. the motion

Mr. Gerry. this is committing too much to chance. If the lot should fall on a sett of unworthy men, an unworthy Executive must be saddled on the Country. He thought it had been demonstrated that no possible mode of electing by the Legislature could be a good one.

Mr. King—The lot might fall on majority from the same State which wd. ensure the election of a man from that State. We ought to be governed by reason, not by chance. As no body seemed to be satisfied, he wished the matter to be postponed

Mr. Wilson did not move this as the best mode. His opinion remained unshaken that we ought to resort to the people for the election. He seconded the postponement.

Mr. Govr. Morris observed that the chances were almost infinite agst. a majority of electors from the same State.

On a question whether the last motion was in order, it was determined in the affirmative; 7. ays. 4 noes.

5

James Madison to Thomas Jefferson
24 Oct. 1787

Papers 10:208–9

(See vol. 1, ch. 17, no. 22)

6

Cato, no. 4
8 Nov. 1787

Storing 2.6.25–32

It is remarked by Montesquieu, in treating of republics, that *in all magistracies, the greatness of the power must be compensated by the brevity of the duration; and that a longer time than a year, would be dangerous.* It is therefore obvious to the least intelligent mind, to account why, great power in the hands of a magistrate, and that power connected, with a considerable duration, may be dangerous to the liberties of a republic—the deposit of vast trusts in the hands of a single magistrate, enables him in their exercise, to create a numerous train of dependants—this tempts his *ambition,* which in a republican magistrate is also remarked, *to be pernicious* and the duration of his office for any considerable time favours his views, gives him the means and time to perfect and execute his designs—*he therefore fancies that he may be great and glorious by oppressing his fellow citizens, and raising himself to permanent grandeur on the ruins of his country.*—And here it may be necessary to compare the vast and important powers of the president, together with his continuance in office with the foregoing doctrine—his eminent magisterial situation will attach many adherents to him, and he will be surrounded by expectants and courtiers—his power of nomination and influence on all appointments—the strong posts in each state comprised within his superintendance, and garrisoned by troops under his direction—his controul over the army, milita, and navy—the unrestrained power of granting pardons for treason, which may be used to screen from punishment, those whom he had secretly instigated to commit the crime, and thereby prevent a discovery of his own guilt—his duration in office for four years: these, and various other principles evidently prove the truth of the position—that if the president is possessed of ambition, he has power and time sufficient to ruin his country.

Though the president, during the sitting of the legislature, is assisted by the senate, yet he is without a constitutional council in their recess—he will therefore be unsupported by proper information and advice, and will generally be directed by minions and favorites, or a council of state will grow out of the principal officers of the great departments, the most dangerous council in a free country.

The ten miles square, which is to become the seat of government, will of course be the place of residence for the president and the great officers of state—the same observations of a great man will apply to the court of a president possessing the powers of a monarch, that is observed of that of a monarch—*ambition with idleness—baseness with pride—the thirst of riches without labour—aversion to truth—flattery—treason—perfidy—violation of engagements—contempt of civil duties—hope from the magistrate's weakness; but above all, the perpetual ridicule of virtue*—these, he remarks, are the characteristics by which the courts in all ages have been distinguished.

The language and the manners of this court will be what distinguishes them from the rest of the community, not what assimilates them to it, and in being remarked for a behaviour that shews they are not *meanly born,* and in adulation to people of fortune and power.

The establishment of a vice-president is as unnecessary as it is dangerous. This officer, for want of other employment, is made president of the senate, thereby blending the executive and legislative powers, besides always giving to some one state, from which he is to come, an unjust pre-eminence.

It is a maxim in republics, that the representative of the people should be of their immediate choice; but by the manner in which the president is chosen he arrives to this office at the fourth or fifth hand, nor does the highest vote, in the way he is elected, determine the choice—for it is only necessary that he should be taken from the highest of five, who may have a plurality of votes.

Compare your past opinions and sentiments with the present proposed establishment, and you will find, that if you adopt it, that it will lead you into a system which you heretofore reprobated as odious. Every American whig, not long since, bore his emphatic testimony against a monarchical government, though limited, because of the dangerous inequality that it created among citizens as relative to their rights and property; and wherein does this president, invested with his powers and prerogatives, essentially differ from the king of Great-Britain (save as to name, the creation of nobility and some immaterial incidents, the offspring of absurdity and locality)[. T]he direct prerogatives of the president, as springing from his political character, are among the following:—It is necessary, in order to distinguish him from the rest of the community, and enable him to keep, and maintain his court, that the compensation for his services; or in other words, his revenue should be such as to enable him to appear with the splendor of a prince; he has the power of receiving embassadors from, and a great influence on their appointments to foreign courts; as also to make treaties, leagues, and alliances with foreign states, assisted by the senate, which when made, become the supreme law of the land: he is a constituent part of the legislative power; for every bill which shall pass the house of representatives and senate, is to be presented to him for approbation; if he approves of it, he is to sign it, if he disapproves, he is to return it with objections, which in many cases will amount to a complete negative; and in this view he will have a great share in the power of making peace, coining money, etc. and all the various objects of legislation, expressed or implied in this Constitution: for though it may be asserted that the king of Great-Britain has the express power of making peace or war, yet he never thinks it prudent so to do without the advice of his parliament from whom he is to derive his support, and therefore these powers, in both president and king, are substantially the same: he is the generalissimo of the nation, and of course, has the command and controul of the army, navy and militia; he is the general conservator of the peace of the union—he may pardon all offences, except in cases of impeachment, and the principal fountain of all offices and employments. Will not the exercise of these powers therefore tend either to the establishment of a vile and arbitrary aristocracy, or monarchy? The safety of the people in a republic depends on the share or proportion they have in the government; but experience ought to teach you, that when a man is at the head of an elective government invested with great powers, and interested in his re-election, in what circle appointments will be made; by which means *an imperfect aristocracy* bordering on monarchy may be established.

You must, however, my countrymen, beware, that the advocates of this new system do not deceive you, by a fallacious resemblance between it and your own state government, which you so much prize; and if you examine, you will perceive that the chief magistrate of this state, is your immediate choice, controuled and checked by a just and full representation of the people, divested of the prerogative of influencing war and peace, making treaties, receiving and sending embassies, and commanding standing armies and navies, which belong to the power of the confederation, and will be convinced that this government is no more like a true picture of your own, than an Angel of darkness resembles an Angel of light.

7

AN OLD WHIG, NO. 5
Fall 1787

Storing 3.3.31

If we pass over the consideration of this subject so essential to the preservation of our liberties, and turn our eyes to the *form* of the government which the Convention have proposed to us, I apprehend that changing the prospect will not wholly alleviate our fears.—A few words on this head, will close the present letter. In the first place the office of President of the United States appears to me to be clothed with such powers as are dangerous. To be the fountain of all honors in the United States, commander in chief of the army, navy and milita, with the power of making treaties and of granting pardons, and to be vested with an authority to put a negative upon all laws, unless two thirds of both houses shall persist in enacting it, and put their names down upon calling the yeas and nays for that purpose, is in reality to be a KING as much *a King as the King of Great-Britain,* and a King too of the worst Kind;—an elective King.—If such powers as these are to be trusted in the hands of any man, they ought for the sake of preserving the peace of the community at once to be made hereditary.—Much as I abhor kingly government, yet I venture to pronounce where kings are admitted to rule they should most certainly be vested with hereditary power. The election of a King whether it be in America or Poland, will be a scene of horror and confusion; and I am perfectly serious when I declare that, as a friend to my country, I shall despair of any happiness in the United States until his office is either reduced to a lower pitch of power or made perpetual and hereditary.—When I say that our future President will be as much a king as the king of Great-Britain, I only ask of my readers to look into the constitution of that country, and then tell me what important prerogative the King of Great-Britain is entitled to, which does not also belong to the President during his continuance in office.—The King of Great-Britain it is true can create nobility which our President cannot; but our President will have the power of making all the *great men,* which comes to the same thing.—All the difference is that we shall be embroiled in contention about the choice of the man, whilst they are at peace under the security of an hereditary succession.—To be tumbled headlong from the pinnacle of greatness and be reduced to a shadow of departed royalty is a shock almost too great for human nature to endure. It will cost a man many struggles to resign such eminent powers, and ere long, we shall find, some one who will be very unwilling to part with them.—Let us suppose this man to be a favorite with his army, and that they are unwilling to part with their beloved commander in chief; or to make the thing familiar, let us suppose, a future President and commander in chief adored by his army and the militia to as great a degree as our late illustrious commander in chief; and we have only to suppose one thing more, that this man is without the virtue, the moderation and love of liberty which possessed the mind of our late general, and this country will be involved at once in war and tyranny. So far it is from its being improbable that the man who shall hereafter be in a situation to make the attempt to perpetuate his own power, should want the virtues of General Washington; that it is perhaps a chance of one hundred millions to one that the next age will not furnish an example of so disinterested a use of great power. We may also suppose, without trespassing upon the bounds of probability, that this man may not have the means of supporting in private life the dignity of his former station; that like Caesar, he may be at once ambitious and poor, and deeply involved in debt.—Such a man would die a thousand deaths rather than sink from the heights of splendor and power into obscurity and wretchedness. We are certainly about giving our president too much or too little; and in the course of less than twenty years we shall find that we have given him enough to enable him to take all. It would be infinitely more prudent to give him at once as much as would content him, so that we might be able to retain the rest in peace; for if once power is seized by violence not the least fragment of liberty will survive the shock. I would therefore advise my countrymen seriously to ask themselves this question;—Whether they are prepared TO RECEIVE A KING? If they are[,] to say so at once, and make the kingly office hereditary; to frame a constitution that should set bounds to his power, and, as far as possible secure the liberty of the subject. If we are not prepared to *receive a king,* let us call another convention to revise the proposed constitution, and form it anew on the principles of confederacy of free republics; but by no means, under pretence of a republic, to lay the foundation for a military government, which is the worst of all tyrannies.

8

JAMES WILSON, PENNSYLVANIA RATIFYING CONVENTION
4 Dec. 1787
Elliot 2:480

The next good quality that I remark is, that the *executive authority is one.* By this means we obtain very important advantages. We may discover from history, from reason, and from experience, the security which this furnishes. The executive power is better to be trusted when it has no screen. Sir, we have a responsibility in the person of our President; he cannot act improperly, and hide either his negligence or inattention; he cannot roll upon any other person the weight of his criminality; no appointment can take place without his nomination; and he is responsible for every nomination he makes. We secure *vigor.* We well know what numerous executives are. We know there is neither vigor, decision, nor responsibility, in them. Add to all this, that officer is placed high, and is possessed of power far from being contemptible; yet not a *single privilege* is annexed to his character; far from being above the laws, he is amenable to them in his private character as a citizen, and in his public character by *impeachment.*

9

James Iredell, Marcus, Answers to Mr. Mason's Objections to the New Constitution 1788

Pamphlets 344–50

V. *Objection.*

"The President of the United States has no constitutional Council (a thing unknown in any safe and regular government), he will therefore be unsupported by proper information and advice, and will generally be directed by minions and favorites—or he will become a tool to the Senate—or a Council of State will grow out of the principal officers of the great departments; the worst and most dangerous of all ingredients for such a Council in a free country, for they may be induced to join in any dangerous or oppressive measures, to shelter themselves, and prevent an inquiry into their own misconduct in office: Whereas, had a constitutional Council been formed (as was proposed) of six members, viz., two from the eastern, two from the middle, and two from the southern States, to be appointed by a vote of the States in the House of Representatives, with the same duration and rotation of office as the Senate, the Executive would always have had safe and proper information and advice: The President of such a Council might have acted as Vice-President of the United States, *pro tempore,* upon any vacancy or disability of the Chief Magistrate, and long-continued sessions of the Senate would in a great measure have been prevented. From this fatal defect of a constitutional Council has arisen the improper power of the Senate, in the appointment of public officers, and the alarming dependence and connection between that branch of the legislature and the Supreme Executive. Hence also sprung that unnecessary and dangerous officer, the Vice-President of the Senate; thereby dangerously blending the Executive and Legislative powers; besides always giving to some one of the States an unnecessary and unjust pre-eminence over the others."

Answer.

Mr. Mason here reprobates the omission of a particular Council for the President, as a thing contrary to the example of all safe and regular governments. Perhaps there are very few governments now in being deserving of that character, if under the idea of safety he means to include safety for a proper share of personal freedom, without which their safety and regularity in other respects would be of little consequence to a people so justly jealous of liberty as I hope the people in America ever will be. Since however Mr. Mason refers us to such authority, I think I cannot do better than to select for the subject of our inquiry in this particular, a government which must be universally acknowledged to be the most safe and regular of any considerable government now in being (though I hope America will soon be able to dispute that preeminence). Every body must know I speak of Great Britain, and in this I think I give Mr. Mason all possible advantage, since in my opinion it is most probable he had Great Britain principally in his eye when he made this remark, and in the very height of our quarrel with that country, so wedded were our ideas to the institution of a Council, that the practice was generally if not universally followed at the formation of our governments, though we instituted Councils of a quite different nature, and so far as the little experience of the writer goes, have very little benefited by it. My inquiry into this subject shall not be confined to the actual present practice of Great Britain; I shall take the liberty to state the Constitutional ideas of Councils in England, as derived from their ancient law subsisting long before the Union, not omitting however to show what the present practice really is. By the laws of England the King is said to have four Councils,—1, The High Court of Parliament; 2, The Peers of the realm; 3, His Judges; 4, His Privy Council. By the first, I presume is meant, in regard to the making of laws; because the usual introductory expressions in most acts of Parliament, viz., "By the King's most excellent Majesty, by and with the advice and consent of the Lords spiritual and temporal, and Commons," &c., show that in a constitutional sense, they are deemed the King's laws, after a ratification in Parliament. The Peers of the realm are by their birth hereditary Counsellors of the Crown, and may be called upon for their advice, either in time of Parliament, or when no Parliament is in being: They are called in some law books *Magnum Concilium Regis* (the King's Great Council). It is also considered the privilege of every particular Peer to demand an audience of the King, and to lay before him anything he may deem of public importance. The Judges, I presume, are called "Council of the King," upon the same principle as the Parliament is, because the administration of justice is in his name, and the Judges are considered as his instruments in the distribution of it. We come now to the Privy Council, which I imagine, if Mr. Mason had any particular view towards England when he made this objection, was the one he intended as an example of a *Constitutional Council* in that kingdom. The Privy Council in that country is undoubtedly of very ancient institution, but it has one fixed property invariably annexed to it, that it is a mere creature of the Crown, dependent on its will both for number and duration, since the King may, whenever he thinks proper, discharge any member, or the whole of it and appoint another. If this precedent is of moment to us, merely as a precedent, it should be followed in all its parts, and then what would there be in the regulation to prevent the President being governed by "minions and favorites?" It would only be the means of riveting them on constitutional ground. So far as the precedents in England apply, the Peers being constitutionally the *Great Council* of the King, though also a part of the legislature, we have reason to hope that there is by no means such a gross impropriety as has been suggested in giving the Senate, though a branch of the legislature, a strong control over the Executive. The only difference in the two cases is, that the Crown in England may or may not give this consequence to the

Peers at its own pleasure, and accordingly we find that for a long time past this great Council has been very seldom consulted; under our constitution the President is allowed no option in respect to certain points wherein he cannot act without the Senate's concurrence. But we cannot infer from any example in England, that a concurrence between the Executive and a part of the legislative is contrary to the maxims of their government, since their government allows of such a concurrence whenever the Executive pleases. The rule, therefore, from the example of the freest government in Europe, that the Legislative and Executive powers must be altogether distinct, is liable to exceptions; it does not mean that the Executive shall not form a part of the Legislative (for the King, who has the whole Executive authority, is one entire branch of the legislature, and this Montesquieu, who recognizes the general principle, declares is necessary); neither can it mean (as the example above evinces) that the Crown must consult neither House as to any exercise of the Executive power. But its meaning must be, that one power shall not include *both authorities*. The King, for instance, shall not have the sole Executive and sole Legislative authority also. He may have the former, but must participate the latter with the two Houses of Parliament. The rule also would be infringed were the three branches of the legislature to share jointly the Executive power. But so long as the people's representatives are altogether distinct from the Executive authority, the liberties of the people may be deemed secure. And in this point surely, there can be no manner of comparison between the provisions by which the independence of our House of Representatives is guarded, and the condition in which the British House of Commons is left exposed to every species of corruption. But Mr. Mason says, for want of a Council, the President may become "a tool of the Senate." Why? Because he cannot act without their concurrence. Would not the same reason hold for his being "a tool to the Council," if he could not act without their concurrence, supposing a Council was to be imposed upon him without his own nomination (according to Mr. Mason's plan)? As great care is taken to make him independent of the Senate as I believe human precaution can provide. Whether the President will be a tool to any persons will depend upon the man, and the same weakness of mind which would make him pliable to one body of control, would certainly attend him with another. But Mr. Mason objects, if he is not directed by minions and favorites, nor becomes a tool of the Senate, "a Council of State will grow out of the principal officers of the great departments; the worst and most dangerous of all ingredients for such a Council in a free country; for they may be induced to join in any dangerous or oppressive measures, to shelter themselves, and prevent an inquiry into their own misconduct in office." I beg leave to carry him again to my old authority, England, and ask him, what efficient Council they have there but one formed of their great officers. Notwithstanding their important *Constitutional Council*, everybody knows that the whole movements of their Government, where a Council is consulted at all, are directed by their *Cabinet Council*, composed entirely of the principal officers of the great departments; that when a Privy Council is called, it is scarcely ever for any other purpose than to give a formal sanction to the previous determinations of the other, so much so that it is notorious that not one time in a thousand one member of the Privy Council, except a known adherent of administration, is summoned to it. But though the President under our constitution may have the aid of the "principal officers of the great departments," he is to have this aid, I think, in the most unexceptionable manner possible. He is not to be assisted by a Council summoned to a jovial dinner perhaps, and giving their opinions according to the nod of the President; but the opinion is to be given with the utmost solemnity *in writing*. No after equivocation can explain it away. It must for ever afterwards speak for itself, and commit the character of the writer, in lasting colors, either of fame or infamy, or neutral insignificance, to future ages, as well as the present. From those *written reasons*, weighed with care, surely the President can form as good a judgment, as if they had been given a dozen formal characters, carelessly met together on a slight appointment; and this further advantage would be derived from the proposed system (which would be wanting if he had constitutional advice to screen him), that the President must be *personally responsible* for everything—for though an ingenious gentleman has proposed, that a Council should be responsible for *their opinions*, and the same sentiment of justice might be applied to these opinions of the great officers, I am persuaded it will in general be thought infinitely more *safe*, as well as more *just*, that the President who *acts* should be responsible for his *conduct*, following advice at his peril, than that there should be a danger of punishing any man for an erroneous opinion which might possibly be sincere. Besides the morality of this scheme, which may well be questioned, its inexpediency is glaring, since it would be so plausible an excuse and the insincerity of it so difficult to detect, the hopes of impunity this avenue to escape would afford would nearly take away all dread of punishment. As to the temptation mentioned to the officers joining in dangerous or oppressive measures to shelter themselves, and prevent an inquiry into their own misconduct in office, this proceeds upon a supposition that the President and the great officers may form a very wicked combination to injure their country, a combination that in the first place it is utterly improbable, in a strong respectable government should be formed for that purpose, and in the next, with such a government as this constitution would give us, could have little chance of being successful, on account of the great superior strength and natural and jealous vigilance of one at least, if not both the weighty branches of legislation. This evil, however, of the possible depravity of *all public officers*, is one that can admit of no cure, since in every institution of government the same danger in some degree or other must be risked; it can only be guarded against by strong checks, and I believe it be difficult for the objectors to our new Constitution to provide stronger ones against any abuse of the Executive authority then will exist in that. As to the Vice President, it appears to me very proper he should be chosen much in the same manner as the President, in order that the States may be secure, upon any accidental loss by death or otherwise of the

President's service, of the services in the same important station of the man in whom they repose their second confidence. The complicated manner of election wisely prescribed would necessarily occasion a considerable delay in the choice of another, and in the mean time the President of the Council, though very fit for the purpose of advising, might be very ill qualified, especially in a critical period, for an active Executive department. I am concerned to see, among Mr. Mason's other reasons, so trivial a one as the little advantage one State might accidentally gain by a Vice President of their country having a seat, with merely a casting vote, in the Senate. Such a reason is utterly unworthy of that spirit of amity, and rejection of local views, which can alone save us from destruction. It was the glory of the late Convention, that by discarding such they formed a general government upon principles that did as much honor to their hearts as to their understandings. God grant, that in all our deliberations, we may consider America as *one* body, and not divert our attention from so able a prospect to small considerations of partial jealousy and distrust. It is in vain to expect upon any system to secure an exact equilibrium of power for all the States. Some will occasionally have an advantage from the superior abilities of its members; the field of emulation is however open to all. Suppose any one should now object to the superior influence of Virginia (and the writer of this is not a citizen of that State), on account of the high character of General Washington, confessedly the greatest man of the present age, and perhaps equal to any that has existed in any period of time; would this be a reason for refusing a union with her, though the other States can scarcely hope for the consolation of ever producing his equal?

10

Federal Farmer, no. 14
17 Jan. 1788
Storing 2.8.177–80

By art. 2. sect. 1. the executive power shall be vested in a president elected for four years, by electors to be appointed from time to time, in such manner as the state legislatures shall direct—the electors to be equal in numbers to the federal senators and representatives: but congress may determine the time of chusing senators, and the day on which they shall give their votes; and if no president be chosen by the electors, by a majority of votes, the states, as states in congress, shall elect one of the five highest on the list for president. It is to be observed, that in chusing the president, the principle of electing by a majority of votes is adopted; in chusing the vice-president, that of electing by a plurality. Viewing the principles and checks established in the election of the president, and especially considering the several states may guard the appointment of the electors as they shall judge best, I confess there appears to be a judicious combination of principles and precautions. Were the electors more numerous than they will be, in case the representation be not increased, I think, the system would be improved; not that I consider the democratic character so important in the choice of the electors as in the choice of representatives: be the electors more or less democratic, the president will be one of the very few of the most elevated characters. But there is danger, that a majority of a small number of electors may be corrupted and influenced, after appointed electors, and before they give their votes, especially if a considerable space of time elapse between the appointment and voting. I have already consdidered the advisory council in the executive branch: there are two things further in the organization of the executive, to which I would particularly draw your attention; the first, which, is a single executive, I confess, I approve; the second, by which any person from period to period may be re-elected president, I think very exceptionable.

Each state in the union has uniformly shewn its preference for a single executive, and generally directed the first executive magistrate to act in certain cases by the advice of an executive council. Reason, and the experience of enlightened nations, seem justly to assign the business of making laws to numerous assemblies; and the execution of them, principally, to the direction and care of one man. Independent of practice, a single man seems to be peculiarly well circumstanced to superintend the execution of laws with discernment and decision, with promptitude and uniformity: the people usually point out a first man—he is to be seen in civilized as well as uncivilized nations—in republics as well as in other governments. In every large collection of people there must be a visible point serving as a common centre in the government, towards which to draw their eyes and attachments. The constitution must fix a man, or a congress of men, superior in the opinion of the people to the most popular men in the different parts of the community, else the people will be apt to divide and follow their respective leaders. Aspiring men, armies and navies, have not often been kept in tolerable order by the decrees of a senate or an executive council. The advocates for lodging the executive power in the hands of a number of equals, as an executive council, say, that much wisdom may be collected in such a council, and that it will be safe; but they agree, that it cannot be so prompt and responsible as a single man—they admit that such a council will generally consist of the aristocracy, and not stand so indifferent between it and the people as a first magistrate. But the principal objection made to a single man is, that when possessed of power he will be constantly struggling for more, disturbing the government, and encroaching on the rights of others. It must be admitted, that men, from the monarch down to the porter, are constantly aiming at power and importance; and this propensity must be as constantly guarded against in the forms of the government. Adequate powers must be delegated to those who govern, and our security must be in limiting, defining, and guarding the exercise of them, so that those given shall not be abused, or made use of for openly or secretly seizing more. . . . Admitting that moderate and even well defined powers, long in the hands of the same man or family, will probably, be unreasonably increased, it will not follow that even extensive powers placed in the hands of a man only for a few years will be abused. . . . The great object is, in a republican government, to guard effectually against perpetuating any portion of power, great or small, in the same man or family; this perpetuation of power is totally uncongenial to the true spirit of republican governments: on the one hand the first executive magistrate ought to remain in office so long as to avoid instability in the execution of the laws; on the other, not so long as to enable him to take any measures to establish himself. The convention, it seems, first agreed that the president should be chosen for seven years, and never after to be eligible. Whether seven years is a period too long or not, is rather matter of opinion; but clear it is, that this mode is infinitely preferable to the one finally adopted. When a man shall get the chair, who may be re-elected, from time to time, for life, his greatest object will be to keep it; to gain friends and votes, at any rate; to associate some favourite son with himself, to take the office after him: whenever he shall have any prospect of continuing the office in himself and family, he will spare no artifice, no address, and no exertions, to increase the powers and importance of it; the servile supporters of his wishes will be placed in all offices, and tools constantly employed to aid his views and sound his praise. A man so situated will have no permanent interest in the government to lose, by contests and convulsions in the state, but always much to gain, and frequently the seducing and flattering hope of succeeding. If we reason at all on the subject, we must irresistably conclude, that this will be the case with nine-tenths of the presidents; we may have, for the first president, and, perhaps, one in a century or two afterwards (if the government should withstand the attacks of others) a great and good man, governed by superior motives; but these are not events to be calculated upon in the present state of human nature.

A man chosen to this important office for a limited period, and always afterwards rendered, by the constitution, ineligible, will be governed by very different considerations: he can have no rational hopes or expectations of retaining his office after the expiration of a known limited time, or of continuing the office in his family, as by the constitution there must be a constant transfer of it from one man to another, and consequently from one family to another. No man will wish to be a mere cypher at the head of the government: the great object of each president then will be, to render his government a glorious period in the annals of his country. When a man constitutionally retires from office, he retires without pain; he is sensible he retires because the laws direct it, and not from the success of his rivals nor with that public disapprobation which being left out, when eligible, implies. It is said, that a man knowing that at a given period he must quit his office, will unjustly attempt to take from the public, and lay in store the means of support and splendour in his retirement; there can, I think, be but very little in this observation. The same constitution that makes a man eligible for a given period only, ought to make no man eligible till he arrive to the age of forty or forty-five years: if he be a man of fortune, he will retire with dignity to his estate; if not, he may, like the Roman consuls, and other eminent characters in republics, find an honorable support and employment in some respectable office. A man who must, at all events, thus leave his office, will have but few or no temptations to fill its dependant offices with his tools, or any particular set of men; whereas the man constantly looking forward to his future elections, and, perhaps, to the aggrandizement of his family, will have every inducement before him to fill all places with his own props and dependants. As to public monies, the president need handle none of them, and he may always rigidly be made account for every shilling he shall receive.

On the whole, it would be, in my opinion, almost as well to create a limited monarchy at once, and give some family permanent power and interest in the community, and let it have something valuable to itself to lose in convulsions in the state, and in attempts of usurpation, as to make a first magistrate eligible for life, and to create hopes and expectations in him and his family, of obtaining what they have not. In the latter case, we actually tempt them to disturb the state, to foment struggles and contests, by laying before them the flattering prospect of gaining much in them without risking any thing.

11

Thomas Jefferson to Alexander Donald
7 Feb. 1788

Papers 12:571

There is another strong feature in the new constitution which I as strongly dislike. That is the perpetual re-eligibility of the President. Of this I expect no amendment at present because I do not see that any body has objected to it on your side the water. But it will be productive of cruel distress to our country even in your day and mine.

12

Alexander Hamilton, Federalist, no. 67, 452–53
11 Mar. 1788

The Constitution of the executive department of the proposed government claims next our attention.

There is hardly any part of the system which could have been attended with greater difficulty in the arrangement of it than this; and there is perhaps none, which has been inveighed against with less candor, or criticised with less judgment.

Here the writers against the Constitution seem to have

taken pains to signalize their talent of misrepresentation, calculating upon the aversion of the people to monarchy, they have endeavoured to inlist all their jealousies and apprehensions in opposition to the intended President of the United States; not merely as the embryo but as the full grown progeny of that detested parent. To establish the pretended affinity they have not scrupled to draw resources even from the regions of fiction. The authorities of a magistrate, in few instances greater, and in some instances less, than those of Governor of New-York, have been magnified into more than royal prerogatives. He has been decorated with attributes superior in dignity and splendor to those of a King of Great-Britain. He has been shown to us with the diadem sparkling on his brow, and the imperial purple flowing in his train. He has been seated on a throne surrounded with minions and mistresses; giving audience to the envoys of foreign potentates, in all the supercilious pomp of majesty. The images of Asiatic despotism and voluptuousness have scarcely been wanting to crown the exaggerated scene. We have been almost taught to tremble at the terrific visages of murdering janizaries; and to blush at the unveiled mysteries of a future seraglio.

Attempts so extravagant as these to disfigure, or it might rather be said, to metamorphose the object, render it necessary to take an accurate view of its real nature and form; in order as well to ascertain its true aspect and genuine appearance, as to unmask the disingenuity and expose the fallacy of the counterfeit resemblances which have been so insidiously as well as industriously propagated.

In the execution of this task there is no man, who would not find it an arduous effort, either to behold with moderation or to treat with seriousness the devices, not less weak than wicked, which have been contrived to pervert the public opinion in relation to the subject. They so far exceed the usual, though unjustifiable, licenses of party-artifice, that even in a disposition the most candid and tolerant they must force the sentiments which favor an indulgent construction of the conduct of political adversaries to give place to a voluntary and unreserved indignation. It is impossible not to bestow the imputation of deliberate imposture and deception upon the gross pretence of a similitude between a King of Great-Britain and a magistrate of the character marked out for that of the President of the United States. It is still more impossible to withhold that imputation from the rash and barefaced expedients which have been employed to give success to the attempted imposition.

13

Alexander Hamilton, Federalist, no. 70, 471–80
15 Mar. 1788

There is an idea, which is not without its advocates, that a vigorous executive is inconsistent with the genius of republican government. The enlightened well wishers to this species of government must at least hope that the supposition is destitute of foundation; since they can never admit its truth, without at the same time admitting the condemnation of their own principles. Energy in the executive is a leading character in the definition of good government. It is essential to the protection of the community against foreign attacks: It is not less essential to the steady administration of the laws, to the protection of property against those irregular and high handed combinations, which sometimes interrupt the ordinary course of justice, to the security of liberty against the enterprises and assaults of ambition, of faction and of anarchy. Every man the least conversant in Roman story knows how often that republic was obliged to take refuge in the absolute power of a single man, under the formidable title of dictator, as well against the intrigues of ambitious individuals, who aspired to the tyranny, and the seditions of whole classes of the community, whose conduct threatened the existence of all government, as against the invasions of external enemies, who menaced the conquest and destruction of Rome.

There can be no need however to multiply arguments or examples on this head. A feeble executive implies a feeble execution of the government. A feeble execution is but another phrase for a bad execution: And a government ill executed, whatever it may be in theory, must be in practice a bad government.

Taking it for granted, therefore that all men of sense will agree in the necessity of an energetic executive; it will only remain to inquire, what are the ingredients which constitute this energy—how far can they be combined with those other ingredients which constitute safety in the republican sense? And how far does this combination characterise the plan, which has been reported by the convention?

The ingredients, which constitute energy in the executive, are first unity, secondly duration, thirdly an adequate provision for its support, fourthly competent powers.

The circumstances which constitute safety in the republican sense are, 1st. a due dependence on the people, secondly a due responsibility.

Those politicians and statesmen, who have been the most celebrated for the soundness of their principles, and for the justness of their views, have declared in favor of a single executive and a numerous legislature. They have with great propriety considered energy as the most necessary qualification of the former, and have regarded this as most applicable to power in a single hand; while they have with equal propriety considered the latter as best adapted to deliberation and wisdom, and best calculated to conciliate the confidence of the people and to secure their privileges and interests.

That unity is conducive to energy will not be disputed. Decision, activity, secrecy, and dispatch will generally characterise the proceedings of one man, in a much more eminent degree, than the proceedings of any greater number; and in proportion as the number is increased, these qualities will be diminished.

This unity may be destroyed in two ways; either by vesting the power in two or more magistrates of equal dignity and authority; or by vesting it ostensibly in one man, subject in whole or in part to the controul and co-operation of others, in the capacity of counsellors to him. Of the first the two consuls of Rome may serve as an example; of the last we shall find examples in the constitutions of several of the states. New-York and New-Jersey, if I recollect right, are the only states, which have entrusted the executive authority wholly to single men. Both these methods of destroying the unity of the executive have their partisans; but the votaries of an executive council are the most numerous. They are both liable, if not to equal, to similar objections; and may in most lights be examined in conjunction.

The experience of other nations will afford little instruction on this head. As far however as it teaches any thing, it teaches us not to be inamoured of plurality in the executive. We have seen that the Achaeans on an experiment of two Praetors, were induced to abolish one. The Roman history records many instances of mischiefs to the republic from the dissentions between the consuls, and between the military tribunes, who were at times substituted to the consuls. But it gives us no specimens of any peculiar advantages derived to the state, from the circumstance of the plurality of those magistrates. That the dissentions between them were not more frequent, or more fatal, is matter of astonishment; until we advert to the singular position in which the republic was almost continually placed and to the prudent policy pointed out by the circumstances of the state, and pursued by the consuls, of making a division of the government between them. The Patricians engaged in a perpetual struggle with the Plebians for the preservation of their antient authorities and dignities; the consuls, who were generally chosen out of the former body, were commonly united by the personal interest they had in the defence of the privileges of their order. In addition to this motive of union, after the arms of the republic had considerably expanded the bounds of its empire, it became an established custom with the consuls to divide the administration between themselves by lot; one of them remaining at Rome to govern the city and its environs; the other taking the command in the more distant provinces. This expedient must no doubt have had great influence in preventing those collisions and rivalships, which might otherwise have embroiled the peace of the republic.

But quitting the dim light of historical research, and attaching ourselves purely to the dictates of reason and good sense, we shall discover much greater cause to reject than to approve the idea of plurality in the executive, under any modification whatever.

Wherever two or more persons are engaged in any common enterprize or pursuit, there is always danger of difference of opinion. If it be a public trust or office in which they are cloathed with equal dignity and authority, there is peculiar danger of personal emulation and even animosity. From either and especially from all these causes, the most bitter dissentions are apt to spring. Whenever these happen, they lessen the respectability, weaken the authority, and distract the plans and operations of those whom they divide. If they should unfortunately assail the supreme executive magistracy of a country, consisting of a plurality of persons, they might impede or frustrate the most important measures of the government, in the most critical emergencies of the state. And what is still worse, they might split the community into the most violent and irreconcilable factions, adhering differently to the different individuals who composed the magistracy.

Men often oppose a thing merely because they have had no agency in planning it, or because it may have been planned by those whom they dislike. But if they have been consulted and have happened to disapprove, opposition then becomes in their estimation an indispensable duty of self love. They seem to think themselves bound in honor, and by all the motives of personal infallibility to defeat the success of what has been resolved upon, contrary to their sentiments. Men of upright, benevolent tempers have too many opportunities of remarking with horror, to what desperate lengths this disposition is sometimes carried, and how often the great interests of society are sacrificed to the vanity, to the conceit and to the obstinacy of individuals, who have credit enough to make their passions and their caprices interesting to mankind. Perhaps the question now before the public may in its consequences afford melancholy proofs of the effects of this despicable frailty, or rather detestable vice in the human character.

Upon the principles of a free government, inconveniencies from the source just mentioned must necessarily be submitted to in the formation of the legislature; but it is unnecessary and therefore unwise to introduce them into the constitution of the executive. It is here too that they may be most pernicious. In the legislature, promptitude of decision is oftener an evil than a benefit. The differences of opinion, and the jarrings of parties in that department of the government, though they may sometimes obstruct salutary plans, yet often promote deliberation and circumspection; and serve to check excesses in the majority. When a resolution too is once taken, the opposition must be at an end. That resolution is a law, and resistance to it punishable. But no favourable circumstances palliate or atone for the disadvantages of dissention in the executive department. Here they are pure and unmixed. There is no point at which they cease to operate. They serve to embarrass and weaken the execution of the plan or measure, to which they relate, from the first step to the final conclusion of it. They constantly counteract those qualities in the executive, which are the most necessary ingredients in its composition, vigour and expedition, and this without any counterballancing good. In the conduct of war, in which the energy of the executive is the bulwark of the national security, every thing would be to be apprehended from its plurality.

It must be confessed that these observations apply with principal weight to the first case supposed, that is to a plurality of magistrates of equal dignity and authority; a scheme the advocates for which are not likely to form a numerous sect: But they apply, through not with equal, yet with considerable weight, to the project of a council, whose concurrence is made constitutionally necessary to the operations of the ostensible executive. An artful cabal in the council would be able to distract and to enervate the whole system of administration. If no such cabal should exist, the mere diversity of views and opinions would alone be sufficient to tincture the exercise of the executive authority with a spirit of habitual feebleness and dilatoriness.

But one of the weightiest objections to a plurality in the executive, and which lies as much against the last as the first plan, is that it tends to conceal faults, and destroy responsibility. Responsibility is of two kinds, to censure and to punishment. The first is the most important of the two; especially in an elective office. Man, in public trust, will much oftener act in such a manner as to render him unworthy of being any longer trusted, than in such a manner as to make him obnoxious to legal punishment. But the multiplication of the executive adds to the difficulty of detection in either case. It often becomes impossible, amidst mutual accusations, to determine on whom the blame or the punishment of a pernicious measure, or series of pernicious measures ought really to fall. It is shifted from one to another with so much dexterity, and under such plausible appearances, that the public opinion is left in suspense about the real author. The circumstances which may have led to any national miscarriage or misfortune are sometimes so complicated, that where there are a number of actors who may have had different degrees and kinds of agency, though we may clearly see upon the whole that there has been mismanagement, yet it may be impracticable to pronounce to whose account the evil which may have been incurred is truly chargeable.

"I was overruled by my council. The council were so divided in their opinions, that it was impossible to obtain any better resolution on the point." These and similar pretexts are constantly at hand, whether true or false. And who is there that will either take the trouble or incur the odium of a strict scrutiny into the secret springs of the transaction? Should there be found a citizen zealous enough to undertake the unpromising task, if there happen to be a collusion between the parties concerned, how easy is it to cloath the circumstances with so much ambiguity, as to render it uncertain what was the precise conduct of any of those parties?

In the single instance in which the governor of this state is coupled with a council, that is in the appointment to offices, we have seen the mischiefs of it in the view now under consideration. Scandalous appointments to important offices have been made. Some cases indeed have been so flagrant, that ALL PARTIES have agreed in the impropriety of the thing. When enquiry has been made, the blame has been laid by the governor on the members of the council; who on their part have charged it upon his nomination: While the people remain altogether at a loss to determine by whose influence their interests have been committed to hands so unqualified, and so manifestly improper. In tenderness to individuals, I forbear to descend to particulars.

It is evident from these considerations, that the plurality of the executive tends to deprive the people of the two greatest securities they can have for the faithful exercise of any delegated power; first, the restraints of public opinion, which lose their efficacy as well on account of the division of the censure attendant on bad measures among a number, as on account of the uncertainty on whom it ought to fall; and secondly, the opportunity of discovering with facility and clearness the misconduct of the persons they trust, in order either to their removal from office, or to their actual punishment, in cases which admit of it.

In England the king is a perpetual magistrate; and it is a maxim, which has obtained for the sake of the public peace, that he is unaccountable for his administration, and his person sacred. Nothing therefore can be wiser in that kingdom than to annex to the king a constitutional council, who may be responsible to the nation for the advice they give. Without this there would be no responsibility whatever in the executive department; an idea inadmissible in a free government. But even there the king is not bound by the resolutions of his council, though they are answerable for the advice they give. He is the absolute master of his own conduct, in the exercise of his office; and may observe or disregard the council given to him at his sole discretion.

But in a republic, where every magistrate ought to be personally responsible for his behaviour in office, the reason which in the British constitution dictates the propriety of a council not only ceases to apply, but turns against the institution. In the monarchy of Great-Britain, it furnishes a substitute for the prohibited responsibility of the chief magistrate; which serves in some degree as a hostage to the national justice for his good behaviour. In the American republic it would serve to destroy, or would greatly diminish the intended and necessary responsibility of the chief magistrate himself.

The idea of a council to the executive, which has so generally obtained in the state constitutions, has been derived from that maxim of republican jealousy, which considers power as safer in the hands of a number of men than of a single man. If the maxim should be admitted to be applicable to the case, I should contend that the advantage on that side would not counterballance the numerous disadvantages on the opposite side. But I do not think the rule at all applicable to the executive power. I clearly concur in opinion in this particular with a writer [DeLolme] whom the celebrated Junius pronounces to be "deep, solid and ingenious," that, "the executive power is more easily confined when it is one": That it is far more safe there should be a single object for the jealousy and watchfulness of the people; and in a word that all multiplication of the executive is rather dangerous than friendly to liberty.

A little consideration will satisfy us, that the species of

security sought for in the multiplication of the executive is unattainable. Numbers must be so great as to render combination difficult; or they are rather a source of danger than of security. The united credit and influence of several individuals must be more formidable to liberty than the credit and influence of either of them separately. When power therefore is placed in the hands of so small a number of men, as to admit of their interests and views being easily combined in a common enterprise, by an artful leader, it becomes more liable to abuse and more dangerous when abused, than if it be lodged in the hands of one man; who from the very circumstance of his being alone will be more narrowly watched and more readily suspected, and who cannot unite so great a mass of influence as when he is associated with others. The Decemvirs of Rome, whose name denotes their number, were more to be dreaded in their usurpation than any ONE of them would have been. No person would think of proposing an executive much more numerous than that body, from six to a dozen have been suggested for the number of the council. The extreme of these numbers is not too great for an easy combination; and from such a combination America would have more to fear, than from the ambition of any single individual. A council to a magistrate, who is himself responsible for what he does, are generally nothing better than a clog upon his good intentions; are often the instruments and accomplices of his bad, and are almost always a cloak to his faults.

I forbear to dwell upon the subject of expence; though it be evident that if the council should be numerous enough to answer the principal end, aimed at by the institution, the salaries of the members, who must be drawn from their homes to reside at the seat of government, would form an item in the catalogue of public expenditures, too serious to be incurred for an object of equivocal utility.

I will only add, that prior to the appearance of the constitution, I rarely met with an intelligent man from any of the states, who did not admit as the result of experience, that the UNITY of the Executive of this state was one of the best of the distinguishing features of our [New York] constitution.

14

Alexander Hamilton, Federalist, no. 71, 481–85
18 Mar. 1788

Duration in office has been mentioned as the second requisite to the energy of the executive authority. This has relation to two objects: To the personal firmness of the Executive Magistrate in the employment of his constitutional powers; and to the stability of the system of administration which may have been adopted under his auspices. With regard to the first, it must be evident, that the longer the duration in office, the greater will be the probability of obtaining so important an advantage. It is a general principle of human nature, that a man will be interested in whatever he possesses, in proportion to the firmness or precariousness of the tenure, by which he holds it; will be less attached to what he holds by a momentary or uncertain title, than to what he enjoys by a durable or certain title; and of course will be willing to risk more for the sake of the one, than for the sake of the other. This remark is not less applicable to a political privilege, or honor, or trust, than to any article of ordinary property. The inference from it is, that a man acting in the capacity of Chief Magistrate, under a consciousness, that in a very short time he *must* lay down his office, will be apt to feel himself too little interested in it, to hazard any material censure or perplexity, from the independent exertion of his powers, or from encountering the ill-humors, however transient, which may happen to prevail either in a considerable part of the society itself, or even in a predominant faction in the legislative body. If the case should only be, that he *might* lay it down, unless continued by a new choice; and if he should be desirous of being continued, his wishes conspiring with his fears would tend still more powerfully to corrupt his integrity, or debase his fortitude. In either case feebleness and irresolution must be the characteristics of the station.

There are some, who would be inclined to regard the servile pliancy of the executive to a prevailing current, either in the community, or in the Legislature, as its best recommendation. But such men entertain very crude notions, as well of the purposes for which government was instituted, as of the true means by which the public happiness may be promoted. The republican principle demands, that the deliberate sense of the community should govern the conduct of those to whom they entrust the management of their affairs; but it does not require an unqualified complaisance to every sudden breese of passion, or to every transient impulse which the people may receive from the arts of men, who flatter their prejudices to betray their interests. It is a just observation, that the people commonly *intend* the PUBLIC GOOD. This often applies to their very errors. But their good sense would despise the adulator, who should pretend that they always *reason right* about the *means* of promoting it. They know from experience, that they sometimes err; and the wonder is, that they so seldom err as they do; beset as they continually are by the wiles of parasites and sycophants, by the snares of the ambitious, the avaricious, the desperate; by the artifices of men, who possess their confidence more than they deserve it, and of those who seek to possess, rather than to deserve it. When occasions present themselves in which the interests of the people are at variance with their inclinations, it is the duty of the persons whom they have appointed to be the guardians of those interests, to withstand the temporary delusion, in order to give them time and opportunity for more cool and sedate reflection. Instances might be cited, in which a conduct of this kind has saved the people from very fatal consequences of their own mistakes, and has procured lasting monuments of their gratitude to the men, who had courage and magnanimity enough to serve them at the peril of their displeasure.

But however inclined we might be to insist upon an unbounded complaisance in the executive to the inclinations of the people, we can with no propriety contend for a like complaisance to the humors of the Legislature. The latter may sometimes stand in opposition to the former; and at other times the people may be entirely neutral. In either supposition, it is certainly desirable that the executive should be in a situation to dare to act his own opinion with vigor and decision.

The same rule, which teaches the propriety of a partition between the various branches of power, teaches us likewise that this parition ought to be so contrived as to render the one independent of the other. To what purpose separate the executive, or judiciary, from the legislative, if both the executive and the judiciary are so constituted as to be at the absolute devotion of the legislative? Such a separation must be merely nominal and incapable of producing the ends for which it was established. It is one thing to be subordinate to the laws, and another to be dependent on the legislative body. The first comports with, the last violates, the fundamental principles of good government; and whatever may be the forms of the Constitution, unites all power in the same hands. The tendency of the legislative authority to absorb every other, has been fully displayed and illustrated by examples, in some preceding numbers. In governments purely republican, this tendency is almost irresistable. The representatives of the people, in a popular assembly, seem sometimes to fancy that they are the people themselves; and betray strong symptoms of impatience and disgust at the least sign of opposition from any other quarter; as if the exercise of its rights by either the executive or judiciary, were a breach of their privilege and an outrage to their dignity. They often appear disposed to exert an imperious controul over the other departments; and as they commonly have the people on their side, they always act with such momentum as to make it very difficult for the other members of the government to maintain the balance of the Constitution.

It may perhaps be asked how the shortness of the duration in office can affect the independence of the executive on the legislature, unless the one were possessed of the power of appointing or displacing the other? One answer to this enquiry may be drawn from the principle already remarked, that is from the slender interest a man is apt to take in a short lived advantage, and the little inducement it affords him to expose himself on account of it to any considerable inconvenience or hazard. Another answer, perhaps more obvious, though not more conclusive, will result from the consideration of the influence of the legislative body over the people, which might be employed to prevent the re-election of a man, who by an upright resistance to any sinister project of that body, should have made himself obnoxious to its resentment.

It may be asked also whether a duration of four years would answer the end proposed, and if it would not, whether a less period which would at least be recommended by greater security against ambitious designs, would not for that reason be preferable to a longer period, which was at the same time too short for the purpose of insiring the desired firmness and independence of the magistrate?

It cannot be affirmed, that a duration of four years or any other limited duration would completely answer the end proposed; but it would contribute towards it in a degree which would have a material influence upon the spirit and character of the government. Between the commencement and termination of such a period there would always be a considerable interval, in which the prospect of annihilation would be sufficiently remote not to have an improper effect upon the conduct of a man endued with a tolerable portion of fortitude; and in which he might reasonably promise himself, that there would be time enough, before it arrived, to make the community sensible of the propriety of the measures he might incline to pursue. Though it be probable, that as he approached the moment when the public were by a new election to signify their sense of his conduct, his confidence and with it, his firmness would decline; yet both the one and the other would derive support from the opportunities, which his previous continuance in the station had afforded him of establishing himself in the esteem and good will of his constituents. He might then hazard with safety, in proportion to the proofs he had given of his wisdom and integrity, and to the title he had acquired to the respect and attachment of his fellow citizens. As on the one hand, a duration of four years will contribute to the firmness of the executive in a sufficient degree to render it a very valuable ingredient in the composition; so on the other, it is not long enough to justify any alarm for the public liberty. If a British House of Commons, from the most feeble beginnings, *from the mere power of assenting or disagreeing to the imposition of a new tax,* have by rapid strides, reduced the prerogatives of the crown and the privileges of the nobility within the limits they conceive to be compatible with the principles of a free government; while they raised themselves to the rank and consequence of a coequal branch of the Legislature; if they have been able in one instance to abolish both the royalty and the aristocracy, and to overturn all the ancient establishments as well in the church as State; if they have been able on a recent occasion to make the monarch tremble at the prospect of an innovation attempted by them; what would be to be feared from an elective magistrate of four years duration, with the confined authorities of a President of the United States? What but that he might be unequal to the task which the Constitution assigns him? I shall only add that if his duration be such as to leave a doubt of his firmness, the doubt is inconsistent with a jealousy of his encroachments.

15

ALEXANDER HAMILTON, FEDERALIST, NO. 72, 468–92
19 Mar. 1788

The administration of government, in its largest sense, comprehends all the operations of the body politic, whether legislative, executive or judiciary, but in its most usual and perhaps in its most precise signification, it is limited to executive details, and falls peculiarly within the province of the executive department. The actual conduct of foreign negotiations, the preparatory plans of finance, the application and disbursement of the public monies, in conformity to the general appropriations of the legislature, the arrangement of the army and navy, the direction of the operations of war; these and other matters of a like nature constitute what seems to be most properly understood by the administration of government. The persons therefore, to whose immediate management these different matters are committed, ought to be considered as the assistants or deputies of the chief magistrate; and, on this account, they ought to derive their offices from his appointment, at least from his nomination, and ought to be subject to his superintendence. This view of the subject will at once suggest to us the intimate connection between the duration of the executive magistrate in office, and the stability of the system of administration. To reverse and undo what has been done by a predecessor is very often considered by a successor, as the best proof he can give of his own capacity and desert; and, in addition to this propensity, where the alteration has been the result of public choice, the person substituted is warranted in supposing, that the dismission of his predecessor has proceeded from a dislike to his measures, and that the less he resembles him the more he will recommend himself to the favor of his constituents. These considerations, and the influence of personal confidences and attachments, would be likely to induce every new president to promote a change of men to fill the subordinate stations; and these causes together could not fail to occasion a disgraceful and ruinous mutability in the administration of the government.

With a positive duration of considerable extent, I connect the circumstance of re-eligibility. The first is necessary to give to the officer himself the inclination and the resolution to act his part well, and to the community time and leisure to observe the tendency of his measures, and thence to form an experimental estimate of their merits. The last is necessary to enable the people, when they see reason to approve of his conduct, to continue him in the station, in order to prolong the utility of his talents and virtues, and to secure to the government, the advantage of permanency in a wise system of administration.

Nothing appears more plausible at first sight, nor more ill founded upon close inspection, than a scheme, which in relation to the present point has had some respectable advocates—I mean that of continuing the chief magistrate in office for a certain time, and then excluding him from it, either for a limited period, or for ever after. This exclusion whether temporary of perpetual would have nearly the same effects; and these effects would be for the most part rather pernicious than salutary.

One ill effect of the exclusion would be a diminution of the inducements to good behaviour. There are few men who would not feel much less zeal in the discharge of a duty, when they were conscious that the advantages of the station, with which it was connected, must be relinquished at a determinate period, then when they were permitted to entertain a hope of *obtaining* by *meriting* a continuance of them. This position will not be disputed, so long as it is admitted that the desire of reward is one of the strongest incentives of human conduct, or that the best security for the fidelity of mankind is to make their interest coincide with their duty. Even the love of fame, the ruling passion of the noblest minds, which would prompt a man to plan and undertake extensive and arduous enterprises for the public benefit, requiring considerable time to mature and perfect them, if he could flatter himself with the prospect of being allowed to finish what he had begun, would on the contrary deter him from the undertaking, when he foresaw that he must quit the scene, before he could accomplish the work, and must commit that, together with his own reputation, to hands which might be unequal or unfriendly to the task. The most to be expected from the generality of men, in such a situation, is the negative merit of not doing harm instead of the positive merit of doing good.

Another ill effect of the exclusion would be the temptation to sordid views, to peculation, and in some instances, to usurpation. An avaricious man, who might happen to fill the offices, looking forward to a time when he must at all events yield up the emoluments he enjoyed, would feel a propensity, not easy to be resisted by such a man, to make the best use of the opportunity he enjoyed, while it lasted; and might not scruple to have recourse to the most corrupt expedients to make the harvest as abundant as it was transitory; though the same man probably, with a different prospect before him, might content himself with the regular perquisites of his station, and might even be unwilling to risk the consequences of an abuse of his opportunities. His avarice might be a guard upon his avarice. Add to this, that the same man might be vain or ambitious as well as avaricious. And if he could expect to prolong his honors, by his good conduct, he might hesitate to sacrifice his appetite for them to his appetite for gain. But with the prospect before him of approaching and inevitable annihilation, his avarice would be likely to get the victory over his caution, his vanity or his ambition.

An ambitious man too, when he found himself seated on the summit of his country's honors, when he looked forward to the time at which he must descend from the exalted eminence forever; and reflected that no exertion of merit on his part could save him from the unwelcome reverse: Such a man, in such a situation, would be much more violently tempted to embrace a favorable conjuncture for attempting the prolongation of his power, at every personal hazard, than if he had the probability of answering the same end by doing his duty.

Would it promote the peace of the community, or that stability of the government, to have half a dozen men who had had credit enough to be raised to the seat of the supreme magistracy, wandering among the people like discontented ghosts, and sighing for a place which they were destined never more to possess?

A third ill effect of the exclusion would be the depriving the community of the advantage of the experience gained by the chief magistrate in the exercise of his office. That experience is the parent of wisdom is an adage, the truth of which is recognized by the wisest as well as the simplest of mankind. What more desirable or more essential than this quality in the governors of nations? Where more desirable or more essential than in the first magistrate of a nation? Can it be wise to put this desirable and essential quality under the ban of the constitution; and to declare that the moment it is acquired, its possessor shall be compelled to abandon the station in which it was acquired, and to which it is adapted? This nevertheless is the precise import of all those regulations, which exclude men from serving their country, by the choice of their fellow citizens, after they have, by a course of service fitted themselves for doing it with a greater degree of utility.

A fourth ill effect of the exclusion would be the banishing men from stations, in which in certain emergencies of the state their presence might be of the greatest moment to the public interest or safety. There is no nation which has not at one period or another experienced an absolute necessity of the services of particular men, in particular situations, perhaps it would not be too strong to say, to the preservation of its political existence. How unwise therefore must be every such self-denying ordinance, as serves to prohibit a nation from making use of its own citizens, in the manner best suited to its exigences and circumstances! Without supposing the personal essentiality of the man, it is evident that a change of the chief magistrate, at the breaking out of a war, or at any similar crisis, for another even of equal merit, would at all times be detrimental to the community; inasmuch as it would substitute inexperience to experience and would tend to unhinge and set afloat the already settled train of the administration.

A fifth ill effect of the exclusion would be, that it would operate as a constitutional interdiction of stability in the administration. *By necessitating* a change of men, in the first office in the nation, it would necessitate a mutability of measures. It is not generally to be expected, that men will vary; and measures remain uniform. The contrary is the usual course of things. And we need not be apprehensive there will be too much stability, while there is even the option of changing; nor need we desire to prohibit the people from continuing their confidence, where they think it may be safely placed, and where by constancy on their part they may obviate the fatal inconvenience of fluctuating councils and a variable policy.

These are some of the disadvantages, which would flow from the principle of exclusion. They apply most forcibly to the scheme of a perpetual exclusion; but when we consider that even a partial exclusion would always render the re-admission of the person a remote and precarious object, the observations which have been made will apply nearly as fully to one case as to the other.

What are the advantages promised to counterballance these disadvantages? They are represented to be 1st. Greater independence in the magistrate: 2dly. Greater security to the people. Unless the exclusion be perpetual there will be no pretence to infer the first advantage. But even in that case, may he have no object beyond his present station to which he may sacrifice his independence? May he have no connections, no friends, for whom he may sacrifice it? May he not be less willing, by a firm conduct, to make personal enemies, when he acts under the impression, that a time is fast approaching, on the arrival of which he not only MAY, but MUST be exposed to their resentments, upon an equal, perhaps upon an inferior footing? It is not an easy point to determine whether his independence would be most promoted or impaired by such an arrangement.

As to the second supposed advantage, there is still greater reason to entertain doubts concerning it. If the exclusion were to be perpetual, a man of irregular ambition, of whom alone there could be reason in any case to entertain apprehensions, would with infinite reluctance yield to the necessity of taking his leave forever of a post, in which his passion for power and pre-eminence had acquired the force of habit. And if he had been fortunate or adroit enough to conciliate the good will of people he might induce them to consider as a very odious and unjustifiable restraint upon themselves, a provision which was calculated to debar them of the right of giving a fresh proof of their attachment to a favorite. There may be conceived circumstances, in which this disgust of the people, seconding the thwarted ambition of such a favourite, might occasion greater danger to liberty, than could ever reasonably be dreaded from the possibility of a perpetuation in office, by the voluntary suffrages of the community, exercising a constitutional privilege.

There is an excess of refinement in the idea of disabling the people to continue in office men, who had entitled themselves, in their opinion, to approbation and confidence; the advantages of which are at best speculative and equivocal; and are overbalanced by disadvantages far more certain and decisive.

16

DEBATE IN VIRGINIA RATIFYING CONVENTION
5, 10, 17–18 June 1788
Elliot 3:59–60, 201–2, 220–22, 483–96

[*5 June*]

[Mr. HENRY.] If your American chief be a man of ambition and abilities, how easy is it for him to render himself absolute! The army is in his hands, and if he be a man of address, it will be attached to him, and it will be the subject of long meditation with him to seize the first auspicious moment to accomplish his design; and, sir, will the American spirit solely relieve you when this happens? I would rather infinitely—and I am sure most of this Convention are of the same opinion—have a king, lords, and commons, than a government so replete with such insupportable evils. If we make a king, we may prescribe the rules by which he shall rule his people, and interpose such checks as shall prevent him from infringing them; but the President, in the field, at the head of his army, can prescribe the terms on which he shall reign master, so far that it will puzzle any American ever to get his neck from under the galling yoke. I cannot with patience think of this idea. If ever he violates the laws, one of two things will happen: he will come at the head of his army, to carry every thing before him; or he will give bail, or do what Mr. Chief Justice will order him. If he be guilty, will not the recollection of his crimes teach him to make one bold push for the American throne? Will not the immense difference between being master of every thing, and being ignominiously tried and punished, powerfully excite him to make this bold push? But, sir, where is the existing force to punish him? Can he not, at the head of his army, beat down every opposition? Away with your President! we shall have a king: the army will salute him monarch: your militia will leave you, and assist in making him king, and fight against you: and what have you to oppose this force? What will then become of you and your rights? Will not absolute despotism ensue?

> [Here Mr. HENRY strongly and pathetically expatiated on the probability of the President's enslaving America, and the horrid consequences that must result.]

[10 June]

[Gov. RANDOLPH.] . . . Let us consider whether the federal executive be wisely constructed. This is a point in which the constitution of every state differs widely as to the mode of electing their executives, and as to the time of continuing them in office. In some states the executive is perpetually eligible. In others he is rendered ineligible after a given period. They are generally elected by the legislature. It cannot be objected to the federal executive that the power is executed by one man. All the enlightened part of mankind agree that the superior despatch, secrecy, and energy, with which one man can act, render it more politic to vest the power of executing the laws in one man, than in any number of men. How is the President elected? By the people—on the same day throughout the United States—by those whom the people please. There can be no concert between the electors. The votes are sent sealed to Congress. What are his powers? To see the laws executed. Every executive in America has that power. He is also to command the army: this power also is enjoyed by the executives of the different states. He can handle no part of the public money except what is given him by law. At the end of four years, he may be turned out of his office. If he misbehaves he may be impeached, and in this case he will never be reëlected. I cannot conceive how his powers can be called formidable. Both houses are a check upon him. He can do no important act without the concurrence of the Senate. In England, the sword and purse are in different hands. The king has the power of the sword, and the purse is in the hands of the people alone. Take a comparison between this and the government of England.

It will prove in favor of the American principle. In England, the king declares war. In America, Congress must be consulted. In England, Parliament gives money. In America, Congress does it. There are consequently more powers in the hands of the people, and greater checks upon the executive here, than in England. Let him pardon me, when I say he is mistaken in passing a eulogium on the English government to the prejudice of this plan. Those checks which he says are to be found in the English government, are also to be found here. Our government is founded upon real checks. He ought to show there are no checks in it. Is this the case? Who are your representatives? They are chosen by the people for two years. Who are your senators? They are chosen by the legislatures, and a third of them go out of the Senate at the end of every second year. They may also be impeached. There are no better checks upon earth. Are there better checks in the government of Virginia? There is not a check in the one that is not in the other. The difference consists in the length of time, and in the nature of the objects. Any man may be impeached here—so he may there. If the people of Virginia can remove their delegates for misbehavior, by electing other men at the end of the year, so, in like manner, the federal representatives may be removed at the end of two, and the senators at the end of six years.

. . . . .

[Mr. MONROE.] . . . Let us now consider the responsibility of the President. He is elected for four years, and not excluded from reëlection. Suppose he violates the laws and Constitution, or commits high crimes. By whom is he to be tried?—By his own council—by those who advise him to commit such violations and crimes? This subverts the principles of justice, as it secures him from punishment. He commands the army of the United States till he is condemned. Will not this be an inducement to foreign nations to use their arts and intrigues to corrupt his counsellors? If he and his counsellors can escape punishment with so much facility, what a delightful prospect must it be for a foreign nation, which may be desirous of gaining territorial or commercial advantages over us, to practise on them! The certainty of success would be equal to the impunity. How is he elected? By electors appointed according to the directions of the state legislatures. Does the plan of government contemplate any other mode? A combination between the electors might easily happen, which would fix on a man in every respect improper. Contemplate this in all its consequences. Is it not the object of foreign courts to have such a man possessed of this power as would be inclined to promote their interests? What an advantageous prospect for France and Great Britain to secure the favor and attachment of the President, by exerting their power and influence to continue him in the office! Foreign nations may, by their intrigues, have great influence, in each state, in the election of the President; and I have no doubt but their efforts will be tried to the utmost. Will not the influence of the President himself have great weight in his reelection? The variety of the offices at his disposal will acquire him the favor and attachment of those who aspire after them, and of the officers and their friends. He will have some connection with the members of the different branches of government. They will esteem him, because they will be acquainted with him, live in the same town with him, and often dine with him. This familiar and frequent intercourse will secure him great influence. I presume that when once he is elected, he may be elected forever. Besides his influence in the town where he will reside, he will have very considerable weight in the different states. Those who are acquainted with the human mind, in all its operations, can clearly foresee this. Powerful men in different states will form a friendship with him. For these reasons, I conceive, the same President may always be continued, and be in fact elected by Congress, instead of independent and intelligent electors. It is a misfortune, more than once experienced, that the representatives of the states do not pursue the particular interest of their own state. When we take a more accurate view of the principles of the Senate, we shall have grounds to fear that the interest of our state may be totally neglected; nay, that our legislative influence will be as if we were actually expelled or banished out of Congress. The senators are amenable to, and appointed by, the states. They have a negative on all laws, may originate any except money bills, and direct the affairs of the executive. Seven states are a majority, and can in most cases bind the rest; from which reason, the interest of certain states alone will be consulted. Although the House of Representatives is calculated on national principles, and should they attend (contrary to my expectations) to the general interests of the Union, yet the dangerous exclusive powers given to the Senate will, in my opinion, counterbalance their exertions. Consider the connection of the Senate with the executive. Has it not an authority over all the acts of the executive? What are the acts which the President can do without them? What number is requisite to make treaties? A very small number. Two thirds of those who may *happen* to be present, may, with the President, make treaties that shall sacrifice the dearest interest of the Southern States—which may relinquish part of our territories—which may dismember the United States. There is no check to prevent this; there is no responsibility, or power to punish it. He is to nominate, and, by and with the advice and consent of the Senate, to appoint, ambassadors, other public ministers and consuls, judges of the Supreme Court, and all other officers of the United States. The concurrence of a bare majority of those who may be present will enable him to do these important acts. It does not require the consent of two thirds even of those who may be present. Thus I conceive the government is put entirely into the hands of seven states; indeed, into the hands of two thirds of a majority. The executive branch is under their protection, and yet they are freed from a direct charge of combination.

[*17 June*]

Mr. GEORGE MASON. Mr. Chairman, there is not a more important article in the Constitution than this. The great fundamental principle of responsibility in republicanism is here sapped. The President is elected without rotation. It may be said that a new election may remove him, and place another in his stead. If we judge from the experience of all other countries, and even our own, we may conclude that, as the President of the United States may be reëlected, so he will. How is it in every government where rotation is not required? Is there a single instance of a great man not being reëlected? Our governor is obliged to return, after a given period, to a private station. It is so in most of the states. This President will be elected time after time: he will be continued in office for life. If we wish to change him, the great powers in Europe will not allow us.

The honorable gentleman, my colleague in the late federal Convention, mentions, with applause, those parts of which he had expressed his disapprobation, he says not a word. If I am mistaken, let me be put right. I shall not make use of his name; but, in the course of this investigation, I shall use the arguments of that gentleman against it.

Will not the great powers of Europe, as France and Great Britain, be interested in having a friend in the President of the United States? and will they not be more interested in his election than in that of the king of Poland? The people of Poland have a right to displace their king. But do they ever do it? No. Prussia and Russia, and other European powers, would not suffer it. This clause will open a door to the dangers and misfortunes which the people of Poland undergo. The powers of Europe will interpose, and we shall have a civil war in the bowels of our country, and be subject to all the horrors and calamities of an elective monarchy. This very executive officer may, by consent of Congress, receive a stated pension from European potentates. This is not an idea altogether new in America. It is not many years ago—since the revolution—that a foreign power offered emoluments to persons holding offices under our government. It will, moreover, be difficult to know whether he receives emoluments from foreign powers or not. The electors, who are to meet in each state to vote for him, may be easily influenced. To prevent the certain evils of attempting to elect a new President, it will be necessary to continue the old one. The only way to alter this would be to render him ineligible after a certain number of years, and then no foreign nation would interfere to keep in a man who was utterly ineligible. Nothing is so essential to the preservation of a republican government as a periodical rotation. Nothing so strongly impels a man to regard the interest of his constituents as the certainty of returning to the general mass of the people, from whence he was taken, where he must participate their burdens. It is a great defect in the Senate that they are not ineligible at the end of six years. The biennial exclusion of one third of them will have no effect, as they can be reëlected. Some stated time ought to be fixed when the President ought to be reduced to a private station. I should be contented that he might be elected for eight years; but I would wish him to be capable of holding the office only eight years out of twelve or sixteen years. But, as it now stands, he may continue in office for life; or, in other words, it will be an elective monarchy.

Gov. RANDOLPH. Mr. Chairman, the honorable gentleman last up says that I do not mention the parts to which I object. I have hitherto mentioned my objections with freedom and candor. But, sir, I considered that our critical situation rendered adoption necessary, were it even more defective than it is. I observed that if opinions ought to lead the committee on one side, they ought on the other. Every gentleman who has turned his thoughts to the subject of politics, and has considered the most eligible mode of republican government, agrees that the greatest difficulty arises from the executive—as to the time of his election, mode of his election, quantum of power, &c. I will acknowledge that, at one stage of this business, I had embraced the idea of the honorable gentleman, that the reëligibility of the President was improper. But I will acknowledge that, on a further consideration of the subject, and attention to the lights which were thrown upon it by others, I altered my opinion of the limitation of his eligibility. When we consider the advantages arising to us from it, we cannot object to it. That which has produced my opinion against the limitation of his eligibility is this—that it renders him more independent in his place, and more solicitous of promoting the interest of his constituents; for, unless you put it in his power to be reelected, instead of being attentive to their interests, he will lean to the augmentation of his private emoluments. This subject will admit of high coloring and plausible arguments; but, on considering it attentively and coolly, I believe it will be found less exceptionable than any other mode. The mode of election here excludes that faction which is productive of those hostilities and confusion in Poland. It renders it unnecessary and impossible for foreign force or aid to interpose. The electors must be elected by the people at large. To procure his reëlection, his influence must be coextensive with the continent. And there can be no combination between the electors, as they elect him on the same day in every state. When this is the case, how can foreign influence or intrigue enter? There is no reason to conclude, from the experience of these states, that he will be continually reëlected. There have been several instances where officers have been displaced, where they were reëligible. This has been the case with the executive of Massachusetts, and I believe of New Hampshire. It happens, from the mutation of sentiments, though the officers be good.

There is another provision against the danger, mentioned by the honorable member, of the President receiving emoluments from foreign powers. If discovered, he may be impeached. If he be not impeached, he may be displaced at the end of the four years. By the 9th section of the 1st article, "no person, holding an office of profit or trust, shall accept of any present or emolument whatever, from any foreign power, without the consent of the representatives of the people;" and by the 1st section of the 2d article, his compensation is neither to be increased nor diminished during the time for which he shall have been elected; and he shall not, during that period, receive any emolument from the United States or any of them. I consider, therefore, that he is restrained from receiving any present or emolument whatever. It is impossible to guard better against corruption. The honorable member seems to think that he may hold his office without being reëlected. He cannot hold it over four years, unless he be reëlected, any more than if he were prohibited. As to forwarding and transmitting the certificates of the electors, I think the regulation as good as could be provided.

Mr. GEORGE MASON. Mr. Chairman, the Vice-President appears to me to be not only an unnecessary but dangerous officer. He is, contrary to the usual course of parliamentary proceedings, to be president of the Senate. The state from which he comes may have two votes, when the others will have but one. Besides, the legislative and executive are hereby mixed and incorporated together. I cannot, at this distance of time, foresee the consequences; but I think that, in the course of human affairs, he will be made a tool of in order to bring about his own interest, and aid in overturning the liberties of his country. There is another part which I disapprove of, but which perhaps I do not understand. "In case of removal of the President from office, or of his death, resignation, or inability to discharge the powers and duties of the said office, the same shall devolve on the Vice-President; and the Congress may by law provide for the case of removal, death, resignation, or inability, both of the President and Vice-President, declaring what officer shall then act as President, and such officer shall act accordingly, until the disability be removed, or a President shall be elected." The power of Congress is right and proper so far as it enables them to provide what officer shall act, in case both the President and Vice-President be dead or disabled. But gentlemen ought to take notice that the election of this officer is only for four years. There is no provision for a speedy election of another President, when the former is dead or removed. The influence of the Vice-President may prevent the election of the President. But perhaps I may be mistaken.

Mr. MADISON. Mr. Chairman, I think there are some peculiar advantages incident to this office, which recommend it to us. There is, in the first place, a great probability this officer will be taken from one of the largest states; and, if so, the circumstance of his having an eventual vote will be so far favorable. The consideration which recommends it to me is, that he will be the choice of the people at large. There are to be ninety-one electors, each of whom has two votes: if he have one fourth of the whole number of votes, he is elected Vice-President. There is much more propriety in giving this office to a person chosen by the people at large, than to one of the Senate, who is only the choice of the legislature of one state. His eventual vote is an advantage too obvious to comment upon. I differ from the honorable member in the case which enables Congress to make a temporary appointment. When the President and Vice-President die, the election of another President will immediately take place; and suppose it would not,—all that Congress could do would be to make an appointment between the expiration of the four years and the last election, and to continue only to such expiration. This can rarely happen. This power continues the government in motion, and is well guarded.

[*18 June*]

Mr. Monroe, after a brief exordium, in which he insisted that, on the judicious organization of the executive power, the security of our interest and happiness greatly depended; that, in the construction of this part of the government, we should be cautious in avoiding the defects of other governments; and that our circumspection should be commensurate to the extent of the powers delegated,—proceeded as follows: The President ought to act under the strongest impulses of rewards and punishments, which are the strongest incentives to human actions. There are two ways of securing this point. He ought to depend on the people of America for his appointment and continuance in office; he ought also to be responsible, in an equal degree, to all the states, and to be tried by dispassionate judges; his responsibility ought further to be direct and immediate. Let us consider, in the first place, then, how far he is dependent on the people of America. He is to be elected by electors, in a manner perfectly dissatisfactory to my mind. I believe that he will owe his election, in fact, to the state governments, and not to the people at large. It is to be observed that Congress have it in their power to appoint the time of choosing the electors, and of electing the President. Is it not presumable they will appoint the times of choosing the electors, and of electing the President. Is it not presumable they will appoint the times of choosing the electors, and electing the President, at a considerable distance from each other, so as to give an opportunity to the electors to form a combination? If they know that such a man as they wish—for instance, the actual President—cannot possibly be elected by a majority of the whole number of electors appointed, yet if they can prevent the election, by such majority, of any one they disapprove of, and if they can procure such a number of votes as will be sufficient to make their favorite one of the five highest on the list, they may ultimately carry the election into the general Congress, where the votes, in choosing him, shall be taken by states, each state having one vote. Let us see how far this is compatible with the security of republicanism. Although this state is to have ten, and Massachusetts eight representatives, and Delaware and Rhode Island are to have but one each, yet the vote is to be by states only. The consequence will be that a majority of the states, and these consisting of the smallest, may elect him; this will give an advantage to the small states. He will depend, therefore, on the states for his reëlection and continuance in office, and not on the people. Does it not bear the complexion of the late Confederation? He will conduct himself in accommodation to them, since by them he is chosen, and may be again. If he accommodates himself to the interest of particular states, will they not be obliged, by state policy, to support him afterwards? Le me inquire into his responsibility if he does not depend on the people. To whom is he responsible? To the Senate, his own council. If he makes a treaty, bartering the interests of his country, by whom is he to be tried? By the very persons who advised him to perpetrate the act. Is this any security? I am persuaded that the gentleman who will be the first elected may continue in the office for life.

The situation of the United States, as it applies to the European states, demands attention. We may hold the balance among those states. Their western territories are contiguous to us. What we may do, without any offensive operations, may have considerable influence. Will they not, then, endeavor to influence his general councils? May we not suppose that they will endeavor to attach him to their interest, and support him, in order to make him serve their purposes? If this be the case, does not the mode of election present a favorable opportunity to continue in office the person that shall be President? I am persuaded they may, by their power and intrigues, influence his reëlection. There being nothing to prevent his corruption but his virtue, which is but precarious, we have not sufficient security. If there be a propriety in giving him a right of making leagues, he ought not to be connected with the Senate. If the Senate have a right to make leagues, there ought to be a majority of the states.

The Vice-President is an unnecessary officer. I can see no reason for such an officer. The Senate might of their own body elect a president who would have no dangerous influence. He is to succeed the President, in case of removal, disability, &c., and is to have the casting vote in the Senate. This gives an undue advantage to the state he comes from, and will render foreign powers desirous of securing his favor, to obtain which they will exert themselves in his behalf. I am persuaded that the advantage of his information will not counterbalance the disadvantages attending his office.

The President might be elected by the people, dependent upon them, and responsible for maladministration. As this is not the case, I must disapprove of this clause in its present form.

Mr. Grayson. Mr. Chairman, one great objection with me is this: If we advert to this democratical, aristocratical, or executive branch, we shall find their powers are perpetually varying and fluctuating throughout the whole. Perhaps the democratic branch would be well constructed, were it not for this defect. The executive is still worse, in this respect, than the democratic branch. He is to be elected by a number of electors in the country; but the principle is changed when no person has a majority of the whole number of electors appointed, or when more than one have such a majority, and have an equal number of votes; for then the lower house is to vote by states. It is thus changing throughout the whole. It seems rather founded on accident than any principle of government I ever heard of. We know that there scarcely ever was an election of such an officer without the interposition of foreign powers. Two causes prevail to make them intermeddle in such cases:—one is, to preserve the balance of power; the other, to preserve their trade. These causes have produced interferences of foreign powers in the election of the king of Poland. All the great powers of Europe have interfered in an election which took place not very long ago, and would not let the people choose for themselves. We know how much the powers of Europe have interfered with Sweden. Since the death of Charles XII., that country has been a republican government. Some powers were willing it should be so; some were willing her imbecility should continue; others wished the contrary; and at length the court of France brought about a revolution, which converted it into an absolute government. Can America be free from these interferences? France, after losing Holland, will wish to make America entirely her own. Great Britain will wish to increase her influence by a still closer connection. It is the interest of Spain, from the contiguity of her possessions in the western hemisphere to the United States, to be in an intimate connection with them, and influence their deliberations, if possible. I think we have every thing to apprehend from such interferences. It is highly probable the President will be continued in office for life. To gain his favor, they will support him. Consider the means of importance he will have by creating officers. If he has a good understanding with the Senate, they will join to prevent a discovery of his misdeeds.

Whence comes this extreme confidence, that we disregard the example of ancient and modern nations? We find that aristocracies never invested their officers with such immense powers. Rome had not only an aristocratical, but also a democratical branch; yet the consuls were in office only two years. This quadrennial power cannot be justified by ancient history. There is hardly an instance where a republic trusted its executive so long with much power; nor is it warranted by modern republics. The delegation of power is, in most of them, only for one year.

When you have a strong democratical and a strong aristocratical branch, you may have a strong executive. But when those are weak, the balance will not be preserved, if you give the executive extensive powers for so long a time. As this government is organized, it would be dangerous to trust the President with such powers. How will you punish him if he abuse his power? Will you call him before the Senate? They are his counsellors and partners in crime. Where are your checks? We ought to be extremely cautious in this country. If ever the government be changed, it will probably be into a despotism. The first object in England was to destroy the monarchy; but the aristocratic branch restored him, and of course the government was organized on its ancient principles. But were a revolution to happen here, there would be no means of restoring the government to its former organization. This is a caution to us not to trust extensive powers. I have an extreme objection to the mode of his election. I presume the seven Eastern States will always elect him. As he is vested with the power of making treaties, and as there is a material distinction between the carrying and productive states, the former will be disposed to have him to themselves. He will accommodate himself to their interests in forming treaties, and they will continue him perpetually in office. Thus mutual interest will lead them reciprocally to support one another. It will be a government of a faction, and this observation will apply to every part of it; for, having a majority, they may do what they please. I have made an estimate which shows with what facility they will be able to reëlect him. The number of electors is equal to the number of representatives and senators; viz., ninety-one. They are to vote for two persons. They give, therefore, one hundred and eighty-two votes. Let there be forty-five votes for four different candidates, and two for the President. He is one of the five highest, if he have but two votes, which he may easily purchase. In this case, by the 3d clause of the 1st section of the 2d article, the election is to be by the representatives, according to states. Let New Hampshire be for him,—a majority of its

	3	representatives is	2
Rhode Island, ...	1	....	1
Connecticut, ...	5	....	3
New Jersey, ...	4	....	3
Delaware, ...	1	....	1
Georgia, ...	3	....	2
North Carolina, ...	5	....	3
A majority of seven states is		....	15

Thus the majority of seven states is but 15, while the minority amounts to 50.

The total number of voices (91 electors and 65 representatives) is	156
Voices in favor of the President are, 2 state electors and 15 representatives, ...	17
	139

So that the President may be reëlected by the voices of 17 against 139.

It may be said that this is an extravagant case, and will never happen. In my opinion, it will often happen. A person who is a favorite of Congress, if he gets but two votes of electors, may, by the subsequent choice of 15 representatives, be elected President. Surely the possibility of such a case ought to be excluded. I shall postpone mentioning in what manner he ought to be elected, till we come to offer amendments.

Mr. GEORGE MASON contended that this mode of election was a mere deception,—a mere *ignis fatuus* on the American people,—and thrown out to make them believe they were to choose him; whereas it would not be once out of fifty times that he would be chosen by them in the first instance, because a majority of the whole number of votes was required. If the localities of the states were considered, and the probable diversity of the opinions of the people attended to, he thought it would be found that so many persons would be voted for, that there seldom or never could be a majority in favor of one, except one great name, who, he believed, would be unanimously elected. He then continued thus:—A majority of the whole number of electors is necessary, to elect the President. It is not the greatest number of votes that is required, but a majority of the whole number of electors. If there be more than one having such majority, and an equal number, one of them is to be chosen by ballot of the House of Representatives. But if no one have a majority of the actual number of electors appointed, how is he to be chosen? From the five highest on the list, by ballot of the lower house, and the votes to be taken by states. I conceive he ought to be chosen from the two highest on the list. This would be simple and easy; then, indeed, the people would have some agency in the election. But when it is extended to the five highest, a person having a very small number of votes may be elected. This will almost constantly happen. The states may choose the man in whom they have most confidence. This, in my opinion, is a very considerable defect. The people will, in reality, have no hand in the election.

It has been wittily observed that the Constitution has *married* the President and Senate—has made them man and wife. I believe the consequence that generally results from marriage will happen here. They will be continually supporting and aiding each other: they will always consider their interest as united. We know the advantage the few have over the many. They can with facility act in concert, and on a uniform system: they may join, scheme, and plot, against the people without any chance of detection. The Senate and President will form a combination that cannot be prevented by the representatives. The executive and legislative powers, thus connected, will destroy all balances: this would have been prevented by a constitutional council, to aid the President in the discharge of his office, vesting the Senate, at the same time, with the power of impeaching them. Then we should have real responsibility. In its present form, the guilty try themselves. The President is tried by his counsellors. He is not removed from office during his trial. When he is arraigned for treason, he has the command of the army and navy, and may surround the Senate with thirty thousand troops. It brings to my recollection the remarkable trial of Milo at Rome. We may expect to see similar instances here. But I suppose that the cure for all evils—the virtue and integrity of our representatives—will be thought a sufficient security. On this great and important subject, I am one of those (and ever shall be) who object to it.

Mr. MADISON. Mr. Chairman, I will take the liberty of making a few observations, which may place this in such a light as may obviate objections. It is observed that none of the honorable members objecting to this have pointed out the right mode of election. It was found difficult in the Convention, and will be found so by any gentleman who will take the liberty of delineating a mode of electing the President that would exclude those inconveniences which they apprehend. I would not contend against some of the principles laid down by some gentlemen, if the interests of some states only were to be consulted. But there is a great diversity of interests. The choice of the people ought to be attended to. I have found no better way of selecting the man in whom they place the highest confidence, than that delineated in the plan of the Convention; nor has the gentleman told us. Perhaps it will be found impracticable to elect him by the immediate suffrages of the people. Difficulties would arise from the extent and population of the states. Instead of this, the people choose the electors.

This can be done with ease and convenience, and will render the choice more judicious. As to the eventual voting by states, it has my approbation. The lesser states, and some large states, will be generally pleased by that mode. The deputies from the small states argued (and there is some force in their reasoning) that, when the people voted, the large states evidently had the advantage over the rest, and, without varying the mode, the interest of the little states might be neglected or sacrificed. Here is a compromise; for in the eventual election, the small states will have the advantage. In so extensive a country, it is probable that many persons will be voted for, and the lowest of the five highest on the list may not be so inconsiderable as he supposes. With respect to the possibility that a small number of votes may decide his election, I do not know how, nor do I think that a bare calculation of possibility ought to govern us. One honorable gentleman has said that the Eastern States may, in the eventual election, choose him. But, in the extravagant calculation he has made, he has been obliged to associate North Carolina and Georgia with the five smallest Northern States. There can be no union of interest or sentiments between states so differently situated.

The honorable member last up has committed a mistake in saying there must be a majority of the whole number of electors appointed. A majority of votes, equal to a majority of the electors appointed, will be sufficient. Forty-six is a majority of ninety-one, and will suffice to elect the President.

Mr. MASON arose, and insisted that the person having the greatest number of votes would not be elected, unless such majority was one of the whole number of electors appointed; that it would rarely happen that any one would have such a majority, and, as he was then to be chosen from the five highest on the list, his election was entirely taken from the people.

Mr. MADISON expressed astonishment at the construction of the honorable member, and insisted that nothing was necessary but a number of votes equal to a majority of the electors, which was forty-six; for the clause expressly said that "the person having the greatest number of votes shall be President, if such number be a majority of the whole number of electors appointed." Each had two votes, because one vote was intended for the Vice-President. I am surprised, continued Mr. Madison, that the honorable member has not pointed out a more proper mode, since he objects to this.

But the honorable gentleman tells us that the President and Senate will be in alliance against the representatives, and that, from the advantage of the few over the many, they may seduce or overrule the representatives. But if this be the case, how can he contend for the augmentation of the number of the latter? for the more you increase their number, the more danger in the disproportion. The diversity of circumstances, situation, and extent, of the different states, will render previous combination, with respect to the election of the President, impossible.

17

JOHN ADAMS TO TIMOTHY PICKERING
31 Oct. 1797
Works 8:560

The worst evil that can happen in any government is a divided executive; and, as a plural executive must, from the nature of men, be forever divided, this is a demonstration that a plural executive is a great evil, and incompatible with liberty. That emulation in the human heart, which produces rivalries of men, cities, and nations, which produces almost all the good in human life, produces, also, almost all the evil. This is my philosophy of government. The great art lies in managing this emulation. It is the only defence against its own excesses. The emulation of the legislative and executive powers should be made to control each other. The emulation between the rich and the poor among the people, should be made to check itself by balancing the two houses in the legislature, which represent these two classes of society, so invidious at all times against each other.

18

ST. GEORGE TUCKER,
BLACKSTONE'S COMMENTARIES
1:APP. 316–25, 328–29
1803

The author of the Treatise on the English Constitution, considers the unity of the executive among the advantages peculiar to that, as a free government. The advantages ordinarily attributed to that circumstance, are supposed to be a necessary and unavoidable unanimity; promptitude and dispatch, as a consequence of it: and, immediate and obvious, responsibility. If such are the real advantages of a single executive magistrate, we may contend that they are found in a much greater degree in the federal government, than in the English. In the latter it exists, only theoretically, in an individual; the practical exercise of it, being devolved upon ministers, councils, and boards. The king, according to the acknowledged principles of the constitution, not being responsible for any of his acts, the minister upon whom all responsibility devolves, to secure his indemnity acts by the advice of the privy council to whom every measure of importance is submitted, before it is carried into effect. His plans are often digested and canvassed in a still more secret conclave, consisting of the principal officers of state, and stiled the cabinet council, before they are communicated to the privy council: matters are frequently referred to the different boards, for their advice thereon, previously to their discussion, and final decision, in the council. Thus, in fact, the unity of the executive is merely ideal, existing only in the theory of the government; whatever is said of the unanimity, or dispatch arising from the unity of the executive power, is therefore without foundation. And with respect to responsibility, we have already observed that the nominal executive, is absolved from it by the constituion: all the responsibility that the government admits, is shared between the different ministers, privy council, and boards. The unity of the nominal executive, therefore, so far from ensuring responsibility, destroys it. If then the constitution of England be relied on as proving the superior advantages of unity in the executive department, it does not support any part of the position.

In the United States the unity of the executive authority is practically established, in almost every instance. For, the senate are constituted a council, rather for special, than for general purposes. It may reasonably be doubted, whether they have a right to advise the president, in any case, without being first consulted; and whether, when consulted, he is obliged to carry into effect any measure which they may advise: the constitution is perhaps defective in both these cases. To illustrate them, let it be supposed, that the senate, without being consulted should advise the sending an ambassador to a foreign court: is the president bound to nominate one to them for that purpose? Or, suppose an ambassador to have concluded a treaty, which the president disapproves, but, which the senate advise him to ratify; is he bound to do so? The constitution says, "*He shall have power*, by, and with, the advice and consent of the senate, to make treaties, provided two thirds of the senators present, concur; and shall nominate, and by, and with, the advice and consent of the senate shall appoint ambassadors." These words appear rather to confer a discretionary authority, that to impose a mandate, or obligation. . . . But although the president may perhaps constitutionally decline the ratification of a treaty, or the appointment of an ambassador, notwithstanding the advice of the senate, yet he cannot adopt any measure, which they may advise him to reject, if the constitution requires their advice, or assent: so that, in general, whatever he does must have the sanction of the senate for it's support: whatever he omits doing, is chargeable upon him, only, unless the measure shall have been submitted to the senate and rejected by them. The conduct of the first magistrate of a nation is as frequently liable to censure for his omissions, as for his acts. Whatever, therefore, is left undone, which the public safety may require to have been done, is chargeable upon the neglect of the president, exclusively: whatever may be done amiss is likewise chargeable upon him, in the first instance, as the author and propounder of the measure: although it should afterwards receive the approbation and consent of the senate. Responsibility, then, pursues him in every situation: whether active or passive; sleeping, or awake.

But although a king of England be not responsible, it is said that his ministers are; for they may be impeached: so may a president of the United States. . . . But I lay no stress upon this point, as a practical means of enforcing responsibility, for reasons that will be more fully explained hereafter. The true point of responsibility rests upon the shortness of the period for which a president of the United States is elected, and the power which the people possess, of rejecting him at a succeeding election: a power, the more formidable, and energetic, as it remains in their hands, is untramelled by forms, and the exercise of it depends more upon opinion, than upon evidence. When brought before such a tribunal, in vain would a culpable president seek shelter under the flimsy veil, of advice of council; such a cobweb, like the net of Vulcan, would only expose him, more effectually.

On the ground of responsibility, then, an immense preference is due to the constitution of the United States: it is at least equal to that of Great-Britain on the ground of unanimity: for, as every executive measure must originate in the breast of the president, his plans will have all the benefit of uniformity, that can be expected to flow from the operations of any individual mind: let it be supposed that the senate reject one of his proposed measures; possessing a perfect acquaintance with the whole system of his own administration, he will naturally be led to adopt some other course, which shall neither retard, nor counteract any other part of his system. No British minister, whose measures are opposed in the cabinet, can do more; probably not so much: for a substitute may, perhaps, be obtruded upon him, by some other influential minister. But no such substitute can be obtruded upon a president of the United States; the power of the senate consisting rather in approving, or rejecting, than in advising or propounding, as already hinted.

The advantages of information, and dispatch, are probably equally in favour of the constitution of the American executive. The constitution of the United States has made ample provision for his aid in these respects, by assigning to him ministers to whom the conduct of each of the executive departments may be committed; from whom he may require all necessary information, as also their opinions in writing, upon any subject relating to the duties of their respective offices; and whom, he may, moreover, remove at pleasure. Here we find a single executive officer substituted for a numerous board, where responsibility is divided, 'till it is entirely lost, and where the chance of unanimity lessens in geometrical proportion to the number that compose it.

The perpetuity of the office, is another boasted advantage of the constitution of the supreme executive magistrate in Great Britain. "The king never dies." . . . But Henry, Edward, or George may die, may be an infant in swaddling clothes, a superannuated dotard, or a raving maniac. Of what benefit is the immortality of the kingly office, in any of these instances? Can the puling infant, or the feeble hand of palsied age wield the sceptre, or can it be entrusted to the raving Bedlamite? A president of the United States cannot be the first: it is highly improbable that he will ever be the second; the constitution has provided for the third case; and for all others, of a similar kind. For, in the case of the removal of the president of the United States from office, or of his death, resignation, or inability to discharge the powers and duties of his office, the same shall devolve on the vice-president; and congress may by law provide for the case of removal, death, resignation, or inability, both of the president and vice-president, declaring what officer shall then act as president, and such officer shall act accordingly, until the disability be removed, or a president shall be elected. Such provision has been accordingly made by law, and the executive authority in such a case, would immediately devolve upon the president of the senate *pro tempore;* or if there be no president of the senate, upon the speaker of the house of representatives, for the time being. Nothing is wanting to the perpetuity of the office, but a provision for it's continuance in case no president shall be elected at the period prescribed by the constitution. Such a case will probably not happen, until the people of the United States shall be weary of the present constitution and government, and adopt that method of putting a period to both. And it is, perhaps, among the recommendations of the constitution, that it thus furnishes the means of a peaceable dissolution of the government, if ever the crisis should arrive that may render such a measure eligible, or necessary. A crisis to be deprecated by every friend to his country.

To pursue the parallel between a king of England, and the president of the United States, a little further. A king of England is the fountain of honour, of office, and of privilege. Honours, as distinct from offices, are unknown in the U. States; so likewise are privileges. At least there are none, which a president of the United States can constitutionally create, or bestow. It is not so with respect to offices; these he can not constitutionally create; they must first be established by law. But when established, he has the exclusive right of nomination to all offices, whose appointments are not otherwise provided for by the constitution, or by some act of congress, to which his assent may be necessary, or may have been previously given. The influence which this power gives him, personally, is one of those parts of the constitution, which assimilates the government, in its administration, infinitely more nearly to that of Great Britain, than seems to consist with those republican principles, which ought to pervade every part of the federal constitution: at least so long as the union is composed of democratic states. On this subject we shall offer some further remarks hereafter.

The heir of a king of England may be born with all the vices of a Richard; with the tyrannical disposition, and cruelty of the eighth Henry; with the empty pride and folly of a James; with the cowardice and imbecility of a John; or with the stupid obstinacy, bigotry, or other depravity of temper, of any of his successors; he must nevertheless succeed to the throne of his fathers; his person is sacred and inviolable as if he were an Alfred; and unless his misdeeds are so rank as to bring him to the block, or force him to an abdication, he continues the lord's anointed all his days. A president of the United States must have attained the middle age of life, before he is eligible to that office: if not a native, he must have been fourteen years a resident in the United States: his talents and character must consequently be known. The faculties of his mind must have attained their full vigour: the character must be formed, and formed of active, not of passive materials, to attract, and secure the attention, and approbation of a people dispersed through such a variety of climate and situation, as the American people are. This activity of mind and of talent must have manifested itself on the side of virtue, before it can engage the favour of those who acknowledge no superiority of rights among individuals, and who are conscious that in promoting to office, they should choose a faithful agent, not a ruler, without responsibility. And should it happen, that they are after all deceived in their estimate of his character and worth, the lapse of four years enables them to correct their error, and dismiss him from their service. What nation governed by an hereditary monarch has an equal chance of happiness!

But, the tumult of popular elections, and the danger in elective monarchies, will be insisted on, as counterbalancing the advantage which we claim in behalf of the constitution of the executive magistrate in the United States. With regard to the latter, something will be said hereafter, when we examine the mode of electing a president of the United States. As to the former: if the sovereignty of the people of the United States, like that of the Roman and Grecian republics, resided in the inhabitants of a single city, or a small territory, the influence of men of popular talents would doubtless produce in certain conjunctures, similar events to those recorded in the annals of those republics. But nature herself seems to be enlisted on the side of the liberty and independence of the citizens of United America. Our cities are few; the population inconsiderable, compared with many of the capitals of ancient, or modern Europe: that population (from the unfavorable influence of climate for some years past) seems not likely to be extended very far beyond its present bounds, and probably will never bear any great proportion to the population of the country at large. This circumstance alone, would probably defeat any attempt to establish an undue influence in any part of the union. Agriculture is, and probably will for ages continue to be, the principal object of pursuit in the United States; and the period seems to be yet very far removed, when their population will be equal to the extent, and fertility of the soil. Europe has so far got the start of us in manufactures, that it is also probable, our population will not depend upon, nor derive any great increase from, them. Until it does, our towns will be principally confined to the sea coast, and, the interior of the United States will continue, as at present, the nurse of a hardy, independent yeomanry. A strong barrier between the United States and the countries which abound in the precious metals is devoutly to be wished by all, who can appreicate, properly, the blessings of liberty and peace. Whilst the ambition of America is limited to the cultivation of the arts of peace, and the science of free government; to the improvement, instead of the extention of her territory, and to the fortefying herself against enemies from within, as well as from without, by fostering, and encouraging the principles of genuine liberty; local influence can never be so formidable as to endanger the peace or happiness of the union, on any occasion. But, whenever our evil genius shall prompt us to aspire to the character of a military republic, and invite us to the field of glory: when rapacity, under the less odious name of ambition, shall lead us on to conquest; when a bold, though raw, militia shall be exchanged for a well trained, well disciplined and well appointed army; ready to take the field at the nod of an ambitious president, and to believe that the finger of heaven points to that course which his directs; then, may we regard the day of our happiness as past, or as hasting rapidly to its decline.

That provision in the constitution which requires that the president shall be a native-born citizen (unless he were a citizen of the United States when the constitution was adopted,) is a happy means of security against foreign influence, which, where-ever it is capable of being exerted, is to be dreaded more than the plague. The admission of foreigners into our councils, consequently, cannot be too much guarded against; their total exclusion from a station to which foreign nations have been accustomed to, attach ideas of sovereign power, sacredness of character, and hereditary right, is a measure of the most consummate policy and wisdom. It was by means of foreign connections that the stadtholder of Holland, whose powers at first were probably not equal to those of a president of the United States, became a sovereign hereditary prince before the late revolution in that country. Nor is it with levity that I remark, that the very title of our first magistrate, in some measure exempts us from the danger of those calamities by which European nations are almost perpetually visited. The title of king, prince, emperor, or czar, without the smallest addition to his powers, would have rendered him a member of the fraternity of crowned heads: their common cause has more than once threatened the desolation of Europe. To have added a member to this sacred family in America, would have invited and perpetuated among us all the evils of Pandora's Box.

The *personal* independence of the president is secured by that clause, which provides that he shall receive a compensation at stated periods, which shall not be diminished during his continuance in office. To guard against avarice, corruption, and venality, it is also provided, that it shall not be encreased during the same period, nor shall he receive within that period any other emolument from the United States, or either of them. His salary, as now fixed by law, seems to be fully adequate, though far below the income of many private persons in England, and even in America.

The *political* independence of the president of the United States, so far as it is necessary to the preservation, protection, and defence of the constitution, is secured, not only by the limitations and restrictions which the constitution imposes upon the legislative powers of congress, but by a qualified negative on all their proceedings, as has been already mentioned elsewhere. This share in the proceedings of the federal legislature, which the constitution assigns to him, consists, like that of a king of England, in the power of rejecting, rather than resolving; a circumstance on which both judge Blackstone, and de Lolme, lay considerable stress; and is one of the grounds upon which the latter founds his preference of that constitution to the republican system. In republics, he tells us, the laws usually originate with the executive; it is otherwise in all the American states. In England, the laws do, in fact, originate with the executive: a revenue bill is always proposed by the chancellor of the exchequer, or some member of that department; and it is understood to be the practice, that every other measure of considerable magnitude and importance is first discussed in the privy council, before it is brought into parliament; where it is generally introduced, and the bill prepared by some of the officers of the crown. The preference which de Lolme gives to the English constitution, therefore, is not altogether well founded. The negative of the president of the United States is not final, like that of the king of England, but suspensive. Neither is the expression of his assent absolutely necessary to the establishment of a law, for if he witholds his decision beyond the period of ten days (exclusive of Sundays) his assent shall be presumed. He may retard for a few days, but cannot prevent any beneficial measure, provided two-thirds of both houses concur in the opinion of its expediency. Thus, the part assigned to him by the constitution is strictly preventative, and not creative; yet this preventative is so modified as never to operate conclusively, but in those cases where it may be presumed the congress have acted unadvisedly through haste or oversight: and we may safely conclude, that where the deliberate sense of two-thirds of both houses of congress shall induce them to persist in any measure to which the president shall have given his negative, it will neither militate with the constitution, nor with the interest of their constituents. There is one instance (besides a question of adjournment) in which his assent appears not to be required; this is, when two-thirds of both houses have concurred in proposing to the states any amendment of the constitution: in this case, the concurrence of two-thirds of both houses being required in the first instance, his assent is dispensed with, as his dissent would be unavailing.

. . . . .

Nothing in the constitution prohibits the re-election of a president as often as the approbation of his country may confer that distinction upon him. If his re-election were to depend entirely upon a majority of votes in the first instance, I should think the argument would be in favour of the principle. But what if a president of the United States should so far have lost the confidence of the people of the respective states, as not to have a majority of the votes of the state electors, in his favour? What, if he should so far have forfeited their esteem, as to be the lowest of five candidates, on the list, neither of whom should have such a majority, as to decide the election? Should we not, in such a case, with indignation behold him continued in office, by the votes of one fourth part of the house of representatives, against the other three? This might be sufficiently guarded against, by an amendment, providing that no president, for the time being, should ever be re-elected, unless he had not only the greatest number of votes in his favour, but a majority of the votes of all the electors appointed. As corruption can only be dreaded on the part of bad men, and is always to be dreaded from them, a president who may have lost the confidence of the citizens of the United States at large, would be the first person with whom the practice of corruption may be expected to commence.

The period for which a president is elected, as has been already noticed, is four years. By many it is thought too long: it seems long enough to give him an opportunity of bringing to a mature conclusion any measures which he may have undertaken for the good of the nation; and it has been thought short enough, for the people to displace him in sufficient time, where his conduct may not have merited approbation, on the one hand, or impeachment, on the other. Much evil, however, may be generated, and even matured, in the compass of four years. . . . Of removal from office by impeachment, no president will ever be in danger. But of this hereafter. I can see no inconvenience that would result from more frequent elections; there may be danger, if the constitution be not so amended as to provide for them. . . . The convention of this state proposed as an amendment to the constitution, That no person should be capable of being president of the United States for more than eight years, in any term of sixteen years. It might have been better to have selected the half of these periods, respectively.

19

UNITED STATES V. BURR

25 Fed. Cas. 30, no. 14,692d (C.C.D.Va. 1807)

[Tuesday, June 9, 1807. The grand jury were adjourned to the following Thursday.]

Mr. Burr then addressed the court. There was a proposition which he wished to submit to them. In the president's communication to congress, he speaks of a letter and other papers which he had received from Mr. Wilkinson, under date of 21st of October. Circumstances had now rendered it material that the whole of this letter should be produced in court; and further, it has already appeared to the court, in the course of different examinations, that the government have attempted to infer certain intentions on my part from certain transactions. It becomes necessary, therefore, that these transactions should be accurately stated. It was, therefore, material to show in what circumstances I was placed in the Mississippi territory; and of course, to obtain certain orders of the army and the navy which were issued respecting me. I have seen the order of the navy in print; and one of the officers of the navy had assured me that this transcript was correct. The instructions in this order were, to destroy my person and my property in descending the Mississippi. Now I wish, if possible, to authenticate this statement; and it was for this purpose, when I passed through Washington lately, that I addressed myself to Mr. Robert Smith. That gentleman seemed to admit the propriety of my application, but objected to my course. He informed me that if I would apply to him through one of my counsel, there could be no difficulty in granting the object of my application. I have since applied in this manner to Mr. Smith, but without success. Hence I feel it necessary to resort to the authority of this court to call upon them to issue a subpoena to the president of the United States, with a clause, requiring him to produce certain papers; or, in other words, to issue the subpoena duces tecum. The attorney for the United States will, however, save the time of this court, if he will consent to produce the letter of the 21st October, with the accompanying papers, and also authentic orders of the navy and war departments.

Mr. Hay declared that he knew not for what this information could be wanted; to what purpose such evidence could relate; and whether it was to be used on the motion for commitment or on the trial in chief.

Mr. Burr, Mr. Wickham, and Mr. Martin observed that perhaps it would be used on both, according as circumstances might require.

Mr. Hay declared that all delay was unnecessary; but he pledged himself, if possible, to obtain the papers which were wanted; and not only those, but every paper which might be necessary to the elucidation of the case.

After considerable of conversation between counsel as to the objects of applying for the subpoena, and the probability of obtaining the papers without it, Mr. Wickham remarked that as to the order from the navy department, a copy might be sufficient, but as to Wilkinson's letter, "We wish to see itself here; and surely it may be trusted in the hands of the attorney for the United States."

Mr. Hay then said: It seems, then, that copies of papers from the government of the United States will not be received! After such an observation, sir, I retract everything that I have promised; let gentlemen, sir, take their own course.

Mr. Wickham explained, disavowing any insinuation against the fairness of the conduct of the government. But he wanted the highest possible degree of evidence, and to confront General Wilkinson with his own letter.

Mr. Hay was satisfied with the explanation, and renewed his promise to apply for the papers if the court deemed them material.

After some further conversation which did not result in any arrangement satisfactory to Mr. Burr's counsel—

The Chief Justice said: If the attorney for the United States is satisfied that the court has a right to issue the subpoena duces tecum, I will grant the motion.

Mr. Hay. I am not, sir.

Chief Justice. I am not prepared to give an opinion on this point, and therefore I must call for argument.

After some further conversation, the court adjourned.

Wednesday, June 10, 1807.

The court met according to adjournment. The subject of the subpoena duces tecum was resumed.

The following affidavit, drawn up and sworn to by Mr. Burr, was read in support of the motion for the subpoena.

"Aaron Burr maketh oath, that he hath great reason to believe that a letter from General Wilkinson to the president of the United States, dated 21st October, 1806, as mentioned in the president's message of the 22d January, 1807, to both houses of congress, together with the documents accompanying the said letter, and copy of the answer of said Thomas Jefferson, or of any one by his authority, to the said letter, may be material in his defence, in the prosecution against him. And further, that he hath reason to believe the military and naval orders given by the president of the United States, through the departments of war and of the navy, to the officers of the army and navy, at or near the New Orleans stations, touching or concerning the said Burr, or his property, will also be material in his defence.

"Aaron Burr.

"Sworn to in open court, 10th June, 1807."

Upon this motion a protracted debate arose, occupying two entire days, and extending into the third, in which the motion was supported by Messrs. Wickham, Botts, Randolph, Martin, and Burr, and opposed by Messrs. Hay, MacRae, and Wirt. Much ability and eloquence were displayed on both sides. But few points of law were contested in the argument, and these are all clearly stated in the opinion of the court, which is here given in full. The arguments turned more upon the propriety of granting the motion, than upon any strictly legal question; although the right of the accused to apply to the court for process to obtain any testimony whatever, at this stage of the case, was denied by the counsel for the United States. The discussion took a wide range, and the course of the government towards Col. Burr, and the conduct of Gen. Wilkinson in respect to him, were animadverted upon with much severity by counsel for the defence, and zealously defended by the counsel for the United States.

On the part of the prosecution it was insisted that the subpoena was unnecessary, because certified copies of any documents in the executive departments could be obtained by a proper application. It was said to be improper to call upon the president to produce the letter of Gen. Wilkinson, because it was a private letter, and probably contained confidential communications, which the president ought not and could not be compelled to disclose. It might contain state secrets, which could not be divulged without endangering the national safety. It was argued that the documents demanded could not be material to the defence, and objected that the affidavit did not even state, in positive terms, that they would be material.

On the part of the defence it was denied that any affidavit whatever was necessary to support the motion. The proposition that the president could withhold a paper material to the defence, merely because it contained confidential communications, was denied, and pronounced wholly untenable in law. If the letter contained state secrets which it would be inconsistent with the public safety to disclose, the president could say so in the return to the subpoena; but it was not to be assumed until he did say so. Or, if the letter contained anything of a confidential character, not relating to the case, the president could point out such parts as he did not wish to have exposed, and they need not be read in court. A copy of the letter, it was said, would not answer the purposes of the defence. Gen. Wilkinson was admitted to be the witness upon whom the prosecution mainly depended. His relation to the prosecution was such, that he had the strongest possible motive for bolstering it up; and if he failed in it, he would himself sink into irreparable disgrace. When he should come upon the stand to sustain a prosecution in which he had so much at stake, it might be of the utmost importance to confront him with his letter in his own handwriting. A copy would not do, because he might deny it; and no confidence was reposed by the defence in his integrity. The contents of the letter were only known to the defence in so far as they had been divulged by the president in a communication to congress. In that communication the president had stated that he had received a letter from Gen. Wilkinson in relation to the transactions of Mr. Burr, "of whose guilt," he says, "there can be no doubt." The president was severely censured (by Mr. Randolph) for thus assuming the functions of a judge, and pronouncing judgment against Mr. Burr in transacting his executive duties. The president had stated in said communication that Gen. Wilkinson had written at large to him respecting Mr. Burr. The defence wanted this letter, and had no doubt that in some of those things which Gen. Wilkinson had stated to the president, they would be able to trip him up.

As to the orders of the war and navy departments, it was said that certified copies would answer. But the secretary of the navy had already refused to furnish copies to one of Mr. Burr's counsel, on an application to him therefor, and they could not run the risk of another refusal. One of these orders (or what purported to be one) had been published in the Natchez Gazette, and it amounted to an order calling forth a military force to attack Mr. Burr and his associates, and destroy their property. It was contended that the president had no legal or constitutional power to issue such an order as this was represented to be; and if an unconstitutional and illegal order had been issued to destroy any man and his property, that man was justified in resisting it. Authenticated copies of these orders, therefore, might be necessary to defend Mr. Burr against any attempt to prove that he had resisted, or made any preparation to resist, the military forces called forth against him. If no orders had been issued calling forth a military force to attack him, then he had a right to resist any such force as being a mere unauthorized mob. On these grounds it was of the utmost importance to the defence to know exactly what orders had been issued in relation to Col. Burr.

At the close of the discussion Mr. Hay said he had in his possession a copy of the very paper which had been so denounced by the counsel for cruelty and severity; the order issued by the secretary of the navy, which he proposed to read in order to show that there was no such thing in it. The opposite counsel desired to look at the paper, to ascertain whether it was the same they had seen in the Natchez Gazette; but Mr. Hay refused to let them take it. He finally put it up again, declaring that he believed it to be the same, but gentlemen did not want it to be read.

Before MARSHALL, Chief Justice, and GRIFFIN, District Judge.

MARSHALL, Chief Justice. The object of the motion now to be decided is to obtain copies of certain orders, understood to have been issued to the land and naval officers of the United States for the apprehension of the accused, and an original letter from General Wilkinson to the president in relation to the accused, with the answer of the president to that letter, which papers are supposed to be material to the defence. As the legal mode of effecting this object, a motion is made for a subpoena duces tecum, to be directed to the president of the United States. In opposition to this motion, a preliminary point has been made by the counsel for the prosecution. It has been insisted by them that, until the grand jury shall have found a true bill, the party accused is not entitled to subpoenas nor to the aid of the court to obtain his testimony. It will not be said that this opinion is now, for the first time, advanced in the United States; but certainly it is now, for the first time, advanced in Virginia. So far back as any knowledge of our jurisprudence is possessed, the uniform practice of this country has been, to permit any individual, who was charged with any crime, to prepare for his defence, and to obtain the process of the court, for the purpose of enabling him so to do. This practice is as convenient and as consonant to justice as it is to humanity. It prevents, in a great measure, those delays which are never desirable, which frequently occasion the loss of testimony, and which are often oppressive. That would be the inevitable consequence of withholding from a prisoner the process of the court, until the indictment against him was found by the grand jury. The right of an accused person to the process of the court to compel the attendance of witnesses seems to follow, necessarily, from the right to examine those witnesses; and, wherever the right exists, it would be reasonable that it should be accompanied with the means of rendering it effectual. It is not doubted that a person who appears before a court under a recognizance, must expect that a bill will be preferred against him, or that a question concerning the continuance of the recognizance will be brought before the court. In the first event, he has the right, and it is perhaps his duty, to prepare for his defence at the trial. In the second event, it will not be denied that he possesses the right to examine witnesses on the question of continuing his recognizance. In either case it would seem reasonable that he should be entitled to the process of the court to procure the attendance of his witnesses. The genius and character of our laws and usages are friendly, not to condemnation at all events, but to a fair and impartial trial; and they consequently allow to the accused the right of preparing the means to secure such a trial. The objection that the attorney may refuse to proceed at this time, and that no day is fixed for the trial, if he should proceed, presents no real difficulty. It would be a very insufficient excuse to a prisoner, who had failed to prepare for his trial, to say that he was not certain the attorney would proceed against him. Had the indictment been found at the first term, it would have been in some measure uncertain whether there would have been a trial at this, and still more uncertain on what day that trial would take place; yet subpoenas would have issued returnable to the first day of the term; and if after its commencement other subpoenas had been required, they would have issued, returnable as the court might direct. In fact, all process to which the law has affixed no certain return day is made returnable at the discretion of the court. General principles, then, and general practice are in favor of the right of every accused person, so soon as his case is in court, to prepare for his defence, and to receive the aid of the process of the court to compel the attendance of his witnesses.

The constitution and laws of the United States will now be considered for the purpose of ascertaining how they bear upon the question. The eighth amendment to the constitution gives to the accused, "in all criminal prosecutions, a right to a speedy and public trial, and to compulsory process for obtaining witnesses in his favor." The right given by this article must be deemed sacred by the courts, and the article should be so construed as to be something more than a dead letter. What can more effectually elude the right to a speedy trial than the declaration that the accused shall be disabled from preparing for it until an indictment shall be found against him? It is certainly much more in the true spirit of the provision which secures to the accused a speedy trial, that he should have the benefit of the provision which entitles him to compulsory process as soon as he is brought into court. This observation derives additional force from a consideration of the manner in which this subject has been contemplated by congress. It is obviously the intention of the national legislature, that in all capital cases the accused shall be entitled to process before indictment found. The words of the law are, "and every such person or persons accused or indicted of the crimes aforesaid, (that is, of treason or any other capital offence,) shall be allowed and admitted in his said defence to make any proof that he or they can produce by lawful witness or witnesses, and shall have the like process of the court where he or they shall be tried, to compel his or their witnesses to appear at his or their trial as is usually granted to compel witnesses to appear on the prosecution against them." This provision is made for persons accused or indicted. From the imperfection of human language, it frequently happens that sentences which ought to be the most explicit are of doubtful construction; and in this case the words "accused or indicted" may be construed to be synonymous, to describe a person in the same situation, or to apply to different stages of the prosecution. The word "or" may be taken in a conjunctive or a disjunctive sense. A reason for understanding them in the latter sense is furnished by the section itself. It commences with declaring that any person who shall be accused and indicted of treason shall have a copy of the indictment, and at least three days before his trial. This right is obviously to be enjoyed after an indictment, and therefore the words are, "accused and indicted." So with respect to the subsequent clause, which authorizes a party to make his defence, and directs the court, on his application, to assign him counsel. The words relate to any person accused and indicted. But, when the section proceeds to authorize the compulsory process for witnesses, the phraseology is changed. The words are, "and every such person or persons accused or indicted," &c., thereby adapting the expression to the situation of an accused person both before and after indictment. It is to be remarked, too, that the person so accused or indicted is to have "the like process to compel his or their witnesses to appear at his or their trial, as is usually granted to compel witnesses to appear on the prosecution against him." The fair construction of this clause would seem to be, that with respect to the means of compelling the attendance of witnesses to be furnished by the court, the prosecution and defence are placed by the law on equal ground. The right of the prosecutor to take out subpoenas, or to avail himself of the aid of the court, in any stage of the proceedings previous to the indictment, is not controverted. This act of congress, it is true, applies only to capital cases; but persons charged with offences not capital have a constitutional and a legal right to examine their testimony; and this act ought to be considered as declaratory of the common law in cases where this constitutional right exists.

Upon immemorial usage, then, and upon what is deemed a sound construction of the constitution and law of the land, the court is of opinion that any person charged with a crime in the courts of the United States has a right, before as well as after indictment, to the process of the court to compel the attendance of his witnesses. Much delay and much inconvenience may be avoided by this construction: no mischief, which is perceived, can be produced by it. The process would only issue when, according to the ordinary course of proceeding, the indictment would be tried at the term to which the subpoena is made returnable; so that it becomes incumbent on the accused to be ready for his trial at that term.

This point being disposed of, it remains to inquire whether a subpoena duces tecum can be directed to the president of the United States, and whether it ought to be directed in this case? This question originally consisted of two parts. It was at first doubted whether a subpoena could issue, in any case, to the chief magistrate of the nation; and if it could, whether that subpoena could do more than direct his personal attendance; whether it could direct him to bring with him a paper which was to constitute the gist of his testimony. While the argument was opening, the attorney for the United States avowed his opinion that a general subpoena might issue to the president; but not a subpoena duces tecum. This terminated the argument on that part of the question. The court, however, has thought it necessary to state briefly the foundation of its opinion, that such a subpoena may issue. In the provisions of the constitution, and of the statute, which give to the accused a right to the compulsory process of the court, there is no exception whatever. The obligation, therefore, of those provisions is general; and it would seem that no person could claim an exemption from them, but one who would not be a witness. At any rate, if an exception to the general principle exist, it must be looked for in the law of evidence. The exceptions furnished by the law of evidence, (with one only reservation,) so far as they are personal, are of those only whose testimony could not be received. The single reservation alluded to is the case of the king. Although he may, perhaps, give testimony, it is said to be incompatible with his dignity to appear under the process of the court. Of the many points of difference which exist between the first magistrate in England and the first magistrate of the United States, in respect to the personal dignity conferred on them by the constitutions of their respective nations, the court will only select and mention two. It is a principle of the English constitution that the king can do no wrong, that no blame can be imputed to him, that he cannot be named in debate. By the constitution of the United States, the president, as well as any other officer of the government, may be impeached, and may be removed from office on high crimes and misdemeanors. By the constitution of Great Britain, the crown is hereditary, and the monarch can never be a subject. By that of the United States, the president is elected from the mass of the people, and, on the expiration of the time for which he is elected, returns to the mass of the people again. How essentially this difference of circumstances must vary the policy of the laws of the two countries, in reference to the personal dignity of the executive chief, will be perceived by every person. In this respect the first magistrate of the Union may more properly be likened to the first magistrate of a state; at any rate, under the former Confederation; and it is not known ever to have been doubted, but that the chief magistrate of a state might be served with a subpoena ad testificandum. If, in any court of the United States, it has ever been decided that a subpoena cannot issue to the president, that decision is unknown to this court.

If, upon any principle, the president could be construed to stand exempt from the general provisions of the constitution, it would be, because his duties as chief magistrate demand his whole time for national objects. But it is apparent that this demand is not unremitting; and, if it should exist at the time when his attendance on a court is required, it would be shown on the return of the subpoena, and would rather constitute a reason for not obeying the process of the court than a reason against its being issued. In point of fact it cannot be doubted that the people of England have the same interest in the service of the executive government, that is, of the cabinet counsel, that the American people have in the service of the executive of the United States, and that their duties are as arduous and as unremitting. Yet it has never been alleged, that a subpoena might not be directed to them. It cannot be denied that to issue a subpoena to a person filling the exalted position of the chief magistrate is a duty which would be dispensed with more cheerfully than it would be performed; but, if it be a duty, the court can have no choice in the case. If, then, as is admitted by the counsel for the United States, a subpoena may issue to the president, the accused is entitled to it of course; and whatever difference may exist with respect to the power to compel the same obedience to the process, as if it had been directed to a private citizen, there exists no difference with respect to the right to obtain it. The guard, furnished to this high officer, to protect him from being harassed by vexatious and unnecessary subpoenas, is to be looked for in the conduct of a court after those subpoenas have issued; not in any circumstance which is to precede their being issued. If, in being summoned to give his personal attendance to testify, the law does not discriminate between the president and a private citizen, what foundation is there for the opinion that this difference is created by the circumstance that his testimony depends on a paper in his possession, not on facts which have come to his knowledge otherwise than by writing? The court can perceive no foundation for such an opinion. The propriety of introducing any paper into a case, as testimony, must depend on the character of the paper, not on the character of the person who holds it. A subpoena duces tecum, then, may issue to any person to whom an ordinary subpoena may issue, directing him to bring any paper of which the party praying it has a right to avail himself as testimony; if, indeed, that be the necessary process for obtaining the view of such a paper. When this subject was suddenly introduced, the court felt some doubt concerning the propriety of directing a subpoena to the chief magistrate, and some doubt also concerning the propriety of directing any paper in his possession, not public in its nature, to be exhibited in court. The impression that the questions which might arise in consequence of such process, were more proper for discussion on the return of the process than on its issuing, was then strong on the mind of the judges; but the circumspection with which they would take any step which would in any manner relate to that high personage, prevented their yielding readily to those impressions, and induced the request that those points, if not admitted, might be argued. The result of that argument is a confirmation of the impression originally entertained. The court can perceive no legal objection to issuing a subpoena duces tecum to any person whatever, provided the case be such as to justify the process. This is said to be a motion to the discretion of the court. This is true. But a motion to its discretion is a motion, not to its inclination, but to its judgment; and its judgment is to be guided by sound legal principles. A subpoena duces tecum varies from an ordinary subpoena only in this; that a witness is summoned for the purpose of bringing with him a paper in his custody. In some of our sister states whose system of jurisprudence is erected on the same foundation with our own, this process, we learn, issues of course. In this state it issues, not absolutely of course, but with leave of the court. No case, however, exists as is believed, in which the motion has been founded on an affidavit, in which it has been denied, or in which it has been opposed. It has been truly observed that the opposite party can, regularly, take no more interest in the awarding a subpoena duces tecum than in the awarding an ordinary subpoena. In either case he may object to any delay, the grant of which may be implied in granting the subpoena; but he can no more object regularly to the legal means of obtaining testimony, which exists in the papers, than in the mind of the person who may be summoned. If no inconvenience can be sustained by the opposite party, he can only oppose the motion in the character of an amicus curiae, to prevent the court from making an improper order, or from burthening some officer by compelling an unnecessary attendance. This court would certainly be very unwilling to say that upon fair construction the constitutional and legal right to obtain its process, to compel the attendance of witnesses, does not extend to their bringing with them such papers as may be material in the defence. The literal distinction which exists between the cases is too much attenuated to be countenanced in the tribunals of a just and humane nation. If, then, the subpoena be issued without inquiry into the manner of its application, it would seem to trench on the privileges which the constitution extends to the accused; it would seem to reduce his means of defence within narrower limits than is designed by the fundamental law of our country, if an overstrained rigor should be used with respect to his right to apply for papers deemed by himself to be material. In the one case the accused is made the absolute judge of the testimony to be summoned; if, in the other, he is not a judge, absolutely for himself, his judgment ought to be controlled only so far as it is apparent that he means to exercise his privileges not really in his own defence, but for purposes which the court ought to discountenance. The court would not lend its aid to motions obviously designed to manifest disrespect to the government; but the court has no right to refuse its aid to motions for papers to which the accused may be entitled, and which may be material in his defence. These observations are made to show the nature of the discretion which may be exercised. If it be apparent that the papers are irrelative to the case, or that for state reasons they cannot be introduced into the defence, the subpoena duces tecum would be useless. But, if this be not apparent, if they may be important in the defence, if they may be safely read at the trial, would it not be a blot in the page which records the judicial proceedings of this country, if, in a case of such serious import as this, the accused should be denied the use of them? The counsel for the United States takes a very different view of the subject, and insist that a motion for process to obtain testimony should be supported by the same full and explicit proof of the nature and application of that testimony, which would be required on a motion, which would delay public justice, which would arrest the ordinary course of proceeding, or would in any other manner affect the rights of the opposite party. In favor of this position has been urged the opinion of one, whose loss as a friend and as a judge I sincerely deplore; whose worth I feel, and whose authority I shall at all times greatly respect. If his opinions were really opposed to mine, I should certainly revise, deliberately revise, the judgment I had formed; but I perceive no such opposition.

In the trials of Smith and Ogden [U. S. v. Smith, Case No. 16,342], the court in which Judge Patterson presided, required a special affidavit in support of a motion made by the counsel for the accused for a continuance and for an attachment against witnesses who had been subpoenaed and who had failed to attend. Had this requisition of a special affidavit been made as well a foundation for an attachment as for a continuance, the cases would not have been parallel, because the attachment was considered by the counsel for the prosecution merely as a means of punishing the contempt, and a court might certainly require stronger testimony to induce them to punish a contempt, than would be required to lend its aid to a party in order to procure evidence in a cause. But the proof furnished by the case is most conclusive that the special statements of the affidavit were required solely on account of the continuance. Although the counsel for the United States considered the motion for an attachment merely as a mode of punishing for contempt, the counsel for Smith and Ogden considered it as compulsory process to bring in a witness, and moved a continuance until they could have the benefit of this process. The continuance was to arrest the ordinary course of justice; and, therefore, the court required a special affidavit, showing the materiality of the testimony before this continuance could be granted. Prima facie the evidence could not apply to the case; and there was an additional reason for a special affidavit. The object of this special statement was expressly said to be for a continuance. Colden proceeded: "The present application is to put off the cause on account of the absence of witnesses, whose testimony the defendant alleges is material for his defence, and who have disobeyed the ordinary process of the court. In compliance with the intimation from the bench yesterday, the defendant has disclosed by the affidavit which I have just read, the points to which he expects the witnesses who have been summoned will testify. If the court cannot or will not issue compulsory process to bring in the witnesses who are the objects of this application, then the cause will not be postponed. Or, if it appears to the court, that the matter disclosed by the affidavit might not be given in evidence, if the witness were now here, then we cannot expect that our motion will be successful. For it would be absurd to suppose that the court will postpone the trial on account of the absence of witnesses whom they cannot compel to appear, and of whose voluntary attendance there is too much reason to despair; or, on account of the absence of witnesses who, if they were before the court, could not be heard on the trial." See the trials of Smith and Ogden [supra]. This argument states, unequivocally, the purpose for which a special affidavit was required.

The counsel for the United States considered the subject in the same light. After exhibiting an affidavit for the purpose of showing that the witnesses could not probably possess any material information, Mr. Standford said: "It was decided by the court yesterday that it was incumbent on the defendant, in order to entitle himself to a postponement of the trial on account of the absence of these witnesses, to show in what respect they are material for his defence. It was the opinion of the court that the general affidavit, in common form, would not be sufficient for this purpose, but that the particular facts expected from the witnesses must be disclosed in order that the court might, upon those facts, judge of the propriety of granting the postponement."

The court frequently treated the subject so as to show the opinion that the special affidavit was required only on account of the continuance; but what is conclusive on this point is, that after deciding the testimony of the witnesses to be such as could not be offered to the jury, Judge Patterson was of opinion that a rule, to show cause why an attachment should not issue, ought to be granted. He could not have required the materiality of the witness to be shown on a motion, the success of which did not, in his opinion, in any degree depend on that materiality; and which he granted after deciding the testimony to be such as the jury ought not to hear. It is, then, most apparent that the opinion of Judge Patterson has been misunderstood, and that no inference can possibly be drawn from it, opposed to the principle which has been laid down by the court. That principle will therefore be applied to the present motion.

The first paper required is the letter of General Wilkinson, which was referred to in the message of the president to congress. The application of that letter to the case is shown by the terms in which the communication was made. It is a statement of the conduct of the accused made by the person who is declared to be the essential witness against him. The order for producing this letter is opposed:

First, because it is not material to the defense. It is a principle, universally acknowledged, that a party has a right to oppose to the testimony of any witness against him, the declarations which that witness has made at other times on the same subject. If he possesses this right, he must bring forward proof of those declarations. This proof must be obtained before he knows positively what the witness will say; for if he waits until the witness has been heard at the trial, it is too late to meet him with his former declarations. Those former declarations, therefore, constitute a mass of testimony, which a party has a right to obtain by way of precaution, and the positive necessity of which can only be decided at the trial. It is with some surprise an argument was heard from the bar, insinuating that the award of a subpoena on this ground gave the countenance of the court to suspicions affecting the veracity of a witness who is to appear on the part of the United States. This observation could not have been considered. In contests of this description, the court takes no part; the court has no right to take a part. Every person may give in evidence, testimony such as is stated in this case. What would be the feelings of the prosecutor if, in this case, the accused should produce a witness completely exculpating himself, and the attorney for the United States should be arrested in his attempt to prove what the same witness had said upon a former occasion, by a declaration from the bench that such an attempt could not be permitted, because it would imply a suspicion in the court that the witness had not spoken the truth? Respecting so unjustifiable an interposition but one opinion would be formed.

The second objection is, that the letter contains matter which ought not to be disclosed. That there may be matter, the production of which the court would not require, is certain; but, in a capital case, that the accused ought, in some form, to have the benefit of it, if it were really essential to his defence, is a position which the court would very reluctantly deny. It ought not to be believed that the department which superintends prosecutions in criminal cases, would be inclined to withhold it. What ought to be done under such circumstances presents a delicate question, the discussion of which, it is hoped, will never be rendered necessary in this country. At present it need only be said that the question does not occur at this time. There is certainly nothing before the court which shows that the letter in question contains any matter the disclosure of which would endanger the public safety. If it does contain such matter, the fact may appear before the disclosure is made. If it does contain any matter which it would be imprudent to disclose, which it is not the wish of the executive to disclose, such matter, if it be not immediately and essentially applicable to the point, will, of course, be suppressed. It is not easy to conceive that so much of the letter as relates to the conduct of the accused can be a subject of delicacy with the president. Everything of this kind, however, will have its due consideration on the return of the subpoena.

Thirdly, it has been alleged that a copy may be received instead of the original, and the act of congress has been cited in support of this proposition. This argument presupposes that the letter required is a document filed in the department of state, the reverse of which may be and most probably is the fact. Letters addressed to the president are most usually retained by himself. They do not belong to any of the departments. But, were the facts otherwise, a copy might not answer the purpose. The copy would not be superior to the original, and the original itself would not be admitted, if denied, without proof that it was in the handwriting of the witness. Suppose the case put at the bar of an indictment on this letter for a libel, and on its production it should appear not to be in the handwriting of the person indicted. Would its being deposited in the department of state make it his writing, or subject him to the consequence of having written it? Certainly not. For the purpose, then, of showing the letter to have been written by a particular person, the original must be produced, and a copy could not be admitted. On the confidential nature of this letter much has been said at the bar and authorities have been produced which appear to be conclusive. Had its contents been orally communicated, the person to whom the communications were made could not have excused himself from detailing them, so far as they might be deemed essential in the defence. Their being in writing gives no additional sanctity; the only difference produced by the circumstance is, that the contents of the paper must be proved by the paper itself not by the recollection of the witness.

Much has been said about the disrespect to the chief magistrate, which is implied by this motion, and by such a decision of it as the law is believed to require. These observations will be very truly answered by the declaration that this court feels many, perhaps, peculiar motives for manifesting as guarded a respect for the chief magistrate of the Union as is compatible with its official duties. To go beyond these would exhibit a conduct which would deserve some other appellation than the term respect. It is not for the court to anticipate the event of the present prosecution. Should it terminate as is expected on the part of the United States, all those who are concerned in it should certainly regret that a paper which the accused believed to be essential to his defence, which may, for aught that now appears, be essential, had been withheld from him. I will not say, that this circumstance would, in any degree, tarnish the reputation of the government; but I will say, that it would justly tarnish the reputation of the court which had given its sanction to its being withheld. Might I be permitted to utter one sentiment, with respect to myself, it would be to deplore, most earnestly, the occasion which should compel me to look back on any part of my official conduct with so much self-reproach as I should feel, could I declare, on the information now possessed, that the accused is not entitled to the letter in question, if it should be really important to him.

The propriety of requiring the answer to this letter is more questionable. It is alleged that it most probably communicates orders showing the situation of this country with Spain, which will be important on the misdemeanor. If it contain matter not essential to the defence, and the disclosure be unpleasant to the executive, it certainly ought not to be disclosed. This is a point which will appear on the return. The demand of the orders which have been issued, and which have been, as is alleged, published in the Natchez Gazette, is by no means unusual. Such documents have often been produced in the courts of the United States and the courts of England. If they contain matter interesting to the nation, the concealment of which is required by the public safety, that matter will appear upon the return. If they do not, and are material, they may be exhibited. It is said they cannot be material, because they cannot justify any unlawful resistance which may have been employed or meditated by the accused. Were this admitted, and were it also admitted that such resistance would amount to treason, the orders might still be material; because they might tend to weaken the endeavor to connect such overt act with any overt act of which this court may take cognizance. The court, however, is rather inclined to the opinion that the subpoena in such case ought to be directed to the head of the department in whose custody the orders are. The court must suppose that the letter of the secretary of the navy, which has been stated by the attorney for the United States, to refer the counsel for the prisoner to his legal remedy for the copies he desired, alluded to such a motion as is now made.

The affidavit on which the motion is grounded has not been noticed. It is believed that such a subpoena, as is asked, ought to issue, if there exist any reason for supposing that the testimony may be material, and ought to be admitted. It is only because the subpoena is to those who administer the government of this country, that such an affidavit was required as would furnish probable cause to believe that the testimony was desired for the real purposes of defence, and not for such as this court will forever discountenance.

20

Thomas Jefferson to George Hay
12 June 1807

Works 10:398–99

Your letter of the 9th is this moment received. Reserving the necessary right of the President of the U S to decide, independently of all other authority, what papers, coming to him as President, the public interests permit to be communicated, & to whom, I assure you of my readiness under that restriction, voluntarily to furnish on all occasions, whatever the purposes of justice may require. But the letter of Genl Wilkinson, of Oct 21, requested for the defence of Colonel Burr, with every other paper relating to the charges against him, which were in my possession when the Attorney General went on to Richmond in March, I then delivered to him; and I have always taken for granted he left the whole with you. If he did, & the bundle retains the order in which I had arranged it, you will readily find the letter desired, under the date of it's receipt, which was Nov 25; but lest the Attorney General should not have left those papers with you, I this day write to him to forward this one by post. An uncertainty whether he is at Philadelphia, Wilmington, or New Castle, may produce delay in his receiving my letter, of which it is proper you should be apprized. But, as I do not recollect the whole contents of that letter, I must beg leave to devolve on you the exercise of that discretion which it would be my right & duty to exercise, by withholding the communication of any parts of the letter, which are not directly material for the purposes of justice.

With this application, which is specific, a prompt compliance is practicable. But when the request goes to "copies of the orders issued in relation to Colo Burr, to the officers at Orleans, Natchez, &c., by the Secretaries of the War & Navy departments," it seems to cover a correspondence of many months, with such a variety of officers, civil & military, all over the U S, as would amount to the laying open the whole executive books. I have desired the Secretary at War to examine his official communications; and on a view of these, we may be able to judge what can & ought to be done, towards a compliance with the request. If the defendant alleges that there was any particular order, which, as a cause, produced any particular act on his part, then he must know what this order was, can specify it, and a prompt answer can be given. If the *object* had been specified, we might then have had some guide for our conjectures, as to what part of the executive records might be useful to him; but, with a perfect willingness to do what is right, we are without the indications which may enable us to do it. If the researches of the Secretary at War should produce anything proper for communication, & pertinent to any point we can conceive in the defence before the court, it shall be forwarded to you.

21

Thomas Jefferson to George Hay
17 June 1807

Works 10:400–402

In answering your letter of the 9th, which desired a communication of one to me from Genl Wilkinson, specified by it's date, I informed you in mine of the 12th that I had delivered it, with all other papers respecting the charges against Aaron Burr, to the Attorney Genl, when he went to Richmond; that I had supposed he had left them in your possession, but would immediately write to him, if he had not, to forward that particular letter without delay. I wrote to him accordingly on the same day, but having no answer, I know not whether he has forwarded the letter. I stated in the same letter, that I had desired the Secretary at War to examine his office, in order to comply with your further request, to furnish copies of the orders which had been given respecting Aaron Burr and his property; and in a subsequent letter of the same day, I forwarded to you copies of two letters from the Secretary at War, which appeared to be within the description expressed in your letter. The order from the Secretary of the Navy, you said, you were in possession of. The receipt of these papers had, I presume, so far anticipated, and others this day forwarded will have substantially fulfilled the object of a subpoena from the District Court of Richmond, requiring that those officers & myself should attend the Court in Richmond, with the letter of Genl Wilkinson, the answer to that letter, & the orders of the departments of War & the Navy, therein generally described. No answer to Genl Wilkinson's letter, other than a mere acknolegement of it's receipt, in a letter written for a different purpose, was ever written by myself or any other. To these communications of papers, I will add, that if the defendant supposes there are any facts within the knolege of the Heads of departments, or of myself, which can be useful for his defence, from a desire of doing anything our situation will permit in furtherance of justice, we shall be ready to give him the benefit of it, by way of deposition, through any persons whom the Court shall authorize to take our testimony at this place. I know, indeed, that this cannot be done but by consent of parties; & I therefore authorize you to give consent on the part of the U S. Mr. Burr's consent will be given of course, if he supposes the testimony useful.

As to our personal attendance at Richmond, I am persuaded the Court is sensible, that paramount duties to the nation at large control the obligation of compliance with their summons in this case; as they would, should we receive a similar one, to attend the trials of Blannerhassett & others, in the Mississippi territory, those instituted at St. Louis and other places on the western waters, or at any place, other than the seat of government. To comply with such calls would leave the nation without an executive branch, whose agency, nevertheless, is understood to be so constantly necessary, that it is the sole branch which the constitution requires to be always in function. It could not then mean that it should be withdrawn from it's station by any co-ordinate authority.

With respect to papers, there is certainly a public & a private side to our offices. To the former belong grants of land, patents for inventions, certain commissions, proclamations, & other papers patent in their nature. To the other belong mere executive proceedings. All nations have found it necessary, that for the advantageous conduct of their affairs, some of these proceedings, at least, should remain known to their executive functionary only. He, of course, from the nature of the case, must be the sole judge of which of them the public interests will permit publication. Hence, under our Constitution, in requests of papers, from the legislative to the executive branch, an exception is carefully expressed, as to those which he may deem the public welfare may require not to be disclosed; as you will see in the enclosed resolution of the H of Representatives, which produced the message of Jan 22, respecting this case. The respect mutually due between the constituted authorities, in their official intercourse, as well as sincere dispositions to do for every one what is just, will always insure from the executive, in exercising the duty of discrimination confided to him, the same candor & integrity to which the nation has in like manner trusted in the disposal of it's judiciary authorities. Considering you as the organ for communicating these sentiments to the Court, I address them to you for that purpose, & salute you with esteem & respect.

22

Thomas Jefferson to George Hay
20 June 1807
Works 10:404–5

I did not see till last night the opinion of the Judge on the *subpoena duces tecum* against the President. Considering the question there as *coram non judice,* I did not read his argument with much attention. Yet I saw readily enough, that, as is usual where an opinion is to be supported, right or wrong, he dwells much on smaller objections and passes over those which are solid. Laying down the position generally, that all persons owe obedience to subpoenas, he admits no exception unless it can be produced in his law books. But if the Constitution enjoins on a particular officer to be always engaged in a particular set of duties imposed on him, does not this supersede the general law, subjecting him to minor duties inconsistent with these? The Constitution enjoins his constant agency in the concerns of 6. millions of people. Is the law paramount to this, which calls on him on behalf of a single one? Let us apply the Judge's own doctrine to the case of himself & his brethren. The sheriff of Henrico summons him from the bench, to quell a riot somewhere in his county. The federal judge is, by the general law, a part of the *posse* of the State sheriff. Would the Judge abandon major duties to perform lesser ones? Again; the court of Orleans or Maine commands, by subpoenas, the attendance of all the judges of the Supreme Court. Would they abandon their posts as judges, and the interests of millions committed to them, to serve the purposes of a single individual? The leading principle of our Constitution is the independence of the Legislature, executive and judiciary of each other, and none are more jealous of this than the judiciary. But would the executive be independent of the judiciary, if he were subject to the *commands* of the latter, & to imprisonment for disobedience; if the several courts could bandy him from pillar to post, keep him constantly trudging from north to south & east to west, and withdraw him entirely from his constitutional duties? The intention of the Constitution, that each branch should be independent of the others, is further manifested by the means it has furnished to each, to protect itself from enterprises of force attempted on them by the others, and to none has it given more effectual or diversified means than to the executive. Again; because ministers can go into a court in London as witnesses, without interruption to their executive duties, it is inferred that they would go to a court 1000. or 1500. miles off, and that ours are to be dragged from Maine to Orleans by every criminal who will swear that their testimony "may be of use to him." The Judge says, "*it is apparent* that the President's duties as chief magistrate do not demand his whole time, & are not unremitting." If he alludes to our annual retirement from the seat of government, during the sickly season, he should be told that such arrangements are made for carrying on the public business, at and between the several stations we take, that it goes on as unremittingly there, as if we were at the seat of government.

23

Joseph Story, Commentaries on the Constitution 3:§§ 1407–10, 1413, 1429–36, 1444–46
1833

§ 1407. Under the confederation there was no national executive. The whole powers of the national government were vested in a congress, consisting of a single body; and that body was authorized to appoint a committee of the states, composed of one delegate from every state, to sit in the recess, and to delegate to them such of their own powers, not requiring the consent of nine states, as nine states should consent to. This want of a national executive was deemed a fatal defect in the confederation.

§ 1408. In the convention, there does not seem to have been any objection to the establishment of a national executive. But upon the question, whether it should consist of a single person, the affirmative was carried by a vote of seven states against three. The term of service was at first fixed at seven years, by a vote of five states against four, one being divided. The term was afterwards altered to four years, upon the report of a committee, and adopted by the vote of ten states against one.

§ 1409. In considering this clause, three practical questions are naturally suggested: First, whether there should be a distinct executive department; secondly, whether it should be composed of more than one person; and, thirdly, what should be the duration of office.

§ 1410. Upon the first question, little need be said. All America have at length concurred in the propriety of establishing a distinct executive department. The principle is embraced in every state constitution; and it seems now to be assumed among us, as a fundamental maxim of government, that the legislative, executive, and judicial departments ought to be separate, and the powers of one ought not to be exercised by either of the others. The same maxim is found recognised in express terms in many of our state constitutions. It is hardly necessary to repeat, that where all these powers are united in the same hands, there is a real despotism, to the extent of their coercive exercise. Where, on the other hand, they exist together, and yet depend for their exercise upon the mere authority of recommendation, (as they did under the confederation,) they become at once imbecile and arbitrary, subservient to popular clamour, and incapable of steady action. The harshness of the measures in relation to paper money, and the timidity and vacillation in relation to military affairs, are examples not easily to be forgotten.

. . . . .

§ 1413. The most distinguished statesmen have uniformly maintained the doctrine, that there ought to be a single executive, and a numerous legislature. They have considered energy, as the most necessary qualification of the power, and this as best attained by reposing the power in a single hand. At the same time, they have considered with equal propriety, that a numerous legislature was best adapted to the duties of legislation, and best calculated to conciliate the confidence of the people, and to secure their privileges and interests. Montesquieu has said, that "the executive power ought to be in the hands of a monarch, because this branch of government, having need of despatch, is better administered by one, than by many. On the other hand, whatever depends on the legislative power is oftentimes better regulated by many, than by a single person. But if there were no monarch, and the executive power should be committed to a certain number of persons, selected from the legislative body, there would be an end to liberty; by reason, that the two powers would be united, as the same persons would sometimes possess, and would always be able to possess, a share in both." De Lolme, in addition to other advantages, considers the unity of the executive as important in a free government, because it is thus more easily restrained. "In those states," says he, "where the execution of the laws is entrusted to several different hands, and to each with different titles and prerogatives, such division, and such changeableness of measures, which must be the consequence of it, constantly hide the true cause of the evils of the state. Sometimes military tribunes, and at others consuls bear an absolute sway. Sometimes patricians usurp every thing; and at other times those, who are called nobles. Sometimes the people are oppressed by decemvirs; and at others by dictators. Tyranny in such states does not always beat down the fences, that are set around it; but it leaps over them. When men think it confined to one place, it starts up again in another. It mocks the efforts of the people, not because it is invincible, but because it is unknown. But the indivisibility of the public power in England has constantly kept the views and efforts of the people directed to one and the same object." He adds, in another place, "we must observe a difference between the legislative and executive powers.

The latter may be confined, and even is the more easily so, when undivided. The legislature on the contrary, in order to its being restrained, should absolutely be divided."

. . . . .

§ 1429. What should be the proper duration of office is matter of more doubt and speculation. On the one hand, it may be said, that the shorter the period of office, the more security there will be against any dangerous abuse of power. The longer the period, the less will responsibility be felt, and the more personal ambition will be indulged. On the other hand, the considerations above stated prove, that a very short period is, practically speaking, equivalent to a surrender of the executive power, as a check in government, or subjects it to an intolerable vacillation and imbecility. In the convention itself much diversity of opinion existed on this subject. It was at one time proposed, that the executive should be chosen during good behaviour. But this proposition received little favour, and seems to have been abandoned without much effort.

§ 1430. Another proposition was (as has been seen) to choose the executive for seven years, which at first passed by a bare majority; but being coupled with a clause, "to be chosen by the national legislature," it was approved by the vote of eight states against two. Another clause, "to be ineligible a second time," was added by the vote of eight states against one, one being divided. In this form the clause stood in the first draft of the constitution, though some intermediate efforts were made to vary it. But it was ultimately altered upon the report of a committee so, as to change the mode of election, the term of office, and the re-eligibility, to their present form, by the vote of ten states against one.

§ 1431. It is most probable, that these three propositions had a mutual influence upon the final vote. Those, who wished a choice to be made by the people, rather than by the national legislature, would naturally incline to a shorter period of office, than seven years. Those, who were in favour of seven years, might be willing to consent to the clause against re-eligibility, when they would resist it, if the period of office were reduced to four years. And those, who favoured the latter, might more readily yield the prohibitory clause, than increase the duration of office. All this, however, is but conjecture; and the most, that can be gathered from the final result, is, that opinions, strongly maintained at the beginning of the discussion, were yielded up in a spirit of compromise, or abandoned upon the weight of argument.

§ 1432. It is observable, that the period actually fixed is intermediate between the term of office of the senate, and that of the house of representatives. In the course of one presidential term, the house is, or may be twice recomposed; and two-thirds of the senate changed, or re-elected. So far, as executive influence can be presumed to operate upon either branch of the legislature unfavourable to the rights of the people, the latter possess, in their elective franchise, ample means of redress. On the other hand, so far, as uniformity and stability in the administration of executive duties are desirable, they are in some measure secured by the more permanent tenure of office of the senate, which will check too hasty a departure from the old system, by a change of the executive, or representative branch of the government.

§ 1433. Whether the period of four years will answer all the purposes, for which the executive department is established, so as to give it at once energy and safety, and to preserve a due balance in the administration of the government, is a problem, which can be solved only by experience. That it will contribute far more, than a shorter period, towards these objects, and thus have a material influence upon the spirit and character of the government, may be safely affirmed. Between the commencement and termination of the period of office, there will be a considerable interval, at once to justify some independence of opinion and action, and some reasonable belief, that the propriety of the measures adopted during the administration may be seen, and felt by the community at large. The executive need not be intimidated in his course by the dread of an immediate loss of public confidence, without the power of regaining it before a new election; and he may, with some confidence, look forward to that esteem and respect of his fellow-citizens, which public services usually obtain, when they are faithfully and firmly pursued with an honest devotion to the public good. If he should be re-elected, he will still more extensively possess the means of carrying into effect a wise and beneficent system of policy, foreign as well as domestic. And if he should be compelled to retire, he cannot but have the consciousness, that measures, long enough pursued to be found useful, will be persevered in; or, if abandoned, the contrast will reflect new honour upon the past administration of the government, and perhaps reinstate him in office. At all events, the period is not long enough to justify any alarms for the public safety. The danger is not, that such a limited executive will become an absolute dictator; but, that he may be overwhelmed by the combined operations of popular influence and legislative power. It may be reasonably doubted, from the limited duration of this office, whether, in point of independence and firmness, he will not be found unequal to the task, which the constitution assigns him; and if such a doubt may be indulged, that alone will be decisive against any just jealousy of his encroachments. Even in England, where an hereditary monarch with vast prerogatives and patronage exists, it has been found, that the house of commons, from their immediate sympathy with the people, and their possession of the purse-strings of the nation, have been able effectually to check all his usurpations, and to diminish his influence. Nay, from small beginnings they have risen to be the great power in the state, counterpoising not only the authority of the crown, but the rank and wealth of the nobility; and gaining so solid an accession of influence, that they rather lead, than follow, the great measures of the administration.

§ 1434. In comparing the duration of office of the president with that of the state executives, additional reasons will present themselves in favour of the former. At the time of the adoption of the constitution, the executive was chosen annually in some of the states; in others, biennially; and in others, triennially. In some of the states, which have been subsequently admitted into the Union, the executive is chosen annually; in others, biennially; in others, triennially; and in others quadriennially. So that there is a great diversity of opinion exhibited on the subject, not only in the early, but in the later state constitutions in the Union. Now, it may be affirmed, that if, considering the nature of executive duties in the state governments, a period of office of two, or three, or even four years, has not been found either dangerous or inconvenient, there are very strong reasons, why the duration of office of the president of the United States should be at least equal to the longest of these periods. The nature of the duties to be performed by the president, both at home and abroad, are so various and complicated, as not only to require great talents, and great wisdom to perform them in any manner suitable to their importance and difficulty; but also long experience in office to acquire, what may be deemed the habits of administration, and a steadiness, as well as comprehensiveness, of view of all the bearings of measures. The executive duties in the states are few, and confined to a narrow range. Those of the president embrace all the ordinary and extraordinary arrangements of peace and war, of diplomacy and negotiation, of finance, of naval and military operations, and of the execution of the laws through almost infinite ramifications of details, and in places at vast distances from each other. He is compelled constantly to take into view the whole circuit of the Union; and to master many of the local interests and other circumstances, which may require new adaptations of measures to meet the public exigences. Considerable time must necessarily elapse before the requisite knowledge for the proper discharge of all the function of his office can be obtained; and, after it is obtained, time must be allowed to enable him to act upon that knowledge so, as to give vigour and healthinesss to the operations of the government. A short term of office would scarcely suffice, either for suitable knowledge, or suitable action. And to say the least, four years employed in the executive functions of the Union would not enable any man to become more familiar with them, than half that period with those of a single state. In short, the same general considerations, which require and justify a prolongation of the period of service of the members of the national legislature beyond that of the members of the state legislatures, apply with full force to the executive department. There have, nevertheless, at different periods of the government, been found able and ingenious minds, who have contended for an annual election of the president, or some shorter period, than four years.

§ 1435. Hitherto our experience has demonstrated, that the period has not been found practically so long, as to create danger to the people, or so short, as to take away a reasonable independence and energy from the executive. Still it cannot be disguised, that sufficient time has scarcely yet elapsed to enable us to pronounce a decisive opinion upon the subject; since the executive has generally acted with a majority of the nation; and in critical times has been sustained by the force of that majority in strong measures, and in times of more tranquillity, by the general moderation of the policy of his administration.

§ 1436. Another question, connected with the duration of office of the president, was much agitated in the convention, and has often since been a topic of serious discussion; and that is, whether he should be re-eligible to office. In support of the opinion, that the president ought to be ineligible after one period of office, it was urged, that the return of public officers into the mass of the common people, where they would feel the tone, which they had given to the administration of the laws, was the best security the public could have for their good behaviour. It would operate as a check upon the restlessness of ambition, and at the same time promote the independence of the executive. It would prevent him from a cringing subserviency to procure a re-election; or to a resort to corrupt intrigues for the maintenance of his power. And it was even added by some, whose imaginations were continually haunted by terrors of all sorts from the existence of any powers in the national government, that the re-eligibility of the executive would furnish an inducement to foreign governments to interfere in our elections, and would thus inflict upon us all the evils, which had desolated, and betrayed Poland.

. . . . .

§ 1444. The remaining part of the clause respects the Vice-President. If such an officer was to be created, it is plain, that the duration of his office should be co-extensive with that of the president. Indeed, as we shall immediately see, the scheme of the government necessarily embraced it; for when it was decided, that two persons were to be voted for, as president, it was decided, that he, who had the greatest number of votes of the electors, after the person chosen as president, should be vice-president. The principal question, therefore, was, whether such an officer ought to be created. It has been already stated, that the original scheme of the government did not provide for such an officer. By that scheme, the president was to be chosen by the national legislature. When afterwards an election by electors, chosen directly or indirectly by the people, was proposed by a select committee, the choice of a vice-president constituted a part of the proposition; and it was finally adopted by the vote of ten states against one.

§ 1445. The appointment of a vice-president was objected to, as unnecessary and dangerous. As president of the senate, he would be entrusted with a power to control the proceedings of that body; and as he must come from some one of the states, that state would have a double vote in the body. Besides, it was said, that if the president should die, or be removed, the vice-president might, by his influence, prevent the election of a president. But, at all events, he was a superfluous officer, having few duties to perform, and those might properly devolve upon some other established officer of the government.

§ 1446. The reasons in favour of the appointment were, in part, founded upon the same ground as the objections. It was seen, that a presiding officer must be chosen for the senate, where all the states were equally represented, and where an extreme jealousy might naturally be presumed to exist of the preponderating influence of any one state. If a member of the senate were appointed, either the state would be deprived of one vote, or would enjoy a double vote in case of an equality of votes, or there would be a tie, and no decision. Each of these alternatives was equally undesirable, and might lay the foundation of great practical inconveniences. An officer, therefore, chosen by the whole Union, would be a more suitable person to preside, and give a casting vote, since he would be more free, than any member of the senate, from local attachments, and local interests; and being the representative of the Union, would naturally be induced to consult the interests of all the states. Having only a casting vote, his influence could only operate exactly, when most beneficial; that is, to procure a decision. A still more important consideration is the necessity of providing some suitable person to perform the executive functions, when the president is unable to perform them, or is removed from office. Every reason, which recommends the mode of election of the president, prescribed by the constitution, with a view either to dignity, independence, or personal qualifications for office, applies with equal force to the appointment of his substitute. He is to perform the same duties, and to possess the same rights; and it seems, if not indispensable, at least peculiarly proper, that the choice of the person, who should succeed to the executive functions, should belong to the people at large, rather than to a select body chosen for another purpose. If (as was suggested) the president of the senate, chosen by that body, might have been designated, as the constitutional substitute; it is by no means certain, that he would either possess so high qualifications, or enjoy so much public confidence, or feel so much responsibility for his conduct, as a vice-president selected directly by and from the people. The president of the senate would generally be selected from other motives, and with reference to other qualifications, than what ordinarily belonged to the executive department. His political opinions, might be in marked contrast with those of a majority of the nation; and while he might possess a just influence in the senate, as a presiding officer, he might be deemed wholly unfit for the various duties of the chief executive magistrate. In addition to these considerations, there was no novelty in the appointment of such an officer for similar purposes in some of the state governments; and it therefore came recommended by experience, as a safe and useful arrangement, to guard the people against the inconveniences of an interregnum in the government, or a devolution of power upon an officer, who was not their choice, and might not possess their confidence.

SEE ALSO:

Generally 2.1; 2.2; 2.3; 2.4
Records of the Federal Convention, Farrand 2:108, 132, 134, 145–46, 171–72, 401–2, 597
Alexander Hamilton's Proposals, Farrand 3:395–96
Cato, no. 1, 27 Sept. 1787, Storing 5.10.2
Charles Pinckney, Observations on the Plan of Government, 1787, Farrand 3:110–11
Ezra Stiles, Diary, 21 Dec. 1787, Farrand 3:169
Luther Martin, Genuine Information, Jan. 1788, Storing 2.4.80–84
Charles Cotesworth Pinckney, South Carolina House of Representatives, 18 Jan. 1788, Elliot 4:315
George Washington to LaFayette, 28 April 1788, Farrand 3:298
James Monroe, Some Observations on the Constitution, 1788, Storing 5.21.24–25
Native of Virginia, Observations on the Proposed Plan of Federal Government, 1788, Monroe Writings 1:378–80
William R. Davie, North Carolina Ratifying Convention, 26 July 1788, Elliot 4:102–4
Benjamin Franklin to Duc de la Rochefoucauld, 22 Oct. 1788, Writings 9:666
James Wilson, Of Government, Lectures on Law, 1791, Works 1:293–94, 295–96
John Adams to Elbridge Gerry, 6 Apr. 1797, Works 8:538–40
James Kent, Commentaries 1:253–55 (1826)
William Rawle, A View of the Constitution of the United States 288–94 (2d ed. 1829)

Article 2, Section 1, Clauses 2 and 3

Each State shall appoint, in such Manner as the Legislature thereof may direct, a Number of Electors, equal to the whole Number of Senators and Representatives to which the State may be entitled in the Congress: but no Senator or Representative, or Person holding an Office of Trust or Profit under the United States, shall be appointed an Elector.

The Electors shall meet in their respective States, and vote by Ballot for two Persons, of whom one at least shall not be an Inhabitant of the same State with themselves. And they shall make a List of all the Persons voted for, and of the Number of Votes for each; which List they shall sign and certify, and transmit sealed to the Seat of the Government of the United States, directed to the President of the Senate. The President of the Senate shall, in the Presence of the Senate and House of Representatives, open all the Certificates, and the Votes shall then be counted. The Person having the greatest Number of Votes shall be the President, if such Number be a Majority of the whole Number of Electors appointed; and if there be more than one who have such Majority, and have an equal Number of Votes, then the House of Representatives shall immediately chuse by Ballot one of them for President; and if no Person have a Majority, then from the five highest on the List the said House shall in like Manner chuse the President. But in chusing the President, the Votes shall be taken by States, the Representation from each State having one Vote; a quorum for this Purpose shall consist of a Member or Members from two thirds of the States, and a Majority of all the States shall be necessary to a Choice. In every Case, after the Choice of the President, the Person having the greatest Number of Votes of the Electors shall be the Vice President. But if there should remain two or more who have equal Votes, the Senate shall chuse from them by Ballot the Vice President.

1

WILLIAM BLACKSTONE, COMMENTARIES 1:185–86
1765

It must be owned, an elective monarchy seems to be the most obvious, and best suited of any to the rational principles of government, and the freedom of human nature: and accordingly we find from history that, in the infancy and first rudiments of almost every state, the leader, chief magistrate, or prince, hath usually been elective. And, if the individuals who compose that state could always continue true to first principles, uninfluenced by passion or prejudice, unassailed by corruption, and unawed by violence, elective succession were as much to be desired in a kingdom, as in other inferior communities. The best, the wisest, and the bravest man would then be sure of receiving that crown, which his endowments have merited; and the sense of an unbiassed majority would be dutifully acquiesced in by the few who were of different opinions. But history and observation will inform us, that elections of every kind (in the present state of human nature) are too frequently brought about by influence, partiality, and artifice: and, even where the case is otherwise, these practices will be often suspected, and as constantly charged upon the successful, by a splenetic disappointed minority. This is an evil, to which all societies are liable; as well those of a private and domestic kind, as the great community of the public, which regulates and includes the rest. But in the former there is this advantage; that such suspicions, if false, proceed no farther than jealousies and murmurs, which time will effectually suppress; and, if true, the injustice may be remedied by legal means, by an appeal to those tribunals to which every member of society has (by becoming such) virtually engaged to submit. Whereas, in the great and independent society, which every nation composes, there is no superior to resort to but the law of nature; no method to redress the infringements of that law, but the actual exertion of private force. As therefore between two nations, complaining of mutual injuries, the quarrel can only be decided by the law of arms; so in one and the same nation, when the fundamental principles of their common union are supposed to be invaded, and more especially when the appointment of their chief magistrate is alleged to be unduly made, the only tribunal to which the complainants can appeal is that of the God of battels, the only process by which the appeal can be carried on is that of a civil and intestine war. An hereditary succession to the crown is therefore now established, in this and most other countries, in order to prevent that periodical bloodshed and misery, which the history of antient imperial Rome, and the more modern experience of Poland and Germany, may shew us are the consequences of elective kingdoms.

2

Records of the Federal Convention

[*1:68; Madison, 1 June*]

The next clause in Resolution 7, relating to the mode of appointing, & the duration of, the Executive being under consideration,

Mr. Wilson said he was almost unwilling to declare the mode which he wished to take place, being apprehensive that it might appear chimerical. He would say however at least that in theory he was for an election by the people; Experience, particularly in N. York & Massts, shewed that an election of the first magistrate by the people at large, was both a convenient & successful mode. The objects of choice in such cases must be persons whose merits have general notoriety.

Mr. Sherman was for the appointment by the Legislature, and for making him absolutely dependent on that body, as it was the will of that which was to be executed. An independence of the Executive on the supreme Legislative, was in his opinion the very essence of tyranny if there was any such thing.

. . . . .

The *mode of appointing* the Executive was the next question.

Mr. Wilson renewed his declarations in favor of an appointment by the people. He wished to derive not only both branches of the Legislature from the people, without the intervention of the State Legislatures but the Executive also; in order to make them as independent as possible of each other, as well as of the States;

Col. Mason favors the idea, but thinks it impracticable. He wishes however that Mr. Wilson might have time to digest it into his own form.—the clause "to be chosen by the National Legislature"—was accordingly postponed.—

Mr. Rutlidge suggests an election of the Executive by the second branch only of the national Legislature—

[*1:80; Madison, 2 June*]

Mr. Wilson made the following motion, to be substituted for the mode proposed by Mr. Randolph's resolution.

"that the Executive Magistracy shall be elected in the following manner: That the States be divided into   districts: & that the persons qualified to vote in each district for members of the first branch of the national Legislature elect   members for their respective districts to be electors of the Executive magistracy. that the said Electors of the Executive magistracy meet at   and they or any   of them so met shall proceed to elect by ballot, but not out of their own body   person   in whom the Executive authority of the national Government shall be vested."

Mr. Wilson repeated his arguments in favor of an election without the intervention of the States. He supposed too that this mode would produce more confidence among the people in the first magistrate, than an election by the national Legislature.

Mr. Gerry, opposed the election by the national legislature. There would be a constant intrigue kept up for the appointment. The Legislature & the candidates wd. bargain & play into one another's hands. votes would be given by the former under promises or expectations from the latter, of recompensing them by services to members of the Legislature or to their friends. He liked the principle of Mr. Wilson's motion, but fears it would alarm & give a handle to the State partizans, as tending to supersede altogether the State authorities. He thought the Community not yet ripe for stripping the States of their powers, even such as might not be requisite for local purposes. He was for waiting till people should feel more the necessity of it. He seemed to prefer the taking the suffrages of the States instead of Electors, or letting the Legislatures nominate, and the electors appoint. He was not clear that the people ought to act directly even in the choice of electors, being too little informed of personal characters in large districts, and liable to deceptions.

Mr Williamson could see no advantage in the introduction of Electors chosen by the people who who would stand in the same relation to them as the State Legislatures, whilst the expedient would be attended with great trouble and expence. On the question for agreeing to Mr. Wilson's substitute, it was negatived: Massts. no. Cont. no. N. Y. no. Pa. ay. Del. no. Mard. ay. Virga. no. N. C. no. S. C. no. Geoa. no. [Ayes—2; noes—8.]

On the question for electing the Executive by the national legislature, for the term of seven years, it was agreed to Massts. ay. Cont. ay. N. Y. ay. Pena. no. Del. ay. Maryd. no. Va. ay. N. C. ay. S. C. ay. Geo. ay. [ayes—8; noes—2.]

[*1:175; Madison, 9 June*]

Mr. Gerry, according to previous notice given by him, moved "that the National Executive should be elected by the Executives of the States whose proportion of votes should be the same with that allowed to the States in the election of the Senate." If the appointmt. should be made by the Natl. Legislature, it would lessen that independence of the Executive which ought to prevail, would give birth to intrigue and corruption between the Executive & Legislature previous to the election, and to partiality in the Executive afterwards to the friends who promoted him. Some other mode therefore appeared to him necessary. He proposed that of appointing by the State Executives as most analogous to the principle observed in electing the other branches of the Natl. Govt.; the first branch being chosen by the *people* of the States, & the 2d. by the Legislatures of the States; he did not see any objection agst. letting the Executive be appointed by the Executives of the States. He supposed the Executives would be most likely to select the fittest men, and that it would be their interest to support the man of their own choice.

Mr. Randolph urged strongly the inexpediency of Mr. Gerry's mode of appointing the Natl. Executive. The confidence of the people would not be secured by it to the Natl. magistrate. The small States would lose all chance of an appointmt. from within themselves. Bad appointments would be made; the Executives of the States being little conversant with characters not within their own small spheres. The State Executives too notwithstanding their constitutional independence, being in fact dependent on the State Legislatures will generally be guided by the views of the latter, and prefer either favorites within the States, or such as it may be expected will be most partial to the interests of the State. A Natl. Executive thus chosen will not be likely to defend with becoming vigilance & firmness the national rights agst. State encroachments. Vacancies also must happen. How can these be filled? He could not suppose either that the Executives would feel the interest in supporting the Natl. Executive which had been imagined. They will not cherish the great Oak which is to reduce them to paltry shrubs.

On the question for referring the appointment of the Natl. Executive to the State Executives as propd. by Mr. Gerry Massts. no. Cont. no. N. Y. no. N. J. no. Pa. no. Del. divd. Md. no. Va. no. S. C. no. Geo. no. [Ayes—0; noes—9; divided—1.]

[*1:236; Madison, 13 June*]

9. Resolved that a National Executive be instituted to consist of a single person, to be chosen by the Natl. Legislature for the term of seven years, with power to carry into execution the national laws, to appoint to offices in cases not otherwise provided for—to be ineligible a second time, & to be removeable on impeachment and conviction of malpractices or neglect of duty—to receive a fixed stipend by which he may be compensated for the devotion of his time to public service to be paid out of the national Treasury.

[*1:244; Madison, 15 June*]

4. Resd. that the U. States in Congs. be authorized to elect a federal Executive to consist of persons, to continue in office for the term of years,

[*2:29; Madison, 17 July*]

9th. Resol: "that Natl. Executive consist of a single person." Agd. to nem. con.

"To be chosen by the National Legisl:"

Mr. Governr. Morris was pointedly agst. his being so chosen. He will be the mere creature of the Legisl: if appointed & impeachable by that body. He ought to be elected by the people at large, by the freeholders of the Country. That difficulties attend this mode, he admits. But they have been found superable in N. Y. &. in Cont. and would he believed be found so, in the case of an Executive for the U. States. If the people should elect, they will never fail to prefer some man of distinguished character, or services; some man, if he might so speak, of continental reputation. If the Legislature elect, it will be the work of intrigue, of cabal, and of faction: it will be like the election of a pope by a conclave of cardinals; real merit will rarely be the title to the appointment. He moved to strike out "National Legislature" & insert "citizens of U. S."

Mr. Sherman thought that the sense of the Nation would be better expressed by the Legislature, than by the people at large. The latter will never be sufficiently informed of characters, and besides will never give a majority of votes to any one man. They will generally vote for some man in their own State, and the largest State will have the best chance for the appointment. If the choice be made by the Legislre. A majority of voices may be made necessary to constitute an election.

Mr. Wilson. two arguments have been urged agst. an election of the Executive Magistrate by the people. 1 the example of Poland where an Election of the supreme Magistrate is attended with the most dangerous commotions. The cases he observed were totally dissimilar. The Polish nobles have resources & dependents which enable them to appear in force, and to threaten the Republic as well as each other. In the next place the electors all assemble in one place: which would not be the case with us. The 2d. argt. is that a *majority* of the people would never concur. It might be answered that the concurrence of a majority of people is not a necessary principle of election, nor required as such in any of the States. But allowing the objection all its force, it may be obviated by the expedient used in Masts. where the Legislature by majority of voices, decide in case a majority of people do not concur in favor of one of the candidates. This would restrain the choice to a good nomination at least, and prevent in a great degree intrigue & cabal. A particular objection with him agst. an absolute election by the Legislre. was that the Exec: in that case would be too dependent to stand the mediator between the intrigues & sinister views of the Representatives and the general liberties & interests of the people.

Mr. Pinkney did not expect this question would again have been brought forward; An Election by the people being liable to the most obvious & striking objections. They will be led by a few active & designing men. The most populous States by combining in favor of the same individual will be able to carry their points. The Natl. Legislature being most immediately interested in the laws made by themselves, will be most attentive to the choice of a fit man to carry them properly into execution.

Mr. Govr. Morris. It is said that in case of an election by the people the populous States will combine & elect whom they please. Just the reverse. The people of such States cannot combine. If their be any combination it must be among their representatives in the Legislature. It is said the people will be led by a few designing men. This might happen in a small district. It can never happen throughout the continent. In the election of a Govr. of N. York, it sometimes is the case in particular spots, that the activity & intrigues of little partizans are successful, but the general voice of the State is never influenced by such artifices. It is said the multitude will be uninformed. It is true they would be uninformed of what passed in the Legislative Conclave, if the election were to be made there; but they will not be uninformed of those great & illustrious characters which have merited their esteem & confidence. If the Executive be chosen by the Natl. Legislature, he will not be independent on it; and if not independent, usurpation & tyranny on the part of the Legislature will be the consequence. This was the case in England in the last Century. It has been the case in Holland, where their Senates have engrossed all power. It has been the case every where. He was surprised that an election by the people at large should ever have been likened to the polish election of the first Magistrate. An election by the Legislature will bear a real likeness to the election by the Diet of Poland. The great must be the electors in both cases, and the corruption & cabal wch are known to characterize the one would soon find their way into the other. Appointments made by numerous bodies, are always worse than those made by single responsible individuals, or by the people at large.

Col. Mason. It is curious to remark the different language held at different times. At one moment we are told that the Legislature is entitled to thorough confidence, and to indefinite power. At another, that it will be governed by intrigue & corruption, and cannot be trusted at all. But not to dwell on this inconsistency he would observe that a Government which is to last ought at least to be practicable. Would this be the case if the proposed election should be left to the people at large. He conceived it would be as unnatural to refer the choice of a proper character for chief Magistrate to the people, as it would, to refer a trial of colours to a blind man. The extent of the Country renders it impossible that the people can have the requisite capacity to judge of the respective pretensions of the Candidates.—

Mr. Wilson. could not see the contrariety stated (by Col. Mason) The Legislre. might deserve confidence in some respects, and distrust in others. In acts which were to affect them & yr. Constituents precisely alike confidence was due. In others jealousy was warranted. The appointment to great offices, where the Legislre. might feel many motives, not common to the public confidence was surely misplaced. This branch of business it was notorious, was most corruptly managed of any that had been committed to legislative bodies.

Mr. Williamson, conceived that there was the same difference between an election in this case, by the people and by the legislature, as between an appt. by lot, and by choice. There are at present distinguished characters, who are known perhaps to almost every man. This will not always be the case. The people will be sure to vote for some man in their own State, and the largest State will be sure to succede. This will not be Virga. however. Her slaves will have no suffrage. As the Salary of the Executive will be fixed, and he will not be eligible a 2d. time, there will not be such a dependence on the Legislature as has been imagined.

Question on an election by the people instead of the Legislature; which passed in the negative.

Mas. no. Cont. no. N.J. no. Pa. ay. Del. no. Md. no. Va. no. N.C. no. S.C. no. Geo. no. [Ayes—1; noes—9.]

Mr. L. Martin moved that the Executive be chosen by Electors appointed by the several Legislatures of the individual States.

Mr. Broome 2ds. On the Question, it passed in the negative.

Mas. no. Cont. no. N.J. no. Pa. no. Del. ay. Md. ay. Va. no. N.C. no. S.C. no. Geo. no. [Ayes—2; noes—8.]

On the question on the words "to be chosen by the Nationl. Legislature" it passed unanimously in the affirmative.

[*2:57; Madison, 19 July*]

On the question on Mr. Govr. Morris motion to reconsider generally the Constitution of the Executive—

Mas. ay. Ct. ay. N.J. ay. & all the others ay.

Mr. Elseworth moved to strike out the appointmt. by the Natl. Legislature, and insert "to be chosen by electors appointed by the Legislatures of the States in the following ratio; towit—one for each State not exceeding 200,000 inhabts. two for each above yt. number & not exceeding 300,000. and, three for each State exceeding 300,000.—Mr. Broome 2ded. the motion

Mr. Rutlidge was opposed to all the modes except the appointment by the Natl. Legislature. He will be sufficiently independent, if he be not re-eligible

Mr. Gerry preferred the motion of Mr. Elseworth to an appointmt. by the Natl. Legislature, or by the people; tho' not to an appt. by the State Executives. He moved that the electors proposed by Mr. E. should be 25 in number, and allotted in the following proportion. to N.H. 1. to Mas. 3. to R.I. 1. to Cont. 2-to N.Y. 2-N.J. 2. Pa. 3. Del. 1. Md. 2. Va. 3. N.C. 2. S.C. 2. Geo. 1.

The question as moved by Mr. Elseworth being divided, on the 1st. part shall ye. Natl. Executive be appointed by Electors?

Mas-divd. Cont. ay. N.J. ay. Pa. ay. Del. ay. Md. ay. Va. ay- N.C. no. S.C. no. Geo. no. [Ayes—6; noes—3; divided—1.]

On 2d. part shall the Electors be chosen by State Legislatures?

Mas. ay. Cont. ay. N.J. ay. Pa. ay. Del. ay. Md. ay. Va. no. N.C. ay. S.C. no. Geo. ay. [Ayes—8; noes—2.]

The part relating to the ratio in which the States sd. chuse electors was postponed nem. con.

Mr. L. Martin moved that the Executive be ineligible a 2d. time.

Mr. Williamson 2ds. the motion. He had no great confidence in the Electors to be chosen for the special purpose. They would not be the most respectable citizens; but persons not occupied in the high offices of Govt. They would be liable to undue influence, which might the more readily be practiced as some of them will probably be in appointment 6 or 8 months before the object of it comes on.

Mr. Elseworth supposed any persons might be appointed Electors, excepting solely, members of the Natl. Legislature.

On the question shall he be ineligible a 2d. time?

Mas. no. Ct. no. N.J. no. Pa. no. Del. no. Md. no. Va. no. N.C. ay. S.C. ay. Geo. no. [Ayes—2; noes—8.]

On the question shall the Executive continue for 7 years? It passed in the negative Mas. divd. Cont. ay. N—J. no. Pa. no. Del. no. Md. no. Va. no. N.C. divd. S.C. ay. Geo. ay. [Ayes—3; noes—5; divided—2.]

Mr. King was afraid we shd. shorten the term too much.

Mr. Govr Morris was for a short term, in order to avoid impeachts. which wd. be otherwise necessary.

Mr. Butler was agst. a frequency of the elections. Geo & S.C. were too distant to send electors often.

Mr. Elseworth was for 6 years. If the elections be too frequent, the Executive will not be firm eno'. There must be duties which will make him unpopular for the moment. There will be *outs* as well as *ins*. His administration therefore will be attacked and misrepresented.

Mr. Williamson was for 6 years. The expence will be considerable & ought not to be unnecessarily repeated. If the Elections are too frequent, the best men will not undertake the service and those of an inferior character will be liable to be corrupted.

On question for 6 years?

Mas. ay. Cont. ay. N.J. ay. Pa. ay. Del. no. Md. ay. Va. ay. N.C. ay. S.C. ay. Geo. ay. [Ayes—9; noes—1.]

[*2:63; Madison, 20 July*]

The postponed Ratio of Electors for appointing the Executive; to wit 1 for each State whose inhabitants do not exceed 100,000, &c. being taken up.

Mr. Madison observed that this would make in time all or nearly all the States equal. Since there were few that would not in time contain the number of inhabitants entitling them to 3 Electors; that this ratio ought either to be made temporary, or so varied as that it would adjust itself to the growing population of the States.

Mr. Gerry moved that in the *1st instance* the Electors should be allotted to the States in the following ratio: to N.H. 1. Mas. 3. R.I. 1. Cont. 2. N.Y. 2. N.J. 2. Pa. 3. Del. 1. Md. 2. Va. 3. N.C. 2. S.C. 2. Geo. 1.

On the question to postpone in order to take up this motion of Mr. Gerry. It passed in the affirmative.

Mas. ay. Cont. no. N.J. no. Pa. ay. Del. no. Md. no. Va. ay. N.C. ay. S.C. ay. Geo. ay. [Ayes—6; noes—4.]

Mr. Elseworth moved that 2 Electors be allotted to N.H. Some rule ought to be pursued; and N.H. has more than 100,000 inhabitants. He thought it would be proper also to allot 2. to Georgia.

Mr. Broom & Mr. Martin moved to postpone Mr. Gerry's allotment of Electors, leaving a fit ratio to be reported by the Committee to be appointed for detailing the Resolutions.

On this motion.

Mas.-no. Ct. no. N.J. ay. Pa. no. Del. ay. Md. ay. Va. no. N.C. no. S.C. no. Geo. no. [Ayes—3; noes—7.]

Mr. Houston 2ded. the motion of Mr. Elseworth to add another Elector to N.H. & Georgia. On the Question:

Mas. no. Ct ay. N.J. no. Pa. no. Del. no. Md. no. Va. no. N.C. no. S.C.-ay-Geo-ay. [Ayes—3; noes—7.]

Mr. Williamson moved as an amendment to Mr. Gerry's allotment of Electors in the 1st. instance that in future elections of the Natl. Executive, the number of Electors to be appointed by the several States shall be regulated by their respective numbers of Representatives in the 1st. branch pursuing as nearly as may be the present proportions.

On question on Mr. Gerry's ratio of Electors

Mas. ay. Ct ay. N.J. no. Pa. ay. Del. no. Md. no. Va. ay-N.C. ay. S.C. ay. Geo. no. [Ayes—6; noes–4.]

. . . . .

Mr. Gerry & Govr. Morris moved "that the Electors of the Executive shall not be members of the Natl. Legislature, nor officers of the U. States, nor shall the Electors themselves be eligible to the supreme Magistracy." Agreed to nem. con.

[*2:73; Madison, 21 July*]

Mr. Williamson moved "that the Electors of the Executive should be paid out of the National Treasury for the Service to be performed by them". Justice required this: as it was a national service they were to render. The motion was agreed to nem.—con.

[*2:95; Madison, 23 July*]

Mr. Houston & Mr. Spaight moved "that the appointment of the Executive by Electors chosen by the Legislatures of the States, be reconsidered." Mr. Houston urged the extreme inconveniency & the considerable expense, of drawing together men from all the States for the single purpose of electing the Chief Magistrate.

On the question which was put without any debate

N.H. ay. Mas. ay. Ct. ay. Pa. no. Del—ay. Md. no. Virga. no. N.C. ay. S.C. ay. Geo. ay. [Ayes—7; noes—3.]

Ordered that to morrow be assigned for the reconsideration. Cont & Pena. no.—all the rest ay—

[*2:99; Madison, 24 July*]

The appointment of the Executive by Electors reconsidered.

Mr. Houston moved that he be appointed by the "Natl. Legislature," instead of "Electors appointed by the State Legislatures" according to the last decision of the mode He dwelt chiefly on the improbability, that capable men would undertake the service of Electors from the more distant States.

Mr. Spaight seconded the motion.

Mr. Gerry opposed it. He thought there was no ground to apprehend the danger urged by Mr. Houston. The election of the Executive Magistrate will be considered as of vast importance and will excite great earnestness. The best men, the Governours of the States will not hold it derogatory from their character to be the electors. If the motion should be agreed to, it will be necessary to make the Executive ineligible a 2d. time, in order to render him independent of the Legislature; which was an idea extremely repugnant to his way of thinking.

Mr. Strong supposed that there would be no necessity, if the Executive should be appointed by the Legislature, to make him ineligible a 2d. time; as new elections of the Legislature will have intervened; and he will not depend for his 2d. appointment on the same sett of men as his first was recd. from. It had been suggested that *gratitude* for his past appointment wd. produce the same effect as dependence for his future appointment. He thought very differently. Besides this objection would lie agst. the Electors who would be objects of gratitude as well as the Legislature. It was of great importance not to make the Govt. too complex which would be the case if a new sett of men like the Electors should be introduced into it. He thought also that the first characters in the States would not feel sufficient motives to undertake the office of Electors.

Mr. Williamson was for going back to the original ground; to elect the Executive for 7 years and render him ineligible a 2d. time. The proposed Electors would certainly not be men of the 1st. nor even of the 2d. grade in the States. These would all prefer a seat either in the Senate or the other branch of the Legislature. He did not like the Unity in the Executive. He had wished the Executive power to be lodged in three men taken from three districts into which the States should be divided. As the Executive is to have a kind of veto on the laws, and there is an essential difference of interests between the N. & S. States, particularly in the carrying trade, the power will be dangerous, if the Executive is to be taken from part of the Union, to the part from which he is not taken. The case is different here from what it is in England; where there is a sameness of interest throughout the Kingdom. Another objection agst. a single Magistrate is that he will be an elective King, and will feel the spirit of one. He will spare no pains to keep himself in for life, and will then lay a train for the succession of his children. It was pretty certain he thought that we should at some time or other have a King; but he wished no precaution to be omitted that might postpone the event as long as possible.—Ineligibility a 2d. time appeared to him to be the best precaution. With this precaution he had no objection to a longer term than 7 years. He would go as far as 10 or 12 years.

Mr. Gerry moved that the Legislatures of the States should vote by ballot for the Executive in the same proportions as it had been proposed they should chuse electors; and that in case a majority of the votes should not center on the same person, the 1st. branch of the Natl. Legislature should chuse two out of the 4 candidates having most votes, and out of these two, the 2d. branch should chuse the Executive.

Mr. King seconded the motion—and on the Question to postpone in order to take it into consideration, The *noes* were so predominant that the States were not counted.

Question on Mr. Houston's motion that the Executive be appd. by Nal. Legislature

N. H. ay. Mas. ay. Ct. no. N. J. ay. Pa. no. Del. ay. Md. no. Va. no. N. C. ay. S. C. ay. Geo. ay. [Ayes—7; noes—4.]

Mr. L. Martin & Mr. Gerry moved to reinstate the ineligibility of the Executive a 2d. time.

Mr. Elseworth. With many this appears a natural consequence of his being elected by the Legislature. It was not the case with him. The Executive he thought should be reelected if his conduct proved him worthy of it. And he will be more likely to render himself worthy of it if he be rewardable with it. The most eminent characters also will be more willing to accept the trust under this condition, than if they foresee a necessary degradation at a fixt period.

[*2:109; Madison, 25 July*]

Mr. Gerry repeated his remark that an election at all by the Natl. Legislature was radically and incurably wrong; and moved that the Executive be appointed by the Governours & Presidents of the States, with advice of their Councils, and when there are no Councils by Electors chosen by the Legislatures. The executives to vote in the following proportions; viz—

Mr. Madison. There are objections agst. every mode that has been, or perhaps can be proposed. The election must be made either by some existing authority under the Natil. or State Constitutions—or by some special authority derived from the people—or by the people themselves.—The two Existing authorities under the Natl. Constitution wd be the Legislative & Judiciary. The latter he presumed was out of the question. The former was in his Judgment liable to insuperable objections. Besides the general influence of that mode on the independence of the Executive, 1. the election of the Chief Magistrate would agitate & divide the legislature so much that the public interest would materially suffer by it. Public bodies are always apt to be thrown into contentions, but into more violent ones by such occasions than by any others. 2. the candidate would intrigue with the Legislature, would derive his appointment from the predominant faction, and be apt to render his administration subservient to its views. 3. The Ministers of foreign powers would have and make use of, the opportunity to to mix their intrigues & influence with the Election. Limited as the powers of the Executive are, it will be an object of great moment with the great rival powers of Europe who have American possessions, to have at the head of our Governmt. a man attached to their respective politics & interests. No pains, nor perhaps expence, will be spared, to gain from the Legislature an appointmt. favorable to their wishes. Germany & Poland are witnesses of this danger. In the former, the election of the Head of the Empire, till it became in a manner hereditary, interested all Europe, and was much influenced by foreign interference—In the latter, altho' the elective Magistrate has very little real power, his election has at all times produced the most eager interference of forign princes, and has in fact at length slid entirely into foreign hands. The existing authorities in the States are the Legislative, Executive & Judiciary. The appointment of the Natl Executive by the first was objectionable in many points of view, some of which had been already mentioned. He would mention one which of itself would decide his opinion. The Legislatures of the States had betrayed a strong propensity to a variety of pernicious measures. One object of the Natl. Legislre. was to controul this propensity. One object of the Natl. Executive, so far as it would have a negative on the laws, was to controul the Natl. Legislature, so far as it might be infected with a similar propensity. Refer the appointmt of the Natl. Executive to the State Legislatures, and this controuling purpose may be defeated. The Legislatures can &

will act with some kind of regular plan, and will promote the appointmt. of a man who will not oppose himself to a favorite object. Should a majority of the Legislatures at the time of election have the same object, or different objects of the same kind, the Natl Executive, would be rendered subservient to them. —An appointment by the State Executives, was liable among other objections to this insuperable one, that being standing bodies, they could & would be courted, and intrigued with by the Candidates, by their partizans, and by the Ministers of foreign powers. The State Judiciarys had not & he presumed wd. not be proposed as a proper source of appointment. The Option before us then lay between an appointment by Electors chosen by the people—and an immediate appointment by the people. He thought the former mode free from many of the objections which had been urged agst. it, and greatly preferable to an appointment by the Natl. Legislature. As the electors would be chosen for the occasion, would meet at once, & proceed immediately to an appointment, there would be very little opportunity for cabal, or corruption. As a further precaution, it might be required that they should meet at some place, distinct from the seat of Govt. and even that no person within a certain distance of the place at the time shd. be eligible. This mode however had been rejected so recently & by so great a majority that it probably would not be proposed anew. The remaining mode was an election by the people or rather by the qualified part of them at large. With all its imperfections he liked this best. He would not repeat either the general argumts. for or the objections agst this mode. He would only take notice of two difficulties which he admitted to have weight. The first arose from the disposition in the people to prefer a Citizen of their own State, and the disadvantage this wd. throw on the smaller States. Great as this objection might be he did not think it equal to such as lay agst. every other mode which had been proposed. He thought too that some expedient might be hit upon that would obviate it. The second difficulty arose from the disproportion of qualified voters in the N. & S. States, and the disadvantages which this mode would throw on the latter. The answer to this objection was 1. that this disproportion would be continually decreasing under the influence of the Republican laws introduced in the S. States, and the more rapid increase of their population. 2. That local local considerations must give way to the general interest. As an individual from the S. States he was willing to make the sacrifice.

Mr. Elseworth. The objection drawn from the different sizes of the States, is unanswerable. The Citizens of the largest States would invariably prefer the Candidate within the State: and the largest States wd. invariably have the man.

Question on Mr. Elseworth's motion as above.

N. H. ay. Mas. no. Ct. ay. N. J. no. Pa. ay. Del. no-Md. ay. Va no. N- C. no. S. C. no. Geo. no. [Ayes—4; noes—7.]

Mr. Pinkney moved that the election by the Legislature be qualified with a proviso that no person be eligible for more than 6 years in any twelve years. He thought this would have all the advantage & at the same time avoid in some degree the inconveniency, of an absolute ineligibility a 2d. time.

Col. Mason approved the idea. It had the sanction of experience in the instance of Congs. and some of the Executives of the States. It rendered the Executive as effectually independent, as an ineligibility after his first election, and opened the way at the same time for the advantage of his future services. He preferred on the whole the election by the Natl. Legislature: Tho' Candor obliged him to admit, that there was great danger of foreign influence, as had been suggested. This was the most serious objection with him that had been urged.

Mr Butler. The two great evils to be avoided are cabal at home, & influence from abroad. It will be difficult to avoid either if the Election be made by the Natl Legislature. On the other hand, the Govt. should not be made so complex & unwieldy as to disgust the States. This would be the case, if the election shd. be referred to the people. He liked best an election by Electors chosen by the Legislatures of the States. He was agst. a re-eligibility at all events. He was also agst. a ratio of votes in the States. An equality should prevail in this case. The reasons for departing from it do not hold in the case of the Executive as in that of the Legislature.

Mr. Gerry approved of Mr Pinkney's motion as lessening the evil.

Mr Govr. Morris was agst. a rotation in every case. It formed a political School, in wch. we were always governed by the scholars, and not by the Masters — The evils to be guarded agst in this case are. 1. the undue influence of the Legislature. 2. instability of Councils. 3. misconduct in office. To guard agst. the first, we run into the second evil. we adopt a rotation which produces instability of Councils. To avoid Sylla we fall into Charibdis. A change of men is ever followed by a change of measures We see this fully exemplified in the vicissitudes among ourselves, particularly in the State of Pena. The selfsufficiency of a victorious party scorns to tread in the paths of their predecessors. Rehoboam will not imitate Solomon. 2. the Rotation in office will not prevent intrigue and dependence on the Legislature. The man in office will look forward to the period at which he will become re-eligible. The distance of the period, the improbability of such a protraction of his life will be no obstacle. Such is the nature of man, formed by his benevolent author no doubt for wise ends, that altho' he knows his existence to be limited to a span, he takes his measures as if he were to live forever. But taking another supposition, the inefficacy of the expedient will be manifest. If the magistrate does not look forward to his re-election to the Executive, he will be pretty sure to keep in view the opportunity of his going into the Legislature itself. He will have little objection then to an extension of power on a theatre where he expects to act a distinguished part; and will be very unwilling to take any step that may endanger his popularity with the Legislature, on his influence over which the figure he is to make will depend. 3. To avoid the third evil, impeachments will be essential, and hence an additional reason agst an election by the

Legislature. He considered an election by the people as the best, by the Legislature as the worst, mode. Putting both these aside, he could not but favor the idea of Mr. Wilson, of introducing a mixture of lot. It will diminish, if not destroy both cabal & dependence.

Mr. Williamson was sensible that strong objections lay agst an election of the Executive by the Legislature, and that it opened a door for foreign influence. The principal objection agst. an election by the people seemed to be, the disadvantage under which it would place the smaller States. He suggested as a cure for this difficulty, that each man should vote for 3 candidates. One of these he observed would be probably of his own State, the other 2. of some other States; and as probably of a small as a large one.

Mr. Govr. Morris liked the idea, suggesting as an amendment that each man should vote for two persons one of whom at least should not be of his own State.

Mr Madison also thought something valuable might be made of the suggestion with the proposed amendment of it. The second best man in this case would probably be the first, in fact. The only objection which occurred was that each Citizen after havg. given his vote for his favorite fellow Citizen wd. throw away his second on some obscure Citizen of another State, in order to ensure the object of his first choice. But it could hardly be supposed that the Citizens of many States would be so sanguine of having their favorite elected, as not to give their second vote with sincerity to the next object of their choice. It might moreover be provided in favor of the smaller States that the Executive should not be eligible more than   times in   years from the same State.

Mr. Gerry—A popular election in this case is radically vicious. The ignorance of the people would put it in the power of some one set of men dispersed through the Union & acting in Concert to delude them into any appointment. He observed that such a Society of men existed in the Order of the Cincinnati. They were respectable, United, and influencial. They will in fact elect the chief Magistrate in every instance, if the election be referred to the people.—His respect for the characters composing this Society could not blind him to the danger & impropriety of throwing such a power into their hands.

Mr. Dickenson. As far as he could judge from the discussion which had taken place during his attendance, insuperable objections lay agst an election of the Executive by the Natl. Legislature; as also by the Legislatures or Executives of the States—He had long leaned towards an election by the people which he regarded as the best and purest source. Objections he was aware lay agst this mode, but not so great he thought as agst the other modes. The greatest difficulty in the opinion of the House seemed to arise from the partiality of the States to their respective Citizens. But, might not this very partiality be turned to a useful purpose. Let the people of each State chuse its best Citizen. The people will know the most eminent characters of their own States, and the people of different States will feel an emulation in selecting those of which they will have the greatest reason to be proud—Out of the thirteen names thus selected, an Executive Magistrate may be chosen either by the Natl Legislature, or by Electors appointed by it.

On a Question which was moved for postponing Mr. Pinkney's motion, in order to make way for some such proposition as had been hinted by Mr. Williamson & others. it passed in the negative.

N. H. no. Mas. no. Ct. ay. N. J. ay. Pa. ay. Del. no. Md. ay. Va ay. N. C. no. S. C. no. Geo. no. [Ayes—5; noes—6.]

On Mr. Pinkney's motion that no person shall serve in the Executive more than 6 years in 12. years, it passed in the negative.

N. H. ay. Mas. ay. Ct. no. N. J. no. Pa. no. Del. no. Md. no. Va. no. N. C. ay. S. C. ay. Geo. ay [Ayes—5; noes—6.]

[*2:118; Madison, 26 July*]

Col. Mason. In every Stage of the Question relative to the Executive, the difficulty of the subject and the diversity of the opinions concerning it have appeared. Nor have any of the modes of constituting that department been satisfactory. 1. It has been proposed that the election should be made by the people at large; that is that an act which ought to be performed by those who know most of Eminent characters, & qualifications, should be performed by those who know least. 2 that the election should be made by the Legislatures of the States. 3. by the Executives of the States. Agst these modes also strong objections have been urged. 4. It has been proposed that the election should be made by Electors chosen by the people for that purpose. This was at first agreed to: But on further consideration has been rejected. 5. Since which, the mode of Mr Williamson, requiring each freeholder to vote for several candidates has been proposed. This seemed like many other propositions, to carry a plausible face, but on closer inspection is liable to fatal objections. A popular election in any form, as Mr. Gerry has observed, would throw the appointment into the hands of the Cincinnati, a Society for the members of which he had a great respect; but which he never wished to have a preponderating influence in the Govt. 6. Another expedient was proposed by Mr. Dickenson, which is liable to so palpable & material an inconvenience that he had little doubt of its being by this time rejected by himself. It would exclude every man who happened not to be popular within his own State; tho' the causes of his local unpopularity might be of such a nature as to recommend him to the States at large. 7. Among other expedients, a lottery has been introduced. But as the tickets do not appear to be in much demand, it will probably, not be carried on, and nothing therefore need be said on that subject. After reviewing all these various modes, he was led to conclude– that an election by the Natl Legislature as originally proposed, was the best. If it was liable to objections, it was liable to fewer than any other. He conceived at the same time that a second election ought to be absolutely prohibited. Having for his primary object, for the pole star of his political conduct, the preservation of the rights of the people, he held it as an essential point, as the very palladium of Civil liberty, that the great officers of State, and particularly the Executive should at fixed periods return to that mass from which they were at first taken, in order that they may feel & respect those rights & interests, Which are again to be personally valuable to them. He concluded with moving that the constitution of the Executive as reported by the Come. of the whole be re-instated, viz. "that the Executive be appointed for seven years, & be ineligible a 2d. time,"

Mr. Davie seconded the motion

Docr. Franklin. It seems to have been imagined by some that the returning to the mass of the people was degrading the magistrate. This he thought was contrary to republican principles. In free Governments the rulers are the servants, and the people their superiors & sovereigns. For the former therefore to return among the latter was not to *degrade* but to *promote* them– and it would be imposing an unreasonable burden on them, to keep them always in a State of servitude, and not allow them to become again one of the Masters.

Question on Col. Masons motion as above; which passed in the affirmative

N. H. ay. Masts. not on floor. Ct. no. N. J. ay. Pa. no. Del. no. Md. ay. Va. ay. N. C. ay. S. C. ay. Geo. ay. [Ayes—7; noes—3; absent—1.]

Mr. Govr. Morris was now agst. the whole paragraph. In answer to Col. Mason's position that a periodical return of the great officers of the State into the mass of the people, was the palladium of Civil liberty he wd. observe that on the same principle the Judiciary ought to be periodically degraded; certain it was that the Legislature ought on every principle– yet no one had proposed. or conceived that the members of it should not be re-eligible. In answer to Docr. Franklin. that a return into the mass of the people would be a promotion. instead of a degradation, he had no doubt that our Executive like most others would have too much patriotism to shrink from the burden of his office, and too much modesty not to be willing to decline the promotion.

On the question on the whole resolution as amended in the words following—"that a National Executive be instituted—to consist of a single person—to be chosen by the Natl. legislature—for the term of seven years—to be ineligible a 2d. time—with power to carry into execution the natl. laws—to appoint to offices in cases not otherwise provided for—to be removeable on impeachment & conviction of mal-practice or neglect of duty—to receive a fixt compensation for the devotion of his time to the public service, to be paid out of the Natl. Treasury"—it passed in the affirmative

N. H. ay. Mas. not on floor. Ct. ay. N. J. ay. Pa. no. Del. no. Md. no. Va. divd. Mr. Blair & Col. Mason ay. Genl. Washington & Mr Madison no. Mr. Randolph happened to be out of the House. N- C- ay. S. C. ay. Geo. ay. [Ayes—6; noes—3; divided—1; absent—1.]

[*2:185; Madison, 6 Aug.*]

Sect. 1. The Executive Power of the United States shall be vested in a single person. His stile shall be "The President of the United States of America;" and his title shall be, "His Excellency". He shall be elected by ballot by the Legislature. He shall hold his office during the term of seven years; but shall not be elected a second time.

[*2:196; Madison, 7 Aug.*]

Mr. Ghorum contended that elections ought to be made by *joint ballot.* If separate ballots should be made for the President, and the two branches should be each attached to a favorite, great delay, contention & confusion may ensue. These inconveniences have been felt in Masts. in the election of officers of little importance compared with the Executive of the U. States. The only objection agst. a joint ballot is that it may deprive the Senate of their due weight; but this ought not to prevail over the respect due to the public tranquility & welfare.

Mr. Wilson was for a joint ballot in several cases at least; particularly in the choice of the President, and was therefore for the amendment. Disputes between the two Houses, during & concerng the vacancy of the Executive, might have dangerous consequences.

[*2:401; Madison, 24 Aug.*]

Art X. sect. 1. "The executive power of the U—S—shall be vested in a single person. His stile shall be "The President of the U—S. of America" and his title shall be "His Excellency". He shall be elected by ballot by the Legislature. He shall hold his office during the term of seven years; but shall not be elected a second time.

On the question for vesting the power in a *single person*—It was agreed to nem: con: So also on the *Stile* and *title*—

Mr. Rutlidge moved to insert "joint" before the word "ballot", as the most convenient mode of electing.

Mr. Sherman objected to it as depriving the *States* represented in the *Senate* of the negative intended them in that house,

Mr. Ghorum said it was wrong to be considering, at every turn whom the Senate would represent. The public good was the true object to be kept in view— Great delay and confusion would ensue if the two Houses shd vote separately, each having a negative on the choice of the other.

Mr. Dayton. It might be well for those not to consider how the Senate was constituted, whose interest it Was to keep it out of sight.—If the amendment should be agreed to, a *joint* ballot would in fact give the appointment to one House. He could never agree to the clause with such an amendment. There could be no doubt of the two Houses separately concurring in the same person for President. The importance & necessity of the case would ensure a concurrence.

Mr. Carrol moved to strike out, "by the Legislature" and insert "by the people"—Mr Wilson 2ded. him & on the question

N. H. no. Massts. no. Cont. no. N. J. no. Pa. ay. Del. ay. Md no. Va. no N. C. no. S. C. no. Geo. no. [Ayes—2; noes—9.]

Mr Brearly was opposed to the motion for inserting the word "joint". The argument that the small States should not put their hands into the pockets of the large ones did not apply in this case.

Mr. Wilson urged the reasonableness of giving the larger States a larger share of the appointment, and the danger of delay from a disagreement of the two Houses.

He remarked also that the Senate had peculiar powers balancing the advantage given by a joint balot in this case to the other branch of the Legislature.

Mr. Langdon. This general officer ought to be elected by the joint & general voice. In N. Hampshire the mode of separate votes by the two Houses was productive of great difficulties. The Negative of the Senate would hurt the feelings of the man elected by the votes of the other branch. He was for inserting "joint" tho' unfavorable to N. Hampshire as a small State.

Mr. Wilson remarked that as the President of the Senate was to be the President of the U—S. that Body in cases of vacancy might have an interest in throwing dilatory obstacles in the way, if its separate concurrence should be required.

Mr. Madison. If the amendment be agreed to the rule of voting will give to the largest State, compared with the smallest, an influence as 4 to 1 only, altho the population is as 10 to 1. This surely cannot be unreasonable as the President is to act for the *people* not for the *States*. The President of the *Senate* also is to be occasionally President of the U.S. and by his negative alone can make ¾ of the other branch necessary to the passage of a law— This is another advantage enjoyed by the Senate.

On the question for inserting "joint", it passed in the affirmative

N. H. ay. Masts ay—Ct. no. N. J. no. Pa. ay—Del. ay. Md. no. Va. ay. N. C. ay. S. C. ay. Geo. no. [Ayes—7; noes—4.]

Mr. Dayton then moved to insert, after the word "Legislatures" the words "each State having one vote" Mr Brearly 2ded. him, and on the question it passed in the negative

N. H. no. Mas. no. Ct. ay. N. J. ay. Pa. no. Del. ay. Md ay. Va. no. N. C. no. S. C. no. Geo. ay [Ayes—5; noes—6.]

Mr. Pinkney moved to insert after the word "Legislature" the words "to which election a majority of the votes of the members present shall be required" &

On this question, it passed in the affirmative

N. H. ay. Mas. ay. Ct. ay. N. J. no. Pa. ay. Del. ay—Md. ay—Va. ay—N. C. ay—S. C. ay—Geo. ay. [Ayes—10; noes—1.]

Mr Read moved "that in case the numbers for the two highest in votes should be equal, then the President of the Senate shall have an additional casting vote", which was disagreed to by a general negative.

Mr. Govr Morris opposed the election of the President by the Legislature. He dwelt on the danger of rendering the Executive uninterested in maintaining the rights of his Station, as leading to Legislative tyranny. If the Legislature have the Executive dependent on them, they can perpetuate & support their usurpations by the influence of tax-gatherers & other officers, by fleets armies &c. Cabal & corruption are attached to that mode of election: so also is ineligibility a second time. Hence the Executive is interested in Courting popularity in the Legislature by sacrificing his Executive rights; & then he can go into that Body, after the expiration of his Executive Office, and enjoy there the fruits of his policy. To these considerations he added that rivals would be continually intriguing to oust the President from his place. To guard against all these evils he moved that the President "shall be chosen by Electors to be chosen by the people of the several States" Mr Carrol 2ded. him & on the question it passed in the negative

N. H. no. Mas. no. Ct. ay. N—J—ay. Pa. ay. Del. ay. Md. no—Va. ay. N—C—no—S—C—no—Geo— no. [Ayes—5; noes—6.]

Mr. Dayton moved to postpone the consideration of the two last clauses of sect. 1. art. X. which was disagreed to without a count of the States.

Mr Broome moved to refer the two clauses to a Committee of a Member from each State. & on the question, it failed the States being equally divided.

N—H— no— Mas—no. Ct. divd. N— J— ay. Pa. ay. Del. ay. Md. ay—Va. ay. N—C—no. S. C. no—Geo. no. [Ayes—5; noes—5; divided—1.]

On the question taken on the first part of Mr. Govr Morris's Motion to wit "shall be chosen by electors" as an abstract question, it failed the States being equally divided—

N—H—no. Mas. abst. Ct. divd. N. Jersey ay Pa ay. Del. ay. Md. divd. Va ay—N—C— no. S. C. no. Geo. no. [Ayes—4; noes—4; divided—2; absent—1.]

The consideration of the remaining clauses of sect 1. art X. was then posponed till tomorrow at the instance of the Deputies of New Jersey—

[*2:497; Madison, 4 Sept.*]

[Report of the Committee of Eleven:] "(4) After the word 'Excellency' in sect. 1. art. 10. to be inserted. 'He shall hold his office during the term of four years, and together with the vice-President, chosen for the same term, be elected in the following manner, viz. Each State shall appoint in such manner as its Legislature may direct, a number of electors equal to the whole number of Senators and members of the House of Representatives, to which the State may be entitled in the Legislature. The Electors shall meet in their respective States, and vote by ballot for two persons, of whom one at least shall not be an inhabitant of the same State with themselves; and they shall make a list of all the persons voted for, and of the number of votes for each, which list they shall sign and certify and transmit sealed to the Seat of the. Genl. Government, directed to the President of the Senate—The President of the Senate shall in that House open all the certificates; and the votes shall be then & there counted. The Person having the greatest number of votes shall be the President, if such number be a majority of that of the electors; and if there be more than one who have such a majority, and have an equal number of votes, then the Senate shall immediately choose by ballot one of them for President: but if no person have a majority. then from the five highest on the list, the Senate shall choose by ballot the President. And in every case after the choice of the President, the person having the greatest number of votes shall be vice-president: but if there should remain two or more who have equal votes, the Senate shall choose from them the vice-President. The Legislature may determine the time of choosing and assembling the Electors, and the manner of certifying and transmitting their votes.' "

. . . . .

The (4) clause was accordingly taken up.

Mr. Gorham disapproved of making the next highest after the President, the vice-President, without referring the decision to the Senate in case the next highest should have less than a majority of votes. as the regulation stands a very obscure man with very few votes may arrive at that appointment

Mr Sherman said the object of this clause of the report of the Committee was to get rid of the ineligibility, which was attached to the mode of election by the Legislature, & to render the Executive independent of the Legislature. As the choice of the President was to be made out of the five highest, obscure characters were sufficiently guarded against in that case: And he had no objection to requiring the vice-President to be chosen in like manner, where the choice was not decided by a majority in the first instance

Mr. Madison was apprehensive that by requiring both the President & vice President to be chosen out of the five highest candidates, the attention of the electors would be turned too much to making candidates instead of giving their votes in order to a definitive choice, Should this turn be given to the business, the election would in fact be consigned to the Senate altogether. It would have the effect at the same time, he observed, of giving the nomination of the candidates to the largest States.

Mr Govr Morris concurred in, & enforced the remarks of Mr. Madison.

Mr Randolph & Mr Pinkney wished for a particular explanation & discussion of the reasons for changing the mode of electing the Executive.

Mr. Govr. Morris said he would give the reasons of the Committee and his own. The 1st. was the danger of intrigue & faction if the appointmt. should be made by the Legislature. 2 the inconveniency of an ineligibility required by that mode in order to lessen its evils. 3 The difficulty of establishing a Court of Impeachments, other than the Senate which would not be so proper for the trial nor the other branch for the impeachment of the President, if appointed by the Legislature, 4. No body had appeared to be satisfied with an appointment by the Legislature. 5. Many were anxious even for an immediate choice by the people— 6— the indispensable necessity of making the Executive independent of the Legislature.—As the Electors would vote at the same time throughout the U.S. and at so great a distance from each other, the great evil of cabal was avoided. It would be impossible also to corrupt them. A conclusive reason for making the Senate instead of the Supreme Court the Judge of impeachments, was that the latter was to try the President after the trial of the impeachment.

Col: Mason confessed that the plan of the Committee had removed some capital objections, particularly the danger of cabal and corruption. It was liable however to this strong objection, that nineteen times in twenty the President would be chosen by the Senate, an improper body for the purpose.

Mr. Butler thought the mode not free from objections, but much more so than an election by the Legislature, where as in elective monarchies, cabal faction & violence would be sure to prevail.

Mr. Pinkney stated as objections to the mode 1. that it threw the whole appointment in fact into the hands of the Senate. 2— The Electors will be strangers to the several candidates and of course unable to decide on their comparative merits. 3. It makes the Executive reeligible which will endanger the public liberty. 4. It makes the same body of men which will in fact elect the President his Judges in case of an impeachment.

Mr. Williamson had great doubts whether the advantage of reeligibility would balance the objection to such a dependence of the President on the Senate for his reappointment. He thought at least the Senate ought to be restrained to the *two* highest on the list

Mr. Govr. Morris said the principal advantage aimed at was that of taking away the opportunity for cabal. The President may be made if thought necessary ineligible on this as well as on any other mode of election. Other inconveniences may be no less redressed on this plan than any other.

Mr. Baldwin thought the plan not so objectionable when well considered, as at first view. The increasing intercourse among the people of the States, would render important characters less & less unknown; and the Senate would consequently be less & less likely to have the eventual appointment thrown into their hands.

Mr. Wilson. This subject has greatly divided the House, and will also divide people out of doors. It is in truth the most difficult of all on which we have had to decide. He had never made up an opinion on it entirely to his own satisfaction. He thought the plan on the whole a valuable improvement on the former. It gets rid of one great evil, that of cabal & corruption; & Continental Characters will multiply as we more & more coalesce, so as to enable the electors in every part of the Union to know & judge of them. It clears the way also for a discussion of the question of re-eligibility on its own merits, which the former mode of election seemed to forbid. He thought it might be better however to refer the eventual appointment to the Legislature than to the Senate, and to confine it to a smaller number than five of the Candidates. The eventual election by the Legislature wd. not open cabal anew, as it would be restrained to certain designated objects of choice, and as these must have had the previous sanction of a number of the States: and if the election be made as it ought as soon as the votes of the electors are opened & it is known that no one has a majority of the whole, there can be little danger of corruption— Another reason for preferring the Legislature to the Senate in this business, was that the House of Reps. will be so often changed as to be free from the influence & faction to which the permanence of the Senate may subject that branch—

Mr. Randolph preferred the former mode of constituting the Executive, but if the change was to be made, he wished to know why the eventual election was referred to the *Senate* and not to the *Legislature?* He saw no necessity for this and many objections to it. He was apprehensive also that the advantage of the eventual appointment would fall into the hands of the States near the Seat of Government.

Mr Govr. Morris said the *Senate* was preferred because fewer could then, say to the President, you owe your appointment to us. He thought the President would not depend so much on the Senate for his re-appointment as on his general good conduct

[*2:511; Madison, 5 Sept.*]

The Report made yesterday as to the appointment of the Executive being then taken up. Mr. Pinkney renewed his opposition to the mode, arguing 1. that the electors will not have sufficient knowledge of the fittest men, & will be swayed by an attachment to the eminent men of their respective States— Hence 2dly the dispersion of the votes would leave the appointment with the Senate, and as the President's reappointment will thus depend on the Senate he will be the mere creature of that body. 3. He will combine with the Senate agst the House of Representatives. 4. This change in the mode of election was meant to get rid of the ineligibility of the President a second time, whereby he will become fixed for life under the auspices of the Senate

Mr. Gerry did not object to this plan of constituting the Executive in itself, but should be governed in his final vote by the powers that may be given to the President.

Mr. Rutlidge was much opposed to the plan reported by the Committee. It would throw the whole power into the Senate. He was also against a re-eligibility. He moved to postpone the Report under consideration & take up the original plan of appointment by the Legislature. to wit. "He shall be elected by joint ballot by the Legislature to which election a majority of the votes of the members present shall be required: He shall hold his office during the term of Seven years; but shall not be elected a second time"

On this motion to postpone

N— H— divd. Mas. no— Ct no— N— J. no. Pa. no— Del— no. Md. no— Va. no. N. C. ay— S. C. ay— Geo. no. [Ayes—2; noes—8; divided—1.]

Col. Mason admitted that there were objections to an appointment by the Legislature as originally planned. He had not yet made up his mind; but would state his objections to the mode proposed by the Committee. 1. It puts the appointment in fact into the hands of the Senate, as it will rarely happen that a majority of the whole votes will fall on any one candidate: and as the Existing President will always be one of the 5 highest, his re-appointment will of course depend on the Senate. 2. Considering the powers of the President & those of the Senate, if a coalition should be established between these two branches, they will be able to subvert the Constitution. — The great objection with him would be removed by depriving the Senate of the eventual election. He accordingly moved to strike out the words "if such number be a majority of that of the electors"

Mr. Williamson 2ded. the motion. He could not agree to the clause without some such modification. He preferred making the highest tho' not having a majority of the votes, President, to a reference of the matter to the Senate. Referring the appointment to the Senate lays a certain foundation for corruption & aristocracy.

Mr. Govr Morris thought the point of less consequence than it was supposed on both sides. It is probable that a majority of the votes will fall on the same man, As each elector is to give two votes, more than ¼ will give a majority. Besides as one vote is to be given to a man out of the State, and as this vote will not be thrown away, ½ the votes will fall on characters eminent & generally known. Again if the President shall have given satisfaction, the votes will turn on him of course, and a majority of them will reappoint him, without resort to the Senate: If he should be disliked, all disliking him, would take care to unite their votes so as to ensure his being supplanted.

Col: Mason those who think there is no danger of there not being a majority for the same person in the first instance, ought to give up the point to those who think otherwise.

Mr Sherman reminded the opponents of the new mode proposed that if the Small States had the advantage in the Senate's deciding among the five highest candidates, the Large States would have in fact the nomination of these candidates

On the motion of Col: Mason

N. H. no— Mas. no. Ct. no. N. J. no. Pa. no. Del. no. Md. ay. Va. no— N. C. ay. S— C. no. Geo. no [Ayes—2; noes—9.]

Mr. Wilson moved to strike out "Senate" and insert the word "Legislature"

Mr Madison considered it as a primary object to render an eventual resort to any part of the Legislature improbable. He was apprehensive that the proposed alteration would turn the attention of the large States too much to the appointment of candidates, instead of aiming at an effectual appointment of the officer, as the large States would predominate in the Legislature which would have the final choice out of the Candidates. Whereas if the Senate in which the small States predominate should have the final choice, the concerted effort of the large States would be to make the appointment in the first instance conclusive.

Mr Randolph. We have in some revolutions of this plan made a bold stroke for Monarchy. We are now doing the same for an aristocracy. He dwelt on the tendency of such an influence in the Senate over the election of the President in addition to its other powers, to convert that body into a real & dangerous Aristocracy—

Mr Dickinson was in favor of giving the eventual election to the Legislature, instead of the Senate— It was too much influence to be superadded to that body—

On the question moved by Mr Wilson

N. H— divd. Mas. no— Ct no— N— J— no. Pa. ay. Del— no. Md. no. Va. ay— N— C. no— S. C. ay. Geo. no. [Ayes—3; noes—7; divided—1.]

Mr Madison & Mr. Williamson moved to strike out the word "majority" and insert "one third" so that the eventual power might not be exercised if less than a majority, but not less than 1/3 of the Electors should vote for the same person—

Mr. Gerry objected that this would put it in the power of three or four States to put in whom they pleased.

Mr. Williamson. There are seven States which do not contain one third of the people— If the Senate are to appoint, less than one sixth of the people will have the power—

On the question

N. H— no. Mas. no— Ct no— N. J— no. Pa. no. Del. no. Md. no— Va. ay. N— C. ay. S. C no Geo. no. [Ayes—2; noes—9.]

Mr Gerry suggested that the eventual election should be made by six Senators and seven Representatives chosen by joint ballot of both Houses.

Mr King observed that the influence of the Small States in the Senate was somewhat balanced by the influence of the large States in bringing forward the candidates, and also by the Concurrence of the small States in the Committee in the clause vesting the exclusive origination of Money bills in the House of Representatives.

Col: Mason moved to strike out the word "five" and insert the word "three" as the highest candidates for the Senate to choose out of —

Mr. Gerry 2ded. the motion

Mr. Sherman would sooner give up the plan. He would prefer seven or thirteen.

On the question moved by Col Mason and Mr Gerry

N. H. no— Mas. no— Ct. no. N— J. no. Pa no. Delaware Md. no Va ay— N— C— ay— S. C. no— Geo— no. [Ayes —2; noes—9.]

Mr Spaight and Mr. Rutlidge moved to strike out "five" and insert "thirteen"—to which all the States disagreed — except N— C. & S— C—

Mr Madison & Mr. Williamson moved to insert after "Electors" the words "who shall have balloted" so that the non voting electors not being counted might not increase the number necessary as a majority of the whole—to decide the choice without the agency of the Senate—

On this question

N. H— no. Mas-- no. Ct. no. N. J— no. Pa ay. Del. no. Md. ay. Va ay— N— C. ay. S— C— no. Geo. no [Ayes—4; noes—7.]

Mr. Dickinson moved, in order to remove ambiguity from the intention of the clause as explained by the vote, to add, after the words "if such number be a majority of the whole number of the Electors" the word "appointed"

On this motion

N. H. ay. Mas— ay— Con: ay N— J— ay— Pa ay. Delaware Md. ay— Va. no. N. C. no. S— C. ay— Geo. ay. [Ayes—9; noes—2.]

Col: Mason. As the mode of appointment is now regulated, he could not forbear expressing his opinion that it is utterly inadmissible. He would prefer the Government of Prussia to one which will put all power into the hands of seven or eight men, and fix an Aristocracy worse than absolute monarchy.

The words "and of their giving their votes" being inserted on motion for that purpose, after the words "The Legislature may determine the time of chusing and assembling the Electors"

[2:521; *Madison, 6 Sept.*]

Mr. King and Mr. Gerry moved to insert in the (5) clause of the Report (see Sepr 4) after the words "may be entitled in the Legislature" the words following— "But no person shall be appointed an elector who is a member of the Legislature of the U.S. or who holds any office of profit or trust under the U.S." which passed nem: con:

Mr. Gerry proposed, as the President was to be elected by the Senate out of the five highest candidates, that if he should not at the end of his term be re-elected by a majority of the Electors, and no other candidate should have a majority, the eventual election should be made by the Legislature—This he said would relieve the President from his particular dependence on the Senate for his continuance in office.

Mr. King liked the idea, as calculated to satisfy particular members & promote unanimity; & as likely to operate but seldom.

Mr Read opposed it, remarking that if individual members were to be indulged, alterations would be necessary to satisfy most of them—

Mr Williamson espoused it as a reasonable precaution against the undue influence of the Senate.

Mr Sherman liked the arrangement as it stood, though he should not be averse to some amendments. He thought he said that if the Legislature were to have the eventual appointment instead of the Senate, it ought to vote in the case by States, in favor of the small States, as the large States would have so great an advantage in nominating the candidates—

Mr. Govr Morris thought favorably of Mr. Gerry's proposition. It would free the President from being tempted in naming to Offices. to Conform to the will of the Senate, & thereby virtually give the appointments to office, to the Senate.

Mr Wilson said that he had weighed carefully the report of the Committee for remodelling the constitution of the Executive; and on combining it with other parts of the plan, he was obliged to consider the whole as having a dangerous tendency to aristocracy; as throwing a dangerous power into the hands of the Senate, They will have in fact, the appointment of the President, and through his dependence on them, the virtual appointment to offices; among others the offices of the Judiciary Department. They are to make Treaties; and they are to try all impeachments. In allowing them thus to make the Executive & Judiciary appointments, to be the Court of impeachments, and to make Treaties which are to be laws of the land, the Legislative, Executive & Judiciary powers are all blended in one branch of the Government. The power of making Treaties involves the case of subsidies, and here as an additional evil, foreign influence is to be dreaded— According to the plan as it now stands, the President will not be the man of the people as he ought to be, but the Minion of the Senate. He cannot even appoint a tide-waiter without the Senate— He had always thought the Senate too numerous a body for making appointments to office. The

Senate, will moreover in all probability be in constant Session. They will have high salaries. And with all those powers, and the President in their interest, they will depress the other branch of the Legislature, and aggrandize themselves in proportion. Add to all this, that the Senate sitting in Conclave, can by holding up to their respective States various and improbable candidates, contrive so to scatter their votes, as to bring the appointment of the President ultimately before themselves— Upon the whole, he thought the new mode of appointing the President, with some amendments, a valuable improvement; but he could never agree to purchase it at the price of the ensuing parts of the Report, nor befriend a system of Which they make a part—

Mr. Govr. Morris expressed his wonder at the observations of Mr. Wilson so far as they preferred the plan in the printed Report to the new modification of it before the House, and entered into a comparative view of the two, with an eye to the nature of Mr. Wilsons objections to the last. By the first the Senate he observed had a voice in appointing the President out of all the Citizens of the U.S. —by this they were limited to five candidates previously nominated to them, with a probability of being barred altogether by the successful ballot of the Electors. Here surely was no increase of power. They are now to appoint Judges nominated to them by the President. Before they had the appointment without any agency whatever of the President. Here again was surely no additional power. If they are to make Treaties as the plan now stands, the power was the same in the printed plan— If they are to try impeachments, the Judges must have been triable by them before. Wherein then lay the dangerous tendency of the innovations to establish an aristocracy in the Senate? As to the appointment of officers, the weight of sentiment in the House, was opposed to the exercise of it by the President alone; though it was not the case with himself— If the Senate would act as was suspected, in misleading the States into a fallacious disposition of their votes for a President, they would, if the appointment were withdrawn wholly from them, make such representations in their several States where they have influence, as would favor the object of their partiality.

Mr. Williamson. replying to Mr. Morris: observed that the aristocratic complexion proceeds from the change in the mode of appointing the President which makes him dependent on the Senate.

Mr. Clymer said that the aristocratic part to which he could never accede was that in the printed plan, which gave the Senate the power of appointing to Offices.

Mr. Hamilton said that he had been restrained from entering into the discussions by his dislike of the Scheme of Govt in General; but as he meant to support the plan to be recommended, as better than nothing, he wished in this place to offer a few remarks. He liked the new modification, on the whole, better than that in the printed Report. In this the President was a Monster elected for seven years, and ineligible afterwards; having great powers, in appointments to office & continually tempted by this constitutional disqualification to abuse them in order to subvert the Government— Although he should be made re-eligible, Still if appointed by the Legislature, he would be tempted to make use of corrupt influence to be continued in office— It seemed peculiarly desirable therefore that Some other mode of election should be devised. Considering the different views of different States, & the different districts Northern Middle & Southern, he concurred with those who thought that the votes would not be concentered, and that the appointment would consequently in the present mode devolve on the Senate. The nomination to offices will give great weight to the President— Here then is a mutual connection & influence, that will perpetuate the President, and aggrandize both him & the Senate. What is to be the remedy? He saw none better than to let the highest number of ballots, whether a majority or not, appoint the President. What was the objection to this? Merely that too small a number might appoint. But as the plan stands, the Senate may take the candidate having the smallest number of votes, and make him President.

Mr. Spaight & Mr. Williamson moved to insert "seven" instead of "four" years for the term of the President—

On this motion

N. H. ay. Mas. no. Ct. no— N. J. no— Pa no. Del— no. Md. no. Va. ay. N. C— ay. S. C. no. Geo— no. [Ayes—3; noes—8.]

Mr. Spaight & Mr. Williamson then moved to insert "six" instead of "four". On which motion

N. H. no. Mas. no. Ct no. N. J. no. Pa. no. Del. no. Md. no. Va. no, N. C— ay. S. C. ay— Geo. no [Ayes—2; noes—9.]

On the term "four" all the States were ay, except N. Carolina, no.

On the question (Clause 4. in the Report) for Appointing President by electors—down to the words,—"entitled in the Legislature" inclusive.

N. H— ay— Mas: ay. Cont: ay N. J. ay— Pa. ay. Del— ay. Md ay, Va ay. N. C. no— S— C— no— Geo— ay. [Ayes —9; noes—2.]

It was moved that the Electors meet at the seat of the Genl. Govt. which passed in the Negative. N. C. only being ay.

It was moved to insert the words "under the seal of the State" after the word "transmit" in 4th clause of the Report which was disagreed to; as was another motion to insert the words "and who shall have given their votes" after the word "appointed" in the 4th Clause of the Report as added yesterday on motion of Mr. Dickinson.

On several motions. the words "in presence of the Senate and House of Representatives" were inserted after the word "Counted" and the word "immediately" before the word "choose"; and the words "of the Electors" after the word "votes".

Mr. Spaight said if the election by Electors is to be crammed down, he would prefer their meeting altogether and deciding finally without any reference to the Senate and moved "That the Electors meet at the seat of the General Government—"

Mr Williamson 2ded. the motion, on which all the States were in the negative except N: Carolina.

On motion the words "But the election shall be on the same day throughout the U— S—" were added after the words "transmitting their votes." N. H. ay. Mas. no. Ct. ay. N. J. no. Pa. ay. Del. no. Md. ay. Va. ay. N. C. ay. S. C. ay. Geo. ay [Ayes—8; noes—3.]

On a question on the sentence in clause (4). "if such number be a majority of that of the electors appointed."

N— H— ay— Mas. ay. Ct ay. N. J. ay— Pa no— Del— ay. Md. ay. Va no— N. C. no. S— C. ay Geo. ay. [Ayes—8; noes—3.]

On a question on the clause referring the eventual appointment of the President to the Senate

N— H— ay. Mas. ay. Ct. ay. N. J. ay. Pa ay. Del— ay— Va ay. N. C. no Here the call ceased.

Mr Madison made a motion requiring ⅔ at least of the Senate to be present at the choice of a President— Mr. Pinkney 2ded, the motion

Mr. Gorham thought it a wrong principle to require more than a majority in any case. In the present case it might prevent for a long time any choice of a President On the question moved by Mr M— & Mr. P.

N. H. ay: Mas. abst Ct. no. N. J. no. Pa. no. Del. no. Md. ay. Va. ay. N— C. ay. S— C. ay. Geo. ay [Ayes—6; noes—4; absent—1.]

Mr. Williamson suggested as better than an eventual choice by the Senate, that this choice should be made by the Legislature, voting *by States* and not *per capita*.

Mr. Sherman suggested the House of Reps. as preferable to "the Legislature", and moved, accordingly,

To strike out the words "The Senate shall immediately choose &c." and insert "The House of Representatives shall immediately choose by ballot one of them for President, the members from each State having one vote."

Col: Mason liked the latter mode best as lessening the aristocratic influence of the Senate.

On the motion of Mr. Sherman

N. H. ay. Mas. ay— Ct. ay— N. J. ay. Pa ay. Del. no. Md. ay. Va ay. N— C. ay— S— C. ay. Geo. ay, [Ayes—10; noes—1.]

Mr. Govr Morris suggested the idea of providing that in all cases, the President in office, should not be one of the five Candidates; but be only re-eligible in case a majority of the electors should vote for him—(This was another expedient for rendering the President independent of the Legislative body for his continuance in office)

Mr. Madison remarked that as a majority of members wd. make a quorum in the H— of Reps. it would follow from the amendment of Mr Sherman giving the election to a majority of States, that the President might be elected by two States only, Virga. & Pena. which have 18 members, if these States alone should be present

On a motion that the eventual election of Presidt. in case of *an equality* of the votes of the electors be referred to the House of Reps.

N. H. ay. Mas. ay. N. J. no. Pa. ay. Del. no. Md. no. Va. ay. N— C. ay. S. C. ay— Geo— ay, [Ayes—8; noes—3.]

Mr. King moved to add to the amendment of Mr. Sherman "But a quorum for this purpose shall consist of a member or members from two thirds of the States," and also of a majority of the whole number of the House of Representatives."

Col Mason liked it as obviating the remark of Mr Madison—The motion as far as "States" inclusive was agd. to

On the residue to wit. "and also of a majority of the whole number of the House of Reps. it passed in the Negative

N. H. no. Mas. ay. Ct. ay. N. J. no. Pa. ay. Del. no. Md. no. Va. ay— N— C— ay— S— C— no— Geo— no. [Ayes—5; noes—6.]

The Report relating to the appointment of the Executive stands as amended, as follows,

"He shall hold his office during the term of four years, and together with the vice-President, chosen for the same term, be elected in the following manner.

Each State shall appoint in such manner as its Legislature may direct, a number of electors equal to the whole number of Senators and members of the House of Representatives, to which the State may be entitled in the Legislature:

But no person shall be appointed an Elector who is a member of the Legislature of the U.S. or who holds any office of profit or trust under the U.S.

The Electors shall meet in their respective States and vote by ballot for two persons, of whom one at least shall not be an inhabitant of the same State with themselves; and they shall make a list of all the persons voted for, and of the number of votes for each; which list they shall sign and certify, and transmit sealed to the Seat of the General Government, directed to the President of the Senate.

The President of the Senate shall in the presence of the Senate and House of Representatives open all the certificates & the votes shall then be counted.

The person having the greatest number of votes shall be the President (if such number be a majority of the whole number of electors appointed) and if there be more than one who have such a majority, and have an equal number of votes, then the House of Representatives shall immediately choose by ballot one of them for President, the Representation from each State having one vote— But if no person have a majority, then from the five highest on the list, the House of Representatives shall in like manner choose by ballot the President— In the choice of a President by the House of Representatives, a Quorum shall consist of a member or members from two thirds of the States, (and the concurrence of a majority of all the States shall be necessary to such choice-)—And in every case after the choice of the President, the person having the greatest number of votes of the Electors shall be the vice-president: But, if there should remain two or more who have equal votes, the Senate shall choose from them the vice-President.

The Legislature may determine the time of choosing the Electors, and of their giving their votes; and the manner of certifying and transmitting their votes—But the election shall be on the same day throughout the U—States."

[*2:535; Madison, 7 Sept.*]

Mr. Gerry moved "that in the election of President by the House of Representatives, no State shall vote by less than three members, and where that number may not be allotted to a State, it shall be made up by its Senators; and a concurrence of a majority of all the States shall be necessary to make such choice". Without some such provision five individuals might possibly be competent to an election, these being a majority of two thirds of the existing number of States; and two thirds being a quorum for this business.

Mr. Madison 2ded. the motion

Mr. Read observed that the States having but one member only in the House of Reps. would be in danger of having no vote at all in the election: the sickness or absence either of the Representative or one of the Senators would have that effect

Mr. Madison replied that, if one member of the House of Representatives should be left capable of voting for the State, the states having one Representative only would still be subject to that danger. He thought it an evil that so small a number at any rate should be authorized, to elect. Corruption would be greatly facilitated by it. The mode itself was liable to this further weighty objection that the representatives of a *Minority* of the people, might reverse the choice of a *majority* of the *States* and of the *people*— He wished some cure for this inconveniency might yet be provided—

Mr Gerry withdrew the first part of his motion; and on the, — . . .

Question on the 2d. part viz, "and a concurrence of a majority of all the States shall be necessary to make such choice" to follow the words "a member or members from two thirds of the States" —It was agreed to nem: con:

[*2:572; Committee of Style*]

Sect. 1. The Executive power of the United States shall be vested in a single person. His stile shall be, "The President of the United States of America;" and his title shall be, "His Excellency." He shall hold his office during the term of four years, and together with the Vice President, chosen for the same term, be elected in the following manner.

Each State shall appoint, in such manner as it's legislature may direct, a number of Electors equal to the whole number of Senators and Members of the House of representatives to which the State may be entitled in the Legislature. But no Person shall be appointed an Elector who is a member of the Legislature of the United States, or who holds any office of profit or trust under the United States.

The Electors shall meet in their respective States and vote by ballot for two Persons of whom one at least shall not be an inhabitant of the same State with themselves.— and they shall make a list of all the Persons voted for, and of the number of votes for each, which list they shall sign and certify, and transmit sealed to the seat of the general Government, directed to the President of the Senate.

The President of the Senate shall in the presence of the Senate and House of representatives open all the certificates and the votes shall then be counted.

The Person having the greatest number of votes shall be the President (if such number be a majority of the whole number of the Electors appointed) and if there be more than one who have such a majority, and have an equal number of votes, then the House of representatives shall immediately choose by ballot one of them for President, the representation from each State having one vote—But if no Person have a majority, then from the five highest on the list, the House of representatives shall, in like manner, choose by ballot the President—In the choice of a President by the House of representatives a quorum shall consist of a Member or Members from two thirds of the States, and the concurrence of a majority of all the States shall be necessary to such choice.—and, in every case after the choice of the President, the Person having the greatest number of votes of the Electors shall be the vice-President: But, if there should remain two or more who have equal votes, the Senate shall choose from them the Vice President

The Legislature may determine the time of chusing the Electors and of their giving their votes—But the election shall be on the same day throughout the United States

The Legislature may declare by law what officer of the United States shall act as President in case of the death, resignation, or disability of the President and Vice President; and such Officer shall act accordingly, until such disability be removed, or a President shall be elected

3

Alexander Hamilton, Federalist, no. 68, 457–61
12 Mar. 1788

The mode of appointment of the chief magistrate of the United States is almost the only part of the system, of any consequence, which has escaped without severe censure, or which has received the slightest mark of approbation from its opponents. The most plausible of these, who has appeared in print, has even deigned to admit, that the election of the president is pretty well guarded. I venture somewhat further; and hesitate not to affirm, that if the manner of it be not perfect, it is at least excellent. It unites in an eminent degree all the advantages; the union of which was to be desired.

It was desireable, that the sense of the people should operate in the choice of the person to whom so important a trust was to be confided. This end will be answered by committing the right of making it, not to any pre-established body, but to men, chosen by the people for the special purpose, and at the particular conjuncture.

It was equally desirable, that the immediate election should be made by men most capable of analizing the qualities adapted to the station, and acting under circumstances favourable to deliberation and to a judicious combination of all the reasons and inducements, which were proper to govern their choice. A small number of persons, selected by their fellow citizens from the general mass, will be most likely to possess the information and discernment requisite to so complicated an investigation.

It was also peculiarly desirable, to afford as little opportunity as possible to tumult and disorder. This evil was not least to be dreaded in the election of a magistrate, who was to have so important an agency in the administration of the government, as the president of the United States. But the precautions which have been so happily concerted in the system under consideration, promise an effectual security against this mischief. The choice of *several* to form an intermediate body of electors, will be much less apt to convulse the community, with any extraordinary or violent movements, than the choice of *one* who was himself to be the final object of the public wishes. And as the electors, chosen in each state, are to assemble and vote in the state, in which they are chosen, this detached and divided situation will expose them much less to heats and ferments, which might be communicated from them to the people, than if they were all to be convened at one time, in one place.

Nothing was more to be desired, than that every practicable obstacle should be opposed to cabal, intrigue and corruption. These most deadly adversaries of republican government might naturally have been expected to make their approaches from more than one quarter, but chiefly from the desire in foreign powers to gain an improper ascendant in our councils. How could they better gratify this, than by raising a creature of their own to the chief magistracy of the union? But the convention have guarded against all danger of this sort with the most provident and judicious attention. They have not made the appointment of the president to depend on any pre-existing bodies of men who might be tampered with before hand to prostitute their votes; but they have referred it in the first instance to an immediate act of the people of America, to be exerted in the choice of persons for the temporary and sole purpose of making the appointment. And they have excluded from eligibility to this trust, all those who from situation might be suspected of too great devotion to the president in office. No senator, representative, or other person holding a place of trust or profit under the United States, can be of the number of electors. Thus, without corrupting the body of the people, the immediate agents in the election will at least enter upon the task, free from any sinister byass. Their transient existence, and their detached situation, already taken notice of, afford a satisfactory prospect of their continuing so, to the conclusion of it. The business of corruption, when it is to embrace so considerable a number of men, requires time, as well as means. Nor would it be found easy suddenly to embark them, dispersed as they would be over thirteen states, in any combinations, founded upon motives, which though they could not properly be denominated corrupt, might yet be of a nature to mislead them from their duty.

Another and no less important desideratum was, that the executive should be independent for his continuance in office on all, but the people themselves. He might otherwise be tempted to sacrifice his duty to his complaisance for those whose favor was necessary to the duration of his official consequence. This advantage will also be secured, by making his re-election to depend on a special body of representatives, deputed by the society for the single purpose of making the important choice.

All these advantages will be happily combined in the plan devised by the convention; which is, that the people of each state shall choose a number of persons as electors, equal to the number of senators and representatives of such state in the national government, who shall assemble within the state and vote for some fit person as president. Their votes, thus given, are to be transmitted to the seat of the national government, and the person who may happen to have a majority of the whole number of votes will be the president. But as a majority of the votes might not always happen to centre on one man and as it might be unsafe to permit less than a majority to be conclusive, it is provided, that in such a contingency, the house of representatives shall select out of the candidates, who shall have the five highest numbers of votes, the man who in their opinion may be best qualified for the office.

This process of election affords a moral certainty, that the office of president, will seldom fall to the lot of any man, who is not in an eminent degree endowed with the requisite qualifications. Talents for low intrigue and the little arts of popularity may alone suffice to elevate a man to the first honors in a single state; but it will require other talents and a different kind of merit to establish him in the esteem and confidence of the whole union, or of so considerable a portion of it as would be necessary to make him a successful candidate for the distinguished office of president of the United States. It will not be too strong to say, that there will be a constant probability of seeing the station filled by characters pre-eminent for ability and virtue. And this will be thought no inconsiderable recommendation of the constitution, by those, who are able to estimate the share, which the executive in every government must necessarily have in its good or ill administration. Though we cannot acquiesce in the political heresy of the poet who says—

> "For forms of government let fools contest—
> That which is best administered is best."

—yet we may safely pronounce, that the true test of a good government is its aptitude and tendency to produce a good administration.

4

JAMES MADISON, OBSERVATIONS ON JEFFERSON'S DRAFT OF A CONSTITUTION FOR VIRGINIA
15 Oct. 1788
Papers 11:289

Executive Governour. An election by the Legislature is liable to insuperable objections. It not only tends to faction intrigue and corruption, but leaves the Executive under the influence of an improper obligation to that department. An election by the people at large, as in this & several other States—or by Electors as in the appointment of the Senate in Maryland, or indeed by the people through any other channel than their legislative representatives, seem to be far preferable. The ineligibility a second time, though not perhaps without advantages, is also liable to a variety of strong objections. It takes away one powerful motive to a faithful & useful administration, the desire of acquiring that title to a re-appointment. By rendering a periodical change of men necessary, it discourages beneficial undertakings which require perseverance and system, or, as frequently happened in the Roman Consulate, either precipitates or prevents the execution of them. It may inspire desperate enterprizes for the attainment of what is not attainable by legitimate means. It fetters the judgment and inclination of the Community; and in critical moments would either produce a violation of the Constitution, or exclude a choice which might be essential to the public safety. Add to the whole, that by putting the Executive Magistrate in the situation of the tenant of an unrenewable lease, it would tempt him to neglect the constitutional rights of his department, and to connive at usurpations by the Legislative department, with which he may connect his future ambition or interest.

5

Alexander Hamilton to James Wilson
25 Jan. 1789
Papers 5:247–49

A degree of anxiety about a matter of primary importance to the new government induces me to trouble you with this letter. I mean the election of the President. We all feel of how much moment it is that Washington should be the man; and I own I cannot think there is material room to doubt that this will be the unanimous sense. But as a failure in this object would be attended with the worst consequences I cannot help concluding that even possibilities should be guarded against.

Every body is aware of that defect in the constitution which renders it possible that the man intended for Vice President may in fact turn up President. Every body sees that unanimity in Adams as Vice President and a few votes insidiously withheld from Washington might substitute the former to the latter. And every body must perceive that there is something to fear from machinations of Antifoederal malignity. What in this situation is wise?

By my accounts from the North I have every reason to believe that Adams will run there universally. I learn that he is equally espoused in Jersey Pennsylvania & Delaware & that Maryland is not disinclined to him. I hear of no persons thought of to the South, but Rutlege in South Carolina and Clinton in Virginia. As the accounts of the appointments of electors will satisfy the partisans of those Gentlemen in each of those States that they will have no coadjustors elsewhere, it seems not improbable that they will relinquish the attempt in favour of their intended candidates. Here then is a *chance* of unanimity in Adams. Nothing [is] so apt to beget it as the opinion that the current sets irresistibly towards him. Men are fond of going with the stream. Suppose personal caprice or hostility to the new system should occasion half a dozen votes only to be witheld from Washington—what may not happen? Grant there is little danger. If any, ought it to be run?

The votes from New Hampshire to Delaware inclusively & exclusive of New York are 41 South of Delaware 32. Here supposing equal unanimity on each side in a different candidate the chance is that there will be Eight votes to spare from Adams leaving him still a majority. Take the probability of unanimity in the North in Adams & of division in the South between different candidates and the chances are almost infinite in his favour. Hence I conclude it will be prudent to throw away a few votes say 7 or 8; giving these to persons not otherwise thought of. Under this impression I have proposed to friends in Connecticut to throw away two to others in Jersey to throw away an equal number & I submit it to you whether it will not be well to lose three or four in Pensylvania. Your advices from the South will serve you as the best guide; but for God's sake let not our zeal for a secondary object defeat or endanger a first. I admit that in several important views and particularly to avoid disgust to a man who would be a formidable head to Antifoederalists—it is much to be desired that Adams may have the plurality of suffrages for Vice President; but if risk is to be run on one side or on the other can we hesitate where it ought to be preferred?

If there appears to you to be any danger, will it not be well for you to write to Maryland to *qualify* matters there?

6

[Selection of Electors, 1796–1832], McPherson v. Blacker
146 U.S. 1 (1892)

Fifteen States participated in the second presidential election, in nine of which electors were chosen by the legislatures. Maryland, (Laws Md. 1790, c. 16, [2 Kelty]; Laws 1791, c. 62, [2 Kelty],) New Hampshire, (Laws N. H. 1792, 398, 401,) and Pennsylvania (Laws Penn. 1792, p. 240,) elected their electors on a general ticket, and Virginia by districts. Laws Va. 1792, p. 87, [13 Hening, 536]. In Massachusetts the general court by resolution of June 30, 1792, divided the State into four districts, in each of two of which five electors were elected, and in each of the other two three electors. Mass. Resolves, June, 1792, p. 25. Under the apportionment of April 13, 1792, North Carolina was entitled to ten members of the House of Representatives. The legislature was not in session and did not meet until November 15, while under the act of Congress of March 1, 1792, (1 Stat. 239, c. 8,) the electors were to assemble on December 5. The legislature passed an act dividing the State into four districts, and directing the members of the legislature residing in each district to meet on the 25th of November and choose three electors. 2 Iredell N. Car. Laws, 1715 to 1800, c. 15 of 1792. At the same session an act was passed dividing the State into districts for the election of electors in 1796, and every four years thereafter. Id. c. 16.

Sixteen States took part in the third presidential election, Tennessee having been admitted June 1, 1796. In nine States the electors were appointed by the legislatures, and in Pennsylvania and New Hampshire by popular vote for a general ticket. Virginia, North Carolina, and Maryland elected by districts. The Maryland law of December 24, 1795, was entitled "An act to alter the mode of electing electors," and provided for dividing the State into ten districts, each of which districts should "elect and appoint one person, being a resident of the said district, as an elector." Laws Md. 1795, c. 73, [2 Kelty]. Massachusetts adhered to the district system, electing one elector in each Congressional district by a majority vote. It was provided that if no one had a majority, the legislature should make the appointment on joint ballot, and the legislature also appointed two electors at large in the same manner. Mass. Resolves, June, 1796, p. 12. In Tennessee an act was passed August 8, 1796, which provided for the election of three electors, "one in the district of Washington, one in the district of Hamilton, and one in the district of Mero," and, "that the said electors may be elected with as little trouble to the citizens as possible," certain persons of the counties of Washington, Sullivan, Green, and Hawkins were named in the act and appointed electors to elect an elector for the district of Washington; certain other persons of the counties of Knox, Jefferson, Sevier, and Blount were by name appointed to elect an elector for the district of Hamilton; and certain others of the counties of Davidson, Sumner, and Tennessee to elect an elector for the district of Mero. Laws Tenn. 1794, 1803, p. 109; Acts 2d Sess. 1st Gen. Assembly Tenn. c. 4. Electors were chosen by the persons thus designated.

In the fourth presidential election, Virginia, under the advice of Mr. Jefferson, adopted the general ticket, at least "until some uniform mode of choosing a President and Vice-President of the United States shall be prescribed by an amendment to the Constitution." Laws Va. 1799, 1800, p. 3. Massachusetts passed a resolution providing that the electors of that State should be appointed by joint ballot of the senate and house. Mass. Resolves, June, 1800, p. 13. Pennsylvania appointed by the legislature, and upon a contest between the senate and house, the latter was forced to yield to the senate in agreeing to an arrangement which resulted in dividing the vote of the electors. 26 Niles' Reg. 17. Six States, however, chose electors by popular vote, Rhode Island supplying the place of Pennsylvania, which had theretofore followed that course. Tennessee, by act of October 26, 1799, designated persons by name to choose its three electors as under the act of 1796. Laws Tenn. 1794–1803, p. 211; Acts 2d Sess. 2d Gen. Ass. Tenn. c. 46.

Without pursuing the subject further, it is sufficient to observe that, while most of the States adopted the general ticket system, the district method obtained in Kentucky until 1824; in Tennessee and Maryland until 1832; in Indiana in 1824 and 1828; in Illinois in 1820 and 1824; and in Maine in 1820, 1824 and 1828. Massachusetts used the general ticket system, in 1804, (Mass. Resolves, June, 1804, p. 19,) chose electors by joint ballot of the legislature in 1808 and in 1816, (Mass. Resolves, 1808, pp. 205, 207, 209; 1816, p. 233;) used the district system again in 1812 and in 1820, (Mass. Resolves, 1812, p. 94; 1820, p. 245;) and returned to the general ticket system in 1824, (Mass. Resolves, 1824, p. 40.) In New York the electors were elected in 1828 by districts, the district electors choosing the electors at large. N.Y. Rev. Stat. 1827, Part I, Title vi, c. 6. The appointment of electors by the legislature, instead of by popular vote, was made use of by North Carolina, Vermont and New Jersey in 1812.

In 1824 the electors were chosen by popular vote, by districts, and by general ticket, in all the States excepting Delaware, Georgia, Louisiana, New York, South Carolina, and Vermont, where they were still chosen by the legislature. After 1832 electors were chosen by general ticket in all the States excepting South Carolina, where the legislature chose them up to and including 1860. Journals 1860, Senate pp. 12, 13; House, 11, 15, 17. And this was the mode adopted by Florida in 1868, (Laws 1868, p. 166,) and by Colorado in 1876, as prescribed by § 19 of the schedule to the constitution of the State, which was admitted into the Union August 1, 1876. Gen. Laws Colorado, 1877, pp. 79, 990.

7

Senate, Electoral College
23 Jan. 1800
Annals 10:29–32

Mr. C. Pinckney, of South Carolina, . . . remembered very well that in the Federal Convention great care was used to provide for the election of the President of the United States, independently of Congress; to take the business as far as possible out of their hands. The votes are to be given by Electors appointed for that express purpose, the Electors are to be *appointed* by each State, and the whole direction as to the manner of their appointment is given to the State Legislatures. Nothing was more clear to him than that Congress had no right to meddle with it at all; as the whole was entrusted to the State Legislatures, they must make provision for all questions arising on the occasion.

Mr. Baldwin, of Georgia . . . must say, for himself, that he did not agree that the present provisions on this subject were so defective and absurd as had been represented. His general respect for those who had gone before him in this House, and especially for the venerable assembly of the most experienced statesmen of the country by whom the Constitution had been formed, forbade him to entertain the belief that this subject, which is the strong feature that characterizes this as an Elective Government, could have been till now so entirely out of sight and neglected. Gentlemen appeared to him, from their observations, to forget that the Constitution in directing *Electors* to be appointed throughout the United States equal to the whole number of the Senators and Representatives in Congress, for the express purpose of entrusting this Constitutional branch of power to them, had provided for the existence of as respectable a body as Congress, and in whom the Constitution on this business has more confidence than in Congress. Experience had proved that a more venerable selection of characters could not be made in this country than usually composed that electoral body. And what are the questions which can arise on the subject entrusted to them to which they are incompetent, or to which Congress is so much more competent? The questions which present themselves seem to be:

1. Those which relate to the elections, returns and qualifications, of their own members. Shall these be taken away from that body, and submitted to the superior decision and control of Congress, without a particle of authority for it from the Constitution?

2. The legality or constitutionality of the different steps of their own proceedings, as, whether they vote for two persons both of the same state; whether they receive votes for a person under thirty-five years of age, or one who has not been fourteen years a citizen of the United States &c. It is true they, as well as any other Constitutional branch of this Government acting under that instrument, may be guilty of taking unconstitutional or corrupt steps, but they do it at their peril. Suppose either of the other branches of the Government, the Executive or the Judiciary, or even Congress, should be guilty of taking steps which are unconstitutional, to whom it is submitted, or who has control over it, except by impeachment? The Constitution seems to have equal confidence in all the branches on their own proper ground, and for either to arrogate superiority, or a claim to greater confidence, shows them in particular to be unworthy of it, as it is in itself directly unconstitutional.

3. The authentication of their own acts. This would seem to be as complete in them, as in either of the other branches of the Government. Their own authentication of their act finishes the business entrusted to them. It is true this must be judged of by the persons who are concerned in carrying it into execution; as in all laws and official acts under this Government, they to whom they are directed, and who are to be bound by them, must judge, and judge at their peril, whether they are duly authenticated or whether they are only a forgery.

If this be the just view of the subject, (and he could see no other which did not involve inextricable difficulties,) it leaves no possible question for the Senators and Representatives, when met together to count the votes agreeably to the Constitution, but to judge of the authentication of the act of the Electors, and then to proceed and count the votes as directed. If this body of the Electors of all the States had been directed by the Constitution to assemble in one place, instead of being formed into different Electoral colleges, he took it for granted none of the questions on which this resolution had been brought forward, would have occurred; every one would have acknowledged that they were to be settled in that assembly. It having been deemed more safe by the Constitution to form them into different Electoral colleges, to be assembled in the several States, does not at all alter the nature or distinctness of their powers, or subject them any more to the control of the other departments of the Government.

He observed further, on the other points to which gentlemen had spoken, that if such radical and important changes were to be made on this subject, as seemed to be in contemplation under this resolution, he thought they must be made by proposing an amendment to the Constitution to that effect; and that they could not be made by law, without violating the Constitution. He did not agree with the gentleman from Massachusetts, (Mr. Dexter,) that the clause at the close of the 8th section of the Constitution, which gives to Congress power to pass all laws necessary and proper to carry into effect the foregoing powers of that section, and all other powers vested by the Constitution in the Government of the United States, or in any department or officer thereof, could be extended to this case; that speaks of the use of the powers vested by the Constitution—this resolution relates to the formation of a competent and essential part of the Government itself: that speaks of the movements of the Government after it is organized; this relates to the organization of the Executive branch, and is therefore clearly a Constitutional work, and to be done, if at all, in the manner pointed out by the Constitution, by proposing an article of amendment to the Constitution on that subject. His own opinion, however, was, what he had before stated, that the provisions on this subject were already sufficient; that all the questions which had been suggested were as safely left to the decision of the assemblies of Electors, as of any body of men that could be devised; and that the members of the Senate and of the House of Representatives, when met together in one room, should receive the act of the Electors as they would the act of any other Constitutional branch of the Government, to judge only of its authentication, and then to proceed to count the votes, as directed in the second article of the Constitution.

8

GOUVERNEUR MORRIS TO PRESIDENT OF NEW YORK SENATE
25 Dec. 1802
Life 3:174–75

When this article was under consideration in the National Convention it was observed, that every mode of electing the chief magistrate of a powerful nation hitherto adopted is liable to objection. The instances where violence has been used, and murders committed, are numerous; those, in which artifice and fraud have succeeded against the general wish and will, are innumerable. And hence it was inferred, that the mode least favorable to intrigue and corruption, that in which the unbiassed voice of the people will be most attended to, and that which is least likely to terminate in violence and usurpation, ought to be adopted. To impress conviction on this subject, the case of Poland was not unaptly cited. Great and ambitious Princes took part in the election of a Polish King. Money, threats, and force were employed; violence, bloodshed, and oppression ensued; and now that country is parcelled out among the neighboring Potentates, one of whom was but a petty Prince two centuries ago.

The evils, which have been felt in the present mode of election, were pointed out to the Convention; but, after due advisement, the other mode appeared more exceptionable. Indeed, if the present be changed, it might be better to abolish the office of Vice President, and leave to legislative provision the case of a vacancy in the seat of the first magistrate.

The Convention was aware, that every species of trick and contrivance would be practised by the ambitious and unprincipled. It was, therefore, conceived, that if in elections the President and Vice President were distinctly designated, there would generally be a vote given for one of only two rival Presidents, while there would be numerous candidates for the other office; because he, who wished to become President, would naturally connect himself with some popular man of each particular district, for the sake of his local influence, so that the Vice Presidency would be but as a bait to catch state gudgeons. The person chosen would have only a partial vote, be perhaps unknown to the greater part of the community, and probably unfit for those duties, which the death of a President might call on him to perform.

The Convention not only foresaw, that a scene might take place similar to that of the last presidential election, but even supposed it not impossible, that at some time or other a person admirably fitted for the office of President might have an equal vote with one totally unqualified, and that, by the predominance of faction in the House of Representatives, the latter might be preferred. This, which is the greatest supposable evil of the present mode, was calmly examined, and it appeared that, however prejudicial it might be at the present moment, a useful lesson would result from it for the future, to teach contending parties the importance of giving both votes to men fit for the first office.

9

RUFUS KING, AMENDMENT TO THE CONSTITUTION, SENATE
20 Mar. 1816

Life 6:4–7

Mr. King said that, so far as regarded the manner and time of choosing Representatives and Senators to Congress, a majority of the Congress may by law now establish the very manner of choosing Representatives, which was now proposed to be erected into a constitutional rule. It seemed to him, therefore, unnecessary to alter the Constitution by imposing a rule, when, according to the Constitution, a competent power can now make the same regulation by law. Not so with the part of the amendment before the Senate, which the gentleman from Virginia (Mr. Barbour) proposed to strike out. The States may now severally direct the manner of choosing their own Electors; it is proposed that the manner shall be prescribed by the Constitution. That, Mr. K. thought, would be an important change, and the only change suggested in the Constitution which he deemed an improvement. He thought he might venture to say, that if there was any part of the Constitution deemed by its framers and advocates to be better secured than any other against the enterprises which have since occurred, it was the very provision on the subject of elections to the Presidency. The idea was, that the action of that particular agency, that has since controlled it, was as much displaced by the constitutional plan of election of President and Vice-President as could possibly be desired. The opinion had been that all undue agency or influence was entirely guarded against; that the men selected by the people from their own body would give their votes in such a manner as that no opportunity would be afforded for a combination to change the freedom and popular character which naturally belonged to the electoral bodies. Such had been the idea at the time of the adoption of the Constitution. We all know, said he, the course which this thing had taken. The election of a President of the United States is no longer that process which the Constitution contemplated. In conformity with the original view of the authors of that instrument, I would restore, as thoroughly as possible, the freedom of election to the people: I would make the mode of election uniform through the country, by throwing the whole nation into as many districts as there are Electors, and let the people of each district choose one Elector. One idea on this subject, he thought worth more than all the arguments against this course; that then all the people of the country would stand precisely on the same footing; and no particular addresses could be made to the special interests and particular views of particular men, or particular sections of the country. The course now pursued in this respect, Mr. King said, was not entitled to that high distinction. On the contrary, those who reflected on it could not help seeing that our progress in Government was not for the better; that it was not likely hereafter to be in favor of popular rights. It was with the people the Constitution meant to place the election of the Chief Magistrate, that being the source least liable to be corrupt. But if, under the name of the liberty of the people, said Mr. K., we put this power into other hands, with different interests, we place it in a situation in which the rights of the people are violated. In this point of view, he said, this particular clause of the proposed amendments of the Constitution was of great value. Let the question of the mode of election of Senators and Representatives rest where it is; if Congress choose to interpose, let them. The other part of the proposition was in favor of the rights of the people, of the freedom of the country; for with regard to these rights and freedom, no man could name a matter so important as the choice of the President of the nation. It is an infirmity of our nature that we look for chiefs and rulers, either for their superior virtue, or their supposed subserviency to the views of those in subordinate situations. It was against the evil of the latter principle Mr. K. desired to guard. The liberties of the people, repeated he, of which we speak much, are more affected by the choice of the President, than by any other ordinary political act. In this point they are vulnerable; here ought the rights of the people and of the States to be guarded. Our existence and the passions of the present day are ephemeral; public liberty should be immortal. Considering that this body should be to the people and States not only the safe guardians of their rights but the protectors of their liberty, he hoped they would adopt a provision he considered so nearly connected with the perpetuation of both.

[Mr. Lacock having moved that instead of the original resolutions, a committee be appointed to inquire into the expediency of proposing an amendment of the Constitution for the election of President & Vice President by the electors of each State qualified to vote for the most numerous branch of the State Legislatures, Mr. King, among others, addressed the senate. He said:]

All experience had shown that the people of any country were most competent to a correct designation of their first magistrate. So far as history affords us light, it leads to this point; that in time of difficulty and peril to a nation, when it is in utmost need of superior talent for its high stations, no tribunal is more competent to discern and select it than the people. Intrigue, turbulence and corruption may have some sway in quiet times, when all is tranquillity in regard to the general situation of the country; but when the Ship of State is in peril and in danger, turbulence ceases, and the best men are by instinctive power fixed on by the people for their governors. That has been wonderfully illustrated by history; and the best designations of magistrates have been produced in this way. My sober view is, said Mr. K., that, as to the election of Chief Magistrate of this nation, nobody is so competent as the great body of freemen to make a proper selection. Whether their first impression should be taken, as now suggested by Mr. Lacock, was a question of great importance. There would be great difficulty in making the returns of the votes; those who collected and compared the votes might defeat the choice of the people, &c. Not that these objections were insuperable. He was persuaded that the course of things under the present mode of choosing a President was in its nature pernicious, and that it had a tendency to prevent the object intended by the Constitution, of a pure elective majority. Men now live who will probably see the end of our system of government; terminate when it will, that termination will not be favorable to public liberty. For five years past he had seen a character developing itself, the predominance of which he feared. Not a people on earth were more capable of high excitement than this people. During the excitement of the passion to which he referred, if a contested election occurs, the gownsmen must stand aside; another character supersedes them; and there can be little difficulty in judging what will be the result. The march from military rule to despotism is certain, invariable. Those who think they see the probable tendency of our present system should interpose something remedial. The people in this particular are the best keepers of their own rights; and any device to remove that power from them weakens the security of it. He was anxious that the Senate should come to this question without the feelings of party; it was one involving all their interests and those of their families and descendants. He knew that this proposition, if agreed to, would break down the power of the great States. He had no objection, if in curtailing their power, the same measure regulated the rights of the whole nation equally. He was willing to let the election for the Presidency rest wholly on the people.

[The further consideration of the matter, after some negative votes on amendments, was postponed.]

10

JAMES MADISON TO GEORGE HAY
23 Aug. 1823
Writings 9:147–55

I have received your letter of the 11th, with the Newspapers containing your remarks on the present mode of electing a President, and your proposed remedy for its defects. I am glad to find you have not abandoned your attention to great Constitutional topics.

The difficulty of finding an unexceptionable process for appointing the Executive Organ of a Government such as that of the U.S. was deeply felt by the Convention; and as the final arrangement of it took place in the latter stage of the Session, it was not exempt from a degree of the hurrying influence produced by fatigue and impatience in all such Bodies, tho' the degree was much less than usually prevails in them.

The part of the arrangement which casts the eventual appointment on the House of Reps. voting by States, was, as you presume, an accommodation to the anxiety of the smaller States for their sovereign equality, and to the jealousy of the larger towards the cumulative functions of the Senate. The agency of the H. of Reps. was thought safer also than that of the Senate, on account of the greater number of its members. It might indeed happen that the event would turn on one or two States having one or two Reps. only; but even in that case, the representations of most of the States being numerous, the House would present greater obstacles to corruption than the Senate with its paucity of Members. It may be observed also, that altho' for a certain period the evil of State votes given by one or two individuals would be extended by the introduction of new States, it would be rapidly diminished by growing populations within extensive territories. At the present period, the evil is at its maximum. Another Census will leave none of the States existing or in Embryo, in the numerical rank of R.I. & Del, nor is it impossible, that the progressive assimilation of local Institutions, laws & manners, may overcome the prejudices of those particular States against an incorporation with their neighbours.

But with all possible abatements the present rule of voting for President by the H. of Reps. is so great a departure from the Republican principle of numerical equality, and even from the federal rule which qualifies the numerical by a State equality, and is so pregnant also with a mischievous tendency in practice, that an amendment of the Constitution on this point is justly called for by all its considerate & best friends.

I agree entirely with you in thinking that the election of Presidential Electors by districts, is an amendment very proper to be brought forward at the same time with that relating to the eventual choice of President by the H. of Reps. The district mode was mostly, if not exclusively in view when the Constitution was framed and adopted; & was exchanged for the general ticket & the legislative election, as the only expedient for baffling the policy of the particular States which had set the example. A constitutional establishment of that mode will doubtless aid in reconciling the smaller States to the other change which they will regard as a concession on their part. And it may not be without a value in another important respect. The States when voting for President by general tickets or by their Legislatures, are a string of beads; when they make their elections by districts, some of these differing in sentiment from others, and sympathizing with that of districts in other States, they are so knit together as to break the force of those geographical and other noxious parties which might render the repulsive too strong for the cohesive tendencies within the Political System.

It may be worthy of consideration whether in requiring elections by districts, a discretion might not be conveniently left with the States to allot two members to a single district. It would manifestly be an important proviso, that no new arrangement of districts should be made within a certain period previous to an ensuing election of President.

Of the different remedies you propose for the failure of a majority of Electoral votes for any one Candidate, I like best that which refers the final choice, to a joint vote of the two Houses of Congress, restricted to the two highest names on the Electoral lists. It might be a question, whether the *three* instead of the *two* highest names might not be put within the choice of Congress, inasmuch as it not unfrequently happens, that the Candidate third on the list of votes would in a question with either of the two first outvote him, and, consequently be the real preference of the voters. But this advantage of opening a wider door & a better chance to merit, may be outweighed by an increased difficulty in obtaining a prompt & quiet decision by Congress with three candidates before them, supported by three parties, no one of them making a majority of the whole.

The mode which you seem to approve, of making a *plurality* of Electoral votes a definitive appointment would have the merit of avoiding the Legislative agency in appointing the Executive; but might it not, by multiplying hopes and chances, stimulate intrigue & exertion, as well as incur too great a risk of success to a very inferior candidate? Next to the propriety of having a President the real choice of a majority of his Constituents, it is desirable that he should inspire respect & acquiescence by qualifications not suffering too much by comparison.

I cannot but think also that there is a strong objection to undistinguishing votes for President & Vice President; the highest number appointing the former the next the latter. To say nothing of the different services (except in a rare contingency) which are to be performed by them, occasional *transpositions* would take place, violating equally the mutual consciousness of the individuals, & the public estimate of their comparative fitness.

Having thus made the remarks to which your communication led, with a frankness which I am sure you will not disapprove, whatever errors you may find in them, I will sketch for your consideration a substitute which has occurred to myself for the faulty part of the Constitution in question

"The Electors to be chosen in districts, not more than two in any one district, and the arrangement of the districts not to be alterable within the period of ——— previous to the election of President. Each Elector to give two votes, one naming his first choice, the other his next choice. If there be a majority of all the votes on the first list for the same person, he of course to be President; if not, and there be a majority, (which may well happen) on the other list for the same person, he then to be the final choice; if there be no such majority on either list, then a choice to be made by joint ballot of the two Houses of Congress, from the two names having the greatest number of votes on the two lists taken together." Such a process would avoid the inconvenience of a second resort to the Electors; and furnish a double chance of avoiding an eventual resort to Congress. The same process might be observed in electing the Vice President.

Your letter found me under some engagements which have retarded a compliance with its request, and may have also rendered my view of the subject presented in it more superficial than I have been aware. This consideration alone would justify my wish not to be brought into the public discussion. But there is another in the propensity of the Moment, to view everything, however abstract from the Presidential election in prospect, thro' a medium connecting it with that question; a propensity the less to be excused as no previous change of the Constitution can be contemplated, and the more to be regretted, as opinions and commitments formed under its influence, may become settled obstacles at a practicable season.

11

JOSEPH STORY, COMMENTARIES ON THE CONSTITUTION 3:§§ 1449–52, 1454–60, 1462–67
1833

§ 1449. It has been already remarked, that originally in the convention the choice of the president was, by a vote of eight states against two, given to the national legislature. This mode of appointment, however, does not seem to have been satisfactory; for a short time afterwards, upon a reconsideration of the subject, it was voted, by six states against three, one being divided, that the president should be chosen by electors appointed for that purpose; and by eight states against two, that the electors should be chosen by the legislatures of the states. Upon a subsequent discussion, by the vote of seven states against four, the choice was restored to the national legislature. Towards the close of the convention the subject was referred to a committee, who reported a scheme, in many respects, as it now stands. The clause, as to the mode of choice by electors, was carried, by the vote of nine states against two; that respecting the time, and place, and manner of voting of the electors, by ten states against one; that respecting the choice by the house of representatives, in case no choice was made by the people, by ten states against one.

§ 1450. One motive, which induced a change of the choice of the president from the national legislature, unquestionably was, to have the sense of the people operate in the choice of the person, to whom so important a trust was confided. This would be accomplished much more perfectly by committing the right of choice to persons, selected for that sole pupose at the particular conjuncture, instead of persons, selected for the general purposes of legislation. Another motive was, to escape from these intrigues and cabals, which would be promoted in the legislative body by artful and designing men, long before the period of the choice, with a view to accomplish their own selfish purposes. The very circumstance, that the body entrusted with the power, was chosen long before the presidential election, and for other general functions, would facilitate every plan to corrupt, or manage them. It would be in the power of an ambitious candidate, by holding out the rewards of office, or other sources of patronage and honour, silently, but irresistibly to influence a majority of votes; and thus, by his own bold and unprincipled conduct, to secure a choice, to the exclusion of the highest and purest, and most enlightened men in the country. Besides; the very circumstance of the possession of the elective power would mingle itself with all the ordinary measures of legislation. Compromises and bargains would be made, and laws passed, to gratify particular members, or conciliate particular interests; and thus a disastrous influence would be shed over the whole policy of the government. The president would, in fact, become the mere tool of the dominant party in congress; and would, before he occupied the seat, be bound down to an entire subserviency to their views. No measure would be adopted, which was not, in some degree, connected with the presidential election; and no presidential election made, but what would depend upon artificial combinations, and a degrading favouritism. There would be ample room for the same course of intrigues, which has made memorable the choice of a king in the Polish diet, of a chief in the Venetian senate, and of a pope in the sacred college of the Vatican.

§ 1451. Assuming that the choice ought not to be confined to the national legislature, there remained various other modes, by which it might be effected; by the people directly; by the state legislatures; or by electors, chosen by the one, or the other. The latter mode was deemed most advisable; and the reasoning, by which it was supported, was to the following effect. The immediate election should be made by men, the most capable of analyzing the qualities adapted to the station, and acting under circumstances favourable to deliberation, and to judicious combination of all the inducements, which ought to govern their choice. A small number of persons, selected by their fellow citizens from the general mass for this special object, would be most likely to possess the information, and discernment, and independence, essential for the proper discharge of the duty. It is also highly important to afford as little opportunity, as possible, to tumult and disorder. These evils are not unlikely to occur in the election of a chief magistrate directly by the people, considering the strong excitements and interests, which such an occasion may naturally be presumed to produce. The choice of a number of persons, to form an intermediate body of electors, would be far less apt to convulse the community with any extraordinary or violent movements, than the choice of one, who was himself the final object of the public wishes. And as the electors chosen in each state are to assemble, and vote in the state, in which they are chosen, this detached and divided situation would expose them much less to heats and ferments, which might be communicated from them to the people, than if they were all convened at one time in one place. The same circumstances would naturally lessen the dangers of cabal, intrigue, and corruption, especially, if congress should, as they undoubtedly would, prescribe the same day for the choice of the electors, and for giving their votes throughout the United States. The scheme, indeed, presents every reasonable guard against these fatal evils to republican governments. The appointment of the president is not made to depend upon any pre-existing body of men, who might be tampered with beforehand to prostitute their votes; but is delegated to persons chosen by the immediate act of the people, for that sole and temporary purpose. All those persons, who, from their situation, might be suspected of too great a devotion to the president in office, such as senators, and representatives, and other persons holding offices of trust or profit under the United States, are excluded from eligibility to the trust. Thus, without corrupting the body of the people, the immediate agents in the election may be fairly presumed to enter upon their duty free from any sinister bias. Their transitory existence, and dispersed situation would present formidable obstacles to any corrupt combinations; and time, as well as means, would be wanting to accomplish, by bribery or intrigue of any considerable number, a betrayal of their duty. The president, too, who should be thus appointed, would be far more independent, than if chosen by a legislative body, to whom he might be expected to make correspondent sacrifices, to gratify their wishes, or reward their services. And on the other hand, being chosen by the voice of the people, his gratitude would take the natural direction, and sedulously guard their rights.

§ 1452. The other parts of the scheme are no less entitled to commendation. The number of electors is equal to the number of senators and representatives of each state; thus giving to each state as virtual a representation in the electoral colleges, as that, which it enjoys in congress. The votes, when given, are to be transmitted to the seat of the national government, and there opened and counted in the presence of both houses. The person, having a majority of the whole number of votes, is to be president. But, if no one of the candidates has such a majority, then the house of representatives, the popular branch of the government, is to elect from the five highest on the list the person, whom they may deem best qualified for the office, each state having one vote in the choice. The person, who has the next highest number of votes after the choice of president, is to be vice-president. But, if two or more shall have equal votes, the senate are to choose the vice-president. Thus, the ultimate functions are to be shared alternately by the senate and representatives in the organization of the executive department.

. . . . .

§ 1454. The mode of election of the president thus provided for has not wholly escaped censure, though the objections have been less numerous than those brought against many other parts of the constitution, touching that department of the government.

§ 1455. One objection was, that he is not chosen directly by the people, so as to secure a proper dependence upon them. And in support of this objection it has been urged, that he will in fact owe his appointment to the state governments; for it will become the policy of the states, which cannot directly elect a president, to prevent his election by the people, and thus to throw the choice into the house of representatives, where it will be decided by the votes of states. Again, it was urged, that this very mode of choice by states in the house of representatives is most unjust and unequal. Why, it has been said, should Delaware, with her single representative, possess the same vote with Virginia, with ten times that number? Besides; this mode of choice by the house of representatives will give rise to the worst intrigues; and if ever the arts of corruption shall prevail in the choice of a president, they will prevail by first throwing the choice into the house of representatives, and then assailing the virtue, and independence of members holding the state vote, by all those motives of honour and reward, which can so easily be applied by a bold and ambitious candidate.

§ 1456. The answer to these objections has been already in a great measure anticipated in the preceding pages. But it was added, that the devolution of the choice upon the house of representatives was inevitable, if there should be no choice by the people; and it could not be denied, that it was a more appropriate body for this purpose, than the senate, seeing, that the latter were chosen by the state legislatures, and the former by the people. Besides; the connexion of the senate with the executive department might naturally produce a strong influence in favour of the existing executive, in opposition to any rival candidate. The mode of voting by states, if the choice came to the house of representatives, was but a just compensation to the smaller states for their loss in the primary election. When the people vote for the president, it is manifest, that the large states enjoy a decided advantage over the small states; and thus their interests may be neglected or sacrificed. To compensate them for this in the eventual election by the house of representatives, a correspondent advantage is given to the small states. It was in fact a compromise. There is no injustice in this; and if the people do not elect a president, there is a greater chance of electing one in this mode, than there would be by a mere representative vote according to numbers; as the same divisions would probably exist in the popular branch, as in their respective states.

§ 1457. It has been observed with much point, that in no respect have the enlarged and liberal views of the framers of the constitution, and the expectations of the public, when it was adopted, been so completely frustrated, as in the practical operation of the system, so far as relates to the independence of the electors in the electoral colleges. It is notorious, that the electors are now chosen wholly with reference to particular candidates, and are silently pledged to vote for them. Nay, upon some occasions the electors publicly pledge themselves to vote for a particular person; and thus, in effect, the whole foundation of the system, so elaborately constructed, is subverted. The candidates for the presidency are selected and announced in each state long before the election; and an ardent canvass is maintained in the newspapers, in party meetings, and in the state legislatures, to secure votes for the favourite candidate, and to defeat his opponents. Nay, the state legislatures often become the nominating body, acting in their official capacities, and recommending by solemn resolves their own candidate to the other states. So, that nothing is left to the electors after their choice, but to register votes, which are already pledged; and an exercise of an independent judgment would be treated, as a political usurpation, dishonourable to the individual, and a fraud upon his constituents.

§ 1458. The principal difficulty, which has been felt in the mode of election, is the constant tendency, from the number of candidates, to bring the choice into the house of representatives. This has already occurred twice in the progress of the government; and in the future there is every probability of a far more frequent occurrence. This was early foreseen; and, even in one of the state conventions, a most distinguished statesman, and one of the framers of the constitution, admitted, that it would probably be found impracticable to elect a president by the immediate suffrages of the people; and that in so large a country many persons would probably be voted for, and that the lowest of the five highest on the list might not have an inconsiderable number of votes. It cannot escape the discernment of any attentive observer, that if the house of representatives is often to choose a president, the choice will, or at least may, be influenced by many motives, independent of his merits and qualifications. There is danger, that intrigue and cabal may mix in the rivalries and strife. And the discords, if not the corruptions, generated by the occasion, will probably long outlive the immediate choice, and scatter their pestilential influences over all the great interests of the country. One fearful crisis was passed in the choice of Mr. Jefferson over his competitor, Mr. Burr, in 1801, which threatened a dissolution of the government, and put the issue upon the tried patriotism of one or two individuals, who yielded from a sense of duty their preference of the candidate, generally supported by their friends.

§ 1459. Struck with these difficulties, it has been a favourite opinion of many distinguished statesmen, especially of late years, that the choice ought to be directly by the people in representative districts, a measure, which, it has been supposed, would at once facilitate a choice by the people in the first instance, and interpose an insuperable barrier to any general corruption or intrigue in the election. Hitherto this plan has not possessed extensive public favour. Its merits are proper for discussion elsewhere, and do not belong to these Commentaries.

§ 1460. The issue of the contest of 1801 gave rise to an amendment of the constitution in several respects, materially changing the mode of election of president. In the first place it provides, that the ballots of the electors shall be separately given for president and vice-president, instead of one ballot for two persons, as president; that the vice-president (like the president) shall be chosen by a majority of the whole number of electors appointed; that the number of candidates, out of whom the selection of president is to be made by the house of representatives, shall be three, instead of five; that the senate shall choose the vice-president from the two highest numbers on the list; and that, if no choice is made of president before the fourth of March following, the vice-president shall act as president.

. . . . .

§ 1462. This amendment has alternately been the subject of praise and blame, and experience alone can decide, whether the changes proposed by it are in all respects for the better, or the worse. In some respects it is a substantial improvement. In the first place, under the original mode, the senate was restrained from acting, until the house of representatives had made their selection, which, if parties ran high, might be considerably delayed. By the amendment the senate may proceed to a choice of the vice-president, immediately on ascertaining the returns of the votes. In the next place, under the original mode, if no choice should be made of a president by the house of representatives until after the expiration of the term of the preceding officer, there would be no person to perform the functions of the office, and an *interregnum* would ensue, and a total suspension of the powers of government. By the amendment, the new vice-president would in such case act as president. By the original mode, the senate are to elect the vice-president by ballot; by the amendment, the mode of choice is left open, so that it may be *vivâ voce.* Whether this be an improvement, or not, may be doubted.

§ 1463. On the other hand, the amendment has certainly greatly diminished the dignity and importance of the office of vice-president. Though the duties remain the same, he is no longer a competitor for the presidency, and selected, as possessing equal merit, talents, and qualifications, with the other candidate. As every state was originally compelled to vote for two candidates (one of whom did not belong to the state) for the same office, a choice was fairly given to all other states to select between them; thus excluding the absolute predominance of any local interest, or local partiality.

§ 1464. In the original plan, as well as in the amendment, no provision is made for the discussion or decision of any questions, which may arise, as to the regularity and authenticity of the returns of the electoral votes, or the right of the persons, who gave the votes, or the manner, or circumstances, in which they ought to be counted. It seems to have been taken for granted, that no question could ever arise on the subject; and that nothing more was necessary, than to open the certificates, which were produced, in the presence of both houses, and to count the names and numbers, as returned. Yet it is easily to be conceived, that very delicate and interesting inquiries may occur, fit to be debated and decided by some deliberative body. In fact, a question did occur upon the counting of the votes for the presidency in 1821 upon the re-election of Mr. Monroe, whether the votes of the state of Missouri could be counted; but as the count would make no difference in the choice, and the declaration was made of his re-election, the senate immediately withdrew; and the jurisdiction, as well as the course of proceeding in a case of real controversy, was left in a most embarrassing situation.

§ 1465. Another defect in the constitution is, that no provision was originally, or is now made, for a case, where there is an equality of votes by the electors for more persons, than the constitutional number, from which the house of representatives is to make the election. The language of the original text is, that the house shall elect "from the five highest on the list." Suppose there were six candidates, three of whom had an equal number; who are to be preferred? The amendment is, that the house shall elect "from the persons having the highest numbers, not exceeding three." Suppose there should be four candidates, two of whom should have an equality of votes; who are to be preferred? Such a case is quite within the range of probability; and may hereafter occasion very serious dissensions. One object in lessening the number of the persons to be balloted for from five to three, doubtless was, to take away the chance of any person having very few votes from being chosen president against the general sense of the nation. Yet it is obvious now, that a person having but a very small number of electoral votes, might, under the present plan, be chosen president, if the other votes were divided between two eminent rival candidates; the friends of each of whom might prefer any other to such rival candidate. Nay, their very hostility to each other might combine them in a common struggle to throw the final choice upon the third candidate, whom they might hope to control, or fear to disoblige.

§ 1466. It is observable, that the language of the constitution is, that "each state shall appoint in such manner, as the legislature thereof may direct," the number of electors, to which the state is entitled. Under this authority the appointment of electors has been variously provided for by the state legislatures. In some states the legislature have directly chosen the electors by themselves; in others they have been chosen by the people by a general ticket throughout the whole state; and in others by the people in electoral districts, fixed by the legislature, a certain number of electors being apportioned to each district. No question has ever arisen, as to the constitutionality of either mode, except that of a direct choice by the legislature. But this, though often doubted by able and ingenious minds, has been firmly established in practice, ever since the adoption of the constitution, and does not now seem to admit of controversy, even if a suitable tribunal existed to adjudicate upon it. At present, in nearly all the states, the electors are chosen either by the people by a general ticket, or by the state legislature. The choice in districts has been gradually abandoned; and is now persevered in, but by two states. The inequality of this mode of choice, unless it should become general throughout the Union, is so obvious, that it is rather matter of surprise, that it should not long since have been wholly abandoned. In case of any party divisions in a state, it may neutralize its whole vote, while all the other states give an unbroken electoral vote. On this account, and for the sake of uniformity, it has been thought desirable by many statesmen to have the constitution amended so, as to provide for an uniform mode of choice by the people.

§ 1467. The remaining part of the clause, which precludes any senator, representative, or person holding an office of trust or profit under the United States, from being an elector, has been already alluded to, and requires little comment. The object is, to prevent persons holding public stations under the government of the United States, from any direct influence in the choice of a president. In respect to persons holding office, it is reasonable to suppose, that their partialities would all be in favour of the re-election of the actual incumbent, and they might have strong inducements to exert their official influence in the electoral college. In respect to senators and representatives, there is this additional reason for excluding them, that they would be already committed by their vote in the electoral college; and thus, if there should be no election by the people, they could not bring to the final vote either the impartiality, or the independence, which the theory of the constitution contemplates.

SEE ALSO:

Generally 2.1.1; Amend. XII
Records of the Federal Convention, Farrand 1:91, 180, 254, 292; 2:132, 134, 135, 145, 158, 171, 406–7, 530–31, 597–98, 626
James McHenry, Maryland House of Delegates, 29 Nov. 1787, Farrand 3:150
Luther Martin, Maryland House of Delegates, 29 Nov. 1787, Farrand 3:158
James Wilson, Pennsylvania Ratifying Convention, 11 Dec. 1787, Elliot 2:510–14
James Iredell, North Carolina Ratifying Convention, 28 July 1788, Elliot 4:106–7
James Wilson, Executive Department, Lectures on Law, 1791, Works 1:438–39
Jonathan Dayton, Amendment to the Constitution, Senate, 29 Nov. 1803, Annals 13:109
Gouverneur Morris to Lewis R. Morris, 10 Dec. 1803, Life 3:194
Rufus King to C. King, 29 Sept. 1823, Life 6:532–34
Rufus King, Amendments to the Constitution, Senate, 18 Mar. 1824, Annals 41:356, 357–58
Rufus King to C. King, 23 Mar. 1824, Life 6:557–58
James Kent, Commentaries 1:255–60, 261–62 (1826)

Article 2, Section 1, Clause 4

The Congress may determine the Time of chusing the Electors, and the Day on which they shall give their Votes; which Day shall be the same throughout the United States.

1

DEBATE IN NORTH CAROLINA RATIFYING CONVENTION
26 July 1788
Elliot 4:104–6

Mr. J. TAYLOR objected to the power of Congress to determine the time of choosing the electors, and to determine the time of electing the President, and urged that it was improper to have the election on the same day throughout the United States; that Congress, not satisfied with their power over the time, place, and manner of elections of representatives, and over the time and manner of elections of senators, and their power of raising an army, wished likewise to control the election of the electors of the President; that by their army, and the election being on the same day in all the states, they might compel the electors to vote as they please.

Mr SPAIGHT answered, that the time of choosing the electors was to be determined by Congress, for the sake of regularity and uniformity; that, if the states were to determine it, one might appoint it at one day, and another at another, &c.; and that the election being on the same day in all the states, would prevent a combination between the electors.

Mr. IREDELL. Mr. Chairman, it gives me great astonishment to hear this objection, because I thought this to be a most excellent clause. Nothing is more necessary than to prevent every danger of influence. Had the time of election been different in different states, the electors chosen in one state might have gone from state to state, and conferred with the other electors, and the election might have been thus carried on under undue influence. But by this provision, the electors must meet in the different states on the same day, and cannot confer together. They may not even know who are the electors in the other states. There can be, therefore, no kind of combination. It is probable that the man who is the object of the choice of thirteen different states, the electors in each voting unconnectedly with the rest, must be a person who possesses, in a high degree, the confidence and respect of his country.

Gov. JOHNSTON expressed doubts with respect to the persons by whom the electors were to be appointed. Some, he said, were of opinion that the people at large were to choose them, and others thought the state legislatures were to appoint them.

Mr. IREDELL was of opinion that it could not be done with propriety by the state legislatures, because, as they were to direct the manner of appointing, a law would look very awkward, which should say, "They gave the power of such appointments to themselves."

Mr. MACLAINE thought the state legislatures might direct the electors to be chosen in what manner they thought proper, and they might direct it to be done by the people at large.

Mr. DAVIE was of opinion, that it was left to the wisdom of the legislatures to direct their election in whatever manner they thought proper.

Mr. TAYLOR still thought the power improper with respect to the time of choosing the electors. This power appeared to him to belong properly to the state legislatures, nor could he see any purpose it could answer but that of an augmentation of the congressional powers, which, he said, were too great already; that by this power they might prolong the elections to seven years, and that, though this would be in direct opposition to another part of the Constitution, sophistry would enable them to reconcile them.

Mr. SPAIGHT replied, that he was surprised that the gentleman objected to the power of Congress to determine the time of choosing the electors, and not to that of fixing the day of the election of the President; that the power in the one case could not possibly answer the purpose of uniformity without having it in the other; that the power, in both cases, could be exercised properly only by one general superintending power; that, if Congress had not this power, there would be no uniformity at all, and that a great deal of time would be taken up in order to agree upon the time.

2

JOSEPH STORY, COMMENTARIES ON THE CONSTITUTION 3:§§ 1469–70
1833

§ 1469. The propriety of this power would seem to be almost self-evident. Every reason of public policy and convenience seems in favour of a fixed time of giving the electoral votes, and that it should be the same throughout the Union. Such a measure is calculated to repress political intrigues and speculations, by rendering a combination among the electoral colleges, as to their votes, if not utterly impracticable, at least very difficult; and thus secures the people against those ready expedients, which corruption never fails to employ to accomplish its designs. The arts of ambition are thus in some degree checked, and the independence of the electors against external influence in some degree secured. This power, however, did not escape objection in the general, or the state conventions, though the objection was not extensively insisted on.

§ 1470. In pursuance of the authority given by this clause, congress, in 1792, passed an act declaring, that the electors shall be appointed in each state within thirty-four days, preceding the first Wednesday in December in every fourth year, succeeding the last election of president, according to the apportionment of representatives and senators then existing. The electors chosen are required to meet and give their votes on the said first Wednesday of December, at such place in each state, as shall be directed by the legislature thereof. They are then to make and sign three certificates of all the votes by them given, and to seal up the same, certifying on each, that a list of the votes of such state for president and vice-president is contained therein, and shall appoint a person to take charge of, and deliver, one of the same certificates to the president of the senate at the seat of government, before the first Wednesday of January then next ensuing; another of the certificates is to be forwarded forth-with by the post-office to the president of the senate at the seat of government; and the third is to be delivered to the judge of the district, in which the electors assembled. Other auxiliary provisions are made by the same act for the due transmission and preservation of the electoral votes; and authenticating the appointment of the electors. The president's term of office is also declared to commence on the fourth day of March next succeeding the day, on which the votes of the electors shall be given.

Article 2, Section 1, Clause 5

No Person except a natural born Citizen, or a Citizen of the United States, at the time of the Adoption of this Constitution, shall be eligible to the Office of President; neither shall any person be eligible to that Office who shall not have attained to the Age of thirty five Years, and been fourteen Years a Resident within the United States.

1

RECORDS OF THE FEDERAL CONVENTION

[*2:116; Journal, 26 July*]

Resolved That it be an instruction to the Committee to whom were referred the proceedings of the Convention for the establishment of a national government, to receive a clause or clauses, requiring certain qualifications of landed property and citizenship in the United States for the Executive, the Judiciary, and the Members of both branches of the Legislature of the United States;

[*2:367; Journal, 22 Aug.*]

at the end of the 1st section 10 article add

"he shall be of the age of thirty five years, and a Citizen of the United States, and shall have been an Inhabitant thereof for Twenty one years"

[*2:494; Journal, 4 Sept.*]

Sect. 2. No Person except a natural born Citizen, or a Citizen of the U. S. at the time of the adoption of this Constitution shall be eligible to the office of President: nor shall any Person be elected to that office, who shall be under the age of 35 years, and who has not been in the whole, at least 14 years a resident within the U. S.

[*2:574, 598; Committee of Style*]

Sect. 2. No Person except a natural born Citizen, or a Citizen of the U. S. at the time of the adoption of this Constitution shall be eligible to the office of President: nor shall any Person be elected to that office, who shall be under the age of 35 years, and who has not been in the whole, at least 14 years a resident within the U. S.

. . . . .

(*d*) No person except a natural born citizen, or a citizen of the United States, at the time of the adoption of this constitution, shall be eligible to the office of president; neither shall any person be eligible to that office who shall not have attained to the age of thirty-five years, and been fourteen years a resident within the United States.

2

JOSEPH STORY, COMMENTARIES ON THE CONSTITUTION 3:§§ 1472–73 1833

§ 1472. Considering the nature of the duties, the extent of the information, and the solid wisdom and experience required in the executive department, no one can reasonably doubt the propriety of some qualification of age. That, which has been selected, is the middle age of life, by which period the character and talents of individuals are generally known, and fully developed; and opportunities have usually been afforded for public service, and for experience in the public councils. The faculties of the mind, if they have not then attained to their highest maturity, are in full vigour, and hastening towards their ripest state. The judgment, acting upon large materials, has, by that time, attained a solid cast; and the principles, which form the character, and the integrity, which gives lustre to the virtues of life, must then, if ever, have acquired public confidence and approbation.

§ 1473. It is indispensable, too, that the president should be a natural born citizen of the United States; or a citizen at the adoption of the constitution, and for fourteen years before his election. This permission of a naturalized citizen to become president is an exception from the great fundamental policy of all governments, to exclude foreign influence from their executive councils and duties. It was doubtless introduced (for it has now become by lapse of time merely nominal, and will soon become wholly extinct) out of respect to those distinguished revolutionary patriots, who were born in a foreign land, and yet had entitled themselves to high honours in their adopted country. A positive exclusion of them from the office would have been unjust to their merits, and painful to their sensibilities. But the general propriety of the exclusion of foreigners, in common cases, will scarcely be doubted by any sound statesman. It cuts off all chances for ambitious foreigners, who might otherwise be intriguing for the office; and interposes a barrier against those corrupt interferences of foreign governments in executive elections, which have inflicted the most serious evils upon the elective monarchies of Europe. Germany, Poland, and even the pontificate of Rome, are sad, but instructive examples of the enduring mischiefs arising from this source. A residence of fourteen years in the United States is also made an indispensable requisite for every candidate; so, that the people may have a full opportunity to know his character and merits, and that he may have mingled in the duties, and felt the interests, and understood the principles, and nourished the attachments, belonging to every citizen in a republican government. By "residence," in the constitution, is to be understood, not an absolute inhabitancy within the United States during the whole period; but such an inhabitancy, as includes a permanent domicil in the United States. No one has supposed, that a temporary absence abroad on public business, and especially on an embassy to a foreign nation, would interrupt the residence of a citizen, so as to disqualify him for office. If the word were to be construed with such strictness, then a mere journey through any foreign adjacent territory for health, or for pleasure, or a commorancy there for a single day, would amount to a disqualification. Under such a construction a military or civil officer, who should have been in Canada during the late war on public business, would have lost his eligibility. The true sense of residence in the constitution is fixed domicil, or being out of the United States, and settled abroad for the purpose of general inhabitancy, *animo manendi,* and not for a mere temporary and fugitive purpose, *in transitu.*

Article 2, Section 1, Clause 6

In Case of the Removal of the President from Office, or of his Death, Resignation, or Inability to discharge the Powers and Duties of the said Office, the Same shall devolve on the Vice President, and the Congress may by Law provide for the Case of Removal, Death, Resignation or Inability, both of the President and Vice President, declaring what Officer shall then act as President, and such Officer shall act accordingly, until the Disability be removed, or a President shall be elected.

1

Records of the Federal Convention

[*1:292; Madison, 18 June*]

V. On the death resignation or removal of the Governour his authorities to be exercised by the President of the Senate till a Successor be appointed.

[*2:146, 172; Committee of Detail, IV, IX*]

The Presidt of ye Senate to succeed to the Executive in Case of (death) Vacancy untill the Meeting of the Legisle*

. . . . .

In Case of his Impeachment, (Dismission) Removal, Death, Resignation or Disability to discharge the Powers and Duties of his (Department) Office; the President of the Senate shall exercise those Powers and Duties, until another President of the United States be chosen, or until the President impeached or disabled be acquitted, or his Disability be removed.

[*2:186; Madison, 6 Aug.*]

In case of his removal as aforesaid, death, resignation, or disability to discharge the powers and duties of his office, the President of the Senate shall exercise those powers and duties, until another President of the United States be chosen, or until the disability of the President be removed.

[*2:427; Madison, 27 Aug.*]

Mr. Govr. Morris objected also to the President of the Senate being provisional successor to the President, and suggested a designation of the Chief Justice.

Mr. Madison added as a ground of objection that the Senate might retard the appointment of a President in order to carry points whilst the revisionary power was in the President of their own body, but suggested that the Executive powers during a vacancy, be administered by the persons composing the Council to the President.

Mr. Williamson suggested that the Legislature ought to have power to provide for occasional successors. & moved that the last clause (of 2 sect. X art:) relating to a provisional successor to the President be postponed.

Mr. Dickinson 2ded. the postponement. remarking that it was too vague. What is the extent of the term "disability" & who is to be the judge of it?

The postponement was agreed to nem: con:

[*2:495; Journal, 4 Sept.*]

The latter part of the 2 sect 10 art to read as follows.

He shall be removed from his office on impeachment by the House of representatives, and conviction by the Senate, for treason or bribery, and in case of his removal as aforesaid, death, absence, resignation or inability to discharge the powers or duties of his office the Vice President shall exercise those powers and duties until another President be chosen, or until the inability of the President be removed.

On the question to agree to the first clause of the report.

it passed in the affirmative

[*2:535; Madison, 7 Sept.*]

The mode of constituting the Executive being resumed, Mr- Randolph moved to insert in the first Section of the report made yesterday

"The Legislature may declare by law what officer of the U.S—shall act as President in case of the death, resignation, or disability of the President and Vice-President; and such officer shall act accordingly until the time of electing a President shall arrive."

Mr. Madison observed that this, as worded, would prevent a supply of the vacancy by an intermediate election of the President, and moved to substitute—"until such disability be removed, or a President shall be elected—" Mr. Governr. Morris 2ded. the motion, which was agreed to.

It seemed to be an objection to the provision with some, that according to the process established for chusing the Executive, there would be difficulty in affecting it at other than the fixed periods; with others, that the Legislature was restrained in the temporary appointment to *"officers"* of the *U. S:* They wished it to be at liberty to appoint others than such.

On the motion of Mr. Randolph as amended, it passed in the affirmative

N. H. divided. Mas. no. Ct. no. N.J. ay. Pa. ay. Del—no. Md. ay. Va. ay. N—C—no—S. C. ay—Geo. ay [Ayes—6; noes—4; divided—I.]

[*2:573, 575, 598; Committee of Style*]

The Legislature may declare by law what officer of the United States shall act as President in case of the death, resignation, or disability of the President and Vice President; and such Officer shall act accordingly, until such disability be removed, or a President shall be elected

. . . . .

. . . and in case of his removal as aforesaid, death, absence, resignation or inability to discharge the powers or duties of his office the Vice President shall exercise those powers and duties until another President be chosen, or until the inability of the President be removed.

. . . . .

(*e*) In case of the removal of the president from office, or of his death, resignation, or inability to discharge the powers and duties of the said office, the same shall devolve on the vice-president, and the Congress may by law provide for the case of removal, death, resignation or inability, both of the president and vice-president, declaring what officer shall then act as president, and such officer shall act accordingly, until the disability be removed, or the period for chusing another president arrive.

[*2:626; Madison, 15 Sept.*]

Art II. sect. I. (paragraph 6) "or the period for chusing another president arrive" was changed into "or a President shall be elected" comformably to a vote of the [seventh] day of [September]

*[Editors' note.—Words in parentheses were crossed out in the original.]

2

Federal Farmer, no. 14
17 Jan. 1788
Storing 2.8.181

The constitution provides only that the president shall hold his office during the term of four years; that, at most, only implies, that one shall be chosen every fourth year; it also provides, that in case of the removal, death, resignation, or inability, both of the president and vice-president, congress may declare what officer shall act as president; and that such officers shall act accordingly, until the disability be removed, *or a president shall be elected:* it also provides that congress may determine the time of chusing electors, and the day on which they shall give their votes. Considering these clauses together, I submit this question—whether in case of a vacancy in the office of president, by the removal, death, resignation, or inability of the president and vice-president, and congress should declare, that a certain officer, as secretary for foreign affairs, for instance, shall act as president, and suffer such officer to continue several years, or even for his life, to act as president, by omitting to appoint the time for chusing electors of another president, would it be any breach of the constitution? This appears to me to be an intended provision for supplying the office of president, not only for any remaining portion of the four years, but in cases of emergency, until another president shall be elected; and that at a period beyond the expiration of the four years: we do not know that it is impossible; we do not know that it is improbable, in case a popular officer should thus be declared the acting president, but that he might continue for life, and without any violent act, but merely by neglects and delays on the part of congress.

3

James Madison to Edmund Pendleton
21 Feb. 1792
Papers 14:235–36

The Bill concerning the election of a President & Vice President and the eventual successor to both, which has long been depending, has finally got thro' the two Houses. It was made a question whether the number of electors ought to correspond with the new apportionment or the existing House of Reps. The text of the Constitution was not decisive, and the Northern interest was strongly in favor of the latter interpretation. The intrinsic rectitude however of the former turned the decision in both houses in favor of the Southern. On another point the Bill certainly errs. It provides that in case of a double vacancy, the Executive powers shall devolve on the Presidt. pro. tem. of the Senate & he failing, on the Speaker of the House of Reps. The objections to this arrangement are various. 1. It may be questioned whether these are *officers,* in the constitutional sense. 2. If officers whether both could be introduced. 3. As they are created by the Constitution, they would probably have been there designated if contemplated for such a service, instead of being left to Legislative selection. 4. Either they will retain their *legislative* stations, and their incompatible functions will be blended; or the incompatibility will supersede those stations, & then those being the substratum of the adventitious functions, these must fail also. The Constitution says, Congs. may declare *what officers* &c. which seems to make it not an appointment or a translation; but an annexation of one office or trust to another office. The House of Reps. proposed to substitute the Secretary of State, but the Senate disagreed, & there being much delicacy in the matter it was not pressed by the former.

4

Joseph Story, Commentaries on the Constitution 3:§§ 1475–78
1833

§ 1475. The original scheme of the constitution did not embrace (as has been already stated) the appointment of any vice-president, and in case of the death, resignation, or disability of the president, the president of the senate was to perform the duties of his office. The appointment of a vice-president was carried by a vote of ten states to one. Congress, in pursuance of the power here given, have provided, that in case of the removal, death, resignation, or inability of the president and vice-president, the president of the senate *pro tempore,* and in case there shall be no president, then the speaker of the house of representatives for the time being shall act as president, until the disability be removed, or a president shall be elected.

§ 1476. No provision seems to be made, or at least directly made, for the case of the non-election of any president and vice-president at the period prescribed by the constitution. The case of a vacancy by removal, death, or resignation, is expressly provided for; but not of a vacancy by the expiration of the official term of office. A learned commentator has thought, that such a case is not likely to happen, until the people of the United States shall be weary of the constitution and government, and shall adopt this method of putting a period to both, a mode of dissolution, which seems, from its peaceable character, to recommend itself to his mind, as fit for such a crisis. But no absolute dissolution of the government would constitutionally take place by such a non-election. The only effect would be, a suspension of the powers of the executive part of the government, and incidentally of the legislative powers, until a new election to the presidency should take place at the next constitutional period, an evil of very great magnitude, but not equal to a positive extinguishment of the constitution. But the event of a non-election may arise, without any intention on the part of the people to dissolve the government. Suppose there should be three candidates for the presidency, and two for the vice-presidency, each of whom should receive, as nearly as possible, the same number of votes; which party, under such circumstances, is bound to yield up its own preference? May not each feel equally and conscientiously the duty to support to the end of the contest its own favorite candidate in the house of representatives? Take another case. Suppose two persons should receive a majority of all the votes for the presidency, and both die before the time of taking office, or even before the votes are ascertained by congress. There is nothing incredible in the supposition, that such an event may occur. It is not nearly as improbable, as the occurrence of the death of three persons, who had held the office of president, on the anniversary of our independence, and two of these in the same year. In each of these cases there would be a vacancy in the office of president and vice-president by mere efflux of time; and it may admit of doubt, whether the language of the constitution reaches them. If the vice-president should succeed to the office of president, he will continue in it until the regular expiration of the period, for which the president was chosen; for there is no provision for the choice of a new president, except at the regular period, when there is a vice-president in office; and none for the choice of a vice-president, except when a president also is to be chosen.

§ 1477. Congress, however, have undertaken to provide for every case of a vacancy both of the offices of president and vice-president; and have declared, that in such an event there shall immediately be a new election made in the manner prescribed by the act. How far such an exercise of power is constitutional has never yet been solemnly presented for decision. The point was hinted at in some of the debates, when the constitution was adopted; and it was then thought to be susceptible of some doubt. Every sincere friend of the constitution will naturally feel desirous of upholding the power, as far as he constitutionally may. But it would be more satisfactory, to provide for the case by some suitable amendment, which should clear away every doubt, and thus prevent a crisis dangerous to our future peace, if not to the existence of the government.

§ 1478. What shall be the proper proof of the resignation of the president, or vice-president, or of their refusal to accept the office, is left open by the constitution. But congress, with great wisdom and forecast, have provided, that it shall be by some instrument in writing, declaring the same, subscribed by the party, and delivered into the office of the secretary of state.

SEE ALSO:

An Act Relative to the Election of a President and Vice-President, 1 Stat. 239 (1792)

William Rawle, A View of the Constitution of the United States 55–57 (2d ed. 1829)

Article 2, Section 1, Clause 7

The President shall, at stated Times, receive for his Services, a Compensation, which shall neither be encreased nor diminished during the Period for which he shall have been elected, and he shall not receive within that Period any other Emolument from the United States, or any of them.

1

MASSACHUSETTS CONSTITUTION OF 1780, PT. 2, CH. 2, SEC. 1, ART. 13

Thorpe 3:1903

XIII. As the public good requires that the governor should not be under the undue influence of any of the members of the general court by a dependence on them for his support, that he should in all cases act with freedom for the benefit of the public, that he should not have his attention necessarily diverted from that object to his private concerns, and that he should maintain the dignity of the commonwealth in the character of its chief magistrate, it is necessary that he should have an honorable stated salary, of a fixed and permanent value, amply sufficient for those purposes, and established by standing laws; and it shall be among the first acts of the general court, after the commencement of this constitution, to establish such salary by law accordingly.

Permanent and honorable salaries shall also be established by law for the justices of the supreme judicial court.

And if it shall be found that any of the salaries aforesaid, so established, are insufficient, they shall, from time to time, be enlarged, as the general court shall judge proper.

2

RECORDS OF THE FEDERAL CONVENTION

[*1:21; Madison, 29 May*]

7. Resd. that a National Executive be instituted; to be chosen by the National Legislature for the term of years, to receive punctually at stated times, a fixed compensation for the services rendered, in which no increase or diminution shall be made so as to affect the Magistracy, existing at the time of increase or diminution,

[*1:81; Madison, 2 June*]

Docr. Franklin moved that what related to the compensation for the services of the Executive be postponed, in order to substitute—"whose necessary expences shall be defrayed, but who shall receive no salary, stipend fee or reward whatsoever for their services"—He said that being very sensible of the effect of age on his memory, he had been unwilling to trust to that for the observations which seemed to support his motion, and had reduced them to writing, that he might with the permission of the Committee, read instead of speaking them. Mr. Wilson made an offer to read the paper, which was accepted—

The following is a literal copy of the paper.

Sir.

It is with reluctance that I rise to express a disapprobation of any one article of the plan for which we are so much obliged to the honorable gentleman who laid it before us. From its first reading I have borne a good will to it, and in general wished it success. In this particular of salaries to the Executive branch I happen to differ; and as my opinion may appear new and chimerical, it is only from a persuasion that it is right, and from a sense of duty that I hazard it. The Committee will judge of my reasons when they have heard them, and their judgment may possibly change mine.—I think I see inconveniences in the appointment of salaries; I see none in refusing them, but on the contrary, great advantages.

Sir, there are two passions which have a powerful influence on the affairs of men. These are ambition and avarice; the love of power, and the love of money. Separately each of these has great force in prompting men to action; but when united in view of the same object, they have in many minds the most violent effects. place before the eyes of such men a post of *honour* that shall at the same time be a place of *profit,* and they will move heaven and earth to obtain it. The vast number of such places it is that renders the British Government so tempestuous. The struggles for them are the true sources of all those factions which are perpetually dividing the Nation, distracting its councils, hurrying sometimes into fruitless & mischievous wars, and often compelling a submission to dishonorable terms of peace.

And of what kind are the men that will strive for this profitable pre-eminence, through all the bustle of cabal, the heat of contention, the infinite mutual abuse of parties, tearing to pieces the best of characters? It will not be the wise and moderate, the lovers of peace and good order, the men fittest for the trust. It will be the bold and the violent, the men of strong passions and indefatigable activity in their selfish pursuits. These will thrust themselves into your Government and be your rulers. And these too will be mistaken in the expected happiness of their situation: For their vanquished competitors of the same spirit, and from the same motives will perpetually be endeavouring to distress their administration, thwart their measures, and render them odious to the people.

Besides these evils, Sir, tho' we may set out in the beginning with moderate salaries, we shall find that such will not be of long continuance. Reasons will never be wanting for proposed augmentations. And there will always be a party for giving more to the rulers, that the rulers may be able in return to give more to them.—Hence as all history informs us, there has been in every State & Kingdom a constant kind of warfare between the Governing & Governed: the one striving to obtain more for its support, and the other to pay less. And this has alone occasioned great convulsions, actual civil wars, ending either in dethroning of the Princes or enslaving of the people. Generally indeed the ruling power carries its point, the revenues of princes constantly increasing, and we see that they are never satisfied, but always in want of more. The more the people are discontented with the oppression of taxes; the greater need the prince has of money to distribute among his partizans and pay the troops that are to suppress all resistance, and enable him to plunder at pleasure. There is scarce a king in a hundred who would not, if he could, follow the example of Pharoah, get first all the peoples money, then all their lands, and then make them and their children servants forever. It will be said, that we don't propose to establish Kings. I know it. But there is a natural inclination in mankind to Kingly Government. It sometimes relieves them from Aristocratic domination. They had rather have one tyrant than five hundred. It gives more of the appearance of equality among Citizens, and that they like. I am apprehensive therefore, perhaps too apprehensive, that the Government of these States, may in future times, end in a Monarchy. But this Catastrophe I think may be long delayed, if in our proposed system we do not sow the seeds of contention, faction & tumult, by making our posts of honor, places of profit. If we do, I fear that tho' we do employ at first a number, and not a single person, the number will in time be set aside, it will only nourish the foetus of a King, as the honorable gentleman from Virginia very aptly expressed it, and a King will the sooner be set over us.

It may be imagined by some that this is an Utopian Idea, and that we can never find men to serve us in the Executive department, without paying them well for their services. I conceive this to be a mistake. Some existing facts present themselves to me, which incline me to a contrary opinion. The high Sheriff of a County in England is an honorable office, but it is not a profitable one. It is rather expensive and therefore not sought for. But yet, it is executed and well executed, and usually by some of the principal Gentlemen of the County. In France the office of Counsellor or Member of their Judiciary Parliaments is more honorable. It is therefore purchased at a high price: There are indeed fees on the law proceedings, which are divided among them, but these fees do not amount to more than three per Cent on the sum paid for the place. Therefore as legal interest is there at five per Ct. they in fact pay two per Ct. for being allowed to do the Judiciary business of the Nation, which is at the same time entirely exempt from the burden of paying them any salaries for their services. I do not however mean to recommend this as an eligible mode for our Judiciary department. I only bring the instance to shew that the pleasure of doing good & serving their Country and the respect such conduct entitles them to, are sufficient motives with some minds to give up a great portion of their time to the Public, without the mean inducement of pecuniary satisfaction.

Another instance is that of a respectable Society who have made the experiment, and practiced it with success more than an hundred years. I mean the Quakers. It is an established rule with them, that they are not to go to law; but in their controversies they must apply to their monthly, quarterly and yearly meetings. Committees of these sit with patience to hear the parties, and spend much time in composing their differences. In doing this they are supported by a sense of duty, and the respect paid to usefulness. It is honorable to be so employed, but it was never made profitable by salaries, fees, or perquisites. And indeed in all cases of public service the less the profit the greater the honor.

To bring the matter nearer home, have we not seen the great and most important of our officers, that of General of our armies executed for eight years together without the smallest salary, by a Patriot whom I will not now offend by any other praise; and this through fatigues and distresses in common with the other brave men his military friends & companions, and the constant anxieties peculiar to his station? And shall we doubt finding three or four men in all the U. States, with public spirit enough to bear sitting in peaceful Council for perhaps an equal term, merely to preside over our civil concerns, and see that our laws are duly executed. Sir, I have a better opinion of our country. I think we shall never be without a sufficient number of wise and good men to undertake and execute well and faithfully the Office in question.

Sir, The saving of the salaries that may at first be proposed is not an object with me. The subsequent mischiefs of proposing them are what I apprehend. And therefore it is that I move the amendment. If it is not seconded or accepted I must be contented with the satisfaction of having delivered my opinion frankly and done my duty.

The motion was seconded by Col. Hamilton with the view he said merely of bringing so respectable a proposition before the Committee, and which was besides enforced by arguments that a certain degree of weight. No debate ensued, and the proposition was postponed for the consideration of the members. It was treated with great respect, but rather for the author of it, than from any apparent conviction of its expediency or practicability.

[*1:236; Madison, 13 June*]

9. Resolved that a National Executive be instituted . . . to receive a fixed stipend by which he may be compensated for the devotion of his time to public service to be paid out of the national Treasury.

[*1:244; Madison, 15 June*]

4. Resd. that the U. States in Congs. be authorized to elect a federal Executive to consist of persons, to continue in office for the term of years, to receive punctually at stated times a fixed compensation for their services, in which no increase or diminution shall be made so as to affect the persons composing the Executive at the time of such increase or diminution, to be paid out of the federal treasury,

[*2:61; Journal, 20 July*]

It was moved and seconded to agree to the following clause namely

"to receive a fixed compensation for the devotion of his time to public service"

which passed unan: in the affirmative [Ayes—10; noes—0.]

It was moved and seconded to agree to the following clause, namely

"to be paid out of the national Treasury"
which passed unan: in the affirmative [Ayes—10; noes—0.]

[*2:121; Madison, 26 July*]

[That a national executive be instituted] . . . to receive a fixt compensation for the devotion of his time to the public service, to be paid out of the Natl. Treasury"—it passed in the affirmative

N. H. ay. Mas. not on floor. Ct. ay. N. J. ay. Pa. no. Del. no. Md. no. Va. divd. Mr. Blair & Col. Mason ay. Genl. Washington & Mr Madison no. Mr. Randolph happened to be out of the House. N.– C– ay. S. C. ay. Geo. ay. [Ayes—6; noes—3; divided—1; absent—1.]

[*2:132, 134, 146, 172; Committee of Detail*]

to receive a fixed Compensation for the Devotion of his Time to public Service—to be paid out of the public Treasury.

. . . . .

7. to receive a fixed compensation for
the devotion of his time to public service
the quantum of which shall be settled
by the national legislature
to be paid out of the national
treasury no Increase or decrease during
the Term of Service of the Executive

. . . . .

He shall, at stated Times, receive for his Services, a fixed Compensation, which shall neither be encreased nor diminished during his Continuance in Office.

[*2:335; Journal, 20 Aug.*]

No person holding the Office of President of the United States,—a Judge of their supreme Court—Secretary for the Department of foreign affairs—of Finance—of Marine—of War—or of
shall be capable of holding at the same time any other office of trust or emolument under the United States, or an individual State.

[*2:575, 599; Committee of Style*]

He shall, at stated times, receive for his services, a compensation, which shall neither be encreased nor diminished during his continuance in office.

. . . . .

(*f*) The president shall, at stated times, receive a fixed compensation for his services, which shall neither be encreased nor diminished during the period for which he shall have been elected.

[*2:626; Madison, 15 Sept.*]

Mr. Rutlidge and Docr Franklin moved to annex to the end paragraph 7. sect. 1. art II—"and he (the President) shall not receive, within that period, any other emolument from the U. S. or any of them." on which question

N—H. ay—Mas. ay. Ct. no. N. J. no. Pa ay. Del. no. Md. ay—Va. ay. N. C. no. S—C. ay. Geo—ay. [Ayes—7; noes—4.]

[*2:636; Mason, 15 Sept.*]

In the 7th clause of the 1st section of the 2nd Article—strike out the words *during the period for which he shall have been elected*—and instead of them insert—so as in any manner to affect the person in office at the time of such increase or diminution.

3

Alexander Hamilton, Federalist, no. 73, 492–94
21 Mar. 1788

The third ingredient towards constituting the vigor of the executive authority is an adequate provision for its support. It is evident that without proper attention to this article, the separation of the executive from the legislative department would be merely nominal and nugatory. The Legislature, with a discretionary power over the salary and emoluments of the Chief Magistrate, could render him as obsequious to their will, as they might think proper to make him. They might in most cases either reduce him by famine, or tempt him by largesses, to surrender at discretion his judgment to their inclinations. These expressions taken in all the latitude of the terms would no doubt convey more than is intended. There are men who could neither be distressed nor won into a sacrifice of their duty; but this stern virtue is the growth of few soils: And in the main it will be found, that a power over a man's support is a power over his will. If it were necessary to confirm so plain a truth by facts, examples would not be wanting, even in this country, of the intimidation or seduction of the executive by the terrors, or allurements, of the pecuniary arrangements of the legislative body.

It is not easy therefore to commend too highly the judicious attention which has been paid to this subject in the proposed Constitution. It is there provided that "The President of the United States shall, at stated times, receive for his services a compensation, *which shall neither be increased nor diminished, during the period for which he shall have been elected,* and he shall *not receive within that period any other emolument* from the United States or any of them." It is impossible to imagine any provision which would have been more eligible than this. The Legislature on the appointment of a President is once for all to declare what shall be the compensation for his services during the time for which he shall have been elected. This done, they will have no power to alter it either by increase or diminution, till a new period of service by a new election commences. They can neither weaken his fortitude by operating upon his necessities; nor corrupt his integrity, by appealing to his avarice. Neither the Union nor any of its members will be at liberty to give, nor will he be at liberty to receive any other emolument, than that which may have been determined by the first act. He can of course have no pecuniary inducement to renounce or desert the independence intended for him by the Constitution.

4

House of Representatives, Compensation of President
16 July 1789
Annals 1:646–51

The House then proceeded to the second part of the report, viz: "That there be paid in like quarterly payments to the Vice President of the United States, 5,000 dollars per annum."

Mr. White.—I do not like the principle on which this provision is made for the Vice President; there is nothing, I believe, in the constitution which gives him a right to an annual sum; it fixes no duty upon him as Vice President, requiring a constant attendance. He may be called upon to act as President, and then I would give him the salary of the President; at other times, he is to preside as President of the Senate, then I would pay him for his services in that character. On this principle, I shall move to strike out the clause; if that is agreed to, I propose to offer one, allowing him the pay of President, when he acts as President; and a daily pay during the time he acts as President of the Senate.

Mr. Page would second the motion for striking out five thousand dollars, but with a different view from what had been intended by his worthy colleague. He wished it struck out, in order to introduce a larger sum. His idea was, that a proper proportion was not observed between the salary of the First and Second Magistrates. As to the utility of the office, he had nothing to say. He had no hand in forming the constitution; if he had, perhaps he should never have thought of such an officer; but as we have got him, we must maintain him; and those gentlemen who talk of respectability being attached to high offices, must admit, in a comparative view, that he is not supported with dignity, provided a situation derives its dignity from the money given him by way of salary; for his part, he thought money, abstractedly considered, could not bestow dignity. Real dignity of character proceeds from a much nobler source; but he apprehended the people of the United States, whose representative the Vice President was, would be displeased to see so great a distinction made between the President and him.

Mr. Sedgwick said, the arguments of the honorable gentleman from Virginia, (Mr. White,) did not strike him with any force, nor did he see the impropriety spoken of. One reason why the pay of the members of the Senate and House is per diem is, because they contemplate their being together but a very inconsiderable part of their time; but I suppose, said he, that every gentleman who has considered the subject, has determined in his own mind that the Vice President ought to remain constantly at the seat of Government; he must always be ready to take the reins of Government when they shall fall out of the hands of the President; hence it will be necessary that he should, for this cause, if not for any other, preclude himself from every object of employment, and devote his whole time to prepare himself for the great and important charge for which he is a candidate. Under these circumstances, it is necessary that he should be provided with a constant salary, to support that rank which we contemplate for him to bear; I therefore conceive it must be such a perpetual salary as the President is entitled to receive. If the principles of the motion are inadmissible, it cannot be supported by argument, because very little information can be obtained on which to ground our reasoning.

Mr. Seney said, that, according to the constitution, a compensation is to be made for services performed. The Vice President may absent himself the whole time. He proposed giving him a handsome allowance while employed, but thought he ought to be paid per diem.

Mr. Sherman adverted to the circumstance of salaries being allowed to Lieutenant Governors in the several States where such officers are appointed; so that, according to this mode, the grant made to the Vice President would correspond with the practice of the States individually. It appeared also, he said, to be necessary, inasmuch as this officer would be taken from all other business.

Mr. White.—If I thought, sir, the attendance of the Vice President as necessary as that of the President, I would not hesitate to allow him an annual salary; but I do not conceive it to be so necessary; it is not made so by the constitution. If he had been appointed Vice President as a perpetual counsel for the President, it would have altered the case; he would then have had services to render, for which we ought to compensate him. The honorable gentleman from Massachusetts (Mr. Sherman) has intimated that he will be precluded from following any other business; there is nothing in the constitution which precludes him from following what profession he thinks proper. I am willing to pay him a full and liberal allowance for all the services he renders; but I do not think we are authorized to institute sinecures for any man.

It ought to be considered that the Vice President has personal advantages from the appointment to that office; it holds him up as the successor of the President; the voice of the people is shown to be considerably in his favor; and if he be a deserving person, there will be but little doubt of his succeeding to the presidential chair; not that I would make this an argument to diminish his compensation. I would pay him amply for all the services he renders, at least as amply as the Government and circumstances of the people will admit. When performing the duties of President, he should receive the salary as such.

The constitution has stipulated, that the President shall be compensated for his services, that we shall ascertain it by law; but it has not said one syllable with respect to the pay of the Vice President; hence I consider it would be improper to pay him on any other principle than in proportion to his services. If these require five thousand dollars a year, it may be made to amount to that sum, at so much per diem.

As to the observations of the gentleman from Connecticut, (Mr. Sherman,) that Lieutenant Governors receive salaries in the several States, and therefore it will be proper to grant one to the Vice President, in order to comport with the practice of the States individually, I shall only remark, that in some States they have no such officer; in others, where they have such an officer, they give him no pay at all; in some, they are paid according to their attendance on business, in the manner that I propose to pay the Vice President. But admitting that every State had an officer of this kind, and that they paid him a salary like that proposed in the report, it would be no argument why the General Government should pursue a practice inconsistent with that economy and sense of propriety which it ought to be the study of the Representatives of the people of the United States to preserve to their constituents.

Mr. Madison.—I do not concur, Mr. Speaker, in sentiment, with my colleague on this subject. I conceive, sir, if the constitution is silent on this point, that it is left to the Legislature to decide according to its nature and its merits. The nature of the office will require that the Vice President shall always be in readiness to render that service which contingencies may require; but I do not apprehend it to be in our power to derive much advantage from any guides furnished by the examples of the several States; because we shall find them differently provided for by the different Governments. If we consider that the Vice President may be taken from the extremity of the continent, and be from the nature of his office obliged to reside at or within the convenient reach of the seat of Government, to take upon him the exercise of the President's functions, in case of any accident that may deprive the Union of the services of their first officer, we must see, I think, it will often happen that he will be obliged to be constantly at the seat of Government. No officer under a State Government can be so far removed as to make it inconvenient to be called upon when his services are required; so that, if he serve without a salary, it may be he can reside at home, and pursue his domestic business; therefore the application in that case does not appear to me to be conclusive.

My colleague says that he will derive advantages from being in the line of appointment to the presidential chair. If he is to be considered as the apparent successor of the President, to qualify himself the better for that office, he must withdraw from his other avocations, and direct his attention to the obtaining a perfect knowledge of his intended business.

The idea that a man ought to be paid only in proportion to his services, holds good in some cases, but not in others. It holds good in legislative business, but not in the executive or judicial departments. A judge will be sometimes unemployed, as in the case of the Vice President; yet it is found necessary to claim the whole of his time and attention to the duties for which he is appointed. If the principle of proportioning the allowance to the quantum of services performed obtains, it will be found that the Judiciary will be as dependent on the legislative authority, as if the Legislature was to declare what shall be their salary for the succeeding year; because, by abridging their services at every session, we could reduce them to such a degree, as to require a very trifling compensation indeed. Neither do I, Mr. Speaker, consider this as a sinecure; but that will appear from the reasons already given. The office of a judge is liable, in some degree, to the same objection; but these kinds of objections are levelled against the institutions themselves. We are to consider his appointment as a part of the constitution; and if we mean to carry the constitution into full effect, we ought to make provision for his support, adequate to the merits and nature of the office.

Mr. Ames said that the Vice President's acceptance of his appointment was a renunciation of every other avocation. When a man is taken from the mass of the people for a particular office, he is entitled to a compensation from the public; during the time in which he is not particularly employed, he is supposed to be engaged in political researches for the benefit of his country.

Every man is eligible, by the constitution, to be chosen to this office; but if a competent support is not allowed, the choice will be confined to opulent characters. This is an aristocratic idea, and contravenes the spirit of the constitution.

Mr. Seney.—This, sir, is a subject of a delicate nature, and the discussion of it rather disagreeable; but I think it my duty to declare my sentiments freely upon it. No argument has been adduced to convince me that the Vice President ought to receive an allowance any more than the other members of the Legislature. He cannot be compelled to perform any duty. This is an important subject, and ought to be maturely considered, as a great deal depends on the decision which will now take place.

Mr. Burke observed that the situation of our finances was so much embarrassed, as to disempower us from giving such ample salaries as we might, under different circumstances, think necessary; that it was but reasonable the Vice President should receive a compensation adequate to the second officer in the Government. He will be subject to extra expenses by living at the seat of Government, and will be obliged to maintain his dignity. Mr. B. further suggested that the sum might not be fully sufficient, but in our present situation, it was as much as we could afford.

Mr. Ames, in his reply to Mr. Seney's observations, pointed out the difference of the situation of the Vice President and the members of the Legislature.

Mr. Sedgwick made some additional remarks of a similar nature, and further observed, it would be necessary that the members of the House should return and associate with their constituents, in order to learn their sentiments and their feelings, and witness their situation and wants, that they may consequently resume their former occupations: but with respect to the Vice President, his acceptance must be considered as an abandonment of every other pursuit; he must reside at the seat of Government, and will necessarily incur extra expenses in consequence of his office.

Mr. Stone.—I am for giving such salaries to the officers of this Government, as will render them easy in their situation. But we are confined by the constitution; salaries are to be given for services performed; they are considered in no other light. The Vice President cannot be viewed in any other light than that of the President of the Senate. I am for his being paid per diem, but would allow him a generous support. I do not think five thousand dollars are sufficient; I would allow him a larger sum, which allowance, per diem, would amount to what would be fully adequate.

Mr. SMITH, of South Carolina, said, that by the constitution, the Vice President could not be considered as a Senator, and therefore could not, with any propriety, be paid as such. Considering him as an officer in the Government, next in dignity to the President, and particularly designated by the constitution, he must support a correspondent dignity in his style of living, and consequently ought to have a competent allowance for that purpose. He did not think five thousand dollars would be considered too much, and would vote for that sum. The idea of a daily allowance must be given up, as inapplicable to the situation assigned him by the constitution. He is there recognised as Vice President, and as such ought to be provided for. A daily pay of twenty-five or thirty dollars would appear a large compensation; yet if Congress sat but one hundred days, which, in all probability, would be the length of their future sessions, it would be insufficient for his support. But suppose it one hundred and fifty days; this, at thirty dollars per day, would come so near the proposed salary, that the saving would be an inconsiderable trifle; but if the session was longer, it might amount to more than is contemplated by any gentleman.

Mr. PAGE was clearly for making the allowance by annual salary, because the office was permanent; a daily allowance could not be relied upon, because if the Senate sat but a few days, it would be incompetent, even at one hundred dollars per day; whereas, if the session was of long continuance, that sum would be more than the services could require, if they are to hold a comparison with those of the President. If the House agreed to strike out the five thousand dollars, he would propose eight thousand, which was not one-third of what was given the President.

Mr. BOUDINOT.—The question seems to turn merely on this point, whether the Vice President shall receive a per diem allowance, or an annual salary? The constitution ought to serve as the ground on which to determine it; therefore we are to consider the point of view in which this office is placed by that instrument. The second article calls him into view with the President; he is to be elected in the same manner as the President, in order to obtain the second best character in the Union to fill the place of the first, in case it should be vacated by any unforeseen accident. The constitution considers him a respectable officer; he is to supersede the President, when it shall happen that the First Magistrate dies, or is removed on impeachment and conviction. These are the great objects of his appointment. His duty as President of the Senate is only collateral; consequently he ought to be respected, and provided for according to the dignity and importance of his principal character. If still inferior duties were attached to him, would it be an argument for reducing the compensation to an equality with what ought to be granted, if he performed such inferior duties only? I apprehend it is a principle of this nature which urges gentlemen on to press the amendment. I cannot see any reason for differing with the constitution on a point in which I think it ought to guide our decision.

I think there is an affinity between the duration of the office and the compensattion. The constitution establishes the office for four years; the compensation ought to be made commensurate with that idea.

The question on Mr. WHITE's motion was taken and lost, as was Mr. PAGE's motion for striking out 5,000 and inserting 8,000 dollars.

The proposition being then agreed to. . . .

Article 2, Section 1, Clause 8

Before he enter on the Execution of his Office, he shall take the following Oath or Affirmation:—"I do solemnly swear (or affirm) that I will faithfully execute the Office of President of the United States, and will to the best of my Ability, preserve, protect and defend the Constitution of the United States."

1

RECORDS OF THE FEDERAL CONVENTION

[*2:146, 172; Committee of Detail, IV, IX*]

9. and shall swear fidelity to the union, (as the legislature shall direct.) by taking an oath of office*

. . . . .

[EDITORS' NOTE.—Words in parentheses were crossed out in the original.]

Before he shall enter on the Duties of his Department, he shall take the following Oath or Affirmation, "I ——— solemnly swear,—or affirm,—that I will faithfully execute the Office of President of the United States of America."

[*2:427; Madison, 27 Aug.*]

Col: Mason & Mr. Madison, moved to add to the oath to be taken by the supreme Executive "and will to the best of my judgment and power preserve protect and defend the Constitution of the U. S."

Mr. Wilson thought the general provision for oaths of

office, in a subsequent place, rendered the amendment unnecessary—

On the question

N.H. ay—Mas—abst Ct ay—Pa ay. Del. no. Md. ay. Va. ay—N. C. abst S. C. ay. Geo. ay. [Ayes—7; noes—1; absent—2.]

[*2:575, 599; Committee of Style*]

Before he shall enter on the duties of his department, he shall take the following Oath or Affirmation, "I ——— solemnly swear (or affirm) that I will faithfully execute the Office of President of the United States of America, and will to the best of my judgment and power, preserve, protect and defend the Constitution of the United States."

. . . . .

(*g*) Before he enter on the execution of his office, he shall take the following oath or affirmation: "I ———, do solemnly swear (or affirm) that I will faithfully execute the office of president of the United States, and will to the best of my judgment and power, preserve, protect and defend the constitution of the United States."

Constitution of the United States and the First Twelve Amendments

We the People of the United States, in Order to form a more perfect Union, establish Justice, insure domestic Tranquility, provide for the common defence, promote the general Welfare, and secure the Blessings of Liberty to ourselves and our Posterity, do ordain and establish this Constitution for the United States of America.

Article. I.

SECTION 1. All legislative Powers herein granted shall be vested in a Congress of the United States, which shall consist of a Senate and House of Representatives.

SECTION 2. The House of Representatives shall be composed of Members chosen every second Year by the People of the several States, and the Electors in each State shall have the Qualifications requisite for Electors of the most numerous Branch of the State Legislature.

No person shall be a Representative who shall not have attained to the Age of twenty five Years, and been seven Years a Citizen of the United States, and who shall not, when elected, be an Inhabitant of that State in which he shall be chosen.

Representatives and direct Taxes shall be apportioned among the several States which may be included within this Union, according to their respective Numbers, which shall be determined by adding to the whole Number of free Persons, including those bound to Service for a Term of Years, and excluding Indians not taxed, three fifths of all other Persons. The actual Enumeration shall be made within three Years after the first Meeting of the Congress of the United States, and within every subsequent Term of ten Years, in such Manner as they shall by Law direct. The Number of Representatives shall not exceed one for every thirty Thousand, but each State shall have at Least one Representative; and until such enumeration shall be made, the State of New Hampshire shall be entitled to chuse three, Massachusetts eight, Rhode-Island and Providence Plantations one, Connecticut five, New-York six, New Jersey four, Pennsylvania eight, Delaware one, Maryland six, Virginia ten, North Carolina five, South Carolina five, and Georgia three.

When vacancies happen in the Representation from any State, the Executive Authority thereof shall issue Writs of Election to fill such Vacancies.

The House of Representatives shall chuse their Speaker and other Officers; and shall have the sole Power of Impeachment.

SECTION 3. The Senate of the United States shall be composed of two Senators from each State, chosen by the Legislature thereof, for six Years; and each Senator shall have one Vote.

Immediately after they shall be assembled in Consequence of the first Election, they shall be divided as equally as may be into three Classes. The Seats of the Senators of the first Class shall be vacated at the Expiration of the second Year, of the second Class at the Expiration of the fourth Year, and of the third Class at the Expiration of the sixth Year, so that one third may be chosen every second Year; and if Vacancies happen by Resignation, or otherwise, during the Recess of the Legislature of any State, the Executive thereof may make temporary Appointments until the next Meeting of the Legislature, which shall then fill such Vacancies.

No Person shall be a Senator who shall not have attained to the Age of thirty Years, and been nine Years a Citizen of the United States, and who shall not, when elected, be an Inhabitant of that State for which he shall be chosen.

The Vice President of the United States shall be President of the Senate, but shall have no Vote, unless they be equally divided.

The Senate shall chuse their other Officers, and also a President pro tempore, in the Absence of the Vice President, or when he shall exercise the Office of President of the United States.

The Senate shall have the sole Power to try all Impeachments. When sitting for that Purpose, they shall be on Oath or Affirmation. When the President of the United States is tried, the Chief Justice shall preside: And no Person shall be convicted without the Concurrence of two thirds of the Members present.

Judgment in Cases of Impeachment shall not extend further than to removal from Office, and disqualification to hold and enjoy any Office of honor, Trust or Profit under the United States: but the Party convicted shall nevertheless be liable and subject to Indictment, Trial, Judgment and Punishment, according to Law.

SECTION 4. The Times, Places and Manner of holding Elections for Senators and Representatives, shall be prescribed in each State by the Legislature thereof; but the Congress may at any time by Law make or alter such Regulations, except as to the Places of chusing Senators.

The Congress shall assemble at least once in every Year, and such Meeting shall be on the first Monday in December, unless they shall by Law appoint a different Day.

SECTION 5. Each House shall be the Judge of the Elections, Returns and Qualifications of its own Members, and a Majority of each shall constitute a Quorum to do Business; but a smaller Number may adjourn from day to day, and may be authorized to compel the Attendance of absent Members, in such Manner, and under such Penalties as each House may provide.

Each House may determine the Rules of its Proceedings, punish its Members for disorderly Behaviour, and, with the Concurrence of two thirds, expel a Member.

Each House shall keep a Journal of its Proceedings, and from time to time publish the same, excepting such Parts as may in their Judgment require Secrecy; and the Yeas and Nays of the Members of either House on any question shall, at the Desire of one fifth of those Present, be entered on the Journal.

Neither House, during the Session of Congress, shall, without the Consent of the other, adjourn for more than three days, nor to any other Place than that in which the two Houses shall be sitting.

SECTION 6. The Senators and Representatives shall receive a Compensation for their Services, to be ascertained by Law, and paid out of the Treasury of the United States. They shall in all Cases, except Treason, Felony and Breach of the Peace, be privileged from Arrest during their Attendance at the Session of their respective Houses, and in going to and returning from the same; and for any Speech or Debate in either House, they shall not be questioned in any other Place.

No Senator or Representative shall, during the Time for which he was elected, be appointed to any civil Office under the Authority of the United States, which shall have been created, or the Emoluments whereof shall have been encreased during such time; and no Person holding any Office under the United States, shall be a Member of either House during his Continuance in Office.

SECTION 7. All Bills for raising Revenue shall originate in the House of Representatives; but the Senate may propose or concur with Amendments as on other Bills.

Every Bill which shall have passed the House of Representatives and the Senate, shall, before it become a Law, be presented to the President of the United States; If he approve he shall sign it, but if not he shall return it, with his Objections to that House in which it shall have originated, who shall enter the Objections at large on their Journal, and proceed to reconsider it. If after such Reconsideration two thirds of that House shall agree to pass the Bill, it shall be sent, together with the Objections, to the other House, by which it shall likewise be reconsidered, and if approved by two thirds of that House, it shall become a Law. But in all such Cases the Votes of both Houses shall be determined by yeas and Nays, and the Names of the Persons voting for and against the Bill shall be entered on the Journal of each House respectively. If any Bill shall not be returned by the President within ten days (Sundays excepted) after it shall have been presented to him, the Same shall be a Law, in like Manner as if he had signed it, unless the Congress by their Adjournment prevent its Return in which Case it shall not be a Law.

Every Order, Resolution, or Vote to which the Concurrence of the Senate and House of Representatives may be necessary (except on a question of Adjournment) shall be presented to the President of the United States; and before the Same shall take Effect, shall be approved by him, or being disapproved by him, shall be repassed by two thirds of the Senate and House of Representatives, according to the Rules and Limitations prescribed in the Case of a Bill.

SECTION 8. The Congress shall have Power To lay and collect Taxes, Duties, Imposts and Excises, to pay the Debts and provide for the common Defence and general Welfare of the United States; but all Duties, Imposts and Excises shall be uniform throughout the United States;

To borrow Money on the credit of the United States;

To regulate Commerce with foreign Nations, and among the several States, and with the Indian Tribes;

To establish an uniform Rule of Naturalization, and uniform Laws on the subject of Bankruptcies throughout the United States;

To coin Money, regulate the Value thereof, and of foreign Coin, and fix the Standard of Weights and Measures;

To provide for the Punishment of counterfeiting the Securities and current Coin of the United States;

To establish Post Offices and post Roads;

To promote the progress of Science and useful Arts, by securing for limited Times to Authors and Inventors the exclusive Right to their respective Writings and Discoveries;

To constitute Tribunals inferior to the supreme Court;

To define and punish Piracies and Felonies committed on the high Seas, and Offences against the Law of Nations;

To declare War, grant Letters of Marque and Reprisal, and make Rules concerning Captures on Land and Water;

To raise and support Armies, but no Appropriation of Money to that Use shall be for a longer Term than two Years;

To provide and maintain a Navy;

To make Rules for the Government and Regulation of the land and naval Forces;

To provide for calling forth the Militia to execute the Laws of the Union, suppress Insurrections and repel Invasions;

To provide for organizing, arming, and disciplining, the Militia, and for governing such Part of them as may be employed in the Service of the United States, reserving to the States respectively, the Appointment of the Officers, and the Authority of training the Militia according to the discipline prescribed by Congress;

To exercise exclusive Legislation in all Cases whatsoever, over such District (not exceeding ten Miles square) as may, by Cession of particular States, and the Acceptance of Congress, become the Seat of the Government of the United States, and to exercise like Authority over all Places purchased by the Consent of the Legislature of the State in which the Same shall be, for the Erection of Forts, Magazines, Arsenals, dock-Yards, and other needful Buildings;—And

To make all Laws which shall be necessary and proper for carrying into Execution the foregoing Powers, and all other Powers vested by this Constitution in the Government of the United States, or in any Department or Officer thereof.

SECTION 9. The Migration or Importation of such Persons as any of the States now existing shall think proper to admit, shall not be prohibited by the Congress prior to the Year one thousand eight hundred and eight, but a Tax or duty may be imposed on such Importation, not exceeding ten dollars for each Person.

The Privilege of the Writ of Habeas Corpus shall not be suspended, unless when in Cases of Rebellion or Invasion the public Safety may require it.

No Bill of Attainder or ex post facto Law shall be passed.

No Capitation, or other direct, Tax shall be laid, unless in Proportion to the Census or Enumeration herein before directed to be taken.

No Tax or Duty shall be laid on Articles exported from any State.

No Preference shall be given by any Regulation of Commerce or Revenue to the Ports of one State over those of another: nor shall Vessels bound to, or from, one State, be obliged to enter, clear, or pay Duties in another.

No Money shall be drawn from the Treasury, but in Consequence of Appropriations made by Law; and a regular Statement and Account of the Receipts and Expenditures of all public Money shall be published from time to time.

No Title of Nobility shall be granted by the United States: And no Person holding any Office of Profit or Trust under them, shall, without the Consent of the Congress, accept of any present, Emolument, Office, or Title, of any kind whatever, from any King, Prince, or foreign State.

SECTION 10. No State shall enter into any Treaty, Alliance, or Confederation; grant Letters of Marque and Reprisal; coin Money; emit Bills of Credit; make any Thing but gold and silver Coin a Tender in Payment of Debts; pass any Bill of Attainder, ex post facto Law, or Law impairing the Obligation of Contracts, or grant any Title of Nobility.

No State shall, without the Consent of the Congress, lay any Imposts or Duties on Imports or Exports, except what may be absolutely necessary for executing it's inspection Laws: and the net Produce of all Duties and Imposts, laid by any State on Imports or Exports, shall be for the Use of the Treasury of the United States; and all such Laws shall be subject to the Revision and Controul of the Congress.

No State shall, without the Consent of Congress, lay any Duty of Tonnage, keep Troops, or Ships of War in time of Peace, enter into any Agreement or Compact with another State, or with a foreign Power, or engage in War, unless actually invaded, or in such imminent Danger as will not admit of delay.

Article. II.

SECTION 1. The executive Power shall be vested in a President of the United States of America. He shall hold his Office during the Term of four Years, and, together with the Vice President, chosen for the same Term, be elected as follows

Each State shall appoint, in such Manner as the Legislature thereof may direct, a Number of Electors, equal to the whole Number of Senators and Representatives to which the State may be entitled in the Congress: but no Senator or Representative, or Person holding an Office of Trust or Profit under the United States, shall be appointed an Elector.

The Electors shall meet in their respective States, and vote by Ballot for two Persons, of whom one at least shall not be an Inhabitant of the same State with themselves. And they shall make a List of all the Persons voted for, and of the Number of Votes for each; which List they shall sign and certify, and transmit sealed to the Seat of the Government of the United States, directed to the President of the Senate. The President of the Senate shall, in the Presence of the Senate and House of Representatives, open all the Certificates, and the Votes shall then be counted. The Person having the greatest Number of Votes shall be the President, if such Number be a Majority of the whole Number of Electors appointed; and if there be more than one who have such Majority, and have an equal Number of Votes, then the House of Representatives shall immediately chuse by Ballot one of them for President; and if no Person have a Majority, then from the five highest on the List the said House shall in like Manner chuse the President. But in chusing the President, the Votes shall be taken by States, the Representation from each State having one Vote; A quorum for this Purpose shall consist of a Member or Members from two thirds of the States, and a Majority of all the States shall be necessary to a Choice. In every Case, after the Choice of the President, the Person having the greatest Number of Votes of the Electors shall be the Vice President. But if there should remain two or more who have equal Votes, the Senate shall chuse from them by Ballot the Vice President.

The Congress may determine the Time of chusing the Electors, and the Day on which they shall give their Votes; which Day shall be the same throughout the United States.

No Person except a natural born Citizen, or a Citizen of the United States, at the time of the Adoption of this Constitution, shall be eligible to the Office of President; neither shall any Person be eligible to that Office who shall not have attained to the Age of thirty five Years, and been fourteen Years a Resident within the United States.

In Case of the Removal of the President from Office, or of his Death, Resignation, or Inability to discharge the Powers and Duties of the said Office, the Same shall devolve on the Vice President, and the Congress may by Law provide for the Case of Removal, Death, Resignation or Inability, both of the President and Vice President, declaring what Officer shall then act as President, and such Officer shall act accordingly, until the Disability be removed, or a President shall be elected.

The President shall, at stated Times, receive for his Services, a Compensation, which shall neither be encreased nor diminished during the Period for which he shall have been elected, and he shall not receive within that Period any other Emolument from the United States, or any of them.

Before he enter on the Execution of his Office, he shall take the following Oath or Affirmation:—"I do solemnly swear (or affirm) that I will faithfully execute the Office of President of the United States, and will to the best of my Ability, preserve, protect and defend the Constitution of the United States."

SECTION 2. The President shall be Commander in Chief of the Army and Navy of the United States, and of the Militia of the several States, when called into the actual Service of the United States; he may require the Opinion, in writing, of the principal Officer in each of the executive Departments, upon any Subject relating to the Duties of their respective Offices, and he shall have Power to grant Reprieves and Pardons for Offences against the United States, except in Cases of Impeachment.

He shall have Power, by and with the Advice and Consent of the Senate, to make Treaties, provided two thirds of the Senators present concur; and he shall nominate, and by and with the Advice and Consent of the Senate, shall appoint Ambassadors, other public Ministers and Consuls, Judges of the supreme Court, and all other Officers of the United States, whose Appointments are not herein otherwise provided for, and which shall be established by Law: but the Congress may by Law vest the Appointment of such inferior Officers, as they think proper, in the President alone, in the Courts of Law, or in the Heads of Departments.

The President shall have Power to fill up all Vacancies that may happen during the Recess of the Senate, by granting Commissions which shall expire at the End of their next Session.

SECTION 3. He shall from time to time give to the Congress Information of the State of the Union, and recommend to their Consideration such Measures as he shall judge necessary and expedient; he may, on extraordinary Occasions, convene both Houses, or either of them, and in Case of Disagreement between them, with Respect to the Time of Adjournment, he may adjourn them to such Time as he shall think proper; he shall receive Ambassadors and other public Ministers; he shall take Care that the Laws be faithfully executed, and shall Commission all the Officers of the United States.

SECTION 4. The President, Vice President and all civil Officers of the United States, shall be removed from Office on Impeachment for, and Conviction of, Treason, Bribery, or other high Crimes and Misdemeanors.

Article. III.

SECTION 1. The judicial Power of the United States, shall be vested in one supreme Court, and in such inferior Courts as the Congress may from time to time ordain and establish. The Judges, both of the supreme and inferior Courts, shall hold their Offices during good Behaviour, and shall, at stated Times, receive for their Services, a Compensation, which shall not be diminished during their Continuance in Office.

SECTION 2. The judicial Power shall extend to all Cases, in Law and Equity, arising under this Constitution, the Laws of the United States, and Treaties made, or which shall be made, under their Authority;—to all Cases affecting Ambassadors, other public Ministers and Consuls;—to all Cases of admiralty and maritime Jurisdiction;—to Controversies to which the United States shall be a Party;—to Controversies between two or more States;—between a State and Citizens of another State;—between Citizens of different States,—between Citizens of the same State claiming Lands under Grants of different States, and between a State, or the Citizens thereof, and foreign States, Citizens or Subjects.

In all Cases affecting Ambassadors, other public Ministers and Consuls, and those in which a State shall be Party, the supreme Court shall have original Jurisdiction. In all the other Cases before mentioned, the supreme Court shall have appellate Jurisdiction, both as to Law and Fact, with such Exceptions, and under such Regulations as the Congress shall make.

The Trial of all Crimes, except in Cases of Impeachment, shall be by Jury; and such Trial shall be held in the State where the said Crimes shall have been committed; but when not committed within any State, the Trial shall be at such Place or Places as the Congress may by Law have directed.

SECTION 3. Treason against the United States, shall consist only in levying War against them, or in adhering to their Enemies, giving them Aid and Comfort. No Person shall be convicted of Treason unless on the Testimony of two Witnesses to the same overt Act, or on Confession in open Court.

The Congress shall have Power to declare the Punishment of Treason, but no Attainder of Treason shall work Corruption of Blood, or Forfeiture except during the Life of the Person attainted.

Article. IV.

SECTION 1. Full Faith and Credit shall be given in each State to the public Acts, Records, and judicial Proceedings of every other State. And the Congress may by general Laws prescribe the Manner in which such Acts, Records and Proceedings shall be proved, and the Effect thereof.

SECTION 2. The Citizens of each State shall be entitled to all Privileges and Immunities of Citizens in the several States.

A Person charged in any State with Treason, Felony, or other Crime, who shall flee from Justice, and be found in another State, shall on Demand of the executive Authority of the State from which he fled, be delivered up, to be removed to the State having Jurisdiction of the Crime.

No Person held to Service or Labour in one State, under the Laws thereof, escaping into another, shall, in Consequence of any Law or Regulation therein, be discharged from such Service or Labour, but shall be delivered up on

Claim of the Party to whom such Service or Labour may be due.

SECTION 3. New States may be admitted by the Congress into this Union; but no new State shall be formed or erected within the Jurisdiction of any other State; nor any State be formed by the Junction of two or more States, or Parts of States, without the Consent of the Legislatures of the States concerned as well as of the Congress.

The Congress shall have Power to dispose of and make all needful Rules and Regulations respecting the Territory or other Property belonging to the United States; and nothing in this Constitution shall be so construed as to Prejudice any Claims of the United States, or of any particular State.

SECTION 4. The United States shall guarantee to every State in this Union a Republican Form of Government, and shall protect each of them against Invasion; and on Application of the Legislature, or of the Executive (when the Legislature cannot be convened) against domestic Violence.

Article. V.

The Congress, whenever two thirds of both Houses shall deem it necessary, shall propose Amendments to this Constitution, or, on the Application of the Legislatures of two thirds of the several States, shall call a Convention for proposing Amendments, which, in either Case, shall be valid to all Intents and Purposes, as Part of this Constitution, when ratified by the Legislatures of three fourths of the several States, or by Conventions in three fourths thereof, as the one or the other Mode of Ratification may be proposed by the Congress; Provided that no Amendment which may be made prior to the Year One thousand eight hundred and eight shall in any Manner affect the first and fourth Clauses in the Ninth Section of the first Article; and that no State, without its Consent, shall be deprived of it's equal Suffrage in the Senate.

Article. VI.

All Debts contracted and Engagements entered into, before the Adoption of this Constitution, shall be as valid against the United States under this Constitution, as under the Confederation.

This Constitution, and the Laws of the United States which shall be made in Pursuance thereof; and all Treaties made, or which shall be made, under the Authority of the United States, shall be the supreme Law of the Land; and the Judges in every State shall be bound thereby, any Thing in the Constitution or Laws of any State to the Contrary notwithstanding.

The Senators and Representatives before mentioned, and the Members of the several State Legislatures, and all executive and judicial Officers, both of the United States and of the several States, shall be bound by Oath or Affirmation, to support this Constitution; but no religious Test shall ever be required as a Qualification to any Office or public Trust under the United States.

Article. VII.

The Ratification of the Conventions of nine States, shall be sufficient for the Establishment of this Constitution between the States so ratifying the Same.

> The Word, "the," being interlined between the seventh and eighth Lines of the first Page, The Word "Thirty" being partly written on an Erazure in the fifteenth Line of the first Page, The Words "is tried" being interlined between the thirty second and thirty third Lines of the first Page and the Word "the" being interlined between the forty third and forty fourth Lines of the second Page.
> Attest WILLIAM JACKSON Secretary

done in Convention by the Unanimous Consent of the States present the Seventeenth Day of September in the Year of our Lord one thousand seven hundred and Eighty seven and of the Independance of the United States of America the Twelfth In witness whereof We have hereunto subscribed our Names,

Go: WASHINGTON—Presidt. and deputy from Virginia

New Hampshire	John Langdon Nicholas Gilman
Massachusetts	Nathaniel Gorham Rufus King
Connecticut	Wm. Saml. Johnson Roger Sherman
New York	Alexander Hamilton
New Jersey	Wil: Livingston David Brearley. Wm. Paterson. Jona: Dayton
Pensylvania	B Franklin Thomas Mifflin Robt Morris Geo. Clymer Thos. FitzSimons Jared Ingersoll James Wilson Gouv Morris
Delaware	Geo: Read Gunning Bedford jun John Dickinson Richard Bassett Jaco: Broom
Maryland	James McHenry Dan of St Thos. Jenifer Danl Carroll
Virginia	John Blair— James Madison Jr.
North Carolina	Wm. Blount Richd. Dobbs Spaight. Hu Williamson
South Carolina	J. Rutledge Charles Cotesworth Pinckney Charles Pinckney Pierce Butler.
Georgia	William Few Abr Baldwin

Amendments to the Constitution

Article I

Congress shall make no law respecting an establishment of religion, or prohibiting the free exercise thereof; or abridging the freedom of speech, or of the press; or the right of the people peaceably to assemble, and to petition the Government for a redress of grievances.

Article II

A well regulated Militia, being necessary to the security of a free State, the right of the people to keep and bear Arms, shall not be infringed.

Article III

No Soldier shall, in time of peace be quartered in any house, without the consent of the Owner, nor in time of war, but in a manner to be prescribed by law.

Article IV

The right of the people to be secure in their persons, houses, papers, and effects, against unreasonable searches and seizures, shall not be violated, and no Warrants shall issue, but upon probable cause, supported by Oath or affirmation, and particularly describing the place to be searched, and the persons or things to be seized.

Article V

No person shall be held to answer for a capital, or otherwise infamous crime, unless on a presentment or indictment of a Grand Jury, except in cases arising in the land or naval forces, or in the Militia, when in actual service in time of War or public danger; nor shall any person be subject for the same offence to be twice put in jeopardy of life or limb; nor shall be compelled in any criminal case to be a witness against himself, nor be deprived of life, liberty, or property, without due process of law; nor shall private property be taken for public use, without just compensation.

Article VI

In all criminal prosecutions, the accused shall enjoy the right to a speedy and public trial, by an impartial jury of the State and district wherein the crime shall have been committed, which district shall have been previously ascertained by law, and to be informed of the nature and cause of the accusation; to be confronted with the witnesses against him; to have compulsory process for obtaining witnesses in his favor, and to have the Assistance of Counsel for his defence.

Article VII

In Suits at common law, where the value in controversy shall exceed twenty dollars, the right of trial by jury shall be preserved, and no fact tried by a jury, shall be otherwise re-examined in any Court of the United States, than according to the rules of the common law.

Article VIII

Excessive bail shall not be required, nor excessive fines imposed, nor cruel and unusual punishments inflicted.

Article IX

The enumeration in the Constitution, of certain rights, shall not be construed to deny or disparage others retained by the people.

Article X

The powers not delegated to the United States by the Constitution, nor prohibited by it to the States, are reserved to the States respectively, or to the people.

Article XI

The Judicial power of the United States shall not be construed to extend to any suit in law or equity, commenced or prosecuted against one of the United States by Citizens of another State, or by Citizens or Subjects of any Foreign State.

Article XII

The Electors shall meet in their respective states, and vote by ballot for President and Vice-President, one of whom, at least, shall not be an inhabitant of the same state with themselves; they shall name in their ballots the person voted for as President, and in distinct ballots the person voted for as Vice-President, and they shall make distinct lists of all persons voted for as President, and of all persons voted for as Vice-President, and of the number of votes for each, which lists they shall sign and certify, and transmit sealed to the seat of the government of the United States, directed to the President of the Senate;—The President of the Senate shall, in the presence of the Senate and House of Representatives, open all the certificates and the votes shall then be counted;—The person having the greatest number of votes for President, shall be the President, if such number be a majority of the whole number of Electors appointed; and if no person have such majority, then from the persons having the highest numbers not exceeding three on the list of those voted for as President, the House of Representatives shall choose immediately, by ballot, the President. But in choosing the President, the votes shall be taken by states, the representation from each state having one vote; a quorum for this purpose shall consist of a member or members from two-thirds of the states, and a majority of all the states shall be necessary to a choice. And if the House of Representatives shall not choose a President whenever the right of choice shall devolve upon them, before the fourth day of March next following, then the Vice-President shall act as President, as in the case of the death or other constitutional disability of the President. The person having the greatest number of votes as Vice-President, shall be the Vice-President, if such number be a majority of the whole number of Electors appointed, and if no person have a majority, then from the two highest numbers on the list, the Senate shall choose the Vice-President; a quorum for the purpose shall consist of two-thirds of the whole number of Senators, and a majority of the whole number shall be necessary to a choice. But no person constitutionally ineligible to the office of President shall be eligible to that of Vice-President of the United States.

Short Titles Used

Documentary citations given in short-title forms as "Life," "Papers," "Works," etc., are to be understood as referring to editions of the author of that particular document. Exceptions are clearly noted.

John Adams, Diary *Diary and Autobiography of John Adams.* Edited by L. H. Butterfield et al. 4 vols. Cambridge: Belknap Press of Harvard University Press, 1961.

John Adams, Papers *Papers of John Adams.* Edited by Robert J. Taylor et al. Cambridge: Belknap Press of Harvard University Press, 1977–.

John Adams, Works *The Works of John Adams.* Edited by Charles Francis Adams. 10 vols. Boston: Little, Brown & Co., 1850–56.

See also: Butterfield; Cappon; Warren-Adams Letters

J. Q. Adams, Writings *Writings of John Quincy Adams.* Edited by Worthington Chauncey Ford. 7 vols. New York: Macmillan Co., 1913–17.

Samuel Adams, Writings *The Writings of Samuel Adams.* Edited by Harry Alonzo Cushing. 4 vols. New York: G. P. Putnam's Sons, 1904–8.

American Archives *American Archives.* Edited by M. St. Clair Clarke and Peter Force. 4th ser., 6 vols. Washington, D.C., 1837–46. 5th ser., 3 vols. Washington, D.C., 1848–53.

American Colonial Documents Jensen, Merrill, ed. *American Colonial Documents to 1776.* English Historical Documents, edited by David C. Douglas, vol. 9. New York: Oxford University Press, 1969.

Annals *Annals of Congress. The Debates and Proceedings in the Congress of the United States.* "History of Congress." 42 vols. Washington, D.C.: Gales & Seaton, 1834–56.

Bailyn Bailyn, Bernard, ed. *Pamphlets of the American Revolution, 1750–1776.* Vol. 1, *1750–1765.* Cambridge: Belknap Press of Harvard University Press, 1965.

Blackstone, Commentaries Blackstone, William. *Commentaries on the Laws of England: A Facsimile of the First Edition of 1765–1769.* Chicago: University of Chicago Press, 1979.

Boyd Boyd, Julian P., ed. *Fundamental Laws and Constitutions of New Jersey, 1664–1964.* New Jersey Historical Series, vol. 17. Princeton: D. Van Nostrand Co., Inc., 1964.

Bradford, Of Plymouth Plantation Bradford, William. *Of Plymouth Plantation, 1620–1647.* Edited by Samuel Eliot Morison. New York: Modern Library, 1967.

Burgh [Burgh, James.] *Political Disquisitions: or, An Enquiry into Public Errors, Defects, and Abuses. . . .* 3 vols. London, 1774–75.

Burke, Works *The Works of the Right Honourable Edmund Burke.* 6 vols. London: Henry G. Bohn, 1854–56.

Burnett Burnett, Edmund C., ed. *Letters of Members of the Continental Congress.* 8 vols. Washington: Carnegie Institution of Washington, 1921–36.

Butterfield Adams, Abigail Smith. *The Book of Abigail and John: Selected Letters of the Adams Family, 1762–1784.* Edited by L. H. Butterfield et al. Cambridge: Harvard University Press, 1975.

Cannon *The Letters of Junius.* Edited by John Cannon. Oxford: At the Clarendon Press, 1978.

Cappon *The Adams-Jefferson Letters: The Complete Correspondence between Thomas Jefferson and Abigail and John Adams.* Edited by Lester J. Cappon. 2 vols. Chapel Hill: University of North Carolina Press for the Institute of Early American History and Culture, Williamsburg, Virginia, 1959.

Chase Chase, Frederick. *A History of Dartmouth College and the Town of Hanover New Hampshire.* Edited by John K. Lord. 2 vols. Cambridge: John Wilson & Son, 1891.

Colonial Records *The Colonial Records of North Carolina.* Edited by William L. Saunders. 10 vols. Raleigh: Josephus Daniels, 1886–90.

Crèvecoeur Crèvecoeur, J. Hector St. John. *Letters from an American Farmer.* New York: Albert & Charles Boni, 1925.

Documentary History *Documentary History of the Constitution of the United States of America, 1786–1870.* 5 vols. Washington, D.C.: Department of State, 1901–5.

Dumbauld Dumbauld, Edward. *The Bill of Rights and What It Means Today.* Norman: University of Oklahoma Press, 1957.

Early History *Early History of the University of Virginia, as Contained in the Letters of Thomas Jefferson and Joseph C. Cabell, Hitherto Unpublished. . . .* Richmond: J. W. Randolph, 1856.

Elliot Elliot, Jonathan, ed. *The Debates in the Several State Conventions on the Adoption of the Federal Constitution as Recommended by the General Convention at Philadelphia in 1787. . . .* 5 vols. 2d ed. 1888. Reprint. New York: Burt Franklin, n.d.

Emlyn Hale, Sir Matthew. *Historia Placitorum Coronae. The History of the Pleas of the Crown.* Edited by Sollom Emlyn. 2 vols. London, 1736. Reprint. Classical English Law Texts. London: Professional Books, Ltd., 1971.

Essays Ford, Paul Leicester, ed. *Essays on the Constitution of the United States, Published during Its Discussion by the People, 1787–1788.* Brooklyn: Historical Printing Club, 1892.

Farrand Farrand, Max, ed. *The Records of the Federal Convention of 1787.* Rev. ed. 4 vols. New Haven and London: Yale University Press, 1937.

Federalist Hamilton, Alexander; Madison, James; and Jay, John. *The Federalist.* Edited by Jacob E. Cooke. Middletown, Conn.: Wesleyan University Press, 1961.

Foster Foster, Sir Michael. *A Report of Some Proceedings on the Commission . . . for the Trial of the Rebels in the Year 1746 . . . , and of Other Crown Cases.* London, 1762. Reprint. Classical English Law Texts. Abingdon, England: Professional Books, Ltd., 1982.

Four Letters on Interesting Subjects *Four Letters on Interesting Subjects.* Philadelphia: 1776. Evans 14759.

Franklin, Papers *The Papers of Benjamin Franklin.* Edited by Leonard W. Labaree et al. New Haven: Yale University Press, 1959–.

Franklin, Writings *The Writings of Benjamin Franklin.* Edited by Albert Henry Smyth. 10 vols. New York: Macmillan Co., 1905–7.

Gerry, Life Austin, James T. *The Life of Elbridge Gerry. With Contemporary Letters.* 2 vols. Boston, 1828–29.

Gray Hale, Sir Matthew. *The History of the Common Law of England.* Edited by Charles M. Gray. Classics of British Historical Literature. Chicago: University of Chicago Press, 1971.

Gwyn Gwyn, W. B. *The Meaning of the Separation of Powers: An Analysis of the Doctrine from Its Origin to the Adoption of the United States Constitution.* Tulane Studies in Political Science, vol. 9. New Orleans: Tulane University, 1965.

Hamilton, Papers *The Papers of Alexander Hamilton.* Edited by Harold C. Syrett et al. 26 vols. New York and London: Columbia University Press, 1961–79.

See also: Federalist

Handlin Handlin, Oscar, and Handlin, Mary, eds. *The Popular Sources of Political Authority: Documents on the Massachusetts Constitution of 1780.* Cambridge: Belknap Press of Harvard University Press, 1966.

Harrington *The Political Writings of James Harrington: Representative Selections.* Edited by Charles Blitzer. New York: Liberal Arts Press, 1955.

History of Congress *History of Congress; Exhibiting a Classification of the Proceedings of the Senate, and the House of Representatives, from March 4, 1789, to March 3, 1793. . . .* Philadelphia: Lea & Blanchard, 1843.

Hume Hume, David. *Essays Moral, Political and Literary.* 1742, 1752.

Hurst Hurst, James Willard. *The Law of Treason in the United States: Collected Essays.* Westport, Conn.: Greenwood Publishing Corp., 1971.

Iredell, Life *Life and Correspondence of James Iredell.* Edited by Griffith J. McRee. 2 vols. New York: D. Appleton & Co., 1857.

Iredell, Papers *The Papers of James Iredell.* Edited by Don Higginbotham. Raleigh: North Carolina Division of Archives and History, 1976–.

Jacobson Trenchard, John, and Gordon, Thomas. *Cato's Letters.* In *The English Libertarian Heritage,* edited by David L. Jacobson. American Heritage Series. Indianapolis: Bobbs-Merrill, 1965.

Jamestown, The Three Charters of the Virginia Company of London *The Three Charters of the Virginia Company of London.* Jamestown 350th Anniversary Historical Booklet, no. 4. 1957

Jay, Correspondence *The Correspondence and Public Papers of John Jay.* Edited by Henry P. Johnston. 4 vols. New York and London: G. P. Putnam's Sons, 1890–93.

Jay, Unpublished Papers *John Jay: Unpublished Papers.* Edited by Richard B. Morris et al. New York: Harper & Row, 1975–.

See also: Federalist

Jefferson, Notes on the State of Virginia Jefferson, Thomas. *Notes on the State of Virginia.* Edited by William Peden. Chapel Hill: University of North Carolina Press for the Institute of Early American History and Culture, Williamsburg, Virginia, 1954.

Jefferson, Papers *The Papers of Thomas Jefferson.* Edited by Julian P. Boyd et al. Princeton: Princeton University Press, 1950–.

Jefferson, Works *The Works of Thomas Jefferson.* Collected and edited by Paul Leicester Ford. Federal Edition. 12 vols. New York and London: G. P. Putnam's Sons, 1904–5.

Jefferson, Writings *The Writings of Thomas Jefferson.* Edited by Andrew A. Lipscomb and Albert Ellery Bergh. 20 vols. Washington: Thomas Jefferson Memorial Association, 1905.

Jensen *The Documentary History of the Ratification of the Constitution.* Edited by Merrill Jensen et al. Madison: State Historical Society of Wisconsin, 1976–.

Journals *Journals of the Continental Congress, 1774–1789.* Edited by Worthington C. Ford et al. 34 vols. Washington, D.C.: Government Printing Office, 1904–37.

Kent Kent, James. *Commentaries on American Law.* 4 vols. New York, 1826–30.

King, Life *The Life and Correspondence of Rufus King.* Edited by Charles R. King. 6 vols. New York: G. P. Putnam's Sons, 1894–1900.

Land Eddis, William. *Letters from America.* Edited by Aubrey C. Land. Cambridge: Belknap Press of Harvard University Press, 1969.

Leake Leake, Isaac Q. *Memoir of the Life and Times of General John Lamb.* Albany, N.Y., 1857.

Lee, Letters *The Letters of Richard Henry Lee.* Edited by James Curtis Ballagh. 2 vols. New York: Macmillan Co., 1911–14.

Lincoln, Collected Works *The Collected Works of Abraham Lincoln.* Edited by Roy P. Basler et al. 8 vols. New Brunswick, N.J.: Rutgers University Press, 1953.

Locke, Second Treatise Locke, John. *Two Treatises of Government.* Edited by Peter Laslett. New York: Mentor Books, New American Library, 1965.

See also: Montuori

Machiavelli Machiavelli, Niccolò. *Discourses on the First Ten Books of Titus Livius.* Translated by Christian E. Detmold. New York: Modern Library, 1940.

McMaster McMaster, John Bach, and Stone, Frederick D., eds. *Pennsylvania and the Federal Constitution, 1787–1788.* Lancaster: Published for the Subscribers by the Historical Society of Pennsylvania, 1888.

Madison, Letters *Letters and Other Writings of James Madison.* Published by order of Congress. 4 vols. Philadelphia: J. B. Lippincott & Co., 1865.

Madison, Papers *The Papers of James Madison.* Edited by William T. Hutchinson et al. Chicago and London: University of Chicago Press, 1962–77 (vols. 1–10); Charlottesville: University Press of Virginia, 1977– (vols. 11–).

Madison, W. & M. Q. Fleet, Elizabeth. "Madison's 'Detached Memoranda.' " *William and Mary Quarterly,* 3d ser., 3 (1946): 534–68.

Madison, Writings *The Writings of James Madison.* Edited by Gaillard Hunt. 9 vols. New York: G. P. Putnam's Sons, 1900–1910.

See also: Federalist

Marshall, Life Beveridge, Albert J. *The Life of John Marshall.* 4 vols. Boston: Houghton Mifflin Co., 1916–19.

Marshall, Papers *The Papers of John Marshall.* Edited by Herbert A. Johnson et al. Chapel Hill: University of North Carolina Press, in association with the Institute of Early American History and Culture, Williamsburg, Virginia, 1974–.

Maryland Archives *Archives of Maryland: Proceedings and Acts of the General Assembly of Maryland.* Edited by William Hand Browne. Vol. 1. Baltimore: Maryland Historical Society, 1883.

Mason, Papers *The Papers of George Mason, 1725–1792.* Edited by Robert A. Rutland. 3 vols. Chapel Hill: University of North Carolina Press, 1970.

Meade Meade, Robert Douthat. *Patrick Henry: Patriot in the Making.* Philadelphia: J. B. Lippincott Co., 1957.

MHS Collections *Collections of the Massachusetts Historical Society.*

Monroe, Writings *The Writings of James Monroe.* Edited by Stanislaus Murray Hamilton. 7 vols. New York and London: G. P. Putnam's Sons, 1898–1903.

Montesquieu *The Spirit of Laws.* 1748. Translated by Thomas Nugent, 1750.

Montuori Locke, John. *A Letter concerning Toleration.* Latin and English texts revised and edited by Mario Montuori. The Hague: Martinus Nijhoff, 1963.

Gouverneur Morris, Amerikastudien Adams, Willi Paul. " 'The Spirit of Commerce Requires that Property be Sacred': Gouverneur Morris and the American Revolution." *Amerikastudien* 21 (1976): 309–31.

Gouverneur Morris, Life *The Life of Gouverneur Morris, with Selections from His Correspondence and Miscellaneous Papers.* Edited by Jared Sparks. 3 vols. Boston, 1832.

Robert Morris, Papers *The Papers of Robert Morris, 1781–1784.* Edited by E. James Ferguson et al. Pittsburgh: University of Pittsburgh Press, 1973–.

New England Federalism Adams, Henry, ed. *Documents Relating to New-England Federalism.* Boston: Little, Brown & Co., 1877.

Niles Niles, Hezekiah, *Principles and Acts of the Revolution in America.* Centennial Offering. New York: A. S. Barnes & Co., 1876.

Old Family Letters Biddle, Alexander. *Old Family Letters.* Ser. A. Philadelphia: J. B. Lippincott Co., 1892.

Otis, Political Writings "Some Political Writings of James Otis." Collected by Charles F. Mullett. *University of Missouri Studies* 4 (1929): 257–432.

Paine, Life *The Life and Works of Thomas Paine.* Edited by William M. Van der Weyde. Patriots' Edition. 10 vols. New Rochelle, N.Y.: Thomas Paine National Historical Association, 1925.

Pamphlets Ford, Paul Leicester, ed. *Pamphlets on the Constitution of the United States, Published during Its Discussion by the People, 1787–1788.* Brooklyn, 1888. Reprint. New York: De Capo Press, 1968.

Penn, Select Works *The Select Works of William Penn.* 5 vols. 3d ed. London, 1782.

Pickering, Life Upham, Charles W. *The Life of Timothy Pickering.* 2 vols. Boston: Little, Brown & Co., 1873.

Pinkney Wheaton, Henry. *Some Account of the Life, Writings, and Speeches of William Pinkney.* Baltimore: E. J. Coale, 1826.

Randolph, History of Virginia Randolph, Edmund. *History of Virginia.* Edited by Arthur H. Shaffer. Charlottesville: University Press of Virginia for the Virginia Historical Society, 1970.

Rawle Rawle, William. *A View of the Constitution of the United States of America.* 2d ed. Philadelphia, 1829. Reprint. New York: Da Capo Press, 1970.

Read, Life Read, William Thompson. *Life and Correspondence of George Read.* Philadelphia: J. B. Lippincott & Co., 1870.

Records of the Federal Convention. *See* Farrand

Remonstrance and Petition, W. & M. Q. Schmidt, F. T., and Wilhelm, B. R. "Early Proslavery Petitions in Virginia." *William and Mary Quarterly,* 3d ser., 30 (1973): 133–46.

Richardson Richardson, James D., comp. *A Compilation of the Messages and Papers of the Presidents, 1789–1897.* 10 vols. Washington, D.C.: Government Printing Office, 1896–99.

Robertson Robertson, C. Grant, ed. *Select Statutes, Cases and Documents to Illustrate English Constitutional History, 1660–1832.* 4th ed., rev. London: Methuen & Co., Ltd., 1923.

Rush, Letters *Letters of Benjamin Rush.* Edited by L. H. Butterfield. 2 vols. Memoirs of the American Philosophical Society, vol. 30, parts 1 and 2. Princeton: Princeton University Press, for the American Philosophical Society, 1951.

Rush, Selected Writings *The Selected Writings of Benjamin Rush.* Edited by Dagobert D. Runes. New York: Philosophical Library, 1947.

Scribner *Revolutionary Virginia: The Road to Independence.* Vol 6, *The Time for Decision, 1776: A Documentary Record,* edited by Robert L. Scribner and Brent Tarter. Charlottesville: University Press of Virginia for the Virginia Independence Bicentennial Commission, 1981.

Sidney, Works *The Works of Algernon Sydney. A New Edition.* London, 1772.

Sources *Sources of Our Liberties.* Edited by Richard L. Perry under the general supervision of John C. Cooper. [Chicago:] American Bar Foundation, 1952.

State Trials *State Trials of the United States during the Administrations of Washington and Adams.* Edited by Francis Wharton. Philadelphia: Carey & Hart, 1849.

Stokes Stokes, Anton Phelps, ed. *Church and State in the United States.* 3 vols. New York: Harper & Bros., 1950.

Storing Storing, Herbert J., ed. *The Complete Anti-Federalist.* 7 vols. Chicago: University of Chicago Press, 1981.

Story Story, Joseph. *Commentaries on the Constitution of the United States.* 3 vols. Boston, 1833.

Tansill *Documents Illustrative of the Formation of the Union of the American States.* Edited by Charles C. Tansill. 69th Cong., 1st sess. House Doc. No. 398. Washington, D.C.: Government Printing Office, 1927.

Taylor Taylor, Robert J., ed. *Massachusetts, Colony to Commonwealth: Documents on the Formation of Its Constitution, 1775–1780.* Chapel Hill: University of North Carolina Press for the Institute of Early American History and Culture, Williamsburg, Virginia, 1961.

Thorpe Thorpe, Francis Newton, ed. *The Federal and State Constitutions, Colonial Charters, and Other Organic Laws of the States, Territories, and Colonies Now or Heretofore Forming the United States of America.* 7 vols. Washington, D.C.: Government Printing Office, 1909.

Tucker, Blackstone's Commentaries Tucker, St. George. *Blackstone's Commentaries: With Notes of Reference to the Constitution and Laws of the Federal Government of the United States and of the Commonwealth of Virginia.* 5 vols. Philadelphia, 1803. Reprint. South Hackensack, N.J.: Rothman Reprints, 1969.

Walker, U. Pa. L. Rev. Radin, Max. "The Doctrine of the Separation of Powers in Seventeenth Century Controversies." *University of Pennsylvania Law Review* 86 (1938): 842–66.

Warren, Life Frothingham, Richard. *Life and Times of Joseph Warren.* Boston: Little, Brown & Co., 1865.

Warren-Adams Letters *Warren-Adams Letters, Being Chiefly a Correspondence among John Adams, Samuel Adams, and James Warren.* Vol. 2, 1778–1814. Collections of the Massachusetts Historical Society, vol. 73. [Boston:] Massachusetts Historical Society, 1925.

Washington, Writings *The Writings of George Washington from the Original Manuscript Sources, 1745–1799.* Edited by John C. Fitzpatrick. 39 vols. Washington, D.C.: Government Printing Office, 1931–44.

Webster, Collection Webster, Noah. *A Collection of Essays and Fugitiv Writings on Moral, Historical, Political and Literary Subjects.* Boston, 1790. Reprint. Delmar, N.Y.: Scholars' Facsimiles & Reprints, 1977.

Webster, Political Papers Webster, Noah. *A Collection of Papers on Political, Literary and Moral Subjects.* New York, 1843. Reprint. New York: Burt Franklin, 1968.

Wharton Wharton, Francis, ed. *The Revolutionary Diplomatic Correspondence of the United States.* 6 vols. Washington, D.C.: Government Printing Office, 1889.

Wilson, Works *The Works of James Wilson.* Edited by Robert Green McCloskey. 2 vols. Cambridge: Belknap Press of Harvard University Press, 1967.

Winthrop Winthrop, John. *The History of New England from 1630 to 1649.* Edited by James Savage. 2 vols. Boston: Little, Brown & Co., 1853.

Woodhouse Woodhouse, A. S. P., ed. *Puritanism and Liberty, Being the Army Debates (1647–9) from the Clarke Manuscripts with Supplementary Documents.* 2d ed. London: J. M. Dent & Sons Ltd., 1951.

Index of Constitutional Provisions

Table of Cases

Index of Authors and Documents

References are to chapter or to constitutional section, and to document number. References to volume 1 are by chapter and document number (e.g., ch. 15, no. 23); references to constitutional provisions in volumes 2–4 are by article, section, clause, and document number (e.g., 1.8.8, no. 12); and references to volume 5 are by Amendment and document number (e.g., Amend. I [religion], no. 66). In the case of documents whose several clauses are ranged under a large number of headings (e.g., the Bill of Rights of 1689, the Massachusetts Constitution of 1780, and the like), reference is made only to appearances of the complete text.